Part 4

Pay, Benefits, Terms and Conditions of Employment

- Wages

- Benefits

- Unions

- Safety and Health

Part 5

Managing Performance

- Appraisals

- Training

- Development

- Privacy

Part 6

Terminating Employment

- Employment at Will with Exceptions

- Just Cause

- Due Process

- Downsizing

WEST LEGAL STUDIES IN BUSINESS
ACADEMIC SERIES

EMPLOYMENT LAW FOR HUMAN RESOURCE PRACTICE

SECOND EDITION

DAVID J. WALSH
Miami University

THOMSON

™

WEST

Australia · Brazil · Canada · Mexico · Singapore · Spain · United Kingdom · United States

THOMSON
SOUTH-WESTERN

Employment Law for Human Resource Practice, Second Edition
David J. Walsh

VP/Editorial Director:
Jack W. Calhoun

Publisher:
Rob Dewey

Acquisitions Editor:
Steven Silverstein

Associate Developmental Editor:
Todd McKenzie

Executive Marketing Manager:
Lisa Lynse

Content Project Manager:
Juli A. Cook

Manager of Technology, Editorial:
Vicky True

Technology Project Editor:
Pam Wallace

Manufacturing Coordinator:
Charlene Taylor

Production House:
Interactive Composition Corporation

Printer:
Thomson-West
Eagan, MN

Art Director:
Michelle Kunkler

Internal Designer:
Design Matters/Diane and Nick Gliebe

Cover Designer:
Paul Neff Design

Cover Images:
© Getty Images, Inc.

Library of Congress Control Number: 2005938147

For more information about our products, contact us at:

Thomson Learning
Academic Resource Center
1-800-423-0563

Thomson Higher Education
5191 Natorp Boulevard
Mason, Ohio 45040
USA

Brief CONTENTS

CONTENTS

PART 2 *The Hiring Process*

PART 3 *Managing a Diverse Workforce*

PART 4 Pay, Benefits, Terms and Conditions of Employment

Preface

Five courses, six chapters to read by next week, two team meetings to attend, fixing the problem that is causing your computer to make scary noises . . . and the semester has just started! At least you can skip over this introduction and get to the important stuff.

Let's make a deal. You'll take just a few minutes to peruse this introduction and I'll keep it brief, confining myself to a few matters that will enable you to make better use of this book.

This is a book about employment law, the set of legal requirements that govern the workplace. A distinction is often made between "employment law" and "labor law" (the latter describing laws related to unions and collective bargaining), but I will generally use the term *employment law* to refer to both. This book has two main objectives. The first is to *explain the major issues and rules of employment law*. What things are legal matters? What does the law say about those matters? The second objective is to *explain what employment law means for human resource practice*. What is it that employers should be doing to comply with the law? What is the legal reasoning behind this practical advice?

EMPLOYMENT LIFE CYCLE APPROACH

These dual purposes of understanding the substance of employment law and its implications for human resource practice account for the way that chapters are organized in this book. The first three chapters provide broad overviews. The remainder of this book traces the steps in the employment process and addresses the particular human resource practices associated with them. We start with issues that lead up to hiring and promotion decisions, including recruitment, interviewing, background checks, references, and employment testing. We then turn to a range of issues that arise when a person is on the job, including harassment, reasonable accommodation of disability, compensation, benefits, performance appraisal, and occupational safety and health. The last two chapters of the book deal with issues related to the termination of employment. This structure is intended to highlight the legal issues that arise within particular areas of human resource practice.

CONTENTS OF A TYPICAL CHAPTER

Clippings Each chapter begins with a few brief synopses of recent cases, events, or reports that illustrate the issues dealt with in the chapter. The intent of the clippings is to pique your interest and begin to show how employment law relates to real things that are happening in the world around us.

The Changing Workplace Under this banner, recent changes in the workplace, human resource practices, and the workforce that have particular implications for the law are highlighted. Changes in the workplace raise new legal questions and point to the types of legal disputes that we can expect to see more of in the future.

Case Excerpts A central part of each chapter is excerpts from decisions in court cases. One of the things that is unusual (and admirable) about legal decision making

is that the decision makers (e.g., judges, members of administrative agencies like the Equal Employment Opportunity Commission) set down in writing their rationales for the decisions they make in the cases that are brought before them. This gives us the opportunity to read firsthand accounts of legal disputes, to have the decision makers explain the relevant rules of law to us, and to see how those principles were applied to the facts of particular cases. I'll be describing the law and other cases for you as well, but there is nothing like reading cases to get a feel for the law.

The words in the case excerpts are the same as those you would find if you looked up the cases on-line or in print. However, to maximize readability, I have shortened the case decisions by focusing on a brief statement of the facts, the legal issue, and (at greatest length) the explanation of the decision maker's rationale. Where part of a sentence is removed, you will see three dots (. . .). Where more than part of a sentence is removed, you will see three stars (* * *). This is to alert you that text has been removed from the full case decision. Legal decisions are replete with numerous footnotes and citations to previous cases that addressed similar questions. In most instances, I have removed the citations and footnotes from the case excerpts. Occasionally, I have included in brackets [] a brief explanation of a legal term.

Practical Implications of the Law Suggestions for carrying out human resource activities in a lawful manner are discussed within the chapters (in italics) and summarized at the end of each chapter. I have endeavored to present this practical advice in a way that makes the legal grounds for the advice clear. *It is important to know not only what to do, but why those things should be done.*

Translating the law into guidelines for practice can be tricky. There are some things that the law clearly requires of employers (e.g., pay at least the minimum wage); there are other things that are not requirements per se, but that will avert legal problems in specific situations (e.g., use only valid employment tests); and there are still other things that are not required, but are legally prudent because they might avoid legal problems in the long run or increase the likelihood that legal claims could be successfully defended (e.g., have an internal grievance procedure). The suggestions offered in this book fall into all three of these categories, but focus on those that are most closely tied to specific legal requirements. *The guidelines are general principles for sound human resource practice. They cannot be—and do not purport to be—specific legal advice for particular situations that you might encounter. Only a trained legal professional thoroughly familiar with the details of your case can provide the latter.*

Not everything is a legal issue, and few things are solely legal issues. The law is a basic determinant of human resource practice and one that cannot be ignored; but simply because the law allows an employer to do something does not mean that it should be done. The law is best conceived as providing a "floor" for human resource practices, rather than a "ceiling." It establishes minimum standards of acceptable treatment of employees, but often it is sensible for employers—based on motivational, pragmatic, or ethical considerations—to go well beyond the bare minimum legal requirements. Thus, our purpose in understanding what the law requires is not to draw a line in the sand between legal requirements and jealously guarded employer prerogatives (everything else). Nor is it to identify "loopholes" that can be exploited or, as one legal scholar[1] has put it, to "bulletproof the workplace" with

superficial measures that look good on paper and make employers less susceptible to lawsuits, but fail to realize the real purposes (e.g., equal employment opportunity) of the law. Instead, *this book encourages you to think about the underlying purposes or "spirit" of the law, and not merely the "letter" of the law. It invites you to consider how to achieve these important social purposes by implementing policies and practices that also make sense given the operational realities of the workplace.*

End-of-Chapter Materials These include a list of key terms, a brief summary of major points in the chapter, and a set of discussion questions. All of these are intended to help with checking understanding of the chapter and reviewing for exams. Additionally, there are Internet resources listed that should enable further research into the topics discussed in the chapter.

FOCUS OF COVERAGE

Since I have been touting the contents of this book, it is only fair to acknowledge material that is largely omitted. Beyond a glancing blow struck in Chapter 1, this book provides relatively little information about such matters as the legislative process, specific procedures for raising different types of legal claims, and the historical development of employment laws. These are all very worthwhile topics, but they are not emphasized because the focus of this book is on the current substance of employment law and its implications for human resource practice. The treatment of labor law in this book does not reach a number of the more specialized issues in this area, but I do attempt to show how labor law continues to be quite relevant to both unionized and nonunion workplaces. Additionally, while cross-national comparisons can enhance our understanding of U.S. law, a comparative perspective is beyond the scope of this book.

ANCILLARY MATERIAL

For more information about this text and its ancillaries, contact your Thomson/West Legal Studies business sales representative or visit this book's Web site (www.thomsonedu.com/westbuslaw).

Instructor's Manual/Test Bank

(ISBN: 0-324-37524-7) Originally prepared by text author David Walsh, the Instructor's Manual includes chapter outlines, answers to case questions and end-of-chapter exercises, and summaries of key chapter material. The second edition Test Bank has been edited and updated by Michael Katz, of Delaware State University.

INTRODUCTION TO THE SECOND EDITION

This edition of *Employment Law for Human Resource Practice* retains the essential structure and focus of the first edition. Linking a thorough understanding of principles of employment law to advice on how to conduct human resource practice remains the central aim of this book. Consistent with this aim, the book continues to be organized around stages in the employment process, from the formation of an

employment relationship on through the termination of that relationship. As in the first edition, substantial excerpts from leading employment law cases and discussions in the text of how different types of employment law cases are decided aim at improving the analytical skills of students. Employment law issues are made more relevant by special features found in each chapter, including "Clippings" of recent events that illustrate the application of employment laws and "The Changing Workplace," which highlights new employment law problems presented by contemporary changes in the workforce and management practices.

Enhancements to this edition include the following:

- A new "Elements of a Claim" feature, in which information about how particular types of employment law claims (e.g., negligent hiring, adverse impact) are analyzed is set apart from the rest of the text and made more prominent. Students can now easily refer to this information when presented with hypotheticals, such as the chapter end case questions.

- An almost entirely new set of "Clippings" and updates to "The Changing Workplace" features to help the book remain as current and relevant as possible. Information about significant cases and other developments in employment law will be posted periodically on the Web page for this book (http://walsh. westbuslaw.com).

- Over half of the excerpted cases in chapters are new from the first edition. Classic cases are still discussed in the text, but the emphasis is on presenting recent cases that capture the current state of the law. New cases in this edition include *Smith v. City of Jackson, Miss.*; *IBP v. Alvarez*; *Pennsylvania State Police v. Suders*; *Cloutier v. Costco*; *Petrosino v. Bell Atlantic*; and *Roquet v. Arthur Anderson*, among many others.

- Coverage of a number of issues is expanded or substantially revised, including limitations on the use of mandatory arbitration agreements, retaliation, the affirmative defense in harassment cases, DOL regulations for the "white-collar exemptions" to the Fair Labor Standards Act, sex-stereotyping, whistle-blower claims under Sarbanes-Oxley, and fiduciary responsibilities under ERISA.

- A substantial number of new chapter end questions have been added.

Thanks to the many faculty and students that have used *Employment Law for Human Resource Practice*. I hope that this edition will serve your needs even better. If you are not presently using this book, I hope that you will consider adopting it. Please do not hesitate to contact me regarding any questions that you have about the book (and ancillary materials) or suggestions for improvement (walshdj@muohio.edu).

Many thanks also to Steve Silverstein, Acquisitions Editor; Todd McKenzie Associate Development Editor; Juli Cook, Content Project Manager; and numerous others at Thomson and its business partners. Being an author provides a small glimpse of the "cast of thousands" who are needed to produce a work of this type.

Lastly, I wish to thank and publicly acknowledge the following individuals who provided valuable comments and suggestions that helped shape this second edition:

Walter A. Bogumil
University of Central Florida

Kabrina K. Chang
Boston University

Elizabeth A. Campbell
Central Michigan University

Amy W. Fellner
Arizona State University

Stephen M. Kociol
Golden Gate University

John McGee
Texas State University

Jim Morgan
California State University, Chico

Joseph J. Solberg
Illinois State University

Ernie Stark
Bellevue University

Pamela P. Stokes
Texas A&M University—Corpus Christi

DEDICATION

In memory of Martin Walsh

PART **1**

Introduction to Employment Law

Chapter **1**
Overview of Employment Law

Chapter **2**
The Employment Relationship

Chapter **3**
Overview of Employment Discrimination

PART 2
The Hiring
Process

PART 3
Managing a
Diverse
Workforce

PART 4
Pay, Benefits,
Terms and
Conditions of
Employment

PART 5
Managing
Performance

PART 6
Terminating
Employment

Overview of Employment Law

CLIPPINGS

▸ Only minutes before a trial was to begin, investment firm Morgan Stanley settled a class-action sex discrimination lawsuit brought by the Equal Employment Opportunity Commission (EEOC) on behalf of several hundred of the firm's female brokers. The charges included harassment, failure to promote qualified women, discrimination in pay, and retaliation against women who complained. Although admitting no wrongdoing, Morgan Stanley agreed to pay $54 million to settle the case. Additionally, the firm will allocate $2 million for diversity programs overseen by an outside monitor and provide antidiscrimination training to managers and employees. Complaints of discrimination and large monetary settlements have been common in recent years at large Wall Street investment firms.[1]

▸ In a case that could dwarf all previous discrimination lawsuits, a federal district court judge has certified a class of some 1.6 million current and former female employees of Wal-Mart as plaintiffs in a massive class-action, sex discrimination lawsuit. It is alleged that women were discriminated against in promotions and pay. Wal-Mart has denied that it discriminates and intends to contest the class certification.[2]

▸ After Donald Lagatree was hired as a legal secretary by the law firm of Luce, Forward, Hamilton & Scripps, he was asked to sign an agreement waiving his right to sue the firm in court. Instead, any dispute he might have with the firm over an employment-related matter would be dealt with through arbitration. Mr. Lagatree refused to sign the agreement and the job offer was withdrawn. He subsequently argued that the firm's action amounted to illegal retaliation for his insisting on retaining his rights under the law. The EEOC took his case to court, but then settled with the firm in June 2004. The settlement allowed the firm to retain, with minor modifications, its arbitration agreement.[3]

▸ Few people would be surprised that the number of cases filed in federal courts has increased markedly over the past several decades. Less well known is that only a small proportion of these cases ever go to trial. In 2002, only 1.8 percent of federal civil cases actually went to trial. The trend in cases going to trial is downward (11.5 percent of civil cases went to trial in 1962). Although settlements are common (occurring in about 35–40 percent of cases), summary disposition of cases by judges based only on papers filed has become even more routine (occurring in about 50 percent of cases).[4]

[1]Patrick McGeehan. "Morgan Stanley Settles Bias Suit With $54 Million." *New York Times* (July 13, 2004), A-1.

[2]Steven Greenhouse and Constance L. Hays. "Wal-Mart Sex-Bias Suit Given Class-Action Status." *New York Times* (June 23, 2004), A-1.

[3]Steven Greenhouse. "Case Challenges Employees' Waiving Right to Sue." *New York Times* (May 5, 2003), A-19; Nancy Montwieler. "EEOC Accord Puts Its Stamp of Approval on Law Firm's Mandatory Arbitration Plan." *Daily Labor Report* 132 (July 12, 2004), AA-1.

[4]Adam Liptak. "Federal Trials Drop as Court Cases Rise in a Longtime Trend." *New York Times* (December 14, 2003), A-1.

HEARD AT THE STAFF MEETING

Congratulations on your new job as human resource manager! You pour a cup of coffee and settle into your seat to hear the following reports from staff members:

> "We have a number of jobs in our production facilities that are physically demanding. To avoid hiring people who cannot do these jobs or might hurt themselves, we have decided to ask all applicants whether they have any health problems that might interfere with their ability to work."

> "Some of our people have been working long hours to develop a new product line. An administrative assistant has complained about not receiving overtime pay for the 50-hour weeks that she has been putting in. Because we pay her a salary, we don't have to worry about overtime, right?"

> "A number of our employees are in the Army Reserves. One of them has been deployed to Iraq twice and has missed over two years of work. She will be returning to the United States soon and has indicated that she wants her job back. Her supervisor feels that since her job skills are now out of date and she might be deployed again at any time, it would be best to not reinstate her."

> "We need to cut employment drastically at one of our facilities. We have asked the supervisors to use their best judgment in deciding who should be let go. To minimize disruption, we'll announce the downsizing two weeks in advance."

You get up to get another—large—cup of coffee and feel very fortunate that you were paying attention during that employment law class you took.

What legal issues emerged during this staff meeting? What should this company be doing differently to better comply with the law? Although you might never encounter this many legal problems in one sitting, employment law pervades virtually every aspect of human resource practice, and managers regularly confront employment law questions.

This book is intended to help you recognize, analyze, and deal effectively with employment law issues when they present themselves. Better yet, a solid grasp of employment law will enable you to put in place policies and practices that will prevent many legal problems from arising in the first place. *Managers need to know about employment law not to "play lawyer," but rather to help them institute policies that prevent violations, recognize legal issues when they arise, and know when to seek advice from legal counsel.* Most often, lawyers get involved after the fact, when bad decisions have already been made and organizations are in damage-control mode. *It is far better to approach legal compliance in a proactive manner, by providing training in proper procedures, carefully selecting supervisors, closely reviewing human resource decisions, establishing grievance procedures, and promptly investigating employee complaints. Given their central role in complying with employment laws, managers—and even more so, human resource managers—must have a solid grasp of employment law.*

The purpose of this chapter is to present a "big picture" of the body of law that we will apply to particular human resource practices throughout this book. The chapter contains an overview of employment laws, the rights they confer on employees, and the processes involved in enforcing these laws. Special attention is given to recent developments in the use of alternatives to litigation to resolve employment disputes.

U.S. EMPLOYMENT LAW IS A FRAGMENTED WORK IN PROGRESS

"Just tell me what the law is and I'll follow it." Were matters only that simple! No single set of employment laws covers all workers in the United States. Instead, the employment law system is a patchwork of federal, state, and local laws. Whether and how laws apply also depend on such things as if the employees work for the government or in the private sector, whether they have union representation, and the size of the employer. Our principal focus will be on federal laws because these reach most widely across U.S. workplaces and often serve as models for state and local laws; however, we will also mention significant variations between employment laws in different areas of the country and types of workplaces.

There is another problem with the idea of just learning the legal rules and adhering to them. Employment law is dynamic. New law is created and old law is reinterpreted continuously. Further, changing workplace practices pose new legal questions. At any point in time, there are "well-settled" legal questions on which there is consensus, other matters that are only partially settled (perhaps because only a few cases have arisen or because courts have issued conflicting decisions), and still other questions that have yet to be considered by the courts and other legal decision makers. Attaining a solid grasp of employment law principles will allow you to make informed judgments in most situations. You must be prepared to tolerate some ambiguity and keep learning, however, as the law of the workplace continues to develop.

SOURCES OF EMPLOYMENT LAW

What comes to mind when you think of the law? Judges making decisions in court cases? Congress legislating? The Constitution? All of these are parts of the law in general and employment law in particular. Legal rules governing the workplace are found in the U.S. Constitution and state constitutions, statutes enacted by legislatures, executive orders issued by presidents and governors, regulations created by administrative agencies, and in judicially authored "common law." All of these pieces of law are regularly interpreted and expanded upon by the courts as they are presented with specific legal disputes (cases) to decide. Distinguishing between these basic sources of law is useful because some forms of law are more authoritative than others, apply to particular groups of employees, or provide for different enforcement mechanisms and remedies.

Constitutions

Constitutions are the most basic source of law in that all other laws must conform or risk being struck down as unconstitutional. **Constitutions** address the relationships between different levels of government (e.g., states and the federal government) and between governments and their citizens. A legal claim based on a constitution must generally assert a violation of someone's constitutional rights by the government (in legal parlance, the element of "state action" must be present). In practical terms, this means that usually only employees of government agencies—and not employees of private corporations—can look to the U.S. Constitution or state constitutions for protection in the workplace. Examples of constitutional protections available to government employees include speech rights, freedom of religion,

protection from unreasonable search and seizure, equal protection under the law, and due process rights.

Statutes

In the U.S. democratic system, voters elect representatives to legislative bodies such as the U.S. Congress. These bodies enact laws, or **statutes,** many of which affect the workplace. Among the many important statutes with implications for human resource practice that we will consider are Title VII of the Civil Rights Act of 1964, the National Labor Relations Act, the Equal Pay Act, the Americans with Disabilities Act, the Family and Medical Leave Act, and the Employee Retirement Income Security Act.

Executive Orders

The executive branch of government has the power to issue executive orders that affect the employment practices of government agencies and companies that have contracts to provide goods and services to the government. **Executive orders** function much like statutes, although they reach fewer workplaces and can be overridden by the legislative branch. The most important example of an executive order affecting employment is Executive Order (E.O.) 11246, which establishes affirmative action requirements for companies that do business with the federal government.

Regulations, Guidelines, and Administrative Decisions

When Congress enacts a statute, it often creates an agency, or authorizes an existing one, to administer and enforce that law. Legislators do not have the expertise (and sometimes do not have the political will) to fill in all the details necessary to put statutes into practice. For example, Congress mandated in the Occupational Safety and Health Act that employers provide safe workplaces, but largely left it to the Occupational Safety and Health Administration (OSHA) to give content to that broad principle by promulgating (creating) safety standards governing particular workplace hazards. Formal **regulations** are put in place only after an elaborate set of requirements for public comment and review have been followed. Regulations are entitled to considerable deference from the courts (generally they will be upheld when challenged), provided that the regulations are viewed as reasonable interpretations of the statutes on which they are based.[5] Agencies also contribute to the law through their decisions in individual cases that are brought before them.

Common Law

Many disputes are resolved through courts interpreting and enforcing the types of law discussed earlier. However, sometimes courts are asked to resolve disputes over matters that have not been objects of legislation or regulation. Over time, courts have recognized certain **common law** claims to remedy harm to people caused by other people or companies. Common law is defined by state courts, but broad similarities exist across states. One branch of common law is the traditional role of the courts in interpreting and enforcing contracts. The other branch is recognition of

[5]Chevron U.S.A., Inc. v. National Resources Defense Council, 467 U.S. 837 (1984).

various **tort** claims for civil wrongs that harm people. Tort claims relevant to employment law include negligence, defamation, invasion of privacy, infliction of emotional distress, and wrongful discharge in violation of public policy.

SUBSTANTIVE RIGHTS UNDER EMPLOYMENT LAWS

Employment laws confer rights on employees and impose corresponding responsibilities on employers. Paradoxically, the starting point for understanding employee rights is a legal doctrine holding that employees do not have any right to be employed or to retain their employment. This doctrine, known as **employment at will**, holds that in the absence of a contract promising employment for a specified duration, the employment relationship can be severed at any time and for any reason not specifically prohibited by law. Statutory and other rights conferred on employees have significantly blunted the force of employment at will, but in the absence of any clear right that employees can assert to not be terminated, employment at will still operates as the "default rule" regarding whether employees can lawfully be terminated.

Broadly speaking, employees have the following rights under employment laws.

Nondiscrimination and Equal Employment Opportunity

A central part of employment law is the set of protections for employees against discrimination based on their race, sex, age, and other grounds. The equal protection provisions of the U.S. Constitution (Fourteenth Amendment), Title VII of the Civil Rights Act of 1964, the Age Discrimination in Employment Act, the Equal Pay Act, and the Americans with Disabilities Act are examples of federal laws that prohibit discrimination in employment and express the societal value of equal employment opportunity.

Freedom to Engage in Concerted Activity and Collective Bargaining

Another approach to protecting workers is to provide them with greater leverage in dealing with their employers and negotiating contractual standards of fair treatment. Labor laws exist to protect the rights of employees to join together to form labor unions and attempt to improve their terms and conditions of employment through collective bargaining with their employers. Important federal labor laws include the National Labor Relations Act, the Railway Labor Act, and the Civil Service Reform Act (covering collective bargaining by federal government employees).

Terms and Conditions of Employment that Meet Minimum Standards

Some employment laws protect workers in a more direct fashion by specifying minimum standards of pay, safety, and other aspects of employment. Federal laws exemplifying this approach include the Fair Labor Standards Act (minimum wage and overtime pay requirements), the Occupational Safety and Health Act (workplace safety standards), and the Family and Medical Leave Act (leave policy requirements).

Protection of Fundamental Rights

Some legal challenges to employer practices are based on broader civil liberties and rights. Public employees have availed themselves of the First Amendment's guarantees of freedom of speech, religion, and association. A variety of privacy protections exist, including the Fourth Amendment (prohibiting unreasonable search and seizure), privacy torts, and the Fair Credit Reporting Act (limiting access to and use of information about employees when gained through third parties).

Compensation for Certain Types of Harm

Employees can take legal action to recover damages where, for example, they are the victims of employer negligence, are defamed, have emotional distress inflicted upon them, their employment contract is breached, or they are wrongfully discharged.

The *Gardner v. Loomis* case that follows is an interesting example of an employee availing himself of legal protection against wrongful discharge. Although it is easy to sympathize with the employee under the facts of this case, the Washington State Supreme Court had to decide whether to hold the employer legally accountable for the termination under one of the recognized exceptions to the employment at-will rule.

GARDNER V. LOOMIS
913 P.2d 377 (Wash. 1996)

● ● ●

OPINION BY JUSTICE DOLLIVER:

The United States District Court for the Eastern District of Washington asks whether an employer contravenes public policy when it terminates an at-will employee who violated a company rule in order to go to the assistance of a citizen who was in danger of serious physical injury or death. We answer in the affirmative.

Plaintiff, Kevin M. Gardner, worked for Defendant, Loomis Armored Inc. (Loomis), as a guard and driver of an armored car. On March 10, 1994, Gardner and his partner, Steffon Sobosky, made a scheduled stop at a Seafirst Bank branch in Spokane. Sobosky got out of the truck and entered the bank while Gardner stayed in the driver's compartment. Gardner then saw a woman, whom he recognized as the bank manager, run out of the bank while pointing behind her and screaming. Gardner looked behind the manager and saw a man with a knife chasing her. The armed man (hereinafter

referred to as the suspect) was approximately fifteen feet behind the manager. While running past the front of the truck, the manager looked straight at Gardner and cried out, "Help me, help me." Gardner described the expression on her face: "It was more than fear. There was a real—it was like a horrified kind of a look, like you—I can't describe it other than that, I mean she—she was horrified, not just afraid."

Gardner looked around the parking lot and saw nobody coming to help the manager. After the manager and the suspect ran past the front of the truck, Gardner got out, locking the door behind him. As he got out of the truck, he temporarily lost sight of the manager and the suspect, who were both on the passenger side of the truck. While out of Gardner's view, the manager reached a drive-in teller booth across the parking lot, where she found refuge. It is unclear whether the manager was safe before Gardner left the truck, but by the time Gardner walked forward to a point where he could see the suspect, the suspect had already grabbed another woman who was walking into the bank.

Gardner recognized the second woman as Kathy Martin. . . . The suspect put the knife to Ms. Martin's throat and dragged her back into the bank. Gardner followed them into the bank where he observed his partner, Sobosky, with his gun drawn and aimed at the suspect. When Sobosky distracted the suspect, Gardner and a bank customer tackled the suspect and disarmed him. The police arrived immediately thereafter and took custody of the suspect. Ms. Martin was unharmed.

Loomis has a "fundamental" company rule forbidding armored truck drivers from leaving the truck unattended. The employee handbook states, "violations of this rule will be grounds for termination." Drivers may not exit the compartment under any circumstance. * * * Gardner was fired for violating this work rule by exiting the truck during the March 10, 1994, incident. * * * Gardner sued Loomis . . . [for] wrongful discharge in violation of public policy. * * *

Henry Perritt Jr., one of this country's foremost scholars on labor and employment law, advocates a comprehensive test for analyzing wrongful discharge claims involving violations of public policy. Perritt proposes four elements of a public policy tort case:

(1) The plaintiffs must prove the existence of a clear public policy (the clarity element).

(2) The plaintiffs must prove that discouraging the conduct in which they engaged would jeopardize the public policy (the jeopardy element).

(3) The plaintiffs must prove that the public–policy-linked conduct caused the dismissal (the causation element).

(4) The defendant must not be able to offer an overriding justification for the dismissal (the absence of justification element).

Perritt's test serves as an excellent guide for analyzing all public policy wrongful discharge torts . . . * * *

Society places the highest priority on the protection of human life. This fundamental public policy is clearly evidenced by countless statutes and judicial decisions. The value placed on human life is demonstrated by the fact that courts have even suspended certain fundamental constitutional rights when a citizen's life is in imminent danger. For example, the Fourth Amendment's protection against warrantless searches is waived under limited exigent circumstances, including situations where the search is necessary "to prevent physical harm to the officers or other persons." Besides subordinating some constitutional rights, the public policy favoring the protection of human life also serves as a defense against most criminal charges. What would otherwise be the illegal use of force becomes lawful when it is done to protect oneself or others from injury. Homicide is justifiable if committed in the lawful defense of oneself or others. * * * Society benefits by a citizen's death being prevented, to the extent that some constitutional rights and criminal laws are suspended when one acts to save another's life. This public policy of saving persons from life-threatening situations satisfies the clarity element. * * *

Under the second element, the employee's discharge must jeopardize the public policy. To establish jeopardy, plaintiffs must show they engaged in particular conduct, and the conduct directly relates to the public policy, or was necessary for the effective enforcement of the public policy. This burden requires a plaintiff to "argue that other means for promoting the policy . . . are inadequate." Additionally, the plaintiff must show how the threat of dismissal will discourage others from engaging in the desirable conduct. * * * [T]he facts of the situation tend to show Gardner reasonably believed the woman's life was in immediate danger, and he was the only source of help. * * * A jury could easily find Gardner believed his conduct was necessary to rescue Ms. Martin from an imminent life-threatening situation. Gardner's being fired for those actions will discourage similar future conduct in other employees. * * *

[The third element, causation, is established by the fact that he was terminated for leaving the armored car, which he needed to do in order to act on behalf of public policy.]

The last element inquires whether the employer has an overriding reason for terminating the employee despite the employee's public–policy-linked conduct. This fourth element of a public policy tort acknowledges that some public policies, even if clearly mandated, are not strong enough to warrant interfering with employers' personnel management.

Loomis has exhaustively defended its work rule as an overriding justification. The rule is allegedly necessary to protect the safety and lives of Loomis employees. The drivers are safe inside the compartments and they can use the available two-way radio, public

address system, and sirens to summon help. A driver's exiting the truck severs the partner's lifeline to safety and renders both employees more vulnerable to harm. . . . Defendant cited a 1991 incident where an armored car driver got out of the truck in response to his partner being robbed. Upon exiting the truck the driver was shot six times and killed. A more specific reason for strictly enforcing the work rule involves the risk of robbers using a ploy to get the driver out of the truck. * * * If robbers knew they could trick drivers out of the truck every time it appeared someone was in need of help, the occurrence of such ploys could increase. A third reason behind Loomis' work rule may involve insurance policies. Some insurance companies will not cover a loss if the truck was robbed while left unattended. * * *

If our society has placed the rescue of a life above constitutional rights and above the criminal code, then such conduct clearly rises above a company's work rule. Loomis' work rule does not provide an overriding justification for firing Gardner when his conduct directly served the public policy encouraging citizens to save persons from serious bodily injury or death.

We find that Gardner's discharge for leaving the truck and saving a woman from an imminent life-threatening situation violates the public policy encouraging such heroic conduct. This holding does not create an affirmative legal duty requiring citizens to intervene in dangerous life-threatening situations. We simply observe that society values and encourages voluntary rescuers when a life is in danger. Additionally, our adherence to this public policy does nothing to invalidate Loomis' work rule regarding drivers leaving the trucks. The rule's importance cannot be understated, and drivers do subject themselves to a great risk of harm by leaving the driver's compartment. Our holding merely forbids Loomis from firing Gardner when he broke the rule because he saw a woman who faced imminent life-threatening harm, and he reasonably believed his intervention was necessary to save her life. Finally, by focusing on the narrow public policy encouraging citizens to save human lives from life-threatening situations, we continue to protect employers from frivolous lawsuits.

CASE QUESTIONS

1. What was the legal issue? What did the court decide?

2. Why did the company have its rule against leaving armored cars unattended? Why is the company liable for enforcing its clear policy?

3. Would it have made any difference if things had not turned out so well (e.g., someone got killed or the armored car was stolen)?

4. Do you agree with the court's decision? Why or why not? How far should the courts go in protecting terminated employees?

Gardner v. Loomis is included here as an illustration of the excerpted employment law cases that you will be reading throughout this text. The words are those of the judge who wrote the decision and are the same words that you would find if you looked the case up (which you can do easily by using an online legal database and searching on either the names of the parties or the citation that appears below the names of the parties). The only difference is that the case has been shortened by selecting only the most essential details and by removing internal citations and footnotes. Notice that the terminated employee is asserting a specific legal claim (wrongful discharge under the public policy exception to employment will); simply showing that the employee was terminated or alleging that the employer acted unfairly is not enough. The elements of a public policy wrongful discharge claim are clearly spelled out in the decision and the court systematically applies those elements to the facts of the case to arrive at a decision. To properly analyze employment laws cases, you must understand the elements of particular legal claims; hence, throughout the text, under the "Elements of a Claim" header, you will find the things that must be established to show that an employee's rights have been violated. By seeing the law applied to particular factual circumstances and reading the court's rationale for its decision, you will gain a fuller understanding of the law.

DETERMINING WHICH EMPLOYMENT LAWS APPLY

Because U.S. employment law is a patchwork of legal protections that apply to some groups of employees but not others, it is necessary to briefly elaborate on some of the key contextual factors that determine which, if any, employment laws apply in a given situation. You will need to consider these factors when presented with situations posing potential legal problems.

Public or Private Sector Employment

The legal environment differs substantially depending on whether **public sector** (i.e., government) employees or **private sector** employees are being considered. Public and private sector does not refer to whether a company trades its stock on the stock market (i.e., publicly traded versus privately held companies), but rather whether the employer is the government or a corporation. Public employees make up roughly 15 percent of the workforce and are a diverse group of workers, including most public schoolteachers and police officers. One reason that public employees are a different case has already been mentioned. In general, constitutional protections pertain only to public employees and not to private sector employees. Beyond this, public employees are often covered by state or municipal civil service laws (regulating hiring, promoting, and discharging practices), and for teachers, by tenure provisions.

Not all the comparisons favor public employees. Public employees are subject to restrictions on their political activities (Hatch Acts), excluded from coverage under the National Labor Relations Act and the Occupational Safety and Health Act, and limited in their ability to sue for violations of federal law. This last point should be underscored. A series of recent U.S. Supreme Court decisions have held, based on the Eleventh Amendment and the broad concept of state sovereignty, that state governments cannot be sued by their public employees, whether in state or federal court, for violations of such federal employment laws as the Fair Labor Standards Act and the Americans with Disabilities Act (however, the Court reached the opposite decision regarding suits under the Family and Medical Leave Act).[6] Thus, even though these federal laws still apply to state government employees, options for enforcement are limited.

Unionized or Nonunion Workplace

When employees opt for union representation and negotiate a collective bargaining agreement with their employer, the employer is contractually committed to live up to the terms of the agreement. In contrast to the vast majority of employees who lack employment contracts, unionized employees have many of their terms and conditions of employment spelled out in enforceable labor agreements. These contractual terms typically go well beyond the minimum requirements of the law (e.g., by providing for daily overtime rather than the weekly overtime required by federal law). Employers in unionized workplaces are also much more limited in their ability to make unilateral changes in workplace practices without first negotiating those changes with unions. Discipline or discharge of a unionized employee is contractually limited to situations where the employer can establish "just cause" for the discipline or discharge, which stands in stark contrast to the at-will employment of most nonunion workers.

[6]Alden v. Maine, 527 U.S. 706 (1999); University of Alabama v. Garrett, 531 U.S. 356 (2001); Nev. Dep't of Human Res. v. Hibbs, 538 U.S. 721 (2003).

TABLE 1–1	Employment Size of Firms (2002)			
Employment Size (No. of employees)	Firms		Employees	
	(*n*)	(%)	(*n*)	(%)
0	770,041	13.5	0	0.0
1–4	2,695,606	47.3	5,697,652	5.1
5–9	1,010,804	17.7	6,639,666	5.9
10–19	613,880	10.8	8,246,053	7.3
20–99	508,249	8.9	19,874,069	17.7
100–499	82,334	1.4	15,908,852	14.2
500+	16,845	0.3	56,034,362	49.8
Total	5,697,759	99.9	112,400,654	100.0

Source: Adapted from U.S. Census Bureau, *Statistics of U.S. Business*, viewed on June 4, 2005 (http://www.census.gov).

Employer Size

The legal environment also varies depending on the size of the employer. Size can be variously construed. For purposes of some statutes, including the Fair Labor Standards Act and the National Labor Relations Act, size is measured in financial terms and coverage is limited to employers that exceed a minimum level of sales (e.g., the general minimum for coverage under the FLSA is $500,000). More often, statutes specify a minimum employer size in terms of number of employees. For instance, both Title VII of the Civil Rights Act and the Americans with Disabilities Act limit coverage to companies that have 15 or more employees; the Age Discrimination in Employment Act applies to employers with 20 or more employees; and the Family and Medical Leave Act applies only to employers with 50 or more employees (within a 75-mile radius, if the company has multiple work sites). These size limitations are not trivial. Consider the following data on firm size (note that these figures pertain to entire companies rather than individual establishments such as offices and plants).

Table 1-1 shows that 89.3 percent of firms have less than 20 employees, which means the major federal employment laws exclude the vast majority of U.S. firms. There are two countervailing factors to consider, however. First, although the major federal employment laws do not cover most firms due to their small size, the minority of companies that are covered nonetheless employ most U.S. workers (because each larger company employs many more people). Thus, the approximately 10 percent of all firms that have 20 or more employees employ fully 81.7 percent of the workforce. The second important fact is that most states have enacted laws that mirror federal employment laws and that apply to smaller workplaces. In Ohio, for example, the Ohio Civil Rights Act[7] covers employees whose employer has 4 or more employees. Thus in Ohio, employers with between 4 and 14 employees would fall under state law, but not federal law, whereas employers with 15 or more employees would be subject to both federal law and state law. Only employers with fewer than 4 employees would not be subject to civil rights statutes.

[7]O.R.C. Ann. § 4112.01(A) (2) (2005).

There is another aspect to the size issue. Counting the number of employees that an employer has is more complex than it first appears. For one thing, employment levels change, often rapidly, and a smaller company could easily vacillate above and below the minimum number of employees specified in a statute. When must the employer have the requisite number of employees then? At the time of the alleged violation? When the claim is filed? An average over some longer period of time?

Another set of questions in regard to size stems from the use of different types of employees. How, for example, should part-time employees be counted? Temporary workers? Congress addressed these questions partially in Title VII of the Civil Rights Act of 1964 (parallel language appears in other employment statutes). An employer is defined as someone "who has fifteen or more employees for each working day in each of twenty or more calendar weeks in the current or preceding calendar year. . . ."[8] The Supreme Court has ruled that the proper method for counting employees is the **payroll method**. An employee is counted for each full week between when she is hired and when she leaves employment, regardless of the number of hours she worked during those weeks.[9] Thus, *employers should use the payroll method to track how many employees they have. Employers should also be aware that growth of their businesses may be accompanied by changes in their legal environments.*

Geographic Location

An employee's rights are affected by where he happens to live. Some states and cities go much further than others and also further than the federal government, in conferring rights on workers. The interrelationship between federal and state laws is a complex legal matter. At the risk of oversimplification, states are free to enact laws pertaining to issues not addressed by federal law. State laws also can match or exceed the protections available under federal laws dealing with the same matters, but they cannot reduce the rights employees have under federal law. Thus, state laws are important not only for reaching smaller workplaces than federal employment laws, but also because they sometimes provide employees with rights not available under federal law. Examples of areas where state laws often exceed federal law include higher minimum wages in some states, laws regulating the handling of personnel records, limitations placed on drug and HIV testing, and prohibitions against discrimination based on sexual orientation. *Lack of uniformity in legal requirements across states also adds complexity for employers with multistate operations. The choices are either to tailor practices to the particular location, or more feasibly, implement the higher standard uniformly.*

Government Contracts

Federal, state, and local governments sometimes use the contracting process as leverage to get employers to implement desired workplace practices. Employers that contract to do business with the federal government (e.g., defense contractors, construction companies, computer suppliers) and that meet certain other criteria are required to engage in affirmative action as a condition of their contracts. Likewise, both the Drug-Free Workplace Act (requiring that employers take certain actions to stop workplace drug use) and the Rehabilitation Act (prohibiting discrimination against and requiring affirmative action on behalf of disabled persons) apply to private employers based on their contracts with the federal government.

[8]42 U.S.C.A. § 2000e(b) (2005).
[9]Walters v. Metropolitan Educational Enterprises, Inc., 117 S. Ct. 660 (1997).

Industry and Occupation

Most employment laws apply to any industry, but some are more narrowly targeted. For example, the Omnibus Transportation Employees Testing Act of 1991 mandates extensive drug (and alcohol) testing, but only for employees in industries regulated by the Department of Transportation (e.g., airlines, railroads, trucking companies). Likewise, employees in the historically very dangerous mining industry are not covered under the Occupational Safety and Health Act, but instead under a separate statute, the Mine Safety and Health Act. Agricultural workers, despite their generally poor working conditions, are wholly or partly excluded from the protection of many employment laws, including the National Labor Relations Act, the Fair Labor Standards Act, and state workers' compensation statutes. An important example of an occupation-based distinction is the National Labor Relations Act's exclusion of supervisors and managers.

Historical Development of U.S. Employment Law

Detailing what the law said previously and how it has changed over time is beyond the scope of this book. However, you should have some sense of when employment laws came into existence. Figure 1-1 is a time line of major employment laws (ignoring, for the most part, amendments to these laws).

At the turn of the twentieth century, employment law was virtually nonexistent in the United States. The first significant departure from an unregulated workplace was the adoption of state workers' compensation laws to deal with the severe problem of injured and disabled workers. A major breakthrough came in the 1930s when the National Labor Relations Act and the Fair Labor Standards Act were enacted. Employment law took large strides forward in the 1960s with the passage of major antidiscrimination statutes, including the Civil Rights Act of 1964, the Age Discrimination in Employment Act, and the Equal Pay Act. Common-law claims, particularly for wrongful discharge, came into vogue in the late 1970s and throughout the 1980s. Benefits have been the object of a number of employment laws since the 1970s, with health insurance being at the center of recent legislative efforts.

Legislation does not emerge in a vacuum. Nor do legislators simply wake up one day and see the need for it. Many of our employment laws reflect the work of **social movements,** organized efforts to create needed changes in workplaces and society. The workers' compensation statutes adopted in the early part of the twentieth century were influenced by the progressive movement that addressed the social problems of that time. The National Labor Relations Act was enacted in 1935 during the early part of the New Deal and in the depths of the Depression. The act both reflected and furthered the efforts of ordinary workers and their unions, joined together in the labor movement, to gain some control over their work lives. Likewise, the Civil Rights Act of 1964 was a crowning achievement of the civil rights movement. The civil rights movement had to overcome enormous opposition to obtain legislation protecting the basic civil rights of all people, and the struggle to realize this law's promise continues. Thus, although we will focus on the effects of employment laws on the human resource practices of companies, the major employment laws mean much more than that; they are windows into important periods in our history, express basic societal values, and represent hard-won accomplishments that should not be taken for granted.

The time line in Figure 1-1 covers the entire twentieth century, but most of the laws are clustered in the second half of this period. As a consequence, many interesting legal questions have yet to be resolved by the courts. Is there "too much"

FIGURE 1-1	**Timeline of Major U.S. Employment Laws**

1900 Workers' Compensation (most states between 1911 and 1920)

1920 Railway Labor Act (1926)

National Labor Relations Act (Wagner Act) (1935)

Social Security Act (1935)

Fair Labor Standards Act (1938)

1940 Labor-Management Relations Act (Taft-Hartley Act) (1947)

1960 Equal Pay Act (1963)

Title VII of the Civil Rights Act (1964)

Executive Order 11246 (1965)

Age Discrimination in Employment Act (1967)

1970 Occupational Safety and Health Act (1970)

Rehabilitation Act (1973)

Employee Retirement Income Security Act (1974)

Pregnancy Discrimination Act (1978)

1980 Common Law Wrongful Discharge Claims (majority of states adopted one or more of these from the late 1970s through the 1980s)

Consolidated Omnibus Budget Reconciliation Act (COBRA) (1985)

Immigration Reform and Control Act (1986)

Employee Polygraph Protection Act (1988)

Worker Adjustment and Retraining Notification Act (1988)

1990 Older Workers Benefit Protection Act (1990)

Americans with Disabilities Act (1990)

Civil Rights Act of 1991 (1991)

Family and Medical Leave Act (1993)

Uniformed Services Employment and Reemployment Rights Act (1994)

Health Insurance Portability and Accountability Act (1996)

2000

employment law now? Opinions differ on this point. Certainly, in comparison to the not-so-distant past, the workplace is far more regulated than it used to be. On the other hand, U.S. employers enjoy considerably more freedom to carry out human resource decisions as they see fit than do employers in most of the other major industrialized nations in the world, particularly in Europe.

PROCEDURES FOR ENFORCING EMPLOYMENT LAWS

Simply conferring rights on employees is not enough. Means of enforcing those rights must be available when employers do not comply with the requirements of the law. TV lawyers get cases and emerge victorious—largely by dint of their rousing courtroom oratory—in the space of single episodes. In the real world, the process of resolving employment disputes is anything but simple and quick. No single process exists for enforcing employees' rights, but it is possible to convey some of the various ways employment law claims proceed.

What Does an Employee Decide to Do When She Believes That Her Rights Were Violated?

In a few situations, employment laws are enforced by government agencies at their own initiative, such as when OSHA elects to inspect a workplace based on the occurrence of a serious accident or because it operates in a particularly dangerous industry. However, as a general rule, both the courts and government agencies rely on individual employees to come forward with complaints before enforcement actions are undertaken. Thus, the decision of an employee to challenge some action of her employer is a key part of the enforcement process.

Some maintain that an avalanche of frivolous employee lawsuits is making the workplace unmanageable and needlessly clogging the courts.[10] Although every case is different, and some frivolous claims are brought against employers, it is a mistake to assume that most employee complaints are baseless and rooted in opportunism. In fact, contesting an employer in the legal system is an expensive, protracted, uncertain, and emotionally draining process. Most likely, the cases that are brought, even though their number has increased substantially, are just the tip of the iceberg. Most employees who have their rights violated by their employers do something other than take legal action; they quit, join a union, withhold commitment and discretionary effort, just let it go, or talk it over with the employer and work things out. Ultimately, although no employer can be expected to like it, the system of employment law depends on employees being willing to come forward and assume the burden of taking legal action against their employers to both remedy the harm that was done to them as individuals and to uphold public policy.[11]

How Long Does the Employee Have to Bring a Case?

An important feature of any **enforcement procedure** is the length of time that an aggrieved person has to come forward with a complaint (the "statute of limitations"). Time limits for filing lawsuits or charges with administrative agencies vary. Unfair labor practice charges must be brought to the National Labor Relations Board within 6 months of their occurrence. In discrimination cases, employees generally have 300 days to file a charge with the EEOC (180 days in states that do not have their own state civil rights agencies), but only 90 days to file suit if the EEOC's efforts to resolve the case conclude unsuccessfully. Wage and hour cases brought

[10]Walter Olson. *The Excuse Factory: How Employment Law Is Paralyzing the American Workplace.* (New York: Free Press, 1997).

[11]McKennon v. Nashville Banner Publishing Co., 115 S. Ct. 879, at 884 (1995).

under the Fair Labor Standards Act can go back as far as 3 years. State laws typically allow tort claims to be brought based on events that occurred several years in the past. A major practical consequence is that *employers must be prepared to defend actions taken well in the past and by individuals who might no longer work for their companies. The only way to do this is to maintain solid documentation regarding all human resource decisions.*

Employees who fail to bring charges in a timely fashion generally lose their right to pursue legal action. However, if an employee is unaware of her rights because she was actively misled by her employer or the employer failed to meet its legal obligation to post information in the workplace,[12] a court might excuse an untimely filing (known as equitable tolling). Additionally, prior actions that occurred too long ago to be the basis for a legal claim might still be legally relevant if they form part of a single unlawful employment practice that unfolds over a period of time (e.g., numerous acts of harassment that create a "hostile environment").[13]

Can a Lawsuit Be Brought? By Whom?

Most employment laws enable employees to enforce their rights through lawsuits against their employers. The Occupational Safety and Health Act is an exception in this regard. When an employee believes that a safety hazard exists in his workplace, he needs to contact OSHA and get an inspector to come. If the inspector does not agree that there is a problem and the employer is not cited, no course of legal action is available to the employee. Likewise, if the General Counsel of the National Labor Relations Board declines to bring a complaint regarding an alleged unfair labor practice, the employee is out of luck. Suits in discrimination cases can be brought either by individuals or the EEOC. However, because the Commission goes to court in only a very small percentage of the cases it receives, the burden of taking legal action to enforce antidiscrimination laws falls mainly on individual employees. Finding an attorney willing to take an employment law case, particularly on a contingent fee basis (the attorney incurs most of the cost of litigation with the promise of a substantial share of any award if the litigation is successful), can be difficult. Employment lawyers accept only an estimated 5 percent of the employment discrimination cases brought to them. Lower-wage workers, for whom provable damages are relatively low, are particularly likely to have their cases turned away.[14]

A great deal happens between when a lawsuit is filed and when the case is actually heard in court (if the action proceeds that far). Considerable managerial time is spent responding to requests for records, answering interrogatories (sets of questions), and giving sworn depositions (statements) regarding the facts of the case. If you are involved in making human resource decisions, you can expect to experience this part of the litigation process firsthand. *The best advice is to testify truthfully and succinctly, and to have documentation to back you up.* Settlement negotiations are likely, both at this point and throughout the course of the litigation. Settlements are a common outcome of litigation.

Employment law cases are brought in both state and federal courts. Where the case will end up depends on such factors as the legal basis for the claim, where the

[12]Mercado v. The Ritz-Carlton San Juan Hotel, Spa & Casino, 2005 U.S. App. LEXIS 9899.

[13]National Railroad Passenger Corporation v. Morgan, 536 U.S. 101 (2002).

[14]Elizabeth Hill. "Due Process at Low Cost: An Empirical Study of Employment Arbitration Under the Auspices of the American Arbitration Association." *Ohio State Journal on Dispute Resolution,* 18 (2003), 777–783.

parties to the case reside or are incorporated, and the strategic choices of the parties. A case that goes into the federal court system starts at the **district court** (trial court) level. The role of the district court is to establish the facts of the case and to reach a decision about the merits of the employee's claim. However, many cases filed against employers are thrown out (the employer is granted **summary judgment**) because the court determines that even if the **plaintiff's** (the employee who is suing) allegations are accepted as true, they are not sufficient to support a legal claim. The increasing tendency of courts to dispose of cases in this manner is an important factor in the declining proportion of cases that go to trial (see the "Clippings" section earlier in this chapter). If the case makes it to trial, the plaintiff bears the **burden of proof** to show, generally by a "preponderance (the majority) of the evidence," that his rights were violated. Cases that go to trial are sometimes decided by juries and other times by judges. District court decisions can be appealed by either party to a federal **appeals court** (circuit court). Appeals courts typically accept the facts of cases as given and focus on whether the lower courts properly applied the law in deciding cases. Appeals court decisions can be appealed to the U.S. **Supreme Court.** However, because the Supreme Court exercises its discretion as to which cases it hears (when the court decides to hear a case, it grants **certiorari**), and it hears relatively few cases each year, rarely does the case go that far. Thus, although you will read many U.S. Supreme Court cases in this book, these cases are included because they raise important employment law issues and decide them authoritatively, not because they are typical cases.

Is There an Administrative Prerequisite to a Lawsuit?

Many employment laws require that a charge be filed with an administrative agency (e.g., the Equal Employment Opportunity Commission, the Wage and Hour Division of the Department of Labor) and that the agency be given the chance to resolve the matter before an employee can go to court. In discrimination cases, an employee usually starts by filing a charge with either the EEOC or a state fair employment practice agency. If the EEOC dismisses the case or fails to achieve **conciliation** (a settlement agreement) between the parties, it issues a **right to sue letter** to the employee alleging discrimination. Only then is the employee able to commence a lawsuit. Other types of legal claims, such as breach of contract or negligence, can proceed directly to court.

Must the Employee Exhaust Internal Dispute Resolution Mechanisms Before Proceeding?

If an employer has a complaint or grievance procedure, the employee does not usually have to use the internal procedure before taking the case to an enforcement agency or court; however, this is an area of the law where profound changes are taking place. The Supreme Court has held that an employer may be able to escape liability for harassment engaged in by a supervisor when an employee unreasonably refuses to avail herself of the employer's complaint procedure.[15] An even more fundamental change has been the rise of alternative dispute resolution procedures intended to take the place of lawsuits (see "The Changing Workplace").

[15]Faragher v. City of Boca Raton, 524 U.S. 775 (1998).

THE CHANGING WORKPLACE

Alternative Dispute Resolution Procedures

There is great interest in **alternative dispute resolution (ADR)** procedures in all areas of the law. Alternative dispute resolution procedures are alternatives to going to court to resolve disputes. Enthusiasm for ADR stems from the belief that these procedures are cheaper, quicker, and less damaging to relationships than litigation. There are many different types of ADR. Two of the most frequently used types are **mediation** and **arbitration**. In mediation, a neutral third party (the mediator) facilitates negotiations between the disputing parties to help them reach an agreement, but does not have the authority to decide the dispute or impose a settlement. In arbitration, a neutral third party (the arbitrator) functions more like a private judge. Arbitrators hear disputes and render decisions that are almost always final and binding on the parties.

The EEOC encourages the parties to discrimination charges to use mediation. Rather than decide whether there has been a violation of the law, the mediator (a trained EEOC staff member or contractor) focuses on helping the parties "jointly explore and reconcile their differences." Typically undertaken prior to EEOC investigation of a charge, mediation is voluntary and confidential. If it proves unsuccessful, the case reverts to the typical EEOC enforcement procedure of investigation, conciliation, and possible litigation. The EEOC's mediation program achieved a 69 percent settlement rate (self-reported) in fiscal year 2003.[1]

Arbitration has for decades been the principal means of enforcing employee rights under collective bargaining agreements in unionized workplaces. This use of arbitration amounts to establishing through collective bargaining a private system for resolving disputes about violations of private contractual agreements. What is new in the last decade or so is that some employers are requiring arbitration agreements as a condition of employment (hence, the term "mandatory" or "employer promulgated" arbitration), and arbitration is being used to resolve all employment law disputes—not simply contractual ones. To get (or keep) the job, employees have to surrender the ability to go to court to vindicate their rights as employees, and they have to do so prior to any dispute arising.

Precise, current estimates of the extent of ADR use in the workplace are lacking. A study by the U.S. General Accounting Office (GAO) found that about 19 percent of large employers were using arbitration to resolve discrimination complaints of their nonunion employees in 1997, up from 10 percent in 1994.[2] An estimated six million nonunion employees were covered by arbitration agreements in 2002, double the number covered in 1997.[3] Whatever the exact number of arbitration agreements in use, the consensus is that the use of arbitration agreements is increasing. But are these agreements that bar employees from going to court enforceable?

[1]U.S. Equal Employment Opportunity Commission. "Questions and Answers About Mediation." Viewed August 26, 2004. (http://www.eeoc.gov/mediate/mediation_qa.html).

[2]U.S. General Accounting Office. *Alternative Dispute Resolution: Employers' Experiences with ADR in the Workplace.* GAO/GGD-97-157 (1997). Viewed June 12, 2005 (http://www.gao.gov).

[3]Elizabeth Hill. "Due Process at Low Cost: An Empirical Study of Employment Arbitration Under the Auspices of the American Arbitration Association." *Ohio State Journal on Dispute Resolution,* 18 (2003), 777, 780

ENFORCEABILITY OF MANDATORY ARBITRATION AGREEMENTS

Recent Supreme Court cases have made it clear that mandatory arbitration agreements, requiring employees to use arbitration rather than the courts as the means of resolving employment law claims, are generally enforceable. In a case involving an arbitration agreement between a broker and the New York Stock Exchange, the Supreme Court ruled that the broker would have to use the NYSE's arbitration procedure rather than the courts to pursue an age discrimination claim against his employer. Quoting an earlier case, the Court minimized the differences between arbitration and litigation: "by agreeing to arbitrate a statutory claim, a party does not forgo the substantive rights afforded by the statute; it only submits to their

resolution in an arbitral, rather than a judicial, forum."[16] In a subsequent case, the Supreme Court decided that arbitration agreements between employers and employees are covered under the Federal Arbitration Act (FAA) and thus generally enforceable (but not when transportation workers are involved, owing to exclusionary language included within the FAA).[17] The Federal Arbitration Act, enacted by Congress in 1925, requires courts to enforce most written arbitration agreements.

The Court's evident enthusiasm for arbitration does not mean that arbitration agreements will always be enforced. In a case involving a disability discrimination suit brought by the EEOC on behalf of an employee who had signed an arbitration agreement as a condition of employment, the Supreme Court decided that the agency's suit was not barred by the agreement and that it could seek to recover victim-specific remedies, including back pay and reinstatement.[18] Thus, even with a signed arbitration agreement in hand, an employer in a discrimination case is still subject to EEOC proceedings and possibly a lawsuit brought on behalf of an employee by the agency. Another issue is that, based on previous Supreme Court decisions,[19] unionized employers are not able to insist that arbitration provisions in collective bargaining agreements bar litigation over violations of individuals' legal rights. And the retaliation theory advanced in the case of the legal secretary who was fired for refusing to sign an arbitration agreement (see "Clippings") has not been definitively tested because his case was settled.

The complicated story of mandatory arbitration agreements does not end here. Fundamentally, an arbitration agreement is a contract. Courts decline to enforce contracts when fraud is involved, the contract was entered into under extreme duress, or where the contract is unconscionable. Contracts are unconscionable when the process of contract formation essentially involves a "take it or leave it" offer of an agreement drafted by a more powerful party (a "contract of adhesion") and when the content of the agreement unreasonably favors the more powerful party. Mandatory arbitration agreements have *sometimes* not been enforced by courts (i.e., the employee was allowed to go to court despite the existence of the agreement) on the grounds that they are unconscionable. *Ingle v. Circuit City Stores* is one such case.

As in *Ingle,* courts have looked at the details of particular arbitration agreements and sometimes found the agreements to be unconscionable and/or not capable of effectively vindicating the legal rights of employees. One area of particular concern is the procedure for selecting an arbitrator. An essential requirement for a fair arbitration is neutrality. Arrangements that give the employer effective control over who can arbitrate a case (e.g., the employer determines who is in the pool of arbitrators from which selections are made) are unlikely to be enforced.[20] Likewise, courts have closely scrutinized arbitration agreements that require employees to bear a significant part of the arbitration cost. Although some courts hold that any fee-splitting arrangement is objectionable, most courts look at the facts of the situation and the likelihood that high cost would deter employees from bringing claims.[21] Remedies that are markedly different from those available through litigation (e.g., reinstatement or punitive damages are not allowed) are also problematic. More generally,

[16]Gilmer v. Interstate/Johnson Lane Corporation, 500 U.S. 20, at 26 (1991).

[17]Circuit City Stores v. Adams, 121 S. Ct. 1302 (2001).

[18]Equal Employment Opportunity Commission v. Waffle House, Inc., 534 U.S. 279 (2002).

[19]Alexander v. Gardner-Denver Co., 415 U.S. 36 (1974); Wright v. Universal Maritime Service Corp., 525 U.S. 70 (1998).

[20]Hooters of America v. Phillips, 173 F.3d 933 (4th Cir. 1999); McMullen v. Meijer, 355 F.3d 485 (6th Cir. 2004).

[21]Blair v. Scott Specialty Gases, 283 F.3d 595, at 609–10 (3d Cir. 2002); Morrison v. Circuit City Stores, 317 F.3d 646 (6th Cir. 2003).

INGLE V. CIRCUIT CITY STORES

328 F.3d 1165 (9th Cir. 2003); *cert. denied*, 2004 U.S. LEXIS 839

● ● ●

OPINION BY CIRCUIT JUDGE PREGERSON:

This appeal arises from the district court's denial of . . . Circuit City Stores, Inc.'s (Circuit City) motion to compel arbitration. Circuit City moved to compel arbitration in response to the action . . . Catherine Ingle filed . . . in which she alleged employment discrimination in violation of state and federal civil rights statutes. Circuit City argues on appeal that the district court erred in declining to enforce an arbitration agreement requiring Ingle and Circuit City to arbitrate employment-related legal claims. We . . . affirm. ***

Circuit City compels all of its employees and job applicants to sign an arbitration agreement requiring arbitration of all employment-related legal claims. The "Circuit City Dispute Resolution Rules and Procedures" (Rules and Procedures) determine the substance and procedures of the arbitration agreement. * * *

The Federal Arbitration Act (FAA) provides that arbitration agreements generally "shall be valid, irrevocable, and enforceable." But when grounds "exist at law or in equity for the revocation of any contract," courts may decline to enforce such agreements. It is a settled principle of law that "arbitration is a matter of contract." * * * Arbitration agreements, accordingly, are subject to all defenses to enforcement that apply to contracts generally. To evaluate the validity of an arbitration agreement, federal courts "should apply ordinary state-law principles that govern the formation of contracts." * * * Ingle was employed in California; we therefore evaluate Circuit City's arbitration agreement under the contract law of that state.

Because unconscionability is a generally applicable defense to contracts, California courts may refuse to enforce an unconscionable arbitration agreement. Unconscionability refers to "an absence of meaningful choice on the part of one of the parties together with contract terms which are unreasonably favorable to the other party." Thus, a contract to arbitrate is unenforceable under the doctrine of unconscionability when there is "both a procedural and substantive element of unconscionability." Significantly, the California Supreme Court has noted that procedural and substantive unconscionability "need not be present in the same degree." In *Armendariz*, the court held that:

> . . . [e]ssentially a sliding scale is invoked which disregards the regularity of the procedural process of the contract formation, that creates the terms, in proportion to the greater harshness or unreasonableness of the substantive terms themselves.' In other words, the more substantively oppressive the contract term, the less evidence of procedural unconscionability is required to come to the conclusion that the term is unenforceable, and vice versa.

To determine whether the arbitration agreement is procedurally unconscionable the court must examine "the manner in which the contract was negotiated and the circumstances of the parties at that time." An inquiry into whether Circuit City's arbitration agreement involves oppression or surprise is central to that analysis. A contract is oppressive if an inequality of bargaining power between the parties precludes the weaker party from enjoying a meaningful opportunity to negotiate and choose the terms of the contract. "Surprise involves the extent to which the supposedly agreed-upon terms of the bargain are hidden in the prolix printed form drafted by the party seeking to enforce the disputed terms."

There is no doubt that Circuit City's arbitration agreement is oppressive. * * * Circuit City, which possesses considerably more bargaining power than nearly all of its employees or applicants, drafted the contract and uses it as its standard arbitration agreement for all of its new employees. The agreement is a prerequisite to employment, and job applicants are not permitted to modify the agreement's terms—they must take the contract or leave it.

* * * Ingle had no meaningful opportunity to opt out of the arbitration agreement, nor did she have any power to negotiate the terms of the agreement. Therefore, because Circuit City presented the arbitration agreement to Ingle on an adhere-or-reject basis, we conclude that the agreement is procedurally unconscionable.

Substantive unconscionability centers on the "terms of the agreement and whether those terms are so one-sided as to shock the conscience." * * * Several

substantive terms of Circuit City's arbitration agreement are one-sided. The provisions concerning coverage of claims, the statute of limitations, the prohibition of class actions, the filing fee, cost-splitting, remedies, and Circuit City's unilateral power to modify or terminate the arbitration agreement all operate to benefit the employer inordinately at the employee's expense. Because these one-sided provisions grossly favor Circuit City, we conclude that, under California law, these terms are substantively unconscionable, and address each term in turn.

* * * Circuit City's arbitration agreement applies only to "any and all employment-related legal disputes, controversies or claims of an Associate," thereby limiting its coverage to claims brought by employees. By the terms of this agreement, Circuit City does not agree to submit to arbitration claims it might hypothetically bring against employees. Without a reasonable justification for such a glaring disparity based on "business realities," "it is unfairly one-sided for an employer with superior bargaining power to impose arbitration on the employee as plaintiff but not to accept such limitations when it seeks to prosecute a claim against the employee." * * * Thus, we conclude that, under California law, a contract to arbitrate between an employer and an employee, such as the one we evaluate in this case, raises a rebuttable presumption of substantive unconscionability. Unless the employer can demonstrate that the effect of a contract to arbitrate is bilateral—as is required under California law—with respect to a particular employee, courts should presume such contracts substantively unconscionable.

The Circuit City arbitration agreement states that the form by which an employee requests arbitration

> shall be submitted not later than one year after the date on which the Associate knew, or through reasonable diligence should have known, of the facts giving rise to the Associate's claim(s). The failure of an Associate to initiate an arbitration within the one-year time limit shall constitute a waiver with respect to that dispute relative to that Associate.

We have already expressly criticized Circuit City's statute of limitations provision, finding that Circuit City's "strict one year statute of limitations on arbitrating claims . . . would deprive [Associates] of the benefit of the continuing violation doctrine available in FEHA suits." * * * While Circuit City insulates itself from potential damages, an employee forgoes the possibility of relief under the continuing violations doctrine. Therefore, because the benefit of this provision flows only to Circuit City, we conclude that the statute of limitations provision is substantively unconscionable.

Circuit City's arbitration agreement directs arbitrators not to consolidate claims of different employees into one proceeding and generally prohibits the arbitrator from hearing an arbitration as a class action. We find that this bar on class-wide arbitration is patently one-sided, and conclude that it is substantively unconscionable. * * * We cannot conceive of any circumstances under which an employer would bring a class proceeding against an employee. Circuit City, through its bar on class-wide arbitration, seeks to insulate itself from class proceedings while conferring no corresponding benefit to its employees in return. This one-sided provision proscribing an employee's ability to initiate class-wide arbitration operates solely to the advantage of Circuit City. Therefore, because Circuit City's prohibition of class-action proceedings in its arbitral forum is manifestly and shockingly one-sided, it is substantively unconscionable. * * *

Under the terms of the arbitration agreement, to initiate a complaint against Circuit City, an employee must submit an "Arbitration Request Form with a required filing fee of $75 (made payable with a cashier's check or money order to Circuit City Stores, Inc.)." Under California law, "when an employer imposes mandatory arbitration as a condition of employment, the arbitration agreement or arbitration process cannot generally require the employee to bear any *type* of expense that the employee would not be required to bear if he or she were free to bring the action in court." Though denominated a "filing fee," the employee-claimant must pay the required seventy-five dollars here directly to Circuit City, rather than to the arbitration service Circuit City identifies in the arbitration agreement. It thus appears that the employee is required to pay Circuit City for the privilege of bringing a complaint. While a true filing fee might be appropriate under *Armendariz*, the fee required by Circuit City is not the "*type*" of expense that the employee would be required to bear" in federal court, and is therefore inappropriate Moreover, by requiring employees to pay the fee to the very entity against which they seek redress, Circuit City may very well deter employees from initiating complaints. * * *

[The Circuit City arbitration agreement contains the] provision that "each party shall pay one-half of the costs of arbitration following the issuance of the

arbitration award." Moreover, the arbitration agreement provides that "the Arbitrator may require the Associate to pay Circuit City's share of the costs of arbitration and incidental costs" should Circuit City prevail at arbitration. Under Circuit City's arbitration agreement, even an employee who has succeeded on her claim against Circuit City could be held liable for her share of the costs of the arbitration, because the arbitrator's authority to require Circuit City to pay in such circumstances is discretionary. Furthermore, the Circuit City arbitration agreement provides that if an employee does not succeed on her claim, the arbitrator has the discretion to charge the employee for Circuit City's share of the arbitrator's services.

* * * The arbitration agreement we evaluate in this case . . . "fails to provide for all the types of relief that would otherwise be available in court." The Circuit City arbitration agreement delimits what relief is available to employees who succeed in arbitration claims against Circuit City. The agreement grants the arbitrator the discretion to award (1) injunctive relief, including reinstatement; (2) one year of full or partial back pay, subject to reductions by interim earnings or public or private benefits received; (3) two years of front pay; (4) compensatory damages in accordance with applicable law; and (5) punitive damages up to $5,000 or the equivalent of a claimant's monetary award (back pay plus front pay), whichever is greater. * * * Because the remedies limitation improperly proscribes available statutory remedies, we . . . conclude that it is substantively unconscionable.

Circuit City's arbitration agreement provides that "Circuit City may alter or terminate the Agreement and these Dispute Resolution Rules and Procedures on December 31st of any year upon giving 30 calendar days written notice to Associates." Circuit City, then, may modify or terminate any and all dispute resolution

agreements with its employees unilaterally. * * * By granting itself the sole authority to amend or terminate the arbitration agreement, Circuit City proscribes an employee's ability to consider and negotiate the terms of her contract. Compounded by the fact that this contract is adhesive in the first instance, this provision embeds its adhesiveness by allowing only Circuit City to modify or terminate the terms of the agreement. Therefore, we conclude that the provision affording Circuit City the unilateral power to terminate or modify the contract is substantively unconscionable.

California law grants courts the discretion either "to sever an unconscionable provision or refuse to enforce the contract in its entirety." * * * While it is within this court's discretion to sever unconscionable provisions, because an "insidious pattern" exists in Circuit City's arbitration agreement "that functions as a thumb on Circuit City's side of the scale should an employment dispute ever arise between the company and one of its employees," we conclude that the agreement is wholly unenforceable. * * *

CASE QUESTIONS

1. What was the legal issue in this case? What did the Court of Appeals decide?

2. What does it mean for a contract to be "unconscionable?" "Procedurally unconscionable?" "Substantively unconscionable?"

3. Why might Ingle have preferred to go to court rather than use the employer's arbitration mechanism?

4. What would you advise Circuit City to do in light of this decision (which was one of several cases in which courts have declined to enforce various versions of its arbitration agreement)?

courts have been reluctant to enforce arbitration agreements that impose markedly different requirements on employees than employers or which reserve to the employer the right to alter the details of the agreement at any time.

Besides delving into the contents of arbitration agreements, courts have considered whether enforceable agreements actually existed. For example, job applicants at Prudential Insurance were directed to sign an application form that referred obliquely to arbitration. The applicants were not told about the arbitration agreement, not given copies of the manual containing the terms of the agreement, and not allowed sufficient time to even read the application form. Under these circumstances, a "knowing" agreement to arbitrate rather than go to court did not exist.[22] Other

[22]Prudential Ins. Co. of America v. Lai, 42 F.3d 1299 (9th Cir. 1994).

courts do not set the bar as high, but still require, as with any valid contract, that a clear offer is made and accepted. An employee who was handed a booklet describing her employer's *Dispute Resolution Procedure* was not held to the arbitration provisions of that procedure because she never provided any written assent to the policy; "For an arbitration agreement to be binding, it must be an agreement, not merely a company policy. Moreover, pursuant to the FAA, the agreement must be in writing." [23] *Campbell v. General Dynamics* considers a related issue: the distribution of a mandatory arbitration agreement in a mass e-mail to company employees.

[23]Lee v. Red Lobster Inns of America, 92 Fed. Appx. 158 at 161 (6th Cir. 2004).

CAMPBELL V. GENERAL DYNAMICS
2005 U.S. App. LEXIS 9360

● ● ●

OPINION BY CIRCUIT JUDGE SELYA:

This appeal calls upon us to consider the enforceability of a mandatory arbitration agreement, contained in a dispute resolution policy linked to an e-mailed company-wide announcement, insofar as it applies to employment discrimination claims brought under the Americans with Disabilities Act (ADA). Our analysis turns on whether the employer provided minimally sufficient notice of the contractual nature of the e-mailed policy and of the concomitant waiver of an employee's right to access a judicial forum. Weighing all the attendant circumstances, we conclude that the notice was wanting and that, therefore, enforcement of the waiver would be inappropriate. Consequently, we uphold the district court's denial of the employer's motion to stay proceedings and compel the employee to submit his claim to arbitration. * * *

On April 30, 2001, at 1:54 p.m., General Dynamics sent an e-mail announcement to its entire workforce regarding the implementation of a new dispute resolution policy (the Policy). * * * The message consisted of a page-long letter from Gerard DeMuro, the president of General Dynamics. In the introductory paragraphs, DeMuro pointed out that General Dynamics was "a leader in a very competitive marketplace," that its success depended on its employees, and that it was committed to "open, forthright and honest communication," especially in the context of "addressing and resolving employee issues concerning legally protected rights and matters." Subsequent paragraphs explained

that the company had developed the Policy as a means to handle legal issues arising out of workplace disputes. The e-mail then limned the Policy's four-step approach to dispute resolution, describing the last step as "arbitration by a qualified and independent arbitrator."

The e-mail made no mention of whether (or how) the Policy would affect an employee's right to access a judicial forum with respect to workplace disputes. Moreover, it neither specified that the Policy contained an agreement to arbitrate that would become binding upon continued employment nor indicated whether the term "workplace disputes" included those giving rise to federal statutory claims. The text of the Policy was not part of the e-mail proper, although the company posted the Policy on its intranet (its internal corporate network). The e-mail did state that the Policy would become effective on May 1, 2001 (the day following its transmission). It also urged recipients to "review the enclosed materials carefully, as the [Policy] is an essential element of your employment relationship." Those with questions were invited to contact the company's vice-president of human resources.

The phrase "enclosed materials" was an apparent reference to two embedded links located at the bottom of the e-mail. * * * The first link . . . provided access to a two-page brochure that detailed how the Policy worked. Upon reading the second page of that brochure, the recipient would have learned that company employees who "continue [their] current employment after the effective date of the [Policy's] adoption" would be "covered" by its terms and that the Policy would encompass, among other things, "employment discrimination and harassment claims, based on, for

example, age, race, sex, religion, national origin, veteran status, citizenship, disability, or other characteristics protected by law." In a shaded box in the lower-right hand corner of that page, the recipient would have found the following statement:

> The Company has adopted this four-step policy as the exclusive means of resolving workplace disputes for legally protected rights. If an employee files a lawsuit against the Company, the Company will ask the court to dismiss the lawsuit and refer it to the [Policy]. Clicking on the second link . . . would have provided access to a dispute resolution handbook, which contained the full text of the Policy, a flow chart illustrating how the Policy worked, forms for filing claims at each of the four levels, and a compendium of questions that the company thought might arise.

No part of the e-mail communication required a response acknowledging receipt of the Policy or signifying that a recipient had read and understood its terms. Although General Dynamics set up a tracking log to monitor whether each of its employees opened the e-mail—the record indicates that the plaintiff opened the e-mail two minutes after it was sent—it did not take any steps to record whether its employees clicked on the embedded links to peruse either the brochure or the handbook. Moreover, General Dynamics has not supplied any evidence to contradict the plaintiff's claim that he never read or saw the brochure, the handbook, or the Policy prior to his termination. * * *

In this appeal, the parties dispute . . . whether a valid agreement to arbitrate exists. This element recognizes that, "though a person may, by contract, waive his or her right to adjudication, there can be no waiver in the absence of an agreement signifying an assent." * * * The appropriateness of enforcing an agreement to arbitrate an ADA claim hinges on whether, under the totality of the circumstances, the employer's communications to its employees afforded "some minimal level of notice" sufficient to apprise those employees that continued employment would effect a waiver of the right to pursue the claim in a judicial forum. In many cases, an employer will be able to satisfy this relatively light burden by producing evidence demonstrating that the employee had actual notice of the agreement. Here, however, General Dynamics did not bother to elicit from any employee an affirmation that he or she had read the e-mail (much less the Policy) or that he or she had

become aware that arriving for work the next morning would constitute binding acceptance of a new contractual term replacing court access with arbitration. . . . Accordingly, the sufficiency of the notice turns on whether, under the totality of the circumstances, the employer's communication would have provided a reasonably prudent employee notice of the waiver. . . . Factors relevant to this analysis include, but are not limited to, the method of communication, the workplace context, and the content of the communication.

As an initial matter, this case requires us to consider the proper weight that the choice of a mass e-mail as a means of communication bears on this multifactor inquiry. * * * [I]n our view, an e-mail, properly couched, can be an appropriate medium for forming an arbitration agreement. * * * [T]he Electronic Signatures in Global and National Commerce Act (E-Sign Act), . . . (codified at 15 U.S.C. §§ 7001–7031), likely precludes any flat rule that a contract to arbitrate is unenforceable under the ADA solely because its promulgator chose to use e-mail as the medium to effectuate the agreement. * * * By its plain terms, the E-Sign Act prohibits any interpretation of the FAA's "written provision" requirement that would preclude giving legal effect to an agreement solely on the basis that it was in electronic form.

Having clarified that the choice of mass e-mail is not determinative of the appropriateness of the notice, we consider the relevance of that means of notification within the context of General Dynamics' workplace routines and conventions. We start by inquiring whether the e-mail announcement was typical in comparison to other significant communications transmitted to the plaintiff over the course of his employment. * * *

Conspicuously absent is the identification of any other instance in which the company relied upon either an e-mail or an intranet posting to introduce a contractual term that was to become a condition of continued employment. We think that there is a qualitative difference between such a term and a policy that informs the employment relationship but imposes no enforceable obligations upon either party. This defect weighs all the more heavily because it could so easily have been remedied. One way that General Dynamics could have set this particular communication apart from the crowd would have been to require a response to the e-mail. Instead, the company opted for a "no response required" format. Within the context of this particular employment relationship, in which significant personnel matters historically had been transacted via signed

documents, this choice disguised the import of the communication. * * *

The upshot is that the record supports the conclusion that e-mail was a familiar format for many forms of intraoffice communication, but it does not suggest that e-mail was a traditional means either for conveying contractually binding terms or for effectuating waivers of employees' legal rights. Given that circumstance, we cannot say that delivery of an e-mail heralding the birth of a new policy would raise a red flag vivid enough to cause a reasonable employee to anticipate the imposition of a legally significant alteration to the terms and conditions of his employment. Therefore, within the context of this case, the e-mail communication, in and of itself, was not enough to put a reasonable employee on inquiry notice of an alteration to the contractual aspects of the employment relationship.

This leaves the content of the communication, which had two components: the e-mail announcement and the ancillary documents that were accessible via computer link. * * *

One fundamental flaw is that the e-mail did not state directly that the Policy contained an arbitration agreement that was meant to effect a waiver of an employee's right to access a judicial forum. Nor did the e-mail contain anything to put the recipient on inquiry notice of that possibility by conveying the Policy's contractual significance. * * *

A second flaw relates to tone and choice of phrase. While the Policy itself spoke in clear, contractual language (e.g., "continuation of employment by an individual shall be deemed [an] acceptance" of the provisions of the Policy, that "the mutual obligations set forth in [the] Policy shall constitute a contract between the Employee and the Company," and that "[the] Policy shall constitute the entire agreement between the Employee and the Company for the resolution of covered Claims"), the e-mail announcement descanted in an entirely different vocabulary, downplaying the obligations set forth in the Policy. The text of the e-mail did not state either that the Policy contained contractually binding terms or that the employer would treat continued employment as an acceptance of those terms. Perhaps most telling, the e-mail's description of the four-step dispute resolution procedure omitted the crucial fact that, as a matter of law, the regimen would become an employee's exclusive remedy for

employment-related claims of virtually every kind and description. Finally, while the e-mail announcement communicated the notion that arbitration is a kinder, gentler alternative to litigation and had the company's blessing, it did not suggest that arbitration was to become mandatory and thereby extinguish an employee's access to a judicial forum as a means for dispute resolution. * * *

To be blunt, the e-mail announcement undersold the significance of the Policy and omitted the critical fact that it contained a mandatory arbitration agreement. The result was that a reasonable employee could read the e-mail announcement and conclude that the Policy presented an optional alternative to litigation rather than a mandatory replacement for it. Because that primary communication lends itself to such a conclusion—rather than cluing in the reader by including a simple statement of the kind contained in the Policy itself that "the mutual obligations set forth in [the] Policy shall constitute a contract between the Employee and the Company"—we conclude that it failed to put the recipient on inquiry notice of the unilateral contract offer contained in the linked materials. * * *

In the absence of minimally sufficient notice, we conclude that it would not be appropriate to enforce the Policy's purported waiver of the right to litigate ADA claims. Consequently, the district court did not err in denying the motion to stay the litigation and compel recourse to an arbitral forum.

CASE QUESTIONS

1. What was the legal issue in this case? What did the Appeals Court decide?

2. What were the defects in how this employer went about "offering" (communicating) the mandatory arbitration program to its employees? What do you conclude from this case regarding how employers that want to institute arbitration agreements should proceed?

3. Do you agree with the decision? Why or why not? Is clicking on the links contained in an e-mail message really too much for an employer to reasonably expect?

No doubt, future court decisions will further clarify the ingredients that render arbitration agreements enforceable. For now, *employers who want to use arbitration agreements should clearly communicate those agreements to employees in written form and obtain written statements of assent. Employers should provide for a fair arbitration process and avoid the temptation to draft one-sided agreements that place burdens on employees, without imposing corresponding limitations on themselves. As much as possible, the agreements should provide employees with the same opportunity to vindicate their legal rights, including remedies for violations of those rights, that they would have enjoyed had their day in court been available to them.*

REMEDIES FOR VIOLATIONS OF EMPLOYMENT LAWS

If an employee takes legal action against her employer and is successful, what does she get for her trouble? A partial list of **remedies** available in employment cases includes attorneys' fees, court orders, back pay, front pay, reinstatement, hiring, liquidated damages (awarded for serious, intentional violations in amounts up to twice the actual damages incurred), compensatory damages (a wide range of damages beyond loss of wages, including pain and suffering), and punitive damages (intended to punish the employer in cases of serious, intentional violations and to create an example to affect the behavior of others). In large, high profile, discrimination cases such as the Morgan Stanley case (see "Clippings"), the EEOC has increasingly sought agreements from defendant employers to have their employment practices overseen by external monitors and to institute wide-ranging diversity programs. Not all remedies are available for every legal claim (nor are all the remedies for which a successful plaintiff is eligible necessarily awarded by the courts). Under the National Labor Relations Act, for example, employees are eligible for "make-whole" remedies, including reinstatement and back pay, but not compensatory and punitive damages. In contrast, common law tort claims can yield monetary damages, but not reinstatement.

You have probably heard stories of huge awards won by employees in lawsuits against their employers. Anecdotes of this sort influence thinking about employment law and certainly help attorneys get the attention of their corporate clients; however, remember that most cases never survive motions to dismiss and go to trial, much less result in plaintiff victories with hefty awards. Headline grabbing and multifigure awards for plaintiffs, as in the Morgan Stanley case (see "Clippings"), are the exceptions rather than the rule. Sometimes, awards or settlements are large because they are for **class-action lawsuits,** in which many plaintiffs had their rights violated in the same manner and share in the award. Class-action lawsuits are controversial, with plaintiffs' counsel seeing them as an efficient means for pursuing the claims of many individuals who would not otherwise be able to take legal action, whereas corporate defendants see them as collections of disparate claims strung together by attorneys seeking to maximize their earnings. Whether a group of employees have claims that are sufficiently similar to justify certification as a "class" is a key determination in these cases, as the massive Wal-Mart class-action suit illustrates (see "Clippings").

Judges routinely slash jury awards by half or more, and employees often settle for considerably less to avoid further delay in getting their money. Victorious plaintiffs in employment law cases have good reason to be concerned about how their cases will fare on appeal. Recent research suggests that employers frequently succeed in

having plaintiffs' victories reversed in employment discrimination cases.[24] Nor is the sky necessarily the limit in terms of potential awards. Under Title VII of the Civil Rights Act, for example, compensatory and punitive damages are capped (a maximum of $300,000 for large employers) and only available in particular types of discrimination cases.

The costs of employment law claims are potentially significant, somewhat unpredictable, and well worth avoiding. Some of the cost related to legal compliance is hidden because employers choose to settle rather than risk litigation. Insurers that provide employment practice liability insurance are raising their premiums substantially as they discover that the number and size of awards in employment cases are far greater than they had anticipated.[25] Additionally, many of the costs associated with legal regulation of the workplace stem not from litigation, but from the things employers must do to comply with the law.

IMPLICATIONS OF THE CHANGING WORKPLACE FOR U.S. EMPLOYMENT LAW

Workplaces in the United States have changed enormously over the past few decades and this transformation will continue. Nostalgic views of a "traditional" workplace characterized by a high degree of employment security, lengthy career ladders, an emphasis on internal equity, and rewards directed at loyal, senior workers tend to ignore the fact that such arrangements were most characteristic of large firms and prevailed only for a relatively short time following World War II.[26] We need to be similarly cautious about creating a caricature of contemporary workplace practices out of anecdotal accounts that ignore the wide variation that exists across firms. Nevertheless, the overall thrust of workplace change over the past few decades seems to be in the direction of less employment stability, greater employee responsibility for their own careers and financial outcomes, intensification of work and performance expectations, reorganization of work processes placing more emphasis on teams, far greater workforce diversity, and the application of technologies with the potential to transform how work is performed and monitored.

These and other changes are mirrored in the types of legal disputes between firms and their workers that we see now—and are likely to see more of in the future.[27] Less stable, more market-driven relationships between firms and workers are manifested in disputes over the status of contingent workers such as independent contractors and temporary workers, but also in legal challenges to downsizing and how people are selected for termination. When workers are encouraged to view themselves as free agents, disputes over the likes of noncompetition agreements and trade secrets are likely. Shifting risk to employees fosters disputes over such things as training and skill acquisition, employer handling of 401(k) plans, and pay equity under pay-for-performance schemes.

[24]Kevin M. Clermont, Theodore Eisenberg, and Stewart J. Schwab. "Proceeding: Show Employment-Discrimination Plaintiffs Fare in the Federal Courts of Appeals." *Employee Rights & Employment Policy Journal* 7 (2003), 547–566 (Over 42 percent of plaintiff victories were reversed on appeal, a figure that is much higher than for other types of civil litigation and that dwarfs the 7 percent reversal rate for defendant trial victories).

[25]Reed Abelson. "Surge in Bias Cases Punishes Insurers, and Premiums Rise." *New York Times* (January 9, 2002), C-1.

[26]Peter Cappelli. *The New Deal at Work.* (Boston: Harvard Business School Press, 1999).

[27]Katherine V. W. Stone. *From Widgets to Digits: Employment Regulation for the Changing Workplace.* (New York: Cambridge University Press, 2004).

Intensified work hours and output expectations lead to disputes over work hours and overtime pay, leave policies, and even occupational safety and health issues such as ergonomic injuries. Reorganizing work processes has prompted challenges to the legal status of employee-involvement teams. The greater diversity of the workforce, with increasing representation of women and persons of color in the workplace, is the backdrop to a host of legal issues, including harassment, accommodation of disabled persons, "English-only" rules, and the treatment of immigrant workers. Technological changes have especially profound effects in the area of privacy, as employees have their computer use monitored or are subjected to genetic testing. The alternative dispute resolution procedures discussed in this chapter are one response by employers to these legal implications of change.

Don't worry if you are not familiar with all the workplace developments that were mentioned in this chapter. They will be explained further in later chapters and are highlighted in the "Changing Workplace" features. The essential point for now is that as workplace practices change, new and interesting questions of employment law are inevitably raised.

Chapter SUMMARY

The body of law that governs human resource practice consists of many different pieces, including constitutions, statutes, executive orders, regulations, common law, and court decisions interpreting all of these. Because the applicable legal rules differ, it is important to determine whether the employer in question is in the public sector or private sector, whether the employees are unionized, the size of the employer, the geographic location of the employer, whether the employer is a government contractor, and the industry and occupation involved. Most employment laws came into being within the last 40 years. These laws confer on employees rights to be protected from discrimination and to enjoy equal employment opportunity, to form unions and engage in collective bargaining with their employers, to have terms and conditions of employment that at least meet minimum standards, to have basic liberties respected, and to receive compensation for certain types of harm done by their employers. However, the starting point for analyzing employees' rights on the job is employment at will. In the absence of a contract of employment for a specified duration, employment can be terminated at any time and for any reason that is not specifically prohibited by law.

The process by which these important rights are enforced varies, but is rarely quick. Employees make choices about whether to undertake legal action, and if they do so, face varying time limits, administrative prerequisites, and court proceedings. Most cases are resolved prior to a trial. A significant development is the increased use of mandatory arbitration agreements, under which employees must agree to take all employment disputes to arbitration rather than court. These agreements have generally been deemed legal and enforceable. However, important questions remain regarding the contents of the agreements and their application in unionized workplaces.

Legal protections for employees and the number of legal claims being brought by employees have clearly increased. Employment laws serve important purposes and express societal values. Anecdotal accounts of frivolous lawsuits and employee windfalls capture our attention, but do not do justice to the far more complex reality of enforcing fair treatment in the workplace.

The workplace and the employment relationship are being transformed. Changes in the workplace over the past few decades—including less stable employment, the shifting of responsibility to employees, intensification of work, reorganization of the work process, diversification of the workforce, and technological developments—are increasingly reflected in the resulting legal controversies.

Practical Advice SUMMARY

- *Managers need to be well versed in employment law and remain up-to-date in the face of ongoing changes.*

- *Managers should learn about employment law so they can*

 –institute sound policies that prevent violations.

 –recognize legal issues when they arise.

 –know when to seek advice from legal counsel.

- *Legal compliance should emphasize proactive measures such as*

 –training in proper procedures.

 –careful selection and oversight of supervisors.

 –careful review of human resource decisions.

 –establishment of grievance procedures.

 –prompt investigation of complaints.

- *Creating and maintaining good documentation of the reasons for human resource decisions is essential.*

- *If mandatory arbitration agreements are used, such agreements should*

 –be in writing.

 –clearly notify employees that they are waiving their right to sue.

 –obtain evidence of employee acceptance in writing.

- *Mandatory arbitration agreements should not*

 –place restrictions on employees without corresponding restrictions on the employer.

 –unreasonably limit the remedies available to employees.

 –burden employees with payments for the arbitration.

 –allow undue employer control over the selection of arbitrators.

 –be subject to change at any time by the employer.

Key TERMS

constitution
statute
executive order
regulation
common law
tort
employment at will
public sector
private sector

payroll method
social movement
enforcement procedures
district court
summary judgment
plaintiff
burden of proof
appeals court
Supreme Court

certiorari
conciliation
right to sue letter
alternative dispute resolution
 (ADR)
mediation
arbitration
remedies
class-action lawsuit

Chapter QUESTIONS

1. Do you think that most employees who take legal action against their employers have valid claims or are looking to "get something for nothing"? What is the basis for your opinion?

2. The XYZ Company had 12 employees for the first half of 2005. It signed a contract with a major retailer in June 2005 and hired an additional 8 employees to handle the extra work. The contract was cancelled in January of 2006 and the company laid off the 8 new hires. In March 2006, an employee was fired. If the employee believed that the termination was discriminatory, could the employee have brought a case under Title VII of the Civil Rights Act?

3. An employee signed an arbitration agreement when he was hired. The agreement provided that the costs of the arbitration would be split equally between the parties, with the employee payment capped at the amount earned in the employee's highest earnings month during the previous year; remedies could not include either punitive damages or reinstatement; all claims must be brought forth within a year; and various limits were imposed on prehearing information gathering, including no more than one deposition for each side. The employee was fired after getting hurt on the job and filing a workers' compensation claim. He sued for retaliation and the company went to court to compel arbitration. What should the court decide? Why? (In *Re Johnny Luna*, 2004 Tex. App. LEXIS 8241)

4. An employee of Olive Garden attended a mandatory weekly restaurant meeting. At the meeting, employees were given copies of the new dispute resolution procedure (DRP). The DRP required arbitration of any unresolved employment disputes. The employee signed an attendance sheet acknowledging receipt of the materials. Three months later the employee was terminated. He sued for discrimination. The company went to court to compel arbitration. What should the

court decide? Why? (*Hightower v. GMRI, Inc.*, 272 F.3d 239 [4th Cir. 2001])

5. An Assistant Manager at a restaurant signed an arbitration agreement providing that "both of us agree that . . . we will settle all claims or disputes about work exclusively through the Company Open Door Policy, and if this procedure fails, then by final and binding arbitration." When the employee was demoted after returning from parental leave, she invoked the open door policy with her supervisor, who laughed at her and told her that she "was being hormonal." Higher management refused to get involved and said that she had to work out the problem with her supervisor. She sued for violation of her rights under the Family and Medical Leave Act and the company sought to compel arbitration. What should the court decide? Why? (*Darrah v. Friendly Ice Cream*, 328 F.Supp. 2d 319 [N.D.N.Y. 2004])

6. Should employers institute mandatory arbitration agreements? What are the pros and cons?

7. What legal issues did you identify in the "staff meeting" discussion that opened the chapter? What should this company be doing differently? What aspects of the situation are you unsure of and would want to learn more about?

Internet RESOURCES

- The Cornell University Law School maintains a site that contains or links to extensive employment law materials: http://www.law.cornell.edu/topics/employment.html

- The U.S. Department of Labor has an employment law guide: http://www.dol.gov/asp/programs/guide.htm

- Site created by the U.S. Small Business Administration featuring "plain-English" guides to a variety of employment and business law issues: http://www.business.gov/topics/business_laws/employment_laws/index.html

- A joint site of *Human Resource Executive Magazine* and Cornell University's School of Industrial and Labor Relations, which contains information relevant to legal and practical issues in human resource management and an extensive set of links to other sites: http://www.business.gov/topics/business_laws/employment_laws/index.html

- American Arbitration Association site providing information on ADR: http://www.adr.org

The Employment Relationship

CLIPPINGS

▸ Graduate students who work at New York University (NYU) as research and teaching assistants formed a labor union in 2000 and subsequently negotiated a labor agreement providing for increased pay and benefits. Graduate students at a number of other private universities have attempted to do the same, but the National Labor Relations Board has thrown these efforts into doubt by reversing itself and ruling that graduate students at private universities are not employees with the right to unionize. At NYU, the university says that it will no longer recognize the union after the current contract expires.[1]

▸ Supermarket chains Safeway, Albertsons, and Ralphs have agreed to pay $21.5 million to settle a class-action lawsuit brought on behalf of janitors in their Southern California stores. The janitors were employees of a building services contractor used by the supermarket chains and were allegedly forced by the contractor to work seven days a week without overtime pay. Although the supermarkets all denied wrongdoing or liability, the plaintiffs' attorney suggested that the settlement was "an important step in the fight to establish joint employment liability for companies that subcontract with firms which then mistreat employees."[2]

▸ Video game company Sega of America and staffing firm Spherion Corp. have agreed to settle a discrimination suit brought by the Equal Employment Opportunity Commission (EEOC) on behalf of Filipino game testers who claimed they had been fired due to their national origin. Spherion had placed the employees with Sega and later terminated them at Sega's request. The two firms will both contribute toward the $600,000 settlement. EEOC District Director H. Joan Ehrlich noted that "Temp agencies have an obligation to oppose and remedy discrimination at client work sites when they learn that the client has discriminated against the staffing firm's workers."[3]

▸ The EEOC has filed an age discrimination suit against the law firm of Sidley, Austin, Brown, & Wood. The agency contends that 31 partners were discriminatorily demoted or forced to leave the firm during an organizational restructuring. Many other former partners were victims of a mandatory retirement policy. The law firm maintains that, as partners, the affected attorneys were not employees entitled to protection under the Age Discrimination in Employment Act.[4]

[1]Daniel Duane. "Eggheads Unite." *New York Times Magazine* (May 4, 2003), 54-7; Eric Lekus. "NYU Proposes to End Recognition of Union Representing Graduate Assistants." *Daily Labor Report* 117 (June 20, 2005), A-10.

[2]Tom Gilroy. "California Supermarket Chains Agree to Pay Janitors $21.5 Million in Overtime Settlement." *Daily Labor Report* 194 (October 7, 2004), A-15.

[3]Equal Employment Opportunity Commission. "Sega, Spherion Settle Suit Alleging Bias Against Filipinos, Retaliation." *News Release,* March 25, 2004 (http://www.eeoc.gov/press/3-25-04.html).

[4]Michael Bologna. "EEOC Files Class-Based Age Bias Suit Against International Law Firm Sidley Austin." *Daily Labor Report* 10 (January 14, 2005), A-7.

THE CHANGING WORKPLACE

Contingent and Alternative Work Arrangements

Employment laws premised on the existence of employment relationships run up against the increasing variety of arrangements under which work is performed. This variety in work arrangements is often captured by the terms **contingent**, alternative, or nonstandard work. In general, these terms are used to contrast full-time, year-round employment with a single employer that is expected to continue indefinitely, with looser (i.e., more flexible or less secure, depending on where you sit) relationships that may exist only as long as some particular project or piece of work needs to be done. Continuation of these latter relationships is thus contingent upon an immediate need for the specific services performed, and there is no expectation that the relationships will be ongoing or long term.

The most expansive definitions of contingent or alternative work arrangements include all part-time employees (roughly 20 percent of the workforce), on the grounds that they are subject to greater variability in hours. More commonly, contingent or alternative work arrangements are deemed to include independent contractors (about 6–7 percent of the workforce in recent years), temp workers provided through an agency (1–2 percent of the workforce), temp workers who are directly hired by companies but not given permanent employee status (2–3 percent of the workforce), contract company workers (e.g., security guards supplied to a particular company) (less than 1 percent of the workforce), on-call (e.g., substitute teachers) or day laborers (1–2 percent of the workforce), and other self-employed workers not classified as independent contractors (about 5 percent of the workforce).[1]

Not everyone is becoming a contingent worker, and agency temp workers in particular still comprise a rather small portion of the workforce. However, the number of contingent workers has grown over the past two decades. Established high-tech firms such as Microsoft, Intel, and Hewlett-Packard, as well as many Silicon Valley "start-ups," have been particularly heavy users of independent contractors and temp workers.[2] The growth of the contingent workforce has forced the courts to wrestle with how our employment laws apply to such workers.

[1]Susan N. Houseman. "The Policy Implications of Nonstandard Work Arrangements." *Employment Research*. W.E. Upjohn Institute (Fall 1999) 5–7; U.S. Bureau of Labor Statistics. "Contingent and Alternative Employment Arrangements, February 2001." BLS News Release. Viewed June 16, 2005. http://www.bls.gov/news.release/conemp.nr0.htm.
[2]Abby Ellin. "A Start-Up's Hiring Attracts Unwanted Attention." *New York Times* (October 11, 2000), C-5.

You are likely either currently employed or have been employed in the past, if only at a summer job or part-time during the school year. Many of you might also be in the process of forming new employment relationships, interviewing for jobs, and receiving offers of employment. Most work gets done through the establishment of employment relationships, but this is not always the case. This chapter delves into the meaning behind the terms **employee** and **employer** and the legal significance of determining whether an employment relationship exists. You might be surprised by how slippery the definitions of *employee* and *employer* turn out to be—and how recent changes in the structure of employment have complicated matters. Regular full-time employment by a single employer is still the norm, but there are many variations on this theme, which can affect the legal rights of persons performing work.

THE IMPORTANCE OF DETERMINING WHETHER AN EMPLOYMENT RELATIONSHIP EXISTS

One reason it is important to correctly determine whether someone performing work is actually an employee is because the Internal Revenue Service (IRS) cares about this—a lot. If someone is an employee, her employer is required to withhold income taxes and to pay the employer's share of Social Security and Medicare taxes.

Additional payments must be made to provide workers' compensation and unemployment insurance for employees. The IRS estimated in 1994 that about 15 percent of all U.S. businesses were misclassifying some of their workers, resulting in more than three million employees being incorrectly labeled independent contractors.[5] A more recent study focusing on Massachusetts found that almost 19 percent of employers in the state had misclassified employees as independent contractors between 2001 and 2003.[6] The misclassifications affected 248,000 workers and resulted in losses to the state of $152 million in income tax revenues and $35 million in unemployment insurance taxes. Employers who misclassify their employees and fail to comply with their responsibilities under the tax code may be subject to payment of back taxes and substantial penalties.

The second reason it is important to determine whether an employment relationship exists is that most employment laws confer rights on employees specifically and do not apply in the absence of an employment relationship. Thus, a threshold issue in many employment law cases, highlighted in this chapter, is whether an employment relationship exists. Employee status may also be a prerequisite for a claim on contractual benefits stemming from an employer's own policies and benefit programs. Remember also that coverage by employment laws often depends on a firm meeting minimum size requirements. Because only employees are counted, whether particular individuals are employees can determine whether other individuals who clearly are employees will have legal rights to assert.

The other side of the employment relationship must also be considered. Even when a person doing work is clearly an employee, there can still be questions about the identity of the employer. Complexities in corporate structure and practices such as leasing employees or obtaining them through temp agencies can cloud the issue of what entity is liable if employees' rights are violated.

Ascertaining who is an employee and who is the employer is clearly important; but is it problematic? Don't we know an employee when we see one? And surely, Congress and other legislative bodies that write employment laws must have defined the intended beneficiaries of those laws. In Title VII of the Civil Rights Act of 1964, which is typical of other employment laws in this regard, Congress defined an employee as "an individual employed by an employer. . . ."[7] Definitions of this sort are hopelessly circular and fail to provide any criteria for discerning who is an employee.

But perhaps Congress neglected to be more specific because the meaning of *employee* is self-evident. Isn't an employee simply a person who performs work for someone else and receives pay in return? In fact, this commonsense definition goes a long way. However, this definition is insufficient to distinguish between employees and independent contractors, because both do work in exchange for pay. Difficulties may also arise in distinguishing employees from temps, interns, students, volunteers, and partners.

WHO IS AN EMPLOYEE?

There is no single answer to this question. The applicable criteria differ somewhat, depending on the legal basis for an employee's claim (e.g., Fair Labor Standards Act, National Labor Relations Act, Workers' Compensation statute) and the particular

[5]"GAO Official Tells House Committee That Changes Needed in Employee Status Rules." *Daily Labor Report* 150 (August 8, 1994), D-10.

[6]Diane E. Lewis. "UMass-Harvard Study Finds Thousands of Workers Misclassified." *Boston Globe* (December 13, 2004), C1.

[7]42 U.S.C.A. § 2000e(f) (2005).

alternative to employee status (e.g., independent contractor, volunteer, partner) being considered. A finding that a worker is an employee covered by wage and hour laws, for example, does not automatically mean that the same worker will be considered an employee for purposes of bringing a discrimination suit or joining a union.

Independent Contractors

Distinguishing between **independent contractors** and employees is the central—and most contentious—issue surrounding employee status. This is due to the relatively large number of independent contractors in use, the keen interest of the IRS in this matter, and the fact that in recent years, numerous employees have had their status changed by the companies that they worked for from employee to independent contractor—often with little apparent change in the nature of their work.

Because both employees and independent contractors perform work in exchange for pay, what are the essential features that differentiate an employment relationship from an independent contractor relationship? In *Baker v. Flint Engineering & Construction*, a federal appeals court considers the employment status of welders performing work for a construction company. The decision clearly sets out the criteria for the **economic realities test** used to ascertain employee status in Fair Labor Standards Act cases. These criteria are helpful in distinguishing employees and independent contractors, but notice that many judgment calls still go into applying these criteria to the facts of particular cases.

BAKER V. FLINT ENGINEERING & CONSTRUCTION
137 F.3d 1436 (10th Cir. 1998)

● ● ●

OPINION BY CIRCUIT JUDGE BRISCOE:

Plaintiffs are a group of rig welders in the natural gas pipeline construction industry. They filed this action against Flint Engineering & Construction Company for overtime compensation under the Fair Labor Standards Act (FLSA). Flint appeals the district court's entry of summary judgment in favor of plaintiffs, contending the court erred in concluding plaintiffs were employees of Flint rather than independent contractors. We . . . affirm.

Flint is a corporation engaged in the construction, installation, and servicing of oil and gas pipelines and related facilities for the oil and gas industry. . . . Flint is routinely hired as a general contractor by oil and gas companies to build natural gas pipelines and compressor stations which transport natural gas from the wellheads to the owner's main processing plants. When Flint is the successful bidder on a project . . . it hires a variety of workers, including rig welders, to assist in completion of the project. Rig welders (a/k/a pipe welders) perform skilled welding on pipes, sheet metal, and other portions of gas industry facilities. They are routinely tested and certified by project owners to insure they can perform their jobs. They provide their own welding equipment, which is typically mounted on flatbed pickup trucks. The equipped trucks are referred to as "welding rigs," and each welding rig costs between $35,000 and $40,000. Rig welders are also responsible for costs of stocking their welding rigs with supplies, as well as for necessary repairs to the rigs. Rig welders do not bid on jobs and do not have contractor's licenses that would enable them to do so. Flint simply hires rig welders at a set hourly rate to work on particular projects. Flint does not negotiate the hourly rate, and sometimes pays

on a "straight contract" basis at approximately $27 to $30 per hour, and sometimes on a "split check" basis at a rate of $10 per hour for labor and $17 per hour for rig rental.

Work on a project is typically conducted six days a week, twelve to fourteen hours per day. Rig welders are supervised by Flint foremen and are required to arrive, take breaks, and leave at times specified by the foremen. They are not allowed to complete their work when they want and, in most cases, it would be impossible for them to do so because they must coordinate their work with the other crafts and because other equipment and workers are necessary to move pipe for welding. Rig welders are not provided project blueprints. Instead, the foremen map out what pipes they want built and in what order. The foremen do not establish the welding specifications and standards, nor do they tell rig welders how to weld or how long a particular weld should take. Welding specifications and standards are established by the customer (i.e., the project owner) and the quality of welding is overseen by an inspector hired by the customer. Because of the nature of their work, rig welders (and other pipeline workers) would be unemployed after completion of a project if they did not seek work on new projects. Accordingly, it is common for rig welders to work for several different companies during the course of a year.

Prior to July 1, 1991, Flint considered rig welders as independent contractors and asked each rig welder to sign a document entitled "Agreement With Independent Contractor," which stated:

> "It is the intent of the parties involved to establish and maintain an 'independent relationship' rather than an employer-employee relationship. All Federal, State and Local laws, regulations, and guidelines should be adhered to accordingly. The Independent Contractor is responsible for maintaining adequate amounts of insurance." * * *

[I]n determining whether an individual is covered by the FLSA . . . the economic realities of the relationship govern, and "the focal point is 'whether the individual is economically dependent on the business to which he renders service . . . or is, as a matter of economic fact, in business for himself.'" * * * In applying the economic reality test, courts generally look at (1) the degree of control exerted by the alleged employer over the worker; (2) the worker's opportunity for profit or loss; (3) the worker's investment in the business; (4) the permanence of the working relationship; (5) the degree of skill required to perform the work; and (6) the extent to which the work is an integral part of the alleged employer's business. * * * None of the factors alone is dispositive; instead, the court must employ a totality-of-the-circumstances approach. * * *

Control

The district court found Flint's "degree of control over the rig welders, and the Plaintiffs' lack of independence over setting their work hours, work crews, and other details of their welding work, is more consistent with employee rather than independent contractor status." . . . [W]e conclude this finding is not clearly erroneous. * * * Flint's foremen tell the rig welders when to report to work, when to take breaks, on what portion of the project they will be working, and when their workday ends. The record indicates rig welders cannot perform their work on their own schedule; rather, pipeline work has assembly line qualities in that it requires orderly and sequential coordination of various crafts and workers to construct a pipeline. The record further indicates plaintiffs work on only one project at a time and do not offer services to third parties while a project is ongoing. Indeed, the hours plaintiffs are required to work on a project (ten to fourteen hours a day, six days a week), coupled with driving time between home and often remote work sites each day, make it practically impossible for them to offer services to other employers. In short, very little about plaintiffs' work situation makes it possible to view plaintiffs as persons conducting their own businesses.

Opportunity for profit or loss

In analyzing the second factor, the district court found plaintiffs are paid at a fixed hourly rate, plaintiffs have no opportunity to experience a loss on the job site, plaintiffs' ability to control costs of welding supplies does not necessarily enable them to make a profit, and plaintiffs' ability to maximize their wages by "hustling" new work is not synonymous with making a profit. * * * If plaintiffs could bid on jobs at a set amount and correspondingly set their own hours or schedule, they would have the opportunity for profit or loss. However, plaintiffs are hired on a per-hour basis rather than on a flat-rate-per-job basis. There is no incentive for plaintiffs to work faster or more efficiently in order to increase their opportunity for profit. Moreover, there is absolutely no risk of loss on plaintiffs' part. * * * "In

short, the [rig welders] have no control over the essential determinants of profits in a business, and no direct share in the success of the business."

Investment in business

The district court found plaintiffs have substantial investments in their welding rigs. . . . Although the court further found Flint's investment in the overall business far exceeds plaintiffs' investments, it nevertheless found "Plaintiffs' investment in this industry, and their compensation which is based on this investment, is more consistent with finding the rig welders independent contractors." * * * In making a finding on this factor, it is appropriate to compare the worker's individual investment to the employer's investment in the overall operation. The district court is clearly correct in finding plaintiffs' investments in their welding rigs are significant (at least when compared to other workers), and in finding a significant portion of plaintiffs' pay is based on their furnishing rigs. However, plaintiffs' investments are disproportionately small when compared to Flint's investment in the overall business. Several witnesses testified that Flint routinely had hundreds of thousands of dollars of equipment at each work site. Compared to Flint's investment in the overall business, plaintiffs' investments are not so significant as to indicate they are independent contractors.

Permanency of working relationship

The district court found plaintiffs rarely work for Flint more than two months at any one time, and rarely for more than three months during any twelve-month period. However, the court found plaintiffs remain on the job site until the necessary welding is done. Thus, the court found "Plaintiffs' lack of permanence is due to natural characteristics in the industry, and not the independent choice usually exhibited by one who intentionally chooses to be in business for oneself. Therefore, while rig welders are temporary workers, this finding is of little relevance in determining whether these Plaintiffs are employees or independent contractors."

Generally speaking, "'independent contractors' often have fixed employment periods and transfer from place to place as particular work is offered to them, whereas 'employees' usually work for only one employer and such relationship is continuous and of indefinite duration." However, "many seasonal businesses necessarily hire only seasonal employees, [and] that fact alone does not convert seasonal employees into seasonal independent contractors." We agree with the district court's findings on this factor. Although plaintiffs exhibit characteristics generally typical of independent contractors as regards the short duration of their employment relationships and their frequent relocation to find employment, these characteristics of plaintiffs' employment are clearly due to the intrinsic nature of oil and gas pipeline construction work rather than any choice or decision on the part of plaintiffs. Notably, the record indicates the majority of workers employed by Flint (e.g., pipefitters, laborers, etc.) work on the same basis as plaintiffs and are nevertheless treated as employees. We conclude it is appropriate to characterize plaintiffs' relationship with Flint as "permanent and exclusive for the duration of" the particular job for which they are hired.

Degree of skill required to perform work

The district court found plaintiffs "are highly skilled individuals" and are, in fact, "the most skilled employees on a transmission systems project." However, the court further found plaintiffs do not "make any independent judgments on the job site," and thus do not exercise their skills "in any independent manner." The court further found Flint does not attempt to hire the most skilled available rig welders nor does it negotiate pay depending on the level of skill possessed. * * * In light of the fact that the Plaintiffs do not exercise any initiative or make any judgment decisions on the job site, the Court finds that Plaintiffs' skills are not indicative of independent contractor status. * * *

Integral part of business

After noting this factor focuses on whether workers' services are a necessary component of the business, the district court found "rig welders are necessary in the construction of all transmission systems projects," and, although "they do not remain on the job site from start to finish, their work is a critical step on every transmission system project." * * * The evidence in the record on appeal clearly indicates rig welders' work is an important, and indeed integral, component of oil and gas pipeline construction work.

Economic dependence of plaintiffs

Our final step is to review the findings on each of the above factors and determine whether plaintiffs, as a matter of economic fact, depend upon Flint's business for the opportunity to render service, or are in business for themselves. Although Flint urges us to focus on whether plaintiffs rely on Flint for their subsistence, we believe the question is whether plaintiffs are

economically dependent upon Flint during the time period they work for Flint, however long or short that period may be. In other words, "the dependence at issue is dependence on that job for that income to be continued and not necessarily for complete sustenance." * * *

Ultimately, we agree with the district court and conclude plaintiffs are employees of Flint, rather than independent contractors, for purposes of the FLSA. In most respects, plaintiffs are no different from any other workers hired by Flint and treated as employees. Plaintiffs are hired to complete a job, are told their working hours, are told their hourly pay rate, and are told on what portion of the project they will be working during a given workday. Although plaintiffs are the most skilled workers on the job site, they are not asked to exercise their discretion in applying their skills; they are told what to do and when to do it. The only substantial difference between plaintiffs and the other workers on the job site is that plaintiffs are required to supply equipment to perform their jobs. This fact alone, however, does not alter the realities of their working situation. Nor does it allow them to make any type of substantial profit above wages they are paid. Ultimately, plaintiffs, like other workers hired by Flint, are dependent upon Flint for the opportunity to render services for however long a particular project lasts.

CASE QUESTIONS

1. What issue did the court decide in this case? What was its decision?

2. What is the economic realities test? What factors do courts consider in applying it? How does each of these factors help us distinguish an employee from an independent contractor?

3. What is the court's rationale for its decision?

4. Do you agree with the court's decision? Why or why not?

Courts use not only the economic realities test, but also a **common law test** and a **hybrid test** (combining elements of the other tests) to determine employee status. The common law test considers the following factors:[8]

1. The hiring party's right to control the manner and means by which the work is done

2. The level of skill required

3. Source of necessary tools and materials

4. Where the work is done

5. The duration of the relationship

6. Whether the hiring party has the right to assign additional projects to the hired party

7. The extent of the hired party's discretion over when and how long to work

8. The method of payment

9. The hired party's role in hiring and paying assistants

10. Whether the work is part of the regular business of the hiring party

11. Whether the hiring party is in business

12. Whether benefits of any kind are provided to the hired party

13. The tax treatment of the hired party

The common law and hybrid tests place greatest emphasis on the element of right of control, whereas the economic realities test focuses more on the market for the

[8]*Nationwide Mutual Insurance Co. v. Darden*, 503 U.S. 318, at 323–24 (1992).

contractor's services and the question of whether the person performing work is in business for herself. When the **right-of-control** factor is considered, the most relevant fact is that the hiring party has the authority to control where, when, and how the work gets done, even if that party chooses not to fully exercise its authority or to delegate certain decisions to the person doing the work. Also, control over how the work gets done—and not what gets done—is the primary issue. After all, even in a pure independent contractor relationship, the hiring party still retains the ability to specify the outcomes desired and negotiate the cost of the work.

Nelson v. Yellow Cab Co. is a good example of a case in which the element of right of control is central to a court's decision about employee status.

NELSON V. YELLOW CAB CO.
564 S.E. 2d 110 (S.C. 2002)

OPINION BY JUSTICE WALLER:

Nelson, a cab driver for Yellow Cab, was murdered while driving his cab on January 6, 1998. His estate filed for Workers' Compensation benefits. * * * The sole question to be determined on appeal is whether Nelson was an employee or an independent contractor of Yellow Cab at the time of his death.

Yellow Cab requires taxi drivers to file an application for employment. The application form reads [in its most relevant part]:

> This is to certify that although I drive a taxicab owned and/or operated by Yellow Cab Company . . . I am in no way employed by the company: that I receive [sic] no salary or other compensation from the company, and that my only financial relationship with the company is to pay rent on the cab I drive, to pay for the gasoline used by me on my shift, and to return the cab with all keys and equipment in good condition at the end of my shift.

All drivers must sign the application before working for Yellow Cab. * * *

Whether a worker is an employee or independent contractor is a fact-specific matter resolved by applying certain established principles. "The general test applied is that of control by the employer. It is not the actual control then exercised, but whether there exists the right and authority to control and direct the particular work or undertaking, as to the manner or means of its accomplishment." * * * There are four elements which determine the right of control: 1) direct evidence of the right or exercise of control; 2) furnishing of equipment; 3) right to fire; and 4) method of payment. * * *

A. EXERCISE OF CONTROL

Yellow Cab contends it lacked control over Nelson, asserting that once Nelson paid his $79.00 per day lease fee, he could work as little or as much as he wanted, and he could take the cab and drive it wherever he wanted. He could also decide which zone he wanted to drive on a given day and could set his own schedule. While these facts show that Yellow Cab exercised little control over Nelson's determination of when and where to drive his cab, we find the record abundantly demonstrates that, when and if Nelson did choose to drive his cab, Yellow had the right to control the method and means of his doing so.

Yellow Cab required Nelson use his meter on all runs except charge accounts and/or authorized flat rate runs; he was not authorized to charge "flat rates" except for plantation tours. Yellow also directed the fares to be charged. He was not allowed to "deadhead," i.e., have any nonpaying passengers with him in the cab. He was prohibited by company rules from driving on the docks and picking up passengers at the airport. He was required to comply with the company dress code while driving the cab, including no sleeveless shirts, no flip-flop shoes, and no unbuttoned shirts. He was required to keep a proper manifest sheet, and prohibited from carrying any weapons in the car. Yellow Cab had certain policies and procedures drivers were to follow if dispatched to a charge account fare, and set

certain fare minimums. Drivers were awarded "free days" and "vacation days" upon driving a sufficient number of days, and were required to bring cabs in for servicing and to purchase all gas from the "point." They were also required to report any accidents, and were prohibited from "stealing calls," "long-mixing," and "freezing stands." According to the testimony of Yellow Cab's manager, Kenneth Halley, if Nelson was operating as a cab driver for them, he was required to have his radio on and respond to the dispatcher. Drivers were not allowed to sleep while on duty and were subject to being sent home for the remainder of the shift to get some sleep if they did so. They were not allowed to use profanity or would be "off the air" for three days. Yellow Cab did all the advertising for the drivers, and Nelson was given business cards with the company's name on them. Yellow Cab also obtained the annual business license authorizing its drivers to operate a taxi in Charleston. Yellow Cab maintained insurance on the cabs (which was included in the drivers' lease payments). * * * The Court of Appeals correctly held this factor leans heavily in favor of a finding of a right of control by Yellow Cab.

B. FURNISHING EQUIPMENT

On this factor, although Nelson paid a $79.00 per day lease fee, the cabs were furnished by Yellow Cab. Drivers were required to have maintenance and oil changes performed by Yellow Cab, and to purchase gas from it. Yellow Cab provided insurance, which was included in the $79.00 per day fee. Yellow Cab did the advertising and gave Nelson business cards. Yellow Cab also obtained the business license permit to operate cabs. Nelson was allowed to purchase a Yellow Cab t-shirt if he wanted. We find the furnishing of equipment element relatively neutral.

C. RIGHT TO FIRE

This factor weighs in Nelson's favor. Yellow Cab had the right to terminate Nelson for a number of reasons, to wit: drinking and driving, too many accidents, failure to deliver packages, failure to comport with the dress code. They also had the right to fire him for providing any false or incomplete information on his application. It was within Yellow Cab's discretion whether to accept him as a driver. Yellow Cab's manager, Halley, testified it would be grounds for termination if Nelson were caught charging a flat rate instead of a meter rate, deadheading, carrying a weapon in the cab, or failing to abide by the rules and regulations of Yellow Cab. He also testified that, at any time Yellow Cab wanted, it was free to decide not to lease a cab to Nelson. In addition to the right to fire, Yellow Cab had the right to discipline him. . . . * * * [T]he right of Yellow Cab to terminate Nelson went far beyond the right to simply terminate an independent contractor relationship.

D. METHOD OF PAYMENT

This factor weighs in favor of Yellow Cab. Once Nelson paid his $79.00 per day, he was entitled to keep all fares earned during the day. * * * Yellow Cab did not provide him any W-2 forms or 1099s. Nelson's Income Tax Returns for 1996 and 1997 indicate he was self-employed. Although this factor weighs in favor [of] Yellow Cab, it had some degree of control over payment inasmuch as it dictated the amounts Nelson could charge fares and required him to use a meter.

Under the specific facts of this case, . . . we find the Court of Appeals correctly held Nelson was an employee rather than an independent contractor. * * *

CASE QUESTIONS

1. What is the legal issue in this case? What did the court decide?

2. What criteria did the court use to assess right of control? How did the court apply these criteria to the facts of this case?

3. Why didn't the court pay more attention to the statement on the application form that drivers are "in no way employed by the company"?

How Useful are Independent Contractor Agreements? One of the clearest practical implications of the foregoing is that a company cannot establish independent contractor status simply by labeling its workers as contractors. Nor do independent contractor agreements suffice to show that workers are not employees. The details of working relationships measured against the criteria of the applicable tests of employee status are what matter—not labels or self-perceptions.

This does not mean that agreements are useless. *Companies using independent contractors should have signed agreements spelling out the terms of these relationships.* Clarifying the nature of relationships at the outset can avert misunderstandings. Agreements also serve to document the nature of the relationship when that relationship is disputed, provided that the agreements are accurate and demonstrate genuine independent contractor status. Just don't assume that a signed piece of paper agreeing to independent contractor status is the end of the story.

In light of the particular importance of right of control as an indicator of employee status, firms have to be prepared to relinquish most of their control over how the work is done if they want to use independent contractors rather than employees. This includes refraining from close supervision of independent contractors, directing or scheduling their activities, providing training, or requiring them to attend staff meetings.

The criteria for distinguishing between employees and independent contractors point to several other things that employers should do (or not do) to establish the independent contractor (IC) status of persons performing work. It is not essential that every one of these requirements be met, but if several cannot be met, that is a good indication that the worker should not be treated as an independent contractor:

- *Require that ICs supply their own tools, materials, and equipment, and pay their own business expenses.*
- *Require that ICs hire their own assistants.*
- *Pay ICs a flat fee for the work performed rather than an hourly or weekly rate.*
- *Closely review long-term ICs, and do not assign new projects without renewing agreements.*
- *Don't have ICs doing the same work that regular employees are doing or work that is central to the business that the company is in.*
- *Don't provide benefits to ICs, including paid time off.*
- *Make it clear that ICs are free to offer their services to others.*

The criteria for determining employee status are numerous and vary across laws and agencies. Worse, applying those criteria to the facts of particular cases necessarily involves considerable subjectivity. The outcomes of these cases are not easily predicted. What should employers do in the face of this uncertainty? *Given the potential penalties, particularly for violation of tax laws, it seems prudent when in doubt to err on the side of caution and treat the worker as an employee.* "Misclassifying" independent contractors as employees should not place firms in legal jeopardy or diminish the rights of workers, whereas doing the opposite will.

Temporary Workers

Another variety of contingent worker is the temporary worker, or temp. **Temporary workers** are procured individually through temporary staffing agencies, via contract agencies that generally "lease" multiple personnel and supervise some entire operation (e.g., security, janitorial services) for a client company, or directly hired. Legal problems can arise when temp workers, particularly those kept on for long periods of time and doing the same work as regular employees, challenge their exclusion from the benefits available to a company's regular employees.

The story of Microsoft's "permatemps" is a case in point. The tale begins in the mid-1980s when a rapidly expanding Microsoft enlisted the services of numerous programmers and systems analysts, classifying them as independent contractors.

These arrangements came to the attention of the IRS and led to enforcement actions against Microsoft in 1989. Microsoft settled with the IRS, conceding that its independent contractors were really employees. However, rather than abandon its use of workers that it distinguished from regular, permanent employees, Microsoft increasingly turned to temporary staffing firms to supply such workers. The workers continued to be excluded from valuable benefits available to permanent employees of Microsoft, including the company's "Savings Plus Plan" and its "Employee Stock Purchase Plan."

In 1992, a group of temp workers, many of whom had been with Microsoft for more than a year and performed the same work as permanent employees, filed suit challenging their exclusion from these benefits. The lengthy litigation that followed culminated in a 1997 decision in which the Ninth Circuit Court of Appeals ruled against Microsoft.[9] The company was under no legal requirement to provide such benefits to any of its employees, but once it undertook to do so, the common law definition of employee applied, and the company was not free to arbitrarily exclude a group of workers who met that definition. The fact that the temps signed agreements stating that they were not regular employees of Microsoft did not alter their status under common law. The 1997 decision did not completely resolve the dispute, but the handwriting was on the wall for Microsoft. In December 2000, the company agreed to pay $97 million to settle the claims of more than 8,000 temp workers it employed between 1987 and 2000.[10]

In a related case, the Metropolitan Water District of Southern California was sued by a group of workers that had been hired through labor supply firms and excluded from certain benefits of employment, including participation in the public employees' pension plan (CalPERS). A number of these "agency temporary employees" had worked for years alongside other employees, doing the same work and under the same conditions. The California Supreme Court decided that if, in fact, the temps were common-law employees and were not excluded by the language of the state law that governs the public employee pension plan (e.g., the statute expressly excludes workers employed for less than six months at a time), they were entitled to participate in the plan.[11] The legislature could choose to make the law more restrictive in terms of coverage, but the water district was not free to disadvantage workers who qualified as employees simply because they were procured through staffing firms.

Employers need to be precise in defining eligibility for company benefits. Employers cannot arbitrarily exclude some workers from benefits of employment by designating them as temps when they are employed on a long-term basis, do the same work as regular employees, and meet other legal criteria for establishing employee status.

Students and Interns

Not all the issues surrounding who is an employee involve contingent workers. Students and interns sometimes perform work for pay, raising questions about their employment status. If work is performed for educational institutions and serves, at least partly, an educational purpose, are persons performing such work employees, students, or both? In arriving at its current position on the employment status of

[9]*Vizcaino v. Microsoft*, 120 F.3d 1006 (9th Cir. 1997), *cert. denied*, 118 S. Ct. 899 (1998).

[10]Steven Greenhouse. "Temp Workers at Microsoft Win Lawsuit." *New York Times* (December 13, 2000), C-1.

[11]*Metropolitan Water District of Southern California v. The Superior Court of Los Angeles County*, 84 P.3d 966 (Cal. 2004).

graduate teaching and research assistants at private universities (see "Clippings"), the National Labor Relations Board found that graduate student assistants ". . . are primarily students and have a primarily educational, not economic, relationship with their university."[12] Factors cited by the NLRB in support of its decision to not treat graduate assistants as employees with the right to unionize include the fact that service as a TA or RA is contingent on continued enrollment as a student; the payment received by graduate assistants is the same as that received by graduate fellows who do not work and is thus more akin to financial aid than pay for work; and teaching is a degree requirement for graduate students in some (but not all) departments. The Board also evinced concern that collective bargaining would be "detrimental to the educational process." The *Brown University* decision implicitly treats employee status as an "either or" proposition (i.e., one is either an employee or student, but not simultaneously both) and suggests that the NLRB might also be poised to revisit an earlier decision in which it found medical interns and residents to be employees with the right to unionize and engage in collective bargaining with hospitals.[13]

That graduate assistants are not currently considered employees for purposes of the National Labor Relations Act does not necessarily mean that they are denied protection under other laws. For example, a graduate student who worked in a university lab was found to be an employee covered by Title VII of the Civil Rights Act and entitled to bring a sex discrimination claim.[14] Even though most of the work was related to completion of her dissertation and degree requirements, the court found her to be an employee because she received a stipend and benefits for her work, she received sick days and annual leave, the University provided her with equipment and training, she was covered under a collective bargaining agreement (she worked for a public university and graduate assistants at public universities have generally been allowed to unionize), and the termination of her services was for employment, rather than academic, reasons.

What about student athletes who perform services (play on teams) and receive payment (scholarships)? Especially at schools with major sports programs, these students generate significant revenue and spend a great deal of time preparing for and participating in athletic contests. Are student athletes employees? The courts have generally said no, but the door might not be closed on this issue. In a relevant case, a former football player at Texas Christian University (TCU) suffered a severe spinal cord injury during a football game.[15] Some time after the injury, the former player applied for and was awarded workers' compensation benefits. This decision was appealed on the grounds that the player was not an employee of TCU, and hence was not eligible to receive workers' compensation for his injury. A Texas appeals court eventually heard the case and agreed that the player was not an employee. The court relied heavily upon the rules of the National Collegiate Athletics Association (NCAA) and its insistence that college athletes remain amateurs. The court dismissed the argument that the scholarship amounted to pay. However, it also cautioned that college athletics has been changing and that future cases might not be decided in the same manner.

[12]*Brown University,* 342 NLRB No. 42, at 5 (2004).

[13]*Boston Medical Center,* 330 NLRB No. 30 (1999).

[14]*Cuddeback v. Florida Board of Education,* 381 F.3d 1230 (11th Cir. 2004).

[15]*Waldrep v. Texas,* 21 S.W.3d 692 (Tex. App. 2000).

Volunteers

Disputes occasionally arise regarding whether someone performing work is an employee or a **volunteer**. At first blush, disputes of this kind seem unlikely to occur because the element of payment (or expectation of payment) for services that lies at the core of an employment relationship is usually absent in volunteer work. However, in a case that went to the Supreme Court, a nonprofit agency serving addicts and the homeless also ran several commercial businesses to raise its operating funds. The businesses were staffed by the agency's clients ("associates") who received food, clothing, shelter, and medical care, but not cash wages. Despite the fact that many of the clients testified that they regarded themselves as volunteers and that payment was in noncash forms, the Supreme Court agreed with the lower courts that the clients were, in fact, employees entitled to the minimum wage. The Court concluded that as a matter of economic reality, the "associates" often worked for long periods of time and were dependent on the agency for food, clothing, housing, and medical care. That the expected compensation took the form of benefits rather than wages was irrelevant.[16] A subsequent appeals court decision held that benefits received by volunteers must amount to "significant remuneration" rather than "inconsequential incidents of an otherwise gratuitous relationship" in order to conclude that there is an employment relationship.[17]

The nonprofit Seattle Opera ran into problems with its "auxiliary choristers." The opera maintains a pool of individuals with singing ability that can be called upon if the number of regular choristers and alternates available for a production is not sufficient. Auxiliary choristers can decline a production without consequence, but if they agree to perform, they must follow the opera's rules and show up consistently at rehearsals and performances. They receive a flat sum of $214 for each production. The opera claims that this is reimbursement for transportation expenses, rather than wages. The issue of whether the auxiliary choristers are employees or volunteers arose because a union that represents other opera employees sought to negotiate on behalf of the auxiliary choristers, and the opera refused. The case hinged primarily upon whether the nominal payment could be viewed as substantial remuneration for work performed. In light of the fact that the amount had no clear relationship to transportation costs incurred, the court agreed with the National Labor Relations Board in concluding that the auxiliary choristers were employees who received payment in exchange for performing work controlled by the opera.[18]

In a case involving police officers (referred to as "nonpaid regulars") who performed occasional police work without pay for a small town in Texas, the court decided that the officers were volunteers rather than employees.[19] The primary motive for performing this service was that, under Texas law, the officers needed to have their police commissions maintained by a law enforcement agency to keep their licenses. The court applied the Department of Labor's regulation defining a volunteer as "[a]n individual who performs hours of service for a public agency for civic, charitable, or humanitarian reasons, without promise, expectation or receipt of compensation for services rendered . . ."[20] to the police officers. However, the court declined to scrutinize the motives of individuals and based its decision instead on the

[16]*Tony and Susan Alamo Foundation v. Secretary of Labor,* 471 U.S. 290 (1985).

[17]*Haavistola v. Community Fire Co. of Rising Sun, Inc.,* 6 F.3d 211, at 222 (4th Cir. 1993).

[18]*Seattle Opera v. National Labor Relations Board,* 292 F.3d 757 (D.C. Cir. 2002).

[19]*Cleveland v. City of Elmendorf, Texas,* 388 F.3d 522 (5th Cir. 2004).

[20]29 C.F.R. 553.101(a) (2005).

inherently civic nature of police work and the absence of significant remuneration. That the officers benefited by maintaining their licenses and gaining experience was not sufficient to render them employees.

Do these cases involving nonprofit and governmental agencies have any bearing on the use of "volunteers" by for-profit firms? America Online (AOL) provides an interesting case in point. AOL used large numbers of individuals to monitor activities in its many chat rooms and bulletin boards. The monitors received free or discounted subscriptions to AOL. In return, they followed rules established by AOL for carrying out their activities, worked a minimum of four hours each week (sometimes considerably more), were trained, and completed paperwork. Suits have been filed alleging that chat room monitors were employees and that AOL failed to pay them the minimum wage and maintain proper wage and hour records. AOL contends that they were volunteers. The Department of Labor has indicated that it does not intend to use its limited resources pursuing the matter, but litigation continues. Although courts are rightly skeptical of arrangements that purport to have persons volunteering their services to profit-making businesses—even if that service is maintaining a cyber community—there may be room for AOL to make this argument. In a decision denying class status to the plaintiffs (i.e., they will now have to pursue their claims individually), a California appeals court refused to rule out the possibility of individuals volunteering their services to profit-making corporations and stated that the focus must be on whether there was any promise or expectation of compensation for the services rendered to AOL.[21]

Partners

Partners, officers, board members, and major shareholders generally are not employees. However, the nature of the individual's relationship to the organization is significant, not the individual's title. The EEOC uses the following criteria to distinguish between employees and **partners:**[22]

1. Whether the organization can hire or fire the individual or set rules and regulations controlling the individual's work

2. Whether, and to what extent, the organization supervises the individual's work

3. Whether the individual reports to someone higher in the organization

4. Whether, and to what extent, the individual is able to influence the organization

5. Whether the parties intend for the individual to be an employee or partner as expressed in written agreements or contracts

6. Whether the individual shares in the profits, losses, and liabilities of the organization

The dominant theme expressed in these criteria is the extent to which the individual acts autonomously and participates in the management of the organization.

The Supreme Court approved the use of these criteria in a case involving the status of physician-shareholders who simultaneously worked for a medical clinic and served as its board of directors.[23] The issue arose because determining the employment status of the physicians was necessary to determine whether the clinic met the

[21] *America Online Cases*, 2005 Cal. App. Unpub. LEXIS 4663.

[22] Equal Employment Opportunity Commission. *Compliance Manual*, § 605:0009.

[23] *Clackamas Gastroenterology Associates v. Wells*, 538 U.S. 440 (2003).

minimum size requirements for a suit by another employee under the American's with Disabilities Act. Applying the criteria to the facts of the case, it was consistent with partner status that the physicians ran the clinic, shared in its profits, and were personally liable for malpractice claims. On the other hand, the fact that the physicians received salaries, reported to a personnel manager, and were required to comply with clinic rules suggested employee status. The Supreme Court remanded the case for further consideration of these issues.

The ongoing age discrimination case against Sidley, Austin, Brown, & Wood (see "Clippings") hinges on the question of whether the plaintiffs were true partners or merely glorified employees. The EEOC is attempting to show that most of the "partners" in the firm had no influence over the workings of the firm and were never given the opportunity to vote on such matters as promotions to partnership, removal from partnership, division of profits, and the composition of the management committee. The situation of the partners at Sidley contrasts with another case in which a court determined that a partner was not an employee.[24] In that case, the plaintiff was one of only four general partners, exercised substantial control over allocation of the firm's profits, could be removed only be unanimous vote of the other partners, shared in the firms profits, attended partnership meetings, had access to private financial information, and served as trustee of the firm's 401(k) account. Even where true partnerships are involved, persons seeking to become partners can still bring claims based on the rights of employees if there is discrimination in the process of promoting employees to partner.[25]

Other Issues Concerning Employee Status

Managers and supervisors, despite being part of management, are generally considered employees and have the same rights under most employment laws as other employees. (The National Labor Relations Act is a significant exception.)

As for undocumented workers (noncitizens who cannot establish their legal right to work in the United States), the general policy of federal agencies is to enforce employment laws without inquiring into the immigration status of workers.[26] Thus, undocumented workers are treated the same as other employees and allowed to pursue their legal claims. However, the remedies to which they are entitled might be affected by their immigration status. An employee whose rights under the National Labor Relations Act were violated admitted during a hearing that he was a Mexican citizen and was in the United States illegally.[27] The Court held that it would contradict national immigration policy to allow undocumented workers who are working illegally to be awarded back pay. Thus, the NLRB could issue a "cease and desist" order based on the violation of these workers' rights, but not award them back pay.

In a subsequent case, an undocumented worker toiled almost three years without pay because he had been promised that he would eventually be made a business partner. After the employee filed a claim for unpaid wages, the former employer apparently reported him to federal authorities that took the employee into custody. In considering the employee's retaliation claim under the Fair Labor Standards Act, the court distinguished pay for work already performed from back pay based on

[24]*Solon v. Kaplan,* 398 F.3d 629 (7th Cir. 2005).

[25]*Hishon v. King & Spalding,* 467 U.S. 69 (1984).

[26]*Patel v. Quality Inn South,* 846 F.2d 700 (11th Cir. 1988), *cert. denied,* 489 U.S. 1011 (1989) (undocumented workers covered by the Fair Labor Standards Act).

[27]*Hoffman Plastic Compounds, Inc. v. National Labor Relations Board,* 122 S. Ct. 1275 (2002).

prospective earnings lost due to an employer's illegal act. Although the Supreme Court had ruled out back pay awards to employees in the country illegally, the lower court determined that the purposes of the Fair Labor Standards Act are best served by not allowing employers to get away with cheating undocumented workers out of pay for work already performed.[28] Likewise, state courts have generally held that undocumented workers are covered and entitled to workers' compensation when they are hurt on the job. In one such case, the Georgia Court of Appeals stated that "[i]n as much as the goal of the IRCA [Immigration Reform and Control Act—the federal law prohibiting employment of undocumented workers] is to reduce the incentives for employers to hire illegal aliens, that goal would be subverted by allowing employers to avoid workers' compensation liability for work-related injuries to those employees since such would provide employers with a financial incentive to hire illegal aliens."[29]

WHO IS THE EMPLOYER?

Even when it is agreed that an individual performing work is, in fact, an employee, disputes sometimes arise concerning the identity of the employer. This is important mainly because employer status generally determines who will be held liable (legally responsible for and required to provide any award or damages) if an employee's rights are violated. We will consider three aspects of this issue. First, to what extent is an employer liable for the actions of its employees (**agents**)? Second, what parts of far-flung corporate structures are sufficiently interrelated to constitute single employers? Third, under what circumstances can firms be deemed joint employers of the same employees?

Agency

As a general rule, employers are legally responsible for the actions of their employees. When an employer confers the authority to make or significantly influence employment decisions on supervisors and other managers, the employer is liable if those employees use that authority to make employment decisions in ways that violate the law. The argument that the employer was not aware of the employee's actions or that the employee's actions were contrary to company policy, will not save an employer from liability. *Employers need to carefully select, train, monitor, and review the actions of their agents, especially those responsible for human resource decisions.*

There are bounds to the responsibility of employers for the actions of their agents. Employer liability is usually limited to employee actions taken within the scope of their employment. Actions are within the **scope of employment** to the extent that they relate to the kind of work the employee was hired to perform, take place substantially within the workplace and during work hours, and serve, at least partially, the interests of the employer. Harmful employee actions taken outside the scope of employment might still form the basis for employer liability if the employer intended the harm to occur, was negligent or reckless in allowing it to occur, impermissibly delegated an employer duty, or if the employee's harmful actions were aided by the existence of apparent or actual authority conferred by the employer.[30]

[28]*Singh v. Jutla,* 214 F.Supp 2d 1056 (N.D. Cal. 2002).

[29]*Continental Pet Technologies v. Palacias,* 604 S.E.2d 627 (Ga. App. 2004).

[30]*Restatement of the Law (Second) Agency* §§ 219, 228 (1958).

In some circumstances, a supervisor or manager can be held individually liable for violating an employee's rights, but this is generally in addition to, rather than in lieu of, employer liability. Individual liability is most likely for intentional, harmful actions, such as infliction of emotional distress.

Single, Integrated Enterprise

The organizational structures of corporations are often very complex. An intricate network of relations exists between parent companies, subsidiaries, merger and alliance partners, and other entities. In light of all these overlapping, connected, and embedded organizational units, what exactly is the employing organization? The EEOC uses the following criteria to determine whether two or more ostensibly separate entities should be considered parts of an **integrated enterprise:**[31]

1. Degree of interrelation between the operations
2. Degree to which the entities share common management
3. Degree to which there is centralized control of human resource and labor relations policies
4. Degree of common ownership or financial control over the entities.

The element of centralized control over human resource and labor relations policy is usually given the greatest weight. Indicators of centralized control include the existence of a single corporate human resource department or other unit with authority to develop personnel policy, maintenance of personnel records in a single location, common screening and testing of applicants for employment, and the same individuals making employment decisions for the involved entities.

In one relevant case, U-Haul International attempted to argue that it was not liable for sex discrimination engaged in by employees of the U-Haul Company of Maine. The court identified numerous grounds for concluding that the two entities were closely intertwined: U-Haul International owns the Maine subsidiary in its entirety; the two companies share three directors; U-Haul International receives revenues from the subsidiary's transactions, as well as daily revenue reports; it establishes equipment rental rates for the subsidiary; and it provides legal, marketing, accounting, and training services to the subsidiary. In the key area of integration in human resource policies, it was shown that there was an interchange of personnel between the two entities and that U-Haul International established wage scales, pay dates, and benefit plans. It also had to approve any deviations from established pay practices and the rehiring of former employees. Employees were directed to present complaints regarding discrimination and other matters to the U-Haul International's HR (Human Resources) Department. All of this was more than enough to demonstrate that human resource policymaking was centralized and that U-Haul International and its Maine subsidiary were an integrated enterprise for purposes of complying with antidiscrimination laws.[32]

Finding that a single, integrated enterprise exists affects not only the pockets that will be dipped into if liability is established, but also the size of the employer. An entity that has too few employees to be covered by a certain law might find that it is part of a larger integrated enterprise with enough employees to fall within the coverage of the statute. For example, an employee of a small company sued her

[31]Equal Employment Opportunity Commission. *Compliance Manual.* "Section 2: Threshold Issues," 2-III B, iii (a).

[32]*Romano v. U-Haul International, U-Haul Co. of Maine, Inc.,* 233 F.3d 655, at 667–68 (1st Cir. 2000).

employer for pregnancy discrimination. The company had fewer than 15 employees, but she was allowed to proceed with her Title VII suit because she presented sufficient evidence that her employer was part of an integrated enterprise with another corporate entity that took care of its human resources and other functions.[33]

Joint Employers

Sometimes companies are linked not because they are parts of integrated enterprises, but because they maintain employment relationships with the same employees. Courts sometimes find that **joint employers** exist and that two (or more) companies share in the liability for violation of an employee's rights. One important circumstance under which joint employment is sometimes found to exist is when a company producing a good or service contracts with another company to produce part of that good or service. Although the settlement did not definitively determine the issue of joint employment, the effort to hold the supermarket chains liable for the wrongdoing of a contract firm that supplied them with janitorial services is emblematic of current trends (see "Clippings").

In *Zheng v. Liberty Apparel Co.*, the court discusses the criteria used to determine whether a manufacturer of apparel is a joint employer of garment workers whose services had been obtained through small contractors. In this Fair Labor Standards Act case, the "economic reality" of the relationship between the workers and the alleged employer must again be examined. However, the question here is not whether the garment workers are employees or independent contractors, but whether they are the employees of a particular firm. The broader question is the legal responsibility of a firm for the actions of its subcontractors.

ZHENG V. LIBERTY APPAREL CO.
355 F. 3d 61 (2d Cir. 2003)

● ● ●

OPINION BY CIRCUIT JUDGE CABRANES:

This case asks us to decide whether garment manufacturers who hired contractors to stitch and finish pieces of clothing were "joint employers" within the meaning of the Fair Labor Standards Act of 1938 ("FLSA") and New York law. Plaintiffs, garment workers in New York City who were directly employed by the contractors, claim that the manufacturers were their joint employers because they worked predominantly on the manufacturers' garments, they performed a line-job that was integral to the production of the manufacturer's product, and their work was frequently and directly supervised by the manufacturers' agents. The manufacturers respond that the contractors, who, among other things, hired and

paid plaintiffs to assemble clothing for numerous manufacturers, were plaintiffs' sole employers. * * * The United States District Court for the Southern District of New York . . . granted the manufacturers' motion, and held that the manufacturers could not be held liable for violations of the FLSA or its New York statutory analogues. * * * We conclude that the District Court erred . . . [and remand the case to the lower court]. * * *

Plaintiffs-Appellants are 26 non-English-speaking adult garment workers who worked in a factory . . . in New York's Chinatown. They brought this action against both (1) their immediate employers, six contractors doing business at 103 Broadway ("Contractor Corporations") . . . and (2) Liberty Apparel Company, Inc. ("Liberty"). Because the Contractor Defendants either could not be located or have ceased doing business, plaintiffs have voluntarily dismissed their claims

[33]*Smith v. K&F Industries, Inc. and Loral Space & Communications*, 190 F. Supp. 2d 643 (S.D.N.Y. 2002).

against those defendants with prejudice. Accordingly, plaintiffs now seek damages only from the Liberty Defendants. * * *

From March 1997 through April 1999, Liberty entered into agreements with the Contractor Corporations under which the Contractor Corporations would assemble garments to meet Liberty's specifications. During that time period, Liberty utilized as many as thirty to forty assemblers, including the Contractor Corporations. Liberty did not seek out assemblers; instead, assemblers came to Liberty's warehouse looking for assembly work. In order to obtain such work, a prospective assembler was required by Liberty to sign a form agreement.

Plaintiffs claim that approximately 70–75% of their work during the time period at issue was for Liberty. They explain that they knew they were working for Liberty based on both the labels that were sewn into the garments and the specific lot numbers that came with the garments. Liberty's co-owner, Albert Nigri, asserts that the percentage of the Contractor Corporations' work performed for Liberty was closer to 10–15%. He derives that figure from individual plaintiffs' handwritten notes and records.

The parties do not dispute that Liberty employed people to monitor Liberty's garments while they were being assembled. However, the parties dispute the extent to which Liberty oversaw the assembly process. Various plaintiffs presented affidavits to the District Court stating that two Liberty representatives—a man named Ah Sen and "a Taiwanese woman"—visited the factory approximately two to four times a week for up to three hours a day, and exhorted the plaintiffs to work harder and faster. In their affidavits, these plaintiffs claim further that, when they finished working on garments, Liberty representatives—as opposed to employees of the Contractor Corporations—inspected their work and gave instructions directly to the workers if corrections needed to be made. One of the plaintiffs also asserts that she informed the "Taiwanese woman" that the workers were not being paid for their work at the factory.

Albert Nigri, on the other hand, avers that Liberty's quality control person made brief visits to assemblers' factories and was instructed to speak only with Lai Huen Yam, a co-owner of the Contractor Corporations, or with his wife. Furthermore, Nigri asserts in his affidavit that Liberty representatives were expected to spend just thirty minutes at each of the assemblers'

work sites. Finally, Nigri states that Liberty did not employ two quality control persons simultaneously; did not employ a quality control person during some of the relevant time period; and did not employ a man as a quality control person. * * *

Liberty Defendants moved for summary judgment on all claims against them on the ground that plaintiffs were not their employees. * * * The District Court determined that Liberty Defendants were not joint employers under the FLSA because, based on the plaintiffs' own admissions, these defendants did not (1) hire and fire the plaintiffs, (2) supervise and control their work schedules or conditions of employment, (3) determine the rate and method of payment, or (4) maintain employment records. * * *

The regulations promulgated under the FLSA expressly recognize that a worker may be employed by more than one entity at the same time. In the present case, it is undisputed that the Contractor Defendants, who are no longer parties to this suit, employed plaintiffs. The issue is whether the Liberty Defendants also employed them. * * *

We conclude . . . that the District Court erred when, based *exclusively* on the four factors . . . , it determined that the Liberty Defendants were not, as a matter of law, joint employers under the FLSA. In our view, the broad language of the FLSA . . . demands that a district court look beyond an entity's formal right to control the physical performance of another's work before declaring that the entity is not an employer under the FLSA. * * * Accordingly, the District Court's judgment in favor of the Liberty Defendants must be vacated. * * *

On remand, the District Court must determine whether the Liberty Defendants should be deemed to have been the plaintiffs' joint employer. * * * The factors we find pertinent in these circumstances, listed in no particular order, are (1) whether Liberty's premises and equipment were used for the plaintiffs' work; (2) whether the Contractor Corporations had a business that could or did shift as a unit from one putative joint employer to another; (3) the extent to which plaintiffs performed a discrete line-job that was integral to Liberty's process of production; (4) whether responsibility under the contracts could pass from one subcontractor to another without material changes; (5) the degree to which the Liberty Defendants or their agents supervised plaintiffs' work; and (6) whether plaintiffs worked exclusively or predominantly for the Liberty Defendants. * * *

The first factor—namely, whether a putative joint employer's premises and equipment are used by its putative joint employees—is relevant because the shared use of premises and equipment may support the inference that a putative joint employer has functional control over the plaintiffs' work. Similarly, the second factor—namely, whether the putative joint employees are part of a business organization that shifts as a unit from one putative joint employer to another—is relevant because a subcontractor that seeks business from a variety of contractors is less likely to be part of a subterfuge arrangement than a subcontractor that serves a single client. Although neither shared premises nor the absence of a broad client base is anything close to a perfect proxy for joint employment (because they are both perfectly consistent with a legitimate subcontracting relationship), the fact finder can use these readily verifiable facts as a starting point in uncovering the economic realities of a business relationship.

The other factors we have pointed out are less straightforward. [The third factor is] the extent to which plaintiffs performed a line-job that is integral to the putative joint employer's process of production. Interpreted broadly, this factor could be said to be implicated in *every* subcontracting relationship, because all subcontractors perform a function that a general contractor deems "integral" to a product or a service. However, we do not interpret the factor quite so broadly. * * * [W]e are mindful of the substantial and valuable place that outsourcing, along with the subcontracting relationships that follow from outsourcing, have come to occupy in the American economy. We are also mindful that manufacturers, and especially manufacturers of relatively sophisticated products that require multiple components, may choose to outsource the production of some of those components in order to increase efficiency. Accordingly, we resist the temptation to say that any work on a so-called production line—no matter what product is being manufactured—should attract heightened scrutiny. Instead, in determining the weight and degree of factor (3), we believe that both industry custom and historical practice should be consulted. Industry custom may be relevant because, insofar as the practice of using subcontractors to complete a particular task is widespread, it is unlikely to be a mere subterfuge to avoid complying with labor laws. * * *

The fourth factor . . . is whether responsibility under the contracts could pass from one subcontractor to another without material changes. * * * [T]his factor weighs in favor of a determination of joint employment when employees are tied to an entity . . . rather than to an ostensible direct employer In such circumstances, it is difficult *not* to draw the inference that a subterfuge arrangement exists. Where, on the other hand, employees work for an entity (the purported joint employer) only to the extent that their direct employer is hired by that entity, this factor does not in any way support the determination that a joint employment relationship exists.

The fifth factor listed above—namely, the degree to which the defendants supervise the plaintiffs' work—also requires some comment, as it too can be misinterpreted to encompass run-of-the-mill subcontracting relationships. * * * [E]xtensive supervision weighs in favor of joint employment only if it demonstrates effective control of the terms and conditions of the plaintiff's employment. By contrast, supervision with respect to contractual warranties of quality and time of delivery has no bearing on the joint employment inquiry, as such supervision is perfectly consistent with a typical, legitimate subcontracting arrangement.

Finally, [it must be] considered whether the purported joint employees worked exclusively or predominantly for the putative joint employer. In describing that factor, we use the words "exclusively or predominantly" on purpose. * * * In those situations, the joint employer may *de facto* become responsible, among other things, for the amount workers are paid and for their schedules, which are traditional indicia of employment. On the other hand, where a subcontractor performs merely a majority of its work for a single customer, there is no sound basis on which to infer that the customer has assumed the prerogatives of an employer.

In sum, by looking beyond a defendant's formal control over the physical performance of a plaintiff's work, the "economic reality" test—which has been distilled into a nonexclusive and overlapping set of factors—gives content to the broad language [defining employee] in the statute. However, by limiting FLSA liability to cases in which defendants, based on the totality of the circumstances, function as employers of the plaintiffs rather than mere business partners of plaintiffs' direct employer, the test also ensures that the statute is not interpreted to subsume typical outsourcing relationships. The "economic reality" test, therefore, is intended to expose outsourcing relationships that lack a substantial economic purpose, but it is manifestly not intended to bring normal, strategically-oriented contracting schemes within the ambit of the FLSA. * * *

Agriculture is another industry where "middlemen," in the form of farm labor contractors (FLCs), are used extensively to provide seasonal labor. These arrangements raise questions about who is legally responsible for the often substandard conditions under which farmworkers toil. In one such case, a farm was found to be the joint employer of farmworkers harvesting cucumbers, sharing liability for a host of employment law violations with a farm labor contractor.[34] The court emphasized the indirect control exerted by the farm; although the FLC chose employees and was responsible for the picking operation, the farm controlled the harvest schedule, had a representative present during picking who inspected the work for quality, and influenced the pay level of the pickers. More broadly, the harvesting occurred on land leased by the farm, and picking the cucumbers was an integral part of its business. A case involving employees recruited by a farm labor contractor to plant seedlings for a paper company had the opposite outcome.[35] Although the planters worked on the paper company's forestland and performed the type of repetitive, less-skilled tasks conducive to economic dependence, they were not directly controlled or supervised by personnel from the paper company (the presence of company personnel at the work site for the purpose of ensuring compliance with contract specifications was deemed not sufficient to show control); decisions about pay, hiring, and firing were made by the FLC; the duration of the relationship between the planters and the paper company was usually only a matter of several weeks; the hand planting of seeds was not integral to the paper company's business as the paper company purchased most of the timber it needed and could use machines to plant; and the paper company did not keep records on the employees, deal with taxes, or engage in any of the other activities common for employers. Under these circumstances, the court concluded that the paper company was not a joint employer of the planters.

The issue of joint employment is particularly important to the garment and agriculture industries, given their long histories of exploitative contracting arrangements, but it is not at all exclusive to those industries. Consider temp workers supplied by temporary staffing firms. Arrangements between temporary staffing firms and client firms vary considerably, but the temp agency usually assumes a number of the client company's human resource functions, including initial hiring of the temps, assignment, some general training, payroll administration, and

[34]*Torres-Lopez v. May,* 111 F.3d 633 (9th Cir. 1997).

[35]*Martinez-Mendoza v. Champion International Corp.,* 340 F.3d 1200 (2003).

arranging workers' compensation coverage. Under these circumstances, a temp agency is most often considered an employer of its temps. Thus, a temp agency's argument that it was not an employer was unavailing when the agency was solely responsible for hiring temps, controlling assignments to employers, establishing work schedules, giving instructions about appropriate dress and work habits, determining the rate and method of payment, maintaining time sheets, and issuing paychecks.[36] The court also pointed to the agency's own promotional materials in which it promised to handle for client companies "'all the burdensome paperwork, bookkeeping, record keeping, payroll costs, and government reporting'" as further confirmation of the staffing agency's status as employer. However, in another case, the role of the temp staffing firm was so minimal that only the client company was deemed an employer.[37] The client company "leased" its entire workforce from the staffing company. It was concluded that the client company was the employer because, among other things, it assigned workers to jobs and supervised their work; it did most of the hiring and firing of workers; it provided workers with equipment, materials, and transportation; and it set pay rates and hours of work. Although the staffing firm performed payroll administration duties, handled job applications, conducted drug tests, and provided some safety training, it exerted no direct control over the workers and was indifferent to how they performed their jobs. Thus, the leasing agreement notwithstanding, the client company was the sole employer. As the employer, it was financially responsible for providing workers' compensation coverage.

A client company might also be deemed a joint employer of employees that it procures through a temporary staffing firm. In one such case, the client firm responded to employee complaints by deciding to obtain all part-time and temporary employees through temporary staffing firms, rather than hire them directly. If the client firm thought that this maneuver would absolve it of any legal responsibilities to these employees, it was wrong. The temp agency hired all the former employees of the client firm that would accept the new arrangement and the client firm continued to manage those employees pretty much as it had before. It exerted substantial control, including requesting and receiving the assignment of particular employees; arranging for particular employees to work consecutive days at the client firm; training and supervising the employees; determining work hours; and supplying time cards. The client firm was found to be a joint employer sharing liability with the temp agency for violations of the National Labor Relations Act.[38]

The message is clear. *Employers cannot assume that simply because they obtain workers from temporary staffing agencies or use the services of employees from contract firms, that they are free of legal obligations to those workers.* The degree of control exerted over the workers is again a key factor, although courts sometimes look beyond obvious indicators of direct control. *The only way to not be deemed an employer (singly or jointly) is to avoid acting like an employer. Actions such as closely supervising, training, setting pay rates for, disciplining, and selecting individual temps for hire or fire are all strong indicators that a client company is an employer of temps.*

[36]*Baystate Alternative Staffing v. Herman,* 163 F.3d 668 (1st Cir. 1998).

[37]*Sonners, Inc. v. Department of Labor & Industries,* 3 P.3d 756 (Wash. App. 2000), *review denied,* 2000 Wash. LEXIS 856.

[38]*NLRB v. Western Temporary Services and the Classic Company,* 821 F.2d 1258 (7th Cir. 1987).

Like much legal advice, this is easier said than done. Carolyn Koenig, Vice President of Human Resources at MasterCard International, a company with a workforce that is more than 20 percent contingent workers, has observed:

> You always have to be very conscious of that [the distinction between temps and employees]. . . . You don't want to direct their work or treat them like an employee, but at the same time, you want to treat them like a person and keep them motivated. It takes a lot of manager awareness and savvy to walk the line appropriately.[39]

The notion of "auditioning" temps for possible hire as permanent employees also runs into problems. No doubt this is an effective way to screen employees, and the prospect of being hired as regular employees makes temps more motivated, but *if "promotion" to regular employee status is a standard practice, a client company is again more likely to be viewed as an employer of its temps.*

A joint employer cannot afford to be indifferent to the treatment of an employee by his other employer(s). For example, if managers at a temporary staffing agency learn that one of their temps is being harassed at a client firm, the temp agency has to take whatever actions it can to stop the harassment.[40] It will not do for them to say that this is the client firm's problem or that the temp should work things out with the client firm. Spherion Corporation erred by carrying out Sega's directions to discriminatorily terminate a number of its temps (see "Clippings"). *Joint employers are liable if they participate in the violation of an employee's rights by another employer of that employee or fail to take appropriate actions to stop violations of their employee's rights by another employer.*

Other Issues Concerning Employer Status

Occasionally firms can be liable for violations of the rights of workers who are employees of other firms and not employees of their own. One important example is in the area of occupational safety and health. Workplaces such as construction sites and aircraft assembly facilities typically bring together the employees of multiple companies to work in close proximity. Inattention by one firm to safety and health standards can create hazards that affect employees of other companies. For example, a contractor responsible for erecting steel at a construction site ignored warnings that its employees were using improper methods to connect beams. Part of the structure collapsed killing two workers, one of them an employee of another company. The contractor's argument that it should not be held responsible for safety violations leading to the death of an individual who was not its employee failed. The court applied the **multi-employer doctrine,** which holds that "on multi-employer work sites, an employer who creates a safety hazard can be liable under the Act regardless of whether the employees threatened are its own or those of another employer on the site."[41] *Thus, the responsibility of employers to provide safe and healthy workplaces extends to protecting employees of other companies who work in or have regular access to those sites.*

[39]Linda Micco. "Employment in the 21st Century: Technology, Outsourcing, Contingent Work." *Daily Labor Report* 1 (January 3, 2000), C-1.

[40]Equal Employment Opportunity Commission. "Enforcement Guidance: Application of EEO Laws to Contingent Workers Placed by Temporary Employment Agencies and other Staffing Firms." No. 915.002 (December 3, 1997).

[41]*United States of America v. Pitt-DesMoines, Inc.,* 168 F.3d 976, at 982 (7th Cir. 1997).

U.S. employment laws generally apply to foreign-owned firms that operate in the United States (but are sometimes subject to treaty limitations). What about the overseas operations of U.S. firms? In general, U.S. laws, including employment laws, apply only within the territorial boundaries of the United States. Thus, a court rejected the overtime claims of employees of a federal contractor because they were stationed in Antarctica, which the court found to be a foreign country for purposes of applying the Fair Labor Standards Act.[42] However, Congress has determined that Title VII of the Civil Rights Act, the Americans with Disabilities Act (ADA), and the Age Discrimination in Employment Act (ADEA) apply **extraterritorially.** That is, these laws apply to U.S. citizens who are employees of U.S. employers operating outside of the United States, provided that complying with U.S. law would not cause employers to violate other nations' laws. However, in a case involving an American company that recruited farm laborers from Mexico, a court decided that foreign nationals seeking employment in the United States are not protected from discrimination under U.S. law.[43] Specifically, a Mexican citizen had applied to a U.S. company with an office in Mexico from which it hired farm laborers to work in North Carolina. The applicant was informed that no one over 40 years of age would be considered for employment, unless they had worked for this outfit previously. Even though the persons hired would be working in the United States and for U.S. employers, the court held that the ADEA does not protect citizens of other countries who apply outside the United States for work in this country.

Chapter SUMMARY

Most of the employment laws discussed in this book apply only if an employment relationship exists. Yet, work is sometimes performed for pay outside of traditional employer-employee relationships. Distinguishing between independent contractors and employees is the central issue in determining who is an employee. Courts use a variety of criteria to make this distinction. These criteria are combined into the economic realities, common law, and hybrid tests of employee status. The economic realities test used to determine coverage under the Fair Labor Standards Act focuses on whether there is a market for the worker's services. Although all the tests consider the issue of right of control over how, when, and where the work is done, this criterion is emphasized most heavily in the common law test. Regardless of the test used, the basic question is whether, on the whole, the worker looks more like someone who is in business for himself and directing his own work or someone who is part of an ongoing employment relationship.

Questions about employee status also arise in other contexts, although the criteria for distinguishing employees from these other statuses are not as well established. When temps are used to perform the same work as permanent employees and do so over a substantial period of time, employers run the risk that they will be considered employees under the common law definition and eligible for benefits available to other employees. Volunteers can be construed as employees if they receive significant remuneration for their services, even if the payment is not in cash. Students and interns that perform paid work might also be deemed employees, although the most recent NLRB decision in this area treats these as mutually exclusive categories. Criteria for distinguishing employees from partners center on the degree to which individuals act autonomously and participate in managing organizations. Undocumented workers in the United States illegally are considered employees with rights under employment laws, but are subject to

[42]*Smith v. Raytheon,* 297 F. Supp. 2d 399 (D. Mass. 2004).

[43]*Reyes-Gaona v. North Carolina Growers Ass'n Inc.,* 250 F.3d 861 (4th Cir. 2001), *cert. denied,* 2001 U.S. LEXIS 10008.

limitations on the individual remedies they can receive for violations of their rights.

On the other side of the employment relationship, the identity of the employer is not always clear. Employers are generally responsible for the actions of their agents that occur within the scope of employment. When supervisors and managers make human resource decisions that violate the rights of employees, liability typically rests with the employing firm rather than the individual actors. Organizational entities that are presented as separate might be deemed parts of single, integrated enterprises. Entities are sufficiently integrated to warrant their treatment as the same employer when they have closely interrelated operations, shared management, centralized human resource and labor relations policies, and shared financial ownership or control. An employee can have more than a single employer, and thus, more than one firm can be responsible for violations of that employee's rights. Possibilities for joint employment abound as firms increasingly contract with other firms for labor. Joint employment is particularly likely when temporary staffing agencies provide workers to client firms that then closely manage the temps. Several major federal antidiscrimination laws apply extraterritorially to U.S. citizens employed by U.S. firms overseas, provided that complying with U.S. law does not require violation of foreign law.

Practical Advice SUMMARY

- *The status of each person performing work for a company has to be determined using the appropriate legal criteria. Simply labeling workers "independent contractors," "interns," or "partners" does not establish their employment status.*

- *Independent contractor agreements should be used, but they matter only insofar as they document actual independent contractor relationships.*

- *Employers that want to use independent contractors (ICs) must be prepared to relinquish most of their control over how the work is done, including refraining from*

 –close supervision of ICs.

 –directing or scheduling ICs' activities.

 –providing ICs with training.

 –requiring or expecting ICs to attend staff meetings.

- *Employers that want to use independent contractors also should be prepared to do at least most of the following:*

 –require that ICs supply their own tools, materials, and equipment, and pay their own business expenses.

 –require that ICs hire their own assistants.

 –pay ICs a flat fee for the work performed, rather than an hourly or weekly rate.

 –closely review the status of long-term ICs.

 –make it clear that ICs are free to offer their services to others.

 –not assign new projects without renewing agreements.

 –not have ICs doing the same work that regular employees are doing or work that is central to the business that the company is in.

 –not provide benefits to ICs, including paid time off.

- *Given the potential penalties, particularly for violation of tax laws, it is prudent when in doubt to err on the side of caution and treat workers as employees.*

- *Be particularly cautious about changing the status of workers from employees to contingent workers or having workers with different statuses perform the same work for long periods of time.*

- *Companies that use workers supplied by temporary staffing agencies must avoid acting like employers if they desire to avoid liability for the mistreatment of temps. This includes refraining from*

 –closely supervising temps.

 –providing training.

 –setting pay rates.

 –selecting individual temps for hire or fire.

 –regularly offering permanent employment to temps.

Key TERMS

employee	hybrid test	scope of employment
employer	right of control	integrated enterprise
contingent worker	temporary worker	joint employers
independent contractor	volunteer	multiemployer doctrine
economic realities test	partner	extraterritoriality
common law test	agent	

Chapter QUESTIONS

1. A company that sells subscriptions to magazines enlisted persons to research the telephone numbers of potential subscribers. These "home researchers" worked out of their own homes, set their own hours, and were subject to relatively few requirements as to how they carried out their tasks. They were given index cards with names and addresses and were paid according to the number of cards returned with telephone numbers. Each was asked to sign an "independent contractors agreement" before beginning to work for the company. The home researchers generally performed their services only for this company and a number of them did so for several years. The company also used in-house researchers to find telephone numbers. Overall, the home researchers accounted for about 4–5 percent of the total telephone numbers obtained by the company. Most of the home researchers used the job as a secondary source of income. Some of the home researchers claimed that they were not being paid the minimum wage for their hours of work. The company contended that they were independent contractors and not employees with rights under the Fair Labor Standards Act. What should the court decide? (*Donavan v. DialAmerica Marketing*, 757 F.2d 1376 (3d Cir.), *cert. denied*, 474 U.S. 919 (1985))

2. A restaurant employee sued for harassment. For the restaurant to have the minimum number of employees required for coverage under Title VII of the Civil Rights Act, delivery drivers would have to be employees. The drivers are assigned schedules identical to those maintained for other employees at the restaurant, paid an hourly rate, expected to work all the hours in their shifts, record their hours of work on the restaurant's computer system, are prohibited from working for other employers during their shifts, and occasionally do other work at the restaurant when not making deliveries. The drivers are not listed on the restaurant's payroll, have no deductions made from their pay, and do not accrue annual leave or retirement benefits. The drivers use their own vehicles and are responsible for insuring and maintaining them. In addition to their hourly rate, drivers receive tips and an incentive bonus based on the total value of deliveries made during shifts. Drivers often work "off and on" at the restaurant and many make deliveries for other companies when off duty. Drivers choose their own routes when making deliveries. Are the drivers employees or independent contractors? (*Arbaugh v. Y&H Corp.*, 380 F.3d 219 (5th Cir. 2004))

3. An attorney and member of the New York Bar Association became actively involved with international environmental issues. She proposed and developed a program and then presented it under the auspices of the association. She engaged in other efforts, including creating a new Bar Association committee on international environmental law, making presentations, and participating at the first United Nations Conference on Environment and Development. In return, the association provided her with workspace, clerical support, publicity, and reimbursement for out-of-pocket expenses. The attorney experienced harassment by a Bar Association official and sued. Was she a volunteer or an employee? (*York v. Association of the Bar of the City of New York*, 286 F.3d 122 (2d Cir. 2002))

4. Several participants in New York City's Work Experience Program, a mandatory welfare work program, experienced harassment at their worksites. When they sued under Title VII, the

city argued that they were not employees. The women worked at a number of different city agencies. For their work, they received cash public assistance, food stamps, transportation, childcare expenses, and eligibility for workers' compensation. Recipients who unjustifiably refuse to work lose a portion of their family's grant. Are participants in this "welfare-to-work" program employees? (*United States of America v. City of New York*, 359 F.3d 83 (2d Cir. 2004))

5. A supermarket and drug store chain in New York City contracted with another company to provide personnel to make home deliveries to customers. This arrangement remained in place for a number of years. The delivery workers operated directly out of the stores. The stores directed the delivery workers in their tasks and instructed them concerning what to pick up, where to go, how to log their deliveries, and how much to receive in payment. The delivery workers worked as individuals, and not as a group shifting from store to store in accordance with demand for delivery workers. Is the supermarket/drug store chain a joint employer liable for violations of the delivery workers rights under the Fair Labor Standards Act? (*Ansoumana v. Gristede's Operating Corp.*, 255 F.Supp 2d 184 (S.D.N.Y. 2003))

6. Try your hand at drafting an independent contractor agreement that a company might use. Don't worry about making your agreement sound like "legalese." Focus instead on what such an agreement should specify.

7. Legal considerations dictate a relatively hands-off approach to the management of independent contractors and temps, and the maintenance of clear boundaries between these workers and regular employees. Do you see problems with putting this legal advice into practice?

8. What is your view on whether student athletes should be considered employees of the universities they attend?

9. What are the consequences of denying back pay and other individual remedies to undocumented workers? Justice Breyer, dissenting from the majority opinion in *Hoffman Plastic Compounds, Inc. v. NLRB*, writes that denying the NLRB the power to award back pay "lowers the cost to the employer of an initial labor law violation. . . . It thereby increases the employer's incentive to find and to hire illegal-alien employees." Does denying remedies to undocumented workers reinforce or undermine national immigration policies?

10. Commenting on the increasingly widespread use of labor contractors by large companies, attorney Della Bahan claimed "These companies are pretending they're not the employer. The contractor is willing to work people seven days a week, not pay payroll taxes, not pay worker's comp taxes. The companies don't want to do that for themselves, but they're willing to look the other way when their contractors do it." Do you agree? To what extent should companies be held responsible for the employment practices of companies with which they contract? (Steven Greenhouse. "Middlemen in the Low-Wage Economy." *New York Times* (December 28, 2003), WK-10)

Internet RESOURCES

Enforcement guidance from the Equal Employment Opportunity Commission (EEOC) on the application of antidiscrimination laws to contingent workers placed by temporary employment agencies and other staffing firms.

http://www.eeoc.gov/policy/docs/conting.html

Enforcement guidance from the EEOC on the application of the ADA to contingent workers placed by temporary employment agencies and other staffing firms.

http://www.eeoc.gov/policy/docs/guidance-contingent.html

This site for the National Alliance for Fair Employment contains a variety of materials related to contingent workers.

http://www.fairjobs.org/

This Web site of the Internal Revenue Service contains numerous documents discussing the tax status of independent contractors and how to distinguish them from employees.

http://www.irs.gov

Overview of Employment Discrimination

CLIPPINGS

▸ The Equal Employment Opportunity Commission (EEOC) has settled a sex discrimination claim brought on behalf of 200 men who were denied temporary assembly-line jobs at the San Antonio plant of an electrical manufacturer. The EEOC alleged that the employer engaged in a pattern or practice of discriminating against males for assembly-line jobs and that its hiring policy was based on 'sexist myths and stereotypes, such as that men have poor manual dexterity and that women are more subservient workers.' Under the terms of the settlement, the males will share in a $475,000 award.[1]

▸ Rae Ann Good was offered a job as Executive Vice President at Johnson International, a global financial services company. Shortly after accepting the position, Ms. Good informed the company that she had recently learned that she was pregnant. Her start date in the new position was first postponed and then "cancelled." The EEOC sued on her behalf and a monetary settlement was obtained.[2]

▸ Rent-A-Center will pay millions to settle a class-action lawsuit filed on behalf of some 5,000 of their female employees. Managers are alleged to have made statements such as "A woman's place is not in my stores," "In case you didn't notice, we do not employ women," "I regularly throw away women's applications," and "You can do the vacuuming because that's a woman's job."[3]

▸ A jury found in favor of former Federal Express manager Ted Maines and awarded him $1.57 million in a retaliation case. Maines, who is white, was disciplined, subjected to intense surveillance, and ultimately forced to resign, after he spoke out on behalf of African-American and Latino employees that he felt were being discriminated against in promotions.[4]

▸ Researchers at M.I.T. conducted an experiment to gauge the extent of discrimination against African-American job applicants. Responding to newspaper listings for entry-level jobs, the researchers sent resumes that were matched in terms of experience, education, and skills, but differed in terms of the "applicants'" names. Applicants with "white-sounding" names (e.g., Kristen, Laurie) were much more likely to be called for interviews than were applicants with "black-sounding" names (e.g., Lakisha, Tamika), despite equal qualifications. Another study using a similar methodology found that job applicants with names common among Arab or South Asian persons were less likely to receive responses from temporary staffing agencies in California than were applicants whose names did not suggest these backgrounds.[5]

[1]Nancy Montwieler. "Women's Alleged Subservience, Dexterity No Excuse for Excluding Men, EEOC Argues." *Daily Labor Report* 109 (June 8, 2005), A-1.

[2]Equal Employment Opportunity Commission. "EEOC and Johnson International Settle Pregnancy Discrimination Suit for $450,000." (December 28, 2004) Viewed January 22, 2005 (http://www.eeoc.gov/press/12-28-04.html).

[3]Robert Grossman. "Paying the Price." *HR Magazine* 47, no. 8 (August 2002).

[4]Equal Employment Opportunity Commission. "Jury Orders Federal Express to Pay $1.57 Million in Employment Bias Suit by EEOC." (December 22, 2004) Viewed January 22, 2005 (http://www.eeoc.gov/press/12-22-04.html).

[5]Alan B. Krueger. "Sticks and Stones Can Break Bones, But the Wrong Name Can Make a Job Hard to Find." *New York Times* (December 12, 2002), C2; Larry Swisher. "Temporary Job Agencies' Resume Responses Show Discrimination by Ethnicity, Study Says." *Daily Labor Report* 195 (October 8, 2004), A-12.

This chapter delves into the concept of employment discrimination, the various types of discrimination, and the methods used in deciding discrimination cases. Because discrimination is a concern in virtually all areas of human resource practice, the material in this chapter is essential background for understanding cases and issues discussed throughout this entire book.

THE CONTINUING REALITY OF EMPLOYMENT DISCRIMINATION

Many things have changed for the better since the 1960s when our nation's primary antidiscrimination law, the Civil Rights Act of 1964, was enacted. We have made some progress in combating discrimination in the workplace and making equal employment opportunity a reality, but the job is by no means finished. Rooting out the contemporary manifestations of discrimination may prove even more difficult than confronting the overt exclusion and segregation characteristic of earlier years.

Discrimination is inherently difficult to prove. Indeed, much of this chapter is devoted to explaining the methods that courts use to decide these complex cases. One indication that discrimination has not yet been eradicated is found in markedly different employment outcomes, such as higher unemployment rates, concentration in lower-level jobs, and pay disparities across different races, sexes, and national origin groups. Unequal labor market outcomes need not have discrimination as their cause, but they are consistent with the presence of discrimination.

A second type of evidence for the continuing reality of discrimination comes from the large numbers of discrimination cases heard by administrative agencies and courts. The EEOC, for example, received roughly 80,000 new charges of discrimination each year during the period from 1992 through 2004.[6] Federal court cases alleging discrimination have increased substantially and now number more than 20,000 per year.[7] State civil rights agencies and courts handle an additional, and probably significant, number of cases each year. Other discrimination cases are not recorded because they are settled before any official charge is brought. Not every case presents a valid claim, and indeed, the majority of cases do not conclude with a finding of discrimination. But despite plaintiffs' heavy burden in proving discrimination, courts and agencies decide in thousands of cases each year that discrimination has occurred. And since many more violations occur than are reflected in official case statistics, the caseload that we see is just the tip of a discriminatory iceberg.

Third, when "employment testers" (matched job candidates who differ only in their race or sex) are dispatched to test for discriminatory hiring practices, the extent of discrimination that they find is usually extensive. In general, field and laboratory studies of employment discrimination, like the experiments on the effects of applicants' names (see "Clippings"), find discrimination very real and pervasive.[8]

THE CONCEPT OF EMPLOYMENT DISCRIMINATION

Numerous laws exist that aim to advance the goal of equal employment opportunity by prohibiting discrimination. Major federal antidiscrimination statutes include Title VII of the Civil Rights Act of 1964, the Equal Pay Act, the Age Discrimination

[6]EEOC. *All Statutes: FY 1992 – FY 2004.* Viewed July 1, 2005 (http://www.eeoc.gov/stats/all.html).

[7]Hoyt N. Wheeler, Brian S. Klaas, and Douglas M. Mahony. *Workplace Justice Without Unions.* Kalamazoo, Mich.: W.E. Upjohn Institute for Employment Research (2004), 18.

[8]Judith Olans Brown, et al. "Some Thoughts About Social Perception and Employment Discrimination Law: A Modest Proposal for Reopening the Judicial Dialogue." *Emory Law Journal* 46 (1997), 1498–99.

THE CHANGING WORKPLACE

The Contemporary Face of Discrimination

Employment discrimination is a continuing reality, but its nature has shifted in accordance with changes in the workplace and societal attitudes. Overt exclusion and segregation are less common now, although the charges leveled at Rent-A-Center (see "Clippings") and the exclusion of men from a manufacturing facility based on demeaning gender stereotypes (see "Clippings") hark back to an earlier era of crude and obvious discrimination. As women and persons of color have entered the workforce in record numbers and begun to attain positions in occupations and industries from which they were largely absent, other forms of discrimination have loomed large. One of these is harassment. As a form of discrimination, harassment is calculated to impress upon its victims that they are not truly included or welcome in the workplace. Persons subjected to harassment find it more difficult to do their jobs well and frequently quit in disgust. Companies desiring greater diversity end up with turnover and legal problems.

Discrimination also increasingly takes the relatively subtle form of blocked access to better jobs, rather than outright exclusion from workplaces.[1] In this regard, there has been extensive discussion of the **glass ceiling** problem, in which "invisible, artificial, and attitudinal barriers" conspire to limit the access of women and persons of color to higher-level positions.[2] The glass ceiling phenomenon takes on added significance in the context of a decline in stable career ladders. Having access to opportunities for training, development, and meaningful job assignments is critical when employees are expected to construct their own career paths (not necessarily within the same organization), and exhibiting loyalty by staying around for the long haul is less likely to be rewarded.[3] The more that promotions, pay, and other important decisions are linked to performance, the more important it is that performance appraisals provide accurate, unbiased assessments. Yet, performance appraisals, at their best, require considerable subjective judgment. This leaves a large door open for bias or the perception of bias.[4] Getting ahead also depends heavily upon one's "connections." Opportunities for informal mentoring, learning about the availability of jobs, and coming to the attention of those higher up in organizations all rest on social relationships. Work teams and peer review processes—both increasingly important—also place a premium on

workplace relationships. That race, sex, or other characteristics of people can affect social relationships on the job—and by extension, employment opportunities—seems beyond question. Ferreting out discrimination when it lies beneath lukewarm performance appraisals, fewer high-profile assignments, low visibility, or subjective judgments that others would better "fit" positions, is difficult, if not impossible.

Even companies that are generally viewed as progressive experience problems in removing discriminatory obstacles to advancement and taking full advantage of workforce diversity. Kodak regularly appears on lists of top companies for minority employees, has an array of diversity programs in place, and has been forthright in investigating and attempting to remedy discrimination claims; yet the company is facing a race discrimination suit brought by a number of its African-American employees. An external diversity council that the company asked to review its programs concluded that the company needed to formalize succession plans for high-level positions, do more to address turnover among higher-ranked women and persons of color, and try harder to eliminate under-representation of minorities in professional and managerial positions.[5] Likewise, General Electric is facing a possible class-action race discrimination suit. The likely lead plaintiff in the case, if it goes forward, is Marcel T. Thomas. Mr. Thomas attained the position of chief executive of GE Aviation Materials and earned a salary in excess of $200,000, but was given low performance ratings and a minimal pay increase in a year where his unit increased its sales and profits markedly. His view that the incident reflected "pervasive" racism at GE is hotly contested by the company, although current and former employees have mixed views on the subject. Carl Brooks, president of the Executive Leadership Council, an organization of African-American executives aptly observed that 'Every company, even GE is still on a journey when it comes to really getting racism knocked.'[6]

As employees become aware of their rights and increasingly inclined to contest discriminatory practices, retaliation has also become a prominent aspect of the contemporary profile of discrimination. Employers frequently compound initial instances of discrimination with the added infraction of punishing employees who complain about their employer's practices or help other

employees obtain their rights. Whether due to an actual increase in retaliatory conduct by employers or to changes in legal strategy, retaliation claims are increasingly raised by plaintiffs. In 2004, fully 28.6 percent of EEOC charges included an allegation of retaliation, up from 15.3 percent in 1992.[7]

[1]Anne Lawton. "The Meritocracy Myth and the Illusion of Equal Employment Opportunity." *Minnesota Law Review* 85 (December 2000), 605–12.

[2]U.S. Department of Labor, Employment Standards Administration. *OFCCP Glass Ceiling Initiative: Are There Cracks in the Ceiling?*

viewed March 29, 2001 (http://www.dol.gov/esa/media/reports/ofccp/newgc.htm).

[3]Katherine V. W. Stone. *From Widgets to Digits: Employment Regulation for the Changing Workplace.* New York: Cambridge University Press (2004).

[4]Susan Bisom-Rapp. "Bulletproofing the Workplace: Symbol and Substance in Employment Discrimination Law Practice." *Florida State University Law Review* 26 (Summer 1999), 1012–18.

[5]Claudia H. Deutsch. "Race Remains a Difficult Issue for Many Kodak Workers." *New York Times* (August 24, 2004), C-1.

[6]Claudia H. Deutsch. "Black, White or Gray: Statistics and Emotions Clash in Bias Cases." *New York Times* (June 7, 2005), C-1.

[7]Equal Employment Opportunity Commission. "Charge Statistics FY 1992 Through FY 2004." Viewed July 1, 2005 (http://www.eeoc.gov/stats/charges/html).

in Employment Act, the Rehabilitation Act, the Pregnancy Discrimination Act, the Americans with Disabilities Act, and 42 *United States Code* sections 1981 and 1983 (the latter are statutes enacted following the abolition of slavery that are now used to contest intentional employment discrimination). The U.S. Constitution, particularly the Fourteenth Amendment's promise of equal protection under the law, also can be brought to bear to combat discrimination. Executive Order 11246 makes nondiscrimination a requirement for contractors and subcontractors doing government work. States and cities have their own antidiscrimination laws that mirror and sometimes extend federal protections. Clearly, laws prohibiting discrimination comprise a large and absolutely central part of employment law. But what is discrimination?

Employment **discrimination** can be defined as the limitation or denial of employment opportunity based on or related to the protected class characteristics of persons. This definition, though broad to subsume the different types of discrimination discussed in the following text, conveys some important aspects of employment discrimination. The element of limitation or denial of employment opportunities (also referred to as "adverse employment actions") indicates that it is not prejudice alone that subjects employers to liability, but the effects of bias on employment opportunities. It also signals that one must be concerned about discrimination in all areas of human resource decision making, including promotions, compensation, benefits, access to training opportunities, discipline, and terminations—and not only in hiring practices. The definition of discrimination is elastic enough to encompass harassment that does not directly alter a person's employment status, but that makes it more difficult to perform well and stay on the job. On the other hand, minor differences in treatment, stray insensitive comments, or instances of exclusion by coworkers from after-work socializing would not, by themselves, have sufficient impact on employment opportunities (i.e., they are not "materially adverse") to be grounds for discrimination claims. Unwanted transfers and job assignments constitute a "gray area." In one recent case, the involuntary transfer of an employee after she informed her employer that she was pregnant was found to be an adverse employment action.[9] There was evidence, including the fact that existing employees avoided applying for

[9]*Equal Employment Opportunity Commission v. SBC Communications,* 2005 U.S. Dist. LEXIS 6667, at 5.

the position, to support the conclusion that the new position was objectively worse and effectively a demotion. In contrast, a court rejected the sex discrimination claim of a former CIA agent who said that her forced reassignment to a remote and more dangerous location in a Latin American country was a discriminatory act. In the court's view, she was unable to show that, having entered an inherently dangerous line of work, the reassignment had a "significant detrimental effect" on her terms and conditions of employment.[10]

Embedded within this definition is also the idea that discrimination is a relative concept. Unequal treatment and outcomes can be discerned only by comparing what happens to some individuals with what happens to other individuals in a workplace. In contrast to other laws that establish specific, minimum standards that employers must meet, U.S. antidiscrimination laws require consistent, even-handed treatment of employees.

But unequal and unfair treatment of individuals is still not sufficient to establish the existence of discrimination. To have discrimination, the unfair treatment must be based on or related to the **protected class** characteristics of persons. Our society deems certain characteristics of people, such as their race, sex, and age, impermissible grounds for making employment decisions. Linking employment decisions to protected class characteristics is prohibited, whereas unequal treatment based on other types of distinctions (e.g., personality, personal friendships) generally does not provide the basis for a discrimination claim.

Protected Classes

Not all distinctions between people—and not even all those things that have no bearing on a person's ability to do a job—are protected class characteristics. To be sure, protected class characteristics are things that we generally regard as having little or no relationship to the ability to do a job. However, protected class characteristics also are fundamentally objectionable as grounds for making employment decisions. One reason that they are objectionable is that most protected class characteristics are either immutable (unchangeable) or not readily altered. For example, a person cannot change his race and should not have to change or hide his religion just to suit the preferences of an employer. A second reason that some characteristics are particularly objectionable as grounds for making employment decisions is that they relate to longstanding forms of hatred and prejudice, including racism, sexism, nationalism, ageism, anti-Semitism, and homophobia.

The following is a list of protected classes under federal employment statutes:

- *Race, color* (Title VII, Civil Rights Act, 42 U.S.C. § 1981)
- *Sex* (Title VII, Civil Rights Act, Equal Pay Act)
- *National origin* (Title VII, Civil Rights Act, 42 U.S.C. § 1981, Immigration Reform and Control Act)
- *Religion* (Title VII, Civil Rights Act)
- *Citizenship* Citizens or legal aliens (Immigration Reform and Control Act)
- *Age* 40 and over (Age Discrimination in Employment Act)
- *Disability* "Qualified individual with a disability" (Americans with Disabilities Act, Rehabilitation Act)

[10]*Peary v. Goss*, 365 F.Supp.2d 713, at 724-25 (E.D. Va. 2005).

- *Pregnancy* Pregnancy, childbirth, and related medical conditions (Pregnancy Discrimination Act)
- *Veterans, Military Service* (Uniformed Services Employment and Reemployment Rights Act)

Some protected classes are recognized under state law, but not federal law. Examples include the following:

- *Marital status* (about 30 states)
- *Sexual orientation* (about 11 states)
- *Tobacco/alcohol use* (about 25 states)
- *HIV/AIDS* (about 8 states)
- *Arrest/criminal conviction* (about 3 states)
- *Weight, personal appearance* (Michigan, Washington DC)

Notice that some antidiscrimination statutes limit the definition of protected class to a particular group that is most likely to be the object of discrimination. For example, the Age Discrimination in Employment Act protects persons who are 40 years of age and older, but does not prohibit denial of employment opportunity because someone under 40 is "too young." In contrast, the protected class of race under Title VII includes *any* race. Although it is less likely that whites will be subjected to employment discrimination, discrimination against whites is clearly prohibited by Title VII. For example, there was a case in which three employees were charged by their employer with stealing cargo. Two of the employees were white and were discharged for the offense. The third employee was black and was not discharged. The Supreme Court held that "While Santa Fe [the employer] may decide that participation in a theft of cargo may render an employee unqualified for employment, this criterion must be 'applied, alike to members of all races,' and Title VII is violated if, as petitioners alleged, it was not."[11] The electrical manufacturer violated Title VII when it relied on stereotypes in denying assembly-line jobs to men (see "Clippings").

TYPES OF DISCRIMINATION

Discrimination can be further distinguished into four "types" or legal theories: disparate treatment, adverse impact (also known as disparate impact), failure to reasonably accommodate, and retaliation.

Disparate treatment is intentional unequal treatment based on protected class characteristics, which results in the limitation or denial of employment opportunity. As the term implies, there is disparity or inequality in how employees are treated, and the difference in treatment is due to the employee's race, sex, or other protected class characteristic. The key element of disparate treatment is **discriminatory intent.** The meaning of intent is that the decision maker based her decision, in whole or part, on a protected class characteristic of the affected employee. Johnson International engaged in disparate treatment when it withdrew its offer of employment after learning that Rae Ann Good was pregnant (see "Clippings"). The company's decision about who to employ was influenced by knowledge of the applicant's protected class characteristic (her pregnancy). Likewise, the electrical manufacturer engaged in

[11]*McDonald v. Santa Fe Transportation Co.*, 427 U.S. 273, at 283 (1976).

disparate treatment when it made hiring decisions based on sex (see "Clippings"). This employer's preference for women was apparently based on dubious stereotypes about male and female employees, but it would not have made any difference if the employer had been able to show that, "on average," males and females really do differ in terms of dexterity and "subservience." Hiring decisions were based on consideration of applicants' sex (the employer did not purport to measure dexterity or subservience), and this violated the law.

Suppose that an employer believes that tall people make better managers because they are able to command more respect from the employees that report to them. What would happen if that employer required all managers to be at least 6 feet tall? Very likely, many more women than men would be excluded from the opportunity to be managers (because considerably more men than women are at least 6 feet tall). Asian Americans and Latinos might also be disadvantaged by this height requirement. But would it be discrimination? If the employer is really selecting managers based on height and not rejecting qualified women who are over 6 feet tall, it cannot be said that there is disparate treatment. Yet, it is still very troubling that women are being disproportionately excluded from these management jobs on this dubious basis.

In fact, this height requirement would most likely be discriminatory because it creates adverse impact. **Adverse impact** is the disproportionate limitation or denial of employment opportunity for some protected class group that results from the use of a "neutral" requirement or practice that is not "job-related and consistent with business necessity." In adverse impact cases, the focus is on **discriminatory effects**, rather than discriminatory intent. *Requirement* or *practice* (or "selection criterion") simply means any factor that is used as a basis for allocating employment opportunities (e.g., choosing who to hire, deciding who gets a raise). *Neutral* means in this context "anything other than protected class characteristics." In our example, the neutral selection criterion is the height requirement. It does not exclude all women, but it can be expected to exclude substantially more women than men. The employer believes that height is related to managerial ability, but unless the employer is able to present substantial evidence that this connection exists, the employer is guilty of discrimination.

Antidiscrimination laws call for reasonable accommodation of employees under two circumstances: for qualified disabled persons who need such accommodations and for employees whose religious beliefs and practices come into conflict with their employers' requirements. An employer discriminates through **failure to reasonably accommodate** by failing to be flexible and make alternative arrangements to remove obstacles to becoming employed, performing a job, or enjoying the full benefits of employment for persons whose disabilities or religious beliefs require such flexibility, and when doing so would not impose "undue hardship" on the employer. For example, if an employee needs a day off for religious observance, the employer has a legal obligation to attempt to accommodate this need, such as by allowing the employee to switch days with another employee. If the employer simply takes a "hard line," refuses to consider the matter, and disciplines the employee for failing to show up, the employer is failing to reasonably accommodate and is guilty of discrimination.

Retaliation can be defined as the limitation or denial of employment opportunity for the purpose of discouraging or punishing persons who seek to obtain their rights under antidiscrimination laws or to assist others in doing so. Although retaliation resembles disparate treatment, the decision to deny employment opportunity is based not on protected class per se, but rather on the employee's actions. For example, an employee might believe that she is being harassed by coworkers. She tells her boss about it, but the harassment continues unabated. Fed up, she files a charge with

the EEOC. Following the charge filing, she is denied an expected raise and discharged for violating a minor company rule that is never enforced. Under these circumstances, the woman would have a strong claim of retaliation. The retaliation claim would be in addition to, and its outcome independent of, the harassment charge.

Cases involving employer retaliation are increasingly common. Federal Express violated Title VII when it punished one of its managers (by issuing him a letter of warning saying that his next "mistake" would result in immediate termination, subjecting him to intense scrutiny, including electronic monitoring, and ultimately driving him out of the job) for contacting the in-house legal department at corporate headquarters regarding his belief that employees were being discriminated against in promotions (see "Clippings").

In deciding whether discrimination has occurred, the "first cut" is to ask whether an employee has suffered a loss or limitation of employment opportunity and whether any link is apparent between that outcome and the protected class characteristics of the employee. If the case appears to raise an issue of discrimination, the next task is to identify the theory (or sometimes theories) of discrimination that best fits the facts of the case. If the employer has allegedly based an employment decision on the protected class characteristics of the person, we have a disparate treatment case. If employment decisions are based on something other than protected class, but the result is that some protected class groups are substantially disadvantaged, we might have an adverse impact case. If an employer is not willing to alter requirements and procedures on behalf of disabled persons and employees with religious conflicts, this may be evidence of a failure to reasonably accommodate. Lastly, if an employee has suffered a loss of employment opportunity after taking action to enforce his rights, retaliation is indicated. Distinguishing between types of discrimination is important because each type of case is analyzed and decided in a different manner. In the following section, we will look more closely at how disparate treatment, adverse impact, and retaliation cases are decided. In-depth discussion of failure to reasonably accommodate appears in Chapter 10.

The discussion to this point also suggests some basic practical advice on how to avoid discrimination. The fundamental implication of disparate treatment is that *employers must not make employment decisions based on the protected class characteristics of their employees.* As with most things in the law, there are a few exceptions to this rule, but the basic guideline goes a long way. More generally, *employers that strive to be fair and to treat like situations alike regardless of the employees involved will be far less likely to discriminate.* The general strategy for avoiding adverse impact is for employers to *closely scrutinize factors used in making employment decisions for their potential to exclude protected class groups and for evidence of their job-relatedness.* Although employers need to exhibit consistency and even-handed treatment, they also *need to be flexible in accommodating the particular needs of disabled employees and employees whose religious practices conflict with workplace requirements.* Requests for flexibility cannot be ignored or dismissed simply because the requested measures would be a departure from the norm. Lastly, *employers need to exercise particular care in making employment decisions regarding employees who have filed charges or spoken out about discrimination.* Such employees do not become "untouchable" by virtue of their actions, but having solid reasons for any adverse employment decisions made under these circumstances is essential.

DISPARATE TREATMENT—A CLOSER LOOK

The crux of a disparate treatment case is an allegation that an employment decision was intentionally discriminatory, in the sense of being based on protected class. However, there are variations on this theme. We need to again draw some distinctions, this time between different types of disparate treatment cases, because not all disparate treatment cases are analyzed and decided in the same manner. Types of disparate treatment cases include direct evidence, facially discriminatory policies or practices, reverse discrimination, pretext, mixed motives, pattern or practice, and harassment.

Types of Disparate Treatment Cases

Direct Evidence Suppose that a 55-year-old software engineer applies for a job at a software company. Despite his extensive, relevant work experience, the applicant is not hired. When he inquires as to the reason, the 20-something founder of the software company says "You're too old, man! I want hip young people around here, not old-timers. Why don't you go play bingo instead?" "Smoking gun" cases like this are rare. But where an employer clearly articulates a discriminatory motive in the context of making an employment decision, there is **direct evidence** of discriminatory intent, and the employer has discriminated. Thus, there was direct evidence of discrimination when a corporate trainer asked for a raise and his boss rejected the request, stating to another employee that "I'm not going to pay him. He's just a white guy."[12] Likewise, the statement by a supervisor to two coworkers of a 63-year-old property manager that he wanted to "replace her with a young chippie with big tits" was found to be direct evidence of motivation to discriminate based on age.[13]

We don't have to inquire into the existence of a discriminatory motive in these cases because the employers have made it clear that their employment decisions were based on protected class. Direct evidence is most likely to be found where the written or spoken statement is clear, comes from someone involved with making the adverse employment decision, refers specifically to the individual denied the employment opportunity, and is expressed close in time to when the employment decision was made. If sufficient direct evidence exists, the employer has engaged in disparate treatment and discriminated, although there is still a possibility of showing that a legal motive also affected the decision (see the "Mixed Motives" discussion in the following text).

Facially Discriminatory Policy or Practice In direct evidence cases, there is no question about the employer's discriminatory motive because the employer has blundered into expressing it. Another type of disparate treatment case in which the employer's motive is transparent occurs when the employer adopts a **facially discriminatory policy or practice**. In these cases, the employer readily admits to using protected class as a basis for making employment decisions, but insists that there is a sound business reason for doing so. For example, early in its history, Southwest Airlines had a policy of hiring only women as flight attendants. Establishing a protected class requirement of this sort is "facially discriminatory." The only way

[12]*Gagnon v. Sprint Corp.*, 284 F.3d 839, at 846 (8th Cir. 2002).

[13]*Glanzman v. Metropolitan Management Corp.*, 391 F.3d 506, at 510 (3d Cir. 2004).

that an employer can prevail in such cases is by showing that the required protected class characteristic is a **bona fide occupational qualification (BFOQ)** for the job in question. Southwest argued that both its marketing strategy and customer preference dictated that they use only female flight attendants. The BFOQ defense is narrow, however, and the court found that Southwest failed to establish a BFOQ because men can also do the job of flight attendant.[14] Facially discriminatory policies or practices and the BFOQ defense are discussed further in Chapter 7.

Reverse Discrimination In a sense, this term is a misnomer, because protected classes such as race and sex include any race and either sex. However, a scenario found in many **reverse discrimination** cases is that an employer with an affirmative action plan hires a woman or person of color. A white male believes that he should have received the employment opportunity instead and sues. The employer does not deny that race or sex played some part in the hiring, but contends that the decision was made in accordance with a lawful affirmative action plan. The case hinges on whether the particular use of affirmative action was legally permissible. Thus, at least when affirmative action plans are involved, these cases take a different course than other disparate treatment cases. Legal challenges to affirmative action are discussed in Chapter 8.

Pretext A more complex—and common—scenario occurs when an employee is denied an employment opportunity (e.g., not promoted), and the employee believes that the decision was influenced by the employer's consideration of a protected class characteristic (say, being female), whereas the employer contends that the decision was based on some lawful factor other than the woman's sex (e.g., that other candidates were more qualified). **Pretext** cases are so named because if the employee's allegations are true, the employer's stated reason is pretextual—a cover-up for the true discriminatory motive. As you can imagine, sorting out these conflicting claims about why an employment decision was made is no simple task.

Mixed Motives The underlying premise of pretext cases is that employment decisions are made *either* for discriminatory or lawful reasons. Yet, because more than one motive can account for a given decision, it is logically possible for an employer to base an employment decision on *both* discriminatory and lawful grounds. For example, in one well-known case,[15] a woman was denied promotion to partner at an accounting firm. The statements of the partners who made the decision clearly indicated that she was being judged differently because she was a woman. Yet, there was also evidence that she had problems relating to staff members and that this was part of why she did not get promoted. In **mixed motives** cases such as this, where strong evidence exists of both discriminatory and lawful motives affecting an employment decision (and not just conflicting claims as in a pretext case), the employer is guilty of discrimination. However, the plaintiff's award will be minimized if the employer can prove that the same decision would have been made absent the discriminatory motive (in other words, that the lawful motive was strong enough by itself to produce the same result).[16] The Supreme Court has clarified that the evidence relied upon to demonstrate that a discriminatory motive played a part in an employment

[14]*Wilson v. Southwest Airlines*, 517 F. Supp. 292 (N.D. Tex. 1981).
[15]*Price Waterhouse v. Hopkins*, 490 U.S. 228 (1989).
[16]Title VII, Civil Rights Act of 1964, 42 U.S.C.A. § 2000e-5(g)(2)(B) (2001).

decision, justifying a mixed motives analysis, can be either direct or circumstantial.[17] Some legal commentators have suggested that the effect of this holding will be to blur (if not obliterate) the distinction between mixed motive and pretext cases.[18] The intricacies of this issue go beyond the scope of this book, but the number of mixed motives cases will probably increase and prompt further instruction from the Supreme Court on how disparate treatment cases should be decided.

Pattern or Practice Although many disparate treatment cases involve single plaintiffs, the concept of intentional discrimination is not limited to challenges of individual employment decisions. Sometimes intentional discrimination is more systematic and affects numerous employees. Employer policies that have the effect of segregating certain groups into lower paid and less desirable jobs or limiting the advancement of such persons are often at the center of pattern or practice claims. In **pattern or practice** cases, the plaintiffs marshal statistical data showing the systematic effects of an employer's discrimination and evidence of intentional discrimination against individuals within the larger affected group.

Harassment Harassment is a form of disparate treatment because the victim of harassment is subjected to abuse because of her sex, race, or other protected class characteristic. Chapter 9 provides a detailed discussion of harassment. Here, the key point is that harassment is treated as discrimination, rather than some entirely separate type of legal claim.

Analyzing Pretext Cases

Pretext cases, in which the employer's motive in making an employment decision is disputed, present a difficult problem. Proof of discriminatory intent is essential. Yet, although the plaintiff bears the burden of proving that discrimination has occurred, the defendant knows the most about why a particular decision was made. The defendant also has an incentive not to be entirely forthcoming if, in fact, the decision was tainted by consideration of an employee's protected class characteristics.

In *McDonnell Douglas v. Green*, the Supreme Court provided a method for deciding pretext cases.[19] This landmark case arose shortly after passage of the Civil Rights Act of 1964. The plaintiff Green was an African American who had worked for the aerospace company as a mechanic and laboratory technician until he was laid off due to a business downturn. When the company advertised openings for mechanics about a year later, Green applied for a position. McDonnell Douglas refused to rehire Green because of his involvement in an illegal "stall-in" outside the plant. To protest perceived racist hiring practices of the company, Green and other employees stalled their cars and blocked traffic at the time of the morning shift change. Green sued, alleging that the real reason for not rehiring him was his race (and his civil rights protest activities). The approach that the Supreme Court provided for sorting out these difficult cases, which it has refined over the years, is outlined on the next page:

[17]*Desert Palace v. Costa,* 123 S. Ct. 2148 (2003).

[18]Henry L. Chambers, Jr. "The Effect of Eliminating Distinctions Among Title VII Disparate Treatment Cases." *SMU Law Review* 57 (Winter 2004), 83–103; William R. Corbett, "McDonnell Douglas. 1973–2003: May You Rest in Peace?" *University of Pennsylvania Journal of Labor & Employment Law* 6 (Fall 2003), 199–219.

[19]*McDonnell Douglas v. Green,* 411 U.S. 792 (1973).

ELEMENTS OF A CLAIM

Disparate Treatment—Pretext

I. Plaintiff must establish a "prima facie" case of disparate treatment by showing:

 a) the protected class characteristic(s) of the plaintiff that are relevant to the case;

 b) that the employment opportunity was applied for;

 c) that the employment opportunity was available;

 d) that the plaintiff was qualified for the employment opportunity;

 e) that the plaintiff was denied the employment opportunity;

 f) that the employer continued to consider candidates for the employment opportunity or selected someone with contrasting protected class characteristics.

II. If the plaintiff successfully establishes a prima facie case, the employer is required to "produce" evidence of a lawful motive for the employment decision.

III. If the employer successfully produces such a motive, the plaintiff has the opportunity to rebut the employer's claims by:

 a) providing evidence that sheds doubt on the credibility of the employer's claimed motive; and/or

 b) providing other evidence which supports the claim that a discriminatory motive is the most likely explanation for the employer's decision.

The plaintiff bears the ultimate burden of proving that the employer intentionally discriminated.

Prima Facie Case of Disparate Treatment　　The elements of a claim in a pretext case begin with a **prima facie case**. This is a showing by the plaintiff that discrimination is a plausible explanation for the denial or limitation of an employment opportunity. A plaintiff who cannot establish a prima facie case is out of luck. On the other hand, the plaintiff who establishes a prima facie case does not "win" anything. It simply means that there is sufficient likelihood of discrimination to warrant further inquiry. The Court recognized that the employer has most of the relevant information about the motivation behind an employment decision. Thus, the bar was set relatively low for the plaintiff to establish a prima facie case. Yet, this device also incorporates a degree of deference to the autonomy of employers. An employer will not be required to account for an employment decision unless the plaintiff can first provide the court reason to believe that discrimination might have occurred.

It is important to appreciate how the prima facie case allows a plaintiff to create an inference that discrimination has occurred, without having to provide compelling, and difficult to come by, evidence of the employer's state of mind. The main thing that the prima facie case accomplishes is to eliminate some of the most common, nondiscriminatory reasons for denial of an employment opportunity, and thereby render discrimination a more plausible explanation. There is nothing

surprising about an employee not getting a job if he never applied for it, if he sought employment when none was available, if he did not meet the basic qualifications required of all candidates, or if he did not give the employer sufficient time to make a decision. In establishing a prima facie case, the plaintiff is ruling out these other mundane reasons. If, on top of this, the employer continues to seek candidates or hires someone whose protected class characteristics contrast with the plaintiff's (e.g., the plaintiff is black and the person hired is white), discrimination begins to look like a real possibility. Alternatively, if the person chosen for an employment opportunity is the same race or sex as the plaintiff, this is usually a strong indication that race or sex was not a relevant factor; the reason must be something more particular to the individual. An important exception would be where both the person selected and the person rejected are over 40 years of age (and thus both within the protected class for ADEA suits). In this instance, the plaintiff is still able to establish a prima facie case of age discrimination, as long as the person selected is "substantially" younger than the plaintiff.[20]

In *McDonnell Douglas*, the plaintiff was able to establish a prima facie case by showing that he was an African American, that McDonnell Douglas was hiring mechanics, that he had the qualifications to work as a mechanic and had performed well in his previous stint with the company, that he was refused employment, and that the company continued to seek applicants to fill mechanic positions.

Courts are somewhat flexible in how they apply these criteria. Failure to apply might not be fatal to the plaintiff's case if the employer placed unreasonable obstacles in the way of the person desiring to apply. Likewise, if the applicant is just strung along and continuously told that the decision has not yet been made, the plaintiff will be deemed to have been denied employment. Hiring someone of the same race or sex as the person passed over might not be fatal to the plaintiff's case if, for example, the hiring occurred *after* discrimination charges were filed. Also, although this statement of the requirements for a prima facie case is oriented toward initial hiring decisions, courts have modified these requirements to better fit other employment decisions, such as terminations (see Chapter 18).

The requirement of identifying the protected class characteristic(s) relevant to the case is usually easily met by the plaintiff. If, for example, a plaintiff is claiming national origin discrimination, his national origin must be shown. A notable exception is the difficulty plaintiffs have in showing that they are "qualified individuals with a disability," entitled to protection against disability discrimination. A discrimination claim may allege discrimination on the basis of more than a single protected class and also on some combination of protected classes (e.g., discrimination against African-American males). Although the Supreme Court referred in *McDonnell Douglas* to the plaintiff showing "that he belongs to a racial minority"[21] rather than identifying protected class in general, that wording reflected the particular facts of that case. However, courts sometimes require an additional showing by nonminority applicants, such as someone of another race making the employment decision, to establish a prima facie case.[22] As one court put it, nonminority plaintiffs must show "that background circumstances support the suspicion that the defendant is that unusual employer who discriminates against the majority."[23] Plaintiffs might also be required to establish that the employer was aware of the relevant protected class

[20]*O'Connor v. Consolidated Coin Caterers Corp.*, 517 U.S. 308 (1996).

[21]*McDonnell Douglas*, at 802.

[22]*Notari v. Denver Water Department*, 971 F.2d 585 (10th Cir. 1992).

[23]*Murray v. Thistledown Racing Club, Inc.*, 770 F.2d 63, at 67 (6th Cir. 1985).

characteristic. Not all protected class characteristics are readily discernible (e.g., religion, disability), and not all employment decisions are made by personnel who have had direct contact with the affected applicant or employee. It is difficult to argue that an adverse employment action was based on a protected class characteristic when no evidence exists that the decision maker was aware of that characteristic. This issue has arisen in a number of cases in which an employee alleging pregnancy discrimination was not yet visibly pregnant.[24] Likewise, an employee's age discrimination complaint failed because she was not able to show that the decision maker knew that she was significantly older than another employee who took over her duties.[25]

Articulation of a Lawful Motive If a prima facie case is shown, the employer must "produce" evidence of a lawful, nondiscriminatory motive. Because the employer is maintaining that no discrimination occurred, the employer should be able to articulate why the plaintiff was denied an employment opportunity. This is not a heavy burden and the court does not weigh the truthfulness of the employer's claims at this stage of the inquiry. However, the explanation still needs to be reasonably specific and not obviously contrived. In *McDonnell Douglas*, the employer's claim that it refused to rehire Green because of his participation in an illegal action detrimental to the company met the company's burden to produce a nondiscriminatory motive. In contrast, an employer failed to do so when it simply asserted that the plaintiff was "not sufficiently suited" for the position without any further justification or elaboration.[26] The employer in this case also claimed that it had selected the "best qualified" candidate for promotion. Normally, an employer's assessment of relative qualifications, even if wholly subjective, would suffice to meet its burden of articulating a lawful motive. But in this case, the explanation fell into the "obviously contrived" category because it was undisputed that the purportedly more qualified candidate was not even under consideration at the time that the plaintiff was denied promotion. The very real prospect of having to defend against discrimination charges underscores the fact that *employers should maintain good documentation and be prepared to explain the nondiscriminatory reasons for particular employment decisions.*

Evidence of Pretext and/or Discriminatory Motive If the employer meets its burden of articulating a lawful, nondiscriminatory motive, the case does not end. The plaintiff still has the opportunity to present additional evidence of discrimination in two ways. First, the plaintiff can try to show that the employer's stated reason, although sufficient as a response to the prima facie case, is ultimately not credible (i.e., it is pretextual). Second, the plaintiff can try to amass additional circumstantial evidence pointing to the employer's discriminatory motive.

An employer's explanation for an employment decision is pretextual if (1) it has no basis in fact (e.g., the true reason for not hiring the plaintiff could not be poor interview performance because no interview was conducted); or (2) it has a basis in fact, but was not actually a motivating factor (e.g., the plaintiff did poorly on his interview, but the decision maker did not bother to get information from the recruiter about the interview before rejecting the plaintiff); or (3) it was a factor, but one insufficient to motivate the decision (e.g., the employer regularly hires people

[24]*Prebilich-Holland v. Gaylord Entertainment Company,* 297 F.3d 438 (6th Cir. 2002).

[25]*Woodman v. WWOR-TV,* 2005 U.S. App. LEXIS 11060.

[26]*Patrick v. Ridge,* 394 F.3d 311, at 316-16 (5th Cir. 2004).

despite poor interviews).[27] Explanations for employment decisions are pretextual if they are lies or cover-ups for discrimination. When decisions are made for reasons that are "mistaken, ill considered, or foolish, so long as [the employer] honestly believed those reasons, pretext has not been shown."[28] Thus, the function of courts in discrimination cases is not to decide whether the employer made the "correct" employment decision, but rather whether the decision that was made was motivated by discrimination. Accordingly, in cases where an employer claims to have hired the most qualified person and where the plaintiff alleges that she is more qualified, most courts will not conclude that the employer's claim to have hired the most qualified person is pretextual unless the plaintiff's qualifications are so superior to those of the person selected for the job that no reasonable, impartial person could have made the hiring decision that was made.[29]

Additional evidence of a discriminatory motive might include statements made by company officials indicating bias (but not sufficiently specific to constitute "direct evidence"), information about prior mistreatment of the plaintiff or other employees, the employer's track record in complying with antidiscrimination laws, and possibly statistics showing a pattern of discriminatory effects. Although the evidence brought to bear can be wide-ranging and circumstantial, "stray remarks" and comments by individuals not involved with carrying out or influencing challenged employment decisions are not likely to be persuasive. Comparative evidence, in which the employer is shown to have treated the plaintiff worse than another employee under the same circumstances, with the only difference being that the other employee was of a different race or sex, can be powerful. Such evidence simultaneously addresses pretext (e.g., if the plaintiff's actions really warranted termination, why didn't the company also terminate another employee who acted in the same manner?) and discriminatory motive (e.g., if two employees acted in the same manner and differed only in their race, the plaintiff's race is a likely reason for why she was treated more harshly). But the employees being compared must be truly "similarly situated" for comparisons of their treatment to have this force. The plaintiff in the *McDonnell Douglas* case was unable to show that employees of other races had engaged in activities comparable to the stall-in and been retained or rehired. Lacking this and any other strong evidence of a discriminatory motive, Green ultimately lost his case on remand.[30] The importance of comparative evidence underscores the fact that *a general strategy for eliminating disparate treatment is to establish policies, rather than make decisions ad hoc, and to enforce those policies in a consistent manner.* Consistency does not mean rigidity; nor does it preclude consideration of legitimate factors that might make one case different from another. But the basic principle remains: treating like cases alike, regardless of the protected class characteristics of the people involved.

What if pretext is shown, but the plaintiff has little or no additional evidence of a discriminatory motive? In an age discrimination case involving the termination of a 57-year-old employee who had worked for a company for 40 years, the plaintiff was able to show that the employer's stated reason for the termination—that he failed to maintain accurate attendance records and discipline employees who violated the attendance policy—was not credible.[31] The employee was following company policy with respect to timekeeping when the time clock was not working, did not have

[27]*Carberry v. Monarch Marking Systems, Inc.*, 2002 U.S. App. LEXIS 2462, at 6.

[28]*Millbrook v. IBP, Inc.*, 280 F.3d 1169, at 1175 (7th Cir. 2002).

[29]*Millbrook*, at 1180.

[30]*Green v. McDonnell Douglas*, 528 F.2d 1102 (8th Cir. 1976).

[31]*Reeves v. Sanderson Plumbing*, 530 U.S. 133 (2000).

responsibility for disciplinary actions against employees who violated attendance policies, and was in the hospital on a day that he allegedly failed to report an employee as absent. Additionally, although the company maintained that the employee's failings justified discharge, the employer never attempted to assess the cost of the overpayments allegedly attributable to the plaintiff's shoddy record keeping and had received no employee complaints or union grievances based on his record keeping. In ruling for the plaintiff, the Supreme Court explained:

> [T]he trier of fact [judge or jury] can reasonably infer from the falsity of the explanation that the employer is dissembling to cover up a discriminatory purpose. Such an inference is consistent with the general principle of evidence law that the fact finder is entitled to consider a party's dishonesty about a material fact as 'affirmative evidence of guilt.' Moreover, once the employer's justification has been eliminated, discrimination may well be the most likely alternative explanation, especially since the employer is in the best position to put forth the actual reason for its decision. Thus, a plaintiff's prima facie case, combined with sufficient evidence to find that the employer's asserted justification is false, may permit the trier of fact to conclude that the employer unlawfully discriminated.[32]

There is some murkiness in the Court's position that a prima facie case plus a showing of pretext *permits*, but does not require, finding for the plaintiff. But the decision generally reinforces the notion that narrowing the inquiry to the truthfulness of the employer's stated motive is the key to making disparate treatment cases based largely on circumstantial evidence tractable.

Laxton v. GAP Inc. is an interesting pretext case in which the plaintiff primarily relies upon evidence that the employer's stated motive for a termination is not worthy of belief to establish that intentional discrimination has occurred.

[32]*Reeves*, at 147-48.

LAXTON V. GAP INC.
333 F.3d 572 (5th Cir. 2003)

● ● ●

OPINION BY DISTRICT JUDGE VANCE:

Plaintiff-Appellant Joanna Laxton appeals from the district court's order granting defendant-appellee Gap, Inc. judgment as a matter of law in this case brought under the Pregnancy Discrimination Act. For the following reasons, we REVERSE and REMAND.

* * * In March 1999, Gap recruited Laxton, the general manager of a Stein Mart department store in Tyler, Texas, to become the general manager of an Old Navy store that Gap intended to open in Tyler. * * *

After accepting the offer but before starting work, Laxton, aged 39 at the time, learned that she was pregnant. On her first day of work, March 29, 1999, she informed Lisa Haverstick, Gap's Regional Assistant Manager, of her pregnancy. She informed her direct supervisor, Karen Jones, of her pregnancy on June 1, 1999. * * * Jones became visibly angry. Laxton testified that Jones "didn't appreciate the fact, I guess, that she was going to have to have someone come in during the holidays and fill in for me." Jones said, "You realize this means that I have to pull other management out of other stores to cover your store, when, basically, you know, this store should have been taken care of. What

management do you think we're supposed to use?" After this conversation, Jones was "usually unpleasant" toward Laxton.

Under Laxton's management, the store timely opened on June 2, 1999. By all accounts, the store earned strong revenues. It won a national tech vest sales contest, and Laxton received monthly bonuses of over $1,000. On July 8, 1999, the mall notified Laxton that it needed to cut power to her store between 9:00 and 10:00 p.m. The store usually closed at 9:00 p.m, after which time employees served the customers that remained in the store, closed all the registers, counted the money, and opened a back door to receive deliveries. Laxton feared that problems could arise if the store's power was cut while her employees were counting money because the back door would be open for deliveries and the alarm system would be dead. She called Jones to ask for permission to close the store 30 minutes early. Jones told Laxton to keep the store open. Laxton decided to close the store early anyway. For this incident, Jones gave Laxton a "Written Warning," the first strike in Gap's "three-strikes-you're-out" policy.

On July 29, 1999, Jones and Carla Dotto, an employee at Gap's corporate headquarters, told Laxton that a "Final Written Warning"—strike two—was on its way. * * * In the Final Written Warning, Gap charged Laxton with four violations of company policies and procedures: (1) exiting the store by the back door; (2) displaying unacceptable behavior toward an employee, Kerri Vallery, over the store's walkie-talkie system; (3) neglecting to inform the regional office that she had taken a sick day; and (4) hiring a bank robber. The supervisors did not discuss these charges with Laxton in the July 29 conversation. Rather, Laxton learned of the nature of the charges only when she received a copy of the Final Written Warning by fax on Saturday, August 14, 1999, which was a day off for her. * * *

As to the allegation that she exited the store by the back door, Laxton testified that once she learned that this was a violation of store policy, she never did so again. As to the walkie-talkie incident, Laxton testified that Vallery had disobeyed her orders about where to place sales associates on the floor of the store. As to the sick day, Laxton testified that she called in to report the sick day, did not reach anyone, and did not leave a message because she intended to talk with headquarters again soon anyway. When she discovered that her hours for the week had been entered improperly, she made efforts to correct them. Regardless, Laxton, despite her pregnancy, was working over 70 hours a week while being paid on a salary based on 40 hours per week, and Gap produced no records indicating a problem with Laxton's overall attendance at work. Finally, Laxton testified that she never hired a bank robber. Vallery recommended that Laxton invite the job applicant to an orientation session. Before the orientation session, Laxton was "amazed" to discover through a conversation with her husband that the applicant was rumored to have robbed a bank. As soon as she discovered the problem, the applicant withdrew his application himself. At no time was the "bank robber" on Gap's payroll.

Before Laxton received the Final Written Warning on August 14, 1999, Laxton's supervisors sent Peg Inglis, a Zone Trainer, to Laxton's store for a visit on August 9, 1999. Based on conversations with three of the store's four assistant managers, Inglis reported that the store suffered from low employee morale. Inglis also reported violations of store policy, including: (1) exceeding the $75 discretionary spending limit by paying $85 for pizza for employees; (2) asking two employees to wear unpurchased Old Navy tech vests during a sales promotion; and (3) failing to permit employees to take lunch breaks. Inglis's report indicates that termination was on Gap's mind, for she wrote that "if Laxton stays in position. . . ." Inglis spoke with Laxton during the store visit, but she did not raise with Laxton the issues of employee morale or the asserted violations of store policy. Instead, Inglis inquired as to Laxton's plans for maternity leave.

At trial, Laxton provided explanations for the three violations cited by Inglis: (1) she bought the pizza for employees during a busy and profitable Tax-Free Weekend after Jones had directed her to "do whatever it takes" to make the weekend a success; (2) she directed two employees to wear tech vests during a nationwide tech vest sales contest that Laxton's store won and, relatedly, Gap had "sent down a directive" to have employees wear unpurchased backpacks to increase backpack sales; and (3) Laxton explained that the breaks were not recorded properly because the store's automated punch clock system was broken and employees were too busy with Tax-Free Weekend to fill out time sheets manually.

* * * On August 16, Laxton called Chazz Pono, her human resources representative, to discuss her suspicion that she was the target of pregnancy

discrimination. The record reflects that Pono took no action. On August 17, 1999, Carlos Licona, a Gap auditor, arrived at Laxton's store unannounced. Licona testified that he was not aware of Laxton's performance-related issues before his store visit. Inglis's report, however, indicated that the report would be forwarded to Licona. Licona discovered the same violations of store policy that Inglis had identified—the pizza money, the tech vests, and the lunch breaks. Like Inglis, Licona did not discuss the violations with Laxton. He instead called Carr, who, together with Dotto, directed Licona to terminate her. This was the first time that Licona, a store auditor, had ever been asked to fire an employee. Gap replaced Laxton with a male. Laxton filed suit in federal district court on October 10, 2000, charging Gap with violating Title VII of the Civil Rights Act of 1964, as amended by the Pregnancy Discrimination Act of 1978 (the "PDA"). * * *

A claim brought under the PDA is analyzed like any other Title VII discrimination claim. Title VII discrimination can be established through either direct or circumstantial evidence. Laxton's case is built on the latter, which means that it is analyzed under the familiar *McDonnell Douglas* framework. * * *

The parties do not dispute on appeal that Laxton made out a prima facie case of pregnancy discrimination. Instead, the parties dispute whether Laxton produced substantial evidence of pretext. * * * Turning to Laxton's showing of pretext, we begin by defining the contours of our inquiry. Our inquiry is "'whether [Gap's] perception of [Laxton's] performance, accurate or not, was the real reason for her termination.'" It is not whether Gap's proffered reason was an *incorrect* reason for her discharge. Our concern is whether the evidence supports an inference that Gap intentionally discriminated against Laxton, an inference that can be drawn if its proffered reason was not the real reason for discharge. Therefore, to survive Gap's motion for judgment as a matter of law, Laxton must produce evidence permitting the jury to disbelieve that Gap's proffered reason was its true motivation. * * *

First, Laxton rebuts the substance of violations asserted by Gap, including the allegation that Laxton hired a bank robber. * * * The applicant . . . was never on Gap's payroll. A second charge that the jury could have reasonably found to be false is that of employee complaints. * * * Gap produced no contemporaneous written documentation of any employee complaints, despite testimony that the corporation abides by rigorous record-keeping policies. Gap did not even produce

written documentation of the walkie-talkie incident referred to in the Final Written Warning. * * *

Laxton challenges the tech vest violation and the pizza money violation on the grounds that they involved conduct that Gap authorized and that is so trivial as to be unworthy of credence. Gap directed Laxton to have employees wear unpurchased backpacks to increase backpack sales, but then cited Laxton for directing two employees to wear unpurchased tech vests during a tech vest sales contest in which her store placed first in the nation. Additionally, in preparation for Tax-Free Weekend, Jones directed Laxton to "do whatever it takes." Laxton therefore exceeded her $75 discretionary spending authority by a minimal amount by spending $85 on pizza for employees. * * *

Second, in addition to her attack on the substance of these violations, Laxton brings evidence that undermines the credibility of Gap's proffered justification for her discharge. The evidence indicates that if Gap were genuinely concerned about Laxton's asserted performance-related problems, it would have permitted Laxton the opportunity to explain or to improve her conduct, but it did not do so. * * * Only six weeks elapsed between Laxton's first Written Warning and her termination, and during that time her supervisors never gave her the chance to explain her conduct or improve it. * * *

Further, the jury may have determined that Gap's witnesses lacked credibility. The record indicates that Jones may have come across as a difficult witness and that Licona was not credible. Licona testified that he did not know that Laxton was pregnant on the day that he terminated her. On that day, Laxton was visibly pregnant, as a contemporaneous photograph confirms. Licona also identified handwriting on his store visit log as that of Laxton, from which the jury could have inferred that Laxton was on notice of the violations that he found. Laxton, however, denied that it was her handwriting, and her testimony was corroborated by that of an assistant manager who testified that it was *her* handwriting and not Laxton's. Finally, Licona testified that he did not see a copy of Inglis's report before he visited Laxton's store. The jury may have reasonably inferred that he had seen a copy because the report indicated that a copy should be forwarded to him and because he identified the exact violations of store policy that Inglis cited in the report. Upon consideration of all of the evidence, the jury may have reasonably concluded that Jones, Carr, and Dotto solicited and exaggerated complaints from Laxton's assistant

managers, issued a Written Warning and a Final Written Warning, and dispatched Inglis and Licona for store visits in an effort to compile a laundry list of violations to justify a predetermined decision to terminate Laxton. * * *

Gap's proffered justification becomes even less credible when viewed in light of the strength of Laxton's prima facie case. * * * Part of Laxton's prima facie case is that she was qualified for the position of general manager. Before joining Gap, she had a successful career in retail with Wal-Mart and Stein Mart. When Gap recruited Laxton away from Stein Mart to open the new Old Navy store, Laxton declined. Only after Gap offered her a considerable raise did Laxton accept. Laxton's store opened on time and, under her direction, earned strong revenues. Gap rewarded her with monthly bonuses of over $1,000. By mid-August, when she was fired, the store had already surpassed the month's quota to qualify for a bonus. * * * Yet, despite Laxton's qualifications as a general manager and despite her success in making the new Old Navy store profitable, Gap proffers that it terminated her for a laundry list of questionable violations, virtually none of which Gap bothered to discuss with her. Conveniently, Gap left itself just enough time to permit a new general manager to settle into the job before the busy holiday season. * * *

Although Laxton's showing of pretext is . . . sufficient for her to survive Gap's motion for judgment as a matter of law, she supplements her case of discrimination with an oral statement of her supervisor, Karen Jones. When Laxton informed Jones that she was pregnant and was due around Thanksgiving, Jones became visibly angry. * * * Jones said, "You realize this means that I have to pull other management out of other stores to cover your store, when, basically, you know, this store should have been taken care of. What management do you think we're supposed to use?" An oral statement exhibiting discriminatory animus may be used [as evidence]. The remark must, first, demonstrate discriminatory animus and, second, be made by a person primarily responsible for the adverse employment action or by a person with influence or leverage over the formal decision maker. * * *

Laxton produced sufficient evidence to enable the jury to conclude that Jones influenced Carr and Dotto, the individuals principally responsible for the adverse employment action. * * * [T]he discriminatory animus of a manager can be imputed to the ultimate decision maker if the decision maker "acted as a rubber stamp, or the 'cat's paw,' for the subordinate employee's prejudice." The relevant inquiry is whether Jones "had influence or leverage over" Carr and Dotto's decision making. Jones issued Laxton's Written Warning. Carr issued Laxton's Final Written Warning, but Carr testified that Jones served as her primary source of information. Gap makes the somewhat implausible assertion that Carr and Dotto did not rely on the two warnings when they decided to terminate Laxton, but instead relied solely on the "independent investigations" of Inglis and Licona. This position is inconsistent with Gap's proffered justification for Laxton's discharge, namely, the cumulative effect of violations of company policy including those cited in the Written Warning and Final Written Warning. * * *

We find that the parties presented the jury with two competing versions of Laxton's termination. Laxton produced evidence of pretext and a discriminatory remark from which the jury could reasonably infer that intentional discrimination took place. This is legally sufficient evidence that amounts to more than a mere scintilla. It is the province of the jury to judge the credibility of witnesses and resolve conflicts in the evidence, and we will not second-guess its rejection of Gap's proffered justification. Gap asserts that Laxton's case must fail because she produced no evidence that discriminatory animus motivated her termination. . . . [H]owever, when a plaintiff makes a sufficient showing of pretext, no further evidence of discriminatory animus is required to withstand a motion for judgment as a matter of law. * * *

CASE QUESTIONS

1. What was the legal issue in this case? What did the court decide?

2. What reason does the employer provide for Laxton's termination?

3. What is the evidence of pretext in this case?

4. What is the evidence of a discriminatory motive in this case?

5. Do you agree with the court's decision? Why or why not?

ADVERSE IMPACT—A CLOSER LOOK

In adverse impact (also referred to as disparate impact) cases, the plaintiff does not argue that the basis for an employment decision is something other than what the employer claims. Nor does the plaintiff assert that the decision is based on protected class. Instead, the contention is that some "neutral" (not protected class) requirement poses an unnecessary obstacle to employment opportunity, one that harms some protected class group much more than others. The discriminatory effects of the employer's requirements and policies, rather than the employer's intent, are at the core of an adverse impact claim.

In an early case, the Supreme Court was called upon to decide whether an employer's requirements for initial hiring and transfers were discriminatory.[33] The employer (Duke Power) had, like many other employers prior to passage of the Civil Rights Act of 1964, openly discriminated against African Americans. African Americans were hired, but only for low-paying, strenuous positions within the company's Labor Department. Immediately after Title VII went into effect, Duke Power instituted a high school diploma requirement for transfers from the Labor Department to other jobs within the company. Obtaining a passing score on two standardized aptitude tests (with the cut-off for passing geared to the median score for high school graduates) was added as an additional requirement and later offered as a substitute for the high school diploma. The context is critical here. Although employers routinely establish educational and testing requirements for positions, and a high school diploma does not sound like an imposing requirement to contemporary ears, the practical effect of these requirements was to lock into place the prior segregation of African Americans into the worst jobs at Duke Power. This is because in the 1960s in North Carolina, whites were nearly three times as likely as African Americans to have obtained a high school diploma. Only one of the African Americans working for Duke Power at the time of the case had a high school diploma. Although many whites (in fact, the majority of the population) also had not graduated from high school, the diploma requirement disproportionately limited the employment opportunities of blacks. The offer to substitute the test for the diploma requirement was an empty gesture. Setting the cut-off score at the median level for high school graduates (meaning the level at which only half of high school graduates would be expected to pass) meant that the tests were actually a more stringent requirement than the high school diploma.

The Supreme Court was thus presented with a case in which an employer's selection criteria disadvantaged African Americans, but there was no evidence that the requirements were instituted for the purpose of discriminating on the basis of race. Citing the broad purpose of Title VII to promote equal employment opportunity, the Court ruled that discrimination in the form of adverse impact, no less than disparate treatment, violates the law: "Under the Act, practices, procedures, or tests neutral on their face, and even neutral in terms of intent, cannot be maintained if they operate to 'freeze' the status quo of prior discriminatory employment practices."[34] Critical to the Court's decision was that Duke Power had not sought to determine that a high school diploma or a passing score on the aptitude tests was meaningfully related to ability to perform jobs at the company. In fact, there was evidence to the contrary. White employees without high school diplomas who were hired before the

[33]*Griggs v. Duke Power*, 401 U.S. 424 (1971).

[34]*Griggs*, at 430.

high school diploma requirement was put into effect and allowed to stay on the job performed satisfactorily and obtained promotions. How necessary, then, was a high school diploma for these jobs? In the Court's words, "The touchstone is business necessity. If an employment practice which operates to exclude Negroes [the term most commonly used for African Americans at the time of this decision] cannot be shown to be related to job performance, the practice is prohibited."[35]

For several decades that followed, the precedent established by the Supreme Court's decision in this landmark case, *Griggs v. Duke Power*, was the legal basis for adverse impact claims. In 1991, Title VII of the Civil Rights Act was amended to specifically cover adverse impact claims.[36] Perhaps only inadvertently, Congress failed to make parallel changes to the language of the Age Discrimination in Employment Act (ADEA). Appeals courts took different positions on whether adverse impact claims should be recognized under the ADEA. In *Smith v. City of Jackson*, the Supreme Court resolved this controversy. Plaintiffs in age discrimination cases can claim adverse impact, but employers will carry a lighter burden in defending such claims than under Title VII.

(handwritten margin notes: ✳ Age Discrim cases)

[35]*Griggs*, at 431.

[36]Title VII of the Civil Rights Act of 1964, 42 U.S.C.A. § 2000e-2(k) (2005).

SMITH V. CITY OF JACKSON
125 S. Ct. 1536 (2005)

OPINION BY JUSTICE STEVENS:

Petitioners, police and public safety officers employed by the city of Jackson, Mississippi (hereinafter City), contend that salary increases received in 1999 violated the Age Discrimination in Employment Act of 1967 (ADEA) because they were less generous to officers over the age of 40 than to younger officers. Their suit raises the question whether the "disparate-impact" theory . . . is cognizable [applies] under the ADEA. * * *

On October 1, 1998, the City adopted a pay plan granting raises to all City employees. The stated purpose of the plan was to "attract and retain qualified people, provide incentive for performance, maintain competitiveness with other public sector agencies and ensure equitable compensation to all employees regardless of age, sex, race and/or disability." On May 1, 1999, a revision of the plan, which was motivated, at least in part, by the City's desire to bring the starting salaries of police officers up to the regional average,

granted raises to all police officers and police dispatchers. Those who had less than five years of tenure received proportionately greater raises when compared to their former pay than those with more seniority. Although some officers over the age of 40 had less than five years of service, most of the older officers had more. * * *

We . . . now hold that the ADEA does authorize recovery in "disparate-impact" cases. . . . Because, however, we conclude that petitioners have not set forth a valid disparate-impact claim, we affirm. * * *

In determining whether the ADEA authorizes disparate-impact claims, we begin with the premise that when Congress uses the same language in two statutes having similar purposes, particularly when one is enacted shortly after the other, it is appropriate to presume that Congress intended that text to have the same meaning in both statutes. * * * Our unanimous interpretation of . . . Title VII in *Griggs* is therefore a precedent of compelling importance.

In *Griggs*, a case decided four years after the enactment of the ADEA, we considered whether . . . Title VII prohibited an employer "from requiring a high school

education or passing of a standardized general intelligence test as a condition of employment in or transfer to jobs when (a) neither standard is shown to be significantly related to successful job performance, (b) both requirements operate to disqualify Negroes at a substantially higher rate than white applicants, and (c) the jobs in question formerly had been filled only by white employees as part of a longstanding practice of giving preference to whites." Accepting the Court of Appeals' conclusion that the employer had adopted the diploma and test requirements without any intent to discriminate, we held that good faith "does not redeem employment procedures or testing mechanisms that operate as 'built-in headwinds' for minority groups and are unrelated to measuring job capability." We explained that Congress had "directed the thrust of the Act to the *consequences* of employment practices, not simply the motivation." * * * We thus squarely held that . . . Title VII did not require a showing of discriminatory intent. * * *

Griggs, which interpreted the identical text at issue here, thus strongly suggests that a disparate-impact theory should be cognizable under the ADEA. Indeed, for over two decades after our decision in *Griggs*, the Courts of Appeal uniformly interpreted the ADEA as authorizing recovery on a "disparate-impact" theory in appropriate cases. It was only after our decision in *Hazen Paper Co.* v. *Biggins,* that some of those courts concluded that the ADEA did not authorize a disparate-impact theory of liability. Our opinion in *Hazen Paper*, however, did not address or comment on the issue we decide today. In that case, we held that an employee's allegation that he was discharged shortly before his pension would have vested did not state a cause of action under a *disparate-treatment* theory. The motivating factor was not, we held, the employee's age, but rather his years of service, a factor that the ADEA did not prohibit an employer from considering when terminating an employee. * * * In sum, there is nothing in our opinion in *Hazen Paper* that precludes an interpretation of the ADEA that parallels our holding in *Griggs*.

The Court of Appeals' categorical rejection of disparate-impact liability . . . rested primarily on the RFOA provision. . . . * * * The RFOA provision provides that it shall not be unlawful for an employer "to take any action otherwise prohibited . . . where the differentiation is based on reasonable factors other than age discrimination. . . ." In most disparate-treatment cases, if an employer in fact acted on a factor other than age, the action would not be prohibited . . . in the first place. In those disparate-treatment cases, such as in *Hazen Paper* itself, the RFOA provision is simply unnecessary to avoid liability under the ADEA, since there was no prohibited action in the first place. * * * In disparate-impact cases, however, the allegedly "otherwise prohibited" activity is not based on age. ("'[C]laims that stress "disparate impact" [by contrast] involve employment practices that are facially neutral in their treatment of different groups but that in fact fall more harshly on one group than another . . .'" It is, accordingly, in cases involving disparate-impact claims that the RFOA provision plays its principal role by precluding liability if the adverse impact was attributable to a nonage factor that was "reasonable." Rather than support an argument that disparate impact is unavailable under the ADEA, the RFOA provision actually supports the contrary conclusion. * * *

Congress' decision to limit the coverage of the ADEA by including the RFOA provision is consistent with the fact that age, unlike race or other classifications protected by Title VII, not uncommonly has relevance to an individual's capacity to engage in certain types of employment. To be sure, Congress recognized that this is not always the case, and that society may perceive those differences to be larger or more consequential than they are in fact. However . . . "certain circumstances . . . unquestionably affect older workers more strongly, as a group, than they do younger workers." Thus, it is not surprising that certain employment criteria that are routinely used may be reasonable despite their adverse impact on older workers as a group. * * *

Turning to the case before us, we initially note that petitioners have done little more than point out that the pay plan at issue is relatively less generous to older workers than to younger workers. They have not identified any specific test, requirement, or practice within the pay plan that has an adverse impact on older workers. . . . [I]t is not enough to simply allege that there is a disparate impact on workers, or point to a generalized policy that leads to such an impact. Rather, the employee is "'responsible for isolating and identifying the *specific* employment practices that are allegedly responsible for any observed statistical disparities.'" Petitioners have failed to do so. Their failure to identify the specific practice being challenged is the sort of omission that could "result in employers being potentially liable

for 'the myriad of innocent causes that may lead to statistical imbalances. . . .'" In this case not only did petitioners thus err by failing to identify the relevant practice, but it is also clear from the record that the City's plan was based on reasonable factors other than age.

The plan divided each of five basic positions—police officer, master police officer, police sergeant, police lieutenant, and deputy police chief—into a series of steps and half-steps. The wage for each range was based on a survey of comparable communities in the Southeast. Employees were then assigned a step (or half-step) within their position that corresponded to the lowest step that would still give the individual a 2% raise. Most of the officers were in the three lowest ranks; in each of those ranks there were officers under age 40 and officers over 40. In none did their age affect their compensation. The few officers in the two highest ranks are all over 40. Their raises, though higher in dollar amount than the raises given to junior officers, represented a smaller percentage of their salaries, which of course are higher than the salaries paid to their juniors. They are members of the class complaining of the "disparate impact" of the award.

Petitioners' evidence established two principal facts: First, almost two-thirds (66.2%) of the officers under 40 received raises of more than 10% while less than half (45.3%) of those over 40 did. Second, the average percentage increase for the entire class of officers with less than five years of tenure was somewhat higher than the percentage for those with more seniority. Because older officers tended to occupy more senior positions, on average they received smaller increases when measured as a percentage of their salary. The basic explanation for the differential was the City's perceived need to raise the salaries of junior officers to make them competitive with comparable positions in the market.

Thus, the disparate impact is attributable to the City's decision to give raises based on seniority and position. Reliance on seniority and rank is unquestionably reasonable given the City's goal of raising employees' salaries to match those in surrounding communities. In sum, we hold that the City's decision to grant a larger raise to lower echelon employees for the purpose of bringing salaries in line with that of surrounding police forces was a decision based on a "reasonable factor other than age" that responded to the City's legitimate goal of retaining police officers. While there may have been other reasonable ways for the City to achieve its goals, the one selected was not unreasonable. Unlike the business necessity test, which asks whether there are other ways for the employer to achieve its goals that do not result in a disparate impact on a protected class, the reasonableness inquiry includes no such requirement.

CASE QUESTIONS

1. What was the legal issue in this case? What did the Court decide?

2. What reasons does the Court cite for recognizing disparate (adverse) impact claims under the Age Discrimination in Employment Act (ADEA)?

3. How does the officers' claim fit the disparate impact theory? What is the neutral employment practice in question? Evidence that it disadvantaged older workers?

4. What is a "reasonable factor other than age (RFOA)"? Why did the Court decide that the city's pay plan was based on reasonable factors other than age?

Analyzing Adverse Impact Cases

Because the plaintiff in an adverse impact case is claiming that some neutral requirement or practice has discriminatory effects, the plaintiff generally has to point to a specific requirement or practice causally connected to these effects as the culprit. In *Smith*, the Court faulted the plaintiffs for failing to identify "any specific test, requirement, or practice within the pay plan that has an adverse impact on older workers." An exception is where the plaintiff is unable to do so because multiple factors are involved in making the employment decision (such as a hiring process with numerous tests, interviews, and so on), and the scoring and relative weight of each factor is unclear. In such cases, the law (at least under Title VII) allows the bundle of related practices to be challenged as one.

ELEMENTS OF A CLAIM

Adverse Impact

I. Plaintiff must establish a "prima facie" case of adverse impact by showing that:

 a) a "neutral" employment requirement or practice has the effect of disproportionately limiting the employment opportunities of a protected class group (e.g., women, Latinos) of which the plaintiff is a part; and

 b) the difference in outcomes across protected class groups is large enough that it is unlikely to exist by chance.

II. If the plaintiff successfully establishes a prima facie case, the employer must prove that the challenged employment requirement or practice is "job related and consistent with business necessity."

 In age discrimination cases, the employer must defend use of the challenged employment requirement or practice by showing that it is a "reasonable factor other than age."

III. If the employer successfully defends the requirement or practice, the plaintiff can still prevail by showing that a feasible alternative exists that would have less discriminatory impact and the employer nonetheless refuses to adopt it (but not in age discrimination cases).

Although **neutral requirement** or practice sounds mysterious, the phrase refers to anything, other than protected class characteristics (in which case they would not be "neutral"), used as grounds for making employment decisions. To produce adverse impact, a requirement or practice has to fall more heavily on some protected class group than others. The example given earlier was of a minimum height requirement that if set high enough would eliminate from consideration some men, but a much larger proportion of women, due to the fact that women are on average shorter than men. In *Griggs*, the neutral requirements were the high school diploma and the specified level of performance on the intelligence and aptitude tests. These requirements were causally linked to discriminatory effects because of the extremely low rate of high school completion among African Americans in North Carolina at that time.

Examples of neutral requirements or practices that have *sometimes* been shown to have adverse impact include the following:

- A variety of written employment tests
- Height and weight requirements
- Language requirements
- No beard policies
- Physical strength tests
- Military service, type of discharge
- Limitation of employment based on arrests and convictions
- Educational requirements

Note that this is not an exhaustive listing and none of these are discriminatory in every situation.

How "disproportionate" does the limitation of employment opportunity have to be to have a prima facie case? Adverse impact cases most often involve extensive statistical analyses. We are going to sidestep this complexity for now and simply say that the plaintiff has to present the court with evidence that any differences in outcomes across protected class groups are large and consistent enough that they are highly unlikely to have occurred simply by chance.

If the plaintiff fails to establish a prima facie case of adverse impact, the employer is not required to defend the challenged requirement or practice. On the other hand, if a prima facie case is established, the employer bears a relatively heavy burden in showing that the challenged requirement or practice is **job-related** and **consistent with business necessity**. When an employment test is involved, the employer usually must produce statistical evidence that the test is a good measure of ability to do a job. In other circumstances, a more general showing that the requirement is related to safety or efficiency may suffice. "Job related" is not synonymous with "consistent with business necessity." A requirement (e.g., strength) might be related to the ability to perform a job, but the amount of strength required or the particular means used to assess strength might not be consistent with business necessity. In age-based adverse impact claims, the employer has the burden of showing that the challenged practice is a **reasonable factor other than age**. This is a more lenient standard for employers to meet than "job related and consistent with business necessity." A "reasonable factor other than age" avoids liability, even if other factors with less discriminatory effects are available and not used. Thus, employers need to be prepared to defend requirements or practices whose use results in disproportionate outcomes across protected class groups. *Employers should not adopt employment practices simply because they sound good and without meaningful examination of their effects and the evidence supporting their job-relatedness.*

If an employer shows that a challenged practice is job-related and consistent with business necessity, then, even though that practice tends to produce unequal outcomes for different protected class groups, it is still legal. However, if the plaintiff can show that an alternative practice would produce more equal outcomes, and the employer declines to use it, the employer is guilty of adverse impact discrimination (but not in ADEA cases).

RETALIATION—A CLOSER LOOK

In retaliation cases, an employee suffers a loss of employment opportunity due to engaging in protected activity related to civil rights in employment. If civil rights laws are to be more than a hollow pretense, protecting persons who act to uphold their rights, or help others do so, is absolutely essential.

The two broad classes of protected activity are participation and opposition. **Participation** refers to participation in the enforcement of an antidiscrimination law, such as by filing a charge, bringing a lawsuit, giving testimony, and assisting in the investigation of a discrimination charge. **Opposition** refers to activities related to obtaining civil rights apart from participation in formal enforcement procedures. Examples of opposition are complaining about discrimination to supervisors or company officials, contacting civil rights and other organizations, speaking with or writing letters to the media, raising concerns with political representatives, circulating petitions, refusing to carry out an order to discriminate, and picketing.

Gallina v. Mintz Levin provides a good illustration of a successful retaliation claim. Even though the employer in this case was a law firm, the firm apparently succumbed to the all-too-common temptation to "get back at" an employee speaking out against perceived discrimination.

GALLINA V. MINTZ LEVIN
123 Fed. Appx. 558 (4th Cir. 2005)

• • •

OPINION BY CIRCUIT JUDGE SHEDD:

A jury determined that Dawn Gallina suffered a retaliatory discharge from the law firm of Mintz, Levin, Cohn, Ferris, Glovsky, & Popeo, P.C. ("Mintz Levin") in violation of Title VII of the Civil Rights Act of 1964. Mintz Levin now appeals . . . * * * [W]e affirm in part, reverse in part, and remand for further proceedings.

Mintz Levin is headquartered in Boston, Massachusetts, and has offices located throughout the United States. Gallina worked as an associate in the Business and Finance section of Mintz Levin's office in Reston, Virginia. Although based in the Reston office, Gallina worked with attorneys from various offices during the course of her employment. Gallina was employed at Mintz Levin from October 14, 1999, until she was terminated on March 23, 2001, for alleged poor performance.

Gallina's problems at Mintz Levin began in November 1999, when Mark Wishner, then acting as managing partner of the Reston office, discovered that she has a small child. Wishner became disconcerted about why Gallina had not informed him of her child when she interviewed with the firm. Thereafter, Gallina felt that Wishner began to treat her differently than male associates. For example, Wishner was more collegial and cordial with male associates than he was with Gallina. Wishner used unusually harsh language toward Gallina (e.g., "f—king idiot"), and on at least one occasion he called her a "stupid bitch.") Wishner also spoke with Gallina "about the commitment differential between men and women, how women lawyers have more demands place[d] on them, and [how] it's very hard for them to balance when they have a family." Additionally, Wishner told Gallina what she regarded as a "cautionary tale" about his prior experience with a female associate who, upon her return from maternity leave, inquired about achieving partnership. Wishner was "beside himself" that the female associate would make such an inquiry, and the story left Gallina with the impression that "pregnant women don't make partner."

In February 2000, while on a trip to the Boston office, Gallina complained about Wishner's behavior toward her to Cindy Deegan, who was the firm's Business and Finance practice administrator. Gallina told Deegan that Wishner was treating her differently because she is female. Deegan referred Gallina to Stan Twarog, a Mintz Levin partner who served as the Business and Finance section manager. Gallina then met with Twarog and repeated her belief that Wishner was treating her differently because she is female. Twarog expressed concern about Gallina's complaint, and he asked her not to file a formal complaint because he felt that the matter could be dealt with informally. Being new to the firm and trying to be a "team player," Gallina trusted that Twarog would deal with the matter in an appropriate manner.

By May the news of Gallina's complaints to Boston reached the Reston office. Scott Meza, a partner in the Reston office, told Gallina that she had "caused a problem" for, and "embarrassed," the Reston office by complaining about Wishner to the Boston office. Meza told Gallina that "[a]ny dirty laundry that there may be in Reston needs to be handled in Reston. You don't need to go to Boston." During a meeting in July, Meza informed Gallina that she was not perceived as being "as committed" as the other lawyers in the Reston office, and he stated that she needed to decide whether she wanted to be "a successful mommy or a successful lawyer." Also, Meza reiterated how Gallina had "embarrassed us when [she] went to Boston." * * * In September, Gallina took her complaints of gender discrimination to Joan Howland, the Director of Human Resources for the Boston office. Gallina sought an interim performance evaluation from reviewers in Boston because she believed that some of her Reston evaluations were biased. Later, in October, Howland denied Gallina's request for the interim performance evaluation and advised her to "keep [her] head down and do [her] work."

In November, David Barmak, a partner practicing employment law, succeeded Wishner as the managing partner of the Reston office. Shortly afterward, Barmak met with Howland to discuss Gallina's "situation." On January 12, 2001, Barmak withheld Gallina's annual pay increase pending the results of her performance evaluations. The performance evaluations were completed in mid-January. In an e-mail on March 19,

Barmak notified Gallina that the performance evaluations had been assembled. On these performance evaluations, all four reviewers from the Reston office gave Gallina negative reviews, while both reviewers from other offices gave her positive reviews. Notably, two of the negative evaluations from the Reston office came from Wishner and Meza. Four days later, on March 23, Barmak terminated Gallina's employment.

Gallina thereafter brought this action against Mintz Levin alleging claims under Title VII for gender discrimination, sexual harassment, and retaliation. Additionally, Gallina asserted a claim under the Equal Pay Act. * * * Before trial, the district court granted summary judgment in favor of Mintz Levin on Gallina's Title VII claims of gender discrimination and sexual harassment, and her claim under the Equal Pay Act. The case then proceeded to trial on Gallina's Title VII retaliation claim. The jury thereafter returned a verdict in Gallina's favor, awarding her $190,000 in compensatory damages and $330,000 in back pay. * * *

Gallina can prove unlawful retaliation by showing (1) that she engaged in a protected activity, (2) that Mintz Levin took an adverse employment action against her, and (3) that a causal connection links the protected activity and the adverse action. Once Gallina makes this showing, Mintz Levin could defend itself by producing "evidence of a legitimate, non-discriminatory reason for taking the adverse employment action." The jury must then decide whether the adverse action was actually taken for the proffered reason, or whether that reason was merely pretext for retaliation. * * *

Gallina presented sufficient evidence at trial to establish that she engaged in a protected activity. Through Title VII, Congress has forbidden employers to retaliate against employees for engaging in protected activities such as opposing gender discrimination in the workplace. "Employees are thus guaranteed the right to complain to their superiors about suspected violations of Title VII." Gallina made such complaints. The jury heard evidence that Gallina complained to at least four superiors at Mintz Levin about her concerns of gender discrimination, lodging most of her complaints after assurances by a partner that the matter would be dealt with informally. Further, although Mintz Levin contends that Gallina lacked a good faith, reasonable belief that the conduct she complained of violated Title VII, Gallina's repeated complaints and expressions of concern in response to this conduct demonstrate that she actually believed she was being subjected to gender

discrimination. Additionally, Wishner's alleged course of conduct toward Gallina, viewed as a whole and in the light most favorable to Gallina, was sufficiently serious to show that Gallina's belief of illegal discrimination was reasonable.

Mintz Levin does not dispute that it took adverse employment actions against Gallina. Indeed, Mintz Levin deferred Gallina's pay increase and ultimately terminated her. Gallina also presented evidence sufficient for a reasonable jury to find that Mintz Levin's pay deferral and firing were the result of her complaints about gender discrimination. After Gallina complained about Wishner's conduct toward her to Deegan and Twarog in Boston, Twarog asked Gallina not to file a formal complaint and assured her that the matter would be dealt with appropriately. Subsequently, Meza explained on two occasions how Gallina had embarrassed the Reston office by complaining about Wishner to the Boston office—where Gallina had complained about gender discrimination. Further, Meza requested that Gallina bring future complaints to him. Despite these apparent efforts to stifle her attempts to complain of gender discrimination, Gallina continued to complain to Gadiano, Weller [omitted from the recapitulation of facts in this excerpt], and Howland. Within two months of Barmak's becoming the managing partner of the Reston office, he met with Howland to discuss Gallina's "situation" and deferred her pay increase. Then, only two month's after the pay deferral, Barmak fired Gallina. The jury could have reasonably inferred from this evidence that Gallina's pay deferral and firing were manifestations of Mintz Levin's retaliation against her. The reasonableness of this inference is buttressed by Gallina's evidence that Mintz Levin had no other valid reason for deferring her pay or terminating her. Gallina presented evidence that on her performance evaluations all four reviewers from the Reston office (including Wishner and Meza) gave her negative reviews, while both reviewers from other offices gave her positive reviews. This evidence supports the inference that, but for the bias of the Reston office, Gallina's work was acceptable to Mintz Levin, and the firm fired Gallina because of her continued complaints of gender discrimination. We therefore hold that there is sufficient evidence to support the jury's verdict on Gallina's retaliation claim. * * *

Gallina argues that the district court erroneously granted judgment as a matter of law to Mintz Levin on her claim for punitive damages. * * * A Title VII plaintiff

is entitled to punitive damages if her employer engaged in intentional retaliation "with malice or with reckless indifference to [her] federally protected rights." This standard does not require "a showing of egregious or outrageous discrimination," but rather proof that the employer retaliated "in the face of a perceived risk that its actions will violate federal law." However, "in the punitive damages context, an employer may not be vicariously liable for the discriminatory employment decisions of managerial agents where these decisions are contrary to the employer's good-faith efforts to comply with Title VII."

We hold that Gallina presented evidence that is sufficient for a reasonable jury to find that Mintz Levin perceived the risk of violating federal law through its retaliation. A reasonable jury could have found that members of a prominent law firm, and especially a law firm with an employment law section in the relevant office, perceived the risk of violating federal law in retaliating against an employee. Notably, Barmak was an employment lawyer and was aware of Gallina's complaints of gender discrimination, so he undoubtedly could have perceived the risk of violating federal law. * * * We also hold that Mintz Levin did not proffer sufficient evidence such that a reasonable juror could only conclude that the firm engaged in good-faith efforts to comply with Title VII. Although Mintz Levin proffered evidence of the existence of a "Sexual Harassment Prevention Training" manual and a contact person to deal with sexual discrimination issues, there was no evidence that Mintz Levin had any specific policy regarding retaliation. The only evidence of any policy was a reference in the "Sexual Harassment Prevention Training" manual, but there was no evidence that anyone at the firm was aware of that policy, nor that it was implemented or enforced. Particularly condemning is the fact that, assuming any policy existed to deal with gender discrimination and retaliation, the policy completely failed Gallina because her complaints of gender discrimination caused her ultimate termination. * * * Accordingly, the district court erred by disallowing Gallina's punitive damages claim to go to the jury.

CASE QUESTIONS

1. What were the legal issues in this case? What did the court decide?

2. What are the elements of a Title VII retaliation claim? How were these elements satisfied in this case?

3. Why is Gallina able to prevail on her retaliation claim even though her other legal claims failed?

4. When are punitive damages available in a Title VII claim? Why did the court conclude that Gallina's claim for punitive damages should be submitted to a jury?

Analyzing Retaliation Cases

Gallina was able to establish a prima facie case of retaliation because she engaged in protected activity. Over a period of months, she made numerous complaints regarding possible sex discrimination in the firm to a variety of managers and colleagues. Her activity took the form of "opposition," rather than participation. In general, protection against retaliation does not hinge upon the correctness of an employee's perceptions of discrimination. *An employee cannot be punished by an employer for participating in enforcement procedures, even if the employer is correct in believing that the employee has knowingly made false statements.* Protection of employees who engage in opposition is more equivocal. The employee does not have to be correct in thinking that the employer's policies opposed are unlawful; however, the employee must have a reasonable, good faith belief that they are. In a relevant case, the Supreme Court decided that an employee was not protected from retaliation for complaining to her boss about a verbal exchange between two male supervisors that occurred in her presence.[37] Two male employees, reviewing the psychological report in a job applicant's file, came across a statement that the applicant had once made to a coworker: "I hear making love to you is like making love to the Grand Canyon."

[37]*Clark County School District v. Breeden*, 532 U.S. 268 (2001).

ELEMENTS OF A CLAIM

Retaliation

I. Plaintiff must establish a "prima facie" case of retaliation by showing that:

a) the plaintiff engaged in protected activity (i.e., participated in enforcement procedures or otherwise used reasonable means to oppose discrimination);

b) the plaintiff suffered a loss or limitation of employment opportunity; and

c) there is a causal link between engaging in the protected activity and the loss or limitation of employment opportunity.

II. If the plaintiff successfully establishes a prima facie case, the employer has the opportunity to produce evidence of a lawful, non-retaliatory motive for the employment decision.

III. If the employer articulates a lawful, non-retaliatory motive, the plaintiff has the opportunity to rebut the employer's claims by:

a) providing evidence that sheds doubt on the credibility of the employer's claimed motive; and/or

b) providing other evidence which supports the claim that retaliation is the most likely explanation for the employment decision.

The comment was read aloud and prompted laughter from the male employees, although the female employee took objection. Employees need only have a good faith belief that their employer is violating the law, but the Court concluded that no reasonable person could have believed that this exchange, by itself, constituted an unlawful, hostile environment. Hence, she was not protected for making the complaint, even if it was the cause of her termination. In *Gallina*, the law firm argued in its defense that she did not have a reasonable, good faith belief that that firm had engaged in sex discrimination or harassment. Her charges other than retaliation were eventually dismissed, but the court maintained that Gallina's repeated efforts to address issues of discrimination in the firm and the totality of the firm's conduct toward her were sufficient to show a reasonable, good faith belief on her part that she was a victim of discrimination.

The manner of opposition also matters. Employees who oppose their employer's discriminatory practices cannot engage in illegal activities, trespass, disrupt the work of others, disparage the company's product, or release confidential documents and still expect to be protected against retaliation. Recall that in the *McDonnell Douglas* case, Green engaged in an illegal "stall-in" at the plant. Although the case is known primarily for its analysis of disparate treatment, Green also alleged retaliation based on his opposition to the company's civil rights practices. However, that claim was not upheld due to the illegality of his actions. Likewise, a manager who was terminated after he attempted to bolster his own EEOC discrimination complaint by pressuring an employee to sign a statement that the manager had prepared, lost his retaliation claim. The court concluded that "[h]e was fired for pursuing a statement in a highly offensive and disruptive manner after repeated warnings that he needed to change the way in which he dealt with subordinates. . . . Title VII protection from retaliation does not clothe the complainant with immunity for past and present inadequacies, unsatisfactory performance, and uncivil conduct in dealing with

subordinates and peers."[38] Despite the law firm's distaste for her complaints and their efforts to stifle them, there was no evidence that the manner of Gallina's opposition was unreasonable and not worthy of protection.

To establish a prima facie case of retaliation, the plaintiff must also show that an "adverse employment action" occurred and that it was causally linked to protected activity. The adverse employment action need not be a termination, but it is not enough for an employee to claim that she was subjected to rudeness or got the "cold shoulder" as a result of her protected activity. A causal link is usually demonstrated by showing that the employer knew about the employee's protected activity, and the timing of the adverse employment decision closely coincided with the employee engaging in protected activity. Gallina had a pay increase withheld and was subsequently terminated. Managers within the firm were clearly aware of her complaints, and her termination took place shortly after negative performance appraisals were obtained from two managers who had attempted to silence her. The element of timing is critical in retaliation cases. As one court has put it, "If a lengthy period of time elapses between the plaintiff's complaint and her adverse employment action, the inference of causation is weakened."[39] However, in that particular case, the court allowed a retaliation claim to proceed even though more than nine months had elapsed between the employee's sexual harassment claim and her termination because there was evidence that the employer had set the employee up for eventual termination.

If a prima facie case of retaliation is established, the case proceeds essentially like a pretext case. The employer must articulate a nonretaliatory reason for the decision (e.g., Gallina's alleged poor performance). If the employer can do so, the plaintiff can still prevail by showing that it is more likely that the employment decision was motivated by the employer's desire to retaliate. An employee of a company doing contract work for NASA was terminated after he communicated a subordinate's sexual harassment complaint about a higher-level manager to the HR manager and later supported her harassment charge in statements made to state agency investigators. Although the employer claimed that the termination was due to poor performance and insubordination, the timing of the termination (less than a month after speaking to investigators), discussions among upper-level managers about firing him for supporting the "bogus" claim, and a statement by the manager who fired him that it would have "made a hell of a difference" if he had gone to him with the complaint rather than to the HR manager, all pointed to a retaliatory motive.[40] In *Gallina*, the court considered numerous expressions that Gallina had "embarrassed" and caused a problem for the Reston office, attempts to sidetrack her complaints, the rapid decision to terminate, and the conflicting performance appraisals (suggesting that the reviewers at the Reston office were biased) in concluding that the pay deferral and termination were retaliatory actions.

Employers must not terminate or otherwise retaliate against employees because they file charges, complain about discrimination, or otherwise participate in enforcement activities or oppose unlawful discrimination. Retaliation looks bad. Juries are rightly suspicious of the "coincidence" that termination befalls an individual on the heels of a discrimination complaint. As one lawyer has put it, "Retaliation resonates with the jury. They may not believe the employer terminated someone because they are black, but they will believe they terminated someone because they rocked the boat."[41]

[38]*Jackson v. St. Joseph State Hospital*, 840 F.2d 1387, at 1390-91 (8th Cir. 1988); *cert. denied*, 488 U.S. 892 (1988).

[39]*Hall v. Eastman Chemical*, 2005 U.S. App. LEXIS 4987, at 8.

[40]*Kubicko v. Ogden Logistics Services*, 181 F.3d 544 (4th Cir. 1999).

[41]Richard A. Oppel, Jr. "Retaliation Lawsuits: A Treacherous Slope." *New York Times* (September 29, 1999), C-8.

Chapter SUMMARY

Despite real progress, employment discrimination continues to be a serious problem. Contemporary discrimination is expressed less often through outright exclusion and segregation (although these still exist) and more often through harassment, blocked access to advancement, and other relatively subtle obstacles captured by the term *glass ceiling*.

Discrimination can be broadly defined as the limitation or denial of employment opportunity based on or related to the protected class characteristics of persons. Bias and unfairness are the essential nature of discrimination; however, only when unfairness is based on or related to protected class does it constitute discrimination. Protected classes include things like race, sex, national origin, and religion. These are characteristics of people that typically have nothing to do with the ability to perform work, are not readily altered, and are ethically objectionable as grounds for deciding who gets employment opportunities.

It is important to distinguish between different types or legal theories of discrimination. How courts decide whether discrimination has occurred depends upon the type of alleged discrimination. Disparate treatment is unequal treatment that is intentional, based on protected class, and results in the limitation or denial of employment opportunity. The employer's intent or motivation in making the employment decision is key. Distinct varieties of disparate treatment cases include direct evidence, facially discriminatory policies, reverse discrimination, pretext, mixed motives, pattern or practice, and harassment. Proving intent or motivation can be difficult. The method for analyzing pretext cases requires a plaintiff to establish an initial presumption that discrimination has occurred largely by ruling out common, nondiscriminatory motives (the prima facie case); requires the defendant to focus the inquiry by articulating a lawful, nondiscriminatory motive; and then requires the plaintiff to show that discrimination was the most likely reason because the employer's stated motive is not believable and/or there is other evidence of discrimination. In mixed motives cases, the evidence (either direct or circumstantial) of a discriminatory motive is sufficiently strong to conclude that the challenged employment decision was, at least partly, affected by consideration of the plaintiff's protected class characteristic. In such cases (at least under Title VII), the employer has violated the law. The remedies for which the employer will be liable depend on whether the employer can prove that it would have made the same decision regardless of the discriminatory motive.

Another type of discrimination is adverse (or "disparate") impact, which occurs when a "neutral" requirement or practice results in the disproportionate limitation or denial of employment opportunity for some protected class group and is not "job-related and consistent with business necessity." Neutral employment practices with the potential to produce adverse impact include written employment tests, size and physical strength requirements, and educational credential requirements. The focus in adverse impact cases is on discriminatory effects that cannot be justified. Plaintiffs must show, usually through statistics, that some employment requirement or practice affects one protected class group more detrimentally than others. If this showing can be made, the employer must defend its use by showing it to be job-related and consistent with business necessity. In age discrimination cases, the neutral requirement or practice must be shown to be a "reasonable factor other than age."

Two other major types of discrimination are failure to reasonably accommodate and retaliation. An employer discriminates when it fails to be flexible in meeting the needs of disabled employees and those whose religious beliefs and practices come into conflict with workplace requirements. Retaliation occurs when an employee who asserts her rights under the law suffers a loss or limitation of employment opportunity for doing so. Employees enjoy considerable protection when participating in the enforcement process for antidiscrimination laws or otherwise opposing the discriminatory practices of an employer. Employees alleging retaliation must show that they engaged in protected activity, that employment opportunity was denied or limited, and that the adverse employment decision was a consequence of engaging in protected activity. To defend a retaliation charge, the employer must articulate an alternative, nonretaliatory reason.

Practical Advice SUMMARY

- *Employers must*

 –*be concerned about avoiding discrimination in all employment decisions.*

 –*refrain from making employment decisions based, in whole or in part, on the protected class characteristics of employees.*

 –*have policies and be consistent in how they are enforced.*

 –*closely scrutinize employment requirements and practices for their potential to disadvantage protected class groups and for evidence of their job-relatedness and business necessity.*

 –*be flexible in accommodating the particular needs of disabled employees and employees whose religious practices conflict with workplace requirements.*

 –*exercise particular care in making employment decisions regarding employees who have filed charges or spoken out about discrimination.*

 –*not punish employees for participating in enforcement procedures or otherwise opposing discrimination.*

 –*maintain good documentation and be prepared to explain the nondiscriminatory reasons for why particular employment decisions were made.*

Key TERMS

glass ceiling
discrimination
protected class
disparate treatment
discriminatory intent
adverse impact
discriminatory effects
failure to reasonably
 accommodate

retaliation
direct evidence
facially discriminatory
bona fide occupational
 qualification (BFOQ)
reverse discrimination
pretext
mixed motives
pattern or practice of
 discrimination

prima facie case
neutral requirement
job-related and consistent with
 business necessity
reasonable factor other than age
participation
opposition

Chapter QUESTIONS

1. Loretta Wilson was hired by B/E Aerospace as an Engineering Business Manager in 1997 and promoted to Engineering Manager in 1998. In the fall of 1999, Wilson expressed interest in an open Site Vice President position to her boss, Roman Ptakowski. According to Wilson, Ptakowski told her that she was "the obvious candidate" for the position and that "even though women aren't typically in that type of position, we'll see what happens when we throw your name out there to corporate." Ptakowski denied making these statements, although two other employees testified that Ptakowski had made similar statements about Wilson to them. The following criteria were established by Ptakowski for the Site V.P. position: 1) prior profit/loss responsibility; 2) experience with customers; 3) knowledge of the aerospace industry. Two male candidates were interviewed. Wilson was not interviewed and Ptakowski said that she was judged not qualified for the position. A male who was Vice President of Marketing and Sales at one of the company's facilities was promoted instead. In that position, he had profit/loss responsibility, oversaw 70 employees, and had extensive contact with customers. Since 1995, only 2 women had been chosen for Vice President out of 44 open positions. Denied the promotion, Wilson sued for sex

discrimination. (*Wilson v. B/E Aerospace*, 376 F.3d 1079 (11th Cir. 2004))

2. Gwen Owens, an African American, has won awards as a journalist and has a master's degree in broadcasting. At one point in her career, she worked as a show host for QVC. She was terminated and joined a race discrimination suit against QVC's corporate parent Comcast. She took a job at another cable news company. That company was eventually purchased by Comcast. Comcast made plans to consolidate its news operations. Owens interviewed for one of the two evening news anchor positions that would remain. In her interview with the "transition committee," Owens disclosed the fact that she was a party to the QVC suit. The interviewer assured her that the lawsuit would not influence the hiring decision, but the lawsuit was subsequently discussed with and among members of management. The stated selection process consisted of an interview and an audition. The choice of candidates would be made based on "the chemistry between the anchors that auditioned." Owens was judged only "fair" in her audition and criticized for being "forced and mechanical." Many of the candidates for the position were not auditioned, and none of them was paired for an audition with the white male anchor who was the first hired. Comcast said that it desired candidates who had name recognition in the Philadelphia area. Owens was known in Philadelphia. The male hired first had been an anchor in Philadelphia, but several white, female candidates who were offered the second position, and one who was eventually hired, had not worked in the area. Owens did not get the evening news anchor position, nor several other positions she sought. She remains with Comcast as a reporter and back-up anchor, but has filed another suit. (*Owens v. Comcast*, 2004 U.S. Dist. LEXIS 23498)

3. At the time of his termination, Gerald Miller was 62-years-old. He had worked at Aramark Corporation for 12 years, selling vending products and cafeteria services. He had a clean work record until the year before his termination. Following appointment of a new supervisor, Miller was reprimanded for failing to report a minor auto accident that occurred on the job. Shortly thereafter, he was instructed to no longer submit expense reports seeking reimbursement for travel expenses to and from his home. Based on his own estimates of the distances between work sites, the supervisor became convinced that Miller was continuing to overstate his mileage even after being warned. Miller was suspended and eventually terminated. A replacement was not hired for Miller's position. Instead, his territory was divided between two existing employees, one of whom was 28 years old and the other who was 42 years old. A former employee of Aramark attested to the supervisor having said that Miller had "negative appeal as an older, overweight sales person." Miller sued. (2004 U.S. Dist. LEXIS 16023)

4. Frederick Kuehnl was a 56-year-old man who had worked nearly 30 years in the "trimming room" of a casket company. Shortly before his termination, a 33-year-old employee asked Kuehnl how old he was and when he planned to retire. Three weeks later, the same employee terminated Kuehnl. According to Kuehnl, the younger employee said: "You're fired. You're getting too f——ing old, you're making too much f——ing money. Get the f——out." Kuehnl's offer to accept less pay so that he could continue to work until he was 65 was rejected on the spot. When Kuehnl asked why he was being fired rather than the other employee in the "trimming room," the younger employee said that the other employee "could give him more years and he needed a job." The company says that the termination was because it could not afford to pay his salary and because Kuehnl had conflicts with coworkers. Kuehnl sued. (*Equal Employment Opportunity Commission v. Warfield-Rohr Casket Company*, 364 F.3d 160 (4th Cir. 2004))

5. An employee had several run-ins with managers, including a situation in which he threatened a manager with physical harm. There was discussion of terminating him, but it was decided to give him another chance. The employee subsequently filed a race discrimination charge with the EEOC challenging the company's pay practices. In a deposition given by the employee preliminary to litigation of his discrimination claim, the employee admitted to secretly taping phone conversations, disclosing confidential information to competitors, and other offenses. A month after the deposition, the employee was sent a letter stating "As a result of issues raised in your deposition, . . . you are suspended from all duties on behalf of the Company." This was followed

shortly thereafter by a termination letter that stated in part "During the entire term of your employment, you have communicated your deep dissatisfaction with your compensation . . ." The employee filed another suit challenging the termination. (*Medlock v. Ortho Biotech, Inc.*, 164 F.3d 545 (10th Cir. 1999); cert. denied, 528 U.S. 843 (1999))

6. Look at the examples of neutral requirements or practices that are listed in the chapter. Why is each of these a "good candidate" for an adverse impact claim? How are they linked to protected class?

7. Should other protected classes be recognized under the law? If so, which ones? "Bikers" are seeking to obtain legislation in Ohio that would prohibit discrimination against people who ride motorcycles or wear biker colors. Is that a good idea? (John Carpenter, "Tired of Stereotyping, Bikers Turn to Law," *New York Times* (December 26, 2001))

Internet RESOURCES

The Web site of the U.S. Equal Employment Opportunity Commission (EEOC) contains a wealth of legal materials (statutes, agency guidelines, compliance guidance, and manual), statistics, and reports on enforcement actions.

http://www.eeoc.gov/

The Web site of the Citizens' Commission on Civil Rights includes links to a variety of civil rights resources and organizations.

http://www.cccr.org/global/resources.cfm

The Web site of Alfred Blumrosen and the late Ruth Blumrosen uses statistical data from employer reports to the EEOC to estimate the extent of intentional discrimination in employment.

http://www. eeo1.com/

PART **2**

The Hiring Process

Recruitment, Applications, and Interviews

CLIPPINGS

▶ Eight New York City employment agencies have agreed to stop screening candidates according to their race, national origin, and other protected class characteristics. The employment agencies provided domestic workers, including nannies, maids, and butlers. Application forms frequently noted race and ethnicity, and referral requests often included statements like "no Blacks" and "Europeans preferred." Investigators contacted the agencies posing as prospective employers or job applicants. They found that the employment agencies routinely solicited racial preferences from prospective employers and used that information in making assignments. These discriminatory practices occurred even when the agencies earned their fees from job seekers.[1]

▶ The EEOC has settled a race discrimination suit brought against Merrill Gardens, a company that operates senior communities. The suit alleged that a pattern or practice of intentional discrimination prevailed for at least nine years at the company's Georgetowne Place facility in Fort Wayne, Indiana. A former general manager testified that nonwhite job applicants were refused positions based on the belief that the residents of the facility preferred white employees. The general manager had instructed subordinates to place Post-it notes on applications to alert her

that a particular candidate was a person of color. She also admitted to placing a mark similar to a "Z" at the bottom of applications to signify that an individual should be rejected because of his or her race. The company had also failed to keep required employment records, including application forms.[2]

▶ A federal judge has approved a $2.5 million consent decree, ending years of litigation with Carl Buddig & Company. The EEOC alleged that African Americans had been excluded from its meat processing plants in the Chicago area and that women were hired into only one low-paying position. EEOC trial attorney Ethan Cohen pointed to heavy reliance on employee referrals as a problem: "It's important that employers realize that while there are arguably many benefits to using employee referrals when hiring, if the process leads [to] applicants or hires who all share the same race or ethnicity, an employer may be steering into rocky waters."[3]

▶ Wal-Mart has agreed to settle a number of claims based on the Americans with Disabilities Act (ADA). One of the claims concerned a preemployment questionnaire that the chain had used between 1994 and 1998. The EEOC charged that the questionnaire illegally attempted to obtain information about applicants' disabilities.[4]

[1] "Eight Domestic Employment Agencies Reach Settlements in Spitzer Bias Probe." *Daily Labor Report* 106 (June 3, 2005), A-14.

[2] Equal Employment Opportunity Commission. "Georgetowne Place to Pay $650,000 to Settle EEOC Race Discrimination Lawsuit." (June 22, 2004). Viewed June 30, 2005 (http://www.eeoc.gov/press/6-22-05.html).

[3] Equal Employment Opportunity Commission. "EEOC Settles Discrimination Suit Against Carl Buddig for $2.5 Million." (September 7, 2004.) Viewed June 30, 2005 (http://eeoc.gov/press/9-7-04.html).

[4] Laura Mahoney. "Wal-Mart Agrees to Pay $6 million to Settle Pending Disabilities Claims." *Daily Labor Report* 241 (December 18, 2001), A-8.

> ▶ A Department of Labor review board has ruled against the Pegasus Consulting Group, upholding a prior decision that the company is liable for violations related to its treatment of 19 employees under the H-1B visa program. The company had enlisted foreign nationals with H-1B visas to work on software for its business customers. When business slowed down, the company decided to temporarily lay the visa holders off without pay. By failing to either pay the promised amounts to the visa holders or to terminate them and notify immigration authorities, the company violated the law. [5]

RECRUITMENT

To establish an employment relationship, there must be one or more ways in which an employer communicates information about the availability of an employment opportunity and persons interested in pursuing the opportunity make their interest known to the employer. The many **recruitment** mechanisms include want ads placed in newspapers or professional publications; Internet job postings; "help wanted" signs placed in storefronts, employment agencies, executive search firms, union hiring halls, job fairs, college placement offices; referrals from state employment services; and word of mouth. Preliminary information about candidates is typically recorded on application forms or resumes. One or more interviews are likely. Discrimination is the fundamental legal concern surrounding these activities. However, statements made by both employers and employees occasionally raise other legal issues, including breach of contract and fraud.

Recruitment mechanisms create the applicant pools from which employees are selected, and thus are vital to the cause of equal employment opportunity. *Unless an employer's recruiting mechanisms reach a broad spectrum of the available workforce (or at least, do not exclude some protected class groups much more than others) and successfully convey the employer's sincere desire that all qualified candidates apply, the most careful and unbiased selection process will still not result in equal employment opportunity.*

Evidence of Discrimination in Recruitment

Although recruitment is critical to equal employment opportunity, showing discrimination in recruitment is particularly complex. After all, it is difficult enough for an employee to discern whether she has been discriminated against after she applies for a job. How does a prospective employee challenge practices that keep her from learning about the existence of an employment opportunity in the first place? Not surprisingly, relatively few cases focus on challenges to recruitment mechanisms, and most of these are initiated by the EEOC on behalf of employees.

Statistical evidence usually lies at the center of discrimination cases that challenge recruitment procedures. But what kind of statistical evidence demonstrates discriminatory recruiting practices? One court has commented on the difficulty of interpreting statistical evidence in these cases:

> [D]iscrimination affects the applicant pool in a way that makes the discrimination harder to detect. The discriminating employer induces qualified blacks not to apply, and these nonapplicants—victims of discrimination as much as the nonhired applicants—will make the employer's hiring look

[5] "Pegasus Consulting Owes Over $300,000 for Shortchanging H-1B Workers, ARB Rules." *Daily Labor Report* 128 (July 6, 2005), A-6.

"better than it is." An applicant pool is biased against finding discrimination if potential applicants know or suspect that the employer is discriminating.[6]

What is the court saying? If we look only at ultimate hiring decisions, we might miss the fact that relatively few women or persons of color have come forward to be considered for employment. Furthermore, because the employer is known or reputed to be hostile to hiring such persons, job seekers might not want to waste their time by applying.

Most often, statistical evidence of discrimination in hiring consists of a comparison of *selection rates*. For example, in a sex discrimination case, the percentage of male applicants who are hired can be compared to the percentage of female applicants who are hired. If the selection rate for males is considerably higher than the selection rate for females, and that difference in outcome is large enough that it is unlikely to have occurred just by chance, this would be evidence of discriminatory effects. But this method will not work if a recruitment procedure is in question. Because recruitment procedures affect the composition of the applicant pool itself, the necessary comparison must be external, rather than internal. That is, the applicant pool of a particular employer must be compared to the group of persons in the labor market who might have become applicants had they known of the employment opportunity.

The most informative comparison is not with the population as a whole (which, after all, includes retirees, children, and others not in the labor force), nor with the overall labor force (which includes many people without the necessary skills or credentials for the particular job), but instead with persons in the **relevant labor market**.[7] The protected class composition of the employer's applicant pool is compared to the protected class composition of people who are qualified for the type of work in question. If, for example, the applicant pool for an airline pilot position has a much smaller percentage of women than the percentage of women in the workforce who are qualified and work as pilots, this is evidence that a recruitment mechanism is operating in a discriminatory fashion. The relevant labor market may be local, regional, national, or even international in scope, depending on the importance of the job, the availability of people with the needed skills, and the customary hiring practices in the industry. A less refined comparison with the general population or workforce might still be acceptable where the job in question calls for general skills that most people would posess.

In *EEOC v. Joe's Stone Crab*, an employer's recruiting practices and its reputation for discriminating are at issue. But notice the difficulty that the courts have in settling on the legal theory of discrimination that best fits the facts of the case.

[6]*Meister v. Illinois Central Railroad*, 832 F.2d 1427, at 1436 (7th Cir. 1987).
[7]*Hazelwood School District v. United States*, 433 U.S. 299, at 308 (1977).

EEOC V. JOE'S STONE CRAB
220 F.3d 1263 (11th Cir. 2000)

OPINION BY CIRCUIT JUDGE MARCUS:

This is the paradigmatic "hard" case, and we have labored for many months to reach the right result. On appeal, Defendant,

Joe's Stone Crab, Inc. ("Joe's"), challenges the district court's entry of judgment in favor of Plaintiff, the Equal Employment Opportunity Commission (the "EEOC"), on its gender-based disparate impact claims under Title VII. Joe's is a landmark Miami Beach seafood restaurant which from 1986 to 1990 hired 108 male food

servers and zero female food servers. After the EEOC filed its discrimination charge in June 1991, Joe's hired 88 food servers from 1991 to 1995, nineteen, or roughly 21.7%, of whom were female. The district court concluded that while Joe's was not liable for intentional discrimination, it was liable for disparate impact discrimination based on these statistical disparities. After thorough review, we vacate the district court judgment, and remand for reconsideration of the EEOC's intentional discrimination claim consistent with this opinion. * * *

To hire new food servers, Joe's conducts a "roll call" every year on the second Tuesday in October. Although Joe's rarely advertises, significantly, the district court found that the roll call is "widely known throughout the local food server community," and typically attracts over 100 applicants for only a limited number of slots. At a typical roll call, each applicant completes a written application and an individual interview. Selected applicants then enter a three-day training program where they shadow experienced servers. Upon successful completion of the program, they then become permanent hires.

Until the EEOC's charge, roll call interviews and hiring selections were handled exclusively by the daytime maitre d' with occasional interview assistance from other staff members. Hiring decisions were made by the daytime maitre d' on the basis of four subjective factors (appearance, articulation, attitude, and experience) and without upper management supervision or the benefit of instructive written or verbal policies. After the EEOC's discrimination charge in 1991, Joe's changed its roll call format somewhat. All applicant interviews were conducted by three members of Joe's management. In addition, each applicant was required to take and pass a "tray test," which involved the lifting and carrying of a loaded serving tray, or else be automatically disqualified from a food server position. The district court found the tray test to be a "legitimate indicator of an individual's ability to perform an essential component of a food server's job at Joe's," and that "women have the physical strength to carry serving trays." * * *

The first and central issue in this appeal is whether the district court erred in finding that the EEOC had established disparate impact discrimination * * *

[I]t is critical to observe that no statistically-significant disparity exists between the percentage of women who actually applied to Joe's and the percentage of women who were hired as servers by Joe's. The record indicates that for the pre-charge period (October 1986 to June 1991) very few female food servers

applied to Joe's, "perhaps 3% of [all] applicants," out of an actual applicant pool of between 80 and 120 people a year. In this five-year time period, 108 male food servers were hired and no women were hired. Despite the fact that no women were hired during this period, Joe's pre-charge hiring rate demonstrated no significant statistical disparity because so few women actually applied for food server positions. For the post-charge period (July 1991 to December 1995), the district court found that, on average, 22.02% of Joe's food server applicants were women and that Joe's hired roughly 21.7% women for these positions. Both parties admit (as they must) that, based on this record, there is no statistically-significant hiring disparity when the actual number of female applicants is compared to the actual number of female hires for either period. * * *

The district court recognized that the number of women who actually applied for server positions at Joe's was disproportionately low when compared with the number of women in the Miami Beach area who were seemingly qualified for such positions. There was, in fact, a significant statistical disparity between the percentage of female applicants to Joe's during the pre- and post-charge periods and the percentage of female applicants to comparable area restaurants. Joe's female applicant percentage of 3% and 22.02% for the pre and post-charge periods respectively varied sharply from the female applicant percentage of area restaurants which ranged from 29.5% to 42.1%. As a result of these findings, the district court found the actual applicant flow data to be "unreliable because it is skewed." It concluded that the data was skewed because of the pronounced self-selection of women out of Joe's hiring process. The district court then expressly rejected the actual applicant flow data in favor of an alternative labor pool consisting of those local food servers who were theoretically "available" and "qualified" to work at Joe's.

After hearing testimony from the expert witnesses of both parties, the district court arrived at an "eligible" labor pool, based on 1990 census data refined for qualification/experience on the basis of past earning capacity, which was 31.9% female. The district court then used this alternative labor data and compared it to Joe's actual hire statistics. By comparing Joe's pre-charge female hiring percentage (0%) with the percentage of women in the qualified labor market (31.9%), the district court created a legally-cognizable statistical disparity. * * *

The central problem in this case, however, is that the district court has identified no facially neutral employment practice responsible for the gender disparity in Joe's food server population, and we can find none. The EEOC and the district court have identified, at most, two neutral employment practices on which to ground a disparate impact analysis: first, Joe's word-of-mouth recruiting, and second, Joe's "undirected and undisciplined delegation of hiring authority to subordinate staff," resulting in its subjective "roll call" hiring process. Disparate impact analysis fails in this case because neither neutral practice can be causally connected to the gender disparity.

First, there is no evidence that Joe's word-of-mouth recruiting method caused any disparity between the percentage of women in the qualified labor pool and the percentage of women actually hired by Joe's as servers. Notably, this is not a case where Joe's formal recruiting practices or its informal word-of-mouth recruiting network kept women from learning about available jobs at Joe's. Rather, the district court specifically found quite the opposite, namely that local female food servers knew about the availability of positions at Joe's and the logistical details of Joe's hiring roll calls. Indeed, it observed that although the hiring roll calls were "rarely advertised," they were "widely known throughout the local food server community." No woman testified that she failed to apply for a position at Joe's because she was unaware of Joe's roll call method for filling openings. Plainly, the disparity between the percentage of women in the qualified labor pool and the percentage of women actually hired as servers by Joe's cannot be causally linked to Joe's word-of-mouth recruiting process because this practice in no way prevented women from applying to or being hired by Joe's.

Nor is there any evidence that Joe's facially neutral, albeit undisciplined and subjective, hiring practices caused the disparity the district court found between the percentage of women in the qualified labor pool and the percentage of women actually hired as servers by Joe's. There is no evidence that Joe's subjective hiring criteria either caused women not to apply to Joe's or caused those who applied not to be hired. * * *

The district court, recognizing that it could not causally connect Joe's neutral, albeit subjective, recruiting and hiring practices with the disparity between the percentage of women in the qualified labor pool and the percentage of women actually hired as servers by Joe's, identified Joe's reputation as a discriminator against women as the causal agent for the disparity. For the district court, Joe's reputation for not hiring female food servers acted as the essential bridge connecting the neutral practices to the statistical disparity. * * * Because of Joe's reputation for discriminating, the district court essentially found, women did not apply to Joe's and therefore were not hired as servers. * * *

While a company may be held liable for a discriminatory reputation if there is evidence it caused or perpetuated that reputation through some intentional affirmative act, we know of no federal circuit that has found an employer liable under Title VII on the basis of a reputation for discrimination it did not cause. Nor are we prepared to impose on an employer an affirmative duty under Title VII to ameliorate a public reputation not attributable to its own employment conduct. * * *

That said, the record extant and some of the district court's findings of fact can be read to support the alternate conclusion that Joe's management intentionally excluded women from food serving positions in order to provide its customers with an "Old World," fine-dining ambience. Thus, for example, the district court found that "Joe's management acquiesced in and gave silent approbation to the notion that male food servers were preferable to female food servers." At another point in its findings, the district court observed that "Joe's sought to emulate Old World traditions by creating an amience in which tuxedo-clad men served its distinctive menu." Moreover, the district court apparently also credited the testimony of one of Joe's former hiring maitre d', Roy Garrett, who explained that Joe's was "a male server type of job" by tradition. As a result, the district court said that "women have systematically been excluded from the most lucrative entry level position, that of server." Finally, the district court found that this historical practice of hiring only men was responsible for Joe's "male-only" reputation. The district court held that "Joe's reputation in the community, which reflected the restaurant's historical hiring practice, led potential female applicants not to apply for server positions. Joe's reputation, therefore, was largely responsible for the gender skew in the pool of applicants at the annual roll call."

But, these factual findings do not mesh easily with a disparate impact theory because they suggest that Joe's hiring system was not in practice facially neutral, but rather was facially discriminatory on the basis of gender. They suggest the conclusion that in fact Joe's had a desired preference for male servers and that this preference influenced the hiring decisions of Joe's decision

makers, resulting in the deliberate and systematic exclusion of women as food servers. If this were true, Joe's could be found liable for intentional discrimination in violation of Title VII. * * *

At bottom then, this case really centers around the theory that women refrained from making the "futile gesture," of applying to Joe's when they knew that Joe's only hired men as food servers. If Joe's reputation came from anything causally attributable to the restaurant, it emanated from Joe's own purportedly discriminatory hiring practices, not from the specific facially neutral practices identified by the district court. * * * [W]e cannot affirm a disparate impact judgment where the case centers entirely around allegations and evidence of intentional discrimination. The record does not support it, and to do so would unwisely conflate the distinct theories of disparate impact and disparate treatment. * * *

CASE QUESTIONS

1. What did the appeals court decide? Why?

2. What if Joe's customers prefer male waiters? Would it make any difference if Joe's could show that, in general, women have more difficulty carrying the heavy food trays? That Joe's hires women for other jobs, including as managers?

3. How are statistics used in this case? What comparisons are made? Does the statistical evidence show discrimination?

4. Why does the court conclude that this case is better viewed as a disparate treatment case than a disparate (adverse) impact case?

5. What would you suggest that this employer do differently?

The appeals court remanded (sent back for further consideration) this case to the district court. On remand, the district court ruled in favor of the EEOC, holding that Joe's Stone Crab had intentionally discriminated on the basis of sex in recruiting and hiring table servers. In its ruling, the district court said that "Joe's *implicit* policy of hiring only male food servers gave rise to a deserved, well-known reputation that Joe's discriminated against female food servers. This reputation, in turn, caused many qualified females not to apply at Joe's for food server positions."[8] Proving that it's never over 'til it's over in litigation, the case made a second trip back to the appeals court. The appeals court upheld the finding against Joe's but only with respect to two out of the four named plaintiffs in the case. The difference was that evidence proved that these two plaintiffs "possessed a real and present interest" in applying for jobs at Joe's during the period in question and were dissuaded from doing so by acquaintances who told them that Joe's did not hire women as waiters.[9]

Recruitment Mechanisms

We turn now to particular recruitment mechanisms, including want ads, employment agencies, nepotism, and "word of mouth." All are used by employers and none are inherently discriminatory. However, all these mechanisms have the potential to be instruments of discrimination. In light of this, *employers should use multiple recruitment mechanisms rather than rely solely on any one mechanism.* This helps to compensate for the potential exclusionary effects of any single mechanism. Equal employment opportunity is enhanced when employers *disseminate information about employment opportunities as broadly as is feasible,* limited by a reasonable understanding of the geographic extent of the labor market and cost considerations in light of the importance of the position.

[8]*EEOC v. Joe's Stone Crab,* 136 F. Supp 2d 1311, at 1313 (S.D. Fla. 2001).

[9]*Equal Employment Opportunity Commission v. Joe's Stone Crab,* 296 F.3d 1265, at 1275 (11th Cir. 2002).

Want Ads and Job Announcements A typical early step in the recruitment process is to produce documents that announce the availability of a job, describe the job and its requirements, and tell prospective applicants what they must do to apply. These documents are then printed in newspapers or professional magazines, posted on bulletin boards, put on the Internet, or otherwise made available for inspection. Title VII of the Civil Rights Act of 1964 is explicit about employers' obligation in producing such materials:

> It shall be an unlawful practice for an employer . . . to print or publish or cause to be printed or published any notice or advertisement related to employment . . . indicating any preference, limitation, specification, or discrimination, based on race, color, religion, sex, or national origin. . . .[10]

Other discrimination laws contain similar prohibitions. The clear message is that *the wording of want ads and other types of job announcements must be neutral.* It cannot express or imply a preference for some protected class group over another. Sex-linked job titles are not neutral. An employer who advertises for a "waitress" is signaling that it expects to hire a woman and is discouraging males from applying. Terms like *young people* or *recent college grad* imply a preference for persons under 40 and tend to discourage applications from older workers. However, courts will consider whether such terms articulate requirements for particular positions or merely suggest groups of people who might be interested in employment.[11]

The content of want ads and job announcements is one matter; where they are published or posted is another. Employers are free to publish neutrally worded ads in publications that are targeted toward particular protected class groups (e.g., a foreign language newspaper). However, if that is all the employer does to get the word out about an employment opportunity, it is likely to produce discriminatory effects. Thus, *employers using narrowly targeted outlets should use these in conjunction with other media that reach a broader spectrum of employees.*

Employers, particularly those with affirmative action plans, often include in job announcements language to the effect that applications from women and minorities are encouraged. Such statements, although not required, do not violate the neutrality principle. They are intended to address the reluctance that women and persons of color might have to pursue employment opportunities given the history of employment discrimination against members of these groups. They also signal that employers are aware of their legal responsibilities and do not intend to discriminate.

Finally, although we have assumed that the employer has produced and disseminated a job announcement of some kind, this is not a foregone conclusion. Employers are under no specific legal requirement to do so, but when information is orally conveyed to a select few and denied everyone else, the hiring process looks very suspect. Failure to post job information and make it available to broader audiences is a common complaint in discrimination cases. For example, in a case successfully challenging the *Boston Herald*'s practices in hiring pressroom workers, the plaintiffs pointed to the paper's failure to both post job announcements in the workplace and to advertise vacancies to the public.[12] Thus, implicit in all the foregoing, is that *employers should, in fact, create written job announcements and disseminate them.*

[10]42 U.S.C.A. § 2000e-3(b) (2001).

[11]*Hodgson v. Approved Personnel Service, Inc.,* 529 F.2d 760 (4th Cir. 1975).

[12]*Gaines et al. v. Boston Herald,* 998 F. Supp 91, at 106 (Mass. 1998).

Employment Agencies Employees are sometimes recruited and hired through employment agencies. Employment agencies can simply refer employees to employers or function more like temporary staffing firms that continue to be the employers (or joint employers) of the employees that they assign to host companies. In either event, employment agencies are covered by antidiscrimination laws and are expressly prohibited from discriminating against employees in referrals or in any other manner.[13] The difficulty here is that employment agencies are businesses. Businesses do well when they make their customers happy. Employers with discriminatory preferences, however subtly conveyed, can put pressure on employment agencies to comply. If employment agencies do so, they violate the law. The case against the New York City employment agencies supplying domestic workers (see "Clippings"), in which the employment agencies screened referrals on the basis of race and national origin, seemed to go even further; the agencies actively solicited racial and other preferences from prospective employers. Employers who make such requests of employment agencies are also violating the law. *Employers must not request that employment agencies refer employees with particular protected class characteristics, nor should they attempt to obtain through employment agencies information about protected class characteristics of referrals that it would be improper for them to obtain directly.*

In a case involving two employment agencies,[14] the EEOC found evidence that the agencies were using a coding system to convey information about the protected class characteristics of prospective referrals and the discriminatory preferences of client employers. For example, "FLOOR 40" was the code used to designate persons over 40 years of age. "TALK TO ADAM" was one of the codes designating that the employer preferred or required male employees. The EEOC went to court to stop the agencies from erasing the coding data from their computers, after being informed by a former employee that she had been instructed to destroy the evidence in anticipation of an investigation. There were also allegations that one of the agencies had received, and honored, a request from IBM Japan that only Japanese employees be referred. Regarding its own internal hiring practices, there were charges that a supervisor at one of the agencies refused to hire an African American as a receptionist because she was "afraid of them" and thought "they were scarey [sic]." It is telling that the supervisor attempted to justify the discrimination by pointing out that if one of the company's many Japanese clients "saw a black face" at the office, the agency would lose the company's business. However, the discriminatory preferences of a customer or client are not a defense to discrimination charges. Regarding the purported preference of senior community residents for white employees (see "Clippings"), an EEOC official stated "Even if customers might prefer to be served by individuals who are a particular race or color or sex . . . the employer is not entitled to commit discrimination."

Nepotism and Word-of-Mouth Hiring Nepotism refers to a preference for family members and other relatives. Civil service laws typically prohibit nepotism in the hiring practices of government agencies because it is contrary to the principle that jobs should be awarded on the basis of merit. Large private sector companies often have policies discouraging nepotism. On the other hand, nepotism is probably common among smaller, private employers and in certain occupations. Because relatives are most often of the same race or national origin, nepotism

[13]Title VII, Civil Rights Act of 1964, 42 U.S.C.A. § 2000e-2(b) (2001).

[14]*EEOC v. Recruit U.S.A. and Interplace/Transworld Recruit, Inc.*, 939 F.2d 746 (9th Cir. 1991).

results in hiring people who are similar in certain protected class characteristics to the people who already work in the company. The aggregate effect of this practice depends on what proportion of positions are filled in this manner and how racially homogenous the workforce is currently. In one relevant case, a policy of nepotism in hiring schoolteachers (civil service laws either did not exist in this case or were ignored) resulted in the virtual exclusion of African Americans. Teaching positions were posted in each school, but not advertised to the public. Relatives of school employees were both more likely to learn about the availability of jobs and were preferred in the selection process. Finding against the school district on an adverse impact claim, the court stated: "Nepotism is not per se violative of Title VII. Given an already integrated work force, nepotism might have no impact on the racial composition of that work force. * * * However, when the work force is predominantly white, nepotism and similar practices which operate to exclude outsiders may discriminate against minorities as effectively as any intentionally discriminatory policy."[15]

Word-of-mouth recruiting is often allied with nepotism and has similar potential to result in discrimination. In word of mouth, employers depend on current employees to spread the word about jobs to their friends, family members, and other associates. To be sure, networks of contacts are frequently the key to success in the labor market. From an employer's perspective, word of mouth is essentially costless. It can also be effective because current employees are able to provide realistic job previews to prospective employees, and they are unlikely to approach persons whom they think are unsuitable, lest the employer blame them for bad referrals. Again, the threat to equal employment opportunity stems from the fact that people tend to associate with others who are like them, especially in terms of race. If an employer's workforce is racially diverse, current employees referring persons of their own race is not a problem because persons of all races will still be referred. But if the employer's current workforce is racially homogenous, heavy reliance on word-of-mouth recruiting will reproduce a racially skewed workforce. The latter was the case at the Carl Buddig meat processing plants, as the employer relied heavily upon referrals from its existing, all white workforce (see "Clippings").

The discriminatory potential of word-of-mouth recruiting is clear. However, the case law in this area is limited and not entirely consistent. A federal appeals court found that a union that required new members to be "sponsored" by existing members (who were all white) discriminated by creating adverse impact.[16] But another appeals court found a small employer's use of word of mouth to not be discriminatory, despite strong statistical evidence of a skewed applicant pool.[17] The rationale in the latter case was that there was insufficient evidence of discriminatory intent and that the employer's passive reliance on word of mouth was not an "employment practice" suitable for adverse impact analysis. In *Joe's Stone Crab*, the court concluded that heavy reliance on word of mouth to communicate about the annual "roll calls" did not disadvantage women because these recruiting sessions were held at the same time each year and the local community of food service workers was sufficiently aware of them.

Although the courts are not entirely of one mind, a sensible conclusion is that *employers should not rely solely on nepotism and word of mouth, especially where their workforces are already homogenous in terms of race and national origin.*

[15] *Thomas v. Washington County School Board*, 915 F.2d 922, at 925 (4th Cir. 1990).

[16] *Equal Employment Opportunity Commission v. Steamship Clerks Union*, 48 F.3d 594 (1st Cir. 1995).

[17] *EEOC v. Consolidated Service Systems*, 989 F.2d 233 (7th Cir. 1993).

THE CHANGING WORKPLACE

Recruiting Foreign Nationals for U.S. Employment

In an increasingly global labor market, the production of goods and services is often outsourced to workers in other countries. Alternatively, and subject to complex immigration laws,[1] persons who are not citizens can sometimes come to the United States to perform work here. Foreign nationals (citizens of other countries) working in the United States are either immigrants who intend to reside in this country and perhaps become citizens or nonimmigrants who come to the United States to work for specified periods of time. Professional sports teams are not the only U.S. employers looking to recruit foreign nationals. Our growing dependence on persons from other countries to fill positions in the sciences and engineering is a source of concern.[2] Many seasonal resort areas rely heavily on temporary labor from other countries.[3] Heightened national security concerns have added to the uncertainty and complexity of using the foreign national labor pool.

Foreign nationals that do not have permanent resident status (i.e., have a "green card") must obtain **visas** that will permit them to work in the United States. Many visa classifications serve this purpose. Among the most relevant are H-1 visas for persons of distinguished merit and ability, H-2 visas for temporary workers (including thousands of agricultural "guest workers"), L-1 visas for intracompany transfers (allowing the transfer of high-level employees from foreign subsidiaries or branches of the same company), and TN visas for highly skilled employees from Canada or Mexico.[4] Students from other countries are typically here under the F-1 visa classification (for students) or the J-1 classification (for exchange visitors). The latter two statuses allow persons to be employed to receive practical training related to their course of study, although employer sponsorship and conversion to another visa classification is required to continue in longer-term employment.

The **H-1B visa classification** has received much attention recently. Employer groups argue that the number of these visas granted each year must be increased, although others suggest that there is no real shortage of skilled workers in the United States and that employers simply want to drive wages down.[5] H-1B visas are granted to persons in "specialty occupations" that require a bachelor's or higher degree in that field. Typical occupations for recipients of these visas include systems analysts, engineers, architects, and accountants. An H-1B visa limits the employee's stay to six years, regardless of the number of employers for which he worked. Readmission to the United States in the same or another classification can only occur after the employee remains outside of the United States for at least a year. The number of H-1B visas granted each year fluctuates, but is currently capped at about 65,000.

Employers wanting to hire foreign nationals with H-1B visas must first file a Labor Condition Application form with the Department of Labor. Employers must attest that they will pay their H-1B visa holders at least the local prevailing wage or the employer's actual wage, whichever is greater; offer benefits on the same basis as for their U.S. workers; provide working conditions that will not adversely affect those of other workers similarly employed; not use H-1B visa holders to perform work during a strike or lockout; and provide prior notice to existing employees and any union representatives of the intent to use H-1B visa holders. There are additional requirements for so-called "H-1B dependent employers." In general, these are employers for whom H-1B visa holders make up 15 percent or more of their total workforces. H-1B dependent employers must attest that they have not displaced U.S. workers by hiring H-1B visa holders and have attempted to recruit U.S. workers for the jobs. H-1B dependent employers are required to offer jobs to U.S. workers when their qualifications are equal to or better than those of H-1B workers.

Problems sometimes arise when employers that are sponsoring H-1B visa holders decide that they want to temporarily lay those employees off or pay them less than the amounts stated in their filings with the Department of Labor. The Department of Labor's case against the Pegasus Consulting Group illustrates this point (see "Clippings"). The firm had placed H-1B visa holders on temporary layoff and stopped paying them. But the law generally requires that H-1B visa holders must be paid at their specified rates unless they are terminated and their H-1B petitions withdrawn.[6] Employers that want to terminate H-1B visa holders prior to the end of their contracts must notify the

U.S. Citizenship and Immigration Services (formerly the INS) and pay to return them to their home countries.

L-1 visas, designed to allow multinational companies to temporarily transfer staff from foreign facilities or subsidiaries to operations in the United States, have also come under increased scrutiny. These visas are attractive to employers because their number is not capped and they carry fewer restrictions than H-1B visas. For example, there is no requirement that L-1 visa holders be paid at least the prevailing rate. In response to reports that L-1 visas were being routinely used to bring foreign nationals to the United States—who were then contracted out to other companies, displacing American workers—Congress passed the the L-1 Visa Reform Act in 2004. The law now requires that companies using L-1 visa holders must station those employees at the companies' own facilities and retain ultimate supervisory authority over them.[7]

In practice then, *employers who recruit nonimmigrant foreign nationals to perform work in the United* *States must be prepared to comply with the numerous and varying requirements attached to the different visa classifications, to monitor the duration of their workers' employment, and to file the necessary petitions and paperwork.*

[1] Immigration and Nationality Act, 8 U.S.C. §§ 1101, et seq. (2005). American Competitiveness in the 21st Century Act, P.L. 106-313 (2000).

[2] James Glanz. "Study Warns of Lack of Scientists as Visa Applications Drop." *New York Times* (November 20, 2003), A-24.

[3] Denny Lee. "Fewer Visas, Fewer Resort Workers." *New York Times* (June 10, 2005), D-1.

[4] Kenneth A. Jenero and Caterina P. Tassone. "Staying Competitive in the Twenty-First Century: Visa Alternatives for Global Employers." *Employee Relations Law Journal* 27 (Summer 2001), 105–116.

[5] "H-1B Visa Program is Misused to Import Cheap Labor, Analysis of Wage Data Concludes," *Daily Labor Report* 3 (January 5, 2006), A-5.

[6] Marc Topoleski and Greg Siskind. "Cut Down Immigration Downsizing Risks." *HR Magazine* (July 2001), 107-08.

[7] "DHS to Require Employers to Retain Authority Over Certain Foreign Transferees." *Daily Labor Report* 121 (June 24, 2005), A-1.

APPLICATIONS AND INTERVIEWS

Application Process

By and large, employers decide whether applications will be accepted from anyone (they do not have to accept applications if there are no current or anticipated employment opportunities), what must be done to apply (e.g., will a resume suffice or only a completed application form?), the period of time for which applications will be accepted, and how long submitted applications will remain valid. The main guideline here is to avoid disparate treatment by *establishing an application policy and adhering to it consistently.* The application process should be the same for everyone seeking the same job. There should not be, as there was in one case, different application forms for persons applying for the same positions (with friends and relatives of current employees receiving lengthier, "insider" applications).[18] Codes marked on applications designating protected class information, such as in the Georgetown Place case (see "Clippings"), strongly suggest the intent to discriminate and should never be used. Additionally, *if an employer is seeking applications, no individuals wanting to apply should be discouraged from doing so.* Certainly, candidates should be informed about the requirements of jobs, but even candidates who do not at first glance appear promising should be allowed to apply and have their applications treated in the same manner as other applications. A person not

[18]*Gaines,* at 107.

allowed to apply or discouraged from doing so would still be able to establish a prima facie case of disparate treatment, despite having not applied. Further, the basis for this type of preemptory snap judgment about an applicant is open to question. There is a real chance that it was based on some superficial protected class characteristic.

Another consideration is that employers are required to maintain records regarding the protected class characteristics of applicants for such purposes as tracking progress in affirmative action and determining whether selection devices (e.g., employment tests) have adverse impact. The federal government's definition of **applicant** is broad, including any person who indicates an interest in being considered for an employment opportunity. The increased use of Web sites, Internet job banks, and e-mail to search for jobs has prompted employer concerns about having to obtain and maintain information on large numbers of "applicants." Arguably, the low cost and ease of inquiring about or applying for jobs electronically encourages more casual inquiries, many of which may come from unqualified persons or may come in the absence of position openings. Rules are in the process of being finalized that narrow the definition of applicant and corresponding record keeping burden on employers when electronic means are used. An applicant will be deemed to exist only when an employer has acted to fill a particular position, the job seeker has followed the employer's standard procedures for submitting applications, and the job seeker has indicated interest in a particular open position.[19]

Recall that failing to reasonably accommodate qualified disabled persons is also a form of discrimination. The legal obligation to reasonably accommodate begins in the recruitment process and not just after a disabled person is hired. Thus, *employers must be prepared to accommodate disabled persons in the recruitment and application process,* such as by providing job information orally or on cassette, assisting visually impaired persons in completing application forms, or by ensuring that interview sites are accessible to persons in wheelchairs. Accommodation of religion can also be an issue at the application and interview stage. *Inquiries about availability for weekend work should be accompanied by a statement that the employer will attempt to reasonably accommodate religious practices, including observation of Sabbaths, unless doing so would impose undue hardship.* Employers have a legitimate interest in finding workers who can work when they are needed. But simply excluding persons who indicate limitations on their availability or raising the issue without any indication that accommodation might be possible amounts to limitation of employment opportunity based on religion.

Application forms serve a useful function by eliciting standard, basic information from all applicants. Without getting too far ahead of ourselves, we can say that employers are advised to *include on applications statements relating to the conditions under which employment can be terminated.* These statements, and the agreement of prospective employees as indicated by their signatures on application forms, can help employers defend wrongful termination suits by cementing employment at-will status (see Chapter 18). For a different set of legal reasons (see Chapter 5), employers should also *use the application form to obtain the consent of prospective employees to contact and get information from employment references.* EEOC guidelines[20] require that *application forms, and any other documents produced in the hiring process, be kept for at least a year from when a hiring decision is made.*

[19] 69 F.R. 10152, at 10155 (March 4, 2004).
[20] 29 C.F.R. § 1602.14 (2005).

Application forms and other documents related to persons hired should be retained throughout their employment and for at least a year thereafter.

Preemployment Inquiries

To avoid discrimination in hiring, it is essential that employers not ask questions whose answers reveal the protected class characteristics of job candidates. Questions on application forms, during interviews, or in the course of informal chatting with job candidates can all end up divulging information about employees that potentially taints the hiring process. What kinds of questions or inquiries are we talking about? Inadvisable **preemployment inquiries** fall into four general categories.

First, *employers should not directly inquire about protected class characteristics.* Remember that protected class characteristics include race, sex, religion, national origin, age, and disability. If, for example, an application form asks the applicant to check male or female or Mr. or Mrs./Ms, these are direct inquiries about the protected class of sex. Similarly, asking candidates for their age, where they were born (national origin), or whether they have a disability, all constitute direct inquiries into protected class characteristics. This information should not be sought prior to hiring because it can, consciously or not, affect employment decisions and result in disparate treatment. *Information that is needed for other purposes (such as age for participation in a pension plan) can be obtained following the decision to hire (but still kept separate from an employee's regular personnel file).*

Employers who want to track the protected class characteristics of their applicants for affirmative action purposes can do so by providing a voluntary reporting mechanism that is separate from the application form or other materials used by persons deciding whom to hire. Also, as Figure 4-1 illustrates, there are often lawful alternatives to prohibited preemployment inquiries that provide necessary information without crossing the line into questions about protected class. For example, rather than ask for a candidate's age, the employer can ask whether she is at least 18 years of age (which is necessary to perform certain jobs and does not discriminate against persons over 40). Similarly, rather than ask whether a job candidate is a U.S. citizen, it is preferable to ask whether, if hired, he will be able to verify his eligibility to work in the United States. This helps prevent discrimination against those noncitizens who have the legal right to work in the United States (e.g., because they hold "green cards").

Second, and slightly less obvious, *employers should not indirectly inquire about the protected class characteristics of job candidates.* Examples of indirect inquiries include asking for an applicant's date of graduation from high school (age), a listing of all organizational memberships (race, religion, national origin, etc.), and whether the candidate has ever filed a workers' compensation claim for a workplace injury (disability). Again, the concern is with getting information about protected class, leading to disparate treatment. If the employer wants to know *whether* someone has graduated from high school, that is what should be asked, rather than *when* the person graduated. Similarly, questions about professional or work-related organizational affiliations are appropriate, whereas inquiries about all organizational affiliations are not.

Third, *employers should avoid questions about requirements or criteria that are not uniformly applied to job candidates.* This is particularly an issue with respect to sex. Questions about marital status, child-rearing plans, and childcare arrangements, and the answers to those questions, are sometimes treated differently depending upon whether the candidate is a man or a woman. Applying different

FIGURE 4-1	Inadvisable Preemployment Inquiries
Inadvisable:	What is your date of birth?
Alternative:	Are you at least 18 years of age?
Inadvisable:	Are you a U.S. citizen?
Alternative:	After being hired, will you be able to document your eligibility for work in the United States?
Inadvisable:	Do you have any health problems that would affect your employment?
Alternative:	Conduct a medical exam following a conditional offer of employment or ask the candidate to demonstrate how a particular job-related task would be performed.
Inadvisable:	Are you available to work on weekends?
Alternative:	Are you available to work on weekends? We will make an effort to accommodate religious practices.
Inadvisable:	Have you ever been arrested or convicted of any crime?
Alternative:	Have you ever been convicted of a crime? Answering yes will not automatically disqualify you, but you must provide details about the conviction.
Inadvisable:	Please list all organizations to which you belong.
Alternative:	Please list all professional associations and other work-related organizations to which you belong.
Inadvisable:	What was your maiden name?
Alternative:	Please list all names that you have used.
Inadvisable:	How many children do you have?
Alternative:	If number of dependents must be known for benefit plan participation, this information can be obtained after hire.

selection criteria to different protected class groups is again disparate treatment. Additionally, in those states where marital status is a protected class under state law, questions about marital status would be direct inquiries about protected class. Employers with concerns about these matters should clearly explain the requirements of positions and ask all employees if they anticipate any difficulty in meeting them.

Fourth, *employers should avoid questions about requirements that have a high probability of producing adverse impact.* These are requirements that are likely to screen out some protected class groups more than others and for which there is not strong evidence of job-relatedness. Examples include questions about prior arrests, type of military discharge, and height and weight.

Notice what we have *not* said: that employers must only ask questions about things that are job related. Although this is a very good idea, the law does not require it. The law requires the employer to refrain from asking questions eliciting information that could be used to discriminate. For the most part, intrusive inquiries relating to

a candidate's personal life, although objectionable on ethical grounds, will not subject employers to liability.

Clearly, it is important to *train interviewers to conduct employment interviews in a lawful manner.* A structured interview format in which each interviewee is asked the same predetermined questions, although not legally required, can help eliminate questions relating to protected class. However, many individuals are often involved with interviewing or asking questions of job candidates, and other managers or support personnel (e.g., receptionists) can have exchanges with job candidates and say inappropriate things. Thus, recruiters and interviewers are not the only employees who need to be aware of the law.

Is an employer breaking the law if he asks questions relating to protected class, but does not use that information in making hiring decisions? The answer to this question becomes a bit complicated, so let's return to a basic point. The prohibition of certain preemployment inquiries is a device for lessening the influence of protected class characteristics on employment decisions. The device is rather limited, however, because an employer who wants to discriminate can glean much information about protected class (e.g., by viewing candidates at interviews, by looking at the length of a person's work history, or by drawing inferences from a person's name) without ever asking a question. Nevertheless, knowledge of protected class characteristics can creep into employment decisions unconsciously and without any overt racist, sexist, or other discriminatory sentiments on the part of decision makers. Refraining from inquiries related to protected class diminishes the chance of this occurring, especially in the very early part of the recruitment and hiring process before candidates have had the opportunity to have their credentials evaluated.

Although the EEOC strongly discourages employers from making such preemployment inquiries, most federal antidiscrimination laws (with the notable exception of the ADA) do not explicitly prohibit them, and the EEOC will not find reasonable cause of discrimination solely on this basis. On the other hand, many state antidiscrimination laws do expressly prohibit such inquiries. In either case, however, asking questions about protected class is most likely to have legal repercussions when someone is actually denied an employment opportunity. Not only does asking these questions make a job candidate suspicious of an employer's motives and more likely to challenge a rejection, but it also provides evidence that the employer was aware of the candidate's protected class characteristics and interested enough to ask about them. Thus, preemployment inquiries become evidence of discriminatory intent in disparate treatment cases.

Medical Inquiries Prior to a Conditional Offer of Employment The Americans with Disabilities Act (ADA) differs from other federal antidiscrimination laws in directly prohibiting preemployment inquiries related to medical information about job candidates. Wal-Mart's preemployment questionnaire violated the ADA by requiring applicants to provide information about their medical conditions (see "Clippings"). This particular provision of the ADA is necessary; otherwise, it would be all too easy for employers to dismiss disabled persons as unable to work, too costly to insure, and so forth. But does this prohibition also protect employees who are not disabled? *Griffin v. Steeltek* addresses this important question.

Griffin won this important "battle" over the interpretation of the ADA, but he subsequently lost the "war." Although Griffin could sue despite not being a disabled person, he had to show that the adverse employment action (being denied the position) was based on the medical information obtained through the employer's improper inquiries. On remand, the district court decided that the employer had other lawful reasons for not hiring him. He was not entitled to damages based solely

GRIFFIN V. STEELTEK

160 F.3d 591 (10th Cir. 1998), cert. denied, 526 U.S. 1065 (1999)

OPINION BY CIRCUIT JUDGE EBEL:

This case requires us to determine whether a non-disabled individual has a cause of action under the Americans with Disabilities Act (ADA), when as a job applicant he or she is asked questions regarding his or her medical history or condition on an employment application. We conclude that in light of the language of the statute and the purposes of its enactment, a non-disabled job applicant does have such a cause of action. Consequently, we reverse the district court's grant of summary judgment in favor of the employer in this case.

Plaintiff-Appellant Randy Griffin ("Griffin"), a non-disabled individual, applied for a position as a grinder with Defendant-Appellee Steeltek, Inc. ("Steeltek"). Griffin was not hired for the position, allegedly because he did not have the two years of grinding experience required by Steeltek. According to Griffin, he was never told that Steeltek required two years of grinding experience, and in fact was told at the time he applied that he was the best qualified applicant for the position.

After Steeltek declined to hire Griffin, Griffin filed suit in the Northern District of Oklahoma, contending that Steeltek's application process violated the ADA, 42 U.S.C. § 12112(d)(2)(A). That section prohibits employers from asking a job applicant "whether such applicant is an individual with a disability or as to the nature or severity of such disability." Griffin identified two questions on Steeltek's employment application that allegedly violated [the ADA]. The first question asked: "Have you received Worker's Compensation or Disability Income payments? If yes, describe." The second asked: "Have you physical defects which preclude you from performing certain jobs? If yes, describe." In response to the first question, Griffin wrote "3 degree burn to hand & foot, surgery to elbow, spain [sic] in shoulder." He left the answer space blank in response to the second question. Griffin did not contend that he was disabled or that Steeltek perceived him to be disabled. Rather, the sole basis of Griffin's claim was that Steeltek violated the ADA by asking these two questions and then by not hiring him because of his responses to these improper questions. * * *

The district court held that "because [Griffin] has failed to allege either that he was disabled or perceived as disabled as defined under the ADA, he has not established a prima facie case of disability discrimination." Hence, Steeltek was entitled to summary judgment "as a matter of law." Because the district court ruled as a matter of law that Griffin had failed to establish a prima facie case because he was neither disabled nor perceived to be disabled, the court never reached the issue of whether Griffin was causally injured by being required to answer the impermissible questions. Additionally, the court did not rule whether Steeltek's proffered reason for not hiring Griffin—that he lacked two years of grinding experience—was pretextual. * * *

The issue we must decide is whether improper medical questions are actionable under § 12112(d)(2) if asked of a non-disabled applicant. Although we have never had occasion to analyze § 12112(d)(2), this court was recently called upon to construe § 12112(d)(4), the subsection prohibiting medical examinations and inquiries of current employees. See *Roe v. Cheyenne Mountain Conf. Resort, Inc.*, 124 F.3d 1221 (10th Cir. 1997). In *Roe*, defendant employers instituted a broad drug and alcohol testing policy that, inter alia [among other things], required employees to report to their supervisors any type of prescription medication they used. The plaintiff there, who was an employee of the defendant, claimed that this requirement violated § 12112(d)(4) and was granted summary judgment. * * *

Although the *Roe* panel [the group of circuit court judges that heard the case] specifically stated that it was not deciding the issue before us today pertaining to job applicants, we find that the reasoning articulated in *Roe* applies equally to § 12112(d)(2). The language of the two statutes is very similar. Section 12112(d)(2) uses the term "job applicant," while § 12112(d)(4) uses the term "employee." It is important that neither section uses the narrower defined term of "qualified individual with a disability," which is the term Congress used in much of § 12112 but chose not to use in § 12112(d)(2) or § 12112(d)(4). The use of terms in defining a broader class of people than the class specified elsewhere in the ADA (the class of qualified individuals with disabilities) cannot be accidental, and it points inextricably to the broader scope of coverage intended for those two sections.

In addition, the policy of the ADA is to eliminate disability discrimination. This policy is best served by allowing all job applicants who are subjected to illegal medical questioning and who are in fact injured thereby to bring a cause of action against offending employers, rather than to limit that right to a narrower subset of applicants who are in fact disabled. The legislative history of the ADA indicates that Congress wished to curtail all questioning that would serve to identify and exclude persons with disabilities from consideration for employment by drafting "a prohibition on pre-offer medical examinations or inquiries," and allowing non-disabled job applicants who are injured thereby to sue will enhance and enforce the blanket prohibition drafted by Congress. Furthermore, Congress was also concerned with the potential stigmatizing effect of medical inquiries and examinations, noting that individuals with diseases such as cancer "may object merely to being identified, independent of the consequences." If we were to require individuals to make a showing of disability . . . , we would in effect be making individuals with disabilities identify themselves as disabled to prevent potential employers from inquiring whether they have a disability. Such a course makes little sense. * * *

We note that the Fifth Circuit recently held that a non-disabled plaintiff could not proceed with a suit for being asked impermissible medical questions on an employment application. In that case, however, the court assumed without deciding that a non-disabled plaintiff did have a cause of action under § 12112(d)(2) and went on to determine whether a violation of that section alone constituted a compensable injury. The Fifth Circuit concluded that the applicant needed to show "some

cognizable injury in fact of which the violation is a legal and proximate cause for damages to arise from a single violation." Because the non-disabled applicant in that case could not show a cognizable injury caused by being asked the impermissible questions, the court concluded that he had failed to show entitlement to damages and affirmed the dismissal of his suit. However, the court held open the "possibility of liability based on any injuries legally and proximately caused by such a violation." In contrast . . . in our case Griffin has sufficiently alleged that he suffered an injury in fact, specifically that Steeltek did not hire Griffin because of his responses to the impermissible questions, and he seeks damages and injunctive relief to remedy his injury. Consequently, we hold that his suit can go forward. * * *

CASE QUESTIONS

1. What was the legal issue in this case? What did the court decide? Why?

2. What if the court had ruled otherwise? Would the purpose of prohibiting preemployment medical inquiries be defeated if this requirement applied only to disabled job candidates?

3. From this decision, do you think that a job applicant asked for medical information prior to an offer of employment would be able to sue even if he was hired? If he was not hired because of refusing to answer medical inquiries?

4. What should an employer do if it thinks that medical information on job candidates is needed? If it has concerns about whether a particular job candidate is physically able to perform a job?

on his being subjected to the questions, when he could not also prove that this had limited his employment opportunity.[21]

Employers must refrain from seeking medical information from all applicants, disabled or not. **Medical inquiries** include questions about disabilities, medical and psychological conditions, medical histories, medications taken, and workers' compensation claims filed. However, an employer who is concerned about a job candidate's ability to do a job is permitted to ask that candidate to demonstrate how he would do the job. Furthermore, the prohibition on medical inquiries applies only to preemployment inquiries. An employer who extends a "conditional offer of

[21]*Griffin v. Steeltek*, 2001 U.S. App. LEXIS 18917.

employment" to a job candidate (meaning that the person will be hired provided that the results of a medical exam are satisfactory) can make any type of medical inquiry or perform any type of medical exam at that point—provided that all persons hired to perform the same type of work are subjected to the same inquiries or exams. Thus, *employers who desire medical information from job candidates should seek that information only after job candidates have been conditionally offered employment based on their other qualifications*. However, such information still cannot be used to discriminate against qualified disabled persons who can perform the main parts of jobs ("essential functions") with or without reasonable accommodation.

Statements by Employers

Whereas recruiting and interviewing focus on extracting information from job candidates, employers also provide information and make statements that can have legal consequences. It is relatively easy for employers to downplay negative information that would scare away prospective employees or make promises regarding the expected duration of employment, promotions, or pay raises when trying to entice desired candidates to take jobs. Later, when circumstances change and the honeymoon period is over, misrepresentations and unfulfilled promises can give rise to a number of different legal claims, including **fraud, negligent misrepresentation,** and **breach of contract.**

For example, an employer recruited employees to take over the jobs of employees on strike, promising them "permanent" employment. When the strike was over, the strikers were reinstated and the strikebreakers let go. The Supreme Court ruled that they could sue for breach of contract.[22] When a medical practice specializing in coronary care sought to recruit a renowned specialist, assurances were given that the specialist would be allowed to become an equal partner in the firm within a short period of time. These assurances were critical to the specialist's decision to accept the position. However, the practice was reorganized shortly thereafter and the opportunity to become an equal partner did not materialize. A state appeals court affirmed the lower court in finding that the doctor had been fraudulently induced to accept the position and remanded the case for consideration of punitive damages in light of the egregious conduct of the practice's partners.[23]

ELEMENTS OF A CLAIM

Fraud

The elements of a fraud claim:
1. A false representation of a material fact was made to another person.
2. The party making the statement knew that it was false at the time that it was made (or had reckless disregard for the truth).
3. The party making the statement intended the other person to rely on the false representation and to act or refrain from acting in a certain way.
4. The other person was, in fact, induced to act or refrain from acting.
5. The other person was harmed by reliance on the false representation.

[22]*Belknap v. Hale*, 463 U.S. 491 (1983).

[23]*Mkparu v. Ohio Heart Care, Inc.*, 740 N.E.2d 293 (1999).

In *negligent misrepresentation* cases, the second element of a fraud claim—intent to falsify or reckless disregard for the truth—need not be shown. Instead, it is sufficient for the plaintiff to establish that the employer should have known about the falsity of its statement. Misrepresentations that provide the basis for fraud and negligent misrepresentation cases are not limited to outright lies. Silence can constitute misrepresentation when an employer selectively omits material facts with the intent of creating a false impression or fails to correct a previous misrepresentation after becoming aware of its falsity. In the context of recruiting, "material" facts are those that would affect a person's decision to accept or not accept a job.

Stewart v. Jackson & Nash provides a good example of a successful fraud claim that arises in the context of an attorney being "wooed" away from one law firm to another. Pay particular attention to how the court distinguishes between fraud and breach of contract claims.

STEWART V. JACKSON & NASH
976 F.2d 86 (2d Cir. 1992)

● ● ●

OPINION BY CIRCUIT JUDGE WALKER:

Victoria A. Stewart appeals from a . . . Judgment of the United States District Court for the Southern District of New York. . . . We . . . hold that she . . . state[s] a claim for fraudulent inducement. * * *

Stewart . . . is an attorney. . . . Prior to October 1988, she was employed in the environmental law department of the New York law firm of Phillips, Nizer, Benjamin, Krim & Ballon. Ronald Herzog, a partner in the firm of Jackson & Nash, . . . contacted Stewart while at Phillips, Nizer regarding the possibility of employment with his firm. Herzog allegedly "represented to Stewart that Jackson had recently secured a large environmental law client, that Jackson was in the process of establishing an environmental law department, and that Stewart would head the environmental law department, and be expected to service the firm's substantial existing environmental law client." Stewart asserts that, in reliance on these representations, she resigned her position with Phillips, Nizer in October 1988 and the following month began work at Jackson & Nash.

Upon her arrival, Stewart alleges that Jackson & Nash put her to work primarily on general litigation matters. When she inquired about the promised environmental work, Herzog repeatedly assured her that it would be forthcoming and "also consistently advised [her] that she would be promoted to a position as head

of Jackson's environmental law department." The major environmental law client and substantial environmental case work, however, never materialized. Finally, in May 1990, a Jackson & Nash partner allegedly informed Stewart that "Jackson had never 'really' had this 'type' of work, nor had [it], in fact, secured an environmental law client." Jackson & Nash dismissed Stewart on December 31, 1990. Jackson & Nash, in its affidavit in support of the motion to dismiss, asserts that it engaged in a year-long effort to acquire environmental work but concedes that it failed to achieve this end.

Count I of Stewart's complaint . . . alleges that Jackson & Nash fraudulently induced her to enter into and remain in its employ. Stewart asserts that she took the position with the firm in reliance on its knowing misrepresentations, as outlined above. She claims that her "career objective—continuing to specialize in environmental law—was thwarted and grossly undermined during her employment with Jackson," and that she suffered "loss of professional opportunity, loss of professional reputation," and damage to her "career growth and potential." Count II alleges negligent misrepresentation. * * *

The district court found that Stewart's fraud claim arose from her termination from the firm and dismissed Count I on the authority of *Murphy v. American Home Prod. Corp. Murphy* held that because at-will employees "may be freely terminated . . . at any time for any reason or even for no reason," they can neither challenge their termination in a contract action

nor "bootstrap" themselves around this bar by alleging that the firing was in some way tortious. Following *Murphy,* the court concluded that Stewart, an at-will employee, could not state a fraud claim based on facts arising out of her termination.

We find *Murphy* distinguishable. In *Murphy,* the plaintiff, an at-will employee of the defendant, claimed that he had been fired in a tortious manner. He alleged that his firing "'was deliberately and viciously insulting, was designed to and did embarrass and humiliate plaintiff and was intended to and did cause plaintiff severe mental and emotional distress thereby damaging plaintiff.'" These tort allegations, springing as they do directly from the termination itself, are a transparent attempt to restate the forbidden contractual challenge in the guise of tort. Stewart's alleged injuries, on the other hand, commenced well before her termination and were, in several important respects, unrelated to it. According to the complaint, Jackson & Nash's misrepresentations caused Stewart, a budding environmental lawyer, to leave a firm with an environmental practice and spend two years at one in which she was largely unable to work in her chosen specialty. The resulting damage to her career development was independent of her later termination from Jackson & Nash and began while she was still at the firm. As stated in her complaint, Stewart's "career objective—continuing to specialize in environmental law—was thwarted and grossly undermined *during* her employment with Jackson." (Emphasis added). Although *Murphy* precludes an award of damages for injuries caused by her termination, it does not prevent her from recovering for injuries that resulted from her reliance on the defendants' false statements.

Appellees Jackson & Nash urge a second ground for dismissal of Count I. They contend that Stewart's alleged injuries, both pre-termination and termination-related, result in substance from broken contractual promises regarding the terms and conditions of her employment. Such broken promises, they contend, cannot support a fraud claim because "the fraudulent breach of a contract does not give rise to an action for fraud. Thus, where the only fraud charged relates to a breach of the contract and not to its inducement or making, no action for fraud is alleged." Appellees' argument boils down to an assertion that Stewart's claim is nothing more than a contract action, which, since it is based on an oral agreement, is not enforceable under New York's Statute of Frauds. Stewart contends that the firm's misrepresentations are actionable under a theory of fraud

in the inducement. She correctly points out that under New York law "it is elementary that where a contract or transaction was induced by false representations, the representations and the contract are distinct and separable. . . . Thus, fraud in the inducement of a written contract is not merged therein so as to preclude an action for fraud."

Stewart alleges four misrepresentations: (1) "Jackson had recently secured a large environmental law client"; (2) "Jackson was in the process of establishing an environmental law department"; (3) "Stewart would head the environmental law department"; and (4) "[Stewart would] be expected to service the firm's substantial existing environmental law client."

As to representations (1) and (2), we find dispositive the New York Court of Appeals' distinction between a prospective business partner's "promissory statements as to what will be done in the future," which give rise only to a breach of contract claim, and his or her false "'representations of present fact,'" which give rise to a separable claim of fraudulent inducement. In the case of *Coolite Corp. v. American Cyanamid Co,* for example, defendant Cyanamid, a manufacturer of light sticks, represented to Coolite that it had fully tested its product and had developed a means of correcting the product's defects. Coolite, allegedly in reliance on these statements, contracted to become the exclusive distributor of the light sticks. Coolite later found the product not to be of merchantable quality and sued for fraudulent misrepresentation. The Appellate Division let the fraud claim stand on the grounds that "Cyanamid's representations . . . were representations of fact and not merely promises of future action."

In this case Jackson & Nash's declarations that it "had recently secured a large environmental law client" and "was in the process of establishing an environmental law department" were not future promises but representations of present fact. Under *Coolite,* these representations support a claim for fraudulent inducement, which is distinct and separable from any contract action. * * *

[R]egarding representation (3), [Stewart] asserts that Jackson & Nash informed her that she "would be promoted to a position as head of Jackson's environmental law department . . . [although], upon information and belief, *at the time Jackson made the aforesaid representations to Stewart, it knew that it did not intend to make her the head of its environmental law department.*" (Emphasis added). While representation

(3) appears, initially, to be a future promise (Stewart would be made head of the department), the New York Court of Appeals has explained that

> while mere promissory statements as to what will be done in the future are not actionable, . . . it is settled that, *if a promise was actually made with a preconceived and undisclosed intention of not performing it, it constitutes a misrepresentation of material existing fact* upon which an action . . . [based on fraudulent inducement] may be predicated.

Stewart's assertion that Jackson & Nash, at the time it made the promise, "knew that it did not intend" to fulfill it, makes representation (3) an allegation of present fact which gives rise to a claim of fraudulent inducement.

To the extent that representation (4)'s pledge that Stewart would "be expected to service the firm's substantial existing environmental law client" goes beyond representation (1)'s statement of the existence of an environmental law client, it is a future promise and would not be actionable.

In sum, we hold that representation (1) is a representation of present fact and that (2), and (3) included both elements of present fact and future promise. To the extent the representations were of present fact, they are actionable under a theory of fraudulent inducement. * * *

We hold that Count I of Stewart's complaint, alleging fraudulent inducement, survives Jackson & Nash's motion to dismiss.

CASE QUESTIONS

1. What was the legal issue in this case? What did the court decide?

2. How are the elements of a fraud claim satisfied in this case?

3. How does the court distinguish between fraud and breach of contract? Why would the law firm prefer to characterize Stewart's claim as a claim for breach of contract?

4. Why do you think that Herzog made these statements to Stewart?

Breach of contract is sometimes claimed simultaneously with fraud, but as *Stewart* shows, the two are distinct. For one thing, intentional misrepresentation is an essential element of fraud claims, whereas breach of contract is established by a failure to live up to binding promises, regardless of intent. Second, fraud claims usually involve false statements made about current or preexisting facts, whereas breach of contract claims involve promises made about future terms and conditions of employment. An important exception, applicable to Stewart's case, is where the party making promises about future conditions is aware of the falsity of those promises at the time at which they are made.

Thus, *employers should refrain from making promises to job candidates as inducements to accept jobs unless they are willing to live up to those promises. Likewise, employers cannot mislead job candidates by misrepresenting facts that would reasonably be relied upon in deciding whether to accept a position.* Employers cannot get so caught up in the recruitment process that they promise more than they can ultimately deliver or, worse, more than they know that they will be able to deliver. *Nor should interviewers comment on a job candidate's prospects of being hired.* In *Griffin v. Steeltek,* Griffin was told that he was the best qualified applicant for the position. Although making the statement did not obligate the company to hire him, it undoubtedly left Griffin more disposed toward suing when he was not hired.

False Statements by Employees

Employers are not the only ones who have to watch what they say. There are potential legal consequences for applicants who provide prospective employers with false

information or omit important facts in hopes of enhancing their chances of getting hired. First, in cases where employers have to defend their decisions not to hire (such as in discrimination claims), courts regard refusal to hire due to falsification or omission as a legitimate, nondiscriminatory reason. This is particularly true where the employer has a consistently enforced policy to this effect, notifies employees of it (usually on the application form), and the falsification or omission is material rather than trivial. Likewise, employers who discover a falsification or omission after a person has already been hired and discharge that person will generally be able to defend any wrongful discharge claim that arises out of the termination. Thus, *employers are advised to have a policy requiring that job candidates provide complete and truthful information and specifying that the penalty for failing to do so will be either refusal to hire or termination if the falsification or omission is discovered posthiring. As with any genuine policy, this policy needs to be consistently enforced and made known to job candidates.*

Cases involving **after-acquired evidence** show that there is another consequence to employee falsifications and omissions during the hiring process. The consequence is that the legal remedies available to employees in suits against their employers may be limited due to their prior misbehavior. For example, suppose that a job candidate falsely claims to have a college degree. The employer does not discover the falsification at the time and hires the woman. Subsequently, she suffers harassment on the job and is forced to quit. She files a sex discrimination suit. In preparing to defend itself, the company goes over all of its records pertaining to this employee, including her application form. They become suspicious of her statements about her educational credentials, and during the discovery process leading up to litigation, she is forced to admit that she fabricated the information. Pursuant to company policy, she is then officially terminated for providing false information on her application. Thus, the employer "acquired" evidence of previous wrongdoing (falsification on her application form), but only after the employee was discriminated against and filed suit.

Should the prior wrongdoing of the employee negate her ability to sue the employer? After all, had the employer known about the false information she submitted, it might not have hired her in the first place (either because she would have been viewed as unqualified or because of a policy against falsification). The Supreme Court has held that employees do not lose their ability to bring suit simply because they do not have entirely clean hands.[24] Lawsuits serve not only to remedy harm to individual plaintiffs, but also to uphold public policy. However, if the employer can show that it would have not hired her had it been aware of the falsification, her remedies (such as back pay) will generally be limited to the point in time when the wrongdoing was discovered, and reinstatement will not be ordered.

Not all instances of alleged falsification of an application will be treated as after-acquired evidence cases. For example, a woman was fired after becoming pregnant, and the jury concluded that the employer discriminated based on pregnancy. The employer argued that any damages should be limited because the woman had failed to list several previous jobs on her resume, including one from which she had been fired. The court rejected the employer's argument because it was unclear whether she had actually been fired from any previous job; the omissions were on her resume rather than the company's application form; the application form did not even ask for a job history; and, perhaps most importantly, there was no evidence that the company had ever fired or not hired anyone for falsification of a resume.[25] Put

[24]*McKennon v. Nashville Banner Publishing Co.*, 115 S. Ct. 879 (1995).
[25]*Sheehan v. Donlen Corp.*, 173 F.3d 1039 (7th Cir. 1999).

differently, this employer's attempt to limit its damages by invoking the after-acquired evidence doctrine failed because it could not prove that there was falsification, that any falsification that might have occurred related to material facts (if the information was so important to its hiring decision, why was there nothing about it on the application?), and that it had a bona fide policy of firing or refusing to hire persons found to have falsified their resumes. This case underscores the fact that *employers must have consistently enforced policies regarding falsifications and omissions if they want to use them as the basis for employment decisions or in arguing for reduced damages.*

Chapter SUMMARY

The many ways in which employers recruit applicants are vital to the cause of equal employment opportunity. If recruitment mechanisms reach some protected class groups more than others or fail to convey a genuine desire that all interested and qualified candidates apply, equal employment opportunity is doomed at the start. People have to know that jobs are available before they can apply for them, and they have to believe that applying will not be a waste of their time. Recruitment mechanisms affect hiring decisions by determining the composition of applicant pools. Thus, to ascertain whether there is discrimination in recruitment, a comparison must be made between the protected class composition of the applicant pool and the composition of persons with the necessary skills in the relevant labor market. Nepotism and word-of-mouth recruiting are especially likely to produce discriminatory effects because they tend to replicate existing workforces, particularly in terms of race.

Employers wanting to recruit nonimmigrant foreign nationals to work in the United States need to deal with a variety of visa classifications, including H-1B visas for persons of distinguished merit and ability, H-2 visas for temporary workers, L-1 visas for intracompany transfers, and TN visas for highly skilled employees from Mexico and Canada. The use of foreign nationals is subject to numerous requirements related to the number of visas available, the types of jobs that can be performed, payment for services, termination of employment, and the duration of employment.

Employers seek to obtain much information from applicants through application forms, interviews, and other means. The primary legal concern regarding preemployment inquiries is discrimination. Information about the protected class characteristics of job candidates is without a legitimate use and can only lead to discrimination. Although the inquiries themselves generally do not violate federal law, they may violate state laws, and they provide evidence of discriminatory intent. The Americans with Disabilities Act (ADA) is unusual among federal laws in containing an express prohibition against preemployment medical inquiries prior to a job candidate receiving a conditional offer of employment. This prohibition applies regardless of whether the job candidate is disabled.

Employers also make statements to prospective employees. These statements can lead to claims of fraud, negligent misrepresentation, or breach of contract. Fraud occurs in the recruitment and hiring process when an employer knowingly misrepresents a fact that is important to the job candidate deciding to take a job, the employer intends for the job candidate to rely on the false information, the job candidate reasonably relies on that information, and the job candidate is damaged by the misrepresentation. In negligent misrepresentation, it is sufficient to show that the employer should have known of the misrepresentation, even if actual knowledge or reckless disregard for the truth cannot be established. Breach of contract arises out of unfulfilled promises that are made regarding future terms and conditions of employment and is distinct from any fraud that may have induced an employee to enter into a contractual relationship.

False statements by employees also have consequences. Courts have consistently upheld employers who have policies that they will refuse to hire or will terminate employees who have falsified or omitted information used to make hiring decisions. When evidence of a falsification or omission surfaces after an employee has commenced legal action against an employer, this "after-acquired evidence" will likely limit any remedies awarded the employee, but will not cause a suit to be dismissed.

Practical Advice SUMMARY

- *When recruiting, employers should*

 –*use multiple recruitment mechanisms, rather than rely solely on one way of getting the word out about employment opportunities.*

 –*disseminate information about employment opportunities as broadly as is feasible, given the nature of the position and the labor market.*

 –*create written job announcements and disseminate them.*

 –*ensure that the wording of want ads and other types of job announcements is neutral and does not express any preference or requirement based on protected class.*

- *When recruiting, employers should not*

 –*request that employment agencies refer employees with particular protected class characteristics.*

 –*attempt to obtain information about the protected class characteristics of referrals from employment agencies.*

 –*rely heavily on nepotism and word of mouth to recruit employees, particularly where the existing workforce is relatively homogenous in terms of race or national origin.*

- *When using foreign nationals with H-1B visas to perform work in the United States, employers should*

 –*adhere to the terms and conditions of employment provided for in Labor Condition Application forms.*

 –*ensure that they are not employed continuously in the United States for more than six years.*

 –*not lay visa holders off or reduce their pay.*

 –*notify immigration authorities and pay for transportation back to the country of origin for visa holders whose employment is terminated before the end of their contracts.*

 –*not use visa holders to displace or adversely affect the working conditions of U.S. workers.*

- *Establish an application policy and adhere to it consistently. The policy should specify the following*

 –*whether applications will be accepted.*

 –*what must be done to complete the application process and be considered an applicant.*

 –*how long applications will be accepted.*

 –*how long submitted applications will remain valid.*

- *If applications are being accepted, no individual wanting to apply should be discouraged from submitting an application.*

- *Be prepared to accommodate disabled persons by providing*

 –*assistance in completing application forms.*

 –*alternative means of communicating the information in job announcements.*

 –*accessible interview sites.*

- *Application forms should*

 –*include a statement relating to the conditions under which employment can be terminated.*

 –*include a request for applicants' consent to contact and receive information from former employers and other references.*

 –*be signed by applicants and dated.*

 –*be retained for at least one year from when the decision not to hire was made (for applicants who are not hired).*

 –*be kept for the duration of employment and at least a year thereafter (for applicants who are hired).*

- *Whether on application forms, during interviews, or otherwise, employers should refrain from asking questions*

 –*directly or indirectly related to protected class characteristics of job candidates.*

 –*about requirements or criteria not uniformly applied to job candidates.*

 –*about requirements or criteria likely to produce adverse impact.*

- *Requests for medical information of any type should be made only after a conditional offer of employment has been extended to a job candidate.*

- *Provide intensive training on discrimination law to interviewers and recruiters, but also make sure*

that others involved in interviewing and interacting with job candidates have a general understanding of their legal responsibilities.

- *Refrain from making promises about future terms and conditions of employment intended to induce job candidates to take jobs unless those promises will be kept.*

- *Be careful not to present false or misleading information that a job candidate would reasonably rely*

upon in accepting a job. This includes creating a false impression by selectively omitting important facts or failing to correct known prior misrepresentations.

- *Have and enforce a clear policy requiring that job candidates provide complete and truthful information, with the penalty for failing to do so being nonhire or termination.*

Key TERMS

recruitment	visa classifications	breach of contract
relevant labor market	applicant	negligent misrepresentation
neutral wording	preemployment inquiries	after-acquired evidence
nepotism	medical inquiries	
word-of-mouth hiring	fraud	

Chapter QUESTIONS

1. Over a three-year period, a manufacturer hired 128 entry-level workers out of a total of 2,087 applicants. Fifty-three of the applicants (2.5%) were African American, whereas 2,034 of the applicants (97.5%) were non–African Americans (primarily Latinos). Of the 128 workers hired, 8 (6.25%) were African Americans and 120 (93.75%) were not. The hiring rate for African Americans was 15.1% versus 5.7% for all others. During the same time period, the percentage of entry-level manufacturing workers in the city who were African American was estimated to be about 36%. The manufacturer relied almost exclusively on word of mouth. Current employees told friends and relatives about job openings and those interested would come in and apply. The EEOC brought suit against the manufacturer. Did the company discriminate? (*EEOC v. Chicago Miniature Lamp Works*, 947 F.2d 292 (7th Cir. 1991))

2. A truck driver sought employment with a company that hauls new cars. Truckers working for this company had to make expensive investments in new tractor trailers. Before accepting

employment, the truck driver was told that jobs were assigned to truckers without regard to seniority. He was also given a figure for the average monthly gross income of the company's truckers over the past few months. Both of these were true at the time. However, the company was simultaneously involved in negotiations with the union that represents its truck drivers to change to a job assignment system based on seniority, a change that would necessarily lessen the income of new drivers. The company was pushing this, and the manager with whom the prospective truck driver was dealing knew about the proposal. About two months after the truck driver took a job with the company, the new, seniority-based system was put into effect. As a new employee, he received very few assignments and his income sunk far below what he had been told company drivers were making. The driver resigned and sued. What should the court decide? Why? (*Varnum v. Nu-Car Carriers*, 804 F.2d 638 (11th Cir. 1986))

3. A job applicant was required to complete a "Health History Questionnaire" that inquired

about his prior work-related injuries and medical care. The applicant completed the questionnaire and answered truthfully a number of questions related to his medical history, but failed to report a back injury that he suffered on a previous job and for which he was currently receiving workers' compensation benefits. The questionnaire, signed by the applicant, also included the following statement: "I hereby certify that I have answered the above questions to the best of my knowledge and that the answers are complete and true. Any misrepresentation or omission may be justification for refusal of employment, or if employed, termination of employment." The applicant was hired. He subsequently re-aggravated the prior back injury and applied for workers' compensation benefits. Claiming that the employee had submitted false information on the health questionnaire, the company terminated the employee. The employee sued. What should the court decide? Why? (*Carter v. Tennant*, 383 F.3d 673 (7th Cir. 2004))

4. A French citizen received a H-1B visa for a job in the United States in 1995. She changed jobs in 1996, receiving a new H-1B visa. She worked until 1998, when she attended graduate school under an F-1 student visa. While a student, she completed a four-month internship with a company that ultimately offered her a position. Her formal offer letter stated that the company "will sponsor you for your H-1B visa. When you start work we will begin the process of submitting the documentation necessary for you to obtain your H-1B visa." Both parties believed that the visa would be in effect through 2005. It was subsequently discovered that the visa would expire in 2003. A plan to transfer the employee to the company's Dublin office for a year and possibly bring her back thereafter was proposed, but not put into effect because the employee insisted on receiving a statement of the employer's intent in writing. The employee ceased working for the company when her visa expired. Was the employer negligent or otherwise in violation of some legal obligation to the visa holder? Why? (*Lucas v. NCR*, 2005 U.S. Dist. LEXIS 5571)

5. A citizen of India was hired to work in the United States as a computer analyst at a salary of $42,000 per year. He received an H-1B visa and came to the United States. Upon his arrival, he was informed that he would be employed as a gas station cashier and paid at less than the minimum wage. The employee worked for a period of time and then sued. What should the court decide? Why? (*Chopra v. U.S. Professionals*, 2005 Tenn. App. LEXIS 62)

6. During World War II and the Korean War, military recruiters orally promised recruits that they would receive free lifetime medical care for themselves and their dependents. Superiors in the military were aware of and authorized recruiters to make these statements. The promised care was provided until the mid-1990s when changes were made limiting the availability of veterans' treatment facilities and effectively forcing veterans to purchase Medicare coverage. A group of veterans sued, seeking to recover the amounts they were forced to pay for health insurance after being promised free lifetime medical care. What should the court decide? Why? (*Schism and Reinlie v. United States*, 316 F.3d 1259 (Fed. Cir. 2002); *cert. denied*, 2003 U.S. LEXIS 4404)

7. Suppose that an employer has a close working relationship with your college and primarily recruits from there for professional positions. What would be the consequence of that recruiting strategy? Would it tend to result in adverse impact?

8. An employer uses the following application form. What questions would you advise this employer not to ask on the application form? Why?

Name_____ Sex_____
Address_____ Date of Birth_____
City_____ State_____ Zip_____
Are you a U.S. citizen?_____
Place of birth_____
In case of emergency, who should be notified?

Are you single?_____ married?_____
separated? _____ divorced?_____
Number of dependents _____
Do you hold a valid driver's license?_____
Have you ever been employed by this company before? _____ When?_____
Are you a U.S. veteran?____ Years of service?____
Type of discharge?_____
Have you ever filed a workers' compensation claim or been injured on the job? _____

Have you ever been convicted of a crime?_____

List all prior employment, including dates of employment, reason for leaving, address and phone number of employer, and supervisor.

I understand that any misrepresentation or omission of material facts will result in nonhire or termination of employment without notice or recourse.

Signature _____ Date_____

Internet RESOURCES

The Web site of the Census Bureau is a major source of data on the demographic composition of the population and relevant labor markets.

http://www.census.gov

A section of the U.S. Citizenship and Immigration Services' Web site provides information for employers. The USCIS is the successor agency to the Immigration and Naturalization Service (INS) following reorganization under the Department of Homeland Security.

http://www.uscis.gov/graphics/services/
employerinfo/index.htm

The EEOC enforcement guidance on preemployment disability-related questions and medical exams is provided on the EEOC Web site.

http://www.eeoc.gov/policy/docs/preemp.html

Background Checks, References, and Verifying Employment Eligibility

CLIPPINGS

▶ Wal-Mart has agreed to pay $11 million to settle federal government charges that it knowingly used undocumented workers to provide janitorial services in its stores. In October 2003, immigration officers raided 60 Wal-Mart stores in 21 states, resulting in the arrest of 245 undocumented workers and civil enforcement actions against Wal-Mart and the contractors that provided the workers. Wal-Mart, whose spokesperson termed the settlement a "donation" to enforcement efforts, still faces a private lawsuit brought on behalf of the workers.[1]

▶ Two casinos that used credit reports in evaluating applicants for jobs have settled charges by the Federal Trade Commission that they violated the Fair Credit Reporting Act. Contrary to the requirements of this law, the casinos allegedly based hiring decisions on the contents of credit reports, but failed to notify applicants of that fact and to provide rejected applicants with copies of their credit reports and information about their rights under the Fair Credit Reporting Act.[2]

▶ In the aftermath of 9/11, the Transportation Security Administration (TSA) was created and the federal government took over passenger and baggage screening from private companies. Although the move was motivated in part by revelations that the private firms had employed unfit individuals with criminal histories as screeners, the hasty hiring process undertaken by the TSA resulted in many of the same problems. Private firms enlisted to perform background checks were often lax, allowing background check documents to go unprocessed for months. In some cases, screeners were allowed to start work before background checks were completed. Nearly 2,000 screeners were fired after their background checks showed criminal records or falsification of information. Screeners with criminal records were allowed to remain on the job for weeks or months after it was determined that they had criminal records.[3]

▶ National Football League (NFL) teams make major investments in their top draft picks and go to great lengths to assess individuals before selecting them. Louisville running back Eric Shelton, widely expected to be a top pick in the 2005 draft, nearly had his career sidelined by an erroneous background check. InfoMart, a company that provides background checks for some NFL teams, confused Mr. Shelton with another individual of the same name and reported that he had a criminal record, including a conviction for aggravated assault and an arrest for marijuana possession. Quick action by Mr. Shelton's agent appears to have succeeded in setting the record straight and preserving his reputation and career.[4]

[1]Michael R. Triplett. "Wal-Mart to Pay $11 Million to Settle Claims Resulting from Immigration Raids in 2003." *Daily Labor Report* 53 (March 21, 2005), AA-1.

[2]"Casinos Settle Failure to Inform Charges Over Their Use of Credit Reports in Hiring." *Daily Labor Report* 137 (July 19, 2004), A-9.

[3]Philip Shenon. "Report Faults Lax Controls on Screeners at Airports." *New York Times* (February 6, 2004), A-22.

[4]Clifton Brown. "False Report May Affect N.F.L. Draft Pick's Status." *New York Times* (April 15, 2005), C-14.

▶ An August 2004 survey of 345 human resource managers by the Society for Human Resource Management found that 38 percent of respondents had increased the amount of time they spend checking references. Verification of eligibility to work in the United States was the most common type of background check performed, followed by a check of criminal records. More than half of respondents (54 percent) said that their organization has a policy of not providing references regarding current or former employees, due to legal concerns.[5]

BACKGROUND CHECKS

The process of considering job candidates for employment typically includes conducting **background checks.** These checks might entail contacting references; verifying past employment and military service history; confirming that necessary degrees, licenses, or other credentials are possessed; checking driving records; checking for criminal convictions; and examining credit reports. Upon hiring, employers are required to obtain documentation verifying their employees' eligibility to work in the United States. These activities raise a number of legal issues including negligent hiring, defamation, and compliance with the requirements of the Fair Credit Reporting Act and the Immigration Reform and Control Act.

Employer Responsibility for Employee Wrongdoing

Employers are generally responsible for the actions of their employees that are taken within the scope of employment. The common law doctrine of **respondeat superior** ("let the master answer") makes employers liable for harm to others that occurs when employees act within the scope of their employment. Employees are deemed to be acting within the scope of their employment when their actions relate to the kind of work that they were hired to perform, take place substantially within the workplace and during work hours, and serve, at least partially, the interests of the employer. For example, if a stock clerk drops an item and injures a shopper while stocking the shelves, the employer is clearly liable for the customer's injury (although the employer's insurance might cover the costs). In contrast, two drivers of an armored car became enraged at a motorist, repeatedly attempted to run his car off the road, aimed a sawed-off shotgun at the motorist, and threatened to "blow off" his head. Even though the drivers were on duty in the employer's truck and brandished weapons provided by the employer, their actions were judged to be outside the scope of employment. Citing the "unprovoked, unusual, and outrageous" nature of their actions, the court further explained that: "We cannot consider the actions of [the drivers] to be 'of the kind' they were employed to perform. [The drivers] were not acting to protect the cargo entrusted to them during this incident—rather, personal animus motivated their actions."[6]

[5]"SHRM Survey Finds Employers Spending More Time on Worker Background Checks." *Daily Labor Report* 36 (February 24, 2005), A-6.

[6]*Jordon v. Western Distributing Company,* 2005 U.S. App. LEXIS 7566, at 8.

This does not mean that employers are never liable for the harmful acts of employees that occur outside the scope of their employment. One important exception to the principle that employer liability for employee actions is limited to harm that occurs within the scope of employment is when it can be shown that the employer was negligent or reckless in allowing the harm to occur.[7] The legal concept of **negligence** is based on the idea that people sometimes have a duty or responsibility to other people to exercise reasonable care in carrying out certain activities. When that duty or responsibility is not met and this failure is a proximate (relatively direct) cause of harm to others, the party that failed to live up to its responsibilities may be found negligent. It is not necessary to show that the negligent party intended for anyone to be harmed.

Negligent Hiring

Employers can be found negligent with respect to a wide range of human resource activities, including hiring, retention, supervision, and training. Our focus in this chapter is on the concept of **negligent hiring**. The significance of negligent hiring is that it extends the liability of employers for harm caused by their employees beyond actions undertaken within the scope of employment (the subject of *respondeat superior* claims) to harmful actions that lie outside the scope of employment, but for which the careless hiring of an unfit employee "set the stage."

Ponticas v. K.M.S. Investments, with its detailed discussion of the inadequacy of an employer's background checking procedures, is an instructive and oft-cited negligent hiring case.

E L E M E N T S O F A C L A I M

Negligent Hiring

To establish that negligent hiring has occurred, a plaintiff must show the following:

1. A standard of conduct or duty to others exists with respect to an employer taking reasonable steps to avoid hiring unfit employees. The extent of any such duty is based on:

 a. foreseeability of harm to others if an unfit person is hired for a particular job.

 b. knowledge of unfitness that the employer had or should have had if proper hiring procedures were used.

 c. public policy.

2. The employer fails to exercise the proper degree of care and hires an unfit employee.

3. A coworker or other third party is harmed or injured by an unfit employee.

4. The employer's failure to exercise the proper degree of care in hiring is the proximate cause of the harm or injury that occurred.

[7]*Restatement of the Law (Second) Agency,* § 219(2)(b) (1958).

PONTICAS v. K.M.S. INVESTMENTS
331 N.W.2d 907 (Minn. 1983)

● ● ●

OPINION BY JUSTICE KELLEY:

The appellants, the owner and the operator of a residential apartment complex, were found negligent by jury verdict in the hiring of a resident manager who violently sexually assaulted one of the female tenants of the complex. * * * We affirm.

In 1978, appellant K.M.S. Investments owned an apartment complex known as Driftwood Apartments. * * * On or about the 1st of August of that year, Dennis Graffice was employed as apartment manager by appellant Skyline Builders. As apartment manager, Graffice had general supervision over 198 apartment units. He was issued a passkey that would afford him admission into all units. On September 8, 1978, Stephanie Ponticas noticed that her refrigerator was not functioning properly and notified Graffice, who came to the apartment. Jorge Ponticas, Stephanie's husband, was a musician. When Graffice was in the apartment on September 8, he made the observation to Stephanie Ponticas that he had not seen Jorge for some time. In response, she informed him that Jorge was out of town for the week on a band job in northern Minnesota. In the early morning hours of Sunday, September 10, she was violently raped at knifepoint by a person whom she recognized to be Dennis Graffice. During the course of the sexual assault, he attempted to strangle her. Following the assault, she escaped from the apartment through a broken window and reported the incident to police. Dennis Graffice was subsequently arrested and convicted of sexual assault in the first degree and was sentenced to Stillwater State Prison. Stephanie and Jorge Ponticas commenced this lawsuit against the appellants K.M.S. Investments and Skyline Builders, alleging that they were negligent in the hiring of Dennis Graffice as manager of the Driftwood Apartments. . . .

In 1978, Dennis Graffice was 25 years old. When he was 19, he joined the Army and served 14 months until November 3, 1973, when he received a general discharge. After his discharge from the Army, he lived in California. While in California, he was charged with burglary and receiving stolen property and convicted of the latter in 1974 and served 4-1/2 months in jail. Shortly after his release from jail, he moved to Colorado. There he was charged with two counts of

armed robbery, two counts of burglary, three counts of theft and one count of theft of auto parts. As a result of plea negotiations, he was convicted of armed robbery and burglary and sentenced to prison. He was released from prison in Colorado in June of 1977 and returned to California where he lived for approximately 6 months working self-employed as operator of a tree service. In January of 1978, he, his wife and child moved to Minnesota. He obtained a job as a driver for the Spring Lake Park School Bus Company. He and his wife were also caretakers for a 24-unit apartment building where they then lived. He was "fired" from the bus company after only a month and a half for drinking on the job and apparently had also had a fight with his supervisor. In March of 1978, he got a job as a line foreman at Carter's Car Wash where his wife also worked part-time.

In June of 1978, Skyline Builders placed an advertisement in the newspaper for a resident manager for the Driftwood Apartment complex. * * * Graffice and his wife answered the ad that had been placed in the newspaper and completed the standard form of application. Delores Swanson, the property manager for Skyline Builders and the person solely responsible for hiring apartment employees, interviewed the Graffices. Later, a credit check of the Graffices was made in Minnesota and in California. It was normal for Skyline Builders to make a check on the named references, either by telephone or by mail. In the case of the Graffices, Mr. Graffice had put down on his application form two names as references, one of which did not have an address and neither of which had telephone numbers. As it turned out, the two names given were his mother and sister who resided in California. Originally, the Graffices were not the successful applicants for the vacancy. The couple that had been chosen to take over the management notified Skyline Builders that they no longer desired to do so, whereupon the Graffices were called and given 20 minutes within which to give a "yes" or "no" answer. They agreed and were hired without further investigation.

On the initial application form, Dennis Graffice indicated that he had been convicted of a crime but he described the crime as "traffic tickets." Ms. Swanson did not inquire further. She did not consider violation of traffic laws to be a crime. In fact, at the time of the

application Graffice was on parole following his Colorado conviction. . . . * * * Ms. Swanson . . . testified she would not have hired Dennis Graffice had she been aware of his criminal record. * * *

Appellants had the duty to exercise that care that a reasonable landlord would have exercised under the same or similar circumstances. The scope of the duty was commensurate with the risks of the situation. Before a breach of this duty may be found by a jury, it must be established that the employee was in fact unfit, taking into consideration the nature of the employment and the risk posed by the employee to those who foreseeably would come into association with him. It is clear that it was foreseeable that Graffice would, by virtue of his employment, associate with tenants of the complex, including Stephanie Ponticas. Hindsight establishes that he, indeed, was unfit as appellants now candidly admit, but whether appellants breached their duty must be determined by their actions or omissions prior to and at the time of the hiring in ascertaining whether Graffice was a fit person to employ and to entrust with a passkey which would admit him into 198 apartment units. * * *

We have often held that negligence is not to be determined by whether the particular injury was foreseeable. The jury, as finder of fact, could have found, as it did, that it was reasonably foreseeable that a person with a history of offenses of violence could commit another violent crime, notwithstanding the history would not have shown him to ever have committed the particular type of offense. * * *

If the employer "knew or should have known" of the incompetence, and notwithstanding hired the employee, there would exist a breach of duty. Although an employer will not be held liable for failure to discover information about the employee's incompetence that could not have been discovered by reasonable investigation, the issue is whether the employer did make a reasonable investigation. The scope of the investigation is directly related to the severity of risk third parties are subjected to by an incompetent employee. Although only slight care might suffice in the hiring of a yardman, a worker on a production line, or other types of employment where the employee would not constitute a high risk of injury to third persons, "a very different series of steps are justified if an employee is to be sent, after hours, to work for protracted periods in the apartment of a young woman tenant." * * *

We now consider respondents' claim that appellants breached their duty with respect to failing to ascertain

Graffice's criminal record for crimes of violence. At the outset, we reject the contention that, as a matter of law, there exists a duty upon an employer to make an inquiry as to a prospective employee's criminal record even where it is known that the employee is to regularly deal with members of the public. If the employer has made adequate inquiry or otherwise has a reasonably sufficient basis to conclude the employee is reliable and fit for the job, no affirmative duty rests on him to investigate the possibility that the applicant has a criminal record. * * * Were we to hold that an employer can never hire a person with a criminal record at the risk of later being held liable for the employee's assault, it would offend our civilized concept that society must make a reasonable effort to rehabilitate those who have erred so they can be assimilated into the community. * * * Liability of an employer is not to be predicated solely on failure to investigate criminal history of an applicant, but rather, in the totality of the circumstances surrounding the hiring, whether the employer exercised reasonable care. * * *

The jury could have believed evidence presented by the respondents that appellants had made little investigation of references. Appellants did contact the owner of an apartment building where the Graffices had been resident managers for a short period of time, the car wash where Graffice had worked for 3 months, and made a credit check in California and Minnesota on the Graffices. The application shows that the Graffices had resided in Minnesota a very short time; that Graffice had received a general discharge from the Army after only 14 months of service—a period shorter than the normal term of service; and had no work history other than 3 months in Minnesota during the 5 years following his discharge. Notwithstanding the short period of Minnesota residency and voids in post-discharge work history, appellants did not contact the California references listed on the application. Had they done so, they would have learned the "references" were Graffice's mother and sister, persons generally considered to be inappropriate references. These "references" were supposed to have been people that Graffice had done work for in his independent tree service. A contact with those "references" would have indicated that he had not told the truth in that respect. Moreover, the decision to hire Graffice was hurriedly made, after appellants' first choice for the job declined the proffered employment, without further interview or other investigation. The record indicates that appellants were aware of possible risk of hiring a caretaker with a history of criminal

activity in that the application form contained a question concerning the same. From the foregoing, the jury could have concluded that appellants' limited investigation furnished an insufficient basis for a reasonable employer to conclude that Graffice was reliable and, therefore, that reasonable care required appellants to investigate further the possibility that Graffice had a criminal record.

CASE QUESTIONS

1. What was the legal issue in this case? What did the court decide?

2. How are the elements of a negligent hiring case satisfied in this case?

3. What specific failings did the court point to in how the apartment complex owners went about hiring the resident manager?

4. What does the court say about the necessity of inquiring into criminal histories? Is it clear when a criminal background check is legally required?

As in *Ponticas*, negligent hiring cases often hinge on the first element—whether the employer had a duty to do more to screen out an unfit employee. No single standard is applicable in all cases for how careful an employer's background check must be, or whether a background check must be conducted at all. Instead, the degree of care that an employer must exercise in hiring depends on the following factors: public policy (including statutory obligations), foreseeability, and knowledge.

Some industries and occupations have specific legal requirements for screening employees. For example, criminal background checks are mandatory for entities that hire childcare workers.[8] A childcare facility that fails to meet this specific legal requirement, with the failure resulting in the hiring of an unfit employee who harms others, would certainly be negligent in hiring. Even when the law does not specify a particular screening procedure, courts sometimes look to **public policy** as an indication that a particular type of employment is sensitive and calls for greater care in hiring. For example, in a case involving an employer's failure to check the criminal history of a truck driver, the court gave considerable weight to the fact that trucking is a highly regulated industry and one in which employers have an obligation not to entrust unfit persons with large, potentially lethal, vehicles.[9] Public policy also points to airport security as a sensitive type of employment for which greater care must be exercised in hiring. The failings of the TSA and its contractors in hiring persons with criminal records as airport screeners and then retaining them for months after their criminal backgrounds were discovered, takes on added significance in light of the acute passenger safety and national security concerns at stake (see "Clippings").

For most jobs, public policy concerns do not enter the picture. Instead, the degree of care that an employer must exercise in hiring depends heavily upon **foreseeability.** Employers are not expected to be omniscient in anticipating bad things that employees might do. Instead, the question is whether a "reasonable person" of average intelligence would be able to foresee that hiring an unfit person for this particular position would render injury or harm to others likely. Foreseeability thus stems primarily from the nature of the position into which an employee is being hired. The more "sensitive" the position and the greater the foreseeability of harm, the more extensive is the background check that should occur. Characteristics of jobs that create

[8]National Child Protection Act of 1993, 42 U.S.C.A. § 5119 (2001).

[9]*Malorney v. B&L Motor Freight*, 496 N.E.2d 1086 (Ill. App. 1986).

greater foreseeability include contact with children, older persons, the mentally ill, and other vulnerable segments of the public; jobs involving personal care and medical treatment; relatively unsupervised work; positions entailing responsibility for security and/or the use of firearms; transportation work; and jobs affording substantial access to the homes and personal possessions of others.

Foreseeability of harm is a slippery concept and court decisions are not entirely consistent. In *Ponticas*, the position of apartment manager provided the employee with a passkey to all the apartments in the complex. It was thus foreseeable that an unfit person hired as apartment manager could do substantial harm to the persons and property of apartment residents. An expansive view of foreseeability is exemplified by a case involving the hiring of a mail clerk. The clerk had a history of convictions for rape and robbery. He murdered a company secretary in her apartment. Because the position of mail clerk afforded the murderer access to the names and home addresses of employees, allowed him to circulate freely among the company's female employees, and afforded him the opportunity to harass female employees without the company taking action against him, the court concluded that the plaintiff might prevail in a negligent hiring claim and refused to throw out the case.[10] In a case involving a furniture store delivery person who assaulted a woman to whom he had delivered furniture, the court rejected the employer's argument that there was little foreseeability because the job involved only "incidental contact" with customers and did not provide the employee with a passkey or other means of direct access to the apartment. The court focused instead on how the position carried with it "indicia of authority" (e.g., uniform, delivery papers) that led customers to open their doors and readily permit entrance to delivery persons.[11] Likewise, a court concluded that sufficient foreseeability could be shown when a trucking company hired a driver with a history of criminal convictions and the driver raped and beat a female hitchhiker. The court relied on the fact that it is common knowledge that drivers pick up hitchhikers, regardless of the employer's policy against doing so.[12] However, in another truck driver case with similar facts, the court found lack of foreseeability based on the company's explicit policy prohibiting drivers from picking up hitchhikers and the absence of any authority over or special access to the victim (a motorist whose car had broken down on the road).[13] A circumscribed view of foreseeability and employers' responsibilities is also evident in a case involving Internet service provider Prodigy. An employee in charge of its sex chat room became introduced to a customer through the chat room, had sex with her, and infected her with AIDS. Despite evidence that the company knew that the employee had AIDS and was having sex with customers he met on-line, the court held that the employer was not liable for negligent hiring. Under New York State law, liability for negligent hiring is limited to situations in which an unfit employee harmed others while on the employer's premises or while using the employer's property.[14]

Some courts recast the issue of foreseeability in terms of whether a "special relationship" exists between the employer and the person harmed. A special relationship exists when, among other things, the meeting in which harm occurred was a direct consequence of employment and the employer would have received some benefit, if only indirect, from the meeting had the harmful act not occurred. In one case using this

[10]*Gaines & Frazier v. Monsanto Co.*, 655 S.W.2d 568 (Mo. App. 1983).

[11]*Tallahassee Furniture Company v. Harrison*, 583 So. 2d 744, at 752 (Fla. App. 1991); *review denied*, 595 So. 2d 558 (Fla. 1992).

[12]*Malorney*, at 1089.

[13]*Stalbosky v. Three Rivers Trucking Company*, 205 F.3d 890, at 896-7 (6th Cir. 2000).

[14]*Haybeck v. Prodigy Services Co.*, 944 F. Supp. 326 (S.D.N.Y. 1996), *affirmed*, 116 F.3d 465 (2d Cir. 1997).

approach, an employee was hired to deliver pizza coupons door-to-door. The employee had a criminal record of sexual assault that the employer failed to detect. In the course of distributing coupons, the employee happened upon a female college student waiting at a bus stop, explained that he was working for the pizza company, and convinced her to accept a ride with him. The employee then abducted and raped the woman. Despite the fact that the employee was on the job at the time of the meeting and invoked the name of his employer to gain her trust, the court concluded that because the woman was not a customer or in some other special relationship to the employer, the company had no legal obligation to do more to protect her from an unfit employee.[15]

Knowledge refers in this context to the fact that the employer was aware, or should have been if proper screening procedures had been followed, that the person hired was unfit. Thus, in contrast to foreseeability, which focuses on the position, knowledge pertains to those characteristics of the person being hired that render him unfit. Importantly, if an employee is hired without an adequate background check and that person proceeds to harm others, the employer will still not be liable for negligent hiring if information indicating unfitness was not available to be found (e.g., the employee had no prior criminal convictions). In *Ponticas*, there was abundant evidence of unfitness that would have been discovered through an adequate background check, including his discharge from the military under questionable circumstances, several convictions and jail terms for serious crimes, his status as a parolee, and discharge from a recent job for drinking and fighting with a supervisor. The evidence of unfitness must bear a relationship to the nature of the position and the type of harm that occurred to constitute "knowledge." Likewise, the evidence of unfitness must be relatively specific. An employer that hired a salesperson despite results of a preemployment psychological test that placed the salesperson in a "high-aggression" category was not liable when that salesperson got into a fight with a motorist, because high-aggression personality is not the equivalent of "violent."[16] In contrast, when an employer had firsthand knowledge of an employee's violent tendencies because it fired him for threatening to assault a supervisor, its decision to rehire the employee (who said that he would file discrimination charges otherwise) resulted in a finding of negligent hiring when the rehired employee assaulted a coworker.[17]

Although the crux of most negligent hiring cases is whether the employer was obligated to do a more thorough background check, plaintiffs must also show that their employers failed to live up to their duties and that these failures were proximate causes of harm. Foreseeability and **proximity** are clearly related; foreseeability pertains to whether harm could be anticipated before the fact, and proximity involves the connection between events as they actually unfolded. A court found that there was not sufficient proximity to establish negligence in the case of an apartment building porter who sexually abused an infant. In reaching this conclusion, the court noted that the abuse occurred 27 years after the employee's manslaughter conviction and 18 years after he was hired; the child's mother was a friend of the employee and named him the child's godfather; and the mother allowed the employee to have unsupervised visits with the infant. These facts "severed the causal nexus" between any negligence in hiring the porter and harm to the infant.[18] In contrast, a furniture

[15]*Poe v. Domino's Pizza*, 139 F.3d 617 (8th Cir. 1998).

[16]*Thatcher v. Brennan*, 657 F. Supp. 6, at 12 (S.D. Miss. 1986), *affirmed*, 816 F.2d 675 (5th Cir. 1987).

[17]*Tecumseh Products Co. v. Rigdon*, 250 Ga. App. 739 (2001).

[18]*Ford v. Gildin*, 1994 N.Y. App. Div. LEXIS 5634, at 5.

company was liable for negligently hiring a delivery person even though the assault occurred three months after a delivery had been made and the woman allowed the man into the apartment after he asked to use the bathroom. However, the delivery person was in uniform, had returned to the apartment on the pretext that a receipt was needed related to the earlier delivery, and the woman recognized and allowed him in due to the prior delivery.[19]

Conducting Background Checks: General Advice The foregoing discussion of negligent hiring holds some general practical implications for background checks. *Depending on the circumstances, an adequate background check might include contacting references; verifying past employment and military service; verifying the possession of degrees, licenses, and other credentials; checking driving and criminal records; and examining credit reports.* Although none of these measures is legally required in all cases, *employers should at minimum follow their own established background check procedures.* If an unfit employee is hired and hurts someone, it becomes difficult to explain why the employer did not at least follow its own policies that were presumably crafted in recognition of the dangers inherent in hiring unfit employees. *Employers should be especially wary of last-minute, rush hiring decisions* (like the one in the *Ponticas* case) because standard hiring procedures are likely to give way to expediency. Background checks are likely to be fruitless if carried out in a perfunctory, pro forma manner. Instead, a concerted effort to get at the truth is needed. *It is critical that inconsistencies and gaps in information provided by applicants be detected and confronted* (another failing of the employer in the *Ponticas* case). If these gaps and inconsistencies cannot be cleared up in interviews and through corroboration by other sources, the person should not be hired.

Because foreseeability is a key element of negligence claims, *background checks should be more extensive in hiring for those positions in which there is greater chance that unfit employees could do serious harm to others.* Many jobs that present foreseeable harm are not regarded as important or worthy of a great deal of concern. Compounding the problem, many of these jobs are low-paid and experience high turnover, necessitating frequent and rapid hiring.

Because knowledge means that the employer knew or should have known that the person hired was unfit, *it is important for employers to document all efforts at obtaining information on job candidates, even when those efforts are not successful* (e.g., references did not respond or were uninformative). Under these circumstances, it is more difficult to argue that an employer should have known about disqualifying information. Also, *if an employer asks about something that is important and about which the applicant is apt to lie (e.g., criminal background), it is important to attempt to corroborate applicants' answers.* The fact that the information was sought suggests that it was viewed by the employer as material knowledge. *If, despite the inadvisability of doing so, an employer opts to hire a needed employee prior to completing a background check, the employer should still finish the background check—but only if willing to use the information of unfitness that is discovered as a basis for terminating the employee.* Otherwise, the employer is left with actual knowledge of unfitness and even greater vulnerability to a negligent hiring or retention claim.

We turn now to issues surrounding particular aspects of background checks: references, criminal records, and credit reports.

[19]*Tallahassee Furniture,* at 756.

REFERENCES

Failure to check references—particularly recent ones that possess information regarding wrongdoing by an employee at a previous job—can be evidence of negligence in hiring. In fact, in a case involving a home health aide who apparently injected one of her patients with insulin causing a seizure (the patient was not diabetic and the aide was not qualified or authorized to perform any such procedure), failure to check recent references was the sole basis of the negligence claim.[20] However, for the most part, the *former employer* asked to provide information about a former employee has the greatest degree of legal concern about references. The principal concern is that the former employer will be sued for defaming its former employee. Other worries are that the former employer may be viewed as retaliating against its former employee or negligent in providing a misleading referral.

Defamation

Defamation is a possibility any time employers make statements about employees to others, but the focus here is on references. The term is being used here in the broad sense of any information that a former employer provides to a prospective new employer regarding a former employee; the former employer need not be specifically designated by the former employee as a "reference." The gist of a defamation claim is that false statements that reflect badly on a person are communicated to others, which results in damage to the person's reputation. As the case of the college football player wrongly identified as a criminal illustrates (see "Clippings"), erroneous

ELEMENTS OF A CLAIM

Defamation

To prevail in a defamation claim, the plaintiff must show that:

1. A statement is made that purports to be "factual" in nature.
2. The statement is false or substantially false.
3. The statement challenges the integrity, character, or ability of another person.
4. The statement is "published" (communicated), either orally (slander) or in writing (libel).
5. There is harm to the reputation of the person about whom the statement is made.

Statements that are defamatory will still not subject an employer to liability if those statements were privileged. Qualified privilege can be lost if any of the following are true:

1. There was malicious intent to harm the person's reputation.
2. The statement was made with reckless disregard for the truth.
3. Publication of the statement was overly broad.

[20]*Interim Healthcare of Fort Wayne, Inc. v. Moyer*, 746 N.E.2d 429 (Ind. App. 2001).

information conveyed by employers or background checking firms can be highly damaging to both reputations and careers. Defamatory statements are not merely harsh or negative; they must be substantially false. As such, it behooves employers responding to requests for references to *ensure that the information provided is as accurate and objective as possible. Among other things, this means basing responses to requests for information on inspection of documents rather than memory, confining statements to known facts rather than speculation or impressions, and having requests dealt with by designated persons who are accustomed to writing letters of reference and familiar with the location of information regarding former employees.*

Defenses to Defamation Claims: Consent and Qualified Privilege Although truthfulness is an absolute defense to a defamation claim, employers do not want to be in the position of defending the accuracy of all their statements. Other defenses are also available to employers that obviate this problem. One is **consent.** If a former employee consents to her former employer providing information about her to a prospective new employer, statements that might otherwise be defamatory will not subject the former employer to liability. Thus, it makes sense for a former employer to *require that any request for information be accompanied by a written "release of information" form, signed by the former employee and granting permission to communicate information about that employee.* This precludes off-the-cuff responses to telephone inquiries about former employees (which is also desirable from the standpoint of accuracy), but does not impose an unreasonable burden on other employers seeking references. In anticipation of this requirement, most prospective employers ask applicants to sign releases of information on their applications. Although requiring release forms is definitely a good idea, there is a legitimate question as to whether this constitutes informed consent on the part of former employees, because they do not know what their former employers will say. A means of gaining more informed consent is for employers to *negotiate with employees prior to their leaving employment and to mutually agree upon a letter of reference.* Clearly, this will not work in all cases. When the employee's departure is acrimonious, this method is least likely to succeed, but it is still worth doing when possible.

A second and more basic defense against defamation claims is that the statements made, even if otherwise defamatory, were "privileged." The law recognizes that communication between employers about prospective employees serves important social purposes. It also recognizes that if employers have to worry about the strict accuracy of everything they say about former employees, this will choke off the flow of necessary information. Thus, former employers providing references are shielded from defamation claims by **qualified privilege.** This privilege or immunity from liability is conditional rather than absolute. It can be lost if false statements are made with **malice** (i.e., intent to harm a person's reputation), with **reckless disregard for the truth,** or if the statements receive **overly broad publication.**

Defamation cases, including *Sigal Construction v. Stanbury,* often focus on whether the employer's statements were made under circumstances that caused the presumption of immunity to be lost.

Qualified privilege only shields communications with others who have a legitimate need for that information. One way to avoid overly broad publication is to *verify the identity of any party seeking information about former employees* by requiring that requests for references be made in writing on the prospective employer's letterhead (and accompanied by a signed release). The same measures that aid an

SIGAL CONSTRUCTION v. STANBURY
586 A.2d 1204 (D.C. App. 1991)

OPINION BY ASSOCIATE JUDGE FERREN:

In this defamation case, a jury awarded appellee, Kenneth S. Stanbury, $370,440 against his former employer, appellant Sigal Construction Corporation. The jury found that a Sigal project manager, Paul Littman, had slandered Stanbury while giving an employment reference to another construction company after Sigal had terminated Stanbury's employment. * * * Sigal appeals. * * * We affirm.

Stanbury worked as a project manager for Sigal from May 1984 to June 1985. According to Sigal's personnel manager, Pamela Heiber, Sigal terminated Stanbury's employment because he "was not doing his job correctly." Sigal, however, told Stanbury he was let go for "lack of work or reduction in work." According to Heiber, "we felt sympathy for Ken because of his age in life" (he was 63 when Sigal terminated his employment). Stanbury contacted Ray Stevens, a previous employer and Regional Manager at Daniel Construction, to find out whether any work was available. Some time later, Stevens called Stanbury about employment as a project manager on the Pentagon City project. Stanbury was eventually offered the job subject to approval by the owner of the project, Lincoln Properties.

William Janes, a Lincoln Properties general partner, had responsibility for investigating Stanbury's employment references. Janes called David Orr, a former Sigal project executive, who suggested that Janes contact Paul Littman, a current Sigal project executive. Janes did so, and Littman later memorialized the conversation:

[Janes] claimed David [Orr] had told him not to hire Ken [Stanbury] and asked me what I thought. I told him.

1. Ken seemed detail oriented to the point of losing sight of the big picture.
2. He had a lot of knowledge and experience on big jobs.
3. With a large staff might be a very competent P.M. [project manager].
4. Obviously he no longer worked for us and that might say enough.

At trial, Littman acknowledged and Stanbury confirmed that Littman had made these statements without having supervised, evaluated, read an evaluation of, or even worked with Stanbury (other than seeing Stanbury in the halls at the office). According to them both, their contact was entirely casual. More specifically, Stanbury testified without contradiction that he had talked to Littman only once during Stanbury's fourteen months with Sigal, and that this conversation was a general discussion about Stanbury's previous job. According to Littman, in evaluating Stanbury for Janes he relied entirely on the "general impression [he] had developed" from "hearing people talk about [Stanbury's] work at the job," perhaps at "casual luncheons" or "project executive meetings" or "over a beer on a Friday afternoon." Littman did nothing to verify the second-hand knowledge he had acquired about Stanbury. At trial, he could recall no facts or work-related incidents that would support the impressions he reported to Janes. When asked where his information about one of Stanbury's projects came from, Littman testified that "there aren't any real specific instances I can point to. I think it was a general opinion I had just developed in the year or two [Stanbury] had been there." * * *

* * * Sigal does not contest, on appeal, either that the statements were false or were negligently made. Sigal does contend, however—and Stanbury does not dispute—that Littman's negligent statements were subject to a "qualified privilege." According to the Virginia Supreme court:

A communication, made in good faith, on a subject matter in which the person communicating has an interest, or owes a duty, legal, moral, or social, is qualifiedly privileged if made to a person having a corresponding interest or duty.

* * * Once the privilege applies, the plaintiff has the burden of proving the defendant has abused, and thus lost, it. To defeat the privilege, a plaintiff must prove the defendant acted with "common law malice." Such malice implies a greater level of ill will than the mindset reflected by mere negligence. In this jurisdiction, we have equated common law malice with "bad faith." In Virginia the common law malice formulation, which

the trial court used for its instruction, includes "bad faith" but is more comprehensive.*

* * * There was sufficient evidence at trial, viewed in the light most favorable to Stanbury, from which a reasonable jury could find by clear and convincing evidence that Littman and Sigal had abused the qualified privilege under Virginia law by acting with "such gross indifference or recklessness as to amount to wanton and willful disregard of the rights of" Stanbury. Littman testified, and Stanbury's testimony confirmed, that Littman had never supervised, worked with, evaluated, or read an evaluation of Stanbury. Moreover, Littman testified that he had not received information from anyone in particular, let alone anyone who had had a work-related relationship with Stanbury. Littman's sources for his statements to Janes were observations in the company's halls and general office contacts with unnamed third parties, perhaps at "casual lunches" or "project executive meetings" or "over beer on a Friday afternoon." But he could recall none of the conversations or otherwise provide any concrete support for his statements, whether first-hand information or hearsay. Littman admitted that he had no facts to support any of his statements to Janes and that he had never sought to verify the information before giving his evaluation. Littman also testified that he knew Janes wanted to speak with someone who had "interacted" with Stanbury at Sigal, and yet Littman further testified that he did not tell Janes he had never done so. Nor did Littman tell Janes the altogether vague sources of his statements. * * *

In sustaining the conclusion that Sigal (through Littman) abused the qualified privilege, we do not mean to imply that employers are at serious risk when providing employment references in the normal course of business. Nor are we suggesting that employers, when providing such references, may not rely on information from the employee's co-workers, even when hearsay. Our analysis here is limited to an office gossip situation where the recommender (1) has conveyed information which cannot be traced to anyone with personal knowledge of the employee whose reputation is at stake, (2) has not

qualified his statements by disclosing the nebulous source of his information, and (3) has led the prospective employer to believe he has worked on a project with the employee and thus has first-hand information.

Cases holding there was no abuse of the qualified privilege are easily distinguishable. This is not a case, for example, where an employee's supervisor, who has worked directly with the employee, provides a negative reference based on personal experience. Nor is this a case where the reference is based on a careful, thorough investigation, or on the employee's own admission. . . . * * *

On this record, therefore, the jury could find wanton, willful, or reckless conduct that amounted to abuse of the qualified privilege.

CASE QUESTIONS

1. What was the legal issue in this case? What did the court decide?

2. How are the elements of a defamation claim satisfied in this case?

3. Why was the company not shielded by "qualified privilege" in this case?

4. What should this employer have done differently?

** * * The qualified privilege may be overcome by showing the defendant acted—*

1. *With actual malice . . . or*
2. *. . . [He or she] used language which was intemperate or disproportionate in strength and violence to the occasion and which was unnecessarily defamatory to the plaintiff; or*
3. *Not in good faith and without an honest belief in their truth; or*
4. *Deliberately adopted a method of speaking the alleged words which gave unnecessary publicity to such words; or*
5. *. . . purposely arranged to speak the alleged words in the presence of a person or persons who were wholly uninterested in the matter and who had no right to be present and who in the natural course of things would not have been present; or*
6. *For the purpose of gratifying some sinister or corrupt motive such as hatred, revenge, personal spite, ill will, or desire to injure the plaintiff; or*
7. *With such gross indifference or recklessness as to amount to a wanton and willful disregard of the rights of plaintiff. . . .*

employer in producing accurate and objective letters of reference should more than suffice to avoid reckless disregard for the truth. As the *Sigal Construction* case shows, *having a substantive, preferably documentary, basis for references is critical.* Malicious intent is less likely to be inferred if the employer *refrains from drawing conclusions about whether the former employee should be hired.* A statement that

someone should not be hired can sound (especially in court) like a grudge is motivating the speaker.

Negligent Referral

What if references are provided, but are misleading and incomplete? Can an employer be sued for negligence in referring an unfit employee who harms others in his new job? In a growing number of jurisdictions, the answer is yes. In *Davis v. The Board of County Commissioners of Doña Ana County,* New Mexico joins the ranks of states that recognize the legal claim of **negligent referral** (or misrepresentation).

DAVIS v. THE BOARD OF COUNTY COMMISSIONERS OF DOÑA ANA COUNTY
987 P.2d 1172 (N.M. App. 1999)

OPINION BY JUDGE RICHARD C. BOSSON:

As a matter of first impression under New Mexico common law, we decide whether an employer owes prospective employers and foreseeable third persons a duty of reasonable care not to misrepresent material facts in the course of making an employment recommendation about a present or former employee, when a substantial risk of physical harm to third persons by the employee is foreseeable. * * *

Mesilla Valley Hospital (MVH), a psychiatric hospital in Doña Ana County, employs mental health technicians for a variety of patient-care functions, such as restraining patients, taking patients on walks, and providing staff coverage at night. MVH hired Joseph "Tinie" Herrera (Herrera) as a mental health technician on January 20, 1995. Plaintiff, a young woman undergoing psychiatric therapy, was admitted to MVH as a patient on February 26 of that same year, and Herrera was assigned to work with her. Plaintiff asserts that Herrera initially managed to ingratiate himself into her confidence, and then, over a period of about two weeks, Herrera subjected Plaintiff to escalating incidents of sexual harassment, sexual assault, and other physical abuse committed under the guise of psychiatric therapy. * * *

Prior to working at MVH, Herrera was employed for some time as a detention sergeant and classification officer at the Doña Ana County Detention Center (Detention Center). According to Plaintiff, MVH's decision to hire Herrera was based in part on unqualified, favorable recommendations from Herrera's supervisors at the Detention Center, Frank Steele and Al Mochen. Steele was the director and Mochen was the captain and assistant director of the Detention Center, both of whom had supervisory authority over Herrera. The accuracy of these favorable recommendations goes to the heart of Plaintiff's suit against the County.

Of particular importance to the accuracy of the recommendations is a report authored by Steele after Herrera was investigated for allegedly sexually harassing female inmates under his authority at the Detention Center. * * * According to Steele's report, Herrera was accused of inappropriate sexual behavior with female inmates that took various forms. The accusations included making statements with sexual overtones, and stating his desire for sex. Reportedly, Herrera received sexual favors from inmates in return for helping them. * * * While not all the allegations against Herrera could be confirmed, the report concluded that Herrera's conduct and performance of duty had been "questionable" and "suspect." Accordingly, Steele recommended disciplinary action against Herrera seeking to have him suspended without pay as well as demoted and reassigned. On April 5, 1994, Steele informed Herrera that he intended to seek disciplinary action at a hearing scheduled for April 12, 1994.

On April 8, 1994, Herrera resigned rather than proceed with the scheduled hearing. Upon his resignation, Herrera asked Steele for a letter of recommendation for prospective employment. On April 11, 1994, only six days after recommending discipline, Steele wrote a positive endorsement of Herrera that omitted any reference to either the reprimand, the subsequent allegations of sexual harassment, the results of the investigation, or the recommended discipline. The letter was written on

county letterhead, which Steele signed as the Detention Center administrator, and stated:

To Whom It May Concern:

This letter will introduce to you, Joseph V. Herrera. I have had the distinct pleasure of working with Tinie Herrera for the past two years. In my opinion he is an excellent employee and supervisor for the Doña Ana County Detention Center. In developing social programs for the inmate population, he displayed considerable initiative and imagination. Tinie was instrumental in the Department's maintenance program and was involved in remodeling projects.

I know that this Department will suffer for his leaving. Employees of his caliber are difficult to find. I am confident that you would find Tinie to be an excellent employee. Should you need verbal confirmation of his ability, I would deem it a pleasure to respond to any inquiries that you may have. . . .

On December 5, 1994, Herrera applied for employment with MVH and included Steele's letter of recommendation. According to Plaintiff, MVH called the Detention Center seeking further information about Herrera, and Mochen told MVH that Herrera was a good person and a hard worker whom he would definitely rehire. * * *

Plaintiff sued the County for negligent misrepresentation alleging that the misinformation supplied by the Detention Center employees, Steele and Mochen, proximately caused Herrera to be hired at MVH and Plaintiff to be assaulted. * * *

First, we must consider whether employers who do not remain silent, those electing to recommend employees, owe any such duty of reasonable care in regard to what they say and how they say it. If so, then we must decide whether such employers owe a duty of care to third parties as well as the prospective employer to whom the recommendation is given. We limit our discussion to the present circumstances involving a substantial, foreseeable risk of physical harm to third parties by the employee if reasonable care is not exercised about what is said when an employer elects to make an unqualified recommendation, and we decide that employers do owe such a duty to third parties. * * *

As an accepted legal proposition, there is generally no affirmative duty to prevent criminal acts by a third party in the absence of some special relationship or statutory duty. However, it is also a general proposition that "every person has a duty to exercise ordinary care for the safety of others" when that person does choose to act. Assuming other policy considerations are satisfied, a duty to exercise ordinary care, where one otherwise would not exist, may arise when a person voluntarily undertakes a course of conduct which, in the absence of due care, may foreseeably injure others as a natural and probable consequence of the person's conduct. * * *

The recent California Supreme Court opinion in *Randi W.*, 929 P.2d 582, is closely analogous and provides persuasive guidance for our case. In *Randi W.*, various officials at different school districts gave gratuitous recommendations "containing unreserved and unconditional praise" of a former employee, despite their knowledge of complaints involving sexual misconduct at his prior employment. The employee was subsequently hired as a vice-principal where he was accused of sexually assaulting a thirteen-year-old student. A unanimous court adopted Sections 310 and 311 of the Restatement [of torts], holding that the recommending school officials owed a duty of care to third-party students "not to misrepresent the facts in describing the qualifications and character of a former employee, if making these misrepresentations would present a substantial, foreseeable risk of physical injury to the third persons." "Having volunteered this information, defendants were obliged to complete the picture by disclosing material facts regarding charges and complaints of [the teacher]'s sexual improprieties." * * *

[W]e see nothing in the facts as alleged that would make the assault and battery suffered by Plaintiff either too remote as a matter of policy or unforeseeable as a matter of law. The County's agents could have remained silent in response to requests for information about Herrera. Instead, they elected to recommend him in a manner distorted by misrepresentations and half-truths. The employment recommendations of Steele and Mochen provided unqualified praise of Herrera as an excellent employee of a caliber that is "difficult to find," and yet they omitted disciplinary action both taken and recommended by these same officers against Herrera. The disciplinary action came as a result of allegations, a subsequent investigation, and a resulting report in which Steele was directly involved, which constitutes far more than mere gossip or innuendo. The information in the report concerned abuse of power and sexual abuse of women who were directly under Herrera's control at the Detention Center which bears a direct correlation to the

potential risks female patients would incur if they were placed under Herrera's control at MVH. The parallels are compelling. We are not persuaded that reasonable people, who had the information possessed by Steele and Mochen, could not have foreseen potential victims like Plaintiff, and could not have foreseen how the omission of objective information, like Steele's report and the disciplinary actions taken, would not pose a threat of physical harm to persons like Plaintiff. * * *

[We] determine that Steele and Mochen did owe a duty of care, once they elected to make employment recommendations for Herrera, in regard to what they said and what they omitted from their references. We also conclude that such a duty was owed to Plaintiff as a third-party victim, under the circumstances of this case. We intend our holding to be narrow. We decline to speculate on how different facts and circumstances, such as the lapse of time between the referral and the assault, might affect this duty, and where "social policy" might compel us "to draw the line against otherwise unlimited liability." * * *

We acknowledge that, at the margins, the common-law duty we recognize in this opinion may discourage some employment referrals. But that impact should be minimal. The duty not to misrepresent applies only in cases of foreseeable physical harm. The vast majority of cases will involve pejorative information in the hands of an employer that does not create a risk of foreseeable physical harm and accordingly does not implicate this duty to disclose. When physical harm by the employee is foreseeable, the employer who discloses will be protected against defamation by the qualified privilege. However, even if some overly cautious employers are deterred unnecessarily from volunteering helpful information and

elect to remain silent, we determine that silence may be preferable under these circumstances to what Steele and Mochen stand accused of in this case. In the face of silence from a former employer, the prospective employer can still conduct its own investigation; silence renders the employer no worse off. In contrast, the prospective employer who is misled may relax its own guard; it may not investigate as thoroughly, and may end up worse off than if it had received no information at all. On balance, therefore, the policy gains of imposing a duty not to misrepresent under these limited circumstances outweigh the potential consequences of inhibiting employer disclosure. * * *

We reverse the district court's grant of summary judgment for the County. . . .

CASE QUESTIONS

1. What was the legal issue? What did the court decide in this case?

2. Why does the court conclude that Doña Ana County could be held liable for negligent referral (misrepresentation)?

3. Would it have made any difference if the assault occurred several years after Herrera was hired, rather than a few months later?

4. Should it have mattered that the former employer's investigation was not able to confirm all the allegations against Herrera?

5. What are the practical implications of this case? Are you convinced by the court's claim that its ruling should not make employers more reluctant to provide references?

The practical implication of the growing recognition of negligent referral as a cause of action is clear; *employers that choose to respond to requests for information about former employers must not do so in a selective and misleading manner*—at least when referring persons for jobs that pose foreseeable harm to others.

At least one more significant legal concern exists regarding references—retaliation. In one such case, an employee was fired and filed a charge of race discrimination against his former employer. While his case was being investigated by the EEOC, the employee applied for a job with another company. The company asked his former employer for a reference. The former employer provided a damaging reference, which the employee alleged was done in retaliation for his discrimination charge.

The U.S. Supreme Court decided that the former employee could sue his former employer for retaliation under these circumstances.[21] Most (but not all) courts seem to regard the unwarranted negative reference itself as an "adverse employment action" sufficient to sustain a retaliation claim and do not require the plaintiff to show that he would have obtained a specific employment opportunity absent the damaging reference. It is enough that the reference is likely to negatively affect future employment prospects.[22] *References provided for former employees who have legal action pending against an employer require particular care to ensure that they are no more negative than the facts warrant and that they do not urge that a candidate not be hired.*

Should Employers Provide Substantive References? To this point, we have discussed what can be done to minimize the legal problems associated with references. The question remains as to whether references should be provided at all. Many employers have concluded that, in light of the legal jeopardy, either no references or only references of the most skeletal sort—basically confirmation of dates of employment—should be provided. In the 2004 Society for Human Resource Management survey, 54 percent of respondents said their organization has a policy of not providing references due to legal concerns (see "Clippings"). Clearly, if employers do not say anything of substance, there will not be any grounds for defamation or other claims. Nor is there any generally applicable legal requirement that employers respond to requests for references (although some states mandate that "service letters" be provided for former employees). In one case, an employee claimed that his reputation was harmed because his former employer told prospective new employers that it would not provide any information about him, leading those employers to conclude that negative information was being concealed. The court rejected that argument and held that "[w]e agree with Rheem [the employer] that the mere refusal to talk about Saucedo [the former employee] as a matter of law does not constitute a defamation."[23]

The argument can be made that in refusing to provide substantive references, employers are overreacting to what is a relatively minor legal threat. The number of defamation claims based on references is small—and the number of successful claims even smaller. Consent and qualified privilege provide employers with powerful defenses, even when they communicate false and damaging information. Some states have augmented these common law defenses with statutes shielding employers who make references in good faith from defamation claims. However, there are questions about the efficacy of such laws and whether they actually extend or diminish qualified privilege. The basic problem is not that employers lose defamation suits in significant numbers, but that they face thousands of dollars in legal expenses if forced to defend such claims.[24] Although their numbers are also small, negligent referral and retaliation claims based on references provide further incentive for employers to remain mum.

A curious disconnect exists between the information that employers want and what they are willing to provide, however. In light of potential negligent hiring claims and security concerns, not to mention the desire to hire the best people,

[21]*Robinson v. Shell Oil Co.,* 117 S. Ct. 843 (1997).

[22]*Hillig v. Rumsfeld,* 381 F.3d 1028 (10th Cir. 2004).

[23]*Saucedo v. Rheem Manufacturing Co.,* 974 S.W.2d 117, at 122 (Tex. App. 1998).

[24]Deborah A. Ballam. "Employment References—Speak No Evil, Hear No Evil: A Proposal for Meaningful Reform." *American Business Law Journal* 39 (Spring 2002), 445–66.

employers are greatly in need of reliable information about prospective employees. Former employers are often the best or only source of the relevant information. Yet, employers that provide only "name, rank, and serial number" should not expect to get more useful information in return. Some employers apparently resort to "back-channel" communications (off-the-record conversations) as an alternative.[25] Although such communications are less detectable, if they come to light, they can look bad and smack of malice or retaliation.

CRIMINAL RECORDS

One of the clearest indications that a prospective employee might be unfit for a position is a history of criminal activity. Failing to check for a criminal record is probably the surest route to negligent hiring. However, legal issues affect both access to information about criminal histories and the use of that information. Conviction information is not always readily available and should not be used to exclude all persons with criminal histories from hiring.

At the start, a distinction should be drawn between **arrests** and **convictions.** Individuals who are arrested ("picked up" by the police and taken to the police station with the intent of charging them with crimes) are often released without actually being charged. They might be picked up for questioning due to proximity to a crime, mistaken identity, or any of a million other reasons. Even if charged, a grand jury might decline to indict or the government might not be able to prove its case. Our system of law operates on the presumption that persons accused of crimes are innocent until proven guilty. Thus, an arrest does not clearly say anything valid about a person's character or fitness. On the other hand, a conviction of a crime, either following a trial or a guilty plea, is a clearer indication of fitness and character. Even so, the employer would still want to ask questions such as: What crime? Under what circumstances? How long ago? What has the person done since?

Information about convictions, unless the records are sealed or "expunged" (removed from the person's record) by a court, are public records and theoretically accessible. However, a few states limit access to criminal records (and the use of such information in hiring decisions) and allow persons to apply for jobs without revealing their criminal histories. Moreover, retrieving information about convictions is not as simple as just hopping onto the Internet. The main problem is that court systems and record keeping are decentralized. A search for conviction records in the area that the job candidate currently resides will not unearth convictions that occurred in other states (or, for that matter, other countries). People with unsavory pasts also tend to change their names and do other things that confound tracking their records. Most employers do not deal directly with these problems, but instead use the services of background checking companies or private investigators. *When employers rely on these services to check for criminal convictions, the comprehensiveness of the search is an important factor.* A search limited to a single state or county is often not sufficient.

To the extent that good information about criminal history can be obtained, what should employers do with it? If the information indicates unfitness for positions where there is foreseeability of harm to others, the threat of negligent hiring suits (and ethics) clearly indicates that unfit candidates should not be hired. However,

[25]Jeffrey L. Seglin. "Too Much Ado About Giving References." *New York Times* (February 21, 1999), BU-4.

problems arise when employers overreact to this legitimate concern by seeking to exclude anyone with a prior criminal conviction (or worse, who has been arrested). There have been successful legal challenges to such policies based on their potential to create adverse impact. How does this work? Under federal law, not having been arrested or convicted for a crime is a neutral requirement, rather than a protected class characteristic. However, this neutral requirement is likely to exclude persons of color at a much higher rate than whites. African Americans and Latinos are far more likely to be both arrested and convicted for crimes. Statistics show, for example, that African Americans are about six times more likely than whites to be convicted of crimes and imprisoned.[26] Thus, relying on criminal histories is likely to screen out African Americans and Latinos at much higher rates than other races and national origins.

Is the absence of prior arrests or convictions a defensible requirement? Recall that even sharply disproportionate outcomes can be defended in adverse impact claims when the neutral requirements that produce them are "job-related and consistent with business necessity." The job-relatedness of prior arrests is difficult to argue for most jobs (law enforcement jobs perhaps excepted), because it is unclear whether arrests mean anything about a person's prior behavior or character.[27] Convictions have a stronger claim to job-relatedness, but courts have held that rather than simply slam the door of employment opportunity shut on anyone who has a prior conviction, employers need to consider, on an individual basis, the seriousness of the offense, its relation to the job in question, and how long ago the offense occurred.[28] Thus, *employers should not use information related to prior arrests in making hiring decisions. Information about prior convictions can, and often should, be used. However, employers should not exclude all persons with prior criminal convictions. Instead, a more individualized assessment should occur, focusing on the seriousness of the offense, its relation to the job in question, and its recency.*

CREDIT REPORTS—THE FAIR CREDIT REPORTING ACT

Credit report is an amorphous term that refers to what can be rather wide-ranging inquiries into the backgrounds of job applicants. The **Fair Credit Reporting Act (FCRA)**,[29] the major federal law regulating the gathering, sharing, and use of information by employers and consumer reporting agencies, distinguishes two types of credit report: consumer reports and investigative reports. The FCRA defines a **consumer credit report** as:

> any written, oral or other communication of any information by a consumer reporting agency bearing on a consumer's credit worthiness, credit standing, credit capacity, character, general reputation, personal characteristics, or mode of living which is expected to be used or collected in whole or part for the purpose of serving as a factor in establishing the consumer's eligibility for . . . employment purposes.[30]

[26]Fox Butterfield. "Number of Inmates Reaches Record 1.8 Million." *New York Times* (March 15, 1999), A-12.

[27]*Gregory v. Litton Systems,* 316 F. Supp. 401 (C.D. Cal. 1970), *affirmed,* 472 F.2d 631 (9th Cir. 1972).

[28]*Green v. Missouri Pacific Railroad,* 523 F.2d 1290, at 1298 (8th Cir. 1975).

[29]15 U.S.C.A. § 1681 et seq. (2005).

[30]15 U.S.C.A. § 1681a(d)(1) (2005).

An **investigative report** contains similar information but is also based on personal interviews with friends, neighbors, or other associates. The term *consumer* is used rather than *employee* because the law also applies to information used in making loan decisions and other nonemployment matters. Notice that although these reports can contain financial information such as bankruptcy filings and repayment of loans, they can go far beyond financial matters to reach all other aspects of background checks, including contacting references and examining conviction records. To implicate the FCRA, the information must be obtained from a **consumer reporting agency.** This term is also broadly defined and includes any entity that regularly gathers or evaluates information on consumers to furnish reports to third parties. The term clearly encompasses companies that perform background checks for employers.

The FCRA is a response to the problem of inaccurate information being gathered and sold about persons, resulting in their being denied jobs, mortgages, and other opportunities. It has many detailed provisions. One important requirement is that *a prospective employer must obtain from a job applicant his written consent to obtain a consumer report. This consent must be indicated on a written notice of the employer's intent to use credit information in the hiring decision that contains no other information.* A statement on an application form will not suffice for this purpose. Proof of consent is then forwarded to the consumer reporting agency with the request for information. Although the background check cannot proceed without the employee's consent, an employer does not have to consider for employment someone who declines to authorize gathering and sharing of information about him. It also appears that "blanket authorizations," permitting an employer to obtain an employee's credit report again in the future should the need arise, are permissible under the FCRA.[31]

If, based *in any part* on information from a consumer credit report, an employer intends to take an **adverse action** (such as not hiring or promoting) against a job applicant or employee, the *employer must provide the individual with a "pre–adverse action disclosure."* This document must be provided prior to actually taking the adverse action. The disclosure is to include a copy of the individual's consumer credit report and a statement of his rights under the FCRA. The purpose of this requirement is to provide individuals with notice that negative information about them exists and to afford them the opportunity to address possible inaccuracies. However, employers do not have to wait any specific period of time before finalizing their decisions not to hire or promote. *After taking an adverse action based on a consumer credit report, an "adverse action notice" must be provided.* The casinos that rejected applicants based on their credit reports, but did not inform those applicants regarding the basis for their hiring decisions—much less provide copies of their credit reports—were clearly in violation of the FCRA (see "Clippings"). Insofar as reliance on credit reports in making employment decisions triggers employer obligations under the FCRA, the question of what motivated an employment decision is apt to arise. In one such case, the employer failed to provide the requisite disclosures, but argued that falsification of an employee's application, and not the information in her credit report, was the basis for a termination. However, the plaintiff was allowed to go to trial on her FCRA claim because a manager's e-mail message referred to concerns about allowing the woman to manage the organization's assets when she apparently had problems with her own finances and because the woman was told at her termination meeting that her credit report was "terrible."[32]

[31]*Kelchner v. Sycamore Manor Health Center,* 2005 U.S. App. LEXIS 3697, at 8.

[32]*Woodell v. United Way of Dutchess County,* 357 F.Supp. 2d 761, at 773–74 (S.D.N.Y. 2005).

The FCRA places responsibilities on both users of consumer information (e.g., employers) and consumer reporting agencies. A basic responsibility of the latter is to "follow reasonable procedures to assure maximum possible accuracy of the information concerning the individual about whom the report relates."[33] The act also requires that stale information be excluded from consumer reports. Reporting agencies are prohibited from including information relating to civil suits, civil judgments, arrests, paid tax liens, accounts placed for collection, and "any other adverse item of information" when it dates back more than seven years. Information about prior Chapter 11 bankruptcy proceedings can date back no more than 10 years. However, these limitations on the inclusion of dated information in consumer reports do not apply if the job for which a candidate is being considered pays more than $75,000 a year. Importantly, "records of convictions of crimes" are explicitly excluded, allowing conviction information (as opposed to arrests) to go back further than seven years.[34]

A FCRA case was brought against both IBM and a company that it uses to perform background checks. The facts of the case are complicated, but basically IBM decided not to hire an individual as a marketing manager because he failed to report a plea of "no contest" to a misdemeanor charge—a conviction that was subsequently vacated by a court—in his application materials. IBM's policy on criminal history is recounted in the case and worth quoting at length:

> An applicant must also complete a Security Data Sheet ("SDS"), which requests . . . that he identify whether he has pleaded guilty or "no contest" to a crime or other offense within the last seven years. However, the applicant is expressly requested not to include "arrests without convictions" or "convictions or incarcerations for which a record has been sealed or expunged." Both the application form and the SDS provide that "any misrepresentation or deliberate omission of a fact . . . will justify terminating consideration" of the application for employment. Further, IBM policy states that the mere identification of a conviction on the SDS will not subject an applicant to disqualification. Rather, the policy requires that the company perform an analysis of whether the crime is related to the position for which the applicant has applied.[35]

The plaintiff claimed that IBM violated the FCRA by deciding not to hire him prior to providing the requisite pre-adverse action disclosure. However, the court dismissed the case against IBM, noting that the statute does not prohibit an employer from formulating the intent to not hire someone through internal discussions before providing the required notice. In fact, this is the very process that the act contemplates; "[a]fter all, how can an employer send an intent letter without having first formed the requisite intent?"[36] The background checking company Choicepoint was less fortunate. The plaintiff's claim that it failed to take reasonable measures to ensure the accuracy of its report was allowed to continue.

[33]15 U.S.C.A. § 1681e(b) (2005).

[34]15 21 U.S.C.A. § 1681c(5) (2005).

[35]*Obabueki v. IBM and Choicepoint, Inc.*, 145 F. Supp. 2d 371, at 375–76 (S.D.N.Y. 2001); *affirmed*, 319 F.3d 87 (2d Cir. 2003); *cert. denied*, 2003 U.S. LEXIS 7336.

[36]*Obabueki*, at 392.

THE CHANGING WORKPLACE

Immigration and the U.S. Workforce

As of mid-2005, the U.S. population stood at nearly 297 million. The U.S. workforce numbered about 150 million people. According to a study by the Department of Labor, immigration will be the major influence on population growth over the next half century.[1] Fully two-thirds of the projected increase in the U.S. population will be due to net immigration. In 2004, about 36 million people residing in the U.S. were foreign-born.[2] Immigration is a primary reason Latinos now slightly outnumber African Americans as the nation's largest "minority" group.[3]

Immigrants who are not citizens of this country are often referred to as "aliens." Noncitizens sometimes have the legal right to work in the United States. Noncitizens who are eligible to work in the United States are referred to as **legal aliens**, whereas those not eligible to work in the United States are termed **illegal** (or unauthorized or undocumented) **aliens**. Persons from other countries who possess unexpired work-authorizing visas (such as the H-1B visa discussed in the previous chapter) are entitled to work in the United States. Likewise, noncitizens with resident alien registration cards (green cards) are eligible to work in the United States. Of course, citizens, whether born in the United States or naturalized, are eligible to work in the United States. Despite policies intended to discourage illegal immigration, the number of illegal aliens in the United States is estimated to be over 10 million.[4] Illegal immigrants, the majority from Mexico and other Latin American countries, are increasingly found throughout the United States and not only in the large border states of California and Texas. Many undocumented workers are employed and some industries are dependent on their labor. Undocumented workers are particularly likely to occupy such jobs as drywall installers, meat and poultry plant workers, dishwashers, farm workers, and janitors.

The employment law issue that flows most immediately from immigration is compliance with requirements of the Immigration Reform and Control Act. This is discussed in the text that follows. Another legal concern linked to immigration is discriminatory employer policies and requirements pertaining to language. Additionally, immigrants often work under harsh, unsafe, and exploitative conditions, raising questions under minimum wage and safety and health laws. The contractors providing janitors to Wal-Mart are accused of numerous wage and hour violations, including making the employees work seven days a week without overtime pay (see "Clippings").

[1] U.S. Department of Labor. "Futurework: Trends and Challenges for Work in the 21st Century." Viewed on June 27, 2000 (http://www.dol.gov/asp/programs/ history/herman/reports/ futurework/report.htm).

[2] Jeffrey S. Passel. *Estimates of the Size and Characteristics of the Undocumented Population.* Report of the Pew Hispanic Center (March 21, 2005), 2.

[3] Lynette Clemetson. "Hispanic Population Is Rising Swiftly, Census Bureau Says." *New York Times* (June 19, 2003), A-22.

[4] Passel, at 2.

VERIFYING EMPLOYMENT ELIGIBILITY

Many people come to the United States from other countries to work. Employers have the responsibility of verifying that all persons hired have the legal right to work in the United States. Immigration has long shaped the U.S. workforce, but the Immigration Reform and Control Act of 1986 and more recent amendments have moved the workplace to the front lines in the government's efforts to curtail illegal immigration.

The Immigration Reform and Control Act

The **Immigration Reform and Control Act (IRCA)** has two main requirements. First, all *employers are prohibited from knowingly hiring or retaining on the job*

unauthorized aliens.[37] Second, *employers with four or more employees are prohibited from discriminating in hiring or termination decisions on the basis of national origin and citizenship.*[38] Of course, this protection against discrimination applies only to citizens and legal immigrants. It does not conflict with the requirement that employers screen out undocumented workers. Nor does this requirement prohibit employers from preferring U.S. citizens for employment when two individuals are equally qualified. Nondiscrimination provisions were included in this law because Congress did not want employers to respond to IRCA by excluding all "foreigners."

To avoid hiring or retaining persons ineligible to work in the United States, employers need to do a number of things. The following procedures apply only to persons hired, and not to all applicants. *Within three days after a newly hired employee begins work, his employer must verify his eligibility to work in the United States. This must be done for all newly hired workers,* and not simply those whose employment eligibility is questioned. This verification is accomplished by *viewing documents establishing eligibility to work and recording the documents viewed on an "Employment Eligibility Verification" form (I-9 form) provided by the federal government's Office of Citizenship and Immigration Services.* Documents can establish identity, eligibility to work, or both. Documents typically used for these purposes include a Social Security card, driver's license, birth certificate, U.S. passport, certificate of naturalization, resident alien registration card, and an unexpired employment authorization document. A full list of acceptable documents can be found on the back of the I-9 form. A voluntary pilot program by the federal government provides employers with a Web-based system for electronically verifying the work authorization documents of newly hired employees.[39] Other than certified copies of birth certificates, *only original documents should be accepted.* Employers are permitted, but not required, to make copies of documents provided by newly hired employees. Employers are not required to further investigate the authenticity of documents, provided that these "reasonably appear on their face to be genuine." Retaining copies of the documents presented can help prove that the decision to accept them was reasonable. *I-9 forms and any copies of documents must be kept separate from employees' personnel files and retained for three years from the date of hire or one year after employment is terminated, whichever is longer.* Thus, the minimum period of time that these forms must be kept is three years. Employment for more than two years extends this period.

Suits like the one against Wal-Mart and its contractors, alleging that they knowingly employed undocumented workers (see "Clippings"), are becoming more common. A suit alleging that Mohawk Industries engaged in a conspiracy in violation of the Rackateer Influenced and Corrupt Organizations Act (RICO) by knowingly hiring undocumented workers for the purpose of driving down wages and workers' compensation claims has been allowed to go to trial.[40] The plaintiffs still have a difficult road ahead, as evidenced by the acquittal in 2003 of Tyson Foods on charges that it had conspired to bring undocumented workers into its poultry plants.[41]

[37] 8 U.S.C.A. § 1324a(a)(1), (2) (2005).

[38] 8 U.S.C.A. § 1324b(1) (2005).

[39] Fawn H. Johnson. "DHS Expands Pilot Program for Verifying Work Authorization Documents to 50 States." *Daily Labor Report* 242 (December 17, 2004), A-1.

[40] *Williams v. Mohawk Industries,* 2005 U.S. App. LEXIS 10710.

[41] Sherri Day. "Jury Clears Tyson Foods in Use of Illegal Immigrants." *New York Times* (March 27, 2003), A12.

Chapter SUMMARY

Compelling legal (and ethical) reasons exist for employers' concerns about hiring unfit employees. If an employee inadvertently harms someone in the course of doing his job, his employer is generally liable for that harm under the doctrine of respondeat superior. But the responsibility of employers for harmful actions of their employees does not end with actions that are taken within the scope of employment. Negligent hiring claims hold an employer liable for harmful actions that take place outside the scope of employment, but for which inadequate screening procedures set the stage. More exactly, an employer is liable for negligent hiring when the employer fails to exercise the level of care in screening out unfit employees that a reasonable person would have used under the circumstances, and the hiring of an unfit person was the proximate cause of harm to some third party.

No single standard is used for how thorough background checks must be and, thus, how far employers must go to avoid breaching their duty. Instead, courts look to a combination of public policy, foreseeability, and knowledge to determine the extent of an employer's duty to screen out unfit employees. Foreseeability refers to the likelihood of harm to others if an unfit person is hired for the position in question. The greater the potential harm, the more extensive the background check should be. Knowledge refers to the extent to which the employer knew, or should have known, if a proper background check had been done, of the unfitness of the person hired. Employers will not be held liable for failing to do an adequate background check when the evidence of unfitness that a background check would uncover does not exist.

Background checks typically include efforts to obtain information from former employers. The legal issues surrounding references primarily affect the former employers asked to provide information. Employers providing references that are false and damaging to the reputations of former employees may be liable for defamation. However, references (or other communications) that would otherwise be defamatory will not subject an employer to liability if the former employee consented to have information released or if qualified privilege was not lost. Qualified privilege is the legal presumption that employers will be immune from liability for engaging in the socially useful act of conveying information about former employees to others with legitimate need to have that information. This immunity is conditional on the absence of malicious intent to harm the former employee's reputation,

reckless disregard for the truth, or overly broad communication of the false and damaging information. Former employers providing references must also be concerned about suits for retaliation against former employees who have filed discrimination charges and for negligent referral. The latter occurs when a reference is provided, the reference is highly misleading, another employer relies on the reference to hire an unfit employee, and that employee proceeds to harm someone in his new job when it was foreseeable that such harm could occur.

A record of criminal convictions is a key indicator of unfitness for many jobs. Employers seeking to check for criminal records may find that they are constrained by state laws that limit access to this information and/or its use. Heavy reliance on criminal records to screen out unfit employees may also produce adverse impact discrimination. Information about arrests can rarely be used legally, whereas convictions can be taken into account, provided that the severity of the offense, its relationship to the job in question, and its recency are considered.

Consumer credit reports or investigative reports that are compiled by credit reporting agencies and sold to employers are regulated by the Fair Credit Reporting Act (FCRA). Credit reports can contain information about character and lifestyle, and are not limited to financial dealings. The FCRA holds many requirements for both employers and consumer reporting agencies. These include the requirement that employers obtain the consent of employees or applicants before seeking to obtain credit reports and provisions for prior and concurrent notice when denial of an employment opportunity (an adverse action) is based in any part on the contents of a credit report.

Whatever else employers do in terms of background checks, they are legally required to verify the employment eligibility of all persons that they hire. Persons eligible for employment in the United States include U.S. citizens and "legal aliens." The Immigration Reform and Control Act (IRCA) prohibits employers from knowingly hiring or retaining illegal or unauthorized aliens. The law also protects legal aliens by prohibiting discrimination in hiring and firing on the basis of national origin or citizenship. Immigrants, both those with proper documentation and those without, continue to come to the United States in large numbers and are projected to make up a large part of the growth in the population and workforce over the coming decades.

Practical Advice SUMMARY

- Depending on the circumstances, an adequate background check might include

 –contacting references.

 –verifying past employment and military service.

 –verifying possession of degrees, licenses, and other credentials.

 –checking criminal and driving records.

 –examining credit reports.

- Background checks must be more extensive when hiring for positions in which unfit employees could do serious harm to others.

- At minimum, an employer should always follow its own established background check procedures and avoid last-minute, rushed hiring decisions that require deviation from normal procedures.

- Inconsistencies and gaps in information provided by applicants should

 –be detected and confronted.

 –result in nonhire if they cannot be satisfactorily explained.

- In conducting background checks, employers should

 –document all efforts to obtain information on job candidates, even when those efforts are not successful.

 –attempt to corroborate answers, and not merely ask applicants, about important matters such as criminal convictions.

- If, despite the inadvisability of doing so, an employer opts to hire a needed employee prior to completing a background check, the employer should still complete the background check—but only if the employer is willing to use any evidence of unfitness discovered (or application falsification) as a basis for terminating the employee.

- To make references as accurate and objective as possible

 –base them on inspection of documents rather than memory alone.

 –confine comments to known facts rather than speculation or impressions.

 –centralize the provision of references by assigning them to designated persons thoroughly familiar with procedures for researching and writing letters of reference.

- Former employers should

 –require that requests for references be accompanied by written release forms signed by former employees.

 –attempt to reach an agreement with departing employees regarding the content of letters of reference.

 –verify the identities of persons seeking information about former employees by requiring that requests be made on company letterhead.

 –refrain from drawing conclusions about whether former employees should be hired by other prospective employers.

- If former employers respond to requests for references at all, then they must do so in a manner that is not misleading.

- Employers should generally not use information about prior arrests in making hiring decisions.

- Before denying employment based on a criminal conviction, employers should consider the seriousness, job-relatedness, and recency of the offense.

- Employers that rely on other companies or individuals to perform criminal background checks should

 –ascertain and agree upon the comprehensiveness of those searches.

 –get written consent to obtain a consumer credit report and do so on a separate form containing no other information (i.e., not an application form).

 –provide a pre-adverse action disclosure if the employer intends to deny an employment opportunity based in whole or in part on a consumer credit report.

 –provide an adverse action notice if an employment opportunity is denied based in whole or in part on the contents of a consumer credit report.

- Employers must not knowingly hire or retain employees who are unauthorized aliens.

- Employers must not discriminate on the basis of national origin or citizenship in carrying out their responsibility to not hire unauthorized aliens.

- *When hiring new employees, employers must*

 –*verify the employment eligibility of newly hired employees within three days after they begin work.*

 –*view documents (e.g., birth certificate, driver's license, resident alien registration card) to establish identity and eligibility to work in the United States.*

 –*record the documents examined on I-9 forms.*

- *Employers can and should make copies of the original documents examined.*

- *I-9 forms should be*

 –*kept separate from employees' personnel files.*

 –*retained for three years or one year after employment is terminated, whichever is longer.*

Key TERMS

background check	consent	consumer credit report
respondeat superior	qualified privilege	investigative report
negligence	malice	consumer reporting agency
negligent hiring	reckless disregard for the truth	adverse action
public policy	overly broad publication	legal alien
foreseeability	negligent referral	illegal alien
knowledge	arrest	Immigration Reform and Control
proximity	conviction	Act (IRCA)
defamation	Fair Credit Reporting Act (FCRA)	

Chapter QUESTIONS

1. A passenger on a flight was greeted by a flight attendant whom he had never met and told that she liked his smile and that "he would be her #1." During the flight, the flight attendant hit the passenger on the head with her open hand several times to initiate a conversation. The passenger moved to another seat to get away from the flight attendant. The flight attendant subsequently poured water on his lap. She proceeded to place stickers labeled "fragile" on the passenger's arm, cheeks, and crotch. The flight attendant forcibly attempted to kiss the passenger on the lips. She also rubbed her tongue along the rim of a beer can before handing it to the passenger. After the plane landed, the flight attendant grabbed the passenger and kissed his lips in an effort to get "one last kiss" while he was standing in line waiting for a rental car. The passenger sued the airline. What should the court decide? Why?

(*Twardy v. Northwest Airlines*, 2001 U.S. Dist. LEXIS 2112)

2. A 15-year-old from a residential facility for troubled teens was traveling on a Greyhound bus. The driver of the bus conversed with the young woman during the trip. At a stop where the driver was scheduled to go off duty for eight hours of rest as required by law, the driver told the young woman that she would have to come to his motel room to obtain a pass enabling her to reboard the bus. In the room provided to the driver by the bus line, the young woman was sexually assaulted. The driver eventually pled guilty to sexual imposition and was sentenced to prison. The driver had been hired five years earlier. He had denied any criminal history on his application form. In fact, he had been convicted of criminal sexual conduct with a minor

in 1980. Greyhound's criminal background check covered the years of 1987–1997 and did not discover the earlier conviction. A suit was brought against the company on behalf of the young woman. What should the court decide? Why? (*Cromp v. Greyhound Lines*, 2003 U.S. Dist. LEXIS 22921)

3. A female student at Virginia Polytechnic Institute was exiting a restroom when a male janitor accosted her. The attacker pushed her back onto the floor and attempted to strangle her. The student survived the attack, but suffered broken facial bones and required neck surgery. The janitor was an employee of Defender Services, which had a contract to provide janitors for the university. The janitor had worked on and off for the company for several years. The first two times that he was hired, he filled out application forms and attested to having no criminal record. The third time he was hired, no application was required, but several personal references were contacted. On none of these occasions did the company complete a criminal background check on the employee. This was despite the fact that the company's contract with the university called for background checks to be performed on all personnel assigned to the university. Eleven months prior to the attack on the student, a protective order had been issued against the employee, stemming from his physical assault on a woman at a restaurant. The injured student sued the services company. What should the court decide? Why? (*Blair v. Defender Services*, 386 F.3d 623 (4th Cir. 2004))

4. An airline employee had a disagreement with her employer and resigned. She went looking for a new job. The responses that she received from prospective employers made her suspicious that there might be a problem with the references being provided by her former employer. She asked friends to call the airline posing as prospective employers. They were told by two managers that the former employee "could work without supervision on occasion," "did not get along well with other employees," "was somewhat dependable," "is a troublemaker," "was not an accomplished planner," and "would not be a good person to rehire." She sued the airline. What should the court decide? Why? (*Chambers v. American Trans Air*, 577 N.E.2d 612 (Ind. App. 1991))

5. Gail Davis worked as an executive assistant to Motown legend, Diana Ross. After about a year, the woman voluntarily resigned. About a year later, Diana Ross wrote and distributed the following letter:

> To Whom It May Concern:
>
> The following people are no longer in my employment.
>
> [list of former employees including Gail Davis]
>
> If I let an employee go, it's because either their work or their personal habits are not acceptable to me. I do not recommend these people. In fact, if you hear from these people, and they use my name as a reference, I wish to be contacted.

Gail Davis had not used Ms. Ross as a reference, nor had any employer requested information from her about Gail Davis. Ms. Davis sued Ms. Ross. What should the court decide? Why? (*Davis v. Ross*, 754 F.2d 80 (2d Cir. 1985))

6. An employee accepted a job with Hilton Hotels. On his employment application, he truthfully replied "no" to a question asking whether he had ever been convicted of a felony or misdemeanor. A paragraph at the bottom of the application stated that "I authorize Hilton to investigate my background . . ." However, the employee did not initial this paragraph. A background checking company (IMI) was asked to check the employee's background. IMI erroneously reported that the employee had been convicted of a misdemeanor and had served six months in jail. The employee was not informed of the background check. When he was confronted by a supervisor who asked him whether he had ever been in prison, the employee again said that he had not. Hilton did not look into the matter any further. Instead, the employee was terminated for falsifying his application. He sued both Hilton and IMI. What should the court decide? Why? (*Socorro v. IMI Data Search and Hilton Hotels*, 2003 U.S. Dist. LEXIS 7400)

7. What conclusions do you draw regarding the use of criminal histories in hiring? Is there a conflict between the interests of employers in being free from liability for negligent hiring and public policy favoring the reemployment of persons who have paid their debts to society?

8. Should employers provide substantive references or is it just not worth the risk?

Internet RESOURCES

Numerous firms perform background checks for employers and are available on the Internet. Two examples are:

http://www.employeescreen.com

http://www.infolinkscreening.com

The Privacy Rights Clearinghouse's site includes the "Employment Background Checks: A Jobseeker's Guide" fact sheet.

http://www.privacyrights.org/fs/fs16-bck.htm

The Federal Trade Commission is charged with enforcing the Fair Credit Reporting Act, and its Web site contains materials intended to aid compliance with the FCRA.

http://www.ftc.gov/os/statutes/fcra/jump.htm

Employment Testing

CLIPPINGS

▶ The EEOC and the Burlington Northern Santa Fe Railway (BNSF) have settled a disability discrimination case challenging the company's use of genetic testing. The company had required employees who submitted claims of work-related carpal tunnel syndrome to provide blood samples. Without the workers' knowledge or consent, these samples were then tested for a genetic characteristic thought to be related to carpal tunnel syndrome. The railroad denies that it violated the ADA, but it will no longer conduct the genetic tests and it will pay over $2 million to the affected employees.[1]

▶ Major League Baseball has reached an agreement with the union that represents professional baseball players on a stricter policy for regulating the use of steroids and other illegal drugs. The previous policy had been criticized as being overly lenient. The new policy provides that players testing positive for steroids will receive 10-day suspensions, with lengthier suspensions forthcoming for any subsequent positive tests.

Random testing for steroids will occur, including during the off-season.[2]

▶ A federal judge has ruled that a test used to assess candidates for entry-level firefighter positions in Chicago discriminated against African Americans. The city failed to show that the test measured skills essential for performance as a firefighter; it used an arbitrary cutoff score that excluded many qualified candidates; and it declined to use less discriminatory, alternative methods for selecting firefighters.[3]

▶ A strength test used by Dial Corporation for entry-level jobs at one of its meat processing plants has been found to discriminate against women. Ninty-seven percent of male applicants passed the "work tolerance" test, compared to less than 40 percent of female applicants. Prior to implementation of the test in 2000, nearly half of the persons hired for this work were women. Dial's effort to defend the test on the grounds that it was needed to reduce injuries in the plant was not successful.[4]

[1]"Accord on Genetic Tests." *New York Times* (May 9, 2002), A-22.

[2]Tyler Kepner. "Baseball Sets Tougher Policy on Steroid Use." *New York Times* (January 14, 2005), A-1.

[3]"Court Says Chicago Firefighter Exam Had Disparate Impact on African Americans." *Daily Labor Report* 65 (April 6, 2005), A-6.

[4]Equal Employment Opportunity Commission. "Pre-Employment Test by Dial Corp. Discriminates Against Women, Court Rules in EEOC Case." News Release (February 8, 2005). Viewed July 15, 2005 (http://www.eeoc.gov/press/2-8-05.html).

Employers use a bewildering variety of employment tests to make hiring and promotion decisions. Employment tests are also used to ascertain fitness to continue on the job. This chapter considers the legal implications of testing procedures, including drug tests, medical examinations, HIV tests, genetic tests, polygraphs, honesty tests, psychological tests, intelligence and skill tests, and physical fitness tests. Some of these tests are intended to identify disqualifying characteristics (e.g., use of illegal drugs, lack of truthfulness), whereas others focus on measuring the extent to which desirable characteristics (e.g., intelligence, strength) are present. The overriding legal concern with employment tests is discrimination, but invasion of privacy and other claims can also arise.

DRUG TESTS

Many employers require employees or job candidates to provide urine, blood, or hair samples that are sent to laboratories and tested for substances indicating use of illegal drugs. **Drug testing** occurs under a variety of circumstances. Tests are given prior to hiring, in conjunction with periodic medical exams, to verify that employees who have been through drug rehabilitation programs are staying "clean," upon observations of aberrant behavior that create **reasonable suspicion** of drug use, following on-the-job accidents, and randomly. In **random drug testing**, a specified percentage of the workforce is selected for periodic drug testing without prior notice and absent individualized suspicion of drug use. If proper procedures are used, a drug test can determine with reasonable certainty whether specified illegal substances are in a person's system. However, it cannot determine how those substances were ingested, the quantity of drugs taken, and whether the tested individual is currently impaired.

What if a job candidate or employee does not want to be drug tested? Does she have any legal right to refuse drug testing without suffering adverse employment consequences? The general answer is no, with some exceptions. Drug testing is an issue that highlights the fragmented nature of U.S. employment law, as the legal rights of employees vary considerably according to whether they work for the government, are unionized, or live in a state that has chosen to regulate drug testing.

One source of legal limitations on drug testing is state drug testing laws. The majority of states have laws that deal with drug testing, although some of these laws require the drug testing of certain types of employees or under certain circumstances (e.g., post-accident testing), and no state prohibits all drug testing of employees. Random drug testing is subject to the most stringent limitations. Laws in at least 10 states prohibit random testing outright or limit it to the occupants of safety-sensitive jobs.[5] Thus, *employers should be especially careful in deciding whether to use random testing and will not be able to do so for nonsafety-sensitive jobs in a number of states.*

Another consideration affecting all forms of drug testing except prehire screening is that when employees are represented by a labor union, employers are generally required under the National Labor Relations Act (see Chapter 14) to negotiate with the union about whether there will be drug testing and the details of the program. This is because the union is the legal representative of the employees (but not job applicants), and drug testing is a "mandatory topic of bargaining" that, if raised by either party, must be negotiated over (but not necessarily agreed upon). Thus,

[5]Fred S. Steingold. *The Employer's Legal Handbook,* 4th ed. (Berkeley, CA: Nolo, 2000), pp. 1/40–1/49. This source provides a useful summary of state drug-testing laws and is the source for other statements about these laws, unless otherwise noted.

unionized employers cannot unilaterally implement drug-testing programs affecting current employees without first negotiating about them with the employees' unions. Major League Baseball negotiated and reached agreement with the Major League Baseball Players' Association before it instituted its revised drug-testing program focusing on steroids (see "Clippings").

Perhaps the most significant limitation on drug testing is found in the U.S. Constitution and state constitutions. Public employees challenging the drug-testing programs of public employers have argued that it is unconstitutional because it violates the **Fourth Amendment** of the U.S. Constitution (and similar language in state constitutions), which protects against **unreasonable searches and seizures.** The Supreme Court has consistently held that drug testing, in which employees are required to submit bodily fluids and have those fluids examined for the presence of illegal substances, constitutes a "search."[6] Thus, public employers have had to defend the reasonableness of such searches. Drug testing precipitated by an employer's reasonable suspicion that an individual is using drugs is certainly reasonable and constitutional. Drug testing under other circumstances will be upheld if the government shows a "special need" for the testing that outweighs employees' right to privacy. In a case involving the post-accident testing of railroad employees, a history of accidents involving railroad employees under the influence of drugs provided the special need.[7] The Supreme Court also upheld the prepromotion testing of U.S. Customs employees who carry firearms or are involved in the interdiction of illegal contraband (including narcotics). Although there was no known or even suspected problem of drug use among customs agents, their position on the front line in the war against drugs was sufficient to overcome their limited privacy interests in being free from drug testing.[8] However, attempts to apply drug testing to the entire workforces of pubic agencies without regard to their particular functions have been struck down as unconstitutional.[9]

Some doubt remains regarding the constitutionality of random testing programs. The U.S. Supreme Court has not dealt squarely with this issue, although it has upheld random drug testing of high school athletes and students participating in after-school programs.[10] Several state supreme courts have distinguished random testing from other forms of drug testing and found it to be unconstitutional. In a case involving police officers, the Alaska Supreme Court struck down the random component of the Anchorage Police Department's drug testing program, citing among other things its greater intrusiveness:

> An unannounced test's added element of "fear and surprise" and its "unsettling show of authority," make random testing qualitatively more intrusive than testing that is triggered by predictable, job-related occurrences such as promotion, demotion, and transfer.[11]

The Arizona Supreme Court reached the same conclusion regarding random drug testing of firefighters.[12] In contrast, a federal appeals court upheld the constitutionality

[6]*Skinner v. Railway Labor Executives Ass'n,* 489 U.S. 602, at 617 (1989).

[7]*Skinner,* at 606–07.

[8]*National Treasury Employees Union v. Von Raab,* 489 U.S. 656 (1989).

[9]*Bolden v. SEPTA,* 953 F.2d 807 (3d Cir. 1991); *National Treasury Employees Union v. Watkins,* 722 F.Supp. 766 (D.DC 1989).

[10]*Veronia School District 47J v. Acton,* 515 U.S. 646 (1995) (student athletes); *Bd. of Education of Indep. Sch. Dist. No. 92 v. Earls,* 536 U.S. 822 (2002).

[11]*Anchorage Police Department Employees Association v. Municipality of Anchorage,* 24 P.3d 547, at 558 (Alaska 2001).

[12]*Petersen v. City of Mesa,* 83 P.3d 35 (Ariz. 2004); *cert. denied,* 125 S. Ct. 51 (2004).

of a random drug-testing program applied to probation and parole officers and other employees working within the Michigan criminal justice system.[13]

Keep in mind that constitutional protections against unreasonable searches and seizures apply only to government employees (unless there is a law requiring testing of private sector employees). *Public employers must be prepared to defend the reasonableness of their drug-testing programs. The surest way to do this is to focus on safety-sensitive jobs and emphasize testing upon reasonable suspicion. To establish reasonable suspicion, supervisors must be well-trained at identifying signs of impairment.*

Some employers are not only permitted, but legally required, to drug test. The most general statutory requirement for drug testing is found in the **Omnibus Transportation Employee Testing Act** of 1991.[14] This federal law requires drug (and alcohol) testing of employees in transportation-related occupations, including airline, railroad, trucking, and public transport workers. The statute calls for testing under a variety of circumstances, including prehire and on a random basis; specifies that procedures be established to ensure test accuracy; requires that employees testing positive be suspended or dismissed; and provides for the establishment of rehabilitation programs.

Drug-Testing Procedures

One source of legal requirements for drug-testing procedures is the collection of state laws mentioned earlier. Some of the more common procedural requirements are the following:

1. Employees must be provided with written notice that testing is required.
2. Employees must be provided with copies of the employer's substance abuse and drug-testing policy.
3. Employers must use licensed laboratories to analyze samples.
4. Employers must perform confirmatory tests if requested or allow employees access to samples to have their own tests done.
5. Employees must be given test results in writing.
6. Employees who test positive must be given the opportunity to explain the result.
7. Samples must be collected with due regard for employee privacy.

The Department of Transportation's regulations[15] for drug testing under the Omnibus Transportation Employee Testing Act set out exacting standards, including steps to balance privacy in producing the sample with safeguards against adulteration of the sample, use of tamperproof custody seals on specimen containers, documentation of the **chain of custody** (the parties who handle the sample), testing by an independent lab, **confirmatory tests** (second, more sophisticated tests) used when initial screening tests come back positive, use of a qualified **medical review officer** to interpret the results and communicate them to the department, and opportunity for the tested employee to explain possible reasons for a positive result (e.g., other legal medications taken). These are widely recognized as sound drug-testing procedures; but are employers liable if they fail to meet these standards? In *Mission Petroleum Carriers v. Solomon,* the Texas Supreme Court considers whether an employer can be found negligent for not exercising proper care in drug testing.

[13]*International Union, U.A.W. Local 6000 v. Winters,* 385 F.3d 1003 (6th Cir. 2004); *cert. denied,* 125 S. Ct. 1972 (2005).
[14]49 U.S.C.A. §§ 45101–45106 (2005).
[15]49 C.F.R. Part 40 (2005).

MISSION PETROLEUM CARRIERS V. SOLOMON
106 S.W. 3d 705 (Tex. 2003)

● ● ●

OPINION BY JUSTICE JEFFERSON:

Mission Petroleum Carriers, Inc. terminated Roy Solomon, an at-will employee, for failing a random drug test. Solomon sued Mission, contending that it breached a common-law duty by not exercising ordinary care in the manner it collected his urine specimen for testing. * * *

[T]he court of appeals held that an employer owes a duty to an at-will employee to conduct a drug test with reasonable care. * * * [W]e reverse the court of appeals' judgment and render judgment that Solomon take nothing.

Mission required its 520 truck drivers to submit to random drug testing pursuant to DOT regulations. As authorized by these regulations, Mission used its own employees to collect the drivers' urine samples for testing by outside laboratories. On April 3, 1997, Roy Solomon . . . was randomly selected to provide a urine sample for drug testing. When Solomon arrived for the test, his immediate supervisor, terminal manager Ed Hillebrandt, gave Solomon an unsealed collection container that had been sitting exposed on a desk in the terminal dispatcher's office. Solomon went unaccompanied into an adjacent restroom to provide the specimen. Solomon returned to the dispatcher's office and set the collection container on the table. He then went back to the restroom to wash his hands, leaving the container behind.

When he returned from the restroom approximately one minute later, Hillebrandt divided the sample into two separate containers. Solomon then sealed each container, initialed the tamper-proof seals, and placed the containers in a plastic bag. Solomon signed an informed consent form confirming the "identity and integrity of [the] sample throughout the collection and testing process." Mission sent one of the containers to Bayshore Clinical Laboratories . . . for analysis; the other was set aside in the event further testing was required. The Bayshore Laboratory analyzed the specimen and discovered THC metabolite, a chemical produced by the human body after marijuana use.

A Medical Review Officer (MRO), charged with ensuring the accuracy of the test results, informed Solomon that he had tested positive for THC metabolite. Solomon told the MRO that the positive result

could not possibly be accurate because he had never used marijuana. Solomon denied taking medication or any other product that might have caused the THC metabolite to appear in his sample. He did not, however, suggest that the results might have been compromised by Mission's faulty collection procedures. Following his discussion with the MRO, Solomon called Mission and requested a retest. Mission sent the second sample to a different laboratory for analysis. On April 9, 1997, when the second test also confirmed the presence of THC metabolite, Mission terminated Solomon's employment.

The next day, Solomon applied for truck-driving positions at Coastal Transport and MCX Trucking. The DOT regulations require a prospective employer to review the applicant's test results from previous employers for the preceding two years from the date of the application. Consequently, as part of each employment application, Coastal Transport and MCX Trucking asked Solomon to sign a consent form authorizing Mission to release those drug test results. Mission reported Solomon's test results to Coastal and MCX after Solomon consented to the disclosure. Neither Coastal Transport nor MCX Trucking hired Solomon.

Eighty-four days after the urine test, Solomon passed an independent laboratory's hair-follicle test, which was designed to detect marijuana consumption. Although there is evidence that hair follicle testing is a scientifically recognized procedure, the test purports only to reveal the persistent use of marijuana over time, not isolated uses. Solomon concedes that the hair-follicle test would establish at most that he was not a regular user of marijuana, but could not confirm or refute that he smoked marijuana around the time Mission collected his urine sample.

Solomon['s] * * * negligence claim proceeded to trial. Solomon testified that he had never smoked marijuana. He also presented evidence that Mission violated each of the following collection protocols, which are designed to ensure the validity of the drug test result:

(1) DOT regulations prohibit an employee's immediate supervisor from collecting the employee's urine sample unless it is impractical for any other individual to perform the collection. Here, however, Solomon's immediate supervisor collected the

specimen, and Solomon presented evidence that non-supervising employees could easily have performed that task.

(2) Both the employee and the collector must be present when the collection container is removed from a sealed collection kit. In this case, however, the container had been removed from the collection kit before Solomon arrived to provide his specimen.

(3) The collector must tell the employee to wash his hands before providing the sample and not again until after the sample is returned. Hillebrandt did not give Solomon this admonition.

(4) The collector is required to restrict access to the collection site. Mission's collection site, however, was unrestricted.

(5) The collection container must be kept in view of the collector and the employee between the time the employee has urinated and the time the specimen is sealed. But Solomon was separated from the container for at least 60 seconds while he washed his hands.

Solomon argued that Mission's failure to follow these DOT protocols resulted in "false positive" test results. He presented evidence that the test results were the catalyst for a series of adverse consequences, culminating in his inability to find employment as a truck driver. * * *

The jury found that Mission's negligence proximately caused Solomon's injuries and awarded Solomon . . . damages . . . totaling $802,444.22. * * * The court of appeals affirmed, holding that Mission owed its employees a duty of care when collecting urine samples for drug testing. It also held that the evidence was legally and factually sufficient to support the jury's finding that Mission's failure to follow DOT testing protocols proximately caused THC metabolite to be present in Solomon's urine sample. * * *

To prevail on his negligence claim, Solomon must show that (1) Mission owed him a duty, (2) Mission breached its duty, (3) Mission's breach proximately caused his injuries, and (4) damages resulted from this breach. Because duty is the threshold issue, we begin by addressing whether an employer owes a duty to an at-will employee to use reasonable care when collecting an employee's urine sample for drug testing pursuant to DOT regulations. * * *

Congress has not given employees a private cause of action under the DOT regulations at issue here.

Nevertheless, . . . the DOT regulations impose stringent rules for administering and disclosing drug test results and levy civil penalties for violation of these rules. In addition, employees have significant avenues of redress when employers fail or refuse to follow DOT protocol in collecting urine samples. Under the DOT regulations, for example, employers cannot require employees to sign consent or release forms with respect to any part of the drug testing, including collection, when the employer fails to follow statutory requisites for collecting the specimen. When employers do not follow DOT protocol, employees can refuse to initial the seal on the specimen bottle and can refuse to sign the Federal Drug Testing Custody and Control Form. Without this form, the Medical Review Officer (MRO) cannot verify the drug test. The regulations anticipate that positive test results do not necessarily confirm that the employee is guilty of drug use. For that reason, the DOT regulations require not only that an independent MRO review the test results, but also provide the MRO with the authority to examine the procedures by which the sample was collected, including interviewing the employee to determine if positive results can be explained by factors other than drug use.

The MRO must review "the chain of custody to ensure that it is complete and sufficient on its face" before certifying a positive drug test result. The MRO is prohibited from verifying positive results that are not obtained or processed in accordance with quality assurance and control protocols. And, before verifying a positive test result, the MRO must give the employee an opportunity to contend that the result is positive for a legitimate reason. If an employee chooses not to initial or sign the seal or Custody and Control Form, the MRO cannot confirm the chain of custody and must contact the employee to discuss the positive result. And even if the chain of custody is confirmed, the MRO cannot verify a positive test result if aware that the urine sample was not obtained in accordance with the DOT protocols. These protections reduce the risk of harm and likelihood of injury to an employee whose employer negligently collects urine samples for drug testing. Solomon did not attempt to utilize these avenues of redress. * * *

Solomon also could have complained and initiated administrative proceedings challenging Mission's specimen-collection regimen. An Associate Administrator for the Federal Highway Administration is charged with investigating alleged violations of the regulations and determining if employers have complied with the statutory requirements. * * * Accordingly, had Solomon

filed a complaint, Mission could have been fined up to $10,000, lost its ability to obtain insurance, or received an unsatisfactory safety rating. Once given an "unsatisfactory rating," a motor carrier is prohibited from transporting hazardous materials and is ineligible for certain federal contracts. The DOT regulations also give the Associate Administrator authority to fashion relief to the complainant and "assure that the complainant is not subject to harassment, intimidation, disciplinary action, discrimination, or financial loss" for having filed the complaint. Because employees can thereby protect themselves from harm, we have less incentive to create a duty requiring employers to exercise ordinary care in collecting employees' specimens for drug testing. * * *

[W]e agree there is a serious risk that an employee can be harmed by a false positive drug test. However, the risk is reduced by the protection DOT regulations afford to the employees. As we have seen, the DOT's comprehensive statutory and regulatory scheme, coupled with the authority granted to the MRO, affords significant protection to employees who are the subject of random drug tests. Without these protections, the risk of harm resulting from a negligently conducted urinalysis test would be great. But here, the DOT regulations strike an appropriate balance between the need for efficient drug testing and the requirement that each employee have the means to insist on the integrity of the process. While the regulations do not create a private cause of action for an employer's breach of DOT protocols, employees are entitled to compel compliance by invoking regulations already in place. Those regulations serve both as an incentive for employers to carefully abide by those protocols and as a safe harbor for employees whose test results are tainted by unacceptable breaches of collection procedures. We therefore decline to impose a common-law duty on employers

who conduct in-house urine specimen collection under the DOT regulations.

We must also balance any risk to employees against the burden it could place on our employment-at-will doctrine. * * * We agree that the employment-at-will doctrine is not directly implicated here because Solomon has not sued for wrongful discharge. But we must consider his claim in its overall context. Because Solomon's complaint concerns the process by which Mission chose to terminate him, it goes to the core of at-will employment. * * * [A]n employer is "at liberty to discharge [an employee] . . . for a reason based on incorrect information, even if that information [is] carelessly gathered." If a duty of care were to arise every time the harm to an employee transcends the employment agreement, the employment-at-will doctrine would be undermined because an employer's basis for termination would have to be justified by a reasonable investigation, which is contrary to the doctrine. * * *

CASE QUESTIONS

1. What was the legal issue in this case? What did the court decide?

2. What were the alleged deficiencies in the company's drug-testing process?

3. What is the court's rationale for declining to recognize a claim for employer negligence in drug testing?

4. What about drug testing that does not involve transportation employees and is not governed by DOT regulations?

5. If Solomon could prove that he was discharged for a false positive on his drug test, why doesn't he have a claim for wrongful termination?

6. Do you agree with the decision? Why or why not?

Absent statutory requirements, courts are unlikely to impose strict procedural requirements upon employer drug-testing programs and find employers negligent for slipshod testing. Negligence by laboratories conducting drug tests might be another matter. In a case involving a flight attendant, a laboratory was found negligent for a faulty drug-testing procedure.[16] The flight attendant was fired by Delta Airlines after the laboratory concluded that her urine sample had showed signs of "substitution" (it was not sufficiently heavier than water and had too little creatinine) and thus did not allow for a valid test of whether drugs had been used. The procedure used to determine whether adulteration or substitution of a sample has occurred is sensitive to such factors as sex, body size, water intake, and diet. The lab failed to adequately

[16]*Ishikawa v. Delta Airlines*, 343 F.3d 1129 (9th Cir. 2003).

account for these in reaching its finding. The lab's errors were characterized by the court as being "at the simple end of the spectrum, to the point of being crude." Although Delta did not bear liability, it rehired the flight attendant with back pay, suspended its policy of discharging employees based on this "validity test" of samples, and terminated its contract with the laboratory.[17]

State laws requiring that employers provide employees with copies of their substance abuse policies dovetail with the federal **Drug-Free Workplace Act (DFWA)** of 1988.[18] This law applies to companies that have contracts to provide goods or services to the federal government. The DFWA is silent on the subject of drug testing. Instead, it requires that covered employers develop and communicate policies prohibiting drug use, possession, sale, or distribution in the workplace; inform employees about the dangers of drug abuse and options available for drug counseling and treatment; establish penalties for drug abuse violations; and report any convictions relating to drug use or sale in the workplace to the funding agency.

Although no single set of legal requirements exists for how drug tests must be done, and the chances of employers being held liable for sloppy drug testing procedures are remote, prudence and the desire to not unfairly deprive individuals of employment suggest that *employers should have policies notifying employees if they are subject to drug testing, the circumstances under which testing will occur, the procedures used, and the consequences of testing positive. Sound drug-testing procedures include the use of confirmatory tests to verify positive results, careful labeling of specimens and documentation of the chain of custody, respect for the privacy of individuals producing specimens, use of reputable labs and monitoring of their performance, use of a medical review officer to interpret results, and opportunity for employees to provide alternative explanations for positive results.* Information about legal medications that might confound the results of drug tests also should be taken into account. However, because the ADA prohibits preemployment questions about medications taken because they tend to point to disabilities, *information about medications should be sought only after a positive test result has occurred.*

Are there any limitations on how the results of drug tests are used? The *Mission Petroleum Carriers* case makes clear the reluctance of most courts to protect at-will employees from termination based on drug tests, even if the tests were conducted improperly. Employers that discharge unionized employees for positive drug tests *sometimes* find that their decisions are overturned by arbitrators because the testing was not done in conformance with contractual requirements or because mitigating factors called for employees to be given second chances. Even with public policy strongly favoring elimination of illegal drug use, courts have generally upheld the decisions of arbitrators to reinstate unionized employees testing positive.[19] State drug-testing laws typically specify that test results must be kept confidential by employers and cannot be used as grounds for criminal proceedings. As a practical matter, employers are unlikely to seek criminal prosecution, because they can simply terminate employees rather than spend a lot of time in court and have to worry about meeting the higher evidentiary standards for criminal cases. However, *all employers should treat drug-test results as confidential.* False statements about drug-test results can be highly damaging to individuals' reputations and thus are fertile ground for defamation suits. A positive drug test cannot support statements such as the tested employee is "a drug addict" or "came into work high on drugs." The test

[17]"Jury Awards Delta Flight Attendant $400,000 for Drug Laboratory Negligence." *Daily Labor Report* 135 (July 16, 2001), A-11.

[18]41 U.S.C.A. §§ 701 et seq. (2005).

[19]*Eastern Associated Coal Corp. v. Mine Workers*, 531 U.S. 57 (2000).

simply indicates the presence of an illegal substance and nothing more. Because of the sensitive nature of drug-test results, even accurate information should be divulged only to those with a clear need to know. Carelessly sharing information about a positive drug test can be grounds for a privacy tort claim (see Chapter 17). The need to ensure that drug-testing results are accurately stated and handled confidentially is another argument for using a medical review officer.

Employers can salvage valuable human resources by allowing employees who test positive to keep their jobs while they get help from substance abuse programs. Many employers provide employee assistance programs (EAPs) to help employees with substance abuse and other problems and give employees second chances; however, after an employee who is addicted to illegal drugs has been allowed to undergo treatment in a rehabilitation program or has successfully completed such a program, that employee is protected by the Americans with Disabilities Act (ADA). *Employers must not decide to terminate, fail to promote, or otherwise discriminate against an employee who has undergone treatment for drug addiction and is no longer using illegal drugs.*

MEDICAL EXAMINATIONS

A **medical examination** is any "procedure or test that seeks information about an individual's impairments or health."[20] The distinction between medical exams and other tests that broadly relate to health is not always clear. For example, a psychological exam might or might not be a medical exam, depending on whether the test is designed to reveal a mental impairment or merely to assess personality traits. A court considered the status of a psychological exam used by Rent-A-Center to select management trainees. The test incorporated questions from the Minnesota Multiphasic Personality Inventory (MMPI). Even though the test was not scored by a psychologist, the court concluded that:

> Because it is designed, at least in part, to reveal mental illness and has the effect of hurting the employment prospects of one with a mental disability, we think the MMPI is best categorized as a medical examination. And even though the MMPI was only a part (albeit a significant part) of a battery of tests administered to employees looking to advance, its use, we conclude, violated the ADA.[21]

Table 6-1 provides examples of tests that are and are not considered medical exams. The significance of this distinction is that medical exams are subject to a number of limitations under the ADA.

Medical Examinations and the ADA

The ADA governs whether medical exams can be conducted, the types of exams that can be performed, and the uses to which information gleaned from medical exams can be put. These rules are outlined in Table 6-2.

The ADA's requirements differ, depending on the stage in the employment process at which medical testing is desired. *Prior to making a conditional offer of employment, employers are prohibited from requiring that applicants submit to medical exams.*

[20]EEOC. "Enforcement Guidance: Disability-Related Inquiries and Medical Examinations of Employees Under the ADA." no. 915.002 (July 27, 2000).

[21]*Karraker v. Rent-A-Center,* 2005 U.S. App. LEXIS 11142, at 13–14.

TABLE 6-1	Examples of Tests That Are and Are Not Considered Medical Examinations

Medical Examination	**Not a Medical Examination**
Medical checkup	Drug test
Blood pressure screening	Physical fitness/agility test
HIV test	Polygraph exam
Genetic test	Honesty test
Psychological test used to determine mental illness	Psychological test assessing personality in the normal range
Vision test analyzed by an ophtalmologist or optometrist	Vision test for ability to read or recognize objects
Nerve conduction test	Demonstrations of ability to perform specific job tasks
Diagnostic procedure (e.g., MRI)	

TABLE 6-2	Requirements for Medical Examinations Under the ADA

	Pre-Offer	After Conditional Offer	Post-Hire
Can exam occur?	No	Yes	Yes
What type of exam?	NA	Unrestricted	(1) job related and consistent with business necessity or (2) voluntary
Can results be used to deny employment to a disabled person?	NA	Only if: (1) cannot perform essential functions of the job even with reasonable accommodation, or (2) is a "direct threat" to self or others	

This is for the same reason that preemployment inquiries that might reveal information about disabilities are prohibited. But this does not mean that employers must make hiring decisions deprived of information about the health of job candidates. After an employer has considered the nonmedical qualifications of candidates and arrived at a tentative hiring decision, the employer is then free to require a medical exam to verify that the person is physically and mentally capable of performing the job. The offer of employment is thus "conditional" upon satisfactory results from the medical exam. *Leonel v. American Airlines* elaborates further on the meaning of "conditional offer of employment" and underscores the importance of adhering to the proper timing in performing medical exams.

LEONEL V. AMERICAN AIRLINES
400 F.3d 702 (9th Cir. 2005)

OPINION BY CIRCUIT JUDGE FISHER:

Appellants Walber Leonel, Richard Branton and Vincent Fusco, who all have the human immunodeficiency virus ("HIV"), applied for flight attendant positions with American Airlines ("American"). Although they went through the application process at different times, the process was essentially the same for all of them. American interviewed them at its Dallas, Texas, headquarters and then issued them conditional offers of employment, contingent upon passing both background checks and medical examinations. Rather than wait for the background checks, American immediately sent the appellants to its on-site medical department for medical examinations, where they were required to fill out medical history questionnaires and give blood samples. None of them disclosed his HIV-positive status or related medications. Thereafter, alerted by the appellants' blood test results, American discovered their HIV-positive status and rescinded their job offers, citing their failure to disclose information during their medical examinations.

The appellants, all California residents, now challenge American's medical inquiries and examinations as prohibited by the Americans with Disabilities Act ("ADA") and California's Fair Employment and Housing Act ("FEHA"). They argue that American could not require them to disclose their personal medical information so early in the application process—before the company had completed its background checks such that the medical examination would be the only remaining contingency—and thus their nondisclosures could not be used to disqualify them.

* * * The federal Americans with Disabilities Act and California's Fair Employment and Housing Act prohibit employers from refusing to hire job applicants whose disabilities would not prevent them from "performing the essential functions of the job with reasonable accommodation." To this end, the ADA and FEHA not only bar intentional discrimination, they also regulate the sequence of employers' hiring processes. Both statutes prohibit medical examinations and inquiries until after the employer has made a "real" job offer to an applicant. "A job offer is real if the employer has evaluated all relevant non-medical information which it reasonably could have obtained and analyzed prior to giving the offer." To issue a "real" offer under the ADA and FEHA, therefore, an employer must have either completed all non-medical components of its application process or be able to demonstrate that it could not reasonably have done so before issuing the offer.

The ADA recognizes that employers may need to conduct medical examinations to determine if an applicant can perform certain jobs effectively and safely. The ADA requires only that such examinations be conducted as a separate, second step of the selection process, after an individual has met all other job prerequisites. This two-step requirement serves in part to enable applicants to determine whether they were "rejected because of disability, or because of insufficient skills or experience or a bad report from a reference." When employers rescind offers made conditional on both non-medical and medical contingencies, applicants cannot easily discern or challenge the grounds for rescission. When medical considerations are isolated, however, applicants know when they have been denied employment on medical grounds and can challenge an allegedly unlawful denial. * * *

American's offers to the appellants here were by their terms contingent not just on the appellants successfully completing the medical component of the hiring process but also on the completion of a critical non-medical component: undergoing background checks, including employment verification and criminal history checks. Other courts have found offers not real, and medical examinations thus unlawfully premature, when an offer remained contingent upon a polygraph test, personal interview and background investigation or upon completion of an application form, criminal background check and driver's test. Here, it is undisputed that American's offers were subject to both medical and non-medical conditions when they were made to the appellants and the appellants were required to undergo immediate medical examinations. Thus the offers were not real, the medical examination process was premature and American cannot penalize the appellants for failing to disclose their HIV-positive status—unless the company can establish that it could not reasonably have completed the background checks before subjecting the appellants to medical examinations and questioning. It has not done so.

As justification for accelerating the medical examinations, [American claims] that the company found it

important to minimize the length of time that elapsed during the hiring process in order to compete for applicants. But competition in hiring is not in itself a reason to contravene the ADA's and FEHA's mandates to defer the medical component of the hiring process until the non-medical component is completed. The appellants' expert . . . testified that it is "the accepted practice for employers to complete such [background] checks prior to conducting a preemployment medical examination of the job applicant." American has not established that there are no reasonable alternatives that would address its asserted need for expedited hiring of flight attendants that would avoid jumping medical exams ahead of background checks. For instance, it has not shown why it could not expeditiously have issued two rounds of conditional offers—the first, after the interviews, informing applicants that they had reached the final stages of the application process and would be hired absent problems with their background checks or medical examinations; and the second, after completion of the background checks, ensuring employment if the applicant passed the medical examination. American also suggests that it conducted the medical examinations before completing the background checks for the convenience of the applicants. * * *Not only does this testimony undercut American's meeting-competition rationale, applicants' supposed convenience does not justify reordering the hiring process in a manner contrary to that set out by the ADA and FEHA. * * *

American argues in the alternative that even if the offers were not real, the company did not violate the ADA or FEHA because it evaluated the appellants' non-medical information before it considered their medical information. * * * As we have explained, however, the statutes regulate the sequence in which employers collect information, not the order in which they evaluate it. * * * The focus on the collection rather than the evaluation of medical information is important to the statutes' purposes. Both the ADA and FEHA deliberately allow job applicants to shield their private medical information until they know that, absent an inability to meet the medical requirements, they will be hired, and that if they are not hired, the true reason for the employer's decision will be transparent. American's attempt to focus on the evaluation rather than the collection of medical information squares with neither the text nor the purposes of the statutes. Whether or not it looked at the medical information it obtained from the appellants, American was not entitled to get the information at all until it had completed the background checks, unless it can demonstrate it could not reasonably have done so before initiating the medical examination process. As to that question, we hold that there are material issues of fact that require reversal of summary judgment on the appellants' claims that American's hiring process violated the ADA and FEHA.

CASE QUESTIONS

1. What was the legal issue in this case? What did the court decide?

2. Why is the timing of when medical exams are administered so important to the ADA?

3. What should the airline have done differently?

4. Did the airline also engage in disparate treatment by failing to hire the plaintiffs? Invade their privacy?

As a practical matter, *medical tests should generally be the last tests performed and the last information considered prior to finalizing a hiring decision.* However, even at the conditional offer stage, *individuals cannot be required to take medical exams unless the exams are required of all other persons hired into the same job category.* People who are disabled or "look disabled" cannot be singled out for medical exams.

Medical exams conducted following conditional offers of employment are unrestricted in scope. They can be wide-ranging inquiries into the physical and mental health of candidates that are not limited to searches for conditions that are specifically job-related. In contrast, *medical exams of current employees are limited to those that are job-related and consistent with business necessity or voluntary.* The rationale is that employers have ongoing evidence about the job performance of current employees and that should be the primary basis for employment decisions, rather than assessments of medical condition. Medical exams are job-related and

consistent with business necessity when employers have reasonable belief that individuals may be unable to perform their jobs due to their medical conditions or that they may pose a direct threat to their own safety or that of others due to their medical conditions. In some occupations (e.g., pilots), periodic exams or health monitoring may be job-related and required by law. A medical exam can also be required to document the existence of a disability that necessitates an accommodation. Lastly, the law also allows for medical exams of current employees when these are truly voluntary, such as if an employee chooses to use an employer-sponsored blood pressure screening or other wellness program.

Regardless of whether the medical exam is conducted after a conditional offer of employment or during employment, the results of the exam cannot be used to deny an employment opportunity to a disabled person unless that person is unable to perform the "essential functions" of the job or poses a "direct threat" to himself or others, even with some "reasonable accommodation" that the employer could make. Fuller explanation of these concepts will have to await the discussion of reasonable accommodation in Chapter 10. For now, we can say that *only if an employee's disability does not allow him to perform the core parts of a job, even with some help, is an employer justified in denying an employment opportunity to that individual.* An employer cannot simply conclude from a medical exam that an employee is disabled and exclude him.

However, if a medical exam conducted at the proper time uncovers information about a medical condition that does not meet the legal definition of a disability, the ADA does not preclude use of that information to deny an employment opportunity. In one such case, 72 applicants were rejected for entry-level manufacturing jobs on the basis of "nerve conduction tests." The accuracy of these tests is disputed, but they are intended to identify persons susceptible to developing carpal tunnel syndrome (a condition increasingly seen among workers performing repetitive tasks and one that can have debilitating effects on hands, wrists, and arms). The applicants challenged their rejection based on this type of medical exam as a violation of the ADA. However, the employees were unable to show that they were either currently disabled or regarded by the employer as disabled. Thus, they were not protected under the ADA.[22] The outcome of this case notwithstanding, employers are skating on thin ice when they exclude individuals because of their potential to later develop disabling conditions. This is shown by another case in which a job candidate's offer of employment was withdrawn after it was found that he had several prior workplace injuries for which he had received workers' compensation. The court upheld a jury's finding that the man was denied the job based on "unsubstantiated speculation about future risks from a perceived disability."[23]

HIV Tests One specific type of medical exam is an **HIV test**. Some employers want to know whether applicants or employees are HIV-positive (have the human immunodeficiency virus that can develop into AIDS). Under the ADA, an HIV test cannot be conducted until after a conditional offer of employment has been made. If an individual tests positive, that information can be used to deny employment only if it can be shown that the person cannot perform the essential functions of the job, even with accommodation, or is a direct threat. A person who is HIV-positive is generally considered disabled.[24] But unless the person actually develops AIDS and the disease progresses to a severe state, he will still be able to perform most jobs

[22]*EEOC v. Rockwell International,* 2001 U.S. App. LEXIS 3457 (7th Cir. 2001).

[23]*Garrison v. Baker Hughes Oilfield Operations, Inc.,* 287 F.3d 955 (10th Cir. 2002).

[24]*Bragdon v. Abbott,* 524 U.S. 624 (1998).

THE CHANGING WORKPLACE

Genetic Testing and Employment

Genetic information about employees can be obtained through low-tech means such as compiling family medical histories, indirectly through exams and lab tests, and directly through new methods for testing DNA and other genetic material. Genetic testing can take the form of **genetic screening** of job candidates for desirable or undesirable genetic traits and **genetic monitoring** to spot adverse changes in the genetic material of employees exposed to hazardous substances. When used for screening purposes, genetic information can identify individuals who have diseases that are not yet manifest, who are genetically disposed toward developing conditions in the future, or who are at greater risk of having children with inherited conditions. However, relatively few diseases have known and direct genetic links. The genetic predisposition to develop a disease interacts with numerous other environmental and behavioral factors to determine whether a particular disease actually develops. There is no certainty that it will.

As a society, we have said through the Americans with Disabilities Act (ADA) and other legislation that it is unacceptable to exclude qualified disabled persons from employment and other opportunities because of their disabilities. To the extent that genetic testing permits employers to delve even deeper into the health status of employees and to potentially exclude persons based not simply on conditions that they have, but also on conditions that they or their children *might someday have*, it raises troubling questions. In fact, there is considerable survey and anecdotal evidence that discrimination on the basis of genetic information is occurring.[1] There is also a history of employers using genetic tests, frequently without consent, to screen out persons with a gene mutation predisposing them to develop sickle cell anemia, a disease that occurs primarily among African Americans.

The legal status of genetic testing is not clear. To be sure, genetic testing is a type of medical exam subject to the ADA's requirements. The more difficult question is whether employers who use information about genetic predispositions to develop disabling conditions to screen out applicants are discriminating based on disability. The EEOC took that position in its suit against Burlington Northern Santa Fe Railroad (see "Clippings"). However, cases like the one in which Rockwell International excluded applicants based on their *potential* to develop

carpal tunnel syndrome, as assessed by nerve conduction tests, raise doubts about whether courts will treat individuals screened out by genetic tests as disabled persons protected by the ADA.

We can also look at two of the other "usual suspects" determining the legality of employment tests: state laws and the U.S. Constitution. A number of states have chosen to regulate genetic testing. Some of these laws are narrow, pertaining only to particular gene-linked conditions (e.g., sickle cell anemia) or to particular methods of gathering genetic information. A few states (e.g., New Jersey, Wisconsin)[2] broadly prohibit subjecting employees to genetic tests and using genetic information to make employment decisions. The U.S. Constitution also places limits on genetic testing. In an instructive case, a government laboratory was covertly testing employees for, among other things, the sickle cell trait. An appeals court found that the testing was invasive and lacked sufficient consent, raising a valid constitutional issue.[3] The lab settled the case.

Executive Order 13145 prohibits discrimination against applicants and employees of *federal government agencies* based on "protected genetic information." Although the executive order reaches only federal government employees, it is intended as a model for all employers. When former President Clinton signed the order, he stated that "no employer should ever review your genetic records along with your resume."[4] The executive order strictly limits the gathering of genetic information (genetic tests cannot be requested or required), its use (genetic information cannot be used to make adverse employment decisions), and the handling and disclosure of the very limited genetic information that can be gathered lawfully. The primary exceptions to the act's broad prohibitions are the use of family medical histories to investigate *current,* potentially disabling, conditions and genetic monitoring.

Broad federal legislation on genetic testing in employment might be on the way. A bill that would prohibit employers from using genetic information in making employment decisions appears to have wide support in the Senate. However, the House of Representatives has been cooler to the idea, and the long-term prospects for passage of a genetic testing in employment law are uncertain.[5] Perhaps the safest conclusion at this time is that the use of genetic information for screening purposes violates the spirit, if not the letter, of the ADA and

should be avoided. Genetic monitoring of employees for workplace exposures to dangerous substances is more justifiable, provided that it does not become a substitute for attempting to eliminate the hazards to which employees are exposed.

[1]U.S. Department of Labor. "Genetic Information and the Workplace." (January 28, 1998) (http://www.dol.gov/asp/programs/history/herman/reports/genetics.htm).

[2]N.J. Stat. Ann. § 10:5–12; Wis. Stat. § 111.372.

[3]*Norman-Bloodsaw v. Lawrence Berkeley Laboratory,* 135 F.3d 1260 (9th Cir. 1998).

[4]EEOC. "Policy Guidance on Executive Order 13145: To Prohibit Discrimination in Federal Employment Based on Genetic Information." no. 915.002 (July 26, 2000), viewed October 20, 2001 (http://www.eeoc.gov/docs/guidance-genetic.html).

[5]Fawn H. Johnson. "Senate Labor Committee Approves Bill Barring Discrimination Based on Genetics." *Daily Labor Report* 27 (February 10, 2005), A-11.

without endangering himself or others. Thus, the information obtained from an HIV test usually does not have any legal, nondiscriminatory use.

A good example of the pitfalls of HIV testing under the ADA is a case involving a man who was offered a job as an entertainer on a cruise ship, conditional on satisfactory results from a medical exam.[25] The exam included testing his blood for HIV. When the results came back that he was HIV-positive, the cruise line withdrew its offer of employment. The man sued, and the company's argument that he posed a "direct threat" to the safety of others proved unavailing. Given the ways in which HIV is transmitted, it could not be shown through objective evidence that the spread of HIV to others was likely in this type of employment. The cruise line eventually settled the suit and agreed to discontinue its HIV testing.

The legal rationale for refraining from HIV testing does not end with the ADA. For public employees, the constitutionality of HIV testing can be challenged under the Fourth Amendment (just as drug testing has been challenged), with considerable likelihood of success. However, in a few cases, courts have upheld the HIV testing of public employees. In one case, the employees were firefighters, and the court's decision hinged on the dangerous, uncontrolled nature of the environments in which they work and the more than minimal chance of contact with bodily fluids.[26] Such situations, which include the military, boxers, actors in the pornographic film industry, and perhaps surgeons performing invasive procedures, are clearly the exceptions rather than the rule. Lastly, information about HIV test results is highly sensitive, and as such, another good candidate for defamation or privacy claims if the results are communicated falsely or to those without a legitimate need to know. The bottom line on HIV testing in the workplace is clear and simple; *except in those unusual circumstances where there is a genuine possibility of HIV transmission in the workplace, employers should refrain from conducting HIV tests.*

POLYGRAPHS AND HONESTY TESTS

Honesty is a highly desirable quality in employees and people in general. Not surprisingly, employers want to test job applicants to determine whether their representations are credible and whether they could be trusted if hired. A number of tests purport to be able to do so, including polygraphs and voice stress analyzers. A **polygraph** does not "detect lies," but instead measures changes in physiological responses, including respiration, blood pressure, and perspiration (galvanic skin response). Voice stress analyzers focus on changes in vocal patterns. Telling lies is

[25]"Denied Job After AIDS Test, an Entertainer Settles Case." *New York Times* (December 19, 1996), A-17.

[26]*Anonymous Fireman v. City of Willoughby,* 779 F. Supp. 402, at 418 (N.D. Ohio 1991).

thought to be stressful, prompting physiological responses or vocal patterns different from baseline readings established by first asking simple, neutral questions (e.g., What is your name?). Polygraphers administer exams and combine their own observations of tested individuals, the physiological indicators, attempts to elicit admissions from persons tested, and more than a little intuition to determine whether there is "significant deception" or "no significant deception." Individuals can thus be rejected either because it is concluded that they are engaging in significant deception or because they confess to something serious during polygraph exams.

Employee Polygraph Protection Act Concerns have been raised about the accuracy of these tests, intimidation tactics used by polygraphers, and invasive questions. Prior to passage of the **Employee Polygraph Protection Act (EPPA)**,[27] preemployment polygraphs were widely used. The law is now clear: *Private sector employers must not request or require that applicants submit to polygraphs or other mechanical or electrical truth-determining devices (including voice stress analyzers).* There is a limited exception for private sector employers producing or dispensing controlled substances (narcotics) or providing "heavy" security services (e.g., guarding nuclear plants, water supplies). Importantly, the act applies only to private sector employers. Government agencies, including law enforcement and security agencies, are still free to polygraph both applicants and employees.

Although the EPPA negates the use of polygraphs in hiring, the law allows polygraphs to be used by private sector employers in conjunction with investigations of employee theft or other serious wrongdoing—subject to many procedural requirements (see Chapter 17). To fill the void left by the polygraph, many employers have turned to paper-and-pencil **honesty tests,** such as the Reid Report. Although the ability of these tests to accurately assess trustworthiness is open to question, they are not regulated by the EPPA.

SCORED TESTS OF ABILITY

The aforementioned tests are intended to screen out candidates with undesirable traits. Employers also use a variety of tests to assess desired characteristics, such as intelligence, aptitude, specific job skills or knowledge, work-related attitudes, personality traits, strength, and physical fitness. These tests are typically scored in some fashion, and persons who score better, or at least above a specified cutoff point, are those that get hired. The main concern is that the tests not be discriminatory. This necessitates paying attention to the wording of test items, the effects of tests on different protected class groups, evidence that tests are job-related and consistent with business necessity, the appropriateness of scoring methods and cutoff levels, and accommodation of disabled test takers.

Frequently, scored tests of ability are developed by consultants or testing companies that sell the rights to use the tests to employers, score the tests, and interpret the results. This does not absolve employers from responsibility for the tests and from taking reasonable steps to ensure their legality. But what should employers look for?

Examining Test Items

Other than physical fitness or strength tests, most scored tests of ability are given on paper (or on-line) and contain numerous items (questions). *Test items should be*

[27]29 U.S.C.A. §§ 2001–2009 (2005).

examined to see if they relate to protected class characteristics, and tests containing such items should not be used. In an instructive case, the parent company of Target Stores used a psychological test devised by a testing company to screen applicants for store security guard jobs. The test contained many items requiring applicants to divulge the extent to which they held various religious beliefs:[28]

> "My soul sometimes leaves my body."
>
> "I believe in the second coming of Christ."
>
> "I go to church almost every week."
>
> "I believe there is a God."

Other test questions pertained to sexual orientation and behavior:

> "I have been in trouble one or more times because of my sex behavior."
>
> "I am very strongly attracted by members of my own sex."
>
> "I have never indulged in any unusual sex practices."

These questions not only constituted preemployment inquiries about protected class (in California, where this case arose, sexual orientation is a protected class), but they were also scored by the testing company. Thus, some answers to these questions were deemed more desirable than others, and the manner in which an applicant responded affected her ability to be hired. On a variety of grounds, including discrimination based on religion and sexual orientation, the court granted the plaintiffs a court order to stop the testing. The employer eventually settled with the class of plaintiffs for over $2 million.

It does not take a great deal of technical sophistication to examine test questions and to red flag those that pertain to protected class or are otherwise inappropriate. The latter category would include questions that presume the sex of the test taker or that are premised on religious or cultural beliefs that would be more familiar to some protected class groups than others. Tests that contain such items simply should not be used.

Examining Test Results

An overriding legal concern with scored tests is that they can produce adverse impact discrimination. Although the tests are neutral requirements (assuming that the same tests are given to all candidates for the same jobs and that they do not contain the types of items mentioned earlier), they may nonetheless have discriminatory effects. Discriminatory effects of employment tests are best seen by examining **applicant flow data.** Applicant flow data compare the protected class composition of an applicant pool to that of the group of people who pass the test and are successful (or at least still in the running) in obtaining an employment opportunity. The underlying premise is that although individuals vary widely in their abilities, overall, people of different races, sexes, national origins, or other protected classes are equally capable of doing most jobs. Thus, we would expect that if tests actually measure ability to do a job, men and women or whites and blacks should experience similar rates of success in passing the tests and obtaining employment opportunities. If, instead, men pass the test at a much higher rate than women, or whites pass the test much more often than blacks, this indicates that something about the test is producing discriminatory effects.

[28]*Saroka v. Dayton Hudson Corp.*, 1 Cal. Rptr. 2d 77 (Cal. App. 1991), *review dismissed,* 862 P.2d 148 (Cal. 1993).

How different do test outcomes have to be to conclude that discriminatory effects (or "disproportionate selection") are occurring? One simple and useful guideline is the EEOC's **four-fifths rule**.[29] The rule says that if the **selection rate**—the percentage of applicants who pass the test and are hired or continue to be considered for employment—for one race or sex or other protected class group is less than 80 percent (4/5) of the selection rate for the race or sex or other protected class group that was most successful at passing the test, this is evidence of discriminatory effects. Note that the comparison is between selection *rates* and not *absolute numbers* of persons hired.

An example might make this more concrete. A meat processing plant used a "work tolerance test" to assess the strength of candidates for its entry-level jobs (see "Clippings"). Applicants who failed this test received no further consideration for employment. The test was challenged for its adverse impact against women. Male applicants passed the test at a rate of 97 percent. In contrast, the pass rate for female applicants was approximately 40 percent. Applying the four-fifths rule to these pass rates yields evidence of discriminatory effects. The pass rate for female applicants is less than half of the pass rate for males (40%/97% = .412). This is far less than 80 percent (.80), leading to the conclusion that something about this test substantially disfavors women.

The four-fifths rule is a "rule of thumb," rather than a strict legal requirement. It can be misleading when the number of applicants, and thus the number of test takers on which selection rates are based, is small. In one such case, pass rates for whites and African Americans on a promotional test for firefighters violated the four-fifths rule, but because the numbers of candidates taking the exam each year were so small (three to seven), they could not establish a prima facie case.[30] When cases go to court, more sophisticated statistical analyses are typically presented. The precise techniques used vary, depending on such factors as the number of groups compared and the sample size, but they share the aim of showing that the difference in selection rates for protected class groups is "statistically significant." This means that the obtained results are highly unlikely to occur by chance. "Highly unlikely" is usually translated as an outcome that would be expected to occur no more than 5 out of 100 times (i.e., a "p-value" of .05 or less) if there were not a true difference in selection rates.

Thus, *employers need to monitor and maintain records of the effects of testing procedures on different protected class groups. The four-fifths rule should be applied to selection rates generated from applicant flow data to identify possible discriminatory effects. If tests are having discriminatory effects, the tests should be discontinued until less discriminatory alternative tests are found or strong evidence is marshaled to establish test validity.*

Establishing That Tests Are Job-Related and Consistent with Business Necessity

Demonstrating that a test has discriminatory effects establishes a prima facie case of adverse impact, but it does not automatically result in a finding of discrimination. A test can be successfully defended—despite its discriminatory effects—if the employer can show that the test is **job-related and consistent with business necessity.** After all, if we go back to the earlier example, working at the meat processing plant is strenuous

[29]29 C.F.R. § 1607.4 (D) (2005).

[30]*Mems v. City of St. Paul, Dept. of Fire and Safety Services,* 224 F.3d 735, at 740 (8th Cir. 2000).

work, requiring the repetitive lifting of 35 pounds of sausage to an elevated storage area. An employer has a legitimate interest in selecting people with sufficient strength and endurance to perform that work with a minimum of injuries. It might well be that this is work for which more men than women are suited, and the test results simply reflect this fact. How can we tell?

It is incumbent upon employers to have evidence of the **validity** of a test that is producing discriminatory effects. In the most general terms, the validity of a measurement device or test refers to whether it actually measures what it purports to measure. Because employment tests are designed to help employers select people who will perform their jobs well, the validity of an employment test rests on how well it predicts future job performance. Does the test help employers make good selection decisions by measuring job-related criteria, or does it impose a needless obstacle?

There are two primary ways to establish the validity of employment tests. The first is **content validation.** A test has content validity to the extent that it requires the performance of the same behaviors and skills as the job in question. A classic example of a content valid testing procedure is use of a word processing test (e.g., speed, accuracy) to assess candidates for a secretarial job. The test is clearly representative of behaviors and skills that are central to the job. A legal limitation on content validation is that it cannot be used to validate tests of intelligence, personality, or other intangible traits. However, tests of job-specific knowledge or skills can be validated in this manner. Another problem is that the tests assume that candidates already possess and can display the desired skills. But many jobs can be learned relatively quickly. Testing procedures that screen out people who would be capable of performing the job following minimal amounts of on-the-job training and practice are not job-related and consistent with business necessity. *Thus, employers should use content valid tests as much as possible, but not to assess intangible characteristics, such as intelligence, and not for tasks that could readily be learned on the job.*

The state of California was able to successfully defend its California Basic Education Skills Test (CBEST) against an adverse impact claim by showing the test's content validity.[31] A passing score on the test is required to be employed as a public schoolteacher, administrator, librarian, or counselor. It was undisputed that pass rates—and, hence, access to education jobs—differed substantially by race and national origin. The test was passed by 73.4 percent of non-Latino whites, 53 percent of Asian Americans, 49.4 percent of Latinos, and 37.7 percent of African Americans.[32] These pass rates failed to meet the four-fifths rule and established a prima facie case of adverse impact. The state was nonetheless able to establish that the test was valid and job-related. More specifically, the state showed that the test measures specific abilities (reading, writing, and math skills); a job analysis incorporating the input of many current educators was performed and showed these skills to be central to education jobs; and the test was developed and content validated consistent with professional standards. The discriminatory effects of the test, particularly in a state with such a diverse population, remain troubling.

The second primary strategy for validating employment tests is **criterion validation.** *Criterion* refers here to a measure of job performance. The essential project in criterion validation is to demonstrate a statistical association between performance on a test and performance on the job. Criterion validation studies can be "predictive" or "concurrent." In a predictive study, the test is given to applicants, scored, but not used to make hiring decisions (instead, the employer uses other information at its disposal). Six months or a year later, when measures of job performance are

[31]*Association of Mexican American Educators v. California,* 231 F.3d 572 (9th Cir. 2000).

[32]*Association of Mexican American Educators v. California,* 937 F. Supp. 1397 (N.D. Cal. 1996).

available, these are compared to the test results to determine if people who scored higher on the test also tended to be better employees. Conducting a predictive study takes time because an adequate number of job candidates must be tested and hired, and a significant period of time must elapse before performance ratings are available. A concurrent study avoids these problems, but at the expense of having a less representative sample. In a concurrent study, the test that an employer wants to adopt is given to existing employees—a handy sample, but one not necessarily representative of job applicants. Performance measures for those employees are either available or can be devised for the validation study. Evidence of validity again comes from showing a statistical association between test scores and job performance ratings. A typical measure of association is the *correlation coefficient*. Correlation coefficients range between -1.0 and $+1.0$. A positive correlation means that persons who score higher on employment tests also tend to be rated more highly for job performance.

The evidence needed to establish the validity (and hence job-relatedness) of a scored employment test comes from a **validation study**. In *Albermarle Paper Co. v. Moody*, the Supreme Court provided guidance on the requirements for an adequate validation study.[33] The employer conceded that the tests of nonverbal intelligence and general verbal facility that it was using had discriminatory effects based on race, but claimed that it had conducted a validation study and found the test to be valid. The Supreme Court scrutinized the methodology of the "validation study" and found it to be inadequate to meet the employer's burden of defending the test as job related and consistent with business necessity. Major failings of the company's validation study included not performing any meaningful study (job analysis) of the jobs for which the test was being used; focusing on employees in jobs near the top of the wage progression, rather than on the entry-level positions for which the tests were used; nonsignificant correlations between test performance and job performance for five out of eight job lines; an absence of African Americans in the sample of employees used to validate the test; and unguided, highly subjective assessments of job performance by company supervisors. The Court also observed that "It cannot escape notice that Albemarle's study was conducted by plant officials, without neutral, on-the-scene oversight, at a time when this litigation was about to come to trial."[34] Thus, in this early case, the Supreme Court sent a strong message to employers that evidence from a credible and methodologically sound validation study would be required to defend testing procedures that have discriminatory effects. Such evidence is best obtained prior to adoption of a test, rather than under the gun of pending litigation.

In addition to the Supreme Court's guidance in *Albemarle*, the EEOC's *Uniform Guidelines on Employee Selection Procedures*[35] and the American Psychological Association's standards are used to judge the adequacy of validation studies. Without getting bogged down in the intricacies of validation studies, a few basic practical implications for employers can be stated. First, although the law does not strictly require that all tests be validated, a validation study is usually necessary to defend a test that has discriminatory effects. Thus, *it makes sense for employers to have evidence of the validity of all their selection procedures, but particularly scored tests*. Rather than wait to be sued, *validity studies should be undertaken before tests are put into use*. Evidence of validity is specific to jobs or classes of jobs. *Assertions that a test is valid should always be followed with the question: valid for what jobs?* The basic purpose of a validation study—to establish the job-relatedness of a test—presupposes that the party conducting the validation study has detailed knowledge

[33]*Albermarle Paper Co. v. Moody*, 422 U.S. 405 (1975).

[34]*Albemarle*, at 433 (note 32).

[35]29 C.F.R. Part 1607 (2005).

of the job(s) for which the test will be used. Thus, *an adequate validation study should proceed from a thorough **job analysis**, in which the tasks of a job and the knowledge, skills, abilities, and other characteristics needed to perform the job are detailed. The job analysis should incorporate significant input from current employees.*

Other key aspects of validation studies that should be examined, and on which testing companies or consultants should be closely questioned, include the following:

- *How large is the sample size?* Small sample sizes render statistics suspect and make it more difficult to perform separate analyses for different protected class groups.

- *Does the validation study include a mixture of races and both male and female candidates?* It is important to assess the effects of tests and their capability to predict performance on diverse samples that are representative of the people who will actually be taking the tests.

- *How good is the assessment of job performance?* Job performance ratings are often "the weakest link" in criterion validation studies. Are raters given clear performance criteria? If there is more than one rater of job performance, to what extent do their ratings agree?

- *How strong is the evidence of validity?* Validity coefficients can be assessed for both their magnitude and statistical significance. Some courts have adopted the guideline that correlation coefficients must be at least .3 to be sufficient evidence of validity. Coefficients of any magnitude are not informative unless they are also statistically significant (meaning that the true correlation between test scores and job performance in the population of applicants is highly unlikely to be zero).

- *How current is the evidence of validity?* Jobs change and previously validated tests may no longer be sufficiently related to redesigned jobs.

Lastly, *employers should consider whether there are feasible alternatives to tests that have discriminatory effects, even if those tests are job-related.* A plaintiff can prevail in an adverse impact case by showing that a less discriminatory alternative test is available that the employer refuses to adopt. In the meat processing plant case, the court concluded that even if Dial had been able to validate its strength test, there were alternative, less discriminatory means of achieving a reduction in injuries (see "Clippings").

Determining Appropriate Cutoff Levels for Test Scores

For tests to be used in selection decisions, they must be scored in some fashion (even if only pass/fail). Typically, **cutoff scores** are established for tests so that scores below the cutoff are deemed "failing" and disqualify candidates from further consideration. If the employer cares about the degree of the tested-for characteristic possessed—and not merely whether a sufficient level of the characteristic is present—test takers with passing scores can be ranked and candidates with the highest scores chosen. One consideration in treating test scores is that *employers must not "adjust the scores of, use different cutoff scores for, or otherwise alter the results of employment-related tests on the basis of race, color, religion, sex, or national origin."*[36] This prohibition of what has been termed **race norming**, although it is not specific to race, means that employers cannot establish separate minimum standards based on protected class or obscure the existence of different standards by altering scores (e.g., by creating separate percentile scores for whites and persons of color).

[36]Civil Rights Act of 1964, Title VII, 42 U.S.C.A. § 2000e-2(l) (2005).

Clearly, the results of a test are affected by what the employer determines to be a passing score. If a test is job related, are there any legal limitations on how high employers can "set the bar" in terms of cutoff scores? An unnecessarily stringent cutoff score was at the center of an adverse impact suit based on the written exam for Chicago firefighters (see "Clippings"). The passing score of 65 originally established by the city resulted in pass rates for African American and white applicants that came close to meeting the requirements of the four-fifths rule. However, the city then opted to select only candidates deemed "highly qualifed" (i.e., those with scores of at least 89). As a result of this change in cutoff scores, whites were more than five times as likely as African Americans to be hired as firefighters. The court found the higher cutoff to be arbitrary and not supported by evidence that candidates with lower passing scores would not be equally effective as firefighters.

Lanning v. SEPTA deals with the cutoff score used in a physical fitness test given to transit officers. Physical fitness tests tend to disfavor women (as well as older workers and the disabled), yet some level of physical fitness is clearly a legitimate requirement for jobs such as police officers and firefighters. This case was litigated for years and the following case excerpt includes material from the court of appeal's 1999 decision ("*Lanning* (I)") and its final determination in 2002 ("*Lanning* (II)").

Not all courts concur with the Third Circuit's relatively stringent approach to establishing business necessity—that cutoff scores with discriminatory effects must be shown to measure the *minimum* qualifications necessary to successfully perform the job. Certainly, successful performance of a job includes considerations of public safety. A showing by plaintiffs that some individuals with lower scores are able to perform a job successfully is not sufficient to establish that a particular cutoff score lacks business necessity when most persons with the lower score cannot perform the job successfully. As a basic principle, the EEOC maintains that *when cutoffs are used, they should be "reasonable and consistent with normal expectations of acceptable proficiency."*[37] Additionally, requirements for one job must not be set unduly high based on the idea that persons hired will then be qualified to move on to other jobs. *Unless progression to higher-level jobs occurs with relative certainty and within a relatively brief period of time, employers should not establish the requirements for lower-level jobs with higher-level jobs in mind.*[38] This does not preclude employers from hiring management trainees and starting them out learning basic production tasks.

There are no easy answers here. For tests that are known to create adverse impact, such as physical fitness tests, lowering cutoffs and not ranking those with passing scores tends to minimize adverse impact. However, if the score needed to pass is set too low, the very purpose of testing is defeated, because almost everyone will be deemed acceptable. Refraining from ranking candidates may obscure important differences in the abilities of candidates. The court in *Lanning* (II) suggested that prior training can overcome the disadvantage that women face on physical strength/fitness tests, although the experience of the New York City Fire Department in this regard is not encouraging. Even though the city helped provide training for female candidates, relatively few passed the rigorous physical fitness test, and those that did had lower scores that could not be overcome by superior performance on other tests.[39] An alternative approach is to focus on developing physical fitness tests that are content valid, whose elements closely reflect tasks performed on the job, and whose cutoff scores derive from the actual requirements of the job. More generally, employers should not

[37]29 C.F.R. § 1607.5(H) (2005).

[38]29 C.F.R. § 1607.5(I) (2005).

[39]Corey Kilgannon. "Trying to Fill a Fallen Husband's Boots." *New York Times* (April 2, 2003), A-19.

LANNING V. SEPTA (I)

181 F.3d 478 (3d Cir. 1999), *cert. denied*, 528 U.S. 1131 (2000)

● ● ●

OPINION BY JUDGE MANSMANN:

In this appeal, we must determine the appropriate legal standard to apply when evaluating an employer's business justification in an action challenging an employer's cutoff score on an employment screening exam as discriminatory under a disparate impact theory of liability. We hold today that under the Civil Rights Act of 1991, a discriminatory cutoff score on an entry level employment examination must be shown to measure the minimum qualifications necessary for successful performance of the job in question in order to survive a disparate impact challenge. Because we find that the District Court did not apply this standard in evaluating the employer's business justification for its discriminatory cutoff score in this case, we will reverse the District Court's judgment and remand for reconsideration under this standard. * * *

SEPTA is a regional mass transit authority that operates principally in Philadelphia, Pennsylvania. * * * In 1991, SEPTA hired Dr. Paul Davis to develop an appropriate physical fitness test for its police officers. Ultimately, Dr. Davis recommended a 1.5 mile run within 12 minutes. Dr. Davis explained that completion of this run would require that an officer possess an aerobic capacity of 42.5 mL/kg/min, the aerobic capacity that Dr. Davis determined would be necessary to perform the job of SEPTA transit officer. * * * Dr. Davis understood that SEPTA officers would not be required to run 1.5 miles within 12 minutes in the course of their duties, but he nevertheless recommended this test as an accurate measure of the aerobic capacity necessary to perform the job of SEPTA transit police officer. Based upon Dr. Davis' recommendation, SEPTA adopted a physical fitness screening test for its applicants which included a 1.5 mile run within 12 minutes. Beginning in 1991, the 1.5 mile run was administered as the first component of the physical fitness test; if an applicant failed to run 1.5 miles in 12 minutes, the applicant would be disqualified from employment as a SEPTA transit officer.

It is undisputed that for the years 1991, 1993, and 1996, an average of only 12% of women applicants passed SEPTA's 1.5 mile run in comparison to the almost 60% of male applicants who passed. For the years 1993 and 1996, the time period in question in this litigation, the pass rate for women was 6.7% compared to a 55.6% pass rate for men. * * * SEPTA concedes that its 1.5 mile run has a disparate impact on women. * * *

In conjunction with the implementation of its physical fitness screening test, SEPTA also began testing incumbent officers for aerobic capacity in 1991. * * * [S]ignificant percentages of incumbent officers of all ranks have failed SEPTA's physical fitness test. By 1996, however, 86% of incumbent officers reached SEPTA's physical fitness standards. * * * SEPTA has promoted incumbent officers who have failed some or all of the components of the physical fitness test. * * * In addition, due to a clerical error, SEPTA hired a female officer in 1991 who failed the 1.5 mile run. This officer has subsequently been "decorated" by SEPTA and has been nominated repeatedly for awards. . . . * * *

Under Title VII's disparate impact theory of liability, plaintiffs establish a prima facie case of disparate impact by demonstrating that application of a facially neutral standard has resulted in a significantly discriminatory hiring pattern. Once the plaintiffs have established a prima facie case, the burden shifts to the employer to show that the employment practice is "job related for the position in question and consistent with business necessity. . . ." Should the employer meet this burden, the plaintiffs may still prevail if they can show that an alternative employment practice has a less disparate impact and would also serve the employer's legitimate business interest. * * *

The laudable mission begun by the Court in *Griggs* was the eradication of discrimination through the application of practices fair in form but discriminatory in practice by eliminating unnecessary barriers to employment opportunities. In the context of a hiring exam with a cutoff score shown to have a discriminatory effect, the standard that best effectuates this mission is implicit in the Court's application of the business necessity doctrine to the employer in *Griggs*, i.e., that a discriminatory cutoff score is impermissible unless shown to measure the minimum qualifications necessary for successful performance of the job in question. Only this standard can effectuate the mission begun by the Court in *Griggs*; only by requiring employers to demonstrate that their discriminatory cutoff score measures the minimum qualifications necessary for successful performance of the job in question can we be certain to eliminate the use

of excessive cutoff scores that have a disparate impact on minorities as a method of imposing unnecessary barriers to employment opportunities. * * *

Our conclusion that the Act incorporates this standard is further supported by the business necessity language adopted by the Act. Congress chose the terms "job related for the position in question" and "consistent with business necessity." Judicial application of a standard focusing solely on whether the qualities measured by an entry level exam bear some relationship to the job in question would impermissibly write out the business necessity prong of the Act's chosen standard. With respect to a discriminatory cutoff score, the business necessity prong must be read to demand an inquiry into whether the score reflects the minimum qualifications necessary to perform successfully the job in question. See also EEOC Guidelines (noting that cutoff scores should "be set so as to be reasonable and consistent with normal expectations of acceptable proficiency within the work force."). * * *

[T]he [business necessity] standard itself takes public safety into consideration. If, for example, SEPTA can show on remand that the inability of a SEPTA transit officer to meet a certain aerobic level would significantly jeopardize public safety, this showing would be relevant to determine if that level is necessary for the successful performance of the job. Clearly a SEPTA officer who poses a significant risk to public safety could not be considered to be performing his job successfully. * * *

The District Court's application of its understanding of business necessity to SEPTA's business justification further illustrates that the District Court did not apply the correct legal standard. As an initial matter, the District Court seemed to conclude that Dr. Davis' expertise alone is sufficient to justify the 42.5 mL/kg/min aerobic capacity cutoff measured by the 1.5 mile run. This

conclusion . . . alone is insufficient to validate an employer's discriminatory practices. More fundamentally, however, nowhere in its extensive opinion did the District Court consider whether Dr. Davis' 42.5 mL/kg/min cutoff reflects the minimum aerobic capacity necessary to perform successfully the job of SEPTA transit police officer. * * *

Instead, the District Court upheld this cutoff because it was "readily justifiable." The validation studies of SEPTA's experts upon which the District Court relied to support this conclusion demonstrate the extent to which this standard is insufficient under the Act. The general import of these studies is that the higher an officer's aerobic capacity, the better the officer is able to perform the job. Setting aside the validity of these studies, this conclusion alone does not validate Dr. Davis' 42.5 mL/kg/min cutoff under the Act's business necessity standard. At best, these studies show that aerobic capacity is related to the job of SEPTA transit officer. A study showing that "more is better," however, has no bearing on the appropriate cutoff to reflect the minimal qualifications necessary to perform successfully the job in question. * * *

Under the District Court's understanding of business necessity, which requires only that a cutoff score be "readily justifiable," SEPTA, as well as any other employer whose jobs entail any level of physical capability, could employ an unnecessarily high cutoff score on its physical abilities entrance exam in an effort to exclude virtually all women by justifying this facially neutral yet discriminatory practice on the theory that more is better. This result contravenes *Griggs* and demonstrates why, under *Griggs,* a discriminatory cutoff score must be shown to measure the minimum qualifications necessary to perform successfully the job in question. * * *

LANNING V. SEPTA (II)
308 F.3d 286 (3d Cir. 2002)

● ● ●

OPINION BY CIRCUIT JUDGE BARRY:

* * * [W]e assess the sole issue we caused to be resolved on remand: whether or not SEPTA has proven that its 42.5 mL/kg/min aerobic

capacity standard measures the minimum qualifications necessary for the successful performance of the job of SEPTA transit police officers. The District Court concluded that the answer was "yes," and that any lesser standard "would result in officers . . . who were a danger to themselves, other officers, and the public at

large, [and] unable to effectively fight and deter crime." * * *

Neither the District Court nor the parties have explicitly defined the key phrase "minimum qualifications necessary," but a definition is implicit in the parties' respective arguments and the District Court's acceptance of that of SEPTA. SEPTA argued that the run test measures the "minimum qualifications necessary" because the relevant studies indicate that individuals who fail the test will be much less likely to successfully execute critical policing tasks. For example, the District Court credited a study that evaluated the correlation between a successful run time and performance on 12 job standards. The study found that individuals who passed the run test had a success rate on the job standards ranging from 70% to 90%. The success rate of the individuals who failed the run test ranged from 5% to 20%. The District Court found that such a low rate of success was unacceptable for employees who are regularly called upon to protect the public. In so doing, the District Court implicitly defined "minimum qualifications necessary" as meaning "likely to be able to do the job."

Plaintiffs argued, however, that within the group that failed the run test, significant numbers of individuals would still be able to perform at least certain critical job tasks. They argued that as long as some of those failing the run test can do the job, the standard cannot be classified as a "minimum." In essence, plaintiffs proposed that the phrase "minimum qualifications necessary" means "some chance of being able to do the job." Under this logic, even if those failing the test had a 1% chance of successfully completing critical job tasks, the test would be too stringent.

We are not saying, as our distinguished brother in dissent suggests we are saying, that "more is better." While, of course, a higher aerobic capacity will translate into better field performance—at least as to many job tasks which entail physical capability—to set an unnecessarily high cutoff score would contravene Griggs. It would clearly be unreasonable to require SEPTA applicants to score so highly on the run test that their predicted rate of success be 100%. It is perfectly reasonable, however, to demand a chance of success that is better than 5% to 20%. In sum, SEPTA transit police officers and the public they serve should not be required to engage in high-stakes gambling when it comes to public safety and law enforcement. SEPTA has demonstrated that the cutoff score it established measures the minimum qualifications necessary for successful performance as a SEPTA officer. * * *

One final note. While it is undisputed that SEPTA's 1.5 mile run test has a disparate impact on women, it is also undisputed that, in addition to those women who could pass the test without training, nearly all the women who trained were able to pass after only a moderate amount of training. It is not, we think, unreasonable to expect that women—and men—who wish to become SEPTA transit officers, and are committed to dealing with issues of public safety on a day-to-day basis, would take this necessary step. * * *

The judgment of the District Court will be affirmed

CASE QUESTIONS

1. What was the legal issue in this case? What did the court decide?

2. What is the evidence of discriminatory effects in this case?

3. What distinction is the court drawing between "job relatedness" and "business necessity?" What is the evidence that SEPTA's aerobic capicity test is both job related and consistent with business necessity?

4. Because physical fitness is clearly related to doing the job of transit officer, why shouldn't SEPTA be free to set high standards and hire only the most physically fit?

select based on differences in test scores among candidates who possess at least the minimum required ability unless such differences are both statistically and substantively significant. In the Chicago firefighter case, the court stated that the city would have still met its legitimate objective of having a qualified workforce if it had randomly selected from the pool of all candidates that passed the test (see "Clippings").

The "banding" of test scores can also diminish the discriminatory effects of tests without unduly compromising the principle of selecting the most able candidates. In **banding**, test scores are treated as estimates of tested-for characteristics (e.g., verbal

ability, intelligence). Because estimates contain errors from various sources, test scores are treated as different from one another only if the gap between them is sufficiently wide that the different scores are likely to reflect real differences in the tested-for characteristics. Selecting from within bands of test scores (e.g., 82 through 86) that are not statistically different from one another, rather than treating an 89 as necessarily better than an 88, allows employers more discretion in hiring without ignoring real differences in candidates' abilities. Courts have upheld the practice of banding test scores.[40]

Accommodating Disabled Persons in Testing

The legal responsibility to accommodate disabled persons begins prehire and includes testing procedures. However, unless the need for accommodation is obvious (e.g., a visually impaired person comes in with a guide dog), *an employer is not responsible for providing accommodation unless requested by a disabled job candidate.* For this to be possible, *candidates should be informed in advance about the types of employment tests used.* An exception to the general rule prohibiting preemployment inquiries regarding disability is that *employers can require job candidates to document their need for accommodation in the application and testing process.* Accommodations might include substitution of written for oral tests (or vice versa), large-print test forms, provision of sign language interpreters, allowing extra time for test completion, allowing breaks or rest periods during long tests, providing alternative testing locations with fewer distractions, or substituting for testing requirements (e.g., by more extensive interviews). Persons with disabilities that limit their vision, hearing, use of hands, concentration, or reading ability are particularly likely to need accommodation in testing.

[40]*Officers for Justice v. City and County of San Francisco,* 979 F.2d 721 (9th Cir. 1992); *cert. denied,* 507 U.S. 1004 (1993).

Chapter SUMMARY

Drug testing has proven to be relatively impervious to legal challenge. The primary legal limitations on drug testing stem from state drug-testing laws and the U.S. Constitution's protection (for public employees only) against "unreasonable searches or seizures" (Fourth Amendment). Random testing for nonsafety-sensitive positions is the form of drug testing most vulnerable to challenge. State drug-testing laws and the Omnibus Transportation Employees Testing Act contain various requirements for drug-testing procedures. Overall, employers are not held to a high standard in their drug-testing procedures, and employees are unlikely to be successful in suits against their employers for negligent drug testing. Suits against labs that actually conduct drug tests are more feasible. Although drug tests are not medical exams and current users of illegal drugs are not considered disabled, the ADA prohibits

terminating individuals who are no longer using illegal drugs and have been through a rehabilitation program or are currently in such a program. The Omnibus Transportation Employee Testing Act requires the drug (and alcohol) testing of millions of transportation employees and specifies procedural guidelines for those tests. The Drug-Free Workplace Act does not mandate drug testing, but instead requires that employers that have contracts with the federal government adopt and communicate policies prohibiting drug use or sale in the workplace.

Medical exams—including HIV tests and genetic tests—are regulated by the ADA. The ADA prohibits medical exams prior to a conditional offer of employment. Exams given following a conditional offer of employment are unrestricted in scope, whereas exams given to current employees must be job related

and consistent with business necessity or voluntary. The results of medical exams cannot be used to exclude qualified disabled persons. In addition to being subject to ADA requirements, HIV tests are prohibited or limited under some state laws and susceptible to Fourth Amendment challenges. Genetic testing includes both genetic screening of candidates for positions and genetic monitoring of current employees for the effects of exposure to hazardous substances. The legal status of genetic testing is murky, but the ADA, state laws, and the U.S. Constitution again provide likely avenues for legal challenges. Additionally, Executive Order 13145 tightly restricts genetic testing of federal government employees and is intended to be a model for both legislators and private sector employers.

A major concern with employment tests—particularly scored tests that measure abilities like intelligence, skill, aptitude, personality, and physical fitness—is adverse impact discrimination. The discriminatory effects of tests are assessed by examining applicant flow data and comparing selection rates for different protected class groupings. According to the four-fifths rule, if the selection rate for applicants of one race or sex is less than 80 percent of the selection rate for the race or sex enjoying the highest selection rate, that is a preliminary indication of discriminatory effects. When tests have discriminatory effects sufficient to establish a prima facie case of adverse impact, employers must defend those tests as job related and consistent with business necessity. For scored tests, validation studies are generally required to establish job relatedness. A content validation strategy defends a test by showing that the test entails the performance of behaviors and skills that closely mirror important aspects of the job itself. A criterion validation strategy defends a test by demonstrating a statistical association between performance on the test and performance on the job. The adequacy of validation studies, particularly criterion validation, is frequently contested and hinges on such factors as whether a proper job analysis was performed, whether the job for which the test was validated is the same as the job for which the test is used, the number of test takers on which the study is based, how closely the persons in the study mirror the people likely to be taking the test, how well job performance is measured, and whether the magnitude and statistical significance of the validity coefficient are sufficient. If a score below an established minimum cutoff level disqualifies candidates from further consideration, a cutoff score in excess of the minimum level needed to perform the job may not be consistent with business necessity. Even with sufficient evidence that a test is job related and consistent with business necessity, adverse impact will still be found if a feasible alternative testing procedure exists that has less discriminatory impact.

Practical Advice SUMMARY

- *Of the various circumstances for drug testing, employers should be especially careful about using random testing for nonsafety-sensitive positions.*

- *Unionized employers must negotiate with employees' unions over drug testing that affects current employees.*

- *Public employers must be prepared to defend the reasonableness of drug testing. Reasonableness is easiest to demonstrate when drug-testing programs*

 –focus on safety-sensitive jobs.

 –emphasize testing upon reasonable suspicion.

- *Supervisors should be well-trained at identifying signs of drug use and impairment.*

- *Employers should have drug-testing policies notifying employees*

 –if they are subject to drug testing.

 –the circumstances under which testing will occur.

 –the procedures that will be used.

 –the consequences of testing positive.

- *Procedurally sound drug-testing programs provide for the following*

 –confirmatory tests to verify positive results.

 –careful labeling of specimens and documentation of the chain of custody.

 –respect for the privacy of individuals in gathering specimens.

–use of reputable labs and monitoring of their performance.

–use of a medical review officer to interpret results.

–opportunity for employees to provide alternative explanations for positive results.

–information about medications taken to be sought only after positive drug-test results occur.

–handling drug-test results as sensitive and confidential information.

- Employers must not terminate or otherwise discriminate against employees who are in drug-treatment programs or have completed rehabilitation and are no longer using illegal drugs.

- Employers that use medical exams must

–not conduct or require medical exams of job candidates prior to extending conditional offers of employment.

–not conduct or require medical exams of job candidates until all other nonmedical aspects of the hiring process have been carried out.

–require that all persons hired into the same job categories, rather than selected individuals, submit to exams.

–not conduct or require medical exams of current employees unless the exams are either job related and consistent with business necessity or voluntary.

–not exclude disabled persons from employment based on medical exam results unless those persons are unable to perform the essential functions of their jobs or pose a direct threat to the health or safety of themselves or others.

- Except in rare circumstances where transmission of the disease on the job is an objective threat, employers should refrain from conducting HIV tests.

- Private sector employers must not require or suggest that job candidates submit to polygraphs or other similar devices at any point in the hiring process.

- Employers that use scored intelligence, aptitude, skill, or personality tests should

–examine test questions to determine whether they pertain to protected class characteristics and refrain from using tests that contain such questions.

–examine test results by comparing selection rates for different race, sex, and national origin groups in accordance with the four-fifths rule.

–discontinue or find substitutes for tests having discriminatory effects, unless strong evidence of validity exists.

–have evidence of job relatedness (validity) for all tests, but particularly for tests that have discriminatory effects.

- Content valid tests should be used to the extent feasible, but

–not to assess intangible characteristics.

–not for tasks that could readily be learned on the job.

- Criterion validation studies conducted by consultants or testing companies should be assessed by determining whether

–the test is validated for the type of job in question.

–a proper job analysis was conducted.

–the sample size was sufficiently large.

–the sample was representative of the people who will actually take the test, particularly in terms of protected class characteristics.

–the effects of the test on particular protected class groups were analyzed.

–job performance was measured in a reasonable way.

–the validity coefficient is sufficiently large and statistically significant.

–the job has been changed since the validation study was conducted.

- Employers must not use different scoring methods for different protected class groups.

- Employers should not establish cutoff scores for tests

–that exceed the levels needed to hire employees capable of performing jobs with the normal degree of proficiency.

–that are higher than necessary in anticipation of possible future positions, unless promotion to those positions is relatively quick and certain.

- Candidates should be informed in advance of required employment tests.

- When made aware that accommodation is needed, employers must reasonably accommodate disabled persons in the testing process.

Key TERMS

drug test
reasonable suspicion
random drug testing
Fourth Amendment
unreasonable search or seizure
Omnibus Transportation
 Employee Testing Act
chain of custody
confirmatory test
medical review officer
Drug-Free Workplace Act (DFWA)

medical examination
conditional offer of employment
HIV test
genetic screening
genetic monitoring
polygraph
Employee Polygraph Protection
 Act (EPPA)
honesty test
applicant flow data
four-fifths rule

selection rate
job-related and consistent with
 business necessity
validity
content validation
criterion validation
validation study
job analysis
cutoff score
race norming
banding

Chapter QUESTIONS

1. A secretary working at a prison facility was given a tip by her supervisor about a part-time job at an auto parts company. She applied for the job, but was rejected because she failed the drug test. When she later told her supervisor what had happened, the information was passed on to administrators at the prison, and they ordered that she be drug tested. She tested positive and admitted to having smoked some marijuana on the weekend. She was terminated. State regulations call for the discharge of employees for on-the-job use or possession of drugs, but provide for more lenient treatment of off-the-job drug use. She challenges her termination. What should the court decide? Why? (*Bond v. Department of Public Safety and Correctional Services*, 867 A.2d 346 (Ct. Spec. App. MD 2005))

2. An electrician employed by a county in Kentucky was arrested on charges of criminal trespass and possession of drug paraphernalia. Temporarily in prison, he attempted to conceal that fact and call in sick. However, his supervisor learned of the arrest, required the employee to submit to "reasonable cause testing" under the county's Drug-Free Workplace Guidelines, and suspended him. After a series of intervening events, the employee was ordered to attend an Employee Assistance Program (EAP) for evaluation of his drug dependency. The EAP provided counseling and randomly drug tested all participants. Following a positive drug test, the employee was terminated. The employee sued, challenging the legality of the drug testing to which he was subjected. What should the court decide? Why? (*Relford v. Lexington-Fayette Urban County Government*, 390 F.3d 452 (6th Cir. 2004))

3. A government agency that provides residential treatment for mentally retarded and developmentally disabled persons decided to require HIV testing of staff members. Although there had been no known instances of staff members infecting clients (or vice versa), staff members were often in situations where they were scratched or bitten by clients. A staff member objected to the mandatory HIV testing and sued. What should the court decide? Why? (*Glover v. Eastern Nebraska Community Office of Retardation*, 686 F. Supp. 243 (D. Neb. 1988))

4. A timber company used a "physical performance test" to assess candidates for entry-level positions handling lumber and cutting wood. The test was developed by industrial psychologists. In its original version, the test consisted of a "board pull ergometer" (pulling 30 to 70 lb. weights for specified durations to assess strength), a step test (stepping up and down on an 11-inch bench for 6 minutes), and a visual inspection of "gross body coordination." Additionally, the applicant's heart rate was measured during the step test to measure endurance. Applicants whose heart rates exceeded a specified level were stopped and deemed to have failed the test. The revised test consisted solely of a "weight stack" (total weight of 40 lbs.). For the three years that the original test was in effect, 70.2 percent of male applicants and 29.8 percent of the female applicants passed the test. Of female applicants, 24 percent failed because they were stopped due to an excessive heart rate, compared to 3.2 percent of male applicants. With the revised test, 66.9 percent of males passed and 25.8 percent of females passed.

A criterion validation study was conducted for both tests, showing statistically significant correlations between test and job performance. Females rejected for employment sued. What should the court decide? Why? (*Equal Employment Opportunity Commission v. Simpson Timber Company*, 1992 U.S. Dist. LEXIS 5829)

5. In the *Siroka* case involving the personality test that had questions relating to religion and sexual orientation, the company claimed that it had evidence of the test's validity for hiring store security officers. Specifically, the company had given the test to 18 of its most successful store security officers, and they had done well on it. Comment on the adequacy of this "validation study."

6. Was the *Rockwell* case correctly decided? Should employers be able to reject employees who fail "nerve conduction tests" and are viewed as more likely to develop carpal tunnel syndrome? Does it matter that the validity of these tests is in question? Does it matter that carpal tunnel syndrome is much more common among women than men?

7. A number of employers are reportedly asking job candidates for their SAT scores and using this information in making hiring decisions. Is this practice legally advisable? (Rebecca L. Weber. "Want a job? Hand over your SAT results." *Christian Science Monitor* (May 18, 2004) viewed at http://www.csmonitor.com/2004/0518/p13s01-legn.htm)

8. How important is it to have women significantly represented among the ranks of police officers and firefighters? What should cities do about physical fitness/strength testing for these important jobs?

Internet RESOURCES

Hiring and Promotion Decisions

CLIPPINGS

▸ At a hearing before the Senate Aviation Subcommittee, a Federal Aviation Administration (FAA) official defended the agency's long-standing rule that commercial pilots must retire by age 60. Questions have been raised as to whether the age limitation on flying is arbitrary and whether a more individualized medical assessment should be substituted for the blanket rule.[1]

▸ Abercrombie & Fitch stores has agreed to pay $50 million to settle three lawsuits alleging discrimination against nonwhites and females in hiring. The cases centered on the contention that the company refused to hire employees who did not have the "A&F Look"—white, young, male, and preppy. Plaintiffs alleged that nonwhite employees were steered toward stockroom and overnight shift positions and away from sales positions. The settlement also includes benchmarks for hiring women and persons of color; an agreement to refrain from targeting fraternities, sororities, or specific colleges for recruitment; diversity goals for managers; new recruiters; and a requirement that marketing materials reflect diversity by including persons of color.[2]

▸ The Borgata Casino in Atlantic City, New Jersey, has established a new weight policy for all its bartenders and waitresses (termed "Borgata Babes"). Employees are weighed to establish a baseline. If an employee's weight increases by more than 10 percent, that employee is suspended for 90 days. If the employee is unable to lose weight during the suspension and does not have a valid medical reason, the employee is fired. The casino has been sued over its weight policy. It defends the policy by saying that the bartenders and waitresses are costumed performers who help carry out the casino's branding and marketing objectives.[3]

▸ A sex discrimination lawsuit has been brought against Costco, challenging the manner in which promotion decisions are made for managerial positions. The plaintiffs' attorneys allege the existence of a "tap on the shoulder" promotion system in which promotional opportunities are not posted, no formal application process exists, and no written guidelines or criteria exist for deciding who gets promoted. Women comprise almost 50 percent of the company's workforce, but are only 17 percent of its store managers and assistant managers. Brad Seligman, the lead attorney in the suit, summed up the case by saying "It's a classic glass ceiling."[4]

[1] Fawn H. Johnson. "FAA Defends 'Age-60 Rule' Forcing Commercial Pilots to Retire." *Daily Labor Report* 138 (July 20, 2005), A-11.

[2] Joyce E. Cutler. "Abercrombie & Fitch Settles Race, Sex Discrimination Lawsuits for $50 Million." *Daily Labor Report* 218 (November 12, 2004), A-2; Tom Gilroy. "$50 Million Settlement of Bias Suits Includes Changes in Hiring Practices." *Daily Labor Report* 221 (November 17, 2004), A-14.

[3] Iver Paterson. "Casino with Weight Policy Finds Boon in Controversy." *New York Times* (March 14, 2005), A-20.

[4] Joyce E. Cutler. "Suit Charges Costco with Bias in Promoting Women as Managers." *Daily Labor Report* 159 (August 18, 2004), A-10.

This chapter rounds out the discussion of the legal issues involved in selecting employees for initial hire or promotion by considering the legal implications of facially discriminatory requirements, physical appearance standards (e.g., weight), and other subjective criteria (e.g., impressions from interviews). After a selection decision is made, the process through which employment or promotion is offered and accepted requires careful attention. Increasingly, discrimination claims involve not entry into employment, but rather obstacles to advancement. Legal concerns surrounding promotion decisions are highlighted.

CRITERIA FOR HIRING AND PROMOTION DECISIONS

Facially Discriminatory Policies/Practices—BFOQ Defense

Employers that base employment decisions of any kind, including hiring and promotion, on protected class characteristics are engaging in disparate treatment discrimination. When they do so overtly and argue that it is necessary to limit a particular type of employment to persons with specific protected class characteristics, this type of disparate treatment is termed a **facially discriminatory** policy or practice. An important but very limited defense is available to employers that adopt facially discriminatory requirements. If an employer can show that a *particular protected class characteristic* (e.g., being male) is a **bona fide occupational qualification (BFOQ)** for the job in question, the facially discriminatory requirement is legal. Thus, our earlier advice for avoiding disparate treatment should be amended by saying that *employers must not establish protected class requirements for jobs, except in those rare instances where those protected class requirements are BFOQs for the jobs in question.*

Title VII of the Civil Rights Act of 1964, in language that is mirrored in the Age Discrimination in Employment Act, defines the BFOQ defense as follows:

> [I]t shall not be an unlawful employment practice for an employer to hire and employ . . . on the basis of his religion, sex, or national origin in those certain instances where religion, sex, or national origin is a bona fide occupational qualification reasonably necessary to the normal operation of that particular business or enterprise. . . .[5]

Notice that the Title VII protected classes of race and color are omitted. Because racial discrimination was the central problem that motivated passage of the Civil Rights Act, Congress was unwilling to allow for any circumstances in which employment opportunity could be strictly limited on the basis of race or color. Thus, the BFOQ defense is not available for policies that facially discriminate on the basis of race or color, and *employers must not establish racial requirements for jobs.*

Although the phrase *reasonably necessary* might not sound overly exacting, the EEOC and courts have made it clear that this is a very narrow exception to the general rule prohibiting disparate treatment. It is important to distinguish between the requirement that *neutral selection criteria* (e.g., employment tests) be job related and consistent with business necessity and the requirement that *specifications based on protected class* (e.g., "We want to hire only female table servers because that is what our customers want") be bona fide occupational qualifications. These terms apply in different contexts and are *not* synonymous. A neutral requirement with discriminatory

[5]42 U.S.C.A. § 2000e-2(e)(1) (2005).

effects can be defended as job related and consistent with business necessity if it tends to be associated with job performance and appears reasonable given the nature of the business. In contrast, defense of a facially discriminatory policy requires the employer to show that only, or virtually only, persons with the specified protected class characteristic can do the job, and that the job, as it is currently configured, is integral to the operation of the business. In other words, hiring someone without the specified protected class characteristic would not simply lead to lower job performance, but would ultimately undermine the business.

Arguments for BFOQs based on the discriminatory preferences of customers, coworkers, or clients are usually unsuccessful. Otherwise, employers could shirk their responsibilities by blaming others: "I would really like to hire a woman as vice president, but our senior managers are old-fashioned and would not be comfortable dealing with her." This would leave a gaping hole in antidiscrimination laws. An appeals court rejected a company's claim that being male was a BFOQ for the position of vice president of international operations for a petro-chemical manufacturer.[6] The company's stated concerns—that Latin American clients would refuse to deal with a woman holding that position and that a woman would be unable to conduct business from hotel rooms—were insufficient to establish a BFOQ.

Work assignments, as well as hiring decisions, can be challenged as facially discriminatory. A telemarketing company, whose major business was "get-out-the-vote" preelection calls, "race-matched" callers and potential voters. At clients' request, African-American employees were assigned to call black voters, given "black" scripts, and located in separate rooms from white employees assigned to call white voters. The court refused to recognize a race-based BFOQ for these discriminatory job assignments and found that the employer had intentionally discriminated.[7] Thus, the idea that "diversity is good for business" should not be interpreted to mean that employers are free to hire or assign work based on race or other protected class characteristics thought to appeal to or match those of desired customers. This is particularly a problem if client segments differ in size or lucrativeness. Instead, *employers should use alternatives to protected class (e.g., interpersonal skills, cultural sensitivity, foreign language proficiency, prior experience) to identify those who could work best with particular groups of clients or customers.*

Grounds for Recognizing BFOQS So, when is a BFOQ recognized? The courts have recognized three general grounds for establishing BFOQs: authenticity, public safety, and privacy. The classic example of **authenticity** or genuineness is a director casting a movie and limiting a female role to female actors. Authenticity also applies where sex or sex appeal is the essence of the business. Owners of clubs featuring topless dancers need not consider males for those jobs. The more difficult cases involve jobs that contain both sex-linked and sex-neutral aspects. A BFOQ will be recognized only if the sex-linked aspects clearly predominate.[8] Hooters restaurants hired only women for jobs as table servers, bartenders, and hosts. A company attorney defended this practice: "Being female is a bona fide occupational qualification. We don't believe the position is simple food service. It's a multidimensional job. We think of Hooters Girls as something closer to the Dallas Cowgirls than to a waitress whose only job is to serve food."[9] In 1997, Hooters agreed to pay $3.75 million

[6]*Fernandez v. Wynn Oil Co.*, 653 F.2d 1273 (9th Cir. 1981).

[7]*Ferrill v. The Parker Group, Inc.*, 168 F.3d 468 (7th Cir. 1999).

[8]*Wilson v. Southwest Airlines*, 517 F. Supp. 292, at 301 (N.D. Tex. 1981).

[9]"Food Chain Charged with Bias for Hiring Only Females for 'Hooters Girls' Waitstaff," *Daily Labor Report* 248 (December 30, 1993), D-11.

to settle a class action sex discrimination suit brought by males denied employment. The company agreed to open up all host positions and *some* bartender and server positions to men. However, the settlement was a compromise and allowed the restaurant to maintain a "modified Hooters Girl" position, open only to women who would be garbed in Hooters Girl uniforms.[10]

The second basis for establishing a BFOQ is **public safety**. When hiring or assigning employees with particular protected class characteristics is necessary to protect the safety of others, facially discriminatory requirements are legally defensible. The Supreme Court held that Alabama could hire only males for certain prison jobs because conditions in the prisons were so bad that there was a real prospect of violent sexual offenders attacking female guards and prison riots ensuing.[11] Importantly the Court's rationale was based upon potential harm to others, not on a paternalistic impulse to protect individual females from accepting potentially dangerous employment. A public safety BFOQ was not established where an employer's "fetal protection policy" excluded fertile women from jobs that involved exposure to lead.[12] Concerns about the safety of a potential fetus, even if within the realm of "public" safety, were deemed not to be sufficiently related to job performance and the essence of the business to warrant a BFOQ. Although the ADEA generally prohibits mandatory retirement and other maximum age requirements, public safety concerns sometimes allow employers to consider only younger persons for jobs. A BFOQ based on public safety was upheld for an inner-city bus company that limited new hires to persons under 40.[13] Likewise, courts have recognized a BFOQ for the mandatory retirement at age 60 of pilots at commercial airlines (although this policy has been questioned—see "Clippings"). However, an airline was unable to show that public safety demanded that *flight engineers* (who are in the cockpit but do not normally operate the controls of planes) retire at age 60.[14] Courts are relatively receptive to BFOQs for age requirements based on public safety, but *employers must establish that the risks posed by older employees are substantial and that more individualized means (e.g., regular medical exams) of identifying persons who might pose risks are not feasible, before excluding older persons from safety-sensitive jobs.*

The third basis for a BFOQ is customer **privacy**. This primarily relates to requirements for employees of a particular sex. One BFOQ case with a privacy basis concerned a psychiatric facility's rule that at least one person of each sex be available on each shift.[15] The rationale for the rule was that many of the hospital's adolescent clients had been victims of sexual abuse and might only be willing to speak with counselors of a specific sex. The court agreed that scheduling shifts based on sex was facially discriminatory, but held that the sex requirement was a BFOQ due to its close relationship to the therapeutic mission of the hospital. Privacy-based BFOQ's have also been recognized in cases involving delivery nurses[16] and custodians.[17] An interesting issue has arisen regarding the apparent preference of many medical practices—and patients—for female ob-gyns.[18] Would such a preference be justified by a privacy-based BFOQ? Litigation has not yet provided a clear answer to this

[10]Nadya Aswad. "Hooters Chain Agrees to Pay $3.75 Million to Settle Bias Claims by Male Job Applicants." *Daily Labor Report* 190 (October 1, 1997), D-32.

[11]*Dothard v. Rawlinson*, 433 U.S. 321 (1977).

[12]*International Union, UAW v. Johnson Controls*, 499 U.S. 187 (1991).

[13]*Usery v. Tamiami Trail Tours*, 531 F.2d 224 (5th Cir. 1976).

[14]*Western Airlines v. Criswell*, 472 U.S. 400 (1985).

[15]*Healey v. Southwood Psychiatric Hospital*, 78 F.3d 128 (3d Cir. 1996).

[16]*EEOC v. Mercy Health Center*, 1982 U.S. Dist. LEXIS 12256.

[17]*Norwood v. Dale Maintenance* Systems, 590 F.Supp. 1410 (N.D. Ill. 1984).

[18]Tamar Lewin. "Women's Health Is No Longer a Man's World." *New York Times* (February 7, 2001), A-1.

question.[19] In light of the fact that males still predominate among gynecologists, it is difficult to argue that men cannot do the job. On the other hand, the privacy interests of patients concerning this type of work seem particularly acute.

A number of BFOQ cases have arisen in the context of correctional facilities. *Everson v. Michigan Department of Corrections* provides a good example of the difficulties involved in applying antidiscrimination law to this setting.

Except when clear authenticity, public safety, or privacy interests are at stake, employers should not impose protected class requirements for employment based on the demands or needs of customers or coworkers. Overall, the best advice regarding BFOQs is that *even when suitability for a job is associated with protected class characteristics, employers should try to find more individualized means of assessing suitability rather than rely on protected class as a convenient proxy.* For example, if being knowledgeable about contemporary music is a requirement of a job, the employer should directly assess that knowledge, rather than limit hiring to young people on the assumption that older persons are not conversant on the subject. Whether younger people are, in fact, more likely to have the requisite musical acumen is irrelevant. Lastly, because some state antidiscrimination laws require that BFOQs be certified by the state fair employment practice agency before being put into use, *employers might be required to convince state fair employment practice agencies that BFOQs are warranted before putting them into effect.*

"Sex-Plus" Cases

A less obvious form of facially discriminatory policy or practice occurs when neutral criteria are applied to some protected class groups, but not others. In an important Supreme Court case,[20] the employer refused to employ women with children under age five. The company did not concern itself with the ages of the children of male employees. Even though the majority of the company's employees were women and the policy excluded only some women, it was deemed facially discriminatory because it was applied to and limited the employment opportunities of women only. The employer would have to establish a BFOQ to defend not hiring women with young children—an unlikely prospect. Although circumstances may call for sex-specific requirements or policies, the general rule is that *employers must not establish requirements that apply to one protected class group but not others.* These cases are labeled **sex-plus** because they most often involve differential requirements based on sex, but the issue is really "protected class–plus." Thus, an employer's policy of requiring that candidates for a promotional position who were over 40 years of age submit to EKG exams, while younger candidates were not usually required to do so, was facially discriminatory. A BFOQ could not be established because of the fairly minimal public safety dimensions of the job and because it was possible to require EKG testing on a more individualized basis than age.[21]

Weight and Appearance

Getting ahead in the workplace is like entering a beauty contest. Well, not exactly, but research has shown that physical appearance has a pervasive effect on employment outcomes. Persons judged better looking are more likely to get hired, promoted, and

[19]Emily Gold Waldman. "The Case of the Male OB-GYN: A Proposal for Expansion of the Privacy BFOQ in the Healthcare Context." *University of Pennsylvania Journal of Labor & Employment Law* 6 (Winter 2004), 357, at 359.

[20]*Phillips v. Martin Marietta Corp.*, 400 U.S. 542 (1971).

[21]*Epter v. New York City Transit Authority*, 127 F. Supp. 2d 384 (E.D.N.Y. 2001).

EVERSON V. MICHIGAN DEPARTMENT OF CORRECTIONS
391 F.3d 737 (6th Cir. 2004)

OPINION BY CIRCUIT JUDGE ROGERS:

Following separate lawsuits by female prisoners in Michigan and by the Civil Rights Division of the United States Department of Justice, both of which alleged rampant sexual abuse of female prisoners in Michigan, the Michigan Department of Corrections (the "MDOC") barred males from working in certain positions at its female prisons. Specifically, the MDOC designated approximately 250 Correctional Officer ("CO") and Residential Unit Officer ("RUO") positions in housing units at female prisons as "female only." A group of MDOC employees, both males and females, sued the MDOC, alleging that the MDOC's plan violated Title VII of the Civil Rights Act of 1964 and Michigan's Elliott-Larsen Civil Rights Act. Following a bench trial, the district court ruled in the plaintiffs' favor, concluding, among other things, that gender was not a bona fide occupational qualification (a "BFOQ") for the positions in question. * * * Because gender is a BFOQ for the positions in question, we reverse the judgment of the district court. * * *

At the time of trial, the MDOC employed approximately 19,000 persons, about 9400 of whom served as COs and RUOs. The duties of COs and RUOs in the housing units include patrolling the sleeping, shower, and bathroom areas, attending to the basic needs of women prisoners (including the provision of sanitary supplies), monitoring activity in the living quarters, enforcing housing rules and procedures, and assuring that proper standards of care and hygiene are maintained. RUOs staff the housing units on the first and second shifts, while COs staff the housing units on the third shift. CO positions outside the housing units include intake officer and transportation officer. Intake officers shepherd prisoners through the intake process, during which new prisoners are strip searched, fingerprinted, and showered, and during which paperwork is completed on the prisoners. Intake officers examine prisoners while they are naked. Among other things, transportation officers drive inmates to prisons to which they have been transferred and to medical appointments. Sometimes during transportation, female prisoners, who are placed in restraints, require the assistance of a transportation officer to use the bathroom. * * *

The MDOC concedes that it has adopted a facially discriminatory plan, and this case therefore "turns on whether such overt disparate treatment is for some reason justified under Title VII. Title VII permits overt discrimination if the disparate treatment is based on a bona fide occupation qualification, or BFOQ. The BFOQ defense countenances gender-based discrimination "in those certain instances where . . . sex . . . is a bona fide occupational qualification reasonably necessary to the normal operation of that particular business or enterprise." It is true that the BFOQ defense is written narrowly, and is to be read narrowly. Moreover, the burden is on an employer to establish a BFOQ defense.

Courts have offered various formulations of the BFOQ defense and from these decisions we distill the principles that lead us to the conclusion that the defense has been established in this case. First, "it is impermissible under Title VII to refuse to hire an individual woman or man on the basis of stereotyped characterizations of the sexes," and an employer must have a "basis in fact," for its belief that gender discrimination is "reasonably necessary"—not merely reasonable or convenient—to the normal operation of its business. Courts have variously stated that an employer can meet this requirement by showing that "all or substantially all [members of one gender] would be unable to perform safely and efficiently the duties of the job involved," that "it is impossible or highly impractical" to determine on an individualized basis the fitness for employment of members of one gender, or that "the very womanhood or very manhood of the employee undermines his capacity to perform a job satisfactorily," Second, the Supreme Court has stressed that "in order to qualify as a BFOQ, a job qualification must relate to the essence, or to the central mission of the employer's business." Third, this court imposes on employers asserting a BFOQ defense the burden of establishing that no reasonable alternatives exist to discrimination on the basis of sex. * * *

Application of the correct legal standard, which mandates that we give due regard to the professional judgment of the MDOC, makes it clear that the female gender is a BFOQ for the CO and RUO positions in the housing units at female prisons in Michigan. Viewed in proper perspective, the exclusion of males from these positions is "reasonably necessary" to "the normal

operation" of the MDOC's female facilities. The MDOC reasonably concluded that a BFOQ would materially advance a constellation of interests related to the "essence" of the MDOC's business—the security of the prison, the safety of inmates, and the protection of the privacy rights of inmates—and reasonable alternatives to the plan have not been identified.

Unquestionably, the security of the prisons relates to the essence of the MDOC's business, and the MDOC maintains that the presence of male COs and RUOs in female housing units imperils security in a number of ways. First, the presence of males in the housing units necessitates the use of "artificial barriers to security" such as covers for cell windows, doors on the toilet stalls, shower curtains, the moratorium on pat-down searches by male officers, and the "knock and announce" policy. Second, allegations of sexual abuse, whether true or not, create a "poisoned atmosphere" that breeds misconduct on the part of inmates and guards. Third, many male officers, afraid of false accusations of sexual abuse, become "gun-shy" and fail to monitor and discipline inmates in a proactive fashion.

Giving due deference to the judgment of the MDOC, we agree that the MDOC's plan will significantly enhance security at the MDOC's female facilities. Support for the MDOC's position comes from *Dothard v. Rawlinson*, in which the Supreme Court held that the male gender was a BFOQ for prison guards in Alabama's maximum-security men's prisons. The environment in Alabama's penitentiaries was, in the words of the Court, "a peculiarly inhospitable one for human beings of whatever sex," characterized by "rampant violence" and a "jungle atmosphere." * * * The Court concluded,

> The likelihood that inmates would assault a woman because she was a woman would pose a real threat not only to the victim of the assault [but] also to the basic control of the penitentiary and protection of its inmates and other security personnel. The employees very womanhood would thus directly undermine her capacity to provide the security that is the essence of a correctional counselor's responsibility.

* * * The safety of inmates also indisputably relates to the essence of the MDOC's business, and the MDOC believes that it must eliminate males from the CO and RUO positions in the housing units in order to safeguard female inmates from sexual abuse. The defendants state

that males perpetrate most of the sexual abuse in its female facilities, noting that, according to the plaintiffs' calculations, between 1994 and 2000, 189 of 208 allegations of sexual misconduct—including all of the sustained allegations—were made against male (officer and non-officer) employees, while the remaining 19 allegations were made against female employees or non-employees. The defendants also claim that sexual abuse most frequently occurs in the housing units, The defendants further argue that corrections officers commit a majority of the sexual abuse. . . . Finally, while conceding that the vast majority of male COs and RUOs conduct themselves professionally, the MDOC contends that it cannot predict which officers will engage in sexual abuse. The MDOC has established that the exclusion of male COs and RUOs from the housing units will decrease the likelihood of sexual abuse. * * *

The district court erred in concluding that the safety interests of female inmates did not support a BFOQ. The court reasoned that the MDOC's plan was not reasonably necessary because the MDOC had only recently implemented the reforms mandated by [law suit settlement agreements], because improper conduct had decreased since the implementation of the reform, and because only a minuscule percentage of male officers sexually abuse inmates. Further, the court relied on the lack of effort "to enhance pre-employment screening of new CO's and RUO's to lessen the likelihood of employing high risk male CO's and RUO's in the female prisons." The district court applied too restrictive a standard in rejecting the MDOC's safety-based argument. Apparently, the court thought that the MDOC could establish a BFOQ only by showing that "all, or substantially all, males are not able to perform safely and efficiently the duties of a CO and RUO in the housing units in the female prisons." However, as discussed above, the "all or substantially all" standard represents just one formulation of the "reasonable necessity" requirement, and the "impossible or highly impractical" standard better suits the instant case. No amount of sexual abuse is acceptable, and, given the gravity of the harm visited on the victims of sexual abuse, the MDOC permissibly eschewed the "wait-and-see" approach commended by the district court. * * *

The privacy rights of Michigan's female inmates also weigh in favor of a BFOQ. * * * Our court has recognized that "a convicted prisoner maintains some reasonable expectations of privacy while in prison, particularly where those claims are related to forced exposure to strangers of the opposite sex, even though those

privacy rights may be less than those enjoyed by non-prisoners." * * * Courts have recognized that this privacy interest can justify the exclusion of male officers from certain positions in female prisons. In *Robino v. Iranon*, a Hawaii women's correctional center asserted that the female gender was a BFOQ for 6 out of 41 corrections officer positions at a women's correctional center because the restriction was reasonably necessary to accommodate the privacy interests of the inmates, and to reduce the risk of sexual conduct between the officers and inmates. The positions at issue raised privacy concerns in that they were "residential" and required the officer on duty "to observe the inmates in the showers and toilet areas for the prison's own security or provided unsupervised access to the inmates." Accepting the BFOQ argument, the court found the policy "a reasonable response to the concerns about inmate privacy and allegations of abuse by male [officers]." * * *

The MDOC's policy similarly advances the privacy interests of Michigan's female inmates. * * * In the housing units, inmates spend a great deal of time in close contact with the officers, who supervise "the most intimate aspects of an inmate's life in prison, what time they go to sleep, where they sleep, when they get up, brush their teeth, use the restroom, shower, dress." Inmates must request sanitary napkins and other personal items from the officers. Given these circumstances, the MDOC, in Martin's words, determined that "sound correctional practices" and "simple human decency" dictated the exclusion of males from CO and RUO positions in the housing units.

In rejecting the MDOC's argument for a BFOQ, the district court stressed that the MDOC's plan departed from national norms. The court found that "standard practices nationwide provide for the employment of male corrections officers in female prisons" and that "there is nothing unique about the operation of the female prisons in Michigan." The court further found that "the published literature on the presence of male correctional officers in female prisons does not support a female BFOQ for corrections officer in the housing units in a female prison." In short, the court reasoned that, because the MDOC's plan deviated from standard practice, the plan was not reasonably necessary to the normal operation of Michigan's female prisons. The district court committed legal and factual error by using standard practice as a yardstick for the reasonable necessity of the MDOC's plan. In determining whether gender-based discrimination constitutes a BFOQ, a court must examine the particular circumstances of the individual employer, and not simply rely on generalizations about an industry or a group of employers. . . . Additionally, "appraisals need not be based on objective, empirical evidence, and common sense and deference to experts in the field may be used" to establish a BFOQ. Both of these precepts are especially true where the employer is a prison administrator that "must be allowed to adopt innovative solutions to the intractable problems of prison administration." * * * In addition to this legal error, the district court clearly erred in finding "nothing unique" about Michigan's female prisons. In reaching this conclusion, the district court inexplicably failed to address Michigan's deplorable record regarding the care of its female inmates, which, absent evidence to the contrary, we must assume sets it apart from other states. In light of the endemic problem of sexual abuse, it was incumbent upon the MDOC to act decisively and creatively. . . . * * *

The district court also erred in finding that there are "reasonable alternatives" to the MDOC's plan. As noted above, an employer invoking the BFOQ defense has the burden of establishing that there are no reasonable alternatives to discrimination. In addition to pre-employment screening, which is discussed above, the district court identified the following alternatives to female-only staffing of the CO and RUO positions in the housing units: covering vacancies with females; increasing female coverage where necessary with overtime; redeployment of female officers in supervisory positions; and eliminating the policy that each CO and RUO conduct five pat-down searches per shift. The MDOC has demonstrated that the district court erred in deeming these proposals "reasonable alternatives" to gender-specific staffing. First, the proposal to fill vacancies with female officers is simply a watered-down version of the MDOC's plan; the district court did not explain why it is permissible under Title VII to move to female-only staffing in the housing units through attrition but not through the immediate transfer of males to other positions. Second, increasing coverage with overtime is self-evidently expensive and inefficient. * * * Third, neither the district court nor the plaintiffs have explained how the redeployment of female supervisors to the housing units at the female prisons would cure problems stemming from the very presence of male COs and RUOs in the housing units. Fourth, the MDOC has already instituted a moratorium on pat-downs of female inmates by male officers, so this measure would not increase inmate safety or privacy. Moreover, the moratorium on pat-down searches impairs the ability of the male officers to protect the security of the prison and the safety of the inmates.

Before concluding, we emphasize the limited nature of our holding. We do not hold that gender constitutes a BFOQ for corrections officers in female prisons outside of Michigan. Nor do we hold that gender constitutes a BFOQ for positions in Michigan's female prisons beyond the approximately 250 positions we have discussed. Nor do we have occasion to address whether the male gender can ever be a BFOQ for a corrections officer position at a male prison. Rather, we simply conclude that, given the endemic problem of sexual abuse in Michigan's female facilities, given the constellation of issues addressed by the MDOC's plan (security, safety, and privacy), and given the deference accorded the MDOC's judgment, the MDOC's plan is reasonably necessary to the normal operation of its female prisons.

CASE QUESTIONS

1. What was the legal issue in this case? What did the court decide?

2. What general criteria for establishing a BFOQ are discussed in this case?

3. What rationale does the court provide for its decision?

4. The court takes pains in the final paragraph to emphasize that its decision pertains only to the small number of positions in question. But does the court's rationale apply more broadly? Should all jobs involving close contact with female prisoners be restricted to female employees? All jobs involving close contact with male prisoners be restricted to male employees?

5. If most other states do not place sex-based restrictions on employment in correctional facilities, in what sense is Michigan's policy "reasonably necessary?"

even paid more.[22] One aspect of appearance that can affect treatment in the workplace is weight. What are the legal implications of taking weight into account in hiring or promotion decisions?

Except for a very few jurisdictions (e.g., Michigan, the cities of San Francisco and Santa Cruz), weight is not a protected class. However, employers that discriminate against persons because they are "too heavy" might be discriminating on the basis of disability. For example, a hospital for the mentally retarded declined to rehire a 5′ 2″, 320-pound woman as an attendant, despite her good prior work record.[23] The woman argued that her obesity led the hospital to regard her as disabled and deny employment on that basis, even though she could do the job. The hospital's arguments that obesity should not be considered a disabling condition because it is mutable (capable of being altered) and voluntarily incurred, even if supportable, did not impress the appeals court, which ruled on the employee's behalf. Courts have differed in their treatment of disability discrimination claims by obese persons. Protection under disability discrimination laws depends on the individual being not merely overweight, but "morbidly obese" (more than twice the normal body weight or 100 pounds over normal body weight for a person of that height) and is more likely if a physiological basis for the obesity, or serious medical problems stemming from it, can be shown. Should an employer discriminate against someone deemed "underweight," disability discrimination could be claimed if the person was anorexic or had some other disabling condition (e.g., cancer, AIDS) as the cause of the person's thinness.

[22]Daniel S. Hamermesh and Jeff E. Biddle. "Beauty and the Labor Market." *American Economic Review* 84 (December 1994), 1174–94.

[23]*Cook v. State of Rhode Island, Dept. of MHRH*, 10 F.3d 17 (1st Cir. 1993).

What about the merely "chubby"? Is there any legal protection for persons disadvantaged by weight that is more within the normal range of variation? Employer policies or practices that place differentially burdensome weight requirements on men and women have been found to constitute sex-plus discrimination. Weight standards for flight attendants at United Airlines were successfully challanged on this basis.[24] The airline had weight limits for both male and female flight attendants, but the limits for males were based on the assumption of a large body frame, whereas the limits for women were based on the assumption of a medium frame. Consequently, female flight attendants were required to weigh between 14 and 25 pounds less than male peers of the same age and height. United was unable to defend its facially discriminatory weight requirements by showing that it was reasonably necessary to its business that female flight attendants be disproportionally thinner than male flight attendants.

Challenges to weight criteria on sex-plus grounds are not limited to formal policies. A highly qualified, 270-pound woman was turned down for a sales representative position. She was allegedly told by several managers that because this was an outside sales position involving direct contact with customers, she needed to lose weight to get promoted. The court agreed that her allegations raised a question of sex-plus discrimination, but her case failed because she was unable to point to men in sales positions whose excess weight was not objected to by the company.[25]

A sex-plus claim against the weight policy of the Borgata Casino (see "Clippings") would face difficulties. Assuming that there are some male bartenders and table servers and that the policy applies to them in the same fashion, no basis exists for arguing that one sex is being subjected to different and more burdensome requirements. However, if no males are in these positions, and the weight policy is not applied to other customer-service–related positions that are held by males, a sex discrimination claim might still be viable. On its face, the policy is aimed at maintaining one's weight and does not specify weight limits for hiring into these positions (although implicit standards might exist). Insofar as weight gain tends to occur as individuals age, it might also be claimed that the weight policy creates adverse impact against older workers.

Separate appearance or grooming requirements for men and women—such as rules relating to hair length, facial hair, jewelry, and the wearing of dresses—are common, but are they discriminatory? In one influential case,[26] a newspaper refused to hire a man for a copy layout artist job because his hair was too long. The newspaper did not have any requirements for the hair length of women. The appeals court distinguished this situation from other sex-plus cases because the neutral requirement paired with sex in this case was not a fundamental right (e.g., having children, getting married) and was not based on an immutable characteristic (i.e., the applicant could get a haircut). Thus, in the court's view, "a hiring policy that distinguishes on . . . grooming codes or length of hair is related more closely to the employer's choice of how to run his business than to equality of employment opportunity."[27] The court also endorsed the alternative rationale that no differential standard based on sex existed, because both sexes were simply being asked to meet generally accepted standards of appearance.

Sex-Stereotyping

Although courts have not been very receptive to claims based on differential appearance standards for men and women, requirements that are markedly different and

[24] *Frank v. United Airlines*, 216 F.3d 845 (9th Cir. 2000); *cert. denied*, 121 S. Ct. 1247 (2001).

[25] *Marks v. National Communications Association*, 72 F. Supp. 2d 322 (S.D.N.Y. 1999).

[26] *Willingham v. Macon Telegraph Publishing Co.*, 507 F.2d 1084 (5th Cir. 1975).

[27] *Willingham*, at 1091.

that impose sex-stereotypical standards are sometimes a different story. In one case, a retailer required female sales clerks to wear maternal-looking smocks, while male sales clerks wore business attire. The court concluded that these disparate standards reinforced stereotypes about women and were discriminatory.[28] Dress requirements that subject women to harassment have also been judged discriminatory.[29] The U.S. Supreme Court made an important statement about **sex-stereotyping** in a case involving a woman denied partnership at an accounting firm.[30] The comments of partners who participated in the decision process made it clear that they saw her as not sufficiently "feminine." Partners criticized her for using profanity, being "macho," "overcompensat[ing] for being a woman," and being "a somewhat masculine hard-nosed manager." When informed that she was denied partnership, the woman was also told that she should "walk more femininely, talk more femininely, dress more femininely, wear makeup, have her hair styled, and wear jewelry." The court stated the following:

> [W]e are beyond the day when an employer could evaluate employees by assuming or insisting that they matched the stereotype associated with their group. . . . "Congress intended to strike at the entire spectrum of disparate treatment of men and women, resulting from sex stereotypes." An employer who objects to aggressiveness in women but whose positions require this trait places women in an intolerable and impermissible Catch-22; out of a job if they behave aggressively and out of a job if they don't. Title VII lifts women out of this bind.[31]

Sex stereotypes can also affect men. A restaurant employee who was continually harassed because he was viewed by coworkers as "effeminate" had grounds for a sex discrimination claim.[32] An even more sweeping application of sex-stereotyping is found in the case of a transsexual firefighter diagnosed with Gender Identity Disorder. The firefighter began to adopt a more feminine appearance, leading to negative comments from coworkers, efforts by managers to force him to quit, and his subsequent suspension. The court said that the crux of the case was the firefighter's gender nonconforming behavior and appearance. Regardless of the transsexual label, discrimination against an individual because he or she does not conform to stereotypes about how persons assigned a particular sex at birth should act and dress violates Title VII.[33]

The influence of physical appearance on employment decisions is perhaps inevitable. For some jobs, physical appearance is job related. Certainly, employers can establish appearance and grooming requirements that are the same for all employees; however, appearance is very closely intertwined with protected class. How will older persons fare in workplace beauty contests? Pregnant women? Persons whose religious beliefs dictate a particular mode of appearance or dress? The lawsuits against Abercrombie & Fitch (see "Clippings") were settled prior to trial, but serve as a cautionary tale. Whatever the merits of the "A&F Look" as a marketing tool, it does not justify refusing to hire women and persons of color or relegating them to positions out of the public eye. *When grooming or appearance standards are needed, employers should ensure that standards for men and women are not widely different, based on stereotypes, or likely to result in harassment.*

[28]*O'Donnell v. Burlington Coat Factory Warehouse*, 656 F. Supp. 263, at 266 (S.D. Ohio 1987).

[29]*EEOC v. Sage Realty Corp.*, 507 F. Supp. 599 (S.D.N.Y. 1981).

[30]*Price Waterhouse v. Hopkins*, 490 U.S. 228 (1989).

[31]*Price Waterhouse*, at 251.

[32]*Sanchez v. Azteca Restaurant Enterprises*, 256 F.3d 864 (9th Cir. 2001).

[33]*Smith v. City of Salem, Ohio*, 378 F.3d 566 (6th Cir. 2004); *rehearing, en banc, denied* 2004 U.S. App. LEXIS 22668.

Although many sex-stereotyping cases have involved issues of appearance, the concept is broader in its reach. *Back v. Hasting on Hudson Union Free School District* considers whether basing employment decisions on stereotypes about the inability of women with small children to remain sufficiently committed to their jobs violates the law—even in the absence of evidence that fathers with small children were treated more advantageously.

BACK V. HASTING ON HUDSON UNION FREE SCHOOL DISTRICT
365 F.3d 107 (2d Cir. 2004)

● ● ●

OPINION BY CIRCUIT JUDGE CALABRESI:

In 1998, Plaintiff-Appellant Elana Back was hired as a school psychologist at the Hillside Elementary School ("Hillside") on a three-year tenure track. At the end of that period, when Back came up for review, she was denied tenure and her probationary period was terminated. * * * Defendants-Appellees contend that Back was fired because she lacked organizational and interpersonal skills. Back asserts that the real reason she was let go was that the defendants presumed that she, as a young mother, would not continue to demonstrate the necessary devotion to her job, and indeed that she could not maintain such devotion while at the same time being a good mother. This appeal thus poses an important question, one that strikes at the persistent "fault line between work and family—precisely where sex-based overgeneralization has been and remains strongest." It asks whether stereotyping about the qualities of mothers is a form of gender discrimination, and whether this can be determined in the absence of evidence about how the employer in question treated fathers. We answer both questions in the affirmative. We also conclude that the plaintiff has asserted genuine issues of material fact in her gender discrimination claim. . . . * * *

In the plaintiff's first two years at Hillside, Brennan and Wishnie [school principal and Director of Pupil Services respectively] consistently gave her excellent evaluations. In her first annual evaluation, on a scale where the highest score was "outstanding," and the second highest score was "superior," Back was deemed "outstanding" and "superior" in almost all categories, and "average" in only one. "Superior" was, according to the performance instrument, the "standard for consideration for obtaining tenure in Hastings." Narrative evaluations completed by Wishnie and Brennan during this time were also uniformly positive, attesting, for example, that Back had "served as a positive child advocate throughout the year," and had "successfully adjusted to become a valued and valuable member of the school/community."

In her second year at Hillside, Back took approximately three months of maternity leave. After she returned, she garnered another "outstanding" evaluation from Brennan, who noted that she was "very pleased with Mrs. Back's performance during her second year at Hillside." Other contemporaneous observations also resulted in strongly positive feedback, for example, that Back "demonstrated her strong social/emotional skills in her work with parents and teachers, and most especially with students," and that she was "a positive influence in many areas, and continues to extend a great deal of effort and commitment to our work." In her annual evaluation, Back received higher marks than the previous year, with more "outstandings" and no "averages." The narrative comments noted that she "continues to serve in an outstanding manner and provides excellent support for our students," and that her "commitment to her work and to her own learning is outstanding." At the beginning of Back's third year at Hillside, she again received "outstanding" and "superior" evaluations from both Brennan and Wishnie.

Defendant-Appellant John Russell, the Superintendent of the School District, also conducted ongoing evaluations of Back's performance. In January 1999, he observed a Learning Team meeting, and reported that Back had managed the meeting "in a highly efficient and professional manner," and that it was "obvious [that she] was well prepared." He rated her performance "superior." In February 2000, he again sat in on a Learning Team meeting, and again indicated that Back's performance was "superior." He also noted that

she was effective without being overly directive, and worked well with the other members of the team. In addition, according to Back, all three individual defendants repeatedly assured her throughout this time that she would receive tenure.

Back asserts that things changed dramatically as her tenure review approached. The first allegedly discriminatory comments came in spring 2000, when Back's written evaluations still indicated that she was a very strong candidate for tenure. At that time, shortly after Back had returned from maternity leave, the plaintiff claims that Brennan, (a) inquired about how she was "planning on spacing [her] offspring," (b) said "'please do not get pregnant until I retire,'" and (c) suggested that Back "wait until [her son] was in kindergarten to have another child." Then, a few months into Back's third year at Hillside, on December 14, 2000, Brennan allegedly told Back that she was expected to work until 4:30 p.m. every day, and asked "'What's the big deal. You have a nanny. This is what you [have] to do to get tenure.'" Back replied that she did work these hours. And Brennan, after reportedly reassuring Back that there was no concern about her job performance, told her that Wishnie expected her to work such hours. But, always according to Back, Brennan also indicated that Back should "maybe . . . reconsider whether [Back] could be a mother and do this job which [Brennan] characterized as administrative in nature," and that Brennan and Wishnie were "concerned that, if [Back] received tenure, [she] would work only until 3:15 p.m. and did not know how [she] could possibly do this job with children."

A few days later, on January 8, 2001, Brennan allegedly told Back for the first time that she might not support Back's tenure because of what Back characterizes as minor errors that she made in a report. According to Back, shortly thereafter Principal Wishnie accused her of working only from 8:15 a.m. to 3:15 p.m. and never working during lunch. When Back disputed this, Wishnie supposedly replied that "this was not [Wishnie's] impression and . . . that she did not know how she could perform my job with little ones. She told me that she worked from 7 a.m. to 7 p.m. and that she expected the same from me. If my family was my priority, she stated, maybe this was not the job for me." A week later, both Brennan and Wishnie reportedly told Back that this was perhaps not the job or the school district for her if she had "little ones," and that it was "not possible for [her] to be a good mother and have this job." The two also allegedly remarked that it would be

harder to fire Back if she had tenure, and wondered "whether my apparent commitment to my job was an act. They stated that once I obtained tenure, I would not show the same level of commitment I had shown because I had little ones at home. They expressed concerns about my child care arrangements, though these had never caused me conflict with school assignments." They did not—as Back told the story—discuss with her any concerns with her performance at that time. * * *

Back retained counsel in response to Brennan and Wishnie's alleged statements, and in a letter dated May 14, 2001, informed Russell of these comments, and of her fear that they reflected attitudes that would improperly affect her tenure review. On May 29, 2001, Brennan and Wishnie sent a formal memo to Russell informing him that they could not recommend Back for tenure. Their reasons included (a) that although their formal reports had been positive, their informal interactions with her had been less positive, (b) that there were "far too many" parents and teachers who had "serious issues" with the plaintiff and did not wish to work with her, and (c) that she had persistent difficulties with the planning and organization of her work, and with inaccuracies in her reports, and that she had not shown improvement in this area, despite warnings. * * *

On or around June 13, 2001, Wishnie and Brennan filed the first negative evaluation of Back, which gave her several "below average" marks and charged her with being inconsistent, defensive, difficult to supervise, the source of parental complaints, and inaccurate in her reports. Their evaluation, which was submitted to Russell, concluded that Back should not be granted tenure. Around the same time, several parents who had apparently complained about Back were encouraged by Russell to put their concerns in writing. Several parents submitted letters, reporting a range of complaints about Back's work, including that she was defensive, immature, unprofessional, and had misdiagnosed children. On June 18, 2001, Russell informed Back by letter that he had received Wishnie and Brennan's annual evaluation, and was recommending to the Board of Education that her probationary appointment be terminated. * * * In September 2001, the Board notified Back that her probationary appointment would be terminated. * * *

To show sex discrimination, Back relies upon a *Price Waterhouse* [a Supreme Court case establishing a precedent for sex stereotyping claims] "stereotyping" theory. Accordingly, she argues that comments made about a woman's inability to combine work and motherhood

are direct evidence of such discrimination. * * * It is the law . . . that "stereotyped remarks can certainly be evidence that gender played a part" in an adverse employment decision. The principle of *Price Waterhouse,* furthermore, applies as much to the supposition that a woman *will* conform to a gender stereotype (and therefore will not, for example, be dedicated to her job), as to the supposition that a woman is unqualified for a position because she does *not* conform to a gender stereotype.

The instant case, however, foregrounds a crucial question: What constitutes a "gender-based stereotype"? *Price Waterhouse* suggested that this question must be answered in the particular context in which it arises, and without undue formalization. We have adopted the same approach, as have other circuits. Just as "it takes no special training to discern sex stereotyping in a description of an aggressive female employee as requiring 'a course at charm school,'" so it takes no special training to discern stereotyping in the view that a woman cannot "be a good mother" and have a job that requires long hours, or in the statement that a mother who received tenure "would not show the same level of commitment [she] had shown because [she] had little ones at home." These are not the kind of "innocuous words" that we have previously held to be insufficient, as a matter of law, to provide evidence of discriminatory intent. Not surprisingly, other circuit courts have agreed that similar comments constitute evidence that a jury could use to find the presence of discrimination. [e.g., a direct supervisor "specifically questioned whether the plaintiff would be able to manage her work and family responsibilities;" a supervisor stated to a woman known to be pregnant that she was being fired so that she could "spend more time at home with her children;" remarks by the head of plaintiff's department that "she would be happier at home with her children"]. * * *

The defendants argue that stereotypes about pregnant women or mothers are not based upon gender, but rather, "gender plus parenthood," thereby implying that such stereotypes cannot, without comparative evidence of what was said about fathers, be presumed to be "on the basis of sex." . . . [H]owever, . . . at least where stereotypes are considered, the notions that mothers are insufficiently devoted to work, and that work and motherhood are incompatible, are properly considered to be, themselves, gender-based. * * *

Defendants are thus wrong in their contention that Back cannot make out a claim that survives summary judgment unless she demonstrates that the defendants treated similarly situated men differently. Back has admittedly proffered no evidence about the treatment of male administrators with young children. Although her case would be stronger had she provided or alleged the existence of such evidence, there is no requirement that such evidence be adduced. * * *

Defendants also fail in their claim that they are immune from Back's allegations simply because, in the year that Back was hired, 85% of the teachers employed at Hillside were women, and 71% of these women had children. . . . [A]lthough the jury is surely allowed to consider such comparative evidence, what matters is how *Back* was treated. Furthermore, the defendants make no mention of the number of men or women in *administrative* positions, nor of the age of any of the relevant children. Both details are essential if the comparative evidence adduced by the defendants is to be given any weight. . . . [W]e hold that stereotypical remarks about the incompatibility of motherhood and employment "can certainly be *evidence* that gender played a part" in an employment decision. . . . As a result, stereotyping of women as caregivers can by itself and without more be evidence of an impermissible, sex-based motive. * * *

[W]e hold that Back has clearly produced sufficient evidence to defeat summary judgment as to Brennan and Wishnie. She has made out her prima facie case by offering evidence of discriminatory comments, which can constitute "direct evidence," and are adequate to make out a prima facie case, even where uncorroborated. The nondiscriminatory reasons proffered by Brennan and Wishnie for their negative evaluations—namely, Back's poor organizational skills and her negative interactions with parents—are in no way dispositive. Viewing the evidence in the light most favorable to Back, a jury could find that the administrative deficiencies cited by the defendants were minor, and unimportant to the defendants before the development of the purported discriminatory motive. As for the parental complaints, it is unclear which of these Brennan and Wishnie were aware of at the time of their negative recommendations and evaluations. But Back's allegations, in any event, are sufficient to allow a jury to find that these complaints were not the real reason for their proffered criticisms of Back. Back asserts, for example, that "in even the most supportive school setting, whether dealing with a teacher or provider of special services, as I was, a small minority of parents will always be critical of the professional. I had very minor skirmishes with several parents while in Hastings. But . . . Brennan and Wishnie always emphasized

to me that I was doing an excellent job and that the complaining parent had her own problems coping with the reality of having a classified child." If some of these "skirmishes" were in Back's first two years, as she alleges, then her performance evaluations—conducted by Brennan and Wishnie—also tend to support her version of events. Similarly, although Back's second year evaluations indicated that she faced some challenges in dealing with teachers and parents who were resistant to her advocacy for students, they also noted that Back was aware these issues and working to "enhance" this area. Back also alleges that Brennan and Wishnie instructed her not to have parents or supporters submit positive letters for her file. This, and the sudden decline in performance evaluations that occurred between the beginning and end of Back's third year—that is, only after the alleged discriminatory comments began—support a conclusion of pretext.

We conclude that a jury could find, on the evidence proffered, that Brennan and Wishnie's cited justifications for their adverse recommendation and evaluation were pretextual, and that discrimination was one of the "motivating" reasons for the recommendations against Back's tenure. * * * Accordingly we VACATE the district court's grant of summary judgment, and REMAND the case for trial with respect to them.

CASE QUESTIONS

1. What was the legal issue in this case? What did the court decide?

2. What was the evidence of sex stereotyping in this case?

3. Is this a sex-plus case? Why or why not?

4. Judging from the evidence provided, does it appear that Back was discriminated against? Why or why not?

5. What should the school district have done differently?

Subjective Criteria

Employment decisions, especially when choosing from among a group of qualified candidates, often rest on subjective judgments. Appearance is one of these subjective, "in the eye of the beholder" criteria, but there are many others. Does this person seem motivated? Will he be a good "team player"? Is he articulate? Does she have a sense of humor? Good interpersonal skills? Will she be a good leader? And at the most elemental level—do we like this person? Impressions on these and other matters are gleaned from interviews, snatches of conversation over lunch, and who knows what else. No bright line exists between "objective" and "subjective" selection criteria—most assessments of job candidates involve elements of both. The criteria mentioned earlier are relatively **subjective criteria** in that standards and means of assessment are not clearly specified and are likely to vary across decision makers. In short, subjective criteria rely heavily on intuition and "gut" feelings.

Subjective hiring criteria are ubiquitous. Do they present any legal issues? One way to view them is as neutral requirements that might have discriminatory effects. In a case involving a woman who was passed over for promotion four times on the basis of interviews conducted by lower-level managers given little guidance on hiring criteria, the Supreme Court held that subjective assessments of this sort—no less than scored tests—can be challenged for their adverse impact.[34] However, the Court also noted that proof of a subjective assessment being job related and consistent with business necessity does not require a formal validation study. Instead, the focus is on the reasonableness of the subjective criteria in light of the job and whether more objective means of assessment were available but not used.

[34]*Watson v. Fort Worth Bank & Trust,* 487 U.S. 977 (1988).

THE CHANGING WORKPLACE

Legal Implications of Changes in Jobs and Hiring Criteria

Pronouncements about the "end of the job"[1] are, at the very least, premature. Nevertheless, jobs are being transformed as technology and customer demand change. Employers are focusing on processes rather than individual jobs. More work is being done in teams, with team members expected to be capable of taking on each other's functions. Any movement away from clearly defined jobs and job descriptions conflicts with the heavy emphasis of the courts on job relatedness. If the ability to take on multiple and changing tasks is requisite, then what selection criteria are job related and consistent with business necessity?

In a service economy, employers increasingly emphasize the **soft skills** of candidates, even for entry-level jobs. Employers assess the motivational, interpersonal, and communication skills of applicants. The means of assessing these skills are usually subjective—primarily impressions gleaned from interviews. Some argue that the increased emphasis on soft skills is a factor in the labor market difficulties of minorities, whom employers view as lacking in these areas.[2]

Subjective selection criteria have also become more prominent as employers increasingly emphasize **organization fit** in making selection decisions.[3] Devices for assessing whether prospective employees share the values or culture of an organization, although they exist, are certainly less developed and less studied for validity than tests of work skills or aptitude. Consider the following description of a "test" given to candidates for employment at Southwest Airlines:

Southwest uses a novel approach to measure selflessness, a key value of their culture. Interviewers ask a group of applicants to prepare a five-minute presentation about themselves.

During the presentations, Southwest's interviewers watch the audience as well as the speakers. What are they looking for in the audience? They want to determine which applicants are using the time to prepare for their own presentations and which are enthusiastically cheering and providing support for the presenters. Interviewers consider the cheering, supportive applicants a better fit with Southwest's culture than the fastidious applicants who continue to prepare up until their presentations.[4]

The validity of such tests (and whether validity can be established with reference to an organization's culture rather than specific jobs) is unclear. A more basic concern is that the desire to hire persons who "fit" comfortably with an organization's culture might be at odds with the value of diversity, in which the aim is to find people who contribute new and different dimensions to an organization. Hiring for cultural fit and diversity are not necessarily mutually exclusive,[5] but the potential negative implications of maintaining strong cultures for opening up employment opportunity seem quite real.

[1]William Bridges. "The End of the Job." *Fortune* 130 (September 19, 1994), 62–74.

[2]Philip Moss and Chris Tilly. *Stories Employers Tell: Race, Skill, and Hiring in America.* (New York: Russell Sage Foundation, 2001).

[3]Mark L. Lengnick-Hall. "Recruitment and Selections: Hiring for the Job or the Organization?" chap. 13 in Ellen Ernst Kossek and Richard N. Block, eds., *Managing Human Resources in the 21st Century: From Core Concepts to Strategic Choice* (Cincinnati, OH: South-Western College Publishing, 2000), p. 13.11.

[4]Lengnick-Hall, at p. 13.16.

[5]Gary N. Powell. "The Simultaneous Pursuit of Person-Organization Fit and Diversity." *Organizational Dynamics* (Winter 1998), 50–61.

Subjective hiring criteria also raise concerns about disparate treatment. An employer that desires to exclude African Americans might very well claim that an African-American job candidate "didn't do well on his interview" to justify rejection. A study of the labor market experiences of inner-city blacks and Latinos found, as have other studies, that informal, subjective hiring criteria result in fewer blacks and Latinos being hired.[35] Or consider a very different setting—the selection of musicians by orchestras. One study found that the chances of women being selected to

[35]Philip Moss and Chris Tilly. *Stories Employers Tell: Race, Skill, and Hiring in America.* (New York: Russell Sage Foundation, 2001).

play in orchestras increased when the manner of conducting auditions was changed so that judges could no longer see the musician (and thus his or her sex) during auditions.[36] Apparently, judgments about the quality of musicianship displayed in auditions are substantially affected by knowledge of the auditioning musician's sex. Increased use of subjective criteria, including a consideration of a candidate's fit with the organization's culture, has implications for equal employment opportunity.

Clearly, subjective assessments are conducive to disparate treatment and cannot be accepted at face value by the courts. At the same time, they are necessary, and it is not the court's role to second-guess all employment decisions. *Medina v. Ramsey Steel Co.* illustrates the scrutiny given subjective assessments in disparate treatment cases.

[36]Claudia Goldin and Cecilia Rouse. "Orchestrating Impartiality: The Impact of 'Blind' Auditions on Female Musicians." *American Economic Review* 90 (September 2000), 715–41.

MEDINA V. RAMSEY STEEL CO.
238 F.3d 674 (5th Cir. 2001)

OPINION BY CIRCUIT JUDGE REYNALDO G. GARZA:

Arturo P. Medina brought suit against his employer . . . alleging that they refused to promote him because of his age. . . . Medina began working for Ramsey Steel in 1968 when he was thirty-two years of age. Six years later, he left Ramsey Steel in search of other career opportunities which included a job selling real estate for a Century 21 franchise. In 1978, Medina returned to Ramsey Steel and worked as a detailer just as he had prior to leaving the company. * * *

Although Medina worked as a detailer for the balance of his employ at Ramsey Steel, from 1978 to 1994, he sought promotions on three occasions. A few years after his return to Ramsey Steel, Medina expressed interest in an outside sales position. Although Ramsey Steel never officially stated that the position was open, Ramsey Steel awarded the job to Joe Menchey, a man twenty-five years Medina's junior. Sometime in 1989 or 1990, Menchey resigned and Medina again expressed interest in the outside sales position. According to Medina, Ramsey Steel's president, Greg Ramsey, told him that he did not have the right "ingredients" for the job. After offering the job to an employee who declined it, the position remained open for several years until Ramsey Steel hired Fred Chavarria, a man twenty-five years Medina's junior. * * *

Medina's age discrimination claims are based on the fact that he was passed over for promotion on three separate occasions. The district court granted summary judgment against Medina on these claims. * * * [W]e reverse. * * *

The first issue for our discussion is whether Medina has raised a genuine issue of material fact as to each element of his prima facie case. In an age discrimination, failure to promote case, the employee must demonstrate that 1) he belongs to the protected class, 2) he applied to and was qualified for a position for which applicants were being sought, 3) he was rejected, and 4) another applicant not belonging to the protected class was hired.

It is undisputed that Medina is within the protected class, that he sought promotion to the job, that Ramsey Steel rejected him, and that individuals not within the protected class filled the outside sales position both times it came open. The focus of Ramsey Steel's attack on Medina's prima facie case, and the basis for the district court's grant of summary judgment, is that Medina is unqualified for the outside sales position because he failed to meet the "substantial sales experience" requirement. This was the only qualification Ramsey gave for the position; so, the crucial, central issue is whether an employer can defeat an employee's claim via summary judgment at the prima facie case stage by claiming that he failed to meet entirely subjective hiring criteria. We do not think so.

While subjective criteria like that set forth by Ramsey Steel "may serve legitimate functions, they also provide opportunities for unlawful discrimination" because the criteria itself may be pretext for age discrimination. As we have indicated before, an employer may not "utilize

wholly subjective standards by which to judge its employees' qualifications and then plead lack of qualification when its promotion process . . . is challenged as discriminatory."

For these reasons, other circuits have concluded that a prima facie case is established once the plaintiff demonstrates that objective employment qualifications have been met. For example, in *Burrus v. United Telephone Co. of Kansas, Inc.*, the Tenth Circuit concluded that objective qualifications are best treated at the first step of the analytical framework and that subjective criteria and other supporting evidence are best treated at the second and third steps. If a failure to satisfy subjective hiring criteria could defeat an employee's prima facie case, "the court then would not be required to consider evidence of pretext." "Thus the use of the subjective hiring criteria would go unchallenged." * * * For these reasons, it is inappropriate to decide as a matter of law that an employee is unqualified because he has failed to meet entirely subjective hiring criteria. Instead, an employee must demonstrate that he meets objective hiring criteria at the prima facie case stage, and the issue of whether he meets subjective hiring criteria is dealt with at the later stages of the analysis. * * *

In *Lindsey v. Prive Corp.*, a gentlemen's club failed to promote two waitresses to dancers because they were not "beautiful, gorgeous, and sophisticated." The waitresses sued the club claiming age discrimination. The district court granted summary judgment in favor of the club on the ground that the waitresses had failed to meet its subjective hiring criteria. In reversing the district court's decision, we acknowledged that an employer can make employment decisions based on subjective criteria. However, we also said that distinguishing legitimate employment decisions based entirely on subjective criteria and those in which subjective criteria serve as pretext for discrimination can only be made by weighing the employer's credibility. "Beauty is in the eye of the beholder and the beholder in this case" is the employer, but the "question left for the judge or jury will not require second guessing of the [club's] personnel decisions but, rather, will require an evaluation of the credibility of the defendant's testimony about the reasons for that decision." In short, "the trier-of-fact will evaluate truthfulness, not beauty."

Similarly, what constitutes "substantial sales experience" is in the eye of the beholder. While Ramsey Steel is the beholder, it is the trier-of-fact's duty to determine whether Ramsey Steel beheld a man it felt was unqualified for the job or a man it felt was too old for the job.

Because Ramsey Steel's hiring criterion was entirely subjective, Medina's claims could not be defeated on summary judgment at the prima facie case stage.

Thus, the burden shifted to Ramsey Steel to articulate a legitimate, non-discriminatory reason for its decision. Ramsey Steel asserted that Medina is not qualified for the job so the burden shifted to Medina to produce evidence raising a fact issue as to whether Ramsey Steel's reason was pretextual. A review of the record demonstrates that Medina has done so.

Medina offered evidence that he had experience selling real estate for Century 21. He also offered evidence that he had more sales experience and more experience in the industry than the individual promoted over him. When he expressed interest in the job, Medina claims the company president told him that he did not have the right "ingredients" rather than saying he was unqualified. Finally, Medina offered evidence that, near the time Medina was passed over in favor of a younger man, Lupe de la Cruz told the Assistant Vice-President, Ismael Legarreta, that he should "get rid of all the old people." Medina has offered evidence that Legarreta was involved in hiring decisions and that he made no response to De la Cruz's remark. All of this evidence raises a genuine issue of material fact as to whether Ramsey Steel's proffered reason for failing to promote Medina was merely a pretext for age discrimination. Therefore, the district court's decision to grant summary judgment against Medina was inappropriate.

CASE QUESTIONS

1. What was the legal issue in this case? What did the court decide?

2. How was Medina able to establish a prima facie case of disparate treatment? What was the lawful, legitimate reason for not promoting Medina that the employer gave? What evidence did Medina have that this reason was a pretext for age discrimination?

3. What does the court say about the relationship between subjective criteria and a plaintiff's ability to establish a prima facie case of disparate treatment?

4. What is the role of the court in this type of case? To review whether candidates were correctly assessed? To determine whether selection criteria and assessment procedures were reasonable? Something else?

5. What should the employer have done differently in this case?

Subjective assessments of job candidates are clearly lawful, but they are likely to receive close scrutiny when there is reason to believe that the decision maker had a discriminatory motive. There are no hard-and-fast rules here, but in the interest of ensuring equal employment opportunity, employers should consider several measures. First, *interviews and other aspects of the hiring process should be made as standard as possible (such as by using structured interviews and scoring them according to preestablished criteria)*. If impressions are going to be formed in this manner, then everyone should at least be given the same "test." The ease with which prejudice can infect subjective assessments of candidates makes it advisable for employers to *use multiple decision makers, preferably differing in race and sex. Employers should give substantial weight to subjective assessments only if they are specific and clearly grounded in statements or actions of job candidates*. For example, if a member of a hiring committee concludes that a candidate "would not be a good colleague," it should be incumbent on that person to cite the statements made by the candidate or other evidence that supports this judgment. If no specific basis exists to back up a conclusion about a candidate, that conclusion deserves little or no weight. Lastly, *if more objective means are available for assessing candidates, use them*. Objective procedures carry more weight in disparate treatment cases and avoid showing that feasible alternatives were available, but not uused, in adverse impact cases. In the *Medina* case, the criterion of "substantial sales experience" was amenable to objective assessment (e.g., by establishing clear standards for the level of experience needed, systematically reviewing resumes for prior experience), but that did not occur.

OFFERING AND ACCEPTING EMPLOYMENT

The employment relationship is contractual in nature. The terms of that contract are sometimes complex and the product of lengthy negotiations, such as when a new CEO is hired. Much more often, the agreement is rudimentary, with the employer offering a job at a specified wage and the employee accepting the job. Whether elaborate or simple, to be legally enforceable, contracts require an **offer, acceptance of the offer,** and **consideration** (something of value given in exchange for receipt of the other's promise). Employment can be offered in writing or verbally. To clearly state what is being offered and accepted, *employers (with legal help) should put employment offers in writing*. The offer letter should include the salary or wage associated with the position and the start date. Because it is usually in the interest of employers for employment to be "at will" (i.e., the relationship can be terminated at any time for any reason), *the offer of employment should specify whether employment at will is being offered (and explain in simple language what that means)*. The employment offer might reference an employee handbook or other materials as authoritative sources about the terms of the employment relationship. In any event, *the offer should clearly specify what is included in the terms of employment and that no further commitments have been made. If an offer of employment is conditional (e.g., upon a medical exam, or upon acceptance of the offer within a specified period), the condition(s) should be clearly stated*.

An offer of employment can be accepted in writing, orally, or simply by commencing to work under the offered terms. If a job candidate proposes terms different from those offered, that proposal is a counteroffer rather than acceptance. The employer might accept the proposed terms, reject them, or negotiate further. To be enforceable, contracts must be supported by consideration. The notion is that people (at least in a business context) do not undertake obligations to do things for others without realizing

some corresponding benefit for themselves. Contracts providing for employment at will are typically supported by the employee performing work in exchange for the agreed-upon job and pay.

What if an employer offers a job, the candidate accepts, and then the employer withdraws the offer prior to the start of employment? Might persons whose accepted offers of employment are revoked have grounds for legal challenges? One possible claim is fraud (or negligent misrepresentation). However, unless the employer withdrawing an offer knew or should have known, at the time the offer was made, that the job would not materialize, a successful fraud claim is unlikely. What about breach of contract? Most new hires are employed at will. Although an "employment-at-will contract" sounds awkward, courts still treat employment-at-will relationships as contractual; however, a contract to employ at will amounts to nothing more than a promise to pay a specified wage for work actually performed. Because either party remains free to terminate the employment relationship at any time, there is no breach of contract if a person is hired, but not given the chance to commence employment. As one court put it, "It would be absurd to require an employer, which had changed its mind after an offer had been made, to actually employ the applicant for one hour or one day so that the employee could then be discharged."[37]

However, a stronger legal claim is available in this situation. Courts recognize claims for **promissory estoppel** in situations where injustice would otherwise occur because a person has relied to his detriment on the promises of another. The basis for the claim is not a contract, but rather the harm that occurs from reasonably relying on another's promises that there would be a contractual relationship.

Applied to the withdrawal of a job offer, it could be argued that the employer's job offer is an unambiguous promise to employ; the new hire reasonably relies on the promise by doing things like relocating and turning down alternative job offers; the employer should reasonably expect that newly hired persons would act in this manner; and these reasonable actions cause harm (e.g., loss of the other job, a now burdensome lease on an apartment). Some courts have accepted this view. For example, the Supreme Court of Nebraska found that a doctor whose job offer was rescinded after she had quit her previous job, was provided with uniforms for her new job, and was already given the schedule for her first week of work, had a valid claim for promissory estoppel.[38] A Minnesota state court recognized a promissory estoppel claim in the case of a newly hired person who, on the first day of employment,

ELEMENTS OF A CLAIM

Promissory Estoppel

1. One party makes an unambiguous promise to another.

2. The party that receives the promise acts in reasonable reliance upon it.

3. Reliance on the promise is expected and foreseeable by the party making the promise.

4. The party to whom the promise is made is harmed by reliance on it.

[37]*Sartin v. Mazur,* 375 S.E.2d 741, at 743 (Va. 1989).

[38]*Goff-Hamel v. Obstetricians & Gynecologists, P.C.,* 588 N.W.2d 798 (Neb. 1999).

"went through a hostile reinterview process that led to his immediate termination."[39] On the other hand, many courts have refused to protect employees under these circumstances. The rationale is that an offer of employment at will is not really an unambiguous promise because employment can be terminated at any time. Alternatively, courts have maintained that it is not reasonable to rely on the essentially empty promise of employment at will. One court, in rejecting a promissory estoppel claim, conceded "the apparent harshness of [its] ruling, the result of which is that an employee who resigns one job for another does so at his peril," but maintained that any other outcome would contradict the established doctrine of employment at will.[40]

OBSTACLES TO ADVANCEMENT ON THE JOB

Women and persons of color are having greater success obtaining employment in industries where previously they were scarce, but the problem of discrimination does not end with getting in the door. Women and persons of color sometimes experience **segregation** into less desirable jobs and face numerous obstacles to advancement in their careers.

Promotions

Much of the information in this and preceding chapters applies with equal force to both initial hiring and promotion, but some additional facets of promotion cases deserve mention. First, there are lines of progression in work organizations, such that promotions usually occur out of particular positions. Thus, if the effect of initial hiring decisions is to segregate some groups into dead-end jobs from which promotions are not typically made, that will also manifest itself in future promotional decisions. In a case involving Home Depot,[41] stereotypes about what jobs were suitable for women led to the channeling of women into clerk positions and away from merchandising department manager and store manager trainee jobs, which were springboards for becoming store managers. For example, a female applicant with prior experience hauling lumber and as an office manager for a lumber processing plant was told that "girls don't work in the lumber department" and hired as a cashier instead.[42] A class of female plaintiffs successfully challenged the store's initial hiring and promotion decisions.

The process for making promotions is often far more informal and covert than that used for initial hiring decisions. Lawyers suing Costco have referred to a "tap-on-the-shoulder" promotion "system," marked by the *absence* of job posting, an application process, stated criteria, and written guidelines for decision makers (see "Clippings"). The Home Depot case described a promotion process in which the following occurs:

> There are no written guidelines for making decisions about promotions to department supervisor positions, and the company does not provide training to Store Managers and Assistant Managers on how to select employees for promotions. . . . Promotion opportunities in existing stores are not posted, and there is no formal procedure for making vacancies known or

[39]*Gorham v. Benson Optical,* 539 N.W.2d 798, at 801 (Minn. App. 1995).

[40]*White v. Roche Biomedical Laboratories,* 807 F. Supp. 1212, at 1220 (D.S.C. 1992).

[41]*Butler v. Home Depot,* 1997 U.S. Dist. LEXIS 16296.

[42]*Butler,* at 26 (footnote n14).

requesting a promotion. In making decisions about promotion to department supervisor, there is no requirement that the person under consideration meet any minimum rating on recent performance evaluations, or that written performance reviews are consulted at all in making the decision. Nor is there any requirement to record the reasons why an employee is or is not selected for a promotion.[43]

Recall that one element of a prima facie case of disparate treatment is a showing that the plaintiff applied for the employment opportunity in question. If the availability of a promotional position is not communicated and employees are not given the opportunity to apply, this will not defeat a disparate treatment claim. Thus, an African American denied a promotion was able to prevail in a race discrimination suit despite not having formally applied for the position because African Americans were discouraged from applying for the job by the person that would do the hiring, the job was not posted, and the plaintiff had spoken to management in the past concerning his interest in the job.[44] In another case, the employer instituted a formal application process for promotions and informed employees of its existence. In holding that the plaintiff could proceed with her discrimination suit despite not having applied for the promotion in question, the court explained:

> Only an employee who knew about an upcoming promotion selection could avail herself of the self-nomination procedure. Thus, even if Giant Food's promotion selection policy was open and apparent to its employees, Williams might still establish a prima facie case if she can show that she was unaware of promotion opportunities because the company did not follow its own policy [for posting jobs] in her stores.[45]

Another distinctive aspect of promotions is that employers have a great deal to do with determining which individuals possess the qualifications needed for promotion. In contrast to initial hiring decisions, where job candidates have developed their qualifications in schools and while working for other employers, promotional candidates acquire many of their qualifications through their employer's own training and development programs, job assignments, and mentoring. Because not all employees have equal access to these qualification-enhancing opportunities, promotions are to some extent "self-fulfilling prophecies." This is intensified by the flattening of corporate structures in recent years , leaving behind fewer promotional opportunities. Companies increasingly attempt to identify high-potential personnel, both managerial and technical, who need to be retained and developed. These judgments are then reflected in who is prepared and selected for promotion.

Lastly, subjective criteria tend to be relied upon even more heavily in promotion decisions. Characteristics such as leadership ability or potential for growth are difficult to assess objectively. In the suit against Costco (see "Clippings"), the plaintiff's attorneys stressed the lack of written criteria and guidelines: "Without a system, 'what you have is default mode,'". . . . "'Default mode is subjective decision making by a virtually all male managerial apparatus' with gender stereotyping and unconscious bias." An employer's heavily subjective promotion process did not survive a discrimination challenge in the face of strong statistical evidence of the segregation of African Americans into a single department. It did not help the employer's case when the department head, asked why blacks were concentrated in his department,

[43]*Butler*, at 33.

[44]*Lam v. General Waterworks Corp.*, 766 F.2d 386 (7th Cir. 1985).

[45]*Williams v. Giant Food*, 370 F.3d 423, at 431 (4th Cir. 2004).

responded, "I would presume that's the type of work that they like."[46] On the other hand, rejection of a candidate for promotion to a management position, partly on the basis of his "poor" interview that demonstrated lack of sufficient "aggressiveness," did not result in a finding of age discrimination. The court noted the importance of subjective assessments in selecting managers and professionals and held that "[a] subjective reason is a legally sufficient, legitimate nondiscriminatory reason if the defendant articulates a clear and reasonably specific factual basis upon which it based its subjective opinion."[47] In this case, the employer was able to provide specifics about the deficiencies in the plaintiff's interview responses and to point to a particular question that was answered poorly. The court also dismissed the view that the employer's concern about lack of sufficient "aggressiveness" might reflect stereotypes about older persons (the plaintiff was 61):

> In the rough and tumble, highly competitive business world, aggressiveness can be a valuable and much sought after trait. Just because a sought after trait is linked by stereotype to an impermissible consideration does not mean an employer cannot search for and consider the trait itself independently from the stereotype.[48]

What are the practical implications for promotional decisions, apart from those that pertain to all hiring? The "fix" for inequities in advancement starts with initial hiring decisions. *Employers must avoid segregating women and persons of color into "dead-end" positions that offer little prospect of advancement.* Discrimination in promotions is less likely when a formal application process is used for promotional positions. *Employers should establish a formal procedure to apply for promotions, communicate the availability of promotional opportunities, and facilitate applications from all interested employees.* As with any other selection decision, reasonable job-related criteria should be established and applied by decision makers. Because some use of subjective criteria is often unavoidable, *employers relying on subjective assessments (e.g., impressions from interviews) of candidates for promotion should document the grounds for their subjective judgments (e.g., what specific responses led to the conclusion that the candidate did poorly on the interview).* Subjective judgments are far less likely to be deemed pretexts for disparate treatment if they can be supported in this manner. Verbatim written notes from interviews are not required, but the absence of any documentation produced at the time of an interview makes it exceedingly difficult to provide specifics in a deposition a year or two later.

Glass Ceilings

Obstacles to advancement into high-level management and professional positions have received particular attention. The U.S. Department of Labor defines a **glass ceiling** as "those artificial barriers based on attitudinal or organizational bias that prevent qualified individuals from advancing in their organization into upper management positions."[49] These obstacles are relatively subtle and not easily observed, but they impede the advancement of women and persons of color to high-level management and professional positions. "Glass ceiling" is not a legal term or claim, but it succinctly captures the experiences of many highly qualified women and persons

[46]*Lam*, at 392.

[47]*Chapman v. AI Transport*, 229 F.3d 1012, at 1034 (11th Cir. 2000).

[48]*Chapman*, at 1036.

[49]U.S. DOL, OFCCP. *Glass Ceiling Initiative: Are There Cracks in the Ceiling?* (1997). Viewed at http://www.dol.gov/esa/media/reports/ofccp/newgc.htm.

of color. Increasingly, such circumstances have prompted lawsuits alleging a pattern or practice of discrimination or other claims.

Only a small percentage of executive positions are occupied by women. Glass ceiling reviews of 53 companies that hold contracts with the federal government found serious problems at nearly 80 percent of the companies. Even using a very broad definition of "officials and managers," only 25 percent of individuals holding these jobs were women and only 11 percent were persons of color (male and female). The highest-ranked women in these companies averaged two reporting levels below the CEO, whereas the highest-ranked persons of color averaged four levels below the CEO. Based on data such as these, the report concluded "the glass ceiling still exists; and the ceiling is lower for minorities than it is for women."[50]

The glass ceiling phenomenon is also found in the legal profession. Although persons of color have been attending law school in significant numbers and account for about 13 percent of all associates at law firms, they make up 3.4 percent of partners. Women comprise over 40 percent of associates, but less than 20 percent of partners. Nor is the pace of ascension to partnership increasing markedly. Minority lawyers accounted for about 5 percent of the lawyers promoted to partner at the largest firms between 1998 and 2001.[51]

The hallowed halls of academia are not immune from these problems either. Women and persons of color are more likely to be found in untenured positions, and when tenured, below the full-professor level. In 1999, the Massachusetts Institute of Technology (MIT) issued a report acknowledging pervasive discrimination against female faculty in hiring, promotions, awards, inclusion on influential faculty committees, and access to resources such as labs and research funds.[52] The percentage of tenured African-American professors at Ivy League schools remained the same (2 percent) from 1993 through 2003.[53]

Advancing to higher level positions within elite institutions is necessarily a rugged, competitive process. Lack of advancement does not necessarily reflect the workings of unfair, discriminatory obstacles. Evidence suggests, however, that the glass ceiling phenomenon is real.[54] The measures needed to deal with this problem go beyond the general advice for promotions. *Employers should closely monitor the career progress of women and persons of color.* Evidence of a disproportionate lack of advancement should prompt a wide-ranging self-analysis. *Employers should examine the protected class composition of positions from which promotions are made and the manner in which key projects and other developmental opportunities are assigned.* Because many promotions rest upon previous positions and project assignments, it is important that women and persons of color get into "the pipeline" and have access to important positions and developmental experiences. *Employers should provide management development programs, assistance in career planning, and mentoring.* Mentors provide less senior managers and professionals with the benefit of their experience, coaching on career choices, and visibility and advocacy in higher organizational circles. Other important steps involve *removing impediments·to performance, including harassment and aspects of an organization's culture that might be hostile to protected class groups (e.g., heavy emphasis on off-the-job*

[50]U.S. DOL (1997), p. 5.

[51]Jonathan D. Glater. "Law Firms Are Slow in Promoting Minority Lawyers to Partner Role." *New York Times* (August 7, 2001).

[52]Carey Goldberg. "M.I.T. Acknowledges Bias Against Female Professors." *New York Times* (March 23, 1999), A-1.

[53]Karen W. Arenson. "Little Advance Is Seen in Ivies' Hiring of Minorities and Women." *New York Times* (March 1, 2005), A-12.

[54]Christine Jolls. "Is There a Glass Ceiling?" *Harvard Women's Law Journal* 25 (Spring 2002), 1.

socializing). Turnover patterns should be carefully examined, as they might indicate frustration with lack of advancement or responses to harassment. Flexibility in considering less traditional career paths and backgrounds in promotional candidates opens up opportunities and increases the numbers of qualified women and persons of color in the pipeline. A more diverse pool of qualified external candidates for management positions might be obtained by considering persons who have proven their leadership ability in nonprofit organizations, public administration, universities, and the military.

Seniority and the BFSS Defense

Seniority, the length of an individual's service at a particular job or in a department or company, is a criterion used in many employment decisions, including promotions and layoffs. This is particularly true of unionized workplaces, but most employers give at least some consideration to length of service in making employment decisions. Seniority has many advantages as a selection criterion. First, and foremost, it is objective. As long as the relevant unit within which seniority is accrued (e.g., department, companywide) and procedures for dealing with issues such as breaks in service are specified, seniority can be measured down to the minute to determine which candidate has the most seniority. Seniority rewards commitment and allows employees to know where they stand in relation to other employees, which might facilitate on-the-job training by lessening the concerns of veteran employees about training persons who will leapfrog over them. Lastly, there need not be any conflict between seniority and merit. Experience is usually a major asset on the job. If management is doing its job and employees are not just putting in time, the most senior candidate often is the most qualified.

But for all its potential benefits, basing employment decisions on seniority has a downside when it comes to ensuring equal employment opportunity. In many organizations, women and persons of color hold less seniority than white males. If the less senior person is less likely to get promoted or is likely to be the first to be laid off when business slows, reliance on seniority as a selection criterion disproportionately limits the employment opportunities of women and persons of color. As a neutral requirement likely to produce discriminatory effects, seniority might be vulnerable to adverse impact claims.

However, Congress addressed this issue when it included in Title VII of the Civil Rights Act a **bona fide seniority system (BFSS)** defense: "[I]t shall not be an unlawful employment practice for an employer to apply different . . . terms, conditions, or privileges of employment pursuant to a bona fide seniority . . . system . . . provided that such differences are not the result of an intention to discriminate. . . ."[55] Thus, seniority systems can be challenged only if their use involves disparate treatment; any adverse impact that they cause cannot be challenged. The BFSS defense applies only to seniority "systems." The use of seniority must be in accordance with a formal, established set of arrangements for tracking employee seniority. Employment decisions based on ad hoc judgments about which candidate is "more experienced" do not fall within the BFSS defense. The system also must be "bona fide." It must apply equally to all employees, allocate seniority in a reasonable manner, and not be instituted or administered for the purpose of discriminating.[56]

[55]42 U.S.C.A. § 2000e-2(h) (2001).

[56]*International Brotherhood of Teamsters v. United States*, 431 U.S. 324, at 355–56 (1977).

Chapter SUMMARY

Employers sometimes contend that occupants of jobs must have certain protected class characteristics (most often, a specified sex or age group). Such requirements are facially discriminatory and can be defended only if employers can show that the protected class requirements are bona fide occupational qualifications (BFOQs). The BFOQ defense is narrow. A BFOQ cannot be established for racial requirements. For the BFOQ defense to be valid, an employer has to show that all, or virtually all, the persons without the specified protected class characteristic cannot do the job, or (particularly in the case of concerns about the health of older employees with safety-sensitive jobs) that a more individualized assessment of ability to do the job cannot be made. To establish a BFOQ, particular protected class characteristics must be shown as necessary to perform the job, and the job, with its current requirements, must be integral to the nature of the business. The preferences of customers, coworkers, or clients rarely justify BFOQs. However, BFOQs may be recognized where certain protected class characteristics are needed for authenticity, public safety, or privacy.

Pairing protected class requirements with neutral requirements (e.g., no women with children under school age will be hired) is also facially discriminatory and can only be defended by a BFOQ. Because sex is the protected class most often involved in these cases, placing requirements on one protected class group that are not placed on others is often referred to as "sex-plus" discrimination. When the neutral requirements differentially applied to men and women involve appearance and grooming, rather than fundamental rights such as childbearing and marriage, the law is murkier. Discrimination on the basis of one aspect of physical appearance, weight, is susceptible to disability and sex-plus discrimination claims. Courts have also held employers accountable for using separate and sex-stereotypical standards to judge male and female employees. On the other hand, courts have generally allowed employers to establish different grooming and appearance requirements for men and women, provided that the differences are not too great and do not subject one group to harassment or demeaning treatment.

Hiring and promotion decisions often involve subjective judgments about candidates' motivation, leadership ability, interpersonal skills, and likeability. Subjective criteria can be challenged for their adverse impact, although validation studies are not required to defend these assessments as job related and consistent with business necessity. Subjective judgments about candidates are also vulnerable to disparate treatment claims. A claim that a candidate is not qualified based on subjective criteria will not defeat a prima facie case when the candidate meets other objective criteria. To the extent that employers are increasingly concerned with the "soft skills" of employees and their ability to fit in with organizational cultures, subjective criteria loom even larger and stand to affect hiring decisions at all levels. Tension exists between the ideas of selecting employees for "organization fit" and valuing diversity.

Employment relationships are contractual in nature. After deciding whom to hire, an employer offers employment and the selected candidate indicates whether the offer is accepted. The employment contract must be supported by consideration, usually the employee commencing work, to be enforceable. If contract terms are offered and accepted, but then violated, a claim can be made for breach of contract. Courts also recognize claims for promissory estoppel where injustice would otherwise occur because a person has relied to her detriment on the promises of another. The basis for this claim is not violation of the terms of a contract, but rather harm that occurs because of the reasonable belief that a contractual relationship would exist. Promissory estoppel claims are recognized where an unambiguous promise is made, a party reasonably relies on the promise to her detriment, and such reliance was foreseeable.

Promotions have much in common with initial hiring, but are affected by prior hiring decisions that determine who is positioned for promotion; the allocation of developmental opportunities; a tendency toward informal procedures including lack of posting; and heavier reliance on subjective criteria. The term *glass ceiling* is frequently used to convey obstacles that impede the advancement of women and persons of color into high-level management and professional positions. Key barriers include insufficient access to developmental opportunities, exclusion from social networks, lack of advocates in higher management, biased criteria (e.g., availability for socializing after work hours), and exclusionary corporate cultures.

Practical Advice SUMMARY

- Employers must not specify protected class requirements for jobs unless BFOQs can be established for those requirements, based on the need for

 –authenticity.

 –public safety.

 –privacy.

- Employers must not specify racial requirements for jobs.

- Rather than use protected class characteristics to identify persons with desired abilities, employers should find more individualized means of assessing job-related abilities.

- Employers must not exclude older employees from safety-sensitive jobs based on assumptions about health status unless

 –there is evidence that older employees pose greater risk.

 –it is not feasible to adequately assess the health of individuals.

- Employers should generally refrain from matching employees with customers or clients based on protected class characteristics and, instead, consider alternative indicators of ability to relate to customers, including

 –interpersonal skills.

 –cultural sensitivity.

 –language skills.

 –prior experience.

- Depending on state law, BFOQs might have to be certified by state fair employment agencies before they can be put into use.

- Employers must not establish requirements that apply to one protected class group, but not to others.

- Grooming or appearance requirements should not be

 –widely different for men and women.

 –based on stereotypes.

 –likely to result in harassment.

- Interviews and other subjective aspects of the hiring process should be made as standard as possible, such as by using structured interviews and scoring them according to preestablished criteria.

- Hiring and promotion decisions should generally be made with the input of more than one person, and preferably with input from persons who differ in race and sex.

- Employers should give substantial weight to subjective assessments only if they are specific and clearly grounded in statements or actions of job candidates.

- Whenever possible, employers should use objective means instead of subjective measures to assess job candidates.

- Employment offers should

 –be put in writing, with the help of legal counsel.

 –state clearly and unequivocally that employment is "at will" if that is the type of employment relationship desired.

 –clearly specify the terms of employment and that no other commitments have been made.

 –state any conditions attached to the offer (e.g., successful completion of a medical exam).

- Employers should not renege on promises to hire employees when it is reasonable for employees to rely on those promises and they would be harmed by doing so.

- Employers should establish a formal procedure to apply for promotions, communicate the availability of promotional opportunities, and facilitate applications from all interested employees.

- Employers relying on subjective assessments (e.g., impressions from interviews) of candidates for promotion should document the grounds for their subjective judgments.

- Employers must avoid segregating women and persons of color into "dead-end" positions that offer little prospect of advancement.

- Employers should closely monitor the career progress of women and persons of color.

- When there is evidence of blocked advancement for some protected class group(s), employers should closely scrutinize the following

 –the protected class composition of positions from which promotions are made.

 –the manner in which key projects and other developmental opportunities are assigned.

 –the availability of mentoring.

 –the existence of harassment and other impediments to performance.

 –the selection criteria and process used in promotions.

 –aspects of the organization's culture that are hostile to protected class groups.

 –turnover patterns.

- To remove obstacles to attaining high-level positions, employers should

 –provide management development programs, career planning assistance, and mentoring.

 –be open to less traditional career paths and backgrounds for promotional candidates.

Key TERMS

facially discriminatory	sex-plus	acceptance of offer
bona fide occupational qualification (BFOQ)	sex-stereotyping	consideration
	subjective criteria	promissory estoppel
authenticity	soft skills	segregation
public safety	organization fit	glass ceiling
privacy	offer	bona fide seniority system (BFSS)

Chapter QUESTIONS

1. Ninety-five percent of the customers of a weight loss center are women. Counselors at the center sell the weight loss program, interact with customers, provide instruction on diet programs, counsel customers about their individual weight problems, and monitor the progress of customers in losing weight. The latter includes taking measurements of size and body fat using a tape measure and calipers. The measurements involve considerable physical contact with customers and are sometimes taken on bare skin. Arguing that many customers would be uncomfortable and embarrassed having men take their measurements and talk with them about their weight problems, the center hires only women as counselors. Two previous attempts to use male counselors were judged to have been unsuccessful. A male, denied employment as a counselor at the weight center, sues. What should the court decide? Why? (*EEOC v. HI 40 Corp.*, 953 F. Supp. 301 (W.D. Mo. 1996))

2. A state regulation required that female prisoners could not be lodged in county jails unless a female deputy was present. Because no female deputies worked the third shift when most females were brought in, a county jail had to pay overtime to have a female deputy come in or have female inmates transferred to other jails with female deputies on duty. The head of the jail subsequently decided that it was necessary to have a female deputy on the third shift. The female deputy required to work the third shift objected and sued. What should the court decide? Why? (*Reed v. County of Casey, Kentucky*, 184 F.3d 597 (6th Cir. 1999))

3. A taxi cab company changed insurance carriers to save money (about $10,000 per year) on the auto insurance that state law required the company to carry on its employees. The company subsequently learned that the new policy did not cover employees under 23 years of age and over 70 years of age. A 73-year-old driver was terminated because he was not covered under the insurance. It is undisputed that the driver was performing satisfactorily at the time of the termination. However, the parties do not agree on whether the

termination was temporary—an expedient to avoid loss of the cab company's business license until other arrangements could be made—or permanent. Following the termination, the owner of the cab company helped the driver find a job with a different company and had discussions with the insurance company about waiving its age restriction. The terminated cab driver was never reinstated, and he sued. What should the court decide? Why? (*Enlow v. Salem-Keizer Yellow Cab Co.*, 389 F.3d 802 (9th Cir. 2004); *cert. denied*, 125 S.Ct. 1837 (2005))

4. A female bartender had worked at Harrah's Casino for 20 years. During that time, her job performance had consistently been rated as excellent. A "Beverage Department Image Transformation" program was implemented. Under the program, all beverage servers were to be "well-groomed, appealing to the eye, firm, and body toned." Female beverage servers were required to wear stockings, use colored nail polish, and wear their hair "teased, curled, or styled." Additionally, women were required to wear makeup. Male beverage servers were prohibited from wearing makeup or colored nail polish and required to maintain short haircuts and trimmed fingernails. The bartender specifically objected to the makeup requirement. She tried wearing makeup on the job once previously, but found that it made her feel like a sexual object and that it was more difficult to deal with unruly guests. Based on her refusal to comply with the makeup requirement, the bartender was terminated. What should the court decide? Why? (*Jespersen v. Harrah's*, 392 F.3d 1076 (9th Cir. 2004); *rehearing en banc granted by, vacated by*, 409 F.3d 1061 (9th Cir. 2005))

5. A 350-pound man interviewed for a job as a sales counselor for a weight loss center. He was told by the interviewer that he was the "most qualified" applicant, but that the regional manager had concerns about his weight. He was later informed that he would not be hired now because the company is "image conscious," and his weight would "send the wrong message." He was told to reapply for employment after losing 70 pounds. The man sued. What should the court decide? Why? (*Goodman v. L.A. Weight Loss Centers*, 2005 U.S. Dist. LEXIS 1455)

6. An African-American employee sought promotion to a chemist position with supervisory responsibilities. Promotions were based on the results of "certification" (based on education and work experience) and an interview. Because of his extensive experience, the African-American employee received a score of 89 on the certification. The second-ranked candidate scored 28 points lower. A panel of three (all white persons) interviewed the five candidates deemed qualified after the certification process. Interviews were scored and a candidate's score was the average score given by the three interviewers. The highest score on the interview was a 52, and the African-American employee ranked third with a score of 48. The interviewers attributed the lower score to the employee not clearly explaining how his skills would be used on the job and how he planned to move the county's environmental programs forward. The white male who scored highest on the interview was promoted, despite the fact that he had scored 34 points lower in the certification stage. The company has an informal policy of hiring from within for promotional positions, although it did not always do so. The African-American employee sued. What should the court decide? Why? (*Obi v. Anne Arundel County, Maryland*, 142 F. Supp. 2d 655 (D. Md. 2001); *affirmed*, 2002 U.S. App. LEXIS 2716)

7. A 42-year-old police officer with 18 years on the job ("Officer A") sought promotion to the rank of sergeant. The promotion was given to a 36-year-old candidate who had been on the force for seven years ("Officer B"). The promotional exam consisted of a written and oral portion, each of which counted for half of the candidate's total score. Officer A had the second highest score on the written exam (83), behind two officers tied at 85. Officer B scored fifth on the written exam with a 79, but received a score of 96 on the oral portion of the exam. Officer A received a score of 71 on the oral exam. Except for Officer B, all the scores on the oral portion of the exam were between 71 and 77. This was the first time that the police Chief had ever sat in on a sergeant's exam. The Chief selected the members of the oral exam panel and met with them beforehand to select questions and review scoring procedures. The Chief instructed the panelists to ask technology-related questions geared to a specific position, even though the candidates were not informed about the requirements of the specific assignment and past practice had been to hire for the general

position of sergeant. Officer B had previously been given special assignments and training related to the new position. A former police officer stated in an affidavit that the Chief had a history of manipulating promotions in favor of younger candidates. The former officer claimed to have been a beneficiary of this interference on one occasion. The Chief had previously referred to some members of the department as "dinosaurs" and "the old guys." He was also quoted as saying at a meeting that "the way to have good morale in the department would be to get rid of the old guys and hire young ones." The police department maintains that Officer B was promoted because he had the best score on the exam, whereas Officer A was not even among the top three scorers on the exam. Officer A sues. What should the court decide? Why? (*McInnis v. Town of Weston*, 2005 U.S. Dist. LEXIS 12704)

8. How should courts deal with different grooming and appearance requirements for men and women? Can sex-stereotyping be clearly distinguished from requirements based on "generally accepted standards of appearance" for men and women?

9. Interviews are a prime source of subjective impressions about job candidates. What should employers do to ensure that interviews do not become obstacles to equal employment opportunity? Because interviewing is a relationship, to what extent do the behaviors of interviewers determine the outcomes of interviews?

10. Do you think that the glass ceiling phenomenon is primarily a pipeline problem that will disappear over time as women and persons of color acquire the relevant experiences, or is it rooted more deeply in organizational cultures and practices hostile to the advancement of women and minorities? Are some careers inherently ill-suited for women who want to have families?

Internet RESOURCES

Department of Labor site with information on reports of the federal Glass Ceiling Commission.

http://www.dol.gov

PART 3

Managing a Diverse Workforce

Affirmative Action

CLIPPINGS

▶ Jimmy Dean Foods, a division of Sara Lee, has entered into a settlement agreement with the U.S. Department of Labor (DOL) to resolve allegations that the company discriminated against female applicants at one of its meat processing plants. The case arose out of a compliance review conducted by the DOL's Office of Federal Contract Compliance Programs (OFCCP). Under the terms of the agreement, the company will hire and provide back pay to 48 female applicants.[1]

▶ The Boston Police Department had operated under a consent decree mandating affirmative action in hiring since 1973. At that time, African Americans comprised approximately 16 percent of Boston's population, but only about 3.5 percent of its police force. By 2004, over 38 percent of entry-level police officers were African Americans, compared to the approximately 40 percent of Boston's population that is African American. Finding that the "rough parity" called for by the consent decree had been achieved, a federal court released the city from further compliance with the decree.[2]

▶ The Federal Aviation Administration (FAA) has settled a "reverse discrimination" suit brought by a white male employee who charged that he was repeatedly passed over for promotion in favor of women and minority candidates. As part of the settlement, the agency agreed to engage in a comprehensive review of its affirmative action policies and plans to ensure that they comply with the law.[3]

▶ The Office of Federal Contract Compliance Programs (OFCCP) recognizes the efforts of federal contractors in promoting equal employment opportunity. The most prestigious award in 2005 went to the Cinergy Corporation of Cincinnati, Ohio. The company was praised for its "innovative programs and initiatives designed to ensure equal employment opportunities for all applicants and employees." Entergy Corp., Ivey Mechanical Company, and Pride Industries were also cited for exemplary programs.[4]

▶ Attitudes toward affirmative action are complex and often passionate. Although a nationwide survey of 1,258 adults found significant support for the goal of diversity, respondents differed on the appropriate means of diversifying the workforce, and responses were sensitive to the particular wording of questions. The majority of respondents supported "special efforts to help minorities

[1]U.S. Department of Labor. "Labor Department Signs Settlement Agreement with Jimmy Dean Foods that Will Benefit 48 Female Applicants." ESA News Release (April 10, 2003).

[2]"After 30 Years, Boston Police Released From Consent Decree Governing Hiring." *Daily Labor Report* 232 (December 3, 2004), A-6.

[3]Donald G. Aplin. "FAA Settles White Male Worker's Bias Case, Agrees to Review Affirmative Action Policies." *Daily Labor Report* 209 (October 29, 2004), A-5.

[4]U.S. Department of Labor. "U.S. Department of Labor Honors Eight Organizations for Creating Opportunities in the Workplace." ESA News Release (March 17, 2005).

get ahead" and "outreach programs to hire minority workers." On the other hand, a clear majority was opposed to "preference in hiring and promotion" and expressed the belief that affirmative action "at least some of the time" results in the hiring of "less qualified persons." Views of white and black respondents differed markedly on some questions, particularly on whether affirmative action should be continued.[5]

Managers know that important financial and operational outcomes, such as profitability and product quality, require close attention and planning. Managers are taught to be *proactive* and to not wait until losses or consumer complaints mount before taking actions to improve profitability, efficiency, and quality. It is important to have a clear sense of desired outcomes (goals), a strategy for attaining those outcomes, and a way to measure the progress that is being made.

Equal employment opportunity is another very important outcome. Rather than simply refrain from discrimination and react to employee grievances or lawsuits, employers can take initiative in studying their workforces, identifying problem areas, devising reasonable measures to enhance equal employment opportunity, setting goals for improvement, and tracking progress. In short, employers can engage in affirmative action.

Affirmative action has been defined as "those actions appropriate to overcome the effects of past or present practices, policies, or other barriers to equal employment opportunity."[6] It has also been described as "a management tool designed to ensure equal employment opportunity."[7] To qualify as affirmative action, such efforts must be undertaken pursuant to formal affirmative action plans. The particular focus of affirmative action is improving the employment opportunities of groups that historically have been victims of discrimination: women, African Americans, Latinos, Native Americans, Asians, Pacific Islanders, disabled persons, and certain veterans.

This chapter considers the situations in which affirmative action is required, circumstances affecting the legality of affirmative action, the ingredients of affirmative action plans, and evidence on its effects. Affirmative action is clearly controversial. The material in this chapter should help you make an informed appraisal of it. The chapter concludes with some thoughts on the relationship between affirmative action and diversity.

WHEN IS AFFIRMATIVE ACTION REQUIRED?

Affirmative action is required of most companies that have contracts to sell goods or services to the federal government. Many states also have affirmative action requirements for contractors. Besides government contracting, the only other time that employers are required to engage in affirmative action is when a discrimination suit results in a settlement or court order that includes affirmative action as a remedy. Otherwise, employers can determine whether they want to have affirmative action plans. Many employers, in fact, choose to adopt voluntary affirmative action plans.

[5]Sam Howe Verhovek. "In Poll, Americans Reject Means but Not Ends of Racial Diversity." *New York Times* (December 14, 1997), A-1.

[6]29 C.F.R. § 1608.1(c) (2005).

[7]41 C.F.R. § 60-2.10(a)(1) (2005).

Government Contractors

Companies that contract to do business with the federal government are covered by *Executive Order 11246*.[8] This executive order requires that *companies with contracts worth at least $10,000 must have a nondiscrimination clause included in their contracts and abide by its terms*. Importantly, *the same clause must be included in the contracts of subcontractors, and they are also bound by its terms*. Federal contractors and subcontractors include many of the nation's major corporations and employ nearly 22 percent of the civilian workforce.[9] The underlying rationale is that if public funds are being expended, it is legitimate for the government to require that contractors' employment practices support public policy in favor of equal employment opportunity. However, all establishments within contracting corporations—and not merely facilities that actually perform contract work—are required to comply with E.O. 11246.

The **nondiscrimination clause** reads, in its most relevant part:

> During the performance of this contract, the contractor agrees as follows: (1) The contractor will not discriminate against any employee or applicant for employment because of race, color, religion, sex, or national origin. The contractor will take affirmative action to ensure that applicants are employed, and that employees are treated during their employment, without regard to their race, color, religion, sex, or national origin. Such action shall include, but not be limited to the following: employment, upgrading, demotion, or transfer; recruitment or recruitment advertising; layoff or termination; rates of pay or other forms of compensation; and selection for training, including apprenticeship. The contractor agrees to post in conspicuous places, available to employees and applicants for employment, notices to be provided by the contracting officer setting forth the provisions of this nondiscrimination clause.[10]

Because most contractors are already covered by Title VII of the Civil Rights Act, isn't it redundant to incorporate nondiscrimination language in contracts? Executive Order 11246 reinforces federal antidiscrimination laws by providing additional sanctions and enforcement mechanisms. Under E.O. 11246, the federal government can suspend, cancel, or terminate the contracts of noncomplying contractors and bar companies from bidding on future projects. These sanctions are rarely invoked, but they provide another strong incentive for employers to pay attention to equal employment opportunity. The DOL's **Office of Federal Contract Compliance Programs (OFCCP)** monitors compliance with E.O. 11246 and other laws requiring affirmative action by contractors. This agency collects considerable workforce data from employers, conducts compliance reviews, and can initiate suits without needing individual plaintiffs to come forth. In these ways, the OFCCP bolsters the enforcement of antidiscrimination laws. The settlement agreement attained in the sex discrimination case against Jimmy Dean Foods (see "Clippings") is an example of the OFCCP's role in enforcing the law.

The nondiscrimination clause also refers to contractors taking affirmative action. Under E.O. 11246, *contractors and subcontractors that have at least 50 employees and contracts worth at least $50,000 must develop written affirmative*

[8]*Executive Order 11246* of September 24, 1965, 30 FR 12319.

[9]U.S. DOL, OFFCP. *Glass Ceiling Initiative: Are There Cracks in the Ceiling?* (1997), p. 8 (http://www.dol.gov/esa/public/media/reports/ofccp/newgc.htm).

[10]Executive Order 11246, part II, subpart B, § 202(1).

action plans and submit them to the OFCCP (within 120 days of the contract commencing). A preapproved affirmative action plan is required for large contracts (in excess of $1 million). The OFCCP has detailed requirements for contractors' affirmative action plans. Some of these are discussed later in the chapter.

Federal contractors also have affirmative action responsibilities under the *Rehabilitation Act of 1973.*[11] *Contractors or subcontractors with federal contracts worth more than $10,000 are required to take affirmative action to employ qualified individuals with disabilities. Contractors or subcontractors with at least 50 employees and contracts worth at least $50,000 are responsible for preparing and maintaining affirmative action plans.* These plans typically contain some of the same items as affirmative action plans produced under E.O. 11246, but do not include analyses of the availability of qualified disabled workers or the establishment of specific goals and timetables. Instead, the focus is on broadening recruitment efforts to reach qualified disabled persons and systematically reviewing workplace policies and practices to identify and remove barriers to the employment of disabled persons.

One other federal law that contains affirmative action requirements for contractors is the *Vietnam Era Veteran's Readjustment Assistance Act of 1974 (VEVRAA).*[12] The law requires that *employers with federal contracts or subcontracts worth more than $25,000 provide equal employment opportunity and affirmative action on behalf of Vietnam era veterans and certain other disabled veterans.* Vietnam era veterans are generally those that served on active duty at some point between 1964 and 1975. The affirmative action requirements of the law primarily involve listing all employment openings (except top management jobs) with state employment services.

Settlements and Court Orders

Affirmative action is one of the remedies available to courts in discrimination cases. When discrimination has been pervasive and deeply entrenched in an organization, simply halting the unlawful practices might not be enough. It might be necessary to undo the damage of prior discrimination (e.g., a hostile organizational climate, a dearth of women and persons of color in positions that lead to promotion) by requiring the employer to make real progress in providing employment opportunities for members of the discriminated-against group(s). Affirmative action that arises out of legal proceedings can be imposed either as a remedy following a determination by a court that an employer has engaged in a serious pattern or practice of intentional discrimination or as part of a judicially approved settlement between the parties. The latter is called a **consent decree**. Affirmative action that arises out of legal proceedings tends to be the most far-reaching in the use of preferences.

Court-imposed affirmative action is not very common, but many of the nation's police and fire departments operate, or have done so in the past, under the terms of consent decrees mandating affirmative action on behalf of women and persons of color. The Boston Police Department's (see "Clippings") experience is typical in this regard. But consent decrees are not intended to remain in place into perpetuity. When the goals of the affirmative action plan are achieved, as they were in the Boston Police Department case, the municipality is relieved of its obligation to comply with the consent decree.[13]

Absent a government contract or a court order, employers are generally free to choose whether to engage in affirmative action. However, to say that affirmative

[11]29 U.S.C. § 793 (2005).

[12]38 U.S.C. § 4212 (2005).

[13]*Deleo v. City of Boston*, 2004 U.S. Dist. LEXIS 24034.

action is voluntary is not to say that employers are free to do whatever they want under the banner of affirmative action. The legal guidelines for affirmative action plans are stringent and appear to be shifting in the direction of even closer judicial scrutiny.

DISTINGUISHING LEGAL AFFIRMATIVE ACTION FROM REVERSE DISCRIMINATION

Most affirmative action takes the form of the suggestions for enhancing equal employment opportunity made in previous chapters, such as identifying and encouraging more diverse applicants, posting all employment opportunities, eliminating selection criteria that impose unnecessary barriers to employment, offering extensive development and mentoring opportunities, and so on. Measures such as these do not leave anyone worse off and raise no issue of discrimination. Under E.O. 11246, contractors are limited to these measures and required to "make selections in a nondiscriminatory manner. Placement goals do not provide the contractor with a justification to extend a preference to any individual . . . on the basis of that person's race, color, religion, sex, or national origin."[14]

The difficulty with these affirmative action measures is that they are not effective without strong commitment from employers (something that might be in short supply in organizations that have been in the habit of discriminating), and the improvements they produce are likely to be gradual. Employers sometimes go further and apply a **preference** for women or persons of color in hiring or promotion decisions to achieve affirmative action goals. In such cases, the protected class characteristics of applicants or employees are considered in making employment decisions and the outcomes of those decisions might differ from what they would have been in the absence of affirmative action. The use of affirmative action to accord preferences for women and persons of color is the most controversial and legally problematic issue.

In **reverse discrimination** cases, an employee who believes that he was passed over for an employment opportunity because an employer with an affirmative action plan considered the protected class characteristics of applicants and chose a woman or person of color instead, alleges disparate treatment. The white male continually passed over for promotions by the FAA had a meritorious reverse discrimination claim (see "Clippings"). In these cases, the employer has, in fact, taken protected class into account (which is not to say that it was the only factor considered), but argues that doing so was permissible because of its affirmative action plan. The question then is whether this use of affirmative action was legal or discriminatory. In reaching an answer, courts will consider both the justification for the affirmative action plan and the reasonableness of the particular measures used to implement it.

Although the "strong" form of affirmative action includes the extension of preferences based on race or sex, affirmative action is not *a matter of establishing rigid quotas, "checking boxes," or reserving employment opportunities solely for persons with the desired protected class characteristics regardless of their qualifications.* Loaded terms such as *quota system* obscure the reality of affirmative action and make it impossible to engage in objective analysis of the legal issues. The legal questions surrounding affirmative action do not concern whether quotas are legal; the answer to that question is plainly no. Instead, we are confronted with the question of to what extent, if at all, protected class characteristics can be taken into account

[14]41 C.F.R. § 60-2.16(e)(2) (2005).

in making employment decisions for the purpose of undoing the effects of discrimination on women and persons of color.

Before looking at some of the case law on the legality of affirmative action, a few other caveats are in order. Court decisions in this area have been sufficiently ambiguous and inconsistent that reasonable people can disagree about exactly what the law currently says. Cases are brought under both Title VII and the U.S. Constitution (the equal protection provisions of the Fifth and Fourteenth Amendments), and the extent to which these bodies of law impose different requirements is not entirely clear. Likewise, affirmative action has been challenged not only in the context of employment, but also in education (admissions decisions of universities) and public contracting (preferences for minority-owned businesses in the awarding of contracts). Cases considering the legality of affirmative action in education and public contracting are often treated as directly relevant to affirmative action in employment, but drawing distinctions between these settings is possible. Lastly, the law in this area is dynamic and appears to be shifting in the direction of greater restriction, but not outright prohibition, of the use of preferences in affirmative action programs.

The Legality of Affirmative Action Under Title VII

Johnson v. Transportation Agency and *Taxman v. Board of Education* involve legal challenges to voluntary (not court-ordered) affirmative action plans under Title VII. The different outcomes of the cases and their discussions of the affirmative action case law help us distinguish between legal affirmative action and reverse discrimination.

JOHNSON V. TRANSPORTATION AGENCY, SANTA CLARA COUNTY
480 U.S. 616 (1987)

● ● ●

OPINION BY JUSTICE BRENNAN:

Respondent, Transportation Agency of Santa Clara County, California, unilaterally promulgated an Affirmative Action Plan applicable, inter alia [among other things], to promotions of employees. In selecting applicants for the promotional position of road dispatcher, the Agency, pursuant to the Plan, passed over petitioner Paul Johnson, a male employee, and promoted a female employee applicant, Diane Joyce. The question for decision is whether in making the promotion the Agency impermissibly took into account the sex of the applicants in violation of Title VII of the Civil Rights Act of 1964. * * *

In December 1978, Santa Clara . . . adopted an affirmative action plan for the County Transportation Agency. * * * [T]he Agency Plan provides that, in making promotions to positions within a traditionally

segregated job classification in which women have been significantly underrepresented, the Agency is authorized to consider as one factor the sex of a qualified applicant.

In reviewing the composition of its work force, the Agency noted in its Plan that women were represented in numbers far less than their proportion of the County labor force in both the Agency as a whole and in five of seven job categories. Specifically, while women constituted 36.4% of the area labor market, they composed only 22.4% of Agency employees. Furthermore, women working at the Agency were concentrated largely in EEOC job categories traditionally held by women. . . . As for the job classification relevant to this case, none of the 238 Skilled Craft Worker positions was held by a woman. * * *

On December 12, 1979, the Agency announced a vacancy for the promotional position of road dispatcher. * * * Nine of the applicants, including Joyce

and Johnson, were deemed qualified for the job, and were interviewed by a two-person board. Seven of the applicants scored above 70 on this interview, which meant that they were certified as eligible for selection by the appointing authority. The scores awarded ranged from 70 to 80. Johnson was tied for second with a score of 75, while Joyce ranked next with a score of 73. A second interview was conducted by three Agency supervisors, who ultimately recommended that Johnson be promoted. Prior to the second interview, Joyce had contacted the County's Affirmative Action Office because she feared that her application might not receive disinterested review [due to prior disagreements with two of the interviewers]. The Office in turn contacted the Agency's Affirmative Action Coordinator. * * * The Coordinator recommended to the Director of the Agency, James Graebner, that Joyce be promoted. * * * Graebner, authorized to choose any of the seven persons deemed eligible, thus had the benefit of suggestions by the second interview panel and by the Agency Coordinator in arriving at his decision. After deliberation, Graebner concluded that the promotion should be given to Joyce. * * *

The assessment of the legality of the Agency Plan must be guided by our decision in *Weber*. In that case, the Court addressed the question whether the employer violated Title VII by adopting a voluntary affirmative action plan designed to "eliminate manifest racial imbalances in traditionally segregated job categories." The respondent employee in that case challenged the employer's denial of his application for a position in a newly established craft training program, contending that the employer's selection process impermissibly took into account the race of the applicants. The selection process was guided by an affirmative action plan, which provided that 50% of the new trainees were to be black until the percentage of black skilled craftworkers in the employer's plant approximated the percentage of blacks in the local labor force. Adoption of the plan had been prompted by the fact that only 5 of 273, or 1.83%, of skilled craftworkers at the plant were black, even though the work force in the area was approximately 39% black. Because of the historical exclusion of blacks from craft positions, the employer regarded its former policy of hiring trained outsiders as inadequate to redress the imbalance in its work force.

We upheld the employer's decision to select less senior black applicants over the white respondent, for we found that taking race into account was consistent with

Title VII's objective of "[breaking] down old patterns of racial segregation and hierarchy." As we stated:

> It would be ironic indeed if a law triggered by a Nation's concern over centuries of racial injustice and intended to improve the lot of those who had 'been excluded from the American dream for so long' constituted the first legislative prohibition of all voluntary, private, race-conscious efforts to abolish traditional patterns of racial segregation and hierarchy.

We noted that the plan did not "unnecessarily trammel the interests of the white employees," since it did not require "the discharge of white workers and their replacement with new black hirees." Nor did the plan create "an absolute bar to the advancement of white employees," since half of those trained in the new program were to be white. Finally, we observed that the plan was a temporary measure, not designed to maintain racial balance, but to "eliminate a manifest racial imbalance." As JUSTICE BLACKMUN's concurrence made clear, *Weber* held that an employer seeking to justify the adoption of a plan need not point to its own prior discriminatory practices, nor even to evidence of an "arguable violation" on its part. Rather, it need point only to a "conspicuous . . . imbalance in traditionally segregated job categories." Our decision was grounded in the recognition that voluntary employer action can play a crucial role in furthering Title VII's purpose of eliminating the effects of discrimination in the workplace, and that Title VII should not be read to thwart such efforts. * * *

In reviewing the employment decision at issue in this case, * * * [t]he first issue is therefore whether consideration of the sex of applicants for Skilled Craft jobs was justified by the existence of a "manifest imbalance" that reflected underrepresentation of women in "traditionally segregated job categories." In determining whether an imbalance exists that would justify taking sex or race into account, a comparison of the percentage of minorities or women in the employer's work force with the percentage in the area labor market or general population is appropriate in analyzing jobs that require no special expertise. Where a job requires special training, however, the comparison should be with those in the labor force who possess the relevant qualifications. The requirement that the "manifest imbalance" relate to a "traditionally segregated job category" provides assurance both that sex or race will be taken into account in a manner consistent with Title VII's purpose of eliminating

the effects of employment discrimination, and that the interests of those employees not benefiting from the plan will not be unduly infringed. * * *

It is clear that the decision to hire Joyce was made pursuant to an Agency plan that directed that sex or race be taken into account for the purpose of remedying underrepresentation. * * *

[H]ad the Plan simply calculated imbalances in all categories according to the proportion of women in the area labor pool, and then directed that hiring be governed solely by those figures, its validity fairly could be called into question. This is because analysis of a more specialized labor pool normally is necessary in determining underrepresentation in some positions. If a plan failed to take distinctions in qualifications into account in providing guidance for actual employment decisions, it would dictate mere blind hiring by the numbers, for it would hold supervisors to "achievement of a particular percentage of minority employment or membership . . . regardless of circumstances such as economic conditions or the number of available qualified minority applicants. . . ."

The Agency's Plan emphatically did not authorize such blind hiring. It expressly directed that numerous factors be taken into account in making hiring decisions, including specifically the qualifications of female applicants for particular jobs. Thus, despite the fact that no precise short-term goal was yet in place for the Skilled Craft category in mid-1980, the Agency's management nevertheless had been clearly instructed that they were not to hire solely by reference to statistics. The fact that only the long-term goal had been established for this category posed no danger that personnel decisions would be made by reflexive adherence to a numerical standard.

Furthermore, in considering the candidates for the road dispatcher position in 1980, the Agency hardly needed to rely on a refined short-term goal to realize that it had a significant problem of underrepresentation that required attention. Given the obvious imbalance in the Skilled Craft category, and given the Agency's commitment to eliminating such imbalances, it was plainly not unreasonable for the Agency to determine that it was appropriate to consider as one factor the sex of Ms. Joyce in making its decision. The promotion of Joyce thus satisfies the first requirement enunciated in *Weber*, since it was undertaken to further an affirmative action plan designed to eliminate Agency work force imbalances in traditionally segregated job categories.

We next consider whether the Agency Plan unnecessarily trammeled the rights of male employees or created an absolute bar to their advancement. In contrast to the plan in *Weber*, which provided that 50% of the positions in the craft training program were exclusively for blacks, and to the consent decree upheld last Term in *Firefighters v. Cleveland*, which required the promotion of specific numbers of minorities, the Plan sets aside no positions for women. The Plan expressly states that "[the] 'goals' established for each Division should not be construed as 'quotas' that must be met." Rather, the Plan merely authorizes that consideration be given to affirmative action concerns when evaluating qualified applicants. As the Agency Director testified, the sex of Joyce was but one of numerous factors he took into account in arriving at his decision. The Plan thus resembles the "Harvard Plan" approvingly noted by JUSTICE POWELL in *Regents of University of California v. Bakke*, which considers race along with other criteria in determining admission to the college. As JUSTICE POWELL observed: "In such an admissions program, race or ethnic background may be deemed a 'plus' in a particular applicant's file, yet it does not insulate the individual from comparison with all other candidates for the available seats." Similarly, the Agency Plan requires women to compete with all other qualified applicants. No persons are automatically excluded from consideration; all are able to have their qualifications weighed against those of other applicants.

In addition, petitioner had no absolute entitlement to the road dispatcher position. Seven of the applicants were classified as qualified and eligible, and the Agency Director was authorized to promote any of the seven. Thus, denial of the promotion unsettled no legitimate, firmly rooted expectation on the part of petitioner. Furthermore, while petitioner in this case was denied a promotion, he retained his employment with the Agency, at the same salary and with the same seniority, and remained eligible for other promotions.

Finally, the Agency's Plan was intended to attain a balanced work force, not to maintain one. * * * The Agency acknowledged the difficulties that it would confront in remedying the imbalance in its work force, and it anticipated only gradual increases in the representation of minorities and women. It is thus unsurprising that the Plan contains no explicit end date, for the Agency's flexible, case-by-case approach was not expected to yield success in a brief period of time. Express

assurance that a program is only temporary may be necessary if the program actually sets aside positions according to specific numbers. * * * In this case, however, substantial evidence shows that the Agency has sought to take a moderate, gradual approach to eliminating the imbalance in its work force, one which establishes realistic guidance for employment decisions, and which visits minimal intrusion on the legitimate expectations of other employees. * * *

We therefore hold that the Agency appropriately took into account as one factor the sex of Diane Joyce in determining that she should be promoted to the road dispatcher position. The decision to do so was made pursuant to an affirmative action plan that represents a moderate, flexible, case-by-case approach to effecting a gradual improvement in the representation of minorities and women in the Agency's work force. Such a plan is fully consistent with Title VII, for it embodies the contribution that voluntary employer action can make in eliminating the vestiges of discrimination in the workplace. Accordingly, the judgment of the Court of Appeals is [a]ffirmed.

CASE QUESTIONS

1. What was the legal issue in this case? What did the Supreme Court decide? Why?

2. What does this case reveal about the conditions under which affirmative action is legal?

3. What evidence did the county have of the need for affirmative action?

4. Why does the Court conclude that the measures used to implement the county's affirmative action plan do not unduly burden white males like Johnson?

5. Do you agree with this decision? Why or why not?

TAXMAN V. BOARD OF EDUCATION OF THE TOWNSHIP OF PISCATAWAY
91 F.3d 1547 (3d Cir. 1996), *cert. dismissed,* 118 S. Ct. 595 (1997)

OPINION BY CIRCUIT JUDGE MANSMANN:

In this Title VII matter, we must determine whether the Board of Education of the Township of Piscataway violated that statute when it made race a factor in selecting which of two equally qualified employees to lay off. Specifically, we must decide whether Title VII permits an employer with a racially balanced work force to grant a nonremedial racial preference in order to promote "racial diversity."

It is clear that the language of Title VII is violated when an employer makes an employment decision based upon an employee's race. The Supreme Court determined in *United Steelworkers v. Weber,* however, that Title VII's prohibition against racial discrimination is not violated by affirmative action plans which first, "have purposes that mirror those of the statute" and second, do not "unnecessarily trammel the interests of the [non-minority] employees."

We hold that Piscataway's affirmative action policy is unlawful because it fails to satisfy either prong of *Weber.* Given the clear antidiscrimination mandate of Title VII, a nonremedial affirmative action plan, even one with a laudable purpose, cannot pass muster. We will affirm the district court's grant of summary judgment to Sharon Taxman.

In 1975, the Board of Education of the Township of Piscataway, New Jersey, developed an affirmative action policy applicable to employment decisions. * * * In 1983 the Board also adopted a one page "Policy," entitled "Affirmative Action—Employment Practices." * * * The operative language regarding the means by which affirmative-action goals are to be furthered is identical in the two documents. "In all cases, the most qualified candidate will be recommended for appointment. However, when candidates appear to be of equal qualification, candidates meeting the criteria of the affirmative action program will be recommended." * * * The Board's affirmative action policy did not have "any remedial purpose"; it was not adopted "with the intention of remedying the results of any prior discrimination or identified underrepresentation of minorities within the Piscataway Public School System." At all

relevant times, Black teachers were neither "underrepresented" nor "underutilized" in the Piscataway School District work force. Indeed, statistics in 1976 and 1985 showed that the percentage of Black employees in the job category which included teachers exceeded the percentage of Blacks in the available work force.

In May, 1989, the Board accepted a recommendation from the Superintendent of Schools to reduce the teaching staff in the Business Department at Piscataway High School by one. At that time, two of the teachers in the department were of equal seniority, both having begun their employment with the Board on the same day nine years earlier. One of those teachers was intervenor plaintiff Sharon Taxman, who is White, and the other was Debra Williams, who is Black. Williams was the only minority teacher among the faculty of the Business Department.

Decisions regarding layoffs by New Jersey school boards are highly circumscribed by state law; nontenured faculty must be laid off first, and layoffs among tenured teachers in the affected subject area or grade level must proceed in reverse order of seniority. Seniority for this purpose is calculated according to specific guidelines set by state law. Thus, local boards lack discretion to choose between employees for layoff, except in the rare instance of a tie in seniority between the two or more employees eligible to fill the last remaining position.

The Board determined that it was facing just such a rare circumstance in deciding between Taxman and Williams. In prior decisions involving the layoff of employees with equal seniority, the Board had broken the tie through "a random process which included drawing numbers out of a container, drawing lots or having a lottery." In none of those instances, however, had the employees involved been of different races.

In light of the unique posture of the layoff decision, Superintendent of Schools Burton Edelchick recommended to the Board that the affirmative action plan be invoked in order to determine which teacher to retain. Superintendent Edelchick made this recommendation "because he believed Ms. Williams and Ms. Taxman were tied in seniority, were equally qualified, and because Ms. Williams was the only Black teacher in the Business Education Department."

While the Board recognized that it was not bound to apply the affirmative action policy, it made a discretionary decision to invoke the policy to break the tie between Williams and Taxman. As a result, the Board "voted to terminate the employment of Sharon Taxman, effective June 30, 1988. . . ." * * *

Title VII was enacted to further two primary goals: to end discrimination on the basis of race, color, religion, sex or national origin, thereby guaranteeing equal opportunity in the workplace, and to remedy the segregation and underrepresentation of minorities that discrimination has caused in our Nation's work force. * * *

The significance of this second corrective purpose cannot be overstated. It is only because Title VII was written to eradicate not only discrimination per se but the consequences of prior discrimination as well, that racial preferences in the form of affirmative action can co-exist with the Act's antidiscrimination mandate.

Thus, based on our analysis of Title VII's two goals, we are convinced that unless an affirmative action plan has a remedial purpose, it cannot be said to mirror the purposes of the statute, and, therefore, cannot satisfy the first prong of the *Weber* test. * * *

The statute on its face provides that race cannot be a factor in employer decisions about hires, promotions, and layoffs, and the legislative history demonstrates that barring considerations of race from the workplace was Congress' primary objective. If exceptions to this bar are to be made, they must be made on the basis of what Congress has said. The affirmative action plans at issue in *Weber* and *Johnson* were sustained only because the Supreme Court, examining those plans in light of congressional intent, found a secondary congressional objective in Title VII that had to be accommodated—i.e., the elimination of the effects of past discrimination in the workplace. Here, there is no congressional recognition of diversity as a Title VII objective requiring accommodation. * * *

[T]he Board's sole purpose in applying its affirmative action policy in this case was to obtain an educational benefit which it believed would result from a racially diverse faculty. While the benefits flowing from diversity in the educational context are significant indeed, we are constrained to hold, as did the district court, that inasmuch as "the Board does not even attempt to show that its affirmative action plan was adopted to remedy past discrimination or as the result of a manifest imbalance in the employment of minorities," the Board has failed to satisfy the first prong of the *Weber* test.

We turn next to the second prong of the *Weber* analysis. This second prong requires that we determine whether the Board's policy "unnecessarily trammels . . . [nonminority] interests. . . ." Under this requirement, too, the Board's policy is deficient. * * *

The affirmative action plans that have met with the Supreme Court's approval under Title VII had objectives,

as well as benchmarks which served to evaluate progress, guide the employment decisions at issue and assure the grant of only those minority preferences necessary to further the plans' purpose. By contrast, the Board's policy, devoid of goals and standards, is governed entirely by the Board's whim, leaving the Board free, if it so chooses, to grant racial preferences that do not promote even the policy's claimed purpose. Indeed, under the terms of this policy, the Board, in pursuit of a "racially diverse" work force, could use affirmative action to discriminate against those whom Title VII was enacted to protect. Such a policy unnecessarily trammels the interests of nonminority employees.

Moreover, both *Weber* and *Johnson* unequivocally provide that valid affirmative action plans are "temporary" measures that seek to "attain," not "maintain" a "permanent racial . . . balance." The Board's policy, adopted in 1975, is an established fixture of unlimited duration, to be resurrected from time to time whenever the Board believes that the ratio between Blacks and Whites in any Piscataway School is skewed. On this basis alone, the policy contravenes *Weber's* teaching.

Finally, we are convinced that the harm imposed upon a nonminority employee by the loss of his or her job is so substantial and the cost so severe that the Board's goal of racial diversity, even if legitimate under Title VII, may not be pursued in this particular fashion. This is especially true where, as here, the nonminority employee is tenured. In *Weber* and *Johnson*, when considering whether nonminorities were unduly encumbered by affirmative action, the Court found it significant that they retained their employment. We, therefore, adopt the plurality's pronouncement in *Wygant* that "while hiring goals impose a diffuse burden, often foreclosing only one of several opportunities, layoffs impose the entire burden of achieving racial equality on particular individuals, often resulting in serious disruption of their lives. That burden is too intrusive."

Accordingly, we conclude that under the second prong of the *Weber* test, the Board's affirmative action policy violates Title VII. In addition to containing an impermissible purpose, the policy "unnecessarily trammels the interests of the [nonminority] employees."

CASE QUESTIONS

1. What was the legal issue in this case? What did the court decide?

2. Why was the outcome of this case different from *Johnson*?

3. Should diversity be a legitimate basis for affirmative action, especially for educational institutions? Is the role model argument persuasive?

4. What should the school district have done? Would they have been better off flipping a coin?

5. Do you agree with this decision? Why or why not?

Johnson and Taxman are not the last word on affirmative action in employment, but they point to some basic requirements for affirmative action plans under Title VII. First, the only reason that Santa Clara County was able to defend its consideration of candidates' sex in the promotion decision was that it did, in fact, have an affirmative action plan. Absent a formal, written affirmative action plan, it would not have worked for the county to claim that it was just trying to help women, that it was committed to diversity, or some other similar sentiment. Thus, an *employer that wants to consider protected class characteristics when making employment decisions to enhance the employment of women and persons of color can do so only if a formal affirmative action plan is in place.*

The case also makes it clear that *affirmative action must be remedial in nature to be legal.* Although it is not necessary under Title VII to establish that the employer has discriminated prior to instituting affirmative action, the plan must address a "manifest imbalance" in the protected class composition of the employer's workforce. Put differently, the plan must be designed to remedy the "underrepresentation" or "underutilization" of women and persons of color. *Affirmative action cannot be used to maintain the racial or gender balance of an employer's workforce; it can only be used to remedy the underutilization of women and persons of color in particular jobs. Affirmative action is a temporary measure that must not continue*

after the identified underutilization has been eliminated. Although the failure to cite a specific expiration date was not fatal in *Johnson*, the case suggests that plans calling for more aggressive use of preferences require clearer evidence of their temporary nature.

The Court upheld the use of affirmative action in *Johnson* not only because of the clear underutilization of women in skilled crafts, but also because the means used to pursue affirmative action goals were moderate and not unduly burdensome on white males. Specifically, the plan did not establish quotas (i.e., rigid requirements such as a specified number or percentage of new hires that must be women) or set aside positions only for women. Nor did the plan result in the hiring of unqualified persons. Instead, sex was considered among many other factors, and the female candidate selected was judged to be only slightly less qualified through the agency's interview process. Thus, although preferences that border on quotas have occasionally been upheld (primarily in early cases such as *Weber*),[15] *employers must refrain from establishing quotas, setting aside positions, or hiring unqualified candidates with the desired protected class characteristics.*

The *Taxman* case underscores the necessity of affirmative action having remedial purposes. A fatal flaw in the school board's case was the lack of evidence proviing underutilization of African Americans as teachers in the district's schools. Good intentions are not sufficient to justify race-conscious employment decisions. The school district's case also failed because the challenged employment decision was a layoff. *Employers must not invoke affirmative action as a basis for disciplinary or layoff decisions.* Even though downsizing might undermine gains in minority and female employment, the heavy burden of losing employment falls on specific individuals and "unnecessarily trammels [interferes with] the interests" of whites and males.

The Legality of Affirmative Action Under the U.S. Constitution

Even though they concerned government agencies, *Johnson* and *Taxman* were argued as Title VII cases. However, challenges to the use of preferences by public employers and to court-imposed affirmative action plans often allege violations of the U.S. Constitution. In constitutional cases, courts subject the use of racial preferences in affirmative action plans to **strict scrutiny**—the most stringent form of judicial review of government actions. To survive a constitutional challenge to an affirmative action plan that uses racial preferences, a public employer must show that the plan serves a **compelling governmental interest**[16] and that the measures employed are **narrowly tailored.** Put differently, the plan must serve a very important public purpose and harm the interests of nonpreferred persons no more than absolutely necessary. One compelling governmental interest is remedying the effects of actual prior discrimination. Mere underutilization does not appear to be sufficient as a constitutional justification for affirmative action. Racial preferences are more likely to meet the narrow tailoring requirement if they are not applied to layoffs or disciplinary actions,[17] they are no more intrusive than absolutely necessary, if race-neutral methods are tried and prove inadequate,[18] they do not amount to rigid quotas, and their use is temporary and flexible.[19] Thus, although considerable overlap exists

[15]*United Steelworkers of America v. Weber,* 443 U.S. 193 (1979).

[16]*Adirand Constructors, Inc. v. Pena,* 515 U.S. 200 (1995).

[17]*Wygant v. Jackson Board of Education,* 476 U.S. 267 (1986).

[18]*City of Richmond v. J.A. Croson Co.,* 488 U.S. 469 (1989).

[19]*United States v. Paradise,* 480 U.S. 149 (1987).

between the requirements for private employers under Title VII and public employers under the Constitution, the latter requirements are more stringent. Also, public employers in several states, most notably in California under Proposition 209, are prohibited outright from extending preferences in public employment (and education and contracting) based on race and other protected class characteristics.

The most recent statement by the Supreme Court on affirmative action came in two cases involving student admissions to the University of Michigan.[20] The Court endorsed the view that student body diversity can be a compelling state interest that justifies the use of race in university admissions.[21] Although the affirmative action program used in selecting students for the law school was upheld as constitutional, the program used for selecting undergraduates was struck down. The law school's efforts to attain a "critical mass" of minority students through a highly individualized assessment that considered multiple forms of diversity was deemed "narrowly tailored," whereas the undergraduate admission program that automatically awarded sizable bonuses based on race and ethnicity in a largely quantitative selection process was not sufficiently narrowly tailored.

To the extent that the Supreme Court expanded the concept of "compelling governmental interest" in the University of Michigan cases, its rationale was explicitly couched in terms of the requirements of public education. However, *Petit v. City of Chicago* suggests that courts may view the need for diversity as an adequate justification for affirmative action in certain types of employment as well.

[20]*Grutter v. Bollinger,* 539 U.S. 306 (2003); *Gratz v. Bollinger,* 539 U.S. 244 (2003).

[21]*Grutter,* at 328.

PETIT V. CITY OF CHICAGO

352 F.3d 1111 (7th Cir. 2003); *cert. denied,* 2004 U.S. LEXIS 3872

● ● ●

OPINION BY CIRCUIT JUDGE EVANS:

Eighteen years ago, the Chicago Police Department (CPD) conducted an examination that for a fairly brief moment in time formed the basis for promotions of patrol officers to the rank of sergeant. After the examination the raw scores were standardized, most relevantly here for race and ethnicity. What followed was this lawsuit alleging that promotions resulting from the exam violated the plaintiffs' rights under the Equal Protection Clause of the United States Constitution. * * *

We turn . . . to the dispositive issue: the City's defense that the procedures used met an operational need of the police department. Like any racial preference, this one must be justified by a compelling state interest.

In *Grutter v. Bollinger,* [a 2003 Supreme Court decision involving admissions to the University of Michigan law school] . . . the Court endorsed the view that "student body diversity is a compelling state interest that can justify the use of race in university admissions." In arriving at that conclusion, the Court deferred to the law school's educational judgment that "such diversity is essential to its educational mission. . . ." The goal of the law school was to assemble a class that was "exceptionally academically qualified and broadly diverse," and as part of that goal it sought to enroll a "critical mass" of minority students. The Court found that the benefits of diversity were substantial, for which proposition it relied in part on the views of high-ranking retired officers and civilian leaders of the United States military to the effect that a "highly qualified, racially diverse officer corps . . . is essential to

the military's ability to fulfill its principle mission to provide national security." Furthermore, in the Court's words, the "effective participation by members of all racial and ethnic groups in the civic life of our Nation is essential if the dream of one Nation, indivisible, is to be realized." The conclusion was that the "Law School has a compelling interest in attaining a diverse student body."

It seems to us that there is an even more compelling need for diversity in a large metropolitan police force charged with protecting a racially and ethnically divided major American city like Chicago. Under the *Grutter* standards, we hold, the City of Chicago has set out a compelling operational need for a diverse police department. * * *

In this case, the City presented a strong basis to conclude that some rather modest affirmative action promotions were necessary for the effective operation of the police department. Professor Samuel Walker, an expert in criminal justice and police-community relations, testified that all major studies conducted since the 1960's recognized the importance of minority representation. The reality of urban policing is that minorities are frequently mistrustful of police and are more willing than nonminorities to believe that the police engage in misconduct. * * * Distrust and a lack of confidence in the police, in turn, reduce the willingness of some community members to cooperate with the police. On the other hand, when police officers are routinely supervised by minorities, the fears that the police department is hostile to the minority community will naturally abate. Walker's conclusion was that an increase in minorities enhanced the public's perception of the CPD, which in turn enhanced the department's ability to prevent and solve crime.

A former chief of the Portland (Oregon) Police Bureau, Tom Potter, testified to the necessity of diversity among police supervisors, both for the community's perceptions of police departments, but also internally in changing the attitudes of officers. Additionally, a number of high-ranking CPD officials confirmed the need for diversity at the sergeant rank and that sergeants are in a unique position to influence officers on the street. These officials testified that the presence of minority sergeants has not only improved police-community cooperation, but also diffused potentially explosive situations, such as the tense racial situation following riots in the 1980's in a predominately Hispanic community.

These officials also recounted the growth in the minority population of the City and the fact that minority representation at the sergeant rank had not kept pace with that growth. * * *

All in all, we find that, as did the University of Michigan, the Chicago Police Department had a compelling interest in diversity. Specifically, the CPD had a compelling interest in a diverse population at the rank of sergeant in order to set the proper tone in the department and to earn the trust of the community, which in turn increases police effectiveness in protecting the city.

This does not end our inquiry, however, for "even in the limited circumstance when drawing racial distinctions is permissible to further a compelling state interest, government is still 'constrained in how it may pursue that end: The means chosen to accomplish the [government's] asserted purpose must be specifically and narrowly framed to accomplish that purpose.'" It is here that *Grutter* and the other University of Michigan case—*Gratz v. Bollinger,* [a 2003 Supreme Court decision involving undergraduate admissions to the University of Michigan]—diverge. The system for undergraduate admissions at issue in *Gratz* was rejected because it was not narrowly tailored and, for that reason, violated the Equal Protection Clause. The method used by the university was automatically to assign 20 points—or one-fifth of the 100 points need to guarantee admission—to each underrepresented minority applicant solely because of race. The system, which made race the deciding factor for every minimally qualified minority applicant, was found not to be narrowly tailored. On the other hand, the system at the Michigan Law School as described in *Grutter* was constitutional. Rejecting "mechanical, predetermined diversity 'bonuses,'" the Court emphasized that race must be used in "a flexible, nonmechanical way." A race-conscious admissions program cannot use a quota system. It cannot "insulate each category of applicants with certain desired qualifications from competition with all other applicants. However, race can be a 'plus' factor in the context of individualized consideration of each and every applicant." In addition, a program must not unduly harm members of any racial group and must "work the least harm possible to other innocent persons competing for the benefit." Finally, the program must be limited in time; that is, not enshrined as a permanent justification for racial preferences.

In the mid-1980s, when the CPD determined that it would make approximately 500 promotions of patrol officers to the rank of sergeant, it formulated an examination procedure, which any patrol officer was eligible to take and anyone who sought a promotion had to take. The promotions were to be made according to rank order of the scores. A total of 3,416 officers took the examination—2,274 white officers . . . ; 931 African-Americans; and 192 persons classified as Hispanic. * * *

As recounted by Robert T. Joyce of the City of Chicago Department of Personnel, the results were evaluated by employees of his department. * * * The results . . . showed that the test had an adverse impact on African-Americans and Hispanics and would have resulted in far too few promotions to persons in those categories. As we noted, there were 458 officers promoted. Using these test results, only 60 would have been African-American and only 15 would have been Hispanic. At the time the examination was being formulated, the City had experience with two prior examinations for the rank of sergeant and, more importantly, was under a federal court order not to promote officers on rank-order examinations unless it could document the test's validity as a rank order promotional device. * * *

For those reasons, through a rather complicated procedure, the City standardized the scores based on race. As Mr. Joyce explains it, standardization is a recognized statistical method of removing differences between the scores of two or more groups of test-takers. If, for instance, two different groups have different mean scores, and there is no objective reason to assume the two groups should have scored differently, standardization is an acceptable method of equalizing the scores. The process was an attempt to produce results that reflected the score a candidate would have received if the test had not had an adverse racial impact. The standardized scores were then used to place the candidates in rank order. * * *

[A]ccording to the examination results, it would appear that all of the candidates who were promoted, and many who were not promoted were qualified for promotion. The passing score on the examination was 70, and approximately 2000 of the candidates passed. The result of the standardization was that, of the top 500 officers, 332 were white, 138 were African-American,

and 30 were Hispanic. The score of the 332nd white candidate in the pool of 500 eligible candidates was 82.98; the unstandardized score of the 138th African-American candidate was 80.70 and the standardized score was 82.82; the unstandardized score of the 30th Hispanic candidate was 80.95 and the standardized score was 83.43. * * * Based on the examination results, the City made standardized rank-order promotions of 402 candidates—298 were white; 119 were African-American; and 41 were Hispanic. In addition, 56 out-of-rank-order promotions were made. It cannot be said that the process affected every "minimally qualified" candidate as did the blanket award of 20 points per candidate, the procedure found to be unconstitutional in *Gratz*. In fact, standardizing the scores can be seen not as an arbitrary advantage given to the minority officers, but rather as eliminating an advantage the white officers had on the test.

The ultimate result was that of the 82 plaintiffs to this action, some had their promotions delayed and approximately 50 were not promoted. While we do not minimize the loss that those who were not promoted suffered, we find that the procedures met the *Grutter* standard for minimizing harm to members of any racial group. Furthermore, the results of this examination were not used after 1991, and no race-conscious promotions have been made since that time. We are told that, in fact, new examinations have been held in 1993, 1998, and 2002. The affirmative action plan at issue in this case was limited in time, as *Grutter* also requires.

* * * The judgment of the district court is AFFIRMED.

CASE QUESTIONS

1. What was the legal issue in this case? What did the court decide?

2. On what basis did the court conclude that a "compelling interest" existed for the police department to hire more persons of color as sergeants?

3. On what basis did the court conclude that the use of race in these promotion decisions was "narrowly tailored?"

4. Do you agree with the decision in this case? Why or why not?

FIGURE 8-1 **Required Contents for Affirmative Action Plans Under E.O. 11246**

I. Quantitative analyses of the workforce
 A. Organizational profile
 B. Job group analysis
 C. Protected class composition of job group incumbents
 D. Availability of qualified women and persons of color
 E. Comparison of job group incumbents with available, qualified workforce

II. Identification of problem areas
 A. Problems in minority or female utilization or distribution (e.g., glass ceilings)
 B. Personnel activities (e.g., applicant flows, promotions, turnover)
 C. Compensation systems—gender or racial disparities
 D. Selection, recruitment, and referral procedures

III. Placement goals

IV. Action-oriented programs

V. Designation of responsibility for implementation

VI. Procedures for periodic internal audits of progress in meeting goals

INGREDIENTS OF AFFIRMATIVE ACTION PLANS

What do affirmative action plans look like? The EEOC guidelines state that voluntary affirmative action plans must contain three basic elements: a reasonable self-analysis, a reasonable basis for concluding that action is appropriate, and reasonable action.[22] DOL regulations implementing E.O. 11246 contain more detailed requirements for contractors' affirmative action plans[23] as outlined in Figure 8-1. Because most of the requirements for affirmative action plans under E.O. 11246 fall within the EEOC's three broad categories, these are used to organize the following discussion of the contents of affirmative action plans.

Reasonable Self-Analysis

The EEOC guidelines state that the "objective of a self-analysis is to determine whether employment practices do, or tend to, exclude, disadvantage, restrict, or result in adverse impact or disparate treatment of previously excluded or restricted groups or leave uncorrected the effects of prior discrimination, and if so, to determine why."[24] Although the EEOC does not mandate any particular form of **self-analysis**, the requirements for federal contractors with affirmative action plans under E.O. 11246—including an organizational profile, job group analysis, documentation of the protected class characteristics of incumbents, and identification of problem areas—provide a concrete model for a thorough self-analysis.

[22]29 C.F.R. § 1608.4 (2005).

[23]41 C.F.R. § 60-2.10(b) (2005).

[24]29 C.F.R. § 1608.4(a) (2005).

An **organizational profile** portrays the staffing patterns in an organization. DOL regulations allow contractors to provide this information in the form of either an *organizational display* or a *workforce analysis*. An **organizational display** (like an organizational chart) depicts the organizational structure of a company, including the units within it and the relationship of each unit to other units in the organization. *For each unit*, information must be provided on the demographics of the supervisor, the total number of males and females, and the total number of males and females broken down by race and ethnicity (African American, Latino, Asians/Pacific Islanders, Native Americans/Alaskan Natives).

The alternative approach, a **workforce analysis**, requires that individual job titles be listed for each department or other organizational unit, in order of pay level. Separate lines of progression within an organizational unit need to be identified. Then, *for each job title*, the same demographic information is provided as stated for the organizational display. The organizational profile is especially helpful in identifying patterns of segregation in an organization, whereby women or persons of color are concentrated within a few units or job titles.

Because skill levels and the available labor force differ substantially across jobs, relatively refined data should be used. Gross portraits of whole organizations or units are not sufficient. Yet, at the same time, dealing with large numbers of individual job titles, some of which might be closely related, becomes very unwieldy. In a **job group analysis**, the individual job titles in a contractor's workforce are combined into a more parsimonious set of job groups. The criteria for performing a job group analysis are similarity in job content, pay level, and opportunities for advancement. Contractors with fewer than 150 employees are permitted to use a standard set of job groups established by the EEOC: officials and managers, professionals, technicians, sales, office and clerical, craft workers (skilled), operatives (semiskilled), laborers (unskilled), and service workers.

After reasonable job groups are established, the sex, race, and ethnicity of each job group's incumbents (and applicants) can be documented. Employers can accomplish this in a legal and reasonably sensitive manner by asking employees or applicants to *voluntarily* self-identify their protected class characteristics. This information is for affirmative action purposes only and must be kept separate from personnel files, applications, or other such documents. Visual observation can also be used to document the protected class characteristics of employees and applicants, although it is less reliable than self-identification. Analyses of underutilization (see text that follows) and any placement goals that are set for improving the utilization of women and persons of color are at the job group level.

The foregoing analyses document protected class characteristics of an employer's workforce and the location of women and minorities within the organization. The **identification of problem areas** makes the self-analysis more dynamic by examining flows into and out of positions and the organization. It attempts to get at the question of why an employer's workforce looks the way that it does. The identification of problem areas is wide-ranging, touching on all aspects of human resource practice, including compensation.

Reasonable Basis for Affirmative Action

A key concept in determining whether a reasonable basis exists for affirmative action is **underutilization**. Underutilization exists when the percentage of women and persons of color in one or more of an employer's job groups is lower than the percentage of women and persons of color with the necessary skills for that type of employment. Under DOL regulations, contractors need to compare the demographics

of their existing workforce with the availability of women and minorities for each of their job groups. When the percentage of women and minorities in a particular job group is less than would be expected based on their availability, the contractor is required to establish a placement goal. Availability is determined by considering two main factors: "the percentage of minorities or women with requisite skills in the reasonable recruitment area" and "the percentage of minorities or women among those promotable, transferable, and trainable within the contractor's organization."[25] The reasonable recruitment area is the geographical area within which the contractor typically recruits or could reasonably do so for the jobs in question. "Trainable" or "promotable" basically refers to persons who could, with training that the employer could reasonably provide, be rendered qualified within the plan year. The point is simply that *employers embarking on affirmative action need to analyze underutilization by carefully considering the availability of qualified women and persons of color, both in the external labor market and within the organization, and compare availability to current utilization.*

Where does all this information about availability come from? Data for determining the availability of trainable and promotable persons come from an employer's own records, the analysis of which is facilitated if the employer maintains an inventory of employee skills and engages in regular succession planning (i.e., identifying, tracking, and grooming candidates for promotions). Data for determining the availability of women and persons of color in the reasonable recruitment area are more difficult to come by. Principal sources of data are the Census Bureau, Bureau of Labor Statistics publications based on the census and the Current Population Survey (CPS), information from state employment services, and data from colleges and other training institutions. The data used for determining availability need to be as current and as closely matched to the job group and geographic area in question as possible.

How large does the discrepancy between availability and current utilization have to be to conclude underutilization exists? There is no single, precise answer. The Supreme Court has consistently referred to the need for evidence of a "manifest imbalance" to justify affirmative action, but the degree of underutilization need not be so large as to violate the four-fifths rule (and thus constitute a prima facie case of adverse impact). Nor is it necessary, at least for private employers, to show that the underutilization of women and persons of color is the result of actual discrimination. The basic premise is that, absent discriminatory practices in the past or present, the percentage of women and minorities working in jobs should roughly match the percentage of women and minorities available in the relevant labor market (i.e., those with the necessary skills and background). Thus, *it is not necessary that the problematic employment practices be severe enough to violate Title VII or that employers admit to violating the law to have a* **reasonable basis** *for affirmative action.* The very point of the self-analysis and affirmative action is to encourage employers to fix problems before they become more severe and possibly objects of litigation.

In *Johnson,* the county transportation agency had conducted a self-study that found its female employees to be concentrated in traditionally female job groups (office and clerical, paraprofessionals), with no women at all among the agency's skilled craft workers. The agency employed women at a level (22 percent of its workforce) lower than their availability in the area workforce (36 percent). The skilled and traditionally male nature of the job in question undoubtedly meant that the proportion of qualified women available was significantly lower than the overall proportion of women in the

[25]41 C.F.R. § 60-2.14(c) (2005).

surrounding workforce, but it was still greater than zero (after all, the successful candidate, Joyce, was one such qualified female). The Court thus concluded that the underutilization (which it referred to in the case as "underrepresentation") necessary to justify affirmative action was present. In contrast, the school district in the *Taxman* case had not conducted a reasonable self-analysis to establish the underutilization of African Americans. In fact, the percentage of African-American teachers in the school district exceeded the percentage available in the relevant labor market. The court was not willing to accept the notion that the absence of an African American within a single department of the school constituted underutilization.

Reasonable Affirmative Actions

If underutilization of women and persons of color exists, what affirmative actions are warranted? One thing that **reasonable actions** include is identifying **goals** for improvement in the utilization of women and minorities and **timetables** for achieving those goals. The EEOC guidelines counsel that goals should take into account the effects of past discrimination, the need for prompt improvement, the availability of qualified or qualifiable candidates, and the number of employment opportunities likely to be available (e.g., based on anticipated growth, turnover). In essence, the more severe the problem of underutilization and the more opportunity there is to remedy it, the more ambitious an employer's goals should be. DOL regulations require that federal government contractors establish placement goals for all job groups for which evidence exists of underutilization of women or persons of color. The goals set by contractors must be at least equal to the availability of women and minorities for the job groups in question. Unless there are substantial differences in utilization rates for particular minority groups or for men and women within minority groups, contractors are generally required to establish a single goal for minority placement in each job group where underutilization is noted.

DOL regulations stress that goals serve as "objectives or targets" reasonably attainable through **good faith effort**. There is more than a semantic difference between *goals* and *quotas*. Contractors' "[p]lacement goals may not be rigid and inflexible quotas, which must be met, nor are they to be considered as either a ceiling or a floor for the employment of particular groups. Quotas are expressly forbidden."[26] No doubt, it can be difficult for managers, who are accustomed to being evaluated according to attainment of quantitative sales or financial goals, to treat placement goals in a serious, but flexible, manner. In one reverse discrimination case, a university dean refused to hire a male as a professor in the psychology department, despite the department's strong support for the candidate. The dean's statements betrayed a fundamental misunderstanding of the nature of affirmative action goals: "[T]he hiring goals for the [psychology department] is [sic] 61.8 percent women and 9.8 percent minorities. . . . Thus, the department needs 3.23 women to reach its target. . . . We cannot send two male candidates forward, given the targets in the department."[27] The court ruled against the university and mused, "[H]ow it was going to appoint 23/100 of a woman Ross [the dean] did not explain." *Employers with affirmative action plans should establish goals as benchmarks against which improvement in the use of underutilized women or minorities can be measured. A sincere, good faith effort to improve the utilization of women and minorities is called for, not mindless adherence to numerical goals.*

[26]41 C.F.R. § 60-2.16(e)(1) (2005).

[27]*Hill v. Ross*, 183 F.3d 586, at 588–89 (7th Cir. 1999).

At its best, affirmative action involves a creative effort to solve problems and to go beyond the minimum requirements of the law in extending equal employment opportunity. No finite set of measures constitutes reasonable affirmative actions. The measures that are instituted should correspond to the particular problems identified through self-analysis. Figure 8-2 provides examples of reasonable affirmative actions. *Employers should make the most of these improvements in human resource practices before considering the use of preferences to achieve affirmative action goals. Retaining the valuable services of women and persons of color is just as important as hiring a diverse group of new employees. Employers should be very concerned about higher turnover among women and persons of color. Affirmative action should be directed at this problem, particularly by eliminating obstacles to advancement and fostering a more welcoming and inclusive organizational climate.*

Effects of Affirmative Action

Some grounds for opposition to affirmative action, such as the view that it contradicts the basic requirement of antidiscrimination law that protected class characteristics not be considered in making employment decisions, do not rest upon evidence about the effects of affirmative action. However, other grounds, such as the argument that affirmative action harms society by resulting in the hiring of unqualified persons, are based on assumptions about its effects. Survey data suggest that beliefs about the lesser qualifications of persons hired by companies with affirmative action programs are widespread (see "Clippings"). One of the most comprehensive studies[28] of the effects of affirmative action surveyed 3,200 employers and looked at differences between firms that did not use affirmative action, those that used it for recruiting, and those that used it for hiring. Among the major findings were the following:

- Firms using affirmative action used a wider variety of recruitment mechanisms, particularly those likely to reach minority applicants (e.g., community agencies).

- Firms using affirmative action engaged in more intensive screening of applicants, but were also less likely to screen out candidates based on criminal background or lengthy prior unemployment.

- Firms using affirmative action recruited and hired somewhat more women and persons of color, with women being the clearest beneficiaries.

- Firms using affirmative action in recruiting generally hired persons with comparable educational credentials to firms without affirmative action. Firms using affirmative action in hiring hired workers with somewhat lower educational credentials.

- Overall, job performance levels for women and persons of color in firms using affirmative action were equal to, and for some groups exceeded, the typical job performance level of employees in those firms.

- Greater investment in training by firms using affirmative action appears to counteract any lower educational credentials of persons hired.

The overall picture of affirmative action's effects emerging from this study and others is reasonably positive and does not comport with the view that affirmative

[28] Harry J. Holzer and David Neumark. "What Does Affirmative Action Do?" *Industrial and Labor Relations Review* 53 (January 2000), 240–71.

FIGURE 8-2	Examples of Reasonable Affirmative Actions

Recruitment

- Communicate the availability of jobs widely.
- Develop relationships with religious organizations, community development groups, schools, and cultural organizations that can refer qualified persons of color.
- Adjust the geographic scope of recruiting.
- Use internships and summer jobs to identify qualified women and persons of color.
- Work with training institutions, such as by providing scholarships, to diversify the pool of persons with needed skills.
- Establish or maintain facilities in communities with substantial minority populations.

Selection Procedures

- Validate all scored employment tests.
- Eliminate or find alternatives for tests and other requirements that disproportionately screen out women or persons of color.
- Lean toward a compensatory approach in evaluating candidates (considering multiple criteria in a portfolio fashion where weaknesses in one area can be offset by strengths in another) rather than strict cutoff levels or multiple hurdles.
- "Band" test scores and select from within bands, rather than simply choosing the highest score.
- Offer assistance to candidates in preparing for tests that tend to screen out women or minorities.
- Use multiple, well-trained interviewers to conduct structured interviews.
- Limit reliance on highly subjective criteria.

Training and Development

- Provide extensive skills training and development opportunities for employees.
- Fund tuition costs for employees to upgrade their skills.
- Redesign jobs to better prepare employees to move on to other jobs in the organization.
- Provide or arrange for English language and literacy courses.
- Maintain inventories of employee skills and work experiences.
- Provide formal mentoring and career planning assistance for employees.

Organizational Climate

- Actively enforce antidiscrimination and harassment policies.
- Institute work-life programs and do not penalize employees who use them.
- Sponsor company social and recreational events that do not exclude women and persons of color.
- Use inclusive language in reports, memos, and other documents.
- Facilitate support groups for women and persons of color.
- Offer diversity training and programs.

THE CHANGING WORKPLACE

Diversity and Affirmative Action

More and more, issues of equal employment opportunity are subsumed under the banner of **diversity**. Diversity is an attractive concept for many reasons, including its positive tone asserting that differences are to be valued (as opposed to merely tolerated or assimilated into the ways of a dominant group), its inclusiveness (everyone is diverse in some manner, after all), and the notion that diversity is an asset to organizational performance, beyond its role in meeting legal requirements. In contrast, affirmative action has acquired a negative connotation, portrayed as obsessed with head counts, getting people in the door and making them fit in rather than offering their unique contributions, and helping women and minorities at the expense of whites and males. This view of affirmative action certainly does not capture its potential nor, to a considerable extent, actual practice. But in whatever ways managing diversity differs from or goes beyond engaging in affirmative action and ensuring equal employment opportunity, *diversity is not a legal term. And, at least until very recently, the desire to increase diversity has carried little weight in legal proceedings.*

A widely cited analysis of workplace diversity distinguishes between three approaches or "paradigms" for managing diversity: discrimination-and-fairness, access-and-legitimacy, and learning-and-effectiveness.[1] The *discrimination-and-fairness* approach is most akin to the legal compliance and affirmative action issues discussed in this book. This paradigm has been criticized for paying too much attention to getting people in the door and too little to making good use of their diverse talents and perspectives. However, it remains necessary for women and minorities to get hired, advance to higher levels, and be retained for them to meaningfully contribute in organizations. Further, they must be present in more than token numbers if their unique voices are to be heard and heeded. Equal employment opportunity laws focus precisely on those differences (e.g., race, sex, national origin) that are primary sources of identity and distinct perspectives. The *access-and-legitimacy* paradigm treats diversity as a means of accessing increasingly diverse and global markets. The legal constraints on this strategy are very real. If employers are not careful, the aim of matching employees to markets can result in facially discriminatory job assignments and segregation. The *learning-and-effectiveness*

approach is multicultural in nature and views maximizing the distinctive contributions of a diverse workforce as essential to organizational effectiveness. Legal issues arise here as well, because protection from harassment, reasonable accommodation, and other legal responsibilities of employers affect the ability of women, persons of color, and the disabled to fully contribute. In short, one does not avoid grappling with legal issues simply by invoking diversity as a value.

The case for promoting diversity is especially strong in the context of higher education. A leading study of the effects of affirmative action in university admissions found evidence that students of all races benefit from the opportunity to interact with racially and culturally diverse student bodies.[2] In finding that creating a diverse student body can be a compelling governmental interest, the Supreme Court credited the view that being exposed to other students with "'the greatest possible variety of backgrounds'" promotes cross-racial understanding, helps to break down racial stereotypes, enables better understanding between people of different races, and makes classroom discussion livelier, more spirited, and more enlightening.[3] The military and numerous corporations filed "friend of the court" briefs in favor of affirmative action by public universities in the lead-up to the Supreme Court's decisions in the University of Michigan cases. The Court acknowledged this input as persuasive : "... major American businesses have made clear that the skills needed in today's increasingly global marketplace can only be developed through exposure to widely diverse people, cultures, ideas, and viewpoints. What is more, high-ranking retired officers and civilian leaders of the United States military assert that, ... a 'highly qualified, racially diverse officer corps ... is essential to the military's ability to fulfill its principle mission to provide national security.'"[4] It remains to be seen whether a broad diversity rationale for affirmative action will be applied to employment cases, although *Petit v. Chicago* suggests some willingness on the part of the courts to do so.

There are consequences to emphasizing the utility of workforce diversity to employers, rather than the considerations of social justice that have traditionally served as the basic rationale for affirmative action. The primary motivation for employer actions becomes organizational performance, rather than legal compliance. The types of diversity that are relevant expand

beyond those that constitute protected classes under the law. Edelman and her colleagues have observed that:

> Diversity rhetoric, which tends to equate differences based on geography or taste in sports or dress style with differences based on race or sex, offers a conception of equal employment opportunity that is quite different from that embodied in the statutory language of Title VII or other civil rights laws. Diversity rhetoric replaced the legal vision of diversity, which is grounded in moral efforts to right historical wrongs, with a managerial vision of diversity, which is grounded in the notion that organizations must adapt to their environments in order to profit.[5]

If obtaining the benefits of diversity is the primary issue, it can be argued that there are many forms of

diversity, and protected class characteristics like race do not necessarily occupy a privileged place among forms of difference.[6] If, on the other hand, social justice is the fundamental issue, eradicating the corrosive effects of past and current discrimination dictates special concern for women and persons of color.

[1]David A. Thomas and Robin J. Ely. "Making Differences Matter: A New Paradigm for Managing Diversity." *Harvard Business Review* (September–October 1996), 79–90.

[2]William G. Bowen and Derek Bok. *The Shape of the River.* (Princeton, NJ; Princeton University Press, 1998), pp. 266–69.

[3]*Grutter v. Bollinger,* 539 U.S. 306, at 330 (2003).

[4]*Grutter, at* 330–31.

[5]Lauren B. Edelman, Sally Riggs Fuller, and Iona Mara-Drita. "Diversity Rhetoric and the Managerialization of Law." *American Journal of Sociology* 106, 6 (May 2001), 1626.

[6]*Johnson v. Board of Regents of the University of Georgia,* 263 F.3d 1234, at 1253 (11th Cir. 2001).

action has a negative impact on the quality of the workforce. Perhaps this is because there are usually more qualified candidates than jobs and thus, given the opportunity and perhaps some training, people who seem slightly less qualified on paper can still do a good job. Nor should it be assumed—given the prevalence of discrimination, sloppy screening, organizational politics, and favoritism; the limitations of available selection devices; and the idiosyncrasies of hiring decision makers engaging in subjective assessments—that, in the absence of affirmative action, the most able person necessarily gets the job.

Chapter SUMMARY

Affirmative action is a systematic program aimed at overcoming the effects of prior or continuing discrimination and removing barriers to equal employment opportunity. Ad hoc decisions to favor particular groups are not affirmative action. Rigid quota systems are not affirmative action. Because affirmative action aims to overcome the lingering effects of discrimination, it is used only on behalf of groups that have historically been victimized by discrimination: women, African Americans, Latinos, Asians, Pacific Islanders, Native Americans, disabled persons, and certain veterans.

The two situations in which employers are required to engage in affirmative action are when they have contracts to provide goods or services to the federal (and in many cases, state) government and when a lawsuit results in either a consent decree or a court order specifying affirmative action as a remedy for

discrimination. Otherwise, employers decide whether to adopt affirmative action programs. Affirmative action on behalf of women and minorities by federal contractors is governed by E.O. 11246. Enforcement of E.O. 11246 and other nondiscrimination and affirmative action requirements for federal contractors is carried out by the Office of Federal Contract Compliance Programs (OFCCP). Less far-reaching affirmative action requirements also arise under the Rehabilitation Act (for qualified disabled persons) and the Vietnam Era Veterans Readjustment Assistance Act (for Vietnam era and certain disabled veterans).

Much affirmative action focuses on modifying employers' recruiting, selection, training, development, and other human resource practices to facilitate the identification, hiring, advancement, and retention of qualified women and persons of color. Affirmative action plans created in compliance with E.O. 11246

are limited to such measures. Some affirmative action plans go further and use preferences based on protected class in making hiring and promotion decisions, such as by using race as a tie-breaker among relatively equal candidates or as a plus factor. Preferences are sometimes challenged as reverse discrimination. Under Title VII, employers must show that their affirmative action plans were adopted to correct "manifest imbalances" in their workforces, and that the measures used to accomplish this do not unnecessarily infringe upon whites or males. Evidence of a manifest imbalance in Title VII cases typically comes from an analysis of underutilization, in which, for each major job group, the percentages of qualified women and minorities available in the surrounding workforce are compared to the percentages of women and minorities currently used by an employer. The affirmative action plans of public employers are sometimes challenged on constitutional grounds, as violating the equal protection provisions of the Fifth and Fourteenth Amendments of the U.S. Constitution. Government agencies seeking to defend the use of racial preferences must show that their affirmative action plans serve a "compelling governmental interest" and that the measures used are "narrowly tailored" to achieve this important purpose with the least possible harm to nonpreferred groups. The legal status of affirmative action is not entirely clear, but appears to be shifting in the direction of greater restriction—but not outright prohibition—of the use of preferences in affirmative action plans.

Under EEOC guidelines, an affirmative action plan must include a reasonable self-study to document the protected class composition of an employer's workforce and its human resource practices; evidence of a reasonable basis for engaging in affirmative action, including an analysis of underutilization; and reasonable actions that will be taken to correct problems and improve the utilization of women and minorities. There are more extensive requirements for affirmative action plans under E.O. 11246, including quantitative analyses of the contractor's workforce, identification of problem areas, placement goals for each job group evidencing underutilization, action-oriented programs, delegation of responsibility for implementation, and procedures for periodic audits of progress in goal attainment.

The concept of managing diversity is a popular way of thinking about the employment and utilization of women, persons of color, and other groups. The contribution of diversity to organizational effectiveness provides employers with additional incentive—beyond the need for legal compliance—to attend to the presence and experiences of diverse persons in their organizations. However, diversity is not a legal concept and the motive of valuing diversity does not exempt an employer's actions from legal requirements or scrutiny. The business case for diversity should not be confused with or obscure the social justice concerns, rooted in the lengthy history of discrimination against African Americans and other protected classes, that provide the fundamental basis for affirmative action.

Practical Advice SUMMARY

- *Federal contractors and subcontractors with contracts worth at least $10,000 must*

 - *have a nondiscrimination clause in their contracts and abide by its terms.*

 - *take affirmative action to employ qualified persons with disabilities.*

- *Federal contractors and subcontractors with at least 50 employees and contracts worth at least $50,000 must*

 - *develop written affirmative action plans addressing employment of women and minorities and submit them to the OFCCP within 120 days of their contracts commencing.*

 - *develop and maintain affirmative action plans for the employment of qualified disabled persons.*

- *Federal contractors and subcontractors with contracts worth more than $25,000 must*

 - *provide equal employment opportunity and affirmative action on behalf of Vietnam era veterans and certain disabled veterans.*

 - *list all employment openings, other than top management jobs, with state employment services.*

- *Employers wanting to engage in affirmative action must have valid, written affirmative action plans in place.*

- *Employers engaging in affirmative action should*

 –maximize the use of improvements in recruitment, selection, training, development, and organizational climate before considering hiring and promotion preferences.

 –pay particular attention to retaining and advancing women and persons of color already employed.

- *Affirmative action should*

 –not be undertaken until the employer has determined that there is underutilization of women or persons of color.

 –be temporary and discontinued after the identified underutilization has been eliminated.

 –not include the establishment of quotas, set-asides of positions for women or minorities, or the hiring of unqualified candidates to meet affirmative action goals.

 –never be used as a basis for making discipline and termination decisions.

- *All affirmative action plans should include*

 –results of a reasonable self-study.

 –analysis of underutilization establishing the basis for affirmative action.

 –reasonable actions to improve the utilization of women and persons of color.

- *Affirmative action plans of government contractors must include*

 –quantitative analyses of current and available workforces.

 –identification of problem areas, placement goals, and timetables for all job groups showing underutilization.

 –action-oriented programs to improve utilization.

 –delegation of responsibility for the affirmative action program to a particular company official.

 –procedures for auditing progress toward goals.

Key TERMS

affirmative action
nondiscrimination clause
Office of Federal Contract
 Compliance Programs (OFCCP)
consent decree
preferences
reverse discrimination
strict scrutiny

compelling governmental
 interest
narrowly tailored
self-analysis
organizational profile
organizational display
workforce analysis
job group analysis

identification of problem areas
reasonable basis
underutilization
reasonable actions
goals
timetables
good faith effort
diversity

Chapter QUESTIONS

1. A white male applicant took a test for a job at General Motors, which has an affirmative action plan that includes a Pre-Apprentice Program (PAP). Minority applicants can participate in this program, and bonus points are added to their test scores. Two minority applicants who initially scored lower than the white applicant participated in the PAP, received the bonus points, and were hired. The white applicant was rejected and sued. What should the court decide? Why? (*Garnet v. GM Corp.,* 2001 U.S. App. LEXIS 20942 (6th Cir. 2001), *cert. denied,* 2002 U.S. LEXIS 1578)

2. A city fire department has a voluntary affirmative action program. It is not disputed that the department had previously discriminated against women and that only 1 percent of fire department employees were female at the time the plan was adopted in 1984. The plan established a "long-term" goal of 36 percent female utilization, based on the proportion of women in the population (52 percent) but reduced by a third to account for the fact that many women would not have the interest or ability to be firefighters. By 1997, 11.6 percent of firefighters were female. The applicant pool that year was 22 percent

female, and 27 percent of the persons hired were female. The department gives preferences to women in hiring by allowing all women who pass the written test to be included in the applicant pool (for males, there is a lottery due to the large number of applicants) and by treating female gender as a plus in making final hiring decisions. A group of males, unsuccessful in obtaining jobs as firefighters, sued. What should the court decide? Why? (*Danskine v. Miami Dade Fire Department*, 253 F.3d 1288 (11th Cir. 2001))

3. A county fire department, undergoing reorganization due to budget shortfalls, eliminated four Training Captain positions and replaced them with three lieutenant-level Training Instructor positions. The plaintiff, a white male, was one of the displaced Training Captains. He applied for one of the new positions and exceeded the stated qualifications. Interviews were conducted by three persons who were not firefighters or trainers and who had not been given copies of the job description. Two of the interviewers were known to be proponents of affirmative action. The stated policy was to consider interview results as only one factor in hiring. The plaintiff was rejected. One of those hired was a minority person who did not meet the minimum qualifications. The county had an affirmative action plan, but claimed that its decision was based (in conflict with its stated policy) solely on the results of the interview. The rejected candidate sued. What should the court decide? Why? (*Bass v. Board of County Commissioners*, 256 F.3d 1095 (11th Cir. 2001); *rehearing en banc denied*, 273 F.3d 1117 (11th Cir. 2001))

4. The city of Chicago has an affirmative action plan designed to deal with the effects of past discrimination in hiring and promotion by the police department. The plan allows for African Americans, Latinos, and women to be promoted even though they had lower scores than white males on the promotional exam. This was done in 14 out of 232 promotions in 1990 and 1991. A group of white male officers who were not promoted despite their higher test scores challenged the promotions. What should the court decide? Why? (*Reynolds v. City of Chicago*, 296 F.3d 524 (7th Cir. 2002))

5. The San Francisco Police Department operated under a consent decree requring affirmative action. To increase the percentage of minority candidates promoted, the city "banded" scores on the promotional exam. Scores that differed, but not to a degree that the differences were "statistically significant," were treated as equivalent (within the same band). Selection decisions were made from within bands, using race as one of the selection criteria. Of 115 promotion decisions, 100 were made in strict rank order based on test scores and 15 were made using the banding procedure. A group of white officers passed over for promotion sued. What should the court decide? Why? (*Officers for Justice v. City and County of San Francisco*, 979 F.2d 721 (9th Cir. 1992); *cert. denied*, 507 U.S. 1004 (1993))

6. What are some arguments in favor of affirmative action? Against it? What is your current view of affirmative action? Why? Does your view differ depending on the measures used to achieve affirmative action goals?

7. How important is diversity as a goal in university admissions? If you think that it is important, how should universities go about selecting diverse students?

Internet RESOURCES

The Web site for the Office of Federal Contract Compliance Programs can be found through the Department of Labor Web site.

http://www.dol.gov

The Web site of the American Association for Affirmative Action, an organization of professionals involved in the administration of affirmative action and diversity programs, offers a variety of useful resources and links.

http://www.affirmativeaction.org

The Web site of the Leadership Conference on Civil Rights (LCCR) and Leadership Conference on Civil Rights Education Fund provides up-to-date information on a variety of civil rights issues with an emphasis on affirmative action.

http://www.civilrights.org

Harassment

CLIPPINGS

▶ The EEOC has settled a discrimination suit brought against Consolidated Freightways on behalf of 12 African-American dockworkers who had been subjected to a racially hostile environment. The EEOC charged that coworkers had engaged in racial intimidation, including hanging nooses in the workplace, assaulting African-American workers, threatening physical harm, displaying racially offensive graffiti, and damaging property. It was further alleged that the company was aware of the harassment, but did nothing to stop it and, in fact, disciplined an employee who complained about the harassment.[1]

▶ The EEOC has sued the well-known Las Vegas hotel and casino Caesars Palace on behalf of a group of female kitchen workers subjected to years of severe sexual harassment by supervisors. The harassment allegedly included supervisors attempting to have forced sex with workers (including, in one case, a worker who was four months pregnant), exposing themselves to employees, making lewd comments, groping workers, bringing offensive pictures into the workplace, and promising favorable treatment in exchange for sex. Complaints were allegedly met with retaliation in the form of demotions, pay cuts, and disciplinary actions.[2]

▶ The EEOC has filed discrimination suits on behalf of teenage workers at two McDonald's restaurants. In the first case, a male supervisor allegedly engaged in same-sex harassment of male employees, including unwanted touching, requests for sex, and sexual remarks. In the second case, young females were subjected to groping and unwanted physical contact by a male assistant manager. One of the employees allegedly found the work conditions so intolerable that she was forced to resign.[3]

▶ A woman who was a writers' assistant on the television sitcom *Friends* has sued NBC, alleging that she was sexually harassed. The harassment took the form of a constant stream of lude, vulgar, and sexually explicit language used by the show's writers. The comments were not specifically directed at her, but she contends that they resulted in an offensive, sexually charged hostile work environment. The studio acknowledges that her description of the work setting is accurate, but contends that a free, uninhibited flow of language about sex is part and parcel of the creative process used to make the show. The California Supreme Court has agreed to hear the case.[4]

[1]U.S. Equal Employment Opportunity Commission. "Consolidated Freightways to Pay $2.75 Million for Racial Harassment of African Americans." (January 12, 2005). Viewed August 30, 2005 (http://www.eeoc.gov/press/1-12-05.html).

[2]U.S. Equal Employment Opportunity Commission. "Caesars Palace Subjected Class of Kitchen Workers to Sexual Harassment, EEOC Charges." (April 4, 2005). Viewed August 30, 2005 (http://www.eeoc.gov/press/4-4-05.html).

[3]U.S. Equal Employment Opportunity Commission. "EEOC Sues McDonald's Franchises in Arizona and New Mexico for Sexual Harassment of Young Workers." (February 24, 2005). Viewed August 30, 2005 (http://www.eeoc.gov/press/2-24-05.html).

[4]Christopher Noxon. "Television Without Pity." *New York Times* (October 17, 2004), Arts&Leisure, 1, 34.

Harassment is a major obstacle to realizing equal employment opportunity. Harassment can isolate employees, keep them from doing their best work, and ultimately drive them from the workplace. In its own pernicious way, harassment limits employment opportunity every bit as much as other forms of discrimination. Employers are clearly on notice that harassment will no longer fly. Eliminating harassment is among the most pressing legal concerns facing employers today.

Although sexual harassment claims are the most common type—and much of the law discussed in this chapter centers on sexual harassment—harassment also affects other protected classes. Racial harassment, such as that experienced by the dockworkers at Consolidated Freightways (see "Clippings"), is a long-standing and increasingly prevalent problem. Employees also experience and seek legal protection from harassment based on their national origin, age, disabilities, and religious beliefs. There are differences, of course, in the particular ways that harassment is manifested, but the fundamental nature of harassment—and employer liability for it—are the same regardless of the protected class involved.

HARASSMENT AS A FORM OF DISCRIMINATION

Harassment is a form of disparate treatment discrimination, but its unique features call for a somewhat different analysis. Courts have articulated the basic elements of a harassment claim in a variety of ways, but the general outlines are shown here. The following sections of this chapter consider each of these elements in order.

"Because of Sex"

Legal challenges to harassment come under general antidiscrimination laws, such as Title VII of the Civil Rights Act, rather than laws specifically designed to prohibit harassment. Title VII says absolutely nothing about harassment, but courts have recognized the discriminatory nature of harassment. However, just as the mere fact that an employee was terminated does not result in a finding of disparate treatment if the plaintiff cannot show that the termination was based on a protected class characteristic, plaintiffs in harassment cases must ultimately show that they were subjected to harassment because of a protected class characteristic. In sexual harassment cases involving harassers and victims who differ in sex, this requirement is usually met by the overtly sexual or gender-related content of the harassment. However, in one case, the court concluded that the harassment of a female employee by a supervisor who

ELEMENTS OF A CLAIM

Harassment
Plaintiffs must show that:
1. They were subjected to harassment based on a protected class characteristic.
2. The harassment resulted in a tangible employment action or was sufficiently severe or pervasive to alter working conditions and create a hostile environment.
3. The harassment was unwelcome.
4. There is a basis for attributing liability to the employer.

repeatedly said that he wanted to have sex with her teenage daughter, though "deplorable," was based on the supervisor's dislike for her husband rather than the employee's sex.[5] Thus, there was no violation of Title VII. Likewise, when a woman ended a romantic relationship with her male supervisor over his objections and began to receive poor performance appraisals, the court held that any harassment was the result of the relationship gone sour rather than because of her sex.[6]

Questions about the motivation for harassment loom especially large in **same-sex harassment** cases when the harasser and the person harassed are of the same sex. Under this circumstance, can it be said that the harassment occurred because of the sex of the person harassed? The Supreme Court considered the case of a male employee who worked as part of an all-male crew on an oil platform in the Gulf of Mexico. The employee experienced severe harassment at the hands of male coworkers, including physical assaults of a sexual nature and threats of rape. The Court ruled that same-sex harassment cases can be brought under Title VII, but the plaintiffs are still responsible for showing that the harassment is **"because of sex."** This could be done by showing that the harasser is homosexual and motivated by sexual desire for persons of the same sex; the victim is harassed in such sex-specific and derogatory terms that it is clear the harasser is motivated by general hostility to the presence of persons of the same sex in the workplace; or the harasser in a mixed-sex workplace treated persons differently based on their sex.[7]

Although the Supreme Court's decision left the door open for same-sex harassment suits, plaintiffs in subsequent cases have had great difficulty squeezing through that opening.[8] In one case, a male welder was regularly touched in private areas by his male supervisor, stalked, and subjected to the ridicule of coworkers who called him the supervisor's "girlfriend." An appeals court reversed a jury verdict in the employee's favor on the grounds that, although this was a case of "gross, vulgar, male horseplay in a male workplace," the conduct was not motivated by general hostility to men in the workplace.[9] In a comment that reveals much about prevailing judicial views of same-sex harassment, the court opined that if it upheld the verdict in this case, "what's next—towel snapping in the locker room?" Likewise, a male employee at a steel plant was harassed by a male coworker who jumped on the employee's back, stuck his tongue in the employee's ear, groped the employee's private areas, called the employee his "bitch," and made repeated vulgar comments of a sexual nature to him.[10] Concluding that that employee failed to show that he was targeted for this abuse because he was a man, the court rejected his harassment claim.

The three methods offered by the Supreme Court for establishing that same-sex harassment is "because of sex" is not an exhaustive listing. Some courts have also used the theory of *sex-stereotyping* to find evidence of a discriminatory motive in same-sex harassment cases. For example, a male waiter who was harassed by male coworkers and a supervisor because the employee was viewed as effeminate was allowed to take his claim of sexual harassment to trial. Among other intended insults, the employee was repeatedly addressed as "she" or "her" and berated for

[5]*Rizzo v. Sheahan,* 266 F.3d 705, at 708 (7th Cir. 2001).

[6]*Pipkins v. City of Temple Terrace, Florida,* 267 F.3d 1197 (11th Cir. 2001).

[7]*Oncale v. Sundowner Offshore Services,* 523 U.S. 75 (1998).

[8]Reed Abelson. "Targets of Same-Sex Harassment, Men Find Legal Recourse Scarce." *New York Times* (June 10, 2001), A-1.

[9]*EEOC v. Harbert-Yeargin, Inc.,* 266 F.3d 498, at 522 (6th Cir. 2001); *rehearing, en banc, denied,* 2002 U.S. App. LEXIS 18785.

[10]*James v. Platte River Steel Co.,* 2004 U.S. App. LEXIS 22157.

carrying his serving tray "like a woman." The court held that he was being harassed because he did not conform to the sex stereotype of a male, and thus the harassment was "because of sex."[11] In another case with similar facts, a male hotel waiter was subjected to severe harassment by his male coworkers over a two-year period. Actions by the coworkers, including whistling and blowing kisses at the employee and calling him "sweetheart" and "doll," strongly suggested that the harassment was prompted by the coworkers' judgments that the employee was not sufficiently masculine.[12]

Ultimately, grounding legal prohibitions against harassment in discrimination laws means that to be actionable, the harassment must be discriminatory—and not "merely" abusive or inappropriate. Other common law claims (e.g., infliction of emotional distress) or criminal charges (e.g., assault, battery, rape) can be brought to bear in some of these cases, but current legal protections against harassment do not reach the full range of "bullying" and abuse that occurs in the workplace (see "The Changing Workplace").

Another circumstance in which the requirements of antidiscrimination law fit uncomfortably with the reality of workplace harassment regards the "equal opportunity harasser." What happens if the harasser subjects both men and women to harassment? Courts often conclude in these cases that because both men and women are victimized, the harassment does not disadvantage members of one sex relative to the other. Hence, it is not discriminatory treatment based on sex. In a case involving a Wal-Mart supervisor, the plaintiff's claim was denied primarily because the harasser "was just an indiscriminately vulgar and offensive supervisor, obnoxious to men and women alike."[13] However, courts have sometimes found discrimination to exist where equal opportunity harassers harassed men and women in different, sex-specific ways.[14] The requirements of discrimination law may also be met where, although members of both sexes are affected by harassment, one sex is more likely to be subjected to harassment than the other. When a woman charged that her employer, a psychiatric hospital, failed to protect her from sexual harassment in the form of sexual assault by a client, the court concluded that while assaults occurred against both male and female staff, the victims of such assaults were disproportionately female.[15] Thus, the woman had a viable harassment claim under Title VII.

RECOGNIZING HARASSMENT

What Behaviors Constitute Harassment?

Now that it is clear that not all harassment can be linked to protected class in the manner required to prove discrimination, we need to step back and consider more carefully the kinds of behaviors that constitute harassment. The EEOC guidelines define sexual harassment as:

> Unwelcome sexual advances, requests for sexual favors, and other verbal or physical conduct of a sexual nature . . . when (1) submission to such conduct is made either explicitly or implicitly a term or condition of an individual's

[11]*Nichols v. Azteca Restaurant Enterprises,* 256 F.3d 864 (9th Cir. 2001).

[12]*Medina v. MGM Grand Hotel,* 305 F.3d 1061 (9th Cir. 2002); *cert. denied,* 538 U.S. 922 (2003).

[13]*Lack v. Wal-Mart,* 240 F.3d 255, at 262 (4th Cir. 2001).

[14]*Steiner v. Showboat Operating Co.,* 25 F.3d 1459 (9th Cir. 1994); *cert. denied,* 513 U.S. 1082 (1995).

[15]*Turnbull v. Topeka State Hospital,* 255 F.3d 1238, at 1244 (10th Cir. 2001); *cert. denied,* 535 U.S. 970 (2002).

THE CHANGING WORKPLACE

Harassment and Workplace Bullying

Harassment is antithetical to equal employment opportunity and valuing diversity. Rather than being appreciated as persons and coworkers with valuable contributions to make, employees subjected to harassment are singled out for mistreatment, viewed as sexual objects or racial categories, demeaned, and forced to endure abusive working conditions that interfere with their work. In workplaces that increasingly include women and persons of color, harassment ultimately serves the same purpose as old-fashioned exclusion and segregation. Persons threatened by the increased diversity of the workforce seek to demonstrate their contempt for, exercise power over, and isolate or drive from the workplace those who they think do not belong. Harassment is a serious problem and is appropriately viewed as a form of discrimination; however, not all mistreatment and abuse of employees—a phenomenon sometimes termed "workplace bullying"—falls within the ambit of harassment and the protection afforded by discrimination laws.

By all indications, harassment is a pervasive phenomenon. A 1994 study of federal government employees found that 44 percent of female respondents had experienced some form of "unwanted sexual attention" during the previous two years.[1] Jokes and verbal comments were the most common type of unwanted attention, but sizeable numbers of respondents also reported deliberate touching, pressure for dates, pressure for sexual favors, and even assault or rape. A 1999 national survey of 3,000 private sector employees (conducted to provide a baseline for a wide-ranging study of violence in the U.S. Postal Service) found that about 16 percent reported having been subjected to sexually harassing behaviors in the past year.[2] Verbal comments about the victim's body and about the harasser's sexual attributes or behaviors were the most common forms of harassment experienced. Sexual harassment charges brought to the EEOC and state Fair Employment Practice (FEP) agencies increased from 10,532 in 1992 to 15,836 in 2000.[3] That the number of sexual harassment charges has since fallen (to 13,136 in 2004) perhaps signals that employers are now taking the matter seriously, although sexual harassment cases still account for a sizable portion of the EEOC's total caseload. Although principally women are victimized by sexual harassment, the percentage of sexual harassment charges filed by men has increased, reaching 15.1 percent in 2004.[4] Racial and national origin harassment

have also been on the rise, accounting for a combined 8,545 charges in 2003.[5]

Mistreatment and abuse of employees is not limited to harassment. Discussion has increased concerning the more general phenomenon of "workplace bullying" and whether new laws should be devised to deal with it. **Workplace bullying** has been defined as "repeated interpersonal mistreatment that is sufficiently severe as to harm a targeted person's health or economic status."[6] The same national survey of private sector employees cited previously found that 33 percent of respondents reported having been verbally abused at work in the past year, including name calling, provoking arguments, shouting, swearing, threatening, and intimidating. Of the respondents, 5 percent said that they had been physically assaulted at work in the past year, including pushing, grabbing, slapping, kicking, hitting, rape or attempted rape, and the threat or use of weapons.[7] Research suggests that the "bullies" are often bosses and that women frequently bully other women.[8] Bullying is a broader concept than harassment, and victims often lack a legal remedy under current law because the mistreatment tends to be seen as not related to sex (because the bully and victim are often the same sex), as trivial "horseplay," as personally motivated, or simply as the actions of a "tough boss." New laws prohibiting abusive, bullying behavior—*regardless of whether it is directed at others because of their protected class characteristics*—might be needed to effectively deal with this problem, but such laws would mark a fundamental departure from the current approach to dealing with harassment and a large step in the direction of government creation of a "general civility code."[9]

[1]U.S. Merit Systems Protection Board. *Sexual Harassment in the Federal Workplace: Trends, Progress, Continuing Challenges* 3 (1995).

[2]National Center on Addiction and Substance Abuse. *Report of the United States Postal Commission On A Safe and Secure Workplace.* (New York: Columbia University, August 2000), 27.

[3]U.S. Equal Employment Opportunity Commission. "Sexual Harassment Charges EEOC & FEPA's Combined: FY 1992–FY 2004." Viewed September 1, 2005 (http://www.eeoc.gov/stats/harass.html).

[4]"Sexual Harassment Charges . . ."

[5]U.S. Equal Employment Opportunity Commission. "Trends in Harassment Charges Filed With the EEOC." Viewed September 1, 2005 (http://www.eeoc.gov/stats/harassment.html).

[6]Gary Namie and Ruth Namie. "Workplace Bullying: How to Adress America's Silent Epidemic." *Employee Rights & Employment Policy Journal* 8 (2004) 315.

[7]National Center on Addiction and Substance Abuse, 3.

[8]Namie and Namie, 325.

[9]*Oncale v. Sundowner Offshore Services*, 523 U.S. 75, at 81 (1998).

employment, (2) submission to or rejection of such conduct by an individual is used as the basis for employment decisions affecting such individual, or (3) such conduct has the purpose or effect of unreasonably interfering with an individual's work performance or creating an intimidating, hostile, or offensive working environment.[16]

A distinction can be drawn between harassment that results in tangible employment actions (1 and 2 in the preceding) and harassment that alters working conditions by subjecting employees to hostile environments, but does not directly affect tangible employment outcomes (3). This distinction is important because the criteria for finding employers liable differ depending on which of these two types of harassment has occurred.

Harassment That Results in Tangible Employment Actions

Harassment sometimes results in significant changes in the employment status of individuals, such as hiring, firing, promotion, demotion, pay increases or decreases, and work assignments. The classic example is where a manager tells an employee that he wants to date or receive sexual favors from her and that she should comply if she does not want her career to suffer. The employee resists the sexual advance and is demoted or fired shortly thereafter. Under these circumstances, harassment has produced a tangible effect on her employment opportunities, and the woman would likely have a strong harassment claim. **Harassment that results in tangible employment actions** often involves a sexual advance or demand for sexual favors that can be "traded" for some employment outcome. To engage in this type of harassment, the harasser must possess sufficient authority to influence or determine employment outcomes (or, at least, be reasonably perceived as having such authority). However, if a supervisor merely threatens an employment consequence, but does not take any action when the employee refuses his sexual advance, there is no tangible employment action (but there might still be a "hostile environment").[17]

The supervisors at Caesars Palace who promised employees favorable treatment in exchange for sex were clearly conditioning employment opportunities on submission to harassment (see "Clippings"). Similarly, a postal service employee whose supervisor demanded (and received) oral sex as the price for granting a leave of absence had a successful harassment claim.[18] In contrast, Paula Jones's assertions regarding her treatment by former President Clinton were legally insufficient to establish harassment resulting in a tangible employment action.[19] She failed to identify any promotional position that she was prevented or discouraged from seeking and any pay raises that she was denied. Her transfer to a similar position and the fact that she did not receive flowers on Secretary's Day were not the types of substantial changes in employment status that qualify as tangible employment actions.

Hostile Environment Harassment

Often, harassment does not directly alter employment status. Instead, it makes it harder for an employee to perform well or remain on the job because of abuse and

[16]29 C.F.R. § 1604.11(a) (2005).

[17]*Burlington Industries v. Ellerth*, 524 U.S. 742 (1998).

[18]*Nichols v. Frank*, 42 F.3d 503 (9th Cir. 1994).

[19]*Jones v. Clinton*, 990 F. Supp. 657, at 672–74 (E.D. Ark. 1998).

intimidation. A **hostile environment** can result from a wide range of verbal conduct, including insults, epithets, tasteless jokes, profanity, and requests for sexual favors; physical conduct, including touching, exposure, staring, stalking, sexual assault, and rape; and displays of images, including pictures, posters, e-mails, Web sites, and pornography. Hostile environments can be created not only by managers and supervisors, but also by coworkers and third parties (e.g., customers and clients). The offensive conduct in sexual harassment claims alleging hostile environments frequently combines both sexual and gender-related content (e.g., requests for sexual favors and telling "dumb blonde" jokes). Hostile environments also often include sexually charged surroundings—for example, frequent sexual banter, use of profanity, posters of scantily clad women—that, while not directed exclusively at the plaintiffs, nonetheless contribute to the abusive and intimidating environments. Most of the allegations in the suit against Caesars Palace—including supervisors attempting to force sex on workers, exposing themselves, making lewd comments, groping workers, and bringing offensive pictures into the workplace—fall into the hostile environment category (see "Clippings").

The law does not mandate that employees be treated in ways that are "nice" or even "civil." Abrasive, insensitive, and boorish behavior is an unfortunate fact of life. The law does not impose "political correctness" in the workplace or expunge all humor, flirting, and the like. However, when workplaces become "abusive" and "hostile" and interfere with employees' ability to perform their jobs, antidiscrimination laws come into play. But how "hostile" must the workplace become before the law is violated?

"Severe or Pervasive" The Supreme Court has stated in several decisions that a hostile environment must be sufficiently **severe or pervasive** to violate Title VII.[20] The victim of harassment need not (as some courts had required) suffer psychological harm for there to be a hostile environment.[21] Conduct that is "physically threatening or humiliating" or that "unreasonably interferes with an employee's work performance" reaches the threshold of a legally actionable hostile environment sooner than "mere offensive utterance[s]."[22] A trade-off exists between severity and pervasiveness, such that conduct that is more severe need not happen often (once is enough for a sexual assault), whereas less severe conduct (e.g., insults) must occur more frequently or over a long period of time to constitute a hostile environment.[23] In the landmark Supreme Court case *Meritor v. Vinson*, the harasser's conduct was both severe and pervasive: A bank vice president raped the plaintiff several times, in addition to following her into the bathroom, fondling her, and repeatedly pressing her to have sex—behavior that went on for several years. Similarly, the executive director of a community services agency asked a female employee whether she knew what a "sexual perpetrator" was, explained in graphic detail how rape is committed, and told her "how easy it is to rape a woman." The director also came into her office, closed the door, and stood uncomfortably close, ignoring requests that he move away. Presented with these and other allegations, the court concluded that "if proven, they establish that plaintiff was required to endure an environment that 'objectively' was *severely* and *pervasively* hostile."[24]

[20]*Meritor v. Vinson*, 477 U.S. 57 (1986); *Oncale*, at 81.

[21]*Harris v. Forklift Systems*, 510 U.S. 17 (1993).

[22]*Harris*, at 23.

[23]*Ellison v. Brady*, 924 F.2d 872, at 878 (9th Cir. 1991).

[24]*Gregory v. Daly & Community Action Agency of Greene Country*, 243 F.3d 687, at 692 (2d Cir. 2001).

Other successful hostile environment claims have involved actions that, viewed individually, were less severe, but in their totality were sufficiently severe or pervasive to be harassment. A hostile environment was found to exist where a coworker repeatedly asked an employee for dates, sent love letters purporting a romantic relationship that did not exist, and hung around her work area.[25] No physical contact occurred between the parties and the coworker's communications were not explicitly sexual, but the pervasive, ongoing nature of his behavior was sufficient to establish a hostile environment. Likewise, an employee whose sexual advances were rebuffed embarked on a campaign of staring at the woman who spurned him. The employee would park his forklift near her work area and stare at her for minutes at a time. This occurred several times each day and lasted for months. The court concluded that she had a valid hostile environment claim.[26] An African-American employee was allowed to proceed to trial on a hostile environment claim based entirely on verbal conduct. The employee alleged a pattern of supervisors using vile racial epithets to refer to himself and other African-American employees. On a daily basis, supervisors used the term "boy" to refer to African-American, but not white, employees. The plaintiff testified that these terms were "'just the way they speak to you at BFI, like you are less than nothing.'"[27]

Paula Jones's numerous allegations against former President Clinton included a hostile environment claim. Because summary judgment was granted for the defense pretrial, her claims remain mere allegations. However, the grant of summary judgment meant that the court viewed her case as legally insufficient to establish a hostile environment (or any other legal violation), even if she had been able to prove that what she said happened really did occur. Jones's hostile environment case rested primarily on events that transpired during a single meeting between herself (a state government employee) and then Governor Clinton in an Arkansas hotel room. According to Jones, Clinton used a state trooper to summon her to his hotel room, took her hand, pulled her toward him, made comments about her hair and body, put his hand on her leg, and attempted to kiss her. She then pulled away from him and sat down in another location closer to the door. Clinton allegedly moved closer again, exposed himself, and suggested oral sex. Jones said that she rebuffed the advance and left the hotel room at that point. Setting the bar for a hostile environment claim relatively high, the court concluded that:

> While the alleged incident in the hotel, if true, was certainly boorish and offensive, the Governor's alleged conduct does not constitute sexual assault. This is thus not one of those exceptional cases in which a single incident of sexual harassment, such as an assault, was deemed sufficient to state a claim of hostile work environment sexual harassment. . . . Considering the totality of the circumstances, it simply cannot be said that the conduct to which Jones was allegedly subjected was frequent, severe, or physically threatening . . . the kind of sustained and nontrivial conduct necessary for a claim of hostile work environment.[28]

A component of racially hostile environments that has appeared with disturbing frequency in recent years is the display of hangman's nooses. As in the Consolidated

[25]*Ellison.*

[26]*Birschstein v. New United Motor Manufacturing, Inc.*, 92 Cal. App. 4th 994 (2001); *rehearing denied*, 2002 Cal. LEXIS 288.

[27]*White v. BFI Waste Services*, 375 F.3d 288, at 297 (4th Cir. 2004) .

[28]*Jones*, at 675.

Freightways case (see "Clippings"), African Americans and other persons of color have been confronted in the workplace with this vicious symbol of a racially segregated past.[29] Harking back to the lynching of African Americans that extended well into the twentieth century, there is nothing innocent or remotely humorous about such displays. *Employers that do not respond to these odious displays with the strongest disciplinary measures are not living up to their responsibilities.*

Hostile environment claims frequently emanate from conduct that occurs outside of the workplace in settings such as business trips, conferences, and parties. One of the more notorious cases of sexual harassment centering on extracurricular activities is the saga of a pharmaceutical company, Astra USA. With CEO Lars Bildman leading the way, female employees were subjected to what can only be termed an organizational culture of sexual harassment. Starting with their initial training and continuing through conferences, regular after-work partying, and out-of-town excursions, female employees were subjected to incessant sexual demands from top managers. A male manager who resigned in disgust said, "If ever there was a company where sexual harassment was rampant, this is it."[30] A female former manager was more blunt: "If they [senior managers] felt like grabbing a woman by the boob or by the ass, that was OK."[31] The party ended when investigations by the EEOC and the press led to dismissal of the top management team. The company settled the EEOC's suit for $10 million.[32]

Although some cases of harassment are obvious, many cases present difficult questions about whether conduct was sufficiently severe or pervasive to be legally actionable. Determining whether a hostile environment existed is primarily an objective assessment based on whether a **reasonable person** would experience the circumstances as offensive, intimidating, or abusive. That is, would a person of average intelligence and sensitivity feel that the challenged conduct was harassment? Some courts maintain that the existence of a hostile environment should be ascertained using a "reasonable woman" or "reasonable victim of the same sex as the plaintiff" standard.[33] The argument is that men and women tend to view the same conduct differently. Actions seen as innocuous by persons of one sex might be threatening to persons of the other sex. The Supreme Court has not squarely addressed this issue, but consistent references to "reasonable person" in its decisions suggest that it does not view adopting a gendered perspective as the appropriate way to decide whether a hostile environment exists.

A hostile environment can exist even when the objectionable behaviors and surroundings are not directed specifically at the plaintiff. Offensive pictures, grafitti, or constant banter of a sexual nature can form the basis of hostile environment claims, even though the harassment is not targeted at individual victims. The case against the producers of *Friends* (see "Clippings") is interesting to consider in this context. A former writers' assistant for the show has sued based on the admittedly raunchy, sexually explicit verbal conduct of coworkers. If accepted, the "creative necessity" defense offered by the studio implies that the definition of a hostile

[29]Sana Siwolop. "Nooses, Symbols of Race Hatred, at Center of Workplace Lawsuits." *New York Times* (July 10, 2000), A-1.

[30]Mark Maremont. "Abuse of Power: The Astonishing Tale of Sexual Harassment at Astra USA." *Business Week* (May 13, 1996), 88.

[31]Maremont, 87.

[32]Kenneth N. Gilpin. "Firm to Pay $10 Million in Settlement of Sex Case." *New York Times* (February 6, 1998), A-10.

[33]*Ellison,* at 878–79.

environment and the right of employees to be free from harassment varies depending on the type of work and industry involved. The contrary view was articulated by a court stating that "We do not believe that a woman who chooses to work in the male-dominated trades relinquishes her right to be free from sexual harassment. . . . [W]omen working in the trades do not deserve less protection from the law than women working in a courthouse."[34] However, the Supreme Court has stated that determinating whether a hostile environment exists ". . . requires careful consideration of the social context in which particular behavior occurs and is experienced by its target."[35]

In *Petrosino v. Bell Atlantic,* general workplace conditions constitute a significant part of the alleged hostile environment.

[34]*Williams v. General Motors,* 187 F.3d 553, at 564 (6th Cir. 1999).

[35]*Oncale,* at 81.

PETROSINO V. BELL ATLANTIC
385 F.3d 210 (2d Cir. 2004)

● ● ●

OPINION BY CIRCUIT JUDGE RAGGI:

* * * From September 1990 until February 1999, Lisa Petrosino was employed by Bell Atlantic as an Installation and Repairs ("I&R") technician at its Edgewater Garage on Staten Island, New York. For the last seven years of her employment, she was the only female I&R technician at the Edgewater Garage. Petrosino's work consisted of installing and repairing residential and commercial telephone systems, cables, and support systems on Staten Island, both within buildings and on telephone poles. Each morning, Petrosino and her co-workers would meet at the garage with their supervisors for approximately half an hour, during which time they received the day's assignments. Occasional interaction with co-workers and supervisors would also occur throughout the day. Petrosino asserts that throughout her employment at Bell Atlantic's Edgewater Garage, she was subjected to a work environment hostile to women. The hostility took two forms: (1) persistent sexually offensive remarks and sexual graffiti that conveyed a low regard for women, and (2) specific comments or actions toward Petrosino that made plain that this negative view of women extended to her and to her work performance.

Petrosino has adduced evidence demonstrating that the work environment at the Edgewater Garage was more reminiscent of a locker room than a place of business. Profanity was commonplace, and crude humor was routine. But the focus of Petrosino's complaint is not on this conduct but on the sexually demeaning conversations that were also an accepted part of the daily work environment. Although male co-workers often insulted each other in these exchanges, the substance of their remarks always conveyed a profound disrespect for women. Further, when working outdoors, Petrosino would constantly confront crude sexual graffiti scrawled by co-workers inside terminal boxes. Among the images depicted were headless women with their legs in the air, women's legs wide open, men with their penises out, and men having sex with animals. A further theme of the graffiti was that Bell Atlantic employees (male and female) performed sex acts on supervisors to advance their careers.

Petrosino's co-workers made plain that she was not exempted from the generally low view of women communicated by the sexually offensive garage banter and terminal-box graffiti. A few months after she began working at Bell Atlantic, at a December 1990 Christmas party, Petrosino was physically attacked from behind in a parking lot by co-worker Charles Degenhardt, who groped and kissed her. When Petrosino shouted for help, other employees pulled Degenhardt away, but for months thereafter, the incident was a "big joke" at the garage and the subject of terminal-box graffiti. In the ensuing years, frequent disparaging remarks were made with reference to Petrosino's "ass,"

her "tits," her menstrual cycle, her weight, and her eating habits, and at least one terminal-box drawing depicted her performing a sex act on a supervisor. Further, the disparagement was not limited to private exchanges, but extended to supervisors' comments relating to her job performance.

For example, Petrosino's direct supervisor from 1990 to 1992, Robert Sharib, punctuated his conversations with her with hostile gender-based comments, referring to Petrosino as "a damn woman," telling her to calm her "big tits down," and dismissing her job concerns as attributable to her menstrual cycle. . . . On one occasion, Sharib humiliated Petrosino by taking a doctor's note that she had brought to work, enlarging it to poster size, and displaying it in the office. Petrosino also points to gender-hostile remarks by Tom Archdecon, her second- and third-level manager throughout her employment at Bell Atlantic. In discussions with Petrosino about her work, Archdecon not only told her that as an individual, she was "too thin-skinned" to belong in her work assignment, he cast this observation "all the time" in gender-wide terms, stating that women as a group were too "simple," "too sensitive," and "too damn thin-skinned" to work at the garage. Over the years, several first-level managers told Petrosino that she would never be permitted to assume managerial responsibilities as long as Archdecon was an I&R supervisor.

Archdecon's gender hostility toward Petrosino was echoed by Frank Mangiero, Petrosino's direct supervisor from 1996 to 1997. On "many occasions," he called her "a damn woman" and told her that if she could not handle working in I&R, "maybe women can't handle it." * * * Mangiero repeatedly cited Petrosino for minor job infractions, such as using a company vehicle to get coffee for another supervisor and playing her truck radio too loudly, without similarly reporting male employees. He made her repeat tasks unnecessarily. On one occasion, he refused Petrosino's request to use a bucket truck to perform an assignment safely, only to allow a male worker to use the truck when the task was reassigned to him.

Petrosino asserts that throughout her employment she complained informally and formally about the gender-hostile environment at the Edgewater Garage. For example, she repeatedly told co-workers and supervisors that she found the constant sexual banter at the garage offensive and demeaning, but no steps were ever taken to address the problem. To the contrary, offending workers ridiculed her concerns by offering sarcastic

apologies, only to persist thereafter in their vulgar exchanges. In 1992, Petrosino filed a labor grievance charging Robert Sharib with harassment. Although she prevailed, she asserts no actual discipline was imposed. Instead, Sharib and Petrosino were sent to a seminar to help them work out their differences. When Petrosino attempted to use the opportunity to voice her concerns, Sharib told her: "Just keep your mouth shut and do what I tell you." * * *

Sometime in 1997 or 1998, a female administrative manager asked Petrosino why she no longer worked overtime. Petrosino explained that she avoided overtime to "stay away" from her then-supervisor, Mangiero, who "harassed [her] and bothered [her]." Petrosino asserts that no one at Bell Atlantic pursued the matter. Some months later, in May 1997, Petrosino called Bell Atlantic's Ethics Hotline to complain formally that Mangiero harassed her because she was the only female in his group. Petrosino's request to discuss her concerns with a female counselor was rebuffed, and no one from Bell Atlantic ever followed up on this complaint. * * *

An aggrieved employee wishing to bring a Title VII claim in district court must file an administrative complaint with the EEOC within 300 days of the alleged discriminatory act. Petrosino filed her discrimination charge with the EEOC on April 13, 1999; thus, the limitations period in her case began 300 days earlier, on June 17, 1998. When, as in this case, a plaintiff's allegations of discrimination extend beyond the 300-day limitations period, the nature of the claim determines what consideration will be given to the earlier conduct. For example, in the case of a hostile work environment claim, the statute of limitations requires that only one sexually harassing act demonstrating the challenged work environment occur within 300 days of filing; once that is shown, a court and jury may consider "the entire time period of the hostile environment" in determining liability. * * *

In *Meritor Savings Bank, FSB v. Vinson*, the Supreme Court made plain that Title VII's prohibition of sex discrimination extends to sexual harassment. "Sexual harassment includes 'conduct [that] has the purpose or effect of unreasonably interfering with an individual's work performance or creating an intimidating, hostile, or offensive working environment.'" To prevail on a claim of sexual harassment based on a hostile work environment, a plaintiff must establish two elements: "'(1) that the workplace was permeated with discriminatory intimidation that was sufficiently severe

or pervasive to alter the conditions of [his or] her work environment, and (2) that a specific basis exists for imputing the conduct that created the hostile environment to the employer.'"

The first element of a hostile work environment claim has both an objective and subjective component: "the misconduct must be severe or pervasive enough to create an objectively hostile or abusive work environment, and the victim must also subjectively perceive that environment to be abusive." In this case, Bell Atlantic does not contest that Petrosino subjectively experienced her work environment as hostile. Thus, we focus on whether Petrosino's work environment could objectively be deemed hostile to women.

The district court concluded that no jury could reasonably find Petrosino's work environment objectively hostile to women. In so ruling, it decided, first, that evidence of incessant sexually offensive exchanges at the daily assignment meeting and omnipresent sexual graffiti in the terminal boxes could not support Petrosino's claim, because this conduct, while "undeniably boorish and offensive," was not "motivated by hostility toward Petrosino because of her sex." Rather, it applied equally to all employees, male and female. Second, the district court concluded that the remaining alleged incidents of harassment, even when viewed as a whole, were insufficiently severe or pervasive to establish a sexually discriminatory hostile work environment. We disagree.

Title VII prohibits "discrimination . . . because of . . . sex." Thus, a work "environment which is equally harsh for both men and women" cannot support a claim for sex discrimination. The mere fact that men and women are both exposed to the same offensive circumstances on the job site, however, does not mean that, as a matter of law, their work conditions are necessarily equally harsh. The objective hostility of a work environment depends on the totality of the circumstances. Further, the perspective from which the evidence must be assessed is that of a "reasonable person in the plaintiff's position, considering all the circumstances [including] the social context in which particular behavior occurs and is experienced by its target." There is some ambiguity in our case law as to whether, in a case such as this, a "reasonable person in the plaintiff's position" must be a woman or a person drawn from the public at large. In fact, we need not choose between these two options because we conclude that the evidence in this case, viewed in the light most favorable to Petrosino, would permit a jury to conclude that a reasonable person, regardless of gender, would

consider the sexually offensive comments and graffiti here at issue more offensive to women than to men and, therefore, discriminatory based on sex.

The comments and graphics that permeated Petrosino's work environment may have sexually ridiculed both men and women, but there is an important, though not surprising, distinction. The conduct at issue sexually ridiculed some men, but it also frequently touted the sexual exploits of others. In short, the insults were directed at certain men, not men as a group. By contrast, the depiction of women in the offensive jokes and graphics was uniformly sexually demeaning and communicated the message that women as a group were available for sexual exploitation by men. Such workplace disparagement of women, repeated day after day over the course of several years without supervisory intervention, stands as a serious impediment to any woman's efforts to deal professionally with her male colleagues.

The fact that much of this offensive material was not directed specifically at Petrosino—indeed, her male coworkers would likely have traded sexual insults every morning and defaced terminal boxes with sexual graffiti regardless of Petrosino's presence in the I&R department—does not, as a matter of law, preclude a jury from finding that the conduct subjected Petrosino to a hostile work environment based on her sex. Indeed, the Fourth Circuit . . . recently reached this same conclusion in a case involving a work environment strikingly similar to that alleged by Petrosino: an all-male production shop (except for the female plaintiff) suffused with "sex-laden and sexist talk and conduct." The employer contended that the offensive conduct could not be deemed discriminatory based on sex "because it could have been heard [or seen] by anyone present in the shop and was equally offensive to some of the men." The court disagreed, concluding that a jury could find "much of the conduct . . . particularly offensive to women and . . . intended to provoke [plaintiff's] reaction as a woman." * * * In sum, although all Bell Atlantic employees at the Edgewater Garage were routinely exposed to sexually offensive language and graphics, we conclude that a reasonable jury could find this conduct more demeaning of women than men

In reviewing the totality of the evidence adduced by Petrosino in support of her hostile work environment claim, we are mindful that Title VII does not establish a "general civility code" for the American workplace. Simple teasing, offhand comments, or isolated incidents of offensive conduct (unless extremely serious) will not

support a claim of discriminatory harassment. To defeat Bell Atlantic's motion for summary judgment, Petrosino must adduce evidence sufficient to permit a reasonable jury to conclude that her workplace was "permeated with 'discriminatory intimidation, ridicule, and insult,' that [was] 'sufficiently severe or pervasive to alter the conditions of [her] employment.'" As we have already observed, a reasonable jury could conclude that the persistent sexually offensive remarks at the Edgewater Garage and the graffiti at outdoor work sites were particularly insulting to women because these actions cast women in a demeaning role: as objects of sex-based ridicule and subjects for sexual exploitation. It is within this context that the remaining evidence of sexual harassment must be considered. In this light, Petrosino's sexual assault by a drunken co-worker within a few months of joining the I&R department might well be viewed by a reasonable jury not simply as an isolated incident but as a tangible extension of the pervasive demeaning talk to Petrosino personally. The assault communicated to Petrosino that she was perceived, at least by one co-worker, not as a professional colleague, but as one more woman available for sexual exploitation. The fact that for some time thereafter Petrosino's male co-workers treated the assault as a subject for office jokes and graffiti only reinforced this perception. Similarly, the men's sarcastic apologies when Petrosino attempted to limit their sexually offensive exchanges support an inference that they were deliberately attempting "to provoke [her] reaction as a woman." Further, the link the men—including supervisors—routinely drew between their perceptions

of Petrosino's professional defects and her anatomy, especially their vulgar references to her breasts and menstrual cycle, likewise communicated that her gender would always stand as a bar to full acceptance within the workplace. Indeed, Petrosino's work concerns were routinely dismissed in gender-based terms: she, like all women, was simply too "thin-skinned" and "sensitive" to work successfully in I&R. * * *

Accordingly, we reverse the award of summary judgment to Bell Atlantic on Petrosino's claim of sexual harassment in the form of a hostile work environment and remand this portion of the case for trial.

CASE QUESTIONS

1. What is the legal issue in this case? What did the court decide?

2. Why is Petrosino able to base her case on events, some of which occurred more than 300 days before she filed a charge with the EEOC?

3. Because other employees, primarily males, were exposed to the same verbal conduct and pictures, why does the court conclude that these conditions were discriminatory toward women?

4. Why does the court conclude that a jury could reasonably find that the harassment was sufficiently severe or pervasive to constitute a hostile environment?

5. Why do you think that Petrosino's coworkers and supervisors acted as they did? What should Bell Atlantic have done about it?

Rampant sexual favoritism on the part of supervisors or managers might also provide the basis for a hostile environment claim. In one such case, the supervisor of a correctional facility was having sexual affairs with several female employees. The supervisor gave promotions, favorable work assignments, and other privileges to these women. The perception became widespread among employees of the facility that the only way to get ahead was to have an affair with the supervisor. A female employee who was subsequently assaulted by one of the supervisor's girlfriends (the supervisor declined to investigate the incident or discipline the offender) sued for sexual harassment. The California Supreme Court, relying heavily on EEOC regulations that recognize widespread sexual favoritism (as opposed to isolated instances of preferential treatment extended to a girlfriend or "paramour") as a valid basis for a hostile environment claim, ruled for the plaintiff. Even though the supervisor did not request sexual favors from or verbally harass the plaintiff herself, "the demeaning message is conveyed to female employees that they are viewed by management as 'sexual playthings' or that the way required for women to get ahead

in the workplace is by engaging in sexual conduct with their supervisors or the management."[36]

When Are Harassing Behaviors Unwelcome?

Individuals can view the same situations very differently. Verbal and physical conduct that would otherwise constitute egregious harassment might be entirely welcomed when engaged in by two employees who are lovers or even just friends who routinely tease one another. Although the principal focus in harassment cases is on the "objective" existence of harassment viewed through the eyes of the hypothetical reasonable person, plaintiffs also must show that they subjectively perceived their treatment as **unwelcome** harassment. Harassing conduct is unwelcome when the person complaining of the conduct did not solicit or provoke it and that person regarded the conduct as offensive and unwanted (at the time at which it occurred).[37]

A circumstance that can cause the unwelcomeness of conduct to be questioned is when an employee fails to tell the harasser and/or the employer that the conduct is offensive or waits a long time before reporting the conduct. Victims of harassment are not always required to confront their harassers (sometimes they are well advised not to do so). Nor must they always report harassment to their employer to establish that the conduct is unwelcome (establishing employer *liability* for harassment is a separate matter that is discussed later). Some contemporaneous indication of unwelcomeness, even if nonverbal (e.g., appearing disgusted at the harasser's statements, taking obvious steps to avoid the harasser), however, is important to the plaintiff's case. Another problematic situation occurs when a prior romantic relationship goes sour, and a party that no longer desires to maintain the relationship continues to be pursued by the other party. It is particularly important in these cases that the person who no longer desires romantic attention clearly notify the other person of this and act accordingly.

Employers seeking to defend harassment claims also sometimes argue that any harassment was not unwelcome because the "victim" provoked or actively participated in the harassment. An employee's own salty language, flirting, pranks, and even sexually provocative dress and appearance[38] can provide indications that the individual was an active participant in, rather than a victim of, harassment. The harassment claim of a woman who, in the words of the court, "displayed a remarkable lust for those of the opposite sex" failed on these grounds.[39] This individual's antics included displaying her body through seminude photos, lifting her skirt to verify an absence of undergarments, making highly salacious comments, and offering sexual gratification "to employees, customers, and competitors alike" (the court wryly notes that there was "uncontroverted evidence of acceptance of her offers"). The court stopped little short of declaring the plaintiff unharassable in ruling against her:

> From plaintiff's character, it is apparent that she would have welcomed rather than rejected Manning's [her supervisor's] advance, if he did indeed do so. But the court finds that Manning made no sexual advance. * * * . . . [p]laintiff was not subjected to any unwelcome sexual harassment.

[36]*Miller v. Department of Corrections,* 2005 Cal. LEXIS 7606, at 3.

[37]Equal Employment Opportunity Commission. "Policy Guidance on Current Issues of Sexual Harassment." No. N-915-050 (March 19, 1990).

[38]*Meritor,* at 61.

[39]*McLean v. Satellite Technology Services, Inc.,* 673 F. Supp. 1458, at 1459 (E.D. Mo. 1987).

Indeed, . . . [she] bears the responsibility for whatever sexually suggestive conduct is involved in this case.[40]

Although this case featured a decidedly unsympathetic plaintiff, it treads on dangerous ground, lest the requirement that harassment be unwelcome become an occasion for judicial moralizing and denying employees the protection of the law on that basis. It is only conduct that involves the workplace—and principally conduct with respect to the alleged harasser—that is relevant in determining unwelcomeness. The fact that someone has a reputation in the workplace, however well-founded, for being "easy" does not mean that the person welcomes the sexual advances of any particular individual. Nor does conduct off the job generally have any bearing on sexual harassment claims in the workplace. In the case of a woman who had posed nude in a "biker" magazine, the court concluded:

> The plaintiff's choice to pose for a nude magazine outside work hours is not material to the issue of whether plaintiff found her employer's work-related conduct offensive. This is not a case where Burns posed in provocative and suggestive ways at work. Her private life, regardless how reprehensible the trier of fact might find it to be, did not provide lawful acquiescence to unwanted sexual advances at her work place by her employer.[41]

Nor is an employee's voluntary or consensual participation in sexual activity necessarily fatal to her harassment claim. The fact that a plaintiff had consensual sex with her harasser some 40 or 50 times over a period of several years did not negate her hostile environment claim when she was able to credibly claim that she did so out of fear of losing her job. The Supreme Court explained that "the fact that sex-related conduct was 'voluntary,' in the sense that the complainant was not forced to participate against her will, is not a defense to a sexual harassment suit brought under Title VII. The gravamen [core requirement] of any sexual harassment claim is that the alleged sexual advances were 'unwelcome.'"[42] Welcomeness and voluntariness are distinct matters.

LIABILITY FOR HARASSMENT

Protecting employees from harassment presents particular problems for employers because harassment often occurs at times and places where supervision or monitoring by others is absent. The law takes into account the fact that employers are not omniscient. The grounds for attributing liability to employers for harassment differ depending on the type of harassment (i.e., whether or not the harassment results in a tangible employment action) and the organizational position of the harasser (i.e., top official, manager, nonsupervisory employee). Table 9-1 outlines the differing standards for employer liability based on these two factors.

Harassment by Top Officials, Managers, and Supervisors

When harassment is engaged in by someone whose position essentially allows him or her to speak and act for the company—for example, an owner, president, partner, or corporate officer—the company is liable for the harassment. This is true regardless

[40]*McLean*, at 1460.

[41]*Burns v. McGregor Electronic Industries, Inc.*, 989 F.2d 959, at 963 (8th Cir. 1993).

[42]*Meritor*, at 68.

TABLE 9-1 Employer Liability for Harassment

	Type of Harassment	
Position of Harasser	Results in a Tangible Employment Action	No Tangible Employment Action (Hostile Environment)
Top officials	Vicarious liability	Vicarious liability
Managers, supervisors	Vicarious liability	Vicarious liability subject to affirmative defense
Nonsupervisory employees, third parties	NA	Negligence standard for liability

of the type of harassment. The liability is **vicarious**, meaning that if the illegal action occurred, legal responsibility for damages (liability) is automatically and unconditionally placed with the employing organization.

Vicarious liability is the norm in discrimination cases. If a manager discriminates against older workers when deciding whom to lay off, the company is liable for that discrimination, regardless of whether owners or top managers were aware of the practice or encouraged it in any way. In harassment cases, the general rule of vicarious liability for discrimination is adhered to when the harassment results in a tangible employment action. If a manager or supervisor uses the decision-making authority that has been conferred upon him to try to exact sexual favors and then makes employment decisions accordingly, the employer is vicariously liable. Even though the supervisor or manager is likely acting outside of the scope of his employment in doing so, he is still an agent of the employer and aided in carrying out the harassment by being given the authority to make employment decisions.

Sometimes, managers or supervisors engage in harassment that does not result in tangible employment actions. In one such case,[43] supervisors created a hostile environment for the female lifeguards that they supervised, but did not alter their employment status in any way. In another case, a mid-level manager made sexual advances and implied that the employee's life at the company would be affected by her response. However, the manager did not follow through on his threat after the employee rebuffed his advances. When harassment by managers and supervisors does not result in tangible employment actions, employers can avoid vicarious liability by establishing the following **affirmative defense:**[44]

1. The employer exercised reasonable care to prevent and correct promptly any harassment.

and

2. The plaintiff unreasonably failed to take advantage of any preventive or corrective opportunities provided by the employer or to avoid harm otherwise.

[43]*Faragher v. City of Boca Raton*, 524 U.S. 775 (1998).
[44]*Ellerth*, at 765.

Whether "reasonable care" is exercised depends on such things as the existence of a sound **harassment policy** and **complaint procedure,** an effective investigative process, and other measures designed to prevent or remedy harassment (e.g., training). Employers also need to show that they acted reasonably promptly in responding to employee complaints. In the case involving the harassment of lifeguards by their supervisors, the Supreme Court concluded that the city could not establish the first prong of the affirmative defense because it had completely overlooked beach employees when it distributed its harassment policy, it made no efforts to monitor the supervisors, and it did not provide the employees with a clear alternative to complaining to the same supervisors that were perpetrating the harassment. In contrast, a female sales representative's hostile environment claim based on harassment by her supervisor failed because the company had taken reasonable care to prevent harassment. Specifically, the employer had a written antiharassment policy, the policy was published in the employee handbook and reinforced by an annual letter sent to all employees, training was provided to both supervisors and employees, her complaint was responded to promptly, the offending supervisor was immediately placed on administrative leave and later fired, a thorough investigation was launched, and multiple interviews were conducted with the involved parties.[45] In another case involving the affirmative defense, the employer responded to an employee's allegations of harassment by a manager at a Christmas party by launching a prompt investigation, suspending the manager pending the outcome of the investigation, and terminating the manager six days later. The court said that the employer's actions "epitomized how a responsible employer should act when confronted with an allegation of employment discrimination."[46]

Employees also have responsibility under this scheme. If the employer shows that the employee did not use the complaint procedure provided and there was no good reason for this failure (e.g., reasonable fear of retaliation), the employer may be able to establish the second prong of the affirmative defense. This was the fate of a campus police officer who waited seven months to use the university's formal complaint procedure, during which time she had attempted to resolve the harassment problem informally.[47] The case of the sales representative mentioned earlier also failed because she waited three months after the first incident of harassment to report it to the company, a delay that the court deemed an unreasonable failure to take advantage of corrective opportunities.

To determine employer liability for harassment engaged in by supervisors and managers, courts first have to decide whether the harassment resulted in a tangible employment action and, if it did not, whether the requirements of the affirmative defense were met. Both of these can be difficult calls to make. For example, victims of harassment commonly become disgusted and quit their jobs, particularly when employers are unresponsive to their complaints. Courts sometimes treat a resignation as a termination when the circumstances prompting the person to quit would be intolerable to a reasonable person. Is a compelled resignation—a "constructive discharge"—a tangible employment action? The Supreme Court addresses this question in *Pennsylvania State Police v. Suders.* Notice how the Court's decision is tied to the underlying logic for distinguishing tangible employment action cases for purposes of assigning liability to employers.

[45]*Walton v. Johnson & Johnson Services, Inc.,* 2002 U.S. Dist. LEXIS 9741, at 26–30; *affirmed,* 347 F.3d 1272 (11th Cir. 2003); *cert. denied,* 541 U.S. 959 (2004).

[46]*Collette v. Stein-Mart,* 2005 U.S. App. LEXIS 2093, at 23.

[47]*Gawley v. Indiana University,* 2001 U.S. App. LEXIS 27353.

PENNSYLVANIA STATE POLICE V. SUDERS
2004 U.S. LEXIS 4176

OPINION BY JUSTICE GINSBURG:

Plaintiff-respondent Nancy Drew Suders alleged sexually harassing conduct by her supervisors, officers of the Pennsylvania State Police (PSP), of such severity she was forced to resign. The question presented concerns the proof burdens parties bear when a sexual harassment/constructive discharge claim of that character is asserted under Title VII of the Civil Rights Act of 1964. * * *

In March 1998, the PSP hired Suders as a police communications operator for the McConnellsburg barracks. Suders' supervisors were Sergeant Eric D. Easton, Station Commander at the McConnellsburg barracks, Patrol Corporal William D. Baker, and Corporal Eric B. Prendergast. Those three supervisors subjected Suders to a continuous barrage of sexual harassment that ceased only when she resigned from the force. Easton "would bring up [the subject of] people having sex with animals" each time Suders entered his office. He told Prendergast, in front of Suders, that young girls should be given instruction in how to gratify men with oral sex. Easton also would sit down near Suders, wearing spandex shorts, and spread his legs apart. Apparently imitating a move popularized by television wrestling, Baker repeatedly made an obscene gesture in Suders' presence by grabbing his genitals and shouting out a vulgar comment inviting oral sex. Baker made this gesture as many as five-to-ten times per night throughout Suders' employment at the barracks. Suders once told Baker she "'d[id]n't think [he] should be doing this'"; Baker responded by jumping on a chair and again performing the gesture, with the accompanying vulgarity. Further, Baker would "rub his rear end in front of her and remark 'I have a nice ass, don't I?'" Prendergast told Suders "'the village idiot could do her job'"; wearing black gloves, he would pound on furniture to intimidate her.

In June 1998, Prendergast accused Suders of taking a missing accident file home with her. After that incident, Suders approached the PSP's Equal Employment Opportunity Officer, Virginia Smith-Elliott, and told her she "might need some help." Smith-Elliott gave Suders her telephone number, but neither woman followed up on the conversation. On August 18, 1998, Suders contacted Smith-Elliott again, this time stating that she was being harassed and was afraid. Smith-Elliott told Suders to file a complaint, but did not tell her how to obtain the necessary form. Smith-Elliott's response and the manner in which it was conveyed appeared to Suders insensitive and unhelpful.

Two days later, Suders' supervisors arrested her for theft, and Suders resigned from the force. The theft arrest occurred in the following circumstances. Suders had several times taken a computer-skills exam to satisfy a PSP job requirement. Each time, Suders' supervisors told her that she had failed. Suders one day came upon her exams in a set of drawers in the women's locker room. She concluded that her supervisors had never forwarded the tests for grading and that their reports of her failures were false. Regarding the tests as her property, Suders removed them from the locker room. Upon finding that the exams had been removed, Suders' supervisors devised a plan to arrest her for theft. The officers dusted the drawer in which the exams had been stored with a theft-detection powder that turns hands blue when touched. As anticipated by Easton, Baker, and Prendergast, Suders attempted to return the tests to the drawer, whereupon her hands turned telltale blue. The supervisors then apprehended and handcuffed her, photographed her blue hands, and commenced to question her. Suders had previously prepared a written resignation, which she tendered soon after the supervisors detained her. Nevertheless, the supervisors initially refused to release her. Instead, they brought her to an interrogation room, gave her warnings under *Miranda* v. *Arizona,* and continued to question her. Suders reiterated that she wanted to resign, and Easton then let her leave. The PSP never brought theft charges against her.

In September 2000, Suders sued the PSP in Federal District Court, alleging, . . . that she had been subjected to sexual harassment and constructively discharged, in violation of Title VII of the Civil Rights Act of 1964. At the close of discovery, the District Court granted the PSP's motion for summary judgment. Suders' testimony, the District Court recognized, sufficed to permit a trier of fact to conclude that the supervisors had created a hostile work environment. The court nevertheless held that the PSP was not vicariously liable for the supervisors' conduct. * * *

The Court of Appeals for the Third Circuit reversed and remanded the case for disposition on the merits. The Third Circuit agreed with the District Court that Suders had presented evidence sufficient for a trier of fact to conclude that the supervisors had engaged in a "pattern of sexual harassment that was pervasive and regular." But the appeals court disagreed with the District Court in two fundamental respects. First, the Court of Appeals held that . . . , genuine issues of material fact existed concerning the effectiveness of the PSP's "program . . . to address sexual harassment claims." Second, the appeals court held that the District Court erred in failing to recognize that Suders had stated a claim of constructive discharge due to the hostile work environment.

A plaintiff alleging constructive discharge in violation of Title VII, the Court of Appeals stated, must establish:

"(1) he or she suffered harassment or discrimination so intolerable that a reasonable person in the same position would have felt compelled to resign . . . ; and (2) the employee's reaction to the workplace situation—that is, his or her decision to resign—was reasonable given the totality of circumstances. . . ." * * *

The Court of Appeals then made the ruling challenged here: It held that "a constructive discharge, when proved, constitutes a tangible employment action." Under *Ellerth* and *Faragher*, [two 1998 Supreme Court decisions addressing the standard for determining employer liability when the harasser is a supervisor or manager] the court observed, such an action renders an employer strictly liable and precludes employer recourse to the affirmative defense announced in those decisions. . . . The Third Circuit reasoned that a constructive discharge "'constitutes a significant change in employment status' by ending the employer-employee relationship" and "also inflicts the same type of 'direct economic harm'" as the tangible employment actions *Ellerth* and *Faragher* offered by way of example (discharge, demotion, undesirable reassignment). Satisfied that Suders had "raised genuine issues of material fact as to her claim of constructive discharge," the Court of Appeals remanded Suders' Title VII claim for trial. This Court granted certiorari to resolve the disagreement among the Circuits on the question whether a constructive discharge brought about by supervisor harassment ranks as a tangible employment action and therefore precludes assertion of the affirmative defense articulated in *Ellerth* and *Faragher*. * * *

[W]e turn to the key issues here at stake: Into which *Ellerth/Faragher* category do hostile-environment constructive discharge claims fall—and what proof burdens do the parties bear in such cases. In *Ellerth* and *Faragher*, the plaintiffs-employees sought to hold their employers vicariously liable for sexual harassment by their supervisors, even though the plaintiffs "suffer[ed] no adverse, tangible job consequences." Setting out a framework for employer liability in those decisions, this Court noted that Title VII's definition of "employer" includes the employer's "agent[s]," We viewed that definition as a direction to "interpret Title VII based on agency principles." * * * [A]n employer is liable for the acts of its agent when the agent "'was aided in accomplishing the tort by the existence of the agency relation.'" We then identified "a class of cases where, beyond question, more than the mere existence of the employment relation aids in commission of the harassment: when a supervisor takes a tangible employment action against the subordinate." A tangible employment action, the Court explained, "constitutes a significant change in employment status, such as hiring, firing, failing to promote, reassignment with significantly different responsibilities, or a decision causing a significant change in benefits." Unlike injuries that could equally be inflicted by a co-worker, we stated, tangible employment actions "fall within the special province of the supervisor," who "has been empowered by the company as . . . [an] agent to make economic decisions affecting other employees under his or her control." The tangible employment action, the Court elaborated, is, in essential character, "an official act of the enterprise, a company act." It is "the means by which the supervisor brings the official power of the enterprise to bear on subordinates." Often, the supervisor will "use [the company's] internal processes" and thereby "obtain the imprimatur of the enterprise." Ordinarily, the tangible employment decision "is documented in official company records, and may be subject to review by higher level supervisors." In sum, we stated, "when a supervisor takes a tangible employment action against a subordinate[,] . . . it would be implausible to interpret agency principles to allow an employer to escape liability."

When a supervisor's harassment of a subordinate does not culminate in a tangible employment action, the Court next explained, it is "less obvious" that the agency relation is the driving force. We acknowledged that a supervisor's "power and authority invests his or her harassing conduct with a particular threatening

character, and in this sense, a supervisor always is aided by the agency relation." But we also recognized that "there are acts of harassment a supervisor might commit which might be the same acts a coemployee would commit, and there may be some circumstances where the supervisor's status [would] mak[e] little difference." . . . The Court reasoned that tying the liability standard to an employer's effort to install effective grievance procedures would advance Congress' purpose "to promote conciliation rather than litigation" of Title VII controversies. At the same time, such linkage of liability limitation to effective preventive and corrective measures could serve Title VII's deterrent purpose by "encourag[ing] employees to report harassing conduct before it becomes severe or pervasive." Accordingly, we held that when no tangible employment action is taken, the employer may defeat vicarious liability for supervisor harassment by establishing, as an affirmative defense, both that "the employer exercised reasonable care to prevent and correct promptly any sexually harassing behavior," and that "the plaintiff employee unreasonably failed to take advantage of any preventive or corrective opportunities provided by the employer or to avoid harm otherwise." * * *

Unlike an actual termination, which is *always* effected through an official act of the company, a constructive discharge need not be. A constructive discharge involves both an employee's decision to leave and precipitating conduct: The former involves no official action; the latter, like a harassment claim without any constructive discharge assertion, may or may not involve official action. * * * To be sure, a constructive discharge is functionally the same as an actual termination in damages-enhancing respects. As the Third Circuit observed, both "en[d] the employer-employee relationship," and both "inflic[t] . . . direct economic harm." But when an official act does not underlie the constructive discharge, the *Ellerth* and *Faragher* analysis, we here hold, calls for extension of the affirmative defense to the employer. As those leading decisions indicate, official directions and declarations are the acts most likely to be brought home to the employer, the measures over which the employer can exercise

greatest control. Absent "an official act of the enterprise" as the last straw, the employer ordinarily would have no particular reason to suspect that a resignation is not the typical kind daily occurring in the work force. . . . [A]n official act reflected in company records—a demotion or a reduction in compensation, for example—shows "beyond question" that the supervisor has used his managerial or controlling position to the employee's disadvantage. Absent such an official act, the extent to which the supervisor's misconduct has been aided by the agency relation, is less certain. That uncertainty . . . justifies affording the employer the chance to establish, through the *Ellerth/Faragher* affirmative defense, that it should not be held vicariously liable. * * *

We agree with the Third Circuit that the case, in its current posture, presents genuine issues of material fact concerning Suders' hostile work environment and constructive discharge claims. We hold, however, that the Court of Appeals erred in declaring the affirmative defense described in *Ellerth* and *Faragher* never available in constructive discharge cases. Accordingly, we vacate the Third Circuit's judgment and remand the case for further proceedings consistent with this opinion.

CASE QUESTIONS

1. What was the legal issue in this case? What did the Supreme Court decide?

2. Why does the Court distinguish between harassment cases that involve tangible employment actions and those that do not for purposes of assigning liability to employers?

3. From the facts outlined in the case, does it appear that Suders was subjected to a hostile environment? Why or why not? That she was constructively discharged? Why or why not?

4. If the affirmative defense is available in this case, would the employer be able to establish it? Why or why not? Should the employer be held liable for any harassment that Suders experienced? Why or why not?

Holly D. v. California Institute of Technology is another interesting case in which a court had to decide whether the affirmative defense was available and whether the employer met its burden in establishing the defense.

HOLLY D. V. CALIFORNIA INSTITUTE OF TECHNOLOGY
339 F.3d 1158 (9th Cir. 2003)

OPINION BY CIRCUIT JUDGE REINHARDT:

* * * Plaintiff Holly D., a working mother who suffered from depression as well as from serious financial difficulties, . . . was promoted to Senior Division Assistant for Professor Stephen Wiggins. . . . As with all such transfers in the Caltech system, this move entailed a six-month probationary period, which lasted until April 1997. Less than a year after Holly D.'s transfer, she and Professor Wiggins allegedly commenced a sexual relationship. According to Holly D.: During the probationary period, Wiggins occasionally looked at her buttocks and breasts. Also, he sometimes made sexual comments, including references to his preferences with respect to various forms of sexual activity, and on occasion showed her pornographic websites—although he would eventually cease these activities when Holly D. told him that she was not interested. During the same period, Wiggins criticized Holly D.'s work and threatened to extend her probationary period, perhaps indefinitely. In June 1997, two months after the probationary period ended and one month before the first sexual contact, Holly D. received a performance evaluation that she characterized as negative. In her mind, she drew a connection between her failure to respond positively to Wiggins's sexual comments and his subsequent criticism and negative evaluation. Holly D. eventually decided that, if Wiggins were to request that she engage in sex with him, she would have to comply in order to keep her job.

Holly D. does not contend that Wiggins used physical force to coerce sex, or that he explicitly threatened her with job-related consequences if she did not have sex with him. Nor does she assert that he ever stated, directly or indirectly, that there was a connection between his requests for sex, initial or otherwise, and any problem with her past work performance or her prospects for future employment. Nevertheless, Holly D. relies on what she believes to be indications that her job depended on her sexual submission. She states that, after the sexual relationship had begun, there were periods during which she rebuffed his advances. At those times, she alleges, Wiggins became "supercritical" of her work performance, but she could "neutralize[] it by giving in to his sexual demands." Because Holly D.

concluded that she could mitigate what she characterized as unreasonable and potentially job-threatening criticism by performing sexual acts, she asserts that she is able to establish that she was forced to commence and maintain the sexual relationship in order to keep her employment.

The first sexual contact occurred in July 1997. According to Holly D., Wiggins visited her in her office, where they initially engaged in some discussion about sexual matters. * * * From July 1997 through July 1998, and then again . . . on one occasion in January of 1999, Holly D. and Wiggins engaged in various sex acts during work hours in their offices, involving many instances of intercourse and oral sex. * * *

Holly D. first attempted to transfer out of Wiggins's office in July 1998, just about the time that her sexual relations with Wiggins appeared to have come to an end. She applied for another Caltech administrative position at a higher pay rate, but was not hired for that position or the next three positions for which she applied. * * * Holly D. first mentioned the sexual harassment to a Caltech administration official—specifically, to a Caltech ombudsman in a confidential meeting—shortly after the EEOC found her disability charge [based on denial of the positions she applied for] to be without merit. She told the ombudsman of the sexual relationship and reported that Wiggins had not requested sex after the one incident in January 1999 until sometime that May, when he "asked for a threesome," which she declined. On June 15, 1999, Holly D. filed a sexual harassment claim with the EEOC. Holly D. contends that, although she knew that Caltech had a sexual harassment policy, and although she knew she was being harassed, she did not report the harassment to the institution because she felt that it would have been futile, given the administration's "bias[] in favor of its faculty." * * *

When Caltech was notified, by way of the EEOC letter, of the harassment allegations, a neutral committee was promptly formed to conduct an internal investigation and Holly D. was placed on paid administrative leave to separate her from Wiggins. The committee interviewed Holly D. and Wiggins, and other employees suggested by the accuser and by the accused. Throughout the Caltech investigation, Wiggins denied any sexual contact with Holly D. The investigating committee

ultimately found insufficient evidence of sexual harassment. It recommended, however, that Holly D. be transferred to work for a female professor in a different department and location upon her return, and that Wiggins be "reminded" of Caltech's harassment policy. * * *

The first issue that we must consider is whether Holly D. has alleged the type of discriminatory action by her supervisor for which her employer may be held liable without more—the type of discriminatory action to which the employer may not assert a "reasonable care" defense. There is no question that a "tangible employment action" occurs when a supervisor abuses his authority to act on his employer's behalf by threatening to fire a subordinate if she refuses to participate in sexual acts with him, and then actually fires her when she continues to resist his demands. The question in this case is whether a "tangible employment action" occurs when the supervisor threatens the employee with discharge and, in order to avoid the threatened action, the employee complies with the supervisor's demands. We join the Second Circuit . . . in holding that it does. * * *

[A] supervisor's successful coercion of an employee who submits to her supervisor's sexual demands because of the threat of discharge or other material job-related consequence . . . depends on the same abuse of supervisorial authority—the power, for example, to hire and fire—that . . . renders a discharge a "tangible employment action." In such cases, the supervisor successfully brings to bear the weight of the employer's enterprise in order to achieve the unlawful purpose. In the typical "tangible employment action" case that reaches the courts, a supervisor has terminated a subordinate who refused to bow to his threats and declined to have sex with him. Because the discharge was possible only as a result of the supervisor's exercise of the authority to make critical employment decisions on behalf of his employer, the Court has held that in such cases the employer may be held vicariously liable and may not assert a "reasonable care" defense. The same rationale holds true in the less frequently litigated cases in which an employee, anxious to retain her position with the employer—a job that is likely to represent her sole means of earning a living—submits to her supervisor's sexual demands because he has advised her of a critical employment decision that he has made: to discharge her if she refuses to comply with his demands. In such cases, . . . the threat does not simply remain unfulfilled or inchoate, but rather results in a concrete consequence. The supervisor accomplishes the objective of the threat—the coercion of the sexual act—by bringing to bear the authority to make critical employment determinations on behalf of his employer. Specifically, the supervisor in such cases exercises the authority to make the initial conditional decision to discharge, and then to make the subsequent final decision to retain the employee in her position. In doing so, he makes the employee's continued employment contingent on her willingness to accede to his sexual demands. Thus, the participation in unwanted sexual acts becomes a condition of the employee's employment. * * *

Here, although Holly D. has properly alleged a "tangible employment action," we conclude that . . . she failed to present sufficient evidence to raise a genuine issue of material fact as to whether Wiggins implicitly threatened to discharge her or conditioned her continued employment on her submission to his sexual demands. . . . Holly D. need not prove that Wiggins explicitly demanded sex in return for job security Such a claim may lie either when continued employment has been expressly conditioned on participation in sexual acts or when the supervisor's words or conduct would communicate to a reasonable woman in the employee's position that such participation is a condition of employment. * * * Nor must Holly D. prove that Wiggins intended that her continued employment would actually be contingent on her compliance with his requests—that is, she need not offer proof of his subjective intent to fire or demote her if she did not comply. Rather, it would be sufficient to show that a reasonable person in Holly D.'s position would have believed that her job depended on fulfilling Wiggins's demands. * * *

. . . [I]n cases alleging that an employee engaged in sexual relations because her supervisor implicitly demanded that she do so as a condition of her employment, we require more than conclusory allegations that the supervisor proposed a sexual liaison and the employee responded to the overtures in order to protect her employment interests. * * * Even assuming, without deciding, that Wiggins created an uncomfortably sexualized environment and that he was a difficult and demanding boss, the evidence in this case does not permit the inference that his conduct, implicit or explicit, would have caused a reasonable woman in Holly D.'s position to believe that her continued employment was dependent upon her providing him with sexual favors, or that there would be no point in declining his first invitation to engage in sex. Holly D. has produced no evidence whatsoever *connecting* any discussion of her job duties

with Wiggins's requests that she engage in sexual acts with him. Nor is there any evidence that Wiggins ever mentioned any potential change in her employment status, or indeed any job-related matters or problems, during any discussion regarding her participation in sexual acts with him, or while actually engaged in such acts. Indeed, the first time that Wiggins asked Holly D. to engage in a sexual act—to which request she replied simply and directly, "Yes"—he did so in a discussion in which the record reveals no mention of any subject other than sex. The mere fact that Holly D. received a less than enthusiastic initial job evaluation weeks earlier does not, without more, support her contention that her compliance with Wiggins's initial request for sex was necessary to save her job. Moreover, other than her vague and unsupported allegation that during the course of their one-and-a-half-year sexual relationship, Wiggins grew "supercritical" when she rejected his advances, Holly D. has presented no evidence that would cause a reasonable woman in her position to believe that Wiggins suggested, directly or indirectly, the existence of a connection between her job security and his requests for sex.* * *

Even if no "tangible employment action" has been proven, a plaintiff may still recover for severe or pervasive sexual harassment that results in a hostile work environment; unlike in "tangible employment action" cases, however, the employer has the opportunity to avoid liability for such claims by establishing the elements of the "reasonable care" affirmative defense.... * * *

Holly D. first asserts that Caltech did not take reasonable care in the design of its anti-harassment policy. To support this contention, she offers the expert opinion of Professor Brian Kleiner . . . that an effective sexual harassment program could reasonably include each of six components not offered by Caltech—such as peer review of supervisors and mandatory sexual harassment training for employees. Professor Kleiner also states that . . . an employer could reasonably communicate a sexual harassment policy by each of nine means not employed by Caltech, including role-playing sessions and training videos. The legal standard for evaluating an employer's efforts to prevent and correct harassment, however, is not whether any additional steps or measures would have been reasonable if employed, but whether the employer's actions as a whole established a reasonable mechanism for prevention and correction. Caltech had promulgated a written policy which defined prohibited behavior, identified contact personnel, and established procedures to investigate

and resolve any claims. It made this policy available in several publications, at least one of which Holly D. received in 1996, when she began working with Professor Wiggins. Caltech also conducted periodic training on sexual harassment, which it publicized to staff and faculty by email, including at least one email sent in 1998 during the period when Holly D. was allegedly being harassed. Holly D. testified that she knew about this training, and indeed, that she knew that Wiggins's behavior constituted sexual harassment. * * *

Holly D. next contends that even if Caltech's policy was facially reasonable, it was unreasonably implemented, and that Caltech failed promptly to correct harassment when it occurred. She charges, for example, that Caltech gave unfair deference to its faculty such that no administrative employee could expect to prevail on a harassment charge. However, she has offered absolutely no evidence to support this allegation. When Caltech learned about Holly D.'s allegations for the first time in June 1999 as the result of her filing a claim with the EEOC, it promptly convened an investigatory committee, which impartially interviewed every witness suggested by either Holly D. or Wiggins. At first, the investigatory committee found insufficient evidence of harassment, but nevertheless recommended that Holly D. be transferred to work for a female professor in a different department and location and that Wiggins be "reminded" of Caltech's harassment policy. Moreover, although post complaint conduct will not exonerate a party at fault, we note that once Caltech gained access to the physical evidence belying Wiggins's assertion that no sexual contact had occurred—evidence that Holly D. declined to provide to the investigating committee—Wiggins was immediately asked for his resignation and promptly resigned. Professor Kleiner attacks these efforts as "seriously flawed," by contending that during its initial investigation, Caltech should have interviewed Professor Wiggins's former secretary, inspected Professor Wiggins's computer for bookmarks to pornographic websites, and examined Professor Wiggins's "intimate areas" to corroborate Holly D.'s alleged knowledge of his anatomy. Even were we to assume that all of these additional steps were advisable, Caltech's failure to pursue all possible leads does not undermine the substantial showing in this case that its investigation was, in toto, both prompt and reasonable. * * *

To prove its affirmative defense, Caltech must prove *both* that its efforts to provide relief were reasonable and that Holly D.'s decision to forego the available

avenues of relief was unreasonable. * * * Here, it is undisputed that Holly D. sought no relief of any kind from Caltech until June 1999, after a full year of unwelcome sexual activity and almost two years after the first sexual incident. Holly D. explains her hesitation by asserting that she did not feel comfortable pursuing assistance from Caltech's employee relations department because she "went to them on two occasions and [she] was unsatisfied with how they handled" her disability discrimination complaint. Even if Holly D.'s hesitation to engage the employee relations department were reasonable—and we do not believe that it was—she has offered no evidence to explain why she did not seek help through any of the other sources affiliated with Caltech. The Division Administrator, Division Chair, Provost, Dean, Staff and Faculty Consultation Center, Counseling Center, and Women's Center at Caltech were all specifically identified by Caltech's written policy materials as equipped to offer assistance in cases of sexual harassment, but Holly D. made no attempt to seek relief from any person able to help put a stop to the harassment. * * * [T]he only rationale that Holly D. presents to justify her decision to forego relief through Caltech's procedures is Caltech's alleged faculty bias. She does not contend that her depression or financial circumstances contributed to that decision. . . . Holly D.

has offered no facts that would support a reasonable belief that Caltech was so biased that resort to its procedures would have been futile.

Because Holly D. has not presented evidence sufficient to raise a genuine issue of material fact either on her "tangible employment action" claim or on Caltech's affirmative defense to her hostile environment claim, we affirm the district court's grant of summary judgment to Caltech on her Title VII claim.

CASE QUESTIONS

1. What were the legal issue(s) in this case? What did the court decide?

2. What was the reasoning behind the court's conclusion that harassment resulting in a tangible employment action has occurred when a supervisor or manager successfully coerces an employee to provide sexual favors to keep his or her job?

3. Why was the university not held vicariously liable for harassment resulting in a tangible employment action in this particular case?

4. Why was the university able to successfully establish the "affirmative defense?"

5. Do you agree with this decision? Why or why not?

Harassment by Coworkers or Third Parties

Employees or third parties (e.g., clients, customers) without the authority to make or influence employment decisions are effectively precluded from engaging in harassment that results in tangible employment actions. However, coworkers and third parties are capable of creating hostile environments for other employees. Employer liability for hostile environment harassment by coworkers and third parties rests on whether the employer was negligent in not protecting the employee from harassment. Specifically, the employer is liable for harassment by coworkers and third parties where the *plaintiff* can establish that:

1. The employer knew or should have known about the harassment.

and

2. The employer failed to take prompt and effective action to stop the harassment.

Some overlap exists between this **negligence standard** and the affirmative defense allowed in cases of supervisor hostile environment harassment, but here the plaintiff must prove these things, and failure to do so means that the employer is not liable. The first element establishes that the employer had either actual or "constructive" knowledge of the harassment; that is, the employer knew of the harassment or should have known, given its prevalence or visibility. A timely and specific complaint to the employer is the simplest way to establish employer knowledge, but employers

cannot use the "ostrich defense" (sticking their heads in the sand) to ignore blatant harassment even in the absence of specific complaints.[48] Given knowledge of harassment, employers have an obligation to take prompt and effective action to curtail it. Foot-dragging and clearly ineffectual remedies will not meet this responsibility.

Employers have less control over third parties, but must still use available means to protect employees from harassment by clients, customers, and contractors. A psychiatric hospital that failed to protect staff from a known problem of sexual assaults by clients—such as by placing treatment rooms in visible areas and providing self-defense training—was found liable for harassment.[49] Likewise, a female table server was subjected to sexually offensive comments from a group of customers. When she complained to the restaurant manager and requested that someone else be assigned to the table, she was told to go back and take care of her customers. The harassment subsequently escalated, with one of the customers pulling her hair, grabbing her breast, and placing his mouth on her breast. The employer was liable because the manager had a significant degree of control over the working environment and instead chose to acquiesce in the harassment.[50]

ELIMINATING HARASSMENT

Employers have a clear obligation to protect employees from harassment. The fact that liability for harassment is predicated on the adequacy of preventive measures and the employer's response to harassment reports provides added incentive to develop sound policies and procedures. However, *the primary concern should be preventing harassment or at least curtailing it before it becomes more serious, rather than escaping liability for harassment after the fact.* Harassment polices and complaint procedures, responses to reports of harassment, investigations, and remedies for harassment all require close attention.

Harassment Policies and Complaint Procedures[51]

Employers should establish, communicate, and enforce policies prohibiting harassment. Although failure to adopt a policy is not, by itself, a violation of the law, a policy is basic to preventing harassment. In the context of the affirmative defense, employers will generally not be able to show that reasonable care to prevent and correct harassment was exercised in the absence of a formal policy, including a viable complaint procedure. At this juncture, the absence of a harassment policy is a clear sign that, legally speaking, an employer is clueless. *Harassment policies should include, at minimum, the following:*

- *A strong prohibition of harassment, applying to all managers and employees*
- *A clear explanation of the meaning of prohibited harassment*
- *A clear and accessible procedure for reporting harassment*
- *A requirement that employees with knowledge of harassment report it to the appropriate persons*

[48]*Robinson v. Jacksonville Shipyards, Inc.,* 760 F. Supp. 1486, at 1530 (M.D. Fla. 1991).

[49]*Turnbull,* at 1245.

[50]*Lockard v. Pizza Hut,* 162 F.3d 1062 (10th Cir. 1998).

[51]This section draws heavily on EEOC, "Enforcement Guidance: Vicarious Employer Liability for Unlawful Harassment by Supervisors." No. 915.002 (June 18, 1999).

- *Assurance of protection against retaliation for reporting harassment or providing information to investigators*
- *Promise of confidentiality in handling harassment complaints, to the extent that an effective investigation permits*
- *A process for handling complaints and investigating them promptly and thoroughly*
- *Assurance that appropriate corrective action will be taken if it is determined that harassment has occurred*
- *Disciplinary actions to which persons engaging in harassment are subject*
- *Assurance that the rights of persons accused of harassment will also be respected*

Real policies have more than a "paper existence"; they must be communicated, reiterated, adhered to, and enforced. *To communicate harassment policies, employees should be given their own copies. The information should also be included in employee handbooks, posted in visible areas, discussed when orienting new employees, and made the subject of training.* Training is not a magic bullet, but it can be an important piece of prevention efforts if it is done skillfully and not as a one-shot deal.

An adequate *policy must clearly and unequivocally inform all employees (including top officials and managers) that harassment is prohibited by company policy and the law, and will not be tolerated. Both forms of harassment—harassment resulting in tangible employment actions and hostile environment harassment—should be explained and understandable to employees without legal training.* Concrete examples of harassment can be helpful, provided it is made clear that no listing of harassing conduct is exhaustive and that the occurrence of such conduct does not amount to harassment in every case. *Given the high incidence of harassment in settings removed from the principal workplace—for example, conferences, conventions, sales meetings, and company parties—the scope of the policy and examples given should include harassment in such settings. Employees should be alerted that harassment based on other protected class characteristics, such as race and national origin, is also prohibited by company policy and is illegal.*

Employees must be told how to report harassment. A viable complaint procedure is essential to showing that an employer intends to prevent and promptly correct harassment. *There should be multiple, accessible parties to whom harassment can be reported, and under no circumstances should an employee be required to report harassment to a supervisor or manager who is the alleged harasser.*[52] A college's harassment policy was found to be legally inadequate for requiring that complaints not made to supervisors be brought to the Director of Personnel and for not giving the campus police a role in handling off-hours complaints.[53] The director was located elsewhere and, in any event, was not accessible to employees working at night or on weekends. Complaint procedures must take into account the dispersed, 24/7 nature of many workplaces. Rather than assume that all harassment complaints can wait until the administratively convenient time and place, *complaint procedures should specifically provide for reports during all hours of operation.*

Harassment policies should require that supervisors and managers with knowledge of harassment, however gained, report it to the appropriate persons designated to handle investigations. In the case of the college mentioned previously, the court was also critical of the distinction drawn in the policy between "formal" and "informal" complaints, with supervisors not being obligated to act on or pass along

[52]*Meritor*, at 72–73.

[53]*Wilson v. Tulsa Junior College*, 164 F.3d 534 (10th Cir. 1998).

"informal" complaints. Courts do not always impute knowledge of harassment to employers based on informal reports to lower-level managers not specifically designated to receive complaints,[54] but employers who do not act on all reports of harassment are clearly risking that courts will conclude that they knew or should have known about harassment and failed to act. Deficient policies cannot serve as firewalls to insulate employers from knowledge and consequent liability. Some harassment policies make it the responsibility of all employees with knowledge of harassment to report it. Requiring all employees to report reinforces the expectation under the affirmative defense that employees should take steps to avoid harm. However, required reporting of harassment should be supported by sincere efforts to remove obstacles to reporting, most notably, retaliation.

It is vital that harassment policies provide strong and credible assurances that persons reporting harassment will be protected from retaliation. Persons subjected to harassment are often doubly victimized: first by the harassment itself and then by retaliation for complaining. The punishment allegedly metted out to the kitchen workers at Caesars Palace after they complained about their mistreatment at the hands of supervisors is an all too common scenario (see "Clippings"). A complaint process cannot be effective if employees have reason to fear its use. In a particularly egregious case,[55] bad things happened to a police officer who filed an internal complaint of harassment against her former supervisor. Transferred to a new precinct, the officer had her work scrutinized much more vigilantly than other officers, was subjected to repeated shift and work assignment changes, was transferred to undesirable work locations, had baseless disciplinary charges brought against her, was required to undergo psychological exams, and, on at least one occasion, was ordered to go on patrol without proper equipment. The retaliation apparently continued even after the woman quit the force. She was subsequently arrested for a traffic violation, brought to her former precinct, detained for 27 hours, strip-searched, given a Breathalyzer test (despite the absence of any indication that she was under the influence of alcohol or concealing anything on her person), and told that the precinct did not "need commotion by a woman like you." A jury believed that the woman was retaliated against (among other claims) and awarded her $1.25 million.

Responding to Reports of Harassment

The employer response to reports of harassment is critical. *Employers must respond promptly and in a manner reasonably calculated to stop and correct any harassment.* A complaint of harassment is not something to be placed on the "back burner." Courts can be tough on employers that do not respond promptly to complaints of harassment. In one case, a woman being harassed by a coworker complained on several instances to the individual designated to receive complaints under the company's harassment policy, only to have the complaints laughed off and to be told that the coworker is such a "'ladies man.'" Even though the manager who failed to act was terminated after a higher-level manager became aware of the situation and steps were then taken to end the harassment, the four-month delay in acting raised "a question of material fact whether defendant's response was sufficiently prompt."[56] The promptness and adequacy of an employer's response is assessed in light of the seriousness of the alleged harassment. In a case involving harassment that resulted in

[54]*Madray v. Publix Supermarkets,* 208 F.3d 1290 (2000); *cert. denied,* 531 U.S. 926 (2000).

[55]*Gonzalez v. Police Commissioner Bratton,* 147 F. Supp. 2d 180 (S.D.N.Y. 2001); *affirmed,* 2002 U.S. App. LEXIS 21521.

[56]*Prindle v. TNT Logistics,* 331 F. Supp. 2d 739 (W.D. Wis. 2004).

criminal charges against the harasser, the court found the employer's response to not be sufficiently timely when the employer delayed the start of its investigation to later in the same day.[57] *Once informed of possible harassment, employers must look into the matter despite any misgivings that the employee has about going forward with a complaint.* This is because the employer has been made aware of possible harassment and has a responsibility to protect employees from harassment, even if they are not sure that they want protection. An employer cannot avoid liability by simply claiming that the victim of harassment did not want any action taken against the harasser. Solid assurances of discrete handling of information and protection from retaliation are particularly important in cases with reluctant complainants. For larger employers, it should be possible to establish mechanisms for employees to receive information about harassment anonymously before deciding whether to make reports to their employers. An adequate response to a report of harassment includes a thorough investigation of the facts and adoption of measures necessary to curtail and correct the harassment.

Investigating Reports of Harassment In a case that focused on the adequacy of an employer's response to an employee's harassment complaint, the court observed:

> The most significant immediate measure an employer can take in response to a sexual harassment complaint is to launch a prompt investigation to determine whether the complaint is justified. . . . By opening a sexual harassment investigation, the employer puts all employees on notice that it takes such allegations seriously and will not tolerate harassment in the workplace. An investigation is a warning, not by words but by action. [H]owever, . . . the "fact of investigation alone" is not enough. An investigation that is rigged to reach a pre-determined conclusion or otherwise conducted in bad faith will not satisfy the employer's remedial obligation.[58]

A police department's **investigation** of a sexual harassment complaint was held to be inadequate when the investigators failed to interview the alleged harasser promptly, gave him time to concoct an elaborate defense, accepted the alleged harasser's claims as true without making any effort to verify them, failed to interview a witness whose account was known to be favorable to the complainant, and discounted evidence favorable to the complainant.[59] Similarly, an employer's grudging investigation, conducted only after repeated complaints and concluded without interviewing an eyewitness to a serious incident of harassment or consulting with the complaining employee, was inadequate to meet the employer's legal responsibility.[60] In contrast, an investigation that took three to four months to complete, and in which the investigator apparently failed to interview several coworkers with material information, was judged to be sufficient. The court held, "Where, as here, the employer takes prompt steps to stop the harassment, liability cannot be premised on perceived inadequacies in the investigation."[61] Thus, although employers are not held to a very high standard in investigating harassment complaints—particularly if they do not use the lack of definitive evidence as an excuse for doing nothing—*it is important that investigations be free of bias, that all pertinent witnesses be*

[57] *Wilson*, at 543.

[58] *Swenson v. Potter*, 271 F.3d 1184, at 1193 (9th Cir. 2001).

[59] *Fuller v. City of Oakland*, 47 F.3d 1523, at 1529 (9th Cir. 1995).

[60] *Hathaway v. Runyon*, 132 F.3d 1214 (8th Cir. 1997).

[61] *Swenson*, at 1198.

interviewed, that complainants be kept informed, and that evidence be weighed fairly. Another basic requirement for a fair investigation is that the *investigator(s) should not be under the supervision or control of any of the involved parties.*

Questions that investigators should pose to employees complaining of harassment include the following:

1. To obtain a detailed description of what has happened: Who harassed you? What exactly did they do? When did it happen? Is it still happening? Where did it occur? How often did it occur?

2. To determine whether the conduct was unwelcome: How did you react? What did you say to the harasser or coworkers at the time of the harassment?

3. To determine the effects of the harassment: How did the harassment affect you? Has there been any effect on your employment status?

4. To ascertain whether someone else has relevant information: Was anyone present when the harassment occurred? Did you tell anyone about the harassment? When? Did you see anyone else nearby when the harassment occurred? Do you know of anyone else who might have been harassed by this person?

5. To determine whether other evidence is available: Do you have any notes, e-mails, pictures, and so on that relate to the harassment?

6. To determine the complainant's preferred outcome: How would you like to see this situation resolved?

Questions that should be asked of persons accused of harassment include the following:

1. What is your response to each of the allegations?

2. Are there any reasons why the complainant might make false allegations?

3. Is there any reason to believe that the conduct was welcomed by the complainant?

4. Are there any other persons with relevant information?

5. Do you have any other evidence related to the alleged incidents?

Investigators need to remain neutral and resist any pressure from the parties to draw conclusions before all the evidence is gathered. Discretion, but not absolute confidentiality, should be promised. An effective investigation necessarily means that others will become aware of the allegations, but *information should be strictly limited to those with a legitimate need to know.* Allegations of harassment can be highly damaging. If they are false and indiscriminately "published," the wrongly accused employee can have a defamation claim. *Employers need to take harassment complaints very seriously, but balance this against respect for the rights of the accused.* This is not always an easy balance to maintain. Some employers include specific warnings against false claims in their harassment policies. Although knowingly false allegations of harassment, to whatever extent they may occur, are clearly reprehensible, the most likely effect of such policy language is to further chill the reporting of harassment. Thus, such statements are best omitted from harassment policies.[62]

Remedies for Harassment *Employers should take initial, temporary measures upon being presented with harassment complaints, and then long-term remedial measures based on the outcomes of investigations.* The thrust of the initial measures

[62]Anne Lawton. "The Emperor's New Clothes: How the Academy Deals with Sexual Harassment." *Yale Journal of Law and Feminism* 11, no. 1 (1999), 75–154.

is to separate the parties and prevent harassment, if any, from continuing. Transfers, reassignments, leaves of absence, and closer supervision of the parties are among the possible initial measures. *In general, the alleged harasser, not the victim of harassment, should be transferred or reassigned.* The employer might also offer to refer the complaining employee to an EAP program or other source of counseling. Particular care is required in responding to harassment claims that involve credible allegations of sexual assault or rape. Despite the fact that an employer immediately suspended and later discharged an employee who sexually assaulted a coworker, a court faulted the employer's initial response because the victim was not allowed to call the police and was not given time off to obtain a protective order.[63]

Wrongdoing discovered through investigation need not be so severe as to establish a legal finding of harassment to justify employer action. The hope is that corrective measures will stop offensive conduct before it deteriorates into illegal harassment. If, upon conclusion of a thorough investigation, discipline is warranted, possibilities include an oral or written reprimand, demotion, suspension, wage reduction, or discharge. *The discipline or other **remedies** used should correspond to the severity of the harassment and be reasonably calculated to end it.* In some cases, discharging harassers is necessary. However, *terminations for harassment need to be conducted in the same careful manner as all other terminations and fully take account of any legal protections that might be available to the discharged employee.* A university breached the due process and contractual rights of a professor when it terminated him for sexually harassing a graduate student without following the procedure for terminating tenured faculty specified in the university policy manual.[64] Another court has cautioned employers against overzealousness:

> Where an employee is not punished even though there is strong evidence that he is guilty of harassment, such failure can embolden him to continue the misconduct and encourage others to misbehave. But where the proof of harassment is weak and disputed, . . . the employer need not take formal disciplinary action simply to prove that it is serious about stopping sexual harassment in the workplace.[65]

Transfers or reassignments can also be used as longer-term measures. Although a transfer is often the most expedient way to deal with harassment, *victims of harassment should not be made to bear the burden of being transferred to less desirable locations or positions.* If instead the harasser is transferred, *employers should be wary of simply transferring a problem employee who continues to harass other employees in new surroundings. If conclusive evidence of harassment is not found, the employer should continue to closely monitor treatment of the complainant.*

An employer that responded to complaints of harassment simply by promising to do spot-checks for the next two weeks and requesting that the employee report future instances of harassment—without questioning the alleged harassers, demanding that any harassment stop, or threatening future disciplinary action—"placed virtually all of its remedial burden on the victimized employee."[66] Likewise, an employer that transferred the harasser to another work site, but then allowed him to transfer back, did not do enough to correct the hostile environment to avoid liability.[67] In a

[63]*Becker v. Ulster County,* 167 F. Supp. 2d 549, at 555 (N.D.N.Y. 2001).

[64]*Chan v. Miami University,* 652 N.E.2d 644 (Ohio 1995).

[65]*Swenson,* at 1197.

[66]*Azteca,* at 876.

[67]*Ellison,* at 882.

case involving a teenage restaurant worker subjected to both verbal harassment and physically threatening acts, the court found the employer's remedy of continually warning male kitchen workers to be inadequate:

> Considering the severity of the incidents, a reasonable jury could determine that simply talking to the people involved in the first two aggressive incidents was not a sufficient response. * * * [The employer] needed to stop merely issuing warnings and start taking disciplinary action against the offending employees.[68]

On the other hand, an employer is not liable for failing to do all that could possibly be done, as long as its actions were reasonably calculated to end the harassment and prevent it from recurring.[69] Adequate remedial measures not only stop harassment, but also seek to undo the damage it causes. In tangible employment action cases, this might mean providing reinstatement, promotion, or some other employment opportunity lost due to harassment. In other cases, correction might mean restoration of leave that was used because of harassment or an apology from the harasser.

There are conflicting views about what, if any, written records should be kept of sexual harassment investigations and, if an attorney is involved, whether attorney-client privilege should be claimed. However, *it is important that records be kept of harassment charges and their disposition.* This not only helps an employer document that it took effective action to deal with harassment, but also permits the employer to identify patterns of harassment by particular individuals or in particular departments.

[68]*Loughman v. Malnati Organization,* 395 F.3d 404, 407-08 (7th Cir. 2005); *rehearing, en banc, denied,* 2005 U.S. App. LEXIS 2562.

[69]*Berry v. Delta Airlines,* 260 F.3d 803, at 813 (7th Cir. 2001).

Chapter SUMMARY

Sexual harassment is unwelcome sexual advances, requests for sexual favors, and other verbal or physical conduct of a sexual nature. Although sexual harassment is especially prevalent, harassment can be based on any protected class characteristic. Harassment is discrimination because it is unwanted treatment to which employees are subjected because of their sex, race, or other protected class characteristic, and it either results in a tangible employment action or has a detrimental effect on working conditions. The basic elements of a sexual harassment claim are that the harassment (1) was based on sex, (2) resulted in a tangible employment action or was sufficiently severe or pervasive to interfere with job performance or create an abusive or hostile environment, and (3) was unwelcome. It is also necessary to show that there is basis for holding the employer liable for the harassment.

That sexual harassment was "because of sex" is typically demonstrated in mixed-sex cases by the explicitly sexual or gender-related content of the harassment. Same-sex harassment (e.g., male-male) can also be because of sex and violate Title VII. This conclusion can be reached if the harasser is a homosexual, the harassment is carried out in a sex-specific manner in a mixed-sex workforce, or evidence exists that the harasser was hostile to the presence of persons of the same sex in the workforce. Additionally, a plaintiff might prevail in a same-sex harassment case if it is shown that the harassment occurred because the victim was viewed as not conforming to the gender stereotype for persons of his or her sex. In practice, however, it is difficult for plaintiffs to prove that same-sex harassment is sex discrimination.

Harassment resulting in tangible employment actions is typically sexual harassment perpetrated by a manager or someone else with the authority to influence employment decisions. That individual makes submission to or rejection of sexual advances a basis for employment decisions. In contrast, hostile environment harassment does not directly result in tangible employment actions. Hostile environments can be created by anyone in an organization, including coworkers and clients or customers. For a hostile environment to exist, the harassment must be sufficiently

severe or pervasive that a reasonable person would find it harder to do the job and experience the working conditions as intimidating and abusive. It is not necessary that the harassment inflict psychological harm. Instances of harassment that are severe need not occur frequently to be legally actionable, whereas conduct that is less severe might still constitute harassment in its totality, especially if frequent and ongoing.

Determining whether harassment occurred rests primarily on the objective characteristics of situations as viewed by the reasonable person. However, the subjective experiences of persons alleging harassment are relevant to showing that the harassing conduct was unwelcome. Harassment is unwelcome when the affected employee did not solicit or provoke it, and instead, regarded the conduct as unwanted and offensive. Examination of the conduct of the employee alleging harassment is generally limited to those actions taken in the workplace and directed toward the alleged harasser. Conduct off the job or toward other persons is generally not relevant to determining whether an employee welcomed harassing conduct. Submission to a sexual advance can be unwelcome, even though it was consensual or voluntary.

Employer liability for harassment depends on the organizational position of the harasser and the type of harassment. The employing organization is vicariously liable for all harassment by top officials, regardless of the type. Vicarious liability means that if the harassment occurred, the employing organization is automatically and unconditionally liable for the acts of its agent. Employers are also vicariously liable for harassment by managers or supervisors that results in tangible employment actions. Liability for hostile environment harassment by managers and supervisors is vicarious, but subject to an affirmative defense. The employer can avoid vicarious liability if it shows that it exercised reasonable care to prevent and promptly correct harassment and that the employee unreasonably failed to take advantage of these preventive or corrective opportunities. Liability for hostile environment harassment by coworkers and third parties is based on negligence. The employer is liable if the plaintiff can show that the employer knew or should have known of the harassment and failed to take prompt and appropriate action to stop it.

Practical Advice SUMMARY

- *Employers are strongly advised to establish, communicate, and enforce policies prohibiting harassment.*

- *Harassment policies should*

 –apply to all officials, managers, and employees.

 –clearly explain the meaning of and strongly prohibit harassment.

 –provide a clear and accessible complaint procedure.

 –require reporting of harassment to the appropriate persons.

 –protect employees against retaliation for reporting harassment.

 –promise careful handling of information, but not absolute confidentiality.

 –specify how complaints will be handled and investigated.

 –promise that appropriate corrective action will be taken and outline potential discipline for those who violate the policy.

 –provide assurance that the rights of persons accused of harassment will be respected.

 –be adequately disseminated, such as by providing employees with copies of policies and training in their use.

 –explicitly apply to conduct in settings such as conventions, business travel, and company parties.

 –specify that harassment based on any protected class characteristic, and not only sexual harassment, is prohibited.

- *Complaint procedures should*

 –provide employees with multiple, accessible parties to whom reports of harassment can be made.

 –not require that harassment be reported to the alleged harasser.

 –require that all employees with knowledge of harassment, but especially supervisors and low-level managers, report it to persons able to take corrective action.

- *Employers must respond to reports of harassment*

 –promptly and in a manner reasonably calculated to end the harassment.

 –by commencing an investigation, even if the complaining employee asks the employer not to act.

- *Investigators should*

 –be free of bias.

 –interview all pertinent witnesses.

 –weigh evidence fairly.

 –avoid drawing conclusions prematurely.

 –keep complainants apprised of the progress of the investigation.

 –never be under the supervision or control of an involved party.

- *In responding to harassment complaints, employers should*

 –be careful not to be overzealous or assume guilt before the facts are in.

 –adopt temporary measures, such as granting leaves of absence or transfers, upon being presented with serious allegations of harassment.

- *–institute permanent measures if they are warranted following completion of investigations.*

 –take corrective action if there is evidence of offensive conduct, even if that conduct does not amount to a legal violation.

- *In remedying harassment*

 –the extent of any discipline imposed against the harasser should correspond to the severity of the harassment.

 –terminations or other discipline imposed against harassers must be conducted in the same careful manner as any other terminations or disciplinary actions.

 –transfers or reassignments should not leave the victim of harassment worse off or permit the harasser to continue harassment in a new setting.

- *If investigations of harassment are inconclusive, employers should continue to closely monitor treatment of the complaining employees.*

- *Employers should maintain records of harassment charges and their disposition.*

Key TERMS

harassment	severe or pervasive	complaint procedure
same-sex harassment	reasonable person	negligence standard
"because of sex"	unwelcome	investigation
harassment with tangible	vicarious liability	remedies
employment action	affirmative defense	workplace bullying
hostile environment	harassment policy	

Chapter QUESTIONS

1. A male engineer claimed that he experienced the following treatment at the hands of his male coworkers: numerous comments implying that the employee is homosexual; touching; "staring very intently at my backside while others were looking"; public posting of profane, sexually explicit notes regarding the employee; lewd comments in telephone calls to his home; theft of some personal belongings; and the "greasing" of his locker. The engineer reported the conduct to his supervisors, but the treatment continued. He eventually quit the job and sued. What should the court decide? Why? (*Ciccotto v. LCOR, Inc.,* 2001 U.S. Dist. LEXIS 1125)

2. Over a period of about 12 months, a female employee at a car dealership was subjected to four

incidents of unwanted touching. On each occasion, a manager of the dealership sat down next to her at a meeting, placed his hand on her knee, slid his hand under her skirt, and moved his hand up and down her thigh. The employee complained to several managers and was told to keep a record of the incidents, but no other action was taken. The employee sued. What should the court decide? Why? (*Parrish v. Sollecito*, 2003 U.S. Dist. LEXIS 2225)

3. A female attorney alleged that at her law firm, male associates engaged in frequent banter of a sexual nature that was offensive to her and in which she did not participate. Coworkers talked about their sex lives, speculated about others' sex lives, joked about masturbation, used slang terms to refer to sex organs, and used profanity. Despite the fact that the attorney is heterosexual, she was called "dyke" and "butch" on several occasions. A number of other comments were made to the attorney that contained apparent sexual references or innuendos. The general relationship of the attorney with her colleagues remained friendly, and she socialized with them throughout her tenure at the firm. What should the court decide? Why? (*Fitzgerald v. Ford Marrin Esposito Witmeyer & Gleser*, 2002 U.S. App. LEXIS 3363; *cert. denied*, 2002 U.S. LEXIS 6538)

4. A woman hired as a prison librarian complained about harassment by a supervisor from another agency that operated within the prison. The behavior that was the subject of her complaint, some of which was witnessed by other employees, occurred about four times a week from the time that she was hired in July 2000 to October 2001. Her complaints about the supervisor included his comments to another male supervisor that the woman should be "spanked" every day; insistent compliments on her appearance and "how attractive" she was; staring at her breasts during conversations; measuring her skirt for the purported purpose of determining whether it complied with the prison's dress code; and repeatedly remarking that if he had such an attractive wife, he would never allow her to work in a prison around so many inmates. Allegedly for safety reasons, the supervisor had a security camera installed in the librarian's office, permitting him to observe her as she worked at her desk. Right after the objectionable conduct

began, the librarian complained to her immediate supervisor who said that "boys will be boys" and took no action. She never filed a formal complaint. She believed that she was ineligible to file a formal complaint during her first year of employment due to her probationary status. After she had been on the job for more than a year, she complained to another manager and an internal investigation was undertaken at that point. The woman sued. What should the court decide? Why? (*Singleton v. Department of Correctional Education*, 2004 U.S. App. LEXIS 24059)

5. An African-American employee complained of two incidents in which supervisors used racial epithets in referring to him and four other incidents in which coworkers had made racially offensive remarks, most of them directed specifically at the employee. Additionally, graffiti depicting burning crosses and the letters KKK appeared in a shower and on a wall of the facility. The graffiti on the shower was in close proximity to other graffiti stating "H.J. [the plaintiff's initials] slept here." The employee sued. What should the court decide? Why? (*Jackson v. Flint Ink*, 382 F.3d 869 (8th Cir. 2004))

6. A convenience store cashier was subjected to the following behavior by a coworker over a period of eight to nine weeks: throwing objects at her; sneaking up behind her and touching her; smacking her buttocks; discussing his sex life, inability to sleep, and need for a girlfriend; commenting that the woman looked "hot" in her uniform and would look good as a "biker chick"; commenting on his sexual desire for female customers; referring to women as dumb and stupid; and standing over the woman as she counted her register and calling her a "dumb blonde" if she made a mistake. The woman complained to managers. They responded by changing her to the third shift, which she did not like. The coworker would then hang around after his shift to see her. Eventually, she was told by the manager that it was not possible to always schedule the two employees for different shifts. A manager spoke to the coworker about his behavior, but there was no investigation or review of store videotapes. Another female coworker had complained to managers about the coworker's behavior six months earlier, but

did not go into detail because she was embarassed. The cashier sues. What should the court decide? Why? (*Speedway America v. Dupont*, 2005 Fla. App. LEXIS 10129)

7. The married owner of a company touched and kissed a female salesperson at work, made comments about oral sex, and suggested that they be alone together. A few months later, the woman began making hotel arrangements and meeting the owner in hotel rooms. The two had sex approximately 10 times during their relationship. The woman testified that she felt that she had to have sex with the owner to keep her job. She admitted that the owner never explicitly threatened her with loss of her job if she did not go to hotels with him. After about a year, the woman decided that she couldn't take it anymore and told him that she would not continue with the affair. At that point, the owner told her that she would be fired if she stopped seeing him. The owner then informed his wife (the co-owner of the business) about the affair, and the salesperson was fired. She sues. What should the court decide? Why? (*Miles v. DDF, Inc.* 2004 Minn. App. LEXIS 524; *review denied*, 2004 Minn. LEXIS 409)

8. A 17-year-old female supermarket employee was being severely harassed by a coworker. Twice she complained about the harassment to her fiancé, who also worked at the supermarket. Twice, the fiancé reported the harassment to the store manager. Both times the manager informed him that under company policy, the woman had to report the harassment herself and make the report directly to the human resources (HR) department. The woman did not make the report to the HR department and later sued. What should the court decide? Why? (*Varner v. National Super Markets*, 94 F.3d 1209 (8th Cir. 1996), *cert. denied*, 519 U.S. 1110 (1997))

9. A woman was hired as parks maintenance foreperson. She was the first female to occupy this position. Other employees questioned her competence and decisions on a daily basis, were insubordinate, called her names such as "bitch," spread rumors about her relationships with other employees and alleged sexual promiscuity, made daily comments about her appearance and clothing, slipped a note addressed to "superbitch"

under her door, keyed her personal and work vehicles, and evaluated her more harshly than other probationary employees. Following her complaint to city officials, the woman had her door glued shut on three occasions, her shift changed, and faced numerous allegations of wrongdoing. The city's HR Department handled her complaint and concluded that she was a victim of harassment. The HR Department held a two-hour training session on the harassment and discrimination policy for Parks Department employees, had numerous meetings with supervisors and employees about the city's policy, provided personal counseling and other assistance to the woman, transferred an employee, disciplined a manager and two supervisors, and terminated a seasonal employee. However, the HR Department itself concluded that "despite all of these actions, selected supervisory personnel and hourly employees are increasingly directing harassing comments and initiating extremely negative rumors towards [the woman]." The woman sues. What should the court decide? Why? (*Nievaard v. City of Ann Arbor*, 2005 U.S. App. LEXIS 3690)

10. Should hostile environment sexual harassment be assessed from a gendered perspective (e.g., the reasonable woman standard)?

11. In light of workplace bullying and the difficulties plaintiffs face in same-sex harassment cases, would it be better to have antiharassment statutes aimed at prohibiting unwelcome, offensive treatment, regardless of whether the motive behind the treatment is discriminatory?

12. Complaint procedures will not work unless employees are given credible assurances that they will not experience retaliation for reporting harassment. What can employers do to assure employees that they will not be retaliated against?

13. The College of William and Mary has adopted a policy strictly prohibiting "amorous relations" between faculty and students. Is that a good idea? Should employers attempt to limit romantic relations between employees as a means of preventing sexual harassment? (Diana Jean Schemo. "William & Mary? Not If She's His Student." *New York Times* [December 2, 2001], A-23)

Internet RESOURCES

Find the Women's Studies database (sexual harassment) at this University of Maryland Web site.

http://www.mith2.umd.edu

NOW's (National Organization for Women) Web page on harassment can be found via this Web site.

http://www.now.org

This Web site, created by UCLA law professor Eugene Volokh, focuses on materials related to his concern that enforcing laws against harassment violates free speech rights.

http://www.law.ucla.edu

This Web site includes EEOC's enforcement guidance regarding vicarious employer liability for harassment by supervisors.

http://www.eeoc.gov

Sample antidiscrimination and harassment policies are available via this Web site.

http://public.findlaw.com

Reasonably Accommodating Disability and Religion

▸ A jury found that Echostar, a provider of digital televsion services, violated the American's with Disabilities Act (ADA) by failing to reasonably accommodate a qualified blind employee. The company failed to accommodate the employee when he originally applied for a customer service representative position, did not use proper testing devices to assess his skills, and failed to install software that would have enabled the employee to perform the job. A computer program (Job Access) is available that allows visually impaired persons to process written language at a speed faster than many sighted persons read.[1]

▸ A jury verdict has been upheld for a lab clerk with severe scoliosis who sued under the ADA when she was terminated from her job. Her employer, DuPont, claimed—to no avail—that the woman was a "direct threat" to herself because she could not evacuate the chemical factory on her own by walking.[2]

▸ Amtrak has agreed with the EEOC to not implement a policy that would have denied employment to all persons with monocular vision (i.e., are legally blind in one eye). Except for positions (such as locomotive engineer) where federal regulations require binocular vision, Amtrak will conduct individualized assessments to determine whether applicants with monocular vision can perform the essential functions of the positions sought, with or without reasonable accommodation.[3]

▸ The Air Force has issued new guidelines on religious issues. The guidelines caution against public prayers at official events other than worship services and the promotion of particular faiths—or religion in general—in official communications. Allegations have surfaced that chaplains at the Air Force Academy in Colorado Springs engaged in religious proselytizing among cadets and fostered an atmosphere of religious harassment.[4]

▸ Some pharmacists are claiming a right to refuse to dispense the "morning after" pill and other drugs related to contraception or abortion. State legislators have entered the fray. Some states are considering proposals to allow pharmacists to exercise their consciences in this matter, whereas other states are seeking to enact legislation requiring pharmacies to fill any legal prescription.[5]

[1]Equal Employment Opportunity Commission. "EEOC Wins $8 Million Jury Verdict for Blind Worker in Disability Bias Case Against Echostar." (May 6, 2005). Viewed September 15, 2005 (http://www.eeoc.gov/press/5-6-05.html).

[2]"Federal Court Backs $591,000 Judgment for Former DuPont Lab Worker in ADA Case." *Daily Labor Report,* 112 (June 13, 2005), A-12.

[3]"Amtrak, EEOC Settle Dispute Over Monocular Vision." *Daily Labor Report,* 77 (April 22, 2005), A-14.

[4]Laurie Goodstein. "Air Force Bans Leaders' Promotion of Religion." *New York Times* (August 30, 2005), A-10.

[5]Monica Davey and Pam Belluck. "Pharmacies Balk on After-Sex Pill and Widen Fight." *New York Times* (April 19, 2005), A-1.

Protection against discrimination means little to disabled persons if workplaces remain full of barriers—sometimes physical obstacles, such as the absence of wheelchair accessibility, but more often inflexible policies and practices—that effectively preclude employment. Likewise, employers with requirements (such as schedules, job duties, and appearance standards) that conflict with the sincere religious beliefs and practices of employees place those persons in the untenable position of choosing between their jobs and their faiths. In mandating reasonable accommodation of disability and religion, the law requires employers to be more flexible and supportive than they might otherwise be, provided that any accommodations are reasonable and do not impose undue hardship.

The obligation to reasonably accommodate is unique to the protected classes of disability and religion. However, the legal basis and nature of this obligation differ, depending on whether disability or religion is involved. Thus, the two forms of accommodation are discussed separately in this chapter. The obligation to reasonably accommodate disabled persons is more extensive than the requirement to accommodate religion. Yet, at the same time, it is more difficult for employees to establish entitlement to reasonable accommodation for their disabilities than for their religious beliefs and practices.

REASONABLE ACCOMMODATION OF DISABILITY

The obligation of employers to reasonably accommodate disability arises under two similar laws: **the Americans with Disabilities Act (ADA)** (Title I)[6] and the **Rehabilitation Act.**[7] The ADA was explicitly modeled after the Rehabilitation Act. We will focus on the ADA because of its broader coverage (private sector employers with at least 15 employees, state and local governments). The protected class under the ADA is **qualified individuals with disabilities.** The interpretation of this phrase is complex, so we must delve deeper into the meaning of *disability* and *qualified* to understand who is entitled to accommodation (and nondiscrimination). But, for all its complexity, this phrase captures an essential premise of the ADA: People can have disabilities and still be capable of work, particularly if flexibility and support are available to them. Although some legal definitions of disability (such as that used by the Social Security Administration to decide who can receive Social Security disability payments) are based on the inability to engage in gainful employment, the view of disabled persons under federal antidiscrimination laws is very different.

Disability

The definition of **disability** under the ADA includes the following:

- A physical or mental impairment that substantially limits one or more major life activities

or

- A record of such an impairment

or

- Being regarded as having such an impairment

[6]42 U.S.C.A. §§ 12101–12213 (2005).
[7]29 U.S.C.A. §§ 701–796i (2005).

Current Disability The first prong of the ADA's definition of disability refers to persons who are currently disabled. *Not all serious medical problems meet the legal definition of disability.* The ADA does not list specific impairments or disorders that are considered disabilities. The definition of disability is based on an individualized assessment of the effects of health problems on a person's functioning, rather than diagnostic labels. Both **physical and mental impairments** are incorporated into the definition of disability. Thus, psychiatric disorders (e.g., depression, schizophrenia), mental retardation, and learning disabilities that meet the other elements of the definition are disabilities protected under the law. However, certain conditions or behaviors are expressly *excluded* from the definition of disability, including homosexuality, bisexuality, transvestism, transsexualism, pedophilia, exhibitionism, voyeurism, gender-identity disorders, compulsive gambling, kleptomania, and pyromania. Significantly, persons who are current users of illegal drugs, regardless of whether they suffer from drug addiction, are not considered disabled under the ADA. However, persons who are undergoing or have completed rehabilitation for drug addiction and are not currently using illegal drugs are protected by the ADA.

To be a disability, a physical or mental impairment must substantially limit an individual in the performance of a one or more **major life activities**. There is no definitive listing of major life activities. According to EEOC guidelines interpreting the ADA, major life activities include, but are not limited to, walking, seeing, hearing, speaking, breathing, learning, and working.[8] Elsewhere, the EEOC has cited caring for oneself, sitting, standing, lifting, concentrating, thinking, and interacting with others as additional major life activities.[9] Supreme Court cases have treated reproduction[10] and performing manual tasks[11] as major life activities.

The third piece to the definition of current disability—that the individual is **substantially limited** in the performance of a major life activity—means that the impairment must be severe and generally either chronic (lasting many months or years rather than days or weeks) or expected to have a long-term impact on functioning. A woman who suffered from intermittent pain and dizziness related to ovarian cysts was deemed not to be disabled because the impairment lasted "only" for about eight months until the cysts were removed and because the condition was judged not sufficiently severe.[12] Similarly, a surgical resident who became depressed, had problems with the antidepression medications he was given, and was subsequently terminated from his residency was unable to convince the court that he was disabled.[13] Although depression can be a protected disability, his depression was relatively short-lived. Additionally, the fact that he was able to go on to another residency elsewhere and do well was viewed by the court as evidence that his impairment was not substantially limiting. In a case involving an autoworker with carpal tunnel syndrome, the Supreme Court held that ". . . to be substantially limited in performing manual tasks, an individual must have an impairment that prevents or severely restricts the individual from doing activities that are of central importance to most people's daily lives. The impairment's impact must also be permanent or long-term."[14] It does not suffice

[8]29 C.F.R. § 1630.2(i) (2005).

[9]EEOC. *Technical Assistance Manual on the Employment Provisions (Title I) of the Americans with Disabilities Act* (January 1992). p. II-3; EEOC. *Enforcement Guidance on the Americans with Disabilities Act and Psychiatric Disabilities.* no. 915.002 (March 25, 1997), pp. 6–7.

[10]*Bragdon v. Abbott,* 524 U.S. 624 (1998).

[11]*Toyota Motor Manufacturing v. Williams,* 534 U.S. 184 (2002).

[12]*Guzman-Rosario v. United Parcel Service,* 397 F.3d 6 (1st Cir. 2005).

[13]*Swanson v. University of Cincinnati,* 268 F.3d 307 (6th Cir. 2001).

[14]*Toyota Motor Manufacturing,* at 198.

for the plaintiff to show limitation in performing some of the manual tasks associated with her job; she must show limitation in performing "tasks of central importance to people's daily lives"—such as bathing, brushing one's teeth, and completing household chores.

When work is the major life activity at which the individual is limited, the impairment must substantially limit performance of either a class of jobs similar in skill requirements or a broad range of jobs in various classes and skill levels, as compared to the average person with comparable skills, ability, and training. To be considered disabled, it is not enough that the individual is unable to perform a single, specialized job. For example, a Major League Baseball pitcher who develops a sore arm and is unable to continue pitching would not be considered disabled on the basis of inability to perform this one job. Similarly, a woman who was fired after she developed cognitive problems following chemotherapy was deemed not disabled because the condition was relatively mild; she was able to perform well in a subsequent job, and she failed to present evidence from a vocational expert documenting her substantial limitation at a broad range of jobs.[15] However, a police officer with severe depression who was unable to carry a firearm was found to be substantially limited in the major life activity of working due to the condition restricting his ability to perform a *class* of jobs in law enforcement.[16]

In *Emory v. Astrazeneca Pharmaceuticals*, the court must determine whether an employee with cerebral palsy is "disabled" under the ADA. Notice the fact-intensive nature of this inquiry, which is only the first of many hurdles that plaintiffs must surmount in ADA cases.

[15] *Whitney v. Greenberg, Rosenblatt, Kull & Bitsoli*, 258 F.3d 30 (1st Cir. 2001).

[16] *Williams v. Philadelphia Housing Authority*, 380 F.3d 751 (3d Cir. 2004); *cert. denied*, 125 S. Ct. 1725 (2005).

EMORY V. ASTRAZENECA PHARMACEUTICALS
401 F.3d 174 (3d Cir. 2005)

● ● ●

OPINION BY CIRCUIT JUDGE RENDELL:

Alvin "Rob" Emory brought suit against his longtime employer, AstraZeneca Pharmaceuticals LP ("AstraZeneca"), alleging disability discrimination in the form of failure to promote and failure to provide reasonable accommodations in violation of the Americans with Disabilities Act ("ADA"). Moving for summary judgment, AstraZeneca urged that Emory's substantive claims of discrimination need not be addressed because Emory, as a threshold matter, was not "disabled" under the ADA. The District Court agreed and granted AstraZeneca's motion on that basis. We disagree. * * *

Emory, who was born with cerebral palsy, has worked as a custodian at AstraZeneca (and its predecessor companies) for more than 27 years. * * * Among the physical impairments Emory endures as a result of his cerebral palsy are permanent partial paralysis on his right side, and a right hand, arm and leg he describes as "deformed." Dr. Stephen Rodgers, M.D. . . . recently evaluated Emory and found that "the percentages of permanent impairment are right upper extremity—50% [and] right lower extremity—25%." * * * Though cerebral palsy left Emory with some use of his right side, he cannot lift anything heavy, or open and close his right thumb, which interferes with activities that involve the use of both hands as well those requiring right-handed gripping or dexterity. As a result, Emory cannot tie his shoes or a tie, roll his sleeves, close buttons, or put on a belt. In addition, among other tasks, he is unable to cut his fingernails or toenails, screw the top on a toothpaste tube, cut his own meat, open a jar, pull heavy dishes

and pans in or out of the oven, change diapers, carry his children up the stairs, hold a pen or pencil in his right hand, or perform certain basic household chores and repairs. * * *

In addition to these physical inabilities, Emory also experiences mental limitations stemming from his cerebral palsy. As a result, he was placed in Special Education classes from an early age. He ultimately obtained a diploma from this track; though, as a tenth grade student, Emory's word recognition and math skills were at a second grade level. * * * In 2003, Emory scored a Full Scale I.Q. of 77, placing him in the borderline range of intellectual performance and in the 6th percentile of the general population. * * * Tests administered in 2003 revealed that in reading, arithmetic and spelling, Emory tested at or below 99 out of 100 adults in his age group. * * * Rather than reading test questions for himself, he needs to have the questions read aloud for him. Even verbal instructions often leave Emory confused. * * * Emory cannot learn new skills from a training manual, rather, he must learn via a "hands-on" or combination visual and verbal approach, but still at a pace substantially slower than his colleagues. * * *

Notwithstanding the frequent professional frustrations wrought by his limitations, Emory has, since adolescence, consistently endeavored to challenge himself and to participate in various civic and community activities. Though he could not lift a gurney, climb a ladder to rescue someone, operate a fire hose without assistance, or "mask-up" on his own, Emory became a volunteer firefighter as a teenager. * * * As an adult, Emory has volunteered to join a team responsible for mediating local disputes at the Center for Justice in Wilmington, Delaware. . . . And, most recently, Emory, who was hired to perform part-time cleaning work for the Newark Temple, formed "Rob's Cleaning Service." He and his partner share cleaning duties and, besides the temple, have one other contract. * * *

Despite undertaking various other commitments, Emory remained undeterred in his pursuit to advance at AstraZeneca. After numerous failed attempts at advancement, in 1999, he assumed a temporary role as acting Second Shift Supervisor following the promotion of another employee. That assignment lasted almost two years—Emory claims that, during that two year period, he was frequently criticized for math errors, spelling and grammar mistakes, and the length of time it took him to complete administrative tasks. When he

asked his supervisors if he could use a calculator to add and subtract overtime and work hours (and offered to buy it himself), he was refused on the ground that it would embarrass him "because everyone should know basic subtraction and adding." One of these same supervisors routinely referred to Emory as "Rainman" in reference to the autistic character in the movie by the same name. Yet still, in an effort to improve his performance in the Second Shift Supervisor position, Emory approached HR Director Hampel and asked for an assessment at Sylvan Learning Center. He was refused. He later asked for and received from AstraZeneca a block of time for Easter Seals computer training. His instructor at Easter Seals, Phyllis Gourdin, issued a report to AstraZeneca with recommendations that voice-activated software be installed on Emory's computer and that additional instruction on grammar, spelling and writing be afforded. No action was taken on these recommendations. Following a reorganization of the Maintenance Department in 2001, Emory, who believed he was the "heir-apparent" to the job after having performed it for close to two years, was passed over for the permanent Second Shift Supervisor position. * * *

The ADA prohibits discrimination against qualified individuals who suffer a "disability." The statute defines "disability," in part, as "a physical or mental impairment that substantially limits one or more of the major life activities of such individual." The parties here agree that cerebral palsy is an impairment. And, Emory has identified those major life activities in which he claims to be substantially limited, which include the performance of manual tasks and learning. AstraZeneca, however, denies that Emory's limitations are substantial. * * * The Supreme Court has made clear that "the Act addresses substantial limitations on major life activities, *not utter inabilities*. When evaluating substantial limitation, courts must consider a plaintiff's ability to compensate for his disability through mitigating measures, but the essence of the inquiry regards comparing the conditions, manner, or duration under which the average person in the general population can perform the major life activity at issue with those under which an impaired plaintiff must perform. * * *

1. Performing Manual Tasks

* * * [T]he paramount inquiry remains—does Emory "have an impairment that prevents or severely restricts [him] from doing activities that are of central importance to most people's daily lives"? If so, then he is

substantially limited in the performance of manual tasks and has established disability under the ADA. The record is replete with references to the severe restrictions imposed by Emory's impairments. Emory has been, since childhood, either unable to perform, or only able to perform with significant difficulty, a range of manual tasks central to daily life. * * * As he cannot perform activities that require him to grasp and hold with two hands, he is also unable to perform a number of more personal manual tasks involving dressing, eating and maintaining personal hygiene. These limitations have interfered with Emory's ability to care for his children and prevent him from performing many ordinary household tasks central to the lives of most people. So, while the District Court stressed that Emory could "operate a cleaning business, perform as a clown, counsel families as a mediator, and assist his community as a firefighter," it ignored evidence that Emory cannot tie his shoes or necktie, open a jar, cut his nails, perform various household chores and repairs, remove heavy dishes from the oven, change a diaper, carry his children up the stairs, or cut his own meat with a knife and fork. These latter activities, which are but a few examples demonstrative of how very manually impaired Emory is, are "of central importance to people's daily lives," and Emory is either completely without ability or severely restricted in his ability to perform them.

The crux of the inquiry lies in comparing the way in which Emory is able to perform activities, if at all, with the way in which an average member of the general population performs the same activities. An average person, for example, thinks nothing of getting dressed, whether or not the task includes buttons, zippers, laces or sleeves. For Emory, the act of dressing presents huge hurdles, some of which he can overcome through accommodations or the help of another person, and many of which he cannot. "That [a plaintiff], through sheer force of will, learned accommodations, and careful planning, is able to perform a wide variety of activities despite his physical impairments does not mean that those activities are not substantially more difficult for him than they would be for an unimpaired individual." What a plaintiff confronts, not overcomes, is the measure of substantial limitation under the ADA. * * * A rational factfinder could reasonably conclude that, when compared to an average individual in the general population, Emory is substantially limited in his ability to perform manual tasks. Therefore, Emory

has established a genuine issue of fact as to his entitlement to protection under the ADA.

2. Learning

The District Court concluded that Emory's "learning impairments" should not be considered substantially limiting because "the record indicates that Mr. Emory graduated from high school and updated his computer skills through occupational training, [passing] the certification requirements to become both a family mediator and a fireman, and . . . consistently earn[ing] positive performance evaluations during his 26 years of employment with AstraZeneca." However, again, "The key question is not whether a handicapped person accomplishes [his] goals, but whether [he] encounters significant handicap-related obstacles in doing so." Further, when compared to others, his learning impairments are clearly severe.

Emory presented evidence in the record that he completed high school, but on a special education track; during his sophomore year of high school he was reading at a second-grade level. He has had his I.Q. tested three times, with the highest score registering in the mid-eighties (the two other scored registered in the seventies), falling into the borderline range of intellectual functioning. Emory's limitations interfere with his ability to read and process information, as well as basic math skills or the filling out of paperwork. Emory can complete exams only if given orally, and even then, requires additional time—this seems to be a result of both his own difficulty with reading and his inability to express himself in writing. Experience has proven that Emory is incapable of learning as do other employees, through manuals or brief instruction or training. Diagnostic tests administered over a span of years establish that Emory's math, reading and cognitive skills are far below those possessed by average persons in the general population—test results reveal poor calculation and computational abilities, literacy skills which place him in the bottom of the first percentile according to one test, and a deficient learning curve.

These manifestations of Emory's mental impairment are significant. The "nature and severity," of Emory's learning impairments are such that he cannot intake or process basic information the way average individuals do, often unconsciously. And, the "expected duration" of these impairments is no less than "permanent." The fact that he is able, through an often laborious combination of non-traditional methodologies, to learn

certain skills does not obscure the substantial limitations imposed by his impairments on his ability to learn. * * * Under both the EEOC guidelines and the Supreme Court's articulation of "substantial limitation" . . . , Emory has created a genuine issue of fact as to whether he is disabled in the major life activities of performing manual tasks and learning.

CASE QUESTIONS

1. What was the legal issue in this case? What did the court decide?

2. What does the court consider in deciding whether Emory is a disabled person protected by the ADA? Are you surprised at the elaborate, fact-intensive analysis involved in determining whether this individual with severe cerebral palsy is "disabled?"

3. Do you think that Emory is a "qualified" individual with a disability with respect to the Second Shift Supervisor position that he sought?

4. What, if any, reasonable accommodations could be made that would enable him to successfully perform this job?

Persons with disabling conditions often take medication, use prosthetic devices (e.g., an artificial leg), wear corrective lenses, and, in general, employ a variety of means to lessen or eliminate the impairing effects of their disabilities. Should these corrective devices be taken into account when determining whether persons are "substantially limited"? In one case that raised this issue, twin sisters were denied employment as pilots at United Airlines because they did not meet the airline's minimum standard for *uncorrected* vision.[17] Both sisters were severely myopic (nearsighted), but could see perfectly well with glasses or contact lenses. The Supreme Court held that whether a person is substantially limited must be assessed in light of any corrective devices used by the individual. Because the twins' corrected vision was fine, they were not disabled persons and not protected by the ADA. Part of the rationale for the Court's decision was the principle that the determination of disability should rest on individualized assessments of functioning, rather than on assumptions about the usual effects of particular conditions. But the Court's decision also evidenced considerable concern about the potentially large number of people that would be protected under the ADA (and thus, potential litigants) if it decided that the uncorrected condition was the relevant state for determining disability.

Although it might be easy to accept that myopic persons who need to wear glasses are not the sort of people that Congress had in mind when it passed the ADA, the effects of this ruling could be far-reaching. For example, is a person who is severely epileptic, but currently free from seizures due to medication, not a disabled person? In one case involving an employee with severe diabetes, the court found that the employee was disabled because despite injecting insulin 3 times a day and testing his blood sugar 10 times a day, the employee continued to suffer from unpredictable and possibly life-threatening hypoglycemic episodes.[18] However, in another case involving a severely diabetic employee, the court concluded that the employee was not disabled—and hence, not entitled to protection under the ADA—because his diabetes was sufficiently controlled through insulin and diet to not be substantially limiting.[19] A particularly troubling aspect of the latter case is that the employee's

[17]*Sutton v. United Airlines,* 527 U.S. 471 (1999).

[18]*Nawrot v. CPC International,* 277 F.3d 896 (7th Cir. 2002).

[19]*Orr v. Wal-Mart,* 297 F.3d 720 (8th Cir. 2002); *cert. denied,* 541 U.S. 1070 (2004).

successful management of his condition rested precisely on his abiliity to take uninterrupted breaks at the appropriate times. When the Wal-Mart that he worked for as a pharmacist decided that its pharmacy must remain continuously open throughout his 10-hour shift, the conditions under which the employee had functioned were fundamentally altered. However, his employer was under no obligation to continue to provide breaks as a reasonable accommodation because the breaks previously provided had mitigated his condition and made him not "disabled."

Whatever its merits, the *Sutton* decision (the case involving the myopic twins) appears to deny protection of the ADA to precisely those persons with serious medical problems who are most likely to be able to succeed in the workplace because their symptoms are controlled or controllable. Only those for whom corrective devices are unavailable or ineffective will be considered disabled. But will the latter individuals be able to show that they are "qualified" disabled persons?

Record of a Disability Employees are sometimes discriminated against not because they are currently disabled (or in addition to that), but on the basis of a prior disability. This might be due to the stigma associated with the condition (e.g., drug addiction, mental illness) or fears that the condition (e.g., cancer) will recur. Sometimes people are misclassified (e.g., as learning disabled), and the record of an erroneous diagnosis stays with them. Persons who have **records of disabling impairments**, whether due to their medical history or misclassification, are protected. In one case, a teacher who had been hospitalized for tuberculosis was terminated due to fears that she would have relapses and infect others with the disease.[20] The court found that she had both a record of disability and a current disability.

Perceived Disability Persons who are erroneously **regarded as being disabled** are also protected by the ADA. Many stereotypes, fears, and misconceptions exist regarding people with disabilities. Persons might be regarded as disabled even though they are not disabled at all (e.g., because of unfounded rumors) or treated as substantially limited even though their conditions (e.g., high blood pressure) are under control. Again, plaintiffs must show that their employers perceived them to be disabled. Thus, in the case involving the twins who were rejected as pilots by United Airlines, their bid to show that the airline regarded them as substantially limited failed for essentially the same reason that they could not establish a current disability. The Court maintained that there was no evidence that United viewed them as unable to perform a range of jobs for which they were qualified, rather than only the specific job for which they applied. Because employers typically consider applicants for only one, or at most, a few specific positions and usually do not comment on their general employability, it is very difficult for plaintiffs to show that they were regarded by employers as substantially limited in performing a wide range of jobs. However, a woman with vertigo was able to show that her employer perceived her to be disabled even though her condition was not actually substantially limiting. Although the woman's condition made it difficult for her to work on a conveyor belt for prolonged periods of time, managers erroneously regarded her as being unable to occupy any position in the vicinity of moving equipment.[21] Likewise, the commanding officers of a police officer suffering from depression wrongly believed that the officer could not hold any job where firearms were present,

[20]*School Board of Nassau County v. Arline*, 480 U.S. 273 (1987).

[21]*D'Angelo v. Conagra Foods*, 2005 U.S. App. LEXIS 18639.

although the actual restriction imposed by the employee's doctors was only that he himself not carry a weapon.[22]

"Qualified Individual with a Disability"

To be protected under the ADA, individuals must not only be disabled, but also **qualified**. A qualified individual with a disability satisfies the skill, education, experience, and other job-related requirements for the job held or sought, and is able, with or without reasonable accommodation, to perform the essential functions of that job.[23] However, an individual who can perform the essential functions of a job, but whose condition is such that she poses a "direct threat" to the health and safety of herself or others—a threat that cannot be eliminated by reasonable accommodation—is not considered qualified.

Able to Perform the Essential Functions of the Job Jobs consist of bundles of tasks. Some of those tasks are central to why the job exists; others are more peripheral. For example, word processing, filing, and answering phones are essential functions for many clerical workers, but going out to get coffee for others or lifting boxes of copier paper are probably marginal functions. Under the ADA, *a disabled person's ability to perform a job must be judged only in relation to the essential functions of the job in question; inability to perform marginal functions cannot be the basis for adverse employment decisions.* Thus, *it is important that employers determine the essential functions of jobs.* Following are the criteria for identifying **essential functions**:

- The position exists to perform this function.
- Few other employees are available to perform this function.
- The function is highly specialized.

Evidence of essential functions includes the employer's own judgment, written job descriptions, documentation of the amount of time spent performing particular functions, analyses of the consequences of not requiring position occupants to perform the functions, job duties listed in collective bargaining agreements, and statements based on the work experience of job occupants. Tasks that are performed infrequently are less likely to be considered essential, but this is not always the case. For example, a firefighter must be able to enter a burning building and carry out a victim, even though most firefighters are called upon to do so only infrequently.

The ADA does not require that employers perform job analyses (systematic studies of jobs to document the major tasks involved and the knowledge, skill, abilities, and other traits needed for successful job performance) or have job descriptions. However, the importance of documenting essential functions for compliance with the ADA provides employers with a clear reason—beyond the general need to defend the job-relatedness of testing procedures in adverse impact cases—to carefully study jobs and document them in up-to-date job descriptions. *Job analyses should include input from both managers and occupants of the jobs in question. Job descriptions should distinguish essential functions from marginal functions and specifically state all essential job functions.* An employer that rejects a disabled job candidate because he is unable to perform some function that was not important enough to warrant mention in a job description is in an unenviable legal position. Additionally, *job*

[22]*Williams,* at 766–67.

[23]29 C.F.R. § 1630.2(m) (2005).

descriptions, and employers deciding whether disabled persons can perform the essential functions of jobs, should focus on what needs to be accomplished, rather than on how tasks are accomplished. Disabled persons are often able to devise alternative ways of doing things. Absent important safety or productivity concerns that dictate adherence to a particular method, employers should be open to different means of producing the same outcomes. Lastly, when *assessing the ability of disabled persons to perform the essential functions of jobs, employers must consider not only whether these individuals can do so unaided, but also whether they can do so with any reasonable accommodations that could be provided without undue hardship.*

Meets Job-Related Qualification Standards To be "qualified," disabled persons must meet the same requirements for education, skill, experience, and background that apply to all other job candidates and employees. However, *if a requirement screens out, or tends to screen out, an individual with a disability or a class of such persons, the employer must be prepared to prove that the requirement is job related and consistent with business necessity.* Only those requirements that relate to ability to perform the essential functions of a job are "consistent with business necessity." Requirements related to physical and mental ability, and the tests used to assess these (e.g., physical agility tests), are the most likely to have discriminatory effects on disabled persons. Reasonable accommodation in the testing process and use of alternative means to establish the necessary qualifications is often sufficient to negate the discriminatory effects of these requirements.

Especially problematic are standards that result in the blanket exclusion (usually on the basis of safety concerns) of all persons with particular disabilities. Similar to Amtrak (see "Clippings"), UPS had vision standards for drivers that excluded all persons with good vision in one eye, but little or no vision in the other, without consideration of actual safety records or driving ability. Persons with monocular vision do not always meet the definition of disability,[24] and UPS ultimately prevailed on these grounds, but its vision requirements have been an ongoing source of legal problems.[25] The type of individualized assessment of functioning that Amtrak agreed to is preferrable and generally required by the ADA. However, if federal or state laws establish health requirements for particular types of jobs (e.g., school bus drivers) that exclude persons with particular disabilities, employers do not violate the ADA by complying with these legal requirements.

Not a Direct Threat In contrast to standards that apply generally to all employees, employers sometimes identify individuals as unfit for employment because their disabilities present a direct threat to safety and health. Such individuals can perform the essential functions of the jobs in question but, for reasons such as the contagious nature of their conditions (e.g., food handlers with hepatitis) or the episodic and unpredictable character of their symptoms (e.g., some persons with epilepsy or mental illness), pose a substantial risk of harm. Does the direct threat standard apply to potential harm to disabled individuals themselves or only potential harm to others (e.g., coworkers, customers)? An employee who had worked in oil refineries for years and who sought employment at a Chevron refinery was rejected due to a liver condition that might be worsened by contact with toxic chemicals. The Supreme Court ruled for the employer, holding that risk to an employee's own safety or health falls within the meaning of "direct threat."[26]

[24]*Albertson's v. Kirkingburg,* 527 U.S. 555 (1999).

[25]*EEOC v. United Parcel Services,* 149 F. Supp. 2d 1115 (N.D. Cal. 2000); *affirmed in part, reversed in part, remanded,* 366 F.3d 794 (9th Cir. 2002); 2005 U.S. App. LEXIS 19823.

[26]*Chevron, U.S.A, Inc. v. Echazabal,* 536 U.S. 73 (2002).

However, to establish that a person's disability constitutes a **direct threat,** the employer must show that the employee *currently* poses a *specific risk* of *significant harm.* This judgment must be made on the basis of *objective medical evidence,* and not on stereotypes or fears. Although inability to evacuate during an emergency might render an employee a direct threat to her own safety and health in some settings, DuPont was unable to convince a jury that the threat posed by a lab clerk with severe scoliosis was sufficiently specific and imminent (see "Clippings"). Likewise, in the vast majority of workplaces, persons who are HIV-positive do not pose direct threats to themselves or others and cannot be excluded on those grounds. However, there have been cases where employers were upheld in excluding HIV-positive health-care workers whose jobs involved performing invasive medical procedures.[27] An outbreak in 2004 of HIV among actors in the Southern California pornographic film industry[28] suggests that this is another venue in which being HIV-positive might pose a direct threat. An employer was also able to successfully argue that a disabled person posed a direct threat when the employee, on medical leave for a psychiatric disability, expressed in graphic terms (to a doctor) her desire to kill her supervisor.[29] Threats to safety or health need not be as certain if the potential consequences are severe. A diabetic chlorine-finishing operator at a chemical plant experienced occasional diabetic seizures. The court concluded that despite the relatively low frequency of seizures, his condition made him a direct threat because of the potentially catastrophic consequences of a chlorine spill.[30] Although the employer usually bears the burden of proving that an employee's disability poses a direct threat, that burden may shift to plaintiffs to show that they will not endanger others in cases involving jobs with public safety functions.[31]

Reasonable Accommodation

The extra flexibility and support to which qualified individuals with disabilities are entitled serve the following purposes: ensuring equal employment opportunity by enabling full participation in the hiring process (e.g., providing additional time on an employment test for an applicant with a learning disability); enabling performance of the essential functions of jobs (e.g., providing voice recognition software for a visually impaired employee); and allowing equal enjoyment of the benefits and privileges of employment (e.g., installing a ramp that affords an employee in a wheelchair access to the staff dining facility). Echostar violated the ADA by failing to accommodate a blind employee during the application process and then by refusing to purchase software that would have allowed him to perform the job of customer service representative (see "Clippings"). Examples of **reasonable accommodation** specifically mentioned in the ADA include the following:

- Making facilities accessible to and usable by disabled persons (e.g., removing physical barriers such as narrow aisles, deep carpeting that hinders wheelchair use)

- Restructuring jobs (e.g. redistributing marginal functions, allowing tasks to be performed in alternative ways)

- Devising part-time or modified work schedules (e.g., flexible start times, liberal medical leave policies)

[27]*Doe v. University of Maryland Medical System Corp.,* 50 F.3d 1261 (4th Cir. 1995).

[28]"California: Sex Film Industry Lifts Moratorium." *New York Times* (May 13, 2004), A-17.

[29]*Collins v. Blue Cross Blue Shield of Michigan,* 579 N.W.2d 435 (Mich. Ct. App. 1998); *appeal denied,* 590 N.W.2d 571 (Mich. 1999).

[30]*Hutton v. Elf Atochem North America,* 273 F.3d 884 (9th Cir. 2001).

[31]*McKenzie v. Benton,* 388 F.3d 1342 (10th Cir. 2004); *cert. denied,* 125 S. Ct. 2294 (2005).

- Acquiring or modifying equipment or devices (e.g., telephone amplifier, voice recognition software, telephone headset)
- Adjusting or modifying exams, training materials, and policies (e.g., providing training materials in large print, allowing guide dogs in the workplace, altering emergency evacuation procedures)
- Providing qualified readers or interpreters (e.g., sign language interpreters)
- Reassigning disabled individuals to vacant positions (e.g., lateral transfer to an open job)

Reasonably accommodating employees with psychiatric disabilities can be especially challenging for employers. Major life activities that are sometimes impaired by mental illness include learning, thinking, concentrating, sleeping, caring for oneself, speaking, interacting with others, and working. *Accommodations that might be particularly helpful in meeting the needs of employees with psychiatric disabilities include leaves of absence; part-time schedules; dividers, partitions, and other sound-proofing or visual barriers to aid concentration; modified supervisory methods, including adjusting means of communication and the level of supervision and struc-ture provided; and modified work rules.*[32] Aberrant behavior that violates standards of employee conduct need not be ignored and can be the basis for discipline. How-ever, such behavior should be taken as a signal of the need for reasonable accommo-dation to help avoid future behavioral problems.

The Process of Reasonably Accommodating Disability

Not all disabled employees require accommodation. When accommodation is called for, employers are not left to their own devices. Many governmental and nongovern-mental agencies can provide advice and assistance to employers seeking to accommo-date disabled employees. Disabled employees themselves are often the best sources of information regarding their needs and what will work for them. *Employers should rely on disabled employees as key sources of information regarding reasonable ac-commodation.* This, in turn, presupposes the existence of an **interactive process** through which employers become aware of an employee's need for accommodation and then work with that person to find a mutually acceptable accommodation.

Disabled employees should be involved early and continuously in the process of identifying and choosing accommodations. The EEOC has suggested a simple methodology for this process. First, *the job in question should be examined and its essential functions determined.* Second, *the individual with a disability should be consulted with to determine his specific physical or mental abilities and limitations.* Third, *together with the disabled individual, potential accommodations should be identified and assessed.* Fourth, *an accommodation that serves the needs of the em-ployee and employer should be selected.*

What matters is a good faith effort by the employer to engage in the interactive process to identify possible accommodations. There is no specific number of meetings that must occur. In a relevant case, an employee claimed that his employer failed to properly engage in the interactive process by meeting only once with the employee in a meeting that did not include his attorney and vocational counselor. Although the presence of others with relevant expertise might be helpful, there is no legal requirement to this effect. And a single meeting was sufficient in this case because the employee had the opportunity to propose an accommodation, was told that if he

[32]EEOC. *Enforcement Guidance . . . Psychiatric Disabilities*, pp. 12–15.

thought of other possibilities to let his boss know, and a number of meetings occurred among managers to discuss whether the employee could be accommodated.[33]

Many employers have policies to guide managers in responding to requests for reasonable accommodation. Under E.O. 13164, agencies of the federal government are required to implement formal policies to facilitate reasonable accommodation.[34] *Reasonable accommodation policies should address the manner in which the reasonable accommodation process is initiated, requirements for medical information to document the need for accommodation, the process for identifying reasonable accommodations, and the choice and notification of the outcome. Employers must document all aspects of the accommodation process.*

In general, the disabled employees or applicants are responsible for making employers aware of their need for reasonable accommodation. Such notification need not be in writing; nor is it necessary for the employee or applicant to say the magic words *reasonable accommodation* or *ADA*. The individual just needs to indicate problems with doing a job or complying with other employment requirements and link this difficulty to a serious health problem. Thus, *it is critical that managers listen carefully to employees and recognize when an accommodation is being requested.* Also, where the need for accommodation is obvious because the individual's disability is visible and his difficulty performing essential functions of his job apparent, the employer should initiate a discussion regarding accommodation.

The obligation of employers to reasonably accommodate qualified disabled persons is ongoing. Whether an employee requests accommodation when hired or has received other accommodations in the past does not matter. Due to the nature of disabilities, persons who were not previously disabled may be so now, and impairments may improve or worsen over time. Nor can employers arbitrarily decide that they have accommodated employees long enough and discontinue accommodation. An employee who had been accommodated with a part-time schedule for more than 10 years had a valid ADA claim when his employer discontinued this accommodation and fired him.[35]

When presented with requests for accommodation, *employers should acknowledge receipt of the requests and act on them as quickly as possible.* If a disability was previously unknown to an employer, law allows the employer to require documentation of the need for accommodation. The primary source of such information should be the employee's own medical care provider. *Inquiries from employers to medical care providers should be restricted to information needed to document the need for accommodations (rather than open-ended excursions into the health status of employees) and should focus on the functional limitations imposed by disabilities.* If the information provided is inadequate to assess the need for accommodation, employers can require employees to be seen by another health professional, at the employer's expense. Although employers can legitimately seek documentation, care should be taken to prevent requests for help that could easily be granted from deteriorating into power struggles.

Some larger employers have ADA coordinators or standing committees (including managers, employees, and/or union representatives) that evaluate requests for accommodation. *The accommodation of reassignment to a vacant position should be considered only if the individual cannot be accommodated in her present job.* Employers need to consider the cost of potential accommodations, as well as their

[33]*Ammons v. Aramark Uniform Services*, 368 F.3d 809 (7th Cir. 2004).

[34]EEOC. "Policy Guidance on Executive Order 13164: Establishing Procedures to Facilitate the Provision of Reasonable Accommodation." no. 915.003 (October 20, 2000).

[35]*Larson v. Seagate Technology, Inc.*, 2001 U.S. Dist. LEXIS 20489.

effects on production and safety. Other things being roughly equal, *employers should adopt the accommodations preferred by disabled employees.* After all, the accommodations are intended to meet their needs. *However, the accommodation selected need not be the one preferred by the employee, provided that an effective accommodation is offered.* Although accommodations might appear to be "special treatment" and prompt questions from coworkers, *employers are obligated under the ADA to keep medical information about employees confidential, and that principle applies to divulging the reasons for reasonable accommodation as well.*

What Makes an Accommodation Reasonable?

Under the ADA, employers are required to make "reasonable" accommodation unless doing so would impose undue hardship. Most often, the interactive process results in a mutually acceptable accommodation. But in cases where an employer's capability to provide a reasonable accommodation is disputed, the exact meaning of the terms *reasonable* and *undue hardship* becomes important. The ADA does not define reasonable accommodation beyond providing examples. Case law and EEOC guidance[36] suggest a number of criteria for the reasonableness of proposed accommodations. Most of these are stated negatively—as bounds to how far employers must go. Employers remain free, of course, to *exceed* minimum legal requirements in meeting the needs of employees. The following are criteria for determining the reasonableness of a proposed accommodation:

- Effective (i.e., removes or sufficiently reduces the barrier to employment opportunity)
- Need not be the employee's preferred option
- Limited to measures that are work related and not primarily for personal use (e.g., eyeglasses)
- Need not be as far-reaching as accommodations made previously if these exceeded legal requirements
- Need not render the working conditions of disabled persons strictly equal to those of nondisabled persons; effective removal of barriers is sufficient
- Does not require creating a new position or making a promotion
- Does not require providing paid leave not available to other employees
- Does not require eliminating essential functions from a job or lowering production standards
- Does not require excusing or refraining from disciplining misconduct related to a disability
- Generally does not require making exceptions to established seniority rules

The Supreme Court addressed the issue of making exceptions to seniority systems in a case involving an airline employee whose injured back limited him to working in the mailroom.[37] When, under the airline's seniority rules, his mailroom position was opened for bidding and more senior employees indicated an interest in his position, the disabled employee requested that the airline accommodate him by making an

[36]EEOC. *Revised Enforcement Guidance: Reasonable Accommodation and Undue Hardship under the Americans with Disabilities Act* (Updated October 2002). Viewed at http://www.eeoc.gov/policy/docs/accommodation.html.
[37]*U.S. Airways v. Barnett*, 535 U.S. 391 (2002).

THE CHANGING WORKPLACE

Telework as a Reasonable Accommodation

Changes in technology and the nature of work have made the place in which work is performed less relevant for some jobs. For example, when employees primarily work on-line and use computers or other communications technology to interact with customers or coworkers, it makes very little difference where those employees are physically situated. Many employers are experimenting with telework (also know as telecommuting), allowing employees to perform some or all of their work at home. One survey found that nearly one in five U.S. employees participates in some type of teleworking arrangement, although most of these employees do so for only part of their work hours.[1] The Census Bureau's estimate that 4.2 million people worked at home in 2000 is far smaller, although the Bureau counted only those who work at home "on most days," and this figure still represented an increase of 23 percent from 1990.[2] The federal government is aiming toward making telecommuting an option for all of its employees. But are employers required to reasonably accommodate persons whose disabilities impair their mobility or otherwise substantially limit their ability to regularly attend work by allowing them to work at home? Answering this question in the affirmative could make a large difference in the number of employment opportunities available to disabled persons, but it goes against traditional ways of thinking about work.

The EEOC regards attendance and punctuality as conditions placed upon when and where work is done, but not essential functions of jobs. In this view, working at home can be a reasonable accommodation to which a disabled person is entitled if it would be an effective accommodation and would not impose undue hardship on the employer.[3] To be an effective accommodation, the essential functions of the job must be capable of being performed at home. Thus, food servers, construction workers, and assembly-line workers, among many others, could not be effectively accommodated by being allowed to work at home. Telemarketers, proofreaders, programmers, and other types of employees often could be effectively accommodated in this fashion. Key issues in determining whether the essential functions of a job can be performed at home include whether employees can be adequately supervised if working at home, whether specialized tools or equipment are needed

for the job, whether in-person interaction and close coordination with other employees is needed, whether direct interaction with customers and clients is an important part of the job, and whether immediate access to documents and other materials available only in the workplace is required to perform the job.[4]

In one significant case,[5] a medical transcriptionist that suffered from obsessive-compulsive disorder had difficulties with attendance and tardiness. Her psychiatric disability led her to obsessively engage in rituals, such as repeatedly washing and brushing her hair for hours at a time, that kept her from getting to work on time or at all. The woman received good performance appraisals for her work when in the office, but was disciplined for her poor attendance. The agency allowed her a "flexible start-time" (she could begin work at any time within a 24-hour period on days that she was scheduled to work) as an accommodation, but summarily refused her request to work at home. Other transcriptionists were allowed to work at home, but because it was agency policy not to provide this option to persons with disciplinary records, her request was denied. The woman was eventually terminated due to her attendance problems. The appeals court held that at least two reasonable accommodations were available that the agency failed to make or even adequately explore with the plaintiff: allowing her to work at home as she requested, or granting her a leave of absence to receive more intensive treatment. The court explicitly endorsed the EEOC's view that allowing work at home might be a reasonable accommodation for employees whose disabilities affect their attendance. And if teleworking would allow a disabled person to perform the essential functions of her job, the employer might be obligated to provide the equipment needed to make that possible.[6]

Although a few other courts[7] have ruled that disabled employees with attendance problems must be allowed to work at home if doing so does not impose undue hardship, many have held otherwise. One appeals court, although allowing that there might be exceptions and that circumstances could change in the future, held that working at home is generally not required as a reasonable accommodation:

Most jobs in organizations public or private involve teamwork under supervision rather

than solitary unsupervised work, . . . and cannot be performed at home without a substantial reduction in the quality of the employee's performance. This will no doubt change as communications technology advances, but is the situation today. Generally, therefore, an employer is not required to accommodate a disability by allowing the disabled worker to work, by himself, without supervision at home.[8]

A number of courts have differed with the EEOC in holding that attendance and punctuality are *themselves* essential functions of jobs on which employers can insist, and not merely conditions under which work is performed.[9] The predominant view of the courts is perhaps best captured by the Tenth Circuit's statement that:

[A] request to work at home is unreasonable if it eliminates an essential function of the job; however, summary adjudication may be improper when the employee has presented evidence she could perform the essential functions of her position at home thereby making the at-home accommodation at least facially reasonable. . . . [W]e think the determination of whether a request for an at-home accommodation is reasonable must . . . be made on a case-by-case basis.[10]

By not categorically rejecting the possibility that an employer could be required to allow a disabled employee to work at home as a reasonable accommodation, courts have left the door open to an arrangement that is sometimes the only way that many disabled persons can continue to be employed. But there remains a strong tendency for the courts to assume that work needs to be performed in a workplace, at specified times, and under close supervision. Whether this view will shift as work itself changes and telework continues to expand as a practice remains to be seen.

[1]Simon J. Nadel. "Increasing Number of Employees Work Outside Office, Telework Association Says." *Daily Labor Report* 204 (October 24, 2001), A-9.

[2]"Number of People Working at Home Increased 23 Percent From 1990 to 2000." *Daily Labor Report* 203 (October 21, 2004), A-7.

[3]Equal Employment Opportunity Commission. *Revised Enforcement Guidance: Reasonable Accommodation and Undue Hardship Under the Americans with Disabilities Act* (updated October 2002) (http://www.eeoc.gov/policy/docs/accommodation.html).

[4]Equal Employment Opportunity Commission. "Work At Home/ Telework as a Reasonable Accommodation." Viewed February 5, 2003 (http://www.eeoc.gov/facts/telework.htm).

[5]*Humphrey v. Memorial Hospitals Ass'n*, 239 F.3d 1128 (9th Cir. 2001); 122 S. Ct. 28 (2001) (U.S. Solicitor General invited to submit brief regarding the issues raised by this case).

[6]*Smith v. Bell Atlantic*, 829 N.E.2d 228, at 241-42 (Mass. App. 2005).

[7]E.g., *Langdon v. Department of Health & Human Services*, 959 F.2d 1053 (D.C. Cir. 1992); *Powers v. Polygram Holding, Inc.*, 40 F. Supp. 2d 195 (S.D.N.Y. 1999).

[8]*Vande Zande v. State of Wisconsin Department of Administration*, 44 F.3d 538, at 544 (7th Cir. 1995).

[9]E.g., *Tyndall v. National Education Centers*, 31 F.3d 209 (4th Cir. 1994); *Hypes v. First Commerce Corp.*, 134 F.3d 721 (5th Cir. 1998).

[10]*Mason v. Avaya Communications*, 357 F.3d 1114, at 1124 (10th Cir. 2004).

exception to the usual rule that more senior employees had first choice of positions. The airline ultimately declined to deviate from its seniority system and the employee was fired. The Supreme Court ruled that the advantages of a seniority system are sufficiently important that, in the usual case, requiring employers to make exceptions for disabled employees would not be "reasonable." However, a plaintiff might still be able to show the existence of "special circumstances"—such as a seniority system that already provides for numerous exceptions or whose rules are frequently changed—that would overcome the presumption that requiring the employer to bend seniority rules to accommodate a disabled person is not reasonable.

When Does an Accommodation Impose Undue Hardship?

The reasonableness of an accommodation is distinct from whether that accommodation would impose undue hardship on a particular employer. An employer can refuse to provide an otherwise reasonable accommodation if the employer can show

that providing it would require "significant difficulty or expense" in relation to the size of the company, its resources, and the nature of its operations. In general, larger employers are required to go further in accommodating disabled employees than are smaller employers. Accommodations imposing **undue hardship** are those that are unduly costly, extensive, substantial, or disruptive; or that would require fundamental alteration of the nature or operation of the business.

Congress expected that employers would incur some cost and difficulty in opening up their workplaces to disabled persons. Employers claiming undue hardship must produce evidence of significant difficulty or expense and cannot rely on mere speculation about potential costs or problems. *One way to convincingly show undue hardship is to try out an accommodation and document any problems.* (In the process, the employer might learn that providing the accommodation is not such a big deal after all.) Studies have shown that the financial costs to employers of providing reasonable accommodations are often minimal.[38] Furthermore, a variety of tax breaks and grants are available to assist employers with the costs of accommodating disabled workers. *An employer that cannot meet the cost of a proposed accommodation, even considering external funding, should offer the disabled employee the option of paying for the portion of the cost that is beyond the employer's means.*

In *Smith v. Henderson,* the court considers the claim of a disabled employee that her employer failed in its obligation to accommodate her. The case is brought under the Rehabilitation Act because her employer is the U.S. Postal Service, but the analysis would be the same under the ADA.

[38]"ADA Accommodations Costs Average $121 for Sears, Study Shows." *BNAC Communicator* (Winter 1995), 21.

SMITH V. HENDERSON
376 F.3d 529 (6th Cir. 2004)

OPINION BY CIRCUIT JUDGE CLAY:

Plaintiff Mary Christine Smith appeals the . . . order of the United States District Court . . . , granting Defendant United States Postal Service's motion for summary judgment on her claims for . . . disability discrimination, in violation of the Rehabilitation Act of 1973. . . . [T]he district court erred in granting summary judgment. . . .

In July, 1979, Plaintiff Mary Christine Smith began her career for the USPS as a distribution clerk in Evansville, Indiana. In September, 1986, Smith was transferred to Elizabethtown, Kentucky, where her title remained distribution clerk. At some point in 1986, Smith disclosed to her supervisors that she has rheumatoid arthritis, which "affects the mobility of [her] hands, legs and feet." In 1997, Smith's physician limited her work time to 8 hours per day, 40 hours per week, and limited her lifting to no more than 20 pounds. The USPS's physicians and supervisory personnel approved of these work restrictions.

In early 1998, a panel of postmasters from the area surrounding Elizabethtown, Kentucky recommended Smith for promotion to customer service supervisor, Tour I, effective March 15, 1998. Tour I is the night shift at the post office when all mail must be off-loaded from the trucks, sorted and dispatched out to the associate post offices. * * * Smith . . . accepted the promotion.

According to Smith, after she became the Tour I Supervisor, she suffered through a series of events that ultimately left her no choice but to quit her job only four months later. * * * [Among other complaints] Smith . . . complains that Mullin refused to permit her to delegate

the duty of facility-wide financial accounting to a subordinate employee, as he had permitted the male Tour I supervisors who had preceded her in that position. As a result, Smith's work day was lengthened, requiring her to work between 10 and 12 hours a day, in contravention of her medical restriction. For one stretch of time (between June 5 and July 5, 1998), Smith worked for thirty days straight without a day off. For another stretch (between July 2 and 17, 1998), Smith was required to work with only one or two days off.

The USPS concedes that the Tour I Supervisor's accounting duties are time-consuming. It points out that Conklin, Smith's male predecessor as Tour I Supervisor, used to spend two to three hours per day on the accounting function. The USPS argues that Mullin would have permitted Smith to delegate the accounting functions to a subordinate, as long as "the assignment did not result in mail being delayed, if it did not violate the terms of the union contract, if it did not cause an increase in work hours and if it did not cause Elizabethtown to incur unnecessary overtime." Mullin did not permit Smith to delegate these duties because Smith's mail production numbers were down, while the costs were up. Smith has acknowledged that production was down on Tour I because she was pulling a subordinate from the production line to perform the accounting work. * * *

On July 17, 1998, Mullin directed Smith to report for duty the following Monday, which was one of Smith's scheduled days off. "Exhausted and in constant pain," Smith resigned her position. * * *

Smith is alleging that the USPS failed to reasonably accommodate her disability as required by the Rehabilitation Act and that the failure-to-accommodate precipitated her involuntary resignation. Thus, the central issue is whether the USPS's alleged rescission of, or refusal to provide, a reasonable accommodation converted her resignation into a constructive discharge. The EEOC's regulations pursuant to Title I of the Americans with Disabilities Act ("ADA") set forth the relevant legal standards for a Rehabilitation Act claim against the USPS. Under these regulations, it would have been unlawful for the USPS not to make reasonable accommodation to Smith's known physical limitations, unless the accommodation would have imposed "an undue hardship on the operation of its business." A reasonable accommodation means, among other things, "modifications or adjustments . . . to the manner or circumstances under which the position held or desired is customarily

performed." Smith was entitled to a reasonable accommodation at the USPS so long as she was a "qualified" individual with a disability, meaning that the modifications and adjustments she sought would have enabled her to perform the "essential functions" of the Tour I Supervisor job. The essential functions means the "fundamental job duties" of the position, not "marginal functions."

The USPS has conceded that Smith, who suffers from rheumatoid arthritis, is disabled and that it provided her a reasonable accommodation in 1997 so that she could perform her non-management position as a distribution clerk. That accommodation limited her work to no more than eight hours per day, 40 hours per week. It can be inferred from the record that the Tour I Supervisor position that Smith assumed in 1998 generally demanded more than 40 hours of work per week due in part to the accounting responsibilities. Further, . . . a reasonable jury could infer that, after Smith became Tour I Supervisor, Mullin rescinded the hours-of-work accommodation that she had enjoyed as a distribution clerk and/or refused to extend this accommodation to her new job. ([Smith testified] that Mullin reminded her numerous times after she became a supervisor that she "was an exempt employee and [she] could work over 40 hours and *[her] medical restrictions didn't apply because [she] was an exempt employee*").

Additionally, . . . after Mullin refused to honor the hours-of-work accommodation, he subsequently denied Smith another form of accommodation that effectively would have reduced her work hours in the Tour I Supervisor position. Via a letter dated May 3, 1998, Smith asked Mullin if she could delegate her financial accounting duties to a subordinate, as other Tour I Supervisors had done in the past. Since it is undisputed that the accounting duties were time-consuming and Mullin was aware of Smith's disability and her need to work restricted hours, a factfinder could infer that Smith's letter constituted a request for an accommodation that would have substantially shortened her work day, in line with her medical restrictions. Such an inference would be reasonable even though Smith's letter did not use the word "accommodation" or specifically mention that she was seeking to delegate the accounting function because of her disability. The context in which the letter was written permits an inference that Mullin knew or should have known that Smith sought to delegate her accounting duties in order to make her job conform with her medical restrictions. * * * [T]hese

facts create a genuine issue of material fact as to whether the May 3, 1998 letter, which sought to delegate the accounting duties, was a request for a reasonable accommodation that triggered the USPS's obligation to participate, in good faith, in an "interactive process" with Smith as to potential reasonable accommodations. According to Smith, Mullin rejected her proposed accommodation, telling her that she was "now in a man's world" and accusing her of "always whining." Thus, if a jury were to find that Smith's May 3, 1998, letter constituted a request for a reasonable accommodation, there appears to be little dispute that the USPS flatly denied that request.

The USPS argues that Smith waived her right to request a delegation-of-accounting-duties accommodation because "she was told before she assumed the duties she would not be allowed to delegate. . . ." * * * [A] qualified individual with a disability does not waive her right to an accommodation in the form of a modification of job duties simply by being apprised of the job duties before she commences work. If this were the rule of law, it is difficult to see how a disabled individual ever would be entitled to a reasonable accommodation, since people usually are aware of what their duties will be before they start a new job.

Given the precedent of prior Tour I Supervisors delegating the accounting function to subordinate employees (including to Smith before she was promoted), there also is a genuine issue of material fact as to whether the accounting duty was an essential function of the Tour I Supervisor position. As a non-essential function, the accounting duty potentially could have been reassigned to subordinate employees as a "reasonable" accommodation of Smith's disability. And if a factfinder reasonably could infer that the accounting duty was a non-essential job function that could have been reassigned, there also is a genuine issue of material fact as to whether this accommodation would have imposed an "undue hardship" on the USPS, a circumstance that would have justified the USPS's denial of that accommodation. The USPS bears the burden of providing undue hardship, but it has not set forth specific facts indisputably demonstrating that such an accommodation would have resulted in "significant difficulty or expense." Mullin states generally that he did not want Smith to delegate her accounting duties because "production was down and costs were up" due to Smith's use of clerks to perform the accounting. But it is not clear from the record that the lower production and increased costs amounted to

significant difficulty or expense, especially when the USPS had permitted other Tour I Supervisors to use subordinate employees for the accounting function. The USPS further argues that Smith was not permitted to delegate the accounting function because she did not know how to do it correctly. But the fact that Smith could not adequately perform a marginal job function suggests that it would have benefitted the USPS to assign that function to another employee. Ironically, the USPS's argument tends to show that the accommodation Smith requested was reasonable. The USPS also has presented no evidence regarding other factors relevant to the "undue hardship" defense, such as the overall financial resources of the Elizabethtown Post Office, the overall financial resources of the USPS, and the impact on the Elizabethtown Post Office's ability to conduct business. * * *

Assuming that Smith was denied a reasonable accommodation that forced her to work well in excess of her medical restrictions, a jury reasonably could infer that the USPS (through Mullin) knew that Smith's working conditions would become intolerable to a reasonable person suffering from her particular disability. * * * The district court erred in ruling, as a matter of law, that Smith had not suffered a constructive discharge.

We do not believe that Smith's situation is comparable to that of employees who prematurely quit their jobs in apprehension that their situations would not improve. Those cases do not involve an individual like Smith, who allegedly was worked to exhaustion and poor health by an employer who was aware of the individual's disability, but nevertheless refused to honor a reasonable accommodation, and denied another, that would have precluded such an overwhelming workload. We also do not believe that Smith had an affirmative duty under the Rehabilitation Act to request her old job back as a distribution clerk (along with the hours restriction that accompanied it) once she realized that she could not work the hours of a Tour I Supervisor. * * * Requiring a disabled employee to relinquish a promotion because an employer refuses to comply with the law by looking beyond the disability and providing a reasonable accommodation would flout this fundamental goal.

CASE QUESTIONS

1. What are the legal issues in this case? What did the court decide?

2. Is Smith a "qualified individual with a disability"?

3. In your view, did Smith request accommodation for her disability?

4. If so, were the requested accommodations "reasonable"? Would they likely pose "undue hardship" for the Postal Service?

5. Is it relevant that Smith did not request accommodation at the time that she accepted the promotion?

6. What is the relationship between failure to accommodate and "constructive discharge"?

REASONABLE ACCOMMODATION OF RELIGION

Under Title VII, *employers are required to reasonably accommodate religion, unless doing so would impose undue hardship*. The essential nature of this requirement, including engaging in an interactive process with the employee or applicant and being flexible when administering policies, is much the same as that for accommodating a disability. However, courts have interpreted the requirement to reasonably accommodate religion as being much more limited than the responsibility to accommodate disability.

Religion

Religion is not only membership in or affiliation with a particular church, congregation, or denomination. Title VII defines **religion** to encompass:

> [A]ll aspects of religious observance and practice, as well as belief, unless an employer demonstrates that he is unable to reasonably accommodate to an employee's or prospective employee's religious observance or practice without undue hardship on the conduct of the employer's business.[39]

Thus, unlike other protected classes, religion is not only something that a person "is" (e.g., a Jew, a Muslim), but also something that is expressed through words and deeds. This behavioral aspect of religion sometimes requires accommodation.

 What makes a belief or practice "religious," as opposed to "philosophical," "political," or "ideological"? The EEOC treats as religious "moral and ethical beliefs as to what is right and wrong which are sincerely held with the strength of religious views."[40] Courts have struggled to distinguish between the secular and the religious. Belief in a particular God or deity is not a necessary element of religion. In fact, atheism and agnosticism are forms of religious belief.[41] To be considered religious, however, courts generally require that such beliefs or practices perform a function in the individual's life comparable to that of traditional religions. Courts have recognized the religious basis of a broad range of beliefs. For example, opposition to abortion,[42] military draft registration,[43] and nuclear power[44] all have been treated

[39]42 U.S.C.A. § 2000e(j) (2005).

[40]29 C.F.R. § 1605.1 (2005).

[41]*EEOC v. Townley Engineering & Manufacturing Co.*, 859 F.2d 610 (9th Cir. 1988), *cert. denied,* 489 U.S. 1077 (1989).

[42]*Wilson v. U.S. West Communications*, 58 F.3d 1337 (8th Cir. 1995).

[43]*American Postal Workers Union v. Postmaster General*, 781 F.2d 772 (9th Cir. 1986).

[44]*Best v. California Apprenticeship Council*, 207 Cal. Rptr. 863 (Cal. App. 1984).

by courts as religious beliefs. The espoused religion does not have to be popular, well known, or even organized. An individual's own sincere beliefs about what his religion requires, even when these go beyond the formal teachings and requirements of his religion, are still aspects of religious belief and practice that potentially require accommodation.

In one recent case, a court considered whether veganism is a religious creed. A job offer at a pharmaceutical warehouse was withdrawn when a candidate who is a strict vegan refused to be immunized for mumps (the vaccine for mumps is grown in chicken embryos). The candidate refused to be immunized because his vegan beliefs dictated that it is immoral to kill or exploit animals, whether for food, clothing, vaccines, or any other purpose. The court concluded that veganism is not a religious creed within the meaning of the California antidiscrimination statute in question, but rather "a personal philosophy, albeit shared by many others, and a way of life."[45] The court based its decision on the fact that the statutory definition of religious creed is narrower than the EEOC's broad concept, but also on criteria distilled from other court cases. Those criteria emphasize that religions address fundamental questions about human existence, entail comprehensive belief systems rather than isolated precepts, and often display formal and external signs such as leaders, ceremonies, and holidays. Veganism's claim to status as a religious practice failed because it was seen as not addressing ultimate questions of meaning, being narrowly focused on the single issue of the treatment of animals, and lacking the external trappings typical of religion.

A religious belief also must be "sincerely held" to be protected. The tendency of the courts is to accept plaintiffs' assertions about their religious beliefs, at least absent clear evidence to the contrary (e.g., prior behavior inconsistent with the alleged religious practice, nonmembership in the relevant religious group). As a general rule, *employers should accept the sincerity of employees' stated religious beliefs and practices and focus on whether it is possible to reasonably accommodate them without undue hardship.* However, in a case involving an employee who claimed religious objections to paying union dues, the union's efforts to verify the sincerity of his beliefs did not violate Title VII.[46] Both the National Labor Relations Act and Title VII require labor unions to allow employees whose sincerely held religious beliefs dictate that they not belong to or financially support unions to contribute an equivalent sum to charity. Suspicious because the employee had worked for years without raising any objection and was being provided with information by an organization hostile to unions, the union required that he provide some independent confirmation of the sincerity of his stated beliefs. The court stressed the very limited extent to which employers can inquire into the sincerity of employees' beliefs, but held that the union's actions were not illegal.

Failure to Reasonably Accommodate Religion

Religious beliefs and practices can clash with workplace requirements under a variety of circumstances. One of the most common is when an employee's *work schedule* conflicts with a Sabbath, holy day, or other religious observance. Likewise, religious practices regarding the wearing of particular clothing, facial hair, or symbols sometimes run up against employer *grooming, uniform, and appearance requirements.* Sometimes, the very *tasks required of employees* conflict with religious

[45]*Friedman v. Southern California Permanente Medical Group*, 102 Cal. App. 4th 39, at 70 (2nd App. Dist. 2002).

[46]*Bushhouse v. Local Union 2209, UAW*, 164 F. Supp. 2d 1066 (N.D. Ind. 2001).

ELEMENTS OF A CLAIM

Failure to Reasonably Accommodate Religion

An applicant or employee can establish a **prima facie case of failure to reasonably accommodate religion** by showing the following:

* The existence of a sincere religious belief or practice that conflicts with an employment requirement
* That the employer was informed of the conflicting belief or practice
* That the employee or applicant suffered an adverse employment outcome due to adhering to the religious belief or practice

If a prima facie case is established, the employer must show one of the following:

* A reasonable accommodation was offered, but not accepted.
* No reasonable accommodation without undue hardship was available.

Inability to establish one of these circumstances will result in a finding that the employer has violated Title VII by failing to reasonably accommodate religion.

beliefs. Examples include a Pentecostal nurse's refusal to assist in occasional abortions[47] and an evangelical Christian counselor's refusal to counsel clients who were homosexual or living together outside of marriage.[48] Whether pharmacists should have the right, on religious grounds, to refuse to dispense certain medications, such as the "morning after" pill intended to terminate pregnancy, is a hotly contested issue (see "Clippings"). Employers are also frequently asked to accommodate employees by allowing them to decorate office space for religious holidays and by providing special meals at company events.[49] There is anecdotal evidence that employees (and perhaps employers as well) exhibit a wider range of religious practices than in the past and are more likely to assert strong religious beliefs and practices in the workplace. If this is true, employers can expect to see more conflicts emerge for which reasonable accommodations will have to be considered. *Maintaining policies that are flexible (e.g., a fixed number of days off that can be used for different reasons) may prevent conflicts from arising in the first place.*

Employers are not expected to be aware of the religious affiliations and practices of their employees. To be entitled to accommodation, employees must inform their employers regarding the presence of conflicts between their religious practices and workplace requirements—and do so before disciplinary action is taken. In one case,[50] an employee with evangelical Christian beliefs was terminated for mailing upsetting letters to other employees' homes. All the letters conveyed the basic sentiment that the employees were sinners who needed to repent. The court agreed that her letters were religiously motivated and that she was punished for doing what she felt her religion required (again, it is not necessary that others of the same faith

[47]*Shelton v. University of Medicine & Dentistry of New Jersey,* 223 F.3d 220 (3d Cir. 2000).
[48]*Bruff v. North Mississippi Health Services, Inc.,* 244 F.3d 495 (5th Cir. 2001), *cert. denied,* 122 S. Ct 348 (2001).
[49]"Religious Discrimination: Survey Finds Employers Have Greater Need to Accommodate Diverse Needs of Employees." *Daily Labor Report,* 127 (July 3, 2001), A-6.
[50]*Chalmers v. Tulon Company of Richmond,* 101 F.3d 1012 (4th Cir. 1996).

would have felt compelled to act in the same manner). However, she was unable to establish a prima facie case of failure to reasonably accommodate because she did not notify the employer, before the fact, of the conflict arising out of her need to send the letters.

Although employees are responsible to make conflicts with their religion known, *employers should listen carefully to employees and be prepared to consider accommodation when alerted to the fact that an employee is having problems with a policy or other workplace requirement related to her religion.* Employees will rarely use terms like *reasonable accommodation,* so it is up to employers to recognize the issue.

The final element of a prima facie case of failure to reasonably accommodate is a showing that the employee was subjected to an adverse employment decision (e.g., suspension, demotion, termination) due to following his beliefs. Most courts appear to require actual loss of employment opportunity, not merely the threat. Thus, in a case involving a hospital clerk whose work schedule conflicted with her Sabbath, the hospital was not liable for failing to accommodate her because she suffered no actual adverse employment consequences. Perhaps fearing discipline or termination, the woman had continued to work the assigned hours that made it impossible to observe her Sabbath. The court observed that "Plaintiff's failure to insist upon strict adherence to these beliefs, even at the cost of negative job consequences, effectively absolved her employer of the responsibility to reasonably accommodate her beliefs."[51]

When presented with timely requests for accommodation of sincere religious beliefs or practices, *employers must take requests for reasonable accommodation seriously and make good faith efforts to identify reasonable accommodations that do not impose undue hardship.* Although a good faith effort to find an accommodation might come up empty, employers are in a better position if some accommodation is offered rather than none. As with disability, *a reasonable accommodation of religion need not be the employee's preferred or suggested accommodation,*[52] *but providing the employee's preference/suggestion should be the first inclination.* Employees who reject reasonable accommodations offered to them are out of luck. The courts also expect that employees will cooperate in the reasonable accommodation process. Thus, the claim of a nurse who refused to assist in abortions failed because she rejected a transfer to the newborn unit and did not work with the hospital human resource staff to locate an alternative position.[53]

How far must employers go in accommodating religion? *Cloutier v. Costco* is an interesting case in which the court expresses some skepticism as to whether a genuine religious conflict exists, but ultimately decides the case on the basis of whether the employee's proposed accommodation would constitute an "undue hardship."

The measures that must be taken to accommodate religion are not extensive. The Supreme Court has characterized the obligation to accommodate religion as "de minimis."[54] In contrast to the ADA's requirement that reasonable accommodations be made absent "significant expense or difficulty," employers need incur no more than minimal expense or operational problems in accommodating religion. In a case involving an employee seeking a work schedule accommodation to allow

[51]*Stone v. West,* 133 F. Supp. 2d 972, at 986 (E.D. Mich. 2001).

[52]*Ansonia Board of Education v. Philbrook,* 479 U.S. 60 (1986).

[53]*Shelton,* at 228.

[54]*TWA v. Hardison,* 432 U.S. 63, at 84 (1977).

CLOUTIER V. COSTCO

390 F. 3d 126 (1st Cir. 2004); cert. denied, 2005 U.S. LEXIS 4923

OPINION BY CIRCUIT JUDGE LIPEZ:

Kimberly Cloutier alleges that her employer, Costco Wholesale Corp. (Costco), failed to offer her a reasonable accommodation after she alerted it to a conflict between the "no facial jewelry" provision of its dress code and her religious practice as a member of the Church of Body Modification. She argues that this failure amounts to religious discrimination The district court granted summary judgment for Costco, concluding that Costco reasonably accommodated Cloutier by offering to reinstate her if she either covered her facial piercing with a band-aid or replaced it with a clear retainer. We affirm the grant of summary judgment, but on a different basis. We hold that Costco had no duty to accommodate Cloutier because it could not do so without undue hardship.

* * * Kimberly Cloutier began working at Costco's West Springfield, Massachusetts store in July 1997. Before her first day of work, Cloutier received a copy of the Costco employment agreement, which included the employee dress code. When she was hired, Cloutier had multiple earrings and four tattoos, but no facial piercings. * * * In 1998, Costco revised its dress code to prohibit food handlers, including deli employees, from wearing any jewelry. Cloutier's supervisor instructed her to remove her earrings pursuant to the revised code, but Cloutier refused. Instead, she requested to transfer to a front-end position where she would be permitted to continue wearing her jewelry. Cloutier did not indicate at the time that her insistence on wearing her earrings was based on a religious or spiritual belief. Costco approved Cloutier's transfer back to a front-end position in June 1998, and promoted her to cashier soon thereafter. Over the ensuing two years, she engaged in various forms of body modification including facial piercing and cutting. Although these practices were meaningful to Cloutier, they were not motivated by a religious belief. In March 2001, Costco further revised its dress code to prohibit all facial jewelry, aside from earrings, and disseminated the modified code to its employees. Cloutier did not challenge the dress code or seek an accommodation, but rather continued uneventfully to wear her eyebrow piercing for several months. Costco began enforcing its no-facial-jewelry policy in June 2001. On June 25, 2001, front-end supervisors Todd Cunningham and Michele Callaghan informed Cloutier and another employee, Jennifer Theriaque, that they would have to remove their facial piercings. Cloutier and Theriaque did not comply, returning to work the following day still wearing their piercings. When Callaghan reiterated the no-facial-jewelry policy, Cloutier indicated for the first time that she was a member of the Church of Body Modification (CBM), and that her eyebrow piercing was part of her religion.

The CBM was established in 1999 and counts approximately 1000 members who participate in such practices as piercing, tattooing, branding, cutting, and body manipulation. Among the goals espoused in the CBM's mission statement are for its members to "grow as individuals through body modification and its teachings," to "promote growth in mind, body and spirit," and to be "confident role models in learning, teaching, and displaying body modification." The church's website, apparently its primary mode for reaching its adherents, did not state that members' body modifications had to be visible at all times or that temporarily removing body modifications would violate a religious tenet. Still, Cloutier interprets the call to be a confident role model as requiring that her piercings be visible at all times and precluding her from removing or covering her facial jewelry. She does not extend this reasoning to the tattoos on her upper arms, which were covered at work by her shirt.

After reviewing information that Cloutier provided from the CBM website, Callaghan's supervisor, Andrew Mulik, instructed Cloutier and Theriaque to remove their facial jewelry. They refused. * * * Although Cloutier learned during the week of July 2, 2001 that Theriaque had returned to work with retainers, she chose to wait for her EEOC complaint to be resolved rather than following suit. During the week of July 7, 2001, Cloutier inquired of her superiors whether she could use vacation time to cover her absences and was told that she had been suspended. The following week, on July 14, Cloutier received notice in the mail that she had been terminated

for her unexcused absences resulting from noncompliance with the dress code. She claims that this was her first notice that Costco had decided not to grant her request for an accommodation that would reconcile the dress code with her religious requirement of displaying her facial jewelry at all times.

The parties remained in contact after Cloutier's termination through the EEOC mediation process. During a meeting on August 10, 2001, Costco offered to let Cloutier return to work wearing either plastic retainers or a Band-Aid over her jewelry (the same accommodation that Cloutier had suggested prior to her termination). Shevchuk repeated the offer in a letter dated August 29, 2001, asking Cloutier to respond by September 6, 2001.

Although there is some dispute as to whether Cloutier attempted to respond to Costco's offer before the deadline, she now maintains that neither of the proffered accommodations would be adequate because the CBM's tenets, as she interprets them, require her to display all of her facial piercings at all times. Replacing her eyebrow piercing with a plastic retainer or covering it with a Band-Aid would thus contradict her religious convictions. Cloutier asserts that the only reasonable accommodation would be to excuse her from Costco's dress code, allowing her to wear her facial jewelry to work. Costco responds that this accommodation would interfere with its ability to maintain a professional appearance and would thereby create an undue hardship for its business. * * *

On appeal, Cloutier vigorously asserts that her insistence on displaying all her facial jewelry at all times is the result of a sincerely held religious belief. Determining whether a belief is religious is "more often than not a difficult and delicate task," one to which the courts are ill-suited. Fortunately, as the district court noted, there is no need for us to delve into this thorny question in the present case. Even assuming, arguendo, that Cloutier established her prima facie case, the facts here do not support a finding of impermissible religious discrimination. * * * We find dispositive that the only accommodation Cloutier considers reasonable, a blanket exemption from the no-facial-jewelry policy, would impose an undue hardship on Costco. In such a situation, an employer has no obligation to offer an accommodation before taking an adverse employment action.

Title VII of the Civil Rights Act of 1964 prohibits employers from discriminating against employees on the basis of, among other things, religion. Under Title VII, an employer must offer a reasonable accommodation to resolve a conflict between an employee's sincerely held religious belief and a condition of employment, unless such an accommodation would create an undue hardship for the employer's business. * * *

Cloutier was terminated on July 14, 2001. She maintains that Costco did not extend any offer of accommodation until August 10, 2001, approximately one month later, during a meeting that was part of the EEOC mediation process. * * * Courts in at least two of our sister circuits have ruled that an accommodation offered after an adverse employment action does not shield an employer from liability under Title VII. Courts have also acknowledged that the opposite rule, treating as reasonable a post-termination offer extended during the EEOC mediation process, would "encourage the making of such offers, thus furthering [Title VII's] important statutory policy favoring voluntary reconciliation." Yet, as the Tenth Circuit has noted, this rule would also leave employers' conduct "virtually unregulated" when conflicts first arise. As a consequence, "Title VII would provide employees no protection until after the fact, an important consideration given the impact a suspension, termination, or rejection may have on an individual's life." * * * We have yet to consider this question directly and decline to do so here. . . . Our affirmance rests instead on an alternative ground advanced by Costco—namely, that the only accommodation Cloutier considers reasonable would impose an undue hardship on Costco. * * *

An accommodation constitutes an "undue hardship" if it would impose more than a de minimis cost on the employer. This calculus applies both to economic costs, such as lost business or having to hire additional employees to accommodate a Sabbath observer, and to noneconomic costs, such as compromising the integrity of a seniority system. Cloutier argues that Costco has not met its burden of demonstrating that her requested accommodation would impose an undue hardship. She asserts that she did not receive complaints about her facial piercings and that the piercings did not affect her job performance. Hence, she contends that any hardship Costco posits is merely hypothetical and therefore not sufficient to excuse it from accommodating her religious practice under Title VII. Courts are "somewhat skeptical of hypothetical hardships that an employer thinks might be caused by an accommodation that

RULE *

never has been put into practice." "Nevertheless, it is possible for an employer to prove undue hardship without actually having undertaken any of the possible accommodations. . . ." It can do so by "examining the specific hardships imposed by specific accommodation proposals." Here, Costco has only one proposal to evaluate (allowing Cloutier to wear and display her body jewelry as she demands) and has determined that it would constitute an undue hardship.

* * * It is axiomatic that, for better or for worse, employees reflect on their employers. This is particularly true of employees who regularly interact with customers, as Cloutier did in her cashier position. Even if Cloutier did not personally receive any complaints about her appearance, her facial jewelry influenced Costco's public image and, in Costco's calculation, detracted from its professionalism. Costco is far from unique in adopting personal appearance standards to promote and protect its image. * * *

Courts have long recognized the importance of personal appearance regulations, even in the face of Title VII challenges. * * * Courts considering Title VII religious discrimination claims have also upheld dress code policies that, like Costco's, are designed to appeal to customer preference or to promote a professional public image. The majority of religious discrimination cases in this arena appear to involve policies regulating facial hair. But we are not the first court to consider a religious discrimination claim involving jewelry. In *Daniels v. City of Arlington* 246 F.3d 500 (5th Cir. 2001), a former police officer claimed that his dismissal for wearing a gold cross pin on his uniform in violation of the police department's no-pin policy violated Title VII. The only reasonable accommodation that Daniels cited was to exempt him from the no-pin policy. The Fifth Circuit granted summary judgment for the police department, concluding that "the only accommodation Daniels proposes is unreasonable and an undue hardship for the city as a matter of law." * * * The assessment of what constitutes an undue hardship may be somewhat different for a private employer than for a police department. Still, we are faced with the similar situation of an employee who will accept no accommodation short of an outright exemption from a neutral dress code. Granting such an exemption would be an undue hardship because it would adversely affect the employer's public image. Costco has made a determination that facial piercings, aside from earrings, detract from the "neat, clean and professional image" that it

aims to cultivate. Such a business determination is within its discretion. * * *

Cloutier argues that regardless of the reasons for the dress code, permitting her to display her facial jewelry would not be an undue hardship because Costco already overlooks other violations of its policy. In support of her position, she cites affidavits from two Costco employees identifying co-workers who "were allowed to wear facial piercings . . . and were not disciplined." Costco responds that any employees who displayed facial jewelry did so without its permission or knowledge, noting that constant monitoring is impossible in a facility with several hundred employees. * * * [T]here is an important distinction between an employee who displays facial jewelry unnoticed in violation of the dress code and one who does so under an exemption from the dress code. In the first scenario, Costco can instruct an employee to remove facial jewelry as soon as it becomes aware of a violation. In the second scenario, Costco forfeits its ability to mandate compliance and thus loses control over its public image.

That loss, as we have discussed, would constitute an undue hardship.

CASE QUESTIONS

1. What is the legal issue in this case? What did the court decide?

2. In your view, is Cloutier able to establish a prima facie case of failure to reasonably accommodate? Does she show the existence of a sincere *religious* belief or practice that conflicts with the employer's appearance requirements?

3. Comment on the *process* of reasonable accommodation in this case. How might Costco have handled the process better? Cloutier?

4. Should courts consider accommodations offered after an adverse employment action has been taken in determining whether an employer has failed to offer a reasonable accommodation?

5. Does Costco meet its burden of showing that no accommodation is acceptable to Cloutier that it could provide without undue hardship? Under the logic of this decision, would employers ever have to make exceptions to established dress and appearance codes to accommodate religious practice?

observance of a Sabbath, the Court concluded that the employer was not required to bear the cost of paying other employees a premium to accept his shift, nor to place the burden of accommodation onto other employees by changing seniority rules or forcing them to work the shift.[55] *To deal with scheduling conflicts, employers should allow and facilitate private swaps between employees; allow employees to use available personal time; permit flexible schedules; and, within normal job assignment procedures, explore the possibility of changes in position that might lessen conflicts. Making exceptions to grooming and appearance requirements will, in many cases, be reasonable and not impose undue hardship.* Note that the accommodation that might be required is making an exception, rather than eliminating, the underlying policy. To settle a suit brought by the EEOC, Federal Express agreed to make exceptions to its no-beard policy for employees whose religious beliefs require them to be bearded.[56] However, safety concerns (e.g., the need to be clean shaven, to wear a respirator), effects on coworkers or the public, or the nature of the job (e.g., police) might render granting exceptions to grooming and appearance policies an undue hardship. In *Cloutier,* the possibility of an adverse effect on the company's public image was sufficient to establish undue hardship—even in the absence of any evidence that employing a clerk who wore facial jewelry would have such an effect. *Conflicts arising from objectionable job duties might require employers to provide assistance in arranging transfers to alternative positions.*

RELIGIOUS ADVOCACY AND RELIGIOUS HARASSMENT

As the allegations concerning the Air Force Academy illustrate (see "Clippings"), employees sometimes convey their religious beliefs to others in the workplace. Often, the aim is to interest coworkers or customers in a particular religion. Such **religious advocacy** or "proselytizing" puts employers in a difficult position. On the one hand, it is part of the proselytizing employee's religious beliefs and practices, potentially requiring accommodation. At the same time, employers are obligated to protect employees from **religious harassment**. The religious advocacy of one employee can be the hostile environment—based on unwelcome, pervasive religious communications—of others. In one illuminating case, a Catholic woman made a solemn vow to wear a large button graphically depicting an aborted fetus during all of her waking hours, until abortion was no more. This disturbed a number of her coworkers and created an uproar in the workplace. The employer, and the court, accepted her button wearing as a sincere religious practice. The employer offered three accommodations to the employee: (1) wear the button when in her own cubicle, but remove it when circulating throughout the office; (2) wear a smaller, less graphic button; or (3) wear the same button at all times, but conceal it in some manner (e.g., by wearing a sweater) when outside of her cubicle. The employee rejected all three proposals. The court held that one of the proposed accommodations, the third one, allowed her to keep her vow and was thus a reasonable accommodation. Because the woman turned it down, her termination was legal.[57] Notice that although coworker preferences generally do not justify employment decisions based on protected class, the nature of the religious practice involved here

[55]*Hardison,* at 77–81.

[56]"Religious Discrimination: FedEx Will Moderate No-Beard Policy to Oblige Muslims Under Consent Decree." *Daily Labor Report* 118 (June 20, 2001), A-2.

[57]*Wilson,* at 1342.

and the employer's simultaneous obligation to prevent religious harassment made consideration of coworker sentiments necessary. The religious advocacy was also actually interfering with employees' ability to work, as opposed to just prompting a few complaints.

In another significant case,[58] an employee who described himself as a "devout Christian" objected to a series of posters displayed by Hewlett-Packard as part of its workplace diversity campaign. The employee particularly objected to what he saw as the company's approval of homosexual activities that his faith instructed him were sinful. The employee responded by posting two biblical passages condeming homosexuality. The quotes from the Bible were visible to coworkers, customers, and other passersby. The employee admitted that the quotes were intentionally "hurtful" toward gays and lesbians to prompt them to repent. Numerous meetings were held with the employee. When the employee continued to refuse to remove the posted material, he was terminated. Regarding the employee's failure-to-accommodate claim, the court expressed "doubt that the doctrines to which [the employee] professes allegiance compel any employee to engage in either expressive or physical activity designed to hurt or harass one's fellow employees," but decided that accommodating the employee would impose undue hardship in any event. The employee indicated that the only acceptable arrangements were to either allow him to continue to post the biblical verses or for the company to remove its "gay posters," in which case he would reciprocate by removing the biblical verses. The court concluded that:

> [The] first proposed accommodation would have compelled Hewlett-Packard to permit an employee to post messages intended to demean and harass his coworkers. His second proposed accommodation would have forced the company to exclude sexual orientation from its workplace diversity program. Either choice would have created undue hardship for Hewlet-Packard because it would have inhibited its efforts to attract and retain a qualified, diverse workforce, which the company reasonably views as vital to its commercial success . . .[59]

The court also distinguished between actions that some coworkers find irritating or unwelcome and actions that "demean or degrade," holding that although employers might have to tolerate the former when they entail religious expression, the latter constitute undue hardship.

These are difficult situations. As a starting point, *employers should not attempt to stifle all religious communication in the workplace. Nor should employers have different policies for more familiar faiths and less familiar ones. Channeling religious communications into forums that allow other employees to receive or ignore the messages as they wish (e.g., postings on bulletin boards, providing private meeting areas for those interested in discussion) will sometimes prove to be a workable solution.*

Sometimes employers rather than employees are the ones expressing their religious views. In one important case,[60] the owners of a company wanted it to be a "Christian, faith-operated business." The company required all employees to attend a weekly devotional service that lasted up to 45 minutes and included prayer and Scripture reading (as well as some business matters). An employee who was an atheist objected to this requirement. The court ruled that although an employer could hold such services, it needed to reasonably accommodate employees who found participation contrary to their own religious beliefs, unless doing so would impose undue hardship

[58]*Peterson v. Hewlett-Packard*, 358 F.3d 599 (9th Cir. 2004).

[59]*Peterson*, at 607.

[60]*EEOC v. Townley Engineering & Manufacturing Co.*, 859 F.2d 610 (9th Cir. 1988), *cert. denied*, 489 U.S. 1077 (1989).

on the operation of the business. Because the employer could have simply excused objecting employees, the employer violated Title VII. In contrast, the Massachusetts Supreme Court held that a mandatory, week-long, nondenominational seminar for managers that used references to Scripture was not discriminatory.[61]

Public employers are subject to the U.S. Constitution, as well as Title VII. This further complicates the handling of religion in the workplace for government agencies. A detailed discussion of the First Amendment's protections of speech and religion is not possible here. Suffice it to say that the First Amendment protects the "free exercise" of religion from infringement by the government (the **free exercise clause**), but also prohibits governmental entities from "establishing" (i.e., sponsoring, supporting) religion (the **establishment clause**). Thus, *public employers need to be especially careful to not unduly limit the religious speech and conduct of employees, while at the same time not allowing the workplace to become infused with religious content.* The importance of striking the right balance is illustrated by a case in which a computer analyst at the California State Department of Education incorporated the phrase "Servant of the Lord Jesus Christ" into all of his work.[62] The department responded by disciplining him and issuing rules prohibiting all religious advocacy in the workplace, as well as the storage or display of religious materials anywhere except in a person's own office or cubicle. The court concluded that the agency's rules restricting religious expression went too far and were unconstitutional. In contrast, a state government agency was upheld in disciplining two employees who, as "born-again Christians," proselytized to agency clients.[63] One of the salient differences between the two cases is that the latter employees were in the position of representing their agency to external clients. Thus, the state's concerns about meeting its responsibility under the establishment clause to remain neutral played a larger role in their case.

RELIGIOUS ORGANIZATION EXEMPTION

If it is illegal to discriminate based on religion, does that mean that churches must hire persons of other faiths and attempt to reasonably accommodate their divergent practices? Title VII contains a **religious organization exemption** that absolves churches of any liability for discriminating *on the basis of religion.* Thus, religious organizations can limit employment to, or have a preference for, persons sharing the same faith. And they can facially discriminate in these ways without bearing the burden of establishing BFOQs based on religion. This exemption includes not only church activities, but also more secular endeavors (e.g., church-sponsored schools, hospitals), at least insofar as the latter are nonprofit entities.[64] Furthermore, for constitutional reasons, discrimination on other grounds is not contested where positions with spiritual functions, such as clergy, are involved. Because the definition of religion is fuzzy, it should not be surprising that it is also difficult to pin down exactly what constitutes a religious organization. However, the mere fact that the owners of a company hold strong religious beliefs is not sufficient to convert a profit-making company into a religious organization.[65]

[61]*Kolodziej v. Smith,* 588 N.E.2d 634 (Mass. 1992); *cert. denied,* 522 U.S. 1029 (1997).

[62]*Tucker v. California Department of Education,* 97 F.3d 1204 (9th Cir. 1996).

[63]*Knight v. Connecticut Department of Public Health,* 275 F.3d 156 (2d Cir. 2001).

[64]*Corporation of the Presiding Bishop of the Church of Jesus Christ of Latter-Day Saints v. Amos,* 483 U.S. 327 (1987).

[65]*Townley,* at 619.

Chapter SUMMARY

The Americans with Disabilities Act entitles "qualified individuals with disabilities" to nondiscrimination and to reasonable accommodation. A fundamental premise of the ADA is that being disabled does not necessarily mean being unable to work, particularly if barriers to employment are removed through reasonable accommodation. Determining who is a qualified disabled person is complex. To be considered disabled under the ADA, an individual must have a physical or mental impairment that substantially limits the performance of a major life activity, have a record of such an impairment, or be regarded as having such an impairment. The emphasis of the ADA is on individualized assessments of functioning rather than on diagnostic labels. To substantially limit a major life activity, a disabling condition must be severe and have long-term duration or effects. When the major life activity that is limited is work, substantial limitation must exist for a range of jobs in comparison to the average person with similar skills and qualifications. Judgments regarding substantial limitation must take into account any corrective devices (e.g., medication, prosthesis) used by the individual.

Disabled individuals must also be qualified to be entitled to reasonable accommodation. Qualified disabled persons have the skills, education, experience, and other requirements for a job and can perform the essential functions of that job, with or without reasonable accommodation. The "essential functions" of a job are the main reasons the position exists, are relatively specialized, and are not readily distributed to other employees. Not all the tasks attached to jobs are essential functions. Inability to perform marginal functions of a job does not render a disabled person unqualified for that job. An individual can be capable of carrying out essential functions, but still not be qualified if his disability is such that he poses a "direct threat" to the health and safety of himself or others.

Qualified disabled persons are entitled to reasonable accommodation, provided that this does not impose undue hardship on the employer. Accommodations are provided to make it possible for disabled persons to participate in the recruitment and hiring process, enable disabled persons to perform essential functions of jobs, and allow disabled persons to enjoy the benefits and privileges of employment. The accommodations that must be provided are limited to those that are "reasonable." Provided that an effective accommodation is offered, employers need not implement the employee's preferred accommodation, provide items that are primarily for personal rather than work use, eliminate essential functions from the job or lower production standards, create new jobs that disabled employees can perform, excuse or refrain from disciplining conduct stemming from a disability, and provide paid leave not available to all employees. Courts disagree about whether or under what circumstances allowing a disabled employee to telecommute is a reasonable accommodation that an employer could be required to make. Accommodations that are reasonable in general might still impose undue hardship on particular employers. If a proposed reasonable accommodation causes an employer to incur "significant difficulty or expense," that accommodation is an undue hardship and the employer does not have to provide it.

Employers are required to reasonably accommodate religion unless doing so would impose undue hardship. Religion is defined broadly under Title VII to include all sincerely held religious beliefs and practices. To show that an employer has violated Title VII by failing to reasonably accommodate religion, a plaintiff must establish a prima facie case by showing the existence of a sincere religious belief or practice that conflicts with an employment requirement, that the employer was notified regarding the conflicting belief or practice, and that the employee was subjected to adverse employment action for failing to comply with the conflicting workplace requirement. The legal obligation to reasonably accommodate religion is far more limited than for disability. Employers need not incur more than minimal expense or difficulty in accommodating religion. Nevertheless, employers are required to engage in good faith efforts to accommodate employees whose religious beliefs conflict with workplace requirements and to be flexible in scheduling and the administration of policies.

Employees who engage in religious advocacy in the workplace pose a difficult problem for employers. Religious speech is an aspect of religion that requires at least an effort at accommodation. Yet, employers also have a legal obligation to protect other employees from religious harassment. This issue is particularly challenging for public employers that must abide by the Constitution's mandates to both permit the "free exercise" of religion and to avoid sponsoring religion. Religious organizations are exempt from Title VII to the extent that they are permitted to discriminate based on religion.

Practical Advice SUMMARY

- *Employers must consider only the ability to perform essential functions of jobs in determining whether disabled persons are qualified for employment.*

- *Employers must identify and document the essential functions of jobs. This is best done through a job analysis, the results of which are used as the basis of a job description.*

- *Job descriptions should*

 –distinguish essential from marginal functions.

 –include all essential functions.

 –specify what needs to be accomplished, rather than particular means of task accomplishment.

- *If employment requirements tend to screen out individuals with disabilities, employers must be prepared to show that these requirements are job related and consistent with business necessity.*

- *Employers can deny employment opportunities to disabled persons on the grounds that they pose a threat to the health or safety of themselves and others only if the threat is significant, current, and based on objective medical evidence.*

- *If a disabled person is unable to perform the essential functions of a job, the employer must consider whether any reasonable accommodation would enable the disabled person to perform the job.*

- *Employers must reasonably accommodate qualified disabled persons unless doing so would impose undue hardship.*

- *Employers should consider these measures, among others, when presented with the need for reasonable accommodation of disability*

 –making facilities accessible and usable.

 –restructuring jobs.

 –devising part-time or modified work schedules.

 –acquiring or modifying equipment.

 –modifying policies.

 –adjusting exam procedures.

 –providing readers or interpreters.

 –reassignment to vacant positions.

- *Employers must recognize when requests for accommodation are being made and cannot insist that requests be made in writing or use legal terminology.*

- *In responding to a request for accommodation, an employer should*

 –act on requests for accommodation as expeditiously as possible.

 –fully engage in the interactive process.

 –work closely with the disabled employee to identify potential accommodations.

 –select a mutually acceptable accommodation.

 –appraise whether the accommodation provided is effective.

 –document all aspects of the accommodation process.

- *Reasonable accommodation policies are helpful to managers and should address*

 –the manner in which requests for accommodation are to be initiated.

 –any required medical documentation of the need for accommodation.

 –the process for identifying reasonable accommodations.

 –criteria for choosing among possible accommodations.

 –procedures for formally notifying employees of the outcome.

- *Inquiries from employers to medical care providers should be limited to information needed to document the functional limitations imposed by an individual's disability.*

- *Requests for reasonable accommodation must be considered regardless of whether other accommodations have been provided in the past. Accommodations must be maintained for as long as they are needed.*

- *Absent strong reasons for preferring alternatives, employers should lean toward providing disabled employees' preferred reasonable accommodations.*

- *Reassignment to vacant positions should be considered only if disabled employees cannot be accommodated in their present jobs.*

- *Information about reasonable accommodations and the reasons they are needed should not be shared with other employees, beyond notifying supervisors.*

- *Employers claiming undue hardship from a proposed accommodation of disability must*

 –*be prepared to document the significant expense or difficulty.*

 –*consider the availability of external funding.*

 –*offer the disabled person the opportunity to pay for the portion of the cost that would create undue hardship.*

- *Employers are required to reasonably accommodate the sincere religious beliefs and practices of employees, unless doing so would cause undue hardship.*

- *Employers should generally accept the sincerity of employees' stated religious beliefs and practices and focus on whether reasonable accommodation can be made.*

- *Religious conflicts can be minimized by making workplace policies as flexible as possible.*

- *Although employers do not have to incur more than minimal expense or difficulty in accommodating religion, it is still necessary to*

 –*take requests for accommodation of religion seriously.*

 –*engage in an interactive process.*

 –*make good faith efforts to identify reasonable accommodations.*

- *To accommodate scheduling conflicts, employers should*

 –*allow and facilitate private swaps between employees.*

 –*permit employees to use available personal time.*

 –*allow flexible schedules.*

 –*consider changes in shifts or positions when these would not adversely affect other employees.*

- *Employers should attempt to accommodate religious advocacy by providing forums for such communication that allow other employees to choose whether they want to listen.*

- *Employers must not allow religious communication that is unwelcome to other employees to become severe or pervasive and interfere with the ability to do their jobs.*

Key TERMS

Americans with Disabilities Act (ADA)
Rehabilitation Act
qualified individual with a disability
disability
physical/mental impairment
major life activities
substantially limited

record of an impairment
regarded as disabled
qualified
essential functions
direct threat
reasonable accommodation
interactive process
undue hardship
religion

prima facie case of failure to reasonably accommodate religion
religious advocacy
religious harassment
free exercise clause
establishment clause
religious organization exemption

Chapter QUESTIONS

1. A nurse whose rheumatoid arthritis worsened was told by her doctor that she needed a "totally sedentary sit-down job." The nurse requested that the nursing home provide her with a motorized cart to use in the workplace. The facility refused the request, maintaining that the job required her to sometimes push patients in wheelchairs and lift them. The nurse's job description did not mention pushing patients in wheelchairs and that task was primarily performed by "transport aides." The nurse sued. What should the court decide? Why?

 (*Stafne v. Unicare Homes*, 266 F.3d 771 (8th Cir. 2001))

2. A delivery person injured his back on the job, resulting in a serious disc problem that required surgery. Following surgery, the employee's doctor imposed a lifting restriction of 23 pounds. This restriction precluded a return to his former position. The employee requested reasonable accommodation, which in this case meant reassignment. The employer's established procedure was to post all job openings and to require

that employees initiate any requests for transfer. The employee completed one transfer request for a computer/clerical position, but was judged to be unqualified due to his limited computer and office skills. The company also considered him for a telephone sales position and contacted him to set up an interview. At the interview it was determined that the employee did not have sufficient motivation for sales. Shortly thereafter, the employee was fired. The employee sued. What should the court decide? Why? (*Burns v. Coca-Cola,* 222 F.3d 247 (6th Cir. 2000))

3. The director of human resources at a hospital typically worked between 50 and 70 hours per week. She began to experience chest pains and other symptoms of a heart problem. After a period of time away from work, the employee offered to return to her position, but with the proviso that she would gradually increase her hours up to 40 per week. She would not be able to work the longer hours that she had previously worked. She was offered a part-time position as a recruiter, but the hospital refused her request to return as director working fewer hours. She sued. What should the court decide? Why? (*Tardie v. Rehabilitation Hospital of Rhode Island,* 168 F.3d 538 (1st Cir. 1999))

4. A sanitation worker suffered from "congenital stationary night blindness" which prevented him from driving at night and made it difficult for him to see in dim light. The condition cannot be corrected by surgery, glasses, or any other means. After only 20 minutes in the darkness, this employee needed 100 times as much light as the average sighted person to see properly. The doctor who examined him concluded that he should not be allowed to drive at night. The employee was initially assigned to a truck on the day shift. After his medical problem became known, he was temporarily transferred to a clerical position. In discussing the employee's situation with other managers, one of the managers said that the employee had "myopic macular degeneration" and that his condition would likely deteriorate. At the end of his probationary period, the employee was terminated. The sanitation worker sued. What should the court decide? Why? (*Capobianco v. City of New York,* 2005 U.S. App. LEXIS 18981)

5. A letter carrier who became disabled with a severe back injury went on disability leave. He repeatedly requested a less strenuous, light-duty assignment. At one point, he was told that under the postal service's "substantiation rule" he would have to provide documentation that his work restrictions persisted during the time that he had been off work (about two years). The letter carrier failed to provide the documentation and was subsequently terminated. He sued. What should the court decide? Why? (*Peebles v. Potter,* 354 F.3d 761 (8th Cir. 2004))

6. A program analyst for the IRS was exposed to a chemical spill that contaminated the ventilation system at the building in which she worked. She developed numerous medical conditions, including severe respiratory problems, asthma, and multiple chemical sensitivity. She tried relocating to other buildings, but experienced the same symptoms. Her doctor recommended that she be allowed to work from home. Other program analysts worked from home, although none on a full-time basis. The IRS claims that it cannot allow her to work from home full-time because the job requires office meetings, personal interaction with customers, and travel. The woman sued. What should the court decide? Why? (*Nanette v. Snow,* 343 F.Supp. 2d 465 (D. Md. 2004))

7. A department store clerk is a devout Catholic. The employee decided that she needed to make a religious pilgrimage to a site in Yugoslavia where several persons have claimed that the Virgin Mary appeared to them. The department store grants unpaid leave at management's discretion and prohibits the use of vacation time between October and December—the store's busiest season. The employee requested unpaid leave for the period from October 17 to October 26 to make the pilgrimage. The employee felt that she had to go at that time, although the dates held no other particular religious significance. Citing general policy against taking time off during the busy season, her boss refused the leave. She went anyhow and was terminated. She sued. What should the court decide? Why? (*Tiano v. Dillard Department Stores,* 139 F.3d 679 (9th Cir. 1998))

8. A devoutly religious office coordinator used the phrase "Have a Blessed Day" in many of her workplace communications (conversations, e-mails, phone calls) with coworkers, managers, and customers/vendors. Employees at one of her company's largest customers, Microsoft, objected to the practice. The company modified its policy by allowing the employee to use this phrase in internal communications, but not in contacts with outside customers/vendors. The employee found

this arrangement unacceptable and sued. What should the court decide? Why? (*Anderson v. U.S.F. Logistics,* 2001 U.S. App. LEXIS 26566 (7th Cir. 2001))

9. A teacher at a public school was required to attend training sessions held at a local college sponsored by a Christian demonination. The sessions included a prayer. Additionally, the district superintendent conducted prayers at mandatory teacher training sessions and displayed a personal Bible and a framed Scriptural quotation in his office. The superintendent refuses to stop these practices. The teacher sues. What should the court decide? Why? (*Warnock v. Archer,* 380 F.3d 1076 (8th Cir. 2004); *rehearing, en banc, denied,* 2004 U.S. App. LEXIS 20529)

10. AT&T employees were presented with a new employee handbook and required to sign a form certifying their receipt of the handbook and willingness to abide by the policies contained therein. An employee objected to the following statement in the handbook: "Each person at AT&T Broadband is charged with the responsibility to fully recognize, respect and value the differences among all of us." The employee felt, based on his religious convictions, that some behaviors and beliefs are sinful and not things that he could promise to "value." The employee sent a letter explaining that he was willing to be respectful and professional toward coworkers and customers, but that he could not in good faith sign the form if it meant agreeing to value conduct contrary to his religious beliefs. Several meeting ensued, but when the employee persisted in not signing the form, he was terminated. The employee sued. What should the court decide? Why? (*Buonanno v. AT&T Broadband,* 2004 U.S. Dist. LEXIS 6218)

Internet RESOURCES

Work-Life Conflicts and Other Diversity Issues

CLIPPINGS

▶ The Family and Medical Leave Act has increased the availability of leave to employees and not proved overly burdensome for most employers, although problems remain. Labor Department surveys of employers and employees found that 16.5 percent of employees had taken leave for family or medical reasons during the previous 18 months; the median duration of leave was 10 days; the most common reason for taking leave was an employee's own health problem; and parental leaves and leaves to care for sick parents are increasing in frequency. Slightly over one-third of leave-takers received no pay during their leaves, and financial concerns kept many employees from taking or remaining on leave. About a third of employers complained about problems in administering leave, but the vast majority reported no adverse effects on productivity and profitability.[1]

▶ Pratt & Whitney has agreed to pay $30,000 to settle a charge that it violated the Uniformed Services Employment and Reemployment Rights Act. An employee of the company had been called into active duty in April 2002 to serve in Kuwait. When he returned six months later, he was told that his position had been eliminated. Additionally, the company failed to offer any comparable positions.[2]

▶ The EEOC has filed a national origin discrimination lawsuit on behalf of a group of Navajo-speaking Native-American employees who were subjected to a strict "English-only" policy in their workplace and terminated if they refused to sign agreements accepting the policy's terms. Mary O'Neill, Acting Regional Attorney for the EEOC's Phoenix office, stated that "It is amazing that, in a country that cherishes diversity, an employer will prohibit the use of indigenous languages in the workplace and terminate Native American employees who question whether that is lawful."[3]

▶ The Government Accountability Office (GAO) estimates that the military spent more than $200 million over the past decade recruiting and training replacements for troops discharged from the military for being openly gay. Roughly 10,000 service men and women were discharged on this basis between 1994 and 2004.[4]

[1]Jane Waldfogel. "Family and Medical Leave: Evidence from the 2000 Surveys." *Monthly Labor Review* (September 2001), 17–23.

[2]Drew Douglas. "Pratt & Whitney to Pay $30,000 Settlement to Army Reservist Whose Job Was Eliminated." *Daily Labor Report* 131 (July 11, 2005), A-3.

[3]Equal Employment Opportunity Commission. "EEOC Sues Arizona Diner for National Origin Bias Against Navajos and Other Native Americans." September 30, 2002 (http://eeoc.gov/press/9-30-02-c.html).

[4]John Files. "Rules on Gays Exact a Cost in Recruiting, A Study Finds." *New York Times* (February 24, 2005), A-16.

This chapter concludes our discussion of managing diversity by examining several other employment law issues posed by diverse workforces. Workforces that are more female, older, and include disabled persons have greater need to take leave from employment for parenting and medical problems. Work-life conflicts can also arise from responsibilities that employees have as citizens, such as serving in the military. Diverse workforces include a wide variety of national origins and languages. Employer language requirements, such as English-only policies, can clash with this basic aspect of diversity and raise legal issues. No discussion of diversity would be complete without considering the treatment of gays and lesbians in the workplace.

WORK-LIFE CONFLICTS AND EMPLOYER LEAVE POLICIES

Employees are also parents, relatives, community members, and citizens. The responsibilities attached to these various roles sometimes conflict with employment requirements. Leave policies are one of the major ways in which the work-life conflicts of employees can be managed. But what, if anything, does the law require in terms of employer leave policies?

Family and Medical Leave Act

The **Family and Medical Leave Act (FMLA)**[5] is the principal federal law governing the provision of leave to employees for parental and medical reasons. All government agencies, regardless of their size, are covered by the law, as are private sector employers with at least 50 employees. Many states have their own laws, some of which have looser eligibility requirements or provide for longer periods of leave. The FMLA provides a minimum standard for employer leave policies—at least for those employers and employees covered by its provisions. *Parental and medical leave policies must be consistent with the provisions of the FMLA* outlined in this chapter, although employers are free to exceed the law's minimum requirements. We will consider eligibility requirements under the FMLA, the responsibility of employees to notify their employers regarding the need for leave, and what the law requires of employers.

Who Is Entitled to FMLA Leave? An employee is *entitled to FMLA leave* if the following are true:

- The employee works for a covered employer (i.e., a government agency or a private company with at least 50 employees).
- The employee worked for that employer for at least 12 months prior to taking leave.
- The employee worked at least 1,250 hours during the 12 months prior to taking leave.
- The employer has at least 50 employees at the employee's work site or within a 75-mile radius of that work site.
- The employee experiences a "qualifying event" and provides timely notification of the need for leave to the employer.

[5]29 U.S.C.A. §§ 2601–2654; 29 C.F.R. §§ 825.100–825.800 (2005).

THE CHANGING WORKPLACE

Workforce Diversity and Work-Life Conflicts

More than anything else, the increased labor force participation of women provides the demographic backdrop to heightened concerns about work-life conflicts. The substantial presence of women in most workplaces is thoroughly unremarkable when viewed from a contemporary perspective but, in fact, represents a major social transformation. In 1940, 28 percent of women were in the workforce, compared to slightly over 60 percent in 2000.[1] Almost three out of four women with children are in the workforce,[2] including well over half of women with infants less than one year old. The rate of growth in female participation in the labor force has slowed in recent years, and there has recently been a small decline in the percentage of women with infants who work,[3] but the longer-term trends have produced a workforce that is about half female, including a large number of mothers with young children. Dual wage earner families have become the norm. Both husband and wife were employed in over 53 percent of married couple families in 2000, compared to the 19 percent of married couple families in which only the husband was employed.[4] Additionally, the proportion of families headed by single parents has increased substantially and stands at nearly 25 percent. And to no one's great surprise, a recent survey by the DOL documents that, on average, working women spend about twice as much time on household chores and childcare as do working men.[5]

It is little wonder that people experience difficulty in managing child care and the rest of their life activities. Congress explicitly cited as "findings" providing the rationale for the Family and Medical Leave Act (FMLA) that:

(1) the number of single-parent households and two-parent households in which the single parent or both parents work is increasing significantly;

(2) it is important for the development of children and the family unit that fathers and mothers be able to participate in early child-rearing and the care of family members who have serious health conditions;

(3) the lack of employment policies to accommodate working parents can force individuals to choose between job security and parenting;

(4) there is inadequate job security for employees who have serious health conditions that prevent them from working for temporary periods;

(5) due to the nature of the roles of men and women in our society, the primary responsibility for family caretaking often falls on women, and such responsibility affects the working lives of women more than it affects the working lives of men; and

(6) employment standards that apply to one gender only have serious potential for encouraging employers to discriminate against employees and applicants for employment who are of that gender.[6]

The intimate connection between leave for family purposes and sex discrimination in employment was highlighted by the Supreme Court in a decision upholding the enforceability of the FMLA against state government agencies. In the words of late Chief Justice William Rehnquist:

Stereotypes about women's domestic roles are reinforced by parallel stereotypes presuming a lack of domestic responsibilities for men. Because employers continued to regard the family as the woman's domain, they often denied men similar accommodations or discouraged them from taking leave. These mutually reinforcing stereotypes created a self-fulfilling cycle of discrimination that forced women to continue to assume the role of primary family caregiver, and fostered employer's stereotypical views about women's commitment to work and their value as employees. These perceptions, in turn, Congress reasoned, lead to subtle discrimination that may be difficult to detect on a case-by-case basis.[7]

Thus, the FMLA is about more than simply helping individuals "manage work-life conflicts." It is aimed at

one of the core issues leading to the discriminatory treatment of men and women in the workplace.

[1]Eva E. Jacobs, ed. *Handbook of U.S. Labor Statistics* 5th ed. (Lanham, MD: Bernan Press, 2001), p. 11.

[2]Jacobs, at 83.

[3]Tamar Lewin. "More Mothers of Babies Under 1 Are Staying Home." *New York Times* (October 19, 2001).

[4]Jacobs, at 80.

[5]Edmund L. Andrews,. "Survey Confirms It: Women Outjuggle Men." *New York Times* (September 15, 2004), p. A-22.

[6]29 U.S.C. § 2601(a) (2005).

[7]*Nevada Department of Human Resources v Hiibbs*, 538 U.S. 721, at 736 (2003).

Thus, eligibility for leave depends on the overall size of the employer, the number of employees at an employee's own workplace, the duration of employment, and the number of hours worked during the previous year. The separate workplace size requirement means that it is possible for an employee to work for a company that has more than 50 total employees, but still not be eligible for FMLA leave because his particular work site is small and geographically remote from the employer's other establishments.

The employment duration and hours requirements must be met as of when leave would commence, rather than at the point in time at which leave is requested. Thus, *an employee cannot be deemed ineligible for leave that would commence in the future simply because the duration or hours requirement is not currently met.* However, a schoolteacher whose annual contract of employment was not renewed after she requested parental leave was not protected by the FMLA because she had not been working for a year at the time that she first requested leave *and* at the point at which the requested leave would have commenced.[6] Tallying the number of hours worked during the past 12 months is not always a straightforward proposition. In a case involving a part-time radiological technician, the court allowed the employee's FMLA claim to proceed even though the employer's time sheets showed that she had worked about 65 hours less than the 1,250 hours required for coverage.[7] The reason was that she had a good chance of being able to show that time spent each day prior to her shift preparing equipment for use and time spent at employer-mandated continuing education courses were work hours that should have been counted.

An employee that is otherwise eligible for FMLA leave must still experience a qualifying event to be entitled to take leave.

What Are FMLA Qualifying Events? Qualifying events are circumstances under which eligible employees are entitled to take FMLA leave. The following are **qualifying events** under the FMLA:

- The birth of a son or daughter of the employee
- Placement of a son or daughter with the employee by adoption or foster care
- The serious health condition of an employee's spouse, son, daughter, or parent
- The serious health condition of an employee that makes him unable to perform the functions of his job

[6]*Walker v. Elmore County Board of Education*, 379 F.3d 1249 (11th Cir. 2004).

[7]*Kosakow v. New Rochelle Radiology Associates, P.C.*, 274 F.3d 706 (2d Cir. 2001).

The "family" portion of family and medical leave is limited to childbirth, adoption, or foster care placement. It does not include time off for other family-related activities, such as attending parent-teacher conferences or obtaining counseling for marital problems. Both males and females are entitled to parental leave. Entitlement to parental leave under the FMLA generally expires 12 months from the date of the birth, adoption, or foster care placement. If an expectant mother's medical condition warrants that leave begin before the birth of a child, such leave is available under the qualifying event of a serious health condition.

The definition of *serious health condition* is complex. This term is far more inclusive than *disability,* but still does not encompass all medical problems of an employee or family member. Basically, **serious health conditions** are medical conditions that involve inpatient care in a hospital (or similar medical facility) or continuing treatment by a health-care provider. A *serious health condition involving inpatient care* includes not only the actual period of hospitalization, but also any **period of incapacity** (inability to work, attend school, or engage in other regular daily activities) and time needed for subsequent treatment of the condition. Serious health conditions involving **continuing treatment** by a health-care provider include the following:

- Conditions that result in periods of incapacity of more than three consecutive calendar days and either two or more treatments by health-care providers or one treatment followed by a regimen of continuing care supervised by a health-care provider
- Any periods of incapacity relating to pregnancy or prenatal care
- Any periods of incapacity, including subsequent treatment, due to chronic, serious health conditions (e.g., asthma, diabetes)
- Long-term periods of incapacity due to conditions for which treatment may not be effective (e.g., stroke, terminal diseases)
- Any absences to receive multiple treatments from health-care providers for conditions that would likely result in periods of incapacity of more than three consecutive calendar days if left untreated

Employers may, and generally should, require that requests for leave based on serious health conditions be supported by certifications from health-care providers. Employees must be given at least 15 days to obtain this medical documentation. However, in the case of an employee whose health-care provider apparently failed to send the required medical information to the employer in a timely fashion, the court ruled for the employer who denied FMLA leave. The court said that the employer was not under any legal obligation to inform the employee that the documentation had not been received.[8] The process of documenting a serious health condition should not be made onerous, and the information provided by an employee's own doctor should generally be sufficient. However, when the information provided is inadequate, employers are permitted, at their own expense, to require employees to obtain second medical certifications from other doctors. If the first and second opinions conflict, employers have the option of requiring a third assessment by a different health-care provider approved by both parties. The third opinion is final and binding. Employers may contact employees while they are on leave to receive information on their status and verify their intent to return to work following leave. An employee on FMLA leave for an anxiety condition was disciplined by his employer when the employee violated a policy requiring employees with bad sick leave records

[8]*Urban v. Dolgencorp of Texas, Inc.,* 393 F.3d 572 (5th Cir. 2004); *clarified by,* 398 F.3d 699 (5th Cir. 2005).

to notify their employer if they were leaving the home. The court stated that while employers' sick leave policies cannot conflict with the FMLA, "Nothing in the FMLA prevents employers from ensuring that employees who are on leave from work do not abuse their leave, particularly those who enter leave while on the employer's Sick Abuse List."[9]

Employers are also permitted to require medical certification of fitness upon an employee's return to work, provided that this is their general practice. However, an employer ran afoul of the law when it subjected an employee returning from FMLA leave to repeated requests for proof of his fitness to work, failed to inform the employee as to precisely what information was needed, and arbitrarily refused to accept the documentation he provided.[10]

Not surprisingly, the existence of a serious health condition is sometimes disputed and must be decided by a court. Department of Labor (DOL) regulations state the following:

> Ordinarily, unless complications arise, the common cold, the flu, earaches, upset stomach, minor ulcers, headaches other than migraine, routine dental or orthodontia problems, periodontal disease, etc. are examples of conditions that do not meet the definition of a serious health condition and do not qualify for FMLA leave.[11]

Although these are useful examples, ultimately the criteria mentioned earlier determine the existence of a serious health condition. In a case involving a woman who was absent with the flu, the court concluded that she nonetheless had a serious health condition because she was incapacitated for more than three days and had several treatments from a health-care provider.[12] Importantly, the court emphasized that "treatments" include visits to doctors for purposes of diagnosis and evaluation.

The right to take leave for the serious health conditions of family members is limited to immediate family members. Thus, employers are not required to grant leave so that employees can provide care to grandparents, aunts or uncles, or even in-laws. Leave to care for sons or daughters applies only to children under 18 years of age, unless the children are disabled and incapable of self-care. The element of "caring for" is also important here. A person taking leave based on the serious health condition of a family member must actually be involved in the ongoing treatment of the condition by providing physical or psychological care. An airline employee who took leave due to the medical complications of his wife's pregnancy was not protected by the FMLA when he was terminated for unexcused absences.[13] The employee's vehicle broke down shortly after the leave commenced and he flew to another city where he owned a second car. He then drove the car back cross-country. The car trip lasted four days. Although the employee's sister-in-law stayed with his wife and the employee remained in regular contact with his wife via cell phone, the court concluded that this was not the type of actual care required by the FMLA. Lastly, the FMLA does not provide leave for periods of bereavement or funeral attendance.

[9]*Callison v. City of Philadelphia*, 2005 U.S. App. LEXIS 6770, at 9-10; *cert. denied*, 126 S. Ct. 389 (2005).

[10]*Stevens v. Coach U.S.A.*, 2005 U.S. Dist. LEXIS 19889.

[11]29 C.F.R. § 825.114(2)(v)(c) (2005).

[12]*Miller v. AT&T Corp.*, 250 F.3d 820 (4th Cir. 2001).

[13]*Tellis v. Alaska Airlines*, 414 F.3d 1045 (9th Cir. 2005).

What Must Employees Do to Obtain Leave? Employees are responsible for notifying their employers that a qualifying event has occurred for which leave is needed. This notification can be verbal and need not specifically refer to the FMLA, but it must provide enough information to alert the employer that the FMLA might apply. *If the need for leave is foreseeable, such as a birth or planned medical treatment where at least the approximate leave dates are known, employees can be required to provide 30 days advance notice.* Failure to provide adequate notice when the need for leave is foreseeable can result in delay of the leave until the 30-day notice requirement is satisfied. *If the need for leave is not foreseeable, such as when a serious health problem suddenly emerges, employees are responsible for providing notice "as soon as practicable."* This phrase is interpreted by the DOL to mean at least verbal notice within one or two business days from when employees learn of the need for leave. What is "practicable" ultimately hinges on the particular facts of the situation. In the case of serious medical emergencies, notification might be made after, rather than before, periods of absence. When leave is needed for planned medical treatment(s), employees are expected to first consult with their employers regarding the timing of the treatment and attempt to schedule leave to lessen its disruptiveness.

The adequacy of employee notification of the need for FMLA leave has been at issue in a number of cases, with somewhat inconsistent results. For example, an employee without a telephone had her mother deliver a note to her employer. The note said that the woman "was having a lot of pain in her side" and would not be able to come to work. The court concluded that the woman had not provided enough information for the employer to be aware that she was requesting FMLA leave for a serious health condition.[14] In contrast, an employee's report that he missed work because he "had a headache" was deemed sufficient notice of need for FMLA leave when the employer had prior knowledge that he suffered from migraines.[15] Employees who provide prior notice of the need for leave (rather than providing it after the fact) and who maintain contact with their employers during leave appear to fare better legally than those who do not.[16]

Walton v. Ford Motor Company is another case centering on whether the employee provided sufficient notification of his need for FMLA leave.

What Does the FMLA Require Employers to Provide? The FMLA requires that employers provide the following to eligible employees who experience qualifying events:

1. Up to a total of 12 workweeks of leave over a 12-month period

2. Maintenance of health insurance under the same conditions as if the employee had not taken leave

3. Restoration to the same position held before leave commenced or to an equivalent position with the same pay, benefits, and other terms and conditions of employment

These three core requirements reinforce one another. The right to take leave would be rendered meaningless if employees did not retain their health insurance. After all,

[14]*Satterfield v. Wal-Mart*, 135 F.3d 973 (5th Cir. 1998), *cert. denied*, 525 U.S. 826 (1998).

[15]*Ware v. Stahl Specialty Co.*, 1998 U.S. Dist. LEXIS 5506.

[16]*Brannon v. OshKosh B'Gosh*, 897 F. Supp. 1028 (M.D. Tenn. 1995); *Collins v. NTN-Bower Corp.*, 272 F.3d 1006 (7th Cir. 2001).

WALTON V. FORD MOTOR COMPANY
424 F.3d 481 (6th Cir. 2005)

OPINION BY CIRCUIT JUDGE BATCHELDER:

Terry D. Walton appeals the district court's grant of summary judgment in favor of Visteon Corporation ("Visteon") on Walton's claim that Visteon interfered with his attempt to exercise his rights under the Family Medical Leave Act of 1993 ("FMLA") by terminating him. . . . Because we find that no reasonable jury could conclude that Walton provided Visteon with adequate notice of his intent to take leave for an FMLA-qualifying injury, we AFFIRM. * * *

On April 18, 2001, Walton suffered a knee injury while working in his yard at home after work. Following a briefing in his department on the morning of April 19, Walton informed his supervisor, Pat Nolan, that he had twisted his knee the day before and that he intended to visit the medical department to have his knee evaluated. During his visit to the medical department, the Milan Plant's nurse, Susan Kinnick, made a preliminary diagnosis of a sprain/strain to the left knee and she gave Walton a cold compress, ibuprofen, and an elastic bandage. Walton neither requested leave nor did he obtain leave of absence forms from the medical department.

Following his visit to the medical department, Walton returned to work for the remainder of the morning. At around noon, he informed Nolan that he had scheduled a doctor's appointment for the afternoon of April 19. Nolan cleared Walton to leave for his appointment, and Walton went to the office of Dr. Rex Figy. Dr. Figy examined Walton and gave him a note instructing him to remain off work until he could be evaluated by Dr. Thomas Merritt, an orthopedic surgeon. Walton did not return to work on April 19 or contact anybody at Visteon to inform them of his status.

On April 20, Walton called the Milan Plant's security office and informed security that he had visited the doctor and had been told to stay off work until he could see a specialist on April 24. Security recorded Walton's call in the Hourly Personnel Absence Call-In Log Sheet. The entry indicates that the reason for Walton's absence was that he was "sick" and that his expected date of return was April 24. Floor supervisors and the labor relations

department receive a periodic distribution of the Hourly Personnel Absence Call-In Log Sheet, but Walton made no attempt to contact directly his supervisor, the labor relations department, or the medical department to inform them of the actual reason for his absence, and he did not provide anyone at Visteon with any medical documentation supporting his absence.

At his appointment with Dr. Merritt on April 24, Walton was diagnosed with having torn the superficial medial collateral ligament in his left knee. As a result, Dr. Merritt disabled Walton from working until May 28. On April 25, Walton again contacted the Milan Plant's security office and informed security that he had attended his scheduled doctor's appointment on April 24 and had been told to stay off work for the next four weeks. The entry in the Hourly Personnel Absence Call-In Log Sheet on this date also indicates that the reason for Walton's absence was that he was "sick" and that his expected date of return was May 28. Once again, Walton made no attempt to contact his supervisor, the labor relations department, or the medical department, and he did not submit any medical paperwork memorializing Dr. Merritt's disability finding to Visteon.

Consequently, on April 27, Visteon sent Walton a letter by registered mail informing him that he had five business days to contact Visteon's labor relations department or his employment would be terminated. * * * Although Walton admits that he received a note from the post office notifying him of the certified letter, he maintains that he did not receive the notice until May 8, the same day that he actually retrieved the letter from the post office. Postal records confirm, however, that although Walton did retrieve the 5-day quit letter from the post office on May 8, he was first notified by mail on April 30 that a certified letter awaited him.

Meanwhile, on May 4, Visteon notified Walton's union that Walton's employment was terminated because he had not provided evidence of a qualified leave for his absence between April 20 and May 4, or responded to the 5-day quit notice. On May 9, one day after Walton claims to have received the 5-day quit letter and five days after his termination, he contacted Visteon's labor relations department and he drove to the Milan Plant and gave a copy of the medical notes he had

received from his doctors to his UAW representative, Fred Probst, who eventually forwarded the medical documentation to Visteon. * * * Visteon nevertheless refused to reinstate Walton.

Visteon's internal procedures generally require that in order properly to request medical leave an employee must notify the labor relations department within two business days of his initial absence and then complete the requisite FMLA forms to be returned to the medical department. Over the course of Walton's employment with Ford and Visteon, the companies issued multiple notices to employees at the Milan Plant that informed them how to obtain an FMLA leave. The notices were posted on bulletin boards located in the medical office, outside the union benefits office, and near the labor relations office. Visteon also posted and attached a bulletin to hourly employees' paychecks in July 2000 entitled "Family Medical Leave Act of 1993." This particular bulletin recited the proper procedures for requesting FMLA leave and it specifically stated, "Do not request FMLA through security." Because Walton had taken several prior medical leaves, for which he had provided proper notice and submitted the medical certification forms properly, he was aware of Visteon's policy.

Walton nevertheless maintains that throughout his nine years of employment at the Milan Plant it was standard procedure for hourly employees to contact the Milan Plant's security office to report absences for any reason. Several Visteon employees, however, explained that while it was proper to call security to report an absence, the primary purpose of such a rule was to allow shift managers to properly staff the assembly lines and related positions when an employee is calling in for an unscheduled absence. * * * Walton himself conceded that he knew security could not grant a medical leave of absence. Visteon's express prohibition against contacting security to request FMLA leave flows, in part, from the fact that the security guards at the Milan Plant are not Visteon employees, but independent contractors leased from a temporary agency, who are given no FMLA training. * * *

The FMLA entitles qualifying employees to up to twelve weeks of unpaid leave each year if, among other things, an employee has a "serious health condition that makes the employee unable to perform the functions of the position of such employee." * * * Walton argues on appeal that Visteon interfered with his rights under the FMLA by refusing to recognize his absence from

April 20 to May 4 as FMLA-qualifying leave. To succeed on his FMLA-interference claim, Walton must demonstrate that: (1) he was an eligible employee; (2) the defendant was an employer as defined under the FMLA; (3) the employee was entitled to leave under the FMLA; (4) the employee gave the employer notice of his intention to take leave; and (5) the employer denied the employee FMLA benefits to which he was entitled. Because the first three factors are not in dispute, the sole issue in this appeal is whether Walton provided adequate notice to Visteon of his need for FMLA leave. . . .

When the need for FMLA leave is unforeseeable, such as here, the pertinent regulations require that an employee should give notice to the employer of the need for FMLA leave as soon as practicable. . . . It is expected that an employee will give notice to the employer within no more than one or two working days of learning of the need for leave, except in extraordinary circumstances where such notice is not feasible. Visteon's internal procedures require that in order to properly request medical leave an employee "must notify Labor Relations within two business days of [his] absence, or at least within 48 hours of [his] return to work," and then complete the requisite FMLA forms to be returned to the medical department within 15 days of receiving such forms. Visteon's internal procedures are therefore consistent with the FMLA's timing requirements for unforeseeable leave.

It is not disputed that by merely calling the Milan Plant's security office to inform Visteon of his absence, Walton did not comply with Visteon's internal policy for requesting and receiving FMLA leave. Nevertheless, . . . "employers cannot deny FMLA leave on grounds that an employee failed to comply with internal procedures as long as 'the employee gives timely verbal or other notice.'" Accordingly, . . . [because] Visteon could not terminate Walton simply for failing to comply with internal company policy requiring that he notify the labor relations department of his absence, our focus turns to whether by making two calls to the Milan Plant's security office to report his absences Walton provided Visteon with sufficient notice that he was invoking the protection of the FMLA. We conclude that he did not.

"To invoke the protection of the FMLA, an employee must provide notice and a qualifying reason for requesting the leave." "The critical question is whether the information imparted to the employer

is sufficient to reasonably apprise it of the employee's request to take time off for a serious health condition." While an "employee need not expressly assert rights under the FMLA or even mention the FMLA," the employee must give "the employer enough information for the employer to reasonably conclude that a [qualifying] event . . . has occurred." * * * On April 19, 2001, Walton informed his supervisor, Pat Nolan, that he had "twisted his knee" and that he planned to get his knee evaluated at the Milan Plant's medical department. During his visit to the medical department, he never indicated that he would need time off and he did not request FMLA certification forms. After receiving an ice pack and ibuprofen from Nurse Kinnick, Walton then *returned to work*. While Walton informed Nolan later that he had scheduled a doctor's appointment for the afternoon of April 19, he never requested leave as a follow up to that conversation. Based on these facts, Walton's supervisor did not have sufficient notice as of April 19 that Walton had suffered a "serious health condition" requiring FMLA leave.

Walton admits that prior to his termination the only other contact he had with Visteon regarding his absence was through his calls to security on April 20 and April 25. These contacts were likewise insufficient to impart notice to Visteon that Walton required FMLA leave. * * * Importantly, the entries in the Hourly Personnel Absence Call-In Log Sheet on both April 20 and April 25 indicate that the reason for Walton's absence was that he was "sick." In fact, the record reveals that, at least on April 20, Walton specifically told security to list him as taking a "sick day." The district court properly concluded that even if the Hourly Personnel Absence Call-In Log Sheet was forwarded to Walton's supervisor and the labor relations department, the information contained in the log was not sufficient to impart notice to Visteon that Walton required FMLA leave.

We recognize that under the applicable regulations "the employee need not expressly assert rights under the FMLA or even mention the FMLA, but may only state that leave is needed. The employer will be expected to obtain any additional required information through informal means." But we find that by sending Walton a 5-day quit letter by registered mail on April 27, Visteon complied with the FMLA regulations. The letter specifically provided: "If you are unable to work because of illness or injury, and so report to the Employment Office within the time stated above, you will

be granted a sick leave of absence to cover the period of your disability upon presenting satisfactory evidence thereof." Postal records show that Walton received notice of the letter on April 30, but that he chose to ignore Visteon's inquiry until after he was terminated. The regulation requires that an employer may sometimes need to seek additional information concerning an absent employee's condition; it does not seek to punish the employer when the employee fails to respond to such an inquiry. * * *

In *Cavin* [*v. Honda of Am. Mfg*], we concluded that the fact that the plaintiff informed Honda's security department (rather than complying with internal company policy by notifying the Leave Coordination Department) that he had been in a motorcycle accident which required hospitalization and that he would be unable to perform his job because of the injuries he sustained was sufficient as a matter of law to impart notice to Honda of an FMLA-qualifying decision . . . * * * [But], Visteon's policies differ from Honda's policies in one very important respect. Visteon explicitly informed its employees, "Do not request FMLA through security." * * *. In contrast to the plaintiff in *Cavin*, therefore, Walton knowingly and repeatedly violated Visteon's express prohibition against requesting FMLA leave through the Milan Plant's security office. * * * [Also] unlike *Cavin*, it is undisputed that the security guards working at the Milan Plant were not Visteon employees, but independent contractors. * * * Clearly then, Walton never informed his *employer* of the reason for his absence until after his employment had already been terminated. * * *

CASE QUESTIONS

1. What was the legal issue in this case? What did the court decide?

2. What was Visteon's internal procedure for requesting medical leave? How did Walton go about trying to request leave?

3. Why is it not sufficient under the FMLA for the company to show that Walton failed to comply with its established procedure for requesting medical leave?

4. Why does the court conclude that Walton was not protected by the FMLA?

entitlement to leave is predicated on events (serious illnesses, childbirth) that are necessarily accompanied by medical services and bills. Likewise, the promise of a right to take leave would be illusory if employees had to take leave without a reasonable guarantee that their jobs would be still be there upon returning from leave. The FMLA's provisions are further buttressed by requirements that employers refrain from discriminating against employees for taking FMLA leave or otherwise interfering with, restraining, or denying the exercise of FMLA rights.

Bachelder v. America West Airlines considers both whether an employee is entitled to FMLA leave and whether her employer violateed the act's prohibition against interference with the exercise of FMLA rights.

BACHELDER V. AMERICA WEST AIRLINES
259 F.3d 1112 (9th Cir. 2001)

● ● ●

OPINION BY CIRCUIT JUDGE BERZON:

Penny Bachelder claims that her employer, America West Airlines, violated the Family and Medical Leave Act of 1993 ("FMLA" or "the Act") when it terminated her in 1996 for poor attendance. The district court granted partial summary judgment to America West, holding that Bachelder was not entitled to the Act's protection for her 1996 absences. * * * This appeal requires us to interpret both the Act and the regulations issued pursuant to it by the Department of Labor. * * *

[T]he regulations provide employers with a menu of choices for how to determine the "twelve-month period" during which an employee is entitled to twelve weeks of FMLA-protected leave:

(1) The calendar year;

(2) Any fixed 12-month "leave year," such as a fiscal year, a year required by State law, or a year starting on an employee's "anniversary" date;

(3) The 12-month period measured forward from the date an employee's first FMLA leave begins; or,

(4) A "rolling" 12-month period measured backward from the date an employee uses any FMLA leave.

This "leave year" regulation is at the heart of Bachelder's appeal.

Bachelder began working for America West as a customer service representative in 1988. From 1993 until her termination in 1996, she was a passenger service supervisor. . . . From 1994 to 1996, Bachelder was often absent from work for various health- and family-related reasons. In 1994, she took five weeks of medical leave to recover from a broken toe, and in mid-1995, she took maternity leave for approximately three months. It is undisputed that these two leaves were covered by, and protected by, the FMLA. In addition to these extended absences, Bachelder also called in sick several times in 1994 and 1995.

On January 14, 1996, one of America West's managers had a "corrective action discussion" with Bachelder regarding her attendance record. Among the absences that concerned the company were several occasions on which Bachelder had called in sick and the 1994 and 1995 FMLA leaves. Bachelder was advised to improve her attendance at work and required to attend pre-scheduled meetings at which her progress would be evaluated.

In February 1996, Bachelder was absent from work again for a total of three weeks. During that time, she submitted two doctor's notes to America West indicating her diagnosis and when she could return to work. Bachelder's attendance was flawless in March 1996, but in early April, she called in sick for one day to care for her baby, who was ill. Right after that, on April 9, Bachelder was fired. * * *

Bachelder filed this action, alleging that America West impermissibly considered her use of leave protected by the FMLA in its decision to terminate her. In response, America West maintained that it had not relied on FMLA-protected leave in firing Bachelder, because none of her February 1996 absences were protected by the Act, and because her 1994 and 1995 FMLA leaves

did not factor into its decision. None of Bachelder's February 1996 absences were covered by the Act, argued America West, because the company used the retroactive "rolling" year method—the fourth of the four methods permitted by the leave year regulation—to calculate its employees' eligibility for FMLA leave. If that method was used, Bachelder had exhausted her full annual allotment of FMLA leave as of June 1995, and was entitled, according to the company, to no more such leave until twelve months had elapsed from the commencement of her 1995 maternity leave. * * *

Bachelder countered that according to the regulations implementing the FMLA, she was entitled to have her leave eligibility calculated by the method most favorable to her. Under a calendar year method of calculating leave eligibility, she contended, her February 1996 absences were protected by the FMLA, and America West had violated the Act by relying on those absences in deciding to fire her. * * *

Congress made it unlawful for an employer to "interfere with, restrain, or deny the exercise of or the attempt to exercise, any right provided" by the Act. The regulations explain that this prohibition encompasses an employer's consideration of an employee's use of FMLA-covered leave in making adverse employment decisions:

> Employers cannot use the taking of FMLA leave as a negative factor in employment actions, such as hiring, promotions or disciplinary actions; nor can FMLA leave be counted under "no fault" attendance policies.

* * * [E]mployer actions that deter employees' participation in protected activities constitute "interference" or "restraint" with the employees' exercise of their rights. . . . [A]ttaching negative consequences to the exercise of protected rights surely "tends to chill" an employee's willingness to exercise those rights: Employees are, understandably, less likely to exercise their FMLA leave rights if they can expect to be fired or otherwise disciplined for doing so. The Labor Department's conclusion that employer use of "the taking of FMLA leave as a negative factor in employment actions," violates the Act is therefore a reasonable one. * * *

In the case before us, there is direct, undisputed evidence of the employer's motives: America West told Bachelder when it fired her that it based its decision on her sixteen absences since the January 1996 corrective action discussion. If those absences were, in fact, covered by the Act, America West's consideration of those absences as a "negative factor" in the firing decision violated the Act.

The FMLA "leave year" regulation, while allowing employers flexibility in deciding how to comply with the Act, also includes various safeguards for employees. First, the employer must apply its chosen calculating method consistently to all employees. Second, if the employer has failed to select a calculating method, the regulations state that the method "that provides the most beneficial outcome for the employee will be used." By preventing employers from calculating FMLA leave eligibility in their own favor on an ad hoc, employee-by-employee basis, the "leave year" regulation encourages the employer to choose its calculating method prospectively. By doing so, the regulation not only prevents unfairness to employees through retroactive manipulation of the "leave year," but also encourages a system under which both employees and employers can plan for future leaves in an orderly fashion.

The regulations allow employers to choose among four methods for calculating their employees' eligibility for FMLA leave, but they do not specifically state how an employer indicates its choice. America West contends, correctly, that the FMLA's implementing regulations do not expressly embody a requirement that employers inform their employees of their chosen method for calculating leave eligibility. The regulations nonetheless plainly contemplate that the employer's selection of one of the four calculation methods will be an open one, not a secret kept from the employees, the affected individuals. * * *

The question remains whether America West adequately notified its employees that it had chosen the retroactive rolling "leave year" calculation method. America West contends, and the district court agreed, that, because its employee hand book states that "employees are entitled to up to twelve calendar weeks of unpaid [FMLA] leave within any twelve month period," it provided sufficient notice to its employees that it uses the "rolling method" for calculating leave eligibility. We disagree. * * * [T]he very fact that the regulation permits employers to use any of four calculating methods is fatal to America West's argument: Because the statute can reasonably be read to allow the four different methods spelled out, merely parroting the statutory language cannot possibly inform employees of the method the employer has chosen. By paraphrasing the statutory language, in other words, America West has done no more than announce its intention to comply with the Act.

Because choosing a calculating method carries with it an obligation to inform employees of that choice and America West has failed to fulfill this obligation, it has "failed to select" a calculating method. Thus, "the option that provides the most beneficial outcome for the employee" must be used to determine whether Bachelder's 1996 absences were covered by the FMLA. The calendar year method provides the most favorable outcome to Bachelder. Under this approach, it is immaterial that Bachelder had utilized her full allotment of FMLA-protected leave between April and June 1995.... Because she began 1996 with a fresh bank of FMLA-protected leave, Bachelder's February 1996 absences were covered by the Act. * * *

[I]t is the employer's responsibility, not the employee's, to determine whether a leave request is likely to be covered by the Act. Employees must notify their employers in advance when they plan to take foreseeable leave for reasons covered by the Act, and as soon as practicable when absences are not foreseeable. Employees need only notify their employers that they will be absent under circumstances which indicate that the FMLA might apply. * * * [T]he employer is responsible, having been notified of the reason for an employee's absence, for being aware that the absence may qualify for FMLA protection.

Bachelder provided two doctor's notes to America West regarding her absences in February 1996. The company was therefore placed on notice that the leave might be covered by the FMLA, and could have inquired further to determine whether the absences were likely to qualify for FMLA protection.

Because we hold that Bachelder's February 1996 absences were protected by the FMLA, and because America West used these absences as a negative factor in its decision to fire her, we reverse the district court's grant of summary judgment for America West.

CASE QUESTIONS

1. What were the legal issues in this case? What did the court decide? Why?

2. What errors did the airline make in this case? What does this case tell us about things that employers must do to comply with the FMLA?

3. Why are "no-fault" attendance policies in conflict with the FMLA?

4. The court selected the calendar year as the method most favorable to Bachelder. Would any of the other three methods have entitled Bachelder to leave for her 1996 absences?

The FMLA establishes a "floor," or set of minimum requirements, for employer leave policies. *If an eligible employee experiences a qualifying event and notifies her employer that she needs to take leave, the employer must grant the leave.* The FMLA creates an entitlement to leave, regardless of if or when an employer would prefer to grant leave. *The amount of leave that must be provided is the amount needed by the employee, up to a total of 12 workweeks over a 12-month period.* As the *Bachelder* case illustrates, employers have four basic options for defining the 12-month period: (1) the calendar year; (2) any other fixed 12-month period; (3) a 12-month period measured forward from the first day that any FMLA leave is taken by the employee; and (4) a rolling 12-month period measured backward from the most recent day in which leave was used. The latter two methods are more complex, but prevent employees from stacking periods of leave on top of one another (e.g., 12 weeks at the end of a calendar year followed by 12 weeks at the beginning of the next year). *Employers must adopt one of these methods, use it consistently, and notify employees regarding their choice of method.*

"Leave" means just that; the employee is relieved of all work duties and the obligation to come to work. Although employers can require that employees on FMLA leaves comply with reasonable, nondiscriminatory policies applied to ensure that leaves are not being abused, *employers are not free to assign work duties to employees on FMLA leave.* An employee who took FMLA leave to have a child received regular phone calls regarding various accounting and payroll problems at work,

beginning when she was still in the hospital. In one of these calls, the employee was "chewed out" for deficient training procedures in the accounting department. On another occasion, the employee was asked to come to work to help resolve some problems, and she went in for three to four hours. The employee was then laid off upon her return to work. The court concluded that "By essentially requiring Plaintiff to work while on leave, and by terminating her for failing to do so, Defendant has 'interfered' with Plaintiff's attempts to take leave, and 'discriminated' against her for taking it."[17]

Whether leave must be taken on a **continuous** basis (i.e., all in one block with no work occurring between the beginning and end of leave) or whether it can be **intermittent** (i.e., periods of leave mixed with periods of work) depends on which qualifying event necessitated the leave. Leaves for childbirth, adoption, or foster care placement must be continuous, unless the employer allows otherwise. Leaves for serious health conditions of employees or their family members can be either continuous or intermittent, depending on the employee's needs. For example, intermittent leave might be needed to receive ongoing treatments or to deal with chronic conditions that occasionally flare up. One particular type of intermittent leave is a **reduced leave schedule**. This means that the employee's normal daily or weekly hours of work are reduced. Periods of intermittent leave can be as short as one hour, and *employees cannot be required to take longer periods of leave than they need simply for the administrative convenience of employers.*

A critical issue for employees is whether the time off from work comes with pay. Surveys of FMLA use by employees show that a substantial percentage of employees end up taking unpaid leave, and that lack of paid leave is a deterrent to leave usage (see "Clippings"). Under the FMLA, *employees may choose—or their employers may require them—to substitute available paid leave for unpaid FMLA leave.* Thus, although the FMLA does not entitle employees to paid leave, many employees are able to use vacation, personal days, sick days, or other paid leave to cover some or all of their FMLA leaves. California law differs from the FMLA in requiring that up to six weeks of a person's family and medical leave be paid leave, regardless of the availability of paid leave under the employer's policies.[18] Any paid leave that is substituted must fit the qualifying event that necessitated FMLA leave. Whether, for example, an employee can use sick leave to stay home and care for a family member with a serious health condition depends on whether the employer customarily permits sick leave to be used for that purpose or only for an employee's own illness.

The FMLA specifically requires that health benefits be maintained under the same conditions that would pertain if the employee did not take leave. Thus, *assuming that the employer offers a group health plan, that coverage must remain in place, including any coverage of family members, with the employer paying what it usually pays for the coverage, and the employee on leave paying whatever employee share is normally paid.* The FMLA permits employers to recover health insurance premiums paid if the leave-taker does not return to work for reasons other than inability to work due to a serious medical condition or other circumstances beyond the employee's control. Seniority and benefits related to time of service, including paid time off, need not continue to accrue while an employee is on unpaid FMLA

[17]*Sherman v. AI/FOCS, Inc.*, 113 F. Supp. 2d 65, at 70-1 (D. Mass. 2000).

[18]John M. Broder. "Family Leave in California Now Includes Pay Benefit." *New York Times* (September 24, 2002), A-18.

leave. However, an employee cannot lose seniority or other benefits that were accrued prior to taking leave. Also, although benefits such as life insurance need not be maintained during periods of leave, the requirement that employees be restored following leave usually means, as a practical matter, that these other benefits must be kept in place.

Upon return from FMLA leave, an employee must be **restored** *or reinstated to the same position held when leave was taken or to a position that is equivalent in pay, benefits, terms, and conditions of employment.* To be equivalent, a position should be generally located in the same work site as the previous position; entail the same work schedule; offer equivalent opportunity for bonuses, profit-sharing, and other payments; and be similar in duties and authority. A store manager who, upon returning from FMLA leave, was offered positions in the procurement office or as a sacker/stocker at $7/hr and with increased health insurance premiums and no life insurance coverage, was clearly not restored to an equivalent position.[19] In contrast, a laundry worker who was restored to a different position that involved somewhat more standing, lifting, and exposure to foul odors was unable to show that she had not been placed in a position equivalent to her preleave position. This was true even though the employee was told that although her pay would remain the same for about a month, it "might go down" thereafter.[20] The DOL regulations specifically allow employers to temporarily transfer employees on intermittent leave or reduced leave schedules to positions equivalent in pay and benefits to their existing jobs, but for which the intermittent leave would be less disruptive.

Taking leave does not immunize an employee from a layoff or termination that would have occurred anyway. "An employee has no greater right to reinstatement . . . than if the employee had been continuously employed during the FMLA leave period."[21] If, for example, an employer can show that the leave-taker's position was eliminated due to restructuring or that the project for which the employee was hired is now completed, restoration would not be required. But notice that the fact of leave-taking raises legal questions that would not otherwise arise in terminating the employment of at-will employees. Thus, *decisions adversely affecting employees on FMLA leave should be very closely scrutinized.*

A common issue in FMLA cases, including *Bachelder,* is employees being disciplined or terminated based on absences due to FMLA leave. Whether framed as "interference" or "discrimination," *employers cannot base adverse employment decisions on the taking of FMLA leave.* After the court determined that Bachelder was entitled to FMLA leave for her absences in 1996, her termination for excessive absences that included those in 1996 violated the FMLA. *"No-fault" attendance policies, which count absences without regard to the reasons for them, are inherently in conflict with the FMLA and must be either eliminated or allow for exceptions.*

What if the vice president of the finance department is having a baby? Is she entitled to FMLA leave and restoration following leave? There is a narrow exception to the restoration requirement when "key employees" take leave. **Key employees** are salaried employees who are among the top 10 percent of a company's employees (i.e., those within a 75-mile radius of the employee's workplace) in pay.

[19]*Hanna v. Pay-and-Save, Inc.,* 2001 U.S. Dist. LEXIS 20095.

[20]*Vasquez v. Northern Illinois Hospital Services,* 2002 U.S. Dist. LEXIS 5257.

[21]29 C.F.R. § 825.216 (2005).

Employers cannot refuse leave to key employees, but can decline to restore them if restoration would "cause substantial and grievous economic injury" to the employer's operation. One of the main reasons for denying restoration is that it was necessary to find a permanent replacement for the key employee on leave. An employee denied restoration on the grounds of being a key employee was allowed to go to trial because there was evidence that his replacement as county tax assessor was hired on an interim basis and could have been returned to his prior position without cost to the county.[22] *Key employees must be informed of their status when they seek leave and, if the employer decides that their restoration would cause substantial and grievous economic injury, be given a reasonable amount of time to return from leave.*

How Should Employers Respond to Requests for FMLA Leave?

Employers presented with requests for time off related to childbirth or medical problems must carefully consider whether the leave is required under the FMLA and respond promptly. "The FMLA envisions a cooperative dialogue between employers and employees through which a balance between their competing needs can be struck. . . . [M]ost litigation arising under the FMLA results from a breakdown of that hoped-for cooperative dialogue."[23] However, this "dialogue" must proceed from the basic premise that employees have an entitlement to leave under the FMLA. Generally, employers do not have the right to deny or delay FMLA leave. Thus, a court held that an employer's effort to get an employee to delay a continuous period of leave until a less busy time could constitute interference with FMLA rights, even though the employer subsequently relented.[24]

The DOL regulations call for employers to *provide written notice to employees requesting leave that the leave is being designated as FMLA leave, generally within one or two business days after notification of the need for leave.* The Supreme Court has determined that the DOL cannot punish employers who fail to provide the timely notification by not allowing them to count the days of leave against an employee's maximum entitlement under the FMLA,[25] but the basic principle remains: *the employer is responsibile for promptly designating leave as FMLA leave and for informing employees of their rights under the FMLA.* In a relevant case, an employee who needed time off due to a serious health condition was not told his leave would be designated FMLA leave or that such leave is limited to a maximum of 12 workweeks. The employee was eventually fired based on his absences. The court concluded that the employee could go to trial on this claim that the employer interfered with his FMLA rights by failing to properly advise him. This failure impaired the employee's exercise of his rights because he was apparently not aware that FMLA leave is limited to a maximum duration of 12 workweeks over a 12-month period.[26]

What should this notification to employees look like? The DOL's Wage and Hour Division has a form that can be used for this purpose. Whether the government's form or an employer's own document is used, *employer notices designating leave as FMLA leave should contain the following:*

- *A specific statement that the leave is designated FMLA leave and will be counted against the employee's leave entitlement*

[22]*Kephart v. Cherokee County,* 2000 U.S. App. LEXIS 18924.

[23]*Shtab v. Greate Bay Hotel and Casino,* 173 F. Supp. 2d 255, at 257 (D.N.J. 2001).

[24]*Shtab,* at 268.

[25]*Ragsdale v. Wolverine Worldwide, Inc.,* 122 S. Ct. 1155 (2002).

[26]*Conoshenti v. Public Service Electric & Gas Company,* 364 F.3d 135 (3d Cir. 2004).

- *Any requirements for producing medical certification of a serious health condition and the consequences of failing to do so*
- *A statement of the employee's right to substitute paid leave for FMLA leave, whether the employer will require that to be done, and any conditions related to the substitution*
- *Any requirements for payment of the employee share of health insurance premiums, arrangements for making those payments, and the right of the employer to recover premium payments if the employee chooses not to return from leave*
- *Any requirements for the employee to present fitness-for-duty certification prior to being restored*
- *A statement of the employee's right of restoration to the same job or an equivalent position*
- *Designation of key employee status if the employee meets the criteria and explanation of the circumstances under which restoration might be denied*

These issues are best determined as matters of policy. *Employers are well advised to have explicit family and medical leave policies, including a clear statement of the 12-month period that will be used in calculating leave entitlement.* The DOL regulations require that *if employers provide written guidance to their employees regarding employee benefit and leave programs—matters often discussed in employee handbooks—information must also be included concerning employee rights and responsibilities under the FMLA.*

Pregnancy Discrimination Act

Because of the relatively high employer size threshold for coverage under the FMLA, many employees do not receive its protection. In 2000, about 58 percent of employees worked in establishments large enough to be covered by the FMLA, with about 47 percent also meeting the hours and duration requirements for eligibility.[27] In light of the limited coverage of the FMLA, the **Pregnancy Discrimination Act (PDA)** continues to have a significant influence on leave policies. The PDA confirms that discrimination based on "pregnancy, childbirth, or related medical conditions" is sex discrimination and violates Title VII.[28] The PDA does *not* require that employers provide leave for childbirth or medical problems associated with pregnancy. However, employers must treat persons with pregnancy-related conditions in the same manner as persons with other medical conditions who are similar in their ability or nonability to work. *If sick leave, disability leave, or other forms of paid or unpaid time off are available to a company's employees, the same forms of leave must be available to its pregnant employees, and on the same terms.* This is also true regarding reassignment to light-duty positions or other alternative working arrangements if these are made available to employees with other temporarily disabling conditions.

Pregnant employees are entitled to continue working for as long as they can perform their jobs (except in those rare cases where not being pregnant is a BFOQ). *Employers are prohibited from requiring pregnant employees who can perform their jobs to take leave or from establishing arbitrary timelines for when parental leave must commence or end.* Pregnancy-related conditions cannot be singled out for

[27]Waldfogel, 19–20.

[28]Civil Rights Act of 1964, Title VII, 42 U.S.C.A. § 2000e(k) (2005).

special procedures for determining ability to work. However, *any medical certification that is generally required prior to granting leave or to document fitness for duty upon return from leave can also be required of employees who take leave for pregnancy-related conditions.* There is no specific restoration requirement under the PDA. Instead, parity is again the rule. *Jobs must be held open for employees on pregnancy-related leave as least as long as they are for employees who take sick or disability leave for other medical conditions.*[29]

Leave to Perform Civic Duties

As citizens, employees are sometimes called upon to perform duties that require their absence from work. One example of this is serving on a jury. The federal **Jury System Improvements Act**[30] protects persons who serve on federal juries from discharge, intimidation, or coercion by their employers. Most states also have laws protecting employees who serve on juries from discharge. Some states require that employees be paid while on jury duty, but that is not always the case. Voting is another civic duty addressed by state laws. Most states require that employees be given a specified number of hours off to vote when there is not sufficient nonwork time to do so. Thus, although the details vary between states, *employers must generally provide employees with time off to serve on juries and vote.*

Uniformed Services Employment and Reemployment Rights Act (USERRA)

Extensive legal requirements surround military service, which are detailed in the **Uniformed Services Employment and Reemployment Rights Act (USERRA)**.[31] Employers of any size are prohibited from discriminating against persons who are members of, apply to become members of, or have obligations to serve in a uniformed military service. Often, complying with this law means allowing an employee in the National Guard to attend scheduled annual drill training and treating the employee as if he had not been absent. However, in a time of ongoing military and peacekeeping operations, National Guard members and reservists are increasingly being called into active duty and required to perform lengthy military service—sometimes on multiple tours.[32] Employers must be aware that such employees retain many important rights under the USERRA. Aircraft manufacturer Pratt & Whitney apparently failed to keep this in mind when it eliminated the position of an Army Reservist who served for six months in Kuwait and failed to re-instate him to a comparable position (see "Clippings").

As a general rule, *employees are entitled to reemployment following up to five years of cumulative absence* (not counting periods of required training) for military service. An employee taking leave for military service is required to notify his employer to that effect, but is not required to await permission or to decide at that time whether reinstatement will be sought following the period of military service. *Provided that an honorable discharge is received and a timely request made for reemployment, an employee returning from military service must be reemployed.* Service

[29]Equal Employment Opportunity Commission. "Facts About Pregnancy Discrimination." (January 1994).

[30]28 U.S.C.S. § 1875(a) (2005).

[31]38 U.S.C.S. §§ 4301–4324 (2005).

[32]Sue Darcy. "Re-Employment Issues, Filling Open Jobs Among Challenges as Tours of Duty Lengthen." *Daily Labor Report* 65 (April 6, 2005), C-1.

members have to report more or less immediately following service periods of less than 31 days and within 90 days of discharge when the service period exceeds 180 days. Service members injured or disabled during service are given up to 2 years to return to their jobs. The main exceptions to this reinstatement requirement are where 1) the employer's circumstances have changed, rendering reemployment "impossible or unreasonable" (e.g., a business closure); 2) the necessary training or other accommodations needed to successfully reemploy the individual would impose "undue hardship;" or 3) the prior employment was for a brief, nonrecurrent period and carried no expectation of continued employment (e.g., temporary employment to complete a specific project).[33]

Under the **escalator principle**, *employers must attempt to place individuals returning from military service into the positions, including promotions, they likely would have attained absent the service.* Employers must make reasonable efforts, such as by providing training, to permit returning service members to perform their jobs. If individuals are not qualified to perform the jobs that they would otherwise have attained, reinstatement to the position held prior to military service or an equivalent position must be considered. Reemployment under the USERRA also means that an employee returns with the seniority he would have had if he were continuously employed and any other benefits related to length of service (e.g., pay raises). Benefits unrelated to seniority must be maintained on the same basis as for other employees receiving comparable, nonmilitary leaves of absence.[34]

Employers are not required to pay employees while they are gone performing military service, although some do so. *Health insurance must be maintained for short (less than 31 days) stints of service and for longer periods (up to 24 months) if the employee pays the full cost of group coverage.*[35] Pension benefits generally continue to accrue while employees are in the military service, although employee contributions might still be required.

The substantial nature of service members' reemployment rights is underscored by the fact that, after they are reemployed, service members can be subsequently terminated only "for cause" for the next six months to a year (depending on length of service). Thus, employees are protected against "sham" reemployment that attempts to circumvent the law.

LANGUAGE REQUIREMENTS AND NATIONAL ORIGIN DISCRIMINATION

One of the more obvious manifestations of diversity is a workforce in which a variety of languages and accents are heard. Language is closely tied to national origin. Legal issues can arise when employers make employment decisions based on English fluency or the presence of an accent and when employers adopt English-only rules to curtail the use of other languages in the workplace.

English Fluency and Accents

As if calculus was not hard enough by itself, you're crammed into a lecture hall, staring at a jumble of strange symbols, and straining to comprehend the heavily accented

[33]38 U.S.C.S. § 4312 (d) (1) (2005).
[34]38 U.S.C.S. § 4316 (a) (2005).
[35]38 U.S.C.S. § 4317 (a) (2005).

words of your foreign-born instructor. That experiences like this might be viewed as real-world lessons in diversity—preparation for a world in which not everyone we work or do business with speaks in a familiar manner—is understandably lost on frustrated students. But is it national origin discrimination for universities or other employers to insist that employees be fluent in English and not speak with heavy accents?

Courts have recognized the close nexus between language and national origin and the ease with which subjective assessments of language can merge into national origin discrimination. In one important case, a Filipino emigrated to Hawaii and scored highest in the state on a civil service exam for motor vehicle bureau clerks. The exam included, among other things, word usage, grammar, and spelling. However, when the man was interviewed for the position, the two interviewers concluded that he had a "heavy accent" and would be difficult for customers to understand, particularly over the phone. The Filipino man was not hired. The court found for the employer because of the following:

> The record conclusively shows that Fragante [the plaintiff] was not selected because of the deleterious effect his Filipino accent had upon his ability to communicate orally, not merely because he had such an. This is a crucial distinction. Employers may lawfully base an employment decision upon an individual's accent when—but only when—it interferes materially with job performance.[36]

Thus, *an employee or job applicant's accent can be lawfully considered in making employment decisions when communication is a significant part of the job in question and the individual's accent substantially interferes with the ability to communicate.* The critical issue is comprehension and not that the person sounds different or "foreign" or that understanding the person requires extra effort on the part of listeners.

Universities have been upheld by the courts in cases where they reasonably took into account the communication skills of faculty. For example, the termination of a professor from Trinidad was upheld, despite the fact that the university's evaluation of his teaching was based on student evaluations that included negative comments about the professor's accent (among other complaints). The court wrote the following:

> [R]equiring that a professor speak the native tongue in order to convey his ideas is not any form of discrimination. . . . This sentence [one student evaluation said "hire a professor who speaks English"] merely expresses the frustration of a student stymied by a professor not conversant in the language of his students.[37]

However, where complaints about an accent were combined with derogatory comments about foreign faculty, inconsistent evaluations of the faculty member, and a highly subjective evaluation system, they supported a finding of national origin discrimination.[38] Likewise, a bank discriminated when it refused to promote an employee because of his Cambodian accent. The employee had completed management training, had taken English classes to improve his language skills, and had good performance appraisals, but he was told that he could not be promoted because of his "foreign" accent.[39]

[36]*Fragante v. City and County of Honolulu*, 888 F.2d 591, at 596 (9th Cir. 1989), *cert. denied*, 494 U.S. 1081 (1990).

[37]*Jiminez v. Mary Washington College*, 57 F.3d 369, at 380 (4th Cir. 1995), *cert. denied*, 516 U.S. 944 (1995).

[38]*Saleh v. Upadhyay*, 2001 U.S. App. LEXIS 11322.

[39]*Xieng v. Peoples National Bank*, 844 P.2d 389, at 392 (Wash. 1993).

English-Only Rules

Employers with bilingual or multilingual employees sometimes institute **English-only rules** that prohibit or restrict the speaking of languages other than English in the workplace. These policies vary in breadth, from total bans to time and place restrictions on speaking other languages in the workplace. The impetus for establishing these policies is often the complaints of monolingual, English-speaking employees or supervisors who believe that they are being denigrated. Safety concerns, customer preferences, and problems in supervision are also cited as motives. Given the demographics of the U.S. workforce, these policies most often have the effect of limiting Latino employees from speaking Spanish on the job. But as the case brought by the EEOC on behalf of Navajo-speaking Native Americans shows, these policies can affect other groups as well (see "Clippings").

The EEOC's guidelines hold that broad English-only rules applied at all times are presumptively discriminatory. More narrowly tailored policies applied only at certain times are legal, provided that employers can demonstrate their business necessity. The EEOC also maintains that unless employers notify employees of the existence of an English-only rule, any disciplinary actions taken against noncomplying employees will be viewed as evidence of discrimination.[40]

Courts have not always concurred with the EEOC's position. However, in *EEOC v. Premier Operator Services,* the court makes a strong statement about the discriminatory character of an employer's English-only rule.

[40]29 C.F.R. § 1606.7 (2005).

EEOC V. PREMIER OPERATOR SERVICES
113 F. Supp. 2d 1066 (N.D. Tex. 2000)

OPINION BY JUDGE STICKNEY:

The Charging Parties and similarly situated aggrieved individuals (hereinafter "class members") for whom the EEOC seeks relief are of Hispanic national origin—they or their parents were born in Mexico or another country in which Spanish is the primary or predominant language. The record also shows that the class members are bilingual. . . . Nevertheless, their primary language or language of national origin is Spanish. * * *

The class members worked as Operators for defendant, Premier Operator Services, Inc. ("Premier"). The recruitment and hiring of the class members was based or conditioned upon their bilingual ability, and in particular, their ability to speak Spanish because of a need for the defendant's business to service Spanish-speaking customers in connecting long distance telephone calls. * * *

Premier enacted a "Speak-English-Only" policy prohibiting the speaking of Spanish on the company premises. The policy was posted on the door at the entrance of the "DNSI" building in which Premier was located. This sign specifically warns about defendant's language policy. The same sign also conspicuously couples the policy with a warning about weapons, implying a combined concern about the conduct of those persons who speak a language other than English, Hispanic employees in this case, and setting the scene for stigmatization of those to whom the policy is directed:

> Absolutely No Guns, Knives or Weapons of any kind are allowed on these Premises at any time! English is the official language of Premier Operator Services, Inc. All conversations on these premises are to be in English. Other languages may be spoken to customers who cannot speak English.

This policy prohibited the speaking of Spanish at all times, including the time during free moments operators had between calls, during lunch, in the employee break

room, when making personal telephone calls, and before and after work if inside the building. Under defendant's policy, the only time it was acceptable to speak Spanish was when assisting a Spanish-speaking customer. Confined to the close quarters of a small work area in which, before the hire of non-Hispanic Operators starting in mid-January 1996, everyone spoke Spanish, the employees of Premier were required to refrain from speaking in Spanish to their co-workers at all times. Working shoulder to shoulder, workers experiencing free time between calls, including those persons working on the night shift, were required to speak to their Hispanic colleagues in English or face discipline or dismissal. Lunchroom conversations—even between a Hispanic husband and wife—could not include Spanish words or phrases. Defendant stipulated and thereby admits that it went as far as to plan installation of a public telephone outside of the building, so that Hispanic employees would have to go outside to make personal phone calls during which they might speak Spanish.

On January 16, 1996, defendant required the class members to sign a memo detailing defendant's English-only policy as a pre-requisite to continued employment. Class members testified and former Vice President Marvin McCroy admitted that it was understood that if the employees did not agree to the prohibitions imposed by the policy, their employment would be terminated.

Six employees who refused to sign the memo— Edgar Lira, Mardia Lira, Marcella Mendez, Lauren Peralta, Ruth Torres and Lupe Torres—were immediately terminated. Two employees who signed the memo under protest and then filed EEOC charges of discrimination alleging the policy to be discriminatory— Francisco Gracia and Albert Estrada—were terminated within 24 hours of defendant's receipt of the charges. * * * Class members who signed the English-only memo under protest or voiced their opposition to the policy were soon "laid off" without notice. * * *

Expert witness Dr. Susan Berk-Seligson, a professor of linguistics . . . testified that adhering to an English-only requirement is not simply a matter of preference for Hispanics, or other persons who are bilingual speakers, but that such restraint can be virtually impossible in many cases. Bilinguals whose original language is a language other than English unconsciously switch from English to their original or primary language when speaking informally with fellow members of their cultural group. This switching back and forth, formally known as "code-switching," can occur in conversation even within a sentence or between sentences.

The expert's findings that the class members in this case were subject to code-switching was based not only on her knowledge and research in the field of linguistics, but also on her review of information elicited from the class members. * * *

The policy was not job-related or consistent with any business necessity for the performance of the job duties and functions of the position of Operator with Premier Operator Services, Inc. To the contrary, the evidence is clear that the speaking of Spanish was a job requirement. Even if the Court were to assume that office "harmony" were properly considered to be a business necessity that would justify an English-only policy, there is no credible or persuasive evidence that there was "discord" amongst the employees of Premier which required harmonization in this manner. Further, there is no evidence that the subject policy and its enforcement promoted "harmony" in the workplace. Quite the opposite, the evidence shows that the policy served to create a disruption in the work place and feelings of alienation and inadequacy by Hispanic employees who had up to that time been proven performers for the company. Likewise, there is no evidence sufficient to establish that there was any inability of the employees, all of whom were bilingual, to communicate with their supervisors and managers, such as Maria Gaytan or Marvin MacCroy, in carrying out their job duties and responsibilities. * * *

Defendant's enactment and implementation of the speak-English-only rule or policy constitutes disparate treatment of Hispanic employees based upon their national origin, in violation of Title VII of the Civil Rights Act of 1964, as amended. A blanket policy or practice prohibiting the speaking of a language other than English on an employer's premises at all times, except when speaking to a non-English speaking customer, violates Title VII's prohibition against discrimination based on national origin. The EEOC Guidelines state that a blanket English-only rule is presumed to violate Title VII:

> A rule requiring employees to speak only English at all times in the work place is a burdensome term and condition of employment. The primary language of an individual is often an essential national origin characteristic. Prohibiting employees at all times, in the workplace, from speaking their primary language or the language they speak most comfortably, disadvantages an individual's employment opportunities on the basis of national origin.

It may also create an atmosphere of inferiority, isolation and intimidation based on national origin which could result in a discriminatory working environment. Therefore, the Commission will presume that such a rule violates Title VII and will closely scrutinize it.

Speak-English-only rules tend to impact people whose national origin is from non-English speaking countries more heavily than it affects others. While English-only rules may be seen as facially neutral, they disproportionately burden national origin minorities because they preclude many members of these groups from speaking the language in which they are best able to communicate, while rarely, if ever, having that effect on non-minority employees. Blanket English-only rules have a significant adverse impact on national origin groups whose primary language or language of national origin is not English. Further, even a tailored English-only rule must be justified by business necessity, if there is one that could conceivably exist, and in this case there is not.

The two appellate cases addressing the legality of English-only rules [both of which upheld the rules] involved prohibitions confined to the work area, excluding free time and break areas. In *Garcia v. Spun Steak Co.*, 998 F.2d 1480 (9th Cir. 1993), the English-only policy stated: "During lunch, breaks, and employees' own time, [employees] are obviously free to speak Spanish if they wish." The Fifth Circuit Court of Appeals, in *Garcia v. Gloor*, 618 F.2d 264 (5th Cir. 1980), *cert. denied*, 449 U.S. 1113 (1981), specifically excluded from its ruling English-only rules covering employees' personal time. * * * Gloor was also decided prior to the extensive research . . . regarding "code switching" and the fact that speaking only English is not simply a matter of preference for bilingual persons whose primary language or language of national origin is other than English. Based on the most recent and

directly relevant state of research on this subject, it is evident that lapsing or switching from English to Spanish is often inadvertent and unconscious on the part of bilingual Spanish speakers such as the class members in this case. * * *

Employees at Premier who did not speak Spanish, and who were not of Hispanic national origin, were not subject to the same oppressive monitoring or potential discipline and discharge as were the Hispanic employees. The Hispanic class members were forced to be constantly on guard to avoid uttering their native language, even in their most private moments in the lunch room or on a break. Nevertheless, as testified by class members including Mardia Lira, once reprimanded for speaking in Spanish to her husband while at lunch in the break room, the policy was strictly enforced. Since the family members of Hispanic employees in most cases speak primarily Spanish or are monolingual, the requirement that all employees speak only English adversely impacted Hispanic employees who sometimes needed to make personal calls to home. The non-Hispanic employees did not similarly risk inadvertently switching to Spanish and the discipline or discharge that could and did result. This difference in working conditions not only constitutes disparate treatment, but also demonstrates the disparate impact of the policy on a protected class of employees, persons of Mexican or other Hispanic national origins. * * *

CASE QUESTIONS

1. What is the legal issue in this case? What did the court decide? Why?

2. Would the policy have been legal if it was less broad?

3. Based on this case, what would you advise employers regarding English-only rules?

Despite the strong tone of the court's opinion in *Premier Operator Services*, the legal status of English-only rules remains unclear. Some courts have held in adverse impact claims that English-only rules do not adversely affect the employment opportunities of bilingual employees because they are able to comply with the policies. Consequently, there was no need for the employers to even show the business necessity for their English-only policies.[41] Courts have also found for employers when the English-only rules were not as broad and rigidly enforced as in the *Premier*

[41]*Garcia v. Spun Steak*, 998 F.2d 1480, at 1488 (9th Cir. 1993), *cert. denied*, 512 U.S. 1228 (1994).

Operator Services case. In one such case, retail store employees were required to speak English when on the sales floor and in the presence of customers—and expressly permitted to speak other languages in the workplace at all other times. The court agreed with the employer that the policy served the business necessity of promoting customer service by rendering salespeople more polite and approachable.[42] But none of this amounts to blanket authorization for English-only rules. Monolingual employees who speak languages other than English are clearly unable to comply and are disadvantaged if the policies are enforced against them. Combined with other forms of hostility to "foreigners," rigidly enforced English-only policies contribute to hostile environments and national origin harassment. Public employees may be able to assert First Amendment speech rights if their government employers limit them to speaking English on the job.[43] And, of course, the EEOC will continue its close scrutiny.

If used at all, English-only rules should be no broader than absolutely necessary to accomplish legitimate business purposes. Enforcement of the rules should not be rigid, and employees must be clearly notified that the rules are in effect.

DISCRIMINATION BASED ON SEXUAL ORIENTATION

A form of difference that this society has certainly become more aware of is sexual orientation. Whether a person identifies himself as heterosexual, homosexual, or bisexual often has real consequences for that individual—both in the larger society and in the workplace. Gays and lesbians face outright exclusion from some workplaces, but more often harassment, demeaning comments, and denial of benefits available to their heterosexual coworkers. What, if any, laws protect employees from discrimination based on their sexual orientation?

Protection Under Federal Law

Title VII of the Civil Rights Act of 1964 refers to "sex" as a protected class, but courts have consistently held that protection against discrimination based on sexual orientation cannot be read into the Act.[44] Efforts to amend Title VII to include sexual orientation as a protected class have thus far been rejected.

The U.S. Constitution offers somewhat more protection, albeit only to public employees. When government agencies make adverse employment decisions based on a person's sexual orientation, those decisions or policies can be challenged as unconstitutional (as denials of equal protection of the law or perhaps violations of associational rights) if they are not "rationally related to a legitimate government purpose or interest." As one court has described the **rational relationship standard** of constitutional scrutiny:

> [T]he state [government] action must still bear a rational relationship to the legitimate state objectives and interest. Under the rational relationship standard, a court presumes that the classification is constitutional and the Plaintiff bears the burden of demonstrating that the classification at issue bears no legitimate purpose. Although most state actions survive legal analysis because of at least some tenuous rational relationship between the class distinction and the state interest, the rational relationship test is not

[42]*Equal Employment Opportunity Commission v. Sephora USA*, 2005 U.S. Dist. LEXIS 20014.

[43]*Ruiz et al. v. Hull, Governor of Arizona*, 957 P.2d 984 (Ariz. 1998), *cert. denied*, 525 U.S. 1093 (1999).

[44] *DeSantis v. Pacific Telephone & Telegraph*, 608 F.2d 327 (9th Cir. 1979); *overruled in part by, Nichols v. Azteca Restaurant Enterprises*, 256 F.3d 864, at 875 (9th Cir. 2001).

entirely toothless. The Supreme Court has used the Equal Protection Clause to protect individuals . . . from "invidious discrimination" and "irrational prejudice."[45]

Though not inherently "toothless," constitutional challenges to sexual orientation discrimination by government agencies generally have not fared well. Many of these cases have involved government agencies with security or law enforcement missions. For example, the FBI's refusal to hire a lesbian was upheld as constitutional[46] (based on concerns that homosexuals would be more subject to blackmail to prevent themselves or their partners from being "outed"). Courts also upheld the Georgia Attorney General's decision to rescind an offer of employment upon learning that a woman had engaged in a commitment ceremony with her female partner[47] (based on the state's claims that citizens would be confused about what the law is regarding same-sex marriage and that the Office's public image would be harmed).

Gays in the Military: "Don't Ask, Don't Tell" More than any other governmental institution, the military has experienced ongoing controversy and legal challenges regarding its treatment of homosexuals. The stated concern of the military is that people who engage in homosexual behavior and are known to be homosexuals might undermine the group cohesion and morale that is vital to military service. A compromise, revised policy—dubbed **"don't ask, don't tell"**—was crafted in 1993. The gist of the policy is that homosexual service members are expected to be discreet and not talk about or openly engage in homosexual behavior. In return, the military must refrain from unwarranted fishing expeditions to ferret out homosexuals in the ranks. Citing their traditional deference to the military and the rational basis for the military's concerns with maintaining morale and cohesion, courts have upheld the legality of the new policy.[48] However, the Navy was enjoined from discharging a serviceman when it violated the "don't ask, don't tell" policy by conducting an extensive investigation absent credible information pointing to the likelihood of homosexual conduct.[49] Furthermore, the Supreme Court's decision, on broad privacy grounds, to strike down as unconstitutional a state law criminalizing consensual sodomy[50] may have implications for future cases involving the military.[51]

Concerns about how the military's revised policy regarding homosexuals is being administered are more than academic. Despite the fact that the policy was intended to be more liberal in allowing homosexuals to serve in the military, discharges of gays and lesbians surged following adoption of the "don't ask, don't tell" policy.[52] The volume of these discharges has dropped off since 9/11 and the military's increased need for service members, but there are still hundreds of discharges each year—resulting in substantial cost and the loss of important skills (including desperately needed Arabic language skills) (see "Clippings").

Protection Under State and Local Laws

For most employees, the availability of legal protection from discrimination based on sexual orientation depends on the geographic location of their workplaces.

[45]*Baumgardner v. County of Cook*, 108 F. Supp. 2d 1041, at 1054 (E.D. Ill. 2000).

[46]*Padula v. Webster*, 822 F.2d 97 (D.C. Cir. 1987).

[47]*Shahar v. Bowers*, 114 F.3d 1097 (11th Cir. 1997), *cert. denied*, 522 U.S. 1049 (1998).

[48]*Able v. United States*, 155 F.3d 628 (2d Cir. 1998).

[49]*McVeigh v. Cohen*, 983 F. Supp. 215 (D.C. 1998).

[50]*Lawrence v. Texas*, 539 U.S. 558 (2003).

[51]John Files. "Gays Ousted from Military Challenge Policy in Lawsuit." *New York Times* (December 7, 2004), A-17.

[52]John Files. "Rules on Gays Exact a Cost in Recruiting a Study Finds." *New York Times* (February 24, 2005), A-16.

Employees in about a dozen states, plus the District of Columbia, enjoy protection under state law. In seven other states, public, but not private sector employees, are covered by state laws prohibiting discrimination based on sexual orientation.[53] A sizeable number of cities address sexual orientation discrimination under municipal laws. *Employers must be aware of and abide by any state and local laws prohibiting discrimination based on sexual orientation.*

Not surprisingly, laws addressing sexual orientation discrimination are controversial. Although the number of states and cities with statutes has slowly grown (New York State added itself to the list in 2002), some jurisdictions have moved in the opposite direction. Voters in Maine, for example, repealed the state's sexual orientation discrimination law in 1998. A second statute was enacted and voted down in 2000. In 2005, opponents failed to win a referendum on yet another Maine law prohibiting discrimination based on sexual orientation.[54] Some groups opposing legal protection for gays and lesbians have gone beyond merely seeking the repeal of existing legislation and tried to ensure that laws addressing sexual orientation discrimination will never be passed. In Colorado, several cities had passed sexual orientation discrimination statutes. Rather than undertake campaigns to repeal the laws, a constitutional amendment was presented to voters and passed that made it unconstitutional for the state or any city in Colorado to pass or keep in place laws protecting against sexual orientation discrimination. The Supreme Court reviewed the constitutionality of the amendment and struck it down. The amendment amounted to a sweeping disenfranchisement of a discriminated-against minority and lacked a rational relationship to any legitimate government purpose.[55]

Subsequent developments have muddied the water, however. A similar strategy was employed in Cincinnati, where the city charter was amended to forbid the city from enacting or enforcing any law that would provide homosexuals with "any claim of minority or protected status, quota preference or other preferential treatment."[56] Despite the apparent similarity to the Colorado amendment, an appeals court discerned relevant differences (including that a city charter rather than the entirety of state law was involved) and upheld the constitutionality of the Cincinnati charter amendment. The Supreme Court declined to review the case. The saga of the Cincinnati charter battle took yet another turn in the 2004 election, when the city's voters gave their approval to abolition of the charter amendment that had prohibited protection of gays and lesbians[57] (confused yet?). The only safe prediction is that legal protections for gays and lesbians will continue to be a volatile political issue and a dynamic area of the law.

Transgender and Transsexual Persons

Whatever their sexual orientation, some persons ("transsexuals") feel that the gender assigned them at birth does not comport with their gender identity and they seek to live as members of the opposite sex (sometimes undergoing hormonal treatments and surgical procedures in the process). "Transgender" is an umbrella term that

[53]Barbara Kate Repa. *Your Rights in the Workplace* 5th ed. (Berkeley, CA: Nolo, 2000), p. 8/50.

[54]Rick Valliere. "Maine Voters Refuse to Nix Measure Adding Sexual Orientation to Bias Law." *Daily Labor Report* 217 (November 10, 2005), A-6.

[55]*Romer v. Evans,* 517 U.S. 620 (1996).

[56]*Equality Foundation of Greater Cincinnati v. City of Cincinnati,* 128 F.3d 289, at 291 (6th Cir. 1997), *cert. denied,* 525 U.S. 943 (1998).

[57]"Cincinnati Voters Reject Law That Barred Enactment of Job Bias Protections for Gays." *Daily Labor Report* 213 (November 4, 2004), A-7.

includes transsexual persons, but also persons who cross-dress while retaining their established gender identities and androgynous persons with ambiguous, shifting, or unconventional gender identities. Discrimination claims by transsexuals have generally been rejected by the courts, on the grounds that any such discrimination is not "because of sex." However, in a recent case involving a firefighter who was subjected to adverse employment actions after he informed his employer regarding his Gender Identity Disorder and began assuming a more feminine appearance in the workplace, the court found that there was sex discrimination in violation of Title VII:

> Sex stereotyping based on a person's gender non-conforming behavior is impermissible discrimination, irrespective of the cause of that behavior; a label, such as "transsexual" is not fatal to a sex discrimination claim where the victim has suffered discrimination because of his or her gender non-conformity.[58]

The court distinguished this case from the earlier decisions because, in the interim, the Supreme Court had firmly endorsed the theory of sex-stereotyping in Title VII cases. A second case involving a transsexual police officer removed from a promotional position for being "not masculine enough" was also decided in favor of the plaintiff, and the Supreme Court opted to not review the decision.[59] Whether other courts will follow the Sixth Circuit's lead on this issue is still unclear.

[58]*Smith v. City of Salem, Ohio*, 378 F.3d 566, at 575 (6th Cir. 2004).

[59]*Barnes v. City of Cincinnati*, 401 F.3d 729 (6th Cir. 2005), *cert. denied*, 2005 U.S. LEXIS 8238.

Chapter SUMMARY

The Family and Medical Leave Act (FMLA) is the principal federal law affecting the provision of leave for parental and medical reasons. The FMLA entitles employees to up to a total of 12 weeks of leave over a 12-month period, maintenance of health insurance benefits during leave, and restoration from leave to the same position held prior to leave or an equivalent position. Employees are entitled to leave if they work at a site where the employer has at least 50 employees within a 75-mile radius, have worked at least 12 months for that employer, have worked at least 1,250 hours within the past 12 months, and have experienced a "qualifying event." Qualifying events for FMLA leave include the birth, foster care placement, or adoption of a child; the serious health condition of the employee; and the serious health condition of a spouse, child, or parent. Serious health conditions involve either inpatient care in a medical facility or continuing treatment by a health-care provider that meets certain other criteria.

Leave policies also must meet the requirements of the Pregnancy Discrimination Act (PDA). The PDA prohibits discrimination based on pregnancy, childbirth, and related medical conditions. Although the PDA does not require that employers offer parental leave, it does mandate that pregnant women be treated the same under employer leave programs as others employees who are similar in their ability or nonability to work.

Employees sometimes need time off to attend to civic duties, and there is some legal protection for employees who perform these services. The rights of persons who serve in the military are protected by the Uniformed Services Employment and Reemployment Act (USERRA). The USERRA protects employees from discrimination based on military service and provides for extensive reinstatement rights upon return from military service.

Language is an important aspect of diversity. Employer requirements related to language can result

in national origin discrimination and violations of Title VII. Accents can lawfully be considered in making employment decisions to the extent that communication is an important aspect of the job in question and the accent interferes with comprehension of the person's words. English-only rules, particularly when broadly applied, are potentially discriminatory, either for their adverse impact or as evidence of harassment or other disparate treatment.

Neither Title VII nor any other federal statute prohibits discrimination based on sexual orientation. Public employees have some protection under the equal protection provisions of the Constitution, but only to the extent that the public employer's discrimination based on sexual orientation or behavior bears no rational relationship to a legitimate government purpose. The treatment of gays and lesbians by the military has been the focus of controversy and legal challenges. The military's current "don't ask, don't tell" policy has thus far withstood constitutional challenges, but legal questions remain. Any protection for private-sector employees from discrimination based on sexual orientation comes under state and city laws. The creation of such laws is a politically charged issue and has spawned campaigns aimed at preventing their passage. The Supreme Court has ruled against one such effort, but the limits are not yet clearly defined. Transsexual persons might now receive protection under Title VII by arguing that, under the theory of sex-stereotyping, discrimination against them is due to their nonconformance with established gender definitions.

Employers are confronted with many questions of how best to deal with differences. Some of these are matters of employment law. However, the law does not and cannot mandate inclusive organizations that genuinely respect and value diverse people. It's up to employers and employees to do this.

Practical Advice SUMMARY

- *For employees who experience qualifying events, request leave, and meet the other eligibility requirements for FMLA leave, employers must*

 – *provide up to 12 workweeks of leave over a 12-month period.*

 – *maintain the health insurance of employees on FMLA leave under the same terms that would have prevailed had leave not been taken.*

 – *restore employees from FMLA leave by reinstating them to their same jobs or to positions that are equivalent in pay, benefits, and working conditions.*

- *Employees must be allowed to use any applicable paid leave provided by their employers to substitute for unpaid FMLA leave.*

- *Employees must be allowed to take leaves on an intermittent basis or as reduced leave schedules when needed to care for serious health conditions.*

- *In responding to requests for leave, employers must*

 – *not attempt to discourage eligible employees from taking leave or attempt to delay the taking of leave.*

 – *assess eligibility for leave as of the point in time when leave would commence, rather than when leave is initially requested.*

 – *promptly respond to employees.*

 – *notify employees in writing whether any leave will be designated as FMLA leave.*

- *If medical certification is required to document the existence of a serious health condition*

 – *employees' own doctors should be the primary sources for this information.*

 – *if they provide inadequate information, certification by another health-care provider can be required at employer expense.*

- *Employers can require that employees*

 – *provide at least 30 days advance notice when the need for leave is foreseeable.*

 – *cooperate in minimizing disruptiveness when scheduling medical treatments.*

- *If certification of fitness for duty is required of other employees returning from medical leaves, an employer should require the same for employees taking FMLA leave.*

- *Key employees must*

 –be informed of their status.

 –be told if the employer does not intend to restore them.

 –be given adequate opportunity to decline or return from leave.

 –be restored unless restoration would cause substantial and grievous economic injury to the employer.

- *Adverse employment decisions should be scrutinized very closely if they involve employees on or recently returned from FMLA leave.*

- *Employers cannot base adverse employment decisions on the taking of FMLA leave. "No-fault" attendance policies must either be discontinued or include exceptions for FMLA leave.*

- *Employer leave policies*

 –must be included in any employee handbooks that are provided.

 –must be consistent with the requirements of the FMLA (although they can exceed these).

 –should spell out the employer's choices about how to administer FMLA leave, including how the relevant 12-month period is defined.

- *If an employer provides sick leave, disability leave, and other forms of leave to persons with medical conditions, the same forms of leave must be available to pregnant employees, and on the same terms.*

- *Employers must generally allow pregnant employees to work for as long as they can perform their jobs and cannot specify when parental leaves will commence or terminate.*

- *Employers generally must allow employees time off to vote and serve on juries.*

- *Employees who have served in the military for up to five years, have been honorably discharged, and have made a timely request for reemployment*

 –must be reinstated by their employers.

 –must be reinstated into positions they would have attained had they been continuously employed, unless they are unable to perform those jobs.

 –must be provided with training needed to be able to perform their jobs.

 –must be reemployed with accrued seniority and benefits.

 –cannot be terminated for up to a year unless "for cause."

- *Employers should consider an applicant or employee's accent only to the extent that*

 –communication is a significant part of the job in question.

 –the individual's accent interferes with the ability to communicate and be understood.

- *If employers use English-only rules at all*

 –employees should be clearly informed that these policies are in effect.

 –the rules should be no broader than necessary to accomplish business purposes.

 –enforcement should not be rigid.

- *Employers need to be aware of and abide by any state or local laws that prohibit discrimination based on sexual orientation.*

Key TERMS

Family and Medical Leave Act (FMLA)	intermittent leave	Uniformed Services Employment and Reemployment Rights Act (USERRA)
qualifying events	reduced leave schedule	
serious health condition	restoration	escalator principle
period of incapacity	key employee	English-only rule
continuing treatment	Pregnancy Discrimination Act (PDA)	rational relationship standard
continuous leave	Jury System Improvement Act	"don't ask, don't tell" policy

Chapter QUESTIONS

1. An employee missed four days of work because of her four-year-old son's ear infection. She took the boy to the doctor the day after he began showing symptoms. The doctor diagnosed his condition, gave him an antibiotic, and told the mother to keep him home from day care for two days to monitor his temperature and to bring him back to the doctor in two weeks. Upon returning from work, the woman was discharged for the absences. What should the court decide? Why? (*Seidle v. Provident Mutual Life Insurance Co.*, 871 F. Supp. 238 (E.D. Pa. 1994))

2. An engineering supervisor at an auto plant became highly upset at his treatment by a manager and left work early. He did not ask permission to leave, explain the reason, or seek treatment at the plant's medical clinic. He drove home and went to bed. On the next work day, he had an appointment to see a doctor and left a voicemail message with the HR department, saying that he would be seeing a physician later that day and would not be at work. The doctor gave him some samples of an antidepressant medication and a note indicating that the employee was advised to stay out of work for at least a week, pending further evaluation and treatment. On the next day, the employee left a second voicemail message, stating that he had seen a physician and would be mailing the physician's note. A letter was sent from the company to the employee threatening disciplinary action if he did not report immediately to the HR department. The employee did not respond immediately, but later wrote a letter stating that he had been absent because he "was so stressed that I felt my health and well-being were at risk." The employee was eventually terminated for unexcused absences. The employee sued. What should the court decide? Why? (*Woods v. DaimlerChrysler*, 409 F.3d 984 (8th Cir. 2005))

3. An autoworker who had been on FMLA leave for a serious health condition was given clearance by her doctor and reported to work on June 27, 2000. She had previously worked on the engine line in a position that accommodated physical restrictions that she had from a back injury. The employee was told that no such positions were currently available. A "placement review" was conducted, but a position was not found until July 26. She returned to the engine line on July 31. However, this was a part-time position, and she did not resume full-time work on the engine line until September 18. The employer contends that this delay was due to the combination of her unexpected return, a changeover in models that affected the production process, and the difficulty of finding a position that accommodated her physical restrictions. The employee sues. What should the court decide? Why? (*Hoge v. Honda of America Mfg.*, 384 F.3d 238 (6th Cir. 2004))

4. A company's employees were offered "stay bonuses" as an inducement to remain with the firm during an acquisition by another company. The bonus was offered in 2000 and predicated on employees remaining "employed and actively working for the company as of September 30, 2001." On May 7, 2001, an employee of the company was granted 12 weeks of FMLA leave for the adoption of a child. The employee returned from leave in early August 2001 and remained with the company. However, her stay bonus was prorated to reflect the 12 weeks that she had been on FMLA leave, resulting in a reduction of some $8,000. The employee sues. What should the court decide? Why? (*Dierlam v. Wesley Jessen Corp.*, 222 F. Supp. 2d 1052 (N.D. Ill. 2002))

5. A manager was the only full-time employee at a gas station. Although he also had administrative tasks, he spent much of his time pumping gas and taking payments from customers. The manager took FMLA leave for a medical condition in October 2001. Concerned about falling revenues at the station, the owner had made plans to change from a full-service to a self-service operation. This change was implemented in fall 2001. Some of the administrative duties previously performed by the manager were transferred to an employee who had been working in another capacity for the company. When the manager returned from leave he was informed that, in light of the operational changes, the store manager position had been eliminated. He was offered a position as an attendant. The position was part-time, paid about $6.50/hr, and included no benefits. The former manager sues. What should the court decide? Why? (*Sylvester v. Dead River Company*, 260 F. Supp. 2d 181 (D. Maine 2003))

6. A couple is having a child. They both work for the same employer. Several months before the anticipated birth date, both inform the employer of their need for leave. The employer says that they are limited to a total of 12 weeks leave between them for the birth. Is the employer correct? (29 C.F.R. § 825.202)

7. A part-time employee works 30 hours a week. The employee is granted FMLA leave in the form of a reduced leave schedule (down to 20 hours per week) to receive treatments for a serious health condition. The HR director informs her she will be able to continue with this reduced schedule for up to 36 weeks. She contends that because she is only using 10 hours of leave per week, she should be entitled to up to 48 weeks of the reduced schedule. Who is right? (29 C.F.R. § 825.205(b))

8. An employee who is expecting a child is eligible and makes a timely request for parental leave. Draft a letter responding to her request for leave and notifying her that it will be considered FMLA leave. What should be included in this letter?

9. An Army Reservist, on his way home in the evening following weekend military duties in another state, stopped by his place of employment to pick up his paycheck and to obtain his schedule for the following week. The shift manager of the grocery store ordered him to stay and work the late shift. He did so. On the drive home, the employee fell asleep at the wheel, crashed, and died from his injuries. His estate is suing the employer, claiming that it violated the law by not providing the employee with a rest period following his return from military exercises. What should the court decide? Why? (*Gordon v. Wawa, Inc.*, 388 F.3d 78 (3d Cir. 2004))

10. A delivery truck driver was in the Army National Guard. He was required to report for drills one weekend per month and for at least two weeks in the summer. His requests for time off were routinely met with resistance by managers. He was told that he should get out of the National Guard and that it was placing a burden on others to cover his shifts. At his supervisor's insistence, the driver had his weekend obligations changed to Wednesdays, his usual day off. However, after 9/11, the National Guard no longer allowed this, and he had to report on weekends. When the driver informed his employer that he would be taking time off to fulfill his two week summer Guard duty, he was told again to "get out" of the Guard. He was given the time off only after the intervention of the HR department. While the driver was away on military duty, an incident was reported in which the driver had hugged an employee of a nursing home that was on his delivery route and left a bruise on her arm. Although the employee said that he was "just fooling around," the nursing home insisted that he not be allowed to deliver to them. The driver was informed upon his return from summer drills that he had been terminated, based on this incident. The driver sued. What should the court decide? Why? (*Mills v. Earthgrains Baking Companies*, 2004 U.S. Dist. LEXIS 14582)

11. Even where it is legally permissible, should employers adopt English-only policies? What are some practical alternatives?

12. Should Title VII be ammended to prohibit discrimination on the basis of sexual orientation? Why or why not?

13. Is "don't ask, don't tell" a sound policy? If not, what should the military do regarding gays and lesbians?

Internet RESOURCES

The DOL site has information on the FMLA and compliance assistance materials for the USERRA.

http://www.dol.gov/esa/whd/fmla

American Federation of State, County, and Municipal Employees (AFSCME) site also has information on the FMLA. AFSCME is a large labor union that represents many public employees.

http://www.afscme.org/wrkplace/fmla.htm

The EEOC site provides the "Facts About National Origin Discrimination" article.

http://www.eeoc.gov/origin/

PART **4**

Pay, Benefits, Terms and Conditions of Employment

○— **Chapter 12**
Wages, Hours, and Pay Equity

○— **Chapter 13**
Benefits

○— **Chapter 14**
Unions and Collective
Bargaining

○— **Chapter 15**
Occupational Safety and Health

Wages, Hours, and Pay Equity

CLIPPINGS

▸ Humana, Inc. will pay $1 million to settle a complaint brought by the Department of Labor (DOL) on behalf of the company's call-center workers. The DOL charged that Humana failed to pay the employees for time spent waiting for computers to power up, logging on to the network, and bringing up the programs needed to perform their jobs.[1]

▸ Cintas has been ordered by a state court to pay $800,000 for violating a Hayward, California, "living wage" ordinance. The city ordinance requires contractors providing services to the city to pay no less than $8/hr (with paid health insurance) or $9.25/hr (without benefits). These amounts are increased each year according to changes in the CPI (consumer price index).[2]

▸ Electronic Arts will pay $15.6 million to settle a claim that it failed to pay required overtime to its graphic artists, animators, and modelers. The employees said that the video game maker misclassified them as managers or creative professionals, but that they lacked the degree of creative control over their work to qualify as exempt. Two other lawsuits against EA for unpaid overtime work are still pending.[3]

▸ Some managers at Starbucks might be owed a "latte" of overtime pay. Managers at Starbucks across the country are attempting to bring a class-action suit for unpaid overtime work. The managers charge that they have been misclassified as "exempt" employees. They spend only about 10 percent of their time doing managerial work, while the bulk of their time is spent performing the same tasks as other store employees. In 2002, Starbucks paid $18 million to settle a similar claim by its managers in California.[4]

▸ New regulations establishing the criteria for the "white collar" exemptions to the Fair Labor Standards Act (FLSA) went into effect in August 2004. Critics claim that the changes will result in millions of workers losing their right to receive overtime pay, whereas the DOL claims that there should be a net gain in the number of employees entitled to overtime pay.[5]

▸ The median weekly earnings of full-time female workers was 79.5 percent of the weekly earnings for full-time male workers in 2003. The male-female earnings gap has been narrowing over the past several

[1]"Humana Agrees to $1 Million Settlement of Shortchanged Call-Center Workers' Claims." *Daily Labor Report* 134 (July 14, 2005), A-1.

[2]Michael R. Triplett. "Cintas Owes $800,000 for Shorting Workers Under Living Wage Ordinance, Court Rules." *Daily Labor Report* 187 (September 28, 2005), A-1.

[3]Michael R. Triplett. "Electronic Arts Agrees to Pay $15.6 Million to Settle Claims by Video Game Employees." *Daily Labor Report* 194 (October 7, 2005), A-9.

[4]Michael R. Triplett. "Court OK's Nationwide Collective Action in Starbucks Managers' Overtime Claims." *Daily Labor Report* 8 (January 12, 2005), A-6.

[5]Steven Greenhouse. "Controversial Overtime Rules Take Effect. " *New York Times* (August 23, 2004), A-11.

decades, as the earnings of women have grown faster than the earnings of men at all levels of education. However, women in professional occupations are more likely to be employed in lower paying professions such as education and library services than in such higher-paying professions as engineering and computer science.[6]

"A fair day's work for a fair day's pay." But what is "fair"? The law does not resolve the question of what is fair pay or impose a general requirement that employees be paid fairly. Instead, employers are prohibited from paying below certain legislatively determined minimum levels of pay and discriminating in pay. The law has even less to say about what is a fair amount of work time and effort. Rather than regulate hours directly, U.S. employment law affects work hours primarily by requiring premium pay for overtime work. This chapter focuses on the Fair Labor Standards Act (FLSA), the principle federal statute regulating wages and hours. It also discusses the Equal Pay Act and briefly mentions other laws bearing on wages, hours, and pay equity.

FAIR LABOR STANDARDS ACT—WAGE AND HOUR STANDARDS

The **Fair Labor Standards Act (FLSA)**[7] establishes a federal minimum wage and requires premium pay for overtime work. It also sets out certain work-hour limitations for minors. The FLSA's main requirements are straightforward. The law's complexity derives from problems in applying its general provisions to the enormous variety that exists among workplaces.

Minimum Wage

Under the FLSA, *employers must pay employees at a rate no less than the minimum wage for each hour worked during a workweek*. The federal minimum wage as of 2005 remains at $5.15/hr (unchanged since 1997). The fact that the **minimum wage** is stated as an hourly rate does not mean that other rates (e.g., weekly pay, piece rates) are prohibited; it only means that when the amount paid for each workweek is converted to an hourly rate, that rate must be equal to or greater than the minimum wage. Nor does the FLSA specify any particular pay period. Payment of the minimum wage and overtime must be prompt, but that generally means in the paycheck covering the relevant workweek (unless state law says otherwise). To determine whether the minimum wage has been paid, total straight-time (i.e., not overtime) pay for a workweek is divided by total hours worked during that workweek. For example, if an employee worked 35 hours in the previous workweek and received $175 in pay for the week, the employee did not receive the full payment due under the FLSA because $175/35 = $5.00/hr. The employer would have had to pay at least $180.25 (35 * $5.15) to comply with the FLSA's minimum wage requirement.

An exception to the general requirement of hourly pay at least equal to the minimum wage is the **opportunity wage**. Employers are permitted to pay employees

[6]"BLS Says Wage Gap Narrowed in 2003 As Women Earned 79.5% of Men's Pay." *Daily Labor Report* 207 (October 27, 2004), A-5.

[7]29 U.S.C.A. §§ 201–219 (2005); 29 C.F.R. §§ 516–794 (2005).

under 20 years of age at the rate of $4.25/hr for their first 90 calendar days on the job. A condition of the opportunity wage is that it cannot be used to displace or reduce the hours of existing employees.

The minimum wage requirement applies to gross pay. Employers are required to withhold income taxes from employees' gross pay, as well as the employee share of Social Security. With employees' consent, deductions can be made for items such as employee contributions to insurance plans, union dues, or savings plans. Additional sums (generally limited to 25 percent of disposable earnings) may be deducted because a court or government agency has ordered an employee's pay to be "garnished" to recover money owed for obligations such as child support, alimony, and student loans. Although deductions for these and other purposes do not affect compliance with the FLSA, *employers are not free to charge employees for items that primarily benefit the employer (e.g., uniforms or the laundering of uniforms, fees to cover breakage), when the effect of those deductions would be to push an employee's hourly wage rate below the minimum wage.*

Overtime Pay

Under the FLSA, *employers must pay at least one and one-half times an employee's regular rate of pay for each hour worked in excess of 40 in a workweek.* Other than for minors, the FLSA does not limit the number of hours employees can be required to work. Instead, the act gives employers a financial incentive to limit **overtime** because those hours of work must be compensated at a premium. That premium is expressed in terms of an employee's **regular rate of pay**. If an employee is paid an hourly wage, the hourly wage is the regular rate (barring receipt of certain other payments). An employee who earns $8/hr and works 44 hours in a workweek would be entitled to $8/hr for the first 40 hours of work ($8 * 40 = $320) plus $12/hr for the 4 overtime hours ($12 * 4 = $48), for a total of $368 for the week. If an employee is paid a weekly sum based on a specified number of hours such as 40, the regular rate would be the weekly pay divided by 40. However, if the employee is paid a weekly salary for a fluctuating number of hours, the regular rate would be the weekly salary divided by the number of hours actually worked each week. Under this scenario, the regular rate varies from week to week and decreases as the number of overtime hours increases. Computing the regular rate in this manner is nonetheless legal (although a potential labor relations nightmare), provided that the employer has previously informed the employee that overtime pay will be calculated in this manner.[8]

The basic unit of time for determining compliance with both the FLSA's minimum wage and overtime requirements is the **workweek**. The workweek is any fixed and recurring period of 7 consecutive days (168 hours). The workweek does not necessarily correspond to the calendar week or begin at the start of a workday. Work does not necessarily occur on each and every day of the workweek. With just a few exceptions, FLSA overtime is earned on a weekly basis. It does not matter how many hours an employee works on a particular day; the relevant issue is the number of hours worked in the workweek. (However, daily overtime might be required under a collective bargaining agreement or state law.) Just as there is no daily overtime under the FLSA, *hours of work generally cannot be averaged across workweeks (e.g., a long workweek followed by a short one) to avoid overtime liability.* However, employers can rearrange hours *within* workweeks (e.g., a long day followed by a shorter day or day off in the same workweek) to avoid incurring overtime liability.

[8]*Samson v. Apollo Resources*, 242 F.3d 629 (5th Cir. 2001), *cert. denied*, 122 S. Ct. 63 (2001).

THE CHANGING WORKPLACE

Work Hours and the Intensification of Work

With employers under constant pressure to improve profitability, employees are being pressed to work harder and longer. According to the International Labor Organization (ILO), U.S. employees have the dubious distinction of working the longest hours among industrialized nations. Employees in the United States averaged 100 more hours of work than Japanese workers in 2000 and fully 500 more hours than German workers.[1] Work hours per employee have not increased markedly (about an extra hour and a half per week since 1980), but work hours for households (largely due to the increased labor force participation of women) have seen substantial increases.

Increased work hours and overtime have many ramifications. Work-life conflicts are exacerbated by escalating work demands. More work hours pose a threat to occupational safety and health, as longer workdays are associated with increases in injuries and stress-related conditions.[2] The percentage of employees reporting that they work very hard and do not have enough time has risen significantly over the past few decades.[3] Job stress is linked to a number of maladies, including high blood pressure and coronary heart disease.

As hours of work rise, conflict over work hours and pay for those hours also becomes more likely. One observer has stated: "As a labor lawyer, I've recently begun to notice that a lot of Americans are working for nothing. By that I mean . . . well, free. Off the books. As in 'This hour doesn't count, so I don't have to pay you.'"[4] Alfred Robinson, Director of the Wage and Hour Division of the DOL concurs that off-the-clock work "is prevalent" and "one of the more common violations of the Fair Labor Standards Act."[5] Workers are often required to work through breaks, perform tasks during unpaid down times, record fewer hours than actually worked, continue working after clocking out, and complete a variety of setup tasks before beginning paid work. Some employers use the even cruder approach of "shaving time." The term refers to the practice of altering work hours by simply deleting them—a ploy that is facilitated by computerized payroll records.[6] Such unlawful acts have contributed to a tide of wage and hour litigation in recent years.

[1] "U.S. Workers Put in Longer Hours But Were Outpaced in Production, Says Study." *Daily Labor Report* 169 (August 31, 2001), A-6.

[2] "Study Links Long Working Hours to Increased Risk of Injury, Illness." *Daily Labor Report* 163 (August 24, 2005), A-7.

[3] Lauren Couillard. "Stress Rising in U.S. Workplaces, Increasing Negative Health Effects." *Daily Labor Report* 212 (November 3, 2004), C-2.

[4] Thomas Geoghegan. "Tampering with the Time Clock." *New York Times* (January 24, 1999), WK-15.

[5] Steven Greenhouse. "Forced to Work Off the Clock, Some Fight Back." *New York Times* (November 19, 2004), A-1.

[6] Steven Greenhouse. "Time Records Often Altered, Job Experts Say." *New York Times* (April 4, 2004), A-1.

Compensatory Time What if an employee who has been working long hours would rather have more time off rather than overtime pay? We have already said that an employer cannot avoid overtime liability by averaging hours across workweeks, but what if the right to overtime is acknowledged, but the overtime is provided in the form of paid time off? The legality of **comp time**—that is, paying for overtime work with compensatory time off rather than overtime pay—depends on whether the employer is in the private or public sector. *Private employers cannot pay for overtime required under the FLSA with compensatory time off in the future, whereas government agencies can do so.* The explanation for this difference is essentially that public employers were not originally covered by the FLSA, and Congress seized upon comp time as a means of softening the fiscal impact when public employers became subject to the law.

The ability of public employers to provide comp time in lieu of cash payment for overtime work is subject to certain restrictions. First, it must be in accordance with an agreement to that effect, either with individual employees or with their collective bargaining representative when the public employees are unionized. For most public employees, the maximum amount of comp time that can be banked is capped at

240 hours. Any additional overtime must be paid for in cash. Public employees have the right to use their accrued comp time "within a reasonable period after making the request," but not if taking the compensatory time off would "unduly disrupt the operations of the public agency."[9] The right to use comp time within a reasonable period apparently does not require that the public employer provide time off on the specific day(s) requested, as long as it is provided within a reasonable amount of time.[10] However, the need to pay overtime to other employees to provide requested time off does not by itself show that operations of a public agency are being unduly disrupted.[11] Public employers are allowed to cash out employees' accrued comp time if they so choose, and employees terminating their employment are entitled to be paid for their unused comp time.

Although comp time agreements are ostensibly "voluntary," public employers are allowed to make acceptance of comp time a condition of employment and of receiving overtime work. Nor is the use of comp time necessarily up to employees. Some public employees, particularly police and firefighters, tend to work a great deal of overtime. This causes them to accrue comp time at levels near or above the maximum (even though the cap for public safety personnel is set much higher at 480 hours). Eager to avoid having to pay for overtime in cash, public employers sometimes insist that their employees "spend down" their comp time within a specific period, regardless of need or desire, or that they use comp time before any other paid time off (e.g., vacation) is used. The Supreme Court has ruled that public employers can require that their employees use up accrued comp time against their will.[12]

DETERMINING COMPLIANCE WITH WAGE AND HOUR STANDARDS

Determining whether the minimum wage and overtime pay requirements of the FLSA have been met requires accurate information on compensation received, compensable work hours, and the exempt or nonexempt status of employees.

Compensation Received

Compensation takes many forms. Employees receive not only hourly wages or salaries, but also tips, commissions, piecework earnings, bonuses, and merit pay; lodging and meals; pay for holidays, vacations, and sick days; premium pay for working on weekends or night shifts; and profit sharing and benefits—among other forms of payment for work. Atlhough wages must generally be paid in cash (i.e., a paycheck), the "reasonable cost" of goods customarily provided by employers for their employees' benefit, such as lodging and meals, can be credited against minimum wage and overtime pay obligations.

Some forms of compensation are subject to special rules under the FLSA. For example, employees who customarily and regularly receive at least $30 per month in tips are considered **tipped employees**. *Employers can meet their minimum wage obligations to tipped employees by paying them at least $2.13/hr, provided that this amount plus tips equals at least the minimum wage. However, to take advantage of the tip credit, employers must inform employees about it beforehand and allow*

[9]29 U.S.C.A. § 207(o)(5)(B) (2005).

[10]*Mortensen v. County of Sacramento*, 368 F.3d 1082 (9th Cir. 2004).

[11]*Beck v. City of Cleveland*, 390 F. 3d 912 (6th Cir. 2004); *cert. denied*, 125 S. Ct. 2930 (2005).

[12]*Christensen v. Harris County*, 529 U.S. 576 (2000).

employees to retain all tips, either individually or pooled among employees. If tips do not bring employees up to the minimum wage, employers must make up the difference. "Pools" should only include those employees who customarily participate in the sharing of tips and not persons unrelated to the services provided. There appears to be considerable leeway in structuring tip pools. A pooling arrangement, in which table servers were required to contribute 3 percent of their gross sales was upheld, despite the servers' claim that low tipping rates and the sale of merchandise for which tips were not obtained (e.g., T-shirts) effectively required them to surrender over a third of their tips.[13] Because pooling of tips is permitted, and none of the servers earned less than the minimum wage, it was legal. However, compulsory service charges (e.g., 18 percent added to the bill) are not considered tips and cannot be used for purposes of the tip credit.

Depending on what types of compensation are considered, some of which may be occasional (e.g., certain bonuses) or not attached to work performed (e.g., paid sick days), an employee's regular rate of pay might vary substantially. When calculating the regular rate of pay on which overtime pay is based, most forms of compensation must be included. The primary *exclusions* are the following:

- Most paid absences (e.g., vacation, holiday, illness)
- Discretionary bonuses (e.g., not based on merit or attendance) and prizes
- Reimbursements for expenses (e.g., travel, materials)
- Employer payments for pensions and other employee benefits
- Profit-sharing plans
- Many forms of premium pay (e.g., extra pay for working on holidays)
- Daily or other non-FLSA required overtime pay

Not surprisingly, the FLSA contains substantial record keeping requirements regarding payments to workers and their hours of work. Because FLSA claims can go back as far as three years (for willful violations), *records of wages paid and hours worked must be kept for at least three years.* Shoddy or nonexistent records do not redound to an employer's benefit in court. Inadequate record keeping is a violation in itself, and in the absence of employer documentation, courts will accept employee's reasonable estimates of what they are owed.[14]

Compensable Time

Besides compensation received, the number of hours worked in a workweek must also be known to apply the FLSA's requirements. This can be more complicated than simply consulting timesheets. Questions about **compensable time** arise because the workday is often punctuated with breaks, periods of waiting or downtime, and other activities different from the principal work duties of an employee. Conversely, work duties sometimes intrude on time off. Further, it is not always obvious when work begins or ends. Table 12-1 provides examples of activities that are generally treated as compensable time and those that are not compensable.

There are a few basic principles for determining whether activities are compensable. A starting point is that employers are required to compensate all work that they "suffer or permit." Employer claims that employees have contributed work without their knowledge and against their will are rightly viewed with skepticism. This does

[13]*Kilgore v. Outback Steakhouse of Florida,* 160 F.3d 294 (6th Cir. 1998).
[14]*Marshall v. Partida,* 613 F.2d 1360, at 1363 (5th Cir. 1980).

TABLE 12-1	Examples of Compensable and Noncompensable Time*
Generally Compensable	**Generally Noncompensable**
Rest periods of 20 minutes or less	Meal periods free of duties (and usually at least 30 minutes)
Meal periods when not substantially relieved from duties	
Meetings during work hours about employee grievances	Preemployment tests
Employer-required training	Voluntary training not related to regular duties, outside work hours, and during which work is not performed
Traveling between work sites	Traveling from home to work site
Changing clothes or washing up if required by the nature of the work	Changing or washing up if not required by the nature of the work
Waiting while on duty	Waiting to start work
	Waiting after being relieved from duty for a definite and useful period
Restrictive on-call arrangements	Most on-call duty performed outside the workplace

*29 C.F.R. §§ 785.14–785.45 (2005).

not mean that employers are expected to be aware of everything that employees do or that employees can simply perform work anywhere or at any time and present their employers with the bill. *If employers do not want to have extra hours worked and incur overtime liability, they must communicate and enforce policies prohibiting employees from working outside of assigned work hours without prior authorization.* For these policies to be genuine, *supervisors cannot ignore workers starting work early, staying late, or coming in on scheduled days off. Nor should employees be assigned work and given deadlines that effectively require them to work late or take work home. Similarly, employees should not be pressured or allowed to underreport hours worked.* The amount of time *actually* spent performing work duties—not norms or expectations (e.g., "it usually takes an hour to clean up after the restaurant closes")—determines compensable time. An employee "taking too long" to carry out some task is a performance issue and not an excuse for violating the FLSA.

Many questions about compensable hours hinge on whether the time in question was or was not spent "predominantly for the benefit of the employee." In cases involving periods of waiting during work hours, courts focus on whether waiting periods were sufficiently long and the surrounding circumstances (e.g., was the employee out in nowhere without a vehicle or next door to a mall?) conducive to employees using the time for their own benefit. Situations in which employees are required to remain on-call often raise the same issue. In one such case, nurses required to be on-call while at home were not entitled to compensation for that time because they remained largely free to

pursue their own interests.[15] Calls were relatively infrequent. The nurses did not have to remain in their homes provided that they could be contacted (e.g., by cell phone) and report to the hospital within 20 minutes. The primary restriction on their activities was that they could not use alcohol.

Employers that need to have employees available for call-in and who want to minimize the chance that time spent on-call will be deemed compensable should do the following for on-call employees:

- Provide a cell phone, pager, or beeper.
- Allow on-call time to be spent outside the workplace.
- Limit the number of calls received.
- Give the employee a reasonable amount of time in which to respond.
- Allow calls to be dealt with over the phone or via computer as much as possible.
- Refrain from disciplining isolated instances of nonresponse.

The overall purpose of these measures is to allow on-call employees as much freedom as possible to use the time for their own benefit. Intrusions on employee time away from the workplace raise questions about compensable time that are likely to become more common as communications technology advances and further blurs the boundaries between work and nonwork time (e.g., requiring employees to read and respond to e-mail on the weekends).

Another principle used by courts is that activities must be sufficiently related to employees' primary job duties to be deemed compensable. Time spent performing activities that are clearly preliminary or postliminary to the employee's main activities is not compensable unless made so by "contract, custom, or practice."[16] Thus, time spent commuting to and from work is usually not compensable. In contrast, the call-center workers who were not paid for time spent logging on to the computer network and bringing up the programs needed to perform their jobs had a strong argument that this time is compensable (see "Clippings"). The activities are integral and indispensable to their work at the call center. What about time spent putting on ("donning") and taking off ("doffing") protective clothing and safety equipment? Time spent walking to and from work areas under these circumstances? In *IBP v. Alvarez/Tum v. Barber Foods* (the two cases were consolidated for review), the Supreme Court addresses these questions.

[15]*Reimer v. Champion Healthcare*, 258 F.3d 720 (8th Cir. 2001).

[16]Portal-to-Portal Act, 29 U.S.C.S. § 254(a) (2005).

IBP V. ALVAREZ/TUM V. BARBER FOODS

126 S. Ct. 514 (2005)

● ● ●

OPINION BY JUSTICE STEVENS:

These consolidated cases raise questions concerning the coverage of the Fair Labor Standards Act of 1938 (FLSA), as amended by the Portal-to-Portal Act of 1947, with respect to activities of employees who must don protective clothing on the employer's premises before they engage in the productive labor for which they are primarily hired. The principal question, which is presented in both cases, is whether the time employees spend walking between the changing area and the production area is compensable under the FLSA. The second question, which is presented only in [*Tum v. Barber Foods*], is whether the time

employees spend waiting to put on the protective gear is compensable under the statute. * * *

[T]he Portal-to-Portal Act * * * narrowed the coverage of the FLSA by excepting two activities that had been treated as compensable under our cases: walking on the employer's premises to and from the actual place of performance of the principal activity of the employee, and activities that are "preliminary or postliminary" to that principal activity. * * * Other than its express exceptions for travel to and from the location of the employee's "principal activity," and for activities that are preliminary or postliminary to that principal activity, the Portal-to-Portal Act does not purport to change this Court's earlier descriptions of the terms "work" and "workweek," or to define the term "workday." A regulation promulgated by the Secretary of Labor shortly after its enactment concluded that the statute had no effect on the computation of hours that are worked "within" the workday. That regulation states: "To the extent that activities engaged in by an employee occur after the employee commences to perform the first principal activity on a particular workday and before he ceases the performance of the last principal activity on a particular workday, the provisions of [the Portal-to-Portal Act] have no application" Similarly, consistent with our prior decisions interpreting the FLSA, the Department of Labor has adopted the continuous workday rule, which means that the "workday" is generally defined as "the period between the commencement and completion on the same workday of an employee's principal activity or activities." These regulations have remained in effect since 1947 and no party disputes the validity of the continuous workday rule.

In [*Steiner v. Mitchell*], we were confronted with the question whether workers in a battery plant had a statutory right to compensation for the "time incident to changing clothes at the beginning of the shift and showering at the end, where they must make extensive use of dangerously caustic and toxic materials, and are compelled by circumstances, including vital considerations of health and hygiene, to change clothes and to shower in facilities which state law requires their employers to provide. . . ." After distinguishing "changing clothes and showering under normal conditions" and stressing the important health and safety risks associated with the production of batteries, the Court endorsed the Court of Appeals' conclusion that these activities were compensable under the FLSA. In reaching this result, we specifically agreed with the Court of Appeals that "the term 'principal activity or activities' in . . . the Portal-to-Portal Act embraces all activities which are an 'integral and indispensable part of the principal activities,' and that the activities in question fall within this category." Thus, under *Steiner*, activities, such as the donning and doffing of specialized protective gear, that are "performed either before or after the regular work shift, on or off the production line, are compensable under the portal-to-portal provisions of the Fair Labor Standards Act if those activities are an integral and indispensable part of the principal activities for which covered workmen are employed. . . ." * * *

IBP, Inc. (IBP), is a large producer of fresh beef, pork, and related products. * * * All production workers . . . must wear outer garments, hardhats, hairnets, earplugs, gloves, sleeves, aprons, leggings, and boots. Many of them, particularly those who use knives, must also wear a variety of protective equipment for their hands, arms, torsos, and legs; this gear includes chain link metal aprons, vests, Plexiglas armguards, and special gloves. IBP requires its employees to store their equipment and tools in company locker rooms, where most of them don their protective gear. * * *

IBP argues that, even though the court below concluded that donning and doffing of unique protective gear are "integral and indispensable" to the employees' principal activity, this means only that the donning and doffing of such gear are themselves covered by the FLSA. According to IBP, the donning is *not* a "principal activity" that starts the workday, and the walking that occurs immediately after donning and immediately before doffing is not compensable. * * * IBP's submission is foreclosed by *Steiner*. * * * Accepting the necessary import of our holding in *Steiner*, we conclude that the locker rooms where the special safety gear is donned and doffed are the relevant "place of performance" of the principal activity that the employee was employed to perform. . . . Walking to that place before starting work is excluded from FLSA coverage, but the statutory text does not exclude walking from that place to another area within the plant immediately after the workday has commenced.

IBP emphasizes that our decision in *Anderson* v. *Mt. Clemens Pottery Co.* may well have been the proximate cause of the enactment of the Portal-to-Portal Act. In that case we held that the FLSA mandated compensation for the time that employees spent walking from time clocks located near the plant entrance to their respective places of work prior to the start of their productive labor. In IBP's view, Congress' forceful repudiation of that holding reflects a purpose to exclude

what IBP regards as the quite similar walking time spent by respondents before and after their work slaughtering cattle and processing meat. * * * This argument is also unpersuasive. There is a critical difference between the walking at issue in *Anderson* and the walking at issue in this case. In *Anderson* the walking preceded the employees' principal activity; it occurred before the workday began. The relevant walking in this case occurs after the workday begins and before it ends. * * * Moreover, there is a significant difference between the open-ended and potentially expansive liability that might result from a rule that treated travel before the workday begins as compensable, and the rule at issue in this case. Indeed, for processing division knife users, the largest segment of the work force at IBP's plant, the walking time in dispute here consumes less time than the donning and doffing activities that precede or follow it. It is more comparable to time spent walking between two different positions on an assembly line than to the prework walking in *Anderson*. * * *

For the foregoing reasons, we hold that any activity that is "integral and indispensable" to a "principal activity" is itself a "principal activity" under the Portal-to-Portal Act. Moreover, during a continuous workday, any walking time that occurs after the beginning of the employee's first principal activity and before the end of the employee's last principal activity is excluded from the scope of that provision, and as a result is covered by the FLSA.

Barber Foods, Inc. (Barber), operates a poultry processing plant in Portland, Maine. . . . These employees . . . perform a variety of tasks that require different combinations of protective clothing. * * * Petitioners are Barber employees and former employees who * * * claimed that Barber's failure to compensate them for (a) donning and doffing required protective gear and (b) the attendant walking and waiting violated the statute. * * *

The time spent waiting to don—time that elapses *before* the principal activity of donning integral and indispensable gear—presents the quite different question whether it should have the effect of advancing the time when the workday begins. * * * [P]etitioners . . . maintain that the predonning waiting time is "integral and indispensable" to the "principal activity" of donning, and is therefore itself a principal activity. However, unlike the donning of certain types of protective gear, which is *always* essential if the worker is to do his job, the waiting may or may not be necessary in particular situations or for every employee. It is certainly not "integral and indispensable" in the same sense that the

donning is. It does, however, always comfortably qualify as a "preliminary" activity.

We thus do not agree with petitioners that the predonning waiting time at issue in this case is a "principal activity". . . . As Barber points out, the fact that certain preshift activities are necessary for employees to engage in their principal activities does not mean that those preshift activities are "integral and indispensable" to a "principal activity" under *Steiner*. For example, walking from a time clock near the factory gate to a workstation is certainly necessary for employees to begin their work, but it is indisputable that the Portal-to-Portal Act evinces Congress' intent to repudiate *Anderson*'s holding that such walking time was compensable under the FLSA. We discern no limiting principle that would allow us to conclude that the waiting time in dispute here is a "principal activity" . . . without also leading to the logical (but untenable) conclusion that the walking time at issue in *Anderson* would be a "principal activity" . . . and would thus be unaffected by the Portal-to-Portal Act.

The Government also relies on a regulation promulgated by the Secretary of Labor as supporting petitioners' view. That regulation states that when an employee "is required by his employer to report at a particular hour at his workbench or other place where he performs his principal activity, if the employee is there at that hour ready and willing to work but for some reason beyond his control there is no work for him to perform until some time has elapsed, waiting for work would be an integral part of the employee's principal activities." That regulation would be applicable if Barber required its workers to report to the changing area at a specific time only to find that no protective gear was available until after some time had elapsed, but there is no such evidence in the record in this case. More pertinent, we believe, is the portion of [this regulation] that characterizes the time that employees must spend waiting to check in or waiting to receive their paychecks as generally a "preliminary" activity covered by the Portal-to-Portal Act.

In short, we are not persuaded that such waiting—which in this case is two steps removed from the productive activity on the assembly line—is "integral and indispensable" to a "principal activity" that identifies the time when the continuous workday begins. Accordingly, we hold that . . . the time employees spend waiting to don the first piece of gear that marks the beginning of the continuous workday [is excluded from the scope of the FLSA].

Exemptions from FLSA Requirements

Thus far, the FLSA's requirements have been stated as though they apply to all employees. They do not. Employers are exempted (excused) from having to follow some or all of the FLSA's rules for certain types of employees. Some of these exemptions are full exemptions (i.e., the rule can be completely disregarded for exempt employees) and other exemptions are partial (i.e., something other than the general rule applies to exempt employees). The terms **exempt** and **nonexempt** employees are used to contrast employees for whom employers do not have to follow FLSA requirements (exempt) with employees entitled to the act's protections (nonexempt).

Figure 12-1 lists examples of FLSA exemptions. This listing is not exhaustive. Some exemptions not listed apply to very narrowly defined groups. For example, an employer is exempted from paying overtime for "any employees engaged in the processing of maple sap into sugar (other than refined sugar) or syrup."[17] "Homeworker[s] engaged in the making of wreaths composed principally of natural holly, pine, cedar, or other evergreens"[18] are excluded from any of the FLSA's protections. This hodgepodge of exemptions is testimony to both the difficulty of applying "one size fits all" standards to a wide range of businesses and the nature of the legislative process.

White-Collar Exemptions The most significant exemptions are for executive, administrative, and professional employees. These occupations are found in all types of businesses and comprise an estimated 20 to 27 percent of the full-time U.S. workforce.[19] Employees holding these jobs often work long hours and earn relatively high rates of pay. That the so-called **white-collar exemptions** (which also include "outside" salespersons) free employers from the obligation to pay overtime to these employees is no small matter. But who is an exempt executive, administrative, or professional employee?

In August 2004, the DOL implemented revisions to its long-standing regulations on the white-collar exemptions (see "Clippings"). Many of the changes were subtle, but given the complex, fact-intensive nature of cases determining exempt status, there might still be an appreciable affect on case outcomes. It is too early to know.

Given the stakes, it is not surprising that employers tend to take a broad view of which employees fit under the umbrella of the white-collar exemptions, whereas employees are apt to claim that they are nonexempt and entitled to overtime pay. In the

[17]29 U.S.C. § 213(b)(15) (2005).

[18]29 U.S.C. § 13(d) (2005).

[19]United States General Accounting Office. *Fair Labor Standards Act: White-Collar Exemptions in the Modern Work Place.* GAO/HEHS-99-164 (September 1999), p. 8.

FIGURE 12–1 | **Examples of FLSA Exemptions***

Full Minimum Wage Exemptions	Outside salespersons
	Employees of amusement or recreational establishments having seasonal peaks
	Employees engaged in the fishing industry
	Agricultural employees who work on certain types of farms
Partial Minimum Wage Exemptions	Certain workers with disabilities (subminimum wage allowed with DOL certification)
	Students employed at colleges and universities (payment at 85 percent of the minimum wage is allowed with DOL certification)
Full Overtime Exemptions	Executive, administrative, or professional employees
	Outside salespersons
	Most transportation employees (e.g., motor carriers, railroads, and airlines)
	Taxicab drivers
	Agricultural employees
	Employees of motion picture theatres
Partial Overtime Exemptions	Commission-paid employees of retail and service establishments (commissions take the place of overtime pay if the regular rate of pay is greater than one and a half times the minimum wage and commissions make up at least half of the employee's total compensation)
	Hospital and nursing home employees (14-day period, rather than the workweek, can be used to calculate overtime if the employee is paid overtime for biweekly hours in excess of 80 and for daily hours in excess of 8)

*29 U.S.C. §§ 207(i), (j), 213–214 (2005).

face of legal challenges, employers bear the burden of proving that employees denied the act's protections are in fact exempt. A common misconception is that whether an employee is exempt turns solely on whether that employee is paid a salary. This is not true—or at best it is incomplete. To determine whether an individual is or is not an exempt **executive, administrative,** or **professional employee,** the nature of that individual's duties and responsibilities must be closely examined (duties test), as well as the manner in which the person is paid (salary-basis test). Not everyone paid a salary is an exempt employee. Criteria for determining whether employees fit within the white-collar exemptions are listed in Figure 12-2.

Duties Test As Figure 12-2 shows, exempt status rests in part on applying a **duties test** to determine whether employees' duties are genuinely executive, administrative,

FIGURE 12–2	Tests for Executive, Administrative, and Professional Employee Status*
Executive Employees	• Have as their primary duty the management of an enterprise, department, or other customarily recognized subunit of a company. • Customarily and regularly direct the work of two or more full-time employees or their equivalent. • Have the authority to hire or fire other employees or have particular weight given to suggestions and recommendations concerning hiring, firing, advancement, promotion, or any other change in the status of other employees. • Paid a salary of at least \$455/wk. • "Highly compensated" employees paid at least \$100,000 annually (which must include at least \$455/wk paid on a salary basis) are exempt if they have an identifiable executive function, even if they do not meet all the duties test criteria. • Employees who have at least a 20 percent ownership interest in the enterprises that employ them and who are actively engaged in management of those enterprises are exempt without regard to the above criteria.
Administrative Employees	• Primary duty is performing office or nonmanual work directly related to the management or general business operations of an employer or the employer's customers. • Primary duty includes the exercise of discretion and independent judgment with respect to matters of significance. • Paid a salary of at least \$455/wk. • "Highly compensated" employees paid at least \$100,000 annually (which must include at least \$455/wk paid on a salary basis) are exempt if they have an identifiable administrative function, even if they do not meet all of the duties test criteria.
Professional Employees	• Primary duty is work that requires advanced knowledge, is predominantly intellectual in character, and entails the consistent exercise of discretion and judgment. The advanced knowledge must be in a field of science or learning and be customarily acquired by a prolonged course of specialized intellectual instruction ("learned professionals") *or* have as their primary duty work that requires invention, imagination, originality, or talent in a recognized field of artistic or creative endeavor ("creative professionals"). • Paid a salary of at least \$455/wk (or for skilled computer employees only, an hourly rate of at least \$27.63).

(continued)

| FIGURE 12–2 | (Continued) |

- Teachers are exempt without regard to other criteria if their primary duty is teaching, tutoring, instructing, or lecturing in the activity of imparting knowledge and if they are employed in this activity by an educational establishment.

- Computer employees are exempt if they are employed as systems analysts, programmers, software engineers, or other similarly skilled occupations. Their primary duties must include the likes of applying systems analysis techniques, consulting with users, and designing or developing computer systems and programs.

- Employees holding valid licenses or certificates to practice law or medicine and who are actively engaged in such practice are exempt without regard to other criteria.

- "Highly compensated" employees paid at least $100,000 annually (which must include at least $455/wk paid on a salary basis) are exempt if they have an identifiable professional function, even if they do not meet all the duties test criteria.

*29 C.F.R. §§ 541.119, 541.214, 541.303, 541.314, 541.315 (2005).

or professional in nature. Job titles, by themselves, mean nothing. Calling a secretary an "Administrative Assistant I" does not transform that person into an exempt employee. The burden on employers to establish exempt status provides yet another reason to maintain accurate and up-to-date job descriptions. *An employee's job description should clearly support the determination that he or she is an exempt employee.* The same occupation can be either exempt or nonexempt depending on the particular circumstances. For example, reporters, producers, and directors for a TV news program were determined to be nonexempt employees.[20] The court's rationale was lengthy, but it basically came down to the fact that they did not manage other employees (hence, they were not executives), their work was directly related to producing the station's product (hence, they were not administrators), and the news program they worked on was more formulaic than creative or original (hence, they were not creative professionals). Yet, in another case involving TV news writers and producers at a different station, the court found that their duties were sufficiently original and creative to warrant exemption as professionals.[21]

The duties test is complicated by the fact that the same persons sometimes perform a mix of both exempt and nonexempt duties. The suits against Starbucks illustrate this point (see "Clippings"). These employees carry managerial titles and perform managerial duties, but the majority of their time is spent serving customers.

[20]*Dalheim v. KDFW-TV,* 918 F.2d 1220 (5th Cir. 1990).

[21]*Freeman v. National Broadcasting Co.,* 80 F.3d 78 (2d Cir. 1996).

Federal cases involving the restaurant industry have tended to look beyond the relative amounts of time spent performing executive and nonexecutive functions. Instead, they focus on the fact that these employees are in charge of the restaurants and these managerial duties are of principal value to their employers. Thus, despite the mixed nature of their duties, restaurant managers have often been considered exempt executives.[22] The revised regulations for FLSA exemptions appear to deemphasize the proportion of time spent performing exempt and nonexempt work as a factor in deciding whether an employee's primary duty is management, treating it as only one factor to consider among others.[23]

Correctly identifying "administrative" employees poses particular problems. Merely performing office work or brushing shoulders with managers is not enough to confer exempt status. The fundamental criterion is whether the individual primarily performs office or nonmanual duties that relate to the general operations and policies of the company, as opposed to producing the goods or services that it sells. In a case involving a woman who was the "office manager" and "bookkeeper" for a consulting firm, the court decided that her job included enough exempt activities to make her a bona fide administrative employee.[24] The woman spent much of her time keeping the books, an activity that DOL regulations indicate is not sufficient to demonstrate exempt administrative work. However, she was also involved in policy decisions and supervised accounts receivable and payable, purchase orders, and payroll records.

Another important criterion for identifying administrative employees is the "exercise of discretion and independent judgment with respect to matters of significance."[25] This is often a telling factor in distinguishing bona fide administrative employees from glorified secretaries and clerical workers. Determining whether sufficient discretion and judgment are being exercised is also difficult. To exercise discretion and independent judgment, an employee must have the authority to consider possible courses of action and make independent choices, free from immediate supervision or direction, regarding significant matters. The employee must do more than merely use skill "in applying well-established techniques, procedures, or specific standards described in manuals or other sources."[26] In the case of the office manager mentioned earlier, the court found evidence of independent judgment in the fact that the woman participated in senior staff meetings and made recommendations in the areas of insurance policies, hiring, firing, and banking. Likewise, "team leaders" that lead a group of other employees in completing "major projects" (e.g., negotiating a labor agreement, selling a part of the business) will generally meet the duties requirements for the administrative exemption even where such employees do not have direct supervisory authority over other employees on the team.[27] In contrast, an interviewer who merely screens candidates for hiring according to preestablished criteria is not exercising discretion and independent judgment.

In *Martin v. Indiana Michigan Power Company*, the court considers an employer's attempt to invoke the computer professional and administrative employee exemptions to defend an employee's FLSA claim for unpaid overtime work. The court's decision rests squarely on its application of the duties test criteria.

[22]*Donovan v. Burger King Corp.*, 675 F.2d 516 (2d Cir. 1982); *Murray v. Stuckey's Inc.*, 50 F.3d 564 (8th Cir. 1995), *cert. denied*, 516 U.S. 863 (1995).

[23]29 C.F.R. § 541.700 (2005).

[24]*Gagnon v. Resource Technology, Inc.*, 2001 U.S. App. LEXIS 18290.

[25]29 C.F.R. § 541.202(a) (2005).

[26]29 C.F.R. § 541.202 (e) (2005).

[27]29 C.F.R. § 541.203 (c) (2005).

MARTIN V. INDIANA MICHIGAN POWER COMPANY

381 F.3d 574 (6th Cir. 2004)

● ● ●

OPINION BY CIRCUIT JUDGE COLE:

Plaintiff-Appellant Anthony Martin claims that his employer, Indiana Michigan Power Company, d/b/a American Electric Power ("AEP"), violated the Fair Labor Standards Act ("FLSA") by failing to pay him time-and-a-half for hours worked in a given week in excess of forty hours. * * * [T]he district court granted summary judgment for AEP, holding that Martin was exempt from overtime pay requirements because he was both an administrative employee and a computer professional. For the reasons below, we REVERSE the judgment of the district court and REMAND for entry of summary judgment in favor of the plaintiff. . . .

Prior to AEP's reorganization of its Information Technology ("IT") department, Martin held the position of "Computer Security/Standards Technician," which AEP classified as nonexempt. On November 1, 1998, when the department was reorganized, Martin's title was changed to "IT Support Specialist," which AEP classified as an exempt position. * * *

Mike Thornburg, Martin's supervisor, describes the function of his IT Support team as follows: "Maintaining the computer workstation software, troubleshooting and repairing, network documentation. . . ." The computers that Martin works on are workstations (or "PCs") at individual desks connected to a local area network ("LAN"); Martin does not work on the plant process computer—"which deals with the plant, what's going on as far as the reactor operators"—which is a different system. When people at the plant have problems with their computers, they call the help desk where the help desk employees put the problems into a database as "help desk tickets," which Martin prints out. Martin responds to these help desk tickets. He goes to the location indicated where he attempts to determine the nature of the problem, to "troubleshoot" it to determine how to proceed, and to repair the problem if possible. Martin installs software . . . on individual workstations. He troubleshoots . . . problems and installs provided software patches.

If Martin cannot fix a problem, he will report the problem and how he tried to fix it to Thornburg. Thornburg will decide whether to request service from the manufacturer or order a replacement part or unit. Martin, however, does not decide or make recommendations as to whether a piece of equipment must be serviced or replaced. Nor has he written reports on his troubleshooting or repair activities. He has not recommended the purchase of any equipment, hardware, or software, although Thornburg considers Martin's comments on printers and problems "valuable" in his own decision making process. * * *

Shortly before Thornburg's February 28, 2001, deposition, Martin received another assignment. According to Thornburg, he assigned Martin "to review a Windows 2000 operating system that we have just developed." At the time of the deposition, Thornburg explained that Martin was in the "process" of "preparing" to do the review. For the assignment, Martin was supposed to "review the desktop operating system in our applications to make sure they work as he uses them in the field. And if not, I expect him to make recommendations for corrections." This assignment—apparently made after the litigation commenced—is the first of this type for Martin. As Thornburg put it, Martin's duties were "evolving."

Martin has no computer certifications and no degree beyond high school. He has taken one course in microcomputing, a class in using Windows 2000, and four week-long hands-on computer training classes. Martin has a work bench located in a common work area—also referred to as a "workshop" in the depositions. Martin does not have his own phone line; everyone in the area shares a "shop phone." * * *

The FLSA requires employers to pay their employees time-and-a-half for work performed in excess of forty hours per week, but exempts employers from this requirement with respect to individuals "employed in a bona fide executive, administrative, or professional capacity." To avoid paying overtime to Martin, AEP must prove that he falls within one of these exempt categories. AEP argues that Martin is exempt as both an "administrative" employee and a "computer professional," which is a subclass of "professional" employees. * * *

To establish that Martin is a "computer professional" under the regulations and therefore not entitled to overtime, AEP must demonstrate that (1) the employee "is compensated on a salary or fee basis at a rate of not less than $250 per week" [the new regulations

were not yet in effect at the time that this case arose] or that the employee "is compensated on an hourly basis at a rate in excess of 6 1/2 times the minimum wage"; (2) the employee's "primary duty consists of the performance of . . . work that requires theoretical and practical application of highly-specialized knowledge in computer systems analysis, programming, and software engineering, and [the employee is] employed and engaged in these activities as a computer systems analyst, computer programmer, software engineer, or other similarly skilled worker in the computer software field . . ."; and (3) the employee's primary duty "includes work requiring the consistent exercise of discretion and judgment." * * *

The evidence establishes that Martin is paid a salary. [However], AEP must raise a genuine issue of fact regarding whether Martin's "primary duty consists of the performance of . . . work that requires theoretical and practical application of highly-specialized knowledge in computer systems analysis, programming, and software engineering, and [whether he is] employed and engaged in these activities as a computer systems analyst, computer programmer, software engineer, or other similarly skilled worker in the computer software field." Thus, although Martin is not a systems analyst, programmer, or software engineer, he could still be exempt from overtime if his work "requires theoretical and practical application of highly-specialized knowledge in computer systems analysis, programming, and software engineering." * * * The district court made an understandable mistake, one that arises from the common perception that all jobs involving computers are necessarily highly complex and require exceptional expertise. However, the regulations provide that an employee's primary duty must require "theoretical and practical application of highly-specialized knowledge in computer systems analysis, programming, and software engineering" not merely "highly-specialized knowledge of computers and software." This is an important difference. The former is a narrower class of jobs that requires a different level of knowledge and training than the latter. Further, it is a distinction which will only become more relevant as the range of computer-related jobs continues to broaden.

Martin does not do computer programming or software engineering; nor does he perform systems analysis, which involves making actual, analytical decisions about how Cook's computer network should function. Rather, Martin's tasks—installing and upgrading hardware and software on workstations, configuring

desktops, checking cables, replacing parts, and troubleshooting Windows problems—are all performed to predetermined specifications in the system design created by others. As Martin testified, he is provided the standard "desktop" for installation on the computers he configures, but he is not involved in determining what the desktop should look like. * * *

AEP selectively identifies certain words from [the DOL's] regulation—particularly "consulting with users" and "testing"—and applies them out of context. There is simply no evidence that Martin "consults with users, to determine hardware, software, or system functional specifications." Martin "consults with users" for purposes of repair and user support, not to determine what "hardware, software, or system functional specifications" the Cook facility will employ, as a systems analyst might. Likewise, when Martin does "testing," he is testing things to figure out what is wrong with a workstation, printer, or piece of cable so that he can restore it to working order. He is not doing the type of testing that is involved in creating a system, determining the desired settings for a system, or otherwise substantively affecting the system. Indeed, he is merely ensuring that the particular machine is working properly according to the specifications designed and tested by other Cook employees. * * * Martin has one project that might fall under the category of systems analysis: the Windows 2000 review. This project was apparently assigned after the instant lawsuit commenced, * * * This single project does not make systems analysis Martin's primary duty. * * *

AEP has not met its burden under the computer professional exemption.

To establish that Martin is a bona fide administrative employee under the applicable Department of Labor ("DOL") regulations, AEP must demonstrate that: . . . the employee's "primary duty consists of . . . the performance of office or nonmanual work directly related to management policies or general business operations of his employer or his employer's customers"; and the employee's primary duty "includes work requiring the exercise of discretion and independent judgment." * * *

AEP's only argument that Martin's work is "directly related to management policies or general business operations of the employer" is that Martin's work is not production work. That is, he is not producing electricity because he is not an "operator" running the nuclear power equipment—and therefore his work is administrative and thus "directly related to management

policies or general business operations of the employer." Under AEP's theory, shippers of radioactive waste, the individuals who don radiation suits and perform maintenance work on the reactors, the janitorial staff, the security guards, the cooks in the company cafeteria, and various other workers including Martin are all doing work "relating to the administrative operations of the business" purely because they do not operate the nuclear reactors. We have rejected the argument that all work that is not production work is automatically "directly related to management policies or general business operations of the employer." * * * The regulations do not set up an absolute dichotomy under which all work must either be classified as production or administrative. Rather, the regulations distinguish production work from the administrative operations of the business—thus production work cannot be administrative—and then go on to define the administrative operations of the business * * *

Martin's primary job duty does not "relate to the administrative operations" at Cook. * * * Martin is in no way involved in "advising the management, planning, negotiating, representing the company, purchasing, promoting sales, and business research and control." Martin's job, instead, is to assist in keeping the computers and network running to the specifications and designs of others. Nor is Martin's work "of substantial importance to the management or operation of the business of his employer." * * *

AEP never presents an argument that Martin's work itself is "of substantial importance to the management or operation of the business of his employer." Indeed, AEP could not successfully argue that Martin's work itself is "of substantial importance to the management or operation of the business of his employer" because Martin makes no decisions that affect even the small segment of the company's operations in which his work is performed. He does not determine what types of workstations, network, hardware, or software AEP employs; he is not involved in the design or development of AEP's network; he does not decide what software will be available to AEP's computer users or determine how that software will be configured; and he does not decide or recommend when equipment must be serviced or replaced. Rather, he sets up and repairs parts of a system wholly designed and approved by others. There is no evidence that he has any input into the nature of the computer resources available to AEP employees. * * *

AEP next argues that Martin's work is of "substantial importance" because of the value of the systems he works on and the consequences of mistakes. The regulations, however, explain that it is the work itself that must be of substantial importance—not the size of the consequences or loss that may result from improper performance of the employee's duties. As the regulations note, an employee operating a very expensive piece of equipment, a messenger boy entrusted with carrying large sums of money, and an inspector for an insurance company can all cause their employers serious loss by failure to perform their jobs properly, but "such employees, obviously, are not performing work of such substantial importance to the management or operation of the business that it can be said to be 'directly related to management policies or general business operations'. . . ." * * *

In sum, the evidence viewed in the light most favorable to AEP neither establishes that nor raises a genuine issue of material fact regarding whether Martin's work is "directly related to management policies or general business operations of his employer or his employer's customers." Thus, not only is AEP not entitled to summary judgment, but Martin is entitled to summary judgment.

CASE QUESTIONS

1. What is the legal issue in this case? What did the court decide?

2. Because Martin spends all his time working with computers, why is he not exempt as a computer professional?

3. Why is Martin not an exempt administrative employee?

4. Why does the court say that defining the boundaries of the computer professional exemption will become increasingly important?

Salary Basis Test To be exempt, executive, administrative, and professional employees must also be paid salaries. Employees must now be paid at least $455/wk to qualify for any of the white-collar exemptions. Pay of over $100,000/yr creates a presumption of exempt status. But the most interesting legal questions surround not the amount of pay, but whether the method of payment is truly a salary.

A salary can be contrasted with an hourly wage in which pay is closely calibrated to time put in, or with a piece-rate system in which pay is directly geared to the volume of output. A **salary** is a prespecified sum that an employee is paid for discharging the responsibilities associated with a position. The amount of time needed to do so and the quality or quantity of work output will likely vary from week to week and are not the bases for payment. Employers certainly benefit when salaried, exempt employees put in long hours for no extra pay. But what about when salaried employees work fewer hours than expected? Certain employer policies can pose questions about whether employees are truly paid on a salary basis and, hence, whether those employees are exempt from the FLSA's overtime pay requirements.

Suppose, for example, that an exempt employee takes the afternoon off to attend to personal business and her employer deducts these hours from her pay. Or suppose that the computer system crashes, the employer sends everyone besides the IT people home, and then reduces the pay of exempt employees. If employees have their pay reduced for time not worked on such occasions, are they really being paid on a **salary basis**? Employers cannot have it both ways—enjoying the benefit of employees' lengthy hours without overtime obligations, but penalizing employees for working fewer hours than expected. And if employees are not paid on a salary basis, they are not exempt from the FLSA's requirements, regardless of how obviously executive, administrative, or professional their duties. This approach to determining whether employees are paid on a salary basis is known as the DOL's **pay docking rule**.

Under the pay docking rule, exempt employees must receive predetermined amounts of pay not subject to reduction due to variations in the quantity or quality of work performed. Employers cannot reduce pay for partial day absences for personal reasons; time missed due to jury duty, court appearances as a witness, and temporary military leave; and for absences occasioned by the employer or the operating requirements of the business when the employee is otherwise ready and able to work. However, exempt status is not jeopardized by deductions for absences of a day or more for personal reasons; for absences due to sickness or accidents (provided that the employer has a policy for compensating employees when days are lost to sickness or accidents); for unpaid disciplinary suspensions of one or more full days "imposed in good faith for infractions of workplace conduct rules"; for hours not worked in the first and last week of employment; and for periods of unpaid leave under the FMLA.[28]

To be absolutely clear, the pay docking rule does not make it illegal for an employer to do any of these things. Rather, the consequence of making prohibited deductions from the pay of exempt employees is that those employees may no longer be considered exempt because they are not paid a genuine salary. If the employer is found to have an actual practice of making improper deductions, exempt status will be lost for all employees who have the same job classification as the employee bringing a complaint for unpaid overtime and who work for the same manager(s) responsible for the deductions. However, an employer can still avoid this outcome by having a clearly communicated policy prohibiting improper deductions and providing a complaint mechanism; reimbursing employees for any improper deductions; and making a "good faith commitment" to comply in the future.[29]

The force of the pay docking rule and the legal consequences for making improper deductions have been greatly diminished by the revised regulations.

[28]29 C.F.R. § 541.602 (2005).
[29]29 C.F.R. § 541.603 (2005).

Nevertheless, payment on a salary basis is still a requirement for exempt status. Thus, *employers should be careful to not dock the pay of exempt executive, administrative, or professional employees for lack of available work to perform, partial-day absences for personal reasons, and time spent on jury duty. Employers should establish and communicate clear policies prohibiting improper deductions from the pay of exempt employees and providing a mechanism for handling complaints about any such deductions. Employees who are nonetheless subjected to improper deductions should be promptly reimbursed.*

OTHER WAGE LAWS

The federal minimum wage is a minimal wage. An individual working full-time, year-round at the minimum wage earns less than $11,000 per year. In recent years, the minimum wage has provided less protection to workers than the labor market, as most employers have needed to pay more than the minimum wage to attract workers. In 2005, the minimum wage stood at only 32 percent of the average wage for private sector, nonsupervisory workers.[30] States have their own wage and hour laws, and the FLSA permits them to establish minimum wages higher than the federal minimum wage. Eleven states (e.g., California, Alaska, Vermont, Massachusetts), mostly in the far west and northeast, have state minimum wages higher than $5.15/hr. Several states (e.g., Ohio, New Mexico, Kansas) provide for minimum wages lower than the federal minimum, but these apply only to firms not covered by the FLSA (generally, companies with revenues less than $500,000 per year).[31] State wage laws are also important as a basis for suits to recover unpaid wages and in establishing requirements for when wages, including final paychecks, must be paid.

Employers incur additional legal obligations to their employees (e.g., affirmative action) when they contract to provide goods or services to the government. Several federal laws require payment of a **prevailing wage** for government contract work. These laws include the **Davis-Bacon Act** (construction contracts) and the **McNamara-O'Hara Service Contract Act** (contracts for many different types of services). In general terms, the prevailing wage is the average wage paid to a class of employees in the relevant geographic area. This amount is determined by the DOL.

The inadequacy of the minimum wage has sparked **living-wage** campaigns.[32] These campaigns have been successful in obtaining city laws mandating levels of hourly pay more consistent with a dignified existence. Most of these laws specify minimum rates of at least $7.50/hr, and some go considerably higher. The living wage in high-cost Santa Cruz is $12/hr ($11/hr if benefits are provided). More than 100 communities have passed living wage laws, including Baltimore, Chicago, Los Angeles, New York, Milwaukee, Minneapolis, and Cincinnati.[33] However, the reach of these laws is limited. They typically apply only to companies doing business with and/or receiving some form of financial assistance from municipalities (e.g., tax abatements, grants)—and sometimes also to municipal employees. Further, some of the laws require payment of a living wage only for particular types of contracts

[30]Jared Bernstein and Isaac Shapiro. "Unhappy Anniversary." Economic Policy Institute, September 1, 2005 (http://www.epinet.org).

[31]Department of Labor. "Minimum Wage Laws in the States." (http://www.dol.gov/esa/minwage/america.htm).

[32]David Reynolds. "The Living Wage Movement Sweeps the Nation." *Working USA* (September–October 1999), 61–80.

[33]William Carlile. "Santa Fe 'Living Wage' Ordinance Upheld by State District Court Judge." *Daily Labor Report* 123 (June 28, 2004), A-7.

(e.g., janitorial services). The ruling against Cintas for violating Hayward, California's living wage law illustrates the growing importance of these laws (see "Clippings"). Significantly, the judge ruled that the higher wages were required for all the hours of those employees performing work for the city because Cintas was unable to show how many hours were spent specifically on city work. Berkeley, California's living wage ordinance has been upheld against a constitutional challenge.[34] Santa Fe's living wage law, which unlike most such statutes applies to all private businesses in the city with at least 25 employees, has also been upheld.[35]

Thus, employers must be aware that, depending on geographic location and dealings with government entities, they might be required to pay a state minimum wage, prevailing wage, or municipal living wage that exceeds the federal minimum wage.

What About Farmworkers?

The people who put food on our tables, many of them migrant laborers who follow the crops that need harvesting, have historically endured some of the lowest wages and most substandard living and working conditions of all employees. Despite their often wretched working conditions and the fact that many farmworkers are employed by large agribusinesses, the image of bucolic family farms has dominated policy making and left agricultural workers with minimal legal protection. The FLSA does little for farmworkers. Agricultural employees, even if they work for covered firms, are completely exempted from the act's overtime provisions, largely exempted from the minimum wage, and in some cases, even excluded from the FLSA's child labor provisions.

The **Migrant and Seasonal Agricultural Worker Protection Act (MSPA)**[36] covers most seasonal agricultural employees. Its provisions are basic, but nonetheless important to farmworkers. The MSPA requires registration of farm labor contractors with the DOL; full written disclosure of the terms and conditions of employment in the employee's language at the time of recruitment; payment of all wages owed to employees; maintenance and retention of wage and hour records; refraining from the practice of forcing employees to purchase services from their employers (the company store); assurance that any housing provided is safe and sanitary; and provision for the safe transportation of employees. Notably, the MSPA does not establish a minimum pay level, much less an entitlement to overtime pay.

Nor is agriculture the only industry where nonpayment of wages and subhuman workings conditions are problems. The garment industry, both internationally and domestically, has long been known for its **sweatshops**. The term *sweatshop* is not a legal term, but generally refers to firms that pay very low wages for long hours of work, provide unsafe conditions, and staunchly oppose unionization. Consumers, including college students purchasing pricey hats and sweatshirts with university logos, are increasingly questioning the terms and conditions under which those items are produced. Although the FLSA ostensibly applies to many garment workers in the United States, fly-by-night operations and intimidation of immigrant workers undermine the enforcement of basic standards. The point is that for many workers at or near the bottom of the labor market, even the minimum standards of the FLSA and other wage laws remain elusive.

[34]*RUI One Corp. v. City of Berkeley,* 371 F.3d 1137 (9th Cir. 2004); *cert. denied,* 2005 U.S. LEXIS 290.

[35]"Santa Fe 'Living Wage' Ordinance." A-7.

[36]29 U.S.C.A. § 1801 *et seq.* (2005).

LIMITATIONS ON WORK HOURS

The FLSA provides employers with an economic incentive to minimize overtime work (i.e., the premium that must be paid for each overtime hour worked by a nonexempt employee), but does not directly limit the number of hours that most employees can be required to work. Nor does the act require that employers provide rest periods, breaks, or time for meals. There are compelling safety, productivity, and labor relations reasons for doing so anyhow, but with the exception of regulations pertaining to particular groups, such as airline pilots and truck drivers, federal law is silent on this matter. Some states mandate breaks or meal periods, however, and a few have taken first steps toward limiting mandatory overtime.

Although the FLSA does not generally limit hours worked, it does prohibit **oppressive child labor**. This requirement affects hours of work for minors. The federal minimum age for employment is 16. However, to perform certain hazardous occupations (e.g., mining, logging, roofing, using power-driven meat slicers), employees must be at least 18 years of age. *Minors (14–15 years of age) can be employed in certain service or retail occupations, subject to restrictions on their hours of work. When school is in session, minors must be employed outside of school hours, between 7 A.M. and 7 P.M. not more than 3 hours per day, and not more than 18 hours per week. When school is not in session, minors can work up to 8 hours in a day and 40 hours in a week. In the summer, the workday of minors can be extended to 9 P.M.*

To comply with the FLSA's child labor requirements, *employers must ascertain the ages of their youthful employees.* Doing so, even in a preemployment context, does not violate the ADEA because the protected class is employees 40 years of age and older. "Working papers" are not mandated by the FLSA, although some states require them. *Managers putting together work schedules should take into account the lesser flexibility they have in assigning minors* (e.g., minors cannot be asked to "hang around for another hour because it's busy" if doing so would violate the FLSA). Undoubtedly, in many cases the FLSA's hours limitations for minors are winked at by employers and employees alike, but there is evidence that excessive work hours can harm teens (e.g., lower grades, greater alcohol use).[37] No matter how complicit minors are in violating the law, employers are legally responsible for compliance.

DISCRIMINATION IN PAY—EQUAL PAY ACT

Pay disparities based on any protected class characteristics are discriminatory, but pay discrimination based on sex is a particular concern. A substantial gap still exists between the earnings of full-time male workers and full-time female workers. The size of the earnings gap has narrowed over time and varies depending on whether hourly, weekly, or annual pay is considered (the largest gap is for annual pay, whereas the smallest is for hourly). In terms of median weekly pay, full-time female workers earned 79.5 percent of what their male counterparts earned in 2003 (see "Clippings"). Many factors undoubtedly account for the persistent male-female earnings gap. To what extent is discrimination in pay one of these?

Identifying discrimination in pay is particularly challenging. Pay determinations are often highly individualized. Pay is influenced by a multitude of factors, including the going rate in the labor market, an organization's pay policies and pay structure, the conditions under which the job is performed (e.g., shift, location), the demands of the job, and a host of individual characteristics (e.g., seniority, education, merit).

[37]Steven Greenhouse. "Problems Seen for Teenagers Who Hold Jobs." *New York Times* (January 29, 2001), A-1.

ELEMENTS OF A CLAIM

Pay Discrimination

To establish a **prima facie case**, the plaintiff must show the following:

There is someone of the opposite sex working within the same establishment who receives a higher rate of pay for performing work substantially equal to that performed by the plaintiff.

If a prima facie case of pay discrimination is established, the employer must show that the challenged differential in pay is explained by one or more of the following:

- A seniority system
- A merit pay system
- A system that bases pay on the quality or quantity of production
- Some other factor other than sex

More than most other employment decisions, pay determinations are subject to negotiation and are affected by prior decisions (e.g., starting pay, adjustments in pay structures intended to deal with particular problems and carried forward in time). Sorting through these complexities requires an approach somewhat different from that used in other discrimination cases. A methodology for proving pay discrimination has been developed for **Equal Pay Act**[38] cases. The Equal Pay Act is specifically targeted at pay discrimination based on sex. *Employers are prohibited from paying a person of one sex at a lower rate of pay than a person of another sex for performing substantially equal work within the same establishment—unless the differential in pay is accounted for by a legitimate "factor other than sex."*

Proving Pay Discrimination Under the Equal Pay Act

Proving pay discrimination involves, first of all, identifying one or more **comparators**, which are persons of the opposite sex who are in the same workplace and receive a higher rate of pay for performing the same type of work as the plaintiff. Importantly, comparators are usually limited to persons employed within the same establishment. Pay comparisons across companies—or even among personnel in different divisions, offices, or plants of the same company—usually will not suffice. A director of rehabilitation who worked for a company in its Corpus Christi network was unable to base an Equal Pay Act claim on the higher pay of his counterpart holding the same job in the company's San Antonio network. However, the plaintiff was able to bring a case based on his lower rate of pay relative to the female that immediately succeeded him as Director of Rehabilitation.[39]

Equal Work

Equal Pay Act cases often hinge on whether the plaintiff can show that she and the comparator perform substantially equal work. The two jobs do not have to be identical or carry the same job title; however, duties and tasks actually performed on the two jobs must overlap substantially. Given a core of common tasks, the analysis

[38]29 U.S.C.A. § 206(d) (2005).

[39]*Perales v. American Retirement Corp.,* 2005 U.S. Dist. LEXIS 22630.

then focuses on the tasks that differentiate the jobs. At this point, the Equal Pay Act incorporates the logic of job evaluation. **Job evaluation** is a systematic process for rating jobs in terms of certain **compensable factors**. The requirements of jobs, rather than the performance of individuals, is at issue in job evaluation. Jobs that are rated higher are more demanding and valuable to employers and tend to be paid more.

The Equal Pay Act cites four compensable factors to be used in determining whether jobs are substantially equal: skill, effort, responsibility, and working conditions. **Skill** refers to the level of ability, education, training, and experience needed to perform the jobs. **Effort** is the amount of physical and mental exertion required on the jobs. **Responsibility** refers to things such as accountability for outcomes, supervisory duties, and involvement in important decisions. **Working conditions** has a much more restricted interpretation under the Equal Pay Act than it does in other areas of employment law. It refers to "hazards" (how dangerous the job is in terms of physical hazards) and "surroundings" (e.g., elements such as fumes, working outside in cold weather). For jobs to be substantially equal, there must be significant commonality in duties; the jobs must require substantially equal levels of skill, effort, and responsibility; and they must be at least similar in terms of working conditions.

What if there is one or more potential comparators earning a higher rate of pay and others who are not? Courts have generally recognized prima facie cases of pay discrimination where some comparators of the opposite sex, but not all, earned a higher rate of pay than the plaintiff. In one such case, the court explained that:

> Taken literally . . . the "some males made the same or less" rule would force a court to hold that a female employee could not make out a *prima facie* case of wage discrimination where she was one of ten females paid half as much as nine males for "equal work," so long as a tenth male was paid the same or less than the female workers. In such circumstances . . . it seems as least highly likely that the employer is "discriminating between employees on the basis of sex," but the employer would nevertheless be insulated from suit. . . .[40]

Wheatley v. Wicomico County is an Equal Pay Act case that hinges on the question of whether the plaintiffs performed work substantially equal to that of their proposed comparators.

[40]*Hennick v. Schwans Sales Enterprises*, 168 F. Supp 2d 938, at 950 (N.D. Iowa 2001).

WHEATLEY V. WICOMICO COUNTY
390 F.3d 328 (4th Cir. 2004)

● ● ●

OPINION BY CIRCUIT JUDGE WILKINSON:

Sandy Wheatley and Jane Grogan supervise the Wicomico County, Maryland, Emergency Services Department, which includes the 911 call center. In June 2001, they sued the County, alleging violations of the Equal Pay Act and Title VII. Ms. Grogan and Ms. Wheatley claim that male depart-

ment supervisors are paid significantly more than female department supervisors, despite the fact that all perform substantially equal managerial work. * * * We are unpersuaded that "equal work" under the Equal Pay Act can be established when two employees have similar titles but responsibilities that bear no more than the most general resemblance. * * *

Wicomico County employs over 500 people, organized in approximately eleven different departments. The

departments vary in size and function. The Emergency Services Department is comprised of approximately 22 people; it operates the 911 call center 24 hours a day, 365 days a year. Since 1986, Sandy Wheatley has served as director of the Emergency Services Department. Jane Grogan has been the deputy director since 1997. * * *

Beginning in 1999, Wicomico County commissioned a study to evaluate its compensation schedule for all 500 of its employees. The purpose of the study was to ensure that County employees were being paid equally for equal work, and also to guarantee that they were being paid comparably to persons in the same positions in other jurisdictions.

This "Hendricks Study" led Wicomico County to reconfigure its pay schedule. The new plan created 22 separate grades and assigned a numerical grade to all County jobs. Grade assignments were based on seven criteria: education, job complexity, scope and impact, supervision, working relationships, working environments, and physical demands. Mr. Hendricks chose these seven criteria because he found them comparable to the four criteria set forth in the Equal Pay Act. Once the jobs were assigned a grade, individual salaries were set using a mathematical formula, based in part on pre-study salaries. Within each grade, the Hendricks study recommended a minimum, maximum, and mid-point salary. Ms. Wheatley's job was originally classified as Grade 16, though it was re-classified as Grade 17 after she filed a complaint with the County Administrative Director. Although she received an 18% pay increase as a result of the Hendricks study, her salary was set below the mid-point of her grade. Ms. Grogan's job was classified as a Grade 13—her pay increased by a similar proportion, but she too received a salary below the mid-point of her grade. Ms. Wheatley now earns $65,808 annually, and Ms. Grogan earns $49,164.

* * * Ms. Wheatley and Ms. Grogan offered statistical evidence to demonstrate a pay disparity between male department leaders and female department leaders. Both plaintiffs suggested that they are paid, on average, $25,000 a year less than the male directors and deputy directors in other departments. Additionally, plaintiffs submitted statistics indicating that while they were assigned salaries below the midpoint for their Hendricks grades, all male directors and deputy directors were given salaries above their grade midpoints. Ms. Wheatley and Ms. Grogan also attempted to demonstrate that department managers all perform the same general duties. Ms. Wheatley testified that, like herself,

directors of other departments supervise subordinates, conduct staff meetings, prepare budgets, answer to the same County Council, and otherwise manage their departments. She told the jury that, aside from a difference in subject-matter, all department heads bore the same responsibilities. * * *

Ms. Wheatley and Ms. Grogan allege Wicomico County violated the Equal Pay Act ("EPA") which provides:

> No employer . . . shall discriminate . . . between employees on the basis of sex by paying wages to employees . . . at a rate less than the rate at which he pays wages to employees of the opposite sex . . . for equal work on jobs the performance of which requires equal skill, effort, and responsibility, and which are performed under similar working conditions, except where such payment is made pursuant to (i) a seniority system; (ii) a merit system; (iii) a system which measures earnings by quantity or quality of production; or (iv) a differential based on any other factor other than sex.

To make out a prima facie case under the EPA, the burden falls on the plaintiff to show that the skill, effort and responsibility required in her job performance are equal to those of a higher-paid male employee. In interpreting the EPA, "'equal means substantially equal.'" * * *

Ms. Wheatley and Ms. Grogan's strategy was to compare their jobs to jobs held by male department heads. To support their theory, the women relied on evidence that all managers—regardless of department subject matter—ultimately perform the same supervisory duties. They all, for instance, prepare budgets, monitor employees, and conduct meetings. We decline to accept the argument, however, that employees with the same titles and only the most general similar responsibilities must be considered "equal" under the EPA. In actuality, plaintiffs present a classic example of how one can have the same title and the same general duties as another employee, and still not meet two textual touchstones of the EPA—equal skills and equal responsibility.

First, it is simply not the case that all department director positions require equal skills. Both the Director and Deputy Director of Public Works in Wicomico County, for instance, are required to hold graduate degrees in civil engineering. By contrast, Ms. Wheatley and Ms. Grogan perform their jobs well without possessing

any advanced degrees at all. While it is certainly true that plaintiffs provide valuable services to the County, it would be disingenuous to argue that their jobs require skills substantially equal to the jobs which require engineers to direct the Department of Public Works. Indeed, to accept plaintiffs' position would mean that although market demand for different skills may vary greatly, the salaries that employers pay for such skills must be the same.

The case law reveals a helpful analogy. In Soble v. University of Maryland, 778 F.2d 164 (4th Cir. 1985), a female Assistant Professor sought to compare herself, for purposes of the EPA, to other assistant professors in a dental school. Professor Soble, who taught in the field of community dentistry, held degrees in sociology and social work. The vast majority of her colleagues, however, held degrees in dentistry. We found that merely possessing the same title of "assistant professor" was not enough to satisfy the EPA requirement of "equal skills." Because the professorships in other departments were "highly specialized and required distinct skills" we foreclosed Professor Soble from making an EPA comparison to them. Similarly, pointing to the mere appellation of "department head" does not suffice to carry plaintiffs' burden under the skills prong of the EPA.

In addition to their failure to show equal skills, Ms. Wheatley and Ms. Grogan also fall short of satisfying a second major EPA requirement. They fail to establish that their jobs and the jobs of other department heads carry substantially equal responsibilities. We have explained that jobs do not automatically involve equal effort or responsibility even if they "entail most of the same routine duties." Jobs are considered unequal—despite having the same general core responsibilities—"if the more highly paid job involves additional tasks which (1) require extra effort . . . (2) consume a significant amount of the time . . . and (3) are of an economic value commensurate with the pay differential." . . . [I]t is significant that different Wicomico County departments perform completely different functions. The Director of Recreation, Parks & Tourism is, among other things, responsible for park maintenance; the Director of Public Works is responsible for coordinating the dredging of waterways; and the Director of Emergency Services is responsible for coordinating resources in the event of a disaster. Granted, at a high level of abstraction these positions all require directors to do the same thing—supervise, coordinate, and organize. But, the

EPA demands more than a comparison of job functions from a bird's eye view.

In enacting the EPA, Congress chose the word "equal" over the word "comparable" in order "to show that the jobs involved should be virtually identical, that is . . . very much alike or closely related to each other." Here, we have employees whose jobs demand the performance of quite different functions. Ms. Wheatley and Ms. Grogan do not deny that the various County departments differ in subject-matter. In fact, although Ms. Wheatley testified that all directors bear the same type of job responsibilities, she admitted that on a day-to-day basis, they work in "different worlds." It may well be true that all Wicomico County department directors prepare budgets and work schedules. It is certainly not true, however, that all departments have budgets and workforces of equal size. If there is a director or deputy director whose job involves the same responsibilities as does Ms. Wheatley's or Ms. Grogan's, and if any extra tasks performed by this director are indeed inconsequential, plaintiffs certainly failed to identify him.

We do not suggest that Ms. Wheatley and Ms. Grogan's action faltered because it failed to identify one specific individual who constitutes a perfect male comparator. The text of the EPA may not be brushed with such a demanding gloss. However, in choosing a proper comparator position, plaintiffs cannot indiscriminately aim at all department supervisors collectively, and then expect to meet the EPA standard of "substantial equality [in] skill, effort [and] responsibility." The inquiry must be more specific. The comparison to the male employee has to be made "factor by factor" and cannot be made to "a hypothetical male with a composite average of a group's skill, effort, and responsibility." * * * In essence, plaintiffs ask us to convert the EPA equality standard into a similarity test. We decline to hold that having a similar title plus similar generalized responsibilities is equivalent to having equal skills and equal responsibilities. Were we to adopt that position, we would deprive compensation structures of all flexibility and deny employers the chance to create pay differentiations that reflect differing tasks and talents. In passing the EPA, Congress embraced "the principle of equal pay for equal work regardless of sex." Congress did not authorize the courts "to engage in wholesale reevaluation of any employer's pay structure in order to enforce their own conceptions of economic worth." There is no question that Ms. Wheatley and Ms. Grogan

are valuable assets to Wicomico County. But it is not the job of the courts to discard Congress' studied use of the term "equality" and set the price for their services.

For the above reasons, we agree with the district court that plaintiffs' . . . EPA argument lacks merit.

CASE QUESTIONS

1. What was the legal issue in this case? What did the court decide?

2. How was the plaintiffs' case lacking?

3. Does this decision effectively mean that comparators must be selected from within the same department?

4. What role, if any, do you think that the compensation study and instituting of a new pay structure had in prompting this litigation?

Factors Other Than Sex

As in other discrimination cases, establishing a prima facie case creates an inference that pay discrimination has occurred, but does not resolve the matter. The employer in Equal Pay Act cases has the opportunity to justify the differential pay as being due to a seniority system, a merit-pay system, a system that bases pay on the quality or quantity of production (e.g., piece-rate system), or any other **factor other than sex**. Factors other than sex that might justify pay differentials for equal work include differences in educational attainment, experience levels, or training; shift premiums; and differential rates for full- and part-time workers—to cite just a few. Although there are many possible factors other than sex, some justifications raise more questions than others. For example, to the extent that women receive lower pay in the labor market, using prior salary level as a basis for offers tends to perpetuate this problem. Does this violate the Equal Pay Act? Some courts maintain that *any* factor other than sex will suffice to defend a pay discrimination claim, and thus, basing pay on prior salary level is lawful despite its potential discriminatory effect.[41] Other courts have held that the employer must be able to show a business reason for considering prior salary (e.g., particular skills, the desire to woo the employee away from another job).[42] Women may also be disadvantaged by reliance on negotiation demands to determine pay offers, because there is some evidence that women are reluctant to initiate salary negotiations and to drive a hard bargain.[43] Additionally, the claim that a particular employee was paid more because he demanded a higher rate of pay in negotiations with the employer could easily serve as a pretext for discriminatory pay decisions. Because employers do not have to accede to pay demands simply because they are made, *employers justifying differential pay on the basis of individual salary negotiations should be able to point to abilities or experience that justify acceptance of a demand for higher pay.* Differences in the revenues or profits accounted for by positions have also been advanced as a factor other than sex (or as a basis for finding unequal work).[44] *Employers making this claim should ensure that the more lucrative positions are open to both male and female employees and that the differential profitability is not itself a product of discrimination.*

[41]*Wernsing v. Department of Human Services, State of Illinois*, 2005 U.S. App. LEXIS 22725.

[42]*Price v. Lockheed Space Operations*, 856 F.2d 1503 (11th Cir. 1988).

[43]Linda Babcock and Sara Laschever. *Women Don't Ask.* (Princeton, NJ: Princeton University Press) 2003.

[44]*Hodgson v. Robert Hall Clothes*, 473 F.2d 589 (3d Cir. 1973), *cert. denied*, 414 U.S. 866 (1973).

In short, *employers should be prepared to account for pay decisions, particularly when males and females performing similar jobs in the same workplace are paid differently.* Defending pay decisions is much easier if employers *establish and consistently apply specific, job-related criteria for making those decisions.* Employers should *avoid basing pay decisions on the pay level in a prior position or on demands made in negotiations unless these actually reflect the abilities of the individuals in question.* Lastly, *if pay discrimination exists, it must be remedied by raising the pay of the lower-paid individual(s).*

Comparable Worth

A major factor in the male-female earnings gap is that men and women often hold different jobs and that those in female-dominated occupations (e.g., schoolteachers, librarians, social workers, nurses, secretaries) tend to be paid less. If the largely female office and clerical workers at a company are paid less than the company's mostly male stock clerks, is that pay discrimination? What if the office and clerical workers' jobs were shown to be at least as demanding as the stock clerk jobs? There would be no case under the Equal Pay Act because there is not a common core of overlapping tasks to make the jobs substantially equal. However, discrimination in pay based on any protected class, including sex, is also prohibited by Title VII. Violations of the Equal Pay Act are also violations of Title VII. The converse is not necessarily true. The Supreme Court has decided that pay discrimination cases under Title VII are not strictly limited to cases that could be brought and won under the Equal Pay Act.[45] The question is whether Title VII permits employees to challenge pay disparities by comparing their jobs to jobs performed predominantly by members of the opposite sex, where evidence (through job evaluations) shows that the jobs are equally valuable to the employer—even though the jobs are not "equal work."

This is the theory of pay discrimination termed **comparable worth.** Under this theory, pay discrimination occurs if an employer fails to pay women working in female-dominated jobs the same rate of pay as men working in male-dominated jobs, when the jobs are shown through job evaluation to be of comparable worth to the employer. In other words, comparisons could be made between jobs that look different and that involve different combinations of skill, effort, responsibility, and working conditions, but which overall are equally demanding (i.e., would receive the same total scores on a job evaluation). Courts have been unwilling to accept this theory of pay discrimination. In the leading case,[46] Washington State had shown through its own job evaluation studies that employees in female-dominated occupations were substantially underpaid relative to male-dominated jobs of comparable worth. The court noted that employers must take account of many factors, including collective bargaining outcomes and market forces—and not just job evaluation scores—in setting pay rates for jobs. Because there was no evidence that the state had based its pay rates on sex and because the court concluded that consideration of market rates was not the type of specific employment practice that could be analyzed for purposes of showing adverse impact, the plaintiffs comparable worth claim failed. Nonetheless, several states (e.g., Minnesota, Iowa) have implemented comparable worth initiatives for their own public employees.

[45]*County of Washington v. Gunther,* 452 U.S. 161 (1981).

[46]*AFSCME v. Washington,* 770 F.2d 1401 (9th Cir. 1985).

Pay Secrecy Policies

Shhh! Pay secrecy policies discourage employees from sharing information about their pay and sometimes go as far as to require the termination of employees who violate the policies. Whatever the advantages of these policies, they clearly pose obstacles to employees seeking to determine whether they are receiving the same rate of pay as others doing the same work. They also interfere with employees' rights under the National Labor Relations Act (NLRA) to join together and communicate about workplace concerns.

In one case, a dietary aide at a nursing home was told several times by supervisors that employees were not to discuss their paychecks with anyone. Several coworkers came to her with problems that they were having with shortages in their paychecks. She agreed to convey their concerns to the supervisor. Shortly thereafter, she was fired. The National Labor Relations Board (NLRB) decided, and an appeals court affirmed, that the aide's rights had been violated. The court held that "A rule prohibiting employees from communicating with one another regarding wages, a key objective of organizational activity, undoubtedly tends to interfere with the employees' right to engage in protected concerted activity."[47] The home was ordered to reinstate her with back pay. We will discuss the NLRA further in Chapter 14. The point for now is that pay secrecy policies are likely to violate employees' rights, regardless of whether the policy is written or only spoken, whether or not the policy is strictly enforced, and whether the workplace is unionized or not unionized. Thus, *employers should refrain from establishing and enforcing pay secrecy policies.*

[47]*NLRB v. Main Street Terrace Care Center*, 218 F.3d 531 (6th Cir. 2000).

Chapter SUMMARY

The principal federal law regulating wages and hours is the FLSA. The FLSA requires that most employees be paid at least the minimum wage for each hour of work in a workweek. Employers are also required to pay most employees at least one and one-half times their regular rates of pay for hours worked in excess of 40 in a workweek. The FLSA also prohibits oppressive child labor, limiting hours of work for minors under 16 and restricting certain dangerous jobs to persons 18 and over. Under the Davis-Bacon Act and the McNamara-O'Hara Service Contract Act, federal government contractors are sometimes required to pay the "prevailing wage" in a locality to employees performing contract work. States have their own wage and hour laws, and a number of states have established minimum wages in excess of the federal minimum wage. Numerous cities have enacted laws requiring that companies doing business with and/or receiving financial support from the city pay their employees a "living wage" well in excess of the minimum wage.

Enforcement of the wage and hour standards of the FLSA or other statutes requires knowledge of compensation received, hours worked, and whether the particular employees are covered by or exempt from the standards. Disputes frequently arise over the number of hours worked (compensable time) because it is not always clear exactly when work begins and ends, not all work hours are spent performing principal duties, and work duties sometimes intrude upon nonwork time. In general, any work that an employer "suffers or permits" is compensable time. Employers are not required to pay for activities that are clearly preliminary or postliminary to employees' principal duties, but drawing the line between these and setup or cleanup activities integral to the principal duties of a job is difficult. Cases involving breaks in work activity or work demands imposed during nonwork time typically turn on whether the time is spent principally for the employer's or the employee's benefit.

The FLSA contains many exemptions that permit employers to not comply with the act's requirements

when compensating certain types of employees. Groups of employees not covered by particular provisions of the FLSA are labeled "exempt," whereas employees covered by those provisions are termed "nonexempt." The "white-collar exemptions" to the FLSA excuse employers from the obligation of paying overtime to executive, administrative, and professional employees. Whether employees fit these categories depends upon the nature of their duties and responsibilities (the duties test), their salary level, and whether they are genuinely paid on a salary basis (the salary basis test). A salary is not calibrated to the number of hours worked or the quantity or quality of production. Instead, salaried employees are expected to accomplish their tasks and to put in the amount of time and effort needed to do so, in return for a predetermined sum. The DOL's pay docking rule is used to determine whether employees are being paid on a salary basis.

The Equal Pay Act promotes fair pay by prohibiting pay discrimination based on sex. Employers are prohibited from paying an employee of one sex at a lower rate of pay than an employee of the opposite sex when those employees perform substantially equal work within the same establishment. To establish a prima facie case of pay discrimination under the Equal Pay Act, an employee must identify one or more comparators of the opposite sex who work in the same establishment and earn a higher rate of pay for performing substantially equal work. To be substantially equal, jobs must have a significant number of overlapping duties; require substantially equal skill, effort, and responsibility; and be carried out under similar working conditions. If a prima facie case is established, an employer can defend the pay discrimination claim by showing that the pay differential was due to a seniority system, a merit-pay system, a system of compensation based on the quantity or quality of production, or any factor other than sex. Pay discrimination is also prohibited by Title VII. Although cases brought under Title VII are not subject to the strict limitations of the Equal Pay Act, comparable worth claims based on differences in pay between male- and female-dominated jobs of equal value have not been recognized by the courts.

Practical Advice SUMMARY

- *Employers must pay nonexempt employees an hourly rate at least equal to the minimum wage for each hour worked in a workweek.*

- *Deductions must not be made from the pay of employees for items that primarily benefit employers (e.g., uniforms), when the effect of those deductions is an hourly wage rate lower than the minimum wage.*

- *Employers can pay "tipped employees" $2.13/hr, provided that*

 –employees are so informed.

 –they (individually or collectively) retain all their tips.

 –their pay plus tips equals at least the minimum wage.

- *Employers will be required to pay employees at a rate higher than the minimum wage if*

 –they perform contract work for the federal or state governments that requires payment of the prevailing wage for that class of employees in the locality.

 –they perform contract work for, or receive financial assistance from, cities that require payment of a specified living wage.

- *Employers must pay nonexempt employees at least one and one-half times their regular rates of pay for hours worked in excess of 40 in a workweek.*

- *In meeting their overtime pay obligations, employers generally cannot*

 –average work hours over periods of time longer than workweeks for purposes of determining overtime eligibility.

 –provide compensatory time off (comp time) in lieu of overtime pay.

- *However, public employers can use comp time if*

 –it has been agreed to by employees or their representatives.

 –comp time accrual is capped (a maximum of 240 hours for most employees).

 –employees are permitted to use their comp time within a reasonable period after asking to do so,

unless fulfilling the request would disrupt agency operations.

—employees are paid for any unused comp time when they leave employment.

- *Wage and hour records must be maintained and kept for at least three years.*

- *To limit unwanted hours of work and overtime liability, employers should*

 —communicate and enforce policies prohibiting employees from working outside of assigned work hours without prior authorization.

 —not ignore employees starting work early, staying late, or coming in on scheduled days off.

 —not assign work or set deadlines that require work outside of work hours.

 —not pressure or allow employees to underreport work hours.

- *To limit overtime liability, on-call employees should be*

 —provided with cell phones, beepers, or pagers.

 —allowed to spend on-call time outside of the workplace.

 —not called in repeatedly.

 —given a reasonable amount of time to respond to calls.

 —allowed to handle calls from home as much as possible.

 —not disciplined for isolated failures to respond.

- *Job descriptions should be accurate, up-to-date, and clearly support determinations of exempt status.*

- *To maintain the exempt status of executive, administrative, and professional employees, employers should not make deductions from pay for*

 —partial day absences for personal reasons.

 —absences due to jury duty, appearances in court as a witness, and temporary military leave.

 —for lack of available work to perform when the employee is ready and able to work.

- *Employers should establish and communicate clear policies prohibiting improper deductions*

from the pay of exempt employees and providing a mechanism for handling complaints about any such deductions. Employees who are nonetheless subjected to improper deductions should be promptly reimbursed.

- *Employers must verify that young employees are old enough to employ. Employers must not use employees under 18 years of age for certain dangerous jobs. Persons 16 and over can be employed at all other jobs. Those who are 14- and 15-years-old can be used for a range of retail and service jobs.*

- *While school is in session, employers must not permit minors (under 16) to work*

 —during school hours.

 —more than 3 hours a day.

 —more than 18 hours a week.

 —outside the hours of 7:00 A.M. to 7:00 P.M.

- *When school is not in session, employers must not permit minors to work more than 8 hours per day and 40 hours per week.*

- *Employers must not pay persons of one sex at lower rates of pay than persons of the opposite sex for performing substantially equal work within the same establishment, unless the different pay is due to*

 —seniority system.

 —merit-pay system.

 —system for compensating according to the quantity or quality of production.

 —any additional factor other than sex.

- *Employers should*

 —be prepared to explain pay disparities between men and women performing similar jobs in the same workplaces.

 —establish and consistently apply clear criteria for making pay decisions.

- *Employers must correct any pay discrimination by raising the pay of the lower paid individual(s).*

- *Employers should refrain from establishing and enforcing pay secrecy policies.*

Key TERMS

Fair Labor Standards Act (FLSA)
minimum wage
opportunity wage
overtime pay
regular rate of pay
workweek
compensatory ("comp") time
tipped employees
compensable time
exempt employees
nonexempt employees
white-collar exemptions
executive employee
administrative employee

professional employee
duties test
salary
salary basis test
pay docking rule
prevailing wage
Davis-Bacon Act
McNamara-O'Hara Service
 Contract Act
living wage
Migrant and Seasonal
 Agricultural
 Worker Protection Act (MSPA)
sweatshop

oppressive child labor
Equal Pay Act
prima facie case of pay
 discrimination
comparators
job evaluation
compensable factor
skill
effort
responsibility
working conditions
factor other than sex
comparable worth
pay secrecy policy

Chapter QUESTIONS

1. Upon returning to work after a period of absence due to the effects of stress, a police department dispatcher was ordered by her employer to see a psychotherapist for counseling. She was told that this was required to keep her job and that her status would be reevaluated after six months. The employee went to the counseling sessions for six months during nonwork hours. The employee claims that she should have been paid for the time spent scheduling, attending, and traveling to the therapy sessions. If that time is counted, she worked more than 40 hours each week. She sues for unpaid overtime. What should the court decide? Why? (*Sehie v. City of Aurora,* 2003 U.S. Dist. LEXIS 13051)

2. In addition to their normal hours of work, electronic technicians at a power plant were required to remain on-call from 4:30 P.M. to 7:30 A.M. on Monday through Friday and for 24 hours on the weekend. While on-call, the technicians typically responded to 3–5 alarms per evening. Each alarm took, on average, about 45 minutes of work. Technicians were expected to respond to alarms within 15 minutes. Failure to respond was grounds for discipline. The technicians were given pagers, but these did not work properly, forcing the technicians to remain at or near home. The technicians were paid for the time they spent actually responding to problems, but not for the remainder of the on-call time. The technicians sued for unpaid overtime. What should the court decide? Why? (*Pabst v. Oklahoma Gas & Electric,* 228 F.3d 1128 (10th Cir. 2000))

3. The manager of a car wash was paid a salary of $345 for each 48-hour week or $360 for each 54-hour week. The manager took care of customer complaints and performed basic administrative responsibilities with respect to the car wash attendants, including scheduling, training, and discipline. Regarding hiring and firing decisions, and setting the pay rates for new hirees, the manager could make "recommendations," but needed the general manager's authorization before setting an employee's rate of pay, or hiring or firing an employee. The manager spent an estimated 95 percent of his work time performing tasks identical to those of the car wash attendants, including sweeping, window cleaning, gardening, emptying the garbage, cleaning the car wash tunnels, and cleaning booths. The total weekly work hours of all the other employees under his supervision exceeded 80 hours per week only 67 percent of the time during the relevant time period. The manager sued for unpaid overtime. What should the court decide? Why? (*Jackson v. Go-Tane Services,* 2003 U.S. App. LEXIS 949)

4. An employee worked as a "field service engineer" for a company that sells robotic test and inspection equipment. He was paid a salary. He was the company's main contact with one of its largest clients, Max Media. His primary duty was to install, troubleshoot, and maintain the company's equipment used by Max Media. He also acted as a conduit for information between his employer and Max Media. Over the past year, he worked with crews to install 10 machines, accounting for about 40 percent of his work time. He spent the remainder of his work time maintaining machines, responding to customer calls, learning about new systems, and completing paperwork. He was expected to keep his supervisor apprised of all his activities. Replacement parts for machines were stored at the home office and could only be obtained by going through his supervisor. The employee sues for unpaid overtime. The employer says that he is an exempt administrative employee. What should the court decide? Why? (*Bothell v. Phase Metrics*, 299 F.3d 1120 (9th Cir. 2002))

5. A group of "planners" work at a nuclear power facility. Their job is to take job orders for maintenance or construction to be done and to prepare "work packages" giving direction to the plant's craft workers. The packages specify which plant procedures apply to particular repairs and whether any permits must be obtained to perform the work. Although the planners spend most of their time in the office, they also make "field walk downs" to assess repair projects. The power plant's procedures and guidelines are numerous and often dictate how a particular repair job must be done. However, when there is no prescribed method of making a repair, the planners determine the best way to go about it. The planners also make choices about whether to replace or repair equipment. The planners are paid a salary, but are required to make up for partial day absences by working extra time on other days or using some of their paid time off. The planners sue for unpaid overtime work. The utility says that the planners are exempt administrative employees. What should the court decide? Why? (*Renfro v. Indiana Michigan Power Company*, 370 F.3d 512 (6th Cir. 2004))

6. An engineering company employed engineers, architects, accountants, and administrators. It paid them biweekly salaries and required that they work at least 8 hours a day. Employees who worked fewer than 8 hours had to use their personal time for the hours missed or have pro rata amounts deducted from their pay. Over a period of a year and a half, 24 employees had pay deducted for not working full days. The employer decided to cancel its policy of making deductions for less than 8-hour days and refunded the deductions that had been made. Some of the employees sued for unpaid overtime and the company claimed that they were exempt employees. What should the court decide? Why? (*Martin v. Malcolm Pirnie*, 949 F.2d 611 (2d Cir. 1991), *cert. denied*, 506 U.S. 905 (1992))

7. Pharmacists at Wal-Mart were paid a salary based on an expected number of hours of work. During slow times of the year, pharmacists' hours and salaries were reduced in response to lower sales. The pharmacists claim that this practice makes them not exempt. They sue for unpaid overtime work. What should the court decide? Why? (*In Re: Wal-Mart Stores, Fair Labor Standards Act Litigation*, 395 F.3d 1177 (10th Cir. 2005))

8. If there is a snow storm and a company remains open for business, can the employer deduct from the pay of salaried employees who do not come to work without jeopardizing their exempt status? If the employer closes its offices due to the storm, can salaried employees be required to use paid time off (e.g., vacation) to cover the day? (Michael R. Triplett. "DOL Gives Advice on Salary Deductions for Weather-Related Absences, Closures." *Daily Labor Report* 218 (November 14, 2005), A-8)

9. The coach of a women's college basketball team demands to receive the same salary as the (male) coach of the men's basketball team. Are these jobs "equal work?" If they are, what "factors other than sex" might justify paying one coach more than the other? (*Stanley v. University of Southern California*, 178 F.3d 1069 (9th Cir. 1999); Equal Employment Opportunity Commission. "Enforcement Guidance on Sex Discrimination in the Compensation of Sports Coaches in Educational Institutions." No. 915.002 (October 29, 1997))

10. Look at Table 12-1 shown earlier. Can you explain *why* each of these activities is generally compensable or noncompensable?

11. Should private-sector employers be allowed to use comp time to meet their overtime pay obligations? What are the potential benefits? Problems? (David J. Walsh. "The FLSA Comp Time Controversy: Fostering Flexibility or Diminishing Worker Rights?" *Berkeley Journal of Employment and Labor Law* 20, 1 (1999))

12. Does the Equal Pay Act go far enough in prohibiting pay discrimination? If not, should courts rethink their rejection of the theory of comparable worth?

Internet RESOURCES

Materials on the DOL's Web site provide guidance on compliance with the many wage and hour laws administered by the DOL.

http://www.dol.gov

The Web site of the Economic Policy Institute contains useful research and other information pertaining to wages, living standards, and labor market conditions.

http://www.epinet.org

Living Wage Resource Center Web site is sponsored by ACORN (Association of Community Organizations for Reform Now).

http://www.livingwagecampaign.org

Materials related to pay equity are available through the Web site of the AFL-CIO (American Federation of Labor—Congress of Industrial Organizations).

http://www.aflcio.org

Benefits

CLIPPINGS

▶ I.B.M. has announced that it will freeze its defined benefit pension plan—the third largest corporate pension plan in the U.S.—as of 2008. When a pension plan is frozen, employees retain accrued benefits, but no additional benefits are earned. I.B.M. had previously decided that new employees would receive 401(k)s, rather than participate in the defined benefit pension plan. In the mid-1990s, I.B.M. converted from a traditional defined benefit pension plan to a cash balance plan. However, the cash balance plan was challenged as discriminatory against older workers, and a district court ruled against I.B.M. in 2003. I.B.M. is still appealing that decision.[1]

▶ The Pension Benefit Guarantee Corporation (PBGC) is struggling to keep up with a growing tide of failed pension plans. The agency insures defined benefit pension plans. It currently pays benefits to more than a million retirees and is responsible for the pension benefits of 43 million employees. An analysis of the PBGC's financial situation found that, without an injection of new funds, the agency will likely run out of money by 2020.[2]

▶ A suit brought under the Employee Retirement Income Security Act (ERISA) against WorldCom has been settled. The plaintiffs were participants in the company's 401(k) plan who charged that the company's directors, officers, and other parties breached their fiduciary duties by failing to accurately disclose WorldCom's financial situation. The employees lost several hundred million dollars when WorldCom stock in which they had invested became worthless and the company filed for bankruptcy.[3]

▶ The Montana State Supreme Court has ruled that public agencies in the state must provide health insurance coverage for the domestic partners of gay and lesbian employees. The court based its ruling on the equal protection provisions of the Montana Constitution.[4]

[1]Mary Williams Walsh. "I.B.M. to Freeze Pension Plans to Trim Cost," *New York Times* (January 6, 2006), A-1.

[2]Mary Williams Walsh. "An Outsider's Grim Prognosis for Pension Agency." *New York Times* (September 14, 2004), C-1.

[3]Jo-el J. Meyer. "Court Approves $47 Million Settlement of WorldCom 401(k) Plan Class Action." *Daily Labor Report* 203 (October 21, 2004), A-5.

[4]Adam Liptak. "Montana Universities Must Offer Health Insurance to Gay Employees' Partners, Court Rules." *New York Times* (February 31, 2005), A-18.

Benefits are an important part of employee compensation. The availability of benefits, such as pensions and health insurance, matters a great deal to employees. For employers, benefit plans are a significant part of labor costs and require considerable expertise to administer. Many laws, both employment and tax laws, affect benefit plans. This chapter focuses on the Employee Retirement Income Security Act (ERISA), the principal federal law regulating benefit plans. Laws specifically regulating group health insurance plans will also be discussed, as will the application of general antidiscrimination statutes to benefit plans.

The law surrounding benefits is very much in flux. Significant public policy questions are being debated about how best to provide and pay for the health care and retirement income needs of an aging population. Employer-provided benefits will no doubt remain central to how most people in the United States meet these basic needs, but employers are clearly seeking to minimize benefit costs and to shift some of the risk and cost associated with them to employees and the public.

WHAT BENEFITS MUST EMPLOYERS PROVIDE?

Employers are required to make contributions on behalf of employees into several social insurance programs. These include Social Security, unemployment insurance, and workers' compensation (for replacement income and medical expenses arising from workplace injuries). Leave required under the Family and Medical Leave Act can also be thought of as a type of legally mandated benefit, although the FMLA does not require that any more paid time off be provided than is already available under an employer's own leave policy. But these programs are exceptions to the general rule that employers are *not* legally required to provide health insurance, pensions, paid sick days, severance pay, or any other benefits. Thus, although the laws discussed in this chapter come into play after an employer decides to have benefits plans, employers decide which, if any, benefit plans they will offer to their employees.

WHAT DOES ERISA REQUIRE?

Despite its name, the **Employee Retirement Income Security Act (ERISA)**[5] governs benefit plans broadly and is not concerned only with pensions. ERISA covers most employer- and labor union–sponsored benefit plans, but not government employer plans. The social insurance programs mentioned earlier are also not covered by ERISA. Under ERISA, benefit plans are classified as either pension plans or welfare plans. **Pension plans** are designed to provide retirement income to employees or to otherwise defer income until after employment ends (e.g., defined benefit pensions, 401(k)s, ESOPs, profit-sharing). **Welfare plans** are essentially any other benefit plans covered by ERISA that are not pension plans (e.g., health insurance, childcare subsidies, prepaid legal services). There are a number of exclusions from this broad category. Without attempting to list them all, the exclusions center on premium pay (e.g., for shift, overtime, or holiday work), payment for nonwork time that comes out of general assets rather than a separate trust fund (e.g., sick pay, vacation pay), scholarship or tuition reimbursement plans, and occasional gifts (e.g., holiday gifts). Benefits that are excluded need not meet ERISA requirements.

[5]29 U.S.C.S. §§ 1001–1461 (2005).

Throughout this book, we have pointed to the important role that state laws play in our system of employment law. States often address issues not covered by federal laws or provide for greater protection of employees. In general, states are free to both fill in where federal law is silent and to mandate greater protection of employees. However, such is not the case when it comes to benefit plans covered by ERISA. ERISA is unusual among employment laws in the sweeping extent to which it preempts (supercedes) state laws even remotely relating to the regulation of benefit plans covered by ERISA. This technical legal issue has real consequences. Because the remedies and requirements of ERISA, particularly those that apply to welfare plans, are more limited than under many state laws, achieving uniformity across states in the legal rules for benefit plans has often come at the price of employee protection. Nowhere is this more evident than in the health insurance arena, where managed care companies have attempted to use ERISA as a shield to ward off legal challenges under state laws. More will be said about managed care later in the chapter, but for now it is enough to point out that ERISA's broad **preemption** language sets it apart from other employment laws.

ERISA is a very complex law that contains four main parts (titles). It combines provisions relating to employee rights with rules relating to the treatment of benefit plans under the tax code. Although the United States relies very heavily on employer-provided benefits (as opposed to government-provided benefits such as national health insurance), employee benefit plans are heavily subsidized through tax deductions. "Qualified" plans receive favorable tax treatment, which provides employers with a strong incentive to conform to ERISA's requirements.

The following overview of ERISA's requirements focuses on the employee rights provisions of Title I. Under ERISA, *employers are required to inform employees about their benefits, deliver promised benefits, provide claims and appeals procedures, manage plans wisely and in employees' interest, and refrain from interfering with or retaliating against beneficiaries.* The main thrust of this law is procedural rather than substantive. ERISA does not require that benefits be offered in the first place or mandate the specific terms or generosity of benefit plans. Instead, it requires that whatever benefits employers offer be made known and actually be provided to employees.

Inform Employees About Their Benefits

A basic premise of ERISA is that informing employees about their benefits will help ensure that employees actually receive the benefits to which they are entitled. Benefit plan administrators are required to periodically (and at no charge) provide employees with reports and respond to employee requests for other information about their benefits. Required reports include the Summary Plan Description (outlining the basic terms of benefit plans), Summary of Material Modifications (listing changes in plans), Summary Annual Report (financial data on pension plans), Individual Benefit Statement (covering individual employees' pension accruals), and Disclosure Notice (alerting employees of certain funding problems with their pension plans).

Summary Plan Descriptions (SPDs) are very important documents. *Summary Plan Descriptions must be provided to employees within 90 days of their becoming covered under benefit plans.* Typically distributed in booklet form (or on-line), *SPDs must be written with a minimum of legalese and be sufficiently comprehensive and accurate to inform employees about their rights and obligations.* In general terms, SPDs must identify the plan administrator, conditions for benefit eligibility, the benefits offered, and procedures for claiming benefits and appealing denials of benefits. Full disclosure of the circumstances under which participants will become ineligible

for or lose benefits is particularly important. The SPD for a health insurance plan should specify any premiums, deductibles, or copayments required of employees; annual or lifetime maximums; limits on coverage for experimental procedures or drugs; limits on choice of health-care providers; conditions for receiving emergency care; and requirements for preauthorization or review of the necessity of medical treatment. The legal importance of SPDs stems from the fact that courts generally rule in favor of employees who reasonably rely on them, even when the SPDs are in conflict with other plan documents. In ruling for a plaintiff whose retirement benefits were unexpectedly reduced due to application of a "phantom account offset," the court acknowledged that SPDs can never contain all the details of benefit plans but that "The impact of the 'phantom account' offset is no minor detail. It resulted in a significant reduction in plaintiff's benefits, compared to . . . what he would reasonably have expected his benefit to be, based on the information provided to him in the SPD."[6]

Apart from reports provided to employees, *ERISA requires that employers detail their benefit plans in written plan documents.* In cases involving disputes over whether promised benefits were provided, courts strongly prefer written plan documents over statements made by company representatives incorrectly advising employees that they were entitled to certain benefits. As one court has put it, "We have made clear . . . that the oral representations of an ERISA plan may not be relied upon by a plan participant when the representation is contrary to the written terms of the plan and those terms are set forth clearly."[7] Thus, employees take risks when they seek and rely on statements about expected benefits. At the same time, employers who misrepresent the terms of benefit plans to employees run afoul of ERISA. In the case cited earlier, the court found for the plaintiff because the combination of an ambiguous SPD and misleading statements by managers and benefits staff led her to the wrong conclusion. *Employers should be careful in advising employees regarding their benefits and refer them to SPDs and other plan documents.*

Deliver on Promised Benefits

Employers are required to provide the benefits they promise. Employees have the right under ERISA to sue their employers for denial of benefits. For example, a health plan might refuse to authorize treatment or decline to pay for care already received because it is deemed "not medically necessary" or "experimental." If a denial-of-benefits case ends up in court, the nature of the review depends on whether the plan gives its administrator discretionary authority to determine eligibility for benefits or to interpret the terms of the plan.[8] Because plan documents typically provide plan administrators with such authority, courts most often confine themselves to determining whether plan administrators abused their discretion by making decisions in an arbitrary and capricious manner, rather than substituting their reading of plans for that of administrators. The relevant question is whether the plan administrator's decision was unreasonable, not whether it was correct.

This **abuse of discretion** standard commonly used in ERISA denial-of-benefits cases is deferential to plan administrators, but does not give them license to unreasonably withhold benefits. A health plan's decision to not authorize high-dosage chemotherapy (HDCT) for an employee with breast cancer was found to be arbitrary and capricious.[9] ERISA was violated because the administrator demanded

[6]*Layaou v. Xerox*, 330 F. Supp. 2d 297, at 303 (W.D.N.Y. 2004).

[7]*Bowerman v. Wal-Mart*, 226 F.3d 574, at 588 (7th Cir. 2000).

[8]*Firestone Tire & Rubber Co. v. Bruch*, 489 U.S. 101 (1989).

[9]*Zervos v. Verizon*, 277 F.3d 635 (2d Cir. 2002).

evidence that HDCT is superior to more conventional treatments to not exclude it as an experimental treatment, even though the plan documents required only that a proposed treatment be recognized by the medical community and have demonstrated effectiveness to be covered. The administrator also erred by ignoring expert medical testimony favorable to the employee. In another case in which the administrator of a health plan abused its discretion, coverage for inpatient treatment in a psychiatric facility was denied, despite the fact that the treating physician saw it as essential to the patient's health. The decision to deny coverage was made by another doctor who had never met the patient and who based her decision on old medical records.[10]

Administrators of benefit plans must base benefit determinations on plan documents, have reasons for their decisions, and use all the current and relevant information available to them.

Provide Claims and Appeals Procedures

Employers are required to provide "reasonable" claims and appeals procedures for their benefit plans.[11] This means meeting certain minimum procedural standards. The standards for handling claims for health benefits are more stringent than those that apply to claims for other types of benefits. To be "reasonable," claims procedures cannot inhibit the filing or processing of claims, such as by imposing filing fees. *Decisions on initial claims generally must be made within 90 days. However, benefit determinations under health plans must be made more quickly.* Urgent-care claims must be decided within 72 hours, whereas claims for treatment already received must be decided within 30 days. These and other time limits on benefit determinations can be extended under certain circumstances.

If a decision is made to deny a benefit claim, the specific reasons for the denial must be provided to the employee in writing. There must be a procedure for appealing adverse benefit determinations, and the procedure must allow at least 60 days (180 days under group health plans) for appeals to be filed. The results of these reviews must be communicated to employees within 60 days (more quickly for some health insurance claims). Reviews of adverse determinations under health plans must not be conducted by the original decision makers or their subordinates.

Unlike most other employment laws, employees are generally required under ERISA to use their employers' claims and **appeals procedures** before going to court to sue for denial of benefits. Thus, an employee was unable to sue his health plan for refusing to pay for a prescription drug that he needed because he had made only a single telephone inquiry about whether the drug was covered and had never used the appeals process.[12] On the other hand, an employee did not fail to exhaust the internal administrative remedy when she sent a number of letters seeking severance pay, but the letters were addressed to the wrong individual in the company's human resources department.[13] The letters could easily have been forwarded to the correct individual, and the employee was never given the correct information about the claims and appeals procedure. Likewise, an insurer's failure to provide a response to an employee's appeal of the decision to end her disability benefits within the time period specified by ERISA meant that the appeal was effectively denied. Having thus exhausted the appeals process, she was free to sue for denial of benefits.[14]

[10]*Salley v. E.I. DuPont de Nemours & Co.*, 966 F.2d 1011 (5th Cir. 1992).

[11]29 C.F.R. § 2560.503-1 (2005).

[12]*Harrow v. Prudential Insurance*, 279 F.3d 244 (3d Cir. 2002).

[13]*Patterson v. J.P. Morgan Chase & Co.*, 2002 U.S. Dist. LEXIS 2014.

[14]*Nichols v. The Prudential Insurance Company of America*, 406 F.3d 98 (2d Cir. 2005).

Manage Plans Wisely and in Employees' Interests—Fiduciary Duties

In general, anyone who exercises discretionary authority or control over the administration of a benefit plan or its funds is considered a **fiduciary**. This usually includes such people as directors, officers, plan administrators, and trustees. Outside parties that regularly render investment advice for a fee are also fiduciaries. The people or entities that control and manage benefit plans have a number of important responsibilities or **fiduciary duties**. First and foremost, *fiduciaries are responsible for managing benefit plans and funds solely in the interest of plan beneficiaries and for the purpose of providing them with benefits. Fiduciaries must manage benefit plans with skill, care, and prudence. They must ensure that plans operate in accordance with plan documents and the requirements of ERISA. With pension plans, fiduciaries are responsible for diversifying plan assets to minimize the risk of large losses, selecting proper investments, monitoring investment performance, and ensuring that plans can meet their obligations. Fiduciaries must also refrain from engaging in certain transactions that have the potential to create conflicts of interest.*

The fiduciary duties of employers extend to information provided to employees regarding their benefits. An employer violated ERISA when it knowingly misled employees, inducing them to make a disadvantageous switch in benefit plans. The employer told employees that their benefits would remain secure if they voluntarily transferred to the benefit plans of its new subsidiary, even though the employer knew full well that the subsidiary was already insolvent. The Supreme Court concluded that there was a clear breach of fiduciary duty: "To participate knowingly and significantly in deceiving a plan's beneficiaries in order to save the employer money at the beneficiaries' expense is not to act 'solely in the interest of the participants and beneficiaries.'"[15] *Employers and other ERISA fiduciaries must provide accurate information about benefit plans and not withhold material facts that would likely affect the choices and interests of plan beneficiaries.*

In *Peralta v. Hispanic Business*, the court considers the fiduciary duty of an employer to provide timely notice regarding the cancellation of a disability insurance plan.

[15] *Varity Corp. v. Howe*, 516 U.S. 489, at 506 (1996).

PERALTA V. HISPANIC BUSINESS
419 F.3d 1064 (9th Cir. 2005)

● ● ●

OPINION BY JUDGE RESTANI:

Carmen Peralta appeals the district court's grant of summary judgment in favor of her former employer, Hispanic Business, Inc. ("HBI"). Peralta alleges that HBI breached its fiduciary duty as an ERISA plan administrator by failing to inform her in a timely manner that her ERISA benefit plan for long-term disability insurance had been cancelled.

We . . . affirm the grant of summary judgment in favor of defendant.

In October 1998, Carmen Peralta began work as a special events manager for HBI, a publisher of business magazines. As part of an effort to enhance its benefits package, HBI introduced a new long-term disability insurance policy ("LTD policy"), effective January 1, 1999, at no cost to its employees, which automatically covered "all regular employees who worked 30 or more

hours per week." The LTD policy was an employee benefits plan, as defined by ERISA, and Peralta was a beneficiary of the plan. In July 2000, Maureen Girouard, the then-Human Resources ("HR") Manager at HBI, wrote to the LTD policy carrier to cancel the policy.

On October 10, 2000, Peralta, while still employed at HBI, was involved in an automobile accident and suffered serious injuries. Believing that she was covered under HBI's LTD policy, Peralta attempted to make a claim for long-term disability benefits. But as the policy had already been cancelled, no benefits were paid. At the time of Peralta's accident, June Wozny was HBI's HR manager. Wozny was in charge of the administration of HBI's employee benefits plan, and one of her projects was to take "a good hard look at the current benefit plan" and try to improve the benefits package, in an attempt to reduce HBI's high employee turnover. During Wozny's investigation into the existing HBI benefits, she discovered . . . "that [someone] had cancelled this long-term disability [policy]." As a result, Wozny sent out an email, on October 18, 2000, informing all HBI employees that the LTD policy had been "cancelled inadvertently" in July 2000 "because of some communication errors." [footnote 2: The email also stated that HBI was obtaining bids from new carriers for the open enrollment period, effective December 1, 2000, and "at that time this policy will be reinstated." Counsel confirmed at oral argument, however, that the policy was not reinstated.] During her deposition, Wozny admitted that prior to these discoveries, based on a summary of HBI's employee benefit plans, she was under the assumption that HBI had an LTD in place. Peralta, who had been in the hospital since October 10, 2000, was initially not aware of Wozny's email. By the time she left the hospital at the end of October 2000, however, Peralta had learned of the cancellation of the LTD policy, which she later verified with the HR manager.

On October 4, 2002, Peralta filed suit in federal district court, alleging breach of fiduciary duty by HBI under the Employee Retirement Income Security Act of 1974 ("ERISA"), Peralta claimed that she had relied on HBI's LTD policy and, believing that she was already covered, did not purchase outside insurance. She further claimed that HBI had a fiduciary duty to "provide complete and accurate information about the status of the employee benefits plan," which included "providing notice of the discontinuation or suspension of coverage." According to Peralta, HBI violated its fiduciary duty to give adequate notice by intentionally concealing the fact that it had cancelled the LTD policy. * * * [T]he district court granted summary judgment for HBI, concluding that no remedy was available. * * * Peralta now appeals. * * *

It is indisputable that an employer has a right to eliminate an ERISA-governed benefit plan. That is not the issue here. The issue is, rather, whether an administrator has a fiduciary duty to notify participants in a timely fashion of the total termination of their coverage, and whether that duty is separate from the reporting and disclosure duty under [ERISA] to notify participants of material changes and modifications. In this case, because HBI's notification of the LTD policy cancellation, per Wozny's October email, occurred approximately three months after Girouard's July cancellation letter, the requirement, that "a summary description of such modification or change shall be furnished not later than 210 days [seven months] after the end of the plan year in which the change is adopted," would be satisfied. Whether there is a more basic duty to provide timely notice of plan cancellation, however, is an issue that few courts have addressed, and for us is an issue of first impression. For the reasons that follow, we conclude that, although the statute does not expressly require timely notice of plan termination, such a requirement is implicit in the purpose and structure of ERISA.

"ERISA seeks 'to safeguard the well-being and security of working men and women and to apprise them of their rights and obligations under any employee benefit plan.'" * * * The statute places a core obligation on an ERISA fiduciary to "discharge [its] duties with respect to a plan solely in the interest of the participants and beneficiaries." . . . [T]he Eleventh Circuit has concluded that "providing notice of the discontinuation or suspension of coverage is a fiduciary responsibility" and that "employees are entitled to prompt notice of the suspension of their plan coverage." We agree with the Eleventh Circuit that the broad fiduciary responsibilities imposed by ERISA require a plan administrator to provide timely notification to employees of termination of their benefits. To conclude otherwise would conflict with ERISA's purpose to safeguard the well-being of employees and apprise them of their rights under an ERISA plan.

In addition to fiduciary duties, ERISA imposes reporting and disclosure obligations on a plan administrator. The reporting and disclosure provisions are set forth separately from the fiduciary duty provisions.

This separation suggests that an administrator's satisfaction of specific reporting requirements does not necessarily satisfy its fiduciary responsibilities. Indeed, to say that compliance with [the reporting and disclosure provisions] of ERISA would also satisfy obligations under [its fiduciary requirements] would render the Act's fiduciary protections a nullity, or at least surplusage. Therefore, in order to give meaning and effect to ERISA's fiduciary purpose, more must be required of an administrator than mere compliance with ERISA's express reporting and disclosure provisions. In other words, "if the fiduciary duty applied to nothing more than activities already controlled by other specific legal duties, it would serve no purpose."

Moreover, although HBI's notice—within approximately three months of the LTD policy cancellation—would satisfy the reporting and disclosure requirements set forth in ERISA, a termination is not the equivalent of a change or modification. Unlike a change or modification, the termination of a plan leaves an employee without any coverage whatsoever. If the statute's 210-day notification period were to apply, employees, unknowingly, would be at risk of having no coverage for seven months. A seven-month notification period hardly can be considered the meaningful disclosure mandated by ERISA . . . * * *

In short, while there is no express statutory requirement to notify participants in a timely fashion of plan cancellation, such a requirement is implicit in the structure and purpose of ERISA, and is more vital than the ordinary technical reporting and disclosure requirements. Employees are entitled to know if they have or do not have an ERISA plan. Failure to so advise employees violates the obligation of a fiduciary to discharge his duties in the interest of the participants with "care, skill, prudence, and diligence."

The remaining issue is whether ERISA's "civil enforcement" provision provides a remedy. * * *

Individual substantive relief under ERISA is available where an employer actively and deliberately misleads its employees to their detriment. * * * Here, however, there is no evidence of such egregious behavior. Despite the lack of clarity regarding the original reason for cancellation, and HBI's policy of promptly notifying its employees in advance of benefit changes, there is no evidence of a scheme either to hide the fact of cancellation or to affirmatively misrepresent the facts. The uncontroverted evidence is that the HR manager, upon learning of the earlier cancellation, gave immediate notice of the cancellation to HBI employees. * * * The evidence is simply of negligently inadequate communications about a policy cancellation. While the effect on Peralta may be the same, whether the cause is deceit or merely a break-down in the channels of communication, the culpability is not. [Thus,] while the ERISA fiduciary had an obligation to provide timely notification to the participants of the termination of coverage, no remedy is available here. It is for Congress to provide a remedy where merely negligent administration results in the termination of coverage without timely notice, and no plan exists under which benefits may be paid.

CASE QUESTIONS

1. What was the legal issue in this case? What did the court decide?

2. What does it mean that employers and others involved with the administration of benefit plans have a fiduciary duty under ERISA?

3. How did the employer violate its fiduciary duty under ERISA in this case?

4. Why did the court nonetheless rule for the employer?

Refrain from Interference or Retaliation

ERISA prohibits discrimination against a benefit plan participant or beneficiary "for exercising any right to which he is entitled" under a benefit plan or "for the purpose of interfering with the attainment of any right to which such participant may become entitled" under a benefit plan.[16] An employer must not, for example, fire an employee to prevent him from becoming entitled to receive a pension.[17] Moreover, this

[16] 29 U.S.C.S. § 1140 (2005).

[17] *Ingersoll-Rand Co. v. McClendon*, 498 U.S. 133 (1990).

protection applies to both pension and welfare plans.[18] Although the statutory language appears relatively broad, courts have restricted this protection to cases in which an adverse employment decision was made for the express purpose of interfering with benefit entitlement. The mere fact that a loss of benefits accompanies a termination does not render that termination a violation of ERISA.

In one case, an employee with AIDS began filing health insurance claims and informed his employer about his condition. The employer responded by cutting the $1 million lifetime maximum under the health plan for other conditions to $5,000 for treatment of AIDS. Despite the facts that this person was the only employee known to have AIDS, and the cut was made immediately after he started to file claims, the court concluded that ERISA was not violated. The reduction would affect all persons with AIDS and not just this individual. More importantly, the employer was free to change the plan at any time. Thus, there was no continuing entitlement to the higher level of coverage.[19] In contrast, when a real estate company terminated its salespersons and offered to allow them to continue as independent contractors without benefits, ERISA was violated.[20] The employer's stated purpose was to avoid paying for health insurance and a 401(k). A key distinction between this and the prior case is that the employer did not change the terms of or discontinue its benefit plans. Instead, it used the terminations to deny to the salespersons benefits that remained in place for other employees.

Employers must not discharge or otherwise discriminate against employees because they have used benefits to which they are entitled or to prevent them from using benefits to which they are entitled.

PENSIONS

Imagine an employee nearing retirement and looking forward to doing nothing more ambitious than walking on the beach every morning. What if he suddenly learns that the pension he was counting on will not be there for some reason? Individuals depend on the income that is deferred into pension plans to provide for their retirements. If problems with a pension plan are not discovered until retirement is at hand, it is far too late to do anything about it. ERISA was created in large part to prevent such disasters, and it contains many complex requirements specific to pension plans. However, some types of pensions are more closely regulated than others. The less-regulated variety is now the most common.

Vesting and Participation

In general, employers are free to alter or discontinue benefit plans at any time. The reduction or elimination of any benefit can be detrimental to employees, but pensions present a particular problem. ERISA allows pension plans to be modified or discontinued, but it requires that individual plan participants and beneficiaries retain the benefits accrued prior to these changes. Under ERISA, *employers with pension plans are required to provide for the vesting of employee pension rights.* **Vesting** means that after a specified number of years of service, employees covered under a pension plan acquire a nonforfeitable right to receive a pension. That period of time

[18]*Inter-Modal Rail Employees Ass'n v. Atchison, Topeka and Santa Fe Railway Co.,* 520 U.S. 510 (1997).

[19]*McGann v. H&H Music Co.,* 946 F.2d 401 (5th Cir. 1991), *cert. denied,* 506 U.S. 981 (1992).

[20]*Seaman v. Arvida Realty Sales,* 985 F.2d 543 (11th Cir. 1993), *cert. denied,* 510 U.S. 916 (1993).

is usually either five years (for "cliff vesting," in which vesting occurs all at once at the end of the fifth year of service) or seven years (for "gradual vesting," in which the nonforfeitable portion increases in increments of 20 percent starting in the third year). Vesting pertains to an employer's contributions to a pension plan. Any employee contributions vest immediately.

Once vested, an employee is entitled to a pension from the employer (or, under certain circumstances, to roll the funds over into another retirement fund), even if the employee goes to work for another company. This does not mean that a 28-year-old who works 7 years for a company and then quits is entitled to a pension at that time. It only means that upon reaching the plan's normal retirement age, the former employee would be entitled to a pension. Because the size of a pension is closely related to length of service, the amount would probably be small in this case. Employers are required not only to vest the pension rights of employees, but also to offer benefits to survivors of deceased employees.

Employers are also prohibited from making changes to pension plans that reduce pension benefits already accrued by employees. In one such case, a multi-employer pension plan for construction workers changed its rules for the types of employment in which retired employees could engage and still receive pension benefits. Some former construction workers who had retired and subsequently accepted positions as construction supervisors saw their retirement benefits suspended when the plan broadened its definition of disqualifying work to include supervisory positions in the industry. The Supreme Court ruled for the former employees, holding that greater restriction of the conditions under which benefits could be received, and not merely a change in the dollar amount of the pension benefit, constituted an impermissible reduction in accrued benefits.[21]

In addition to mandatory vesting, ERISA has **participation** requirements for pension plans aimed at broadening coverage. As a general rule, *pension plans cannot exclude employees who are at least 21 and have at least 1 (if gradual vesting) or 2 (if cliff vesting) years of service.* Limitations other than those based on age or years of service (e.g., division, occupation) can still be imposed. However, qualified pension plans enjoying tax-exempt status are subject to the additional participation requirement that the lesser of 50 employees or 40 percent of the workforce must be covered.

Types of Pension Plans

Under ERISA, pension plans are categorized as either defined benefit or defined contribution plans. Legal requirements vary depending on the type of plan, with defined benefit plans being subjected to greater scrutiny. Cash-balance pension plans incorporate some of the features of both types and have raised new legal questions.

As the name suggests, **defined benefit plans** promise a specific pension benefit upon retirement. The size of an individual's pension is typically determined by a formula based on years of service and earnings. In establishing a defined benefit plan, an employer undertakes a long-term obligation to provide a specified level of retirement income to its employees. A pension fund is maintained, separate from the employer's other assets, and benefits are paid from the fund. However, no separate accounts or funds are set aside for individual employees. The employer bears the burden of providing funding sufficient to meet the plan's obligations to its retired employees. If the investments made by the pension fund do well, the employer has

[21]*Central Laborers' Pension Fund v. Heinz,* 541 U.S. 739 (2004).

to contribute less. If the investments do poorly, the employer has to make up the difference. In either case, the pensions received by employees remain the same.

Obviously, adequate financing is key to the operation of a defined benefit plan. ERISA's funding requirements for defined benefit pension plans are well beyond the scope of this book. Suffice it to say that there are many such rules, including minimum funding standards and financial penalties for underfunding. Defined benefit pension plans can be terminated or frozen, but funding has to be maintained to pay the benefits that have already been accrued by vested employees and retirees. In cases where the employer is unable to meet its obligations to retirees, the **Pension Benefit Guaranty Corporation (PBGC)** intervenes. Employers with defined benefit pension plans pay termination insurance, and these funds are used by the PBGC to provide at least partial retirement benefits to retirees and vested employees. Failures of pension funds at large employers such as United Airlines have placed a major strain on the finances of the PBGC (see "Clippings") and will likely result in more stringent rules for employer funding of defined benefit plans.

The many types of **defined contribution plans** include 401(k)s, profit-sharing plans, stock bonus plans, and employee stock ownership plans (ESOPs). In all these plans, contributions are made into individual employee accounts. The pension benefit that employees receive is not specified beforehand, but depends instead on the amounts in these individual employee accounts at the time of retirement. In turn, those amounts are linked to choices about how much income to defer, whether employee contributions are matched by their employers, the investments selected, and gains or losses from those investments. Thus, with defined contribution plans, employers establish plans and define what their own contributions, if any, will be (e.g., match employee contributions up to specified amounts, provide certain amounts of company stock). They make no promises regarding the eventual pay-out to employees.

Legal regulation of 401(k)s and other defined contribution plans will likely tighten. The Sarbanes-Oxley Act[22] was enacted in 2002 and requires (among many other corporate governance measures) that *employees must receive a 30-day notice of blackout periods (i.e., lock-downs) that would affect their ability to direct investments in or receive distributions from their 401(k)s.* The law provides that corporate insiders will also be subject to any blackout periods, meaning that they will be unable to sell shares or exercise stock options when employees with 401(k)s are so restricted.

Defined contribution plans are not governed by the extensive funding and administrative requirements that apply to defined benefit plans, but employers and other decision makers still have a basic fiduciary duty toward participants in defined contribution plans. In one relevant case, the court found that defendents responsible for managing an employee stock ownership plan (ESOP) breached their fiduciary duty to plan participants by purchasing stock on behalf of the ESOP without proper investigation and by overpaying for the stock. Reliance on an outside expert to establish a fair market value for the stock was not sufficient evidence of prudence in this case because the expert was not supplied with complete and accurate information. Beyond the problem of the faulty stock valuation, the court summed up the case as follows:

> [T]he facts demonstrate that the Hall Chemical ESOP was established in an environment where the trustees were unaware of what was going on, the trustees were not consulted on major decisions . . . , there was not negotiation

[22]P.L. 107-204 (2002).

THE CHANGING WORKPLACE

Defined Contribution Plans and Shifting Risk to Employees

Many contemporary workplace developments can be viewed as means of shifting risk and uncertainty from employers to employees. For example, less stable and more contingent forms of employment place the burden of fluctuations in the need for labor squarely on employees and relieve employers from commitments to use corps of relatively permanent employees. Likewise, when employers move toward "variable compensation" linked to the performance of employees (e.g., merit pay) or organizations (e.g., profit-sharing), risk is shifted from employers to employees. In the area of benefits, this trend is most clearly seen in the movement away from defined benefit pensions to defined contribution plans.

Less than half of all employees are covered under pension plans offered by their employers. For those employees fortunate enough to have pension plans, defined contribution plans have become the preeminent type over the past few decades. Between 1975 and 1999, the number of single-employer, defined benefit plans decreased by approximately 60 percent, whereas the number of single employer, defined contribution plans increased by almost 240 percent.[1] Among firms with less than 1,000 employees, there was a 70 percent decline in the number of firms offering defined benefit plans between 1990 and 2004. Overall, 20 percent of private-sector workers were covered by defined benefit pension plans in 2004, compared to 42 percent of workers covered by defined contribution plans.[2]

Does this shift toward defined contribution plans raise legal concerns? One rather pedestrian, but persistent, problem is unwarranted delays in forwarding contributions deducted from employee paychecks to mutual funds or other investments. The DOL regulations require that funds deducted for this purpose be invested as soon as possible, but no later than 15 business days from the end of the month in which the deduction

was made. Some employers have held these funds beyond the maximum allowable time, and in some cases indefinitely, as a form of interest-free loan. The DOL is currently litigating this issue.[3]

Other problems surround defined contribution plans. Although defined benefit plans are generally limited to a maximum of 10 percent of a company's own stock in its pension fund, defined contribution plans are not currently subject to this or any specific limit. Ill-considered employee choices regarding investment portfolios and the practice by many companies of making contributions in the form of company stock compound lack of diversification of assets. As a result, 401(k) plans that include company stock as an investment option have about a third of their assets invested in employer stock.[4] Enron employees had over half of their assets invested in Enron stock at the time of the company's meltdown. Good investment advice might help employees make better choices, but employers generally refrain from offering specific advice, and investment firms might be suspected of pushing their own products. The problems at Enron were exacerbated by the "lock-down" period that was imposed, during which employees were unable to sell their Enron stock despite its plummeting value. And, of course, defined contribution plans are not insured. If investments turn sour or the funds in employees' accounts are otherwise dissipated, there is no recourse to the PBGC.

[1] Dallas L. Salisbury. "The State of Private Pensions." In Sheldon Friedman and David C. Jacobs, eds., *The Future of the Safety Net: Social Insurance and Employee Benefits* (Ubana-Champaign, IL.: Industrial Relations Research Association, 2001), pp. 139–64.

[2] Employment Policy Foundation. *The American Workplace 2005: The Changing Nature of Employee Benefits.* (2005), ix.

[3] "District Court Certifies Class Action Centering on Late 401(K) Plan Deposits." *Daily Labor Report* 86 (May 3, 2002), A-5.

[4] Richard A. Oppel. "The Danger in a One-Basket Nest Egg Prompts a Call to Limit Stock." *New York Times* (December 19, 2001), C-1.

as to the price of the . . . stock, there was more concern for the return on investment for the Master Trust, and the inconvenience of dealing with uneven numbers could justify charging the Hall Chemical ESOP an additional $44,900.00 for the stock it purchased. Such facts demonstrate not only the uniquely careless and haphazard manner in which the Hall Chemical ESOP was created, but also clear violations of defendant's fiduciary duties.[23]

[23] *Chao v. Hall Holding Company,* 285 F.3d 415, at 433-34 (6th Cir. 2002); *cert. denied,* 2003 U.S. LEXIS 887.

Cases are also proliferating in the courts alleging breach of fiduciary duty by employers who continued to offer company stock as an investment option for employee retirement accounts and failed to inform employees of known problems with that stock, resulting in large losses. Like WorldCom (see "Clippings"), numerous other companies (e.g., Enron, K-Mart, CVS) have settled such claims. Other cases are wending their way through the court system. For example, participants in Polaroid's defined contribution plans have alleged that:

> Despite the bleak condition of the Company, the precipitous decline in its stock price, the imminent possibility of financial collapse, and ultimately its actual collapse, . . . Defendants continued to offer Polaroid stock as a Plan investment option for participant contributions, match contributions in Polaroid stock, and . . . contribute Polaroid stock to the Plan.[24]

Defendants have generally not been successful in arguing that they were constrained by plan documents to continue to offer company stock as an investment[25] or that insider-trading laws would prohibit the disclosure of relevant, nonpublic information to plan participants.[26]

Although the courts appear to be increasingly receptive to claims involving breach of fiduciary duty with respect to defined contribution plans, some cases have gone against employees. For example, a group of employees sued under ERISA when their employer offered 401(k) plan participants an investment option (described by the employer as a "conservative" investment intended to return principal and interest) that was based on junk bonds, and the investment subsequently lost money. After several rounds of litigation, the court concluded that the employer had not breached its fiduciary duties to offer prudent investments, diversify (the bad investment comprised 20 percent of the fund), or disclose material information to participants.[27] The court stressed that it is the fiduciary's conduct in arriving at an investment decision (e.g., conducting appropriate research before purchasing investments), and not the financial outcome, that establishes prudence. Likewise, 401(k) participants were unsuccessful in a suit based on the heavy investment of nonvested funds in company stock. The price of that stock had plummeted following the release of negative information to the public. The employees' claim that the employer knew the stock was overvalued, yet did not disclose this to plan participants and continued to allow it to be purchased as a plan investment, foundered largely on the issue that the company itself, as opposed to the plan committee, had little fiduciary responsibility under the plan.[28] The court allowed a separate securities fraud claim to continue, but stressed that a distinction exists between ordinary business decisions that have an effect on benefits and actions specifically directed toward a plan. It is only the latter that implicate fiduciary duties under ERISA.

The law in this area is still developing, but employers should do a few basic things regarding 401(k)s and other defined contribution plans. First, *employers must invest the funds deducted from employees' pay no later than 15 business days after the end of the month in which deductions are made.* Second, *employers should carefully research investments, offer a range of investment types and investment companies from which to choose, and warn employees regarding the dangers of inadequate diversification.* Third, *employers should make impartial investment information*

[24]*In Re: Polaroid ERISA Litigation*, 362 F. Supp. 2d 461, at 467 (S.D.N.Y. 2005).

[25]*Polaroid*, at 473-75.

[26]*Rankin v. Rots*, 278 F.Supp 2d 853 (E.D.Mich. 2003); *In Re: AEP ERISA Litigation*, 327 F. Supp. 2d 812 (S.D.Ohio 2004).

[27]*In Re: Unisys Savings Plan Litigation*, 173 F.3d 145 (3d Cir. 1999); *cert. denied*, 528 U.S. 950 (1999).

[28]*Hull v. Policy Management Systems*, 2001 U.S. District LEXIS 22343.

available to employees. Fourth, *employers should consider placing reasonable limits on the extent to which employee accounts are comprised of company stock and should remove company stock as an investment option when it is no longer a prudent investment.* Fifth, *employers must not violate their fiduciary duty to manage plans in the best interests of employees by imposing lock-downs for illegitimate purposes.*

Cash-Balance Plans Cash-balance plans are defined benefit pensions that also include some features of defined contribution plans (hence, they are often termed *hybrid* plans). Cash-balance plans first appeared in 1985. About one-fourth of large employers with defined benefit plans had converted to cash balance plans by 2003.[29] However, the pace of this change has slowed due to legal uncertainty surrounding these plans. As with other defined benefit plans, employers sponsoring cash-balance plans are responsible for providing a promised level of benefits, employees are entitled to receive their benefits in the form of lifetime annuities if they choose (as opposed to lump-sum distributions), and the plans are insured through the PBGC. Unlike other defined benefit plans, the pension benefit is defined by the accumulation of annual employer contributions based on a percentage of an employee's salary plus a specified interest rate. A hypothetical account is created for each employee to track the accrual of pension benefits over the course of employment. The accounts do not actually exist, and employees do not have the ability to make investment decisions for their pensions funds, but the pension benefit to which employees are entitled upon leaving employment is the amount accrued in these hypothetical accounts (i.e., the cash balance).

So what is the problem that has led employees at IBM (see "Clippings") and other companies to challenge cash-balance plans? The issue is complex, but it comes down to the potentially harmful effects on older workers of conversion from traditional defined benefit plans to cash-balance plans. Most defined benefit plans relate benefits to employees' earnings in the last few years of employment when earnings are usually highest. Thus, much of the pension benefit accrues late in an employee's career. In contrast, benefits accrue more evenly under cash-balance plans and are essentially based on average earnings over an entire career. Older employees who are forced to change to cash-balance plans lose out on the period of time when their traditional defined benefit plans would have grown most in value. Worse, although benefits earned by vested employees prior to the conversion must be retained, employees can be excluded from further accrual under the new plan until the vested benefits no longer exceed what the employees would have been entitled to under the new cash-balance plan (a phenomenon termed *wear away*).

The legal status of conversion to cash-balance plans is unclear. A court has ruled against IBM, stating that the design of such plans inherently violates age discrimination provisions within ERISA.[30] However, other courts have upheld cash-balance plans and the Department of Treasury has also taken the position that such plans are not inherently age discriminatory.[31] The safest conclusion at this point is that *employers should proceed cautiously in converting to cash-balance plans, fully inform employees about the nature of this change, and attempt to minimize the detrimental effects on older workers* (such as by allowing older workers to choose between plans).

[29]Elizabeth White Grover. "Shift to 'Hybrid' Pension Plans Slows; Employers Considering HSAs, EPF Says." *Daily Labor Report* 164 (August 25, 2005), A-10.

[30]*Cooper v. The IBM Personal Pension Plan and IBM Corp.*, 274 F. Supp 2d 1010 (S.D.Ill. 2003).

[31]*Eaton v. Onan Corp.*, 117 F. Supp. 2d 812 (S.D. Ind. 2000); *Register v. PNC Financial Services Group*, 2005 U.S. Dist. LEXIS 29678.

HEALTH INSURANCE

Health insurance is far and away the most important type of welfare plan covered by ERISA. Legal issues surrounding this costly but very necessary benefit include ensuring access to and quality of care in the face of efforts to restrain costs; removing barriers to obtaining coverage, such as preexisting condition exclusions; preventing loss of health insurance; and contesting discrimination—particularly against disabled persons and pregnant women.

Legal Challenges to Managed Care

Much of our health care is now paid for and provided through the activities of health maintenance organizations (HMOs) and other types of managed care such as preferred provider organizations (PPOs) and point of service plans (POSs). Managed care can be contrasted with traditional fee-for-service arrangements. In the latter, physicians chosen by their patients provide medical services, and the bill for those services is passed along to insurers. Doctors have little incentive to restrain the use of medical services. **Managed care** creates a closer linkage between the provision of health care and payment for that health care. Managed care organizations (MCOs) receive sums of money to provide for the health care of insured patients and profit to the extent that costs can be minimized. The insured are required or given financial incentives to use only those care providers employed by the MCO or located within an established network of providers. To be included in provider networks, doctors have to agree to follow managed care companies' rules and accept their established levels of reimbursement. Various financial incentives are provided for physicians to keep the cost of care down. Patients are required to obtain preapproval of many services, have their treatment regimens or hospital stays closely monitored for conformance with established norms, and are otherwise limited in their use of medical services—if they want to have the cost of those services covered.

To what extent can persons covered under group health plans contest the decisions and actions of managed care organizations? Certainly, ERISA claims for denial of benefits are possible, although the abuse of discretion standard discussed earlier in this chapter gives health plan administrators considerable leeway in deciding whether particular treatments should be covered, and damages are generally limited to recovery of the benefits denied. The Supreme Court has considered the question of whether the structure of managed care, particularly bonuses paid by managed care companies to physicians based on their success in keeping costs down by rationing care, is inherently incompatible with the fiduciary duty to manage benefit plans solely in the interest of beneficiaries.[32] In the case in question, a woman experiencing severe pain in the area of her abdomen was examined by a doctor at her HMO and told that she would have to wait eight days to have an ultrasound test performed at another facility (50 miles away) run by the same HMO, rather than be tested immediately at a local hospital. Before the test could be obtained, the woman's appendix ruptured causing peritonitis. The Court decided that, at least with respect to decisions that rely on doctors' medical judgments about patients' conditions to make coverage decisions ("mixed decisions"), managed care companies do not act in a fiduciary capacity. Thus, ERISA was not violated in this case or, more generally, by the profit incentives built into managed care.

[32]*Pegram v. Herdrich*, 530 U.S. 211 (2000).

ERISA is of limited use in challenges to managed care companies. Congress has thus far failed to pass comprehensive federal "patient's bill of rights" legislation, although it has proceeded with piecemeal regulation of the substance of health plans by requiring them to pay (without preauthorization) for at least 48 hours of hospitalization for childbirth (96 hours if the delivery is by cesarean section)[33] and for breast reconstruction surgery if mastectomies are covered.[34] However, state law has been at the center of recent challenges to managed care. Remember that ERISA contains very broad preemption language and generally supercedes state laws in matters relating to benefit plans. In many states, patients can still bring malpractice suits against individual physicians for negligence and serious defects in the *quality* of care provided (as opposed to decisions not to cover particular treatments). The woman whose appendix burst in the case mentioned earlier was successful in a separate malpractice claim against the doctor. States have also passed laws establishing external medical review boards to deal with disputes between managed care companies and patients and other laws requiring that "any willing provider" be allowed to join a managed care company's network. The Supreme Court has found that such laws are not preempted by ERISA.[35] Some states have gone further and enacted laws providing a right to sue managed care companies for damages stemming from their failure to exercise proper care in making health care treatment decisions. However, the Supreme Court held in a case involving the Texas Health Care Liability Act that any such claim was rooted in the terms of the health insurance plan and thus preempted by ERISA.[36] Thus, federal law continues to provide a powerful shield against holding managed care companies liable for the consequences of their actions.

Maintaining Coverage—COBRA and HIPAA

The large number of Americans who are without any health insurance at all is a major concern. The number varies from year to year, but approximately 46 million people lacked health insurance in 2005.[37] Young adults are especially likely to be without coverage. Many persons obtain health insurance coverage through their employer. However, the percentage of private-sector employees covered by employer-sponsored health plans has been slipping and stood at 53 percent in March 2005.[38]

One strategy for dealing with the problem of the uninsured is to focus on circumstances in which individuals would lose their coverage and provide them with a means for staying insured until they become covered under other group health plans. **COBRA (Consolidated Omnibus Budget Reconciliation Act)**[39] requires that employers who have group health insurance plans and at least 20 employees offer continuation coverage under certain circumstances (qualifying events) in which employees (and other beneficiaries if there is family coverage) would otherwise lose their health insurance. COBRA **qualifying events** and the

[33]Newborns' and Mothers' Health Protection Act, 42 U.S.C.S. §§ 300gg–4(a) (2005).

[34]Women's Health and Cancer Rights Act, 29 U.S.C.S. § 1185b(a) (2005).

[35]*Rush Prudential HMO v. Moran,* 536 U.S. 355 (2002); *Kentucky Association of Health Plans,* 538 U.S. 329 (2003).

[36]*Aetna Health v. Davila,* 124 S. Ct. 2488 (2004).

[37]John Broder. "Health Coverage of Young Widens with States' Aid." *New York Times* (December 4, 2005), A-1.

[38]"Employer-Sponsored Health Plans Cover 53 Percent of Private Sector Workers." *Daily Labor Report* 164 (August 25, 2005), D-1.

[39]29 U.S.C.S. §§ 1161–1167 (2005).

periods of time for which coverage (if chosen by an employee or beneficiary) must be maintained are:

- *Continue coverage for up to 18 months*
 - Voluntary or involuntary termination of employment for reasons other than "gross misconduct"
 - Reduced hours of employment
- *Continue coverage for up to 36 months*
 - Divorce or legal separation
 - Death of an employee
 - Loss of dependent child status under the terms of the health plan
 - Covered employee becoming entitled to Medicare

If one of these qualifying events occurs, an employer must offer continuation coverage to the employee and other family members who have been covered under the employee's health insurance. Employees cannot simply be "dropped" from health plans without following COBRA's procedures. The continuation coverage must be the same coverage enjoyed by employees who have not experienced a qualifying event. There is a heavy emphasis under COBRA on providing proper notification. *Information about COBRA rights must be provided to covered employees and their spouses and be included in health plan SPDs at the time health plan coverage begins.* Employers must notify plan administrators of the occurrence of qualifying events within 30 days. Because employers would not necessarily know of divorces, separations, or loss of dependent child status, employees or other beneficiaries are responsible for bringing these events to the attention of plan administrators within 60 days. *After they are alerted that a qualifying event has occurred, plan administrators have 14 days to offer continuation coverage. Notice of the availability of continuation coverage should go to all the affected beneficiaries, and not just to covered employees. Beneficiaries must be given at least 60 days from when their health coverage ends or from when they are notified of their COBRA rights, whichever is later, to elect continuation coverage and an additional 45 days to make the first payment.*

To properly comply with COBRA, employers should document the sending of notification, request that all employees respond to the offer of continuation coverage regardless of whether they are accepting or declining, maintain up-to-date contact information, arrange for how payment will be made, and track coverage periods.

Continuation coverage under COBRA is not free. Beneficiaries can be charged up to 102 percent of the cost to the employer of providing coverage under the group health plan. Although this is a major expense for most employees, it may still be preferable to the options of being uninsured or trying to purchase individual policies from insurance companies, especially if the employee or family members have known health problems. *If an employee elects continuation coverage, the coverage must continue for up to either 18 or 36 months unless the employee fails to make the payments, the employer discontinues offering group health insurance to its employees, or the employee becomes covered under another group health plan (e.g., gets another job).*

McDowell v. Krawchison emphasizes the importance of proper notification to all beneficiaries who stand to lose their health insurance coverage.

Another obstacle to obtaining health benefits or maintaining coverage when changing jobs is the preexisting condition exclusions commonly incorporated into health plans. A **preexisting condition exclusion** denies coverage for a specified period of time for the treatment of conditions that existed before an individual enrolled in

McDOWELL V. KRAWCHISON
125 F.3d 954 (6th Cir. 1997)

OPINION BY CIRCUIT JUDGE MOORE:

Defendants-Appellants John Raymond Krawchison and Winton Road Chiropractic Center, Inc. appeal from the district court's order entering judgment in favor of Plaintiff-Appellee Terry McDowell in this action for failure to provide health insurance benefits under ERISA, as amended by the Comprehensive [sic] Omnibus Budget Reconciliation Act of 1986 ("COBRA").

At the times relevant to this case, Krawchison held an ownership interest in and operated several chiropractic clinics in Ohio, Kentucky, and Indiana. * * * The clinics provided health insurance to their employees through Medical Benefits Mutual Life Insurance Company. * * * In late 1991, Krawchison asked McDowell to work for him at the Winton Road clinic in Cincinnati. McDowell accepted and began work in early January 1992. In September 1992, Dr. Dennis Anderson, who had previously worked at the Winton Road clinic, returned to buy the clinic from Krawchison. He terminated McDowell's employment, effective two days later. McDowell, whose wife, Sidovar, had breast cancer, wanted to continue his and Sidovar's health insurance. * * * McDowell later asked Susan Porter, the office manager for the Winton Road clinic, if he could continue on the health insurance plan. Porter told him that she believed it was possible, but that she would check with Krawchison, which she did. On McDowell's last day of employment, Porter told him that his health insurance would be continued. . . . * * * Neither McDowell nor Sidovar sought coverage for any medical treatment from September 1992 until early June 1993. At that time, Sidovar sought pre-approval for medical treatment and learned that she had no insurance coverage. * * *

COBRA imposes a statutory requirement that a plan administrator notify "any qualified beneficiary" of his or her right to continue health insurance coverage for up to eighteen months after a "qualifying event" (here, McDowell's termination). "Providing appropriate notice is a key requirement under COBRA. If the administrator fails to provide that notice [of triggering of COBRA rights] to the qualified beneficiary, it may be bound to provide coverage to her." * * *

It was undisputed that McDowell and Sidovar received no written notice of their COBRA rights. * * * The statute itself does not prescribe the contents of the required notice. Nevertheless, the notice given must be sufficient to allow the qualified beneficiary to make an informed decision whether to elect coverage. Although the defendants contend that oral notice should be deemed sufficient, we need not decide that issue in this case. Even if the notice to McDowell by way of his conversation with Porter was legally sufficient, it did not meet the statutory requirement as to Sidovar. She was entitled by statute to her own notice of her rights. The statute explicitly requires notice to be given to any qualified beneficiary, and defines a covered spouse to be a qualified beneficiary. A covered spouse has his or her own rights under COBRA, which are not dependent on the covered employee's rights. For example, a covered spouse might choose to elect coverage while the covered employee does not, or they might choose different plans. The covered spouse often may be a qualified beneficiary where the covered employee is not: a covered spouse is specifically defined as a qualified beneficiary; a covered employee, on the other hand, is a qualified beneficiary only when he or she is terminated other than for gross misconduct or experiences a reduction in hours. In fact, the definition of "qualifying event" focuses largely on the resulting loss of coverage to other family members; COBRA coverage for qualified beneficiaries is triggered not only when the covered employee is terminated, but also when he or she dies or becomes covered by Medicare, when the covered spouse is divorced or legally separated from the covered employee, when a dependent child ceases to be a dependent child, or when an employer from whom the covered employee retired files for bankruptcy.

Other COBRA provisions belie the defendants' contention that notice to the covered employee satisfies the administrator's obligation as to a covered spouse. [One provision] states that notification by the administrator "to an individual who is a qualified beneficiary as the spouse of the covered employee shall be treated as notification to all other qualified beneficiaries residing with such spouse at the time such notification is made." In other words, the administrator is not required to notify each covered dependent child living at home, provided that the nonemployee parent, the spouse of the covered

employee, is notified. If the statute eliminates the need to notify certain qualified beneficiaries, but does not explicitly except notification of the spouse—and, in fact, relies upon such notification to provide notice to covered dependents—then we cannot read the statute to eliminate the need to notify a covered spouse.

The statute also provides that "any election of continuation coverage by a qualified beneficiary . . . shall be deemed to include an election of continuation coverage on behalf of any other qualified beneficiary who would lose coverage under the plan by reason of the qualifying event. If there is a choice among types of coverage under the plan, each qualified beneficiary is entitled to make a separate selection among such types of coverage." Perhaps significantly, this provision acts only to preserve coverage for other qualified beneficiaries; it does not, for instance, treat one beneficiary's decision not to continue coverage as eliminating the other beneficiaries' option to elect, and in fact it allows beneficiaries to elect different types of coverage. This election provision is useful as an analogy—it allows one beneficiary to be deemed to have acted on others' behalf only in order to maintain coverage, and it explicitly provides for a separate election by each

beneficiary; it does not allow beneficiaries to be treated as a unit for purposes of denying coverage. Similarly, we do not interpret the statute's notice provisions as treating the covered employee and his or her spouse as a unit for notice purposes, such that the plan administrator is absolved of its duty to notify the spouse. * * *

Therefore, we hold that the plan administrator was required to provide Sidovar with sufficient notice of her rights, and that failure to do so violated COBRA.

CASE QUESTIONS

1. What was the legal issue in this case? What did the court decide?

2. What should the employer have done to properly comply with COBRA?

3. What was the qualifying event? What was the date of the qualifying event? How much continuation coverage were they entitled to?

4. What would have happened if the continuation coverage had been provided, and during that time, the couple divorced?

a health plan. The **Health Insurance Portability and Accountability Act (HIPAA)**[40] greatly restricts, but does not eliminate, the use of preexisting condition exclusions by health plans. First, HIPAA restricts preexisting conditions to those "for which medical advice, diagnosis, care, or treatment was recommended or received within the 6-month period ending on the enrollment date."[41] Pregnancy cannot be deemed a preexisting condition. Second, *exclusionary periods can last no longer than 12 months* (18 months for late enrollees). Third, *exclusionary periods must be reduced by any periods of prior coverage under a group health plan (including COBRA coverage), provided that no more than 63 days elapsed between the prior coverage and enrollment in the new plan.* Prior coverage under a group health plan is documented in a **certificate of creditable coverage.** *Certificates of creditable coverage must be provided automatically and free of charge to employees when they lose coverage or exhaust their COBRA continuation coverage.*

Retiree Health Benefits

The need for medical care generally increases during a person's retirement years. Medicare is designed to be the primary health insurance for retired persons, but it provides only partial coverage of medical costs and is not available to younger retirees. In the face of rapidly rising health costs, many employers are now cutting

[40]42 U.S.C. §§ 300gg-300gg-2 (2005).
[41]U.S.C. § 300gg(a) (2005).

back on or completely eliminating health insurance coverage for their retirees.[42] This has raised the question of whether employers are legally bound to continue providing health insurance coverage to retirees. The principle issue in these cases is whether the employer intended to confer an irrevocable right to receive health benefits on retirees. As *Vallone v. CNA Financial* illustrates, it is difficult for a plaintiff to show that an employer has committed itself to providing health insurance for the duration of retirement.

[42]Mary Williams Walsh. "Another Cloud on the Horizon for Lucent Retirees." *New York Times* (November 20, 2002), C-1.

VALLONE V. CNA FINANCIAL
375 F.3d 623 (7th Cir. 2004); *cert. denied*, 125 S. Ct. 670 (2004)

● ● ●

OPINION BY CIRCUIT JUDGE CUDAHY:

This case involves another episode in the widespread efforts of corporations to reduce their liabilities by cutting back on retiree benefits. The law in this circuit is well-established, but this does nothing to cushion the hardship of pensioners faced with a new drain on their limited resources. In late 1991, The Continental Insurance Company (Continental) offered an early retirement package ["Voluntary Special Retirement Program"—VSRP] to some of its employees as a cost containment initiative. [The plaintiffs] are three of the 347 Continental employees who accepted the early retirement package (the early retirees), which included the "lifetime" welfare benefit at issue in this case, a Health Care Allowance (HCA). In 1995, Continental was acquired by CNA Financial Corporation (CNA). In 1998, CNA notified the early retirees that as of January 1, 1999, their HCA benefit would be terminated. The plaintiffs challenged this decision by complaining to the Plan Administrator of CNA's retirement plan, to no avail. They subsequently brought suit, alleging claims of wrongful denial of benefits under the Employee Retirement Income Security Act (ERISA), breach of contract, estoppel and a breach of fiduciary duty. The district court granted summary judgment to the defendants on all claims, and we now affirm. * * *

The retirement package in this case involves a complicated construction of enhancements to the general retirement plan in effect at the time. Not surprisingly, the parties disagree about which documents (and oral representations) created the VSRP and its enhanced

HCA benefit at issue here. * * * During group and individual meetings that took place in late 1991 between Continental's human resources representatives and eligible employees in various locations around the country, the HCA was consistently described as a "lifetime" benefit. Heidemann, who was an assistant vice president of human resources for the Great Lakes region and an officer of the company at the time of her retirement, testified at deposition that she had been told by her superiors in human resources that the HCA benefit was a "lifetime" benefit. She could not recall anyone ever telling her that the VSRP benefits were irrevocable. She strongly believed the VSRP was separate and distinct from the general retirement plan, and since no one in human resources ever told her the benefits *could* be revoked, and none of the documents specifically discussing the VSRP contained a disclaimer, she assumed that the "lifetime" benefits were irrevocable. When Heidemann presented the VSRP to the eligible employees in her region (including Vallone), she represented the benefits as being for "your lifetime" but did not say anything about their irrevocability. The district court, from the perspective of the evidence most favorable to the plaintiffs, determined that eligible employees were told that the benefits were for their own and their spouses' lifetimes; that they were not told the benefits could be changed or revoked (although they were referred to documents that reserved those rights); that they were not told the "lifetime" benefits were irrevocable, but they nevertheless concluded that the benefits were irrevocable for reasons similar to Heidemann's reasons; that this conclusion was material to their decision to retire; that Continental had no intention at the time of the plaintiffs' retirement of altering the HCA

benefit; and that the intention and decision to change benefits came several years later, after Continental had been acquired by CNA. * * *

We start from the premise that "employers . . . are generally free under ERISA, for any reason at any time, to adopt, modify, or terminate welfare plans." For this reason, if ERISA welfare benefits "vest at all, they do so under the terms of a particular contract." The Supreme Court, followed by several courts of appeals, has indicated that a modification that purports to vest welfare benefits must be contained in the plan documents and must be stated in clear and express language. Given our presumption against the vesting of welfare benefits, silence indicates that welfare benefits are not vested. Moreover, although ERISA itself "left open . . . the possibility that a written plan may be combined with an oral promise, such as an undertaking to give a worker twice the benefits so established," wholly oral promises cannot be used to require the employer to provide irrevocable benefits. If there is some ambiguity in the language of the written agreement that is not disambiguated elsewhere in the document, only then may we consider evidence of the parties' intent that is "extrinsic" to the written documents, such as oral representations. * * *

The plaintiffs argue that the VSRP documents indicate that the HCA is a "lifetime" benefit, and that this had been confirmed in oral representations made to them. * * * That the HCA benefit was a "lifetime" benefit—both for regular retirees and for retirees who accepted the VSRP package—is actually conceded by CNA. The problem for the plaintiffs is that "lifetime" may be construed as "good for life unless revoked or modified." This construction is particularly plausible if the contract documents include a reservation of rights clause (which, as will be shown, is the case here). Reading the document in its entirety, the clauses explain that although the plan in its current iteration entitles retirees to health coverage for the duration of their lives and the lives of their eligible surviving spouses, the terms of the plan—including the plan's continued existence—are subject to change at the will of [the employer]. * * *

The plaintiffs next argue that, as a separate and distinct program, the benefits in the VSRP were not subject to the reservations of rights clauses in the various general retirement plan documents, and that the documents specifically mentioning the VSRP did not contain reservation of rights clauses. However, regardless of how the plaintiffs believe the VSRP was marketed to the early retirees, their initial premise that the

VSRP was separate and distinct from the general retirement plan is incorrect. This is evident from a review of the Brief Description Newsletter, which repeatedly refers to the general retirement plan in discussing the VSRP's enhanced benefits, making clear that the general retirement plan is the baseline program to which the VSRP's enhancements would be made. The plaintiffs themselves admit that the VSRP was a modification of the regular retirement plan. * * * [I]f the plaintiffs had been correct that the reservation of rights clauses in the general retirement plan documents did not apply to the VSRP, the grant of "lifetime" benefits would have created an ambiguity allowing them a trial and allowing us to examine extrinsic evidence of the parties' intent. However, since we determined that this was not the case, there is no ambiguity requiring an examination of extrinsic evidence. * * *

The district court unsurprisingly had difficulty distinguishing this purported contract claim from the plaintiffs' claim that they were wrongfully denied ERISA benefits. * * * [C]laims by a beneficiary for wrongful denial of benefits (no matter how they are styled) have been held by the Supreme Court to "fall[] directly under . . . ERISA, which provides an exclusive federal cause of action for resolution of such disputes." Recent decisions of both this circuit and the Supreme Court have held that state law claims, such as the plaintiffs' breach of common law contract claim here, are pre-empted by ERISA. * * *

In order to prevail on an estoppel claim under ERISA, we ordinarily require that plaintiffs show (1) a knowing misrepresentation; (2) that was made in writing; (3) with reasonable reliance on that misrepresentation by them; (4) to their detriment. * * * But this estoppel claim fails for two reasons. First, the plaintiffs have not shown a knowing misrepresentation of fact. Although "representations about plans and intentions could be false if, at the time the statements were made, the speaker actually had a different intention," the district court found that, at the time the VSRP was offered, Continental had no intention of terminating the "lifetime" HCA benefit. Moreover, the plaintiffs have pointed to no false statements about whether the HCA benefit could be terminated * * * Second, the plaintiffs cannot show reasonable reliance. . . . [E]ven if there were material written misrepresentations as to the nature of the HCA benefit, the plaintiffs unreasonably ignored the reservations of rights clauses in the general retirement plan documents that put them on notice that the HCA benefit could be terminated or modified. * * *

ERISA requires a trustee or other fiduciary to "discharge his duties with respect to a plan solely in the interest of the participants and beneficiaries." In interpreting this statute, the Supreme Court has held that an employer breaches its fiduciary obligation by lying to employees in order to induce them to surrender their benefits. * * * The Second Circuit, which has given the broadest scope to ERISA fiduciary duty claims, has held that representing to plan participants that a plan's benefits are "lifetime" when they are not vested can create a genuine issue of material fact as to whether misrepresentations were made or whether there was a failure to provide complete and accurate information. The Third Circuit has held that a fiduciary duty claim could proceed, despite the employer's reservation of the right to terminate retirement benefits, when oral and written representations were made to employees that the benefits would continue for life and the employer was aware that retirement decisions were being based on the mistaken assumption that the benefits were also vested. And the Sixth Circuit has held that a breach of fiduciary duty claim was made out where a company—both of its own accord and in response to specific employee inquiries—misrepresented to employees that a reservation of rights clause in the plan did not allow retirement benefits to be changed when the legal effect of the clause was precisely the opposite.

In this circuit, a breach of fiduciary duty exists if fiduciaries "mislead plan participants or misrepresent the terms or administration of a plan." "Although not every error in communicating information regarding a plan will be found to violate a fiduciary's duty under ERISA, we have made clear that fiduciaries must communicate material facts affecting the interests of plan participants or beneficiaries and that this duty to communicate exists when a participant or beneficiary 'asks fiduciaries for information, and even when he or she does not.'" * * * The district court was correct that [this circuit has adopted] a narrower interpretation of [the fiduciary's duty to inform] than exists in other circuits. Specifically, while there is a duty to provide accurate information

under ERISA, negligence in fulfilling that duty is not actionable. That is why the employer must have set out to disadvantage or deceive its employees, in order for a breach of fiduciary duty to be made out. * * * There is simply no evidence that Continental set out to deceive its employees by its actions. . . .

In fact, it is not even clear that the information provided was inaccurate. As we found earlier, the general retirement plan documents containing reservation of rights clauses were made part of the VSRP by the documents setting out the VSRP's enhancements. There was no evidence that any employee ever specifically asked about the irrevocability of the HCA benefit, that Continental falsely indicated to any employee that the HCA benefit was irrevocable or that Continental was aware that the early retirees were coming to the mistaken conclusion that "lifetime" equated to "vested." And in this circuit, if accurate written information is provided, as it was here, then the plaintiffs are unfortunately out of luck. In law, the inclusion of reservation of rights clauses in an agreement accurately conveys that benefits may be altered or terminated. Thus, the plaintiffs' fiduciary duty claim fails. * * *

CASE QUESTIONS

1. What were the legal issues in this case? What did the court decide?

2. What does it mean for an employer to offer a "lifetime" benefit? Why was the employer able to present the retiree health insurance benefit in this fashion and then discontinue it?

3. Why is a claim for breach of contract not viable in this case?

4. How does the Seventh Circuit's view of the extent of the fiduciary's duty to inform plan participants differ from that of other appeals courts? Which is the better view?

5. What are the practical implications of this case? For plan administrators? For employees and retirees?

DISCRIMINATION AND BENEFITS

Some benefits, including life insurance, disability insurance, and health insurance, are more expensive to provide for older workers. The **Older Workers Benefit Protection Act**,[43] which amended the ADEA, takes account of this fact. *Employers are permitted*

[43]P.L. 101-433, 104 Stat. 978 (1990).

to provide less extensive coverage for older workers, so long as the amount spent to provide benefits to older workers is at least equal to the amount spent providing those benefits to other workers. This cost-equalization principle applies only to welfare plans whose cost is age-related, and not to pension plans. Certain offsets or deductions from benefits received by older workers in exchange for other benefits (e.g., less severance pay in exchange for retiree health insurance) are also permitted. Regarding pensions, plans can establish minimum ages for receipt of pension benefits (e.g., employees must be at least 52 regardless of how many years of service they have) and "normal" retirement ages (e.g., 65). However, as a general rule, *older workers must be allowed to participate in and continue accruing benefits under pension plans regardless of how old they are when first employed or whether their age now exceeds the normal retirement age under the plans.*

Disabled persons have a particularly great need for health insurance. At the same time, this might provide some employers concerned about the rising cost of health insurance with an incentive to discriminate against them. Clearly, *employers cannot refuse to hire or terminate disabled persons based on the assumption, or even fact, that they are more expensive to insure.* Basing employment decisions on disability is disparate treatment and violates the Americans with Disabilities Act. *Employers are also prohibited from discriminating against an employee because that employee is associated with a disabled family member who might be a heavy user of health benefits. An employer also violates the ADA by refusing to provide health coverage to employees with disabilities if health coverage is provided to nondisabled employees.* Thus, the ADA was violated when an employer changed group health plans and the new insurer refused to cover an employee who previously had cancer and was currently afflicted with AIDS.[44] In addition, HIPAA contains rather sweeping language in which *group health plans are prohibited from limiting eligibility based on the health status, medical condition, claims experience, medical history, genetic information, or disability of an employee or dependent.*

The Pregnancy Discrimination Act is another antidiscrimination statute with implications for the design of health plans. The basic principle of the PDA is that pregnant employees are entitled to the same treatment as nonpregnant employees with similar ability to work. *Health plans must cover expenses for pregnancy-related medical care on the same basis as for other medical conditions.* An exception is that health plans can refuse to pay the cost of abortions where the life of the mother is not endangered. Not only must pregnancy-related medical costs be covered, but *health plans are prohibited from imposing additional deductibles or copayments for pregnancy-related treatments.* Additionally, *coverage of pregnancy-related treatment cannot be limited to married employees, and the same level of coverage must be provided for the spouses of male employees as is provided for the spouses of female employees.*

Would it be discrimination for a health plan to refuse to cover the cost of prescription contraceptives when it covers most other kinds of prescription drugs and devices? The EEOC has taken the position that health plans that do not cover the cost of prescription contraceptives when they cover other prescription items are engaging in sex discrimination. At least one court has agreed:

> Male and female employees have different, sex-based disability and healthcare needs, and the law is no longer blind to the fact that only women can get pregnant, bear children, or use prescription contraception. The special or increased healthcare needs associated with a woman's unique sex-based

[44]*Anderson v. Gus Mayer Boston Store*, 924 F. Supp. 763 (E.D. Tex. 1996).

characteristics must be met to the same extent, and on the same terms, as other healthcare needs. . . . [T]he exclusion of women-only benefits from a generally comprehensive prescription plan is sex discrimination under Title VII.[45]

Domestic Partner Benefits

Many people become entitled to benefits through their associations with others. For example, health insurance plans typically allow employees to opt for family coverage to insure their spouses and dependents. To the extent that eligibility to share benefits is based on a marital relationship, persons who are not married but living with another person are disadvantaged. This is particularly true of gays and lesbians, who do not have the option of becoming legally married to their partners.

Because federal law does not prohibit discrimination based on sexual orientation, it also does not require that benefits be made available to domestic partners. The decision of the Montana Supreme Court on constitutional grounds (equal protection of the law) that public universities must provide gay and lesbian employees with health insurance coverage for their domestic partners (see "Clippings") is noteworthy, but its significance is diminished by the fact that it applies only to Montana and public employees in that state (courts in only a few other states have issued similar rulings). For the most part then, employers decide whether to offer **domestic partner benefits**. A number of state and city governments provide domestic partner benefits voluntarily, as do numerous private employers. The Human Rights Campaign Foundation, an advocacy group for gay, lesbian, bisexual, and transgender employees, found that 49 percent of Fortune 500 companies offered domestic partner benefits in 2005.[46] However, relatively low use rates for domestic partner benefits at companies that offer them suggest that gay employees are reluctant to identify themselves to others. Although domestic partner benefits are often made available to both same-sex and opposite-sex partners, a court has ruled that a program limited to same-sex domestic partners does not constitute sex discrimination.[47]

[45]*Erickson v. Bartell Drug Co.*, 141 F. Supp. 2d 1266, at 1271–72 (W.D. Wash. 2001).

[46]Human Rights Campaign Foundation. *Corporate Equality Index*. Washington, DC (2005).

[47]*Foray v. Bell Atlantic*, 56 F. Supp. 2d 327 (S.D.N.Y. 1999).

Chapter SUMMARY

The Employee Retirement Income Security Act (ERISA) is the principal federal law regulating the benefit plans of private-sector employers. ERISA covers plans that defer income for retirement (pension plans), as well as a host of other benefits such as health insurance and severance pay (welfare plans). Under ERISA, employers must provide reports and other information to employees about their benefits,

ensure that promised benefits are actually provided, establish reasonable claims and appeals procedures, manage plans wisely and solely in the interest of beneficiaries, and refrain from interfering with or retaliating against plan participants. Many ERISA cases involve either claims that promised benefits were denied or that there was a breach of fiduciary duty. Fiduciaries are those parties who exercise

discretionary authority or control over the management or administration of a benefit plan or its assets. They have many responsibilities under ERISA, including managing plans in compliance with ERISA and plan documents, exercising skill and prudence, being loyal to the interests of plan participants and beneficiaries, diversifying investments, avoiding conflicts of interest, and not misrepresenting or knowingly withholding material information about benefit plans.

ERISA regulates pension plans more closely than welfare plans. Unlike other benefits, employee pension rights vest after a specified period of service, resulting in a nonforfeitable right to a pension. ERISA's participation rules encourage pension plans to have broad coverage. The law distinguishes between defined benefit and defined contribution pension plans. Defined benefit plans specify a particular benefit that vested employees will receive upon retirement. Defined contribution plans do not promise any particular level of payment upon retirement. Instead, the size of the pension is determined by the sum of money that has accrued in an employee's account as the result of contributions and the manner in which they were invested. Employers with defined benefit plans must comply with many rules intended to ensure that their plans are adequately funded. The Pension Benefit Guaranty Corporation exists to deal with problems created by the termination of defined benefit pension plans and to ensure that vested employees do not lose their pensions in plan terminations.

With defined contribution plans, the risk of producing adequate retirement income is placed squarely with employees. As employers have shifted away from defined benefit plans to defined contribution plans, particularly 401(k)s, many concerns have arisen regarding lack of diversification in investments, lack of good information about investments, delays in or misappropriation of investments, and misuse of administrative mechanisms such as lock-down periods. Cash-balance plans have also raised concerns. Cash-balance plans are defined benefit pensions that have some of the features of defined contribution plans, most notably a hypothetical individual account that tracks the accumulation of pension funds on an individual basis. The conversion from traditional defined benefit plans to cash-balance plans tends to disadvantage older workers and has been challenged under both the ADEA and ERISA.

Health insurance is the most important type of welfare plan covered by ERISA. Increasingly, health care is paid for and provided through managed care organizations, including HMOs. Managed care places constraints on both health-care providers and patients to limit use of services and costs. The efforts of managed care companies to keep costs down have resulted in abuses and in increasing legal challenges to managed care. States have been active in attempting to regulate managed care companies, but ERISA still provides a powerful shield from liability. ERISA stresses uniformity in the legal requirements for benefit plans and preempts state or local laws relating to employee benefit plans.

A major concern of policy makers is the large number of persons in the United States without any health insurance. Because most people obtain health insurance through group health plans sponsored by employers, legislation has aimed at trying to remove obstacles to obtaining coverage and to prevent loss of coverage. COBRA requires that employers provide the option of continuation coverage when qualifying events occur that would otherwise cause coverage to be lost (for the employee or other beneficiaries). These qualifying events include termination for reasons other than gross misconduct, reduction in hours, legal separation or divorce, death of a covered employee, entitlement of a covered employee to Medicare, and loss of dependent child status by a beneficiary. The Health Insurance Portability and Accountability Act (HIPAA) greatly restricts, but does not eliminate, the use of preexisting condition exclusions. HIPAA also makes it illegal for health plans to base eligibility on any aspect of health status. Retirees are subject to loss of health insurance coverage unless they show that their employer intended to confer an irrevocable benefit.

Discrimination in benefits, like other employment opportunities, can be challenged. The ADEA addresses issues related to the greater cost of providing some benefits for older workers and allows adjustments to be made in benefits, provided that employers pay no less toward the benefits of older workers than is expended for younger workers. Employers are prohibited by the ADA from excluding disabled persons from employment opportunities based on concerns about their use of medical services. Under the PDA, pregnancy must be treated like other medical conditions under health plans. Lastly, it is generally up to employers whether to extend benefit coverage to the domestic partners of gay or other unmarried employees.

Practical Advice SUMMARY

- Benefit plans must be detailed in writing in plan documents.

- Summary Plan Descriptions (SPDs) must be
 - written in plain language.
 - sufficiently comprehensive and accurate to inform employees about their rights and responsibilities under benefit plans.
 - provided to employees within 90 days of their becoming covered under benefit plans.

- Employers should be careful in advising employees about their benefits and refer them back to SPDs and other plan documents.

- Benefit plan administrators must
 - base benefit determination decisions on plan documents.
 - have reasons for their decisions.
 - use all the current and appropriate information available to them.

- Employers must establish "reasonable" claims and appeals procedures for their benefit plans. This requirement includes
 - generally making decisions on benefit claims within 90 days (more quickly for claims under health plans).
 - providing written notice when benefits are denied, including the specific reason(s) for the denial.
 - allowing at least 60 days (180 days for group health plans) to appeal adverse decisions regarding benefit claims.

- Parties acting as fiduciaries are responsible for managing benefit plans and funds solely in the interest of plan participants and beneficiaries, and for the purpose of providing them with benefits.

- The duties of fiduciaries include
 - managing plans with skill, care, and prudence.
 - ensuring that plans comply with plan documents and ERISA.
 - diversifying the assets of pension plans to minimize the risk of large losses.
 - selecting proper investments for pension plans and monitoring their performance.
 - refraining from transactions that would create conflicts of interest.
 - providing accurate information about benefit plans and not withholding material facts that would likely affect the choices and interests of beneficiaries.

- Employers must not discharge or otherwise discriminate against employees because they have used benefits to which they are entitled, or to interfere with their use of benefits to which they are entitled.

- Employers with pension plans must allow
 - participants to vest their rights to receive pensions, usually after no more than five or seven years of service.
 - employees who are at least 21 years of age and have served for at least one (if gradual vesting) or two (if cliff vesting) years to participate in pension plans, although other limitations can be imposed.

- Employers with defined contribution plans
 - must ensure that funds deducted from pay are invested no later than 15 days after the end of the month.
 - should offer a range of investment types and investment companies from which employees can choose.
 - should make impartial investment information available to employees.
 - should consider placing limits on investment in company stock and remove company stock as an investment when it is no longer a prudent investment option.
 - should not impose lock-downs for illegitimate purposes.
 - must provide a 30-day notice of blackout periods (i.e., lock-downs).

- Employers converting to cash balance pension plans should
 - proceed with caution.

-*fully inform employees about the nature of this change.*

-*strive to minimize the detrimental effects on older workers.*

• *With just a few exceptions, employers must not establish mandatory retirement ages.*

• *Older workers cannot be denied benefits, but employers can provide less extensive benefits to older workers when*

-*the cost of providing those benefits is greater for older workers.*

-*the total amount spent on benefits for older workers is at least equal to the amount spent for other employees.*

• *Employers with group health plans and at least 20 employees must offer continuation coverage to employees and other beneficiaries who would otherwise lose their health insurance due to one or more qualifying events*

-*an employee can be charged up to 102 percent of the cost of covering the employee under the group health plan for continuation coverage.*

-*information about COBRA continuation coverage must be provided to covered employees and their spouses at the time health plan coverage begins.*

-*notice of the availability of continuation coverage following occurrence of a qualifying event must go to both covered employees and their spouses.*

-*beneficiaries must be given at least 60 days from when their health coverage would end or notice is received, whichever is later, to elect continuation coverage.*

• *Employers should*

-*carefully document when COBRA notifications are sent.*

-*request that all employees respond regardless of whether they are accepting or declining.*

-*maintain up-to-date contact information.*

-*arrange for how payment will be made.*

-*track coverage periods.*

• *When continuation coverage is chosen, that coverage must continue for up to either 18 or 36 months (depending on the qualifying event) unless*

-*the employer discontinues offering group health insurance.*

-*the employee fails to pay.*

-*the employee obtains coverage under another group health plan.*

• *Preexisting condition exclusionary periods*

-*can be applied only to conditions for which diagnosis, care, or treatment was recommended or received within the 6 months prior to plan enrollment (and never to pregnancy).*

-*can last no more than 12 months (18 months for late enrollment).*

-*must be reduced by any periods of prior coverage under a group health plan that ended no more than 63 days before enrollment in the new health plan.*

• *Certificates of creditable coverage must be provided automatically and free of charge to employees when they lose health insurance coverage or exhaust their COBRA continuation coverage.*

• *Employers cannot refuse to hire or terminate disabled persons, or employees with disabled family members, based on concerns about the cost of providing them with health insurance.*

• *Group health plans must not limit eligibility based on health status, medical condition, claims experience, medical history, genetic information, or the disability of an employee or dependent.*

• *Health plans must*

-*cover costs of pregnancy-related medical treatment (except abortion).*

-*not impose any additional deductibles or copayments for such treatments that are not required for other medical treatments.*

-*provide the same level of coverage for pregnancy-related medical treatment to both married and unmarried employees and for the spouses of both male and female employees.*

Key TERMS

Employee Retirement Income
 Security Act (ERISA)
pension plan
welfare plan
preemption
Summary Plan Description (SPD)
abuse of discretion
appeals procedure
fiduciary
fiduciary duties

vesting
participation
defined benefit plan
Pension Benefit Guaranty
 Corporation (PBGC)
defined contribution plan
cash-balance plan
managed care
COBRA (Consolidated Omnibus
 Budget Reconciliation Act)

qualifying events
preexisting condition exclusion
Health Insurance Portability
 and Accountability Act
 (HIPAA)
certificate of creditable coverage
Older Workers Benefit Protection
 Act
domestic partner benefits

Chapter QUESTIONS

1. A number of employees had been laid off for al-most 10 years. Some of the employees had vested pension rights, and others did not. When business picked up, the employer began hiring again, and the employees sought to be rehired. The employer refused to consider the former employees for rehiring because doing so would create greater future pension liability than if persons without any prior service or pension credits were hired. The former employees sued. What should the court decide? Why? (*Becker v. Mack Trucks*, 281 F.3d 372 (3d Cir. 2002); *cert. denied*, 537 U.S. 818 (2002))

2. A flight attendant got into an altercation with another employee while performing between-flight duties on a plane. The flight attendant threw an apple at the other employee, who then threw it back. The flight attendant used a racial epithet to refer to the other employee, who was African American. The two ended up tussling on the floor of the aircraft with choke holds being applied. The fight was eventually broken up by two first-class passengers boarding the plane. Both employees were fired. The airline failed to notify the flight attendant of her right to continuation health coverage, and she sued. What should the court decide? Why? (*Nakisa v. Continental Airlines*, 2001 U.S. Dist. LEXIS 8952)

3. A company terminated an employee and sent him notification of his COBRA rights via certified mail with return receipt requested. The former employee was out of the house on two occasions when the postal service attempted to deliver the letter. It left a note that he could pick it up at the post office. However, when he went to the post office, the letter could not be found. The letter was later found and sent back to the employer marked "undelivered." The employer made no further attempt to contact the former employee. The employee incurred medical expenses for which he wanted continuation coverage. The employer denied continuation coverage because he did not elect it within the required 60 days. The former employee sued. What should the court decide? Why? (*Degruise v. Sprint Corp.*, 279 F.3d 333 (5th Cir. 2002))

4. DuPont amended its pension plan to create a Temporary Pension System (TPS) that would provide an enhanced retirement benefit to employees who chose early retirement. In a written communication detailing the plan, employees were told that "If taken as a lump sum, all or part of the lump sum can be rolled into the DuPont Savings and Investment Plan (SIP) or any other qualified IRA, within 60 days." The advantage of "rolling over" a lump sum payment of this sort is that the employee is able to avoid a large tax payment. However, the communication failed to mention that not all employees would be entitled, under IRS rules, to roll over the TPS payment. Two weeks before the retirement date of an employee who had opted to accept the offer, largely because of the extra benefit that would be free from tax liability, company personnel processing his paperwork became aware that the employee would not be entitled to roll over the funds. The employee was not informed of this and after retiring, he was assessed approximately $50,000 in taxes on the lump sum that he received. He sued. What should the court decide? (*Griggs v. DuPont*, 237 F.3d 371 (4th Cir. 2001))

5. Under a Force Management Plan (FMP) adopted by Lucent in July 2001, employees who were downsized would receive severance pay and other benefits. Employees were told that the facility that they worked at would be closing and that they "should consider themselves FMP'd at some future date." A couple of months later and prior to closure of the facility, several employees were told that they were under investigation for failing to work 40 hours per week at the facility. The employees subsequently received letters indicating that they were being terminated "for cause" and would not be entitled to FMP benefits. The fact that these employees performed some of their work hours off-site had been known by the company for some time. The company had not warned or taken any previous action against the employees for this alleged violation of company policy. The terminated employees sued. What should the court decide? Why? (*Leszczuk v. Lucent Technologies,* 2005 U.S. Dist. LEXIS 11552)

6. An employer's health plan excluded coverage for infertility treatments. An employee who desires to receive treatments for her infertility sues. What should the court decide? Why? (*Lehman v. Adecco North America,* 2001 U.S. Dist. LEXIS 6391)

7. An employee's wife had a liver disease and eventually received a transplant. The employer is a relatively small company that has a self-insured health plan. The wife's numerous treatments caused the company to incur substantial costs. Managers attempted to convince the couple to accept some alternative arrangement for insuring the wife, but no viable alternative existed, and she remained under the plan. The employee was told at one point that the company's options were to fire him or make him an independent contractor without benefits, but nothing was done at the time. About a year later, the employee was fired, and he sued. What should the court decide? Why? (*Jackson v. Service Engineering,* 96 F. Supp. 2d 873 (S.D. Ind. 2000))

8. Is there a need for stronger legal regulation of managed care companies? If so, what kind?

9. What should be the legal responsibility of employers who offer defined contribution plans to their employees?

Internet RESOURCES

This Cornell University Law School site focuses on pension law.

http://www.law.cornell.edu/topics/pensions.html

The Department of Labor site includes an Employee Benefits Security Administration (EBSA) page.

http://www.dol.gov/ebsa/

The Employee Benefits Research Institute includes much information on benefits.

http://www.ebri.org

This News site for HR professionals focuses on benefits topics.

http://www.benefitnews.com

Unions and Collective Bargaining

CLIPPINGS

▶ A study of union organizing campaigns in the city of Chicago in 2002 is the latest in a series of studies finding widespread violations of the National Labor Relations Act (NLRA) when employees attempt to form unions. The Chicago study found that 30 percent of employers faced with organizing campaigns fired one or more workers who engaged in union activity and 49 percent threatened to close or relocate their business if workers voted to unionize.[1]

▶ A strike by mechanics at Northwest Airlines has been going on for months and shows no signs of ending anytime soon. Members of the Aircraft Mechanics Fraternal Association rejected a proposed contract in December 2005. With their jobs outsourced to contractors or filled by permanent replacements, many of the mechanics are unlikely to be recalled when the strike ends.[2]

▶ The Transport Workers' Union, Local 100, agreed to end a three-day strike by New York City bus and subway employees. Strikes by public employees are illegal under New York state law. The union, its officers, and its members were facing the imposition of fines and other severe penalties for the strike. The union and the transit authority will resume contract negotiations.[3]

▶ Bureau of Labor Statistics (BLS) figures show that 12.5 percent of the wage and salary workers were union members in 2004. Government employees are far more likely to be union members (36.4 percent) than are private-sector employees (7.9 percent). Occupations with relatively high unionization rates include protective services (police and fire), educators, construction workers, and transportation employees. Sales workers are among the least likely to be union members. New York, Hawaii, Michigan, and Alaska had the highest rates of unionization, whereas North Carolina and South Carolina had the lowest.[4]

▶ The federal government agency that enforces the NLRA is being criticized for pro-management bias. The National Labor Relations Board (NLRB) is no stranger to charges of shifting with the political winds, but a number of its recent decisions have been controversial and prompted questions as to whether established principles of labor law are being compromised for political reasons.[5]

[1]Chirag Mehta and Nik Theodore. "Undermining the Right to Organize: Employer Behavior During Union Representation Campaigns." Center for Economic Development, University of Illinois at Chicago (December 2005).

[2]"AMFA Members Turn Down Proposal to Settle Strike Against Northwest Airlines." *Daily Labor Report* 02 (January 4, 2006), A-10.

[3]Steven Greenhouse and Sewell Chan. "60-Hour Transit Strike Ends, and New York Cheers." *New York Times* (December 23, 2005), A-1.

[4]Bureau of Labor Statistics. "Union Members in 2004." *News Release* (January 27, 2005).

[5]Steven Greenhouse. "Labor Board's Detractors See a Bias Against Workers." *New York Times* (January 2, 2005), 12.

Most of the law discussed in this book concerns rights conferred on individual employees, such as the rights not to be discriminated against and to be paid at least the minimum wage. The labor laws discussed in this chapter take a fundamentally different approach to protecting workers. Their focus is on protecting employees who join together in groups and seek to engage in collective bargaining with their employers. Rather than legislators, courts, or administrative agencies deciding what is acceptable treatment of employees, collective bargaining allows for employers and employees to decide many of the rules that will govern their workplaces—and to do so on relatively equal terms. This chapter focuses on the principal federal labor law that governs collective bargaining by private-sector employees, the National Labor Relations Act.

Not all employees have union representation. In fact, as the latest BLS figures demonstrate, the vast majority of private-sector employees are not currently unionized (see "Clippings"). This does not negate the importance of understanding the NLRA and other labor laws. For one thing, employees who are currently not represented by unions might opt for unionization at some point in the future. Nonunion employers often have dealings with contractors and suppliers whose employees are unionized. Mergers or acquisitions might bring unionized employees into the fold. Even if an employer does not have any dealings with unionized employees, nonunion employees still have certain rights under the NLRA that must be respected. This chapter highlights how the NLRA applies to nonunion workplaces, including implications for employee involvement teams. The important point is that the *NLRA and other labor laws also affect nonunion workplaces and cannot be safely ignored by those employers.*

THE IDEA OF COLLECTIVE BARGAINING

When people want to get things done, they organize. Joining together with other like-minded people often makes it possible to accomplish objectives that elude individuals acting alone. This is particularly true when employees seek to influence their powerful and well-organized employers. The institution of **collective bargaining** recognizes both the value of employees banding together to deal with their employers and the fact that the desires of employees and employers sometimes clash. Both employers and employees care a great deal about and are apt to disagree on wages, hours, and many other terms and conditions of employment. Collective bargaining provides employees with representation, greater power in dealing with their employers, and a means of resolving issues in ways that meet the requirements of both parties.

Labor unions play a critical role in collective bargaining. Unions are organizations of employees that represent employees in their dealings with employers. Employees have the opportunity to choose, by majority rule, whether they want to have union representation. Unions negotiate with employers to obtain labor agreements—contracts specifying the wages and many other terms and conditions of employment for the employees they represent. However, the collective bargaining process does not end with the signing of labor agreements. Unions have an ongoing role in representing employees, including filing grievances when disputes arise about whether employees' contractual rights have been violated.

There is much to recommend collective bargaining. Providing employees with a means of influencing important workplace issues that directly affect their well-being is entirely consistent with our democratic values. Rather than having to either accept

their employers' dictates or quit, collective bargaining gives employees the opportunity to exert a strong voice in the workplace. Another laudable feature of collective bargaining is that the parties most directly affected by decisions about terms and conditions of employers—the employees and the employers—get to decide the rules by which they will live. As a consequence, the rules contained in labor agreements can be responsive to the particular needs of individual industries, firms, or workplaces—as opposed to government-mandated, one-size-fits-all standards.

Despite these and other benefits, collective bargaining is wildly unpopular with U.S. employers. The reasons for this are simple enough: money and power. Unions do a reasonably good job of increasing the share of corporate revenues claimed by employees and make it more difficult for employers to implement policies not favored by employees. Certainly, employer views vary concerning collective bargaining, but the typical response is hostility. Thus, even though collective bargaining is a vital piece of U.S. public policy governing the workplace, the process of attempting to form unions and bargain with employers is often contentious and produces many legal claims.

The **National Labor Relations Act (NLRA)** is the principal federal law concerning self-organization and collective bargaining by private-sector employees. The **National Labor Relations Board (NLRB)** is the agency that administers the NLRA, including holding elections to determine whether employees desire union representation and determining whether unfair labor practices (ULPs) have been committed. The **Railway Labor Act (RLA)** is a federal labor law that governs collective bargaining in the highly unionized railroad and airline industries. The RLA is administered by the **National Mediation Board (NMB)**. State laws or executive orders provide for collective bargaining by (some or all) state and local government employees in more than 40 states. Collective bargaining by federal government employees is governed by the **Civil Service Reform Act (CSRA)** and overseen by the **Federal Labor Relations Authority (FLRA)**. The details of these labor laws vary, but they share in common procedures for determining desire for union representation as well as provisions to protect employees' right to engage in collective bargaining.

THE NATIONAL LABOR RELATIONS ACT (NLRA)

Because the framers of the NLRA[6] contemplated at least partially conflicting interests between labor and management, supervisors and managers are excluded from its protections. Determining who is a **supervisor** is sometimes problematic. Under the act, supervisors are individuals who have the authority, in the interest of the employer, to make personnel decisions (e.g., hiring, discharge, discipline, and promotion), to responsibly direct other employees, to settle their grievances, or to effectively recommend such actions. To confer supervisory status, these activities must also entail the use of independent judgment. The statutory definition of supervisor is intended to distinguish positions that are genuinely part of management from lower-level employees with some of the trappings of managerial authority (e.g., "leadpersons" on work teams) and from professionals in general (who are covered by the NLRA when they are not supervisors or managers).

One relevant case involved nurses who did not hold administrative or managerial job titles, but who were often the most senior employees on duty, ensured adequate

[6]29 U.S.C.A. § 151 et seq. (2005).

staffing, made daily work assignments for aides, and monitored the work of the less-skilled aides. The Supreme Court disagreed with the NLRB by holding that actions undertaken in the course of providing care to patients can also be supervisory actions taken "in the interest of the employer."[7] In another nurse case, the Supreme Court agreed with the NLRB that employers bear the burden of proving that particular employees are supervisors or managers excluded from the NLRA's protection. However, the Court rejected the NLRB's position that the use of "independent judgment" requisite for supervisory status is not evidenced by the exercise of "ordinary professional or technical judgment in directing less-skilled employees to deliver services in accordance with employer-specified standards."[8] Although these cases are fact-specific and do not mean that all nurses are supervisors, the effect of the Supreme Court's decisions is to deny the NLRA's protections to a group of employees who have shown considerable interest in unionizing and to raise questions about the coverage of other professional employees.

Managerial employees, who "formulate and effectuate management policies by expressing and making operative the decisions of their employer" are also excluded from coverage.[9] It was no doubt news to many professors at Yeshiva University, a private college, when the Supreme Court ruled that they were managers. The Court reasoned that the faculty's role in making decisions about such basic matters as curriculum, hiring faculty, and granting tenure was managerial authority exercised in the employer's interest.[10] Although the *Yeshiva* decision closed the door to the unionization of most faculty at private universities, state public employee collective bargaining statutes have generally been interpreted as covering faculty members. Thus, if you are a student at a public university, the faculty members at your school might be unionized.

Employee Rights Under the NLRA

The NLRA does not directly affect employment outcomes for workers; instead, it provides employees with a means of acting in their own interest to improve their terms and conditions of employment. The fundamental rights conferred by the NLRA (often termed *Section 7 rights*) include the right to do the following:

- Engage in self-organization
- Form, join, or assist labor organizations
- Bargain collectively with their employer through representatives of the employees' own choosing
- Go on strike
- Engage in other concerted activities for the purpose of collective bargaining or other mutual aid or protection
- Refrain from such activities

Concerted Activity The self-organization and concerted activity protected by the NLRA is broadly construed. Concerted or group activity is not confined to formal collective bargaining conducted by unions. Instead, any efforts of employees

[7]*NLRB v. Health Care & Retirement Corp.*, 114 S. Ct. 1778 (1994).

[8]*NLRB v. Kentucky River Community Care*, 121 S. Ct. 1861, at 1867 (2001).

[9]*NLRB v. Bell Aerospace Co.*, 416 U.S. 267, at 288 (1974).

[10]*NLRB v. Yeshiva University*, 444 U.S. 672 (1980).

to join together for "mutual aid or protection" can qualify as protected **concerted activity**—even if those employees are not represented by or attempting to form a union.

NLRB v. Caval Tool Division provides a good illustration of how concerted activity is protected, even in nonunion workplaces.

NLRB V. CAVAL TOOL DIVISION
262 F.3d 184 (2nd Cir. 2001)

● ● ●

OPINION BY JUDGE UNDERHILL:

[T]he ALJ [Administrative Law Judge] held that the respondent, Caval Tool Division, Chromalloy Gas Turbine Corporation ("Caval"), violated...the NLRA by suspending Diane Baldessari ("Baldessari") without pay and placing her on probation, because she challenged a new break policy at a company meeting. He further determined that Caval violated the NLRA by imposing overly broad probationary terms on Baldessari, who was found to have been prohibited from engaging in "protected concerted activity." * * * Caval argues that the ALJ applied an incorrect legal standard in determining that Baldessari's conduct was "concerted activity." * * * We find Caval's arguments to be without merit and, accordingly, enforce the Order. * * *

On August 14, 1998, Caval held a series of informational meetings for its employees, all of which were conducted by Caval's president, Paul Pace. Each meeting included a period for questions and comments. Baldessari, a computer programmer, attended the 11:30 A.M. meeting with other employees holding similar positions. At that meeting, Pace expressed dissatisfaction with worker productivity and "scrap" rates at Caval. * * * Pace also announced a change in the company's break schedule that was intended, at least in part, to address the concerns about worker productivity. Under the new break policy, employees would receive two ten-minute breaks, one in the morning and one in the afternoon, during which they were to take care of all of their personal business. Under the prior break policy, employees received one fifteen-minute break in the morning, but were free to leave their work areas throughout the day to get coffee from the company's vending machines or to attend to personal business.

After Pace announced the new break policy, Baldessari began to question Pace concerning the specifics of the policy. Baldessari first asked Pace if,

under the new policy, employees would no longer be allowed to get coffee throughout the day outside of the designated break time, and if employees would be "written up" if they did so. Pace responded affirmatively to both questions. Baldessari then asked if the new break policy would apply to office employees. Pace responded by asking Baldessari if she would like the policy to apply to office workers. Baldessari responded affirmatively and stated that "it would be nice if things were fair for a change." Pace then stated that the policy would indeed apply to office workers. Baldessari next asked Pace if the new break policy was meant to punish workers for the high "scrap" rate and downtime. After Pace asked Baldessari what she meant, she explained that she felt management was taking a privilege away from the workers (i.e., the ability to get coffee and conduct personal business outside of the designated break times) despite the fact that they had no control over the amount and timing of the work given them. Baldessari blamed management for scheduling problems leading to poor work flow. Pace responded to these comments by asking Baldessari if, to address her concerns, she would like him to fire all of the managers. Baldessari replied that that would be a start, except for one particular manager whom she considered to be a good manager. At that point, Pace expressed displeasure with Baldessari's continued complaints about management, and suggested a Human Resources employee "come up with a package so [Baldessari could] leave." Baldessari ceased her questioning, and the meeting continued.

That afternoon, Baldessari was escorted out of work and was placed on suspension for an indefinite period of time. After receiving permission from Caval, Baldessari returned to work on September 8, 1998 on probationary status for an indefinite term. By memorandum dated August 30, 1999, Baldessari was informed that her probation would be lifted the next day. * * *

[T]he NLRA was enacted "generally to equalize the bargaining power of the employee with that of his employer by allowing employees to band together in confronting an employer regarding the terms and conditions of their employment." To that end, Section 7 guarantees employees certain rights, including the right "to engage in . . . concerted activities for . . . mutual aid or protection." That right is protected through Section 8(a)(1), which provides that it is an unfair labor practice for an employer to "interfere with, restrain, or coerce employees in the exercise of the rights guaranteed in [Section 7]."

The phrase "concerted activity" clearly "embraces the activities of employees who have joined together in order to achieve common goals." Although one could interpret the phrase, 'to engage in concerted activities,' to refer to a situation in which two or more employees are working together at the same time and the same place toward a common goal, the language of § 7 does not confine itself to such a narrow meaning." Rather, that phrase also includes the actions of a single employee, acting alone, who intends to initiate group activity. This is so because, "to protect concerted activities in full bloom, protection must necessarily be extended to intended, contemplated or even referred to group action, lest employer retaliation destroy the bud of employee initiative aimed at bettering terms of employment and working conditions."

In this case, the Board adopted the ALJ's finding that Baldessari's statements during the August 14, 1998 meeting "had the objective of initiating . . . or . . . inducing group action" in response to the company's new break policy and therefore constituted concerted activity. It further adopted the ALJ's finding that Caval suspended Baldessari and placed her on probation because of her questions and comments at the August 14, 1998 meeting. In so doing, the Board concluded that Caval engaged in unfair labor practices . . . * * *

[A]n individual's action must have "some linkage to group action in order for conduct to be deemed 'concerted' within the meaning of Section 7." * * * "[T]he guarantees of . . . the Act extend to concerted activity which in its inception involves only a speaker and a listener, for such activity is an indispensable preliminary step to employee self-organization." Under this longstanding Board doctrine, the speech of an individual employee is "concerted as long as it is engaged in with the object of initiating or inducing . . . group action." The . . . requisite intent to initiate or induce group action could be inferred in the context of a group meeting held to discuss the terms and conditions of employment. * * *

[I]n order properly to conclude that Caval violated Section 8(a)(1), the Board must have found that "the discharge or other adverse personnel action was motivated by the protected activity." * * * The [NLRB's] Order . . . specifically states that "it is clear that [Caval] would have taken no action against Baldessari absent her questions and comments at the meeting." The Board also examines both "Baldessari's questions and comments" concerning the new break policy and her "comments, in response to Pace's question about firing all the managers," and finds both to have been protected activity. Specifically, the Order states that Baldessari's "comments about the impact of the managers' scheduling on the production employees['] productivity flowed from these concerns that production employees were not being treated fairly," and were, therefore "concerted." The Board found that Baldessari's "comments in response to Pace's question about firing all the managers," were "concerted" because, under the circumstances, they bore a direct relationship to her concern that the change in the break policy was meant as punishment for the workers' reduced productivity. Having found that "Baldessari was engaged in protected concerted activity at the August 14, 1998 meeting," the Board then concluded . . . that "it necessarily followed that her suspension that day was unlawful."

Moreover, the Board's findings are supported by substantial evidence. For example, it was reasonable to conclude from the August 28, 1998 letter from Caval to Baldessari (advising her that her suspension would end and a term of probation would begin), that Baldessari was disciplined for all of her comments at the meeting, not simply those aimed at management. Although the letter specifically admonishes Baldessari for having "accused [Pace] of punishing our workers," and for having "stated that all of the managers, except for Ted Cichy, could not do their jobs and should be fired," Caval also more generally chastises Baldessari for having "intentionally provoked an argument over the new coffee break policy." The letter also references Baldessari's prior dissatisfaction with the company and the fact that Baldessari "repeatedly challenged Chromalloy's right to set and enforce policies . . . Finally, the letter makes clear that Baldessari would be terminated if, during her probation, she "engaged in any disruptive behavior," including "challenging [Pace's] right or the right of managers to set policy [and] openly criticizing management decisions." Thus, the record's only written

expression of Caval's reasons for disciplining Baldessari amply supports the Board's findings.

Caval correctly notes that some testimony indicated that Baldessari was terminated for her disruptive conduct, rather than her questions concerning the new break policy. Specifically, Baldessari testified that Pace told her that she was being disciplined because she made him look like a fool during the meeting and disrupted the meeting. Caval's witnesses similarly testified that Baldessari was disciplined for disparaging Pace in front of the other employees. It is true that "the fact that an activity is concerted . . . does not necessarily mean that an employee can engage in the activity with impunity." Moreover, an employee "may engage in concerted activity in such an abusive manner that he loses the protection of § 7." Nevertheless, in other labor contexts, we have held that employees receive "some leeway since passions may run high and impulsive behavior is common." Other courts, as well as the NLRB itself, have held similarly.

The testimony the ALJ found credible supports the finding that Baldessari's comments concerning management, while perhaps not the model of diplomacy, were, under the circumstances, made only in response to Pace's own question, and were directly related to her concern that the new break policy was being instituted as punishment. Accordingly, even if Baldessari's comments concerning management were part of the motivation for disciplining her, her concerted activity did not exceed the bounds of protected conduct for which she may not be disciplined.

CASE QUESTIONS

1. What was the legal issue in this case? What did the court decide?

2. What is the evidence that the employee (Baldessari) was engaging in protected concerted activity?

3. What is the evidence that she was punished for engaging in concerted activity?

4. Why wasn't the employer successful in arguing that she was insubordinate?

5. What should this employer have done differently?

What makes employee actions "concerted"? In general, conduct must be "engaged in with or on the authority of other employees, and not solely by and on behalf of the employee himself" to be concerted.[11] An employee who voices a personal gripe is not engaging in concerted activity. In *Caval Tool*, the individual employee's statements were deemed concerted activity because they were made at an employee meeting, were directed toward a change in employer policy, and most importantly, had the purpose of initiating group action by employees. In another case, a nonunion employee who distributed fliers criticizing the layoffs of coworkers and asking that red ribbons be worn in support of those laid off was found to have engaged in protected concerted activity for mutual aid or support.[12] Likewise, a financial consultant's complaints about his employer's compensation practices and his meeting with other financial consultants to discuss their concerns was protected concerted activity.[13] Evidence of group activity—such as efforts by an individual employee to rally coworkers, discussions among employees, a group of employees approaching management together, or delegation of an employee to speak with management—is generally necessary to demonstrate that activity is concerted. However, for unionized employees, a complaint or grievance that relates to enforcement of rights under a labor agreement is concerted activity, even if the complaint is raised only by an individual. The reason is that this activity is part of the collective bargaining process and clearly affects the rights of all employees covered by the

[11]*Meyers Industries (II)*, 281 N.L.R.B. 882, at 885 (1986), affirmed sub nom., *Prill v. NLRB*, 835 F.2d 1481 (D.C. Cir. 1987).

[12]*United Services Automobie Association v. NLRB*, 387 F.3d 908 (D.C. Cir. 2004).

[13]*Citizens Investment Services Corp.*, 2005 U.S. App. LEXIS 27711.

contract. Thus, an employer violated the NLRA by firing a truck driver who invoked the protections included in his labor agreement when he refused to drive a truck that he honestly believed was unsafe.[14]

To receive protection, an employee's actions must be both "concerted" *and* for the purpose of "mutual aid or support." These two requirements tend to coincide, but are nonetheless distinct. In one of the NLRB's controversial recent decisions (see "Clippings"), the Board decided that an employee who was fired after she attempted to persuade a coworker to testify before a state agency in her harassment case, was not protected by the NLRA.[15] This was so even though the Board determined that she did engage in concerted activity (seeking support from a coworker) and that it was her concerted activity that was the basis for the termination. However, because she was viewed as acting solely to further *her own legal claim,* the concerted activity was not protected.

Even when it is for mutual aid or support, concerted activity by employees is not always protected. For one thing, the activity must be related to employee concerns regarding their wages, hours, terms, and conditions of employment. Secondly, the manner in which the activity is carried out must not be extreme or abusive. Conduct that is flagrant, egregious, or abusive and speech that is malicious, defamatory, or highly profane are not protected. The occasional use of profanity in emotionally charged situations or the ruffling of managerial feathers is not sufficient to cause a loss of protection. In *Caval Tool,* the employee was protected even though her comments about management were "not the model of diplomacy." Likewise, an employee's persistent hounding of management to answer a question regarding his contractual rights, although perhaps overdone, was "not so flagrant or egregious as to leave him unprotected."[16] In contrast, a nurse who made statements on a television program alleging that the hospital was "jeopardizing the health of mothers and babies" by cutting staff was not protected by the NLRA. Although her conduct (which occurred in the midst of efforts to organize a union) was concerted activity, it was not protected "because her false and disparaging public statements alienated her from her most important coworkers and made her continued employment untenable."[17]

Company policies can run afoul of the NLRA due to the constraints that they place on concerted activity. "Pay secrecy" policies that restrict employees from talking with one another about the central issue of wages are invalid for this reason (see Chapter 12). Policies limiting "solicitation" and access to the workplace are also problematic. A casino restaurant's rules that employees could not report to the "property" more than 30 minutes prior to the start of shifts or remain longer than 30 minutes after shifts, and that employees were prohibited from returning to the "premises" during unscheduled hours other than as paying guests, were struck down by the NLRB.[18] Similarly, a policy prohibiting "negative conversations" about coworkers or managers violated the NLRA due to the likelihood that employees would view the rule as prohibiting complaints about management decisions.[19] However, another employer's more general rules prohibiting "abusive and profane language," "harassment," and "verbal, physical, and mental abuse" were deemed lawful. Although these rules could conceivably be invoked to punish employees

[14]*NLRB v. City Disposal Systems,* 465 U.S. 822 (1984).

[15]*Holling Press,* 343 NLRB No. 45 (2004).

[16]*Union Carbide v. NLRB,* 2001 U.S. App. LEXIS 26594, at 14.

[17]*St. Luke's Episcopal-Presbyterian Hospitals v. NLRB,* 268 F.3d 575, at 582 (8th Cir. 2001).

[18]*Ark Las Vegas Restaurant Corp.,* 343 NLRB No. 126 (2004).

[19]*KSL Claremont Resort,* 344 NLRB No. 105 (2005).

criticizing management or seeking to persuade their coworkers to unionize, the NLRB determined that the rules did not explicitly restrict protected activity. Thus, for the rules to be invalidated, there would have to be evidence that employees would reasonably construe the language to prohibit protected activity, the rules were created in response to protected activity, or the rules had been applied to restrict such activity. None of these were shown.[20] Applying the same principles, the NLRB also upheld a rule prohibiting security guards from at any time fraternizing or "becoming overly friendly" with coworkers or employees of client companies. In the Board's view, "employees would reasonably understand the rule to prohibit only personal entanglements, rather than activity protected by the Act."[21]

Employers, in both unionized and nonunion workplaces, must respect the right of employees to join together in contesting or expressing concerns regarding their terms and conditions of employment. Policies that limit this right should not be maintained or enforced.

Unfair Labor Practices (ULPs)

To protect employees' rights to self-organization and give collective bargaining a chance to work, the NLRA prohibits certain actions by employers and unions. These unfair labor practices (ULPs) are listed here.

Employers must refrain from the following activities:

1. *Interfering with, restraining, or coercing employees in the exercise of their rights under the NLRA*

2. *Dominating or interfering with the formation or administration of a labor organization*

3. *Discriminating against employees for the purpose of encouraging or discouraging membership in any labor organization*

4. *Retaliating against employees for filing charges or giving testimony under the act*

5. *Refusing to engage in collective bargaining*

Labor organizations must refrain from the following activities:

1. *Restraining or coercing employees in the exercise of their rights under the act*

2. *Causing an employer to discriminate against an employee for the purpose of encouraging or discouraging membership in a labor organization*

3. *Refusing to engage in collective bargaining*

4. *Broadening labor disputes to include neutral employers ("secondary boycott")*

5. *Charging excessive or discriminatory initiation fees or dues*

6. *Causing an employer to pay for work not performed ("featherbedding")*

7. *Picketing for more than 30 days for the purpose of obtaining union recognition*

Because our primary concern is with the legal obligations of employers, we will focus on employer ULPs. The first category of employer ULP—interfering with, restraining, or coercing employees in the exercise of their NLRA rights—encapsulates employers' legal obligations under the NLRA. The remaining employer ULPs are

[20]*Lutheran Heritage Village-Livonia*, 343 NLRB No. 75 (2004).

[21]*Guardsmark, LLC*, 344 NLRB No. 97 (2005).

elaborations on this general requirement. The cases discussed earlier involving employees being terminated or otherwise disadvantaged for engaging in protected concerted activity exemplify employer interference with and restraint of NLRA rights.

The prohibition against employer domination of a **labor organization** or interference in its administration (including providing financial support) requires more explanation. The underlying notion is that to be bona fide employee representatives, labor organizations must be independent of employers. The requirement of independence holds not just for labor unions, but also for labor organizations of any kind. The definition of labor organization under the NLRA is broad. A labor organization is "any organization . . . or employee representation committee or plan, in which employees participate and which exists for the purpose, in whole or in part, of dealing with employers concerning grievances, labor disputes, wages, rates of pay, hours of employment, or conditions of work."[22] Clearly, employers are prohibited from creating or controlling "company unions" that do not genuinely represent employees' interests. But does the NLRA also throw into question the wide variety of employee involvement groups and work teams that employers now use?

[22]29 U.S.C.A. §152(5)(2005).

THE CHANGING WORKPLACE

Employee Involvement and the NLRA

Employees have always been "involved" in the workplace; after all, they do the work. The idea of the employee-involvement or participation programs that have proliferated in the past few decades is to improve productivity, quality, and organizational effectiveness by including employees in decisions previously reserved for management and eliciting their active involvement in solving organizational problems. Employee involvement takes many forms but typically involves groups of employees interacting in some fashion with managers to discuss production, safety, and other issues.

The NLRA comes into the picture because employee-involvement groups can be deemed "labor organizations" dealing with employers regarding employment matters. And if the groups are labor organizations, then they will almost certainly be considered "dominated," because they are initiated by employers. Thus, their existence can violate the NLRA.

In one important case, a nonunion employer responded to employee dissatisfaction by creating a number of "action teams." The teams included employee representatives and managers. Separate teams were created to deal with the issues of absenteeism, no-smoking policy, communication, pay progressions, and an attendance bonus program. The teams were eventually disbanded after a union organizing campaign began, but the NLRB ruled, and an appeals court affirmed, that the teams violated the NLRA.[1] The teams constituted labor organizations because employees participated, and they dealt with management regarding the types of issues typically taken up in collective bargaining. The decision stressed that "dealing with" is not limited to formal negotiations. When, as in this case, there is an exchange of views between employees and management and an attempt to influence decision outcomes, there is "dealing." Some board members also attributed particular significance to the fact that employees on the action teams were expected to represent the views of other employees. The action teams were also employer-dominated. The employer initiated the teams, established their purpose, limited the number of teams employees could serve on, provided materials, and paid employees for their time.

A unionized employer also violated the NLRA by setting up company dominated employee-involvement teams that dealt with such issues as safety and benefits. Furthermore, the Board concluded that the employer was bypassing the employee's representative and not meeting its legal obligation to bargain only with the union on these issues.[2] However, the law was not violated when a unionized employer sought employee volunteers to serve on a committee to make recommendations regarding the process for selecting "crew leaders." The recommendation was used by the employer to

formulate its own proposal in bargaining over the issue with the union.[3] Nor was the NLRA violated when a nonunion company created seven employee committees that functioned as "self-managing" work teams. The Board concluded that because the decision-making authority on a range of issues was delegated to the teams and the plant manager rarely overruled committee recommendations ". . . it cannot be doubted that each committee exercises as a group authority that in the traditional plant setting would be considered to be supervisory. . . . [T]he seven committees are not labor organizations because their purpose is to perform essentially managerial functions, and thus they do not "deal with" the [employer]. . . ."[4]

[1] *Electromation, Inc.,* 309 NLRB 990 (1992), *enforced, Electromation, Inc. v. NLRB,* 35 F.3d 1148 (7th Cir. 1994).
[2] *E.I. DuPont & Co.,* 311 NLRB 893 (1993).
[3] *Georgia Power Company,* 342 NLRB No. 18, slip op. (2004).
[4] *Crown Cork & Seal Company,* 334 NLRB 699, at 701 (2001).

So, what should employers do in light of the potential conflict between the NLRA and employee involvement? Legal challenges to employee involvement teams resulting in the NLRB ordering them disbanded have been relatively few in number (one study found an average of less than two such cases per year between 1983 and 1993).[23] The primary strategy for conforming employee involvement teams to the NLRA is to ensure that the teams do not have the characteristics of labor organizations. One way this is done is by delegating substantial decision-making authority to the teams. Because the teams then perform essentially managerial functions, they did not exist to "deal with" the employer. The element of bilateral dealing with an employer is also absent when an employee-involvement mechanism amounts to a one-way transfer of suggestions or ideas, such as with brainstorming groups or "suggestion boxes." On the other hand, groups in which employees represent the views of other employees are more likely to be viewed as labor organizations. The issues dealt with are also relevant. Employee-involvement teams confined to such matters as productivity, quality, and customer satisfaction are unlikely to be viewed as labor organizations. However, it can be difficult to maintain a clear distinction between these issues and employment issues (e.g., discussions of productivity might lead to consideration of work schedules and rules), so employers have to be vigilant in explaining the boundaries of employee-involvement groups and policing those limits.

Thus, *employers that use employee involvement mechanisms should structure them so that employees do not serve in a representative capacity, the teams are given substantial decision-making authority, communication is not bilateral, and/or their focus is on productivity rather than employment issues. Additionally, employee-involvement teams should never be instituted in response to a union organizing campaign as a means of offering an "alternative" to unionization. And when a union already represents a group of workers, employee involvement teams must not be used to decide matters that are properly part of collective bargaining.*

Employers also commit a ULP by discriminating against employees for the purpose of either encouraging or discouraging membership in a labor organization. Thus, employers cannot refuse to hire, fire, demote, or otherwise limit the employment opportunities of employees because they are known or suspected to be union activists or supporters. As in other disparate treatment discrimination cases, proving the motive for a challenged employment decision is crucial. However, a somewhat different approach is used in NLRA cases.[24]

[23] James R. Rundle. "The Debate over the Ban on Employer-Dominated Labor Organizations: What Is the Evidence?" pp. 161–76 in Sheldon Friedman et al., eds., *Restoring the Promise of American Labor Law* (Ithaca, NY: ILR Press, 1994).
[24] *NLRB v. Transportation Management Corp.,* 103 S. Ct. 2469 (1983).

ELEMENTS OF A CLAIM

Discrimination Under the NLRA

To establish a prima facie case of discrimination, the General Counsel of the NLRB must show the following:

1. The employee engaged in protected activity.

2. The employer was aware of the protected activity.

3. The employer demonstrated hostility toward the protected activity.

4. There was a causal connection between this hostility and the decision to deny an employment opportunity.

If a prima facie case is established, the NLRA is violated unless the employer can show that the same decision would have been made regardless of whether the employee engaged in protected activity.

The NLRB bears the burden of establishing a prima facie case that an employee's protected conduct was a motivating factor in the employment decision. If this prima facie showing is made, the employer will be found in violation of the NLRA unless it can show that it would have made the same employment decision absent the illegal motivation (i.e., the employee's union activity). In one such case, a mechanic applied for work on a highway construction project. Despite having been referred from the union hiring hall (the typical procedure for filling such jobs) and being well qualified, the company declined to hire the mechanic. In a letter to the union, the company cited "past performance and personality conflicts" (the mechanic had worked on other projects with this construction company) as its reason for not hiring him. The mechanic questioned the company owner about the alleged personality conflict and the owner said that "maybe you was too union for us." The NLRB found for the mechanic on his discrimination charge, and on appeal, a court agreed.[25]

UNION ORGANIZING AND REPRESENTATION ELECTIONS

Legal claims under the NLRA, particularly charges of interference with self-organization and discrimination against union supporters, are especially common during periods when employees are attempting to form unions. The NLRA places many constraints on employer behavior under these circumstances. The act also spells out a set of procedures for holding representation elections to determine whether employees desire union representation.

Union Organizing Campaigns

Why are there unions in some workplaces but not others? Unions are formed over a period of time—sometimes months, sometimes years—in which employees dissatisfied with their terms and conditions of employment become convinced that unionization is the best way to improve their lot. As an organizing campaign develops momentum,

[25]*Mashuda Corp. v. NLRB*, 135 Fed. Appx. 574 (4th Cir. 2005).

there is typically much discussion and persuasion among workers, distribution of literature, wearing of buttons and other symbols of support for unionization, rallies, and requests to sign petitions or "authorization cards" (indicating desire for representation). Nonemployee organizers from established unions often play an important leadership role, but for the most part, employees organize themselves. At some point, if sufficient support is enlisted, the NLRB might be petitioned to hold an election to determine whether a union will be certified as the legal representative of the employees.

What does the NLRA require of employers when their employees are attempting to organize a union? The basic principle of not interfering with, coercing, or restraining employees in the exercise of their rights has some particular implications for employer conduct during organizing campaigns. *Multi-Ad Services v. NLRB* illustrates some of the actions that employers must avoid when responding to organizing activity by employees.

MULTI-AD SERVICES V. NLRB
255 F.3d 363 (7th Cir. 2001)

OPINION BY CIRCUIT JUDGE RIPPLE:

This petition asks us to review whether Multi-Ad Services, Incorporated ("Multi-Ad") violated the National Labor Relations Act ("Act") by interfering with its employees' efforts to form a union. The National Labor Relations Board ("Board") concluded that Multi-Ad violated . . . the Act by (1) coercively interrogating employee Ted Steele about his interest in forming a union; (2) impliedly promising to help Mr. Steele improve his employment situation without the need for union representation; and (3) threatening to close one of its departments if that department's employees unionized. The Board also concluded that Multi-Ad violated . . . the Act by discharging Mr. Steele because it believed that he might contact a union to organize employees. [W]e deny the petition for review and grant enforcement of the Board's order. * * *

[T]he Act guarantees employees the right to self-organization by forming, joining, or assisting labor organizations. The Board concluded that Multi-Ad's actions violated §§ 8(a)(1) and (a)(3) of the Act. Section 8(a)(1) protects the right to self-organization by prohibiting employers from interfering with, restraining, or coercing employees in the exercise of their right to form a union. It is therefore an unfair labor practice to threaten an employee with shop closure or

discharge or to interrogate coercively an employee in order to discourage union activities. An employer also violates § 8(a)(1) by offering benefits to potential union supporters to prevent them from exercising the right to unionize. In deciding whether an employer's conduct is forbidden by the Act, we must determine whether that conduct reasonably tended to interfere with or coerce employees exercising their protected rights. The words used by the employer, as well as the context in which they were conveyed, must be examined. In determining what an employee reasonably might have inferred from a communication, the Board must consider the employee's economic dependence on the employer and that employee's concomitant tendency to pick up intended implications that might be more readily dismissed by a more disinterested ear.

Section 8(a)(3) makes it an unfair labor practice for an employer to discourage union activity by discriminating against employees with regard to hire or tenure of employment. In evaluating an allegation under § 8(a)(3), the Board must ascertain the employer's motivation in taking a particular action. This determination often must be based on circumstantial evidence. When an employee's statutorily protected activity motivated a discharge, a violation has been established unless the employer demonstrates that it would have taken the same action in the absence of the employee's protected activity. * * *

Whether an employer's questioning of an employee is coercive depends on the factual context in which the questioning occurs. The test is not whether coercion actually occurred, but only whether the employee perceived the employer's actions to be coercive. Factors that ought to be considered in deciding whether a particular inquiry is coercive include the tone, duration, and purpose of the questioning, whether it is repeated, how many workers are involved, the setting, the authority of the person asking the question, and whether the company otherwise had shown hostility to the union. We also consider whether questions about protected activity are accompanied by assurances against reprisal and whether the interrogated worker feels constrained to lie or give noncommittal answers rather than answering truthfully.

Substantial evidence supports the Board's conclusion that management coercively interrogated Mr. Steele on August 16. The closed-door meeting was conducted in a manager's office by Heathcoat and Ireland, two people who had authority to fire Mr. Steele. The two managers questioned Mr. Steele regarding why he would want to bring a union into the company. Moreover, Ireland immediately thereafter asked Mr. Steele about his own career advancement and arranged an interview for a maintenance position, even though no such opening existed. The managers did not assure Mr. Steele that reprisals would not be taken against him for his answers, adding to the potentially coercive nature of the inquiry. Further, this meeting was conducted after company managers had expressed uneasiness over union activity. These circumstances are more than enough evidence to sustain the Board's findings.

Multi-Ad next challenges the Board's finding that it made an implied promise of benefits by asking Mr. Steele how he could help his own situation and by arranging the job interview. An employer violates the Act when it interferes with the employees' exercise of their rights to organize by soliciting grievances when such solicitation is accompanied by implied promises of benefits specifically aimed at deterring union activity. Here, Ireland asked Mr. Steele why he wanted to form a union and then asked Mr. Steele how Mr. Steele could improve his own situation. Mr. Steele expressed an interest in a maintenance position, and Ireland arranged for an interview immediately, even though there were no such openings. The context in which this occurred is significant. Because the managers made this overture during a conversation about the need for a union, the

Board reasonably could have concluded that the company was willing to confer a benefit to deter Mr. Steele from contacting a union. Thus, given the circumstances in which the managers discussed Mr. Steele's career advancement, substantial evidence supports the Board's conclusion that Ireland's remarks constituted an implied promise of benefits to dissuade Mr. Steele from contacting a union.

Next, Multi-Ad argues that substantial evidence does not support the Board's conclusion that Multi-Ad threatened to close the bindery department. Unlike an interrogation, which is coercive only if reasonable employees would perceive it as such, a threat of plant closure is per se a violation of § 8(a)(1). In this case, three employees testified unequivocally that DeRossett said that the bindery department would be the "first to go" if they brought in a union, and this evidence is more than sufficient to establish a violation.

An employer violates §§ 8(a)(1) or (3) of the Act by firing employees because of their union activities. * * * To establish that anti-union animus was a substantial or motivating factor in a discharge, the Board must demonstrate that (1) the employee engaged in union activities; (2) the employer knew of the employee's involvement in protected activities; (3) the employer harbored animus toward those activities; and (4) there was a causal connection between the employer's animus and its decision to discharge. * * * Multi-Ad challenges only the third element, but substantial evidence supports a finding that the company harbored animus, including (1) the timing of Mr. Steele's firing, which coincided with his increased efforts to organize a union; (2) the coercive interrogation of Mr. Steele regarding his interest in forming a union; (3) management's questioning of other employees about their interest in forming a union; and (4) DeRossett's warning that the bindery department would close if employees unionized. Thus, the Board met its burden of establishing anti-union animus.

Multi-Ad claims . . . that it fired Mr. Steele for leaving three meetings without permission. The Board concluded, however, that Multi-Ad's proffered reason was pretextual and that the company fired Mr. Steele because of his efforts to unionize. That conclusion is supported by substantial evidence, including (1) Multi-Ad's written explanation of termination stating a different reason—that he was discharged because he refused to abide by corporate policies; (2) the September 4 encounter was not a "meeting"—Mr. Steele entered

the office to pick up materials to which he was legally entitled and twice denied access; and (3) no manager instructed Mr. Steele to remain at the previous two meetings, both of which occurred after shift hours. Thus, substantial evidence supports the Board's conclusion that Multi-Ad fired Mr. Steele because of his union activity and that its stated reasons for doing so were pretextual.

CASE QUESTIONS

1. What were the legal issues in this case? What did the court decide? Why?

2. What things did the employer do wrong in responding to the nascent union-organizing campaign?

3. What should the employer have done instead?

Employer Responses to Union Organizing

Employers faced with organizing campaigns might be tempted to ask employees about their attitudes toward having a union or whether they intend to vote for a union. In *Multi-Ad Services*, the employer asks Mr. Steele and other employees why they wanted to have a union. Making these types of inquiries is not a per se (automatic) violation of the NLRA,[26] but it tends to be intimidating and coercive, even if not accompanied by explicit threats. Employees are apt to suspect that their employer wants this information to single out union supporters for disadvantageous treatment. Under certain, limited circumstances, systematic polling of employees regarding their union views is allowed, but by and large, *employers should refrain from either interrogating individuals or polling employees to find out who supports unionization, why employees want a union, and how employees intend to vote in a representation election.* Videotaping or photographing employees engaged in lawful organizing activity is also likely to be intimidating and violate the NLRA.[27]

Although some employers agree to remain neutral during organizing campaigns, the NLRA does not require that employers remain on the sidelines. Employers are generally free to make their views about the merits of unionization known to employees. Except for the 24-hour period immediately preceding a NLRB representation election, employers are free to require employees to attend meetings ("captive audience meetings") where the employer's views about unionization are presented.[28] For that matter, employers (and unions) are generally free to engage in another staple of electoral politics—lying. The NLRB does not police the truthfulness of statements made in the course of organizing campaigns, unless the Board's processes are misrepresented, forged documents are presented, or inflammatory appeals based on racism are made.

However, *employers (and unions) are prohibited from making statements that contain threats of reprisal or force or promises of benefit.* In *Multi-Ad Services*, the company's apparent attempt to co-opt the leader of the budding unionization drive by arranging an interview for a job that he desired is an example of promising benefits to interfere with self-organization. Multi-Ad also used the opposite tack; it threatened employees that their department would be closed down if they unionized. Typical threats include claims that unionization will inevitably result in plant closure, loss of employment, diminished wages or benefits, and strikes. More subtle, but

[26]*Hotel & Restaurant Employees, Local 11 v. NLRB,* 760 F.2d 1006 (9th Cir. 1985).

[27]*The Timken Co. v. NLRB,* 29 Fed. Appx. 266 (6th Cir. 2002).

[28]*Peerless Plywood Co.,* 107 N.L.R.B. 427 (1953).

potentially unlawful, are employer claims that unionization will be futile. In one such case, employees were told that bargaining would "start at zero" (implying that the outcome would be inferior to current terms), the union would likely seek to gain control of the 401(k) plan resulting in loss of the plan, and work could be quickly shifted to another facility if a strike occurred. The Board concluded, and a court agreed, that these statements constituted unlawful threats.[29] *Employers must refrain from threatening employees as a means of influencing their decisions regarding unionization.*

Although employees cannot be threatened, employers can make "predictions" about the likely consequences that unionization will have for the business—consequences that are objectively probable due to economic reality that is beyond the employer's control.[30] An employer violated the NLRA by making each of the following statements: that a client company could terminate its contract with the employer if the union won the election; employees might lose their jobs; and the employer would close down the business if employees unionized.[31] Although the first two comments were relatively conditional, the Board viewed them as more akin to threats than predictions because they lacked any objective basis and they were explicitly linked to the unionization decision. Threats that violate the NLRA might still not warrant the holding of a new election. In one case, an employee was told by a production manager shortly before a representation election that, if the employees voted to unionize, the employer would move the facility at the end of the year when the lease expired. The union lost the election by a slim margin and asked the NLRB to order a rerun election due to the illegal threat. The Board decided that in such cases the objecting union bears the burden of proving that the threat made to one or a few employees had spread throughout the larger workforce. Dissemination of the coercive threat would not be presumed.[32]

Providing, rather than merely promising, benefits is also problematic. After *an organizing campaign is underway, and especially if an election has been ordered, employers risk violating the NLRA if they raise wages or make other previously unscheduled changes in employment benefits.* Although this might seem like a reasonable way to respond to dissatisfied employees, it is usually done as a last-ditch effort to sway employees prior to an impending election. Overnite Trucking, faced with organizing campaigns at a number of its service centers, violated the law with a pay raise because the raise was virtually simultaneous with several elections, it was the second pay raise in several months and a departure from the company's usual practice, and it occurred in the context of other ULPs committed by the company. In contrast, a pay increase the following year was not a ULP because it occurred at the usual time for pay increases and few elections were pending.[33]

Multi-Ad's termination of Mr. Steele for his organizing activity illustrates an all-too-common occurrence. *Employers must not discharge or otherwise discriminate against employees because of their efforts to organize a union.* This does not mean that employees can never be terminated in the midst of organizing campaigns. But terminations under these circumstances are suspect, particularly if the employer offers conflicting reasons, the discipline is unusually harsh, or the termination is for behavior that has been condoned in the past. Despite the clear legal requirement to

[29]*Federated Logistics and Operations,* 400 F.3d 920 (D.C. Cir. 2005).

[30]*NLRB v. Gissel Packing Co.,* 395 U.S. 575, at 618 (1969).

[31]*Tellepsen Pipeline Services Co.,* 335 N.L.R.B. 88 (2001).

[32]*Crown Bolt, Inc.,* 343 NLRB No. 86 (2004) (this new rule was applied prospectively, rather than to the case at hand).

[33]*Overnite Transportation Co. v. NLRB,* 280 F.3d 417 (4th Cir. 2002).

refrain from discharging employees for their union organizing activity, studies show that discriminatory discharges of union activists occur regularly (see "Clippings"). These terminations are a clear affront to the rule of law and any sense of fair play. Claims that employees are no longer interested in unionization carry little weight when employers regularly resort to terminations, and the threat of terminations, to defeat employees' desire for unions.

The high degree of control over employee conduct exercised by many employers must give way somewhat to the right of employees to organize. *In general, employers must allow employees to engage in discussions about unionization in the workplace during nonwork time.* However, restriction of organizing to nonwork time presupposes that the employer has a fairly enforced, nondiscriminatory policy prohibiting other forms of "solicitation" during work time. In some workplaces (e.g., hospitals, retail stores), organizing can be restricted to nonwork areas. *In general, employees must be allowed to wear union buttons or display other insignias and to engage in activities such as lunchtime rallies.*

Nonemployee organizers (e.g., union employees, community activists) who assist employees in forming unions are often critical to employees acting on their rights under the NLRA; however, providing outsiders with access to employees often clashes with the property rights of employers. In one important case, nonemployee organizers sought to communicate with the employees of a retail store. The store was located in a shopping center with a parking lot. The store was part-owner of the privately owned lot. When organizers attempted to place handbills on the windshields of employee cars, the store had the organizers removed from the parking lot. The Supreme Court held that as long as the location of a workplace and the living quarters of employees do not place them beyond the reach of reasonable communication means, nonemployee organizers need not be provided with access to employees on the private property of employers.[34] Because the union in this case had some ability to contact employees at their homes and to communicate with employees in a public area located between the parking lot and a highway, the employer did not violate the NLRA by barring the nonemployee organizers. The examples cited by the Court of cases in which private property rights would have to yield to organizing efforts (remote logging and mining camps) suggest that accommodation of nonemployee organizers is rarely required. Thus, *provided that nonemployee organizers have some viable means of communicating with employees, employers with nondiscriminatory no-solicitation policies can deny nonemployee organizers access to workplaces and private property surrounding them.*

The employee/nonemployee dichotomy ignores another significant category of potential union organizers—employees of the same company who work at other facilities. Such "offsite employees" have a direct stake in the success of union organizing at other facilities: "'when offsite employees seek to organize similarly situated employees at another employer facility, the employees seek strength in numbers to increase the power of their union and ultimately to improve their own working conditions.'"[35] The NLRB and courts have generally held that off-site employees must be allowed access to nonwork areas surrounding the workplace, even if these are otherwise treated as private property by the employer.

Questions remain about exactly what areas are private, particularly in workplaces that are open to the public. In a case involving nonemployee organizers distributing literature and picketing in a privately owned parking lot and walkway outside of a grocery store, the court concluded that the grocery store owner violated

[34]*Lechmere Inc. v. NLRB*, 112 S. Ct. 841 (1992).

[35]*ITT Industries v. NLRB*, 413 F.3d 64, at 70-1 (D.C. Cir. 2005).

the NLRA by having the organizers removed.[36] The key difference from the Supreme Court case cited earlier was that, under California state law, the peaceful exercise of free speech is favored over property rights in areas open to the public, such as shopping centers and malls. State property laws, not the NLRA, determine whether employers have property rights to assert in denying access to nonemployee organizers.

Representation Election Procedures

The NLRA (in common with other labor laws) sets out procedures for determining employee choice through **representation elections**. But the next question is which employees will be represented? Employees of a company hold many different job titles and are often spread across numerous workplaces, departments, and divisions. The NLRB is responsible for ensuring that the group of employees for which representation is being sought constitutes an **appropriate bargaining unit**. This determination is very important. As every gerrymandering politician knows, the outcome of an election is often a direct function of how the electorate is defined. Furthermore, if union representation is chosen, the success of collective bargaining is affected by whether the employees in the bargaining unit have sufficient common interests.

For the most part, the NLRB determines the appropriateness of proposed bargaining units on a case-by-case basis. The primary criterion used by the Board is whether the employees "share a community of interest." Among the indicators used to determine community of interest are similarity in skill levels, interrelationship of tasks, and common pay systems, supervision, and personnel policies. Certain provisions of the NLRA also limit the makeup of bargaining units. For example, professional employees cannot be included in bargaining units with nonprofessionals unless a majority of the professional employees choose to be included in such units. Plant guards and other security personnel cannot be included in bargaining units with other employees under any circumstances.

The typical (but not the only) path to union representation under the NLRA proceeds from an organizing campaign to employees (or a union on their behalf) petitioning the NLRB to hold a representation election. One of the main requirements for the Board to order an election is a showing that at least 30 percent of the employees in an appropriate bargaining unit desire union representation. This showing is typically made by employees signing **authorization cards**. To be valid, these cards must be current and indicate a desire for representation by a particular union (as opposed to merely the holding of an election). Under the NLRB's formal certification process, the authorization cards are not the representation election itself, but rather evidence that an election is warranted. The Board will not hold repeated elections for the same group of workers. If there was a prior election within the past 12 months, an election will not be ordered (this is known as the *election bar*). Also, if the employees are already represented by a union and covered by a collective bargaining agreement, an election to change representatives will be ordered only during a brief window period prior to contract expiration or after contract expiration (the *contract bar*).

If an election is ordered, the employer is required to provide to the NLRB within seven days, a list of names and addresses of all employees in the bargaining unit to give the union a chance to contact all employees who might be interested in unionization.

[36]*NLRB v. Calkins*, 187 F.3d 1080 (9th Cir. 1999), *cert. denied*, 529 U.S. 1098 (2000).

During this time between when an election is ordered and when the election is held, employer and union conduct is subject to particularly close scrutiny. Misconduct by an employer or union that upsets the "laboratory conditions" for free choice by employees can cause the NLRB to order a rerun election, even without a finding that the misconduct amounts to a ULP.[37] In rare cases, an employer's misconduct prior to an election is so severe that the Board will certify a union that had shown majority support through authorization cards and require the employer to bargain, even though the union lost the election.[38] Representation elections are secret ballot elections held under the supervision of the NLRB and generally in the workplace during work time. Election observers can be chosen, but these must not be managers or supervisors. If the majority of employees who actually cast votes choose union representation, the NLRB will certify the union as the "exclusive representative" of all employees in the bargaining unit.

Although the usual purpose of elections is to determine whether currently unrepresented employees desire representation, the NLRA also provides for **decertification elections** in which employees decide whether they want to continue to have union representation. *Employers cannot petition for decertification elections to be held, nor interfere by encouraging employees to decertify their unions.*

Voluntary recognition of a union by an employer is also permitted, provided there is evidence of majority support for the union. Frustrated by delays and by what they see as employer manipulation of the representation election process, unions are increasingly seeking to obtain recognition through a **card check procedure**. In general, this entails obtaining the employer's agreement to recognize the union if a majority of employees signs authorization cards. A neutral third party is designated to verify the results. Under this procedure, authorization cards serve as the decisive indicators of employee preference and not merely as means to obtain elections. Use of a card check procedure expedites representation determinations and is associated with a very high union win rate.[39] The NLRB is currently considering the deference that should be given to this type of voluntary recognition,[40] and legislators have drafted various bills both supporting and prohibiting use of the card check procedure.

The union's status as **exclusive representative** is important. In practice, it means that *unionized employers must generally refrain from dealing with individual employees regarding their wages, hours, terms, and conditions of employment.* Even if an individual employee is willing to accept terms other than those provided for under the labor agreement, deals of this sort are not permitted. It also means that the union represents all employees in the bargaining unit, regardless of whether those employees voted for the union or want it now.

Representation by a union is distinct from membership. Many employees choose to become union members. However, because a union is legally required to represent all the employees in a bargaining unit and some employees might be tempted to "free-ride" by receiving representation without paying for it, unions commonly negotiate with employers to include union security provisions in their labor agreements. There are different types of **union security** provisions (e.g., union shop, agency shop), but in general these clauses require all employees in a bargaining unit

[37]*General Shoe Corp.,* 77 N.L.R.B. 124 (1948).

[38]*Gissel Packing.*

[39]Adrienne E. Eaton and Jill Kriesky. "Union Organizing Under Neutrality and Card Check Arrangements." *Industrial & Labor Relations Review* 55, 1 (October 2001), 42–59.

[40]*Dana Corp.,* 341 NLRB No. 150 (2004).

to pay union initiation fees and dues (or equivalent amounts) within a specified period of time (not less than 30 days after hire), under penalty of discharge by the employer. Employees who do not want to be union members and who object to paying full dues can inform their unions of that fact and pay a lesser amount that covers the cost of representation, but not other union activities deemed by the courts to be outside the realm of representation (e.g., political action).[41] For now at least, it appears that costs related to organizing new members can legitimately be passed along as part of representation.[42]

Union security provisions are legal under the NLRA because the section of the law that prohibits discrimination by an employer for the purpose of encouraging or discouraging membership in a labor organization makes an exception for the discharge of employees who do not meet their obligations to financially support their unions. However, the NLRA also permits states to pass laws making it illegal to incorporate union security provisions into labor agreements. These laws are known as **right-to-work laws** and exist in more than 20 states.

BARGAINING

Employees unionize in large part to obtain the legal right to engage in collective bargaining with their employers and to negotiate contracts containing improved wages, hours, terms, and conditions of employment. It is a ULP for an employer (or a union) to refuse to engage in collective bargaining. But what does an employer have to do to meet its obligation to bargain? And if agreement proves elusive, what rights do the parties have to use strikes and other economic weapons?

Duty to Bargain in Good Faith

The law does not, and cannot, ensure that collective bargaining will result in agreement; however, **good faith bargaining** is required. The NLRA does not go very far in defining what this means; it refers to the obligation to *"confer in good faith with respect to wages, hours, and other terms and conditions of employment,"* the *"mutual obligation of the employer and the representative of the employees to meet at reasonable times,"* and the *"execution of a written contract incorporating any agreement reached."*[43] Because parties to a collective bargaining relationship are free to engage in "hard" bargaining and need not reach agreement or even make concessions to the other party, identifying when there is a lack of good faith is difficult. However, *actions such as imposing conditions on the holding of negotiations, attempting to dictate which union representatives can be present at negotiations, inhibiting or delaying negotiations, withdrawing accepted offers, or simply going through the motions of negotiating without making a genuine effort to reach agreement are indicators of lack of good faith and should be avoided.*

Pleasantview Nursing Home v. NLRB illustrates the difficulty of deciding whether an employer has met its legal obligation to bargain in good faith when negotiations fail to produce an agreement.

Good faith bargaining entails sharing information. As a general matter, *employers are required to supply unions with information, if requested, that is "relevant*

[41]*Communication Workers of America v. Beck,* 108 S. Ct. 2641 (1988).

[42]*United Food and Commercial Workers, Local 1036 v. NLRB,* 307 F.3d 760 (9th Cir. 2002); *cert. denied,* 537 U.S. 1024 (2002).

[43]29 U.S.C.A. § 158(d) (2005).

PLEASANTVIEW NURSING HOME V. NLRB
351 F.3d 747 (6th Cir. 2003)

OPINION BY CHIEF JUDGE BOGGS:

Petitioner Pleasantview Nursing Home, Inc. ("Pleasantview"), operated a nursing home organized by the Textile Processors, Service Trades, Health Care, Professional and Technological Employees International Union, Local No. 1 ("Union"). After the 1996 negotiations between Pleasantview and the Union for a new collective bargaining agreement ("CBA") broke down, Pleasantview declared an impasse and unilaterally imposed its final offer. The National Labor Relations Board ("NLRB"), acting on a Union charge, found Pleasantview to have engaged in a series of unfair labor practices in violation of the National Labor Relations Act ("NLRA"): . . . [including] a unilateral increase in wages of some employees during the final negotiations; refusal to negotiate holiday and pension buy-backs in good faith; insistence to an impasse on a change in the initiation fee provision; and unilateral implementation of Pleasantview's final offer without a valid impasse. * * * We enforce the [NLRB's] order in part and grant the petition for review in part.

Pleasantview operates a nursing home on the west side of Cleveland. In 1984, the Union was certified as the collective bargaining representative of Pleasantview's orderlies and other aides. * * * On April 25, 1996, the Union and Pleasantview began negotiations for a new CBA covering the seventy-eight employees represented by the Union. As Pleasantview was facing a serious labor shortage, one of its aims in these negotiations was to provide for a significant increase in the pay of the represented employees. Pleasantview's initial proposal was to increase hourly wages and to finance this increase partially by the elimination of three paid holidays and the company contribution to Union-managed pension and disability funds. In return, employees would receive access to employer-sponsored investment and insurance plans. Pleasantview also wished to be freed . . . of its obligation to collect initiation fees until another area nursing home was required to do so. Alternatively, Pleasantview offered to collect the initiation fees but only if the union-shop clause was replaced by a maintenance-of-membership clause requiring current members to remain in the Union but

giving new hires the option not to join. On May 31, the last written CBA expired, but Pleasantview and the Union orally agreed to extend the CBA while negotiations continued and to apply the new CBA, when agreed to, retroactively to this date. Subsequently, Pleasantview informed the Union that, because of the labor shortage, it was going to increase pay unilaterally for new hires while negotiations were proceeding. According to Pleasantview, the Union negotiator nodded in response. On July 6, Pleasantview did increase the starting hourly wage for new employees and recently hired employees whose wages were still below the new starting wage. * * *

On September 17, after twelve negotiation sessions, Pleasantview, at the suggestion of a federal mediator involved in the negotiations, made a final offer to the Union incorporating the changes to the CBA that Pleasantview sought. The Union rejected this offer and declined to present it to the Union membership for a vote. At this point, Pleasantview declared an impasse and stated its intention to implement its final offer unilaterally on September 22. In response, the Union called a strike for that date and filed an unfair labor practices charge with the NLRB. On September 19, Pleasantview wrote a letter to its represented employees explaining that it would implement its final offer and informing employees that, should they not wish to participate in the strike, they could avoid union fines by withdrawing from the Union. On September 22, the Union struck and began picketing Pleasantview. However, a large majority of represented Pleasantview employees chose to cross the picket line that consisted of three Pleasantview employees and several Union officials. The strike collapsed after one shift. By the time the strike collapsed, more than three-quarters of Pleasantview's represented employees had informed Pleasantview of their withdrawal from the Union. * * *

[One of the] unfair labor practice[s] alleged is Pleasantview's unilateral increase of starting wages during the 1996 contract negotiations. * * * "The Board has taken the position that it is difficult to bargain if, during negotiations, an employer is free to alter the very terms and conditions that are the subject of those negotiations." "If an employer changes wages or other terms without affording the Union an opportunity for adequate consultation, it 'minimizes the influence of

organized bargaining' and emphasizes to the employees 'that there is no necessity for a collective bargaining agent.'" Therefore, "an employer's unilateral change in conditions of employment under negotiation is . . . a violation of [the NLRA], for it is a circumvention of the duty to negotiate which frustrates the objectives of [the NLRA] much as does a flat refusal" to negotiate. In this case, Pleasantview unilaterally increased the wages of some employees during the negotiations with the Union covering that very subject. Even though this unilateral change only affected a handful of current employees and new hires, it was an unfair labor practice.

Pleasantview contends that these wage increases were compelled by economic exigency and hence were exempted from the rule against unilateral imposition of changes during labor negotiations. "When economic exigencies compel prompt action," employers are authorized to make such changes even during negotiations. An employer attempting to prove economic exigency must carry a "heavy burden." Economic exigency requires a "compelling business justification." A mere "business necessity is not the equivalent of compelling considerations which excuse bargaining." * * *

Under this standard, the NLRB's finding that Pleasantview did not face an economic exigency was supported by substantial evidence and hence must be upheld. Undoubtedly, Pleasantview faced intense labor market pressure to increase wages. Its eagerness to do so, rare in any rational employer not under such pressure, attests to that. However, Pleasantview does not demonstrate that this pressure had reached emergency levels. Rather, Pleasantview admits to having suffered this chronic problem since 1985. Pleasantview does not claim that it faced an immediate risk of staff levels so low as to force it to shut down. * * * The conclusion that Pleasantview did not face an economic exigency is supported by the two-month delay between the time it first requested the wage increase and the time it implemented it. * * *

[Another] unfair labor practice alleged was Pleasantview's failure to negotiate with respect to its proposal for the buy-back of pension and paid holiday provisions. The NLRA imposes on unionized employers a duty to bargain collectively. This mutual obligation to bargain collectively is confined to good faith discussions "with respect to wages, hours, and other terms and conditions of employment." Parties are obligated to negotiate on these so-called mandatory subjects "and within that area neither party is legally obligated

to yield." Fringe benefits, such as paid holidays and pensions, "clearly fall within the compass of 'wages,' and are therefore subjects over which employers and employees must bargain." Here, the NLRB alleges that Pleasantview failed to bargain in good faith with respect to the holiday buy-back and pension changes. It bases this conclusion on three facts: that Pleasantview did not alter its initial bargaining position with respect to these issues; that during one negotiation session Pleasantview's negotiator stated that its position regarding holiday and pension buy-backs was non-negotiable; and that Pleasantview unilaterally implemented the wage increase, which it ultimately wished to finance by the holiday and pension buy-back, for a handful of employees while negotiations were still ongoing. . . . [T]hese facts, separately or in combination, were insufficient to allow the NLRB to conclude that Pleasantview refused to negotiate these issues in good faith.

Pleasantview's ultimate refusal to change its position regarding the buy-backs does not constitute bad faith. "Good faith bargaining is all that is required. That the position of one party on an issue prevails unchanged does not mandate the conclusion that there was no collective bargaining over the issue. * * * Where "the failure to execute a contract was not because of a failure or refusal to negotiate, but in the final analysis was because the parties would not agree on one remaining issue, considered by both of them as basically important," no bad faith has been evinced. "To say that the Company should have accepted the Union's proposal on this issue is to ignore the language of the statute that the obligation to bargain collectively 'does not compel either party to agree to a proposal or require the making of a concession.'" Pleasantview's insistence on the buy-backs constituted no more than hard bargaining. "Hard bargaining, the kind countenanced by the NLRA as an inevitable aspect of labor-management relations" is "not unfair bargaining."

The NLRB's most serious factual ground for finding bad faith was the statement by Pleasantview's negotiator during the July 25 session that the buy-backs were "non-negotiable." If this statement had reflected Pleasantview's actual stance regarding this mandatory bargaining subject, it would undisputedly have been sufficient to support a finding of bad faith. "If a party is so adamant concerning its own initial positions on a number of significant mandatory subjects, we may properly find bad faith evinced by its 'take-it-or-leave-it' approach to bargaining." However, to determine the

existence of bad faith, we look to bargaining conduct, not bargaining rhetoric. Pleasantview's conduct both before and after the July 25 session indicates that the "non-negotiable" statement was mere rhetoric and not an accurate reflection of Pleasantview's stance. Negotiations continued for almost two months after July 25. Pleasantview's statement that it "just couldn't come up with a different plan to get the fifty cents" wage increase, cited by the NLRB as further evidence of bad faith, in fact indicates the opposite. It conveys a willingness to listen to alternative ways of reaching agreement. * * * Where the overall bargaining conduct indicates good faith and willingness to negotiate, a stray statement indicating inflexibility will not overcome the general tenor of good faith negotiation. * * *

[Another] unfair labor practice alleged was Pleasantview's insistence to the point of impasse regarding the collection of initiation fees. "Internal affairs of labor organizations are not 'an aspect of the relationship between the employer and the employees,' but rather, by statutory definition are encompassed by the relationship between labor organizations and employees. * * * Hence the collection clause was not a mandatory subject of bargaining. However, "union security is properly a 'condition of employment'... within the statutory area of collective bargaining." Hence the question of whether the CBA would contain a union-shop or a maintenance-of-membership provision was a mandatory subject. As to non-mandatory matters, "each party is free to bargain or not to bargain." However, neither party may "refuse to enter into agreements on the ground that they do not include some proposal which is not a mandatory subject of bargaining." * * *

Pleasantview's negotiation stance combined offers with respect to a mandatory subject, union security, and with respect to a non-mandatory subject, the collection clause. It offered alternatively to agree to a union-shop provision in return for an elimination or modification of the collection clause *or* to agree to the collection clause in return for a change from a union-shop provision to a maintenance-of-membership provision. The NLRB in its analysis chose to sever the mandatory and the non-mandatory subjects. In that analysis, Pleasantview simply insisted to an impasse on a change in the collection-clause, a non-mandatory subject, violating its duty to negotiate the mandatory subjects in good faith. As this severance of the subjects does not reflect the evidence regarding Pleasantview's negotiation stance, we cannot agree. * * *

Pleasantview was concerned that the reduced net wages received by employees because of the deduction of union initiation fees would render its pay package uncompetitive with those offered by other nursing homes that did not have to deduct union initiation fees. Pleasantview saw the elimination of the collection clause, or suspension until competitors operated under similar clauses, as one way of alleviating this concern. An alternative, and from the point of view of Pleasantview equivalent, solution was replacement of the union-shop clause with a maintenance-of-membership clause. Under a maintenance-of-membership provision, new hires could choose whether to join the Union and pay the initiation fees. * * * For both groups of new hires, the collection clause would no longer present a deterrence against coming to work for Pleasantview. Therefore Pleasantview's alternative offers during the labor negotiations represented two reasonably equivalent ways of accommodating its needs. The linkage arose organically out of the economic relationship between the mandatory and non-mandatory subjects and was not an attempt to make an end-run around the distinction between mandatory and non-mandatory subjects. Hence it was permissible.

The final unfair labor practice alleged was the implementation of Pleasantview's final offer without the existence of a valid impasse. Impasse is defined as "that point at which the parties have exhausted the prospects of concluding an agreement and further discussions would be fruitless." "While that state of affairs that constitutes an impasse is not subject to precise definition, at least it encompasses the notion that both sides are aware of precisely what is at issue and that they have made more than a perfunctory attempt to reach a resolution." "Absent a *valid, good-faith impasse,* a company's [unilateral implementation] constitutes a breach of its duty to bargain. . . . * * *

The NLRB, . . . concedes the existence of impasse. Hence, the sole remaining question is whether the impasse was invalid because it was brought about by Pleasantview's failure to bargain in good faith. The NLRB points to Pleasantview's unfair labor practices as evidence of bad faith. However, there is no "presumption that an employer's unfair labor practice automatically precludes the possibility of meaningful negotiations and prevents the parties from reaching a good faith impasse." * * * [T]he unfair labor practices . . . involved minor topics only and [were] far from crucial to the failure of the parties to reach an agreement. [N]egotiations between the Union and Pleasantview continued

along the same lines for more than a month after the Union learned of the wage increase. * * * [A] valid impasse existed on September 17 and Pleasantview was within its rights to implement its final offer on September 22.

. . . Pleasantview also argues that it was under no duty to recognize or negotiate with the Union after the collapse of the strike because the Union has lost majority support. To "withdraw recognition of a union, an employer has the burden of demonstrating (1) that the union in fact did not enjoy majority support; or (2) that it had a good-faith belief, founded on a sufficient objective basis, that the union no longer represented a majority of the employees." "To prove an actual lack of majority support, the employer must make a numerical showing that a majority of employees opposed the union as of the date that union recognition was withdrawn." * * * Pleasantview bases its contention that the Union had lost support of a majority of its members on the fact that the September 22 strike was not honored by the large majority of the represented employees, resulting in its collapse after one shift, and on Pleasantview's receipt, no later than September 23, of letters of withdrawal from the Union by more than three-quarters of the represented employees.* * * Short of a decertification petition signed by a majority of the employees, it is difficult to imagine clearer evidence that most represented employees rejected further representation by the Union. At the very least, these facts supported by clear, cogent, and convincing evidence Pleasantview's good faith belief that the Union no longer represented a majority of employees. * * *

Hence Pleasantview was entitled to cease recognizing or bargaining with the Union no later than September 23 and is not required to reopen bargaining. * * *

CASE QUESTIONS

1. What was the legal issue in this case? What did the court decide?

2. What was the problem with the employer raising the wages of some employees?

3. How do we know whether an employer has bargained in good faith? Why did the court reject the NLRB's conclusion that the nursing home did not bargain in good faith regarding the "buy-backs" of pension and paid holiday provisions?

4. Why did the court conclude that the nursing home did not reject an agreement based on a nonmandatory topic of bargaining (i.e., the collection of initiation fees)?

5. Why was it legal for the employer to cease negotiating and implement its final offer? To withdraw recognition of the union?

6. Was the ill-fated strike an economic or ULP strike?

and necessary" to bargaining effectively. This information is usually limited to wage and other employment data directly related to bargaining issues, rather than financial data. However, if an employer asserts that a union demand cannot be met due to financial constraints, the employer will have to provide financial information to substantiate that claim if it is requested.[44] *Bypassing union representatives and appealing directly to employees constitutes refusal to bargain with the legal representative of employees. Employers also fail to show good faith when they make material changes in employees' terms and conditions of employment without informing and negotiating with unions over these changes.*

Does the duty to bargain extend to each and every issue that might be raised by one of the parties? For example, a union might be concerned about the firm's business strategy, the excessive pay of top management, the prices charged for a company's products, or any of a host of other issues. The duty to bargain pertains to "wages, hours, terms and conditions of employment." This phrase is given a very broad reading under the NLRA, but it does have boundaries. The NLRB distinguishes between "mandatory" and "permissive" (or voluntary) topics of bargaining.[45]

[44]*NLRB v. Truit Manufacturing*, 351 U.S. 149 (1956).

[45]*NLRB v. Wooster Division of Borg-Warner Corp.*, 356 U.S. 342 (1958).

Mandatory topics are issues that, if raised by either party, must be negotiated over. Furthermore, disagreement over a **mandatory topic** is a sufficient reason for failing to reach agreement in negotiations. In contrast, if a permissive topic is raised, the other party can decline to discuss it. And if a **permissive topic** is discussed but not agreed upon, it cannot be the basis for failing to come to terms. However, *Pleasantview Nursing Home* shows that this principle is difficult to apply to real world negotiations where complex mixtures of mandatory and nonmandatory topics are often considered, and reasons for rejecting agreements are not observable. The many mandatory topics of bargaining include wages, bonuses, benefits, work schedules, safety, layoff and recall procedures, and grievance procedures, to cite only a few. Permissive topics are all nonmandatory topics that would not be illegal to incorporate into a labor agreement. The firm's business strategy, CEO pay, and pricing policy are permissive topics that an employer is not required to discuss.

What Happens When Parties Cannot Reach Agreement?

Proposals in collective bargaining come from both unions and employers. When employers are facing severe financial or operational problems, they are usually anxious to reach agreement on terms that will enable them to lower their labor costs or operate more efficiently. Although employers are generally prohibited from making unilateral changes in the terms and conditions of employment for their unionized employees, an employer can unilaterally implement its last, best offer made during negotiations if an impasse is reached (and any existing contract has expired). An **impasse** is reached when negotiations over one or more mandatory topics have become deadlocked and both parties are warranted in assuming that further negotiation would be futile. An impasse is not necessarily a permanent state of affairs and can be broken by one or both parties later relenting and making further concessions to the other.

Determining whether there is a genuine impasse justifying unilateral implementation of terms or an illegal refusal to bargain in good faith is difficult. In one case, the employer and union negotiated over a new contract, made progress in compromising on their differences, but remained far apart on several important issues as the contract expiration date approached. In the last negotiating session, the employer announced that it was making its "last, best, and final offer" and that it intended to implement those terms shortly thereafter if they were not accepted. An appeals court overruled the NLRB and found that the employer had not violated the act. Despite the relatively small number of negotiation sessions (eight) prior to the declaration of impasse and the abruptness of the final offer, the court concluded that the company had reached the point where it was no longer willing to compromise, that it had engaged in good faith bargaining by altering its positions in the direction of union demands previously, that it was experiencing economic duress that necessitated a firm bargaining stance, and that the union's expressed desire to continue negotiations was not accompanied by a concrete indication that it was willing to change its demands.[46] In *Pleasantview Nursing Home*, an impasse had been reached, and the employer was permitted to implement its final offer because the court concluded that the employer's ULPs had not caused the impasse.

Third-Party Intervention For the most part, unions and employers are on their own when it comes to bargaining. The assistance of outside parties can be helpful in

[46]*TruServ Corp. v. NLRB*, 254 F.3d 1105 (D.C. Cir. 2001), *cert. denied*, 122 S. Ct. 1070 (2002).

negotiations, but usually is not legally required. **Mediators** are neutral third parties who, by entering negotiations and exerting control over the bargaining process, help unions and employers reach their own negotiated settlements. Mediators can only facilitate negotiations; they have no authority to impose agreement or any particular terms on the negotiating parties. The NLRA requires that the Federal Mediation and Conciliation Service (FMCS) be notified within 30 days after bargaining is requested if an agreement has not been reached in the negotiations. The agency, at its own initiative or at the request of the parties, is charged with promptly communicating with the parties and using mediation to produce agreements and avoid strikes. However, if the negotiating parties do not want to settle, there is little that a mediator can do.

Mediators have a stronger hand under the Railway Labor Act (RLA). Only when the National Mediation Board (NMB) concludes that further negotiations would be fruitless are the parties released from mediation and allowed to pursue a strike or other "self-help" approaches. Airline industry negotiations overseen by the NMB sometimes take several years to conclude. Fact-finding procedures that delay strikes are used in rare circumstances under the NLRA (in "national emergency" disputes) and somewhat more frequently under the RLA (appointment of "presidential emergency boards"). Only rarely does the law require that negotiating parties turn over unresolved issues for resolution by an arbitrator (e.g., state collective bargaining laws requiring arbitration for contract disputes involving police and firefighters in lieu of the right to strike).

Strikes and Other Economic Weapons Perhaps the most highly publicized and dramatic manifestation of labor relations is the **strike**. However, despite their hold on the public's imagination, the vast majority of negotiations conclude successfully without strikes. In a strike, employees withhold their labor, refusing to resume work until their employer agrees to more favorable terms and conditions of employment or refrains from engaging in ULPs. Strikers are not quitting their jobs. Rather, they are attempting to place pressure on their employers to act differently. Strikes, and the threat of strikes, play a vital role in negotiations. Because employees can credibly threaten to impose unwanted costs on employers through the disruption of production, employers have a strong incentive to bargain seriously, compromise, and attempt to reach agreement. Strikes also impose costs and pose potential dangers for employees and their unions. As the experience of Northwest Airlines' mechanics demonstrates all too well (see "Clippings"), there is no guarantee that strikes will succeed. In *Pleasantview Nursing Home,* the failed strike led to a loss of representation. At the very least, there will be a loss of wages and union dues. Thus, the strike option gives both management and labor good reason to bargain seriously.

Strikes and associated activities, such as picketing, are concerted activity. As such, strikers are generally protected by the NLRA, and *private employers must not terminate employees for engaging in lawful strikes.* Although the right to strike is protected under the NLRA (and the RLA), federal government employees do not have the right to strike. Many state and local government employees are also prohibited from striking. This is why the New York City transit workers faced numerous sanctions for their strike (see "Clippings").

Strikers engaging in lawful strikes cannot be terminated, but they can be "replaced." The rights of strikers hinge on whether the strike is an economic strike or a ULP strike. **Economic strikes** are undertaken to pressure employers to meet employee negotiation demands. The issues in dispute need not be money issues. **Unfair labor practice strikes** are undertaken in response to employer ULPs (e.g., refusal to bargain in good faith), for the purpose of pressuring employers to comply with the

law. In any strike, employers have a number of options. They can, for example, cease operating during the course of a strike or operate using management personnel only. If employers choose to operate by using replacements for the striking employees, the distinction between economic and ULP strikes becomes relevant. In economic strikes, employers can hire either temporary (for the duration of the strike) or permanent replacements.[47] *Strikers who are permanently replaced remain employees and have the right, when the strike is over, to be placed on a recall list, notified of available job vacancies, and rehired if a job substantially equivalent to their previous position becomes available and they do not have substantial employment elsewhere.* Strikers in a ULP strike can be temporarily, but not permanently, replaced.[48] *Employers must reinstate ULP strikers upon their making unconditional requests to return to their jobs.*

Whether a strike is a ULP strike is not certain until after the NLRB, and often the courts, have ruled. This fact creates risk for both employers and unions. If the NLRB decides that a strike was in response to a ULP, replaced strikers are entitled to immediate reinstatement and substantial back pay. At the same time, if employers confer "permanent" status on replacements in strikes that turn out to be ULP strikes, the replacement workers who must be discharged have grounds to sue for breach of contract.[49]

Strikers sometimes lose legal protection due to behavior engaged in during a strike. Picketing is common behavior during strikes (although it also occurs apart from strikes). Picketers establish a presence near their workplace and through words or signs make it known that they have a dispute with their employer. Emotions run high and harsh words can be expected on picket lines. However, picketing that restrains or coerces other employees who have the right to refrain from concerted activity is not protected and, under some circumstances, violates state criminal laws. Thus, mass picketing that does not allow picket lines to be crossed, actual violence or clear threats of violence against nonstrikers, destruction of employer property, and similar conduct is not protected. Picketing generally must be limited to the primary employer. Other secondary, neutral employers cannot lawfully be picketed. For example, a union cannot picket a supplier that provides the major components for a manufacturer's product as a means of placing pressure on the manufacturer. This would be a type of "secondary boycott" that the NLRA makes a union ULP. However, if a secondary employer is not truly neutral because it is performing work on behalf of a struck employer, then it is a business ally who can lawfully be picketed.[50] Also, unions can picket at retailers to urge consumer boycotts of products produced by their primary employer if it is clear that they are not urging a boycott against the retailer generally and the product in question does not account for a substantial portion of the neutral retailer's business.[51]

Under certain circumstances, employers can legally engage in a **lockout** of employees. Following the expiration of any labor agreement, an employer might choose to withhold the opportunity to work from employees despite their willingness to remain on the job and continue negotiating. The employer might do so because it fears that a strike will take place later at a very disadvantageous time (e.g., while the employer has a large inventory of perishable goods), or it might do so to

[47]*NLRB v. Mackay Radio & Telegraph Co.*, 304 U.S. 333 (1938).

[48]*Mastro Plastics Corp. v. NLRB*, 350 U.S. 270 (1956).

[49]*Belknap v. Hale*, 463 U.S. 491 (1983).

[50]*NLRB v. Business Machine & Office Appliance Mechanics Conference Board, IUE, Local 459*, 228 F.2d 553 (2d Cir. 1955), *cert. denied*, 351 U.S. 962 (1956).

[51]*NLRB v. Fruit & Vegetable Packers & Warehousemen, Local 760*, 377 U.S. 58 (1964).

put more pressure to settle on a union that is reluctant to strike. Courts have allowed employers to use temporary replacements for locked-out employees.[52] However, a lockout is illegal if the purpose of the lockout is to defeat employees' right to have a union. In one relevant case, an employer continued to operate in the face of a strike. A number of employees crossed the picket line. The union decided to end the strike and make an unconditional offer to return to work. The employer responded by locking out all of the strikers until a contract was obtained, but allowing the employees who previously crossed the picket line to continue working. This "partial lockout" that punished employees for exercising their right to strike and that did not have a substantial business justification violated the NLRA.[53] The lockout seems to have become a favorite tactic of professional sports leagues. Most recently, it was used by the National Hockey League (NHL) to force significant concessions on the players, albeit at the cost of losing both an entire season and a major television contract.

LABOR AGREEMENTS

Negotiations that conclude successfully, either without or following a strike, result in written, signed labor agreements. Most unions require that agreements be approved or "ratified" by their members before they become final, but ratification procedures are internal to unions and not a legal requirement. Even though their strike was going badly, the mechanics at Northwest Airlines voted to not ratify a proposed agreement that would have ended the strike because it included many of the same, objectionable terms that had prompted the strike in the first place (see "Clippings"). Labor agreements are very important documents. They are the basic source of rules governing the wages, hours, terms, and conditions of employment for unionized employees. The provisions they contain typically go well beyond minimum legal requirements. Labor agreements contain enforceable, contractual protections for employees. *Employers must abide by the terms of labor agreements when making human resource decisions regarding employees represented by unions. Thus, managers must be thoroughly familiar with any labor agreements that cover their employees.*

Enforcing Labor Agreements—Grievance Procedures and Arbitration

What happens when an employee believes that her employer has violated the labor agreement? For example, an employee might be passed over for a promotion and believe that the contract's language regarding criteria for making promotional decisions was not followed. Disputes of this sort are inevitable. Rather than require lawsuits for breach of contract every time an employee's rights have been violated, labor agreements almost universally provide for grievance procedures, ending with arbitration if necessary. Employees who believe that their contractual rights have been violated can file **grievances** (or unions will do so on their behalf). The grievances will be considered by successively higher levels of management and union personnel. The representative role of the union must be respected in the contract administration process, just as during the negotiations. Thus, *although individual employees can choose to file and pursue their own grievances, unions must be notified and given the*

[52]*American Ship Building Co. v. NLRB*, 380 U.S. 300 (1965).

[53]*Local 15, International Brotherhood of Electrical Workers v. NLRB*, 429 F.3d 631 (7th Cir. 2005).

opportunity to have a representative present at any meeting about the grievance. Most importantly, individual employees and employers cannot agree to resolve grievances in ways that would alter or conflict with the labor agreement. The availability of a grievance procedure also means that employees cannot take contract enforcement into their own hands, such as by refusing to follow orders that they believe are contrary to the labor agreement. Instead, they are required to follow the orders and file a grievance (situations threatening employee safety are an exception). If the grievance is upheld, the employee will receive a remedy for the violation.

Grievances that cannot be resolved by conferences between representatives of labor and management are sometimes submitted to arbitration. Ultimately, the union decides whether to take a case to arbitration. Recall that in arbitration, a neutral third party acts like a judge in rendering a decision that is generally final and binding on the parties. In **grievance arbitration**, the arbitrator decides disputes regarding the interpretation and enforcement of an existing labor agreement.

The courts have made it clear that arbitration is the preferred means of resolving disputes about rights under labor agreements and that arbitrator's decisions generally will be final.[54] Arbitrators have a great deal of leeway in interpreting labor agreements, but their decisions must still be grounded in or "draw their essence from" the language of those agreements. One of the circumstances under which courts will overturn an arbitrator's decision is when the arbitrator clearly disregards the contract. In a case involving a dispute over commissions paid to delivery drivers, a court overturned ("vacated") an arbitrator's decision because the arbitrator had ignored the clear and unambiguous language of the contract. The court noted the limited and highly deferential nature of its review:

> [O]ur concern is limited to whether the arbitrator went beyond, or outside the bounds of interpreting the contract before him. . . . The question is not whether the arbitrator misinterpreted the agreement, but only whether the arbitrator's inquiry disregarded the very language of the agreement itself.[55]

The court concluded that the arbitrator had in fact ignored clear contract language in favor of his own view of what would be fair, based on what he took to be the past practice of the parties regarding the payment of commissions.

In another case in which an employer sought judicial review of an arbitrator's decision, the labor agreement provided that part-time employees "are eligible to purchase per diem parking passes [at a discount]." When per diem pass holders were consistently denied access to the parking garage and forced to park elsewhere at their own expense, a grievance was filed. The arbitrator decided that although the contract referred only to the purchase of passes and not actual parking rights, interpreting the contract in such a narrow fashion would be contrary to the plain meaning of "parking pass" and would render the promise to provide them at a discount meaningless. Thus, the arbitrator ruled for the employees, and the court concurred because it found "the arbitrator's decision to be a plausible, commonsense interpretation of the agreement's plain language."[56] This interpretation of the contract was reinforced by the employer's prior practice for many years of ensuring that pass holders had access to the parking garage.

Labor agreements between unions and employers are more than the words written on paper. Grievance procedures and arbitration are critical in defining the rights

[54]*United Steelworkers v. Enterprise Wheel & Car Co.*, 363 U.S. 593 (1960).

[55]*Anheuser-Busch, Inc. v. Teamsters Local 744*, 280 F.3d 1133 (7th Cir. 2002); *cert. denied*, 537 U.S. 885 (2002).

[56]*The Providence Journal Co. v. Providence Newspaper Guild*, 271 F.3d 16, at 20–21 (1st Cir. 2001).

of the parties under a labor agreement. Thus, *employers should handle grievances and arbitration cases very carefully, including gathering the facts and carefully considering which cases should be settled or allowed to go to arbitration.* An adverse arbitration decision can amount to the same thing as negotiating unfavorable terms. For example, whatever the employer in the previous case intended, it is now committed to providing adequate parking space for pass-holding employees. The agreement sometimes extends to ongoing practices of the parties, even when these are not explicitly (or not at all) mentioned in the labor agreement. Arbitrators may find a **binding past practice** to exist when a practice is clear, it has been consistently engaged in over a substantial period of time, and the practice existed with the knowledge and at least tacit consent of both the union and the employer. For example, if an employer has regularly provided coffee or food for employees despite the absence of any contractual requirement to do so, an arbitrator might overrule the discontinuation of this practice. A binding past practice is more likely to be found when some type of employee privilege or benefit is concerned than when work schedules or other managerial decisions are involved.

A change in circumstances (e.g., installation of new equipment) or in contract language would likely invalidate a prior practice. Past practice cannot be cited to create rights that conflict with clear and unambiguous contract language (the mistake made by the arbitrator in the case involving delivery drivers' commissions), but it can be important in supplementing labor agreements when they are silent on a given matter or where there is more than one reasonable interpretation of the contract language. After all, it is reasonable to assume that the issue presented in a grievance has been dealt with before, and the manner in which it was dealt with conveys important information about how the parties understand their agreement. In light of the importance of past practice in arbitration, *unionized employers should not establish informal practices of conferring benefits or privileges not specified in the labor agreement unless they are willing to sustain those practices (or bargain over changes in them). Both employers and unions have a responsibility to actively "police" the contract and ensure that it is being enforced in a manner consistent with the understandings at the time the agreement was reached.*

Chapter SUMMARY

Labor laws protect the rights of employees to join together and engage in collective bargaining with their employers. In collective bargaining, employees are represented by labor unions in negotiating with employers over wages, hours, and a host of other terms and conditions of employment. The rules of the workplace are negotiated and incorporated into enforceable labor agreements, rather than left to management or legal mandates imposed by government. The National Labor Relations Act (NLRA) is the principal federal labor law covering private-sector workplaces. The NLRA is administered by the National Labor Relations Board (NLRB).

The NLRA confers on employees the basic rights to self-organization; to form, join, or assist labor organizations; to bargain collectively with employers

through representatives of employees' own choosing; to go on strike; to engage in concerted activities for the purpose of collective bargaining or other mutual aid or protection; and to refrain from such activities. Concerted or group activity by employees aimed at influencing employers regarding wages, hours, terms, and conditions of employment goes beyond union formation and formal collective bargaining. Employees who are not currently unionized and not seeking to form unions can still engage in protected concerted activity. To be protected, the activity must be engaged in with other employees or with their backing, rather than only by or on behalf of an individual. For unionized employees, conduct related to enforcing rights under a labor agreement can be concerted activity, even if engaged in solely by an individual. Protection

for concerted activity can be lost if the conduct or speech is extreme or abusive.

The NLRA prohibits certain activities by employers and unions and labels these unfair labor practices (ULPs). Employer ULPs include interfering with, restraining, or coercing employees in the exercise of their NLRA rights; dominating or interfering with the administration of a labor organization; discriminating against employees for the purpose of encouraging or discouraging membership in a labor organization; retaliating against employees for filing charges or giving testimony under the act; and refusing to engage in collective bargaining. All employer ULPs have at their core the element of interfering with or restraining employees' NLRA rights. The ULP of dominating a labor organization aims at ensuring the independence of labor organizations by prohibiting company unions established or controlled by employers. The NLRA's broad definition of labor organization includes any organization or committee in which employees participate and which deals with employers regarding employment issues. If care is not taken to limit the issues dealt with or the manner in which employees on employee-involvement teams interact with management, these teams can constitute dominated labor organizations and violate the NLRA. The ULP of discriminating against employees for the purpose of encouraging or discouraging membership in labor organizations requires the NLRB to establish a prima facie case that an employee's protected conduct was the motivation for a discharge or other adverse employment decision. If the NLRB can show this, the employer has violated the NLRA unless it can show that the same decision would have been made absent the discriminatory motive. Although employers are prohibited from discriminating to either encourage or discourage union membership, it is legal under the NLRA, but not state right-to-work laws, to negotiate union security provisions in labor agreements. These clauses obligate employees to pay for the services they receive from unions and require the discharge of employees who fail to meet this obligation.

The NLRB closely polices employer and union conduct during organizing campaigns for ULPs and other conduct that would disturb "laboratory conditions" for the free exercise of employee choice regarding unionization. The NLRA provides for representation elections to determine whether employees desire union representation. These secret ballot elections are overseen by the NLRB. If the majority of employees who vote choose union representation, the union will be certified as the exclusive representative of all the employees in the bargaining unit. The NLRB determines whether a proposed bargaining unit is an appropriate bargaining unit by considering whether the employees share a community of interest.

Employers have a legal obligation to bargain in good faith with the union(s) representing their employees. Good faith bargaining requires a sincere effort to settle but does not necessitate that employers and unions actually reach agreement or make concessions from their stated positions. The duty to bargain pertains to mandatory, but not permissive or illegal topics of bargaining. Third parties such as mediators are available to assist in negotiations, but under the NLRA the negotiating parties determine whether they want to avail themselves of this assistance. The government plays a limited role in private-sector labor negotiations and, in most cases, does not intervene to stop or delay strikes. Private-sector employees have the right to strike and cannot be terminated for going on strike. In contrast, public-sector collective bargaining laws usually require the intervention of third parties if agreement cannot be reached, and many public employees are prohibited from going on strike.

Although private-sector employees cannot be fired for going on strike under the NLRA, they can be replaced. In economic strikes, where the aim is to place pressure on an employer to offer more satisfactory terms and conditions of employment, employees can be either permanently or temporarily replaced. With permanent replacement, strikers need not be restored to their jobs at the end of a strike, but they retain the right to be recalled to their former positions or substantially equivalent ones. In ULP strikes, which are precipitated by employer ULPs and aim to place pressure on an employer to stop breaking the law, employees can be temporarily, but not permanently, replaced. Employees who make an unconditional offer to return to work from a ULP strike must be reinstated, even if that means terminating a replacement worker.

Labor agreements are contracts that govern the wages, hours, terms, and conditions of employment for unionized employees. Labor agreements are enforced through contractual grievance and arbitration procedures. If grievances alleging violations of employee rights under labor agreements cannot be resolved in discussions between unions and employers, the disputes may be submitted to arbitration. The decisions that arbitrators make regarding the meaning

and enforcement of labor agreements are usually final and binding. Arbitrators have considerable leeway in interpreting and enforcing labor agreements, but their decisions must be based on the language of those contracts. Arbitrators often look to evidence of how the parties have dealt with the same issues in the past. A binding past practice can be found where a clear practice has been consistently engaged in over a period of time with the knowledge and consent of both parties. Past practice does not negate unambiguous contract language, but it plays an important role in determining the intent of the parties when a contract is either ambiguous or silent on a matter in dispute.

Practical Advice SUMMARY

- *Employers must respect the right of employees to join together in contesting or expressing concerns regarding their terms and conditions of employment. Employment policies that interfere with these rights must not be maintained or enforced.*

- *Employers must refrain from interfering with, restraining, or coercing employees in the exercise of their NLRA rights. This includes*

 –*refraining from interrogating individual employees or systematically polling employees regarding why they want a union and how they intend to vote in a representation election.*

 –*not responding to organizing efforts by raising wages or making other unscheduled changes in employment benefits.*

 –*not threatening employees or promising them benefits as a means of influencing their decisions regarding unionization.*

 –*allowing employees to engage in discussions about unionization in the workplace during non-work time.*

 –*allowing employees to wear union buttons, display other insignias, and engage in other activities such as lunchtime rallies.*

- *Employers can bar nonemployee organizers from the workplace and surrounding private property, provided that*

 –*the organizers have some viable means of communicating with employees.*

 –*the employer has a nonsolicitation policy.*

 –*the policy is applied in a nondiscriminatory manner to all outside parties.*

- *Employers generally must allow off-site employee organizers access to nonwork areas outside the workplace, even if these are otherwise treated as private property.*

- *Employers must refrain from dominating or interfering with the formation or administration of a labor organization. This includes*

 –*not creating or controlling "company unions."*

 –*not instituting employee involvement in response to union organizing campaigns.*

 –*not using employee-involvement teams to discuss or decide issues that are properly part of collective bargaining, when employees are represented by a union.*

- *Any employee-involvement teams that are used should be structured so that at least one of the following conditions is met*

 –*employees do not serve in a representative capacity.*

 –*substantial decision-making authority is delegated to them.*

 –*communication is not bilateral.*

 –*their focus is on productivity rather than employment issues.*

- *Employers must refrain from discriminating against employees for the purpose of encouraging or discouraging membership in any labor organization.*

- *Employers cannot refuse to hire, fire, demote, or otherwise limit the employment opportunities of employees because they are known or suspected to be union supporters or activists.*

- *Employers must refrain from retaliating against employees who file charges or give testimony in proceedings related to enforcement of the NLRA.*

- *Employers must not encourage or assist employees in decertifying their unions.*

- *Employers must not refuse to engage in collective bargaining with employees' labor representatives.*

- *When employees are represented by a union, employers must refrain from negotiating or otherwise*

dealing with individual employees regarding their wages, hours, terms, and conditions of employment.

- Employers must be willing to bargain in good faith with their employees' representative, including

 –meeting at reasonable times.

 –putting any agreements into writing.

 –refraining from imposing conditions on the holding of negotiations.

 –not attempting to dictate which union representatives can be present at negotiations.

 –not inhibiting or delaying negotiations.

 –not withdrawing accepted offers.

 –not going through the motions of bargaining without a genuine effort to reach agreement.

 –providing unions with information, if requested, that is relevant and necessary to effective bargaining and representation.

 –not making material changes in employees' terms and conditions of employment without first notifying and negotiating with the employees' union.

- Employers can unilaterally implement their final offers on issues only after bargaining in good faith and reaching an impasse.

- Private-sector employers must not terminate employees for engaging in lawful strikes, provided that they do not engage in serious misbehavior during the strikes.

- If strikers in an economic strike are permanently replaced, those employees must be

 –placed on a recall list.

 –notified of available job vacancies.

–rehired if a job substantially equivalent to their previous position becomes available and they do not have substantial employment elsewhere.

- Employers must reinstate strikers in a ULP strike who make an unconditional request to return to their jobs.

- Employers must abide by the terms of labor agreements when making human resource decisions regarding unionized employees.

- Managers must be thoroughly familiar with any labor agreements covering their employees.

- If individual employees want to present their own grievances

 –their union must be notified.

 –the union must be given the opportunity to be present at any meeting about the grievances.

 –resolution of the grievance must not alter or conflict with the labor agreement.

- Employers should handle grievance and arbitration cases very carefully, including carefully researching them and considering which cases should be settled rather than allowed to go to arbitration.

- Unionized employers should not establish informal practices of conferring benefits or privileges not specified in labor agreements unless they are willing to sustain those practices or bargain over changes in them.

- Employers should be vigilant in monitoring whether labor agreements are being enforced in a manner consistent with what was intended when they were negotiated.

Key TERMS

collective bargaining	concerted activity	mandatory topic
labor unions	unfair labor practices (ULPs)	permissive topic
National Labor Relations Act (NLRA)	labor organization	impasse
	representation election	mediator
National Labor Relations Board (NLRB)	appropriate bargaining unit	strike
	authorization cards	economic strike
Railway Labor Act (RLA)	decertification election	unfair labor practice strike
National Mediation Board (NMB)	card check procedure	lockout
Civil Service Reform Act (CSRA)	exclusive representative	labor agreement
Federal Labor Relations Authority (FLRA)	union security	grievance
	right-to-work law	grievance arbitration
supervisor	good faith bargaining	binding past practice

Chapter QUESTIONS

1. Two employees worked as band saw operators at a small, nonunion furniture manufacturer. The band saws were located near the shop's large, overhead door. The two band saw operators complained on a number of occasions about cold, drafty conditions. Many of the other employees who were stationed further away from the door complained about heat in the shop and wanted the door open. On a cold morning, the two employees walked off the job after their request to have the door closed was refused. The company president fired the two employees, saying that he wanted "to set an example" and that he was not "going to have people walking out like that." The terminated employees filed a charge with the NLRB. What should the court decide? Why? (*NLRB v. Jasper Seating Co.*, 857 F.2d 419 (7th Cir. 1988))

2. A company included the following in its employee ("partner") handbook: "We honor confidentiality. We recognize and protect the confidentiality of any information concerning the company, its business plans, its partners [employees], new business efforts, customers, accounting and financial matters." A union attempting to organize the company's workers challenged the policy before the NLRB. What should the Board decide? Why? (*Cintas Corporation*, 344 NLRB No. 118 (2005))

3. A unionized employee filed more than a dozen grievances over a three-year period. His supervisors asked him why he was filing so many grievances and called him a "troublemaker." The employee got into an argument with a coworker and was told that if there was another instance, he would be fired. A few months later, the employee made a derisive comment about another coworker who was not present. When the coworker later heard second-hand what had been said about him, he complained to management. The employee was suspended and then terminated for "comments directed toward another employee that were totally inappropriate, intimidating, antagonistic and offensive and could be construed as sexual harassment towards a fellow employee." Vulgar comments were common in this workplace. No written rule prohibited profanity, and no employee had ever been discharged on this basis before. The employee's case

was brought to the NLRB. What should the Board decide? Why? (*United Parcel Service v. NLRB*, 2005 U.S. App. LEXIS 8982)

4. A store had the following nonsolicitation policy: "Associates may not engage in solicitation . . . during working time." An employee of the store came in while off-duty wearing a tee shirt that said "Union Teamsters" on the front and "Sign a card . . . Ask me how!" on the back. A manager on duty had the employee removed from the store for engaging in solicitation. The next day, while on duty, the employee invited two other employees to attend a union meeting. The employee also said that he would like one of the employees "to consider signing a union authorization card." The employee was given a "coaching session" for violating the nonsolicitation policy. The union filed a ULP charge. What should the Board decide? Why? (*Wal-Mart Stores v. NLRB*, 400 F.3d 1093 (8th Cir. 2005))

5. A hospital adopted a policy prohibiting employees from (1) soliciting and distributing materials to coworkers during work time and in patient care areas (including areas adjacent to patient units) at any time and (2) soliciting and distributing materials to all nonemployees at any time throughout the entire hospital. Additionally, a nonemployee organizer who was sitting on a bench in front of the hospital waiting for a ride from an employee was ordered off the hospital's property. ULP charges were filed. What should the Board decide? (*Stanford Hospital and Clinics v. NLRB*, 325 F.3d 334 (D.C. Cir. 2003))

6. An employer announced a new drug-testing program for employees. The union objected to the policy, and it was not implemented. A year later, the union was presented with a revised policy that the company subsequently implemented. The company refused the union's demand to bargain over the policy or retract it. Charges were filed with the NLRB. What should the NLRB decide? Why? (*Delta Tube & Fabricating Corp.*, 323 NLRB. 153 (1997))

7. An employer entered negotiations by presenting the union with its "firm and fair offer." It refused to modify its position in any way unless the union could demonstrate facts that would cause it to reconsider. Additionally, the employer

mailed information to each of its employees, explaining its offer and urging them to tell their union representatives to accept it. The union filed charges with the NLRB. What should the court decide? Why? (*NLRB v. General Electric Co.*, 418 F.2d 736 (2d Cir. 1969), cert. denied, 397 U.S. 365 (1970))

8. A newly certified union and an employer negotiated over a first contract. Prior to the employees unionizing, the employer had occasionally used temp agency employees to supplement its workforce. During the negotiations, and without informing the union, the employer began to use only temps to replace employees who left. As a result, the number of employees represented by the union dwindled from 42 to 8. When the union discovered what was going on, it demanded information about the temp agencies and the terms of the company's contracts with them. The employer refused to provide the information. The parties met frequently to negotiate the contract and reached agreement on some issues. However, the employer declined to provide any reasons for its rejection of certain union proposals.

The employer rejected a union security clause and proposed a broad management rights clause. On one occasion, two employees who were on the union bargaining committee were not released from work to attend the negotiation. ULP charges were filed. What should the Board decide? Why? (*St. George Warehouse, Inc.*, 341 NLRB No. 120 (2004))

9. Should card-check procedures be allowed to determine employees' desire for union representation or only formal representation elections?

10. Is it fair that employers can permanently replace economic strikers? Does the right to strike mean much if striking employees are subject to permanent replacement?

11. Why does the NLRA require that labor organizations remain independent of employers? Is the current NLRB policy regarding employee-involvement teams reasonable and workable?

12. What can be done about the seeming ineffectiveness of the NLRA in contending with discriminatory discharges and other unlawful responses to organizing activity?

Internet RESOURCES

NLRB case decisions are among the useful materials available at its site.

http://www.nlrb.gov

The AFL-CIO is the principal voice of the labor movement in the United States. The site provides information on issues important to workers and unions, including proposed legislation.

http://www.aflcio.org

This site on labor law is hosted by the Legal Information Institute.

http://www.law.cornell.edu/topics/labor.html

American Rights at Work is an advocacy group focused on the right of workers to unionize.

http://www.americanrightsatwork.org

Occupational Safety and Health

CLIPPINGS

▸ BP Products North America has agreed to pay $21.36 million to the Occupational Safety and Health Administration (OSHA). The company had been cited for more than 300 violations of safety and health standards following a refinery explosion in Texas City that killed 15 employees and injured at least 170 others. Most of the citations were for "willful violations."[1]

▸ OSHA has set out its regulatory agenda for fiscal 2006. Included on this agenda are revisions to the respiratory protection standard intended to protect workers who use respirators to work in areas where it is unsafe to breathe; a final rule on exposure limits for hexavalent chromium, a substance associated with lung cancer and skin disorders; completion of a risk assessment aimed at updating the standard for exposure to crystalline silica, a substance that causes silicosis and other serious diseases; and final action on a regulation that would clarify employers' responsibility to pay for OSHA-required personal protective equipment. The latter regulation was first proposed in 1999. All these items have been on OSHA's agenda for years. Work on the hexavalent chromium standard has proceeded under court order.[2]

▸ The people who inspect U.S. workplaces for safety and health violations have reason to be concerned about their own safety and health. Blood tests of 271 OSHA compliance officers found that 10 (3.7 percent) tested positive for beryllium sensitivity. The positive test does not mean that these inspectors will develop chronic beryllium disease, but it does call for medical monitoring of their health status on an annual basis. No one knows where the exposure occurred, although industries involved with nuclear weapon production, machining, and metals pose particular risk of beryllium exposure.[3]

▸ Buttered popcorn might put more than waistlines in danger. Numerous workers at a Missouri factory that packages microwave popcorn have developed a rare and serious lung disorder. The cause appears to be exposure to artificial butter flavoring while mixing and packaging the microwave popcorn produced by the plant. The National Institute for Occupational Safety & Health (NIOSH) has investigated and found evidence of lung disease in popcorn plant workers in several states. Workers' compensation claims have been filed on behalf of employees, as well as numerous lawsuits

[1]Susanne Pagano. "BP Agrees to $21.36 Million Settlement for Fatal Explosion at Texas Refinery." *Daily Labor Report* 185 (September 26, 2005), AA-1.

[2]"Respiratory Protection, Other Health Rules Identified as High Priority in Regulatory Plan." *Daily Labor Report* 209 (October 31, 2005), AA-3.

[3]Ellen Byerrum. "Ten of 271 at Agency Have Tested Positive for Beryllium Sensitivity, OSHA Confirms." *Daily Labor Report* 57 (March 25, 2005), A-10.

against the company that produced the butter flavoring. A former employee of the Missouri plant recently won a $15 million verdict against the manufacturer of the butter flavoring.[4]

► There were 5,703 fatal workplace injuries recorded in the United States in 2004, a rate of 4.1 deaths per 100,000 workers. Highway accidents were the most common cause of death for workers, followed by falls and being struck by objects. The number of deaths by falls increased by 17 percent from the previous year, whereas workplace homicides saw a 13 percent decline. Workers in the construction and transportation industries suffered the highest numbers of fatalities, but the agriculture, fishing, and mining industries had higher fatality rates.[5]

Providing safe workplaces is one of the most important responsibilities that employers have to their employees. The **Occupational Safety and Health Act (OSH Act)**[6] is the principal federal law requiring private-sector employers to prevent occupational injuries and illnesses by removing hazards from the workplace. A separate statute, the Mine Safety and Health Act, governs safety in the mining industry. A wide variety of other federal laws affect workplace safety, even though that is not their major focus (e.g., Federal Aviation Act, Hazardous Materials Transportation Act, Superfund Amendments and Reauthorization Act). State **workers' compensation** laws provide remedies for employees who suffer injury, illness, or death from their employment.

THE OCCUPATIONAL SAFETY AND HEALTH ACT

Three new agencies were created when the OSH Act was enacted: the **Occupational Safety and Health Administration (OSHA)**, the **National Institute of Occupational Safety and Health (NIOSH)**, and the **Occupational Safety and Health Review Commission (OSHRC)**. OSHA has overall responsibility for administering and enforcing the OSH Act. It establishes safety standards, conducts inspections of workplaces, and provides information to employers and employees about workplace safety and health issues. NIOSH provides scientific and technical support to OSHA, helping it to identify hazards and develop appropriate standards. When requested, NIOSH visits workplaces and conducts health hazard evaluations, as it did in the case of the popcorn packaging plants (see "Clippings"). The OSHRC hears appeals of OSHA enforcement actions.

The OSH Act protects most private-sector employees, but not government employees (at least not directly). The act allows states that prefer to issue and enforce their own safety and health standards to do so, as long as the state programs are certified by OSHA as being at least as effective as the federal program. Another condition for OSHA certification of state plans is that state and local government employees also be covered. About half the states are state plan states. When the OSH Act runs up against other federal laws affecting the safety and health of private-sector employees (e.g., laws regulating transportation, nuclear plants), OSHA is generally prohibited from exercising its jurisdiction.

[4]Christopher Brown. "Jury Awards Popcorn Worker $15 Million for Lung Disease Related to Work at Plant." *Daily Labor Report* 70 (April 13, 2005), A-7.

[5]"Fatal Falls Reach New Series High in 2004; All Workplace Deaths Up Slightly, BLS Says." *Daily Labor Report* 165 (August 26, 2005), D-4.

[6]29 U.S.C.A. §§ 651–678 (2005).

The OSH Act is aimed at eliminating, or at least lessening, safety and health hazards in the workplace. Unsafe conditions violate the law, even if they have not (yet) resulted in injury, illness, or death. The latter might prompt enforcement activities or affect penalties, but unsafe conditions by themselves violate the OSH Act.

How Safe Is "Safe Enough"?

Most agree that workplaces should be safe, but some risk is involved in any activity. (As I sit here typing these words, a projectile might come crashing through the window, my back might go out when I twist to reach for some papers, the air might be full of asbestos, and so on.) How far should employers have to go in protecting employees from hazards to their safety and health? The minimum levels of safety that employers are required to provide are defined in two ways: through standards created by OSHA to address specific hazards and through the OSH Act's general duty clause.

Safety Standards At its own initiative, or at the request of other parties (e.g., NIOSH), OSHA has the authority to create (or "promulgate") **safety standards**. Separate standards are issued for general industry, maritime, construction, and agriculture. General industry standards apply to all industries, unless more specific maritime, construction, or agricultural standards deal with the same issues. Figure 15-1 lists a few examples of OSHA general industry standards. *Employers must become aware of and comply with all standards that apply to their operations.* However, it is possible to obtain a temporary **variance** if there is good reason why an employer is unable to comply with a new standard by its effective date and a permanent variance if an employer can show that it uses alternative means that are equally effective in protecting employees.

Figure 15-2 further illustrates the nature of OSHA standards by outlining the contents of OSHA's occupational noise exposure standard. Exposure to excessive noise on the job is a serious hazard that threatens the hearing of workers in a variety of occupations, from factory workers to rock musicians.

In deciding what standards are applicable, more specific standards take precedence over more general ones. Employees do not actually have to be exposed to the conditions that violated a standard (nor suffer any harm); it is enough that the

FIGURE 15-1	**Examples of OSHA General Industry Standards**
Substances	lead, benzene, asbestos, formaldehyde, blood-borne pathogens
Equipment	woodworking machinery, mechanical power presses, cranes
Work processes	grain handling, arc welding and cutting, pulp and paper mills
Environmental conditions	noise, ventilation, sanitation
Safety practices	control of hazardous energy (lockout/tagout), hazard communication, respirators, eye and face protection, medical services, and first aid

FIGURE 15-2	**Summary of the OSHA Occupational Noise Exposure Standard***

Establishes a *permissible exposure limit* (PEL) of 90 decibels (based on an 8-hour day).

When employees are subjected to sound in excess of the PEL, employers are to use appropriate, feasible engineering (e.g., adjustments to equipment to reduce vibration, sound barriers, mufflers) or administrative (e.g., limitation on work hours, job rotation, quiet break areas) *controls* to lessen the exposure. Personal protective equipment (e.g., ear plugs) must be used if these measures do not reduce the exposure below the PEL.

Establishes an *action level* of 85 decibels (based on an 8-hour day).

A *hearing conservation program* must be established for all employees exposed to noise above the action level. This includes monitoring workplace noise levels; making audiometric (hearing) testing available at no cost to employees; taking, within six months of an employee's first exposure at or above the action level, a baseline audiogram against which subsequent tests can be compared; taking follow-up audiograms on at least an annual basis; and evaluating audiograms for evidence of hearing loss.

Hearing protectors must be made available at no cost to employees exposed to noise at or above the action level. Employers must ensure that protectors are worn, give employees a choice among a variety of suitable protectors, provide training in their proper use, and ensure that they fit properly.

A *training* program must be instituted and repeated annually for all employees exposed to noise at or above the action level.

Records of exposure monitoring must be retained for two years and be made available on request to employees and their representatives. Records of individual audiometric tests must be retained for the duration of an employee's employment.

*29 C.F.R. § 1910.95 (2005).

ELEMENTS OF A CLAIM

Violation of an OSHA Safety Standard

To establish violation of a standard, OSHA must show all the following:

1. An applicable standard exists.
2. The standard was not complied with.
3. One or more employees were exposed or had access to the hazard.
4. The employer knew or should have known of the hazard.

nature of their work and the facility make it reasonable to expect that they might encounter the danger. Knowledge of a hazard that violates an OSHA standard can be either actual or constructive. Employers are not expected to be omniscient, but they cannot evade their responsibilities by ignoring obvious problems. Thus, if a hazard is in plain view, known to supervisors, or is the object of employee complaints, the employer will be deemed to have known of its existence. Because employers are

expected to be aware of applicable standards, professing ignorance that particular conditions violate OSHA standards is of no avail.

An employer might argue that a safety violation was due to unpreventable employee misconduct. To prevail in this argument, the employer must be able to show that it established rules designed to address the hazard, the rules were communicated to employees, efforts were made to discover violations, and persons violating the rule have been disciplined. This defense is also more likely to fly where isolated instances of misconduct by an individual are involved, rather than more widespread or continuous violations. In a case involving the drowning of an employee at a construction site, the employer was unsuccessful in claiming the defense of unpreventable employee misconduct. The employer's safety policies did not address the hazard at hand, the supervisor did not require foremen to report hazards if the foremen thought that they could take of the problems by themselves, and the employer's rules on the use of personal protective equipment were discretionary rather than mandatory.[7]

Congress allowed OSHA to adopt national consensus standards on an expedited basis for the first two years of its existence so that it could "ramp up" quickly. These were drawn from voluntary standards that had been created by a number of nongovernmental organizations (e.g., for use by insurers), and many are still in effect. OSHA also has the authority to bypass normal procedures and adopt emergency temporary standards when there is "grave danger" from exposure to toxic or other harmful substances or from some new hazard. The process of adopting or revising permanent standards is laborious, so the details are not spelled out here. In general terms, OSHA must develop substantial documentation to support proposed rules, make several announcements of its intention to promulgate a new standard, seek public comments in writing, and hold hearings. New standards are initially published in the *Federal Register* and subsequently included with other OSHA standards in the *Code of Federal Regulations* (CFR). The adoption of a new standard typically precipitates a race to the courthouse in which one or more parties associated with industry or labor challenges the standard's legality. Court sometimes stay (put off) the implementation of a standard until legal challenges are concluded. Sometimes Congress gets into the act. In short, the process of adopting new safety standards is lengthy, arduous, litigious, and politicized. OSHA bureaucrats certainly do not create new standards on a whim. In fact, the number of new permanent standards that OSHA has managed to implement since its inception is quite small. Standards are nonexistent (e.g., workplace violence, ergonomics) or outdated (e.g., crystalline silica) for many significant hazards. It is not surprising that the priority items on OSHA's regulatory agenda have already been years in the making. They face a long road still, including possible litigation. OSHA is caught between those who believe that it is doing too little to protect workers and industries that would rather OSHA do less. Some parties in the former camp sued OSHA to compel it to issue a revised standard for hexavalent chromium, and the agency is now under court order to do so (see "Clippings").

Beyond the procedural and political hurdles, courts have placed certain constraints on OSHA's standard setting. The OSH Act says the following about standards:

> The term "occupational safety and health standard" means a standard which requires conditions, or the adoption or use of one or more practices, means, methods, operations or processes, reasonably necessary or appropriate to provide safe or healthful employment and places of employment.[8]

[7]*Davis-Shook Joint Venture XXV v. Secretary of Labor*, 319 F.3d 805, at 812-13 (6th Cir. 2003).

[8]29 U.S.C.A. § 652(8) (2005).

[I]n promulgating standards dealing with toxic materials or harmful agents . . . [OSHA] shall set the standard which most adequately assures, to the extent feasible, on the basis of the best available evidence, that no employee will suffer material impairment of health or functional capacity even if such employee has regular exposure to the hazard . . . for the period of his working life. . . .[9]

When OSHA reduced the **permissible exposure limit (PEL)** (the maximum allowable level of exposure to a hazard) for benzene, the Supreme Court was called upon to determine whether OSHA had exceeded its authority. The Court interpreted the statutory language just quoted here (particularly "reasonably necessary or appropriate") to mean that OSHA bears the burden of demonstrating that any new or revised standard addresses a **significant risk** to the health of employees.[10] The agency is justified in establishing a new standard only if this significant risk can be shown. The revised standard for benzene was struck down because the agency had not done a sufficient risk assessment to establish that workers were endangered by keeping the PEL at the existing, higher level. (OSHA succeeded in lowering the PEL for benzene several years later.) An attempt by OSHA to package a large number of standards covering related hazards into a single, generic ("air contaminants") standard, without showing that each of the individual hazards posed significant risk, was also rejected.[11] However, courts have permitted OSHA to require the medical monitoring of employees as a means of ensuring that they are not being harmed, even where there is not current evidence of significant risk.[12]

OSHA must conduct extensive risk assessments to justify proposed standards. Is it also required to conduct cost-benefit analyses? In a **cost-benefit analysis**, the costs to employers of complying with a standard are compared to the economic value of the expected improvement in worker health (e.g., fewer cases of cancer, fewer deaths). Standards would be adopted only if the projected costs do not exceed the projected benefits. In a case involving the standard for cotton dust, which causes brown-lung disease, the Supreme Court rejected the industry's arguments that OSHA is required to conduct a formal cost-benefit analysis before promulgating standards.[13] Because OSHA is authorized to set standards that eliminate health hazards "to the extent feasible," the focus must be on whether improved safety is achievable, not whether it is economically optimal. Feasibility includes economic considerations, and, in fact, Congress requires OSHA to consider and estimate the cost implications of its proposed regulations (e.g., their potential impact on small businesses). But OSHA is not required to perform a cost-benefit analysis, nor is the agency limited to adopting only those standards whose monetary benefits are demonstrably greater than their costs. A more recent Supreme Court decision concluding that the Environmental Protection Agency (EPA) is not required to perform cost-benefit analysis in adopting environmental regulations suggests that the same continues to be true for OSHA.[14]

General Duty Clause It is impossible for OSHA to develop standards addressing all hazards to which employees might be exposed. The OSH Act's **general duty**

[9]29 U.S.C.A. § 655(b)(5) (2005).

[10]*Industrial Union Department v. American Petroleum Institute*, 448 U.S. 607 (1980).

[11]*AFL-CIO v. OSHA*, 965 F.2d 962 (11th Cir. 1992).

[12]*National Cottonseed Products Ass'n v. Brock*, 825 F.2d 482 (D.C. Cir. 1987), *cert. denied*, 485 U.S. 1020 (1988).

[13]*American Textile Manufacturers Institute, Inc. v. Donovan*, 452 U.S. 490, at 509 (1981).

[14]*Whitman v. American Trucking Ass'ns*, 531 U.S. 457 (2001).

ELEMENTS OF A CLAIM

Violation of the General Duty Clause
To prove a violation of the general duty clause, OSHA must show all the following: 1. A workplace hazard was allowed to exist. 2. The hazard was or should have been recognized by the employer. 3. The hazard caused or was likely to cause death or serious physical injury. 4. Feasible means exist to abate the hazard and were not used.

clause places basic responsibility for workplace safety with employers and can be invoked for enforcement purposes in the absence of specific standards:

> Each employer . . . shall furnish to each of his employees employment and a place of employment which are free from recognized hazards that are causing or are likely to cause death or serious physical harm to his employees. . . .[15]

Hazards are "recognized" when there is reason to believe that they are known to the employer or to the industry in which the employer operates. Recognition refers in this context to awareness that a condition is hazardous to employees, in contrast to the "knowledge" element in standards violation cases, where awareness of the condition is the issue. In a case demonstrating the limited scope of recognized hazards reached by the general duty clause, OSHA cited an employer for failing to keep its workplace free from the hazard of violence.[16] The company operated garden apartment complexes, and its employees were violently attacked by residents on numerous occasions. The administrative law judge (ALJ) deciding the case for the Occupational Safety and Health Review Commission (OSHRC) determined that the employer was not liable because the hazard was not recognized. The decision stressed the differences between violence perpetrated by other people and the typical (and arguably more controllable) hazards regulated by OSHA, as well as the lack of evidence that violence is a particular problem in apartment management.

In general duty clause cases, OSHA must also establish the existence of some feasible means of eliminating or lessening the recognized hazard. This has proven to be an obstacle in OSHA's attempts to use the general duty clause to pursue ergonomic hazards.

Secretary of Labor v. Beverly Enterprises is a case in which OSHA attempts to use the general duty clause to confront serious ergonomic hazards. Much of the decision centers on the question of whether the hazard was "recognized."

While on remand, this case was settled. Beverly agreed to provide further training and purchase more mechanical lifting devices, but did not admit to a violation. Enforcement under the general duty clause remains problematic, but it is clear that ergonomic hazards are a serious problem in many industries, and *employers should use the available, demonstrated means of reducing ergonomic hazards, rather than wait for a clear legal mandate to do so.*

[15]29 U.S.C.A. § 654 (a)(1) (2005).

[16]*Megawest Financial, Inc.*, 17 OSHRC 1337 (1995).

THE CHANGING WORKPLACE

Ergonomic Hazards

Ergonomics deals with the fit between the physical demands of jobs and the physical abilities of people. Work tasks, equipment, and surroundings can pose hazards to employees when they entail such things as frequent use of force, lifting heavy loads, repetitive motions, awkward postures, excessive standing in one place, vibration, and exposure to cold temperatures. These ergonomic risk factors can result in a variety of **musculoskeletal disorders (MSDs)** (also referred to as repetitive stress injuries or cumulative trauma disorders). Particular types of MSDs include carpal tunnel syndrome, rotator cuff syndrome, low back pain, sciatica, and tendonitis. These conditions range in severity, but can be painful and debilitating. The number of reported MSDs suffered by workers increased enormously between the mid-1980s and 1996. The number of reported cases has dropped off somewhat since then, but MSDs still constitute the lion's share of recorded occupational illnesses (in contrast to injuries) and account for a significant proportion of workers' compensation claims. In 2004, MSDs accounted for 32 percent of all injuries and illnesses resulting in lost work time.[1] Not all MSDs are caused by work activities, but substantial evidence exists that many MSDs are work related and that ergonomic interventions in workplaces can reduce the incidence of MSDs.[2]

OSHA's efforts to develop an ergonomics standard are a classic illustration of the highly contentious and politicized standard-setting process. The agency started out in the mid-1980s by offering ergonomics training to employers. It issued voluntary guidelines for the meatpacking industry in 1990. In 1992, OSHA announced that it intended to develop an ergonomic standard (it issued an

"advance notice of proposed rule making"). A draft standard was released in 1995, and as former OSHA head Charles Jeffress put it, "all hell broke loose."[3] OSHA made revisions and held numerous public hearings, but industry prevailed on its allies in Congress to attach riders to OSHA's budget appropriations prohibiting it from adopting an ergonomics standard. OSHA eventually issued an ergonomics standard in November 2000, requiring the establishment of ergonomic programs covering employees in manufacturing and manual handling jobs, and other jobs when an MSD was reported by a job occupant. Congress responded in early 2001 by invoking the never-before-used Congressional Review Act of 1996 to repeal the ergonomic standard. The end result is that there is currently no specific OSHA standard addressing this major workplace safety and health hazard. However, in an approach that sounds remarkably similar to where it started over a decade ago, OSHA is now working on a set of industry-specific voluntary "guidelines."[4] Guidelines have been issued for nursing homes and retail grocery stores.[5]

[1] Lauren Couillard. "Serious Injuries, Illnesses Decline Slightly in 2004, Along with Days Away, BLS Says." *Daily Labor Report* 239 (December 14, 2005), D-15.

[2] National Research Council. *Work-Related Musculoskeletal Disorders: A Review of the Evidence.* (Washington, DC: National Academy Press, 1998).

[3] Charles N. Jeffress. "Ergonomics in the Workplace." Speech at Fitchburg, Massachusetts (September 29, 1999) (http://www.osha.gov).

[4] Department of Labor, Office of Public Affairs. "OSHA Announces Comprehensive Plan to Reduce Ergonomic Injuries." OSHA National News Release (April 5, 2002).

[5] "OSHA Releases Retail Grocery Guidelines Aimed at Reducing Musculoskeletal Disorders." *Daily Labor Report* 104 (June 1, 2004), A-9.

SECRETARY OF LABOR V. BEVERLY ENTERPRISES
2000 OSHRC LEXIS 121

● ● ●

BY THE OCCUPATIONAL SAFETY AND HEALTH REVIEW COMMISSION:

* * * [W]e are asked to consider whether nursing assistants (NA's) who experience LBP [lower

back pain] while lifting and moving residents in nursing homes were exposed to a recognized hazard in violation of [the general duty clause]. [W]e conclude that the Administrative Law Judge . . . erred in concluding that the Secretary of Labor ("Secretary") failed to prove the alleged violations. . . . We reverse and remand. * * *

[An expert witness] showed that the difference between the LWDI [lost work days incidence] of NA's and for other employee groups averaged over three years . . . ranged from 7.4 times greater at Richland Manor to 3.4 times greater at Monroeville, and the LWDI for four of the Beverly facilities exceeded the national average for nursing homes by as much as two to three times. . . . He also observed that the national average for nursing homes was more than twice the average rate for all of general industry. * * *

We find on the scientific evidence presented [including epidemiological studies of the health effects of lifting, computer modeling of the effects of lifting, and application of NIOSH's "lifting equation" used to determine safe lifting weights] that manual lifting of residents is a known and recognized risk factor for LBP. Considering also the evidence showing that the frequency and manner in which Beverly's NA's performed their assigned tasks exposed them to compressive forces in excess of limits well-established and accepted in the scientific community, and that Beverly's working conditions resulted in numerous lost-time incidents and prevented Beverly's NA's from performing their usual daily activities, we conclude that the manual lifting of residents was shown on this record to be a hazardous work practice and that Beverly controls the methods used to perform the lifting. * * *

Beverly's own internal reporting forms contain numerous instances of reports by employees of back pain while moving residents. * * * Beverly's loss control director . . . testified that back injuries were the most common of the workmen's compensation claims and that most of those back injury claims occur from resident lifting and transferring or resident care generally. . . . As part of a settlement with OSHA at a Beverly facility in Connecticut, Beverly hired an ergonomist who studied the injuries reported in the facility and concluded that a primary factor was aggressive or unanticipated movements by residents. In June 1991, Beverly instituted a "lost-time hotline," a program under which each facility was required to report to the corporate . . . and regional office by telephone any injury resulting in lost time of one day or more. * * * The purpose of this program was to increase the awareness of lost-time injuries at the corporate level. . . . * * *

Beverly's response to the numerous workmen's compensation claims, includ[ed] training programs such as "Lift with Care," personal protective equipment, and safety incentive and accident prevention programs. * * * The stated goal of "Lift with Care" is to train NA's how to perform transfers in a manner which would reduce the likelihood both of injury to the resident and back injury to the NA. * * * In October 1991, Beverly's Northeast region was directed by Beverly's corporate headquarters to institute a policy under which it would provide and require all NA's to wear a device known as a "ProFlex Back Support." * * * This memorandum acknowledged the incidence of back injuries in Beverly facilities: "The back support by itself is not the total answer to our back injury problem. . . . However, it should dramatically reduce the number of injuries." * * *

[T]he Secretary must show that the hazard was recognized either by the individual employer or the industry. Beverly's position is that the incident reports, OSHA logs, and workmen's compensation documents as well as the precautions it took do not establish awareness on its part that manually lifting non-weight-bearing residents is hazardous because such lifting practices are normal procedures commonly used in the nursing home industry. * * * The fact that Beverly's work practices are typical of those in the industry as a whole does not necessarily establish that Beverly would not understand those practices to be hazardous. * * * Beverly understood the hazard of lifting a non-weight-bearing resident without some sort of back protection because it attempted to implement a program under which its NA's would wear the Pro-Flex back support. * * * While an employer's safety precautions alone do not establish that the employer believed that those precautions were necessary for compliance with the Act, precautions take by an employer can be used to establish hazard recognition in conjunction with other evidence. Moreover, . . . warnings by or to company personnel regarding the existence of a hazard are more persuasive on the issue of recognition than purely voluntary safety precautions. The record here shows that Beverly's managers at the highest level of the corporation recognized . . . and warned Beverly personnel of the lifting hazard. * * *

The standard for industry recognition is not the knowledge or understanding of experts directly associated with the specific industry in question. So long as the experts who regard the practice or work operation as hazardous are familiar with the conditions in the industry, the Commission does not require that they be employed *in* that industry. * * * [A] preponderance of the evidence supports the conclusion that experts familiar with nursing home industry perceive lifts such as those performed at Beverly to be hazardous. * * *

Under the . . . [general duty clause], the Secretary must show that the recognized harm is one which is "causing" or "likely to cause" "death or serious physical harm." . . . [T]his language does not require the Secretary to show that an accident is likely but rather that *if* an accident were to occur, death or serious physical harm would be the likely result. * * * The question before us, therefore, is whether an employee who experiences LBP is likely to suffer serious physical harm. * * * Beverly's position is that LBP is not serious physical harm because it is merely a symptom, not an injury, and there is no accompanying tissue damage or medical pathology. Beverly also notes that LBP is a common occurrence outside the work environment and that most instances of LBP are of fairly short duration. . . . * * *

LBP has not been shown to have any pathoanatomic association, that is, LBP manifests itself as a type of distress which cannot be linked to any detectable tissue or body damage or injury. * * * [In] the Commission's only other decision involving ergonomics [and] [w]ith respect to injuries resulting from repetitive motion such as upper extremity musculo-skeletal disorders . . . , the Commission concluded that "*physical disorders* that so adversely affect employees that they are disabled from doing their jobs are serious physical harm . . . even if the disability is not permanent." * * * [In] the lead case on the application of the "serious physical harm" criterion to situations in which there is no recognized pathoanatomic damage . . . employees were exposed to excessive levels of airborne silver. The effects of this overexposure included argyria, a permanent and irreversible discoloration of the skin resulting from an increase in melanin levels. * * * [T]he Commission agreed that the evidence failed to show any "systemic implications to silver exposure," but held that an employee's "permanent disfigurement" was a sufficient basis on which to find a serious violation. * * *

The facts here show that LBP has a substantial and significant effect on the affected employees' ability to perform their normal activities and effectively disables employees for periods of time which are extensive in some instances. We conclude that in view of the debilitating effect on employees and the potential duration of the disability, LBP is properly considered serious physical harm.

The last remaining element of proof of a violation . . . is the existence of feasible means of abating or correcting the recognized hazard. The Secretary must specify the proposed abatement measures and demonstrate both that the measures are capable of being put into effect and that they would be effective in materially reducing the incidence of the hazard. * * * "Feasible" means economically and technologically capable of being done. Feasible means of abatement are those regarded by conscientious experts in the industry as ones they would take into account in "prescribing a safety program." In *Pepperidge Farm,* the Commission held that where an ergonomic hazard could not be abated with a single measure, it was permissible for OSHA to require the employer to engage in a "process approach" to abatement "to determine what action or combination of actions will eliminate or materially reduce the hazard." * * *

Here, the Secretary has proposed the following abatement measures: mechanical assist devices, revised policies and work practices, and training. To a limited extent, some of the measures are already in place at the five facilities. . . . The question of whether these abatement measures will eliminate or materially reduce the potential for harm to the back and upper extremities is complicated by numerous evidentiary disputes as to the proper method for lifting certain residents. * * * Similar difficulties are presented by the economic feasibility of the proposed abatements. * * * Once these factual disputes are resolved by the judge on remand, the issue of Beverly's ability to afford the costs of the abatements must be decided. In cases involving the general duty clause, the Commission has generally held that an abatement method is not economically feasible if it "would clearly threaten the economic viability of the employer." * * *

CASE QUESTIONS

1. What was the legal issue in this case? What did the OSHRC decide?

2. What is the evidence that back injuries due to lifting nursing home residents are "recognized hazards"?

3. What is the evidence regarding the severity of these injuries?

4. Does it appear that there are feasible means of lessening this hazard?

5. What are the practical implications of this case for employers? Would employers be better off with a specific standard detailing what is expected of them?

How Is the OSH Act Enforced?

Unlike most other employment laws, the OSH Act is enforced not only by responding to employee complaints of violations, but also by OSHA going out to workplaces and conducting **inspections** to determine whether employers are complying with the law. At the same time, enforcement is not effective without the active involvement of employees or their unions bringing hazards to OSHA's attention, participating in the inspection process, and occasionally taking enforcement into their own hands.

Inspections and Citations OSHA has limited resources. In fiscal year 2004, OSHA conducted approximately 39,000 inspections.[17] If this sounds like a sizeable number of inspections, consider that U.S. workplaces number in the millions. OSHA has to carefully prioritize when selecting sites to inspect. In order of priority, OSHA inspects workplaces where it has reason to believe that there is imminent danger of death or serious physical harm to employees, where it is investigating a catastrophe or fatal accident, where it has received employee complaints of alleged violations, where the workplace was selected as part of a planned effort to conduct inspections in dangerous industries ("programmed inspections"), and where the agency wants to determine whether prior violations have been corrected (follow-up inspections).

Most OSHA inspections are unannounced. When OSHA inspectors (compliance officers) arrive at workplaces, they first locate and present their credentials to the owners or other persons in charge. The OSH Act empowers OSHA inspectors to enter workplaces without delay and at reasonable times to examine records, inspect conditions, and question individuals. However, the Supreme Court has determined that the Fourth Amendment rights of employers to be free from unreasonable search and seizure permit them to refuse entry to OSHA inspectors without a search warrant.[18] This right of refusal does not apply if a clear emergency exists, the hazard in question is in plain view, or an authorized party consents to entry (even though a co-owner disagrees). Refusing entry is at best a delay tactic. OSHA can generally obtain a warrant from a court by establishing probable cause of a violation (e.g., the fatalities that occurred, credible employee complaints) or by showing that selection for a programmed inspection was based on reasonable administrative criteria (e.g., located in a dangerous industry). However, although OSHA inspections generally are not limited to examination of the particular hazards that were the objects of complaints, the scope of searches authorized by warrants might be.[19]

An inspection typically begins with an opening conference where the circumstances of the inspection are explained by the OSHA compliance officer. *An employer representative is entitled to accompany the compliance officer during a workplace inspection, but employers are prohibited from intimidating or interfering with compliance officers as they perform their jobs.* While touring workplaces, compliance officers might write down observations, take photographs, take instrument readings, and ask questions of employees. Apparent violations are pointed out. Although some violations can be corrected on the spot, this does not necessarily preclude issuance of citations for those violations. At a closing conference, the compliance officer goes over the observed violations and the OSHA appeal process.

[17]"OSHA Exceeds FY 2004 Inspection Goal; More Serious, Willful Violations Cited." *Daily Labor Report* 223 (November 19, 2004), A-6.

[18]*Marshall v. Barlow's, Inc.*, 436 U.S. 307 (1978).

[19]*In re: Inspection of Workplace (Carondelet Coke Corp.)*, 741 F.2d 172 (8th Cir. 1984) (broad scope inspection was allowed on the facts of the case).

Citations or fines are not levied by inspectors. Instead, the directors of OSHA area offices issue citations and penalties after reviewing inspection reports. **Citations** for safety violations indicate the nature of the violations, the OSHA standard(s) violated, the monetary penalties associated with the violations, and the amount of time that the employer has to correct the problems (the **abatement** period). Fines vary according to the severity of violations and whether they are deemed willful (intentional). The fines against BP Products NorthAmerica were unusually heavy due to the hundreds of violations alleged and the fact that most were deemed willful violations; but the fines were arguably still light in comparison to the number of serious injuries and lives lost in the refinery explosion (see "Clippings"). Although the OSH Act provides for limited criminal penalties (a maximum of $20,000 in fines and one year in jail, regardless of the number of violations), in cases where employers willfully violate standards and these violations result in employee deaths, criminal penalties are only rarely sought.[20] Stronger enforcement may require OSHA to team up with other federal agencies, particularly the EPA, that have the capability to impose more severe criminal sanctions against employers.[21] Employers that subject their employees to serious workplace hazards are often equally poor stewards of the environment.

Copies of citations received must be posted in the workplace near where the violations occurred and for three working days or until the violations are corrected, whichever is longer. Employers have the right to challenge the existence of violations, penalties, and/or the length of abatement periods. *Employers have 15 days following the receipt of a citation to contest the citation (i.e., file a written Notice of Contest with the OSHA area director who transmits the case to the OSHRC). Although all violations should be corrected promptly, employers are not legally required to correct alleged violations until their appeals have been heard and the OSHRC has issued a final order.* Besides appealing to the OSHRC (and sometimes, subsequently the courts), employers can petition OSHA to modify abatement schedules or meet with OSHA area directors to discuss settlements.

Employee Role in Enforcement Because OSHA visits only a miniscule number of workplaces at its own initiative, employee reports of potential hazards are critical to enforcement. Not surprisingly, some employers take a dim view of such complaints. OSHA does not reveal the identities of employees who make safety complaints, but it does inform employers when inspections are prompted by complaints and provides copies of written complaints (with names deleted). In one case,[22] a machine operator complained to coworkers and her boss about a chemical spray emitted by her machine. She then filed a formal complaint with OSHA, prompting an inspection. The employer pressed the OSHA compliance officer for the identity of the complainant and expressed annoyance when it was not divulged. Three days later, the complainant was fired. The company said that the termination was for tardiness, but they had ignored violations by other employees. The court concluded that the employee was retaliated against in violation of OSHA. It was not necessary to show that the employer had certain knowledge of the identity of the complainant to establish a causal connection between engaging in protected activity and suffering adverse employment consequences. *Employers are prohibited from retaliating against employees for making complaints about safety problems, contacting*

[20]David Barstow. "U.S. Rarely Seeks Charges for Deaths in Workplace." *New York Times* (November 22, 2003), A-1.

[21]David Barstow and Lowell Bergman. "With Little Fanfare, a New Effort to Prosecute Employers that Flout Safety Laws." *New York Times* (May 2, 2005), A-17.

[22]*Reich v. Hoy Shoe Co.*, 32 F.3d 361 (8th Cir. 1994).

OSHA, filing complaints with OSHA, speaking with inspectors, or otherwise participating in the enforcement process.

Employees' lives, health, and well-being are at stake in dangerous workplaces. Under the best of circumstances, there is delay between when OSHA is informed of potential hazards and when any inspections occur. Employees who refuse to work under dangerous conditions have some legal protection from termination or other punishment for their refusal to work. For one thing, walking off the job due to serious safety problems can constitute protected concerted activity under the National Labor Relations Act (NLRA). Also, a section of the NLRA specifically permits employees to stop work because of "abnormally dangerous" conditions. The nonretaliation provisions of OSHA have been interpreted as protecting refusals to engage in very dangerous work, and the Supreme Court has concurred with this interpretation.[23] However, such refusals are protected only where the hazard poses a threat of serious injury or death, the threat is too immediate to rely on the normal enforcement process, and the employer has been informed but has not corrected the hazard. *Employers should take employee safety complaints seriously and must not punish employees for refusing to work under conditions that pose a serious and imminent threat to their health.*

An employee representative must be allowed to participate in the opening conference and to accompany the compliance officer during an inspection. The employee representative must not be chosen by the employer. As a practical matter, this right is most often exercised when employees have union representation.[24] Employees can request informal review in cases where OSHA declines to issue a citation, but only the amount of time that the employer is given to fix problems can be formally contested by employees.

Employees are responsible under OSHA for following health and safety rules, although employees who fail to do so are not subject to any type of enforcement action. The reason is that employers already have available the means of obtaining employee compliance (e.g., discipline, training, supervision).

Recording and Reporting Requirements

Keeping records of occupational injuries and illnesses is important in order to discern patterns that might point to systemic problems and is a requirement of the OSH Act. Exempted from these recording requirements are most employers with 10 or fewer employees and employers in a variety of service and retail industries. *Employers not exempted from record keeping are required to establish and communicate to their employees specific procedures for reporting workplace injuries and illnesses. Employers are required to record (within 6 days of their occurrence) all work-related injuries or illnesses that result in death, days away from work, restricted work, transfer to another job, loss of consciousness, or medical treatment beyond first aid—and any other "significant" injuries or illnesses diagnosed by licensed health care professionals.* Injuries or illnesses are work related when "an event or exposure in the work environment either caused or contributed to the resulting condition or significantly aggravated a preexisting injury or illness."[25]

Because safety and health conditions can vary considerably between individual workplaces, *records must be kept for each separate establishment and not just an entire company.* Employers can use OSHA's Form 300 (Log of Work-Related Injuries

[23]*Whirlpool Corp. v. Marshall,* 445 U.S. 1 (1980).

[24]David Weil. "Enforcing OSHA: The Role of Labor Unions." *Industrial Relations* 30, no. 1 (1991), 28–29.

[25]29 C.F.R. § 1904.5(a) (2005).

and Illnesses) and Form 301 (Injury and Illness Incident Report) or maintain the same information in other comparable formats. *An annual summary of injuries and illnesses must be maintained and posted for employee inspection during the month of February (for the previous year).* (OSHA's Form 300A—Summary of Work-Related Injuries and Illnesses—can be used for this purpose.) *These records must be retained for five years and made available for OSHA inspectors.*

Records must also be maintained for documenting safety training provided and certifying that certain potentially dangerous equipment (e.g., cranes) has been examined and is in safe working order. If employees are given periodic medical tests to screen for adverse health effects or workplace conditions are monitored (e.g., air-quality tests), those records must also be kept. Because occupational diseases often take a long time to develop, medical and exposure records must be retained for many years.

Although logs of injuries and illnesses are not usually sent to OSHA, *employers are required to report to OSHA (within eight hours) any fatal accident or any accident that results in the hospitalization of three or more employees. Employers are also required, if selected, to participate in the Bureau of Labor Statistic's (BLS) annual survey of occupational injuries and illnesses.* This survey is a basic source of data for occupational safety and health statistics. Even firms that are otherwise exempt from OSHA recording requirements have to participate in the BLS survey.

Violations of record-keeping requirements can be costly. A court upheld a penalty of $224,050 imposed against an employer for numerous willful violations in failing to record serious injuries.[26] The employer failed to record some 357 injuries (86 percent of the total) that occurred in one of its facilities during a year. The injuries included finger amputations, broken bones, eye injuries, and severe burns. In light of the seriousness of the injuries, the number of nonrecorded injuries, and evidence that the employer was aware of OSHA's record-keeping requirements, the company's claim that its behavior was not willful was unpersuasive.

PREVENTING OCCUPATIONAL INJURIES AND ILLNESSES

Some OSHA standards are specific about the particular actions that employers must take, but many others leave it to employers to devise a set of **controls** that will effectively make their particular operations safer. For example, the occupational noise exposure standard outlined earlier specifies maximum noise exposure levels and the elements of a hearing conservation program intended to identify and respond to hearing loss, but in terms of abating the noise hazard itself, it says only that "feasible administrative or engineering controls shall be utilized" when exposure is above the maximum allowed. The standard further states that "if such controls fail to reduce sound levels within the [specified] levels, personal protective equipment shall be provided and used to reduce sound levels. . . ."[27] This and other OSHA standards reflect the safety principle of a **hierarchy of controls.**"[28] The hierarchy runs from measures that might eliminate a hazard entirely (e.g., using new equipment, substituting another component for a toxic substance), to engineering controls that do not eliminate hazards but automatically provide protection from them (e.g., machine guards, venting), to administrative measures that limit the extent of exposure

[26]*Kaspar Wire Works, Inc. v. Secretary of Labor,* 268 F.3d 1123 (D.C. Cir. 2001).

[27]29 C.F.R. § 1910.95(b)(1) (2005).

[28]Gerald Wagner. "The Hierarchy of Controls: An Alternative to Behavior-Based Safety." *Occupational Hazards* (May 1999), 95–97.

(e.g., job rotation, additional staffing), to training and warnings that teach employees about how to protect themselves from hazards, to personal protective equipment that is worn by employees and provides the last line of defense between the hazard and the individual. Eliminating or engineering out hazards tends to be more expensive, but is also more effective. *Employers should focus on eliminating hazards or reducing them to the maximum extent possible through use of engineering and administrative controls.* Training and personal protective equipment are clearly necessary and important, but they do not do anything to make unsafe conditions safer, and they are vulnerable to the vicissitudes of employee behavior.

Flexibility and options are desirable in many realms, but not with respect to safety rules. *Safety rules should be clear, specific, consistent with one another, and consistently enforced.* An employer had a rule prohibiting the use of gloves near moving machinery (because gloves tend to get caught in machinery and pull their wearer's hands in with them), but gave employees the option of using gloves near a particular type of moving machinery that presented the threat of cuts and abrasions to the hand. The employer was found to have violated two OSHA standards regarding hand protection and machine guarding. The court observed:

> Rather than adopting a hand protection policy that took into account two simultaneous hazards, Riverdale adopted one policy forbidding use of gloves around moving machinery, but then allowed employees to wear gloves when using the Peck machine in order to avoid cuts. These contradictory policies forced employees to choose which hazard to protect against, thereby exposing them to one hazard or the other, unabated.[29]

The absence of recordable injuries and illnesses does not mean that a workplace is safe. For example, near-misses may occur that, but for luck, would have resulted in serious injury. *Employers should engage in proactive efforts to identify and abate unsafe conditions in their workplaces. One of the best ways to do this is to establish an effective workplace safety program.* OSHA guidelines[30] and contemporary safety practice strongly encourage the implementation of effective **workplace safety programs.** Figure 15-3 outlines the basic elements of a safety program.

One of the ways in which OSHA encourages the implementation of safety programs is through its Voluntary Protection Program (VPP). This program recognizes excellence in employer safety and health practices. Firms that are certified under the VPP as having effective safety and health programs are subject to less frequent inspections. OSHA also provides free consultations, particularly to small businesses; those firms will not be cited for any violations observed, provided that they agree to abate the hazards. However, although safety and health programs are clearly beneficial, OSHA was thwarted when it attempted to give employers with high injury rates the choice of either implementing comprehensive safety and health programs or facing "wall-to-wall" inspections.[31] This strategy, termed the Cooperative Compliance Program, was deemed by the court to be a revision of safety standards that had to be approved through the formal standard-setting process. It was viewed as a change in standards because safety and health programs go beyond the minimum safety levels required by the OSH Act in addressing and abating all identified hazards.

[29]*Riverdale Mills v. OSHRC,* 29 Fed. Appx. 11 (1st Cir. 2002).

[30]Occupational Safety and Health Administration. *Safety and Health Program Management Guidelines* (1989).

[31]*Chamber of Commerce v. Department of Labor,* 174 F.3d 206 (D.C. Cir. 1999).

FIGURE 15-3	Elements of Workplace Safety Programs
Demonstrate Management Commitment	*Develop a safety and health policy statement* *Communicate with employees about safety and health issues* *Establish objectives for safety and health performance; measure performance* *Assign responsibility for health and safety activities and outcomes* *Provide sufficient time, authority, and resources to safety and health of staff* *Reward good safety and health performance* *Enforce safety rules* *Show direct involvement of upper-level managers in safety issues*
Obtain Employee Commitment	*Utilize safety and health committees (structured to also comply with the NLRA)* *Work closely with union representatives on safety issues* *Involve employees in identifying and solving safety problems* *Encourage expression of safety concerns*
Perform Worksite Hazard Analyses	*Consult with outside experts* *Review OSHA-required records for patterns* *Carefully investigate accidents and near-misses, looking for root causes* *Conduct self-inspections, job hazard analyses* *Consider health and safety ramifications of changes in equipment, work processes, and staffing*
Prevent or Control Hazards	*Give priority to eliminating or abating hazards* *Use engineering, work process, and administrative controls; training; personal protective equipment; medical and exposure monitoring* *Properly maintain facilities and equipment* *Engage in emergency planning and preparation* *Ensure that medical surveillance and treatment are readily available*

WORKERS' COMPENSATION

The purpose of the OSH Act is to avoid injuries and illnesses by making workplaces safer; workers' compensation statutes deal with the consequences of those workplace injuries and illnesses that occur. Workers' compensation is generally provided for under state laws. The role of the federal government is limited to providing coverage for longshoring employees, as well as for its own employees.

Workers' compensation statutes require coverage of almost all employees, whether full-time or part-time, private or public sector. The major exclusion from coverage is persons who perform work as independent contractors (some states also limit coverage of farm workers and domestics). However, companies that use the employees of contractors to perform work that would normally be performed by their own employees can be deemed "statutory employers." If a contractor does not provide workers' compensation for its employees, the statutory employer can be required to provide such coverage. Thus, *firms using employees from contract companies should ensure that those contractors are providing workers' compensation*

for their employees. Furthermore, *even if an employer does not pay workers' compensation premiums for its contract employees (or temps), it is still obligated under OSHA to provide a safe workplace for those workers.* And because of their lesser familiarity with the workplace layout and equipment, and the dirty, dangerous tasks for which they are sometimes enlisted (e.g., maintenance of equipment, cleaning), contract employees and temps are at considerable risk of injury or death.[32]

In almost all states, workers' compensation coverage is mandatory. By law, *employers must arrange workers' compensation coverage for their employees.* They do so by contributing to state workers' compensation funds, purchasing coverage from private insurers, or (for larger employers) self-insuring. The available funding options vary by state. The amounts that must be contributed depend largely on the industry in which the employer operates and, to a lesser extent, on experience rating. Under **experience rating,** employers that have worse records of injuries and claims pay more, providing a financial incentive to invest in safety. However, rates only partially reflect claims experience and, with the exception of self-insurance where the employer bears all the costs of claims, incentives to invest in safety are probably less than they need to be.

What do employees who are hurt on the job get through workers' compensation? Benefit levels are fixed by law. The benefits include replacement income (if an employee is unable to work), payment of all medical costs associated with the injury or illness, and rehabilitation services. Workers' compensation statutes provide for only partial income replacement, on the theory that this will give employees greater incentive to return to work. Typical payment levels are replacement of two-thirds of normal pay, up to an amount that is not more than the statewide average weekly wage. Payments depend on whether the individual is judged to be temporarily or permanently disabled and whether the disability is full or partial. Survivors can receive payments for employee deaths. Coverage of medical costs under workers' compensation is separate from any health insurance benefits that an employee receives through her employer.

Workers' compensation is provided, for the most part, on a no-fault basis. Employees receive benefits without having to demonstrate in court that their employers were negligent in allowing them to get hurt. Employees need not fend off employer claims that they contributed to the harm they suffered by being careless, that a coworker caused the injury rather than the employer, or that employees knowingly "assumed risk" by accepting their jobs. These traditional common law defenses to negligence claims—**contributory negligence,** the **fellow servant rule,** and **assumption of risk,** respectively—do not apply under workers' compensation. However, the right to receive workers' compensation without proving employer negligence comes at a price. Workers' compensation is the **exclusive remedy** for injuries and illnesses that arise out of and in the course of employment. Employees who are hurt on the job generally cannot sue their employers. Instead, they are limited to filing workers' compensation claims and accepting the meaningful, but comparatively limited, remedies.

Exclusive Remedy

Laidlow v. Hariton Machinery considers an important exception to the general rule that workers' compensation is the exclusive remedy for workplace injuries. The rule does not hold when an injury is intentional, rather than accidental.

[32]Greg LaBar. "Contingent Worker Safety: A Full-Time Job in a Part-Time World." *Occupational Hazards* (October 1997), 92–99.

LAIDLOW V. HARITON MACHINERY
790 A.2d 884 (N.J. 2002)

OPINION BY JUSTICE LONG:

* * * Rudolph Laidlow (Laidlow) suffered a serious and debilitating injury when his hand became caught in a rolling mill he was operating at his place of employment, (AMI). Laidlow sustained a crush and degloving injury resulting in partial amputations of the index, middle, ring and small fingers of his dominant left hand. Laidlow sued AMI on an intentional tort theory. * * * AMI . . . moved for summary judgment on the basis of the Workers' Compensation bar. * * *

On the day of the accident, Laidlow's glove became caught by the unguarded nip point as he was pushing a bar of silver into the channel. His gloved hand was pulled toward the mill's rollers. An eyewitness, Laidlow's co-worker Steven Smozanek, described the incident as follows: "The rollers are approximately 18 inches in diameter, and as he was feeding the bar into the roller, it pulled his hand against the roller, not into the roller, and as it pulled the hand against the roller, it just ripped the glove and the skin right off his hand."

On a prior occasion, Laidlow's glove had also become hooked on a bar, but he was able to slip his hand out of the glove before it was pulled into the machine. Smozanek described a similar incident when he was working on the mill and his gloved hand had snagged on a bar, but he too was able to pull his hand out of the glove just in time to escape injury. Those close calls were reported to AMI.

After the rolling mill was purchased by AMI in 1978, the company arranged to have a safety guard installed. However, the safety guard was "never" engaged; from 1979 to the date of Laidlow's accident in 1992, the guard always was "tied up." According to Laidlow, the guard was placed in its proper position only when Occupational Safety and Health Administration (OSHA) inspectors came to the plant. On those occasions, Portman, Laidlow's supervisor, would instruct employees to release the wire that was holding up the safety guard. As soon as the OSHA inspectors left, the safety guard would again be disabled.

Laidlow operated the mill without the safety guard in place for approximately twelve to thirteen years.

During that period, except for the "near misses" referred to earlier, there were apparently no accidents with the mill until Laidlow was seriously injured during the incident at issue here. Laidlow spoke to Portman regarding the safety guard three times during the period immediately preceding his accident. * * * According to Laidlow, the guard was never restored. Portman responded to his requests by stating that "it was okay" and "not a problem," and by "walking away." Laidlow never refused to operate the mill without the safety guard in place nor spoke with any other superior in the company about the safety guard.

AMI concedes that the guard was removed for "speed and convenience." In addition, Gerald Barnes, a professional engineer retained by Laidlow, certified that AMI "knew there was a virtual certainty of injury to Mr. Laidlow or a fellow worker arising from the operation of the mill without a guard." * * *

In essence, Laidlow's argument is that the combination of the employer's disabling of the safety guard and deception of OSHA presents a triable issue on whether such conduct meets the definition of an "intentional wrong." AMI counters that under *Millison*, an intentional wrong requires a "deliberate intention to injure" and that Laidlow concedes that no one at AMI harbored such an intention. * * * Our decision in *Millison* is obviously at the root of this case and a review of our holding there is essential. In *Millison*, we were faced with the question of "what categories of employer conduct will be sufficiently flagrant so as to constitute an 'intentional wrong.'" . . * * * [The] exclusive remedy provision of the Workers' Compensation Act [is] often referred to as the Workers' Compensation bar. *Millison* confronted that provision in the context of an occupational disease caused by exposure to asbestos during employment. * * *

[I]n *Millison* . . . we stated . . . that an intentional wrong can be shown not only by proving a subjective desire to injure, but also by a showing, based on all the facts and circumstances of the case, that the employer knew an injury was substantially certain to result. In addition to adopting [a] "substantial certainty" test relative to conduct, in *Millison* we added a crucial second prong to the test: "Courts must examine not only the conduct of the employer, but also the context in which

that conduct takes place. . . ." * * * By the addition of the context prong, *Millison* required courts to assess not only whether the employer acted with knowledge that injury was substantially certain to occur, but also whether the injury and the circumstances surrounding it were part and parcel of everyday industrial life or plainly outside the legislative grant of immunity.

Applying th[is] . . . standard to the facts in *Millison,* we concluded, with respect to the defendant employer, that . . . [a]lthough defendants' conduct in knowingly exposing plaintiffs to asbestos clearly amounts to deliberately taking risks with employees' health, . . . the mere knowledge and appreciation of a risk—even the strong probability of a risk—will come up short of the "substantial certainty" needed to find an intentional wrong resulting in avoidance of the exclusive-remedy bar of the compensation statute. * * * Regarding the defendant physicians' conduct, however, we reached a different conclusion. . . . * * * [A]lthough plaintiffs' physical examinations revealed changes in chest x-rays indicating asbestos-related injuries, du Pont's doctors did not inform plaintiffs of their sicknesses, but instead told them that their health was fine and sent them back to work under the same hazardous conditions that had caused the initial injuries. * * * There is a difference between, on the one hand, tolerating in the workplace conditions that will result in a certain number of injuries or illnesses, and, on the other, actively misleading the employees who have already fallen victim to those risks of the workplace. * * *

The evidence with inferences in favor of Laidlow is powerful. The rolling mill is a dangerous machine because it requires an employee to manually feed material into a nip point. Indeed, it has been held that "an employee who manually feeds material into a machine with an unguarded nip point is at great risk of great injury." Apparently recognizing that principle, after its purchase AMI provided a safety guard for the rolling mill. Yet, for 13 years, from 1979 to 1992 when Laidlow was injured, the guard was inactivated by AMI nearly 100% of the time the machine was in use. During that period, Laidlow and a fellow employee had experienced close calls with the nip point of the unguarded mill. Those were potentially serious accidents in which the employees' gloves were ripped off by the machine and their fingers saved only by the cloth in the gloves. Those close calls were reported to AMI to no avail. They were persuasive evidence that AMI knew not only that injury was substantially certain to occur,

but also that when it did occur it would be very serious, as Laidlow's injury turned out to be. Within the month prior to his accident, Laidlow asked his supervisor three times to restore the guard because the unguarded machine was dangerous and because new and inexperienced employees would be operating it. Nothing was ever done.

Significantly, the only time the guard was ever activated by AMI was when OSHA inspectors came. In fact, AMI systematically deceived OSHA into believing that the machine was guarded, inferentially at least, because it knew that operating the machine without the guard inevitably would cause injury and that OSHA would not allow such a dangerous condition to exist. * * * By its deception, a jury could conclude that AMI evidenced an awareness of the "virtual" certainty of injury from the unguarded mill. * * *

AMI argues that the absence of prior accidents obviates a possible finding of "substantial certainty" by a jury. We disagree. * * * The appreciation of danger can be obtained in a myriad of ways other than personal knowledge or previous injuries. Simply because people are not injured, maimed or killed every time they encounter a device or procedure is not solely determinative of the question of whether that procedure or device is dangerous and unsafe. If we were to accept the appellee's reasoning, it would be tantamount to giving every employer one free injury for every decision, procedure or device it decided to use, regardless of the knowledge or substantial certainty of the danger that the employer's decision entailed. . . . * * *

A finding that the substantial certainty prong was satisfied does not end our inquiry. * * * We have concluded that if Laidlow's allegations are proved, however, the context prong of *Millison* would be met. Indeed, if an employee is injured when an employer deliberately removes a safety device from a dangerous machine to enhance profit or production, with substantial certainty that it will result in death or injury to a worker, and also deliberately and systematically deceives OSHA into believing that the machine is guarded, we are convinced that the Legislature would never consider such actions or injury to constitute simple facts of industrial life. On the contrary, such conduct violates the social contract so thoroughly that we are confident that the Legislature would never expect it to fall within the Worker's Compensation bar. * * *

The judgment of the Appellate Division is reversed. The matter is remanded for trial . . .

CASE QUESTIONS

1. What was the legal issue in this case? What did the court decide? Why?

2. Why was the employer arguing that the injured employee is entitled to workers' compensation, while the employee was arguing against coverage?

3. What facts support the conclusion that there was "substantial certainty" of harm?

4. Would the injured employee have been protected if he had refused to work on the machine without the guard in place?

The New Jersey Supreme Court's interpretation of "intentional" injury in *Laidlow* is relatively liberal; in general, courts are sparing in recognizing this exception to the exclusivity of workers' compensation. In a California case, an employee was told by his supervisor to enter a structure and was not given further instruction or warnings. Entering the structure required bending over to get through a three-foot-high doorway. Immediately upon entering the room, the employee made contact with an operating screw conveyor mounted on the floor next to the door. The injury to the employee's leg resulted in amputation below the knee. Despite evidence of lack of training, violation of OSHA regulations, and supervisor animosity toward the employee, the court concluded that the employer's actions did not evidence the requisite intent to harm or "the kind of violations of law or public policy, fraud, or false imprisonment" necessary to take the case outside the boundaries of workers' compensation.[33] Likewise, in a case involving the death of an employee in a collapsed trench, the Kentucky Supreme Court stated:

> [S]ince the trench was over five feet deep Environmental failed to comply with Kentucky OSHA regulations regarding safety precautions for trench work by not sufficiently sloping the trench, shoring the trench walls, or installing a trench box. Environmental failed to provide the proper means of escape from the trench and failed to report [the employee's] death to Kentucky OSHA officials within the required eight hours. Environmental also failed to have a competent person perform daily inspections of the site. Environmental knew that injury or death could result from a failure to take the proper precautions. Nevertheless, Environmental's violation of OSHA regulations and acknowledgement of the possible consequences does not amount to a deliberate intention to produce [the employee's] death.[34]

Another exception to the exclusivity of workers' compensation as a remedy is that third parties (e.g., equipment manufacturers, suppliers of components) can sometimes be sued for workplace injuries and illnesses, even when employers cannot be. The employees who suffered lung diseases after being exposed to airborne butter flavoring are limited to workers' compensation claims against their employer, but are pursuing lawsuits against the company that made the flavoring (see "Clippings"). The plethora of suits brought by plaintiffs, including employees, against asbestos manufacturers for their failure to warn users of the dangers associated with their product is the leading example of this exception to the exclusivity of workers' compensation. On the other hand, suits by employees against the manufacturers of computer keyboards for ergonomic injuries generally have not succeeded.

[33]*Brutz v. Calmat Co.*, 2002 Cal. App. Unpub. LEXIS 3685.

[34]*Moore v. Environmental Construction Corp.*, 147 S.W. 3d 13 (Ky. 2004).

Arising out of and in the Course of Employment

Workers' compensation is intended to deal with work-related injuries and illnesses—specifically, those that "arise out of and in the course of employment." The requirement that the injury or illness occur **in the course of employment** refers to the time, place, and setting in which it occurs. **Arising out of employment** refers to the underlying causation of the injury or illness. These phrases are deceptively simple. They have been the objects of much litigation. *Wright v. Beverly Fabrics* is one interesting example.

WRIGHT V. BEVERLY FABRICS
95 Cal. App. 4th 346 (2002); *review denied,* 2002 Cal. LEXIS 3206

OPINION BY JUDGE WISEMAN:

A prominent American playwright, journalist, and political figure, Clare Booth Luce, once said, "No good deed goes unpunished." These words seem especially pertinent when considering the plight of plaintiff/respondent Paula Wright. Wright, by all accounts an excellent employee of defendant/appellant Beverly Fabrics, Inc., had come to the store on her day off to sign a condolence card and contribute money for two other employees who had lost family members. Unfortunately, while there, she injured her back as she helped hold up a collapsing shelf containing store merchandise.

Wright filed suit for negligence. Beverly Fabrics made numerous legal attempts to "nip it in the bud," contending Wright's remedy was confined to workers' compensation. The court held, as a matter of law, Wright's damages were not barred by the workers' compensation exclusive remedy rule. A jury found in favor of Wright and awarded her in excess of one-half million dollars.

On appeal, Wright argues the workers' compensation exclusive remedy rule does not apply, as she was on the premises to engage in a voluntary social activity that exempts her from workers' compensation benefits. . . . We sympathize with Wright and the legal "Catch-22" she now faces. However, we conclude the law is clear, and reverse the judgment. * * *

On Wednesday, June 3, 1998, Wright went to work, despite the fact it was her day off, to sign a condolence card and contribute money for two employees who had lost family members. She was not requested by anyone with Beverly Fabrics to make a donation or sign any cards. It was not uncommon for employees to come

into the store on a day off to visit, and they were permitted to shop in the store and assist customers on their days off. However, employees were not paid for working on these days.

Wright was visiting in the back of the store with fellow employees Donna Bell and Colleen Dutro, who were both working at the time. There were no customers in the area. Bell was standing about one foot from a shelving unit when she noticed the shelf move. Heavy clay pots were stacked at the end of the shelf where the three women were standing. * * * Unbeknownst to the three women, the shelf was missing some braces.

* * * When Wright saw the shelf falling, she moved about six feet from where she was standing, positioned herself between Dutro and Bell, straddling boxes, and grabbed the shelf. Wright immediately felt pain down her back. Soon after Wright, Bell and Dutro grabbed the falling shelf, other employees came to assist. Melinda McRee, the store's manager, also grabbed the shelf and told everyone if they could not hold it, to let go. Dutro also advised any person to let go if she was hurting. In response, Wright stated her back was hurting, but she could not let go. While Wright, Dutro and McRee were holding up the shelf, four other employees started taking items off of it. When the shelf was unloaded, it was pushed upright. Bell then released her hold on the shelf and went to find braces for it and a repairman. The other women continued to hold the shelf. During the time the shelf was being held up and unloaded, customers were kept out of the area and precluded from providing any assistance. * * *

[California law] provides that the sole and exclusive remedy of an injured employee against an employer is the right to recover workers' compensation benefits [for]

any injury sustained by his or her employees arising out of and in the course of the employment * * * [subject to conditions including that] the injury does not arise out of voluntary participation in any off-duty recreational, social, or athletic activity not constituting part of the employee's work-related duties, except where these activities are a reasonable expectancy of, or are expressly or impliedly required by, the employment. . . ."

* * * In resolving this issue, we are guided by the Legislature's command . . . that workers' compensation laws "be liberally construed by the courts with the purpose of extending their benefits for the protection of persons injured in the course of their employment." "The requirement [for coverage] is twofold. On the one hand, the injury must occur in the "course of the employment." This concept ordinarily refers to the time, place, and circumstances under which the injury occurs. Thus an employee is in the "course of his employment" when he does those reasonable things which his contract with his employment expressly or impliedly permits him to do.'" * * * [T]he statute [also] requires that an injury "arise out of" the employment. . . . It has long been settled that for an injury to "arise out of the employment" it must "occur by reason of a condition or incident of [the] employment. . . ." That is, the employment and the injury must be linked in some causal fashion.'"

We find Wright was acting in the course of her employment at the time of her injury and her injury arose out of her employment. Injuries sustained while an employee is performing tasks within his or her employment contract but outside normal work hours are within the course of employment. The rationale is that the employee is still acting in furtherance of the employer's business. The combination of a personal act performed outside of regular working hours with the performance of acts in furtherance of the employer's business does not defeat a finding that the employee was acting in the course of his or her employment. * * *

Wright was assisting fellow employees in holding up a collapsing shelf. She was doing no more than what a reasonable employer would expect from a responsible employee in her position. There can be no doubt that Wright was engaged in an activity incidental to her employment in furtherance of her employer's business and protecting its assets. * * *

Wright's reliance on the restriction for social activities . . . is misplaced. [This restriction] precludes recovery of workers' compensation benefits for injuries arising out of voluntary participation in off-duty recreational, social or athletic activities that are not part of an employee's work-related duties. However, there is no preclusion if the activity that resulted in the injury is a reasonable expectancy of the employment. * * * Wright was not engaged in a recreational or social activity at the time of her injury, and her injury did not arise out of participation in any such activity. Wright was not hurt while she was signing a condolence card or visiting with coworkers. She was hurt holding up a shelf in an effort to protect the property of her employer, an activity reasonably contemplated by her employment. Simply put, Wright's actions in assisting her coworkers in holding up the shelf were taken in furtherance of her employer's business and were reasonably expected by her employer. * * *

In sum, we conclude Wright's injuries arose out of and in the course of her employment with Beverly Fabrics. Thus, the court erred in finding Wright's damages were not barred by the workers' compensation exclusive remedy rule.

CASE QUESTIONS

1. What was the legal issue in this case? What did the court decide?

2. What is the evidence that she was injured "in the course of" employment? "Arising out of" employment?

3. Why didn't the restriction on workers' compensation coverage for voluntary participation in social activities apply?

4. What is the effect of this decision on Wright? Was this case correctly decided?

Many circumstances raise questions about whether injuries or illnesses arose out of and in the course of employment. For example, are employees who are injured or killed while commuting to work entitled to workers' compensation? Such injuries are typically not compensable, but if employees are commuting in company-provided transportation, performing duties enroute to work (e.g., picking up materials at a supplier), or being exposed to special hazards stemming from the location

of the workplace (e.g., a dangerous left turn across traffic without a light), their injuries would likely be compensable. Similarly, injuries that occur while entering or leaving the workplace or in company-owned parking lots are usually compensable. However, when a teenage employee who became ill at work was mugged while walking home at 3:00 A.M., the court concluded that his injuries were not compensable because he was not exposed to any special hazard to which the general public was not equally subject in walking home at that time of day.[35]

Travel by employees, outside of commuting to and from work, also raises questions about coverage. In a case with an extraordinary set of facts, an accountant accepted a two-year assignment in the Phillipines and moved to Manila. Four days after his arrival in the country, and on an off-day from work, the employee was abducted after leaving a restaurant and heading back to his hotel. The employee was held by his captors for three weeks, chained to the floor, threatened, and tortured. Despite telling the employee's wife that the company would pay the ransom demand, the employer stalled in doing so out of concern that this would create an incentive to kidnap other employees. Angry that the promised ransom had not been paid, the kidnappers cut off part of the employee's ear and sent a videotape of the event to the employer. The ransom was paid the next day and the employee was released. In response to the numerous legal claims brought by the employee and his wife, the company asserted that workers' compensation was the exclusive remedy for the employee's injuries. The court recognized that a "traveling employee" exception, extending workers' compensation coverage to certain employees who are injured in the course of job-related travel, exists under Washington DC's (the relevant jurisdiction) workers' compensation statute. However the court refused to apply the traveling employee exception to all injuries that might occur anytime an employee relocates outside of the state or country for work. Although the accountant was in the Phillipines because of this work assignment, his injuries did not arise out of or in the course of his employment. He remained free to pursue tort claims against his employer.[36]

What about when employee or coworker misconduct results in injury? An employee who suffered a back injury when she went to sit down in her chair, the height of which had been lowered by a coworker as a prank, was entitled to workers' compensation.[37] In general, nonparticipating employees who are injured by the horseplay or pranks of other employees are entitled to workers' compensation. Even employees who actively participate in such activity can be covered if the employer condoned the conduct. A chicken plant employee who was seriously slashed by a coworker after both had been using their 5-inch knives to try to cut the apron strings of the other was still entitled to workers' compensation for the injury. Playing with deboning knives was customary in this workplace, and the employer had never done anything to stop it.[38] Misbehavior that results in injury but does not constitute a substantial departure from required tasks is likely to be compensable. In an extreme example of this point, a truck driver who was hurt when the truck he was driving was struck by a train was entitled to compensation, even though there was evidence that he had also been engaged in sexual activity with a coworker at the time of the mishap.[39] However, employees who are injured while under the influence of drugs or alcohol on the job are generally viewed as having abandoned their jobs and are not

[35]*Slagle v. White Castle System, Inc.*, 607 N.E.2d 45 (Ohio 1992).

[36]*Khan v. Parsons Global Services, Ltd.*, 428 F.3d 1079 (D.C. Cir. 2005).

[37]*Oliva v. Heath*, 35 Cal. App. 4th 926 (1995).

[38]*Bare v. Wayne Poultry Co.*, 318 S.E.2d 534 (N.C. App. 1984), *review denied*, 325 S.E.2d 484 (N.C. 1985).

[39]*Darco Transportation v. Dulen*, 922 P.2d 591 (Okla. 1996).

entitled to workers' compensation.[40] Consequently, *employers often conduct drug and alcohol tests following accidents, and they may be required to do so by insurers.*

Heart attacks and back injuries present other problems. These conditions clearly have many causes and might be preexisting conditions that become aggravated by the demands of employment. Most courts follow the usual-exertion rule, under which such injuries are compensable if the normal demands of employees' jobs are such that they might reasonably result in injury. Courts that follow the unusual-exertion rule insist that only those injuries resulting from some unusual set of demands over and above what the injured employees' jobs typically entailed are compensable. Preexisting conditions that are aggravated by occupational factors are often compensable. The general principle is that employers take their employees "as they find them"—healthy or not so healthy.

Does workers' compensation cover psychological conditions also? Considerable variability exists regarding this issue. Psychological conditions that follow from physical injuries (e.g., depression following an amputation) and psychological stresses that cause physical harm (e.g., upset or stress precipitating a stroke) are likely to be compensated. In many states, psychological conditions resulting from single, traumatic events at work (e.g., witnessing a coworker's death) are compensated. However, psychological conditions that develop over time and are related to ongoing stresses in the work environment are generally not compensated.

In *McCrone v. Bank One Corporation,* the Ohio Supreme Court considers the constitutionality of the state's workers' compensation statute that excludes from coverage any psychological conditions not linked to physical injuries. The excerpt of this decision includes two dissenting opinions from justices that would have ruled differently than the majority.

[40]*Coleman v. State ex rel. Wyoming Workers' Compensation Division,* 915 P.2d 595 (Wyo. 1996).

McCRONE V. BANK ONE CORPORATION
107 Ohio St. 3d 272 (2005)

● ● ●

OPINION BY JUSTICE LANZINGER:

The question presented is whether [Ohio's workers' compensation statute] violates equal protection by excluding psychological or psychiatric injuries from workers' compensation coverage. We hold that it does not.

Appellee, Kimberly McCrone, was an employee of Bank One Corporation from 1998 to 2001. During her employment, the branch in which she worked was robbed twice. At the first robbery on December 20, 2000, McCrone was present but was not the teller involved; however, she was the teller robbed on August 4, 2001. Although McCrone returned to work without claiming adverse effects after the first robbery, after the

second she was diagnosed with posttraumatic stress disorder and has not worked for the bank since. She filed for workers' compensation benefits for her psychological condition stemming from the second robbery, but benefits were denied because she had not suffered a physical injury. * * *

In 1986, [the workers' compensation statute] was amended to define what constitutes a workers' compensation injury and what does not. "'Injury' includes any injury, whether caused by external accidental means or accidental in character and result, received in the course of, and arising out of, the injured employee's employment. 'Injury' does not include:

"(1) Psychiatric conditions except where the conditions have arisen from an injury or occupational disease."

Both before and after these amendments, courts have held that compensable injuries under the workers' compensation system require a physical component suffered by the claimant. In *Rambaldo v. Accurate Die Casting* (1992), 65 Ohio St.3d 281, we discussed whether nonphysical injuries could be claimed as occupational diseases. . . . We held that "in the absence of a clearly expressed legislative intent to recognize mental conditions caused solely by work-related stress as occupational diseases within the purview of the Workers' Compensation Act, such mental conditions are not compensable as occupational diseases." Similarly, we now hold that psychological or psychiatric conditions that do not arise from a compensable physical injury or occupational disease are excluded from the definition of "injury" . . . and from workers' compensation coverage.

Because the General Assembly has classified mental conditions as compensable under workers' compensation laws only when they are accompanied by physical injury, the question becomes whether that classification violates the Equal Protection Clause of either the United States or Ohio Constitution. Legislative enactments are presumed to be constitutional. However, the constitutional guarantee of equal protection requires that laws operate equally upon persons who are identified in the same class. * * *

The guarantee of equal protection of the laws requires the existence of rational grounds for making a distinction between those within and those outside a designated class. * * *

[T]he BWC [Bureau of Workers' Compensation] argues that it is reasonable to classify psychological and psychiatric conditions differently from those accompanied by physical injury because it is often difficult to prove the existence of, as well as the cause of, mental injuries. * * * Although a physical injury may or may not cause a psychological or psychiatric condition, it may furnish some proof of a legitimate mental claim. * * * The BWC also emphasizes the government's interest in making the most efficient use of a finite fund. Applying the rational-basis test to this justification for the exclusion of psychological or psychiatric conditions, we conclude that the state has a legitimate interest. It is reasonable to expect government to protect the self-supporting nature of the Workers' Compensation Fund, to distribute available resources so that benefit payments are kept at an adequate level for covered injuries rather than at an inadequate level for all potential disabilities, and to maintain a contribution rate not unduly burdensome to participating employers.

The BWC thus offers legitimate reasons that relate to the constitutional purpose underlying the workers' compensation statute. It cannot be said that denying workers' compensation benefits to claimants who simply allege mental disorders or emotional stress due to their jobs is irrational. . . . * * *

Undoubtedly, psychological and psychiatric injuries may arise from an individual's employment, and we do not discount their impact on those who suffer them. The General Assembly, however, is the branch of state government charged by the Ohio Constitution to make public policy choices for the Workers' Compensation Fund. * * * At some point, the General Assembly may determine that psychological or psychiatric conditions arising in the workplace are compensable without regard to attendant physical injury or occupational disease. Until then, however, claims for such conditions are limited. . . . * * *

Dissenting Opinion by Justice Resnick:
Semantics aside, appellee, Kimberly McCrone, was injured in the course of her employment for Bank One Corporation, and her injury arose out of that employment. She was injured as a result of a bank robbery that occurred at her place of employment while she was the teller on duty. Her injury is real and disabling, and its existence is supported by competent medical evidence. It is work-related in every sense of the word, it was accidental in character and result, and it has prevented appellee from returning to her former position of employment. It is not compensable under the Workers' Compensation Act, however, because it is psychological or mental in cause and effect, meaning that it has no "physical component" and was unaccompanied by physical trauma or damage. And yet this same injury—posttraumatic stress disorder—would be fully covered under the statute if only the bank robber had been considerate enough of appellee's compensation position to have shoved her during the robbery so that she could stub her toe and acquire the physical element that is deemed so essential to her right of recovery.

Now what kind of rational explanation or legitimate state interest could possibly justify distinguishing the compensability of one posttraumatic stress disorder from another under equivalent life-threatening circumstances based on the fortuity of a stubbed toe? * * * [I]t is unsatisfactory, to say the least, that the majority is constrained to fall back on the difficulty-of-proof/conservation-of-resources rationale in order to justify the denial of coverage to an entire class of work-related

injuries. Not only are workers' compensation claims routinely amended to include psychological injuries resulting from previously allowed physical injuries, but the time has long since passed when denying recoveries for "purely psychological" injuries can be excused on grounds of evidentiary difficulties or illusory claims. We are no longer living in the 19th century when it was considered impossible to accurately diagnose psychological injuries. * * *

Moreover, the majority's cost-cutting justification rings hollow. Since when is reducing governmental costs sufficient to nullify the basic protections afforded by the Ohio Constitution? Is there a specific dollar amount of savings that must be realized before ignoring the Equal Protection Clause is justified?

Dissenting Opinion by Justice Pfeifer:
This case demonstrates the failure of [Ohio law] to allow a meaningful chance for recovery for workers psychologically harmed by violent workplace attacks. In . . . a case factually similar to this one, Rachel Bunger had been the victim of a holdup while working at a Dairy Mart. She sued her employer in common pleas court for negligence and also sought workers' compensation benefits for her psychological injuries. This court held that while Ohio's workers' compensation statutes did not allow recovery for purely psychological injuries, Bunger could pursue a negligence claim against her employer. * * * Although *Bunger* recognized that a cause of action for negligence in such situations is available, from a practical standpoint such a cause of action is not often useful. The real-world truth is that employers can do only so much to protect their employees from the evil that men do; the fault for the trauma done to an employee in a robbery case usually lies entirely with the thug committing the felonious act. Therefore, a cause of action against an employer for negligence is usually unwinnable, and accordingly, an employee is left with no compensation for her very real workplace injury.

That result is all the more unacceptable because workers' compensation benefits are in fact available for psychological injuries . . . as long as they are accompanied by a physical injury. The majority writes, "Although a physical injury may or may not cause a psychological or psychiatric condition, it may furnish some proof of a legitimate mental claim," that is, a physical injury may be proof of a work-related, cognizable

triggering event causing the psychological trauma. The injury tells us that something happened. A physical injury is merely evidence of the event—it is the triggering event that is significant. But injuries are not the only possible evidence of traumatic events.

If the criminal in this case had given a paper cut to the teller when handing over his holdup note, would that have made her claims of mental distress easier to prove? Certainly not. There is no rational basis to treat injured employees differently when both the physically injured and the nonphysically injured employees each can identify the genesis of their psychological condition. A cognizable triggering event, whether resulting in physical injury or not, is the proper determinant for proof of psychological injury. A professional can evaluate the injury and the event to determine whether compensation is appropriate.

Finding the workers' compensation statutes unconstitutional as they relate to workers psychologically harmed by a cognizable triggering event would not open the floodgates for compensation for all forms of mental distress. * * * We are not dealing in these cases with a person claiming depression because she is bored with her job and really wants to be an actress. This [and similar cases] all present instances in which the psychological injuries were demonstrably tied to a specific traumatic, accidental event in the workplace. They do not present the same issues of proof as "I hate my job"-type depression masquerading as a workers' compensation claim. Allowing benefits in this case does not mean across-the-board compensation for all claims of mental illness. Allowing benefits in this case allows for equal treatment of people with the same, equally provable injuries.

CASE QUESTIONS

1. What was the legal issue in this case? What did the court decide?

2. Why do you think that the case was brought on constitutional grounds?

3. Why does the court uphold the law?

4. Are psychological injuries really so different from physical ones?

5. Are the dissenting opinions persuasive? How would you decide this case?

At least in theory, workers' compensation covers both injuries and illnesses. Injuries generally result from single exposures or accidents that lead to cuts, burns, fractures, sprains, and so on. Illnesses are disorders other than injuries and include skin disorders, respiratory problems, poisoning by toxic substances, and musculoskeletal disorders. Illnesses most often stem from multiple exposures over time and have a gradual onset (often after a change of jobs or retirement). Illnesses are far less likely than injuries to be acknowledged as work related, recorded, and compensated. Recognition of the occupational basis of the lung disorders suffered by the popcorn plant workers was facilitated by the rarity of the condition and the involvement of NIOSH (see "Clippings"). Some of OSHA's inspectors might have been exposed to excessive levels of beryllium in the course of conducting inspections and are at risk of becoming ill in the future (see "Clippings").

RESPONDING TO WORKPLACE INJURIES

Employers should require that employees report all injuries that occur in the workplace as soon as possible. This allows for any needed first aid or other treatment to be provided. *Employers should err on the side of caution in referring injured employees for medical treatment.* Prompt reporting also puts an employer on notice that a workers' compensation claim might be forthcoming and allows for effective investigation. However, most workers' compensation statutes allow employees substantial time to file claims, and the seriousness of some conditions might not become apparent until a later date. *Reports of injuries should be investigated immediately and thoroughly. Hazards that caused the injuries should be identified and abated.* If a claim is filed, a decision must be made about whether to contest the claim. *Workers' compensation claims should not be routinely contested. Reasonable grounds for contesting claims are when the severity of an injury or whether it arose out of and in the course of employment is in question.*

Employees must not be retaliated against for filing workers' compensation claims. Filing a workers' compensation claim is an injured employee's sole remedy under the law. An employer violated a New Jersey's workers' compensation statute when it fired an employee for failing to attend several medical appointments, scheduled during nonwork time, to treat a work-related shoulder injury. The employee had returned to full-time work and missed the appointments because dissatisfaction with his treating physician led him to consult another doctor. Under the employer's policy, missed medical appointments were counted as absences from work, but only for employees with work-related conditions. The court decided that the policy discriminated against workers' compensation claimants by treating them less advantageously than persons with non–work-related conditions. However, the court also opined that a neutral policy counting all absences, regardless of whether the absent employees are receiving workers' compensation, would be legal.[41]

Employers should stay in close contact with injured employees and their medical care providers. Information about job tasks and requirements should be conveyed to medical care providers so they can make accurate assessments about readiness to return to full-time or light-duty work. Light-duty assignments should be available and considered for injured employees who are not yet capable of fulfilling all the duties of their former positions. However, there are some important caveats. The injuries employees suffer on the job might also constitute "serious health conditions"

[41]*Carter v. AFG Industries*, 782 A.2d 967 (N.J. Super. 2001), *cert. denied*, 793 A.2d 718 (2002).

entitling them to FMLA leave. Or they might be disabilities under the ADA, in which case the employees would be entitled to leave or other reasonable accommodations allowing them to perform their regular jobs.[42] Thus, although employers usually require acceptance of light-duty assignments and press for employees to return to work as soon as possible as part of their efforts to control workers' compensation costs, *employers need to be mindful that employees with work-related injuries might also be entitled to take leave or receive accommodations that will allow them to perform the essential functions of their regular jobs.*

[42]Equal Employment Opportunity Commission. "Enforcement Guidance: Workers' Compensation and the ADA." No. 915.002 (1996).

Chapter SUMMARY

The Occupational Safety and Health Act is the principal federal law governing safety in private sector workplaces. The OSH Act is administered by OSHA. OSHA establishes standards, provides information about how to meet those standards, and enforces them by conducting inspections. The National Institute of Occupational Safety and Health NIOSH provides scientific and technical advice to OSHA. The Occupational Safety and Health Review Commission OSHRC hears appeals of OSHA enforcement decisions.

An elaborate process exists for establishing standards. OSHA bears the burden of showing that a dangerous substance or other hazard poses a significant risk to the health of employees. However, proposed standards are not required to pass a strict cost-benefit analysis. To prove a violation of an existing standard, OSHA must show that a relevant standard exists, it was violated, the employer knew or should have known of the violation, and employees were working in or had access to the area of the workplace in which the violation occurred.

The general duty clause covers hazards for which no specific standard exists. To prove a violation of the general duty clause, OSHA must show that a hazard existed, the hazard was recognized by the employer or the industry, the hazard caused or was likely to cause serious physical injury or death, and feasible means existed to abate the hazard. Because OSHA has been unsuccessful in establishing an ergonomic standard, the general duty clause is the only means at OSHA's disposal to address ergonomic hazards that result in musculoskeletal disorders (MSDs).

Situations where there is imminent risk of serious physical harm or death have the highest priority for inspection, followed by inspections in the aftermath of serious accidents, inspections in response to employee complaints, programmed inspections in high-risk industries, and follow-up inspections. Violations observed by compliance officers during inspections are reported to the OSHA area director who decides whether to issue citations. Challenges to citations must be made to the OSHRC within 15 days of receiving citations and can contest whether the violations existed, the penalties, or the period of time given to correct hazards. Employees and their unions play an important role in the enforcement process. Employees are protected for refusing to perform work that poses an imminent threat of death or serious physical harm, when the employer has been informed of the hazard and failed to fix it.

State workers' compensation laws provide remedies to employees who suffer injuries, illnesses, or death from their employment. Workers' compensation provides employees with partial replacement income, medical care, and rehabilitation. Workers' compensation is provided on a no-fault basis and is the exclusive remedy available to employees hurt on the job. Exceptions to exclusivity occur when injuries are intentional rather than accidental, and when third parties are involved. Workers' compensation covers all injuries, illnesses, and deaths that "arise out of and in the course of" employment. However, illnesses or diseases that occur over prolonged periods of exposure and have a delayed onset are much less likely to be covered than injuries sustained from single, identifiable events.

Practical Advice SUMMARY

- Employers must become aware of and comply with all OSHA standards that apply to their operations.

- Employers must provide employees with employment and places of employment that are free from recognized hazards that are causing or are likely to cause death or serious physical harm.

- Employers should use the available, demonstrated means of reducing ergonomic hazards, rather than wait until there is a clear legal mandate to do so.

- When faced with an inspection by OSHA, employers

 –must allow inspectors to enter the workplace and conduct inspections, although they may require that the agency first obtain a search warrant.

 –can and should designate a representative to accompany OSHA compliance officers.

 –must allow an employee representative not chosen by the employer to participate in the inspection process.

 –must not attempt to intimidate or interfere with inspectors as they conduct inspections.

- When cited for a safety violation, employers must

 –correct the violation within the required abatement period, unless the citation is being contested.

 –post a copy of the citation in the workplace near the site of the violation for three working days or until the violation is corrected, whichever is longer.

- Employers must not retaliate against employees for

 –making complaints about safety problems.

 –contacting OSHA.

 –speaking with inspectors or otherwise participating in the enforcement process.

 –refusing to work under conditions that pose a serious and imminent threat to their health and about which the employer has been informed.

- Employers not exempted from record-keeping requirements must

 –establish and communicate procedures for their employees to report workplace injuries and illnesses to them.

 –record, within six days of their occurrence, all work-related injuries or illnesses that meet the established criteria of seriousness.

 –record injuries and illnesses separately for each establishment operated.

 –complete an annual summary of work-related injuries and illnesses to be posted in the workplace during the month of February.

 –retain records of work-related injuries and illnesses for five years and make them available to OSHA upon request.

- All employers must report to OSHA within eight hours

 –all fatal accidents.

 –all accidents that result in the hospitalization of three or more employees.

- All employers must, if selected, participate in the BLS's annual survey of occupational injuries and illnesses.

- Safety rules should be

 –clear and specific.

 –consistent with one another.

 –consistently enforced.

- Employers should engage in proactive efforts to identify and abate unsafe conditions in their workplaces, especially by implementing effective workplace safety programs.

- Employers must provide workers' compensation coverage for their employees.

- Firms using workers from contract companies should ensure that the contract companies are providing workers' compensation for their employees.

- Employers should require that employees report all injuries that occur in the workplace as soon after they occur as possible.

- When employees are hurt on the job, employers should

 –err on the side of caution in referring injured employees for medical treatment.

 –investigate reports of injuries immediately and thoroughly.

–identify and abate any hazards that caused the injuries.

–not routinely contest workers' compensation claims, but contest those in which the severity of injuries or whether they arose out of and in the course of employment is questionable.

–convey information about job tasks and requirements to medical care providers treating work-related injuries.

–make light-duty assignments available to employees who are not yet capable of fulfilling all the duties of their regular positions, provided that this does not conflict with entitlement to leave or other reasonable accommodations.

• Employees must not be retaliated against for filing workers' compensation claims.

Key TERMS

Occupational Safety and Health Act (OSH Act)
workers' compensation
Occupational Safety and Health Administration (OSHA)
National Institute of Occupational Safety and Health (NIOSH)
Occupational Safety and Health Review Commission (OSHRC)
safety standard

variance
permissible exposure limit (PEL)
controls
significant risk
cost-benefit analysis
general duty clause
ergonomics
musculoskeletal disorder (MSD)
inspections
citations

abatement
hierarchy of controls
workplace safety programs
experience rating
contributory negligence
fellow servant rule
assumption of risk
exclusive remedy
in the course of employment
arising out of employment

Chapter QUESTIONS

1. Employees were making repairs on a company's huge forging press using a gear-pulling device. The device had 4 large steel studs, weighing nearly 40 pounds each. A stud broke off during the repair operation, flew 121 feet, and struck an employee in the head. There had been two prior incidents in which studs had broken off and nearly injured persons, including supervisors, in the vicinity. The lead repairman for the day shift had repeatedly requested enhanced safety precautions during repair operations, but the company rejected these measures because they would be too expensive or time-consuming. However, on another occasion, the company did take the lead repairman's suggestion that they post warning signs and cordon off the area. OSHA cited the company under the general-duty clause. The company appealed the citation. What should the court decide? Why? (*Caterpillar v. OSHRC*, 122 F.3d 437 (7th Cir. 1997))

2. For a company-sponsored outdoor barbecue, the employer purchased a gas grill equipped with a 20-pound propane tank. To ensure sufficient gas to complete the grilling, the employer then purchased and installed a 40-pound tank. Doing so was difficult, as the larger tank required use of a special adaptor and had to be tipped at an angle to fit under the grill. The larger tanks have a warning label that cautions against using them with grills ordinarily equipped with 20-pound tanks. Several employees were assigned to operate the grill. When it was determined that the grill was not adequately cooking the meat, two of the employees attempted to improve the flow of gas by checking the regulator and repositioning the tank. This caused fuel to escape and a ball of fire to erupt from the grill. One employee suffered severe burns to his hands and the other had his hair singed. OSHA cited the company under the general-duty clause. The company appealed the citation. What should the court decide? (*Safeway v. OSHRC*, 382 F.3d 1189 (10th Cir. 2004))

3. An employee showed up at work not wearing her proper uniform. This precipitated an argument

with a supervisor that resulted in the employee being told that she was fired. The discussion then escalated into a physical altercation. During the course of the fight, another employee got involved and threw scalding hot water on the combatants. The (now former) employee sued for the burns and other injuries she sustained during the fight. What should the court decide? Why? (*Cook v. AFC Enterprises*, 2002 Ala. Civ. App. LEXIS 12)

4. An employee of a company that manufactures plastic drainage tubing was severely burned by hot plastic in an explosion and died several days later. On the day of the accident, another operator noticed that hot molten plastic appeared to be leaking from a screen changer. The foreman instructed the operator to shut the line down so that certain bolts could be replaced. The plastic extruder was shut down and the electrical heaters in the area of the repair were turned off. However, heaters located approximately five feet away were left on. The manufacturing line was separated at the screen changer, leaving an open end of pipe. The employee came over to where the repairs were being done to offer assistance. It was company policy that employees should do so when their own duties were completed. The offer was declined by the other operator, but while the employee was still within about 3 feet of the open pipe, an explosion occurred and the employee was sprayed with hot plastic, eventually resulting in his death. The deceased employee's widow brought a tort claim against the employer. What should the court decide? Why? (*Gibson v. Drainage Products*, 95 Ohio St. 3d 171 (2002))

5. A secretary who worked for Sea World was asked if she would like to be a model in publicity pictures. The pictures would show her in a bikini, riding Shamu the killer whale. The secretary was warned in general terms that there was danger involved, but she was not told that Shamu had been conditioned to only allow persons in wetsuits to ride her, that the whale had previously attacked persons attempting to ride her wearing regular swimsuits, and that Shamu had been behaving erratically in recent months. During one of the rides on Shamu for the photo shoot, a trainer noticed that the whale was showing signs of agitation. On the next ride, the woman was thrown off and bitten on the legs and hips. Her wounds required over a hundred stitches and left permanent scars. She sued Sea World. What should the court decide? Why? (*Eckis v. Sea World Corp.*, 134 Cal. Rptr. 183 (Cal. App. 1976))

6. An employee worked as a manager at an automotive service and repair shop. Typically, he spent at least 30 percent of each work day talking on the telephone with customers, other managers, and vendors. At the time of his injury, there was a thunderstorm outside. The manager was talking on a corded telephone to another manager and leaning against a metal table. The telephone was struck by lightning. The manager filed a workers' compensation claim based on serious medical problems suffered due to the lightning strike. The employer contested the claim. What should the court decide? Why? (*Ex parte Richard Byrom*, 895 So. 2d 942 (Ala. 2004))

7. A developmentally disabled teenager was hired by a grocery store to work as a part-time courtesy clerk. On three occasions, she was sexually assaulted by an employee of a company providing janitorial services to the grocery store. The employee was unknown to the teenager prior to her becoming employed at the store. The first assault occurred in a cleaning supply room within the store. The other two assaults occurred behind a dumpster, after the teenager had gone out to collect shopping carts from the parking lot. The janitor pled guilty to one count of attempted assault and was sentenced. The teenager became pregnant as a result of the assaults and had a child. The teenager and her parents brought a number of tort and statutory claims against both the store and the janitorial services company. What should the court decide? Why? (*Wood v. Safeway*, 121 P.3d 1026 (Nev. 2005))

8. The "historic bargain" that resulted in workers' compensation laws occurred at a time (the early 1900s) when almost no other employment laws existed, and courts routinely ruled against workers with disabling injuries caused by their employers' negligence. Is workers' compensation a fair bargain now, or does it too often shield employers from the consequences of their negligence?

9. Should OSHA have to prove that their proposed standards pass a cost-benefit analysis?

10. In light of the fact that more and more work is being done out of homes, how, if at all, should the safety and health of those workplaces be ensured? (Steven Greenhouse. "Home Office Isn't Liability for Firms, U.S. Decides." *New York Times* (January 28, 2000), A-13)

Internet RESOURCES

The Occupational Safety and Health Administration (OSHA) Web site offers a great deal of useful information about safety and health hazards as well as legal compliance materials.

http://www.osha.gov

The Occupational Safety and Health Review Commission (OSHRC) Web site provides information on OSHRC procedures and the full text of OSHRC decisions.

http://www.oshrc.gov

The National Institute of Occupational Safety and Health (NIOSH) Web site contains much useful information about safety and health hazards.

http://www.cdc.gov/niosh/homepage.html

This Web site contains a variety of materials related to workers' compensation, including tables comparing workers' compensation statutes in different states.

http://www.workerscompresources.com

The Workers' Compensation Research Institute Web site includes research information about worker's compensation issues.

http://www.wcrinet.org/

The National Council for Occupational Safety and Health (COSH) Web site focuses on practical tools for workers to use in understanding their rights.

http://www.coshnetwork.org/

PART 1
Introduction
to Employment
Law

PART 2
The Hiring
Process

PART 3
Managing a
Diverse
Workforce

PART 4
Pay, Benefits,
Terms and
Conditions of
Employment

PART 6
Terminating
Employment

PART **5**

Managing Performance

Chapter **16**
*Performance Appraisals, Training,
and Development*

Chapter **17**
*Privacy on the Job: Information,
Monitoring, and Investigations*

Performance Appraisals, Training, and Development

▸ A judge in Michigan has given final approval to a $10.5 million settlement of a class-action lawsuit challenging a performance appraisal process that had been used by the Ford Motor Company to rate its managers and supervisors. The system called for employees to be rated as A, B, or C and required that at least 10 percent (later reduced to 5 percent) of employees receive the C rating. Persons in the C category were ineligible for bonuses and were in danger of demotion or termination. The suit alleged age discrimination, as older workers were disproportionately rated as performing in the C category.[1]

▸ The OSHA regulation under which employers were most frequently cited between 2003 and 2005 was the hazard communication standard. The standard applies to chemical manufacturers, importers, and employers that use hazardous chemicals in the workplace. The standard includes broad employee information and training requirements.[2]

▸ Some Burger King employees might not be dancing in the aisles anytime soon. During a team-building retreat attended by more than 100 members of Burger King's marketing department, participants walked barefoot over an 8-foot strip of white-hot coals. The stated intent was to teach participants that they could achieve things they had not thought possible. About a dozen employees suffered first- and second-degree burns to their feet. Some were seen in wheelchairs the next day at the airport. Burger King executives claimed that the retreat was a success, but fire-walking will apparently not be part of future retreats.[3]

▸ A federal judge in Ohio has given final approval to the settlement of another class-action lawsuit against Ford. This suit centered on race discrimination in the selection process for admission to the carmaker's apprenticeship program. The test that had been used for this purpose will be eliminated, positions will be offered to nearly 300 current and former employees who were denied admission to the apprenticeship program, and monetary awards will be paid to several thousand class members.[4]

[1]"Michigan Judge Grants Final Approval to $10.5 Million Age Bias Settlement at Ford." *Daily Labor Report* 51 (March 15, 2002), A-1.

[2]"OSHA Official Discusses Citation Trends at Hazard Communication Conference." *Daily Labor Report* 189 (September 30, 2005), A-2.

[3]Elaine Walker. "Burger King Marketing Team Walks over Coals at Key Largo, Fla., Retreat." *Miami Herald* (October 6, 2001).

[4]Nancy Montwieler. "Judge Gives Final Approval to Ford Decree Settling Bias Charges by Black Apprentices," *Daily Labor Report* 119 (June 22, 2005), AA-1.

Employers care about performance. "Performance management" incorporates all the aspects of an organization that affect employee performance, including rewards, supervision, discipline, performance appraisal, training, and development. This chapter focuses on legal issues surrounding performance appraisals and training and development programs. These important human resource activities raise interesting questions for the application of laws that we have already discussed. Performance appraisals and training and development programs are likely to be the objects of even more legal controversies in the future, as organizations tie employment decisions more closely to assessments of performance, and employees strive to remain marketable in the face of changing skill requirements and less stable employment relationships.

PERFORMANCE APPRAISALS

Performance appraisals are a fact of life for most employees. At their best, they provide welcome recognition of accomplishments and needed feedback on how to improve performance. At their worst, they are pointless exercises or shams perpetrated to justify questionable employment decisions. Performance appraisals hold considerable legal significance. Discrimination is the central legal concern with respect to performance appraisals.

In general, employers do not have a legal duty to conduct performance appraisals or to do so with any particular level of proficiency. However, the failure to evaluate some employees while evaluating others might result in discrimination claims. For example, a female manager sued her employer for age and sex discrimination based on its failure to evaluate her performance, a failure that she contended led to her not being promoted. Despite repeated requests and contrary to the firm's (a management consulting firm no less) stated policy, the woman did not receive any annual, written performance appraisals for 12 years. When she finally received an appraisal, it was negative and lacked the type of development plan typically included in the appraisals of male employees. The plaintiff was able to show that several younger male employees received nine evaluations during the period that she received only one. The company's bid to have her case thrown out failed, and a trial was ordered.[5]

An inaccurate performance appraisal, standing alone, does not give rise to a legal claim. A woman who worked as a tree surgeon at a university was unsuccessful when she sued the school for giving her negative performance evaluations in retaliation for filing a charge with the EEOC. A prima facie case of retaliation includes a showing that the plaintiff suffered an adverse employment action following participation in a protected activity (in this case, charge filing). The court concluded:

> While adverse employment actions extend beyond readily quantifiable losses, not everything that makes an employee unhappy is an actionable adverse action. . . . The dispositive question in our case is not whether [the employee's] performance evaluations were undeservedly negative, but whether even undeserved poor evaluations can alone constitute the second element [adverse employment action] of her prima facie case. . . . [W]e can only conclude that the evaluations alone do not constitute an actionable adverse employment action. . . .[6]

[5]*Esterquest v. Booz-Allen & Hamilton, Inc.*, 2002 U.S. Dist. LEXIS 2545.
[6]*Smart v. Ball State University*, 89 F.3d 437, at 442 (7th Cir. 1996).

Similarly, an employee's claim that excessively negative performance appraisals and inadequate feedback constituted key parts of a racially hostile environment also failed. The court maintained that:

> [W]e do not sit to appraise . . . [the] appraisal. Rather, "our sole concern is whether the reason for which the defendant discharged the plaintiff was discriminatory." . . . There is evidence in the record that suggests Price was a tough, demanding supervisor. . . . Price's criticism of her may have been blunt and even at times unfair. But the types of difficulties that Hawkins encountered with Price arise routinely in employment relationships. . . . Her suit amounts mostly to an effort to seek judicial review of the quantity and quality of workplace criticism. The District Court properly dismissed the action, for employment discrimination law "is not a vehicle for substituting the judgment of a court for that of the employer."[7]

The foregoing does not mean that employers have carte blanche with respect to performance appraisals, however. To the contrary, there are strong legal reasons that *employers should conduct performance appraisals regularly and maintain credible, written documentation of performance.* Performance appraisals affect many different employment decisions, including promotions, training and development, merit pay and bonuses, demotions, layoffs, and terminations. If decisions about employment opportunities are based on biased performance appraisals, those decisions can be challenged as discriminatory. In a recent case involving an African-American woman who lost out on a raise due to performance appraisal ratings that she argued were discriminatorily low, the court stated "We hold that an evaluation that directly disentitles an employee to a raise of any significance is an adverse employment action under Title VII."[8] Thus, performance appraisals are the central focus in many discrimination cases.

Performance Criteria and Standards

Common **performance criteria** include work quality and quantity, attendance and punctuality, judgment, ability to work with others in a team, leadership, and so forth. In general, employers are free to establish the criteria and standards of performance (e.g., the level of work quality regarded as "poor" or "excellent") that they see fit in evaluating employee performance. However, performance criteria and standards must take into account the needs of disabled employees, be consistently applied, be as objective as possible, and be job related and consistent with business necessity.

The ADA and Rehabilitation Act hold several implications for performance appraisals. As a starting point, *employers can and should hold disabled employees to the same standards of performance as nondisabled employees who do the same jobs.* However, if an employee with a disability needs a reasonable accommodation to perform the essential functions of her job with an acceptable degree of proficiency, that accommodation must be provided unless it would impose undue hardship. *The performance of disabled employees should be appraised with any needed accommodations in place. Receipt of an accommodation should not be held in any way against a disabled employee, such as by lowering performance ratings because the individual*

[7]*Hawkins v. Pepsico, Inc.*, 203 F.3d 274, at 280, 282 (4th Cir. 2000), *cert. denied*, 531 U.S. 875 (2000).

[8]*Gillis v. Georgia Department of Corrections*, 400 F.3d 883, at 888 (11th Cir. 2005).

is *"getting help."* If, due to her disability, a disabled employee is unable to perform *a marginal function of a job with an acceptable degree of proficiency, that function should be removed from the job and the failure to perform it should not be reflected in performance ratings.* More generally, *employers should consider whether performance deficits are related to disabilities.* This is particularly true for employees with known disabilities, but sensitive inquiries can also be made to determine whether a previously undisclosed (or newly developed) disability might be playing a role in observed performance problems.

In one relevant case, a woman who suffered serious neurological damage following a car accident saw her condition improve, but still had difficulties with memory, concentration, balance, and mobility. The woman was hired on a probationary basis as a library teacher. Largely on the basis of an unannounced visit to her class by an administrator, during which she remained seated while teaching and was deemed to have not taken sufficient steps to control the class, the school decided not to grant her tenure. She sued under the Rehabilitation Act, claiming that the school district should have provided her with a teacher's aide as a reasonable accommodation. The court remanded the case to gather further facts on the reasonableness of her proposed accommodation. Significantly, and in response to the employer's claim that she was denied tenure on the basis of her poor performance rather than her disability, the court stated:

> Failure to consider the possibility of reasonable accommodation for such disabilities, if it leads to discharge for performance inadequacies resulting from the disabilities, amounts to a discharge solely because of the disabilities.[9]

Performance criteria and standards must be applied in a consistent manner. Using double standards to evaluate members of different protected class groups is clearly disparate treatment. An employee's complaint that he was retaliated against when his employer changed evaluation criteria and gave the employee a low rating that led to the loss of his position was dismissed in large part because the plaintiff "was evaluated using the same standards as the other loss prevention field agents. . . ."[10] In contrast, an accountant was allowed to go to trial on an age discrimination claim based on evidence that the employer set him up for failure by establishing performance objectives that could not be met. E-mails between company managers said that the performance plan given to the accountant "will then enable us to take appropriate action *when* he fails to meet the documented objectives" and "looking at this data (*good job Janice*) can I now put [the accountant] on a verbal warning?" The court took note of the facts that the accountant was given only 30 days to familiarize himself with, and complete an assignment using, a software package not used by anyone else in the company; no training or assistance was provided; and the software was dropped shortly after the accountant was terminated and replaced by a younger employee.[11]

To lessen the chance of disparate treatment, *performance criteria should also be as specific and objective as possible.* Performance appraisal inherently involves an element of subjectivity (the judging of Olympic figure skating illustrates this on a grand scale). Subjective performance criteria (e.g., potential for advancement) are not illegal, but they stand up less well in the face of other facts suggesting a discriminatory motive. Thus, in the case of a Latino police officer who was repeatedly

[9] *Borkowski v. Valley Central School District,* 63 F.3d 131, at 143 (2d Cir. 1995).

[10] *Gresham v. Food Lion,* 31 Fed. Appx. 131 (4th Cir. 2002).

[11] *Andrews v. Glaxo Smithkline,* 2005 U.S. Dist. LEXIS 1021, at 20–22.

(seven times) denied promotions on the basis of performance appraisals that rated his interpersonal skills as poor, the court concluded:

> Considering the facts of this case and the potential for manipulation inherent in the use of subjective evaluations, the district court properly concluded that Officer Jauregui was a victim of disparate treatment.[12]

Likewise, a court denied summary judgment to an employer and criticized the performance appraisal process used to select employees for downsizing in the following terms:

> This process . . . consisted of a single-paragraph string of conclusory subjective judgments wholly without grounding in concrete factual reference. Indeed, . . . the level of reference is in some instances so vague that it is impossible to determine in a meaningful way what the criticism even means.[13]

Consistent with the desirability of specific and objective performance criteria, *"global" or overall performance ratings should be avoided unless they are based on ratings for more specific criteria that are then combined in a reasonable manner to produce the overall scores.* Performance is too multifaceted a construct to capture in a single score without first considering specific dimensions of performance. It is also *important to have criteria that are established and known to employees beforehand.* A court noted with approval that "the subjectivity inherent in such a review is tempered by a requirement that employee goals and objectives be mapped out well in advance, in order to allow the employee the opportunity to meet articulated job expectations."[14]

Lastly, subjectivity can be minimized by *maintaining documentation of performance that is independent of and goes beyond supervisors' ratings on performance appraisals.* Sales records, attendance records, and customer input are just a few examples of such additional documentation.

As "neutral" employment practices that affect employment opportunities, performance appraisals can also be challenged for their adverse impact. For example, a woman claimed that Hewlett-Packard's promotion process based on performance appraisals led to the exclusion of women from management positions. The court found that the disparity between the high ratings she received on more objective criteria (meeting sales quotas) and low ratings on more subjective criteria, combined with the fact that no female sales representatives had ever been promoted to management, was sufficient to warrant a trial on her adverse impact claim.[15] Although an early case suggested that employers had to validate performance appraisal devices in the same manner as formal employment tests,[16] it has since become clear that the courts view performance appraisals as more akin to employment interviews—relatively discretionary devices for which evidence of a "manifest relationship to the employment in question" is required, but not formal validation studies.[17] Thus, although most cases involving performance appraisals allege disparate treatment rather than adverse impact, there are legal grounds for holding that *performance appraisal criteria should be job related and consistent with business necessity.*

[12]*Jauregui v. City of Glendale*, 852 F.2d 1128, at 1136 (9th Cir. 1988).

[13]*Platero v. Baumer*, 98 Fed. Appx. 819, at 821 (10th Cir. 2004).

[14]*Donaldson v. Microsoft*, 2001 U.S. Dist. LEXIS 23396, at 20.

[15]*Victory v. Hewlett-Packard Co.*, 34 F. Supp. 2d 809 (E.D.N.Y. 1999).

[16]*Brito v. Zia Co.*, 478 F.2d 1200 (10th Cir. 1973).

[17]*Watson v. Fort Worth Bank & Trust*, 487 U.S. 977 (1988).

Performance Appraisal Process

In *Thomas v. Eastman Kodak,* the court had to decide whether a company's decision to lay off an employee was based on racially neutral performance appraisal scores or was tainted by consideration of her race.

THOMAS V. EASTMAN KODAK
183 F.3d 38 (1st Cir. 1999), *cert. denied,* 528 U.S. 1161 (2000)

OPINION BY CIRCUIT JUDGE LYNCH:

In 1993, Myrtle Thomas, the only black Customer Service Representative in Eastman Kodak's Wellesley, Massachusetts office, was laid off. Thomas responded with a race discrimination suit against Kodak under Title VII, arguing that Kodak's layoff decision was discriminatory because it resulted from a ranking process that relied on racially biased performance appraisals . . . * * * We decide . . . in favor of Thomas. * * *

Thomas generally performed her job well. Kodak managers who supervised Thomas during her first ten years as a CSR in the Wellesley office reported variously that they were never dissatisfied with her performance, that they were "delighted" with Thomas, that her work was "excellent" and "far superior" to that of some of the other CSRs, that she was "very much on top of things," and that she was "the perfect support person." Co-workers and customers expressed similar sentiments. * * * Because of her high level of performance, Thomas received awards and bonuses from Kodak. * * * Thomas received at least eight other salary increases during her years as a CSR. At the time of the 1993 layoff, Thomas was the fourth most senior CSR in the Wellesley office and earned the third highest salary. * * *

Thomas's appraisals for 1988 and 1989 show that she was performing at a high level. In 1988, when she was responsible for more than 400 machines, Thomas received seven 5 ratings and one 6 rating, for an overall rating of 5, which was a rating "appropriate for individuals who not only achieve results and meet all expectations on a regular basis, but who go beyond these requirements from time to time." Her supervisor's comments were uniformly positive. In 1989, when she was responsible for more than 500 machines, Thomas received even higher ratings—five 6s and three 5s, for

an overall rating of 6, which meant that her "performance consistently exceeded the requirements of the position and [was] characterized by unusual initiative, resourcefulness, and creativity." Once again, the supervisor's comments were uniformly positive.

In 1989, Kodak created the position of Customer Support Manager throughout its Office Imaging organization. Thomas asked to be considered for the Wellesley position, but was told that she was not qualified. Instead, the position went to Claire Flannery. . . . The appointment of Flannery as Customer Support Manager marked a significant downturn in Thomas's fortunes at Kodak. * * * Thomas alleges that Flannery treated her differently from the other five CSRs, all of whom were white (as were, in fact, all of the other CSRs during Thomas's thirteen years in the Wellesley office). * * *

Thomas's most significant and concrete allegation is that Flannery gave her inaccurately low scores on her annual performance appraisals. For example, after receiving only 5s and 6s in 1988 and 1989, Thomas received a 2, four 3s, and a 4 from Flannery in 1990, for an overall score of 3. This was a below-average rating, appropriate for employees who had "a need for further improvement to achieve a middle rating [of 4]" or for employees "whose overall performance has slipped from a higher level." Thomas's performance appraisal scores in 1991 and 1992, while higher than her 1990 scores, were also inappropriately low, in Thomas's estimation—especially when compared to the higher scores that Flannery gave to other CSRs. * * *

In January 1993, Kodak decided to reduce the number of employees in its Office Imaging Division. It selected employees for layoff using a "Performance Appraisal Ranking Process" ("PAR process"), which produced a numerical score for each employee by adding together the employee's overall performance appraisal score for each of the three preceding years, after weighting the most recent score by a factor of 25 and

the second most recent score by a factor of 5. Thomas's PAR ranking, which was derived from the three appraisals conducted by Flannery, was the second lowest of the Wellesley CSRs. Since Kodak had decided to cut two Wellesley CSR positions, as well as the Customer Support Manager position, Flannery, Thomas, and the lowest ranked CSR (Eileen Lavallee) were laid off in March 1993. * * *

The . . . question on appeal is whether a reasonable jury could find, based on Thomas's evidence, that Flannery discriminated against Thomas because of her race when she assigned Thomas's performance appraisal scores. * * * Thomas has established a prima facie case of discrimination by showing that she is a member of a protected class who met Kodak's legitimate performance expectations and was laid off, while Kodak retained persons outside the protected class. * * * Kodak met its burden of production—and eliminated the presumption that it had discriminated—by contending that its layoff decision was based solely on racially neutral performance appraisal scores. At the third stage of the McDonnell Douglas/Burdine framework, the ultimate burden is on the plaintiff to persuade the trier of fact that she has been treated differently because of her race. * * *

As we understand Thomas's argument, she alleges a more subtle type of disparate treatment than the type often used to exemplify the operation of the McDonnell Douglas/Burdine framework. She does not argue that Kodak has articulated a false reason for her layoff (for example, excessive tardiness) in order to disguise the actual, unrelated reason (her race)—what one might describe as a "truth versus lies" claim—rather, she challenges the racial neutrality of the proffered reason itself. The latter type of challenge is also cognizable as a form of disparate treatment: if an employer evaluates employees of one race less favorably than employees of another race who have performed equivalently, and if race, rather than some other factor, is the basis for the difference in evaluations, then the dis-favored employees have been subjected to "discrimination . . . because of . . . race." * * *

The first portion of Thomas's third-stage burden is to produce sufficient evidence to show that she was not evaluated on the same terms as her colleagues, but rather was evaluated more harshly than the other, non-minority CSRs. * * * One strong piece of evidence is the sharp drop in Thomas's overall score (from 6 in 1989 to 3 in 1990) after Flannery became her supervisor. While the drop in score would not demonstrate

uneven treatment if Flannery were simply a "tough grader," this does not appear to have been the case. In 1990, when Thomas received a 3, all of the other CSRs whom Flannery graded received either a 5 or a 6. Furthermore, over her three years as supervisor Flannery gave CSRs other than Thomas a number of 7s in individual categories, a score that earlier supervisors characterized as extremely rare or even unheard of.

The drop in Thomas's score from 1989 to 1990 would also fail to demonstrate uneven treatment if it merely reflected a higher standard imposed upon Thomas due to her grade change in 1989. According to Kodak, "the higher the wage grade and salary, the more Kodak expected from the employee." But Thomas presents deposition testimony from other supervisors suggesting that there was no such rule, and the scores that Flannery assigned to other Wellesley CSRs seem to bear this out: one CSR who received a grade change in 1991 received a 5 in 1992 after receiving a 6 in 1991 (a drop of only one point rather than three after the grade change), and another CSR who received a grade change in 1991 received a higher score the following year (from a 4 in 1991 to a 5 in 1992).

Thomas makes other specific comparisons as well. The strongest of these concern her scores for "quantity of results," which was the most objective of the categories appraised, since it was based directly on the number of machines and installations for which a CSR was responsible. Thomas's scores appear low when compared to the scores for quantity given to other CSRs. In 1990, for instance, Thomas received only a 3 for quantity of results—a below average score—for managing 730 machines and 110 installations, while another CSR, also in the K6 grade, received a 5 for quantity in 1991 for managing far fewer machines (504) and fewer installations (81). * * *

In addition to the performance appraisals themselves, Thomas presents other evidence to show that Flannery treated her differently than she treated the other CSRs. According to Thomas, Flannery used flimsy grounds to prevent her from delivering an important presentation at a Kodak meeting, refused to provide her with computer training, failed to allow her appropriate developmental opportunities, and failed to evaluate her accurately on the basis of her interaction with customers (since she never accompanied Thomas on site in order to observe that interaction, as she did with the other CSRs).

On the whole Thomas has presented enough evidence to survive summary judgment on the question of

disparate treatment. Some of Thomas's scores, and particularly the 1990 scores, appear lower than one would expect given her apparent performance level. * * * Our inquiry does not end with this finding, since even the most blatant unfairness cannot, on its own, support a Title VII claim. "Title VII does not grant relief to a plaintiff who has been discharged unfairly, even by the most irrational of managers, unless facts and circumstances indicate that discriminatory animus was the reason for the decision." Instead, our focus shifts to the question whether Thomas has produced sufficient evidence to support a finding that the apparent disparity in treatment was due to her race.

Thomas can meet her burden with respect to this question using the same evidence used to show unequal treatment. * * * Where the disparity in treatment is striking enough, a jury may infer that race was the cause, especially if no explanation is offered other than the reason rejected as pretextual. That is the case here, since Kodak argues that Thomas's scores were objectively fair, not that they were unfair due to a personality conflict, as the district court surmised. In fact, Thomas does present additional evidence on this point. She describes incidents and situations which suggest that Flannery had a general disregard for her professional abilities and status. It also appears, from the picture that Thomas paints (and which Kodak does not dispute), that Flannery was at times inappropriately upset or angry with Thomas, to the point of behaving

unprofessionally. This, in turn, suggests that she did not respond neutrally to Thomas. A jury might reasonably infer from Thomas's description of these incidents that Thomas's race was an issue for Flannery and that Flannery's evaluations of Thomas were affected by some form of conscious animus or less conscious bias.

Our assessment of the evidence would be quite different if Thomas had been one of several black employees supervised by Flannery, some of whose scores were not low relative to those of the non-minority CSRs. But that was not the case. * * * In the end, Thomas is in a different position than a plaintiff who merely "disagrees with [the employer's] assessment of her relative performance." Thomas has presented "evidence . . . that [her] abilities and qualifications were equal or superior to employees who were retained." It is not an "improbable inference[]" . . . to further conclude . . . that Kodak failed to recognize this fact because it relied on an evaluation procedure that was tainted by racial bias.

CASE QUESTIONS

1. What was the legal issue in this case? What did the court decide?

2. What evidence was there that the company's stated motive for the layoff was pretextual? That her race was the real motive?

3. What should Kodak have done differently?

Performance ratings that suddenly diverge from established track records of performance are apt to attract judicial notice. This is particularly true when the alleged precipitous decline in performance occurs following the filing of a charge (suggesting retaliation) or shortly before a layoff or termination (suggesting the possibility that a "paper trail" is being created to cover up an anticipated discriminatory action). For example, a 57-year-old machinist was fired five days after receiving a performance appraisal describing his work as unsatisfactory over the past five months and recommending termination. He had received consistently favorable performance reviews for years, including one from the same supervisor earlier in the year that stated, "Your work . . . has been exceptional. You have made a positive contribution in work and in adapting to change." In the period intervening between the two evaluations, the company had decided to downsize. Following attendance at a meeting with upper management about the impending terminations, the supervisor had said, "These damn people—they want younger people here." The court found these circumstances more than sufficient to show that the employer's claims regarding poor performance were a pretext for intentional age discrimination.[18]

[18] Woodman v. Haemonetics Corp., 51 F.3d 1087 (1st Cir. 1995).

Likewise, an African-American woman who had been a server for more than 10 years was offered the choice of termination or becoming a busboy following an incident in which a "mystery shopper" from corporate headquarters allegedly experienced inadequate service. The woman had a record of solid performance appraisals at another restaurant in the chain and had recently transferred to a facility where she was the only full-time African-American employee. Despite the employer's claims that she was unable to keep up with the faster pace at her new assignment, she had received a very positive evaluation and a pay raise shortly following her arrival. Within a few weeks of that appraisal, she was effectively terminated ("constructively discharged") for poor performance. The court found that the plaintiff had stated facts sufficient to warrant a trial on her disparate treatment claim.[19] An employer suffered the same fate when its highly subjective performance appraisal, conducted on the eve of a downsizing, was used to terminate a Navajo woman. The court pointed to numerous glaring inconsistencies between the pre-downsizing appraisal and a contemporaneous appraisal by the employee's supervisor (e.g., criticism for not being a "team player" compared to high ratings on "teamwork," including "builds positive collaborative relationships"). Although the inconsistency did not necessarily mean that the appraisal used in the downsizing was biased, it was sufficient to raise doubts about the termination that could only be resolved through a trial.[20]

Sometimes, a recent change in performance ratings works to an employee's disadvantage. An employee whose performance improved markedly in the month prior to his termination was unable to show that his employer's claims of poor performance were pretextual because his record for the majority of his tenure had been poor.[21]

Performance appraisals must not be manipulated and made more negative than actual performance warrants as a means of retaliating against employees who file charges or to justify discriminatory actions.

Who Conducts Performance Appraisals? *Employers should provide training (or at least written instructions) to supervisors and others who conduct performance appraisals.* Training should include not only instruction in applying the particular appraisal device and in using appropriate language, but also in recognizing and countering the many ways in which bias can distort performance appraisals.[22] *Persons conducting appraisals must be thoroughly familiar with the jobs in question and the work of the persons being evaluated.* In concluding that an employer's performance appraisal process could be viewed as a "sham" designed to cover up its retaliatory motive, the court pointed to the fact that two of the evaluators had little firsthand knowledge of the plaintiff's performance and had not troubled themselves to even review his personnel file and previous evaluations.[23]

Coworkers sometimes play a pivotal role in performance appraisals. Tenure decisions by faculty committees are the classic example of peer review of performance and the object of considerable litigation.[24] Both peer review and 360-degree appraisals (in which employees at various organizational levels, and perhaps

[19]*Logan v. Denny's Inc.*, 259 F.3d 558, at 577 (6th Cir. 2001).

[20]*Platero*, at 821.

[21]*Olsen v. Marshall & Ilsley Corp.*, 267 F.3d 597 (7th Cir. 2001).

[22]Susan Bisom-Rapp. "Bulletproofing the Workplace: Symbol and Substance in Employment Discrimination Law Practice." *Florida State University Law Review* 26 (Summer 1999), 959, at 998.

[23]*Woodson v. Scott Paper Co.*, 109 F.3d 913, at 923 (3d Cir. 1997), *cert. denied*, 522 U.S. 914 (1997).

[24]Terry L. Leap. *Tenure, Discrimination, and the Courts, 2nd ed.* (Ithaca, NY: ILR Press, 1995).

customers, participate in evaluating an individual) have the effect of widening the circle of persons conducting, or at least contributing to, performance appraisals. *If these methods are used, the group of employees given training in proper appraisal techniques and legal issues should widen correspondingly.* Employers remain legally responsible for the actions of peer reviewers. An airline terminated an employee near the end of his probationary period. The airline cited unsatisfactory peer-pilot evaluations of his performance as the basis for the termination, but refused to allow the employee the opportunity to review the evaluations. There was evidence that the employee aroused the ire of his fellow pilots by having crossed a picket line. The court upheld an arbitrator's determination that the company was liable for the termination. The employer knew that the employee had been "blacklisted" by his peers and that the outpouring of negative evaluations reflected bias, and yet it nonetheless chose to terminate him based on the tainted evaluations.[25]

Content of Appraisals Performance appraisals are not occasions for "unloading" on employees who have, for good reasons or not, fallen into disfavor. *Appraisers do not have to shy away from criticism, but their tone should be measured and professional.* Shrill, extreme language suggests animus or hostility and makes it less likely that performance appraisals will be deferred to in legal challenges. No less than letters of reference, statements in performance appraisals that are false, damaging to the reputation of an employee, and communicated to others are grist for defamation claims if qualified privilege is lost. Such cases are not very common, but in one case, an employee was allowed to proceed with a defamation claim based on specific allegations of misconduct included in a performance appraisal (but not based on ratings of work performance because these were deemed expressions of opinion rather than purported facts).[26]

Language used in performance appraisals can also betray discriminatory motives. For example, an evaluator who writes, "I doubt whether at this stage in your career you will be able to acquire the new skills we need," reveals stereotypical beliefs about the inability of older workers to learn new things and bias toward older workers. More subtle is the case of an employee whose performance appraisal included a recommendation that he work with an outside consultant to improve his "perception by supervisors." This comment came on the heels of the employee filing a discrimination charge with the EEOC. The court concluded that this comment, in the context of other actions, was evidence of a "pattern of antagonism" and supported the employee's claim of a retaliatory discharge based on his EEOC filing. The fact that the statement was incorporated into a formal performance appraisal reviewed by management made it weightier and something more than a mere "stray comment."[27] Performance appraisals also must not include criticisms for lack of performance during periods when employees are on leaves to which they are legally entitled (doing so raises questions of discrimination under the FMLA or ADA).

Courts have sometimes pointed to the fact that appraisals contain both positive and negative comments as an indicator of lack of bias.[28] Courts also seem impressed when appraisals go beyond checking boxes to *explain behaviors that are the basis for ratings,*[29] and more generally, when employers are able to *cite specific instances of poor performance or wrongdoing.*[30]

[25]*Matthewson v. Aloha Airlines, Inc.*, 919 P.2d 969, at 976 (Haw. 1995).

[26]*Grossman v. Computer Curriculum Corp.*, 131 F. Supp. 2d. 299 (D. Conn. 2000).

[27]*Woodson*, at 921–22.

[28]*Gresham*, at 15.

[29]*Hawkins*, at 279.

[30]*Stovall v. General Electric Co.*, 1999 U.S. Dist. LEXIS 6953.

Feedback on Performance Performance appraisals should be part of a larger process of providing information to employees about their performance, as well as the means and opportunities to correct deficiencies. *Employers should communicate performance appraisals to employees, provide an opportunity for discussion, and allow employees to respond to and appeal them.* Failure to provide adequate, honest feedback sometimes results in legal problems. In one notable case,[31] an African-American female attorney returning from maternity leave was criticized for her low volume of work. Her supervisor also took exception to the number of coworkers who were coming to meet with her "behind closed doors." The supervisor opined that the attorney "was allowing herself to become a black matriarch." The attorney was offended by the remark. Concerned that she might sue, her supervisor was told by a company attorney to avoid confrontations with the employee. Subsequent performance appraisals were not provided to her, but indicated satisfactory performance. Her boss viewed these as overly high ratings given for the sake of expedience. The attorney was eventually terminated in a downsizing and sued. The court concluded that the employer discriminated by giving the employee what it knew to be overly positive reviews. This deprived her of the opportunity to learn that her performance was unsatisfactory and to avail herself of improvement measures that the company offered to other employees.

In contrast, the Veteran's Administration (VA) did not discriminate when it deliberately overrated an employee who had previously filed numerous charges with the EEOC. The VA did so in the hope that this would head off future charges. It didn't. The employee alleged that the overrating kept him from being eligible for a remedial program that might have facilitated his advancement. The court distinguished this case from the case mentioned previously by observing that even in the face of the disingenuous appraisals, this employee had been told on a number of occasions that his performance was unsatisfactory and had been provided with considerable remedial assistance (e.g., several training programs, seminars, mentoring).[32]

Supervisors make choices when writing performance appraisals. Sometimes, a more encouraging and less critical tone will produce a better outcome than a bluntly forthright assessment. The cases discussed earlier do not stand for the proposition that there is legal jeopardy when performance appraisals are written with tact and an eye toward encouragement. However, *employers should not attempt to avoid unpleasant confrontations by failing to provide employees with feedback about their performance and opportunities to improve performance that are routinely provided to other employees.*

Forced Distribution Method If your professor "grades on a curve," a type of forced distribution method is being used to appraise your performance. **Forced distribution methods** require that predetermined percentages of employees be placed into particular performance categories. Forced distribution rankings are often accompanied by fairly rigid policies calling for termination or other adverse employment consequences for those employees unfortunate enough to be ranked in the lowest category. Use of forced distribution methods of performance appraisal appears to be increasing.[33] Not surprisingly, these systems have become the object of legal challenges.[34] Ford initiated such a performance appraisal system for its supervisors and managers in January 2000 (see "Clippings"). A firestorm of complaints

[31]*Vaughn v. Edel*, 918 F.2d 517 (5th Cir. 1990).

[32]*Cullom v. Brown*, 209 F.3d 1035 (7th Cir. 2000).

[33]Mark Lowery. "Forcing the Issue." *Human Resource Executive* (January 26, 2004) (http://www.workindex.com/editorial/staff/sta0401-03.asp).

[34]Reed Abelson. "Companies Turn to Grades and Employees Go to Court." *New York Times* (March 19, 2001), A-1.

and lawsuits ensued, leading to a restructuring of the system in July 2001 that deleted the predetermined percentages (except top-achiever status was limited to 10 percent). The suits, which alleged age discrimination because older employees were disproportionately rated in the lowest category, were settled for a substantial sum in March 2002.

Microsoft has also faced legal challenges to its forced distribution appraisal system. Appraisals are conducted twice per year, and each employee is assigned a score from 1.0 to 5.0. Of employees in a work group, 25 percent must be assigned scores of 3.0 or less, 40 percent must be assigned a score of 3.5, and 35 percent are assigned scores at or above 4.0. The scores primarily affect compensation and promotion decisions. A group of employees sued, claiming that the system discriminates against women and African Americans. Although further legal challenges are possible, the court in this case denied the plaintiffs' motion to bring a class-action lawsuit, stating:

> This rating system, however, is not faulty per se. In order to satisfy the Court that Microsoft's rating system worked to the detriment of Microsoft's employees, plaintiffs would have to come forward with some evidence of either disparate treatment or disparate impact arising from the implementation of that system. Plaintiffs have failed to do either.[35]

Thus, although forced distribution performance rankings are not illegal per se, they are likely to be perceived as unfair and to serve as lightning rods for litigation, particularly when low-ranking performers are summarily terminated and are disproportionately members of the same protected class group(s).

TRAINING AND DEVELOPMENT

Training and development programs can make employees more productive and help them get ahead in their careers. They are a feature of better jobs in which employers are willing to invest in their human resources. The provision of training and development is largely up to employers, but there are circumstances under which training is legally required or at least highly advisable. Significant legal questions also can arise concerning who receives training, payment for training, and the contents of training programs. Training and development opportunities are expected to be at the center of more legal disputes in the future, as less stable employment relationships place a premium on acquiring skills that make employees marketable, and employers attempt to ensure that they receive a return on their training investments.

When Is Training Legally Required?

As a general matter, employers do not have a legal duty to train their employees. One important exception is safety and health training. Circumstances also exist under which employers could be found negligent for failing to adequately train their employees. In other situations, training is not expressly required, but is highly desirable for legal reasons.

Safety and Health Training The OSH Act does not require that all covered employees receive safety and health training. However, well over 100 OSHA standards

[35]Donaldson, at 39.

THE CHANGING WORKPLACE

Training and the New Psychological Contract

There has been much talk in recent years about establishing a "new psychological contract" between employers and employees. This concept refers to beliefs about the mutual obligations that employers and employees have to one another. The "old" psychological contract was an implicit bargain that employers (especially larger ones) would provide long-term employment and career advancement within organizations to employees (particularly white-collar workers) who worked hard and remained loyal. Many employers have concluded that such an arrangement is no longer tenable.[1] In its place, employers have emphasized the responsibility of employees for their own careers and made fairly nebulous promises of trust, honest communication, opportunities to learn, and positive work environments. Some variants of the new psychological contract stress the opportunity to acquire skills and access to experiences that will enable employees to perform well in future positions, within or outside their current organizations, as substitutes for the implicit promise of job security and career ladders.[2]

The new psychological contract thus places a premium on access to training and development opportunities. Legal challenges to denial of training are likely to arise more frequently. Training and developmental assignments that increase skills and marketability are more likely to be viewed, by both employees and courts, as valuable ends in themselves—the denial of which is "materially adverse." In a case involving a chemistry technician who alleged discriminatory denial of training, it is noteworthy that, in allowing her case to go forward, the court gave weight to the plaintiff's testimony that "receiving training on advanced equipment would, at the very least, mean she could command a better salary *at other companies* [emphasis added], because it would mean she would have more experience and skills."[3]

Greater employee mobility presents problems for employers. On the one hand, changes in technology and markets require continual upgrading of skills. On the other hand, employers are reluctant to train if their investments will not be recouped because employees, who have gotten the message that they must manage their own careers, pick up and leave (or worse yet, go to work for competitors). Some employers have entered into "training contracts," requiring employees to either stay for specified periods of time following receipt of training or be liable for repayment of training costs.[4] Enforcement of these agreements has not yet emerged as a major legal issue (perhaps because the "poaching" employers are willing to buy out the contracts), but there are examples of such cases. A nurse who received tuition assistance enabling her to complete a nurse anesthetist program was required to repay the hospital because she left to take a job elsewhere.[5] The contract that she signed called for the loan to be forgiven if she worked at the hospital for five years following completion of her schooling. The court rejected the nurse's argument that the contract was no longer valid because the hospital had previously breached it by not providing her with a nurse anesthetist position upon completion of her studies. However, because the contract did not specifically require that the hospital place the nurse in the position she desired, the court ruled for the hospital. Likewise, apprenticeship programs have successfully sued trainees for breaching their agreements to work at sponsoring companies for a specified period of time after completion of their training.[6]

Employers might also seek to shift training costs to employees by requiring individuals to obtain degrees or certification from external training institutions before they can be considered for employment. The primary legal limitation on this strategy is that hiring requirements must not create adverse impact. If they would tend to produce adverse impact, requirements for prior training must be job related for the positions into which applicants would be hired—and not geared toward future positions (unless advancement is quick and relatively assured).

After an individual is hired, she must be paid for training that is required by her employer and occurs during work hours because this is clearly compensable time under the Fair Labor Standards Act. Training that occurs outside of regular working hours might also be compensable, unless attendance at the training is voluntary, no work is performed for the employer during the training, and the training is not directly related to the employee's current job. If an employer "expects" attendance, and nonattendance would detrimentally affect employment standing, the training is not voluntary. However, probationary campus police officers who were required to receive and retain EMT certification

within one year of their appointment were not entitled to compensation for the many hours (at least 120) they spent in EMT training. The court rejected their FLSA claim even though successfully completing the training within a year was a condition of continued employment. The court explained that:

> One of those [DOL] regulations makes training non-compensable if, [among other things], it is both voluntary and unrelated to the employee's job—conditions that do not appear to be satisfied here. But we doubt that the regulation was meant to cover the peculiar situation presented here—that is, where the training is not continuing education relating to existing job duties, but instead a pre-condition

for employment which the employer tolerantly allows to be satisfied while the employee is working on a probationary basis.[7]

[1]The Conference Board. "Implementing the New Employment Compact." *HR Executive Review* 4 (1997).

[2]Katherine V.W. Stone. *From Widgets to Digits: Employment Regulation for the Changing Workplace.* (Cambridge, UK: Cambridge University Press, 2004), pp. 111–12.

[3]*Scurto,* at 45–46.

[4]Peter Cappelli. *The New Deal at Work.* (Boston: Harvard Business School Press, 1999), pp. 198–201.

[5]*Sweetwater Hospital Association v. Carpenter,* 2005 Tenn. App. LEXIS 63.

[6]*Milwaukee Area Joint Apprenticeship Training Committee v. Howell,* 67 F.3d 1333 (7th Cir. 1995).

[7]*Bienkowski v. Northeastern University,* 285 F.3d 138, at 141 (1st Cir. 2002).

call for training for employees exposed to the particular hazards at which the standards are directed. Failure to provide this training violates the OSH Act. A failure to train could also violate the general duty clause if the hazard is recognized, likely to result in death or serious physical harm, and training is a feasible means of abating the hazard. In one relevant case, a construction company was cited for violating a construction industry standard requiring employers to instruct employees in the recognition and avoidance of unsafe conditions. Specifically, the company failed to train its employees regarding the hazard of crossing multilane highways that are in use. An employee, who was part of a work team digging a trench beside an interstate highway, attempted to cross over to the other side of the road. He was struck by a car and killed. The OSHRC upheld the citation for failure to train, and a court agreed. The court pointed to evidence that the employer had actual knowledge of this hazard and dismissed the employer's argument that the hazard was too obvious to require instruction or training:

> The fact that he attempted to cross a road, as he and other employees had done in the past, . . . suggests that the dangers inherent in crossing an active roadway were not so obvious that employees would not have benefited from systematic instruction. This was not a freak accident, but one that could have been prevented with adequate guidance about when the crossing of the highway should not be attempted and when alternative means of crossing the road should be employed.[36]

One important OSHA standard that contains substantial information and training requirements is the **hazard communication standard**. One of the most frequently violated OSHA regulations (see "Clippings"), this standard is based on the principle of a **right to know**—the idea that employees have a right to receive information about the dangerous chemicals that they encounter on the job. Substances that fall within the standard can pose either health hazards (e.g., carcinogens, toxic agents, irritants) or physical hazards (e.g., flammable liquids, compressed gases, reactive

[36]*W.G. Fairfield Co. v. OSHRC,* 285 F. 3d 499 (6th Cir. 2002).

materials). Both chemical manufacturers/importers and employers have obligations under the standard, which is briefly summarized here:[37]

- *Chemical manufacturers/importers must evaluate the hazards of chemicals that they make or sell in light of the available scientific evidence.*

- *Chemical manufacturers and importers must ensure that each container of hazardous chemicals is properly labeled. Employers using these substances must keep these labels on the containers.*

- *Chemical manufacturers and importers must provide a **material safety data sheet (MSDS)** for each hazardous chemical produced or sold. MSDSs must be provided to downstream employers with or prior to shipment of hazardous chemicals.*

- *Employers must have an MSDS for each hazardous chemical used in the workplace. The MSDS must be accessible to employees for their inspection.*

- *MSDSs must include the chemical name of the substance that appears on the label, the common name, physical and health hazards associated with the substance, the OSHA PEL and other applicable standards, procedures for safe handling and use, and first-aid procedures.*

- *Employers must have written hazard communication plans. These plans must show how the standard's labeling, MSDS, and training requirements will be met. All hazardous chemicals known to be in use in the workplace must be listed in the plan. These plans must also address how chemical information will be provided to contractors.*

- *Employees must be provided with training on hazardous chemicals in their work areas when they are initially assigned and whenever a new hazard is introduced.*

- *Elaborate procedures are set out for providing information about hazardous substances in situations where a trade secret is involved.*

Although some may be inclined to view the hazard communication standard as merely an exercise in paperwork, the U.S. Chemical Safety and Hazard Investigation Board has cited inaccurate data sheets as a factor in six industrial accidents since 2000, resulting in 19 deaths and 96 injuries.[38] Knowledge of chemical hazards is vital to employees working with these substances, to persons responsible for the cleanup of facilities, and to firefighters and other emergency responders.

OSHA standards refer to the type of training that must be provided, but do not spell out exactly what must be covered or how. OSHA has issued voluntary guidelines to assist employers in conducting safety training.[39] *Identifying employees who are at risk, the particular hazards to which they are exposed, and their training needs is critical. Effective training also requires paying attention to trainees' language skills, reading comprehension, and cultural backgrounds.*

Other Circumstances in Which Training Is Legally Required or Advisable
Most employers that have contracts to supply goods or services to the federal government (or that are recipients of federal grants) must comply with the Drug Free Workplace Act (DFWA).[40] The DFWA requires contractors to certify that they are providing drug-free workplaces to their employees. This includes publishing

[37]29 C.F.R. § 1910.1200 (2005).

[38]John Gannon. "Improving Safety Data Communications Focus of Hazard Communications Group." *Daily Labor Report* 58 (March 28, 2005), A-6.

[39]Occupational Safety and Health Administration. *Training Requirements in OSHA Standards and Training Guidelines* (1995).

[40]41 U.S.C.A. § 701 *et seq.*

policies prohibiting drug use, sale, or possession in the workplace; backing up those policies with sanctions against violators; and creating and maintaining drug awareness programs. These programs must *inform employees about the drug-free policy; dangers associated with drug abuse; available options for counseling, rehabilitation, and employee assistance programs; and potential penalties for drug violations.*

Just as it is possible for employers to be negligent by failing to use adequate care to screen out applicants who are likely to harm others (negligent hiring), employers can also be negligent in failing to properly train employees. Like any other negligence claim, **negligent training** occurs where there is a duty to others (in this case to provide adequate training), that duty is breached (no, or clearly inadequate, training is provided), there is harm to one or more parties, and breach of the duty to train is the proximate cause of harm. The key issue is whether there is a duty to train. This rests on whether the employer knew or should have known that the employee did not have the information and skills needed to perform the job without endangering others ("knowledge"), the likelihood that an improperly trained employee would cause harm to others given the nature of the job ("foreseeability"), and any public policies relevant to the provision of training in the industry or occupation. The *duty to train is clearest for jobs where supervision is limited, sound judgment must be exercised, and poor performance can readily result in serious harm to others. Employers should assess jobs for these characteristics to determine who needs training and should provide the necessary training.* Careful selection, clear policies, good supervision, and effective training all play a role in averting harm. *Needed training should be provided before employees are put into sensitive jobs and not just when there is time to get around to it.*

Not surprisingly, a number of cases challenging the adequacy of training have involved police officers. Supervisors cannot regularly be out on the streets with officers; sound judgment is needed to handle tense situations that can readily escalate into violence; and police carry guns and other potentially harmful weapons. In one case, a 21-year-old reserve deputy had been on the job for just a few weeks, received no training from the sheriff's department, held only a high school diploma, and lacked prior experience in law enforcement. The deputy observed a pickup truck turn around at a roadblock, pursued the vehicle, stopped it, and proceeded to force a passenger from the vehicle. His "arm-bar" technique of removing the passenger resulted in severe injuries to her knees. The court concluded:

> [T]he County's provision of no training (and no supervision) to Burns, on these facts, constitutes 'deliberate indifference' to the health and safety of the citizens of Bryan County. . . . [W]e take it as elemental that police officers need at least some training to perform their job safely and effectively. The jury was therefore justified to conclude that it was obvious to Sheriff Moore that officers without any training have a high probability of injuring citizens, routinely and unnecessarily, through use of improper techniques, improper force, and improper judgment calls.[41]

The reference to "deliberate indifference" in this quotation is important. Suits against municipalities based on their alleged failure to adequately train or supervise must show not just negligence (which does not require intent or recklessness), but deliberate indifference to the known or obvious consequences of an action.[42]

[41]*Brown v. Bryan County,* 219 F.3d 450, at 462 (5th Cir. 2000), *cert. denied,* 532 U.S. 1007 (2001).

[42]*Board of County Commissioners v. Brown,* 520 U.S. 397, at 407 (1997).

Thus, in another police case, a woman sued the city after a police officer came to her home in the early morning (after having earlier arrested her husband on drug charges), announced that he was there to strip-search her, and proceeded to conduct a body-cavity and strip search. The officer was convicted on counts of second-degree rape and sexual battery, but the woman's attempt to hold the city liable for violation of her Fourth Amendment right against unreasonable search and seizure failed. She was unable to show that inadequate training led to the violation of her rights because there had been no prior instances of such conduct to alert the city that further supervision or training was needed, the officer's actions directly violated the city's written search policy, employees were trained in the policy, and the policy was customarily followed.[43]

A basic premise of this book is that a good working knowledge of employment law is indispensable for managers, supervisors, and others involved in making employment decisions. *Training in understanding and applying antidiscrimination policies, although not expressly required by the law, is highly advisable.* The advisability of providing training in employment law stems, in the first instance, from the hope that it will prevent violations of employees' rights. If violations occur nonetheless, the existence of policies, training in those policies, and enforcement can lessen the damages for which employers will be liable.

Under Title VII, employees can be awarded punitive damages in cases of intentional discrimination where employers act "with malice or with reckless indifference to the federally protected rights" of their employees.[44] Punitive damages are intended to severely punish the offenders and to send a message to others that engaging in the same unacceptable behavior could subject them to substantial liability. In a case involving egregious hostile environment harassment, much of it perpetrated by a manager, the court pointed squarely to the absence of an antidiscrimination policy and any training on discrimination as grounds for ordering a trial on the issue of punitive damages. The existence of an EEOC poster that no one ever read on a wall in the workplace was not sufficient to show good faith.[45] Similarly, in an age discrimination case, the court upheld the "liquidated damages" (an amount, up to double the award, that can be assessed for "willful" violations in ADEA and FLSA cases) awarded to a plaintiff. In the court's words:

> [A]s this circuit has held, leaving managers with hiring authority in ignorance of the basic features of the discrimination laws is an "extraordinary mistake" for a company to make, and a jury can find that such an extraordinary mistake amounts to reckless indifference.[46]

The employer's pro forma attempt at legal compliance—putting "boilerplate" language about age discrimination being against the law on its employment applications—was to no avail. In fact, the court pointed out that using this language while making no effort to train hiring managers about how to implement it showed that the employer was aware of the law, but was indifferent as to whether its managers followed it.

The Notification and Federal Employees Anti-Discrimination and Retaliation (No FEAR) Act[47], enacted in 2002, requires agencies of the federal government to provide training to employees on their rights under federal antidiscrimination, whistleblower protection, and retaliation laws.

[43]*Crownover v. City of Lindsay, Oklahoma,* 2000 U.S. App. LEXIS 22390.

[44]*Kolstad v. American Dental Ass'n,* 527 U.S. 526, at 534 (1999).

[45]*Anderson v. G.D.C., Inc.,* 281 F.3d 452 (4th Cir. 2002).

[46]*Mathis v. Phillips Chevrolet, Inc.,* 269 F.3d 771, at 778 (7th Cir. 2001).

[47]Pub. L. No. 107-174 (2002).

Selection of Trainees

Many training and development opportunities are offered on a limited basis and present questions of selection. In *Hoffman v. Caterpillar,* an employer's decision to not make training available to a disabled employee was challenged under the ADA.

HOFFMAN V. CATERPILLAR
256 F.3d 568 (7th Cir. 2001)

OPINION BY CIRCUIT JUDGE KANNE:

Shirley Hoffman, who was born without a left arm below the elbow, brought suit alleging that Caterpillar, Inc. unlawfully discriminated against her by failing to provide training on two machines in violation of the Americans with Disabilities Act (ADA). * * *

Hoffman began working for Caterpillar's Optical Services Department ("OSD") in April 1996. * * * Hoffman's primary job responsibility is indexing—entering data relating to a scanned image into the computer. Her job also includes preparing papers to be scanned, maintaining the copy machine, running the flatbed scanner (a low-speed scanner), and ordering office supplies. Due to the fact that she is missing her lower left arm, Hoffman needs several accommodations to perform her job, including a typing stand, poster putty to raise the function key on her computer, and a compound called tacky finger to improve finger grip. It is also sometimes necessary for Hoffman to have the items in her work area rearranged. . . . [I]t is clear that she is now able to perform the essential functions of her job. Caterpillar concedes that, with the exception of her first three weeks on the job, Hoffman's work has been average or better and that she performs her indexing job as fast or faster than a person with two hands.

Although Hoffman already performs all of the required functions of her job, she has repeatedly expressed a desire to be trained . . . to operate the high-speed scanner, a production machine that scans forty to fifty pages per minute. Operation of the high-speed scanner is a key position in the OSD because the overall productivity of the department depends on the speed at which documents are scanned. OSD employees in Hoffman's position are not required to run the high-speed scanner; out of the twenty-one people in the department as of March

1999, only seven are completely trained to operate it. Caterpillar contends that Hoffman's lack of training on the high-speed scanner does not affect her compensation, benefits, work hours, job title, or ability to advance within the OSD. Hoffman disagrees with Caterpillar's claim that the denial of training does not affect her ability to advance; she argues that she will be a more attractive candidate for promotion if she is well-trained. In addition, Hoffman maintains that she should be trained, regardless of whether it affects her ability to advance, because every other employee who has expressed an interest in operating the high-speed scanner has received the necessary training to do so.

Hoffman's supervisor and the head of the OSD, Lynn Cripe, admits that he denied Hoffman training on the high-speed scanner because she only has one hand. He claims that her disability would prevent her from being able to properly run the high-speed scanner because two hands are needed to clear paper jams and to straighten documents as they exit the machine. Paper jams occur frequently on the high-speed scanner—sometimes four to five times an hour—disrupting production for anywhere from a few seconds to fifteen minutes depending on the severity of the jam. Cripe is concerned that Hoffman would be unable to run the machine, and even if she were able to operate it, that she would be unable to maintain an acceptable speed or clear the frequent paper jams without assistance. Although Cripe is not fully trained on the high-speed scanner himself, his observation of the machine leads him to believe that Hoffman, even if able to physically run the machine, would not be able to keep up with the production standards set for the department. * * * Cripe's belief that Hoffman would be unable to run the high-speed scanner was never confirmed, however, because Hoffman was never given a chance to try. * * *

Hoffman claims that Caterpillar's denial of training on the high-speed scanner constitutes both disparate treatment and a failure to accommodate under the

ADA. Because Caterpillar does not challenge Hoffman's claim that she is a qualified individual with a disability within the meaning of the ADA, we turn first to Hoffman's disparate treatment claim.

At the outset, we note that it is quite clear that Caterpillar is not obligated to train Hoffman on the high-speed scanner if she is not capable of running it. The ADA certainly does not require employers to allow employees to use equipment that they are unable to operate. Nor does anything in the ADA mandate that Caterpillar must tolerate a drop in productivity in order to allow Hoffman to run the high-speed scanner. * * *

Viewing the evidence in the light most favorable to Hoffman, we find that there is an issue of fact as to whether Hoffman would be able to operate the high-speed scanner. * * * [T]he ADA discourages employment decisions "'based on stereotypes and generalizations associated with the individual's disability rather than on the individual's actual characteristics.'" The ADA recognizes that a non-disabled person's instincts about the capabilities of a disabled person are often likely to be incorrect. Therefore, a determination that two-handed people use both of their hands to operate the high-speed scanner, or even a determination that most one-handed people would be unable to run it, should not be the end of an employer's inquiry. In this case, it seems doubtful that Cripe made an individualized determination as to whether Hoffman could operate the high-speed scanner because he never gave her a chance to try it. Caterpillar claims that the primary reason that Hoffman lacks the capability to run the high-speed scanner is that she would be unable to effectively clear the frequent paper jams that occur. There is evidence in the record, however, that Hoffman clears paper jams from the copy machine without assistance, and Caterpillar presents no evidence to suggest that clearing paper jams from the high-speed scanner is somehow different. Nor does Caterpillar counter Hoffman's claim that she could use her left arm in a manner similar to a flat hand to hold down the paper as it is being fed into the machine. Therefore, drawing all inferences in favor of Hoffman, we must assume that she is physically capable of running the high-speed scanner. * * *

Hoffman's supervisor, Cripe, admits that he refused Hoffman's requests for high-speed scanner training because of her disability. * * * Caterpillar contends that it is clear that an alleged denial of training must materially affect an individual's employment for it to be actionable. However, none of the authorities that Caterpillar cites for the proposition that a denial of training must be materially adverse deal with denials of job training under the ADA; rather, they address failure to train claims under Title VII and the ADEA. This distinction is relevant because the ADA specifically prohibits discrimination in "regard to job application procedures, the hiring, advancement, or discharge of employees, employee compensation, job training, and other terms, conditions, and privileges of employment," while the parallel provisions of Title VII and the ADEA do not specifically include the term "job training" among the prohibited actions. * * *

While we agree that Congress did not intend the ADA to reach every bigoted act or gesture, we must believe that Congress did intend to reach conduct that it specifically prohibited in the statute. Thus, with respect to employment actions specifically enumerated in the statute, a materially adverse employment action is not a separate substantive requirement. We agree with Hoffman that, because the ADA specifically prohibits discrimination in regard to "job training," and she has direct evidence of discriminatory intent, she need not show that the denial of training was materially adverse. Hoffman is not asking for special training because of her disability, on the contrary, she is merely asking for the same training that is available to all other employees who request it. * * *

We next turn to Hoffman's failure to accommodate claim. At issue is whether Caterpillar must accommodate Hoffman in order to allow her to operate the high-speed scanner if she is unable to do so without accommodation. As we noted above, Hoffman has already been accommodated in order to perform the essential functions of her job. She now requests (assuming she needs it) accommodation so that she may operate the high-speed scanner—a non-essential function of her position. While it is admirable that Hoffman wants to perform job tasks that Caterpillar does not require her to perform, "it is the employer's prerogative to choose a reasonable accommodation; an employer is not required to provide the particular accommodation that an employee requests."

Caterpillar has chosen to accommodate Hoffman's disability by letting other employees run the high-speed scanner; and, if Caterpillar is correct that Hoffman is unable to run the high-speed scanner without assistance, we will not disturb Caterpillar's chosen method of accommodation. The ADA requires "an employer to make whatever accommodations are reasonably possible in the circumstances to perform the functions essential to his position," including removing nonessential

functions from the job, but nothing in the statute requires an employer to accommodate the employee so that she may perform any nonessential function that she chooses. * * *

For the foregoing reasons, the district court erred in requiring the plaintiff to show that the denial of training on the high-speed scanner was a materially adverse employment action. Therefore, we VACATE the district court's grant of summary judgment on Hoffman's disparate treatment claim with respect to the high-speed scanner and REMAND to allow the plaintiff to attempt to show that she is entitled to recover on this claim. We AFFIRM the district court's grant of summary judgment for Caterpillar with respect to Hoffman's failure to accommodate claim. . . .

CASE QUESTIONS

1. What were the legal issues in this case? What did the court decide?

2. Why did Hoffman have a disparate treatment claim based on denial of training?

3. Why is there a discussion of whether denial of training is a "materially adverse employment action"? Why does the court say that it doesn't matter in this case?

4. Why is she not entitled to reasonable accommodation to enable her to successfully complete the training? Is this consistent with the rest of the decision?

5. What should the employer have done differently?

When employers offer training, they must not discriminate in deciding whom to train. In general, discrimination claims require plaintiffs to show loss of employment opportunity (i.e., a **materially adverse employment action**). We saw earlier in this chapter that an undeservedly negative performance appraisal that does not result in an adverse employment outcome cannot be the basis for a discrimination claim. The law is less clear regarding training opportunities. In *Hoffman*, the court decided that the specific reference in the ADA to *job training* (among other employment actions for which disability discrimination is prohibited) means that ADA plaintiffs need not show that a denial of training was materially adverse. Other statutes, including Title VII and the ADEA, do not refer to job training specifically, but arguably encompass it within the phrase *other terms and conditions of employment*. Courts have differed on whether denial of training, by itself, is a valid claim under Title VII and the ADEA.[48] However, in practice, the receipt and successful completion of training is often closely linked to employment opportunities (e.g., promotions, raises).

Much of the training that employees receive is informal, **on-the-job training** from coworkers. An African-American woman was allowed to go to trial on her discriminatory failure to train claim, even though the company did not have a formal training program. It was enough that the typical practice was to provide on-the-job training by experienced coworkers and that she received less of such training than did similarly situated white male employees.[49] Interestingly, the court also ruled that an allegedly retaliatory transfer received by the woman could be viewed as "materially adverse" because it further reduced her opportunity to receive on-the-job training. Even though the woman retained the same job title and pay level, there was:

> . . . a question of fact whether the transfer . . . constituted a materially adverse employment action, particularly in light of [the employer's] admission that one of the goals of a setup operator trainee is to learn to set up various types

[48] *Spencer v. AT&T Network Systems,* 1998 U.S. Dist. LEXIS 10718, at 14 (denial of training not an adverse employment action); *Scurto v. Commonwealth Edison Co.,* 2000 U.S. Dist. LEXIS 16171 (failure to train actionable even if not linked to loss of a promotional opportunity).

[49] *Hamilton v. Spraying Systems,* 2004 U.S. Dist. LEXIS 19398.

of machines and that a trainee could stay a trainee for years (as opposed to becoming a setup operator) if that trainee [fails to acquire this skill].[50]

Another meaningful form of training is **apprenticeship programs**. These programs typically combine classroom instruction with work under the guidance of experienced coworkers. They are most often used to train employees in skilled, manual crafts (e.g., electricians, carpenters). Apprenticeship programs are often sponsored by labor unions, sometimes in conjunction with employer associations. Entry into apprenticeship programs is an important avenue to better paying jobs, but the availability of apprenticeships is often limited. The legal challenge to Ford's apprenticeship progam centered on the Apprenticeship Training Selection System (see "Clippings"). The test used to establish an eligibility list for the apprenticeship program was alleged to be discriminatory against African Americans. As part of the settlement, "Ford will immediately cease the use of the current selection procedure for choosing apprentices at Ford facilities in the U.S." and the "parties will agree upon an industrial psychologist to serve as an expert to devise new apprenticeship selection procedures."[51] Although apprenticeships are often thought of as being for younger workers, apprenticeship programs are subject to the ADEA and cannot discriminate based on age. In a case involving an apprenticeship program for maritime workers that had accepted applications only from persons aged 17–35, the court observed that:

> The stereotype underlying age restrictions in apprenticeships, meanwhile, is that older people are unable to learn the skills of a trade as efficiently as their younger counterparts. Such barrier to entry may also demean the contributions to the human capital of younger workers that their more mature peers can impart. . . . [T]he kind of age discrimination that is alleged here contravenes the reason the statute was enacted.[52]

An employer that denies training to an employee and is charged with discrimination still has the opportunity to offer a lawful reason for the decision. In *Hoffman,* this avenue was precluded because the supervisor openly admitted that the employee's disability was the reason for denying her training. One of the lessons that can be drawn from this case is that *training is particularly well-suited to determining a disabled employee's ability to perform a job and is greatly preferable to indulging in speculation about what disabled employees are capable of doing.* In other cases, employers have successfully defended their decisions to not provide training by showing that the individuals in question did not meet established criteria. For example, a woman who sought entry to her employer's "administrator in training" program was unable to show that the denial of training was due to her religion because she lacked one of the minimum qualifications that state law required nursing home administrators to possess (two years of prior management experience).[53] However, a court refused to throw out the age discrimination claim of a woman who was not given accountancy training, even though she had made it known that she was looking for another job, and company policy appeared to require that employees working in accounting positions have degrees in the field. Evidence that she had been promised training when she took the job and employer statements conveying a discriminatory motive ("it's young women I like to train") were sufficient to avoid summary judgment.[54]

[50]*Hamilton*, at 33.

[51]*Robinson, et al., v. Ford Motor Company,* 2005 U.S. Dist. LEXIS 11673, at 5.

[52]*Equal Employment Opportunity Commission v. Seafarers International Union,* 394 F.3d 197, at 206 (4th Cir. 2005).

[53]*Roh v. Lakeshore Estates, Inc.,* 241 F.3d 491 (6th Cir. 2001).

[54]*Holtz v. Rockefeller & Co., Inc.,* 258 F.3d 62 (2d Cir. 2001).

Contents of Training Programs

What were they thinking? In the name of team-building and motivation, members of Burger King's marketing department were led by consultants through a series of "physical challenges" culminating in an ill-fated stroll over hot coals, but also including the likes of breaking boards and smashing bricks with bare hands, bending steel bars with throats, and walking on nails (see "Clippings"). It has not been reported whether any legal claims stemmed from this episode. At the least, it would appear that the injured employees are entitled to workers' compensation to cover their medical expenses. Suits against the trainers are a possibility, although participants were required to sign waivers acknowledging the possibility of injury. The owner of the consulting company did not find the rate of injury unusual and was quoted as saying "[s]ome people just have incredibly sensitive feet."

Clearly, *employers should choose trainers carefully, ascertain what they are actually going to do before they do it, and carefully evaluate their performance.* Training in job skills presents hazards when the work involves contact with dangerous equipment or substances, or when coworkers must rely on trainees' actions. Training that is aimed at soft skills and attitudes, such as the team-building retreat, poses different kinds of risk. Consultants might have numerous high-powered clients and strings of letters following their names, but their offerings can still be quackery and potentially harmful to employees.

In *Altman v. Minnesota Department of Corrections,* the contents of a diversity training program raised legal questions.

ALTMAN V. MINNESOTA DEPARTMENT OF CORRECTIONS
251 F.3d 1199 (8th Cir. 2001)

OPINION BY CIRCUIT JUDGE LOKEN:

Thomas Altman, Kristen Larson, and Kenneth Yackly are employees of the Minnesota Department of Corrections assigned to the correctional facility in Shakopee, which we will refer to as MCFS. In October 1997, they silently read their Bibles during a mandatory seventy-five-minute training program entitled "Gays and Lesbians in the Workplace." The three received written reprimands, which made Larson and Yackly ineligible for promotions then in progress. They filed this action against the Department and various officials. . . . * * * The district court granted summary judgment. . . . * * * Concluding that Appellants have raised triable free speech, equal protection, and Title VII issues, we reverse.

In mid-1997, MCFS's training director persuaded Warden Connie Roehrich to include in the next regular one-day training session a program dealing with issues of gays and lesbians in the workplace. When the agenda for the training session was published to MCFS staff, Altman sent Roehrich an e-mail objecting to the mandatory nature of this program and protesting that it would "raise deviant sexual behavior for staff to a level of acceptance and respectability." Faced with this protest, and rumors that other staff members objected to this part of the mandatory training session, Roehrich issued a memorandum to all staff explaining that the gays-and-lesbians-in-the-workplace program was part of "the facility's strong commitment to create a work environment where people are treated respectfully, regardless of their individual differences." The training is not "designed to tell you what your personal attitudes or beliefs should be," the memorandum continued, but all employees must attend.

Prior to the training session, Appellants reviewed the training materials for the gays-and-lesbians-in-the-workplace program and concluded the training would be, in the words of their complaint, "state-sponsored indoctrination designed to sanction, condone, promote, and otherwise approve behavior and a style of life

Appellants believe to be immoral, sinful, perverse, and contrary to the teachings of the Bible." Immediately prior to the session, Appellants met and decided to read their Bibles during this program as a silent protest and as support because of the discomforting subject matter. During the program, Appellants read their Bibles, copied scripture, and participated to a limited extent. They did not disrupt the trainers' presentation. Numerous supervisors attended the program; none complained about Appellants' behavior or told them to stop reading their Bibles.

After the program, two of the trainers reported Appellants' behavior, and the MCFS Affirmative Action Officer filed a complaint. Following an internal investigation, written reprimands were issued to Appellants as formal discipline. The reprimands were based on Appellants' conduct during this portion of the training session. The reprimands made Appellants ineligible for promotion for two years. The summary judgment record includes deposition testimony by numerous witnesses that, to their knowledge, prison officials have never disciplined other employees who were inattentive during training sessions, for example, by sleeping or reading magazines.

To prevail on their First Amendment claims, Appellants must prove they were punished for conduct "fairly characterized as constituting speech on a matter of public concern," and that their interest in speaking out on that matter of public concern "outweighs the public employer's interest in promoting its efficiency by prohibiting the conduct." Appellants contend that defendants violated Appellants' right to equal protection of the law because defendants have not disciplined similarly situated persons—employees who have been inattentive for other reasons during MCFS training sessions. In their Title VII claim, Appellants allege they were impermissibly disciplined on the basis of their religious beliefs. * * *

Appellants argue that reading their Bibles during the training program was nonverbal conduct that qualifies as speech for First Amendment purposes. . . . However, the district court concluded that Appellants did not engage in speech on a matter of public interest and concern because they were "concerned only with internal policies or practices which are of relevance only to the employees of that institution." We disagree. Though the issue is inherently "internal," the way in which the Department and MCFS deal with issues of gays and lesbians in the workplace affects the performance of their public duties and is a matter of political and social concern to the general public. By making attendance at the training session mandatory, MCFS created a context in which employees speaking out in opposition to their public employer's handling of this social issue should be considered speech on a matter of public interest and concern.

Even if a public employee's speech addresses a matter of public concern, * * * [t]he public employer will be justified in imposing discipline if the speech impeded the employee's ability to perform his or her responsibilities, or undermined office relationships, or disrupted office operations or efficiencies. In this regard, a public employer may decide to train its employees, it may establish the parameters of that training, and it may require employees to participate. An employee who refuses to be trained has, from the employer's reasonable perspective, impeded his or her ability to do the job.

Defendants argue that Appellants were reprimanded for insubordination—refusing to be trained—not for their nonverbal speech. This is a potentially strong argument . . . but it is not supported by the undisputed facts in this summary judgment record. In our view, the critical fact is that other employees have been similarly inattentive at MCFS training sessions, but none has ever been disciplined. Thus, the only employees disciplined for "insubordination" are those who spoke out in opposition to the training message, despite Warden Roehrich's prior assurance that, "In no way is this training designed to tell you what your personal attitudes or beliefs should be." Moreover, Appellants were selected out for punishment after conveying their opposition by reading the Bible. * * * [S]ummary judgment dismissing their First Amendment, equal protection, and Title VII claims is inappropriate . . . when a trial might establish that the reason for the discipline was Appellants' non-disruptive speech, or their religion, or the fact that they expressed their opposition through religious activity, and that other employees went unpunished who showed equally insubordinate but less constitutionally protected disregard for MCFS training. * * *

CASE QUESTIONS

1. What was the legal issue in this case? What did the court decide? Why?

2. Did the objecting employees engage in speech related to a "matter of public concern"?

3. What, if anything, should this employer have done differently?

This case was decided largely on constitutional (free speech) grounds because the employer was a state government agency. However, Title VII rights are also implicated (both failure to reasonably accommodate sincerely held religious beliefs and disparate treatment in disciplining the employees), so this case has relevance to private employers as well. Diversity training can be very beneficial. By its nature, diversity training is apt to make some individuals uncomfortable. If diversity training is thought to be important, it should not be voluntary. However, diversity training has considerable potential to go awry. *Careful selection of competent diversity trainers and close monitoring of the training is essential.* The legal protection of sincerely held religious beliefs and practices under Title VII necessitates concern for the religious sensitivities of persons required to attend diversity training. The Corrections Department clearly erred in disciplining these employees, while routinely ignoring nonparticipation by others. Even if participation was strictly enforced, the department should have considered possible accommodations because it was on notice that some employees objected on religious grounds to the content of the training.

Chapter SUMMARY

Performance appraisal and training are important aspects of performance management. Both are closely linked to attaining employment opportunities, including bonuses, promotions, and avoiding layoffs. Performance appraisal and training are not the objects of separate laws, but instead raise interesting questions for the application of more general laws. Discrimination is the overriding legal concern.

Employers do not have a legal duty to conduct performance appraisals. Nor will courts recognize claims based solely on undeservedly negative evaluations. However, performance appraisals provide a key source of documentation regarding performance. They become central to disparate treatment claims when employees who suffer the loss of employment opportunities allege discrimination, and their employers attribute the decisions to poor performance. In deciding whether discrimination is the real motive, the credibility of the performance appraisal necessarily becomes an issue. Marked declines in performance ratings shortly before adverse employment decisions are made, highly subjective criteria, lack of familiarity of raters with employees' performance, and language suggesting bias are among the circumstances that will undermine performance appraisals and make it seem more likely that employment decisions were based on protected class. Performance appraisals can also be challenged for adverse impact, although formal validation studies are not required for appraisal devices.

In general, employers do not have a legal duty to provide training and development programs for their employees. However, training in safety and health matters is required under the OSH Act for employees who are exposed to certain hazards and, in general, when recognized hazards likely to result in death or serious physical harm can be feasibly abated through training. OSHA's hazard communication standard requires that employees exposed to dangerous chemicals be given information and training regarding those substances. Negligent training claims can be brought when a lack of needed skills or knowledge is known to an employer or should be known, the employee's position is one that makes serious harm to others foreseeable when occupied by an improperly trained person, harm occurs, and the harm is the proximate result of a failure to train. Employers have strong legal incentives to provide training in legal compliance to persons involved in making employment decisions. Failure to do so can result in greater liability when employees' rights are violated.

The allocation of training and development opportunities is likely to become a larger issue in future years. Under the "new psychological contract," employees are being told that they must assume responsibility for their own careers. Acquiring new skills, experiences, and contacts is necessary to remain marketable. Who pays for training and how training costs can be recouped by employers are also likely to become more frequently contested legal issues. Under the Fair Labor Standards Act, most training must be compensated. However, if the training is voluntary, not directly related to performance of a current job, and does not entail performance of work during the

training, it usually is not compensable. As training moves from particular job skills to efforts to shape broader attitudes and behaviors, concerns over the contents of the training and the credentials of trainers become more acute. Conflicts between training contents and sincerely held religious beliefs, and the need to attempt to accommodate those beliefs, can be anticipated.

Practical Advice SUMMARY

- *Employers are advised to*

 – *conduct performance appraisals regularly.*

 – *maintain credible, written documentation of employee performance.*

 – *have documentation of performance that goes beyond supervisor ratings.*

- *In appraising the performance of disabled employees, employers should*

 – *hold disabled employees to the same standards of performance as nondisabled employees who do the same jobs.*

 – *evaluate performance with any needed accommodations in place.*

 – *not rate performance less positively due to the need for accommodation.*

 – *not require the performance of marginal functions.*

 – *not allow failure to perform marginal functions to result in lower performance ratings.*

 – *consider whether performance deficits are related to disabilities before taking actions against underperforming employees.*

- *Performance criteria and standards should be*

 – *applied in a consistent manner.*

 – *as specific and objective as possible.*

 – *established and communicated to employees before performance is appraised.*

 – *job related and consistent with business necessity.*

- *Global performance ratings should be avoided unless they are derived from combined ratings on more specific criteria.*

- *Employers should carefully consider whether the use of forced distribution methods of rating performance is worth the risk.*

- *Performance appraisals must not be manipulated and made more negative than actual performance warrants as a means of getting back at employees who complain about violations of their rights or to justify discriminatory actions.*

- *Supervisors and others who conduct performance appraisals should:*

 – *receive training or at least explicit written instructions.*

 – *be thoroughly familiar with the jobs in question and the work of the persons being evaluated.*

- *Performance appraisals generally should*

 – *include both positive and negative comments.*

 – *detail the behaviors that are the basis of ratings.*

 – *cite specific instances of good or poor performance.*

 – *be neutral and professional in tone.*

 – *be reviewed by higher-level managers before they are given to employees.*

- *After performance has been appraised, employers should*

 – *communicate performance appraisals to employees.*

 – *provide an opportunity for discussion.*

 – *allow employees to respond to and appeal them.*

- *Employers should not attempt to avoid unpleasant confrontations by failing to provide feedback or opportunities to improve performance when these are provided to other employees.*

- *Safety and health training must be provided when employees are exposed to hazards covered by OSHA standards with training requirements or to other recognized hazards that would likely result in death or serious physical harm and for which training is a feasible means of abatement.*

- Employers whose employees are exposed to hazardous chemicals must

 –maintain material safety data sheets (MSDSs) for each of these substances.

 –have written hazard communication plans.

 –train employees regarding the hazardous chemicals to which they are exposed.

- Employers that have contracts with the federal government must

 –establish drug-free workplace policies.

 –maintain drug awareness programs.

- Employers have a duty to train, closely supervise, or otherwise act to avert harm to others when

 –they employ people who they know do not have the skills or information needed to perform their jobs without endangering others.

 –the nature of those jobs makes it likely that such harm will occur.

- Employers must not discriminate in selecting employees for training.

- Employees must be paid for required training that occurs during work hours. Training during non-work hours must also be compensated, unless

 –it is voluntary.

 –no work is performed during the training.

 –the training is not directly related to the employee's current job.

- Employers should choose trainers carefully, ascertain what they are going to do before they do it, and carefully evaluate their performance.

Key TERMS

performance appraisal
performance criteria
forced distribution method
training
development

hazard communication standard
right to know
material safety data sheet (MSDS)
negligent training

materially adverse employment action
on-the-job training
apprenticeship program

Chapter QUESTIONS

1. A woman of Asian national origin was hired as vice president for human resources by a hospital chain. She received two annual performance appraisals that indicated she was meeting the hospital's standards in most areas. About two years after her hiring, a new president took over, and the woman was terminated. The woman was not told the reason at the time, but the hospital now cites a number of failings relating to inadequate management of legal compliance issues as the basis for the termination. These concerns were not specifically addressed in her performance appraisals. The woman contends that she was discriminated against and that several other employees had received counseling and were allowed time to correct performance deficiencies.

What should the court decide? Why? (*Sakaguchi v. Legacy Health System*, 1999 U.S. Dist. LEXIS 11080)

2. A female customer services manager received a favorable performance appraisal in February. In recognition of her good work, she received a bonus in April and was given an expenses-paid trip to Hawaii in May. Upon returning from the trip, she was discharged because she did not "fit in" and was replaced by a male. She was not charged with violating any rules or engaging in any misconduct during her employment. In addition to suing for sex discrimination, she also filed claims of negligence and fraudulent misrepresentation, based on the performance appraisals that

failed to inform her of any problems with her performance. Was the employer negligent in how it conducted its performance appraisals? Did it engage in fraudulent misrepresentation? (*Mann v. The J.E. Baker Co.*, 733 F. Supp. 885 (M.D. Pa. 1990))

3. A woman received a score of 3.7 (out of 5) on her first performance appraisal. She began to experience severe harassment from a coworker. She complained about it to her supervisor and the human resources department on numerous occasions. On a subsequent appraisal, she received a score of 3.04. The woman was laid off shortly thereafter, with the employer citing the fact that she had the lowest overall performance rating as the basis for the decision. She sued. What should the court decide? Why? (*Winarto v. Toshiba*, 274 F.3d 1276 (9th Cir. 2001))

4. A police department terminated an African-American probationary employee shortly before completion of a one-year training program for troopers. The department cited his subpar performance in report writing and radio communications. A few months before the termination, the department had the employee professionally evaluated. It was determined that he had a possible learning disability, and a remedial training program was devised to help him overcome the problem. However, by the time the remedial efforts were to begin, his probationary period was ending. Due to his performance problems, the department chose to terminate him. The employee claimed race discrimination and pointed to another (white) trainee who had been having similar problems. That employee received special assistance for six months, starting at the outset of his training (although ultimately to no avail). The department attributed the differential treatment to the fact that the other employee's problem became apparent sooner. What should the court decide? Why? (*Kidd v. Illinois State Police*, 2001 U.S. App. LEXIS 27214)

5. Employees of a contractor that manufactures cabinets were delivering cabinets to a house under construction. Two employees were carrying a large cabinet up a stairway to the second floor when one of them fell off the landing and was killed. There were no railings or other guards on the stairway that was still under construction. The contractor

had no written safety rules specifically addressing unguarded stairs or landings. However, delivery crews were instructed that if they encountered an "unsafe condition" while making a delivery, they should leave the cabinet downstairs and call the office. The lead delivery person testified that he had occasionally left cabinets downstairs due to dangerous obstacles, but had never reported it to the office. He also testified that unguarded stairs do not always pose a hazard, depending on how much room there is on the steps. Another delivery person testified that he had delivered cabinets upstairs despite the absence of railings or guards because he never had any problems doing so. The contractor is cited by OSHA for failing to adequately train its employees. What should the commission decide? Why? (*Superior Custom Cabinet Co.*, 18 OSHRC 1019 (1997))

6. An apprenticeship program trains people to become electricians. One of the requirements for entry into the apprenticeship program is possession of a high school diploma or GED. Applicants without a diploma or GED who applied nonetheless were rejected. In the counties where the program operated, 89.2 percent of whites and 68.3 percent of blacks held diplomas or GEDs. Blacks comprised 18.3 percent of the potential applicant pool (defined as people who work as operators or laborers in the surrounding geographic area) but only 12.2 percent of actual applicants. Of actual applicants, blacks were several times more likely than whites to be rejected due to lack of a diploma or GED. The apprenticeship program is sued for race discrimination. What should the court decide? Why? (*EEOC v. Joint Apprenticeship Committee of the Joint Industry Board of the Electrical Industry*, 186 F.3d 110 (2d Cir. 1998))

7. What are the advantages and disadvantages of forced distribution methods of performance appraisal? Are they worth the potential legal and employee relations problems?

8. Was *Bienkowski v. Northeastern University*, the case dealing with payment of campus police officers for required EMT training, decided properly? Can a clear distinction be drawn between the type of training involved in this case and other training needed to perform a job?

Internet RESOURCES

Bacal & Associates maintain this Web site that provides information to employers about performance appraisals and performance management.

http://www.work911.com/performance

ELT specializes in providing employment law training.

http://www.elt-inc.com

The American Society for Training and Development Web site provides information and events related to training.

http://www.astd.org

The Department of Labor's Employment Training Administration Web site provides information on government job training programs.

http://www.doleta.gov

Privacy on the Job: Information, Monitoring, and Investigations

CLIPPINGS

▸ A jury in Florida awarded $1 million to each of two women who had their privacy invaded while working for a financial services company. A coworker placed a camera under their desks and subsequently posted revealing pictures of the women on the Internet. The coworker also peeped on female employees through ceiling tiles in the women's restroom. The company failed to take effective action after receiving numerous complaints about the coworker. Much of the award was based on the jury's finding that there was an intentional infliction of emotional distress.[1]

▸ Employers have had to learn how to comply with new medical privacy regulations under the Health Insurance Portability and Accountability Act (HIPAA). The regulations went into effect in April 2003. They have the greatest impact on companies that self-insure, but all employers that sponsor group health insurance plans and are privy to medical information that can be linked to specific individuals have responsibilities under the law.[2]

▸ As the number of Web logs ("blogs") has proliferated, employees are finding that their employers are taking note. Employers are also sometimes taking disciplinary action against employees with blogs. A flight attendant at Delta Airlines was terminated for appearing on her blog in uniform, and a Google employee was fired for his comments about the company's finances. Few, if any, legal protections are available to employees whose blogging raises the ire of their employers.[3]

▸ A study by the American Management Association and the ePolicy Institute found that 62 percent of responding employers monitor all their employees' Internet activity. Another 14 percent monitor employees in selected jobs. A sizable percentage of respondents (26 percent) had terminated an employee for misusing the Internet. Over half of the respondents reported using video surveillance of the workplace.[4]

[1]Drew Douglas. "Jury Awards $2 Million to Women Taped by Co-Worker's Hidden Camera." *Daily Labor Report* 37 (February 25, 2005), A-3.

[2]Michael W. Wyand. "Practitioners Offer Last Minute Suggestions on HIPAA Privacy Rule for Self-Insured Plans." *Daily Labor Report* 73 (April 16, 2003), A-5.

[3]Tom Zeller Jr. "When the Blogger Blogs, Can the Employer Intervene?" *New York Times* (April 18, 2005), C-1.

[4]"Study Finds 76 Percent of Respondents Monitor Usage of Internet by Employees," *Daily Labor Report* 100 (May 25, 2005), A-8.

Employers gather, generate, and store a great deal of information about their employees. Applications, test results, performance appraisals, attendance and payroll records, Social Security numbers, telephone numbers, medical information, grievance filings, disciplinary actions, and documents generated by investigations of misconduct are among the many records that employers typically maintain. Employers also monitor employees' actions and investigate allegations of wrongdoing. The volume of information available about employees and the means of monitoring their actions have expanded greatly with the proliferation of computers. All these record-keeping and information-gathering activities raise questions of privacy. Most people are under no illusion that they are sacrificing some privacy when they go to work and are screened, supervised, evaluated, and generally watched. What are the legal limits to incursions upon privacy in the workplace?

OVERVIEW OF WORKPLACE PRIVACY PROTECTIONS

Many laws relate to workplace privacy. Legal protections for employee privacy can be found in constitutions, common law, and statutes. However, the protection of employee privacy rights only goes so far; courts generally view the privacy rights of employees as minimal.

Constitutional Protection

The U.S. Constitution does not explicitly provide for a right to privacy (some state constitutions do, such as California's). However, constitutionally protected privacy rights have been fashioned out of the Fourth Amendment's protection against unreasonable search or seizure. *O'Connor v. Ortega* is an important Supreme Court decision that specifically addresses the constitutional privacy rights of public employees, but its approach has influenced the analysis of workplace privacy issues more generally.

O'CONNOR V. ORTEGA
480 U.S. 709 (1987)

OPINION BY JUSTICE O'CONNOR:

This suit . . . presents two issues concerning the Fourth Amendment rights of public employees. First, we must determine whether the respondent, a public employee, had a reasonable expectation of privacy in his office, desk, and file cabinets at his place of work. Second, we must address the appropriate Fourth Amendment standard for a search conducted by a public employer in areas in which a public employee is found to have a reasonable expectation of privacy.

Dr. Magno Ortega, a physician and psychiatrist, held the position of Chief of Professional Education at Napa State Hospital (Hospital) for 17 years, until his dismissal from that position in 1981. As Chief of Professional Education, Dr. Ortega had primary responsibility for training young physicians in psychiatric residency programs. In July 1981, Hospital officials, including Dr. Dennis O'Connor, the Executive Director of the Hospital, became concerned about possible improprieties in Dr. Ortega's management of the residency program. In particular, the Hospital officials were concerned with Dr. Ortega's acquisition of an Apple II computer for use in the residency program. The officials thought that Dr. Ortega may have misled Dr. O'Connor into believing that the computer had been donated, when in fact the computer had been financed by the possibly coerced contributions of residents. Additionally,

the Hospital officials were concerned with charges that Dr. Ortega had sexually harassed two female Hospital employees, and had taken inappropriate disciplinary action against a resident.

On July 30, 1981, Dr. O'Connor requested that Dr. Ortega take paid administrative leave during an investigation of these charges. * * * At some point during the investigation, Mr. Friday [the Hospital Administrator] made the decision to enter Dr. Ortega's office. The specific reason for the entry into Dr. Ortega's office is unclear from the record. The petitioners claim that the search was conducted to secure state property. * * * Dr. Ortega contends that the purpose of the search was to secure evidence for use against him in administrative disciplinary proceedings.

The resulting search of Dr. Ortega's office was quite thorough. The investigators entered the office a number of times and seized several items from Dr. Ortega's desk and file cabinets, including a Valentine's Day card, a photograph, and a book of poetry all sent to Dr. Ortega by a former resident physician. These items were later used in a proceeding before a hearing officer of the California State Personnel Board to impeach the credibility of the former resident, who testified on Dr. Ortega's behalf. * * * [N]o formal inventory of the property in the office was ever made. Instead, all the papers in Dr. Ortega's office were merely placed in boxes, and put in storage for Dr. Ortega to retrieve. * * *

The Fourth Amendment protects the "right of the people to be secure in their persons, houses, papers, and effects, against unreasonable searches and seizures. . . ." Our cases establish that Dr. Ortega's Fourth Amendment rights are implicated only if the conduct of the Hospital officials at issue in this case infringed "an expectation of privacy that society is prepared to consider reasonable." * * *

[W]e reject the contention made by the Solicitor General and petitioners that public employees can never have a reasonable expectation of privacy in their place of work. Individuals do not lose Fourth Amendment rights merely because they work for the government instead of a private employer. The operational realities of the workplace, however, may make some employees' expectations of privacy unreasonable when an intrusion is by a supervisor rather than a law enforcement official. Public employees' expectations of privacy in their offices, desks, and file cabinets, like similar expectations of employees in the private sector, may be reduced by virtue of actual office practices and procedures, or by legitimate regulation. * * * Given the great variety of work environments in the public sector, the question whether an employee has a reasonable expectation of privacy must be addressed on a case-by-case basis. * * *

[T]he undisputed evidence suggests that Dr. Ortega had a reasonable expectation of privacy in his desk and file cabinets. . . . Dr. Ortega did not share his desk or file cabinets with any other employees. Dr. Ortega had occupied the office for 17 years and he kept materials in his office, which included personal correspondence, medical files, correspondence from private patients unconnected to the Hospital, personal financial records, teaching aids and notes, and personal gifts and mementos. The files on physicians in residency training were kept outside Dr. Ortega's office. Indeed, the only items found by the investigators were apparently personal items because, with the exception of the items seized for use in the administrative hearings, all the papers and effects found in the office were simply placed in boxes and made available to Dr. Ortega. Finally, we note that there was no evidence that the Hospital had established any reasonable regulation or policy discouraging employees such as Dr. Ortega from storing personal papers and effects in their desks or file cabinets, although the absence of such a policy does not create an expectation of privacy where it would not otherwise exist. * * *

[W]e must determine the appropriate standard of reasonableness applicable to the search. A determination of the standard of reasonableness applicable to a particular class of searches requires "[balancing] the nature and quality of the intrusion on the individual's Fourth Amendment interests against the importance of the governmental interests alleged to justify the intrusion." In the case of searches conducted by a public employer, we must balance the invasion of the employees' legitimate expectations of privacy against the government's need for supervision, control, and the efficient operation of the workplace. * * *

Balanced against the substantial government interests in the efficient and proper operation of the workplace are the privacy interests of government employees in their place of work which, while not insubstantial, are far less than those found at home or in some other contexts. * * * Government offices are provided to employees for the sole purpose of facilitating the work of an agency. The employee may avoid exposing personal belongings at work by simply leaving them at home.

In sum, we conclude that the "special needs, beyond the normal need for law enforcement make the . . . probable-cause requirement impracticable," for legitimate work-related, noninvestigatory intrusions as well as investigations of work-related misconduct. A standard

of reasonableness will neither unduly burden the efforts of government employers to ensure the efficient and proper operation of the workplace, nor authorize arbitrary intrusions upon the privacy of public employees. We hold, therefore, that public employer intrusions on the constitutionally protected privacy interests of government employees for noninvestigatory, work-related purposes, as well as for investigations of work-related misconduct, should be judged by the standard of reasonableness under all the circumstances. Under this reasonableness standard, both the inception and the scope of the intrusion must be reasonable. * * *

Ordinarily, a search of an employee's office by a supervisor will be "justified at its inception" when there are reasonable grounds for suspecting that the search will turn up evidence that the employee is guilty of work-related misconduct, or that the search is necessary for a noninvestigatory work-related purpose such as to retrieve a needed file. Because petitioners had an "individualized suspicion" of misconduct by Dr. Ortega, we need not decide whether individualized suspicion is an essential element of the standard of reasonableness that we adopt today. The search will be permissible in its scope when "the measures adopted are reasonably related to the objectives of the search and not excessively intrusive in light of . . . the nature of the [misconduct]." * * *

The Court of Appeals concluded that Dr. Ortega was entitled to partial summary judgment on liability. It noted that the Hospital had no policy of inventorying the property of employees on administrative leave, but it did not consider whether the search was otherwise reasonable. Under the standard of reasonableness articulated in this case, however, the absence of a Hospital policy did not necessarily make the search unlawful. A search to secure state property is valid as long as petitioners had a reasonable belief that there was government property in Dr. Ortega's office which needed to be secured, and the scope of the intrusion was itself reasonable in light of this justification. Indeed, petitioners have put forward evidence that they had such a reasonable belief; at the time of the search, petitioners knew that Dr. Ortega had removed the computer from the Hospital. The removal of the computer—together with the allegations of mismanagement of the residency program and sexual harassment—may have made the search reasonable at its inception under the standard we have put forth in this case. * * *

On remand, therefore, the District Court must determine the justification for the search and seizure, and evaluate the reasonableness of both the inception of the search and its scope. * * *

CASE QUESTIONS

1. What was the legal issue in this case? What did the Court decide?

2. What factors did the Court consider in concluding that Dr. Ortega had a reasonable expectation of privacy regarding the contents of his office?

3. Does it appear that the search was reasonable? In its inception? In its scope?

4. Does the Court's approach adequately protect the privacy of public employees? Unduly constrain administrators?

O'Connor shows that government employees can challenge affronts to their privacy on constitutional grounds. Unlike in the law enforcement context, *public employers need not establish probable cause or obtain warrants before conducting workplace searches. However, they must be prepared to defend the reasonableness of searches and other actions that infringe upon employees' reasonable expectations of privacy.* Searches are reasonable at their inception when there are reasonable grounds for believing that they will produce evidence of wrongdoing or when they are necessary for noninvestigatory, work-related purposes (e.g., retrieving files). Searches are reasonable in scope when the measures employed are not excessive in light of the purpose of the search and the seriousness of the suspected misconduct. The Court remanded the case for consideration of whether the search was reasonable. Following over 10 more years of court proceedings, Dr. Ortega prevailed in his Fourth Amendment privacy claim.[5]

[5]*Ortega v. O'Connor*, 146 F.3d 1149 (9th Cir. 1998).

The idea of a **reasonable expectation of privacy** is a key concept in workplace privacy law. Although tied most directly to privacy claims based on the Constitution, this concept is also relevant to common law privacy tort claims. If an employee cannot be said to have had a reasonable expectation of privacy under the circumstances, she will not prevail in either a constitutional or a common law privacy claim. One factor often considered by the courts is the existence of a policy or prior notification to employees regarding the limits of their privacy rights. To a great extent, if employers tell employees that they are subject to monitoring, searches, and other arguably invasive actions, those employees will not be deemed to have any reasonable expectations of privacy. An employee of a public university who objected to a search of his e-mails lacked a reasonable expectation of privacy.[6] The university had a computer policy that allowed for searches relevant to ongoing litigation (which was the case here), the employee was informed in advance of the need for the search, and keywords were used that focused the search on the information needed. However, although the existence of policies often extinguishes privacy claims, the Supreme Court in *O'Connor* makes clear that the absence of such a policy does not create an expectation of privacy where it would not otherwise exist. *Employers should establish privacy polices that alert employees to the limits of their privacy rights in the workplace.*

The constraints on employer privacy policies are more practical than legal. Draconian privacy policies might create employee relations problems and be contrary to an employer's desired image. (Who wants to work in a place that is run like a top-secret weapons installation?). At their core, policies that provide for extensive searches and monitoring convey profound mistrust of employees. Employers can expect that such mistrust will be reciprocated.

Circumstances under which a reasonable expectation of privacy is more likely to be found include intrusions that take place in areas of the workplace (e.g., restrooms, locker rooms) that are usually regarded as private, intrusions upon an employee's person rather than property, intrusions that occur outside of the workplace and not out in public, and intrusions that are effected through deceptive, secretive means (e.g., hidden cameras).

Common Law Protection

Individuals, including employees, have a common law remedy for invasion of privacy. Most states recognize the following *privacy torts*:

- Intrusion upon seclusion
- Public disclosure of private facts
- Placement in a false light
- Appropriation of a name or likeness

One fundamental way in which privacy is violated is by others snooping, prying, or otherwise engaging in unwarranted intrusions into our private affairs. "It's none of your business!" captures the flavor of **intrusion upon seclusion** claims.

To establish that privacy has been invaded in this manner, a plaintiff must show that an intentional intrusion into her solitude or private affairs occurred, and the nature of the intrusion was such that it would be highly offensive to a reasonable person. The objects of intrusions must be truly private (e.g., not in plain sight or divulged by the plaintiff) and the intrusion must be "highly" offensive (generally resulting in

[6]*Biby v. Board of Regents of the University of Nebraska at Lincoln,* 419 F.3d 845 (8th Cir. 2005).

E L E M E N T S O F A C L A I M

Intrusion upon Seclusion

Plaintiffs must show:

1. An intentional intrusion, physical or otherwise;

2. into something truly private; and

3. the intrusion would be highly offensive to a reasonable person.

anguish or suffering). One example of a successful intrusion upon seclusion claim involved a department store employee whose locker—including her purse that was within the locker—was searched by store managers without her consent or awareness. The managers were apparently searching for a watch they suspected another employee of having stolen and some missing price-marking guns (bar codes and scanners were not yet in use). Each employee was provided with a locker to store personal items, but some employees, including the plaintiff, provided their own locks. Although searches regularly occurred, employees were not informed of this policy. The outcome probably would have been different if the store had supplied the locks and clearly informed employees about its search policy, but the plaintiff prevailed in her intrusion upon seclusion claim.[7] Likewise, an intrusion upon seclusion occurred when a manager installed a surveillance camera system to covertly observe female employees using the restroom.[8] The employer's argument that the system was installed to investigate rumors of drug use and sale in the restroom was unavailing, because the observation went on for several years. Certainly, using a concealed camera to take pictures under the skirts of female employees amounted to an intrusion upon seclusion, among other claims (see "Clippings").

Another way privacy can be violated is by taking private and sensitive information and indiscriminately bandying it about. To establish a **public disclosure of private facts** claim, plaintiffs must show that private facts of their lives that are of no legitimate concern to the public were broadly disclosed to others in a manner that would be highly offensive to a reasonable person. The facts must be truly private (e.g., not previously known or available to others), and the disclosure must be broad (to a large enough group that the information essentially becomes public knowledge).

E L E M E N T S O F A C L A I M

Public Disclosure of Private Facts

Plaintiffs must show:

1. A public disclosure occurred;

2. the disclosure involved facts that were truly private;

3. the disclosure would be highly offensive to a reasonable person;

4. the disclosure was intentional; and

5. the matter disclosed is not of legitimate concern to the public.

[7] *K-Mart v. Trotti,* 677 S.W.2d 632 (Tex. App. 1984), *writ denied,* 686 S.W.2d 593 (Tex. 1985).

[8] *Johnson v. Allen et al.,* 613 S.E.2d 657 (Ga. App. 2005).

In an illustrative case, an employee who had undergone a mastectomy and reconstruction surgery had conversations about the procedures with the company nurse. Although she had been assured of confidentiality by the nurse, the woman found out from a coworker that others in the workplace had been informed of her medical condition. In finding that these facts stated a viable claim for public disclosure of private facts, the court emphasized that although the disclosure might not have been very broad in this case, it nonetheless exposed embarrassing private information to a group of people with whom the plaintiff clearly did not want to share the information.[9] Posting pictures of female employees' body parts on the Internet clearly qualifies as public disclosure of private facts (see "Clippings").

Most privacy tort claims arising in the workplace are of the preceding two varieties. However, an individual's privacy can also be violated by placing him in a "false light." In **placement in a false light** claims, the plaintiff must show that characteristics, conduct, or beliefs were falsely attributed to him; this false information was broadly publicized; the individual publicizing the false information knew or should have known that it was false; and being placed in this false light would be highly offensive to a reasonable person. False light claims are similar to defamation but require that the information be broadly disclosed. (Defamation claims only require publication to a third party.) Erroneous statements by company officials that an employee suspected of stealing goods from the company was an "admitted thief" and a highly public investigation that included placement of numerous, allegedly stolen, items on the employee's lawn, supported the employee's false light (and defamation) claims.[10]

Employees also occasionally allege privacy violations through **appropriation of a name or likeness**. In appropriation claims, the symbolic value of one's name or likeness (e.g., prestige, recognition), which others then use for their own commercial or other ends, is at issue. A professor's name was included on a grant application (listing him as a "coinvestigator") without his knowledge or explicit consent. When the school obtained the grant but did not continue to employ the professor because the grant was for substantially less money than had been requested, the professor sued for appropriation of his name. The court concluded that the professor had impliedly consented to being listed on the grant application by virtue of his prior involvement in the research project and the general nature of his duties (carrying out collaborative research).[11] The outcome might well have been different if the professor had been terminated before his name was used on the grant application.

A variety of other common law tort claims are often raised in conjunction with privacy claims. Perhaps the most common of these is intentional infliction of emotional distress.

ELEMENTS OF A CLAIM

Intentional Infliction of Emotional Distress

Plaintiffs must show:

1. Intent to harm;
2. behavior that is so outrageous, shocking, or atrocious as to be beyond the bounds of what is tolerable in a civilized society; and
3. Severe emotional harm or distress.

[9] *Miller v. Motorola*, 560 N.E.2d 900 (Ill. App. 1990).

[10] *Wal-Mart Stores v. Lee*, 74 S.W.3d 634 (Ark. 2002).

[11] *Nemani v. St. Louis University*, 33 S.W.3d 184 (Mo. 2000), *cert. denied*, 532 U.S. 981 (2001).

Some courts recognize negligent or reckless infliction of emotional distress claims. The latter are based not on specific intent to harm but on the existence of a "special relationship" (sometimes including employment) that calls for a higher standard of conduct.

Courts are emphatic that infliction of emotional distress claims are not available for garden-variety insensitivity, abrasiveness, or incivility. The challenged conduct must truly be "outrageous." For example, when a young female cashier was accused of taking some money that a customer had placed on the counter, store personnel proceeded to take her into a restroom and conduct a strip search—in full view of the complaining customer. It is scarcely relevant that the search turned up no money and that the customer later called back saying that she had miscounted her money. This extreme course of action, undertaken to placate a troublesome customer and without the slightest apparent regard for the dignity and sensibilities of the young woman, was more than sufficient to support an infliction of emotional distress claim (against both the store and the customer). Although there was no evidence that the store personnel intended to cause harm, they were reckless in their treatment of the employee. The store's claim that she had consented to the search was contested and ultimately discounted by the court in light of her young age and probable belief that she was required to submit to the search.[12]

Other tort clams that sometimes arise in the context of handling employee information or investigating employee conduct include defamation, false imprisonment, and malicious prosecution. These are discussed further in later sections of this chapter.

Statutory Protection of Privacy

A number of statutes address aspects of workplace privacy. Some of these laws (e.g., Privacy Act, Electronic Communications Privacy Act) have privacy as their central focus. Other statutes—including the ADA, NLRA, and OSH Act—are not privacy laws, but nonetheless have implications for employee privacy and access to records.

HANDLING RECORDS AND EMPLOYEE INFORMATION

Employers gather and store a great deal of information about employees. Some of it (e.g., medical information, drug-testing results, reports on investigations into harassment complaints) is sensitive. Major questions arise as to what information should be kept, the accuracy of that information, whether employees have access to their personnel files, and the circumstances under which information from employee records is released to other parties.

Personnel Records

Many of the records that employers maintain about their employees are incorporated into personnel files that are kept for each employee. To a large extent, the handling of personnel records is a matter of employer policy, rather than law. A number of states, but by no means all, have laws pertaining to personnel records. Most of these state laws give employees the right, under specified circumstances, to review (and perhaps copy) the contents of their personnel files. However, the most comprehensive

[12]*Bodewig v. K-Mart*, 635 P.2d 657 (Or. App. 1981), *review denied,* 644 P.2d 1128 (Or. 1982). But see *Snead v. Metropolitan Property & Casualty Ins.*, 909 F. Supp. 775 (D. Or. 1996) (questioning whether Oregon recognizes reckless infliction of emotional distress claims).

law dealing with personnel records is the federal Privacy Act.[13] The **Privacy Act** regulates the handling of personnel records by agencies of the federal government. The act defines *record* very broadly to include "any item, collection, or grouping of information about an individual that is maintained by an agency. . . ."[14] Federal employees must be given access to their personnel records under reasonable procedures established by federal agencies, allowed to copy materials from their personnel files, and permitted to contest the accuracy of records in written statements that are included with any disclosures of the records to other parties. Importantly, federal agencies must obtain the consent of employees before disclosing information from their personnel records to outside parties. The Privacy Act also limits the kinds of information that federal agencies can keep regarding their employees and imposes a duty on federal agencies to maintain accurate records.

Violations of the Privacy Act can be difficult to prove because plaintiffs must show that the violations were intentional or willful and that there were actual damages, such as an adverse employment determination. However, an applicant for a job at the Postal Service was allowed to proceed to trial on a Privacy Act claim when he listed the name of his current employer on an application, he said that he did not want his current employer contacted, the Postal Service contacted the current employer anyway, and the employee was fired from his job (and, adding insult to injury, was not hired by the Postal Service).[15] Likewise, the Privacy Act was violated when the Department of Labor denied a workers' compensation claim to one of its employees based in part on certain information that the agency had been ordered by a court to discard but had nonetheless retained. The DOL's action was contrary to its Privacy Act obligation to maintain records "with such accuracy . . . as is necessary to ensure fairness in any determination. . . ."[16]

Because the Privacy Act does not apply to private-sector employers, where does this leave them? In terms of access to personnel records, *if an employer operates in a state with a personnel records law, the employer generally has to allow employees access to their personnel files.* Even absent such a law, *employers generally must allow union representatives to see pertinent information in employees' personnel files.* The duty of employers under the National Labor Relations Act (NLRA) to bargain in good faith and to provide union representatives with information relevant to proper topics of negotiations pertains not only to bargaining over new contracts but also to information needed to handle grievances and otherwise represent employees. Both employers and employees have an interest in having personnel files contain only accurate, job-relevant information. *One way to help ensure accuracy is to allow employees to see the contents of their personnel files and to contest records that they believe are inaccurate.*

In terms of divulging information, communication of false, damaging information to third parties without a legitimate need to know might lead to defamation claims. Even information that is true could prompt a legal claim for public disclosure of private facts if the information is genuinely private in nature and effectively made public knowledge. Employee consent is a defense to both defamation and invasion of privacy claims. Thus, *although most private-sector employers are not strictly required to do so, it is sensible to obtain the consent of employees prior to divulging information from their personnel records to third parties.*

[13]5 U.S.C.A. § 552a (2005).

[14]5 U.S.C.A. § 552a(a)(4) (2005).

[15]*Sullivan v. United States Postal Service,* 944 F. Supp. 191 (W.D.N.Y. 1996).

[16]*Louis v. United States Department of Labor,* 19 Fed. Appx. 487 (9th Cir. 2001). Additional Privacy Act issues were considered on remand and the court ruled against the plaintiff in *Louis v. United States Department of Labor,* 419 F.3d 970 (9th Cir. 2005).

Medical Information

Employers, even those that do not self-insure or administer their own health plans, amass a considerable amount of medical information on their employees. For example, preemployment medical exams (following a conditional offer of employment) or periodic exams of employees (to assess job-related conditions) might be conducted. Employees requesting leave for serious health conditions under the FMLA submit medical documentation, and employees hurt on the job file workers' compensation claims. Employees with disabilities might make their conditions known when requesting accommodations. Information about medications paid for under group health plans is available to employers. Employee assistance programs might provide reports to employers on employees experiencing personal or substance abuse problems. Whatever the source of the medical information, this sensitive information is subject to additional legal constraints beyond those applying to personnel records in general.

The Americans with Disabilities Act requires that employers *keep information regarding an employee's medical condition or history in a location apart from other personnel records and treat it as a "confidential medical record."* However, information can and should be made available to managers and supervisors regarding needed accommodations and to first-aid and safety personnel to facilitate emergency medical treatment. The medical confidentiality provisions of the ADA apply regardless of whether an employee is disabled.[17]

The OSH Act provides employees (and unions) with a right of access to medical and exposure records created in compliance with the act. A number of OSHA standards require medical monitoring of individual employees, as well as monitoring of the workplace for levels of exposure to toxic substances and harmful physical agents. Because occupational diseases can take a long time to develop and such records are critical to identifying the occupational basis of these conditions, *exposure records must be maintained for 30 years and medical records for the duration of employment, plus 30 years.* Medical records of short-term employees (less than 1 year) need not be retained as long as they are provided to those employees upon termination of employment. *Access to medical and exposure records produced in compliance with OSHA, which includes the right to examine and copy records, must generally be provided within 15 working days.* Requests need not be in writing, except where trade secrets are involved. Unions and health professionals need the specific written consent of employees to have access to their personal medical records, but they can examine exposure records without obtaining consent.

Medical privacy regulations under the HIPAA are also relevant (see "Clippings"). These regulations[18] primarily affect health care providers and self-insured companies. However, any employer that receives protected health information (i.e., information about medical conditions that can be linked to individuals) from insurers or health care providers has obligations under the law. Parties with access to protected health information must limit the uses and disclosure of that information, train staff on maintaining the privacy of medical information, designate a privacy officer with responsibility for compliance, and notify employees of their rights. Employees have the right to inspect and copy their medical records and propose corrections. However, the regulations do not require that consent be obtained before using or disclosing information in employees' medical records. Additionally, the HIPAA regulations apply only to medical information derived from the administration of group health plans; other sources of medical information are not affected. The HIPAA medical

[17]*Giaccio v. City of New York,* 2005 U.S. Dist. LEXIS 642, at 9.
[18]45 C.F.R. Parts 160, 164 (2005).

privacy regulations underscore the need to handle medical information in an especially careful, confidential manner.

The case mentioned earlier in this chapter regarding unauthorized public disclosure to coworkers of the private fact that an employee had a mastectomy is a good illustration of the need to treat medical information as confidential. In another case, information about a flight attendant's medical condition was given by her gynecologist to a male supervisor who had no need to know the information and who subsequently shared it with the woman's husband. The supervisor also repeatedly pressed her to discuss the details of her condition and raised the subject in front of another manager. Under these circumstances, the court found that the employee's privacy rights had been violated.[19]

However, other courts have required that private information be publicized to persons outside of the workplace to support a public disclosure of private facts claim. For example, an employer did not violate the privacy rights of a nuclear power plant employee when it informed her coworkers that she had a hysterectomy to counter rumors that she was suffering from radiation exposure.[20] In another case, the court acknowledged that medical records fall within constitutional privacy protections, but concluded that the employer did not violate the constitutional rights of an employee by disclosing information about his HIV status to several other managers.[21] The information was inferred from a list of heavy prescription drug users that was provided by the drug chain used under the employer's prescription drug plan. Factors that the court pointed to in reaching this conclusion included that the employer had not requested names of individuals, it had obtained the report for the legitimate purpose of controlling drug costs, and the information was divulged to only a small number of employees involved with benefit administration.

MONITORING AND SURVEILLANCE OF EMPLOYEES

"The boss is coming down the hall. We'd better look busy!" Employees are regularly observed on the job. Electronic means of monitoring and surveillance—including using video cameras, monitoring computer keystrokes, and examining Internet sites visited—are more comprehensive and unrelenting than old-fashioned supervision (after all, you could always slack off when the boss left) and raise new privacy concerns.

Video Surveillance

Video cameras have become increasingly commonplace, with people "starring" on more videotape than they realize as they go about their business using ATMs, shopping, and sometimes just walking down the street. Employers use video cameras to keep tabs on both customers and employees. In general, employers can train video cameras on their employees without significant legal concerns. Thus, a Fourth Amendment challenge to a video surveillance system installed by a public agency failed because the workspace in question was open to public view and did not include private offices; the surveillance was entirely visual and did not include microphones;

[19]*Levias v United Airlines*, 500 N.E.2d 370 (Ohio App. 1985).

[20]*Young v. Jackson*, 572 So. 2d 378 (Miss. 1990).

[21]*Doe v. SEPTA*, 72 F.3d 1133 (3d Cir. 1995), *cert. denied*, 519 U.S. 808 (1996).

employees were informed that the videotaping would occur; and the cameras recorded only what was plainly visible on the surface. In short, the court held that the Fourth Amendment does not prohibit "management from observing electronically what it lawfully can see with the naked eye."[22]

In another case, an employee of a public university was videotaped stealing money from the university box office.[23] Even though the video camera was hidden and she was not warned about being subject to video surveillance, the court concluded that her Fourth Amendment rights had not been violated. In reaching the conclusion that she had no reasonable expectation of privacy, the court relied heavily on the facts that her work area was open to view by both coworkers and the public and her job involved the handling of money. However, *although informing employees that they are subject to surveillance is clearly not necessary in every case, employers are on surer legal ground if they inform employees that they are subject to monitoring and surveillance.*

One circumstance in which videotaping employees has been successfully challenged is when the cameras were trained on individuals engaging in protected concerted activity. Thus, an employer violated the NLRA when it videotaped and photographed employees who were distributing union literature at the entrance to the plant. The surveillance began after a minor confrontation between a human resource manager and a prounion employee, but the fact that it continued regardless of whether any managers were present cast doubt on the employer's stated motive of protecting managers against false claims of assault and battery. The court concluded that the employer cited "no legal justification for its indiscriminate videotaping of employees who handed out union literature; under these circumstances, the NLRB's finding of a violation was proper."[24] The reason is that surveillance under these circumstances tends to be coercive and interferes with the exercise of NLRA rights. When a union is already in place, employers generally have an obligation to bargain with the union over the installation of video surveillance.[25] *Employers must not conduct surveillance of employees engaged in protected concerted activities, including union organizing.*

An employer was also liable when two managers broke into a locked restroom and snapped a revealing photograph of a male employee while he was urinating. The managers refused the employee's demands that they return the photograph. Instead, it was circulated around the office. "Peewee" and "Splinter" were among the names the employee was tagged with after the incident. Upon his transfer to another office, the picture was forwarded by the managers and quickly became common knowledge in his new workplace. The court found that the behavior was sufficiently outrageous to support a finding of intentional infliction of emotional distress.[26]

Video surveillance that occurs off the job is more likely to run afoul of privacy law than surveillance in the workplace. Many of these cases involve employers enlisting investigators to determine whether employees claiming workers' compensation or disability benefits are really unable to work. In one such case, an employee receiving workers' compensation for treatment of a back problem mentioned that his hobby was riding a motorcycle. A private investigator hired by the company videotaped the

[22]*Vega-Rodriguez v. Puerto Rico Telephone Co.*, 110 F.3d 174, at 180 (1st Cir. 1997).

[23]*Cowles v. State of Alaska*, 23 P.3d 1168 (Alaska 2001), *cert. denied*, 122 S. Ct. 1072 (2002).

[24]*The Timken Co. v. NLRB*, 29 Fed. Appx. 266, at 269 (6th Cir. 2002).

[25]*Brewers and Maltsters, Local 6 v. NLRB*, 414 F.3d 36 (D.C. Cir. 2005).

[26]*Fotiades v. Hi-Tech Auto Collision & Painting Services, Inc.*, 2001 Cal. App. Unpub. LEXIS 2559.

employee engaging in various activities around his house, including riding his motorcycle. On the basis of the video, the employer contested the employee's workers' compensation claim, and the employee sued for invasion of privacy (intrusion upon seclusion). The court concluded that the videotaping was legal because it captured him moving about in public.[27] However, if the investigator had trespassed or filmed activities transpiring inside the home, the outcome would have been different. *Surveillance of employees outside of the workplace, if it occurs at all, should be limited to public areas.*

Electronic Communications

Work is increasingly performed using computers and other electronic information processing and communications devices. Attempts by employers to monitor and control these communications have posed profound privacy issues.

The **Electronic Communications Privacy Act (ECPA)**[28] has been used to challenge employer incursions on the privacy of electronic communications. The ECPA amended existing federal wiretapping laws. *Employers (and others) are prohibited from intentionally intercepting (through the use of electronic, mechanical, or other devices) wire, oral, or electronic communications and from disclosing such information. The unauthorized accessing of stored electronic communications is also prohibited.* However, as *Konop v. Hawaiian Airlines* shows, application of this law is tricky, and the ECPA provides only limited protection to employees.

[27] *York v. General Electric Co.*, 759 N.E.2d 865 (Ohio App. 2001).
[28] 18 U.S.C.A. §§ 2510 *et seq.* (2005).

THE CHANGING WORKPLACE

The Electronic Workplace and Employee Privacy

Most employees spend a good part of their workday, and often nonwork time as well, tethered to communications and information-processing devices. These range from the venerable telephone to voicemail systems, pagers, e-mail, the Internet, company computer networks, and wireless tracking systems, among many other items. This reliance on electronic communications devices opens up new vistas for the monitoring and surveillance of employees. It is now relatively easy for employers to monitor every keystroke entered by an employee, the contents of an employee's computer screen at any point in time, stored e-mails, Internet sites visited, and the employee's whereabouts. An American Management Association survey (see "Clippings") of 526 U.S. employers found that 76 percent monitored the Internet sites visited by at least some of their employees, 55 percent retained and reviewed e-mail messages, 51 percent used video monitoring of at least some work areas, 50 percent stored and reviewed computer files, 36 percent tracked content, keystrokes and time spent on computers, 8 percent used GPS to monitor employee IDs or smartcards, and 5 percent used GPS to track cell phones issued to employees.[1] All this monitoring and tracking has had consequences for employees beyond puncturing illusions of privacy. Of the responding employers, 26 percent had terminated workers for misusing the Internet, 25 percent had fired employees for abuse of e-mail, and 5 percent had terminated employees for misuse of office telephones. Although the use of GPS to track employees does not appear to be widespread at this point, many commentators are particularly concerned about the privacy implications of this technology.[2] GPS and other location-detection technology can readily be embedded in cell phones, company vehicles, and ID badges. The possibility that this technology can be used to keep tabs on employees when they are off-the-job or to map the

locations of employees to identify activities such as union organizing seems quite real.

Nor is monitoring employees' activities on-line limited to use of company computer equipment during work time. Employers have taken action against bloggers based on the contents of their blogs, even when the blogging was done on home computers (see "Clippings"). A number of employers have attempted to obtain court orders forcing Internet service providers to divulge the identies of individuals making comments critical of the companies (and arguably defamatory). This is often used as a means of identifying the offending employees, who are then terminated, rather than pursuing the legal claim.[3] In a case involving flight attendants at Northwest Airlines, a court ordered flight attendants to turn over their own personal computers to a neutral third party that would check the contents of their hard drives for evidence in a court case brought by the airline.[4] Northwest had claimed that the flight attendants were using their computers to orchestrate an illegal "sickout" in violation of the Railway Labor Act.

Employers cite numerous reasons for monitoring employees through electronic means, including the need to ensure that work time is being used productively, workplace security is maintained, company equipment is not misused, and trade secrets and other confidential information are not being divulged. Legal concerns—including preventing sexual harassment through the distribution of downloaded pornography or via offensive e-mails from coworkers—are also cited as prime reasons for monitoring computer use. A recent decision by a state court in New Jersey adds some force to this argument. In this sad case, an employee spent large amounts of work time accessing and downloading pictures from pornographic Web sites, including child pornography. The employee took nude pictures of his young step-daughter and transmitted them to a Web site featuring child pornography. The employee's activities went on for several years and were well-known to supervisors and coworkers alike, but no official action was taken against the employee. Following the employee's arrest on child pornography charges, the girl's mother sued the employer. The court concluded that:

> [A]n employer who is on notice that one of its employees is using a workplace computer to access pornography, possibly child pornography, has a duty to investigate the employee's actions and to take prompt and effective action to stop the unauthorized activity, lest it result in harm to innocent third-parties.[5]

Ironically, the employer in this case attempted to argue that it could not conduct such an investigation because doing so would infringe upon the privacy rights of the employee. The court dismissed this argument, holding that "[W]e readily conclude that Employee had no legitimate expectation of privacy that would prevent his employer from accessing his computer to determine if he was using it to view adult or child pornography."[6]

According to the American Management Association survey, most (80–85 percent) employers that engage in electronic monitoring or surveillance inform employees of that fact, often through formal policies. There is general consensus that such policies, while not strictly necessary, are advisable. They provide clear indications of the extent to which any expectations of privacy are reasonable. *In general, policies should place bounds on employee use of electronic communications for purposes other than completing work assignments, rather than attempt to strictly prohibit all such communications.* IBM's "Blogging Policy and Guidelines" encourages blogging, but spells out a set of guidelines for bloggers to follow (e.g., identify yourself, make it clear that you are not speaking on behalf of the company, don't provide confidential or proprietary information, and so on).[7] *Policies should address not only the type of monitoring or surveillance engaged in, but also how the resulting information will be used, how long such information will be stored, and how it will be kept secure.* Lastly, the legitimate business purposes for monitoring and surveillance have to be balanced against the greater stress this places on employees and the negative implications for working relationships based on trust.[8]

[1] American Management Association. "2005 *Electronic Monitoring & Surveillance Survey:* Many Companies Monitoring, Recording, Videotaping—and Firing—Employees." Viewed June 22, 2005 (http://www.amanet.org).

[2] John Sullivan. "Use of GPS Technology Said to be Growing, But Monitoring Leads to Privacy Concerns." *Daily Labor Report* 228 (November 29, 2004), A-5.

[3] Margo E.K. Reder and Christine Neylon O'Brien. "Corporate Cybersmear: Employers File John Doe Defamation Lawsuits Seeking the Identity of Anonymous Employee Internet Posters." *Michigan Telecommunication and Technology Law Review* 8 (2001/2002), 195.

[4] *Northwest Airlines v. International Brotherhood of Teamsters, Local 2000,* 2000 U.S. Dist. LEXIS 22638.

[5] *Doe v. XYC Corporation,* 2005 N.J. Super. LEXIS 377, at 1–2.

[6] *Doe,* at 25.

[7] IBM Corp. "IBM Blogging Policy and Guidelines." May 16, 2005.

[8] Michael R. Triplett. "As Employee Monitoring Expands, Attention Turns to Information, Policies." *Daily Labor Report* 46 (March 10, 2005), C-2.

KONOP V. HAWAIIAN AIRLINES

302 F.3d 868 (9th Cir. 2002); *cert. denied*, 2003 U.S. LEXIS 1186

OPINION BY CIRCUIT JUDGE BOOCHEVER:

Robert Konop brought suit against his employer, Hawaiian Airlines, Inc. ("Hawaiian"), alleging that Hawaiian viewed Konop's secure website without authorization, disclosed the contents of that website, and took other related actions in violation of the federal Wiretap Act [and] the Stored Communications Act.... * * * The district court granted summary judgment against Konop on [these] claims.... * * * We now affirm the judgment of the district court with respect to Konop's Wiretap Act claims ... [but] reverse ... with respect to [his] claims under the Stored Communications Act....

Konop, a pilot for Hawaiian, created and maintained a website where he posted bulletins critical of his employer, its officers, and the incumbent union, Air Line Pilots Association ("ALPA"). Many of those criticisms related to Konop's opposition to labor concessions which Hawaiian sought from ALPA. Because ALPA supported the concessions, Konop, via his website, encouraged Hawaiian employees to consider alternative union representation.

Konop controlled access to his website by requiring visitors to log in with a user name and password. He created a list of people, mostly pilots and other employees of Hawaiian, who were eligible to access the website. Pilots Gene Wong and James Gardner were included on this list. Konop programmed the website to allow access when a person entered the name of an eligible person, created a password, and clicked the "SUBMIT" button on the screen, indicating acceptance of the terms and conditions of use. These terms and conditions prohibited any member of Hawaiian's management from viewing the website and prohibited users from disclosing the website's contents to anyone else.

In December 1995, Hawaiian vice president James Davis asked Wong for permission to use Wong's name to access Konop's website. Wong agreed. Davis claimed he was concerned about untruthful allegations that he believed Konop was making on the website. Wong had not previously logged into the website to create an account. When Davis accessed the website using Wong's name, he presumably typed in Wong's name, created a password, and clicked the "SUBMIT" button indicating acceptance of the terms and conditions. Later that day,

Konop received a call from the union chairman of ALPA, Reno Morella. Morella told Konop that Hawaiian president Bruce Nobles had contacted him regarding the contents of Konop's website. * * * From this conversation with Morella, Konop believed Nobles had obtained the contents of his website and was threatening to sue Konop for defamation based on statements contained on the website. * * *

Konop claims to have learned only later from the examination of system logs that Davis had accessed the website using Wong's name. In the meantime, Davis continued to view the website using Wong's name. Later, Davis also logged in with the name of another pilot, Gardner, who had similarly consented to Davis' use of his name. Through April 1996, Konop claims that his records indicate that Davis logged in over twenty times as Wong, and that Gardner or Davis logged in at least fourteen more times as Gardner. * * *

* * * Congress passed the Electronic Communications Privacy Act (ECPA), which was intended to afford privacy protection to electronic communications. Title I of the ECPA amended the federal Wiretap Act, which previously addressed only wire and oral communications, to "address[]the interception of . . . electronic communications." Title II of the ECPA created the Stored Communications Act (SCA), which was designed to "address[]access to stored wire and electronic communications and transactional records." . . . [T]he intersection of these two statutes "is a complex, often convoluted, area of the law." In the present case, the difficulty is compounded by the fact that the ECPA was written prior to the advent of the Internet and the World Wide Web. As a result, the existing statutory framework is ill-suited to address modern forms of communication like Konop's secure website. Courts have struggled to analyze problems involving modern technology within the confines of this statutory framework, often with unsatisfying results. We observe that until Congress brings the laws in line with modern technology, protection of the Internet and websites such as Konop's will remain a confusing and uncertain area of the law. * * *

While most websites are public, many, such as Konop's, are restricted. * * * The legislative history of the ECPA suggests that Congress wanted to protect electronic communications that are configured to be private, such as email and private electronic bulletin boards. The nature of the Internet, however, is such

that if a user enters the appropriate information (password, social security number, etc.), it is nearly impossible to verify the true identity of that user. We are confronted with such a situation here. Although Konop took certain steps to restrict the access of Davis and other managers to the website, Davis was nevertheless able to access the website by entering the correct information, which was freely provided to Davis by individuals who were eligible to view the website.

Konop argues that Davis' conduct constitutes an interception of an electronic communication in violation of the Wiretap Act. The Wiretap Act makes it an offense to "intentionally intercept[] . . . any wire, oral, or electronic communication." We must therefore determine whether Konop's website is an "electronic communication" and, if so, whether Davis "intercepted" that communication.

An "electronic communication" is defined as "any transfer of signs, signals, writing, images, sounds, data, or intelligence of any nature transmitted in whole or in part by a wire, radio, electromagnetic, photoelectronic or photooptical system." . . . [W]ebsite owners such as Konop transmit electronic documents to servers, where the documents are stored. If a user wishes to view the website, the user requests that the server transmit a copy of the document to the user's computer. When the server sends the document to the user's computer for viewing, a transfer of information from the website owner to the user has occurred. Although the website owner's document does not go directly or immediately to the user, once a user accesses a website, information is transferred from the website owner to the user via one of the specified mediums. We therefore conclude that Konop's website fits the definition of "electronic communication."

The Wiretap Act, however, prohibits only "interceptions" of electronic communications. "Intercept" is defined as "the aural or other acquisition of the contents of any wire, electronic, or oral communication through the use of any electronic, mechanical, or other device." Standing alone, this definition would seem to suggest that an individual "intercepts" an electronic communication merely by "acquiring" its contents, regardless of when or under what circumstances the acquisition occurs. Courts, however, have clarified that Congress intended a narrower definition of "intercept" with regard to electronic communications. In *Steve Jackson Games, Inc. v. United States Secret Service*, 36 F.3d 457 (5th Cir. 1994), the Fifth Circuit held that the government's acquisition of email messages stored on an electronic bulletin board system, but not yet retrieved by the intended recipients, was not an "interception" under the

Wiretap Act. The court observed that, prior to the enactment of the ECPA, the word "intercept" had been interpreted to mean the acquisition of a communication contemporaneous with transmission. The court further observed that Congress, in passing the ECPA, intended to retain the previous definition of "intercept" with respect to wire and oral communications, while amending the Wiretap Act to cover interceptions of electronic communications. The court reasoned, however, that the word "intercept" could not describe the exact same conduct with respect to wire and electronic communications, because wire and electronic communications were defined differently in the statute. Specifically, the term "wire communication" was defined to include storage of the communication, while "electronic communication" was not. The court concluded that this textual difference evidenced Congress' understanding that, although one could "intercept" a *wire* communication in storage, one could not "intercept" an *electronic* communication in storage. . . . The *Steve Jackson* Court further noted that the ECPA was deliberately structured to afford electronic communications *in storage* less protection than other forms of communication. * * *

We agree . . . that the narrow definition of "intercept" applies to electronic communications. * * * We therefore hold that for a website such as Konop's to be "intercepted" in violation of the Wiretap Act, it must be acquired during transmission, not while it is in electronic storage. This conclusion is consistent with the ordinary meaning of "intercept," which is "to stop, seize, or interrupt in progress or course before arrival." More importantly, it is consistent with the structure of the ECPA, which created the SCA for the express purpose of addressing "access to *stored* . . . electronic communications and transactional records." The level of protection provided stored communications under the SCA is considerably less than that provided communications covered by the Wiretap Act. * * * [I]f Konop's position were correct and acquisition of a stored electronic communication were an interception under the Wiretap Act, the government would have to comply with the more burdensome, more restrictive procedures of the Wiretap Act to do exactly what Congress apparently authorized it to do under the less burdensome procedures of the SCA. Congress could not have intended this result. * * * Because we conclude that Davis' conduct did not constitute an "interception" of an electronic communication in violation of the Wiretap Act, we affirm the district court's grant of summary judgment against Konop on his Wiretap Act claims.

Konop also argues that, by viewing his secure website, Davis accessed a stored electronic communication without authorization in violation of the SCA. The SCA makes it an offense to "intentionally access[]without authorization a facility through which an electronic communication service is provided . . . and thereby obtain[] . . . access to a wire or electronic communication while it is in electronic storage in such system." The SCA excepts from liability, however, "conduct authorized . . . by a user of that service with respect to a communication of or intended for that user." The district court found that th[is] exception . . . applied because Wong and Gardner consented to Davis' use of Konop's website. * * *

The parties agree that the relevant "electronic communications service" is Konop's website, and that the website was in "electronic storage." In addition, for the purposes of this opinion, we accept the parties' assumption that Davis' conduct constituted "access without authorization" to "a facility through which an electronic communication service is provided." We therefore address only the narrow question of whether the district court properly found Hawaiian exempt from liability under [the section of the law that] allows a person to authorize a third party's access to an electronic communication if the person is 1) a "user" of the "service" and 2) the communication is "of or intended for that user." A "user" is "any person or entity who— (A) uses an electronic communications service; and (B) is duly authorized by the provider of such service to engage in such use." * * * *

Based on the common definition of the word "use," we cannot find any evidence in the record that Wong ever used Konop's website. There is some evidence, however, that Gardner may have used the website, but it is unclear when that use occurred. At any rate, the district court did not make any findings on whether Wong and Gardner actually used Konop's website—it simply assumed that Wong and Gardner, by virtue of being eligible to view the website, could authorize Davis' access. The problem with this approach is that it essentially reads the "user" requirement out of [the SCA]. Taking the facts in the light most favorable to Konop, we must assume that neither Wong nor Gardner was a "user" of the website at the time he authorized Davis to view it. We therefore reverse the district court's grant of summary judgment to Hawaiian on Konop's SCA claim.

CASE QUESTIONS

1. What are the legal issues in this case? What does the court decide?

2. What does "interception" mean in the context of the ECPA? Given the way in which electronic communications work, would it ever be possible to "intercept" the information on a Web site or in an e-mail?

3. Why does the court reach a different decision under the part of the ECPA that deals with "stored communications?" Does it make any difference which part of the ECPA is violated?

The distinction between intercepting and accessing has proven troublesome to apply to communications such as e-mail and Internet sites. As in *Konop,* courts have generally held that that the stricter penalties associated with interception apply only when a communication is obtained at the same time that it is sent. One such case involved an agent for Nationwide Insurance who allegedly sent e-mails to two competitors inquiring about their interest in obtaining some of Nationwide's policyholders. When Nationwide became aware of the e-mails, it searched the file server on which the agent's e-mails were stored for e-mails to or from the agent that might show similar behavior. On the basis of the two mails and the subsequent search, the agent's contract (he was an independent contractor) was terminated. The court concluded that:

> While Congress's definition of "intercept" does not appear to fit with its intent to extend protection to electronic communications, it is for Congress to cover the bases untouched. We adopt the reasoning of our sister circuits and therefore hold that there has been no "intercept" within the meaning of Title I of ECPA.[29]

[29] *Fraser v. Nationwide Mutual Insurance,* 352 F.3d 107, at 114 (3d Cir. 2003).

Further, and unlike the outcome in *Konop*, the agent was not able to show that the search of his stored e-mails was illegal. Because the e-mail was stored on Nationwide's own system and providers of a communication service are specifically exempted from the ECPA's restrictions on unauthorized accessing of stored communications, there was no ECPA violation.

There are some notable exceptions to the ECPA's general requirements. Interceptions are legal if prior consent to them was granted. Providers of wire or electronic communication services are exempted from the law's requirements to the extent that such activities are necessary to render service or protect their rights and property. Additionally, business users of equipment furnished by providers are exempted to the extent that such equipment is used **in the ordinary course of business.** This term refers to uses that are routine, for legitimate business purposes, and about which employees are notified. In the context of telephone conversations, this means that *employers can use additional extensions on business phones to monitor business calls for service quality or other business purposes, but cannot listen in on personal calls.* (State laws are sometimes more restrictive, including requiring notification to all parties that calls are subject to monitoring.) *Personal calls can be monitored only to the degree needed to determine that they are indeed personal.* Thus, an employer violated the ECPA by intercepting, tape recording, and listening to all of its employees' personal calls.[30] Likewise, the business user exception did not shield a police department from an ECPA violation when, without a warrant, it tapped a police officer's pager because it believed that he was in cahoots with drug dealers. (He wasn't.) This covert monitoring without any notification was not in the ordinary course of the police department's business.[31]

Overall, employees have fared poorly in privacy claims, whether based on the ECPA or other grounds, concerning e-mail or use of employer-provided computers. An intrusion upon seclusion claim based on an employer's review of e-mail stored in a "personal folder" (with a separate password created by the employee) failed. The employee had been accused of sexual harassment and other offenses. While he was suspended, the company decrypted his personal password and gained access to his e-mails. The court likened the arrangement to a locker for which the employer retains the combination or a master key and found that the employee had no reasonable expectation of privacy.[32] Similarly, an employee whose intemperate e-mail remarks about company personnel were read by management, resulting in his discharge, was unsuccessful in his common law privacy (and wrongful discharge) claims. Despite the fact that employees were told by the company that their e-mail communications were confidential and would not be read by management, the employee was deemed not to have had a reasonable expectation of privacy. The court pointed to the voluntary nature of his statements and the fact that they were made on a company-provided network. Further, the court held that "the company's interest in preventing inappropriate and unprofessional comments or even illegal activity over its e-mail system would outweigh [the employee's] claimed privacy interest in those communications" in any event.[33]

In another case, an employee alleged that he was terminated to keep him from obtaining stock to which he was entitled, whereas his employer claimed that he was terminated for repeatedly accessing pornographic sites on his computer at work.

[30]*Smith v. Devers Insurance Agency*, 2002 U.S. Dist. LEXIS 1125.

[31]*Adams v. City of Battle Creek*, 250 F.3d 980, at 984 (6th Cir. 2001).

[32]*McLaren v. Microsoft Corp.*, 1999 Tex. App. LEXIS 4103.

[33]*Smyth v. The Pillsbury Co.*, 914 F. Supp. 97, at 101 (E.D. Pa. 1996).

The employer had provided another computer for him to work on at home and went to court to obtain an order directing the employee to turn over that computer with the contents of its hard drive intact. The court reasoned that the employee had no reasonable expectation of privacy in the contents of the computer because, even though it was used at home, it was still the employer's property and subject to its computer use policy. The court also asserted the existence of a "community norm," in which it is now accepted practice for employers to monitor employee computer use.[34]

Interestingly, the NLRA places certain limits on what employers can do in monitoring and taking action against employees based on their computer use. An employer violated the NLRA when it discharged an employee for e-mail comments distributed to other employees over the company e-mail system.[35] The comments were in response to a proposed change in the company's vacation policy. The Board found the comments to be protected concerted activity intended to persuade other employees that the proposed change was ill-advised. The e-mails did not amount to a "take over" of the e-mail system, employees were permitted by the employer to post e-mails to one another, and there was nothing about the manner in which the activity was engaged in that would cause it to lose legal protection. Although this case did not involve union organizing, the use of e-mail and Web sites as organizing devices, including communications from nonemployee union organizers, is a contested matter.[36] A reasonable argument can be made that, if employers allow other forms of outside solicitation to reach employees via e-mail or allow employees to access other Web sites with their computers, communications regarding forming a union would also have to be permitted.

INVESTIGATION OF EMPLOYEE CONDUCT

The importance of conducting immediate and thorough investigations of allegations of sexual harassment was stressed in Chapter 9. Many other situations also require investigation, including potential violations of employer policies (e.g., misuse of company property, alcohol use), civil law (e.g., discrimination, retaliation), and criminal law (e.g., assaults, drug dealing, embezzlement). Means of investigating include searches, interviews, and even polygraph exams. Decisions must also be made about what, if anything, to disclose regarding the outcomes of investigations and what to do if allegations of wrongdoing are substantiated.

Some investigations are handled by managers or company legal staff. Others involve outside counsel or private investigators. Persons conducting investigations should be credible and convincing if called upon to be witnesses in legal proceedings. The Fair and Accurate Credit Transactions Act of 2003,[37] which amended the Fair Credit Reporting Act, clarified that employers could use outside investigators for workplace investigations of suspected employee misconduct without bringing the prior consent requirements of the FCRA into play. However, if an adverse action is taken based on information from a third party investigator, the employer is still

[34]*TBG Insurance Services v. Zieminski*, 96 Cal. App. 4th 443 (2002).

[35]*Timekeeper Systems, Inc.*, 323 NLRB 30 (1997).

[36]Michael R. Triplet. "Technology Issues Outpace Guidance from NLRB, Attorneys Tell ABA Conference." *Daily Labor Report* 46 (March 10, 2005), C-1.

[37]P.L. 108-159 (2003).

required to disclose to the employee the "nature and substance" of the information that was the basis for the action.[38]

Searches

Investigations sometimes entail searches of work areas, desks, files, lockers, and other venues that might yield evidence of wrongdoing. Searches, by their nature, are intrusive, because they delve into the contents of things that are not in plain view. *O'Connor v. Ortega*, excerpted earlier in this chapter, involved a workplace search. The Supreme Court held that public employees have some constitutional protection from workplace searches, but only to the extent that they have a reasonable expectation of privacy in the items subjected to the search. And even where there is a reasonable expectation of privacy, it must give way to a search that is reasonable in both its inception and scope. *Employers should establish policies notifying employees regarding the circumstances under which searches will occur, communicate these policies, and enforce them by conducting searches only under the stated circumstances. The searches themselves should be conducted in a reasonable (e.g., not overly broad, not resulting in destruction of employee property, nondiscriminatory) manner. Evidence obtained through searches, particularly if it relates to potential criminal activity (e.g., weapons, drugs), must be handled carefully and kept in a secure location.*

Because consent is a defense to privacy claims, *obtaining consent prior to conducting searches is desirable.* However, employers must be careful in how they go about obtaining consent. The case of a Wal-Mart employee whose home was searched for stolen goods provides a cautionary tale.[39] The employee was apparently told that the employer would be looking for missing life jackets and fishing poles when, in fact, the employer suspected theft of tools and equipment. The employee provided initial oral consent for a search of his home based on his understanding of the limited scope of the search. At his home, the employee signed a written consent form presented by a detective (the police had been called to assist Wal-Mart employees in what turned out to be a seven-hour search in which some 400 items were seized). However, there was evidence that the employee felt coerced into signing the consent form, that he was never told that he had the right to not sign, and that he believed that he would be fired if he did not sign. Wal-Mart also argued that the employee tacitly consented to the search by standing by as the marathon search proceeded, but the employee offered evidence that his objections were ignored. In the end, the court upheld a jury's finding that the employee did not give his consent to the highly intrusive search of his home.

Some searches are more problematic than others. Certainly, strip searches, like the one imposed on the young K-Mart employee, are highly intrusive and likely to inflict emotional distress. Except for unusual situations, such as prisons, *strip searches should never be conducted. Contact with employees during searches of their person (e.g., searching pockets for stolen goods or drugs) should be avoided or at least minimized.* To lessen the chance of sexual harassment claims, *any search involving contact with the person searched should be conducted by someone of the same sex.* To the extent possible, *searches should be conducted away from the view of the public and coworkers.* A search conducted in full view of others might falsely communicate to others that an employee has done something bad, occasioning a defamation claim.

[38]P.L. 108–159 § 611 (a) (2) (2003).
[39]*Lee.*

Deceptive means of conducting searches, in which an attempt is made to conceal the fact that a search is taking place, should also be avoided. An employer hired private investigators to "go undercover" and pose as employees. Despite the fact that the focus of the investigation was supposed to be on possible theft, sabotage, and drug use in the facility, the investigators forwarded weekly reports that included considerable amounts of personal information unrelated to the probe. These reports included information about employees' families, sex lives, future employment plans, medical problems, drinking problems, paternity disputes, and complaints about the employer. The employer did nothing to limit the scope of the reports (except instructing the investigators not to report on union organizing that was going on). In finding that the plaintiff's intrusion upon seclusion claim could go to trial, the court observed:

> [T]he act of placing private detectives, posing as employees, in the workplace to solicit highly personal information about defendant's employees was deceptive. A disclosure obtained through deception cannot be said to be a truly voluntary disclosure. Plaintiffs had a reasonable expectation that their conversations with "coworkers" would remain private, at least to the extent that intimate life details would not be published to their employer.[40]

Interviews and Interrogations

Investigations of potential misconduct entail interviewing witnesses and interrogating employees accused or suspected of wrongdoing. As *Dietz v. Finlay Fine Jewelry* illustrates, interrogations that are not skillfully conducted can lead to many legal problems.

[40]*Johnson v. K-Mart Corp.*, 723 N.E.2d 1192, at 1196 (Ill. App. 2000), *appeal granted*, 729 N.E.2d 496 (2000).

DIETZ V. FINLAY FINE JEWELRY
754 N.E.2d 958 (Ind. App. 2001)

● ● ●

OPINION BY JUDGE BROOK:

Appellant-plaintiff Melissa Dittoe Dietz ("Dietz") appeals from the . . . grant of summary judgment in favor of Finlay on Dietz's claims for invasion of privacy, false imprisonment, defamation, [and] intentional infliction of emotional distress. . . . * * * We affirm in part, reverse in part, and remand. * * *

Finlay leases a commercial space in the L.S. Ayres retail store, from which it sells fine jewelry. Finlay did not employ its own security personnel, but instead, utilized the security services provided by L.S. Ayres. In July of 1998, Finlay hired Dietz as a sales clerk. . . . In September of 1998, a customer wanted to purchase a Finlay diamond ring on sale for $1,439.20. The customer intended to charge the purchase to her "top" account, but Dietz did not know how to perform that task. After she mistakenly placed the purchase on the customer's "flex" account, Dietz voided the transaction and then repeatedly sought assistance to complete the sale. Both Dietz and the customer grew frustrated. Eventually, an L.S. Ayres manager assisted Dietz. Without authorization, Dietz gave the then "irate" customer an extra ten percent discount.

L.S. Ayres security manager Dennis Bake ("Bake") learned about the transaction from another employee. He confirmed the unauthorized sales price and spoke with his supervisor. Thereafter, Bake asked Dietz to accompany him to an interview room, and Dietz

complied. Two other employees were present. Kathleen Camp ("Camp"), a sales manager, witnessed the interview because, if a female is interviewed, "they call one of the female managers in on it[.]" A male security employee, Curt Seufert ("Seufert"), allegedly examined video monitors during the first five or ten minutes of the meeting, a task unrelated to the Dietz interview. Dietz sat in a chair, and Bake sat in front of her.

The ensuing interview lasted fifty-seven minutes. Dietz first signed a document acknowledging that she understood she was free to leave at any time. Bake then explained his job title and responsibilities. He told Dietz that he had access to her L.S. Ayres charge account and could determine if she had been late in making her payments. Dietz was "on guard." She described Bake's demeanor as "very gruff, very intimidating." Bake also spoke of mistakes in Dietz's account book and informed Dietz that there were six pieces of jewelry missing. Dietz claims that Bake also accused her of having a drug or alcohol problem and "suggested" that she pawned the jewelry to pay bills or to support her problem. Bake allegedly stated, "It all leads back to you. What are you going to do about it?" Several times, Bake told Dietz not to interrupt him. At one point, he also demanded that Dietz stay in the room. Dietz stated she did not feel free to leave, and she believed if she had attempted to do so, Bake would have verbally intimidated her into staying.

Bake asked Dietz if she had ever given a discount to a friend or relative, or to "anybody." Dietz disclosed the incident involving the discounted ring but insisted she had done nothing wrong. Eventually, Dietz signed a promissory note for $143.92, the amount of the discount. At Bake's direction, she also drafted and signed a document admitting she had given the unauthorized discount. Finlay dismissed Dietz for violating company policy. * * *

We first consider Dietz's invasion of privacy claim, based upon her allegation that Bake disclosed her credit problems to Camp and Seufert. The general tort, invasion of privacy, includes four distinct injuries: (1) intrusion upon seclusion, (2) appropriation of likeness, (3) public disclosure of private facts, and (4) false-light publicity. The public disclosure of private facts . . . occurs when a person gives "'publicity'" to a matter that concerns the "'private life'" of another, a matter that would be "'highly offensive'" to a reasonable person and that is not of legitimate public concern. * * *

[U]nder the . . . view adopted by most courts, a communication to a single person or to a small group of persons is not actionable because the publicity element requires communication to the public at large or to so many persons that the matter is "'substantially certain to become one of public knowledge.'" In this case, Bake allegedly discussed Dietz's credit difficulties in the presence of sales manager Camp. The record does not disclose what co-employee Seufert overheard, but release of the information to even two co-workers does not satisfy the publicity requirement. . . . In contrast, "a few courts, including Indiana's neighbors," have adopted a looser definition of "publicity," finding a disclosure actionable if made to a "'particular public'" with a special relationship to the plaintiff. Here, Camp was present as a female witness, and Seufert was a member of the security staff, watching video monitors. There is no evidence that Dietz had a special relationship with either so that a disclosure to them, under the circumstances, would render them a "particular public." [Because the] publicity element of Dietz's claim [was lacking], the [defendants] were entitled to summary judgment for invasion of privacy. * * *

False imprisonment involves "an unlawful restraint upon one's freedom of locomotion or the deprivation of liberty of another without [her] consent." "False imprisonment may be committed by words alone, or by acts alone, or by both and by merely operating on the will of the individual, or by personal violence, or both." [The defendants] assert immunity under the Shoplifting Detention Act which provides:

(a) An owner or agent of a store who has probable cause to believe that a theft has occurred or is occurring on or about the store and who has probable cause to believe that a specific person has committed or is committing the theft may:

(1) detain the person and request the person to identify [herself]; * * * (3) determine whether the person has in [her] possession unpurchased merchandise taken from the store; * * *

(b) The detention must: (1) be reasonable and last only for a reasonable time; and (2) not extend beyond the arrival of a law enforcement officer or two (2) hours, whichever first occurs.

The Shoplifting Detention Act "permits the merchant's agent to effect a warrantless arrest or detention where the facts and circumstances known to the agent at the time of the arrest would warrant a person of reasonable caution to believe the arrestee has committed or is committing a theft on or about the store." * * *

At the time of the detention, Bake had discovered and verified the unauthorized transaction. Thus, he reasonably believed that Dietz had intentionally sold the diamond ring at a price less than that approved by Finlay with the intent to deprive Finlay of part of its value. That constitutes probable cause for purposes of the Shoplifting Detention Act. That alone, however, does not mean the test of reasonableness in manner and time has been met in this case. * * * In her deposition testimony, Dietz stated that Bake also questioned her about six pieces of missing jewelry. Assuming that questioning occurred, we cannot say as a matter of law that Bake had probable cause to suspect Dietz was involved in those thefts. Without probable cause, there is no immunity under the Shoplifting Detention Act.

Nor can it be determined as a matter of law that Dietz voluntarily remained in the room during the entire interview. Although Dietz had signed a document acknowledging that she was free to leave at any time, she also stated that she did not feel free to leave during the meeting. Allegedly, at one point Bake told Dietz to stay in the room. In addition, Dietz felt that, if she had attempted to leave, Bake would have used "verbal intimidation" to keep her there. Because the designated evidence does not conclusively establish the reasonableness of the detention, we cannot determine whether the Shoplifting Detention Act renders Finlay and Ayres immune for false imprisonment. Summary judgment on that claim was improvidently granted. * * *

[D]efamation consists of the following elements: (1) a communication with defamatory imputation, (2) malice, (3) publication, and (4) damages. A communication is defamatory per se if it imputes criminal conduct. * * * Here, as stated above, Bake was justified in questioning Dietz about the unauthorized discount and, thus, Finlay and Ayres are immunized from claims of defamation based on reasonable communications related to that investigation. Indeed, statements that Dietz gave an unauthorized discount to a customer are true and, thus, not actionable. * * *

Finlay and Ayres also seek immunity under a qualified privilege of common interest, which protects "communications made in good faith on any subject matter in which the party making the communication has an interest or in reference to which he has a duty, either public or private, either legal, moral, or social, if made to a person having a corresponding interest or duty." The privilege does not apply, however, to statements made without belief or grounds for belief in their truth.

As stated above, factual issues remain concerning whether Bake had grounds for belief in the truth of his alleged statements regarding jewelry thefts to support a drug or alcohol problem.

There is a second bar to application of the privilege on the designated evidence. As our supreme court recognized, a statement may lose its privileged character if there is excessive publication of the defamatory statement. "The privilege is lost if the defamation goes beyond the group interest, or if publication is made to persons who have no reason to receive the information." In this case, sales manager Camp was present during the entire interview as a female witness. Thus, Camp was required to be present. The designated evidence, however, does not indicate what Seufert heard and whether he had a corresponding duty to be present. Bake himself stated that Seufert "didn't need to be there[.]" Thus, we cannot say as a matter of law that Seufert had a reason to receive the information.

[T]here are factual disputes regarding whether Bake had grounds to believe his alleged statements concerning additional thefts to support a drug or alcohol problem. There is also a question about whether there was excessive publication of any such statements. * * * Accordingly, the trial court erred when it granted summary judgment on the defamation claim.

We next consider whether the designated material supports a claim for intentional infliction of emotional distress. The tort . . . is committed when a person engages in extreme and outrageous conduct that intentionally or recklessly causes severe emotional distress to another. Rigorous requirements must be met to prove the tort. The conduct at issue must exceed all bounds usually tolerated by a decent society and must cause mental distress of a very serious kind. * * *

In this case, Dietz asserts that Bake accused her of substance abuse, shoplifting, and dishonesty in a gruff and intimidating manner. Even if the interview proceeded as asserted, Dietz's intentional infliction of emotional distress claim fails as a matter of law. Bake's actions occurred in the context of a detainment for the purpose of determining the extent of Dietz's unauthorized conduct. While, at the most, Bake may have unreasonably detained and defamed Dietz, his actions in this case do not constitute outrageous behavior. Taken in context, Bake's conduct did not exceed all bounds usually tolerated by a decent society. The trial court properly entered summary judgment in favor of Finlay and Ayres on Dietz's intentional infliction of emotional distress claim. * * *

CASE QUESTIONS

1. What were the legal issues in this case? What did the court decide?

2. What was the basis of Dietz's privacy tort claim? Her infliction of emotional distress claim? Why were they rejected?

3. What was the basis of her false imprisonment claim? Her defamation claim? Why was she allowed to go to trial on them? Is she likely to prevail at trial?

4. What, if anything, should this employer have done differently?

Interrogations, like the one in *Dietz,* have enormous potential for generating legal claims, especially false imprisonment and infliction of emotional distress. **False imprisonment**—the intentional restraint of the physical liberty of an individual—is "false" because employers are not the police or the courts. Employers do not have the authority to effectively incarcerate other citizens. Confinement can be achieved by physical barriers, physical force, the threat of force, or other forms of duress. In a false imprisonment case with facts less subtle than those in *Dietz,* an employee was taken to a conference room with glass windows, interviewed for more than seven hours while coworkers passed by giving her "dirty looks," followed to the restroom by security personnel, not allowed to make a call to her husband in private, and not permitted to leave to pick up her daughter from school. Her false imprisonment claim was allowed to go to trial.[41]

Shopkeeper statutes and common law allow employers to take reasonable actions to protect their property against theft, but this does not translate into a general right to force employees to submit to interrogations or to remain in the workplace against their will. *Absent the need to stop the theft of employer property, employers should not attempt to detain employees suspected of wrongdoing or force them to submit to interrogations against their will. Instead, the cooperation of employees in investigations should be requested.* If the employee refuses to cooperate, employers have the option of disciplining or terminating the employee or, if a crime has been committed, involving the police. To minimize the chance of false imprisonment or infliction of emotional distress, *make it clear that the employee is free to leave the interview; do not threaten an employee with harm; do not lock or physically obstruct the door; avoid making accusations; allow the employee a chance to answer rather than grilling him with rapid-fire questions; and keep the interrogation as brief as possible.* In other words, persons conducting interrogations of employees should forget all the crime shows they have ever seen with detectives "tuning up" suspects to obtain confessions. Intimidation is undoubtedly part of the art of interrogation, and employers have numerous concerns when dealing with cases of serious misconduct, but poorly trained security personnel conducting heavy-handed interrogations only make bad situations worse.

What if an employee demands to have someone else present during an interview or interrogation? Employees do not have the right to have attorneys present in these situations. However, *employers must allow unionized employees who are called into interviews that they reasonably believe are likely to result in discipline or discharge to have a union representative present.* This is referred to as employees' *Weingarten*

[41]*Johnson v. Federal Express Corp.,* 147 F.Supp 2d 1268, at 1277 (M.D. Ala. 2001).

rights, named after the case in which the Supreme Court decided that such representation must be permitted to unionized employees because it is a form of concerted activity for mutual aid or protection.[42] This right is limited in several ways. The presence of a union representative must be requested by employees; it need not be offered. Routine conversations not likely to result in adverse employment consequences are not covered, nor are situations in which a decision to administer discipline has already been made and the purpose of the meeting is merely to convey that fact. An interview need not be postponed because a particular union representative is not available. Lastly, the union representative's role is circumscribed; she is there as an observer and not to engage in bargaining over the prospective disciplinary action.

What about nonunion employees? The Supreme Court's *Weingarten* decision did not consider them, and the NLRB has vacillated over the years on this question. However, the NLRB's current view is that nonunion employees do not have any right to be accompanied by coworkers when being interviewed by management for possible discipline.[43] The Board reasons that nonunion workplaces should be treated differently because coworkers, unlike union officers, do not represent the interests of the entire workforce, cannot effectively redress the imbalance of power between employees and management, do not have the same level of skill at representation, and are more likely to compromise the confidentiality of investigations. In light of the increased frequency of workplace investigations, the Board viewed it as critical that employers "be allowed to conduct . . . required investigations in a thorough, sensitive, and confidential manner," a task that "can best be accomplished by permitting an employer in a nonunion setting to investigate an employee without the presence of a coworker."[44]

Polygraphs

Although the Employee Polygraph Protection Act (EPPA) prohibits most preemployment polygraph exams by private-sector employers, polygraphs can be used for "ongoing investigations" of theft, embezzlement, sabotage, and related activities that result in economic loss or injury to an employer's business.[45] However, *individuals can be asked to submit to polygraphs in connection with such investigations only if they had access to the property involved in the investigation, the employer has reasonable suspicion of their involvement, and they are given written information (signed by a representative of the employer and retained for at least three years) regarding the specific incident or activity being investigated and the basis for selecting particular employees for testing.* Reasonable suspicion must be based on evidence that goes beyond the mere fact of access or proximity. *Even for investigatory purposes, submission to a polygraph exam cannot be required or made a condition of employment.* Refusal to submit to a polygraph exam, by itself, cannot be the basis for discipline or discharge. Polygraph exams conducted as part of investigations are also subject to numerous procedural requirements:[46]

- *Employees must not be asked questions designed to "degrade or needlessly intrude" on their privacy.*

[42]*NLRB v. J. Weingarten, Inc.,* 420 U.S. 251 (1975).

[43]*IBM Corporation,* 341 NLRB No. 148 (2004).

[44]*IBM Corporation,* at 3.

[45]29 U.S.C.A. § 2006(d) (2005).

[46]29 U.S.C.A. § 2007 (2005).

- *Employees must not be asked questions concerning religious beliefs, opinions about racial matters, political beliefs, sexual behavior, and beliefs or activities regarding labor organizations.*
- *Employees have the right to review all questions beforehand.*
- *Employees must be informed whether any observational (e.g., two-way mirrors) or recording devices are being used.*
- *Employees have the right to terminate a polygraph exam at any time.*
- *Employees must not be tested who have written documentation from a physician that their physical or mental condition might cause abnormal responses.*
- *Employees have the right to a written copy of any opinion or conclusion based on the test.*

Acting on Results of Investigations

Investigations gather information. If the wrong conclusions are drawn and are communicated to others in a manner that causes qualified privilege to be lost, defamation claims are in the offing. In *Dietz,* the alleged defamation took place in the course of the interrogation, as potentially false allegations of drug use and theft were communicated to other staff. In the aforementioned case of the Wal-Mart employee whose home was searched for stolen goods, the employer compounded its error (and liability) by having the allegedly stolen items placed out in the yard in full view of neighbors and, eventually, the media. This resulted in news stories about a mass seizure of stolen equipment. Wal-Mart personnel were shown to be, however indirectly, sources of information for the articles. The problem was that there was never any good evidence that the employee actually stole the seized items. What can be said with certainty is that the county prosecutor refused to bring criminal charges. Defamation (and privacy) claims were upheld, and the employee was awarded $1.65 million.[47] In another case involving Wal-Mart, several employees were fired for eating "claims candy" (candy from open or torn bags that were removed from store shelves and put aside to be discarded or returned). Managers made a number of statements about the employees and the reasons for their termination. Although statements to the effect that the employees had engaged in theft were true (and hence, not defamatory), additional statements implying that there were other, more serious violations ("there was more to it . . . than just claims candy"), were without foundation and defamed the former employees.[48] Even absent false allegations, broad disclosure of employee wrongdoing (such as by speaking to the press) can constitute public disclosure of private facts and an invasion of privacy.

Although all this might suggest a strategy of staying mum about the results of investigations, other employees are usually aware of the incidents in question. To quell rumors and to demonstrate the enforcement of policies, employers often need to say something about the outcomes of investigations. The general advice is to *treat such information as sensitive and limit communication to those with a legitimate need to know.*

[47]*Lee.*

[48]*Stringer v. Wal-Mart Stores,* 151 S.W.3d 781 (Ky. 2004).

In a relevant case, the discharge of an employee for sexually harassing a coworker (the discharged employee denied having done so) led the employer to issue (in part) the following statement:

> The recent sexual harassment incident which resulted in an employee's termination has raised supervisory and employee questions about the subject. This particular incident was determined to be a serious act of employee misconduct, but in deference to the employees involved cannot be discussed in detail. However, deliberate, repeated, and unsolicited physical contact as well as significant verbal abuse was involved in this case.[49]

The statement was distributed to approximately 140 supervisors with instructions for them to discuss it with all their employees. The alleged harasser sued for defamation. The court held that the employer had good reason to communicate with employees regarding enforcement of its harassment policy and that "coworkers have a legitimate interest in the reasons a fellow employee was discharged."[50] The court commended the employer for not describing the events in sensationalistic detail and for including additional language from EEOC guidelines. The court also approved of distribution to the supervisors, but remanded the case for further consideration of whether subsequent communications by supervisors to employees amounted to overly broad publication causing qualified privilege to be lost.

Employee misconduct is sometimes criminal in nature. The evidence used by employers to reach employment decisions and the process of gathering that evidence is different from what is needed to obtain criminal convictions. Employers often choose to deal with arguably criminal activities by terminating employees rather than seeking prosecution. The latter course of action might require court appearances by company personnel and invite unwanted publicity. Occasionally, it can subject employers to claims for malicious prosecution. **Malicious prosecution** occurs when criminal proceedings are initiated against an innocent party, the party initiating criminal proceedings does so without probable cause, the criminal proceedings terminate in favor of the accused party, and the accusing party was motivated by malice. In one such case,[51] a restaurant terminated a chef and then filed a criminal complaint against the chef for allegedly stealing kitchen equipment. The chef was arrested, but the District Attorney's office subsequently went to court to have the case dismissed. The restaurant was not granted summary judgment on the chef's malicious prosecution claim because it had played an active role in prosecuting the employee (simply reporting a possible crime would not be sufficient); the criminal proceeding ended in a manner not inconsistent with innocence (there need not be a trial); the employer lacked probable cause because, despite complaining about the theft of multiple items, the chef had been seen leaving with only one item and it was common for chefs to use their own equipment; and malice was shown by prior threats to have the chef arrested and to use connections in the police department against him. *Employers do not have to be correct or have ironclad evidence that employees have committed crimes to seek their prosecution; but they do have to have reasonable grounds for pursuing legal action and not appear to be out to get an innocent person.* Of course, deciding to terminate an employee is a weighty decision in its own right, as the upcoming chapters demonstrate.

[49]*Garziano v. E.I. DuPont De Nemours & Co.*, 818 F.2d 380, at 384 (5th Cir. 1987).

[50]*Garziano*, at 387.

[51]*Lawson v. New York Billiards Corp.*, 331 F.Supp 2d 121 (E.D.N.Y. 2004).

Chapter SUMMARY

Public employees are protected against unreasonable search and seizure under the Fourth Amendment of the U.S. Constitution. This protection applies only in situations where employees have a reasonable expectation of privacy. By virtue of their employment, public employees have less protection against governmental intrusion than ordinary citizens. Whether there is a reasonable expectation of privacy is a case-by-case determination based on policies, practices, and other circumstances. If a reasonable expectation of privacy is deemed to exist, the reasonableness of a search—both at its inception and in its scope—is considered. Unlike in the law enforcement context, warrants or a showing of probable cause are not required for workplace searches. To be reasonable at their inception, searches should be based on a reasonable belief that they will uncover evidence of wrongdoing or that they are necessary for noninvestigatory, work-related purposes. Searches are reasonable in their scope when the measures employed are commensurate with the purposes of the search and the seriousness of the alleged misconduct.

Under common law, four different types of privacy torts are recognized in most states: intrusion upon seclusion, public disclosure of private facts, placement in a false light, and appropriation of a name or likeness. Intrusion upon seclusion occurs when the solitude or private affairs of an individual are intentionally intruded upon and the nature of the intrusion is such that it would be highly offensive to a reasonable person. Public disclosure of private facts occurs when private facts about a person that are of no legitimate concern to the public are broadly disclosed to others in a manner that would be highly offensive to a reasonable person. Placement in a false light occurs when characteristics, conduct, or beliefs are falsely attributed to an individual; this false information is broadly publicized; the person publicizing the information knew or should have known that it was false; and being placed in this false light would be highly offensive to a reasonable person. In appropriation of a name or likeness, an individual's name or likeness is used by others without consent and for their own commercial or other ends.

Situations that give rise to privacy tort claims, such as searches and interrogations, also tend to lead to other common law claims. In infliction of emotional distress claims, plaintiffs must show intent to harm (or the existence of a "special relationship" in states where negligent infliction of emotional distress is recognized); behavior that is so outrageous, shocking, or atrocious as to be beyond the bounds of what is tolerable in a civilized society; and severe emotional harm or distress. False imprisonment occurs when an individual completely restrains the physical liberty of another person, resulting in harm. Malicious prosecution occurs when criminal proceedings are initiated against an innocent party, the party initiating the proceedings does so without probable cause and with malice, and the criminal proceedings terminate in favor of the accused party.

Privacy protections are also found in statutes. Under the ADA, medical information must be kept separate from other personnel records and treated as confidential. HIPAA imposes a set of requirements aimed at protecting the privacy of medical information obtained through the administration of group health plans. The NLRA protects privacy by prohibiting intrusions that interfere with concerted activity. It also provides unionized employees with a right to representation during disciplinary interviews. Under the OSH Act, employees have a right of access to exposure and medical records kept in compliance with the act. The Employee Polygraph Protection Act allows private employers to use polygraphs to investigate certain types of misconduct, but it also establishes many requirements for the exams. The federal Privacy Act regulates the handling of records regarding federal government employees. Under this law, federal government employees must be allowed access to their personnel records, to make copies, and to contest information they believe to be erroneous. Federal agencies have an obligation to maintain accurate records, to limit the contents of records to appropriate information, and to obtain employee consent before disclosing information from records to outside parties.

Technological changes, particularly the extensive use of electronic communications and information-processing devices, have posed new workplace privacy issues. The Electronic Communications Privacy Act prohibits the interception and disclosure of wire, oral, or electronic communications. However, there are exceptions for service providers, use in the ordinary course of business, and situations where employees have consented to the interception or disclosure. The ECPA also prohibits the unauthorized accessing of stored communications, although this does not apply to the provider of a system. The many exceptions to the ECPA and the reluctance of courts to find that employees have a reasonable expectation of privacy in matters such as their e-mail or Internet use have left employees with relatively little protection in these areas.

Practical Advice SUMMARY

- *Employers should establish privacy policies that alert employees to the limits of their privacy rights in the workplace.*

- *Regarding personnel files, employers*

 –should generally allow employees to view their files.

 –should obtain consent before divulging information about employees to third parties.

 –must allow union representatives access to information needed for representational purposes.

 –must keep medical information separate from other personnel records and handle it as confidential.

- *Regarding medical and exposure records required by the OSH Act, employers must*

 –allow employees (and union representatives) to examine and copy their records (within 15 working days of making a request to do so).

 –retain exposure records for 30 years.

 –retain medical records for the duration of employment, plus 30 years.

- *When engaging in monitoring or surveillance of employees, employers*

 –should inform employees that they are subject to monitoring or surveillance.

 –must not engage in surveillance of employees engaged in protected concerted activities, including union organizing.

 –should limit any surveillance of employees outside of the workplace to public areas.

 –should refrain from surveillance in areas of the workplace typically regarded as private (e.g., restrooms).

- *Employers must not intercept or disclose the contents of telephone conversations, e-mails, and other wire, oral, or electronic communications without consent unless*

 –the interception occurs routinely in the ordinary course of business.

 –there are for legitimate business purposes.

 –employees receive prior notification.

- *Employers must not access stored electronic communications without authorization, unless they are the service providers.*

- *Employers must not listen in on private telephone calls. Employers monitoring business calls must get off the line after it is determined that a personal call is being made or received.*

- *Regarding workplace searches, employers should*

 –establish policies explaining the circumstances under which searches may occur.

 –communicate those policies.

 –enforce search policies in a consistent, nondiscriminatory manner.

 –make searches no more intrusive or extensive than necessary.

 –handle carefully and keep in a secure place any evidence or contraband obtained through searches, particularly if there is potential criminal activity.

 –never conduct strip searches.

 –minimize any physical contact with employees during searches of their person.

 –conduct searches out of the view of coworkers and the public.

- *Public employers, in particular, must be prepared to defend the reasonableness of searches and other actions that infringe upon employees' reasonable expectations of privacy.*

- *Employers can take appropriate action to prevent the theft of their property, but should not otherwise detain employees suspected of wrongdoing or force them to submit to interrogations against their will.*

- *When conducting interrogations of employees, it is important that*

 –employees are told they are free to leave.

 –employees are not threatened with harm.

 –the room is not locked or the path of egress physically obstructed.

 –employees are given the opportunity to explain events rather than being grilled with rapid-fire questions or accusations.

 –interrogations are kept as brief as possible.

- *If requested, unionized employees must be allowed to have a union representative present at meetings that are reasonably likely to result in discipline or discharge.*

- Employers can request that employees submit to polygraph exams in the course of investigating thefts or other events causing economic loss, but only those individuals

 –who had access to the property involved in the investigation.

 –who, on the basis of additional evidence, are reasonably suspected of involvement.

 –who are given written information (signed by a representative of the employer and retained for at least three years) regarding the specific incident or activity being investigated and the basis for selecting particular employees for testing.

- When the polygraph is used for investigatory purposes

 –submission to a polygraph exam cannot be required or made a condition of continued employment.

 –numerous requirements must be met regarding the questions that can be asked and procedures to be followed.

- Information about employee misconduct derived from investigations should be treated as confidential and communicated only to those with a legitimate need to know.

Key TERMS

reasonable expectation of privacy
intrusion upon seclusion
public disclosure of private facts
placement in a false light

appropriation of a name or likeness
intentional infliction of emotional distress
Privacy Act

Electronic Communications Privacy Act (ECPA)
ordinary course of business
false imprisonment
malicious prosecution

Chapter QUESTIONS

1. A research analyst for the Indiana Department of Corrections was told that she would have to submit to a psychological examination to keep her job. She took the exam, which lasted two hours and contained many questions related to details of her personal life. She sued, claiming that the test violated her constitutional rights. What should the court decide? Why? (*Greenawalt v. Indiana Department of Corrections*, 397 F.3d 587 (7th Cir. 2005))

2. At the end of her shift, a 19-year-old shoe salesperson was questioned by two store security officers. She was questioned in a small room for three hours. One of the security officers sat behind her on the right side where she could not see him (she was blind in the right eye). She was asked to sign a document stating that she was voluntarily waiving her "rights," including the right to remain silent. When she asked for further

explanation of the document before she signed it, she was told that it "doesn't mean anything" unless you've "done something wrong." A security officer threatened to call the police and have her jailed unless she signed a confession. She was told that the interrogation could last all night and that if she signed a confession she could probably keep her job. Under these circumstances she signed. She was fired two days later. What should the court decide? Why? (*Smithson v. Nordstrom, Inc.*, 664 P.2d 1119 (Ore. App. 1983))

3. A telephone company employee was on disability leave. Company policy prohibited taking vacation while collecting disability. The employee disregarded the policy and left for his planned fishing trip. Managers became suspicious and went to his house to wait for him, finding no one home. Phone records were checked to verify that the employee had not called in from home, as

he had claimed, or made any other calls. The employer also contacted the kennel where the employee had boarded his dog, the Canadian province where he obtained a fishing license, and the post office that he had instructed to hold his mail. The employee was fired. He was reinstated without back pay by an arbitrator, but he sued for invasion of privacy. What should the court decide? Why? (*Schmidt v. Ameritech*, 768 N.E.2d 303 (Ill. App. 2002); *review denied*, 813 N.E. 2d 229 (Ill. 2004))

4. A woman was beaten by a coworker with whom she was living, resulting in several broken ribs. She filed charges against the coworker, and the coworker's conviction for domestic violence was reported in the newspaper. The woman did not report any of this information to her employer, but managers became aware of the situation due to the newspaper account. A workplace violence team investigated, seeking to determine whether the coworker was dangerous and should be removed from the workplace. On four occasions, they attempted to interview the woman, asking questions regarding her relationship with the coworker, the domestic violence incident, and her physical and mental health. On each occasion, she became angry and left the interview insisting that this was private information that she did not want to share. The woman was eventually terminated for her failure to cooperate with the workplace violence program. She sued. What should the court decide? Why? (*Rowe v. Guardian Automotive Products*, 2005 U.S. Dist. LEXIS 31296.)

5. An employee worked the night shift at a bakery. She was having an affair and sometimes pretended to go to work when she was really visiting with her lover. One evening when she was supposed to be working, her husband called the bakery and learned that she was absent. The next day he went to the bakery and met with a human resources (HR) manager. After consulting her personnel file, the HR manager informed the husband that she had been absent on a number of occasions. Shortly thereafter, the husband committed suicide. He left a note saying that he hoped his wife would be happier without him being in the way. The wife sued the bakery for divulging the information. What should the court decide? Why? (*Kobeck v. Nabisco*, 305 S.E.2d 183 (Ga. App. 1983))

6. An employee worked for a military contractor, performing mailroom services at a naval station. One day, after the end of work and when the mailroom was closed, she returned to retrieve something from the refrigerator. In the process, she discovered 14 opened and undelivered Christmas cards in the wastebasket. She immediately reported the situation to her supervisor. When the supervisor investigated, she found a pay stub among the pieces of undelivered mail. The stub was from the pay check of another employee who had been working at the front desk for most of that day. All the mailroom employees were subsequently asked to submit to a polygraph exam. They were told that the exam was voluntary and they were asked to sign general release forms. These forms were not signed by any official of the company and did not specifically mention the mail incident or provide the basis for testing each employee. All the employees signed the form. The prime suspect was polygraphed first and the exam suggested deception in his responses. The contractor said that it still wanted to polygraph the other employees. By this time, the employee who had discovered the undelivered mail refused to take the exam. Less than a week later, she was fired on the grounds that she had accepted package deliveries through the mailroom's back door in violation of naval security procedures. The employee sued, challenging both the polygraph request and her termination. What should the court decide? Why? (*Polkey v. Transtecs Corp.*, 404 F.3d 1264 (11th Cir. 2005))

7. A nurse was terminated from her job at a hospital for improperly medicating a patient. When she sought to obtain information from the hospital for a hearing on her termination, she was told that the hospital was prohibited by HIPAA from releasing the medical file of the patient in question to her. She sues for release of the information needed for her case. What should the court decide? Why? (*Chapman v. Health and Hospitals Corporation*, 796 N.Y.S. 2d 876 (Sup. Ct. New York County 2005))

8. Is the current privacy protection for e-mail and Internet use sufficient?

9. If you were called on to draft a privacy policy for a company, what would you include in that policy?

Internet RESOURCES

The American Civil Liberties Union (ACLU) site has information on numerous workplace privacy issues.

http://www.aclu.org/workplacerights/

Site of the Privacy Rights Clearinghouse, a non-profit consumer information and advocacy organization, includes useful fact sheets on employment privacy issues.

http://www.privacyrights.org/workplace.htm

Site of the Electronic Privacy Information Center includes links to articles and cases dealing with the privacy of electronic communications

http://www.epic.org/privacy/workplace/

PART **6**

Terminating Employment

Chapter 18
Terminating Individual Employees

Chapter 19
Downsizing and Posttermination Issues

PART 1
Introduction
to Employment
Law

PART 2
The Hiring
Process

PART 3
Managing a
Diverse
Workforce

PART 4
Pay, Benefits,
Terms and
Conditions of
Employment

PART 5
Managing
Performance

Terminating Individual Employees

CLIPPINGS

▸ Barbara Roberts, a grandmother and employee of Positronic Industries, requested time off to care for her grandchildren following the flooding of New Orleans. The parents were stranded in New Orleans, and there was no one else to watch the children. Roberts was told to report to work or be fired. When she failed to report, her employment was terminated.[1]

▸ Jim Alderson, a former accountant at a hospital, refused to adopt the fraudulent practice of keeping two sets of records for Medicare reimbursements and was terminated. The information that he provided to the government resulted in the recovery of $1.7 billion in Medicare funds improperly obtained by Columbia/HCA and the Quorum Health Group. Under the False Claims Act, Mr. Alderson received settlements amounting to tens of millions of dollars. In the approximately two decades since the inception of the False Claims Act, the federal government has recovered about $12 billion dollars of improper payments to contractors, and whistleblowers have received over a billion dollars.[2]

▸ Arbitrator Roger Kaplan ruled that the 25-game suspension of player Jermaine O'Neal by the National Basketball Association (NBA) would be reduced to 15 games. The union for NBA players had challenged the disciplinary actions taken against O'Neal and three of his teammates for brawling with fans. The arbitrator upheld the suspensions of the other players, including a season-long suspension for Ron Artest.[3]

▸ Ester Kartiganer, a former producer of TV news programs, is suing CBS. She was among the employees who had responsibility for a "60 minutes" segment that raised questions about the National Guard service of President Bush. It was concluded shortly thereafter that the report was based on documents that could not be authenticated and that it had been rushed into production without proper vetting. CBS Chairman Leslie Moonves subsequently stated on the network's Web site that Ms. Kartiganer had "abnegated her assigned function" and that "CBS News is the worse for it." Ms. Kartiganer's suit alleges both defamation and age discrimination.[4]

▸ Ward Churchill, a tenured professor at the University of Colorado, is a controversial figure. In the aftermath of 9/11, he wrote an essay in which he referred unsympathetically to employees killed during the attack as "technocrats" and "little Eichmanns." The latter referred to the Nazi, Adolf Eichmann. This has prompted threats of violence against Churchill, calls for his removal, and a special investigation of his scholarly record by the Board of Regents and governor.[5]

[1]Bill Draper. "Grandmother Fired for Katrina Absences." Boston.com (September 15, 2005).

[2]"For Some Whistle-Blowers, Big Risk Pays Off." *New York Times* (November 26, 2004), A-17.

[3]Alex Berenson. "At Pfizer, the Isolation Increases for a Whistle-Blower." *New York Times* (June 8, 2005), C-1.

[4]Jacques Steinberg. "CBS Producer Sues Over Job." *New York Times* (March 10, 2005), A-14.

[5]Kirk Johnson. "Storm of Debate Flares Over Professor's Essay on 9/11." *New York Times* (February 11, 2005), A-11.

"You're fired!" Those dreaded words carry weighty consequences for employees and employers alike. Terminations can drastically affect the ability of employees to provide for themselves and their families, harm future career prospects, and strike devastating blows at reputations and self-esteem. For employers, terminations are stressful, occasionally dangerous, and apt to prompt legal challenges. Terminations are more likely than any other human resource activity to result in legal claims.

The legal standards governing termination differ substantially depending on whether private-sector and nonunion employees or public-sector and unionized employees are being considered. The first, and largest, portion of this chapter deals with the legal protections available to private-sector, nonunion employees. Their legal status is captured by the term "employment at will with exceptions." The latter part of this chapter considers the more stringent "just cause/due process" standard for terminations that generally applies to unionized and public-sector employees. There are also important differences between terminations of individuals for reasons specific to those individuals and the selection of numerous employees for termination in conjunction with downsizings, plant closings, mergers, and the like. This chapter considers individual terminations. Chapter 19 deals with downsizing and plant closings.

DETERMINING WHETHER A TERMINATION HAS OCCURRED— CONSTRUCTIVE DISCHARGE

Disputes over whether an employee quit or was fired are not uncommon. If an employee truly resigns of his own volition, the employee cannot sue for wrongful termination. However, employers cannot avoid the legal consequences of terminations by effectively, but not officially, discharging employees (e.g., "You weren't fired, you were just permanently descheduled"). More importantly, a quit is deemed to be a termination when an employer creates intolerable working conditions with the intention of forcing an employee to quit. This is known as a **constructive discharge**. The quit is construed as a termination if, under the circumstances, a reasonable person would have felt compelled to quit.

Factors that courts examine to determine whether an employee who resigned was constructively discharged include demotions; cuts in salary; reductions in job responsibilities; reassignment to menial or degrading work; reassignment to work under a younger supervisor; badgering, harassment, and humiliation calculated to encourage resignation; and offers of early retirement on terms less favorable than the employee's former status.[6] A resignation that occurs when an employee is presented with the stark option of resigning or being immediately terminated can constitute a constructive discharge. However, a constructive discharge did not exist when a veteran teacher retired after being told by a school superintendent that he would recommend that the school district not renew her contract at the end of the school year (six months from then).[7] The court observed that, despite the superintendent's stated intention, the teacher had numerous avenues to contest nonrenewal, and the likely outcome of that process was unknown. Furthermore, this was not a case where she was assigned demeaning job duties or demoted.

A constructive discharge was found where an employee returned from vacation to find that her desk was empty, all of her belongings were packed up in boxes, and her

[6]*Logan v. Denny's*, 259 F.3d 558, at 569 (6th Cir. 2001).

[7]*Cigan v. Chippewa Falls School District*, 388 F.3d 331 (7th Cir. 2004).

office was being used as storage space. Additionally, the employee had been told by her former supervisor a month earlier to "watch your back." While she was on vacation, her new supervisor had called regarding the whereabouts of some documents. Dissatisfied with her response, the supervisor told her, "This is the last straw." The employee had also received her first negative performance appraisal ever, and some of her job duties had been shifted to a newly hired employee. Under all these circumstances, the court concluded that a reasonable person would have believed that, had she not resigned, she would have been terminated.[8]

As the *Suders* case discussed (see Chapter 9), harassment can be the basis for a constructive discharge. However, courts generally require that the severity of the harassment exceed the minimum level necessary to establish a hostile environment claim. Thus, some cases of harassment, if followed by a quit, become wrongful discharge cases as well.

Note, however, that constructive discharge is not a legal claim in itself. Instead, a finding that an employee who resigned was constructively discharged allows that employee to bring any legal claims for wrongful discharge that would be available had she been formally terminated. The nature of constructive discharges, and the incredible lengths to which employers sometimes go to drive employees out, also lends itself to other legal claims. One strong possibility is infliction of emotional distress. In one such case, a 60-year-old, high-level manager with more than 30 years of experience in the industry was demoted with a reduction in benefits to a warehouse supervisor position. He had no employees to supervise and spent his time sweeping floors and cleaning the cafeteria. He was subjected to the "silent treatment" by other managers, when he was not actively being harassed (e.g., another manager posted a sign in the workplace saying "Wilson is old"). The man suffered severe psychological problems as a result of this mistreatment. Upholding a multimillion dollar jury verdict, the court concluded:

> We find it difficult to conceive a workplace scenario more painful and embarrassing than an executive, indeed a vice-president and the assistant to the president, being subjected before his fellow employees to the most menial janitorial services and duties of cleaning up after entry level employees; the steep downhill push to total humiliation was complete. The evidence . . . will fully support the view . . . that Monarch, unwilling to fire Wilson outright, *intentionally and systematically* set out to humiliate him in the hopes that he would quit. . . . [T]his conduct was, indeed, so outrageous that civilized society should not tolerate it.[9]

Clearly, *employers should not attempt to avoid terminations by creating intolerable conditions designed to force employees to quit*. This strategy is a loser because employees who quit under these circumstances will be deemed constructively discharged, and the process of attempting to force them out might give rise to claims of harassment or infliction of emotional distress.

EMPLOYMENT AT WILL WITH EXCEPTIONS

To understand the legal limitations on termination of most private sector, nonunion employees, it is useful to distinguish among pure employment at will, employment at will with exceptions, and just cause as legal standards governing terminations.

[8]*EEOC v. University of Chicago Hospitals*, 276 F.3d 326 (7th Cir. 2002).
[9]*Wilson v. Monarch Paper Co.*, 939 F.2d 1138, at 1145 (5th Cir. 1991).

Under pure **employment at will,** there is no such thing as a wrongful termination. An employee without a contract of employment for a specified term can be terminated for good reason, bad reason, or no reason. Either party to the relationship can sever the employment relationship at any time. Pure employment at will describes the legal regime that existed in the United States prior to 1937. In 1937, the Supreme Court upheld the constitutionality of the National Labor Relations Act. The NLRA carved out the first major exception to employment at will: Employers could no longer lawfully terminate employees for union organizing or otherwise exercising their rights under the NLRA.

The opposite end of the spectrum, in terms of the ease with which employers can terminate employment relationships, is represented by the just cause/due process standard. Under a just cause/due process standard, employers bear the burden of proving that terminations were carried out properly and based on good reasons. The default rule is that if an employer cannot adequately defend a challenged termination, that termination is wrongful, and the employee is entitled to reinstatement, back wages, or other remedies. This standard applies to roughly 20 percent of the current U.S. workforce, including most public employees, unionized employees, employees with individual employment contracts specifying the term of employment, and employees in Montana (where a "good cause" standard was established by statute).

In contrast to both pure employment at will and just cause, most private-sector, nonunion employees have their employment relationships governed by a legal regime that can best be described as **employment at will with exceptions.** Under this arrangement, employment at will is still the starting point for analyzing an employee's right to not be terminated. However, since 1937, pure employment at will has been substantially modified by legislation and judicial recognition of common law wrongful discharge claims. To some observers, the number of exceptions now overwhelms the rule of employment at will, but that is an overstatement. Under employment at will with exceptions, employees bear the burden of showing that their termination was for an "illegal cause" prohibited by law. But if they fail to do so, the default rule is still employment at will; the termination is legal regardless of how dubious the reasons or circumstances. The decision to terminate Barbara Roberts because she cared for her grandchildren during an emergency rather than coming to work (see "Clippings")—although grossly unfair in the minds of most people—was almost certainly lawful. The available facts do not suggest the applicability of any of the exceptions to employment at will; therefore, the termination of this non-union, private-sector employee was legal. However, her story has a happy ending. The firing was picked up by the news media and prompted a firestorm of criticism that caused the company to relent and reinstate Barbara Roberts.[10]

IMPERMISSIBLE GROUNDS FOR TERMINATION

Table 18-1 lists the primary legal protections against wrongful discharge. Terminations can be challenged on constitutional, statutory, and common law grounds. Common law grounds include both contractual and tort claims. Remedies in contractual claims are intended to restore individuals to the position they would have been in had their contracts not been breached ("make the individual whole"), whereas plaintiffs suing in tort can recover both compensatory and punitive damages

[10]"Company restores job to fired grandmother." *Columbia Daily Tribune* (September 17, 2005).

TABLE 18-1	Legal Protections Against Wrongful Discharge		

		Common Law	
Constitutional	**Statutory**	**Contract**	**Tort**
First Amendment (e.g., speech)	*Civil service, tenure laws*	*Individual (express) employment contract*	Public policy exception
Fifth and Fourteenth amendments (due process, equal protection)	*Antidiscrimination laws* (e.g., ADA, ADEA)	*Labor agreement*	Intentional interference with a contractual relationship
	Noninterference provisions of statutes (e.g., NLRA, FMLA)	Implied contract	
State constitutions		Covenant of good faith and fair dealing	
	Antiretaliation provisions of statutes (e.g., OSHA, ERISA)	Promissory estoppel	Infliction of emotional distress
	Whistleblower protection laws		Defamation
	Civic duty laws (e.g., USERRA)		Privacy torts
	Off-duty conduct laws (e.g., smoking)		False imprisonment
	Montana WDEA		

for the harm done to them. The tort claims listed below the line in Table 18-1 are not wrongful discharge claims per se, but rather claims that can flow out of the circumstances leading up to and following terminations.

It is important to keep this "menu" in mind when analyzing the legality of a termination. Some of the protections listed in Table 18-1 (those in italics) are available only to public-sector employees, unionized employees, and other employees not employed at will. What remains is considerable, although the various protections overlap and states vary in terms of whether and how particular legal protections are recognized. To simplify greatly, the exceptions to employment at will for most private-sector, nonunion employees boil down to the following impermissible grounds for termination: terminations that would breach an implied contract or other contract-related obligation, terminations in retaliation for employee actions that support public policy, terminations that interfere with the exercise of statutory rights, and terminations that are discriminatory.

Breach of an Implied Contract

A small number of employees (e.g., professional athletes, high-level managers) have "express" (i.e., explicit, mutually acknowledged) contracts of employment that are the products of negotiation, executed in writing, signed, and specify a particular

term of employment (or specific grounds under which the contract can be terminated). However, the vast majority of employees do not. Nevertheless, under the **implied contract** exception to employment at will that is recognized in about 38 states,[11] the right of employers to terminate at will can be limited by promises of job security. Even in the absence of an express contract of employment, written or oral statements by employers—and their entire course of conduct in dealing with employees—can give rise to enforceable, contractual rights to something other than employment at will. The "something other" might be employment for a specified term, termination only for certain reasons (e.g., "for cause"), or use of specified procedures when making termination decisions (e.g., progressive discipline). If an implied (or implied-in-fact) contract exists, discharged employees can sue for wrongful discharge based on breach of the implied contract.

Criteria for Determining the Existence of an Implied Contract Not every statement that an employer makes will be contractually binding on the employer. Following are some factors that point to the existence of an implied contract:

- The promise was specific.
- The promise was made frequently and consistently.
- The source of the promise was someone with sufficient authority to offer it.
- The promise was communicated to the employee.
- The promise was not highly conditional (i.e., dependent on the employer's own judgment).
- The employer's entire "course of conduct" (e.g., policies, practices, statements, industry practices, employee tenure) was consistent with the promise.
- There was an exclusive listing of dischargeable offenses in a handbook.
- A change to a less-protective policy was not communicated to employees.
- There was no effective disclaimer.

Vague, stray, or highly conditional promises do not evidence intent to depart from employment at will. Statements such as "you have a promising future with the company" (lack of specificity) or "you will have a job for as long as we like your work" (conditionality) are unlikely to be enforceable. The statements relied on must be sufficiently specific to constitute "offers," rather than mere general statements of policy. Thus, inclusion of a general nondiscrimination provision in an employee handbook did not create an implied contract because it "was not specific and did not make any promises regarding disciplinary procedure or termination decisions."[12] In contrast, an employee handbook that labeled its provisions as "binding" and that outlined specific disciplinary procedures was sufficiently specific and authoritative to form the basis for an implied contract.[13] Listings of dischargeable offenses can limit employment at will if they can fairly be read to restrict terminations to those based on the stated set of reasons.

To understand whether a promise was made, some courts look not only at statements spoken by managers or written in documents, but also to the entire course of

[11]Charles J. Muhl. "The Employment-at-Will Doctrine: Three Major Exceptions." *Monthly Labor Review* (January 2001), 3–11, at 4.

[12]*Hessenthaler v. Tri-County Sister Help, Inc.*, 616 S.E.2d 694, at 699 (S.C. 2005).

[13]*Jones v. Lake Park Care Center*, 569 N.W.2d 369 (Iowa 1997).

an employer's conduct. The course of conduct relevant to determining the existence of an implied contract includes the employer's informal policies, past practice (e.g., practice of not terminating without cause), industry customs, and treatment of the individual employee. However, although longevity, consistent raises, promotions, and positive performance appraisals can bolster an employee's claim that employment is not strictly at will, "they do not, *in and of themselves*, . . . constitute a contractual guarantee of future employment security."[14]

To be contractually enforceable, offers must be communicated by persons authorized to make them. Additionally, statements of employer policy, such as supervisor's manuals, that are not directly communicated to employees usually will not support the finding of an implied contract. Employee handbooks are often at the center of implied contract cases because they represent authoritative statements of employer policies that are communicated to all employees.

Specific promises made to employees regarding their term of employment, permissible reasons for termination, or termination procedures must be honored. Employers that do not want to limit their prerogative to terminate at will should refrain from making such promises. Because of the central role that employee handbooks play in many implied contract cases, *handbooks, applications, and other authoritative documents should be carefully written and vetted (reviewed) by persons with legal expertise before they are put into use.*

If contractual rights limiting employment at will can stem from employer statements in handbooks and other sources, what happens if modifications are made that adversely affect those rights? Many courts permit employers to unilaterally make such changes, provided that employees are given reasonable notice.[15] However, other courts require more. The Arizona Supreme Court, for example, has held that merely providing employees with new handbooks is not legally adequate. Instead, employees must be specifically informed of any new terms, made aware of their effect on the preexisting contract, and affirmatively consent to modifications. Modifications must be supported by separate consideration—that is, some benefit to employees beyond simply being allowed to continue their employment. The court explained its reasoning as follows:

> To those who believe our conclusion will destroy an employer's ability to update and modernize its handbook, we can only reply that the great majority of handbook terms are certainly non-contractual and can be revised, that the existence of contractual terms can be disclaimed in the handbook in effect at the time of hiring and, if not, permission to modify can always be obtained by mutual agreement and for consideration. In all other instances, the contract rule is and has always been that one should keep one's promises.[16]

If changes are made that lessen employees' rights to not be terminated at will, employees should be clearly informed of those specific changes. Do not try to just "slip them by." Some states require employers to obtain a clear indication of employees' assent to those changes and to provide some benefit in exchange.

In *Dillon v. Champion Jogbra*, the court must decide whether an implied contract to use specified termination procedures exists, despite the presence of a "disclaimer."

[14]*Guz v. Bechtel National, Inc.*, 8 P.3d 1089, at 1104 (Cal. 2000).

[15]*Gaglidari v. Denny's Restaurants, Inc.*, 815 P.2d 1362 (Wash. 1991).

[16]*Demasse v. ITT Corp.*, 984 P.2d 1138, at 1148 (Ariz. 1999), *cert. denied*, 528 U.S. 930 (1999).

DILLON V. CHAMPION JOGBRA
819 A. 2d 703 (Vt. 2002)

OPINION BY JUSTICE MORSE:

Plaintiff Linda Dillon appeals an order of the superior court granting summary judgment to defendant Champion Jogbra, Inc. in her action for wrongful termination. Dillon contends that the trial court erroneously concluded as a matter of law that Dillon's at-will employment status had not been modified by Jogbra's employment manual and employment practices, and that the undisputed material facts failed to give rise to a claim for promissory estoppel supporting a claim for wrongful discharge. We affirm with respect to Dillon's claim for promissory estoppel, but reverse and remand on her breach of contract claim. * * *

Jogbra has an employee manual that it distributes to all employees at the time of their employment. The first page of the manual states the following in capitalized print:

> The policies and procedures contained in this manual constitute guidelines only. They do not constitute part of an employment contract, nor are they intended to make any commitment to any employee concerning how individual employment action can, should, or will be handled.

Champion Jogbra offers no employment contracts nor does it guarantee any minimum length of employment. Champion Jogbra reserves the right to terminate any employee at any time "at will," with or without cause. During the period from 1996 to 1997, however, Jogbra developed what it termed a "Corrective Action Procedure." This procedure established a progressive discipline system for employees and different categories of disciplinary infractions. It states that it applies to all employees and will be carried out in "a fair and consistent manner." Much of the language in the section is mandatory in tone.

Linda Dillon . . . was hired on as a full-time employee in August 1997 in the position of "charge-back analyst." In the summer of 1998, the position of "sales administrator" was going to become vacant. Dillon was approached by Jogbra management about applying for the position. * * * In the course of interviewing for the position, Dillon recalls that she was told that she would receive "extensive training." More specifically,

she was told by the human resources manager that she would overlap with her predecessor who would train her during those days. Originally, her predecessor was scheduled to leave August 15. In the course of Dillon's interview with the vice president of sales, who would be her immediate supervisor, he informed her that her predecessor was actually leaving earlier and would be available for only two days of training before Dillon started the job. He reassured her, though, that the predecessor would be brought back sometime thereafter for more training. Dillon also recalls that he told her that "it will take you four to six months to feel comfortable with [the] position," and not to be concerned about it. Dillon was offered and accepted the position. She spent most of her predecessor's remaining two days with her. Her predecessor then returned in early September for an additional two days of training. Dillon stated that she felt that, after the supplemental training, she had received sufficient training for the job.

On September 29, Dillon was called into her supervisor's office. The human resources manager was also present. They informed Dillon that things were not working out and that she was going to be reassigned to a temporary position, at the same pay and benefit level, that ended in December. She was told that she should apply for other jobs within the company, but if nothing suitable became available, she would be terminated at the end of December. According to Dillon, her supervisor stated that he had concluded within ten days of her starting that "it wasn't going to work out." Prior to the meeting, Dillon was never told her job was in jeopardy, nor did Jogbra follow the procedures laid out in its employee manual when terminating her. Dillon applied for one job that became available in the ensuing months, but was not selected for it. She left Jogbra in December when her temporary position terminated. * * *

In the implied contract context, we have noted . . . that . . . when an employer takes steps to give employees the impression of job security and enjoys the attendant benefits that such an atmosphere confers, it should not then be able to disregard its commitments at random. * * * [W]e have noted repeatedly that the presumption that employment for an indefinite term is an "at-will" agreement . . . imposes no substantive limitation on the right of contracting parties to modify terms of their arrangement or to specify other terms that

supersede the terminable-at-will [arrangement]." Additionally, an employer may modify an at-will employment agreement unilaterally. When determining whether an employer has done so, we look to both the employer's written policies and its practices. An employer not only may implicitly bind itself to terminating only for cause through its manual and practices, but may also be bound by a commitment to use only certain procedures in doing so. * * *

When the terms of a manual are ambiguous . . . or send mixed messages regarding an employee's status, the question of whether the presumptive at-will status has been modified is properly left to the jury. This may be the case even if there is a disclaimer stating employment is at-will, as the presence of such a disclaimer is not dispositive in the determination. "The mere inclusion of boilerplate language providing that the employee relationship is at will cannot negate any implied contract and procedural protections created by an employee handbook." Furthermore, an employer's practices can provide context for and help inform the determination. * * *

In this case, we cannot agree with the trial court that the terms of Jogbra's manual are unambiguous such that, as a matter of law, Dillon's status was not modified, especially considered in light of the conflicting record before the court regarding Jogbra's employment practices. Notwithstanding the disclaimer contained on the first page of the manual quoted above, the manual goes on to establish in Policy No. 720 an elaborate system governing employee discipline and discharge. It states as its purpose: "To establish Champion Jogbra policy for all employees." It states that actions will be carried out "in a fair and consistent manner." It provides that "the Corrective Action Policy requires management to use training and employee counseling to achieve the desired actions of employees." It establishes three categories of violations of company policy and corresponding actions to be generally taken in each case. It delineates progressive steps to be taken for certain types of cases, including "unsatisfactory quality of work," and time periods governing things such as how long a reprimand is considered "active." All of these terms are inconsistent with the disclaimer at the beginning of the manual, in effect sending mixed messages to employees. Furthermore, these terms appear to be inconsistent with an at-will employment relationship, its classic formulation being that an employer can fire an employee "for good cause or for no cause, or even for bad cause."

With respect to the record before the court on Jogbra's employment practices, Dillon herself was aware of at least one employee whose termination was carried out pursuant to the terms set forth in the manual. She also testified in her deposition to conversations with the human resources manager, with whom she was friendly, in which the manager had described certain procedures used for firing employees. She stated that the manager had told her that Jogbra could not "just get rid of" people, but instead had to follow procedures. The human resources manager herself testified that, although the progressive discipline system was not generally applied to salaried employees, it was "historically" used for nonsalaried employees. She could only recall two instances in which the portion of the manual providing for documentation of progressive action was not followed, one of which resulted in a legal claim against the company and the other of which involved an employee stealing from the company. In fact, the manual specifically provides that stealing "will normally result in discharge on the first offense." Thus, it is not clear how that discharge deviated from the provisions of the manual.

In conclusion, the manual itself is at the very least ambiguous regarding employees' status, and Jogbra's employment practices appear from the record to be both consistent with the manual and inconsistent with an at-will employment arrangement. Therefore, summary judgment was not proper on Dillon's breach of implied contract claim.

Dillon also argues that the trial court's grant of summary judgment on her claim of promissory estoppel was erroneous. Dillon based her claim on two separate statements: the assurance that she would receive training and the assurance that it would take her four to six months to become comfortable with the sales administrator position. We have held that, even if an employee otherwise enjoys only at-will employment status, that employee may still be able to establish a claim for wrongful termination under a theory of promissory estoppel if that employee can demonstrate that the termination was in breach of a specific promise made by the employer that the employer should have reasonably expected to induce detrimental reliance on the part of the employee, and that the employee did in fact detrimentally rely on the promise. We agree with the trial court in this case, however, that essential elements of promissory estoppel are absent with regard to both statements.

With respect to Jogbra's promise to Dillon that she would receive training, Dillon specifically conceded

that, upon her predecessor's return in September, she had received adequate training to perform the job. In other words, Jogbra had delivered on its promise. Furthermore, even assuming that Jogbra failed to provide the full extent of promised training, Dillon has failed to explain how, as a matter of law, the promise of training modified her at-will status. * * * With respect to the assurance that it would take four to six months to become comfortable with the position, the statement cannot be reasonably relied upon as a promise of employment in the sales administrator position for a set period of time. Courts have generally required a promise of a specific and definite nature before holding an employer bound by it. An estimate of how long it would take a person to adjust to a job cannot be converted into a definite promise of employment for that period of time. Thus, the vague assurance given to Dillon is not sufficient to support her claim of promissory estoppel. * * *

CASE QUESTIONS

1. What were the legal issues in this case? What did the court decide?

2. What was the implied contract in this case? How did the employer breach it?

3. Why does the disclaimer in the employee manual not have the effect desired by the employer?

4. Why does Dillon's promissory estoppel claim fail?

Effect of Disclaimers Employment at will is a harsh arrangement. It is difficult to put a positive "spin" on the message that "We can fire you at any time, for any reason not specifically prohibited by law, and without even the most elementary procedural safeguards." Most employers prefer to gain the motivational and employee relations benefits that come from communicating the desire to treat employees fairly. Most employers probably also intend to treat employees fairly. But employers do not want to be bound by promises of fair treatment and liable for breaches. In short, most employers would like to have it both ways: basking in the warm glow of assurances of fair treatment and remaining entirely free to depart from any self-imposed limitations on the right to terminate at will.

Disclaimers are used to this end. **Disclaimers** are written statements, incorporated into employee handbooks, employment applications, or other important documents, that "disclaim" or deny that any statements in those documents create contractual rights binding on the employer. Language disclaiming the existence of a contract is typically combined with notification to employees in clear terms that their employment is at will. The statement (capitalized) on the first page of the employee manual in *Dillon* informing employees that the manual's provisions constituted guidelines only and that no commitment was being made to employees about how terminations and other decisions would be handled, is a good example of a disclaimer. As another example, a bank included the following in its employee handbook:

> [T]he contents of this handbook DO NOT CONSTITUTE THE TERMS OF A CONTRACT OF EMPLOYMENT. Nothing contained in this handbook should be construed as a guarantee of continued employment, but rather, employment with the bank is on an "at will" basis. This means that the employment relationship may be terminated at any time by either the employee or the Bank for any reason not expressly prohibited by law.[17]

Disclaimers also frequently include language denying the contractual effect of any conflicting statements made elsewhere, reserving the right of the employer to

[17]*Chambers v. Valley National Bank,* 721 F. Supp. 1128, at 1131 (D. Ariz. 1988).

modify policies, and placing that authority solely with designated individuals. For example:

> [M]y employment and compensation can be terminated, with or without cause, and with or without notice, at any time, at the option of either the company or myself. I understand that no store manager or representative of Sears, Roebuck and Co., other than the president or vice-president of the Company, has any authority to enter into any agreement for employment for any specified period of time, or to make any agreement contrary to the foregoing.[18]

But do disclaimers, inserted in the midst of statements and other facts suggesting a departure from employment at will, actually shield employers from wrongful discharge suits based on implied contract? In many cases, yes. *Thus, employers that desire to maintain employment at will should incorporate disclaimers into employee handbooks and other important documents defining the employment relationship.* As the New Jersey Supreme Court put it in a leading implied contract case:

> [I]f the employer, for whatever reason, does not want the manual to be capable of being construed by the court as a binding contract, there are simple ways to attain that goal. All that need be done is the inclusion in a very prominent position of an appropriate statement that there is no promise of any kind by the employer contained in the manual; that regardless of what the manual says or provides, . . . the employer continues to have the absolute power to fire anyone with or without good cause.[19]

Disclaimers will often defeat contractual rights flowing from handbooks and other sources if the disclaimers themselves are clear and unequivocal and if they are presented to employees in a prominent and conspicuous manner. Fine print buried within lengthy documents is not sufficient. A disclaimer placed on the first page of an employee manual, capitalized, and printed in bold is both prominent and conspicuous.[20] *Disclaimers should be communicated to employees, and employees should be asked to acknowledge receipt in writing.* Disclaimers that are included on applications for employment, so that employees know the terms of the relationship upfront, appear to be especially effective.

However, disclaimers—even those carefully crafted and prominently displayed—are not foolproof. Some courts have taken the position that the interspersing of disclaimers and statements that appear to confer rights is inherently ambiguous. Rather than simply allow a disclaimer to override everything else, the case is given to a jury to decide what the contract, as a whole, means.[21] This is precisely the approach that the court took in *Dillon*. The "mixed messages" sent by the disclaimer, the specific "Corrective Action Policy," and the employer's practices created ambiguity as to whether an implied contract existed.

If it is determined that contractual rights limiting an employer's ability to terminate at will do not exist, an implied contract wrongful discharge claim will fail. However, if contractual rights exist, it still remains to be proven that the employer violated those rights in terminating an employee. In a case involving an employee who was hired under an implied contractual agreement to terminate only for "good

[18] *Reid v. Sears, Roebuck & Co.*, 790 F.2d 453, at 456 (6th Cir. 1986).

[19] *Woolley v. Hoffmann-LaRoche, Inc.*, 491 A.2d 1257, at 1271 (N.J. 1985), *modified*, 499 A.2d 515 (N.J. 1985).

[20] *Hessenthaler*, at 697.

[21] *McDonald v. Mobil Coal Producing, Inc.*, 820 P.2d 986 (Wyo. 1991).

cause" and who was subsequently fired for sexual harassment, the California Supreme Court held:

> [T]he question critical to defendant's liability is not whether plaintiff in fact sexually harassed other employees, but whether at the time the decision to terminate his employment was made, defendants, acting in good faith and following an investigation that was appropriate under the circumstances, had reasonable grounds for believing plaintiff had done so.[22]

Thus, under this view—shared by most other courts—the role of the courts in implied contract cases is not to start with a blank slate and decide whether the employer's judgment was correct, but instead to determine whether the employer's decision was reasonable under the circumstances. In one relevant implied contract case, the court upheld a jury's verdict that the employee was not discharged for good cause, as company policy prescribed. The employee had been terminated for violating a strict policy against taking "anything, large or small." His offense was retrieving expired meat that had been disposed of in a barrel for pickup by a salvage company, cooking the meat on a grill, and (along with coworkers) eating it for lunch.[23]

Other Contract-Related Claims Courts have long read into contracts an implied covenant of good faith and fair dealing. Courts in a distinct minority of states (about 11) have applied this covenant to employment relationships. As a type of wrongful discharge claim, the **covenant of good faith and fair dealing** pertains to terminations undertaken in bad faith and having the effect of denying employees the benefits of their contractual employment relationship. The term is potentially misleading. It does *not* amount to a general requirement that employers operate with good faith or terminate employees only for cause. Instead, in most of the states where it is recognized, the covenant applies only where there is an express or implied contract, and the employer has used a termination to deprive an employee of an already-earned benefit. For example, a wrongful discharge in violation of the covenant of good faith and fair dealing was recognized where a long-term employee was fired immediately after obtaining a large order, for the purpose of depriving him of his commission.[24] Overall, although some uncertainty remains about the reach of the covenant of good faith and fair dealing, and a few states (e.g., Alaska) have given it a broader reading, it appears to add relatively little protection against wrongful discharge beyond that already available under implied contract claims.

A second claim occasionally raised in discharge cases is **promissory estoppel.** We previously considered this legal claim in the context of a job applicant accepting employment and then having the offer withdrawn prior to commencing work (see Chapter 7). The key elements are reasonable and detrimental reliance on a clear promise. If, for example, an employee remains on the job due to reasonably relying on an employer's promises of job security, turns down lucrative alternative employment offers or incurs expenses relocating to a new assignment, and is then terminated, promissory estoppel might be invoked by the courts to redress the harm to the terminated employee—even in the absence of an express or implied contract. An employer who reneged on an offer to reinstate an employee if he was found innocent of criminal charges was liable for damages based on this theory.[25] In *Dillon,* the employer's statement that it would probably take four or six months for an employee

[22]*Cotran v. Rollins Hudig Hall International, Inc.,* 948 P.2d 412, at 423 (Cal. 1998).

[23]*Janes v. Wal-Mart Stores, Inc.,* 279 F.3d 883 (9th Cir. 2002).

[24]*Fortune v. National Cash Register Co.,* 364 N.E.2d 1251 (Mass. 1977).

[25]*Mers v. Dispatch Printing Co.,* 529 N.E.2d 958 (Ohio App. 1988).

to become comfortable in her new position was not a sufficiently clear promise of job security to support a promissory estoppel claim when Dillon was terminated for unsatisfactory performance shortly following acceptance of the job.

A third contract-related claim (but one for which tort damages are available) is **intentional interference with a contractual relationship.** This occurs when intentional, improper interference causes a third party to breach or not enter into a contractual relationship (the latter is sometimes referred to as "interference with prospective business advantage") with the plaintiff. In this context, "contractual" means any type of employment relationship, including at-will employment. The interference must be improper or without justification. Additionally, there must be a third party that is induced to breach or not enter into a contractual relationship. Cases where a former employee is blacklisted to prevent him from obtaining other employment clearly fit this requirement. The application of this claim to terminations in which agents of an employer (e.g., supervisors) use improper means to get employees fired is less clear. Is the employer a third party in such cases? The answer depends on whether the supervisor was acting within the scope of his employment when the interference occurred. An intentional interference claim was allowed to proceed to trial in the case of a manager who took actions that led to the constructive discharge of an employee who opposed his romantic relationship with a married, female subordinate. Evidence that the manager was acting from the purely personal motive of maintaining his affair made it plausible to argue that he was a separate party from the employer.[26]

Retaliation for an Act Supporting Public Policy

A variety of laws protect employees against terminations that, broadly speaking, are in retaliation for actions supporting public policy or that interfere with employees' rights under the law. These include common law claims for wrongful discharge under the public policy exception to employment at will, whistleblower protection statutes, antiretaliation and noninterference provisions in employment laws, and civic duty laws.

Public Policy Exception to Employment at Will Employees are also citizens with rights and responsibilities. Sometimes these roles conflict. Employers occasionally find it in their interest to have employees act in ways that are contrary to the public good. Under the **public policy exception to employment at will,** employers are liable in tort for wrongful discharge when they terminate employees for taking actions that public policy requires or commends. Allowing the terminations to stand would offend and undermine public policy. This type of wrongful discharge claim is recognized in about 43 states.

Lloyd v. Drake University is an interesting example of a public policy claim by a terminated employee.

Courts insist that claims be firmly grounded in fundamental and well-established public policies. To be protected, employees' actions must pertain to the public or society at large, and not merely personal interests or internal company matters. Primary sources of public policy are statutes and constitutions, although regulations, court decisions, and even professional codes of ethics are sometimes recognized as grounds for public-policy claims. Although constitutions are the most basic source of law and public policy, courts have generally not permitted private-sector employees

[26]*Kaelon v. USF Reddaway, Inc.,* 42 P.3d 344 (Or. App. 2002).

ELEMENTS OF A CLAIM

Public Policy Exception to Employment at Will

Plaintiffs must show:

1. The existence of a clear public policy relevant to their conduct (*clarity element*).

2 That discouraging the conduct in which they engaged would jeopardize this public policy (*jeopardy element*).

3. That engaging in conduct supportive of public policy resulted in termination (*causation element*).

Plaintiffs that establish these elements will prevail unless the defendant is able to show that there was an overriding justification for the termination (*absence of justification element*).

LLOYD V. DRAKE UNIVERSITY

686 N.W. 2d 225 (Iowa 2004)

● ● ●

OPINION BY JUSTICE STREIT:

A Drake University security guard tried to forcibly subdue a black football player at a university-sponsored street-painting event. The security guard thought the football player was assaulting a female student. The security guard's actions, which were caught on videotape, ignited a media firestorm and inflamed racial passions. He was eventually fired.

The security guard sued for wrongful discharge.... His wrongful-discharge claim was premised upon the theory that, notwithstanding our long tradition of at-will employment, it is wrong as a matter of public policy for an employer to fire a security guard simply for upholding the criminal laws of the state. Because we find the security guard's claims lack merit, we affirm the district court's dismissal of his lawsuit in its entirety. * * *

Nicholas Lloyd was a Drake University security guard on duty at the annual Drake Relays street-painting event on April 20, 2002. A student told Lloyd about an apparent altercation between Phillipe Joseph, a Drake football player, and Erin Kane. Lloyd and Kane were white; Joseph was black. Joseph was holding Kane in the air with her feet kicking. Lloyd and another security guard, Steven Smith, thought Joseph was holding Kane in a headlock. Although Kane later

claimed she and Joseph were just friends engaged in horseplay, Lloyd alleges Joseph's girlfriend called Lloyd and said Joseph had admitted to her that he and Kane were fighting. Lloyd ordered Joseph to release Kane. After Lloyd's second command, Joseph did so. Joseph suddenly made a 180-degree turn and lunged toward Lloyd with his fists raised to his chest and "an angry look on his face." Lloyd feared for his own safety and pepper sprayed Joseph. Smith reached for his pepper spray at the same time and would have sprayed Joseph if Lloyd had not done so first. Another Drake security guard, Sergeant Risvold, attempted to handcuff Joseph, but was unable to do so—Joseph was still writhing from the pepper spray. Lloyd hit Joseph on the thigh with his baton, forcing him to the ground.

Des Moines police officers took Joseph to the police station, where he was charged with disorderly conduct. Meanwhile, witnesses began screaming "racist, racist" at Lloyd. Students immediately discussed the incident with Drake's president, David Maxwell. Maxwell obtained Joseph's release and took him for medical treatment, even though he had not previously complained about any injuries resulting from the arrest. Joseph later pled guilty to disturbing the peace. He also received a settlement from Drake.

As local media reported on the street-painting episode, Lloyd's actions became the subject of a heated

controversy. After the NAACP and Black Student Coalition demanded an investigation, Drake organized a panel to study the incident and related topics. The panel concluded Lloyd had overreacted and used unnecessary force. Although the panel determined Lloyd's actions at the street-painting event were not overtly racially motivated, the panel discovered some prior complaints against Lloyd involving minority students. (Lloyd, however, points out he was never reprimanded on any of those occasions.) The panel also criticized Drake for insufficiently training its security guards and its "ambiguous philosophy for security." During the investigation, Drake assigned Lloyd to a desk job. Maxwell assured Lloyd he would not lose his job. One of Lloyd's supervisors told Lloyd he was still in line for a promotion. Nonetheless, Drake fired Lloyd from his security position on June 16, 2002. * * *

Lloyd does not dispute he was an at-will employee. As a consequence, Drake could fire him for any lawful reason, or for no reason at all. A discharge is not lawful, however, when it violates public policy. Lloyd claims Drake violated public policy and thereby committed the tort of wrongful discharge when it fired him simply for upholding the criminal laws, i.e., attempting to arrest Joseph, a man he thought was assaulting a student.

Having alleged a violation of public policy, to succeed in his wrongful-discharge claim Lloyd must thus prove:

(1) The existence of a clearly defined public policy that protects an activity.

(2) This policy would be undermined by a discharge from employment.

(3) The challenged discharge was the result of participating in the protected activity.

(4) There was lack of other justification for the termination.

The district court dismissed Lloyd's wrongful-discharge claim on causation grounds, ruling Drake had fired Lloyd for a variety of other lawful reasons, including (1) a desire to capitulate to outside pressures in the hopes of forestalling a lack of public confidence in Drake's security system; and (2) a determination—based upon newly rediscovered prior complaints and the panel's conclusion Lloyd used premature and excessive force in subduing Joseph—that Lloyd lacked the appropriate demeanor of a security guard. (On appeal, Drake also points out Lloyd's conduct affected its

relationships with a variety of constituencies, and his retention could have cost it essential financial support.) * * * We take a different route than the district court, but reach the same conclusion. * * * Even assuming Lloyd was fired simply for upholding the law, we think his claim still fails because the public policy against discharge that Lloyd asserts is neither clearly defined nor well recognized.

. . . [I]n order to prevail on his wrongful-discharge claim Lloyd must first identify a clearly defined and well-recognized public policy that would be undermined by his dismissal. To determine whether such a public policy exists, on prior occasions we have generally looked only to our statutes and state constitution. We have also recognized that other states have looked to other sources, such as judicial decisions and administrative rules. Regardless of the source, however, "we proceed cautiously *and will only extend such recognition to those policies that are well recognized and clearly defined.*" Only such policies are weighty enough "to overcome the employer's interest in operating its business in the manner it sees fit," which we have long and vigorously protected. Over the years we have recognized a number of clearly defined public policies. [The court cites Iowa cases finding public policy in favor of providing truthful testimony; reporting suspected child abuse; permitting employees to demand their wages; permitting employees to seek partial unemployment benefits; [and] permitting employees to seek workers' compensation for work-related injuries]. To date, however, we have not held that a private security guard's actions in "enforcing the criminal laws of the state" to be a well-recognized and clearly defined public policy.

Not surprisingly, Lloyd cites little authority, and his argument mostly consists of vague generalizations about the social desirability of upholding the criminal laws of the state. He draws upon our language in [a case] in which we remarked that other courts have recognized a cause of action for discharge in violation of public policy when the termination of the employee "is *in retaliation for performing an important and socially desirable act,* exercising a statutory right, or refusing to commit an unlawful act." Lloyd also points out that there need not be an express statutory prohibition against discharge to underpin the public policy. In a number of cases, we have "found an implied prohibition against retaliatory discharge based on an employee's exercise of a right conferred by a clearly articulated legislative enactment." The gist of Lloyd's argument is

that because upholding the criminal laws is important and socially desirable conduct, this court should find a public-policy exception to the at-will employment doctrine for a private security guard who tried to effectuate an arrest of a suspected criminal.

Lloyd's argument is not well taken. We have little quarrel, however, with one of the basic premises of Lloyd's argument: namely, that the criminal laws of the state reflect a general public policy against crime, and in favor of the protection of the public. That said, the public policy asserted here is far too generalized to support an argument for an exception to the at-will doctrine. In short, the public policy is not *clearly defined*. Apart from a vague reference to the whole of the criminal law, Lloyd cites no statutory or constitutional provision to buttress his claim. Divorced from any such provision or equivalent expression of public policy, we cannot find a well-recognized and clearly defined public policy in such vague generalizations. "Any effort to evaluate the public policy exception with generalized concepts of fairness and justice will result in an elimination of the at-will doctrine itself." "It could unwittingly transform the public policy exception into a 'good faith and fair dealing' exception, a standard we have repeatedly rejected."

Lloyd's best attempt at grounding his claim in a specific legal principle involves citation to a recent federal district court ruling, which references the fact that we have on prior occasions recognized a "special relationship" between peace officers and the members of the public they protect. The line of cases Lloyd refers to, however, is clearly distinguishable; these cases do not create an all-encompassing duty that would require *private* security guards to investigate crime and effect arrests whenever they have probable cause to do so. We have only recognized that peace officers owe a special duty to aid and protect those who are *in their custody.* * * *

Having found no support in our own precedents or other legal authority in this jurisdiction, we note that two other courts have rejected similar arguments. For example, the Oregon Supreme Court wrote:

> Such expressions of a public desire for law and order are far too general We are concerned here with a duty to perform a specific act (the arrest of lawbreakers by private citizens or private security personnel), and the statutes cited have nothing to say about that kind of act. . . . [The statutes] are neutral on the essential issue, which is whether the law encourages law enforcement action by private

individuals or security personnel or otherwise demonstrates that such acts enjoy high social value.

Likewise, the Maryland Court of Special Appeals, in ruling against a store security guard who was fired for investigating whether his store manager was a thief, ruled the criminal statute the employee was upholding "makes theft a crime, but does not impose on citizens a duty to investigate or report theft."

Unlike [another Iowa case], in which we held the law against perjury necessarily implies an inverse corresponding public policy to provide truthful testimony, here the inverse of the policy that the criminal laws ought not be broken is clearly *not* that everyone who sees a crime committed must actively try to stop it. In the absence of any statutory, constitutional, or other expression imposing a duty upon private security personnel to do so, we can find no origin for the well-recognized and clearly defined public policy essential to carve out an exception to the at-will employment doctrine. There is nothing, then, to sustain the tort of wrongful discharge on these facts—however encouraged or frequently beneficial it may be to have private citizens take it upon themselves to enforce the criminal laws. The point is simply this: while we might be persuaded that society would be better off if private security personnel investigated and attempted to stop crimes in progress, we are not convinced it is a clear and well-recognized public policy of this state "that we all become citizen crime fighters."

CASE QUESTIONS

1. What is the legal issue in this case? What did the court decide?

2. On what grounds had the lower court decided the case? How did the Iowa Supreme Court's analysis differ?

3. Isn't the criminal code a basic source of public policy? Why does the court say that Lloyd failed to point to a clearly defined public policy supporting his wrongful termination claim?

4. Could Lloyd have been legally terminated if he had refused to intervene in the apparent assault, and the woman or someone else complained?

5. Did the university handle this situation well? Was termination an appropriate response? Did the university overreact in response to the racially charged situation?

to use constitutions as the basis for public-policy claims. Thus, an employee of a private hospice who was allegedly fired for her speech was not able to ground a public-policy claim in the First Amendment's protection of free speech. The court stated:

> [T]he First Amendment free speech provision expresses a guarantee only against action taken by the government. * * * [It] does not sufficiently describe the type of conduct alleged here, a *private* employer terminating an employee for the exercise of free speech, to enable the employer to know the fundamental public policies expressed by the First Amendment prohibited such a termination.[27]

Lloyd's claim against Drake University failed because he was unable to convince the court that he was acting in furtherance of a clearly defined, well-recognized public policy (the "clarity element") when he was terminated. Criminal laws prohibiting assault did not create a duty for a private security guard to intervene in what he believed was a criminal act. The "jeopardy element" in a public-policy claim points to the fact that even when an employee's actions relate to a clear public policy, the employee will not be protected unless termination would tend to undermine the public policy in question. Courts will inquire into whether alternative means exist to promote the public policy. In a case involving a manager who said that he was fired for correcting an erroneous time card, the court agreed that wage and hour laws establish a clear requirement that employers maintain accurate records of work hours, but held that this public policy was adequately protected through numerous civil and criminal penalties against offending employers. Thus, the policy was not jeopardized by termination of the employee.[28] The "causation element" is common to any type of retaliation claim and would be satisfied by evidence regarding the timing of the termination and other indicators of a motive of retaliating for the action taken in support of public policy. If an employee can establish the first three elements, an employer can still prevail by showing that the termination was also motivated by another overriding factor.

Four varieties of the public policy exception to employment at will are recognized: termination for (1) refusing to commit an illegal act; (2) exercising a legal right; (3) performing a public duty; and (4) reporting illegal activity (i.e., whistle-blowing). *Employees must not be terminated for refusing to commit illegal acts, exercising their legal rights, performing important public duties, or reporting illegal activities of employers and their agents.*

The first case in which the public policy exception to employment at will was recognized involved the termination of an at-will employee for **refusal to commit an illegal act.** Employed by the Teamster's union, the man was called to testify at a state legislative hearing probing the union's activities.[29] When he refused his employer's instructions to give false testimony, he was summarily fired. Citing the state's criminal code and its prohibition of perjury, the court held that allowing the termination would undermine a public policy basic to law enforcement. Employees could be placed in the untenable position of breaking the law or losing their jobs. Other examples of successful public-policy claims based on refusal to commit illegal acts include cases where employees were fired for refusing to pollute a waterway,[30] fill a vehicle designed for unleaded gas with leaded gas,[31] and drive a vehicle without a valid

[27]*Grinzi v. San Diego Hospice,* 120 Cal. App. 4th 72, at 81 (2004).

[28]*White v. Sears, Roebuck & Co.,* 163 Ohio App. 3d 416 (2005).

[29]*Petermann v. International Brotherhood of Teamsters, Local 396,* 344 P.2d 25 (Cal. App. 1959).

[30]*Sabine Pilot Service v. Hauck,* 687 S.W.2d 733 (Tex. 1985).

[31]*Phipps v. Clark Oil & Refining Corp.,* 408 N.W.2d 569 (Minn. 1986).

inspection sticker.[32] In contrast, a nurse's public-policy claim that she was fired for refusing to backdate a Medicare form was rejected because signing a backdated form does not violate the law.[33] This was not a case of Medicare fraud. The services had, in fact, been performed, and a doctor had certified that they were necessary.

Public policy wrongful discharge claims are also recognized when employees are terminated for **exercising legal rights.** Successful claims have been raised by employees fired for such things as filing workers' compensation claims;[34] exercising their voting rights as stockholders in a manner contrary to their employer's wishes;[35] and having wages withheld (garnished) for child support.[36] However, in a troubling case, a cashier who was fired for refusing to drop assault and battery charges against her supervisor failed in her public-policy claim.[37] The supervisor had assaulted her after she made known her suspicions that he was embezzling money from their employer. The employee was terminated a few weeks before the criminal trial (in which the supervisor was convicted). The court held that laws against obstruction of justice are aimed at preserving the integrity of the criminal justice system and not at preventing intimidation of individuals. Hence, the laws did not provide a sufficient public-policy basis for a wrongful discharge claim.

The most nebulous and least often recognized variety of public-policy claims is termination for **performing a public duty.** The duty in these cases is something that is not strictly required by law (if it was, this would place it in the category of termination for refusal to act illegally), but it is clearly an action undertaken in the public interest. In an illustrative case, an employee was terminated for supplying information to the police about possible criminal activity in the plant and agreeing to assist in an investigation. The court found that even though the employee's active participation in law enforcement was not legally mandated, he had been wrongfully discharged in violation of a clear public policy favoring the investigation and prosecution of criminal offenses.[38] *Gardner v. Loomis* (see Chapter 1) is another example of this type of case. As you may recall, the court ruled for the armored car driver who left his armored car to intervene in a likely homicide, even though he had no legal obligation to do so, and he was acting contrary to a strict company policy. However, courts have been very reluctant to protect employees who "do the right thing" absent a specific legal requirement. Although the argument could be made that the security guard in the *Lloyd* case was also assisting in the enforcement of the law, the court ruled against him.

The last type of public-policy claim is termination for reporting illegal activity or **Whistleblowing.** Whistleblowers report activities engaged in by employers or their agents that are illegal or otherwise likely to be injurious to the public. The willingness of insiders to come forward is often critical to bringing corporate wrongdoing to light and enforcing the law. However, society's gratitude for this service is usually not matched by the reaction of employers. To put the matter succinctly, whistleblowers often get hammered by their employers. A high-level manager at Oracle had a successful public-policy claim when she was fired after raising questions regarding possible misappropriation of another company's trade secrets and intellectual property.[39]

[32]*Adams v. G.W. Cochran & Co.,* 597 A.2d 28 (D.C. App. 1991).

[33]*Callentine v. Staff Builders, Inc.,* 271 F.3d 1124 (8th Cir. 2001).

[34]*Taylor v. General Motors Corp.,* 826 F.2d 452 (6th Cir. 1987).

[35]*Bowman v. State Bank,* 331 S.E.2d 797 (Va. 1985).

[36]*Greely v. Miami Valley Maintenance Contractors,* 551 N.E.2d 981 (Ohio 1990).

[37]*Rowan v. Tractor Supply Co.,* 559 S.E.2d 709 (Va. 2002).

[38]*Palmateer v. International Harvester,* 421 N.E.2d 876 (Ill. 1981).

[39]*Baratta v. Oracle Corp.,* 2002 Cal. App. Unpub. LEXIS 4108.

Whether reports of wrongdoing are raised internally or externally can affect the outcome of cases. Some courts have declined to protect internal reports, viewing them as more akin to internal policy disputes than to efforts to enforce public policy (at least in the absence of threats to go public if changes are not made).[40] Other courts require that internal reports occur before employees "go outside" their organizations with their suspicions of wrongdoing.[41] In either event, the subject of the report must be a matter that truly affects the public, rather than simply an alleged violation of company policy. This distinction is sometimes not so easily drawn. Courts have differed, for example, on whether hospital employees reporting problems with patient care are merely disputing internal hospital policies or reporting problems affecting public health.[42]

Whistleblower Protection Statutes

Whistleblowers also enjoy protection under a variety of statutes. Most states have whistleblower protection laws, although some of these statutes apply only to public-sector employees. Some whistleblowers are protected under laws that pertain to specific safety-sensitive industries, including aviation and nuclear power. A variety of federal environmental laws incorporate whistleblower protections for employees reporting environmental violations by their employers. The **Sarbanes-Oxley Act**, passed in response to a wave of corporate scandals, adds to existing whistleblower protections by protecting employees of publicly traded companies (as well as officers, contractors, subcontractors, and agents of such companies) who disclose information, assist in investigations, file charges, testify, or otherwise assist in proceedings related to fraud against shareholders of publicly traded companies.[43] The case law interpreting and applying the whistleblower provisions of Sarbanes-Oxley is in the early stages of its development. *Collins v. Beazer Homes USA* is one such case.

[40]*House v. Carter-Wallace, Inc.,* 556 A.2d 353 (N.J. Super. 1989), *cert. denied,* 564 A.2d 874 (N.J. 1989).
[41]*Baratta,* at 69.
[42]*Wright v. Shriners Hospital for Crippled Children,* 589 N.E.2d 1241 (Mass. 1992) (report about patient care not protected); *Witt v. Forest Hospital,* 450 N.E.2d 811 (Ill. App. 1983) (report about patient care protected).
[43]18 U.S.C.S. § 1514A(a) (2005).

COLLINS V. BEAZER HOMES USA
334 F.Supp. 2d 1365 (N.D.Ga. 2004)

OPINION BY DISTRICT JUDGE STORY:

* * * This case arises out of Plaintiff Judy Collins' employment with and termination from Defendant Beazer Homes Corp. On May 24, 2002, . . . Beazer Homes offered Collins a position as Director of Marketing. . . . Collins would be subject to a ninety day assessment review period during which "either you or the Company may decide to terminate employment without giving a reason." Collins accepted the offer and began work around June 10, 2002.

Soon after starting with the company, Collins began having conflicts with her manager, Division President Bill Mazar, and her coworker, Director of Sales Mary Ann Hashem. Defendants state that many of these conflicts stemmed from the use of the Montello Advertising Agency ("Montello"). * * * Collins was not pleased with Montello's services and around July 11, 2002, she signed a contract with a new advertising agency. * * *

Collins believed that Mazar and Hashem continued to use Montello's services behind her back even after she had terminated the agency.

On July 30, 2002, Collins spoke with Marilyn Gardner, Vice President of Sales and Marketing for Beazer Homes about some problems in Jacksonville. Collins indicated [among other things] that she did not like how they were paying the Montello agency and did not like how marketing costs were being categorized. Gardner responded specifically to Collins' assertion that marketing costs were not being properly categorized. Gardner asked Collins whether there were any other incidents other than marketing when invoices were not being categorized properly and Collins indicated that there were. Gardner informed Collins that her concerns raised issues that were "serious allegations" and that they were "something very important" and that she needed to raise them with human resources. Gardner then arranged for Collins to meet with Jennifer Jones, Vice President of Human Resources for Beazer USA to discuss Collins' concerns. On August 5, 2002, Collins met with Jones. . . . * * * [She again complained that] they were paying Montello for bills that should not be paid and were being forced to use the agency by the President of the Jacksonville division Marty Shaffer Based on Collins' statements to Jones, Jones began to investigate Collins' claims and spoke with various company officials. Jones sought to determine whether the issues that Collins had raised were merely business issues or whether something criminal, against the law or against company policy was taking place. * * *

Regarding the payments to Montello, Jones spoke with Ian McCarthy, Chief Executive Officer of Beazer USA. McCarthy directed Jones to speak directly with Shaffer. Shaffer informed Jones that the president of Montello had called him about a past due invoice that Collins had refused to pay. Shaffer told Mazar to review the invoice, and to pay it if Beazer owed the agency money, and if not, to discuss it with Montello. Mazar reviewed the invoices from Montello and paid them. Collins states that Mazar spoke with Shaffer and then told her that Shaffer wanted her to pay Montello regardless of the amount because Shaffer and Montello's president were friends. * * *

On August 14, 2002, Collins emailed Gardner. In the four page email, Collins again expressed her frustration with the investigation and complained about Montello. She alleged that Mazar told her to pay Montello regardless of the amount, that she suspected kickbacks in lumber purchases, and that marketing costs were not being properly broken-down in order to hide information. Prior to the August 19, 2002 meeting with Collins, Shaffer discussed Collins' complaints with Jones. Jones informed Shaffer that Collins had made a series of complaints including allegations of a break in company policy. Shaffer and Jones also discussed whether they should continue Collins' employment. Shaffer questioned Jones about the circumstances under which he could terminate Collins.

On August 19, 2002, Collins met with Shaffer. Shaffer understood that one of the purposes of the meeting was for him to discuss with Collins possible violations of company policy. * * * Collins did not specifically tell Shaffer that illegal activity was taking place in the company. At the end of the meeting, Shaffer told Collins that "I don't see that this situation is going to work out between [you, Mazar and Hashem]." Shaffer noted that Mazar and Hashem had been with the company for some time, and since it did not appear that the conflict with Collins was going to end, he would have to let her go. Although Shaffer consulted with Jones regarding Collins' termination, he states that he was the sole person responsible for terminating her. Shaffer stated that he terminated Collins for several reasons including Mazar's dissatisfaction with her job performance, a presentation he viewed by Collins that was "way off the mark," but primarily because she could not get along with any of her fellow employees. * * *

Plaintiffs claims arose almost in tandem with the enactment of Sarbanes-Oxley and come before the Court as a matter of first impression. The Sarbanes-Oxley Act of 2002 was enacted on July 30, 2002. Title VIII of Sarbanes-Oxley is . . . the provision that provides "whistleblower" protection to employees of publicly traded companies. . . . [A]n employer may not discriminate against any employee in the terms and conditions of employment because of any lawful act done by the employee:

> (1) to provide information, cause information to be provided, or otherwise assist in an investigation regarding any conduct which the employee reasonably believes constitutes a violation of section 1341, 1343, 1344, or 1348 [laws dealing with various types of fraud], any rule or regulation of the Securities and Exchange Commission, or any provision of Federal law relating to fraud against shareholders, when the information or assistance is provided to or the investigation is conducted by —

(A) a Federal regulatory or law enforcement agency;

(B) any Member of Congress or any committee of Congress; or

(C) a person with supervisory authority over the employee (or such other person working for the employer who has the authority to investigate, discover, or terminate misconduct)

* * * Before an employee may file in federal court, she must file a complaint with the Occupational Safety and Health Administration within ninety days of the date on which the violation occurred. The Regulations governing OSHA's handling of discrimination complaints under Sarbanes-Oxley provide for an investigation, a hearing before an administrative law judge, a review by an administrative review board, and an appeal to the Circuit Court of Appeals. * * * If a final administrative decision is not issued within 180 days of the filing of the complaint and "there is no showing that such delay is due to the bad faith of the claimant," an employee may bring an action . . . in federal court. * * * In this case, Plaintiff was terminated on August 19, 2002. She filed her complaint with OSHA in October 2002, within the required ninety day time period. OSHA did not issue its findings until May 22, 2003. * * * Because OSHA failed to issue findings within 180 days and there was no showing of bad faith, jurisdiction in this case is proper. * * *

[A] plaintiff in federal court must show by a preponderance of the evidence that the plaintiff's protected activity was a contributing factor in the unfavorable personnel action alleged in the complaint. That is, the plaintiff must show by a preponderance of the evidence that (1) she engaged in protected activity; (2) the employer knew of the protected activity; (3) she suffered an unfavorable personnel action; and (4) circumstances exist to suggest that the protected activity was a contributing factor to the unfavorable action. Proximity in time is sufficient to raise an inference of causation. The defendant employer may avoid liability if it can demonstrate by clear and convincing evidence that it "would have taken the same unfavorable personnel action in the absence of [protected] behavior." * * *

[A] plaintiff is not required to show an actual violation of the law, but only that she "reasonably believed" that there was a violation of one of the enumerated laws or regulations. * * * Defendants assert that Plaintiff did not engage in protected activity because she never specifically alleged securities or accounting fraud

and because her complaints were too vague to constitute protected activity. Defendants contrast the type of disclosures made by Sherron Watkins, the former Enron Vice President, to the disclosures made by Plaintiff. Defendants point out that Watkins was an accountant whose job it was to review Enron's securities, that she outlined specific accounting procedures and transactions about which she was concerned, and that she expressed concerns that specific securities laws were being violated. By contrast, Defendants contend, Plaintiff was the Director of Marketing who expressed only vague concerns that amounted to nothing more than personality conflicts and differences in marketing strategies.

Plaintiff points to four specific disclosures which she made that she alleges are within the coverage of Sarbanes-Oxley. Plaintiff states that (1) she alleged that the division was knowingly overpaying invoices to Montello; (2) the division was using Montello because of a personal relationship between management and Montello; (3) Hashem was violating the division's commissions scheme by overpaying sales agents who were her personal friends; and (4) there were kickbacks involving the purchase of lumber. Plaintiff contends that these disclosures are protected because they allege attempts to circumvent the company's system of internal accounting controls and therefore state a violation of Section 13 of the Exchange Act.

The Court finds that Defendants cannot establish as a matter of law that Plaintiff did not engage in protected activity under Sarbanes-Oxley. * * * It is evident that Plaintiff's complaints do not rise to the level of complaints that were raised by Sherron Watkins at Enron. However, the mere fact that the severity or specificity of her complaints does not rise to the level of action that would spur Congress to draft legislation does not mean that the legislation it did draft was not meant to protect her. In short, if Congress had intended to limit the protection of Sarbanes-Oxley to accountants, or to have required complainants to specifically identify the code section that they believe was being violated, it could have done so. It did not. Congress instead protected "employees" and adopted the "reasonable belief standard for those who "blow the whistle on fraud and protect investors." Additionally, though Defendants contend that Plaintiff's complaints were too vague to constitute protected activity, the individuals to whom they were addressed understood the serious nature of Plaintiff's allegations. * * * The Court agrees with Defendants that the connection of Plaintiff's complaints to the substantive law protected in

Sarbanes-Oxley is less than direct. However, Plaintiff's allegations detailed violations of the company's internal accounting controls in favor of preferential treatment based on personal relationships. * * *

Sarbanes-Oxley protects employees who provide information to any "person with supervisory authority over the employee (or such other person working for the employer who has the authority to investigate, discover, or terminate misconduct)." Plaintiff made numerous complaints to her supervisors, including complaints to Gardner, a meeting with Jones, an email to Gardner, an email to McCarthy and her final meeting with Shaffer. Defendants do not contest that they were aware of Plaintiff's complaints. Defendants, however, assert that Shaffer was the sole decision maker in Plaintiff's termination and that he did not know of Plaintiff's letters to Gardner and McCarthy. Shaffer did, however, discuss Plaintiff with Jones including Plaintiff's series of complaints, discussion of payment of the Montello invoices, and the circumstances in which it would be acceptable for him to terminate her. To permit an employer to simply bring in a manager to be the "sole decisionmaker" for the purpose of terminating a complainant would eviscerate the protection afforded to employees by Sarbanes-Oxley. The Court finds that Defendants were aware of Plaintiff's protected activity.

Plaintiff suffered an unfavorable personnel action when she was terminated on August 19, 2002. * * * Plaintiff must also establish that there are circumstances which suggest that the protected activity was a contributing factor to the unfavorable action. Defendants contend that Plaintiff cannot establish the causal connection because the person responsible for firing her, Shaffer, was not aware of Plaintiff's letters to McCarthy and Gardner and because she did not bring any illegal activities to Shaffer's attention. Defendants further state that temporal proximity is not sufficient to create circumstances to suggest causation. Plaintiff responds that Shaffer was in fact aware of prior complaints that she made alleging violations of company policy and that the fact that she was fired fourteen days after complaining to Jones establishes the circumstances sufficient to demonstrate causation. The Court finds that the temporal proximity between the time when Plaintiff made her complaints and the time she was terminated is sufficient to establish circumstances which suggest that protected activity was a contributing factor to the unfavorable personnel action. * * * Here, Plaintiff first complained to Jones on August 5, 2002 and was terminated fourteen days later on August 19, 2002. Therefore, the proximity in time provides the

circumstances to suggest that the protected activity was a contributing factor to the unfavorable personnel action. Moreover, it is clear that Shaffer had discussed Plaintiff's complaints with Jones and was aware that she had complained about violations of company policy when he terminated her. * * *

Only if Defendants can establish by clear and convincing evidence that they would have fired Plaintiff absent her participation in protected activity, would Defendants be entitled to summary judgment. Defendants argue that Shaffer was the sole decision maker with regard to Plaintiffs termination and that she was terminated for three reasons: (1) personality conflicts with her co-worker and manager; (2) Mazar's dissatisfaction with her; and (3) Shaffer's belief that Plaintiff had made a presentation that was "way off the mark." The Court finds that Defendants have not established by clear and convincing evidence as a matter of law that they would have terminated Plaintiff even absent her protected activity. * * * While Plaintiff does admit that there was a conflict among the three of them, Mazar stated that he did not believe he had a personality conflict with Plaintiff. Mazar stated that he had discussed some concerns about Plaintiff's job performance with Shaffer, but he had not yet made the decision to terminate her and was planning to meet with her to discuss the problems. * * * Defendants in their representations to OSHA indicated that reasons for Plaintiff's termination were her "discontent with her job" and her "extreme unhappiness" with the company. It is evident that Plaintiff made numerous complaints to her supervisors, many of which would not constitute protected activity under Sarbanes-Oxley. To allow Defendants to obtain summary judgment by singling out these complaints and insisting that only unprotected complaints were the basis for their action against Plaintiff would thwart the purpose of Sarbanes-Oxley. Again, whether Defendants would have terminated Plaintiff absent her protected activity presents a close question. It appears that she got off on the wrong foot with some of her co-workers from the very beginning, and that her supervisors had some concerns about her ability to adapt to the home building industry. It also appears that Mazar thought she did a good job with respect to Internet marketing and the hiring of the new marketing firm, an area of purported dispute. Though Defendants emphasize that Plaintiff was in her ninety day assessment period, the short history of Plaintiff's employment only makes it more difficult to discern whether the problems that Plaintiff had would have ultimately resulted in her termination absent participation in protected activity

or whether they would have simply been addressed and resolved. Because there is a genuine issue of material fact whether Defendants have established by clear and convincing evidence that they would have fired Plaintiff absent her protected activity, Defendants are not entitled to judgment as a matter of law.

CASE QUESTIONS

1. What was the legal issue in this case? What did the court decide?

2. What does the court mean when it says that this is a case of "first impression?" Does the court seem

to be giving a narrow or relatively broad reading to Sarbanes-Oxley?

3. What actions are protected under the whistle-blower provisions of Sarbanes-Oxley? Did this employee's actions fall within the law's protection?

4. What is the evidence that Collins was discharged for engaging in protected activity?

5. Because Collins had signed an agreement stipulating that her employment could be terminated within the first 90 days "without giving a reason," why is she able to take her wrongful termination case to court?

Federal government employees are covered by the federal **Whistleblower Protection Act** (WPA).[44] The WPA prohibits taking or failing to take a personnel action because an employee or applicant has disclosed information that is reasonably believed to show (1) a violation of a law, rule, or regulation; or (2) gross mismanagement, gross waste of funds, abuse of authority, or a substantial and specific danger to public health or safety. The definition of protected reports is relatively broad under the WPA because the "internal" affairs of federal government agencies nonetheless concern the public. The act's prohibition against retaliation is also broad, extending to decisions to order psychiatric testing and "any other significant change in duties, responsibilities, or working conditions." Not all disclosures relating to these matters trigger the WPA, however. Reports made to a supervisor about the supervisor's own conduct or those made through normal channels as part of an employees' job responsibilities are not covered. On the other hand, complaints made to a supervisor about other employees' misconduct are protected reports.[45] Despite the apparent breadth of the WPA, the federal appeals court hearing these cases has almost always ruled against plaintiffs.[46]

One other federal whistleblower law deserves mention. The **False Claims Act**[47] applies to individuals who come forth with information about a knowingly false or fraudulent claim made against the federal government. The law allows the Department of Justice to join in suits to recover the amounts lost through fraud or for individuals to sue on behalf of the government. Because these cases often involve large amounts of money (e.g., defense contracts, Medicare payments to hospitals) and the act allows recovery of three times the actual damages to the government—with 15 percent to 30 percent going to the individual initiating the action—whistleblowing under the False Claims Act can be lucrative. The False Claims Act suit filed by the former accountant (see "Clippings") involved more than a billion dollars fraudulently charged to the Medicare program by the largest commercial hospital chain in the United States. The False Claims Act also protects employees against retaliation based on their investigating or otherwise pursuing actions intended to uncover fraud

[44]5 U.S.C.S. § 2302 (2005).

[45]*Huffman v. Office of Personnel Management,* 263 F.3d 1341 (D.C. Cir. 2001).

[46]David Cay Johnston. "Court Says Ex-I.R.S. Employee Deserves Whistle-Blower Status." *New York Times* (September 2, 2004), C-4.

[47]U.S.C.S. §§ 3729–3730 (2005).

against the federal government. Employees whose normal job responsibilities include making reports to their employers about issues that are the subject of whistle-blower claims must show that their actions went beyond just doing their jobs. A chief contract negotiator for a defense contractor was protected under the False Claims Act when he was suspended shortly after he told the Navy to "continue to challenge" the contractor's cost data.[48]

Rather than retaliate against the bearers of bad news, *employers should provide employees with a credible internal procedure for reporting suspected wrongdoing by the company or its agents. Reports of wrongdoing should be investigated, and employees should not be punished for making such reports.*

Civic Duty Laws A number of statutes protect employees against discharge for engaging in specific civic duties. One of these is jury service. Under the Jury System Improvements Act,[49] permanent employees are protected from termination because of their service on federal court juries. Most states have similar laws covering employees who serve on state court juries. Another important civic duty is military service. The extensive reinstatement rights of veterans under the Uniformed Services Employment and Reemployment Rights Act (USERRA) were discussed in Chapter 11. A significant addition to these rights is that *uniformed services members who are reinstated cannot be terminated without cause for specified periods of time.* In the case of employees who serve in the military for between 30 and 180 days prior to reinstatement, any termination must be for cause for a period of 180 days. If the military service is for more than 180 days, the period during which termination is limited is a year.[50] An employee who was downsized four months after returning from active duty had a successful USERRA claim. Although the company was losing money and had laid off large numbers of employees, his termination was not "for cause" because he was given a position with less responsibility following his deployment (another violation) and thereby disadvantaged when his performance was compared to that of other employees.[51] Clearly, reinstatement following leave for military service needs to be genuine.

Antiretaliation and Noninterference Provisions of Other Laws Most of the statutes discussed throughout this book contain protections against retaliation. These include Title VII of the Civil Rights Act, Fair Labor Standards Act (FLSA), Occupational Safety and Health Act (OSH Act), National Labor Relations Act (NLRA), Employee Retirement Income Security Act (ERISA), and the Family and Medical Leave Act (FMLA). Employees who file charges, give testimony, and take other actions involved in the enforcement of these laws are protected from all forms of retaliation, including discharge. Under the OSH Act, protection against retaliation extends to situations where employees refuse work that presents an imminent threat of injury or death. The message is simple: *Employers must not terminate employees because they have filed charges, given testimony, or otherwise participated in the enforcement of employment laws.*

Several statutes also prohibit terminations that have the effect of interfering with or restraining employees in the exercise of their statutory rights. For example, it violates the FMLA to "interfere with, restrain, or deny the exercise of" any rights provided by the act. Termination of an employee for requesting or taking leave

[48]*United States of America, ex rel. Williams v. Martin-Baker Aircraft*, 389 F.3d 1251 (D.C. Cir. 2004).

[49]28 U.S.C.S. § 1875 (2005).

[50]U.S.C.S. § 4316(c) (2005).

[51]*Duarte v. Agilent Technologies*, 366 F. Supp. 2d 1039 (D. Co. 2005).

violates the FMLA. Thus, a law that is ostensibly about leave nonetheless confers a right not to be terminated at will under certain circumstances. Does this mean that employees taking family and medical leave are immune from discharge? After all, a basic FMLA right is restoration from leave. Courts have dealt with this issue by holding that employees who take FMLA leave acquire no greater right to retain their jobs than they would have enjoyed had they not taken leave. They can still be terminated, provided that the termination is not motivated by their taking of FMLA leave. Thus, the FMLA was not violated when a nurse who was experiencing psychological problems and who continued to act in an aberrant fashion while on leave for her condition was terminated.[52] In contrast, an employer's attempt to argue that an employee had been "restored" because he was brought back to work for a day before he was terminated failed.[53] In addition to the suspicious timing of his termination on the heels of taking leave, the court also pointed to inconsistent performance standards (other employees were not warned about failures to complete paperwork) and statements made by managers about the inconvenient timing of his leave as evidence sufficient to warrant a trial. Thus, although taking FMLA leave does not shield employees from adverse employment actions that would have occurred anyway, it creates another exception to employment at will, and places employers in the position of having to account for terminations of leave takers. *Employers should be especially careful in terminating employees who are on FMLA leave or have recently returned from leave and must not terminate them because they have taken leave.*

Off-Duty Conduct Laws Most employees believe that their personal lives off the job are none of their employer's business and certainly not something that should affect their employment status. Alas, the legal reality is much different. About half of all states have off-duty conduct laws on the books. However, the reach of these laws is limited. Most of the statutes protect employees only for their use of tobacco and other lawful products when off the job. In states with these laws, smokers cannot be refused hire, terminated, or otherwise discriminated against (although they need not be allowed to smoke in the workplace). Elsewhere, it is legal for employers to discriminate against smokers if they so choose. One of the broadest off-duty conduct laws is New York's. This statute protects against discrimination for using lawful products and for engaging in union activity, political activity, and lawful recreational activity. However, "lawful recreational activity" does not reach romantic relationships and dating. Two employees fired for violating their employer's policy against married employees dating employees to whom they are not married were unsuccessful in pursuing claims for wrongful discharge under New York's off-duty conduct law.[54] A subsequent case in which both parties were unmarried, and there was no policy regarding fraternization had the same outcome.[55]

Discriminatory Termination

Terminations influenced by the protected class characteristics of employees, no less than any other adverse employment decisions, are discriminatory disparate treatment. Discriminatory discharge cases present fundamentally the same issues as other discrimination cases. However, some modifications are required to apply the methodology for analyzing disparate treatment cases to discharges.

[52]*Throneberry v. McGehee Desha County Hospital,* 403 F.3d 972 (8th Cir. 2005).

[53]*Snelling v. Clarian Health Partners,* 184 F. Supp. 2d 838, at 847 (S.D. Ind. 2002).

[54]*State v. Wal-Mart Stores,* 1995 N.Y. App. Div. LEXIS 17.

[55]*McCavitt v. Swiss Reinsurance America Corp.,* 237 F.3d 166 (2d Cir. 2001).

ELEMENTS OF A CLAIM

Disparate Treatment in Termination

To establish a prima facie case of discriminatory discharge, plaintiffs must show:

1. The protected class characteristic(s) relevant to the case.

2. Up to the point of the termination, the employee had been meeting the employer's legitimate performance expectations.

3. The employee was terminated (formally or constructively).

4. The employer sought a replacement or hired one with contrasting class characteristics, or

5. A person with different protected class characteristics engaged in similar conduct, but was not terminated.

If a prima facie case is established, the case is analyzed like other pretext cases with the employer needing to articulate a nondiscriminatory reason for the termination, and the plaintiff having the opportunity to show that the articulated rationale is pretext and that the decision was more likely motivated by discrimination.

Inconsistency in applying disciplinary rules is frequently an issue in discriminatory discharge cases. An African-American employee was terminated for violating a store's "progressive discipline policy" by being written up three times for cash discrepancies. She was the only employee suspended or terminated for violating the policy, even though at least 16 other cashiers, most of them white, had enough discrepancies to warrant suspension or termination under the policy. Even taking account of a change in management, the store could not show that it had been consistent in enforcing the policy and that the alleged violation was not a pretext for race discrimination. Thus, the employee's case was allowed to go to trial.[56]

Courts differ in terms of how strictly comparable the situations of employees must be to show that they are sufficiently **similarly situated** to serve as evidence of disparate treatment. In one case, a lieutenant who worked at a correctional facility was terminated after he was arrested and charged with felony assault in the off-duty stabbing of another person at a bar (the charges were later dismissed). The lieutenant, a Latino, contended that he had been treated more harshly than other, non-Latino employees who had gotten into scrapes with the law. A jury, instructed by the trial court judge that the "quantity and quality of the other employees' misconduct must be of comparable seriousness to the misconduct of the plaintiff" to show that they were similarly situated, found for the plaintiff in his disparate treatment claim.[57] An appeals court vacated the decision on the grounds that the employees' circumstances must be "nearly identical" to conclude that they are similarly situated. There were circumstances that differentiated the employees in question, including that the plaintiff had refused to explain his actions to investigators and that his was the only case involving a formal Internal Affairs investigation.[58] Not all courts set the "bar" so high, and some differentiate between what must be shown to establish

[56]*Curry v. Menard*, 270 F.3d 473 (7th Cir. 2001).

[57]*Perez v. Texas Department of Criminal Justice, Institutional Division*, 395 F.3d 206, at 212 (5th Cir. 2004); *cert. denied*, 2005 U.S. LEXIS 7862.

[58]*Perez*, at 214.

a prima facie case and what must be shown to establish pretext. Thus, in the case of an African-American bank teller, the court found that she had established a prima facie case by showing that she was involved in or accused of conduct similar to that engaged in by employees of other races (violating a bank rule against conducting transactions on a teller's own account), but disciplined more harshly (she was fired and a white employee received no discipline). However, she was ultimately unsuccessful in establishing pretext because she could not show that she and the other employee were similarly situated in "all relevant respects." Her offense had involved a much larger sum of money, there were multiple questionable transactions rather than only one, and the white teller had attempted to immediately correct the mistake that she had made.[59]

Although it can be difficult for plaintiffs to prove discrimination by showing that they were disciplined more harshly than other, similarly situated employees, consistent, even-handed treatment is still the goal. *One of the best ways to avoid discriminatory terminations is to enforce policies in a consistent manner, treating like situations in a like manner, regardless of the individuals involved.*

JUST CAUSE/DUE PROCESS

Employees regularly over-estimate their rights in the workplace, particularly when it comes to terminations. Commonly, employees believe that they have the legal right to not be fired without good reason.[60] We have seen that such is not the case for the vast majority of the workforce. Nonunion, private-sector employees can be terminated for any reason that is not specifically illegal and using whatever decision process the employer deems appropriate. However, some segments of the workforce enjoy much greater protection against wrongful termination than is available under employment at will with exceptions. Broadly speaking, terminations of employees who are unionized, work for government agencies, reside in Montana, or have individual contracts of employment must meet a just cause/due process standard. Under this standard, employers bear the burden of showing that they had good reasons for their termination decisions and followed reasonable procedures.

Unionized Employees

The distinct legal status of unionized employees derives first and foremost from language in labor agreements that limits discipline and discharge to situations in which there is "just cause." Labor agreements almost universally provide for grievance procedures to challenge discipline and discharge (and other employer decisions), with arbitration of grievances that are not otherwise resolved. Arbitrators are typically given broad authority. If an arbitrator decides that a discharge was not for just cause, the arbitrator can overturn the decision entirely or modify it to provide for a lesser penalty. The arbitrator hearing the cases of the basketball players given lengthy suspensions for brawling with spectators in the stands upheld the discipline administered by the NBA commissioner in three of the cases and shortened the suspension of another player (see "Clippings"). A court subsequently upheld the arbitrator's authority to do so.[61]

[59]*Rodgers v. U.S. Bank, N.A.,* 417 F.3d 845 (8th Cir. 2005).

[60]Pauline T. Kim. "Bargaining with Imperfect Information: A Study of Worker Perceptions of Legal Protection in an At-Will World." *Cornell Law Review* 83 (November 1997), 105 at 133–34.

[61]*National Basketball Association v. National Basketball Players Association,* 2004 U.S. Dist. LEXIS 26244.

Just cause is clearly a central concept in understanding the legal rights of unionized employees. But what does just cause actually mean? Arbitrators consider the following factors to determine whether employers had **just cause** for discipline or discharge:

- Was there a rule or standard prohibiting the behavior engaged in by the employee?
- Was the rule or standard clearly communicated to employees?
- Is the rule or standard a reasonable one, related to efficiency and safe operation?
- Has the rule or standard been consistently enforced?
- Was the employee afforded due process?
- Is there sufficient proof that a rule or standard was violated?
- Was progressive discipline applied?
- Was the discipline commensurate with the offense?
- Are there any mitigating factors that call for imposition of a lesser penalty?

Arbitrators are concerned that employees have prior notice that their behavior will subject them to discipline or discharge. Typically, this requires that unionized employers *establish rules, standards, and policies, and communicate these to employees.* This does not apply if the behavior in question is something that any reasonable person would know is wrong. For example, an employee who sprays the office with an AK-47 cannot benefit from the absence of an explicit rule prohibiting the strafing of coworkers with high-powered weapons. However, an arbitrator overturned discipline imposed by the Federal Aviation Administration on a group of air traffic controllers for taking extended breaks (sometimes lasting four hours or more) in their cars during work time because the agency had no rules about breaks, the breaks were taken during periods when air traffic was slow, and supervisors tacitly condoned the breaks.[62] *Rules can be communicated to employees through such means as postings, memos, warnings, and inclusion in labor agreements.*

Policies become real and enforceable not merely by being formalized and communicated in some fashion to employees, but more importantly, by being consistently enforced. *Enforcement of rules must be consistent across both time and different individuals engaging in the same conduct.* Unionized employers cannot decide to "get tough" all of a sudden and make an example of a particular employee when violations of the same rule have been ignored in the past or subjected to only lax enforcement. *Unionized employees must clearly communicate changes in policies before attempting to enforce new, more stringent, standards.* Nor are arbitrators likely to uphold harsh discipline meted out to one employee when other employees committing the same offense at the same time are treated more leniently. The discrimination in such cases need not be along protected class lines; it is enough that one individual is treated differently than others without good reason, regardless of whether his race or sex are the same as those who benefited from leniency.

Although employers have the right to establish rules and these rules are entitled to deference, arbitrators ask whether challenged disciplinary actions are based on reasonable rules related to efficiency, safety, and other important business purposes. Discipline for off-duty conduct sometimes fails this test of reasonableness. In general, arbitrators do not uphold discharges for off-the-job activities unless the misconduct renders the employee unable to perform his job properly (e.g., the employee is

[62]*Federal Aviation Administration, Denver Air Route Traffic Control Center,* 99 L.A. 929 (Corbett 1992).

shunned by coworkers) or has an adverse effect on the employer's business (e.g., harm to the employer's reputation). For example, the termination of an LPN after she pled guilty to shoplifting was reduced to a suspension. In concluding that the employer suffered little harm, the arbitrator relied on the facts that a newspaper account of the incident did not identify the individual as an employee of the hospital, the infraction was a misdemeanor, and shoplifting had little relationship to the job of LPN.[63] Similarly, an employee was reinstated (without back pay), despite having pled guilty to six, off-the-job assaults within a 16-month period. The arbitrator noted that the employee had virtually no contact with the public (he was a relief "coal man" at a power plant), the assaults had not been widely publicized, and the employee was having problems with alcohol and drug addiction for which he subsequently received treatment.[64] In contrast, an arbitrator upheld the termination of a hotel employee who stole four car tires from a service station and served five days in jail for the offense. Even though media coverage was minimal and did not mention the hotel, the employee's job was cleaning air conditioner filters, which meant that he had unsupervised access to guests' rooms and possessions. Given the degree of trust needed to perform his job, it was reasonable for the employer to conclude that the theft rendered him unqualified to perform his job. Additionally, the employer had consistently terminated employees found guilty of off-duty theft.[65]

Grievance procedures and arbitration provide for substantial **due process** following termination. However, arbitrators typically require that elements of due process be present before termination decisions are made as well. *Unionized employers must adequately investigate alleged misconduct, notify employees of charges against them, provide employees with a chance to respond to those charges, and respect the Weingarten rights of employees* (to have union representatives present at meetings likely to result in the imposition of discipline). The aim is to ensure a careful, deliberative process and avoid any "rush to judgment."

To have just cause, the investigation must produce sufficient evidence that the accused employee is actually guilty of wrongdoing. The employer bears the burden of proving a violation. In arbitration, it is not enough that the employer reasonably believed a violation occurred or that the employer was not motivated by unlawful factors in reaching that conclusion; arbitrators will assess an employer's case to determine whether there is sufficient evidence of guilt. There is no single standard for what is "sufficient." Sometimes the standard is a "preponderance of the evidence" (overall, does the evidence weigh in the direction of innocence or guilt?). Other times, arbitrators require "clear and convincing" evidence of guilt; and, in some cases, evidence is required that establishes guilt "beyond a reasonable doubt." The more stringent standards tend to be used when the alleged offense involves criminal activity or acts of moral turpitude, such that termination on these grounds would seriously impair an employee's ability to obtain future employment.

Arbitrators view discipline as corrective, rather than punitive. Although some offenses are so serious that they warrant termination following a single occurrence (e.g., assaults, theft), arbitrators generally expect to see **progressive discipline.** That is, the first instance of a violation is met with a warning or other relatively mild discipline. Subsequent offenses result in progressively more severe discipline and, if the undesirable conduct continues, discharge. The aim is to provide employees with

[63]*Fairmont General Hospital*, 91 L.A. 930 (Hunter, 1988).

[64]*Iowa Public Service Company*, 95 L.A. 319 (Murphy, 1990).

[65]*CSX Hotels, Inc., d/b/a The Greenbrier*, 93 L.A. 1037 (Zobrak, 1989).

the chance to learn what is expected of them and to alter their conduct accordingly. *Unionized employers should generally use progressive discipline. Progressive discipline entails a genuine effort to correct undesirable behavior, not just going through the motions and creating a paper trail before terminating an employee.*

Arbitrators are also concerned that the "punishment fits the crime." An employee might be guilty of violating a rule, but if the penalty of discharge is disproportionate to the nature of the offense, a lesser penalty might be ordered. Lastly, *mitigating factors are considered when imposing discipline.* Mitigating factors do not affect the finding that an employee did something wrong, but can call for a reduction in the severity of the discipline imposed. Arbitrators are empowered to reduce the penalties given offenders when they conclude that these penalties are excessive, but they are not free to substitute their own preference for leniency in the face of otherwise appropriate penalties. Potentially mitigating factors include the employee's past record (e.g., clean or multiple prior infractions), length of service, compelling personal or medical problems that might explain aberrant behavior, and situational factors (e.g., if the employee was in a fight, did he instigate it or engage in self-defense?). The especially lengthy suspension given to Ron Artest for his involvement in the fracas with fans in Detroit was based on Artest's role in precipitating the incident and several prior suspensions he had received (see "Clippings").

Arbitrators do not apply these criteria in a mechanical fashion or insist that every single factor clearly support an employer's position before upholding a termination. However, *unionized employers should carefully consider these just cause factors when making discharge decisions.* These criteria provide excellent guidance for making reasonable and legally defensible termination decisions. Unionized employers that fail to substantially meet these criteria can expect that their termination decisions will be challenged and most likely not upheld in arbitration.

Public Employees

A number of legal protections converge to generally remove public employees from employment at will. For one thing, public employees are far more likely than private-sector employees to have union representation and to be protected by just cause language in labor agreements. Unique to public employees are statutory protections under civil service and tenure laws and constitutional protections generally requiring due process and regard for speech and associational rights.

Civil Service and Tenure Laws

Most cities, counties, and states—as well as the federal government—have **civil service laws** that are intended to ensure that the merit principle, and not political patronage, guides employment decisions. Besides specifying job classification, testing, hiring, and promotion procedures for public employment, civil service laws usually incorporate processes for review of disciplinary decisions. Often, civil service laws provide that nonprobationary employees can be terminated only for cause. The Civil Service Reform Act covers most federal government employees. Disciplinary actions, including terminations, can be appealed to the Merit Systems Protection Board (MSPB). The federal agency imposing the discipline bears the burden of showing, by the preponderance of evidence, that the alleged misconduct actually occurred and that the penalty is reasonable in light of the severity of the offense.

Teachers and professors in public schools and universities sometimes enjoy the protection of tenure laws. In private schools, tenure systems are matters of policy and contract, rather than law. **Tenure** is typically conferred following a relatively lengthy

probationary period and a formal assessment of past and likely future performance. Tenure is not an absolute guarantee of a job for life. Even when tenure is provided for by law, the employment of tenured faculty can be terminated due to financial exigencies or serious misconduct. Tenure recognizes some unique facts of academic life. The freedom to raise questions, express controversial or unpopular ideas, examine chosen research topics, and pursue the truth wherever it leads are central to the purposes of academia. Absent the institution of tenure, faculty would feel less able to do these things. At a time when schools, both public and private, are chasing every dollar that can be wrung out of private sources, the potential for the free exchange of ideas to be inhibited (e.g., "Don't say anything critical of Company X; the CEO is contributing millions for a new business school") is all the more real.

Constitutional Protections

The U.S. Constitution protects public employees from wrongful termination in two ways. The Fifth and Fourteenth amendments generally require that public employees be provided with due process before being deprived of their employment. Public employees also have substantive constitutional rights under the First Amendment—freedom of religion, speech, association—that can be invoked when a termination or other discipline is used to suppress those rights.

Property and Liberty Interests in the Job—Due Process The U.S. Constitution requires that due process be provided before the government can deprive individuals of property rights. The Fourteenth Amendment says, in part, that states shall not "deprive any person of life, liberty, or property without due process of law." The Fifth Amendment places the same restriction on the federal government. Most, but not all (e.g., probationary and temporary employees), public employees can be said to hold a **property interest** in their jobs. The existence of a property interest is defined by state laws, government agency employment policies, and express or implied contracts. The Supreme Court has considered the nature of the due process to which public employees with a property interest in their jobs are entitled prior to termination. Although a *pre-termination* hearing "need not be elaborate" (assuming that a fuller, *post-termination* hearing will be available), the public employee is still "entitled to oral or written notice of the charges against him, an explanation of the employer's evidence, and an opportunity to present his side of the story" prior to discharge.[66] This preliminary due process serves as "an initial check against mistaken decisions."

What about discipline short of termination? A relevant case involved a university police officer who was immediately suspended after being arrested on a felony drug charge.[67] Even though the criminal charges were dropped within several days, the university continued its own investigation and did not hold a meeting with the suspended police officer until almost a month after his suspension. At that meeting, he was not informed of evidence against him. Within a week, he was demoted to a groundskeeper position. The Supreme Court distinguished between the finality of terminations and the "relatively insubstantial" loss to temporarily suspended employees in holding that there is no constitutional obligation to provide suspended employees with presuspension hearings. The Court also emphasized that due process is a flexible concept. The process that is constitutionally due depends on weighing

[66]*Cleveland Board of Education v. Loudermill*, 470 U.S. 532, at 545–46 (1985).

[67]*Gilbert v. Homar*, 520 U.S. 924 (1997).

the significance of the employee interests at stake, the risk of wrongly depriving employees of their rights, the value of additional procedural safeguards, and the interests of the government as an employer. However, although the Court concluded that no presuspension hearing was required, it remanded the campus police officer's case for further consideration of whether the still necessary postsuspension hearing was needlessly delayed.

Public employees are also sometimes deemed to have a **liberty interest** that is jeopardized through termination. The focus of this liberty interest is on maintaining the employee's good name. The charges that are the basis for termination must be stigmatizing (e.g., theft, drug use), false, and made public without a meaningful opportunity for the employee to clear his name.[68] If so, the employee is entitled to due process in the form of an opportunity to establish the falsity of the charges.

In general, public employers are responsible for affording their employees due process, both pretermination and posttermination. Prior to termination, a hearing must be held that provides public employees with notice of the charges against them, explanation of the evidence, and opportunity to present their side of the story. Following termination, a more elaborate hearing with opportunities to confront witnesses and present evidence is required if requested by terminated employees.

Substantive Constitutional Rights—Speech and Associations

Public employees, like other citizens, have rights under the **First Amendment** concerning the manner in which they are treated by the government. These rights include freedom of religion, speech, and association. Terminating or otherwise disciplining employees for exercising these rights is unconstitutional. But because the relationship between the government and individual citizens is different from that between government agencies and their employees, a more delicate balancing of constitutional rights and the government's prerogatives as an employer is required in the latter situation. The government employer's interests in efficient and effective operations provide less room for the play of constitutional rights, but do not completely override those rights.

Pappas v. Giuliani considers the constitutional speech rights of a public employee fired for mailing racist propaganda.

[68]*Wells v. Doland*, 711 F.2d 670, at 676 (5th Cir. 1983).

PAPPAS V. GIULIANI
290 F.3d 143 (2d Cir. 2002); *cert. denied,* 123 S. Ct. 2642 (2003)

OPINION BY CIRCUIT JUDGE LEVAL:

This appeal raises the question whether a municipal police department may, without violating the First Amendment's guarantee of freedom of speech, terminate a police officer by reason of the officer's anonymous dissemination of bigoted racist anti-black and anti-semitic materials. Appellant Thomas Pappas brought this suit . . . against officials of the City of New York and the New York City Police Department (NYPD) alleging that he was unconstitutionally fired from his employment by the police department by reason of his exercising rights of free speech protected by the First Amendment. The United States District Court . . . granted the defendants' motion for summary judgment. We affirm the district court.

Pappas was employed by the New York City Police Department (NYPD) from January 25, 1982 until his termination on August 18, 1999. At the time of his

termination, Pappas worked in the Department's Management Information Systems Division (MISD), which was responsible for maintenance of its computer systems.

On at least two occasions in 1996 and 1997, Pappas received letters from the Mineola Auxiliary Police Department (MAPD) soliciting charitable contributions and enclosing reply envelopes for use in sending contributions. Pappas stuffed the reply envelopes with offensive racially bigoted materials and returned them anonymously. The materials included printed fliers conveying anti-black and anti-semitic messages. The fliers asserted white supremacy, ridiculed black people and their culture, warned against the "Negro wolf . . . destroying American civilization with rape, robbery, and murder," and declaimed against "how the Jews control the TV networks and why they should be in the hands of the American public and not the Jews."

Upon receipt of these materials, the Nassau County Police Department then undertook an investigation in the hope of identifying the sender. * * * The Nassau County Police Department traced the source to . . . a post office box registered under the name "Thomas Pappas/The Populist Party for the Town of North Hempstead." Upon ascertaining that Thomas Pappas was a New York City police officer, the Nassau County Police Department notified the New York City Police Department's Internal Affairs Bureau (IAB), which repeated the investigative experiment, sending Pappas further charitable solicitation mailings, once again with the result that Pappas returned the reply envelopes stuffed with similarly provocative materials. * * *

. . . Pappas's conduct and the subsequent investigation had been the subject of news media reports. Commissioner Martinez issued a 20-page decision, finding Pappas guilty of violating a Departmental Regulation by disseminating defamatory materials through the mails, and recommending his dismissal from the force. Police Commissioner Howard Safir adopted the recommendation and dismissed Pappas.

Where a government employee suing for violation of the First Amendment establishes that he was terminated by reason of his speech "upon a matter of public concern," the Supreme Court has instructed that the court's task is "to arrive at a balance between the interests of the . . . citizen, in commenting on matters of public concern, and the interest of the State, as an employer, in promoting the efficiency of the public services it performs through its employees." Under the balancing test [first articulated in the *Pickering* case], the

governmental employer may defeat the claim by demonstrating that it "reasonably believed that the speech would potentially interfere with or disrupt the government's activities, and can persuade the court that the potential disruptiveness was sufficient to outweigh the First Amendment value of that speech."

There is no dispute that Pappas was terminated because of his speech and would not have been terminated were it not for his speech. The defendants contend that Pappas's anonymous sending of the bigoted materials may not be "fairly characterized as constituting speech on a matter of public concern." * * * "When employee expression cannot be fairly considered as relating to any matter of political, social, or other concern to the community, government officials should enjoy wide latitude in managing their offices, without intrusive oversight by the judiciary in the name of the First Amendment." "Whether an employee's speech addresses a matter of public concern must be determined by the content, form, and context of a given statement, as revealed by the whole record." Because of our resolution of the *Pickering* balancing test, we assume without deciding that Pappas's mailings constituted speech on a matter of public concern.

Pickering's balancing test weighs the plaintiff's interest in freely speaking his mind on a matter of public concern against the State's interest in the performance of its functions. Under our Constitutional doctrines, few values are more carefully and thoroughly protected than the citizen's right to speak his mind on matters of public concern without interference by government. Nonetheless, the right is not absolute. At times, the right of free speech conflicts with other important governmental values, posing the problem which interest should prevail. The effective functioning of entities of government could be seriously undermined by its employees' unrestrained declarations of their views. For this reason, the employee's right of free speech is sometimes subordinated to the interest of the effective functioning of the governmental employer.

The effectiveness of a city's police department depends importantly on the respect and trust of the community and on the perception in the community that it enforces the law fairly, even-handedly, and without bias. * * * For a New York City police officer to disseminate leaflets that trumpet bigoted messages expressing hostility to Jews, ridiculing African Americans and attributing to them a criminal disposition to rape, robbery, and murder, tends to promote the view among New York's citizenry that those are the opinions of

New York's police officers. The capacity of such statements to damage the effectiveness of the police department in the community is immense. Such statements also have a great capacity to cause harm within the ranks of the Police Department by promoting resentment, distrust and racial strife between fellow officers. In these circumstances, an individual police officer's right to express his personal opinions must yield to the public good. The restrictions of the First Amendment do not require the New York City Police Department to continue the employment of an officer whose dissemination of such racist messages so risks to harm the Department's performance of its mission. * * *

Pappas argues that the foregoing considerations should not apply to him because he tried to conceal his identity as the source of the bigoted opinions. He contends he is being punished for his opinions, rather than his actions. The argument misses the mark. Pappas was tried and found to have violated Police Department regulations. That fact is important to our upholding of the lawfulness of the Department's actions. If Pappas had written his bigoted views in a private diary, or revealed them in confidence to his family or intimate friends, and they had become known accidentally, or through a breach of confidence, that case would present different considerations. We do not speculate how such a case would be decided. But those are not the facts we deal with. Here, Pappas deliberately sought to publicize his views. He repeatedly sent leaflets that aggressively pronounced his provocative views to organizations engaged in public solicitation. He admittedly did so with the intention of influencing public opinion. The Department appropriately took action against him not because of his private opinions but because of his conduct in violation of Departmental regulations—conduct that risked to harm the Department in the performance of its governmental mission. Although Pappas tried to conceal his identity as speaker, he took the risk that the effort would fail. * * *

While it is undoubtedly the case that ill-considered public statements of a high policy-making executive often have a higher likelihood of harming the employer's accomplishment of its mission than similar statements made by a file clerk, laborer or a janitorial employee, it by no means follows that rank and file employees are incapable of harming the employer's effectiveness by their speech, or that governmental employers are powerless to sanction lower level employees when their statements do have the capacity to harm the employer's performance of its mission. * * * The public

perception in minority communities that risks to harm the mission of the Police Department is not that the Police Commissioner or his principal deputies are racially biased. It is rather the perception that ordinary cops are biased. An ordinary police officer's distribution of these bigoted hate-filled materials reinforces that perception and thus harms the effectiveness of the Police Department. Furthermore, for police officers of one race to express hatred and scorn for members of another race obviously fans anger, dissension and racial tensions among officers of different races and thus inflicts harm of a second kind on the Department's performance of its mission. * * *

Pappas is not a civilian employee. He is a cop. The fact that he was assigned to work on computers does not make him any less a cop, either in fact or in public perception. His assignment furthermore was subject to change; at any time he could have been assigned to a beat. If the press became aware of his dissemination of racist diatribes, it would report that this was done by a police officer—not that it was done by a person employed to work on Police Department computers. Furthermore, as to the capacity of Pappas's statements to cause racial tension and strife among fellow police officers, it would make no difference whether he was assigned to patrol a beat or to program computers. * * *

It is undoubtedly true that complaints about office policies made away from the office to persons having no connection with the employment would generally have little capacity to harm the employer. It is also true that Pappas's proclamations of bigotry made privately, away from work, during off-duty time, had a lesser likelihood of undermining the Department's effectiveness than if he had passed out his leaflets in uniform to citizens in the streets of New York or to his fellow officers at the workplace. But to say that his statements would have had greater likelihood of causing harm if made in uniform or at work does not mean that they did not have a substantial capacity to cause harm as they were made. Where and when the statements are made is certainly a factor to be considered in the overall assessment, but it is only a factor. * * * While it may be true that the Department could have avoided adverse publicity had it covered up Pappas's misconduct rather than proceeding against him, that does not make it the right thing to do, and the Department did not lose the right . . . to dismiss Pappas for this misconduct merely because the bringing of the disciplinary action brought to public light the fact that it was a police officer who was responsible for the hate mailings. * * *

A governmental employer's right to discharge an employee by reason of his speech in matters of public importance does not depend on the employer's having suffered actual harm resulting from the speech. The employee's speech must be of such nature that the government employer reasonably believes that it is likely to interfere with the performance of the employer's mission. The employer's interest in discharging the employee is demonstrated if the employee's statements create a significant risk of harm, regardless whether that harm actually materializes.

In conclusion, it is indeed possible to imagine changed facts that would make the case against Pappas still stronger. The Department's right to dismiss him would have been even clearer if he were a high ranking policy-maker, or if he had distributed his leaflets to the public while on duty wearing his police uniform. The fact that a stronger case can be imagined does not mean that the actual case for discharge is inadequate. Considering the facts as they are, balancing Pappas's interest in his right to pronounce his views against the interest of the Department as an employer in promoting the efficiency of the public service it performs, we conclude that the Department was entitled to terminate Pappas by reason of his public dissemination of his diatribes. * * *

CASE QUESTIONS

1. What was the legal issue in this case? What did the court decide?

2. Would it have made a difference legally if the NYPD had chosen to suspend Pappas rather than terminate him?

3. What is the evidence that the employee's speech jeopardized the mission of the police department? Does this decision mean that any expression of racist views by a police officer is grounds for termination?

4. In applying the balancing test, does the court give sufficient weight to the speech rights of this public employee? Was this case correctly decided?

Constitutional protection against termination or other disciplinary actions based on public employee speech depends, first of all, on whether the speech is related to a **matter of public concern.** The voicing of private grievances and disputes in the workplace does not implicate the Constitution. A doctor who openly questioned the fitness and decisions of the director of his medical center was not engaging in speech on matters of public concern. The court concluded that comments "arising from a purely private disagreement between colleagues about the manner in which a personnel matter should be handled do not constitute protected speech for purposes of the First Amendment."[69] Instead, speech is on a matter of public concern and potentially protected when it pertains to political or social matters that concern the larger community. The employee is speaking as a citizen about matters relevant to the public, rather than as an employee regarding matters of personal interest. A school teacher whose contract was not renewed after she assigned several classic books to which some parents objected was allowed to go to trial on her constitutional claim.[70] Assignment of the materials was treated as a form of speech by the court and the broad themes of the books (e.g., *To Kill a Mockingbird, Fahreheit 451*) related to matters of public concern. The court in *Pappas* assumed, without explicitly deciding, that the police officer's speech via the dissemination of racist pamphlets was on a matter of public concern. Certainly, race relations can be viewed as a prime example of a public issue; however, one of the judges that agreed with the decision would nonetheless have found that Pappas was not addressing a matter of public concern because his motive in sending the pamphlets was to stop unsolicited mailings from charitable organizations.

[69]*Hellstrom v. United States Department of Veterans Affairs*, 178 F. Supp. 2d 164 (N.D.N.Y. 2001).

[70]*Evans-Marshall v. Board of Education of the Tipp City Exempted Village School District*, 428 F.3d 223 (6th Cir. 2005).

As the *Pappas* case illustrates, protected speech is often speech that we would rather not hear. In another speech case, a prison guard appeared on a local television program to promote a Ku Klux Klan rally. Although the employee's termination was ultimately upheld on other grounds, it was uncontested that the speech related to a matter of public concern and was subject to constitutional protection.[71] Similarly, upon hearing of an attempt to assassinate former President Reagan, an employee in a county constable's office stated, "If they go for him again, I hope they get him."[72] The comment, prompted by a news report of the assassination attempt and uttered in the context of a broader criticism of Reagan's social policies, was deemed to be on a matter of public concern. Ward Churchill's controversial remarks on the victims of 9/11, while distasteful to many, clearly addressed a matter of public concern (see "Clippings").

Words are often uttered quickly and are apt to be misunderstood. Employers, if they hear of statements at all, usually learn about them secondhand and with no enduring record to inspect. What responsibility do public employers have to determine that any speech that they believe warrants discipline was correctly reported? The Supreme Court considered this issue when dealing with the case of a nurse who was fired after several coworkers claimed that she spoke disparagingly of her boss and department and attempted to dissuade another nurse from transferring to her department.[73] The nurse and several other witnesses who overheard the conversation maintained that she had not attempted to discourage the other nurse's transfer and that any criticisms of the boss and department were in the context of her repeatedly voiced concerns that cross-training of staff was detrimental to patient care. The Court did not reach the important question of whether statements about policies that might affect patient care are related to matters of public concern. However, the Court held that a public employer does not have to be correct in its beliefs about what an employee said; instead, it can act on what it reasonably thought was said. For their beliefs to be reasonable, *public employers should conduct some type of inquiry, gather evidence about what was said, and not ignore evidence that is plainly available.*

Public employees who speak out on matters of public concern might still not be protected from termination or other discipline if their employers' interests in efficiently and effectively delivering services outweigh employee speech rights. Speech that harms supervisory relationships, promotes lack of harmony in the workplace, has a detrimental effect on close working relationships requiring loyalty and confidence, or renders employees unable to perform their duties will not be protected. In the case of the prison guard who went on television to promote a Ku Klux Klan rally, the court concluded that "the state's interests in maintaining safety and avoiding racial violence . . . [outweigh the plaintiff's] interests in associating with and promoting the Ku Klux Klan. . . ."[74] The court pointed to the racially charged nature of the prison environment, the negative effect of the statements on inmate perceptions of prison administration, the fact that the employee himself would be at risk for retribution, and that as a sergeant, the employee's statements were more likely to be attributed to the institution itself.

In contrast, the Supreme Court found that the statement of the employee who responded to news of an attempted assassination of President Reagan by saying, "if they go for him again, I hope they get him," did not unduly interfere with the

[71]*Weicherding v. Riegel,* 160 F.3d 1139 (7th Cir. 1998).

[72]*Rankin v. McPherson,* 483 U.S. 378, at 380 (1987).

[73]*Waters v. Churchill,* 511 U.S. 661 (1994).

[74]*Weicherding,* at 1143.

efficient functioning of the constable's office. The Court emphasized the private nature of the conversation (the comment was made to a coworker, but was overheard by another employee and reported to the constable); the employee's low-level, essentially clerical position; the absence of any direct reporting or working relationship with the constable; and the limited law enforcement function of the agency.[75] Under these circumstances, the comment, however impertinent, did not unduly interfere with the functioning of the agency and was constitutionally protected. Despite the unusual post-tenure "review" of Ward Churchill's writings and speeches by the University of Colorado, any action taken against him on the basis of the political content of his work would almost certainly run afoul of the Constitution (see "Clippings"). In *Pappas*, the court pointed to his status as a police officer (albeit one assigned to work on the computer system), the fact that he actively disseminated his materials, and the high potential for disruption stemming from his stated views to differentiate the case from that of the employee in the constable's office and to reach the conclusion that the police department's interests trumped the employee's constitutional rights.

The First Amendment also prohibits the government from restricting "the right of the people to peaceably assemble." This language has been interpreted by the courts to protect a broader range of associations. Associational rights include both intimate relationships and people banding together for speech or other expressive purposes.[76] At the same time, certain categories of public employees, particularly teachers and police officers, have traditionally been held to a high standard of off-the-job conduct. The result of these conflicting forces is limited and somewhat unpredictable constitutional protection of public employees from termination for their off-the-job relationships. A lengthy suspension was upheld for two police officers found to be cohabiting, despite the absence of an explicit policy prohibiting the practice.[77] A state attorney general's office was upheld in revoking an offer of employment to a woman who had participated in a commitment ceremony with her female partner.[78] An instructor at a community college who was terminated for going with students to the World Trade Organization (WTO) protest in 1999, after having been warned by administrators not to do so, was unsuccessful in arguing that her speech and associational rights had been violated.[79] The court found that the legitimate student safety and other interests of the college outweighed any infringement on her rights. On the other hand, the termination of a police officer for cohabiting with a married woman was struck down on constitutional grounds.[80] Likewise, in a case involving the dismissal of a state government official whose wife had successfully sued the state, the court stated: "[t]hough the matter is not free from doubt, we think a spouse's claim that adverse action was taken solely against that spouse in retaliation for conduct of the other spouse should be analyzed as a claimed violation of a First Amendment right of intimate association."[81] *Public employers must respect the constitutional rights of public employees, including their freedoms of religion, speech, and association. Termination or other disciplinary action should be imposed only when the exercise of these rights clearly interferes with an employee's ability to do her job or with accomplishment of the public agency's mission.*

[75]*Rankin*, at 389–91.

[76]*Roberts v. United States Jaycees*, 468 U.S. 609, at 617–18 (1984).

[77]*Shawgo v. Spradlin*, 701 F.2d 470 (5th Cir. 1983), *cert. denied*, 464 U.S. 965 (1983).

[78]*Shahar v. Bowers*, 114 F.3d 1097 (11th Cir. 1997), *cert. denied*, 522 U.S. 1049 (1998).

[79]*Hudson v. Craver*, 403 F.3d 691 (9th Cir. 2005).

[80]*Briggs v. North Muskegon Police Department*, 746 F.2d 1475 (6th Cir. 1984); *cert. denied*, 473 U.S. 909 (1985).

[81]*Adler v. Pataki*, 185 F.3d 35, at 44 (2d Cir. 1999).

Montana Wrongful Discharge from Employment Act

Many employers were alarmed by the growing recognition of common law wrongful discharge claims in the 1970s and 1980s. Outcomes of cases were unpredictable, and damages could be enormous. Although these concerns were widespread and legislation was proposed in a number of states, only Montana enacted a comprehensive wrongful discharge statute. The **Montana Wrongful Discharge from Employment Act (WDEA)**[82] effectively eliminated employment at will in Montana. It replaced a patchwork of common law wrongful discharge claims with a statutory framework that more clearly spelled out the rights of employees, but also limited the liability of employers for wrongful discharge and offered incentives to use alternative dispute-resolution procedures.

Under the Montana WDEA, a discharge is wrongful if any of the following is true:

1. It was in retaliation for an employee's refusal to violate public policy or for reporting a violation of public policy.

2. The discharge was not for good cause, and the employee had completed the employer's probationary period.

3. The employer violated the express provisions of its own written personnel policy.

The WDEA incorporates variants of the public policy exception to employment at will and implied contract into its statutory language, but goes much further in conferring a right on nonprobationary employees to not be terminated except for good cause. "Good cause" is defined in the statute as "reasonable, job-related grounds for dismissal based on a failure to satisfactorily perform job duties, disruption of the employer's operation, or other legitimate business reason."

In a case involving an airline employee terminated for intentionally submitting timesheets overstating her hours of work, the court concluded that it was not enough for the employer to act in good faith and reasonably believe the offense had been committed.[83] Good cause is lacking when a termination rests on an employer's mistaken interpretation of facts, as well as on grounds invalid as a matter of law under the WDEA (e.g., reporting a violation of public policy) or when the stated reason for discharge is a pretext for some other illegitimate reason. A jury found that the airline employee's recording errors were unintentional, and thus, she was terminated without good cause. To have good cause for termination under the WDEA, the airline had to be honest about its reasons for the termination and have its facts straight. The first of these, by itself, was not enough.

The WDEA was passed largely in response to employer concerns. What's in it for employers? The main thing that the WDEA accomplishes for employers in Montana is that it limits their potential liability for wrongful discharge. In contrast to common law tort claims, in which the sky is the limit, damages under the WDEA are limited to the award of lost wages and benefits for a period not to exceed four years from the date of discharge, including interest and reduced by interim earnings. Punitive damages are available only when clear and convincing evidence exists that an employer engaged in actual fraud or malice in terminating an employee for refusing to violate, or for reporting a violation of, public policy. Damages for pain and suffering, emotional distress, and other compensatory and punitive damages are specifically disallowed.

[82]Mont. Code Ann. § 39-2-901 *et seq.* (2005).

[83]*Marcy v. Delta Airlines*, 166 F.3d 1279 (9th Cir. 1999).

Claims brought under the WDEA must be filed within 1 year after the date of discharge, a much shorter period of time than typically allowed for common law suits. The WDEA encourages employers to establish internal appeals procedures. When employers have such procedures in place, they must be used and exhausted (completed) before a suit can be filed under the WDEA. However, this does not give employers license to sit on appeals indefinitely. Appeals not concluded within 90 days are deemed to be denied and employees are allowed to proceed to court under the WDEA. Additionally, employers are required to supply discharged employees with a written copy of their appeals procedures within 7 days of termination. An employee who failed to use his employer's internal appeals procedure after being discharged nonetheless won his case under the WDEA. The employer had orally informed the employee about the procedure, but failed to provide the required written information within the specified time frame.[84]

HANDLING TERMINATIONS

Even when employed at will, employees cannot be terminated for illegal reasons. These illegal reasons have been discussed, and practical advice for avoiding unlawful terminations has been sprinkled throughout this chapter. This chapter concludes with some generally applicable advice for handling the termination process (the much more extensive due process requirements for the termination of unionized employees and public employees are not reiterated here).

A wrongful termination claim cannot be brought absent a termination or constructive discharge. *Alternatives to termination—including retraining, transferring, demoting, suspending, and signing last-chance agreements—should be considered.* To the extent that these are adverse employment actions, they still present legal concerns, but they are less apt to be challenged than terminations. Employees also can be encouraged to resign, although presenting an employee with the stark choice of resigning or being fired, or putting undue pressure on an employee to resign, is apt to be viewed as constructive discharge. The *option of resignation is best pursued when there are growing concerns about the performance or conduct of an employee, but a termination is not yet imminent. Resignations should be documented in written resignation agreements that stipulate the voluntary nature of the resignation.*

Termination decisions should receive careful, higher-level review. Terminations tainted by discriminatory or retaliatory motives are particularly likely to be identified by this type of dispassionate internal review. Termination decisions should not be made on-the-spot by single individuals. *Employees should be placed on administrative leave if circumstances warrant their removal prior to completion of an investigation or proper review of a termination decision.*

Employers do not have to be correct about their reasons for terminating at-will employees; they need only not be motivated by illegal reasons and not be in breach of an enforceable promise not to terminate at will. Nevertheless, an employer without good documentation of the reasons for a termination and the process followed will be at a distinct disadvantage in defending against wrongful discharge claims. In the face of facts suggesting a discriminatory or retaliatory motive, the absence of documentation makes the illegal motive appear much more plausible. Thus, *the reasons for termination decisions and the process followed should be solidly documented.* This documentation includes performance appraisals, prior disciplinary

[84]*Casiano v. Greenway Enterprises, Inc.*, 47 P.3d 432 (Mt. 2002); *cert. denied*, 2002 U.S. LEXIS 8337.

actions, warnings, investigation results, and other pertinent items. *These materials should be in writing, should be produced prior to the termination decision, and should support the decision to terminate.*

Employees should not be kept in the dark about the reason(s) for their termination. For one thing, a number of states have "service-letter" laws mandating that terminated employees be given written documentation of their term of service with the employer and (sometimes) the reasons for termination.[85] In the absence of such requirements, an employee who is being terminated might view the refusal to provide a reason as an indication that the termination is, in fact, wrongful. And if it comes down to a legal challenge, vague or inconsistent explanations look highly suspicious. *Provide employees with a clear and succinct statement of the reason(s) for their termination.* Employers should *generally avoid making public statements about terminated employees and the reason for their termination.* The defamation claim of the CBS News producer who was fired and publicly identified as having failed to fulfill her responsibility to keep erroneous reports off the air (see "Clippings") is a cautionary tale in this regard.

Discharges should be handled in a reasonable, dignified manner. There is no way to make termination pleasant or comfortable. Instead, the aim is to communicate the reality of termination without any ambiguity, keep the situation under control, and possibly dampen the former employee's desire for revenge through litigation or worse. Employees should be notified of termination in person. The meeting should be brief and occur in a private setting away from the view of coworkers. If possible, the meeting should not occur at the very end of the week or immediately before a holiday. *Unless there are compelling security concerns, terminated employees should be allowed a reasonable amount of time to clear out their offices and take care of other business, rather than be ushered out of the workplace.* The fact of termination and the reasons should be clearly communicated but not discussed or debated. Information should be provided regarding final paychecks and benefits. *Final wages should be paid quickly and within any period provided for under state law. Unless termination is for gross misconduct, terminated employees should be notified of their right to continuation health insurance coverage under COBRA.*

Employees do not have a legal right to receive severance pay, absent any contractual agreement to provide it. However, *employers should consider offering severance pay in exchange for releases of legal claims related to terminations.* In general, releases of legal claims by terminated employees are legal and enforceable. Such releases must be knowing, voluntary, and supported by consideration. The consideration can come from severance pay, outplacement services, payment of health insurance premiums, early retirement incentives, or other inducements to accept the detriment of forgoing legal claims. The ADEA, as amended by the Older Workers Benefit Protection Act[86], imposes an exacting *set of requirements for waivers of ADEA claims to be valid: (1) waivers must be plainly worded, written agreements that specifically reference the ADEA and suggest consultation with a lawyer prior to acceptance; (2) consideration must be provided for acceptance; (3) employees must be given at least 21 days to consider waivers (45 days for group early retirement offers); and (4) waiver agreements do not become final—and can be revoked—until 7 days after acceptance.* Only claims that arose prior to the date of the waiver can be waived. An employer that fails to meet these requirements will have an unenforceable waiver and is not entitled to recover the severance pay or other consideration provided to support the agreement.[87]

[85]Barbara Kate Repa. *Your Rights in the Workplace, 5th ed.* (Berkeley, CA: Nolo, 2000), 10/12–10/17.

[86]Pub.L. No. 101-433, Sect. 201 (1990).

[87]*Oubre v. Entergy Operations, Inc.,* 522 U.S. 422 (1998).

Chapter SUMMARY

The legal framework governing the termination of most private-sector, nonunion employees can best be described as employment at will with exceptions. Terminations are presumed to be legal, no matter how dubious the reasons or circumstances, unless plaintiffs can prove that their terminations occurred for reasons or under circumstances that are specifically illegal. The exceptions to employment at will fall into the broad categories of terminations breaching implied contracts or other contract-related rights, terminations in retaliation for acts supporting public policy, terminations that interfere with the exercise of statutory rights, and terminations based on the protected class characteristics of employees.

Quits or resignations that occur when an employer creates intolerable working conditions with the intent of forcing an employee out are constructive discharges. If a reasonable person would have felt compelled to quit under the circumstances, the quit is treated as a termination. Constructive discharge is not a legal claim, but rather a finding that permits an employee who resigned to pursue any claims for wrongful discharge that would have been available had the employee been formally terminated. The behavior involved in creating intolerable working conditions also lends itself to harassment and infliction of emotional distress claims.

The right of employers to terminate at will can be limited by employer policies, handbook provisions, manager's statements, and the entire course of conduct between employers and their employees. The breach of an implied contract to not terminate at will is a type of wrongful discharge claim. Specific promises to terminate only for good reasons or to use specified disciplinary procedures that are communicated to employees and not effectively disclaimed are enforceable and provide a legal basis for challenging terminations in violation of those promises. Apart from any express or implied contract, employees who reasonably rely on clear promises of job security and suffer a specific detriment for doing so can sue under the theory of promissory estoppel. Employees can sometimes also sue (in tort) for intentional interference with a contractual relationship when intentional, improper interference causes termination of employment or inability to establish a new employment relationship.

Under the public policy exception to employment at will, employers are liable in tort for terminating employees in retaliation for their taking actions that public policy requires or commends. The public policy exception has been recognized for terminations based on an employee's refusing to engage in illegal activity, exercising a legal right, performing a public duty, and reporting illegal activity. Public-policy claims must be firmly grounded in fundamental and well-established public policies, as spelled out in statutes, constitutions, and other sources, and not merely in individual judgments about what is right or in the public interest. Reporting illegal activity—whistleblowing—is also protected under a variety of state and federal statutes. The federal Whistleblower Protection Act (WPA) protects federal government employees who make reports about violations of laws, rules, and regulations; gross mismanagement; gross waste of funds; abuse of authority; and substantial and specific dangers to public health and safety. Under the False Claims Act, parties with knowledge of intentional fraud against the federal government can bring suits to recover government funds and share substantially in the recovered funds. The Sarbanes-Oxley Act includes provisions protecting employees who blow the whistle on possible violations of securities laws or other fraud against shareholders of publicly traded companies.

Employees reinstated following military service are protected by the Uniformed Services Employment and Reemployment Rights Act (USERRA). Such employees can be terminated only for cause for up to a year following reinstatement. Most federal employment laws protect employees who file charges or give testimony against termination or other retaliation for participating in the enforcement process. Additionally, the NLRA, ERISA, and the FMLA prohibit employers from interfering with employees by discharging them for exercising their rights.

To establish a prima facie case of disparate treatment in a discharge situation, plaintiffs must show the protected class characteristic(s) relevant to the case; that up to the time of discharge, they were performing acceptably; that they were discharged; that their employer sought or hired a replacement; or that a person outside the protected class engaged in similar conduct but was not terminated. Many discriminatory discharge cases center on whether rules were consistently enforced, raising the question of whether other similarly situated employees with contrasting protected class characteristics were treated less harshly.

The legal framework governing the termination of most employees who are unionized, work for government agencies, reside in Montana, or have express contracts of employments for specified durations can

be described as a just cause/due process standard. For unionized employees, labor agreements typically specify that discipline or discharge must only be for just cause. If a discharge is challenged, an arbitrator decides whether there was just cause, taking into account the following factors: (1) was there a rule prohibiting the behavior? (2) was the rule communicated to employees? (3) is the rule reasonable? (4) was the rule consistently enforced? (5) was the employee afforded due process? (6) is there sufficient proof that the rule was violated? (7) was progressive discipline applied? (8) was the discipline commensurate with the severity of the offense? (9) are there mitigating factors that call for imposition of a lesser penalty? Employers bear the burden of proving that discipline or discharge was for just cause.

Public employees are generally removed from employment at will by virtue of the combination of their high rate of unionization, civil service and tenure laws, and constitutional protections. Public employees deemed to have a property interest in their jobs are entitled under the Fifth and Fourteenth amendments to due process before their employment can be terminated. Due process includes both pretermination and posttermination hearings. Public employees deemed to have a liberty interest in their employment are entitled to an opportunity to clear their names. Like other citizens, public employees also have religious, speech, and associational rights under the First Amendment. Public employers cannot use terminations or other discipline to suppress these rights. However, First Amendment freedoms must be balanced against the government's interests in the efficient operation of public agencies. Public employees' speech is constitutionally protected to the extent that it relates to matters of public concern and is not unduly disruptive. Factors to be weighed include the effects of speech on supervisory relationships, workplace harmony, close working relationships requiring loyalty and confidentiality, and employees' ability to perform their duties. Public employers can act on what they reasonably believe employees have said, even if those beliefs ultimately turn out to be incorrect.

Termination is the human resource decision most likely to result in legal action. The law gives employers, especially nonunion employers in the private sector, considerable latitude in making this decision, but employers still must carefully consider the grounds for any termination and the termination process itself should be as humane and dignified as possible.

Practical Advice SUMMARY

- *Employers should not attempt to avoid terminations by creating intolerable conditions designed to force employees to quit.*

- *When communicating with employees via handbooks and other means, employers should*

 - *refrain from making specific promises to employees regarding duration of employment, grounds for discharge, or termination procedures unless they are willing to honor those promises.*

 - *ensure that employee handbooks, employment applications, and other documents are carefully written and reviewed by someone with legal expertise before they are put into use.*

 - *clearly inform employees regarding changes in policies that have the effect of lessening protection against termination.*

 - *incorporate disclaimers and employment-at-will statements if that is the type of employment relationship desired.*

- *If disclaimers are used they must be*

 - *clear and specific in their language.*

 - *presented in a prominent and conspicuous manner.*

 - *communicated to employees, with receipt of the information acknowledged in writing.*

- *Employees must not be terminated for*

 - *refusing to commit illegal acts.*

 - *exercising their legal rights.*

 - *performing important public duties.*

 - *reporting illegal activities of employers and their agents.*

- *Employers should*

 - *provide credible internal procedures for reporting wrongdoing by the company or its agents.*

 - *investigate reports of wrongdoing and not punish whistleblowers for making them.*

- *Employers must not terminate reinstated military service members without cause for a period of time (180 days or a year, depending on length of service) following reinstatement.*

- *Employers should be cautious about terminating employees who are on or have recently returned from FMLA leave and must not terminate them because they have taken leave.*

- *Employers should enforce disciplinary policies in a consistent manner, treating like situations in a like manner, regardless of the individuals involved.*

- *Employers must not terminate employees because they have filed charges, given testimony, or otherwise participated in the enforcement of employment laws.*

- *If resignation is offered as an alternative to termination*

 - *the employee should not be presented with the stark choice of quitting or being immediately terminated.*

 - *acceptance of the offer should be documented in a written resignation agreement that stipulates the voluntary nature of the quit.*

- *Before arriving at the decision to terminate, employers should*

 - *consider alternatives including retraining, transferring, demoting, suspending, and signing last-chance agreements.*

 - *subject the decision to careful, higher-level review.*

 - *place employees on administrative leave if immediate removal is warranted, but time is needed to properly conduct an investigation.*

 - *have documentation of the process and the reasons for termination that is written, produced prior to termination, and consistent with the decision to terminate.*

- *After a decision to discharge has been made*

 - *the discharge should be handled in a reasonable, dignified manner.*

 - *a brief termination meeting should be held in a private setting.*

 - *a clear, succinct statement of the reason(s) for the termination should be given to the employees (in some states, a service letter is required).*

 - *absent compelling security concerns, terminated employees should be allowed a reasonable amount of time to clear out their offices.*

 - *final wages should be paid quickly and within any period of time specified under state law.*

 - *unless termination is for gross misconduct, terminated employees should be notified of their right to continuation of health insurance coverage under COBRA.*

 - *consideration should be given to offering severance pay in exchange for releases of legal claims.*

- *Waivers of ADEA rights must*

 - *be plainly worded, written documents that specifically refer to the ADEA and suggest consultation with a lawyer prior to acceptance.*

 - *be supported by consideration.*

 - *allow employees at least 21 days to consider acceptance.*

 - *not take effect until at least 7 days after acceptance.*

Key TERMS

employment at will
employment at will with exceptions
constructive discharge
implied contract
disclaimer
covenant of good faith and fair dealing
promissory estoppel
intentional interference with a contractual relationship

public policy exception
refusal to commit an illegal act
exercising legal rights
performing a public duty
whistleblowing
Whistleblower Protection Act (WPA)
Sarbanes-Oxley Act
False Claims Act
similarly situated

Montana Wrongful Discharge from Employment Act (WDEA)
just cause
civil service laws
due process
progressive discipline
Tenure
property interest
liberty interest
First Amendment
matter of public concern

Chapter QUESTIONS

1. An employee was fired after 32 years on the job and working his way up to become a vice president at the company. The employee did not have an express contract of employment. The employee had consistently received bonuses and promotions and was never disciplined or warned that his performance was lacking. The employee had been told by the former company president that "if you are loyal to the company and do a good job, your future is secure." Over the years, the company had a practice of not terminating administrative employees without cause. His termination came after he returned from a business trip and was told by a new company president that his services were no longer needed. When he pressed for further elaboration, he was told to "look deep within" himself to find the answer. The employee believed that he had been terminated at the behest of union officials who wanted him fired because he had objected to certain potentially illegal arrangements between the company and union. What should the court decide? Why? (*Pugh v. See's Candies, Inc.,* 171 Cal. Rptr. 917 (Cal. App. 1981))

2. Who let the Ice Dogs out? Actually, the question is whether the ownership of the Bozeman Ice Dogs, a Junior A hockey team, violated its written contract of employment with the team's coach and general manager when it terminated him for poor performance based on the team's losing record (18 wins, 35 losses, and 7 ties in his last full season). At the time of the termination, the coach had a 5-year contact specifying that he would be entitled to his salary and bonus for a full calendar year if he was terminated for other than cause. The contract did not specify any particular win/loss record or other team performance standard for the coach. The team argued that it was not required to provide the specified payment because the termination was "for cause." What should the court decide? Why? (*Cole v. Valley Ice Garden,* 113 P.3d 275 (Mont. 2005))

3. An employee of a company that provides home care to seniors received an "Employee Warning" threatening discharge if there was not "marked improvement" in her performance at the end of the next four weeks. The employee believed that some of the allegations in the warning were false

and possibly defamatory. She was asked to sign the report, but instead told her supervisors that she had been advised to consult an attorney before making a formal response to the warning. Almost immediately thereafter, she was fired. The employee sued. What should the court decide? Why? (*Porterfield v. Mascari II, Inc.,* 823 A.2d 590 (Md. 2003))

4. The activities director for a nursing home requested and received FMLA leave to have a child. She was temporarily replaced by another employee whom some of the residents seemed to favor. Shortly after the start of the leave, an investigation was begun into the activity director's handling of a checking account that contained residents' funds. Dates and check numbers had not been recorded for every entry, and it was ultimately determined that there was a discrepancy of about $70. While she was still on leave, the nursing home asked the activities director to attend two conferences. She went to the first conference, but declined to go to the second, citing her nursing infant. The director of the nursing home became angry and said "How is that going to change in two weeks when you come back?" Shortly before her return, she was told by another employee that the nursing home was going to give her "a hard time" when she got back and that she should look for another job. On her first day back from leave, the activities director was terminated for "misappropriation or mishandling" of patient funds. The activities director sued. What should the court decide? Why? (*Kohls v. Beverly Enterprises,* 259 F.3d 799 (7th Cir. 2001))

5. An employee of a family-owned car dealership suffered an injury while lifting computer equipment on the job. The employee reported the injury to the personnel department. The owner of the car dealership was convinced that the injury was actually incurred in a stockcar accident and told a supervisor to get the employee to sign a form waiving his right to received workers' compensation for the injury. The supervisor (a brother of the owner) was told that if he didn't get the employee (who happened also to be his son) to sign the waiver, both of them would be fired. A waiver was never signed, and both employees were terminated. They sued. What

should the court decide? Why? (*Rothrock v. Rothrock Motor Sales*, 883 A.2d 511 (Pa. 2005))

6. An employee was hired as general manager of a new assisted living facility. She received positive feedback on her progress for several months. At a meeting, two supervisors inquired about her child-rearing plans. She admitted that she planned to have children and was fired two weeks later. She was replaced by a 60-year-old woman. Her supervisor's manual included a policy on progressive discipline that was generally adhered to. However, she also received and signed a disclaimer that stated in part: "I understand that [neither] the policies and procedures of the facility, nor the Handbook . . . are intended to constitute a contractual agreement. . . . I understand that my employment is 'at will.' . . ." What should the court decide? Why? (*Kuest v. Regent Assisted Living, Inc.*, 43 P.3d 23 (Wash. App. 2002))

7. An employee worked as a lab assistant at a company that manufactures eyeglasses. The employee became aware that the company was not adhering to government regulations requiring that lenses be hardened and tested for resistance to shattering. The employee complained to his boss about the violation, and when nothing was done, complained to the Food and Drug Administration. Shortly thereafter, he was terminated. What should the court decide. Why? (*Boyle v. Vista Eyewear*, 700 S.W.2d 859 (Mo. App. 1985))

8. Does the employment at will with exceptions standard provide sufficient protection for employees? Would it be better if all employers were required to meet a just cause/due process standard for terminations?

Internet RESOURCES

The Fair Measures, Inc. site addresses numerous frequently asked questions about the legality of terminations.

http://www.fairmeasures.com/wrongful.html

The Department of Labor site has links to a variety of environmental laws that incorporate whistleblower protections.

http://www.osha.gov/dep/oia/whistleblower/index.html

The Workplace Fairness site focuses on whistleblower protection

http://www.workplacefairness.org/index.php?page=whistleblowing

The Montana Association of Counties site includes this page that focuses on compliance with the Montana WDFEA

http://maco.cog.mt.us/pages/PERSONNEL.htm

Downsizing and Posttermination Issues

CLIPPINGS

▸ Honeywell International has entered into a consent decree and agreed to pay $2.15 million to end an age discrimination suit brought by the EEOC on behalf of a class of older sales representatives terminated or demoted in 1997 during a reorganization. The sales reps had been employees of AlliedSignal Automotive, a firm acquired by Honeywell in 1999. In its suit, the Commission alleged that the former company president stated, "Anybody over 40 is a dinosaur," and promised to fire older workers and "replace them with people like myself." A vice president allegedly said that long-term employees will be "bugs on AlliedSignal's windshield."[1]

▸ The Yellow Roadway Corporation has agreed to a $7 million settlement of claims by former employees of USF Red Star, a trucking company that it purchased in 2005. USF Red Star had closed all of its terminals without any prior notice, apparently in response to a one-day work stoppage by Teamster truck drivers who were supporting an organizing campaign by clerical workers at the company. The settlement covered claims under the Worker Adjustment and Retraining Notification Act (WARN Act) and the National Labor Relations Act (NLRA).[2]

▸ The Los Angeles City Council has approved a city ordinance that would require large stores that sell primarily household foodstuffs for off-site consumption to retain employees for a least 90 days in the event of a change in ownership. Any terminations during the 90-day period must be for cause, and if the employer subsequently determines that fewer employees are needed, retention decisions must be based on seniority. The ordinance is the first statute of its kind in the nation, and there are questions about whether the city has exceeded its constitutional authority in enacting the law.[3]

▸ Larry Johnson used to have a job cleaning at Windows on the World restaurant. The restaurant and his job disappeared on September 11, 2001. He applied for unemployment insurance, but was rejected because of insufficient earnings over the previous 18 months. Mr. Johnson's experience is far from unique. Employees who work part-time, earn low wages, have irregular employment, or leave employment to care for family members often find they are ineligible for unemployment insurance. In each year since 1980, less than 40 percent of unemployed persons have received unemployment benefits.[4]

▸ Microsoft filed suit against Google, alleging that its hiring of a former Microsoft executive was in violation of a noncompetition agreement that the executive had

[1]"Honeywell Signs $2.15 Million Settlement with EEOC Ending Class Discrimination Suit." *Daily Labor Report* 195 (October 8, 2004), A-4; "EEOC Sues Honeywell for Age Bias against Class of AlliedSignal Sales Reps." *Daily Labor Report* 110 (June 7, 2002), A-3.

[2]Michelle Amber. "$7 Million Settlement Reached for 1,900 Who Lost Their Jobs When Red Star Closed." *Daily Labor Report* 156 (August 15, 2005), A-12.

[3]Tom Gilroy. "Los Angeles City Council Again OKs Supermarket Worker Retention Measure." *Daily Labor Report* 246 (December 27, 2005), A-8.

[4]David Leonhardt. "Out of Work, and Out of the Benefits Loop." *New York Times* (October 17, 2001), C-1.

signed. The former executive, Kai-Fu Lee, was hired to oversee Google's operations in China. According to Microsoft spokespersons, the noncompetition agreement barred Dr. Lee from working for a direct competitor of Microsoft for at least one year and from disclosing Microsoft trade secrets at any time.[5]

DOWNSIZING

Downsizing is not a legal term. It is one of many euphemisms used to describe the fact that employment is being involuntarily terminated. **Downsizing** is used in this chapter to refer to terminations that affect numerous employees and that are based on employers' judgments that the number of employees, positions, or facilities must be reduced. As such, downsizing poses legal issues distinct from those considered in the previous chapter. Questions arise regarding the very decision to downsize, prior notification of downsizing, the selection of individuals for downsizing, and the manner in which downsizing is implemented, including early retirement offers.

The Decision to Downsize

Employers regularly decide to go out of business, close facilities, relocate, subcontract, outsource, reduce staffing to save money, sell businesses, and merge with or acquire other companies. These business decisions typically result in numerous employees losing their jobs (although employment opportunities might thereby be opened up or made more secure for other individuals). The law provides employees with very few options for challenging employment-threatening business decisions. Whatever the eventual fate of the Los Angeles ordinance restricting downsizing for a period of time following the sale of a store (see "Clippings"), this law is very much the exception to the general rule that employers are free to make decisions regarding the size of their workforces. Thus, in ruling against the plaintiffs in a case involving an employer who closed two plants at which the vast majority of workers were over 40 and replaced them with two new plants in other states in which an equally wide majority of the workers were under 40, the court observed:

> The ADEA was not intended to protect older workers from the often harsh realities of common business decisions and the hardships associated with corporate reorganizations, downsizing, plant closings and relocations. Unlike law and social policy in many European countries, the laws of the United States do not prohibit or seriously discourage these plant closings and relocation activities and the attendant dislocation, unemployment and new employment.[6]

Any ability of employees to challenge downsizing decisions derives primarily from the National Labor Relations Act (NLRA). The NLRA affects employment-threatening business decisions in two ways. First, the closure of a facility might be an ULP if it is deemed to interfere with the exercise of employees' NLRA rights or to discriminate against employees based on their union activity. Second, the employer might have a legal obligation to bargain with union representatives over the decision to downsize.

[5]Matt Richtel. "Microsoft Sues Over Google's Hiring of a Former Executive." *New York Times* (July 20, 2005), C-3.
[6]*Allen v. Diebold, Inc.*, 33 F.3d 674, at 677 (6th Cir. 1994).

In a case involving the shutdown of a textile plant by a company that owned a number of textile plants, the Supreme Court observed that "when an employer closes his entire business, even if the liquidation is motivated by vindictiveness toward the union, such action is not an unfair labor practice."[7] But because the employer in question operated multiple plants, this was only a partial closing. The Court concluded that "a partial closing is a ULP . . . if motivated by a purpose to chill unionism in any of the remaining plants of the single employer and if the employer may reasonably have foreseen that such closing will likely have that effect."[8] It was ultimately decided that the plant closing was motivated by antiunion animus and that a chilling effect on other employees at other plants was reasonably foreseeable.[9] Remedies for violations included back pay and opportunities to transfer to other facilities, but not compelled reopening of the closed facility. *Thus, although employers can always choose to go out of business entirely, they must not selectively close facilities for the purpose of inhibiting unionization at their remaining facilities.*

Relocation of work from one facility to another can also violate the NLRA if motivated by hostility toward unions. Following a representation election, an employer transferred part of its operation to another plant and terminated the employment of six employees who had been assigned to operate those machines.[10] The court upheld the National Labor Relations Board's (NLRB) decision that the employer had committed an unfair labor practice (ULP). Evidence of discrimination included the facts that the six discharged employees were known union supporters, the company had threatened employees with a plant closing or job loss throughout the organizing campaign, the owner had vowed to "take care" of the fired employees, and the company offered false and contradictory reasons for the transfer of work. Because the plant where the work was originally performed still existed in this case, the Board ordered that the employer return the operation that had been transferred.

Occasionally, the NLRB intervenes to keep a shop from "running away" in the first place. One day after employees voted to unionize, an employer announced that it was relocating its production facilities to Mexico and terminating most of its employees. The suspicious timing of the announcement (nothing had been said about a possible relocation previously, and the employer had just spent a considerable sum to move to the present location), in conjunction with the company's strident efforts to defeat the union organizing campaign, strongly suggested a discriminatory motive. The company's efforts to justify the relocation decision as a matter of economic necessity did not impress the court, which granted a preliminary injunction to halt the move: "The rhetoric of 'cheap foreign labor' is a shibboleth that employers may not rely upon to justify unlawful, anti-union conduct."[11]

The second way in which labor law is relevant to downsizing decisions is that, in unionized workplaces, these decisions are sometimes mandatory topics of bargaining. If a downsizing decision is a mandatory topic of bargaining, the employer has a legal obligation to bargain in good faith with the union prior to taking any action. In general, business decisions that involve a change in the scope or direction of a business are comparable to decisions to enter or leave a line of business and are not mandatory topics of bargaining. Thus, a company that provided maintenance and housekeeping services under contract with a nursing home did not violate the NLRA

[7]*Textile Workers Union v. Darlington Mfg. Co.*, 380 U.S. 263, at 273–74 (1965).

[8]*Darlington*, at 275.

[9]*Darlington Mfg. Co.*, 165 N.L.R.B. 1074 (1967), *enforced*, 397 F.2d 760 (4th Cir. 1968), *cert. denied*, 393 U.S. 1023 (1968).

[10]*NLRB v. Taylor Machine Products, Inc.*, 136 F.3d 507 (6th Cir. 1998).

[11]*Aguayao v. Quadrtech Corp.*, 129 F. Supp 2d. 1273, at 1278 (C.D. Cal. 2000).

when it terminated the contract (due to dissatisfaction with the low fees paid by the home) and laid off the employees who had performed this work without first negotiating with their union.[12] On the other hand, subcontracting and outsourcing, in which employers continue to produce the same things by substituting the services of the employees of another company for the work of their own employees, are generally mandatory topics of bargaining. The same is true for the relocation of work from one facility owned by an employer to a different facility owned by that employer, particularly if labor cost differentials that might be affected by negotiations played a part in the decision.[13] *To the extent that downsizing decisions are mandatory topics, unionized employers must negotiate in good faith before finalizing such decisions. Regardless of whether employers are legally required to negotiate over the decisions themselves, employers are obligated to negotiate with unions over the effects of downsizing decisions on employees (e.g., transfer rights, retraining, severance pay, extended benefits, and so on).*

The duty to bargain often survives the takeover of one company by another. *Successor employers must bargain with unions that represent employees at acquired companies, although they are generally not bound by the terms of existing labor agreements.* Whether an employer is a "successor" or simply a different firm depends on the degree of continuity between the new operation and the prior operation, including the number of former employees of the acquired firm hired; the extent of similarity in operations, products, and customers; and the length of time between when the old operation ceased and the new one began. In one case, a firm was found to be a successor obligated to bargain even though the original business was closed for seven months before the new operation started and the former employees were rehired through newspaper ads rather than the employment records of the acquired firm.[14]

Informing Employees Prior to Downsizing—WARN Act

Although employers usually have a free hand in deciding to downsize, the implementation of downsizing decisions is sometimes affected by the **Worker Adjustment and Retraining Notification (WARN) Act.**[15] *Employers covered by the WARN Act are prohibited from ordering plant closings or mass layoffs until the end of a 60-day period that follows the provision of written notice to affected employees (or, if the employees are unionized, to union representatives) and to state and local government officials.* "By closing down its terminals without any prior notification to employees and their union, the trucking company clearly violated the WARN Act (see "Clippings"). **Affected employees** are those who are reasonably expected to suffer **employment loss** stemming from a plant closing or mass layoff, including termination (other than a quit, discharge for cause, or retirement), a layoff lasting more than 6 months, or a greater than 50 percent reduction in work hours during each month of any 6-month period. Other measures that might be used by struggling employers—including cuts in pay or benefits, short-term layoffs (less than 6 months), and limited (less than 50 percent) reductions in work hours—do not bring the WARN Act's notification requirements into play.

Only relatively large employers are covered by the WARN Act. Specifically, employers are covered if they have 100 or more full-time employees or have 100 or more full- and part-time employees working in the aggregate at least 4,000 hours

[12]*First National Maintenance Corp. v. NLRB,* 452 U.S. 666 (1981).

[13]*Dubuque Packing Co. v. NLRB,* 1 F.3d 24 (D.C. Cir. 1993); *cert. denied,* 511 U.S. 1138 (1994).

[14]*Fall River Dyeing & Finishing Corp. v. NLRB,* 482 U.S. 27 (1987).

[15]29 U.S.C.A. §§ 2101–2109 (2005).

per week (excluding overtime hours). The usual problems of counting employees to determine statutory coverage are even more acute under the WARN Act because downward fluctuation in employment levels is inherent in the circumstances under which the act is applied. The relevant point in time for determining coverage is the date that the first notice of an impending closing or mass layoff is required to be given (i.e., 60 days prior to the downsizing).

The meanings of the terms *plant closing* and *mass layoff* are central to the act and not self-evident. Under the WARN Act, a **plant closing** is a permanent or temporary shutdown of a single site of employment when that shutdown results in employment loss during any 30-day period for at least 50 full-time employees. A **mass layoff** is a reduction in force that is not caused by a plant closing, but that results in employment loss at a single work site during any 30-day period for at least 500 full-time employees (regardless of the percentage of total employees) or at least 50 full-time employees (when these comprise at least 33 percent of total employment at the work site).

But wait! It gets more complicated still. In the messy real world, closings or layoffs do not necessarily occur at single points in time. The WARN Act provides that when there are employment losses for two or more groups of employees at a single employment site (e.g., several "waves" of layoffs)—and none of these groups are individually large enough to meet the numerical standards for plant closings or mass layoffs, but they do so in the aggregate—the employment losses over any 90-day period can be combined to establish that a plant closing or mass layoff has occurred (unless the employer can show that the employment losses stemmed from separate and distinct causes). A downward spiral of financial problems that eventually ends in the closure of a facility is a single cause. Thus, a hospital that began laying off employees due to funding problems several months before it decided to close its doors was liable for failing to give notice dating back to 60 days before the very first employee was laid off.[16]

Multiple notifications might be required under the WARN Act. In one case, an employer gave notice of a mass layoff but then decided to permanently close the plant. The employer notified the union that the mass layoff was being converted to a permanent shutdown, but it did so on the same day that it closed the plant. The court concluded that although the employees were already laid off, the prior notification was not sufficient because they had incurred the new employment loss of a termination. Thus, the employer had failed to provide the required 60-day notice of a plant closing.[17] An employment loss does not occur if, prior to a plant closing or mass layoff, the employer offers to transfer the employee to another work site within a reasonable commuting distance and with no more than a 6-month break in employment or the employer offers a transfer to another work site regardless of the distance, no more than a 6-month break in employment, and the employee accepts within 30 days. Thus, the WARN Act contains an incentive for employers to offer downsized employees continued employment through transfer to other facilities (i.e., such employees cannot be litigants in WARN Act cases, and the offer of transfers might affect whether notification is even required).

The WARN Act also contains some rather large loopholes. Employers are excused for not providing the full 60-day prior notice when a closure or layoff is due to a natural disaster; when a capital infusion or new business is being sought, which, if obtained, would avoid or postpone a closure, and the employer has a good faith belief that giving notice would make it impossible to obtain the needed capital or business;

[16]*Hollowell v. Orleans Regional Hospital*, 217 F.3d 379 (5th Cir. 2000).

[17]*Graphic Communications International Union, Local 31-N v. Quebecor Printing Corp.*, 252 F.3d 296 (4th Cir. 2001).

and when the closure or layoff is the result of business circumstances not readily foreseeable at the time when notice should have been given. Under these circumstances, the employer is required to provide as much notice as possible and to explain in the notice why the full 60-day prior notice requirement was not met. Likewise, if a layoff is originally thought to last less than 6 months but extends longer, the employer is liable for failure to provide required notice unless the extension is caused by business circumstances not reasonably foreseeable at the time of the initial layoff, and notice is given as soon as it becomes apparent that the layoff will extend beyond 6 months. The closure of facilities or operations understood to be temporary in nature and layoffs that result from strikes or lockouts do not require any prior notice.

Roquet v. Arthur Andersen considers whether a mass layoff stemming from a financial scandal was "reasonably foreseeable," necessitating notice under the WARN Act.

ROQUET V. ARTHUR ANDERSEN
398 F.3d 585 (7th Cir. 2005); *cert. denied*, 126 S. Ct. 375 (2005)

OPINION BY CIRCUIT JUDGE EVANS:

This case involves the Worker Adjustment and Retraining Notification Act, better known by its shortened name, the WARN Act. The Act became law in 1989, and its purpose is to soften the economic blow suffered by workers who unexpectedly face plant closings or mass layoffs. Among other things, the Act requires that companies subject to its reach (generally large employers) give employees 60 days notice in advance of any mass layoffs or plant closings. The notice gives affected workers a little time to adjust to a job loss, find new employment, or, if necessary, obtain retraining.

Our case, however, is not your typical WARN Act fare as it involves hot-button topics like "Enron," "document shredding," and "indictment." And it concerns an exception to the WARN Act's notification requirement: the Act's 60-day-notice obligation is eliminated, or reduced to a shorter term, if a mass layoff or plant closing is "caused by business circumstances that were not reasonably foreseeable as of the time that notice would have been required." * * *

First, a little background. As of early 2002, Andersen had over 27,000 employees in 80 locations throughout the country. * * * One of the firm's major clients was the Enron Corporation, the infamous Houston, Texas, energy marketer that fell like a house of cards in 2001 when it came to light that the company had grossly misstated its earnings. Andersen was at the center of Hurricane Enron—it audited the company's publicly filed financial statements and provided internal counseling. In November of 2001, Andersen received bad news in the form of a subpoena from the SEC requesting Enron-related documents. During the course of its investigation, the SEC discovered that Andersen employees destroyed thousands of relevant documents in the 6 weeks leading up to its receipt of the subpoena. Over the next few months, the media began to speculate about Andersen's continuing viability. Stories also circulated that Andersen's employees were concerned about layoffs and that some of the company's clients were contemplating defection.

During this time, Andersen worked hard to try to resolve its Enron-related ills with the SEC and the Department of Justice (DOJ). As of February 22, 2002, Andersen had not suffered a significant loss of business nor was it giving any thought to a mass layoff. That day, Andersen's lawyers met with lawyers from the DOJ. The next day, counsel briefed Andersen's management team, and a participating manager e-mailed the following update to employees:

> At our meeting on Saturday, February 23, the current status of the investigation into document destruction was presented by the outside lawyers from Davis Polk. They are moving forward as quickly as possible to bring this matter to a conclusion as it relates to the Firm with the Department of Justice. * * *

On March 1, the DOJ delivered dire news—it was going to seek an indictment of the company. Andersen

tried to convince the DOJ to change its mind, but to no avail. On March 7, an Andersen managing partner, Terry Hatchett, sent an e-mail informing employees that the firm was "presently engaged in discussions with the Department of Justice regarding the parties' respective views" and that "no final conclusions have been reached." That very day, however, the DOJ filed a sealed indictment charging the firm with obstructing the SEC investigation by destroying and with-holding documents. * * * [O]n March 14 the indictment was unsealed.

To the surprise of no one, news of the indictment triggered massive client defection. From March 15 to the 31st, Andersen lost $ 300 million in business. During this time period, the practice group on West Monroe Street in Chicago alone lost $ 57 million, roughly 14 percent of its fees. * * * In light of these setbacks, and with additional hemorrhaging expected, Andersen decided to lay off thousands of employees. On April 8, management at West Monroe gave notices of termination to 560 employees, including Nancy Roquet and Coretta Robinson, the named plaintiffs in this suit. After receiving notice, Roquet remained on the payroll for 2 weeks and Robinson for 5 weeks. * * * Roquet and Robinson filed a class-action complaint in federal district court alleging that Andersen violated the WARN Act by failing to give 60 days notice to its workers before laying them off. * * *The district court concluded that the need for lay-offs was not reasonably foreseeable 60 days before the decision was made and entered summary judgment in favor of Andersen. The plaintiffs appeal that decision. . . . * * *

A business circumstance may be reasonably unforeseeable if it was caused by some sudden, dramatic, and unexpected action, or by conditions outside the employer's control. When determining whether a mass layoff was caused by unforeseeable business circumstances, courts evaluate whether a similarly situated employer exercising reasonable judgment could have foreseen the circumstances that caused the layoff. * * * The district court concluded that the need for mass layoffs was caused by the public announcement of the indictment on March 14. We agree. Up until then, Andersen suffered no marked loss of business despite a spate of negative publicity. It is clear that economic hemorrhaging really did not begin until word of the indictment got out. The plaintiffs contend that Andersen's felonious misconduct caused the layoffs, not the indictment. But, while it is true that the illegal acts of some Andersen employees were the root cause of the

firm's ultimate downfall, not until the indictment became public did it feel the pain. * * *

The heart of the dispute in this case centers on foreseeability. In determining whether a crippling business circumstance is foreseeable, we must bear in mind that "it is the 'probability of occurrence that makes a business circumstance "reasonably foreseeable," 'rather than the 'mere possibility of such a circumstance.' "The layoffs began on April 23, which means that Andersen was required to notify employees 60 days earlier, or February 22. The plaintiffs argue that the indictment was reasonably foreseeable on that date because "the DOJ disclosed to Andersen that an indictment was highly probable." But the record does not support this position. The plaintiffs point to Andersen's meeting with the DOJ on February 22 and its subsequent efforts to fight off an indictment. The February 23 e-mail summarizing that meeting, however, makes no mention of the firm being indicted. And Andersen's subsequent negotiations with the government do not mean that it knew an indictment was likely. Possible? Certainly. But probable? No. Indeed, as of February 22 it was not a foregone conclusion that Andersen would be indicted as a company—in the past, the government typically went after culpable individuals, not companies as a whole. By all accounts, this was an unusual move by the DOJ. There is evidence in the record suggesting that Andersen could have reasonably foreseen the indictment by March 1—the date it was told by the DOJ that it was being indicted. But hope still remained that the dreaded act could be stalled if not avoided.

We believe that a reasonable company in Andersen's position would have reacted as it did. Confronted with the possibility of an indictment that threatened its very survival, the firm continued to negotiate with the government until the very end and turned to layoffs only after the indictment became public. The plaintiffs argue that Andersen should have notified employees of layoffs on February 22. We do not agree. At that point, Andersen had not yet lost business or been indicted. Indeed, in our view, a mass layoff at that point would have been a poor business decision. What if the government decided not to indict the firm as a whole, or waited 6 months to make the decision? The only reason for providing notice so early would be to ward off potential WARN Act liability. But, as the Sixth Circuit [has] explained . . . , the WARN Act is not intended to deter companies from fighting to stay afloat:

> WARN was not intended to force financially fragile, yet economically viable, employers to

provide WARN notice and close its doors when there is a *possibility* that the business may fail at some undetermined time in the future. Such a reading of the Act would force many employers to lay off their employees prematurely, harming precisely those individuals WARN attempts to protect. A company that is struggling to survive financially may be able to continue on for years and it was not Congress's intent to force such a company to close its doors to comply with WARN's notice requirement.

These same concerns were at play here. Thus, Andersen's failure to notify employees earlier than it did was not unreasonable.

The plaintiffs argue that the layoffs were foreseeable . . . because the indictment was not sudden, dramatic, and unexpected nor outside the employer's control. In their view, Andersen was long aware of its misconduct, and punishment for that misconduct was inherently foreseeable. But the indictment was certainly sudden and dramatic in that Andersen did not know if it would be indicted as a firm. Nor did Andersen really know when the indictment would be returned until the act occurred. Again, the WARN Act deals in reasonable probabilities, not possibilities. Moreover, an employer does not have to be caught completely off guard by a dire business circumstance for it to be "sudden, dramatic,

or unexpected." Case law reveals that WARN Act defendants need not show that the circumstances which caused a plant closing or mass layoff arose from out of the blue to qualify for the exception. * * *

The lead time in the notice Andersen ended up giving varied from employee to employee. Our two named plaintiffs, for example, got 2 (Roquet) and 5 (Robinson) weeks notice before they were out of work. Given the situation here, and the "business circumstances" exception . . . , Andersen, although deserving of no roses for the acts of some of its agents in the Enron mess, did not violate the WARN Act by giving the notice as it did on April 8. * * *

CASE QUESTIONS

1. What was the legal issue in this case? What did the court decide?

2. From the evidence presented, when were the business circumstances causing the mass layoff "reasonably foreseeable?"

3. Does the court adequately consider whether earlier, but not necessarily 60 days, notice was required?

4. Why might a firm be reluctant to provide information to employees about an impending layoff or closure? Does the WARN Act strike the right balance between employer and employee interests in these circumstances?

For their trouble, plaintiffs in WARN Act cases are entitled to receive back pay for the number of days that they were deprived of timely notice, up to a maximum of 60 days. Courts have differed on whether eligibility for back pay is based on calendar days or only days on which work would have been performed.[18] Employers are also liable for health insurance premiums and pension payments for the period of the WARN Act violation, but not for the likes of holiday and vacation pay.

Selecting Employees for Downsizing

Short of a wholesale business closure, the question remains of which particular employees will be selected for termination. The main legal requirement in this regard is that the means of selecting individuals for downsizing must not be discriminatory. As the EEOC's suit against Honeywell for the discharge of numerous older sales representatives during a reorganization illustrates (see "Clippings"), a particular concern is age discrimination. The EEOC has taken on a number of Age Discrimination in Employment Act (ADEA) cases relating to downsizing, including *EEOC v. Board of Regents of the University of Wisconsin.*

[18]*United Mine Workers of America, International Union v. Eighty-Four Mining Co.*, 2005 U.S. App. LEXIS 25039.

EEOC V. BOARD OF REGENTS OF THE UNIVERSITY OF WISCONSIN
288 F.3d 296 (7th Cir. 2002)

OPINION BY CIRCUIT JUDGE EVANS:

* * * The EEOC alleged that the Board of Regents of the University of Wisconsin System (UW) violated the ADEA when it terminated the employment, on the basis of age, of four persons working for the University of Wisconsin Press. The EEOC prevailed in a jury trial.... * * * The EEOC's case is based on claims by four "charging" parties: Rosalie Robertson, who was 50 years old at the relevant time; Mary Braun, who was 46; Joan Strasbaugh, age 47; and Charles Evenson, who was 54. The university personnel who made the termination decisions were David Bethea, the interim director of the Press, and Steve Salemson, the associate director. * * *

In an age discrimination case, we evaluate whether there is evidence that the employer discriminated against the employees "because of" age. Our task, then, is to examine the record to see whether there was evidence from which a reasonable jury could conclude that the "charging" parties were terminated "because of" their ages. * * *

Soon after Bethea became interim director, he came to the conclusion, as early as February 1999, that the Press was in financial trouble. Concluding that costs had to be cut, he decided it was necessary to terminate some employees. Working with Salemson, he set out to make a list of persons who would be let go. The list was prepared in March and included all of the charging parties, who were the oldest employees at the Press—other than the two decision-makers themselves. An oversight committee approved the list and it was submitted to Ann Marie Lamboley, a senior administrative program specialist, who was the self-described "campus layoff expert." She instructed Bethea and Salemson to provide a written justification of the selection of the four people. As instructed and, notably, after the decisions had already been made, they prepared a document entitled "A Justification for the UW Press's Layoff Proposal." Bethea and Salemson then met with each of the charging parties on May 9, 1999, to inform them of their termination; each was told that the termination was "not in any way related to performance or personality issues." Each one was also given a copy of this document.

The unavoidable fact is that the four oldest employees were the only ones terminated, and the terminations occurred under circumstances from which one could, in fact, draw an inference that they were chosen because of their ages. These workers were terminated and the responsibilities were taken over either by other employees or by replacements brought in from the outside, which supports an inference of discrimination. Robertson was terminated from the acquisitions department, and 2 weeks later the Press hired Sheila McMahon, who was in her mid-twenties, to work in acquisitions. Strasbaugh was 47 when she was terminated as assistant marketing manager. Her duties were assumed by a woman in her twenties or thirties, whose contract was renewed and extended shortly after Strasbaugh's termination. Evenson was 54 years old when he was terminated from his position as a senior marketing specialist, while 23-year-old Rebecca Gimenez was retained. Other people in their twenties and thirties were brought into the acquisitions and marketing departments as well.

The UW tries to distinguish between the charging parties and those retained or hired, saying they were not similarly situated to one another. But the "Justification" itself compares the charging parties and the other individuals working at the Press. For instance, the document discusses the relative skills of Evenson and Gimenez, both of whom worked in marketing. It also compares Robertson and the person retained in acquisitions. Although the "Justification" was said to be an assessment of the skills and experience of the various people working at the Press, neither Bethea nor Salemson spoke with the charging parties about their skills. The two men did not solicit the opinions of managers regarding who should be let go. There were no formal employee evaluations. Documents they did look at included out-of-date resumes which had been on file at the Press, and these were not looked at until April, after the termination decisions had already been made.

The "Justification" can be read to show that they held the charging parties to a higher standard than the younger workers. It claims that Evenson would have to take courses to get "up to speed" on "Webpage programming or the electronic transfer of data and images." In the document there is no indication whether Gimenez, the preferred younger employee, herself had

taken such courses. The facts show she had not. Gimenez also received credit in the "Justification" for things she had not done. It says she created the Webpage, but, in fact, it had been created before she began working at the Press.

A reasonable jury could believe that the "Justification" uses code words which reflect an age bias. It refers to Evenson as having skills suited to the "pre-electronic" era and that he would have to be brought "up to speed" on "new trends of advertising via electronic means."

The UW also justifies the termination decisions by saying that the job titles of the newly hired younger people were different from those of the charging parties. Some of the people were hired as "limited term employees." We do not think that hiring individuals under less desirable terms can necessarily overcome the inference that the persons being replaced were replaced because of their ages.

There was also an interesting concept taking hold at the Press. Both Bethea and Salemson acknowledged during cross-examination that the Press was seeking a "new vision." Salemson conceded that the younger individuals brought into the Press were part of the new vision. Bethea wanted to hire replacements who would fit the new vision if he could jump the "legal hurdle" of the ADEA. He thought that in the past the Press had not "had the vision to be agile enough" and that the terminations of the charging parties would "improve that agility." It is certainly an interesting metaphor, from which the jury could reasonably draw an inference that in Bethea's mind youth and agility go hand-in-hand.

In addition to finding discrimination, the jury also found that the discrimination was willful. Under the ADEA, an employer's violation of the statute is willful if the "employer knew or showed reckless disregard for the matter of whether its conduct was prohibited by the

ADEA." The evidence was sufficient to allow the jury to infer that Bethea knowingly sought to circumvent the ADEA. We have already referred to his desire for agility and his attempt to jump legal hurdles. He conceded that the hurdles included the ADEA. There is also evidence that the UW seemed recklessly to disregard whether its conduct was prohibited. Bethea, for instance, knew the ADEA was a hurdle, but neither he nor Salemson had been given any employment law training and neither man seemed to know the age at which the protections of the Act arose. In addition, even though the charging parties were the oldest people at the Press, Lamboley, the campus layoff expert, did not look at the terminations to see if age discrimination might have been involved. Neither did Associate Dean Mareda Weiss, who also did not know that the floor age of protection under the ADEA was 40. Nor did Dean Virginia Hinshaw, who also reviewed the proposed terminations. We have previously said that "leaving managers with hiring authority in ignorance of the basic features of the discrimination laws is an 'extraordinary mistake'" from which a jury can infer reckless indifference. * * *

The judgment of the district court is AFFIRMED.

CASE QUESTIONS

1. What was the legal issue in this case? What did the court decide?

2. What was the evidence that the discharges were based on age?

3. What should this employer have done differently?

4. What about the "vision" thing? Can't an employer terminate employees because it wants new ideas, to institute a new "culture," and so on?

Although characterized as a downsizing or reduction in force (RIF) necessitated by financial pressures, *Board of Regents* had aspects of a regular discriminatory discharge case, insofar as new personnel were hired (or had contracts extended) to fill at least two of the positions vacated by the discharged employees. Determining whether a discharge is actually part of a RIF is not always straightforward. In a case that raised this issue, the court outlined the relevant considerations for determining whether a RIF has occurred:

A work force reduction situation occurs when business considerations cause an employer to eliminate one or more positions within the company. An employee is not eliminated as part of a work force reduction when he or she is

replaced after his or her discharge. However, a person is not replaced when another employee is assigned to perform the plaintiff's duties in addition to other duties, or when the work is redistributed among other existing employees already performing related work.[19]

Thus, when a 56-year-old manager was terminated in what the company claimed was a RIF, but an employee 24 years younger was hired the day after (and at the same salary) to perform the same managerial duties, it was easily concluded that the company's RIF justification was pretext.[20] Likewise, when an existing employee was changed from part-time to full-time status with fundamentally different responsibilities to cover the duties that had been performed by a terminated employee, a court concluded that this was equivalent to hiring a new employee as a replacement.[21]

Determining whether a termination is part of a RIF matters because, if it is, that fact necessitates a modification of the approach typically used in discriminatory discharge cases. If downsizing is seized upon as an opportunity to rid organizations of older employees, the ADEA is violated. But ferreting out discrimination in this context is problematic. When employers determine, however wisely or foolishly, that jobs have to be cut, courts are loathe to interfere with that business judgment. As one court put it, "when a company exercises its business judgment in deciding to reduce its work force, 'it need not provide evidence of financial distress to make it a legitimate RIF.'"[22] No one deserves to be downsized. In downsizing cases, it is usually not helpful to ask whether the discharged employee was meeting her employer's legitimate performance expectations at the time of discharge, as is typically done in other discriminatory discharge cases. Further, because positions disappear during genuine reductions in force, it is not useful to ask whether the employer sought to fill the vacated position or did so with someone whose protected class characteristics differ from the plaintiff's. As one court put it, "[t]he question in this context is not why members of the group were discharged or whether they were meeting performance expectations, but whether the particular employees were selected for inclusion on the list for discharge because of their age."[23]

Courts accept the general legitimacy of downsizing and the likelihood that many of those who are downsized will be over 40 simply because of the large proportion of the workforce comprised by this age group. A relatively heavy burden is placed on plaintiffs terminated in a RIF to establish a prima facie case of disparate treatment based on age. Notice also that the comparisons being drawn are between terminated employees and others "substantially younger." This is because age discrimination plaintiffs do not have to show that they were treated worse than employees under 40; it is enough that a "substantial" difference exists in age and the plaintiff is the older party.[24] The first approach to defining a prima facie case is tailored to the (typical) situation where an employer claims that performance was a factor in selecting employees for downsizing. This approach asks whether any inference of age discrimination can be drawn from a comparison of the ages and relative performance levels of employees terminated with those retained. The second approach is more general

[19]*Godfredson v. Hess & Clark, Inc.,* 173 F.3d 365, at 372 (6th Cir. 1999).

[20]*Miller v. Eby Reality Group,* 396 F.3d 1105 (10th Cir. 2005).

[21]*Tinker v. Sears, Roebuck & Co.,* 127 F.3d 519, at 522 (6th Cir. 1997).

[22]*Regel v. K-Mart Corp.,* 190 F.3d 876 (8th Cir. 1999).

[23]*Mitchell v. Data General Corp.,* 12 F.3d 1310, at 1315 (4th Cir. 1993).

[24]*O'Connor v. Consolidated Coin Caterers Corp.,* 517 U.S. 308 (1996).

ELEMENTS OF A CLAIM

Discriminatory Discharge in a RIF (Age)

The plaintiff must establish a prima facie case by showing:

1. The downsized employee was age 40 or over.

2. He was selected for termination from a larger group of candidates.

3. He was performing at a level at least substantially equivalent to the lowest level among the group of employees retained.

4. The group of employees retained included some persons who were substantially younger than the terminated employee and who were performing at a lower level than that at which he was performing.

OR

1. The downsized employee was age 40 or over.

2. He was performing his job to his employer's reasonable expectations.

3. He was terminated (or suffered another adverse employment action such as failure to transfer or rehire).

4. Other similarly situated employees (i.e., those with comparable positions, skills, and qualifications) who were substantially younger than him were treated more favorably.

If a prima facie case is established, the employer must articulate the lawful reason(s) for selecting the employee for termination.

The plaintiff has the opportunity to show that the stated reasons are pretext and that it is more likely that the decision was based on the employee's age.

and can be used to analyze situations where, for example, some employees are given the option to transfer and others are not.

Board of Regents is (literally) a "textbook" example of mishandling a RIF. The university was found to have willfully violated the ADEA because older employees were terminated, substantially younger employees were hired or had their contracts extended to perform the duties of some of the discharged employees, the university developed its justification for the RIF after the fact, it failed to use up-to-date information about employee performance and qualifications, higher skill requirements were placed upon the terminated workers than upon their replacements, and a decision maker spoke of getting around the "legal hurdle" of the ADEA. Additionally, statements were made that, in the context of the case, could be interpreted as code words revealing bias toward and stereotyping of older employees. One employee was described as having skills suited to the "pre-electronic era." The directors also used terms like vision and agility to describe the characteristics they were looking for and saw older employees as lacking in those attributes.

In contrast, an employer was able to successfully defend its termination of a marketing director during a RIF. The company decided to close down a pet food business that it had started a few years earlier, but which had lost over $10 million. Of the 18 employees terminated, 10 were under 40 years of age. The 59-year-old plaintiff's claim failed because although he was the oldest person terminated, more than half were under 40; it was uncontroverted that the business he had spent the majority of

his time on had sustained a large loss; and there was, in fact, a genuine reduction in force based on an objective plan to restructure the company.[25] In another case, a 58-year-old quality assurance manager was terminated in a reduction in force. He had only recently moved from a plant-level job to a newly created corporate position. The court placed great emphasis on the fact that, when selected for the job, he was told that he would have to travel regularly, be very energetic in pushing the company's new quality assurance initiative, and produce results in short order. His boss came to the conclusion that he was not sufficiently energetic and committed to change, and placed his name on the list of people to be downsized. Although the court acknowledged that the boss's criticisms hinted at stereotypical views of older employees as slow moving and resistant to change, his expectations were made clear at the outset and were not met. The court also observed that, insofar as the boss had only recently hired the employee into the new position, this created a strong inference that something other than age accounted for the termination.[26]

In another instructive case, an employer was upheld when it terminated two older retail store employees during a RIF. After it was determined that the store would have to eliminate two full-time positions, a plan was developed to select for termination the two least-senior employees in "nonskilled" positions. The rationale was that this would save training costs and have the least detrimental effect on store operations. The ages and identities of the employees selected for termination were not known until after the selection procedure was applied. In ruling for the employer, the court observed that this was a genuine RIF; management, in consultation with the regional human resources director, had developed an objective selection procedure not based on age; alternative procedures were considered but were not feasible; and the employer adhered to its stated procedure.[27]

What conclusions can be drawn regarding how employers should go about conducting reductions in force? Much of the advice that applies to any termination applies equally here, particularly the need for documentation of the reasons for termination, sound performance appraisals, and careful review of termination decisions. More specific to the RIF context, *employers should have clear, objective criteria for deciding who to downsize. These criteria must not include age and should be applied consistently and before the fact of termination. Decisions should not be based on vague criteria related to stereotypical views of older workers, such as potential for growth, acceptance of change, vision, and so on. Statements made to and about downsized older employees should not include code words suggesting bias against older employees. If all, or a disproportionate percentage, of persons initially selected for downsizing are older employees, this should prompt a review of selection procedures and decisions. If a RIF is needed, hiring new, younger employees or substantially changing the duties of existing employees to absorb the duties of terminated employees should generally be avoided.*

Because downsizing is often aimed at cost savings, what if employees are selected not on the basis of age but by taking into account their salary levels? To the extent that salary is related to length of service, and older workers, on average, are likely to have higher seniority, decisions to weed out higher-paid employees tend to disadvantage older workers. Certainly, employers are not free to target older workers as a group on the assumption (correct or incorrect) that they are more expensive to employ or to cite concern over high salary levels as a pretext for decisions actually

[25]*Godfredson*, at 374.

[26]*Mitchell*, at 1317–18.

[27]*Regel*, at 880.

based on age. Either of these would be disparate treatment. But what if decisions really are made on the basis of salary level? Is an adverse impact claim viable? After all, salary level can be viewed as a "neutral" selection criterion that results in the disproportionate selection of older employees for downsizing. If so, its use in downsizing decisions would not necessarily be illegal, but would need to be defended by the employer. The Supreme Court's decision in *Smith v. City of Jackson, Miss.* (see Chapter 3), confirming that adverse impact claims are available under the ADEA, might bolster challenges to downsizing decisions based on salary level or other neutral factors correlated with age. However, plaintiffs must contend with the requirement that their statistical evidence has to demonstrate adverse impact on the entire protected class (all employees 40 and over), and not just some part of it (e.g., employees over 55 years of age).[28] Furthermore, the Court made clear in *Smith* that an employer's burden under the ADEA to defend challenged practices as "reasonable factors other than age" is lighter than the "job-related and consistent with business necessity" showing required under Title VII. Courts might very well view the desire to lower costs as "reasonable," with the only question being whether employers would be required to demonstrate any particular level of financial distress. The availability of alternatives to downsizing that would have less detrimental effect on older workers would not have to be considered.

RIF's frequently present questions of whether downsized employees will be allowed to transfer to other workplaces, change positions, consult, or be rehired. In general, *it makes both practical and legal sense to offer experienced employees the opportunity to retain employment.* Employers are not required to offer downsized employees the opportunity to transfer or otherwise retain employment; "[b]ut when internal job placement services are benefits of employment which are provided to younger employees, an employer must provide roughly the same benefits to ADEA-protected employees, and when an employer responds to a RIF by transferring employees to available positions, it may not refuse to transfer older employees based on their age."[29] A 53-year-old employee who was terminated in a reduction in force was unable to prove that his employer violated the ADEA when it transferred other, younger employees. The court described the shortcomings of his case as follows:

> [A] showing of discrimination requires more—much more than simply identifying employees who obtained jobs around the same time that the plaintiff was looking for a position. A valid comparison would have entailed showing that these employees also encountered a RIF, that they obtained positions for which Radue [the plaintiff] was qualified, and that the supervisors in charge also knew that Radue was looking for such positions. Without this, there's no basis for inferring that the other employees were similarly situated.[30]

In contrast, a woman who was not rehired for a related job after she was terminated from her position as an insurance adjuster during a reduction in force was allowed to go to trial on her age discrimination claim. Although the company president stated that displaced employees "should have preference" for new jobs and would be given training, the woman received only a cursory interview, and a younger employee who had never worked for the company was hired. In addition to throwing doubt on the employer's stated reasons for not rehiring her, the woman was able to show that the interviewer wrote down her age and that the ages of other applicants

[28]*Lowe v. Commack Union Free School District,* 886 F.2d 1364 (2d Cir. 1989); *cert. denied,* 494 U.S. 1026 (1990).

[29]*Radue,* at 615.

[30]*Radue,* at 619.

were circled or underlined on resumes and other documents.[31] Similarly, and just a few months after he was downsized, a 56-year-old employee saw an advertisement from his former employer for a position that was very much like his previous one. The advertisement listed four specific qualifications, all of which were possessed by the former employee. He applied for the job, but a much younger employee who did not possess all the stated qualifications was hired. The court rejected the company's contention that it was free to conclude that the hired employee was a "better fit" despite the failure to meet its own qualifications.[32]

Early Retirement Offers

The ADEA prohibits mandatory retirement (with the exception of certain persons in bona fide executive and high policy-making positions). *Employers must not force employees to retire when they reach a specified age.* However, as an alternative to terminations, downsizing employers often attempt to increase attrition by offering inducements for employees to voluntarily leave employment.

Under the Older Workers Benefit Protection Act, it is legal for employers to offer such incentives, even though the minimum age or service requirements might exclude younger employees. However, *early retirement offers cannot be extended to one age group (e.g., employees between 52 and 56 years of age), but denied to older employees.* A school district's early retirement incentive violated the ADEA when it provided for payment of health insurance premiums until age 65 and then provided a lump sum payment only for employees who retired before age 65. The incentive treated employees between 55 and 65 equally, but by defining "early" retirement in terms of age and denying the benefit to employees who retire after age 65, the plan was discriminatory.[33]

Employees mulling over when to retire obviously have an abiding interest in learning of their employer's intent to offer retirement incentives. Who wants to retire and learn shortly thereafter that if he had remained on the job a few months longer he would have been in line for an enhanced retirement package? On the other hand, employers might prefer to not divulge the existence of early retirement programs until they are a certainty and would rather not provide incentives to employees who are going to leave anyhow. A number of courts have held that, as an aspect of the fiduciary responsibility of employers under ERISA to manage benefit plans in the interest of beneficiaries, *employees must be informed regarding the status of early retirement incentive plans that are under "serious consideration."*[34] Plans are under **serious consideration** when there is a specific proposal, the proposal is being discussed for purposes of implementation, and members of senior management with the authority to implement the plan are engaged in the discussion. Employers can (and should) gather information about plan options and engage in discussions at all levels of management, without triggering the duty to disclose that an early retirement offer is being considered. However, after *the plan solidifies to the point that it is sufficiently concrete to be considered as a proposal, the discussion shifts from strategy to implementation, and high-level managers become involved in reviewing and approving a specific plan, employees must be informed.*

Employers that offer early retirement incentives typically want assurance that employees who accept these benefits will not subsequently sue for age discrimination.

[31]*Corneveaux v. CUNA Mutual Insurance Group*, 76 F.3d 1498 (10th Cir. 1996).

[32]*Carberry v. Monarch Marking Systems, Inc.*, 30 Fed. Appx. 389 (6th Cir. 2002).

[33]*Jankovitz v. Des Moines Independent Community*, 421 F.3d 649 (8th Cir. 2005).

[34]*McAuley v. IBM*, 165 F.3d 1038 (6th Cir. 1999); *cert. denied*, 527 U.S. 1066 (1999).

The Older Workers Benefit Protection Act permits waivers of rights or claims under the ADEA, but it establishes stringent conditions for such waivers.[35] Some of these conditions were outlined in Chapter 18, including a knowing and voluntary waiver, extra benefits beyond those that would normally be available, waivers that are in plain language, waivers that explicitly refer to the ADEA and advise consultation with an attorney, waivers that do not pertain to any claims arising after the date of execution, a sufficient amount of time to consider offers, and 7 days to reconsider acceptance. *In the case of group early retirement offers, employees must be given at least 45 days to consider the offers. Additionally, employees must be informed in writing regarding the class, unit, or group of employees covered by the early retirement incentive offer; any eligibility factors for the program; the time limits applicable to the program; the job titles and ages of all individuals eligible or selected for the program; and the ages of all individuals in the same group who are not eligible or selected for the program.*

Courts strictly apply the conditions for a valid waiver of ADEA rights. A "General Release and Covenant Not to Sue" entered into by an employee terminated in a RIF and his employer, IBM, was deemed not enforceable because it lacked the requisite clarity.[36] The language confused the purpose of the release of claims (to establish that a right or claim has been relinquished) and the covenant not to sue (an agreement not to enforce any right or claim via a lawsuit). The absence of even one of the required elements is sufficient to invalidate a waiver. An otherwise acceptable waiver was not upheld because it was executed in the context of a RIF, and the employer failed to provide details regarding the group of employees targeted for downsizing and the basis for selecting individuals for termination.[37] Although this might seem like nit-picking, such information is critical to employees understanding whether they might have age discrimination cases, and hence, understanding the true nature of any waiver of their rights.

Effects of Bankruptcy on Employee Rights

Financially struggling companies often file for bankruptcy. Such companies are likely to owe wages to their employees, have obligations under benefit programs, and, in unionized workplaces, have contractual obligations to employees under labor agreements. Employees are not considered secured creditors. However, when employers file for bankruptcy under Chapter 11 and continue to operate as they reorganize, the wages and benefits earned following the bankruptcy filing by those employees who are retained have a high priority claim on the company's resources. These payments are treated as administrative expenses necessary to maintain the viability of the enterprise. Employees have a weaker claim for wages and benefits earned prior to petitions for bankruptcy. These claims have lower priority and are limited to amounts earned within 90 days before the filing of the bankruptcy petition.

Nonunion employers are generally free to cancel expected raises or bonuses, cut wages, or reduce benefits as means of lowering costs. What about unionized employers? They can approach union representatives and attempt to convince them to agree to needed concessions. However, failing at that, unionized employers cannot unilaterally alter the terms of labor agreements or conveniently ignore them. *Nor does filing for bankruptcy necessarily absolve an employer of its obligations under a labor agreement.* The Bankruptcy Code contains a set of procedures that must be followed before bankrupt firms can alter or circumvent labor agreements.[38] *Firms*

[35]P.L. No. 101-433, 104 Stat. 978 (1990), Sect. 201.

[36]*Thomforde v. IBM*, 406 F.3d 500 (8th Cir. 2005).

[37]*Kruchowksi v. The Weyerhaeuser Co.*, 423 F.3d 1139 (10th Cir. 2005).

[38]11 U.S.C.A. § 1113 (2005).

must present union representatives with proposals based on the most complete and reliable information available, provide the union with all relevant supporting information, and bargain in good faith. If the union rejects the proposals without good cause, the court may permit the employer to make the desired changes. However, the proposed changes must be truly necessary to allow the company to reorganize (not merely a "wish list"), they must treat employees and other parties equitably (employees should not bear the full brunt of cost-cutting), and they usually cannot be implemented until the court has approved them.

POSTTERMINATION ISSUES

Legal issues do not necessarily end with the termination of employment. For one thing, employees who lose their jobs often file for unemployment insurance and former employers sometimes contest those filings. Former employers might also seek to enforce noncompetition agreements and other forms of restrictive covenants aimed at limiting the ability of former employees to use knowledge or trade secrets obtained through employment to compete against them. Former employers sometimes attempt to restrain the speech of former employees when it is deemed detrimental to the employers' interests.

Unemployment Insurance

Employees who involuntarily become unemployed and are able to work, available for work, and actively looking for it are eligible to receive unemployment insurance. **Unemployment insurance** is intended to partially replace lost earnings during periods of unemployment for persons who have demonstrated an attachment to the workforce. Unemployment insurance is provided for through a combination of federal law, principally the Federal Unemployment Tax Act (FUTA) and state unemployment insurance laws. Federal law governs the funding of unemployment benefits and sets out broad parameters for coverage, whereas state laws contain the details of coverage and benefit levels.

Eligibility Criteria and Benefits The requirement that an individual be out of work **involuntarily** raises many questions. Employees who are laid off or terminated based on business considerations during downsizings are eligible for unemployment insurance. However, if an employee is discharged for misconduct, she might be disqualified. The misconduct usually must be serious and intentional to disqualify an employee from the receipt of unemployment benefits following termination; employer dissatisfaction with performance is generally not enough. However, a court found that an employee's failure to comply with her employer's rule that all workplace injuries be reported during the same shift was intentional misconduct that disqualified the employee from receiving unemployment insurance.[39]

Employees who quit generally are not eligible for benefits, but there are exceptions to this rule. If a quit is actually a constructive discharge, it is not voluntary. Courts consider whether a reasonable person would have felt compelled to quit under the circumstances, such as harassment[40] or extreme verbal abuse by a boss. Employees who leave their jobs due to health hazards might still receive benefits, particularly if they can show that the health problems caused were serious and that their employer was apprised of the situation but did not eliminate the problem. For

[39]*Schmidgall v. FilmTec Corp.,* 644 N.W. 2d 801 (Minn. 2002).
[40]*Munro Holding v. Cook,* 695 N.W. 2d 379 (Minn. App. 2005).

example, a painter was eligible for unemployment insurance when she quit her job after repeatedly suffering chest pains and headaches due to sensitivity to the type of paint being used. The employee had informed her supervisors, and the company had actually purchased safety equipment for her, but for reasons that are not entirely clear, she was not allowed to use the equipment.[41] However, several city government employees who quit their jobs in response to what they saw as inadequate protection against workplace violence were not eligible for unemployment insurance.[42] Although an altercation had occurred in City Hall and police protection that had been provided was removed about a month later, the court decided that the plaintiffs had voluntarily resigned because they had not personally been targets of the violence, the city had allowed them to work at home for three days after the incident, police protection was provided for a meaningful period of time, and the violent employee was not expected to return. Employees who go on strike are not eligible for unemployment insurance for all, or at least a part, of the time they are on strike. However, courts have sometimes found striking employees to be eligible for unemployment insurance when their employer made repeated statements that the employees had been permanently replaced and no longer had jobs.[43]

To receive unemployment benefits, the involuntarily unemployed also have to demonstrate an attachment to the workforce, both prior to and following their loss of employment. Most states establish eligibility for unemployment insurance by examining the claimant's work history over a specified period of time (the **base period**) prior to the job loss (usually the first four out of the five quarters preceding the claim for benefits). Only individuals who meet minimum earnings and hours of work standards during this base period are eligible. Part-time employees or those who have irregular work histories are often unable to meet these criteria and are denied benefits (see "Clippings"). Unemployed persons also must show that they are "able" to work, in the sense that they possess the requisite physical and mental abilities.

Availability for work raises more questions. The unemployed must be willing to seek and accept "suitable employment." In general terms, **suitable employment** is work that does not endanger the health or safety of the employee, work for which the individual has the requisite training and experience, and work that is within a reasonable distance of the individual's residence or last place of employment. Unemployed persons who place excessive restrictions on the types of jobs they will accept or the circumstances (e.g., hours, schedule, location) under which they will work may be deemed unavailable for work and denied benefits. However, unemployed persons are not generally expected to accept employment that is substantially lower paying and less skilled than their usual work. Individuals who refuse to take jobs that are vacant due to a strike are usually still eligible for unemployment benefits. An employee might also reject employment for religious reasons. For example, the Supreme Court found that the constitutional rights of an employee were violated when he was denied unemployment insurance because he turned down a job that would have required working on Sunday.[44]

Unemployment benefits generally last for up to 26 weeks (assuming suitable employment is not located before then). During periods of high unemployment, benefits are usually extended for additional weeks. In many cases, employees exhaust their unemployment benefits before finding new jobs. In 2003, 43 percent of

[41]*Pahl-Jones v. ASI Sign Systems,* 2002 Minn. App. LEXIS 4.

[42]*Adkins v. Gatson,* 2005 W. Va. LEXIS 131.

[43]*Titan Tire Corp. v. Employment Appeal Board,* 641 N.W. 2d 752 (Iowa 2002).

[44]*Frazee v. Illinois Department of Employment Security,* 489 U.S. 829 (1989).

unemployment insurance recipients exhausted their benefits without finding jobs.[45] In most states, unemployment insurance is limited to about 50 percent of weekly earnings. However, because maximum benefit levels are also specified, the actual earnings replacement rate is more like 33 percent.[46] Only about two-thirds of employees who are eligible for benefits collect them. Unemployment benefits might also be reduced by severance pay received.

Responding to Unemployment Insurance Claims Unemployment insurance payments are provided through state agencies. Employers do not have a direct role in administering these benefits. However, employers are required to supply information regarding their former employees' length of employment and the reasons for their job loss. An administrative appeals process can be invoked by both former employees and employers, occasionally resulting in court cases. Unemployment insurance taxes are experience-rated. Employers who have less stable employment and produce more claims pay more taxes. *Employers should not routinely contest unemployment insurance claims. Solid grounds for contesting claims include evidence that the former employee voluntarily quit, was terminated for serious misconduct, is receiving other payments (e.g., workers' compensation), or committed fraud. The former employee's statement to the state agency regarding the circumstances of his termination should be examined for accuracy. Employers must provide clear statements of the reasons for terminations and supporting evidence to state agencies that decide unemployment insurance claims.*

Restrictive Covenants

Restrictive covenants is an umbrella term that refers to a wide variety of contractual agreements that aim to protect employer interests by limiting the ability of former employees to do such things as going to work for competitors, disclosing trade secrets or other sensitive information, soliciting clients or former coworkers to do business with or join other firms, and making disparaging comments about their former employers. The increasing use of restrictive covenants to constrain the activities of former employees raises important legal and public policy questions.

Noncompetition agreements (covenants not to compete) are contracts that restrict the ability of a former employee (or former owner or partner) to compete with his former employer for a specified period of time following employment. Such agreements have become increasingly common, but that does not mean, as *Victoria's Secret Stores v. May Department Stores* shows, that they are always enforceable.

Courts consider a number of factors when deciding whether to enforce noncompetition agreements (by issuing injunctions against former employees or awarding damages for breach of the agreements), and their willingness to do so varies across states. As a starting point, courts regularly state that such agreements are disfavored as restraints on trade, and they will be enforced only if former employers can bear the burden of showing that the restraint is no greater than necessary to protect legitimate business interests. The employer's need for the agreement is balanced against its detrimental effect on the former employee's ability to earn a living and its effect on the public.[47] Valid employer interests in this context include the protection

[45]Economic Policy Institute. "Annual unemployment insurance exhaustion rate at highest level in 60 years." *Economic Snapshots* (September 22, 2004). Viewed October 4, 2004 (http://www.epinet.org).

[46]Christopher J. O'Leary. "U.S. Unemployment Insurance: Progress and Prospects." *Employment Research* (W.E. Upjohn Institute, July 2000), 3.

[47]*Modern Environments v. Stinnett*, 561 S.E. 2d 694, at 695 (Va. 2002).

VICTORIA'S SECRET STORES V. MAY DEPARTMENT STORES
157 S.W. 3d 256 (Mo. App. 2004)

OPINION BY JUDGE CRAHAN:

The May Department Stores Company ("May") appeals a judgment declaring that its former employee, Mark J. Weikel ("Weikel"), would not be in violation of the non-competition provisions of his employment contract by accepting a position with Victoria's Secret Stores, Inc. ("VSS"). We affirm.

Weikel was employed by May as Chairman of its Foley's Department Store ("Foley's") division. In 2000, Weikel and May entered into an Employment Agreement ("Agreement") whereby Weikel would render personal services to Foley's from May 15, 2000 until April 30, 2003 (later extended to April 30, 2005). In the Agreement, Weikel agreed to the following provision:

At all times while you are employed by May and for two years after your employment terminates, you will not directly or indirectly:

(i) own, manage, operate, finance, join, control, advise, consult, render services to, have an interest or future interest in or participate in the ownership, management, operation, financing or control of, or be employed by or connected in any manner with any Competing Business . . .

The section of the agreement defining "Competing Business" provides: "Competing Business" includes, but is not limited to, (i) any (x) retail department store, specialty store or other retail business that sells goods or merchandise of the types sold in May's (or its subsidiaries' or divisions') stores at retail to consumers or (y) any group of such stores or businesses or any other business that (A) competes (for customers, suppliers, employees or any other resource) with May or a May subsidiary, division or store; (B) is located in the United States . . . ; and (C) had annual gross sales volume or revenues . . . in the prior fiscal year of more than $ 25 million . . . ; or . . . (iii) any business in the United States or another country where May or a May subsidiary or division operates a store or stores in which your duties and functions would be substantially similar to your duties and functions under this Agreement and that is in material competition with May or a May subsidiary or division. * * *

In the spring of 2003, VSS made Weikel an offer to become its Chief Operating Officer. Weikel considered this a once-in-a-lifetime opportunity. After negotiations between his counsel and VSS, Weikel entered into an indemnification agreement with VSS, but he did not accept the offer of employment or sign an employment agreement. The following business day, Weikel met with his boss, Drew Pickman ("Pickman"), to tell him of the offer from VSS and to seek May's agreement that his acceptance of VSS's offer would not violate the terms of the restrictive covenant or any other contractual obligations to May because VSS is not a competitor of May. Weikel requested an immediate response because both he and VSS were anxious to begin their relationship. Weikel pledged to continue to faithfully perform all of his duties under the Agreement and offered to assist May with the transition to a new Chairman of Foley's.

Pickman told Weikel that he wanted him to stay and that he would work with the CEO of May to persuade him to stay. Pickman told Weikel that he believed VSS was a competitor of May and asked for more time to respond. Weikel told Pickman he needed an answer that day. Because May would not agree that VSS and May are not competitors, Weikel and VSS filed the underlying declaratory judgment action seeking a declaration that Weikel's employment by VSS would not violate his Agreement with May. On June 9, 2003, upon learning of the filing of the declaratory judgment action, May terminated Weikel from active employment but continued to pay his salary. Weikel did not begin working for VSS, and he remained inactive pending the trial court's judgment. * * *

The trial court found that VSS . . . specializes in the sale of women's intimate apparel. * * * It designs its own lingerie and controls its manufacture and distribution through its own channels. VSS targets younger women, specifically in their mid-twenties, who are willing to pay higher prices for the Victoria's Secret premium brand. VSS markets sex appeal for the fashion conscious. VSS has annual sales of approximately $ 2 billion per year. May and its divisions, including Foley's, are traditional

department stores that sell a broad array of products, consisting of hundreds of merchandise categories and thousands of brands. Intimate apparel constitutes approximately 3% of May's overall sales. May's core customers are women between the ages of 40 and 50 years old. May is considered a branded business in that it sells products manufactured by others as opposed to a private label business. May's bi-annual Market Share report, which breaks down its market share and apparel store competitors, does not mention VSS.

VSS customers are "item specific" and loyal to the Victoria Secret brand. VSS has developed a marketing strategy that is brand-driven as opposed to price-driven. That strategy is separate and distinct from that used by May or other broad-line retailers. VSS promotes its designer image. In contrast, May's business focuses on price advantage and does not trade on brand loyalty. The trial court further found that VSS wanted to hire Weikel solely for his personal skills and not for any information or knowledge he has about May. It is not interested in information he has about how May conducts its business because its business focus, strategy and marketing techniques are not at all similar to May's. VSS does not competitively shop May or study anything May does in terms of sales, products or operations. VSS finds such information to be counterproductive because May is a traditional or horizontal marketer whose retailing approach is markedly different from VSS.

The trial court found no evidence that Weikel had attempted to solicit or contact any other employees or executives of May. There was no evidence of specific customer lists or contacts Weikel would be able to use if employed by VSS and no evidence Weikel had divulged any confidential or proprietary information to VSS. Weikel has signed a non-disclosure agreement with VSS prohibiting solicitation of May employees or disclosure of any of May's confidential information. * * * Although the trial court found no evidence Weikel had solicited May employees or misused confidential or trade secret business information from May, the provision barring such activity was found to be enforceable for one year. . . . * * *

By definition, covenants by employees not to compete with their employers after termination of their employment restrain trade in a free market. Covenants not to compete are presumptively void and are enforceable only to the extent they are demonstrably reasonable. The determination of reasonableness depends upon the competing needs of the parties as well as the needs of the public. These needs are: (1) the employer's need to protect legitimate business interests, such as trade secrets

and customer lists; (2) the employee's need to make a living; and (3) the public's need to secure the employee's presence in the labor pool. A restrictive covenant in an employment agreement is only valid and enforceable if it is necessary to protect trade secrets and customer contacts, and if it is reasonable as to time and place. The burden of demonstrating the covenant's validity is on the party seeking to enforce it.

In its first point, May urges that the trial court's finding that VSS does not compete with May is against the weight of the evidence and erroneously declares and applies the law in that: (1) the covenant defines competition so as to include VSS and its affiliated companies; (2) the evidence overwhelmingly established that both companies sell hundreds of millions of dollars worth of intimate apparel in many of the same markets at comparable price points; (3) there is a substantial amount of cross-shopping by customers and the parties for employees as well as customers; and (4) VSS has repeatedly identified department stores as significant competitors and May's intimate apparel department considers VSS as among its principal competitors. We will briefly examine these contentions in turn.

May's first contention misstates the findings of the trial court. The trial court did not find that VSS and May are not competitors, it found that there was no meaningful or material competition between May and VSS. * * * There is substantial evidence that VSS was not a business that was in "material competition" within the intent of the parties. The trial court specifically found that May's bi-annual Market Share report, which breaks down its market share and apparel store competitors, does not mention VSS. Clearly, not all businesses that offer the "same" products, broadly defined, are necessarily in "material competition." Ritz-Carlton and Motel 6 both offer lodging, but few would characterize the competition between them as "material." Mortons of Chicago and McDonalds both offer food, but it is unlikely that either firm would view the other as a "material" competitor. More importantly, it is highly unlikely that an executive moving from any of these firms to the "competitor" would give the new employer an unfair competitive advantage, which is one of the key stated purposes of the agreement at issue in this case. The trial court specifically found that any confidential information possessed by Weikel would not give VSS a competitive advantage over May. This finding is supported by substantial evidence.

May would apply definition (i) of the term "Competing Business," which includes any retailer of goods or merchandise of the type sold by May with a

sales volume of $ 2 million. The difficulty with this contention is that definition (iii) specifically defines the term as applied to employment in a similar capacity, which is the situation presented in this case. Moreover, if literally applied, definition (i) would preclude employment by virtually every non-automotive or hardware retailer in the United States. On this record, such a broad prescription would appear to be far broader than necessary to protect May from any unfair competitive advantage. * * * It is certainly true, as May urges, that the record establishes that both May and VSS sell hundreds of millions of dollars worth of intimate apparel. There was substantial evidence, however, that they are selling them to essentially different groups of consumers. May's evidence with respect to the amount of cross-shopping did not establish the percentage of customers who actually made purchases of intimate apparel at both stores and was apparently found unpersuasive by the trial court. * * *

In sum, the trial court found that VSS and May are not in material competition for the sale of intimate apparel. * * *

In its second point, May argues the trial court erred in refusing to enforce Weikel's covenant not to compete because the overwhelming evidence established that Weikel had knowledge of and access to numerous types of confidential information concerning May's marketing, pricing, personnel, vendor margins, cost-control efforts, staffing, inventory, expansion plans, and other data that are proprietary to May and would be useful to VSS and its affiliated companies. Covenants not to compete are enforceable only to protect against unfair competitive use of either customer contacts or trade secrets. The Missouri Uniform Trade Secrets Act defines a trade secret as "a formula, pattern, compilation, program, device, method, technique or process" that derives value from not being known and not being readily ascertainable by proper means by others who can obtain economic value from its use and is "the subject of [reasonable] efforts . . . to maintain its secrecy." The protection does not extend to knowledge that is the natural product of the employment or known throughout the industry, but only to trade secrets or influences over customers.

There is no dispute that Weikel did not have customer contacts which could conceivably give VSS an unfair competitive advantage over May. * * * May produced three witnesses on the subject of confidential information. Kay Piper ("Piper"), May's Vice-President of the intimate apparel and hosiery department . . . identified four May company reports she believed might be valuable to a competitor. She had never heard Weikel's name

until the lawsuit was initiated and had no idea whether he had seen any of the reports. Weikel testified that he spent less than 3% of his time on intimate apparel matters at Foley's, concentrating instead on operational matters involving areas such as furniture, mattresses, cosmetics and shoes. He had never reviewed any strategic initiatives regarding intimate apparel at Foley's or May. Kenneth Wilkerson ("Wilkerson") . . . identified several categories of confidential information to which a Chairman at May would have had access. These included two sales reports, the departmental operating report, May's staffing system, May's customer service program and human resource information. Wilkerson had no knowledge that Weikel had any of May's confidential information in his possession and Weikel testified that he did not. Weikel has had no ability to access such information since June 2003.

There was evidence that the confidential information to which Weikel would have had access was not readily susceptible to memorization and had a limited useful life. Wilkerson conceded that he could not recite the actual sales numbers and figures in the sales report without having the document in front of him. The intimate apparel steering committee meets six times per year to generate a business plan setting out the strategic direction for May's sale of intimate apparel. Those plans are updated and changed every couple of months. The confidential reports identified by Piper are generated weekly or monthly. May's seasonal plans and forecasts, discussed at the twice-annual President's Counsel and Chairman's roundtable meetings, cover a six-month period of time. Sales and other reports are generated weekly or monthly. May's merchandising plans are generally for a six-month period, but they are constantly reviewed and updated. Based on this evidence, the trial court could reasonably have found that while the actual reports themselves would be potentially valuable to a competitor when issued, the useful life of the reports is relatively short. The fact that Piper, who is in charge of May's intimate apparel business, has a six-month non-competition agreement supports this inference. The trial court's finding that any confidential May business information known to Weikel would not give VSS a competitive advantage over May is supported by substantial evidence. Point denied. * * *

CASE QUESTIONS

1. What was the legal issue in this case? What did the court decide?

2. Look at the noncompetition agreement in this case. What exactly does it prohibit? Is it reasonable or overly broad?

3. What was the evidence that Mays and Victoria's Secret are not competitors? What companies might Mr. Weikel have been barred from joining? Wal-Mart? Sears? J.C. Penny's?

4. Why did the court reject May's claim that Mr. Weikel possessed information from his employment that could be used against May's and in favor of Victoria's Secret?

THE CHANGING WORKPLACE

Restrictive Covenants and Control of Human Capital

To the extent that there is a new employment relationship or psychological contract between employers and employees in the United States, it is most clearly manifested in employees being counseled to not expect long-term employment relationships, to acquire skills and experiences that will improve their marketability, and to always keep at least one eye toward moving on to another employment opportunity. A looser employment bond benefits employers in many ways, but it also has drawbacks. Knowledge and relationships with customers are key sources of competitive advantage. These assets reside primarily within employees, can leave the organization with them, and can readily be deployed elsewhere. This leads to contests between employers and former employees over who owns and controls **human capital.**[1]

Employers, particularly in technology fields and sales, have turned to an array of contractual devices and common law claims to restrict the actions of former employees. There are no precise data on the number of *noncompetition agreements* and other *restrictive covenants* in use, but the consensus is that this number has increased substantially over the past few decades. Correspondingly, litigation over the enforceability of such agreements has increased and become "one of the most frequently litigated issues in the employment law field."[2] Extending the reach of employer control over employees beyond the end of employment presents troubling and difficult legal questions. The interests of the public in maintaining competition and of employees in using their human capital to pursue their livelihoods must be balanced against the interests of employers in maintaining assets that are inherently difficult to safeguard. It has been argued that, although courts regularly voice their misgivings about such agreements, the trend over the past few decades is that courts have

become more receptive to the use of restrictive covenants and are more likely to enforce them.[3] A significant aspect of this shift has been judicial recognition of legitimate employer interests that extend beyond protection of *trade secrets* to the likes of maintaining customer relationships and recouping investments in training. The definition of trade secret has also expanded. Some courts have accepted the doctrine of "inevitable disclosure," which is the idea that the high likelihood of former employees using trade secrets justifies a broad restriction on competition, even in the absence of explicit noncompete agreements.[4]

Legal scholar Katherine V. W. Stone argues that the wider use and enforcement of restrictive covenants runs counter to the reality of contemporary employment relationships. She writes that:

[C]ourts should develop an approach to human capital cases that prevents employers from violating the tacit understandings of today's employment contract. When forced to decide who owns employees' general human capital, courts should factor the implicit terms of the new psychological contract into their determination. Thus, they should adopt a narrow definition of trade secrets, limit enforcement of noncompete covenants to the protection of trade secrets narrowly defined, reject the doctrine of inevitable disclosure, and thereby give employees broad rights to acquire, retain, and deploy their own human capital.[5]

[1] Katherine V.W. Stone. *From Widgets to Digits: Employment Regulation for the Changing Workplace.* Cambridge, U.K.: Cambridge University Press, 2004.

[2] Stone, at 128.

[3] Stone, at 132-49.

[4] Stone, at 149-52.

[5] Stone, at 156.

of trade secrets and other confidential information, protection of customer relationships, and possibly protection of employers' investments in training employees. The simple desire to be shielded from business competition is not sufficient to justify a restrictive covenant. Agreements are more likely to be deemed overly broad and not enforceable the longer they remain in effect, the wider the geographic area to which they apply, and the more numerous the activities that are restricted. As *Victoria's Secret Stores* demonstrates, noncompetition agreements are only enforced if the employee goes to work for a genuine competitor. Location within the same broad industry is not sufficient to establish competitor status. The enforceability of Microsoft's noncompetition agreement with Dr. Lee will hinge on how his activities for Google in China relate to his prior work at Microsoft and whether it is reasonable to apply such restrictions to someone working on the other side of the world (see "Clippings"). Thus, *employers should use noncompetition agreements only if important business interests are at stake. These agreements should be crafted to be no broader than necessary to protect those important business interests.*

Circumstances surrounding the adoption of noncompetition agreements can also affect whether they are enforceable. Some courts hold that agreements signed after employment has already commenced are not enforceable without additional consideration. In one case, a court refused to enforce a noncompetition agreement that was signed five days after an employee started work.[48] *If noncompetition agreements are used, they should be signed either before employment begins or with provision of some added benefit that constitutes consideration for accepting the limitation on postemployment activities.* Agreements also might not be enforced if the employer's own unlawful motive caused the termination of an employee. A court also refused to enforce a noncompetition agreement that was entered into with another employer that was subsequently acquired.[49]

Nonsolicitation agreements are another variety of restrictive covenant. They sometimes are packaged together with noncompetition agreements and other times appear as stand-alone agreements. Some courts give employers more leeway in using nonsolicitation agreements because they impose a less total restriction on the former employee's actions and ability to earn a living.[50] Nonsolicitation agreements restrict former employees from approaching their former employers' customers, clients, or employees. These agreements are more likely to be upheld where the client relationship is long-standing, the former employee's knowledge of the client rests solely on her work with the former employer, and—again—the restrictions are not overly broad. The Idaho Supreme Court refused to enforce a nonsolicitation agreement against an engineer who changed firms because the agreement barred him from "providing any services to [his former employer's] clients, current, past and potential, without regard to whether [the employee] had any contact with these clients."[51] California law enforces agreements preventing former employees from soliciting clients of a former employer only if doing so is necessary to protect trade secrets. A pension fund investment consulting firm was unsuccessful in obtaining a court order stopping former employees from soliciting clients to take their business to a new firm started by the former employees. The consulting firm argued that knowledge

[48] *Universal Hospital Services, Inc. v. Henderson,* 2002 U.S. Dist. LEXIS 9046.

[49] *Clark Substations, L.L.C. v. Ware,* 838 So. 2d 360 (Ala. 2002).

[50] *Freiburger v. J-U-B Engineers,* 111 P. 3d 100, at 105 (Idaho 2005) (noting that some courts use different standards, but choosing to apply the same "no more restrictive than necessary" standard to all types of restrictive covenants).

[51] *Freiburger,* at 106.

of the particular investment strategies of clients was a type of trade secret, but the court concluded:

> [I]t is not unusual for clients to follow consultants when they switch firms. . . . These kinds of relationships, rather than any special knowledge of the client's investment information or strategy, are the key to competition. But under California law, these kind of personal and professional relationships, developed over time, are not considered a "trade secret" the exploitation of which would prevent an employee from soliciting a former employer's clients.[52]

However, the court did order the former employees to refrain from using or recreating the former employer's custom-designed computer programs, which were trade secrets, disparaging the former employer, and soliciting their former coworkers to quit and come to work with them.

Noncompetition agreements often specifically refer to trade secrets and confidential information, but even in the absence of such agreements, courts have traditionally recognized a duty of employees under common law not to divulge such information. **Trade secret** refers to information (including formulas, programs, devices, methods, and processes) that has actual or potential economic value because it is not generally known to others, and the owner makes reasonable efforts to keep this information secret.[53] The definition of trade secrets used in most states is expansive and not limited to inventions or purely technical matters. Lists of customers can be trade secrets, but the lists cannot be readily compiled through other means, and employers must exert efforts to maintain their secrecy. An employer will not be able to successfully justify restraints on former employees to protect trade secrets when the employer has not previously taken sufficient steps to maintain the secrecy of the information.[54] *Employers that want to ensure that trade secrets and other confidential information will not be divulged or used by former employees must make reasonable efforts to preserve the confidentiality of that information.*

Speech by or about former employees has increasingly become the subject of legal wrangling. **Nondisparagement clauses** are now commonly included in severance pay agreements. These clauses require both parties to refrain from making negative or critical statements about one another. A hefty severance pay package granted to Virginia Buckingham, former director of the Massachusetts Port Authority, was met with an outpouring of criticism from both the public and other agency employees. The Port Authority's chief legal counsel responded by reminding agency employees that the nondisparagement clause in Buckingham's severance agreement required that they "not make any disparaging, critical, or otherwise adverse remarks, relating to, or about, Ginny, her services as an employee of Massport, or the circumstances surrounding her employment and/or separation of employment."[55] Thus, agency employees in this case were prohibited from speaking out on an issue that was of considerable concern to the public.

Former employees are sometimes sued for leveling criticism at their former employers. The Internet has greatly enabled employees who have issues with their former employers to effectively communicate this dissatisfaction—and to do so

[52]*Rogerscasey, Inc. v. Nankof*, 2002 U.S. Dist. LEXIS 7165, at 5–6; *affirmed*, 50 Fed. Appx. 461 (2d Cir. 2002).

[53]*Rogerscasey*, at 4 (citing California law, which incorporates, as have most states, the Uniform Trade Secrets Act).

[54]*Omega Optical v. Chroma Technology Corp.*, 800 A. 2d 1064 (Vt. 2002).

[55]Raphael Lewis. "Memo Tries to Stifle Dissent on Buckingham Deal: Massport Officials Warned on Criticism." *Boston Globe* (November 14, 2001), B1.

anonymously. However, an attempt by Intel to hold a former employee liable for a type of common law trespass was rejected by the California Supreme Court. The employee had sent mass e-mails to Intel employees on six occasions over a nearly two-year period. The e-mails criticized Intel management and particularly its human resource practices. The e-mails did not contain viruses or otherwise compromise the operation of the Intel computer system. Recipients were given the option of removing themselves from the distribution list. The court concluded that:

> [U]nder California law the tort does not encompass . . . an electronic communication that neither damages the recipient computer system nor impairs its functioning. Such an electronic communication does not constitute an actionable trespass to personal property, i.e., the computer system, because it does not interfere with the possessor's use . . . of . . . the personal property itself.[56]

The court hastened to add that, in contrast to cases involving spammers whose unsolicited bulk e-mails overwhelmed computer systems "[i]n the present case, the claimed injury is located in the disruption or distraction caused by the *contents* of the e-mail messages, an injury entirely separate from, and not directly affecting, the possession or value of personal property."[57]

Increasingly, employers have reacted to anonymous criticism posted on the Internet by filing "John Doe" lawsuits alleging defamation and other claims against anonymous employees or former employees. Subpoenas are obtained, which are then served on Internet service providers or bulletin board services to get them to divulge the identities of parties posting objectionable content. There is increasing concern that aggressive efforts by employers to control employees' and former employees' speech on the Internet are interfering with speech rights. Some courts are beginning to question whether John Doe suits are being brought for valid reasons or merely to stifle speech.[58] Additionally, some states have **anti-SLAPP laws** (strategic lawsuit against public participation) that courts have applied in these circumstances. For example, a former vice president of a company used a list of shareholders that he received while still employed and anonymously sent the shareholders articles describing several ongoing lawsuits against the company (including his own). The motive was to place pressure on the company to settle his suit. The company found out who sent the articles and sued him for misappropriation of trade secrets (the shareholder list). Anti-SLAPP laws provide for the dismissal of lawsuits brought to stifle the exercise of free speech regarding matters before the executive, legislative, or judicial branches, unless the parties bringing the suits show that they are likely to succeed in their claims. In this case, the court concluded that the former employee's statement pertained to a judicial proceeding and that the employer's trade secrets claim was unlikely to prevail. Thus, the employer's case was thrown out.[59]

Terminated employees will commence the search for new work and their former employers will seek to fill at least some of the vacated positions. This discussion brings us full circle in our tour of legal issues in employment. You should now have a better idea of how to meet both the spirit and the letter of the law—and to keep your employer's name out of any future editions of this book.

[56]*Intel Corp. v. Hamidi,* 71 P. 3d 296, at 300 (Cal. 2003).

[57]*Intel Corp.,* at 300–301.

[58]Margo E.K. Reder & Christine Neylon O'Brien. "Corporate Cybersmear: Employers File John Doe Defamation Lawsuits Seeking the Identity of Anonymous Employee Internet Posters." *Michigan Telecommunication Technology Law Review* 8 (2001/2001), 195, 202.

[59]*Commonwealth Energy Corp. v. Chappell,* 2002 Cal. App. Unpub. LEXIS 4866.

Chapter SUMMARY

Employers are generally free to go out of business, close facilities, eliminate positions, and reduce the number of people they employ. The primary legal constraint on downsizing decisions is the National Labor Relations Act (NLRA). Employers violate the NLRA when they close facilities or parts of their business if the decision is motivated by a desire to discourage unionization at the employer's remaining facilities and it is reasonably foreseen that the closing would have that effect. Likewise, the relocation of work from one facility to another in an attempt to defeat unionization also violates the NLRA. Many downsizing decisions are mandatory topics of bargaining that unionized employers must bargain in good faith over before implementing. Unionized employers are also required to bargain over the effects of such decisions on employees.

The Worker Adjustment and Retraining Notification (WARN) Act prohibits large employers from ordering plant closings and mass layoffs until the end of a 60-day period following the provision of written notice to affected employees or their union representatives. Employees are affected if they are reasonably expected to suffer employment loss stemming from a plant closing or mass layoff. *Employment loss, plant closing,* and *mass layoff* all have specific definitions under the WARN Act. Less than full notification can be provided when a plant closing or mass layoff is due to a natural disaster, when efforts to obtain a capital infusion or new business would be compromised by notification, or due to business circumstances not readily foreseen. Employees whose rights under the WARN Act are violated are entitled to back pay and benefits for the period of time they were deprived of timely notice, up to a maximum of 60 days.

Antidiscrimination laws prohibit employers from selecting individuals for termination based on their protected class characteristics. Age discrimination is commonly alleged in downsizing or reduction-in-force (RIF) cases. In a true RIF, terminated employees are not replaced. However, allocation of an employee's responsibilities to existing employees who perform the duties in addition to their own duties is not replacement. Terminations in the course of downsizing are analyzed differently, and a somewhat heavier burden is placed on plaintiffs in establishing a prima facie case than with other discriminatory discharges. Most legal challenges to downsizing have been brought as disparate treatment cases. Although adverse impact claims are available under the ADEA,

and basing downsizing decisions on salary level tends to disadvantage older workers, salary level would most likely be considered a reasonable factor other than age and thus not discriminatory. Early retirement offers can be used to reduce employment levels. However, any waivers of ADEA rights associated with acceptance of these offers must meet the requirements of the Older Workers Benefit Protection Act. Under the Employee Retirement Income Security Act (ERISA), employers have a fiduciary duty to inform employees about upcoming early retirement offers when those plans are under serious consideration.

The Federal Unemployment Tax Act (FUTA) and state unemployment insurance laws combine to govern the provision of unemployment benefits to persons who are involuntarily unemployed, able to work, available for work, and actively seeking suitable employment. Employees who quit their jobs or are fired for serious misconduct generally are not eligible for unemployment insurance. Individuals must demonstrate attachment to the workforce, both before and after applying for benefits. Minimum earnings and work duration requirements during a base period prior to applying for benefits must be met to be eligible for benefits. To remain eligible, individuals must be willing to seek and accept suitable employment. Benefits can be received for up to 26 weeks, and this period is sometimes extended when unemployment is high.

Knowledge, customer relationships, and other key sources of competitive advantage reside within employees and can leave with them when they depart for other employment or to pursue business opportunities. Noncompetition agreements are increasingly being used to address this reality, but such agreements are not always enforced. The key issue is whether the agreements are viewed as overly broad and restrictive. Even without any explicit agreements, common law aids employers who want to protect trade secrets and other confidential information from being divulged or otherwise misappropriated by former employees. Employers also have taken action against former employees believed to be disparaging or defaming them, particularly via the Internet. Concerns have been raised about the aggressive use by employers of the courts to stifle the speech of current and former employees. States with anti-SLAPP (strategic lawsuit against public participation) laws have tried to limit the use of lawsuits to suppress free speech.

Practical Advice SUMMARY

- *Employers must not selectively close facilities for the purpose of inhibiting unionization at other sites or relocate work based on antiunion motives.*

- *Before implementing many downsizing decisions, unionized employers must*

 –bargain in good faith over the decisions themselves (particularly subcontracting, outsourcing, and other decisions that involve the relocation, rather than elimination, of work).

 –bargain in good faith over the effects of downsizing on represented employees, including consideration of severance pay and transfer rights.

- *Successor employers must bargain with unions that represent employees at acquired companies, although they are generally not bound by the terms of existing labor agreements.*

- *Large employers must not order plant closings or mass layoffs*

 –until written notice is provided to union representatives (individual employees in nonunion workplaces) and certain government officials.

 –and for at least 60 days thereafter.

- *Employers must not select employees for downsizing based on their protected class characteristics, including age.*

- *Employers terminating employees in the context of downsizing or a reduction in force should*

 –have clear, objective criteria for deciding whom to downsize.

 –have these criteria in place before downsizing decisions are made.

 –apply downsizing selection criteria in a consistent manner.

 –not base downsizing decisions on stereotypical beliefs about older workers (e.g., unable to change).

 –not include code words suggesting bias against older workers in communications about the reasons individuals were selected for downsizing.

 –review selection procedures and decisions if a disproportionate (relative to the age composition of the pre-RIF workforce) percentage of persons selected for downsizing are employees over 40 years of age.

 –not hire additional, younger employees or substantially change the duties of existing employees to absorb the duties of terminated employees.

 –whenever possible, offer employees faced with downsizing the opportunity to transfer or otherwise retain their employment.

- *With a very few exceptions, employers cannot require that employees retire upon reaching some specified age.*

- *Employers can establish a minimum age and other criteria to define eligibility for early retirement offers, but cannot make such offers available to younger employees while excluding older ones.*

- *To be valid, waivers of ADEA rights by employees accepting group early retirement offers must meet the general conditions for ADEA waivers. Additionally, employees must be given*

 –at least 45 days to consider the offer.

 –information in writing regarding the group of employees covered by the program.

 –eligibility factors and time limits for decisions.

 –the job titles and ages of all employees eligible or selected for the program.

 –the job titles and ages of employees in the same group who are not eligible or selected for the program.

- *Employees must be informed regarding the status of early retirement offers that have not yet been finalized but are under "serious consideration," which occurs when*

 –there is a concrete proposal under consideration.

 –implementation of the proposal is being discussed.

 –high-level managers are involved in reviewing and approving the proposal.

- *After filing for bankruptcy, unionized employers*

 –cannot unilaterally alter or ignore the terms of labor agreements.

 –must bargain over any changes to existing labor agreements.

 –if negotiations fail to produce agreement, must receive bankruptcy court approval before instituting changes in terms and conditions of employment.

- *Employers should not routinely contest unemployment insurance claims. Solid grounds for contesting claims (or continuation of benefits) include evidence that the former employee*

 –voluntarily quit.

 –was discharged for serious misconduct.

 –is receiving other payments.

 –has committed fraud.

- *Employers should examine the accuracy of statements provided by former employees to state unemployment insurance agencies explaining the circumstances of their job loss.*

- *Noncompetition agreements should be*

 –used only if important business interests are at stake.

 –crafted to be no broader than necessary to protect those interests.

 –signed before employment begins or with additional consideration provided.

- *Employers that want to ensure that trade secrets and other confidential information will not be divulged or used by former employees must make reasonable efforts to preserve the confidentiality of that information.*

Key TERMS

downsizing	early retirement offer	human capital
Worker Adjustment and Retraining Notification (WARN) Act	serious consideration	noncompetition agreement
	unemployment insurance	nonsolicitation agreement
	involuntary unemployment	trade secrets
affected employee	base period	nondisparagement clause
employment loss	availability for work	anti-SLAPP laws (strategic lawsuit
plant closing	suitable employment	against public participation)
mass layoff	restrictive covenant	

Chapter QUESTIONS

1. In the year prior to its closing, a meat packing plant with 350 employees received numerous (more than 30) "noncompliance records" from the Agriculture Department (USDA) citing serious failures to maintain sanitary conditions and warning of possible "regulatory or administrative action." A handwritten letter delivered on September 17, 2001 carried the same warning. On October 31, 2001 the USDA withdrew inspection after a third incident of rodent droppings, forcing a halt in production. Production had to be stopped again due to unsanitary conditions on November 2. On November 7, the company's request to ship its product was denied, and the company was ordered by the USDA to destroy the suspect meat. The company had made a number of changes in equipment and operating procedures over this period. On November 15, the company detailed plans to spend $3 million for new coolers if the plant would be allowed to operate, but the USDA again refused permission. Later the same day, the owner decided to close the plant. Employees were informed when they showed up for work the next day that their employment had been terminated. A group of employees sued the company for not providing adequate notice of the plant closing. What should the court decide? Why? (*Pena v. American Meat Packing Corp.*, 362 F.3d 418 (7th Cir. 2004))

2. On Friday, November 8, 2002, a company sold a manufacturing plant to another company. The buyer interviewed the plant's 68 employees over the weekend, and 44 were rehired to work in the new plant. The new plant opened without any break in operations on Monday, November 11, 2002. The new plant made the same product, using the same equipment as previously. A group of former employees sued because they had not been provided with proper notice. What should the court decide? Why? (*Smullin v. Mity Enterprises*, 420 F.3d 836 (8th Cir. 2005))

3. During a reduction in force implemented over a two-year period, an employer terminated 13.7 percent of its employees aged 55 and above, compared to 5.4 percent of employees under age 55. Employees over age 55 comprised 14.7 percent of the workforce before the RIF and 13.6 percent afterward. The employer's stated criteria for selecting employees in the RIF included salary level and eligibility for retirement. Other evidence included a videotape in which the company CEO stated that employees over 50 "have trouble changing," a memo soliciting nominations for "high potential/high achiever candidates" that specified candidates must "have NOT reached their 40th birthday," and a number of other statements by top managers regarding the need to retain "young people" to stay competitive. A group of older employees terminated during the RIF sued. What should the court decide? Why? (*EEOC v. McDonnell Douglas Corp.*, 191 F.3d 948 (8th Cir. 1999))

4. A company wanted to reduce the size of its workforce through an early retirement offer. From past experience, the company realized that employees were reluctant to accept such offers because they assumed that a more generous offer would be forthcoming in the future. The company addressed this matter in the Summary Plan Description (SPD) that it issued to employees for its early retirement program. The SPD stated that if any future early retirement plans were offered, "the benefits would not be as good as those contained in this plan." Four years later, the company adopted another early retirement plan that had more generous benefits than the previous plan. A group of employees who left under the earlier plan sued. What should the court decide? Why? (*McCall v. Burlington Northern/Santa Fe Co.*, 237 F.3d 506 (5th Cir. 2000), *cert. denied*, 122 S. Ct. 57 (2001))

5. In 1999, Allstate Insurance decided to no longer sell insurance through its own employees, but rather to use a network of independent contractors. The company terminated all (6,400) of its employee agents in 2000. The former employees were given four options. The first two options offered two different varieties of independent contractor arrangements. The third option was to end the relationship with Allstate and receive a year's pay as severance. The fourth option was to terminate the relationship and receive a maximum of 13 weeks of severance pay. The first three options required the former employees to sign releases of legal claims against Allstate. The fourth option did not require the signing of a release. Two employees, one of whom took option 2 and the other who took option 4, sued Allstate for retaliation, age discrimination, and violations of ERISA. What should the court decide? Why? (*Isbel v. Allstate Insurance*, 418 F.3d 788 (7th Cir. 2005))

6. An employee was hired to drive a car used to transport patients to and from hospitals and nursing homes. In his first three and a half months on the job, the employee had four accidents with the employer's vehicle. Each of the accidents involved striking stationary objects, and none occurred while patients were being transported or caused serious damage. The employee was fired after the fourth accident and the state agency denied unemployment insurance. What should the court decide? Why? (*Pesce v. Board of Review*, 515 N.E.2d 849 (Ill. App. 1987))

7. An employee of a financial information services company located in New York performed her work by "telecommuting" from Florida. The employee had a home office in her residence, was provided with a second telephone line and computer equipment by her employer, and was given access to the company's mainframe computer located in New York. The employee was required to be available during normal business hours, and she maintained daily contact with her supervisor in New York. At some point, the employer decided to end the telecommuting arrangement. The employee was offered employment at the New York office, which she declined. She initially filed for unemployment insurance in Florida. The employer contested this claim on the grounds that she had voluntarily left her job. Subsequently, she was informed that she might be eligible for unemployment insurance (with higher weekly payments) in New York. Her claim for benefits in New York was again contested by the employer, this time on the grounds that she had not been employed in New York. What should the court decide regarding her eligibility for unemployment benefits and from which state any benefits should come? Why? (*Allen v. Commissioner of Labor*, 794 N.E. 2d 18 (Ct. App. N.Y. 2003))

8. Business Designs, Inc. (BDI) uses "digital thermal resin transfer imaging" in its specialty of producing signs and decals advertising car washes for service stations. The founder of the company spent a number of months developing the product. As business grew, he hired two employees who assisted with all phases of the work. The two employees became dissatisfied and joined a former employer who was starting a new company. The employees had not been required by BDI to sign noncompetition agreements, and the company did not have a formal confidentiality policy. The new company used the same imaging process. Within a week, the company was able to ship full sign packages to numerous former customers of BDI. BDI sued the former employees. What should the court decide? Why? (*Business Designs, Inc. v. Midnational Graphics*, 2002 Iowa App. LEXIS 524.)

9. What do you think about the increasing use of restrictive covenants? Should employers who attempt to enforce these agreements against employees that have been fired have to show that the terminations were for cause?

Internet RESOURCES

The Department of Labor (DOL) site provides information about compliance assistance for the WARN Act.

http://www.dol.gov/dol/compliance/comp-warn.htm

The DOL Employment and Training Administration site provides information on unemployment insurance.

http://www.dol.gov/dol/topic/unemployment-insurance/index.htm

The federal government's Office of Personnel Management site provides information on downsizing.

http://www.opm.gov/reduction_in_force/

Glossary

A

Abatement Elimination or lessening of a workplace hazard that puts employees at risk for safety and health problems.

abuse of discretion Standard often used by the courts in reviewing the decisions of benefit plan administrators in denial-of-benefits cases under ERISA.

acceptance of offer Assent, such as when a prospective employee accepts a job offer, that is needed, along with an offer and consideration, to have a contract.

administrative employee An employee who has as his primary duty performing office or nonmanual work directly related to the management policies or general business operations of an employer and meets other DOL criteria.

adverse action An employer's action against a job applicant or employee (e.g., not hiring, not promoting).

adverse impact The disproportionate limitation or denial of employment opportunity for some protected class group that results from the use of a "neutral" requirement or practice that is not "job-related and consistent with business necessity."

affirmative action Formal, planned actions that are appropriate to overcome the effects of past and present barriers to equal employment opportunity for underutilized women, persons of color, persons with disabilities, and certain veterans.

affirmative defense A defense to vicarious liability for hostile environment harassment by managers that shows the employer exercised reasonable care to prevent and correct promptly any harassment, but the plaintiff unreasonably failed to take advantage of the opportunities provided by the employer (or failed to avoid harm in some other way).

after-acquired evidence Evidence of prior misbehavior by an employee that is acquired after the employee sues. The employee does not lose the right to sue, but may have his or her legal remedies limited due to the prior misbehavior (e.g., falsifying information on an application form).

alternative dispute resolution (ADR) A procedure for resolution of disputes that is an alternative to going to court; the two most common types are mediation and arbitration.

Americans with Disabilities Act A federal act that prohibits discrimination against qualified individuals with a disability and obligates employers to reasonably accommodate an employee's disability.

anti-SLAPP laws (strategic lawsuit against public participation) Laws in effect in some states that provide for the dismissal of lawsuits brought to stifle the exercise of free speech regarding matters before the executive, legislative, or judicial branches, unless the parties bringing the suits show that they are likely to succeed in their claims.

appeals court Any state or federal court that hears appeals from judgments and rulings of trial courts or lower appeals courts.

appeals procedure An internal administrative process for addressing employee grievances. ERISA requires that such a procedure be provided for review of benefit determinations.

applicant A person who applies for a job.

applicant flow data Data comparing the protected class composition of an applicant pool with that of the group of people who are successful in passing an employment test; used in adverse impact cases to determine whether a test has discriminatory effects.

appropriate bargaining unit A group of employees with common interests who can be appropriately represented by a labor organization.

appropriation of a name or likeness A privacy tort claim in which the symbolic value of one's name or likeness is used for another's commercial or other ends.

arbitration A dispute resolution procedure in which a neutral third party (the arbitrator) functions like a private judge by hearing disputes and rendering decisions that are almost always final and binding on the parties.

arising out of employment A requirement for workers' compensation that refers to the underlying cause of an employee's injury or illness.

arrest When an individual is "picked up" by the police and taken to the police station with the intent of charging him with a crime; often such individuals are released after questioning without being charged.

association rights Constitutional protection under the First Amendment, covering both intimate relationships and people banding together for speech or other expressive purposes.

assumption of risk A common law defense to negligence claims that does not apply under workers' compensation and holds that an employer is not responsible for an employee's injury if the employee knowingly took on dangerous work.

authenticity A basis for establishing that an employer's qualification based on a particular protected class characteristic is a BFOQ; for example, a movie director's requirement that a female role must be filled by a female actor.

authorization cards Cards that are signed by employees to express their desire for representation by a specific union. These are used to obtain a representation election.

availability for work The unemployed person is willing to seek and accept suitable employment; this is a requirement for receiving unemployment insurance.

B

Background check A potential employer's check of a job candidate's claims about her character and employment history (e.g., contacting references; verifying past employment and military service history; confirming necessary degrees, licenses, and other credentials; checking driving record; checking for criminal convictions; examining credit reports).

banding When an employer, in considering employment test scores, groups all scores within a statistically derived confidence range together and treats them as identical for hiring and promotion purposes; this allows an employer to consider affirmative action criteria with little or no effect on merit.

base period A specified period of time prior to an employee's termination for which the unemployment insurance claimant's work history is examined to determine whether the employee met the minimum earnings and hours of work standards required to be eligible for unemployment insurance.

"because of sex" Because harassment is treated as a form of discrimination, it is necessary to show that the plaintiff in a sexual harassment case was subjected to the unwanted treatment because of his or her sex.

binding past practice An employment practice that is clear, has been consistently engaged in over a substantial period of time, and existed with the knowledge and at least tacit consent of both the union and the employer. An arbitrator may treat this practice as an implied term of the labor agreement.

bona fide occupational qualification (BFOQ) A defense to a facially discriminatory policy or practice. It is found where a protected class requirement is reasonably necessary to the normal operation of a business.

bona fide seniority system (BFSS) A seniority system with a formal, established set of arrangements for tracking employee seniority that may serve as a defense in adverse impact cases.

burden of proof The requirement that a party to a lawsuit meet a specified standard (e.g., "preponderance of evidence") in establishing that all the facts necessary to win a judgment are presented and true.

business necessity A showing that must be made by an employer to defend an adverse impact claim. The challenged requirement or practice must be both job-related and no more stringent than necessary to achieve the employer's legitimate business interests.

C

Cash-balance plan A defined benefit pension plan that also includes some features of a defined contribution plan; often termed a *hybrid* plan.

certificate of creditable coverage A certificate documenting prior coverage under a group health insurance plan that must be provided automatically and free of charge to an employee who loses coverage or exhausts his COBRA continuation coverage; used for compliance with HIPAA.

certiorari A writ (order) of a higher court (most commonly the U.S. Supreme Court) to a lower court, indicating that the court will hear the case and review the lower court's decision.

chain of custody Refers to the parties who handle evidence or, in the case of drug testing, specimens for drug tests; chain of custody must be documented.

citations Notices to employers of safety violations under the OSH Act that include the nature of the violations, the OSHA standard(s) violated, the monetary penalties associated with the violations, and the amount of time the employer has to correct the problems (the abatement period).

civil service laws Laws intended to ensure that the merit principle, and not political patronage, guides employment decisions regarding government

employees; these laws cover job classifications, testing, hiring, and promotion procedures, and usually incorporate processes for review of disciplinary decisions.

class-action lawsuit A lawsuit brought by many plaintiffs who have had their rights violated in a similar fashion by the same defendant; all the plaintiffs in the class action share in any award.

COBRA (Consolidated Omnibus Budget Reconciliation Act) A law that requires employers who have group health insurance plans and at least 20 employees to offer continuation coverage under certain circumstances (qualifying events) in which employees and other beneficiaries would otherwise lose health insurance coverage.

collective bargaining A means of deciding issues related to wages, hours, terms, and conditions of employment. Unions represent employees and negotiate labor agreements with employers.

common law Judge-made law revealed through legal precedents over time, in contrast to statutes enacted by legislatures.

common law test A test used to ascertain employee status that focuses on right of control.

comparable worth A theory under which pay discrimination exists if an employer fails to pay women working in female-dominated jobs the same rate of pay as men working in male-dominated jobs, when the jobs are shown through job evaluation to be equally demanding overall, even though they might involve different combinations of skill, effort, responsibility, and working conditions. This theory has not been accepted by the courts.

comparators Persons of the opposite sex in the same workplace who receive a higher rate of pay for performing the same type of work as the plaintiff.

compelling governmental interest An abiding interest that serves as a defense to a constitutional challenge to a public employer's affirmative action plan that uses racial preferences; necessary to withstand strict scrutiny.

compensable factor A factor (e.g., skill, effort, responsibility) used to rate jobs in a job evaluation.

compensable hours Hours of work for which employees must be compensated.

complaint procedure An established procedure by which someone who experiences harassment can report it.

comp time Compensatory time off work that is substituted for overtime pay.

concerted activity Any effort made by employees to join together for "mutual aid or protection."

conditional offer of employment An offer of employment that is conditional on the job applicant meeting certain standards, for example, passing a medical examination.

confirmatory test A second, more sophisticated drug test that is used when an initial screening comes back positive.

consent A defense available to an employer in a defamation claim in which the employer can show that the employee or former employee gave permission to the employer to provide information about him or her.

consent decree A decree that, as part of a judicially approved settlement between the parties, imposes an affirmative action program on an employer.

consideration Something of value given in exchange for receipt of another's promise. Along with an offer and acceptance of an offer, it is needed for a contract to exist.

constitution A document that addresses the relationships between different levels of government (e.g., states and the federal government) and between governments and their citizens.

constructive discharge Refers to a situation in which an employer creates intolerable working conditions with the intention of forcing an employee to quit.

consumer credit report A communication by a consumer reporting agency of information having to do with a consumer's credit worthiness, character, and general reputation.

consumer reporting agency Any entity that regularly gathers and evaluates information on consumers to furnish reports to third parties; term encompasses companies that perform background checks for employers.

content validation A means of establishing the validity of an employment test; a test has content validity to the extent that it requires the performance of the same behaviors and skills as the job in question.

contingent worker A term used to identify a looser, more flexible, and less secure relationship with an employer that lasts only as long as a particular project or piece of work is being done (e.g., independent contractors, temps), in contrast to full-time, year-round employment by a single employer.

continuing treatment Ongoing treatment by a health care provider for a serious health condition.

continuous leave Leave that is taken all in one block, with no work occurring between the beginning and end of the leave.

contributory negligence A common law defense to negligence claims that does not apply under workers' compensation, which holds that if a person is injured in part due to his own negligence (i.e., his negligence "contributes" to the accident), the injured party is not entitled to damages.

controls Methods by which employers can eliminate or lessen hazards to which employees are subjected (e.g., guards on machines, proper ventilation, rest breaks).

conviction Refers to a court's judgment that a person who was arrested for a crime actually committed it.

cost-benefit analysis An examination of the costs to employers of complying with an OSHA safety standard compared to the economic value of the expected improvement in worker health.

covenant of good faith and fair dealing A type of wrongful discharge claim pertaining to terminations undertaken in bad faith and having the effect of denying employees the benefits of their contractual employment relationship.

criterion validation A means of establishing the validity of an employment test; a test has criterion validation if a statistical association exists between performance on the test and performance on the job.

cutoff score The minimum score needed on an employment test to receive further consideration for a job.

D

Davis-Bacon Act A law covering the prevailing wage for employers who have construction contracts with the U.S. government.

decertification election An election in which employees decide if they want to continue to have representation by a union.

defamation When an employer makes false statements that reflect badly on a person (e.g., while providing a reference) and this results in damage to the person's reputation.

deferral doctrine An NLRB doctrine that usually allows arbitrators to resolve cases that raise both contractual and NLRA issues.

defined benefit plan A pension plan that promises a specific pension benefit to the employee upon retirement, in which the employer maintains a pension fund separately from his or her other assets and pays benefits from this fund.

defined contribution plan A pension plan in which contributions are made into individual employee accounts, and in which the pension benefit that an

employee receives will depend on the amount in his or her individual account at the time of retirement (e.g., 401(k)s, profit-sharing plans, stock bonus plans, ESOPs).

development Programs that help employees further their careers.

direct evidence An employer's clear articulation of a discriminatory motive in the context of making an employment decision.

direct threat A person's disability that poses a specific risk of significant harm to the person or others.

disability A physical or mental impairment that substantially limits one or more major life activities.

disclaimer A written statement, incorporated into an employee handbook or other important document, that denies that any statements in the document create contractual rights that will be binding on the employer.

discrimination The limitation or denial of employment opportunity based on or related to the protected class characteristics of persons.

discriminatory effects Key element of adverse impact; refers to the disproportionate limitation of employment opportunity for some protected class group.

discriminatory intent Key element of disparate treatment; refers to the attitudinal state of an employer who bases an employment decision, in whole or in part, on the protected class characteristics of the affected employee.

disparate treatment Unequal treatment that is intentional, based on protected class characteristics, and that results in the limitation or denial of employment opportunity.

district court A trial court for federal cases in a particular court district (all or a portion of a state) or a local court in some states.

diversity A concept that asserts that differences between people and cultures are to be valued.

domestic partner benefits Employee benefits that are offered to same-sex partners and, in some instances, to unmarried opposite-sex partners.

"don't ask, don't tell" policy Military policy under which homosexual service members are expected to be discreet and not talk about or openly engage in homosexual behavior, and the military must refrain from inquiring about the sexual orientation of service members without good reason.

downsizing Terminations of employment that affect numerous employees and that are based on

employers' judgments that the number of employees, positions, or facilities must be reduced.

drug test A test performed with urine, blood, or hair samples to determine whether a person is using illegal drugs.

due process A protection afforded to employees; this requires that employers adequately investigate alleged misconduct, notify employees of charges against them, provide employees with a chance to respond to those charges, and respect the Weingarten rights of employees to have union representatives present at meetings likely to result in discipline or discharge.

duties test A test used to determine whether an employee's duties are genuinely executive, administrative, or professional in nature. It is one factor used to determine whether the employee is exempt under the FLSA.

duty A responsibility held toward others.

Early retirement offer An offer of enhanced benefits made by an employer to induce employees to retire earlier than they otherwise would be able to in order to promote attrition.

economic realities test A test used to ascertain employee status, particularly in Fair Labor Standards Act cases.

economic strike A strike that is undertaken to pressure the employer to meet employee negotiation demands.

effort The amount of physical and mental exertion required on a job.

Electronic Communications Privacy Act (ECPA) An act that amended existing federal wiretapping laws to prohibit both the intentional interception (through the use of electronic, mechanical, or other devices) and the disclosure of wire, oral, or electronic communications—and which also prohibits the unauthorized accessing of stored electronic communications.

employee A person who is hired for a wage, salary, fee, or payment to perform work for an employer; employee status is distinguished from other forms of paid work by applying the common law or other appropriate test.

Employee Retirement Income Security Act (ERISA) A federal law that governs most employer and labor union sponsored benefit plans, including pensions, but not government employer plans or social insurance programs.

employer A person or entity that hires the services of another; in agency law, the employer is the principal, and the employee is the agent.

employment at will An employment relationship in which either party, the employer or employee, may sever the relationship at any time, for any reason not specifically prohibited by law.

employment at will with exceptions Term describing the legal status of most nonunion, private-sector employees. An increasing number of wrongful discharge claims is available to employees, but unless the terminated employee can prove that one of these applies, the termination is presumed to be legal.

employment loss Under the WARN Act, a loss of employment stemming from a plant closing or mass layoff, including termination (other than a quit, discharge for cause, or retirement), a layoff lasting more than six months, or a greater than 50 percent reduction in work hours during each month of any six-month period.

enforcement procedure A procedure by which employees may seek redress when they believe that their rights have been violated.

English-only rule A rule that prohibits or restricts the speaking of languages other than English in the workplace.

Equal Pay Act (EPA) A law that prohibits employers from paying a person of one sex at a lower rate of pay than a person of another sex for performing substantially equal work within the same establishment, unless the differential in pay is accounted for by a legitimate factor other than sex.

ergonomics Deals with the fit between the physical demands of jobs and the physical abilities of people.

escalator principle Under this rule, employers must attempt to place individuals returning from military service into the positions (including promotions) they likely would have attained absent the service.

essential functions Functions that are necessary to a job; criteria for identifying these are (1) the position exists to perform these functions, (2) few other employees are available to perform these functions, and (3) the functions are highly specialized. Used for determining compliance with the ADA.

establishment clause A clause in the First Amendment to the U.S. Constitution that prohibits governmental entities from sponsoring or supporting religion.

exclusive remedy Workers' compensation is the exclusive remedy for injuries and illnesses that arise out of and in the course of employment. Employees cannot sue their employers under these circumstances.

exclusive representative Status of unions that win a representation election. When a union is thus certified, it is the representative of all employees in the bargaining unit, regardless of membership status.

executive employee An employee who has as her or his primary duty the management of an enterprise, department, or other subunit of a company, and meets other DOL criteria.

executive order A president's or governor's declaration that has the force of law, requiring no action by the Congress or state legislature.

exempt employees Employees for which employers are excused from following some or all of the FLSA's rules.

exercising legal rights A variant of the public policy exception to employment at will in which an employer is held liable for firing an employee because the employee has exercised his legal rights (e.g., filed a workers' compensation claim, refused to work for less than minimum wage).

experience rating An employer's track record regarding the number of injuries that have occurred in the workplace, which is used in determining the amount an employer must contribute to workers' compensation.

express employment contract An explicit, mutually acknowledged contract that specifies a term of employment or the circumstances under which the contract can be terminated.

extraterritoriality Describes laws that apply to U.S. citizens who are employees of U.S. employers operating outside of the United States, provided that complying with U.S. law would not cause employers to violate other nations' laws.

F

Facially discriminatory A policy or practice adopted by an employer who openly uses protected class as a basis for making employment decisions, while insisting that it is necessary (i.e., there is a BFOQ).

factor other than sex Something other than an employee's sex that accounts for disparate pay between the employee and an employee of the opposite sex who is performing substantially equal work in the same workplace.

failure to reasonably accommodate An employer's failure to be flexible and make alternative arrangements to remove obstacles to becoming employed, performing a job, or enjoying the full benefits of employment, for persons whose disabilities or religious beliefs require such flexibility, when doing so would not impose "undue hardship" on the employer.

Fair Credit Reporting Act (FCRA) The major federal law regulating the gathering, sharing, and use of information by employers and consumer reporting agencies.

Fair Labor Standards Act (FLSA) A law that establishes a federal minimum wage and requires premium pay for overtime work; it also sets out certain work-hour limitations for minors.

False Claims Act A federal whistleblower law that protects individuals who come forth with information about a knowingly false or fraudulent claim made against the federal government.

false imprisonment The intentional restraint of the physical liberty of an individual. A type of tort claim.

Family and Medical Leave Act (FMLA) The principal federal law governing the provision of leave to employees for parental and medical reasons.

fellow servant rule A common law defense to negligence claims, which does not apply under workers' compensation, that holds that employers being sued by employees can defend themselves by claiming that fellow workers were responsible instead.

fiduciary Anyone who exercises discretionary authority or control over the administration of a benefit plan or its funds.

fiduciary duties The responsibility of the people or entities (fiduciaries) who control and manage benefit plans to manage those plans solely in the interest of plan beneficiaries.

forced distribution method A method of evaluating employee performance in which predetermined percentages of employees are placed into particular performance categories.

foreseeability Refers to whether a reasonable person of average intelligence would be able to foresee that hiring an unfit person for a particular position would render injury or harm to others likely.

four-fifths rule Equal Employment Opportunity Commission (EEOC) rule that says if the selection rate (the percentage of applicants who pass an employment test and are hired or continue to be considered for employment) for one race or sex or other protected class group is less than 80 percent (4/5) of the selection rate for the race or sex or other protected class group that was most successful at passing the test, this is evidence of discriminatory effects in an adverse impact case.

Fourth Amendment An amendment to the U.S. Constitution that protects citizens against unreasonable searches and seizures.

fraud A situation in which a person makes a false representation of material fact to another party, while knowing it is false or demonstrating a reckless disregard for the truth, in order to induce the other person to act in a certain way, and in which the other person is harmed by reliance on the false representation.

free exercise clause A clause in the First Amendment to the U.S. Constitution that protects citizens' free exercise of religion from infringement by the government.

General duty clause A clause in the OSH Act that places basic responsibility for workplace safety with employers; this clause can be invoked for enforcement purposes in the absence of standards regulating the specific hazard involved.

genetic monitoring Monitoring employees' genetic material to watch for adverse changes, in situations where the employees are exposed to hazardous substances.

genetic screening Screening of job candidates for desirable or undesirable genetic traits.

glass ceiling Invisible, artificial, and attitudinal barriers that conspire to limit the access of women and persons of color to higher-level positions.

goals What an employer hopes to accomplish in an affirmative action program aimed at correcting the underutilization of those in a protected class; to be legal, goals must be flexible and not be rigid quotas.

good faith bargaining The mutual obligation of an employer and union to confer in good faith regarding wages, hours, and other terms and conditions of employment; to meet at reasonable times; and to execute a written contract incorporating any agreement reached.

good faith effort An employer's sincere efforts to correct the underutilization of women and persons of color through an affirmative action plan.

grievance A complaint from an employee who believes her employer has violated a labor agreement.

grievance arbitration A means of resolving a grievance by calling in a neutral third party who acts like a judge in rendering a decision regarding the interpretation and enforcement of an existing labor agreement. Generally the arbitrator's decision is final and binding on the parties.

Harassment A form of disparate treatment discrimination in which an employee is subjected to unwelcome physical or verbal conduct related to a protected class characteristic. It can result in tangible employment actions or creation of a hostile environment.

harassment policy An employer's policy regarding the conduct of employees that prohibits harassment and provides recourse for those who experience it.

harassment with tangible employment actions Harassment that results in significant changes in the employment status of individuals, such as hiring, firing, promotion, demotion, pay increases or decreases, and work assignments.

hazard communication standard An OSHA standard that contains substantial information and training requirements regarding hazardous chemicals.

Health Insurance Portability and Accountability Act (HIPAA) A law that deals with numerous aspects of health insurance plans, including preexisting condition exclusions and the privacy of medical information.

hierarchy of controls Industrial hygiene principle that safety improvement efforts should give highest priority to eliminating or engineering out hazards. Personal protective equipment is viewed as a last resort.

HIV test A medical test to determine whether someone has been infected by the human immunodeficiency virus that can develop into AIDS.

honesty test A paper-and-pencil test used to determine the honesty of job applicants or employees.

hostile environment Harassment that is sufficiently severe or pervasive to interfere with an individual's work performance or that would be experienced by a reasonable person as intimidating, offensive, or abusive. The harassment makes it harder to perform or remain on the job, but does not result in a tangible employment action.

hybrid test A test used to ascertain employee status in court that combines elements of other tests, such as the economic realities test and the common law test.

Identification of problem areas A dynamic analysis of an employer's workforce, including an examination of the flows into and out of positions, in an effort to identify measures that will improve the employer's utilization of persons in protected classes.

illegal alien　A noncitizen who is not eligible to work in the United States; also referred to as being unauthorized or undocumented.

Immigration Reform and Control Act (IRCA)　A federal law requiring that employers (1) refrain from knowingly hiring or retaining on the job unauthorized aliens, and (2) refrain from discriminating in hiring or termination decisions on the basis of national origin and citizenship.

impasse　A point in labor negotiations when the two parties become deadlocked over one or more mandatory topics and both parties are warranted in assuming that further negotiation would be futile at this time.

implied contract　A type of wrongful discharge claim that limits the employer's right to terminate if the employer has made written or oral statements containing promises not to terminate at will, or implied such a contract through his course of conduct with the employee.

independent contractor　A person or business that performs services for another person or entity under a contract that spells out terms such as duties, pay, the amount and type of work, and other matters.

infliction of emotional distress　A common law tort claim in which plaintiffs must show (1) intent to harm (or the existence of a special relationship); (2) behavior that is so outrageous, shocking, or atrocious as to be beyond the bounds of what is tolerable in a civilized society; and (3) severe emotional harm or distress.

inspections　Examinations of workplaces made by OSHA in an effort to enforce its safety and health standards.

integrated enterprise　Two or more ostensibly separate companies that are related enough to be considered a single employer.

intentional interference with a contractual relationship　A tort claim in which intentional, improper interference causes a third party to breach or not enter into a contractual (i.e., employment) relationship with the plaintiff.

interactive process　Where an employer becomes aware of an employee's need for accommodation and works with that person to find a mutually acceptable accommodation.

intermittent leave　Periods of leave are mixed with periods of work.

in the course of employment　A requirement for workers' compensation that refers to the time, place, and setting in which an employee's injury or illness occurred.

intrusion upon seclusion　A privacy tort claim in which a plaintiff must show that an intentional intrusion into his or her solitude or private affairs occurred and that the nature of the intrusion was such that it would be highly offensive to a reasonable person.

investigation　An examination of the circumstances surrounding events described in a harassment complaint to determine whether the complaint is justified.

investigative report　A communication by a consumer reporting agency that is similar to a consumer credit report, but which is also based on personal interviews with friends, neighbors, or other associates.

involuntary unemployment　Condition of eligibility for unemployment insurance; exists where the employee did not voluntarily quit and was not discharged for serious misconduct, but rather was laid off or terminated based on business considerations.

Job analysis　An analysis of a job in which the tasks of the job and the knowledge, skills, abilities, and other characteristics needed to perform the job are detailed.

job evaluation　A systematic process for rating jobs in terms of certain compensable factors; those jobs that are rated higher are defined to be more demanding and valuable to the employer, and hence deserving of higher pay.

job group analysis　The combination of the individual job titles in a contractor's workforce into a more parsimonious set of job groups based on similarity in job content, pay level, and opportunities for advancement. The demographic composition of job groups is documented.

job-related and consistent with business necessity　A defense used in adverse impact cases to justify an employer's requirement or practice that results in disproportionate outcomes as being not discriminatory, but necessary and justified for business purposes.

joint employment　Two or more companies that are not part of an integrated enterprise, but that maintain employment relationships with the same employees (e.g., a company that uses temps and the temporary staffing firm that supplies the temps might be considered joint employers).

Jury System Improvement Act　A federal law that protects persons who serve on federal juries from discharge, intimidation, or coercion by their employers.

just cause　A requirement for discipline or discharge of a unionized employee under a labor agreement;

the employer must show that the discipline or discharge was undertaken for good reasons, that the employee was afforded due process, and that the punishment fit the offense.

Key employee A salaried employee who is among the top 10 percent of a company's employees in pay. Under certain circumstances, these employees can be denied restoration from FMLA leave.

knowledge Refers to the fact that the employer was aware, or should have been if proper screening procedures had been followed, that the person hired was unfit.

Labor agreement The basic source of rules governing the wages, hours, terms, and conditions of employment for unionized employees.

labor organization Any organization, committee, or plan in which employees participate and which exists for the purpose, in whole or in part, of dealing with employers concerning grievances, labor disputes, wages, rates of pay, hours of employment, or conditions of work.

labor unions Organizations that represent employees in their dealings with employers.

legal alien A noncitizen who is eligible to work in the United States.

liberty interest An interest held by most public employees that can be jeopardized through termination of employment; the focus of this interest is on maintaining the employee's good name.

living wage A wage set by local laws that is intended to promote levels of hourly pay that are more consistent with a dignified existence than the federal minimum wage. These laws usually apply only to contractors.

lockout An employer's withholding of the opportunity to work from employees after their labor agreement expires, despite the employees' willingness to remain on the job and continue negotiating.

Major life activities Activities that are necessary to functioning in everyday life, including walking, seeing, hearing, speaking, breathing, learning, and working.

malice Intent to harm a person's reputation.

malicious prosecution A claim against an employer who has wrongfully sought criminal prosecution of an employee.

managed care A health care system in which managed care organizations (MCOs) receive sums of money to provide for the health care of insured patients and profit to the extent that costs can be minimized.

mandatory topic An issue that, if raised by either party in labor negotiations, must be negotiated over in good faith.

mass layoff Under the WARN Act, a reduction in force that is not caused by a plant closing, but that results in employment loss at a single work site during any 30-day period for at least 500 full-time employees (regardless of the percentage of total employees) or at least 50 full-time employees (when these comprise at least 33 percent of total employment at the work site).

material safety data sheet (MSDS) A sheet that chemical manufacturers and importers must provide for each hazardous chemical produced or sold; the sheet must include the chemical name of the substance that appears on the label, the common name, physical and health hazards associated with the substance, the OSHA PEL and other applicable standards, procedures for safe handling and use, and first-aid procedures.

materially adverse employment action A loss of employment opportunity, which generally must be shown in discrimination claims.

matter of public concern Political or social issue that concerns the larger community. The speech rights of public employees under the Constitution apply only to statements made about this type of issue and not to personal concerns or grievances.

McNamara-O'Hara Service Contract Act A law covering the prevailing wage for employers who contract with the U.S. government for many types of services.

mediation A dispute resolution procedure in which a neutral third party (the mediator) facilitates negotiations between the disputing parties to help them reach an agreement, but does not have the authority to decide the dispute or impose a settlement.

mediator A neutral third party who, by entering negotiations and exerting control over the bargaining process, helps unions and employers reach their own negotiated settlements.

medical examination Any procedure or test that seeks information about an individual's health or health impairments.

medical inquiries Questions asked by a potential employer about an applicant's disabilities, medical

and psychological conditions, medical history, medications taken, or workers' compensation claims filed.

medical review officer A person with medical training who is qualified to interpret the results of a drug test and communicate them to the employee's manager.

Migrant and Seasonal Agricultural Worker Protection Act (MSPA) A federal law covering most seasonal agricultural workers that provides some basic safeguards related to pay, housing, and transportation.

minimum wage The lowest wage employers are permitted to pay employees for each hour they work during a workweek.

mitigating factors Circumstances that might call for a diminution in the severity of an employer's discipline (e.g., the employee's past record, length of service, compelling personal or medical problems that might explain aberrant behavior, and situational factors).

mixed motives Refers to cases in which strong evidence exists of both discriminatory and lawful motives affecting an employment decision. The employer with mixed motives is guilty of discrimination.

Montana Wrongful Discharge from Employment Act (WDEA) A broad wrongful discharge statute that protects employees in the state of Montana. The law prohibits the discharge of nonprobationary employees without "good cause."

multiemployer doctrine Holds that on multiemployer work sites, an employer who creates a safety hazard can be liable if an employee is injured or threatened, regardless of whether the employee is its own or that of another employer on the site.

musculoskeletal disorder (MSD) A repetitive stress injury or cumulative trauma disorder that results from employees' interaction with work tasks, equipment, and surroundings in the workplace.

Narrowly tailored Measures used as part of an affirmative action plan that do not harm the interests of nonpreferred persons any more than is absolutely necessary to achieve the plan's goals.

National Institute of Occupational Safety and Health (NIOSH) An agency that provides scientific and technical support to OSHA, helping it to identify workplace hazards and develop appropriate standards.

National Labor Relations Act (NLRA) The principal federal law concerning self-organization and collective bargaining by private-sector employees.

National Labor Relations Board (NLRB) The agency that administers the NLRA, including holding elections to determine whether employees desire union representation, and determining whether unfair labor practices (ULPs) have been committed.

National Mediation Board (NMB) The board that administers the RLA, the labor law governing collective bargaining in the railroad and airline industries.

negligence Refers to the actions of a party who fails to meet his duty or responsibility to other people to exercise reasonable care in carrying out certain activities, where this failure is a proximate cause of harm to others. Intent to harm need not be shown.

negligence standard The standard by which an employer's liability is judged when coworkers or third parties harass an employee; under this standard, the employer is liable if he or she knew (or should have known) about the harassment and failed to take prompt, effective action to stop it.

negligent hiring A form of negligence that extends the liability of employers for harm caused by their employees beyond actions undertaken within the scope of employment (the subject of respondeat superior claims) to harmful actions that lie outside the scope of employment, but for which the careless hiring of an unfit employee "set the stage."

negligent misrepresentation A situation in which a person makes a fraudulent statement that he or she may not have known to be false, but which he or she should have known to be false.

negligent referral A former employer's misrepresentation about an employee in giving a reference; an employer can be sued for negligence if he or she refers an unfit employee for a job and the employee harms others in that new job.

negligent training A negligence claim stating that an employer failed to provide adequate training where there was a duty to others, thereby breaching his or her duty, and that such breach of duty was the proximate cause of harm to one or more third parties.

nepotism Refers to an employer's preference for hiring family members and other relatives of current employees.

neutral requirements Requirements, other than protected class characteristics, used as grounds for making employment decisions.

neutral wording Wording of want ads and other types of job announcements that does not express or imply a preference for some protected class group over another.

noncompetition agreement Also known as a covenant not to compete, this is a contract in which a former employee, owner, or partner agrees not to compete with his former employer for a specified period of time and over a particular geographic area.

nondiscrimination clause A clause that, under E.O. 11246, must be included in employment contracts if a contractor or subcontractor does business with the federal government.

nondisparagement clause Commonly included in severance pay agreements, this is a clause that requires both a former employer and former employee to refrain from making negative or critical statements about one another.

nonexempt employees Employees who are entitled to the protection of the FLSA.

nonsolicitation agreement A contract that restricts former employees from approaching their former employers' customers or clients.

 O

Occupational Safety and Health Act (OSH Act) The principal federal law requiring private-sector employers to prevent occupational injuries and illnesses by removing hazards from the workplace.

Occupational Safety and Health Administration (OSHA) An agency that has overall responsibility for administering and enforcing the OSH Act—which it does by establishing safety standards, conducting inspections of workplaces, and providing information to employers and employees about workplace safety and health issues.

Occupational Safety and Health Review Commission (OSHRC) An agency that hears appeals of OSHA enforcement actions.

offer A promise, such as when an employer offers a prospective employee a job, that if sufficiently clear and definite, is one of the essential requirements for the formation of an employment contract.

Office of Federal Contract Compliance Programs (OFCCP) An agency within the U.S. Department of Labor that monitors compliance with Executive Order 11246 and other laws requiring affirmative action by contractors.

Older Workers Benefit Protection Act An amendment to the Age Discrimination in Employment Act (ADEA) that establishes special rules for the treatment of older workers under benefit plans.

opportunity wage An exception to the general minimum wage requirement under which employers are permitted to pay employees under 20 years

of age at a lower rate for their first 90 calendar days on the job.

opposition Refers to activities related to obtaining civil rights apart from participation in formal enforcement procedures (e.g., protests, speaking with news media).

oppressive child labor Employment of minors (under 16) at types of employment and for hours of work not permitted by the FLSA.

ordinary course of business A term that refers to business activities that are routine, for legitimate business purposes, and about which employees are notified. Activities of this kind are exempt from ECPA requirements.

organizational display An organizational chart that depicts the organizational structure of a company, including the units within it and the relationship of each unit to other units in the organization. The demographic composition of these units is documented.

organizational profile Portrays the staffing patterns in an organization.

organization fit A subjective selection criterion based on how well a prospective employee will share the values of the organization and fit into its corporate culture.

overly broad publication Refers to an employer making a defamatory statement to persons without a legitimate need to know the information.

overtime pay One and one-half times an employee's regular rate of pay for each hour worked in excess of 40 in a workweek.

 P

Participation Refers to participation in the enforcement of an antidiscrimination law (e.g., filing a charge, bringing a lawsuit, giving testimony, assisting in the investigation of a discrimination charge).

partner One of the co-owners and investors in a partnership; partners are distinguished from employees.

pattern or practice of discrimination Refers to cases in which plaintiffs marshal statistical data showing the effects of an employer's discrimination and evidence of intentional discrimination against individuals within the larger affected group.

pay docking rule The Department of Labor's approach to determining whether employees are paid on a salary basis; impermissible deductions from pay can cause a loss of exempt status.

payroll method Under this method for determining employer size, an employee is counted for each

full week between when the employee is hired and when he or she leaves employment, regardless of the number of hours worked during those weeks.

pay secrecy policy An employer's policy that discourages employees from sharing information about their pay and threatens punishment for doing so.

Pension Benefit Guaranty Corporation (PBGC) An independent organization established under ERISA that intervenes and provides at least partial retirement benefits to retirees and vested employees whose employers are unable to meet their pension obligations.

pension plan A benefit plan designed to provide retirement income to employees or to otherwise defer income until after employment ends (e.g., defined benefit pension, 401(k), ESOP, profit-sharing).

performance appraisal A review of an employee's performance in which, ideally, an employer recognizes the employee's accomplishments and provides feedback on how to improve performance.

performance criteria Standards used to judge an employee's performance; common criteria include work quality and quantity, attendance and punctuality, judgment, ability to work with others in a team, leadership, and so forth.

performing a public duty A variant of the public policy exception to employment at will where an employee is terminated for actions that were clearly undertaken in the public interest, but not specifically required.

period of incapacity A period during which a person is unable to work, attend school, or engage in other regular daily activities; relevant to assessing whether a serious health condition exists under the FMLA.

permissible exposure limit (PEL) The maximum exposure to a hazard allowable under the OSH Act.

permissive topic An issue that one party can decline to discuss when the other party raises it in labor negotiations.

physical/mental impairment A physical impairment involves the effects of health on a person's functioning; a mental impairment includes psychiatric disorders, mental retardation, and learning disabilities.

placement in a false light A privacy tort claim in which the plaintiff must show that characteristics, conduct, or beliefs were falsely attributed to him or her; this false information was broadly publicized; the individual publicizing the false information knew or should have known that it was false; and being placed in this false light would be highly offensive to a reasonable person.

plaintiff The party who brings a lawsuit.

plant closing Under the WARN Act, a permanent or temporary shutdown of a single site of employment when that shutdown results in employment loss during any 30-day period for at least 50 full-time employees.

polygraph A test that measures changes in physiological responses (e.g., respiration, blood pressure, perspiration); used to infer whether someone is telling the truth.

preemployment inquiries Questions asked by potential employers on application forms, during interviews, and in the course of informal chatting with job candidates.

preemption The rule of law that if the federal government through Congress has enacted legislation on a subject matter, it shall be controlling over state laws and/or preclude the state from enacting laws on the same subject.

preexisting condition exclusion An exclusion commonly incorporated into health insurance plans that denies coverage for a specified period of time for the treatment of conditions that existed before an individual enrolled in the health plan.

preference When an employer considers protected class as a plus factor in a hiring or promotion decision to achieve affirmative action goals.

Pregnancy Discrimination Act (PDA) A law confirming that discrimination based on pregnancy, childbirth, or related medical conditions is sex discrimination and violates Title VII.

pretext An employer's stated reason for denying an employment opportunity that is no more than a cover-up for a discriminatory motive.

prevailing wage The wage set by several federal laws that employers must pay to their employees if they contract to provide goods or services to the U.S. government. This amount is generally in excess of the minimum wage.

prima facie case A showing by the plaintiff that discrimination is a plausible explanation for the denial or limitation of employment opportunity.

prima facie case of failure to reasonably accommodate religion An applicant or employee can establish such a case by showing that he or she has a sincere religious belief or practice that conflicts with an employment requirement, that the employer was informed of this belief or practice, but that the employee was subjected to an adverse employment outcome because of adhering to this belief or practice.

prima facie case of pay discrimination Established where plaintiff can show that someone of the opposite sex working within the same establishment receives a higher rate of pay for performing work that is substantially equal to that performed by the plaintiff.

privacy A basis for establishing that an employer's qualification based on a particular protected class characteristic is a BFOQ; it is usually argued that the privacy concerns of customers or patients require employees to be a particular sex.

Privacy Act A federal act that regulates the handling of personnel records by agencies of the federal government and allows federal employees to have access to their personnel records under reasonable procedures established by federal agencies.

private sector Refers to profit-making companies, nonprofit organizations, and their employees.

professional employee An employee whose primary duty is performing work that requires an advanced type of knowledge in a field of science or learning (learned professional); that requires invention, imagination, or talent in a recognized field of artistic endeavor (creative professional); or that involves the teaching activity of imparting knowledge (teaching professional); and meets other DOL criteria.

progressive discipline The first instance of a violation is met with a warning or other relatively mild discipline, and then subsequent offenses result in progressively more severe discipline and, if the undesirable conduct continues, discharge. The focus is on correcting undesirable conduct.

promissory estoppel A claim in which the plaintiff has reasonably relied to his or her detriment on the clear promises of another (e.g., that he or she would have employment).

property interest An interest held by most public employees in their jobs that requires public employers to follow due process procedures when disciplining an employee or terminating employment.

protected class Characteristics (e.g., race, sex, age) that society deems to be impermissible grounds for making employment decisions.

proximate cause of harm Something that is a relatively direct cause of harm to others in negligence cases.

proximity Involves the connection between events as they actually unfolded (in negligence cases).

publication Making something about a person public to at least one person through speech or print.

public disclosure of private facts A privacy tort claim in which plaintiffs must show that private

facts of their lives that are of no legitimate concern to the public were broadly disclosed to others in a manner that would be highly offensive to a reasonable person.

public policy Factor used in negligent hiring cases to determine the degree of care that an employer should have exercised in hiring.

public policy exception An exception to the finality of arbitration that allows an arbitrator's decision to be overturned when it is contrary to an explicit and well-defined public policy.

public policy exception to employment at will A type of wrongful discharge claim under which employers are liable in tort for wrongful discharge when they terminate employees for taking actions that public policy requires or commends.

public safety A basis for establishing that an employer's qualification based on a particular protected class characteristic is a BFOQ; the focus is on potential harm to the public, rather than to the individual employee.

public sector Refers to government agencies and their employees.

 Q

Qualified Refers to an individual with a disability who satisfies the skill, education, experience, and other job-related requirements for a job that is held or sought, and who is able, with or without reasonable accommodation, to perform the essential functions of that job.

qualified individual with a disability The protected class under the Americans with Disabilities Act.

qualified privilege A defense available to an employer in a defamation claim; this conditional immunity can be lost if claims are made with malice or reckless indifference to the truth, or if there is overly broad publication of the statement.

qualifying events Circumstances under which eligible employees are entitled to take FMLA leave (e.g., birth of a child).

 R

Race norming Adjusting the scores of, using different cutoff scores for, or otherwise altering the results of employment-related tests on the basis of race, color, religion, sex, or national origin.

Railway Labor Act (RLA) A federal labor law that governs collective bargaining in the railroad and airline industries.

random drug testing A random selection procedure used to test a specified percentage of the workforce when the employer has no individualized suspicion of drug use.

rational relationship standard A standard used to determine whether certain government actions are unconstitutional. Under this standard, government actions are constitutional if they are rationally related to a legitimate government purpose or interest.

reasonable accommodations of disability Employers are expected to be flexible and provide support to qualified individuals with disabilities as long as making the accommodations does not cause the employer undue hardship.

reasonable action An affirmative action taken by an employer, upon discovering the company is underutilizing women or persons of color, to improve the utilization of these groups.

reasonable basis Basic element of an affirmative action plan that documents the underutilization of women or persons of color in the employer's workforce.

reasonable expectation of privacy Whether, under the circumstances, a reasonable person would expect to enjoy privacy. Unless this can be shown, a plaintiff will not prevail in either a constitutional or common law privacy tort claim.

reasonable person The standard by which an objective assessment is made regarding whether or not a hostile environment existed in a plaintiff's workplace: Would a person of average intelligence and sensitivity experience it as offensive, intimidating, or abusive?

reasonable suspicion When an employer reasonably suspects, based on observations of an employee's behavior, that an employee is using illegal drugs.

reckless disregard for the truth Refers to an employer's lack of effort to establish the veracity of her statements about someone.

record of an impairment A medical history or other record that contains information about an employee's disability. Persons not currently impaired, but with a record of a disability, are protected from discrimination on that basis.

recruitment Refers to mechanisms used by employers to communicate information about the availability of employment opportunities (e.g., want ads, Internet job postings, "help wanted" signs, referrals).

reduced leave schedule A type of intermittent leave, in which the employee's normal daily or weekly hours of work are reduced.

refusal to commit an illegal act A variant of the public policy exception to employment at will under which an employer can be held liable for wrongfully discharging an employee when he or she does so because the employee refuses to break the law.

regarded as disabled A person who is not disabled but is regarded as being disabled because of stereotypes, fears, or misconceptions. Persons erroneously regarded as disabled are protected from discrimination on that basis.

regular rate of pay Total pay for a workweek (excluding certain payments) divided by total hours worked.

regulation Rules created by government agencies to elaborate upon statutory requirements.

Rehabilitation Act An act protecting federal government employees with disabilities from discrimination and on which the Americans with Disabilities Act is based.

relevant labor market Group of people who are qualified for the type of work in question and whose geographic location makes them likely applicants for the job.

religion A person's spiritual belief system; it includes all aspects of religious observance, practice, and belief.

religious advocacy The conveyance of religious beliefs to others; proselytizing in the workplace.

religious harassment A hostile environment created by unwelcome, pervasive religious communications.

religious organization exemption An exemption in Title VII that absolves churches of any liability for discriminating in employment on the basis of religion.

remedies Remedial measures instituted to correct a wrong, such as harassment or discrimination.

reporting illegal activity A variant of the public policy exception to employment at will that applies in instances where employers discharge whistleblowers (i.e., employees who report illegal activities by employers or their agents).

representation election An election in which employees express their willingness or unwillingness to be represented by a labor organization.

respondeat superior A common law doctrine that makes employers liable for harm to others that occurs when employees act within the scope of their employment.

responsibility Refers to an employee's accountability for outcomes, supervisory duties, and involvement in important decisions.

restoration An employee's reinstatement to the same position that was held when FMLA leave was taken, or to a position that is equivalent in pay, benefits, terms, and conditions of employment.

retaliation The limitation or denial of employment opportunity as a means of discouraging or punishing persons who seek to obtain their rights under antidiscrimination laws or to assist others in doing so.

reverse discrimination An allegation of disparate treatment where an employer shows a preference for a person from a protected class in a hiring or promotion decision to achieve affirmative action goals.

right of control Refers to the hiring party's authority to control where, when, and how work gets done.

right to know The idea that employees have a right to receive information about the dangerous chemicals they encounter on the job.

runaway shop Relocation of work from one facility to another motivated by hostility toward unions; this is a violation of the NLRA.

S

Salary-basis test A test used to determine whether employees are truly paid on a salary basis. Being paid a salary is one requirement for exempt status.

salary-level test A test used to determine whether an employee's salary level is high enough to make the employee exempt.

same-sex harassment Harassment where both the harasser and the person being harassed are of the same sex.

scope of employment The term for actions that relate to the kind of work an employee was hired to perform, take place substantially within the workplace during work hours, and serve, at least partially, the interests of an employer.

segregation Separating one group from another; for example, the channeling of women and persons of color into less desirable jobs.

selection rate The percentage of applicants who pass an employment test and are hired or continue to be considered for employment; used with the four-fifths rule in determining whether there is evidence of discriminatory effects in an employer's employment practices.

self-analysis Basic element of an affirmative action plan aimed at analyzing the workforce and identifying problem areas.

serious consideration Under ERISA, there is a fiduciary duty to inform employees about the status of any early retirement incentive plans when there is a specific proposal, the proposal is being discussed for purposes of implementation, and members of senior management with the authority to implement the plan are engaged in the discussion.

serious health condition A medical condition that involves inpatient care in a hospital or similar medical facility or a condition that requires continuing treatment by a health care provider.

severe or pervasive A hostile environment in which an employee is harassed either severely, or frequently or over a long period of time; this type of harassment is a violation of Title VII.

sex-plus A form of facially discriminatory policy or practice, where neutral criteria are applied to some protected class groups, but not to others.

sex-stereotyping Disparate standards for men and women that are based on, and reinforce, stereotypes about sex.

significant risk The level of risk to employees that must be established before OSHA is allowed to promulgate new safety standards for the workplace.

skill The level of ability, education, training, and experience needed to perform a job.

social movement An organized effort to create needed changes in workplaces and society.

soft skills Motivational, interpersonal, and communication skills of applicants that are assessed primarily in a subjective manner through interviews.

speech rights Guaranteed under the First Amendment, but not absolute, public employees' right to speak out on matters of public concern is balanced against the interests of public employees.

standards Requirements set by OSHA for employers that pertain to particular hazardous substances, machinery, work processes, environmental conditions, and safety practices. Standards specify the minimum level of safety required by law.

statute A written law passed by Congress or a state legislature and signed into law by the president or a state governor.

strict scrutiny The most stringent form of judicial review of government actions under the Constitution. The action must serve a compelling governmental interest and be narrowly tailored to be defensible.

strike Refers to the situation where employees withhold their labor, refusing to resume work until their employer agrees to more favorable terms and conditions of employment or refrains from engaging in unfair labor practices.

subjective criteria Selection criteria in which standards and means of assessment are not clearly specified and are likely to vary across decision makers.

substantially limited An individual whose impairment is severe or chronic enough to have a long-term impact on functioning and the performance of major life activities.

successor employer An employer who takes over a company and is thus the successor to a previous employer.

suitable employment Work that does not endanger the health or safety of the employee, work for which the individual has the requisite training and experience, and work that is within a reasonable distance of the individual's residence or last place of employment; a standard used in determining whether an unemployment insurance claimant is available for work.

summary judgment A court order ruling that no factual issues remain to be tried, and therefore the cause of action in the complaint can be decided without trial.

summary plan description (SPD) A document that under ERISA must be provided to employees to inform them, comprehensively and accurately, about their rights and obligations under benefit plans.

supervisor Under the NLRA, an individual who has the authority, in the interest of the employer, to make personnel decisions (e.g., hiring, discharge, discipline, promotions), to responsibly direct other employees, to settle their grievances, or to effectively recommend such actions—all of which must also entail the use of independent judgment.

Supreme Court The highest court in the United States; it has the power to decide constitutional questions and other appeals based on its jurisdiction as granted by the Constitution (e.g., cases based on federal statutes, between citizens of different states, or in which the federal government is a party).

sweatshop Refers generally to firms that pay very low wages for long hours of work, provide unsafe conditions, and staunchly oppose unionization.

Temporary worker A type of contingent worker who is hired for a temporary amount of time or to complete a particular project or piece of work; often procured through temporary agencies.

tenure A protection against employment termination afforded to some teachers and professors in public schools and universities; this is typically conferred following a relatively lengthy probationary period and a formal assessment of past and likely future performance.

timetables A schedule for achieving the goals of an affirmative action plan.

tipped employees Employees who customarily and regularly receive at least $30 per month in tips; minimum wage rules differ for these employees.

tort Refers to that body of common law that allows an injured person to obtain compensation from the person who caused the injury.

trade secrets Information (including formulas, programs, devices, methods, and processes) that has actual or potential economic value because it is not generally known to others and that the owner makes reasonable efforts to keep secret.

training Programs that teach employees how to do their jobs or that increase employees' skills and abilities.

U

Underutilization When the percentage of women and persons of color in one or more of an employer's job groups is lower than the percentage of women and persons of color with the necessary skills for that type of employment.

undue hardship Significant difficulty or expense on the part of an employer that excuses the employer from making an accommodation for an employee with a disability.

unemployment insurance Insurance that is intended to partially replace lost earnings during periods of unemployment for persons who have demonstrated an attachment to the workforce.

unfair labor practices (ULPs) Actions that the NLRA prohibits employers and unions from taking; these center on interference, restraint, or coercion of employees in the exercise of their rights.

unfair labor practice strike A strike that is undertaken in response to, or is prolonged by, employer unfair labor practices (e.g., refusal to bargain in good faith), for the purpose of pressuring the employer to comply with the law.

Uniformed Services Employment and Reemployment Rights Act (USERRA) An act containing an extensive set of legal requirements surrounding military service; employers of any size are prohibited

from discriminating against persons who are members of, apply to become members of, or have obligations to serve in a uniformed military service.

union security Provisions in a labor agreement that require all employees in a bargaining unit to pay union initiation fees and dues within a specified period of time, upon penalty of discharge by the employer (e.g., union shop).

unreasonable search or seizure A search or seizure by police or other governmental actors that is undertaken without sufficient justification or in a manner that renders it unconstitutional.

unwelcome harassment Occurs where the person complaining of another's conduct did not solicit or provoke it, and considers it offensive and unwanted.

Validation study A study to determine the validity of an employment test.

validity Refers to whether a measurement device measures what it purports to measure. The validity of an employment test depends on whether it measures characteristics related to job performance.

variance Permission for an employer to not comply, either temporarily or permanently, with an OSHA standard.

vesting An employee's achievement (based on years of service) of a nonforfeitable right to receive a pension.

vicarious liability A company's legal responsibility for damages when the person engaging in harassment is in a position (e.g., owner, president, partner) that allows him to speak or act for the company, or where an agent uses the authority conferred upon him or her to engage in harassment.

visa classifications The various types of visas (e.g., H-1B, L-1, TN, F-1, J-1) that permit foreign nationals who do not have permanent resident status (i.e., a green card) to work in the United States.

volunteer A person who renders a service without being paid or expecting payment.

Welfare plan Any benefit plan covered by ERISA that is not a pension plan (e.g., health insurance, child-care subsidies, prepaid legal services).

Whistleblower Protection Act A law protecting federal government employees who engage in whistleblowing.

whistleblowing An employee's report of illegal activities injurious to the public that are being engaged in by his or her employer or agents.

white-collar exemptions Salaried executive, administrative, and professional employees to whom employers are not obligated to pay overtime.

word-of-mouth hiring Refers to an employer's dependence on current employees to spread the word about jobs to their friends, family members, and other associates.

Worker Adjustment and Retraining Notification (WARN) Act Prohibits employers covered by the act from ordering plant closings or mass layoffs until the end of a 60-day period that follows the provision of written notice to affected employees (or, if the employees are unionized, to union representatives) and to state and local government officials.

workers' compensation State laws that provide the exclusive remedy for employees who suffer accidental injury, illness, or death from their employment.

workforce analysis A listing of individual job titles in each department or organizational unit in order of pay level. The demographic composition is documented for each job title.

working conditions Refers to hazards (how dangerous a job is in terms of physical hazards) and surroundings (elements such as fumes, working outside in cold weather, etc.).

workplace safety programs Comprehensive programs established by employers to identify and abate unsafe conditions in their workplaces.

workweek The basic unit of time for determining compliance with both the FLSA's minimum wage and overtime requirements; any fixed and recurring period of 7 consecutive days (168 hours).

Case INDEX

Subject INDEX